CONCISE
DANTE DICTIONARY

CONCISE DICTIONARY

OF

PROPER NAMES AND NOTABLE MATTERS

IN THE

WORKS OF DANTE

BY

PAGET TOYNBEE

M.A., D.LITT. (OXON.)

'Dietro alle poste delle care piante.'
Inf. xxiii. 148

PHAETON PRESS
NEW YORK
1968

Originally Printed 1914
Reprinted 1968

' Omnium hominum in quos amorem veritatis natura superior impressit, hoc maxime interesse videtur, ut quemadmodum de labore antiquorum ditati sunt, ita et ipsi posteris prolaborent, quatenus ab eis posteritas habeat quo ditetur.'

(DANTIS *De Monarchia,* I. i, 1–7.)

Library of Congress Catalog Card Number 68-15695

Published by Phaeton Press, Inc.

PREFACE

THIS *Concise Dante Dictionary*, based upon my *Dictionary of Proper Names and Notable Matters in the Works of Dante*, which, originally published in 1898, has now for some time been out of print, is offered to students and readers of Dante as a convenient hand-book, and companion to the Oxford edition of the complete works of Dante.

The articles have been carefully revised, and, it is hoped, brought up to date, throughout. A certain number of new articles have been added, comprising the names of persons and places mentioned in the *tenzone*, or poetical correspondence, between Dante and Forese Donati [1] (which was included for the first time in the third edition of the Oxford Dante), and in the Latin poems addressed to Dante by Giovanni del Virgilio. On the other hand, the names which occur in the *canzone*, ' O patria, degna di trionfal fama' (Canz. XVIII in the Oxford Dante), have been omitted, it having been established that this poem is not by Dante. [2]

As the scope of the book does not allow of references to authorities in the body of the work, I am glad to take this opportunity of repeating my acknowledgements to the writers specified in the Preface to the larger work, among whom I may specially mention Prof. Casini, the last edition of whose commentary on the *Divina Commedia* [3] has been

---

[1] In six sonnets, numbered LII, LII*, LIII, LIII*, LIV, LIV*, in the Oxford Dante (third edition, 1904, pp. 179–80). For most of the information concerning the persons and places referred to in this correspondence I am indebted to Prof. Isidoro del Lungo's article on the *tenzone*, published in his volume of studies, *Dante ne' Tempi di Dante*, pp. 437–61.

[2] The same may be said of the *ballata*, ' Fresca rosa novella ' (Ball. IV in the Oxford Dante), which is by Guido Cavalcanti.

[3] Fifth edition, Florence, 1903.

PREFACE

in constant requisition, as has that (published since the issue of the *Dictionary*) of Prof. Torraca.[1]

I am indebted for numerous corrections and additions to various reviews of the previous work, in particular to the instructive article by Prof. Michele Barbi in the *Bullettino della Società Dantesca Italiana*.[2] To this last-named periodical (now in its twenty-fifth year), a veritable storehouse of information on all matters Dantesque, which, under the able editorship, originally of Prof. Barbi, latterly of Prof. E. G. Parodi, has become indispensable to every serious student of Dante, I am under especial obligations.

It may be explained that the reduction in the size of the work has been attained by condensation in the wording of the articles, where condensation was possible; by the omission of the *précis*, or summaries, from various articles dealing with episodes in the *Divina Commedia*; by the substitution of references only for full-length quotations from chroniclers and commentators, and from authors cited or utilized by Dante; by the suppression of certain of the less important articles comprising 'notable matters'; and, lastly, by the omission as far as possible of controversial matter (such as discussions as to the dates of composition of Dante's various works, or as to the interpretation of the details of the mystic Procession in the Terrestrial Paradise, and the like). Though a large amount of interesting illustrative matter has thus necessarily been eliminated, it is hoped that, as far as essential information is concerned, the present book will be found no less useful than its predecessor.

PAGET TOYNBEE.

Fiveways, Burnham, Bucks.
July, 1913.

---

[1] Second edition, Rome-Milan, 1908. To Prof. Torraca, further, I owe the identification of 'il Provenzale' of *Convivio* iv. 11[93] with Giraut de Borneil. (See the article **Gerardus de Borneil.**)

[2] N. S., vol. vi, pp. 201-17.

CONTENTS

LIST OF ABBREVIATIONS

(WITH PAGE-REFERENCES TO THE OXFORD DANTE,
THIRD EDITION, 1904).

A.T.	*Quaestio de Aqua et Terra* (pp. 423-31).	Inf.	*Inferno* (pp. 1-51).
A.V.	*Authorized Version.*	Mon.	*De Monarchia* (pp. 341-76).
B.	Beatrice (in the *D.C.*).	N.T.	*New Testament.*
Ball.	*Ballata* (see p. 180).	O.T.	*Old Testament.*
Canz.	*Canzone* (see p. 180).	Par.	*Paradiso* (pp. 103-53).
Carm.	*Carmen Latinum* (of Giovanni del Virgilio) (pp. 185-6).	Purg.	*Purgatorio* (pp. 52-102).
		ref.	*reference.*
Cent.	*Century.*	Sest.	*Sestina* (see p. 180).
Conv.	*Convivio* (pp. 237-338).	Son.	*Sonetto* (see p. 181) [1].
D.	Dante.	V.	Virgil (in the *D.C.*).
D.C.	*Divina Commedia* (pp. 1-153).	v.	*verse.*
		V.E.	*De Vulgari Eloquentia* (pp. 379-400).
Ecl.	*Ecloga* (pp. 186-7, 188-90).	V.N.	*Vita Nuova* (pp. 205-33).
Ecl.R.	*Ecloga Responsiva* (of Giovanni del Virgilio) (pp. 187-8).	var.	*variant.*
		Vill.	Giovanni Villani (*Cronica*, 8 vols., Florence, 1823).
edd.	*editors* or *editions.*		
Epist.	*Epistola* (pp. 403-20).	Vulg.	*Vulgate.*

[1] The sonnets of Forese Donati in his *tenzone* with Dante (pp. 179-80) are marked with an asterisk : Son. lii*, liii*, liv*.

EXPLANATION OF SIGNS, &c.

References throughout are to the Oxford edition (1904) of the complete works of Dante.

In order to facilitate reference in the case of the prose works, references (indicated by ' superior ' or index-numbers) are given to the *lines* (numbered separately for each chapter) of the several treatises as printed in the Oxford Dante, as well as to *Book* and *Chapter*; thus Conv. i. 12^{19} = Convivio, *Bk.* i, *Ch.* 12, *l.* 19; Mon. ii. 3^{102} = De Monarchia, *Bk.* ii, *Ch.* 3, *l.* 102; V.N. § 25^{76} = Vita Nuova, *Sect.* 25, *l.* 76; and so on. The index-numbers being disregarded, the references hold equally well for other editions of the several treatises.

Cross-references are indicated by printing the name referred to between square brackets and in black type, e.g. [**Buemme**]. Head-words between square brackets, e.g. [**Belluzzo**], [**Altafronte**], [**Pharos**], [**Thestylis**], are names of persons or places mentioned by Forese Donati and Giovanni del Virgilio in their poetical correspondence with Dante. *A single square bracket after a head-word, e.g. **Fedra**], **Imola**], indicates that the person or place in question is alluded to only, not mentioned by name, in Dante's works. Index-numbers are employed for the purpose of distinguishing between several persons or places of the same name, e.g. **Aceste**[1] (Acestes), **Aceste**[2] (Acaste); **Indo**[1] (Indian), **Indo**[2] (Indus) ; **Reno**[1] (Rhine), **Reno**[2] (river of Italy); **Sesto**[1] (Sestos), **Sesto**[2] (Sextus Pompeius), &c.

A

Abate di San Zeno. [Zeno, San.]

Abati], ancient noble family of Florence, thought by some to be referred to by Cacciaguida (in the Heaven of Mars) as *quei che son disfatti Per lor superbia*, Par. xvi. 109–10; but the reference is more probably to the Uberti [Uberti]. The Abati lived in the Porta san Piero (Vill. v. 39); they were Ghibellines, and were among those who were expelled from Florence in 1258 (vi. 33, 65); they took part in the battle of Montaperti, with which their name is associated through the treachery of Bocca degli Abati (vi. 78) [Bocca]; eventually they sided with the Bianchi (viii. 39).

Abati, Bocca degli. [Bocca.]
Abati, Buoso degli. [Buoso.]
Abati, Ciolo degli. [Ciolus.]

Abbagliato, name applied by the Florentine Capocchio (in Bolgia 10 of Circle VIII of Hell) as a nickname ('muddle-head') to a Sienese spendthrift, who has been identified with one Meo (i.e. Bartolommeo), son of Rainieri de' Folcacchieri of Siena, who held high office in Siena between 1277 and 1300, and who was a member of the 'spendthrift brigade', a company of twelve wealthy young Sienese, who vied with each other in squandering their means, Inf. xxix. 130–2 [Brigata Spendereccia].

Abel, Abel, second son of Adam;

mentioned by Virgil among those released by Christ from Limbo, Inf. iv. 56. [Limbo.]

Abido, Abydos, town in the Troad, on the narrowest part of the Hellespont, nearly opposite to Sestos in Thrace; celebrated as the home of Leander, who used to swim nightly across to Sestos to visit Hero, Purg. xxviii. 74 [Leandro: Sesto [1]]; mentioned in connexion with the bridge of boats built by Xerxes across the Hellespont, *Abydos*, Mon. ii. 9^{53-4} [Ellesponto: Serse].

Abile], Mt. Abyla, in N. Africa, opposite Calpe (Gibraltar); alluded to by Ulysses (in Bolgia 8 of Circle VIII of Hell) as one of the Pillars of Hercules, Inf. xxvi. 108. [Colonne di Ercole.]

Abraam, patriarch Abraham; mentioned by Virgil among those released by Christ from Limbo, Inf. iv. 58. [Limbo.]

Absalone, Absalom, son of David, who, encouraged by the evil counsels of Ahithophel the Gilonite, rebelled against his father, but was defeated in Gilead, in the wood of Ephraim, where he met his death (2 *Sam.* xv–xix); he is mentioned by Bertran de Born (in Bolgia 9 of Circle VIII of Hell), who compares his own instigation of the 'Young King' to rebel against his father, Henry II of England, with the similar part played by Ahithophel in encouraging Absalom to rebel against

David, Inf. xxviii. 136–8. [Arrigo[4].]

Abydos. [Abido.]

Academicae Quaestiones], Academic Questions of Cicero; hence D. got the opinion of Zeno that virtue is the highest good, Conv. iv. 6[84–7] (Acad. Quaest. ii. 22, 42) [Zenone]; and also the account of the Academic and Peripatetic schools of philosophy, Conv. iv. 6[115–47] (Acad. Quaest. i. 4).

Acam. [Acan.]

Acan, Achan, son of Carmi, of the tribe of Judah, 'who took of the accursed thing' in appropriating part of the spoil of Jericho, contrary to the commands of Joshua. After the defeat of the Israelites in their attack upon Ai, A. confessed his guilt, and the booty was discovered. Thereupon he and his whole family were stoned to death by command of Joshua, and their remains and property were burned (Josh. vii). D. includes A. among the instances of avarice proclaimed by the Avaricious in Circle V of Purgatory, Purg. xx. 109–11 [Avari].

Accademia, the Academia, a piece of land on the Cephissus, near Athens, so called from having originally belonged to a hero named Academus. It subsequently became celebrated as the scene of Plato's teaching, whence his followers were called Academic philosophers. D. speaks of it as 'lo luogo dove Platone studiava', in connexion with the origin of the name of his school of philosophy, Conv. iv. 6[125–8]. [Accademici: Platone.]

Accademici, Academic or Platonic school of philosophers, so called

from the Academia at Athens, where Plato and Speusippus used to teach, Conv. iv. 6[125–8] [Accademia]; they were succeeded and superseded by the Peripatetics, Conv. iv. 6[142–5] (cf. Cicero, Acad. Quaest. i. 4) [Peripatetici].

Acciaiuoli, Niccola], Florentine Guelf, who in 1299, together with Baldo d'Aguglione (Par. xvi. 56), in order to destroy the evidence of a fraudulent transaction in which, with the connivance of the Podestà, he had been engaged, defaced a sheet of the public records of Florence. This scandal, which is recorded at length by Dino Compagni (i. 19), took place during the period of corruption and maladministration which followed the expulsion of Giano della Bella from Florence. D. alludes to this tampering with the 'quaderno', Purg. xii. 105 [Aguglione].

Accidiosi], the Slothful, supposed by some, on account of the expression 'accidioso fummo' (Inf. vii. 123), to be included with the Wrathful (and perhaps also the Envious) in Circle V of Hell [Invidiosi: Iracondi].

Those who expiate the sin of Sloth (accidia) in Purgatory are placed in Circle IV, Purg. xvii. 46–xix. 43 [Beatitudini: Purgatorio]; their punishment is to be obliged to run continually round and round, urging each other to greater exertion with the cry 'Ratto, ratto, che il tempo non si perda Per poco amore', Purg. xviii. 94–104; those in front recall instances of alacrity, viz. how the Virgin Mary hastened to salute Elisabeth (Luke i. 39), and how

Julius Caesar hastened to subdue Lerida (*vv.* 99–102) [Maria[1]: Cesare[1]]; those behind recall instances of sloth, viz. how the children of Israel lost the promised land, and how some of the companions of Aeneas remained behind in Sicily (*vv.* 131–8) [Ebrei: Aceste[1]]. *Example*: an Abbot of San Zeno at Verona [Zeno, San].

Accorso, Francesco d', son of the famous Florentine jurist, Accorso da Bagnola (commonly known by the Latin name of Accursius), who lectured in the university of Bologna, where he died in 1260; the son, who was born at Bologna in 1225, was himself a celebrated lawyer; he was professor of civil law at Bologna, and in 1273, when Edward I passed through that city on his way back from Palestine, decided, upon the invitation of the latter, to accompany him to England, where he lectured for some time at Oxford; he returned to Bologna in 1281, where he died in 1293.

D. places Francesco d'Accorso, together with Priscian and Brunetto Latini, among the Sodomites in Round 3 of Circle VII of Hell, Inf. xv. 110 [Sodomiti].

Aceste[1], Acestes, Trojan born in Sicily; D. refers to the account given by Virgil (*Aen.* v. 711–18) of how Aeneas on his arrival in Sicily was hospitably entertained by Acestes, with whom he left those of his companions who were unfit to proceed with him to Italy, Conv. iv. 26[92–6]; these latter are mentioned as instances of sluggards by the Slothful in Circle IV of Purgatory, Purg. xviii. 136–8. [Accidiosi.]

Aceste[2], Acaste, nurse of Argia and Deiphyle, the two daughters of Adrastus, King of Argos; mentioned with reference to the account given by Statius in the *Thebaid* (i. 529 ff.) of how she brought the two maidens into the presence of their father when Polynices and Tydeus were with him, Conv. iv. 25[78–84]. [Adrasto.]

Achaemenides, companion of Ulysses, who left him behind in Sicily, when he escaped from the Cyclops. When subsequently the Trojans landed in the island, they found Achaemenides there, and heard from him how his companions had been devoured by Polyphemus. D. refers to this episode (his account of which is derived either from Virgil, *Aen.* iii. 588–691; or from Ovid, *Metam.* xiv. 160–222), Ecl. ii. 82–3. [Polyphemus.]

Acheronte, Acheron, one of the rivers of Hell, which forms the boundary of Hell proper, Inf. iii. 78; xiv. 116; Purg. ii. 105; *gran fiume*, Inf. iii. 71; *trista riviera*, *v.* 78; *fiume*, *v.* 81; *livida palude*, *v.* 98; *onda bruna*, *v.* 118; *mal fiume*, Purg. i. 88; on its shore assemble from every land all those who have died in the wrath of God, Inf. iii. 122–3; Purg. i. 88; ii. 105; here they wait to be ferried across by Charon, Inf. iii. 70–120 [Caron: Inferno]; its origin, and that of the other rivers of Hell, is explained to D. by Virgil, Inf. xiv. 112–19 [Fiumi Infernali].

Achille, Achilles, son of Peleus and Thetis, the foremost hero of the Greeks in the Trojan war. In his youth he was instructed by Chiron the Centaur, from whose charge he was withdrawn by his mother, who placed him in hiding in the island of Scyros, to prevent his going to the Trojan war. While there he became enamoured of Deidamia, daughter of Lycomedes, King of Scyros, but at the instance of Ulysses, who discovered his hiding-place, he deserted her and accompanied him to the war. The spear of Achilles possessed the property of healing the wounds inflicted by it. At the first landing of the Greeks in the Troad, Telephus, son of Hercules, the King of Mysia, was wounded by A.; as the wound did not heal he sought the oracle, and was told that it could only be cured by him who inflicted it : he accordingly sought A., who applied some of the rust of his spear to the wound and healed it.

D. places A., ' il grande Achille ' (cf. Purg. xxi. 92), in Circle II of Hell, among those who met their death through love, and says of him, in allusion to the mediaeval tradition as to his death, ' con amore al fine combatteo,' i.e. he fought with love at the last, Inf. v. 65–6 [Lussuriosi] ; he is mentioned in connexion with his bringing up by Chiron, Inf. xii. 71 [Chirone]; his desertion of Deidamia, Inf. xxvi. 62 [Deidamia]; the healing property of his spear, Inf. xxxi. 5 [Peleus]; his conveyance to Scyros by his mother, Purg. ix. 34 [Schiro]; the (unfinished) poem of Statius (the Achilleid) on the subject of his heroic achievements, Purg. xxi. 92 [Achilleide]; his descent from Aeacus, Conv. iv. 27[192–5] [Eaco].

According to the Homeric story A. was killed before Troy, after having slain Hector. D. follows (Inf. v. 65–6) the later account, current in the Middle Ages, according to which A. was killed by treachery by Paris in the temple of Apollo Thymbraeus in Troy, whither he had been lured by the promise of a meeting with Polyxena, of whom he was enamoured, and who had been offered him in marriage if he would join the Trojans (cf. Servius on Aen. iii. 85, 332).

Achilleide], Achilleid, poem in hexameters on the subject of Achilles and the Trojan war, commenced by Statius, the author of the Thebaid, but left incomplete at his death, only one book and a portion of the second having been written. Statius (in Purgatory) alludes to it, in addressing Virgil, as la seconda somma, 'the second burden', under which he fell by the way, Purg. xxi. 92–3 [Stazio]. D. was indebted to it for the incident of Ulysses' persuasion of Achilles to desert Deidamia, Inf. xxvi. 61–2 (Achill. i. 536 ff.; ii. 1 ff.) [Deidamia : Ulisse]; and for that of Achilles awaking in Scyros, Purg. ix. 34–9 (Achill. i. 198 ff.) [Schiro] ; as well as for certain details in his invocation to Apollo, and his reference to the laurel as the reward of poets and warriors, Par. i. 13 ff., 25–6 (Achill. i. 9–16).

[Achilleus], of Achilles ; Achilleus Chiron (i.e. Chiron who brought up A.), Ecl. R. 79 [Chirone].

Achitofel, Ahithophel the Gilonite, who encouraged Absalom in his rebellion against his father David (2 Sam. xv–xvii) ; he is mentioned by Bertran de Born (in Bolgia 9 of

Circle VIII of Hell), who compares his own evil-doing in stirring up the 'Young King' to rebel against his father Henry II with that of A. in inciting Absalom to rebel against David, Inf. xxviii. 136–8 [Absalone: Bertram dal Bornio].

Acis, shepherd of Sicily, son of Faunus, who was beloved by the nymph Galatea, and was consequently crushed beneath a rock by the Cyclops Polyphemus, who was jealous of him; his blood as it gushed from under the rock was changed by Galatea into the river Acis. The story (which D. got from Ovid, *Metam.* xiii. 860–97) is referred to, Ecl. ii. 78–80. [Galatea: Polyphemus.]

Acone[1], village in Tuscany, in the neighbourhood of Florence, in the Valdisieve, one of the valleys opening out of the upper end of the Valdarno.

Cacciaguida (in the Heaven of Mars) laments that the feud between the Church and the Emperor, among other consequences, brought the Cerchi, the leaders of the Bianchi, from their original home at Acone to settle in Florence, Par. xvi. 65. [Cerchi.]

Acone[2]], Hakon V (VII), King of Norway, 1299–1319; alluded to (probably) by the Eagle in the Heaven of Jupiter as *quel di Norvegia*, Par. xix. 139. [Aquila[2]: Norvegia: Table N.]

Acquacheta ('Still-water'), the name, according to D., of the river Montone ('Ram'), above Forlì, Inf. xvi. 97. D. compares the descent of the infernal river, Phlegethon, to the falls of the Montone near the monastery of San Benedetto in Alpe (*vv.* 94–105); he speaks of the Montone as the first river which, rising on the N. side of the Apennines, flows direct into the Adriatic without entering the Po (*vv.* 94–6) —a description which is no longer true of the Montone, but applies at the present day to the Lamone, which falls into the Adriatic N. of Ravenna [Lamone: Monte Veso].

The Montone rises as a torrent in the district of the Etruscan Apennines known as Muraglione, about six miles from the monastery of San Benedetto; close to the latter it is joined by the torrents of the Acquacheta and Riodestro, and later on, a few miles above Forlì, it receives the waters of the Rabbi; finally at Ravenna it joins the Ronco, and the two, forming one stream under the name of the Fiumi Uniti, enter the Adriatic between Ravenna and S. Apollinare. D. implies that the river was known as the Acquacheta as far as Forlì, and only received the name of Montone on reaching that city. In the present day, at any rate, this is not the case, the name of Montone being applied to it as high up as San Benedetto.

Acquaqueta. [Acquacheta.]

Acquasparta, village in Umbria, about ten miles SW. of Spoleto, at the head of a torrent of the same name, which flows into the Tiber not far from Todi; mentioned by St. Bonaventura (in the Heaven of the Sun), together with Casale (in allusion to Matteo d'Acquasparta and Ubertino da Casale, the leaders of the two sects which arose within the

Franciscan Order soon after the death of St. Francis), Par. xii. 124. [Matteo d' Acquasparta : Ubertino da Casale.]

Acri, Acre, commonly called St. Jean d'Acre by Europeans, town and seaport of Syria, situated on a low promontory at the N. extremity of the Bay of Acre. After having been in the possession of the Saracens since the middle of Cent. vii, Acre was taken by the Crusaders in 1104, who retained it until 1187, when it was recovered by Saladin. In 1191 it was retaken by Richard Cœur-de-Lion and Philip of France, who gave the town to the knights of St. John of Jerusalem, whence it received the name of St. Jean d'Acre. It remained in the possession of the Christians until 1291, when it was besieged with a great host by the Sultan, and carried by assault, 60,000 of the inhabitants being taken prisoners, and either put to the sword or sold into slavery. With this great disaster, by which the last of the Christian possessions in the Holy Land passed back into the hands of the Saracens, the Latin kingdom of Jerusalem came to an end.

The loss of Acre is referred to by Guido da Montefeltro (in Bolgia 8 of Circle VIII of Hell), who reproaches Boniface VIII with carrying on war at home with Christians (meaning the Colonnesi), instead of devoting his resources to the recovery of Acre and the chastisement of the Saracens, Inf. xxvii. 85-9. [Colonnesi : Laterano.]

Actus Apostolorum, Acts of the Apostles, Mon. ii. 8[70] (ref. to *Acts* i. 26); Mon. iii. 13[42-3]; quoted, Conv. iv. 20[28-9] (*Acts* x. 34); Mon. iii. 9[137-9] (*Acts* i. 1); Mon. iii. 13[43-53] (*Acts* xxv. 10; xxvii. 24; xxviii. 19); Epist. v. 4[68] (*Acts* ix. 5).—The book of the Acts of the Apostles is supposed to be symbolized by the elder habited like a physician (in allusion to the description of the author as ' Luke, the beloved physician', *Coloss.* iv. 14) in the mystical Procession in the Terrestrial Paradise, Purg. xxix. 134-8, 145-8.

Adalagia], Alazais (Adelais), wife of Barral, lord of Marseilles, of whom the troubadour Folquet of Marseilles was enamoured ; his love for her is hinted at, Par. ix. 96-9. [Folco.]

Adam. [Adamo.]

Adamo, Adam, the first man, Inf. iii. 115 ; Purg. ix. 10; xi. 44; xxix. 86; xxxii. 37; Conv. iv. 15[28, 32, 68, 70]; *Adam*, Mon. ii.13[2, 6]; V. E. i. 4[24], 6[10, 17, 49]; *il primo parente*, Inf. iv. 55 ; Conv. iv. 15[27]; *il primo generante*, Conv. iv. 15[28]; *radix humanae propaginis*, V.E. i. 8[6]; *l'anima prima*, Purg.xxxiii.62; Par. xxvi. 83 ; V. E. i. 6[41]; *l'anima primaia*, Par. xxvi. 100; *l'uom che non nacque*, Par. vii. 26; *seme dell' umana natura*, Par. vii. 86; *il petto onde la costa Si trasse per formar la bella guancia*, *Il cui palato a tutto il mondo costa*, Par. xiii. 37-9; *la terra degna Di tutta l' animal perfezione*, Par. xiii. 82-3 ; *il primo padre*, Par. xiii. 111 ; *pomo che maturo Solo prodotto fosti*, Par. xxvi. 91-2 ; *padre antico*, Par. xxvi. 92 ; *il padre per lo cui ardito gusto L'umana specie tanto amaro gusta*, Par. xxxii. 122-3 ; *il maggior padre di famiglia*, Par. xxxii. 136; *il primo uomo*, Conv. iv. 5[19];

primus homo, V.E. i. 5³⁻⁴, ¹²; *primus loquens*, V. E. i. 5²⁷, 6⁶⁰; *vir sine matre, vir sine lacte, qui neque pupillarem aetatem nec vidit adultam*, V. E. i. 6⁵⁻⁷; Adam and Eve, *la prima gente*, Purg. i. 24; *l' umana radice*, Purg. xxviii. 142 ; *li primi parenti*, Par. vii. 148; *primi parentes*, Mon. i. 16⁷; Adam and St. Peter, *due radici* (of the Celestial Rose), Par. xxxii. 120.

Il mal seme d' Adamo, i.e. the damned, Inf.iii. 115 ; *quel d'Adamo*, i.e. human nature, Purg. ix. 10 (so *la carne d'Adamo*, Purg. xi. 44); *le figlie d' Adamo*, i.e. womankind, Purg. xxix. 86 ; *figli d'Adamo, figliuoli d' Adamo*, i.e. mankind, Conv. iv. 15⁶⁸⁻⁷⁰ ; *filii Adam*, V. E. i. 6¹⁰.

Adam created as a full-grown man, Par. vii. 26 ; xxvi. 91–2 ; V. E. i. 6⁵⁻⁷; the most perfect of living things, Par. xiii. 82–3 ; V. E. i. 5¹⁴; the father of the human race, Inf. iii. 115 ; iv. 55 ; Purg. ix. 10 ; xi. 44 ; xxix. 86 ; Par. vii. 86, 148; xiii. 111 ; xxvi. 92 ; xxxii. 122, 136 ; Mon. i. 16⁷; his and Eve's eating of the forbidden fruit the cause of all the woes of mankind, Par. xiii. 37–9 ; xxxii. 122–3.

Adam is mentioned by Virgil among those released by Christ from Limbo, Inf. iv. 55 [Limbo]; his name is murmured by those who accompany the mystical Procession in the Terrestrial Paradise in token of their reprobation of his sin of disobedience, Purg. xxxii. 37 ; D. sees his spirit in the Heaven of the Fixed Stars, *quarto lume* (the other three being those of the three Apostles, St. Peter, St. James, and St. John), and converses with him, Par. xxvi.

81–142 ; he informs D. that he was expelled from Paradise for disobedience and pride (*vv.* 97–117); that the Creation took place 5232 (i.e. 4302 + 930) years before the Crucifixion (hence 6498, i.e. 5232 + 1300–34, years before the date of the Vision) (*vv.* 118–20) ; that he lived 930 years upon earth (*Gen.* v. 5) (*vv.* 121–3); that the language he spoke was extinct before the building of the Tower of Babel (*vv.* 124–6) ; that before his death God was called *I* upon earth, but that afterwards man changed the name to *El* (*vv.* 133–8) [El]; lastly, that he abode in Paradise rather more than six hours (*vv.* 139–42); his place in the Celestial Rose, where he is seated on the left hand of the Virgin Mary, as being the first to believe in Christ to come, while St. Peter, the first to believe in Christ come, is seated on her right, is pointed out to D. by St. Bernard, Par. xxxii. 121–6 [Rosa].

In discussing the nature of nobility D. argues that, if it is merely hereditary, then, if Adam was noble, all mankind must be noble, and, if Adam was vile, then all mankind must be vile, Conv. iv. 15¹⁹⁻³⁴ ; Solomon's description (*Eccles*. iii. 21) of mankind, as distinct from beasts, as the sons of Adam, Conv. iv. 15⁶⁵⁻⁷¹ ; the sin of Adam not punished in Christ if the Roman Empire did not exist of right, Mon. ii. 13¹⁻³ ; all mankind sinners through his sin, Mon. i. 16⁶⁻⁸ ; ii. 13⁶⁻⁷ ; Adam the first being endowed with speech, V. E. i. 4²⁴⁻⁶ ; his first utterance addressed to God, V. E. i. 5³⁻⁴ ; the absurd pretensions of those who claim that their mother-tongue was the language spoken by Adam, V. E. i. 6[11]–[17] ; the language spoken by him Hebrew, which survived the confusion of tongues at the building of the Tower of Babel, V. E. i. 6[49]–[61] (an opinion which D. retracts, Par. xxvi. 124–6). [Heber.]

Adamo, Maestro, Master Adam of Brescia, famous coiner, who, at the instigation of the Conti Guidi of Romena, counterfeited the gold florin of Florence, in consequence of which the Florentines caused him to be burned alive (in 1281) at Consuma, on the road between Florence and Romena, in the Casentino.

D. places Maestro Adamo among the Falsifiers in Bolgia 10 of Circle VIII of Hell (Malebolge), Inf. xxx. 61 ; *mastro A., v.* 104 ; *un fatto a guisa di liuto, v.* 49; *l' idropico, v.* 112 ; *quel ch' avea enfiata l'epa, v.* 119; *il monetier, v.* 124 [Falsatori].

Adice, Adige, river of Upper Italy, which rises in the Tyrolese Alps and flows S. through the Tyrol past Trent and Roveredo ; entering Italy it turns SE. towards Verona, which it encloses in a loop, and subsequently flows E. into the Adriatic a few miles below Chioggia.

D. mentions it in connexion with the deflection of its course by a great landslip in the neighbourhood of Trent, Inf. xii. 4–5 [Trento]; the March of Treviso, with Lombardy and Romagna, is described by Marco Lombardo (in Circle III of Purgatory) as *il paese ch' Adice e Po riga*, Purg. xvi. 115 [Marca Trivisiana]; Cunizza (in the Heaven of Venus) refers to the inhabitants of the greater part of the modern province of Venetia, including the towns of Vicenza, Padua, Treviso, Feltro, Belluno (and perhaps Verona and Venice), as *la turba . . . Che Tagliamento ed Adice richiude*, Par. ix. 43–4 [Tagliamento].

Adimari], powerful Florentine family, of which the Aldobrandi (Inf. xvi. 41), Argenti (Inf. viii. 61), and Cavicciuli (Inf. xix. 19), were branches ; they lived in the Porta san Piero and were Guelfs (Vill. iv. 11 ; v. 39) ; after the Ghibelline victory at Montaperti in 1260 they fled from Florence with the rest of their party (vi. 79), and subsequently, when the Guelfs in Florence split up into Bianchi and Neri, they joined the former, with the exception of the Cavicciuli branch, who sided with the Neri (viii. 39). Though actually of ancient stock, they were regarded by D. and his contemporaries (Vill. iv. 11) as of recent origin ; hence Cacciaguida (in the Heaven of Mars), who refers to them as *l' oltracotata schiatta*, Par. xvi. 115, speaks of them as derived from *picciola gente*, and says that in consequence Ubertin Donato, who had married a daughter of Bellincion Berti, was not well pleased when the latter married another daughter to one of the Adimari (*vv.* 118–20) [Bellincion Berti : Donato, Ubertin].

Adoardo. [Edoardo.]

Adolfo, Adolf of Nassau, Emperor (but never crowned) from 1292 to 1298, in which year he was defeated and slain in a battle near Worms by his successor, Albert I. [Alberto Tedesco.] D. mentions him, together with Albert, and his predecessor Rudolf, among the successors

of Frederick II, Conv. iv. 3$^{41-2}$.
[**Federigo**^{2} : **Ridolfo**^{1} : **Table Q.**]

Adrasto, Adrastus, King of
Argos, father of Argia and Deiphyle, whom he respectively married
to Polynices of Thebes, and Tydeus
of Calydon, each of them a fugitive
from his native country. His attempt to restore Polynices to the
throne of Thebes, which had been
usurped by his brother Eteocles, led
to the celebrated war of the Seven
against Thebes, Adrastus, Polynices,
and Tydeus being joined by four
other heroes, Amphiaräus, Capaneus,
Hippomedon, and Parthenopaeus.
D. mentions A., in illustration of
his definitions of 'stupore', 'pudore',
and 'verecundia', in connexion with
three incidents related by Statius in
the *Thebaid* (i. 482 ff., 529 ff., 680
ff.), Conv. iv. 25$^{60-4, 78-88, 107-16}$.

Adria, Adriatic sea; Ravenna
referred to by Tityrus (i.e. D.) as
being in the Emilia on the shores of
the Adriatic, Ecl. ii. 68. [**Mare
Adriano.**]

[**Adriacus**], Adriatic; *litus Adriacum*, shores of the Adriatic, Ecl. R.
11. [**Mare Adriano.**]

Adriano^1, Adriatic; *il lito Adriano*, i.e. the shores of the Adriatic, the
reference being to the situation of the
monastery of Sta. Maria in Porto
fuori at Ravenna, or, perhaps to that
of Sta. Maria in Pomposa near Comacchio, Par. xxi. 122 [**Damiano,
Pier**]; *il mare Adriano*, i.e. the Adriatic sea, Conv. iv. 13^{121}. [**Mare
Adriano.**]

Adriano^2], Adrian V (Ottobuono
de' Fieschi of Genoa), elected Pope
at Rome, in succession to Innocent
V, July 11, 1276; died at Viterbo

on Aug. 16 following, before he had
been crowned. D. places him among
the Avaricious in Circle V of Purgatory, alluding to him as *successor
Petri*, Purg. xix. 99; *l' altro na-
scosto, v.* 84; *quella creatura, v.* 89;
Roman Pastore, v. 107 [**Avari**].

Adrianus, Pope Adrian I (772–
795); mentioned by D. (who erroneously states that Charlemagne was
crowned Emperor by him), in reference to the fact that it was at his invitation that the King of the Franks
attacked and crushed the Lombards
under Desiderius, and thus saved the
Church from destruction, Mon. iii.
11$^{1-5}$ [**Carlo Magno: Desiderio**].

Adriaticum Mare. [**Mare Ad·
riano**.]

Adulatori], Flatterers, placed
among the Fraudulent in Bolgia 2 of
Circle VIII of Hell (Malebolge),
Inf. xviii. 100–36 [**Frodolenti**];
their punishment is to be plunged up
to the lips in filthy excrement, while
they beat their heads with their fists,
vv. 104–8, 112–14, 124. *Examples*:
Alessio Interminei of Lucca [**Ales·
sio Interminei**]; the harlot Thaïs
[**Taide**].

Aeacidae, descendants of Aeacus,
King of Aegina; Pyrrhus, King of
Epirus (who claimed the title of Aea-
cides as being descended from Achilles, grandson of Aeacus), described
by D. as 'tam moribus Aeacidarum,
quam sanguine generosus', Mon. ii.
10$^{57-8}$. [**Eaco: Pirro**^{2}.]

Aegyptii, Egyptians; do not concern themselves with the political
system of the Scythians, Mon. iii.
3$^{12-15}$ (from *Ethics* iii. 3, D. having
by a slip substituted *Egyptians* for
Spartans); as oppressors of the Israel-

ites they typify the opponents of the Emperor Henry VII, Epist. v. i[20].

Aegyptius. [**Aegyptii.**]

Aegyptus. [**Egitto.**]

Aemilis Terra, Emilia,province of N. Italy, corresponding roughly (as regards its present boundaries) with the old province of Romagna ; mentioned by Tityrus (i. e. D.) in connexion with the situation of Ravenna on the Adriatic coast, Ecl. ii. 68. [**Ravenna : Romagna.**]

Aeneas. [**Enea.**]

Aeneis, *Aeneid* of Virgil, epic poem in twelve books, containing an account of the fortunes of Aeneas after the fall of Troy, and of his wanderings until he settled in Italy ; quoted as *Aeneis*, Mon. ii. 3[29], 11[15] ; V. E. ii. 4[7], 8[22] ; *Eneida*, Purg. xxi. 97 ; V. N. § 25[76,83] ; Conv. i. 3[75] ; ii. 6[120] ; iii. 11[159] ; iv. 4[115], 24[96], 26[61, 64, 70] ; D. speaking to Virgil calls it *il tuo volume*, Inf. i. 84 ; V. himself calls it *la mia rima*, Inf. xiii. 48 ; *l' alta miaTragedia*, Inf. xx. 113; *gli alti versi*, Inf. xxvi. 82 ; Statius calls it *la divina fiamma Onde sono allumati più di mille*, Purg. xxi. 95–6; and says of it, *mamma Fummi, e fummi nutrice poetando, vv.* 97–8.

D., whose works are full of echoes, conscious or unconscious, of the *Aeneid*, quotes from or refers to it directly upwards of forty times :—Inf. xx. 112–3 (*Aen.* ii. 114); Purg. xxii. 40–1 (*Aen.* iii. 56–7); Purg. xxx. 21 (*Aen.* vi. 884); Purg. xxx. 48 (*Aen.* iv. 23); V. N. § 25[76–84] (*Aen.* i. 65, 76–7; iii. 94); Conv. i. 3[76–7] (*Aen.* iv. 174–5); Conv. ii. 6[121–3] (*Aen.* i. 664–5); Conv. iii. 11[159–60] (*Aen.* ii. 281); Conv. iv. 4[117–19] (*Aen.* i. 278–9); Conv. iv. 26[60–141]

(*Aen.* iv, v, vi ; iv. 272–82 ; vi. 98 ff. ; v. 715–18; v. 545 ff. ; vi. 162 –84 ; v. 45 ff.) ; V. E. ii. 4[73–5] (*Aen.* vi. 129–31); V. E. ii. 8[23] (*Aen.* i. 1) ; Mon. ii. 3[46–115] (*Aen.* i. 342 ; i. 544–5 ; vi. 166–70; iii. 1–2; viii. 134–7 ; iii. 163–7 ; iii. 339–40 ; iv. 171–2 ; xii. 936–7); Mon. ii. 4[58–7] (*Aen.* viii. 652–6); Mon. ii. 5[97–120] (*Aen.* vi. 844–5 ; vi. 826; vi. 821–2); Mon. ii. 7[71–85] (*Aen.* vi. 848–54; iv. 227–30); Mon. ii. 8[92–4] (*Aen.* v. 337–8); Mon. ii. 9[84–6] (*Aen.* i. 234–6); Mon. ii. 11[8–21] (*Aen.* xii. 697–765 ; xii. 938–52); Epist. vi. 5[130] (*Aen.* ii. 353); Epist. vii. 3[62–3] (*Aen.* i. 286–7); Epist. vii. 4[88–92] (*Aen.* iv. 272–6).

Aeolus. [**Eolo.**]

Aetna, Mt. Aetna, volcano in E. extremity of Sicily, due N. of Catania ; name under which Bologna is figured in D.'s correspondence with G. del Virgilio, Ecl. ii. 27; referred to as *Aetnaeum litus, v.* 69 ; *Trinacriae mons, v.* 71 ; *Aetnica saxa, v.* 74 ; its position near the Gulf of Catania, which it at times overshadows with a thick pall of smoke, Par. viii. 67–70 [**Catania**]; the smoke from its crater caused, not by the buried monster Typhoeus, but by sulphur, Par. viii. 70 [**Tifeo**]; *Mongibello*, Inf. xiv. 56 (where D. alludes to the ancient belief that in the interior of Mt. Aetna Vulcan and the Cyclopes had their forge, where they made the thunderbolts of Jove) [**Mongibello**].

Aetnaeus, Aetnicus. [**Aetna.**]

Affrica, Africa; the scene of the combat between Hercules and Antaeus, Conv. iii. 3[64–5] [**Anteo**]; Hannibal's despatch to Carthage of the rings taken from the Romans slain at Cannae, Conv. iv. 5$^{166-8}$ [**Canne**]; the African campaign of Scipio Africanus Major, Conv. iv. 5$^{169-71}$ [**Scipione**^{1}]; the continent to which belonged Electra, ancestress of Aeneas, and Dido, his second wife, Mon. ii. 3$^{68-77,\ 102-3}$ [**Enea**]; Atlas, the ancestor of Aeneas, of African origin, Mon. ii. 3^{85} [**Atlas**^{1}]; Mt. Atlas in Africa, as testified by Orosius, Mon. ii. 3$^{85-91}$ [**Atlas**^{2}]; the scene of Julius Caesar's victory (at Thapsus), and Cato's death (at Utica), Mon. ii. 5$^{159-70}$ [**Cesare**^{1}: **Catone**]; alluded to as, *le arene*, Purg. xxvi. 44; *la terra che perde ombra* (since in the torrid zone when the Sun is vertically overhead there is no shadow), Purg. xxx. 89; *la terra di Iarba*, Purg. xxxi. 72 [**Iarba**].

Affricani. [**Africani.**]
Affricano. [**Scipione**^{1}.]
Aforismi, *Aphorisms* of Hippocrates, one of the chief medical authorities in the Middle Ages; mentioned, Par. xi. 4; coupled with the *Tegni* of Galen as inappropriate gifts from a physician to a knight, Conv. i. 8$^{31-3}$. [**Ippocrate: Galieno: Taddeo.**]

Afri, Africans, i.e. Carthaginians, their defeat by the Romans, Mon. ii. 11^{61}. [**Cartaginesi.**]
Africa. [**Affrica.**]
Africani, Africans; do not admit the claim of the Church to bestow the Imperial authority, Mon. iii. 14^{59}; i.e. Carthaginians, commanded by Hannibal in their war with the Romans, Mon. ii. 11$^{59-60}$. [**Afri: Cartaginesi.**]

Agábito, Agapetus I, Pope 535–536; mentioned by the Emperor Justinian (in the Heaven of Mercury) as having convinced him of the error of his heretical belief as to there being but one nature in Christ, Par. vi. 14–18 [**Giustiniano**].

Agag, King of the Amalekites, who was spared by Saul contrary to God's command, and afterwards slain by Samuel (1 *Sam.* xv); mentioned as type of the opponents of the Emperor Henry VII in Italy, whom D. urges the latter to destroy as Samuel destroyed Agag, Epist. vii. 5$^{108-12}$ (where D. refers to the supposed meaning of the name, 'festina sollemnitas,' given in the *Explanatio Nominum* in many MSS. of the Vulgate). [**Amalech.**]

Agamemnone], Agamemnon, son of Atreus, and brother of Menelaüs, the leader of the Greeks in the Trojan war; alluded to by Beatrice (in the Heaven of the Moon), in connexion with the sacrifice of Iphigenia, as *lo gran duca dei Greci*, Par. v. 69. [**Ifigenia.**]

Agápito. [**Agábito.**]
Agathon. [**Agatone.**]
Agatone, Agathon, Greek tragic poet, a pupil of Socrates, and friend of Euripides and Plato, born at Athens c. B.C. 448, died c. 400; a tragedy of his is mentioned by Aristotle in the *Poetics*, but none of his works have come down to us.

A. is mentioned by Virgil as being among the Greek poets who are with Homer and himself in Limbo, Purg. xxii. 107 [**Limbo**]; his saying (taken from *Ethics* vi. 2.) that God cannot cause what is, not to have been, *Agathon*, Mon. iii. 6$^{50-3}$.

Aggregazione delle Stelle, Libro dell', the alternative title (*Liber de*

Aggregatione Scientiae Stellarum) of the *Elementa Astronomica* of Alfraganus ; quoted to prove that the motions of the Heaven of Venus are threefold, Conv. ii. 6$^{133-6}$. [**Alfergano : Venere, Cielo di.**]

Aghinolfo da Romena], one of the Conti Guidi who persuaded Maestro Adamo of Brescia to counterfeit the Florentine gold florin ; referred to by Adamo as brother of Guido and Alessandro da Romena, Inf. xxx. 77 ; one of them (Guido, who died before 1292), he says, is already in Hell (*v.* 79) [**Adamo, Maestro**]. This Aghinolfo (who died after 1338) was the father of Uberto and Guido da Romena, to whom D. addressed one of his letters (Epist. ii.) [**Guidi, Conti**].

Aglauro, Aglauros, daughter of Cecrops, King of Athens, who was changed into a stone by Mercury, because she in jealousy tried to prevent him from visiting her sister Herse, whom he loved. D. (who got her story from Ovid, *Metam.* ii. 737–832) introduces her as an instance of envy in Circle II of Purgatory, where her voice is heard proclaiming, ʻ I am Aglauros who was turned into stone,ʼ Purg. xiv. 139 [**Invidiosi**].

Agli, Lotto degli], Florentine judge (one of the Guelf sureties in the peace concluded by Cardinal Latino in 1280, Prior in 1285, and Podestà of Trent in 1287), who after delivering an unjust judgement went home and hanged himself. Lotto (who was still living in 1297) is supposed by some to be the individual placed among the Suicides in Round 2 of Circle VII of Hell,

Inf. xiii. 123–xiv. 3 ; *cespuglio*, xiii. 123, 131 ; *quegli, v.* 139; *colui,* xiv. 3. [**Suicidi.**]

Others think the person intended was one Rocco deʼ Mozzi, who hanged himself in despair at finding himself bankrupt.

Agnèl, Agnello, one of five Florentines (Inf. xxvi. 4–5) placed by D. among the Thieves in Bolgia 7 of Circle VIII of Hell (Malebolge), Inf. xxv. 68 ; *uno (spirito), v.* 51 ; he is one of three spirits seen by D. to undergo transformation, he being blended in form with a serpent (*vv.* 49–78). [**Ladri.**]

Agobbio, Gubbio, town of Central Italy on the slopes of the Apennines in N. of Umbria ; mentioned in connexion with Oderisi, the illuminator, whom D. calls *lʼonor dʼ Agobbio,* Purg. xi. 80. [**Oderisi.**]

Agostino[1], Augustine, one of the earliest followers of St. Francis of Assisi, whom he joined in 1210, and eventually (in 1216) head of the Franciscan Order in Terra di Lavoro ; placed by D., together with Illuminato of Rieti, among the Spirits who loved wisdom (*Spiriti Sapienti*) in the Heaven of the Sun, where they are named to him by St. Bonaventura, Par. xii. 130–2 [**Sole, Cielo del**].

Agostino[2], St. Augustine (Aurelius Augustinus), Father of the Latin Church, born at Tagaste in Numidia, Nov. 13, 354; died at Hippo, during the siege of the town by the Vandals, Aug. 28, 430. His father was a pagan, but he was brought up by his mother in the Christian faith; as he grew up, however, he fell away from his motherʼs influence, and led a dissolute life, but was devoted at the same time to his studies. After studying at Carthage, where for a time he joined the Manichaeans, he went to Rome, whence he was invited to Milan, in his thirtieth year, as teacher of rhetoric. Here he came under the influence of St. Ambrose, Bishop of Milan, and in 386 was converted and baptized. After paying a second visit to Rome, he went to Hippo, where he was ordained presbyter, and finally became Bishop in 396; here he died thirty-four years later at the age of seventy-six. St. A.'s two most famous books are his *Confessions*, written shortly after he became bishop, in which he gives a vivid sketch of his early career, and the *City of God*, an apologetic treatise in vindication of Christianity and the Christian Church.

St. A. is mentioned by St. Thomas Aquinas in the Heaven of the Sun in connexion with Orosius, of whose *Historiae adversum Paganos* he is said to have availed himself in the *De Civitate Dei*, Par. x. 120 [**Orosio**]; his place in the Celestial Rose is pointed out to D. by St. Bernard, Par. xxii. 35 [**Rosa**]; his *Confessions* the kind of work in which it is allowable for the author to speak of himself, Conv. i. 2[101—5] [*Confessioni*]; his saying that 'no man is without stain', Conv. i. 4[67—8] (*Conf.* i. 7); his contention that if men comprehended and practised equity there would be no need of the written law, Conv. iv. 9[82—6]; his advice that men should acquire the habit of self-control, Conv. iv. 21[126—8]; a man may lead a religious life without

assuming the habit of St. Benedict, or St. Augustine, or St. Francis, or St. Dominic, Conv. iv. 28[68—74]; his writings undoubtedly inspired, *Augustinus*, Mon. iii. 3[87—91]; his *De Civitate Dei* and *De Doctrina Christiana* quoted, Mon. iii. 4[51—72] [*Civitate Dei, De: Doctrina Christiana, De*]; his works and those of the other Fathers neglected for those of the Decretalists, Epist. viii. 7[116] [**Decretalistae**]; his treatise *De Quantitate Animae*, Epist. x. 28[556] [*Quantitate Animae, De*]. Some think St. Augustine is alluded to as one of 'the four in humble guise' in the mystical Procession in the Terrestrial Paradise (the other three being St. Ambrose, St. Gregory, and St. Jerome), Purg. xxix. 142.

Agosto[1]. [**Augusto**.]

Agosto[2], month of August; mentioned in connexion with the prevalence of 'vapori accesi' (i.e. meteors and summer lightning) in the twilight of summer evenings, Purg. v. 37—9; *mezzo agosto*, Son. lii. 5; referred to as the period *tra il luglio e il settembre*, in connexion with the crowded state of the hospitals of Valdichiana at that time of year, owing to the malaria generated by its swamps, Inf. xxix. 47 [**Chiana**].

Agubbio. [**Agobbio.**]

Aguglione, castle (now destroyed) formerly called Aquilone, in the Florentine territory in the Val di Pesa to the S. of the city; Cacciaguida (in the Heaven of Mars) laments that owing to the extension of its boundaries Florence has 'to endure the stink' of *il villan d'Aguglion*, i.e. according to the most general interpretation Baldo d'Aguglione, Par. xvi. 56.

Baldo d'Aguglione was one of those who drew up the *Ordinamenti di Giustizia* in Florence in 1293 [**Giano della Bella**]. His family were Ghibellines, and as such were exiled from Florence in 1268. Baldo himself, however, took the other side and remained in Florence, where, after playing an important part in the events of 1293, and in the expulsion of Giano della Bella in 1295, he became Prior in 1298. In 1299, in consequence of the discovery of his share in the fraud of Niccola Acciaiuoli (Purg. xii. 105) he fled from Florence, and was condemned in his absence to a fine and to a year's banishment. [**Acciaiuoli, Niccola.**] In 1302, when through the intervention of Charles of Valois the Bianchi were expelled, he and Bonifazio da Signa (Par. xvi. 56) joined the Neri with certain other renegade Bianchi and Ghibellines. From this time forward he occupied a position of great influence in Florence. In 1311, while he was Prior for the second time, and the city was anxious to present a united front to the Emperor Henry VII, he drew up the decree (dated Sept. 2, 1311) known as the ' Riforma di Messer Baldo d'Aguglione', whereby the sentences against a number of the Guelf exiles were revoked and cancelled, and a number of others, who are all included under the head of Ghibellines, were expressly excepted, among the latter being Dante Alighieri [**Dante**]. When, in the next year, the Emperor Henry VII's army was advancing towards Florence, Baldo fled from the city, and was consequently himself declared an outlaw ; he managed, however, to secure a pardon, and returned to Florence, where he died not long after.

Aiace, Ajax, son of Telamon ; his descent from Aeacus, Conv. iv. 27[194]. [**Eaco.**]

Aimeric. [**Hamericus: Namericus.**]

Alagherius. [**Alighieri.**]

Alaghieri. [**Alighiero**[2].]

Alagia, Alagia de' Fieschi, of Genoa, daughter of Niccolò de' Fieschi, Imperial Vicar in Italy, niece of Pope Adrian V, and wife of Moroello Malaspina [**Malaspina, Moroello**] ; she is mentioned by Adrian V (in Circle V of Purgatory) as being still alive, and the only one of his kin who was virtuous, and whose prayers could avail him, Purg. xix. 142–5 [**Adriano**[2]].

Alagna, Anagni, town in Latium, situated on a hill about forty miles SE. of Rome, celebrated as the birthplace of Pope Boniface VIII, and as the scene of his imprisonment by Philip the Fair ; mentioned by Hugh Capet (in Circle V of Purgatory) in connexion with Philip's outrage on the Pope, Purg. xx. 86–7 ; *quel d' Alagna,* i. e. Boniface VIII, Par. xxx. 148 [**Bonifazio**[1] : **Filippo**[2]].

The long struggle between Philip the Fair and Pope Boniface culminated at length in the employment of open violence on the part of the King of France against the Pope's person. Philip accused Boniface of profligacy and heresy, and demanded the convocation of a General Council 'to remove these scandals from the Church'. Boniface retorted by issuing a Bull, in which the King of France was declared excommunicate, while his subjects were released from their allegiance, and the clergy were forbidden to receive benefices at his hands. This Bull was ordered to be suspended in the porch of the Cathedral of Anagni on Sept.8, 1303; but on the eve of that day Sciarra Colonna, whose house Boniface had so bitterly wronged, and William of Nogaret, the emissary of the King of France, suddenly appeared in Anagni with an armed force, and seizing the person of the Pope, after heaping every indignity upon him, held him a prisoner for three days, while the soldiers plundered his palace. He was at last rescued by the people of Anagni, who expelled the soldiers and forced Sciarra and Nogaret to fly for their lives. Boniface immediately set out for Rome to prepare measures of vengeance against Philip and his accomplices, but the shock he had undergone was too much for him ; he became raving mad, and died at Rome, barely a month after his rescue from prison, Oct. 11, 1303. [Colonna, Sciarra: Guglielmo di Nogaret.]

Alamania. [Lamagna.]
Alamanni. [Tedeschi.]

Alardo, Erard de Valéry, lord of Saint-Valérian and of Marolles, Constable of Champagne, born c. 1200, died 1277; mentioned in connexion with the battle of Tagliacozzo (Aug. 23, 1268), in which by his aid Charles of Anjou defeated Conradin, the last of the Hohenstaufen, Inf. xxviii. 17–18.

Erard accompanied St. Louis on his first expedition to the East in 1248. In 1265, according to the continuators of Guillaume de Tyr, he went a second time to the East. In 1268, finding himself on account of his advancing years unequal to the fatigues and hardships of oriental warfare, he set out from Palestine to return to France. On his way he passed through Italy, where his opportune arrival was hailed with delight by Charles of Anjou, then on the eve of a battle with the young Conradin. The two armies met at Tagliacozzo, and Charles, though inferior in numbers, was enabled, by the superior skill of Erard, to defeat his foe and take him prisoner. The victory was due mainly to the fact that Charles, by Erard's advice, kept his reserves in the background until Conradin's German and Spanish troops, who at the beginning of the day had routed their opponents, were disordered by pursuit and scattered over the field in search of plunder. Charles then suddenly advanced with his fresh troops (consisting of a third of his forces, which Erard had prevailed upon him to hold concealed behind a hill), and, falling upon the enemy, completely routed them. It is in allusion to Charles's victory by means of this stratagem of Erard's that D. speaks of 'Tagliacozzo Ove senz' arme vinse il vecchio Alardo', Inf. xxviii. 17–18. [Curradino : Tagliacozzo.]

Alba, Alba Longa, the most ancient town in Latium, built according to tradition by Ascanius, son of Aeneas ; mentioned by the Emperor Justinian (in the Heaven

of Mercury) in connexion with the
Roman Eagle, which he says re-
mained therefor three hundred years,
until the defeat of the three Alban
Curiatii by the three Roman Horatii,
Par. vi. 37–9. [Albani: Curiatii.]
Albani, inhabitants of Alba
Longa; their descent from Aeneas
and Lavinia, Mon. ii. 3$^{108-9}$; their
defeat by the Romans in the combat
between the Roman Horatii and the
Alban Curiatii, Par. vi. 37–9; Conv.
iv. 5$^{155-60}$; Mon. ii. 11$^{22-36}$.
[Alba : Curiatii.]

Albanus, Alban; *populus A.*,
the Albans, their contest with the
Romans for supremacy, Mon. ii.
11$^{22-7}$. [Albani.]

Alberichi, ancient noble family of
Florence (extinct in D.'s time),
mentioned by Cacciaguida (in the
Heaven of Mars) as having been
already in decline in his day, Par.
xvi. 89.

Alberigo, Frate, Friar Alberigo
(so called because he was one of the
'Jovial Friars', which order he joined
in or before 1267), a member of the
Manfredi family, the Guelf lords of
Faenza (to which also belonged
Tribaldello, Inf. xxxii. 122), and
father of Ugolino Bucciola (V. E. i.
14$^{19-20}$) [Bucciola, Ugolino :
Frati Gaudenti]; placed by Dante
in Tolomea, the third division of
Circle IX of Hell, among those who
betrayed their guests, Inf. xxxiii.
118; *un de' tristi della fredda crosta,*
v. 109; *lui, vv.* 115, 121, 139,
150; *ei, v.* 142 ; *il peggiore spirto*
di Romagna, v. 154 [Tolomea :
Traditori].

The circumstances of Alberigo's
crime were as follows: His younger

brother, Manfred, in order to obtain
the lordship of Faenza, plotted against
him, and in a dispute which occurred
in consequence struck Alberigo; the
latter, however, pretended to forgive
the insult on the ground that it was
the act of an impetuous youth, and
a reconciliation took place. Later
on, when he thought the matter had
been forgotten, Alberigo invited
Manfred and one of his sons to a
banquet (at his house at Cesato,
May 2, 1285); the repast over, he
called out, 'Bring the fruit', at which
signal some assassins, who had been
concealed behind the tapestry, rushed
out and despatched father and son
before his eyes. Hence 'le male
frutta di Frate Alberigo' passed into
a proverb.

Albero da Siena, a noble Sienese
(still living in 1259), said to be the
son or protégé of a bishop of Siena,
whom he persuaded to cause the alchemist Griffolino of Arezzo to be
burned for pretending that he could
teach him to fly; mentioned by
Griffolino (in Bolgia 10 of Circle
VIII of Hell), Inf. xxix. 109; *lui,*
v. 112; *quei, v.* 114 [Griffolino].

Alberti, Alberto degli. [Al-
berto ^{3}.]

Alberti, Alessandro degli.
[Alberto ^{3}.]

Alberti, Napoleone degli.
[Alberto ^{3}.]

Alberti, Orso degli. [Orso,
Cont'.]

Albertino Mussato. [Mus-
sato, Albertino.]

Alberto^1. [Alberto di Cologna.]

Alberto ^{2}. [Alberto Tedesco.]

Alberto^3, Alberto degli Alberti,

Count of Mangona in the Val di Sieve, and of Vernia and Cerbaia in the Val di Bisenzio, a few miles NW. of Florence; mentioned by Camicione de' Pazzi (in Caina) in connexion with his two sons, Alessandro and Napoleone, who killed each other in a dispute about the inheritance, Inf. xxxii. 57. D. places the two brothers in Caina, the first division of Circle IX of Hell, among those who were traitors to their kindred, *i fratei miseri lassi*, Inf. xxxii. 21; *due stretti, v.* 41; *quei, v.* 44; *ei, v.* 50; *cotesti due, v.* 55 [Camicion de' Pazzi: Caina: Traditori].

A son of Napoleone degli Alberti, viz. Count Orso, is placed in Antepurgatory, Purg. vi. 19 [Orso, Cont'].

Alberto della Magna. [Alberto di Cologna.]

Alberto della Scala], lord of Verona, 1277–1301; referred to by the unknown Abbot of San Zeno in Circle V of Purgatory as having 'already (i. e. in 1300, the assumed date of the Vision) one foot in the grave', Purg. xviii. 121; the Abbot goes on to refer to Alberto's appointment of his illegitimate son, Giuseppe, whom he describes as ' deformed in body and mind, and basely born ', to the abbacy of San Zeno (' quel monistero '), an appointment which he will shortly repent in Hell (*vv.* 122–6). [Zeno, San.]

Alberto, who was at that date an old man, died on Sept. 10, 1301. Besides this illegitimate son he had three legitimate sons, who succeeded him one after the other in the lordship of Verona, viz. Bartolommeo,

Alboino, and Can Grande, D.'s host at Verona.

Alberto di Cologna, Albert of Cologne, better known as Albertus Magnus, styled 'Doctor Universalis' on account of his vast learning, was born of noble parents at Lavingen on the upper Danube in Swabia in 1193. After studying at Padua and Paris, he joined the Dominican Order in 1222, and under its rules studied theology at Bologna and elsewhere. Subsequently he was appointed to lecture at Cologne, where the Order had a house, and he taught for several years there and at Ratisbon, Freiburg, Strasburg, and Hildesheim. Among his pupils at Cologne was Thomas Aquinas, who in 1245 accompanied him to Paris, where he received his doctorate; after remaining in Paris for three years he returned to Cologne with Aquinas in 1248. In 1254 he was elected Provincial of the Dominican Order at Worms; and in 1260 was made Grand Master of the Palace at Rome, and Bishop of Ratisbon, by Alexander IV. Three years later he retired to Cologne, where he died at the age of eighty-seven, Nov. 15, 1280. He was a most voluminous writer, his collected works filling twenty-one folio volumes, of which six are devoted to commentaries on Aristotle, five on the Scriptures, two on Dionysius the Areopagite, three on the *Liber Sententiarum* of Peter Lombard, the remaining five containing his *Summa Theologiae*, *Summa de Creaturis*, treatise on the Virgin, and various *opuscula*, one of which is on alchemy.

Albertus is referred to as *Alberto*,

Conv. iii. 7²⁷; iv. 23¹²⁶; *Alberto di Cologna*, Par. x. 98; *Alberto della Magna*, Conv. iii. 5¹¹³; he is placed among the spirits of great theologians and others who loved wisdom (*Spiriti Sapienti*) in the Heaven of the Sun, together with his pupil St. Thomas Aquinas, by whom his spirit is pointed out to D. as having been his 'frate e maestro', Par. x. 97–9 [Sole, Cielo del]; his theory as to the Equator as propounded in the *De Natura Locorum* and the *De Proprietatibus Elementorum*, Conv. iii. 5¹¹¹⁻¹⁵ [**Locorum, De Natura: Proprietatibus Elementorum, De**]; his opinion in the *De Intellectu* as to the distribution of the Sun's light, Conv. iii. 7²⁷⁻⁴⁵ [**Intellectu, De**]; his theory as to the four ages of life and the several 'qualities' appropriated to them, as set forth in the *De Meteoris* (a misreference of D., the passage in question occurring in the *De Juventute et Senectute*), Conv. iv. 23¹¹³⁻²⁶ [**Meteora**²].

D. also refers to the *De Meteoris* for the theory of Albertus as to the nature of comets, his references to Albumazar and Seneca being taken from the same source, Conv. ii. 14¹⁶⁴⁻⁷⁶ [**Albumassar: Seneca**]; from here too he got the account of the various theories as to the nature and origin of the Milky Way, Conv. ii. 15⁴⁵⁻⁷⁷ [**Galassia**]; and his account of the incident which happened to Alexander the Great and his army in India, Inf. xiv. 31–6 [**Alessandro Magno**]. From Albertus Magnus (*De Coelo et Mundo*) are derived also the opinions of Aristotle and Ptolemy as to the number

and order of the several heavens, Conv. ii. 3³⁶⁻⁴⁵ [*Coelo, De*²].

Alberto Tedesco, German Albert, i. e. Albert I of Austria, son of Rudolf of Hapsburg, Emperor (but never crowned), 1298–1308 [**Ridolfo**¹]; he was elected after having defeated and slain his predecessor, Adolf of Nassau, in a battle near Worms, his treason against Adolf having been condoned by Boniface VIII in consideration of the advantages of his alliance against the Pope's mortal enemy, Philip the Fair of France [**Adolfo**].

D. refers to him as *Alberto*, Par. xix. 115; Conv. iv. 3⁴²; *Alberto Tedesco*, Purg. vi. 97; *Cesare*, Purg. vi. 92, 114; he apostrophizes him, reproaching him for his neglect of Italy, and foretells his violent death (which took place on May 1, 1308, when he was assassinated at Königstein, close to the castle of Hapsburg, by his nephew John), Purg. vi. 97–117; rebukes him (by the mouth of the Eagle in the Heaven of Jupiter) for his cruel invasion of Bohemia (in 1304), Par. xix. 115–17 [**Praga**]; mentions him as successor of Rudolf and Adolf, Conv. iv. 3³⁸⁻⁴³ [**Federigo**². **Table Q.**]

Albia, river Elbe, which rises in N. of Bohemia, through which it flows first S., then W., then NW., being joined by the Moldau some 20 miles N. of Prague; it subsequently flows NW. into the North Sea.

D. mentions it in connexion with Bohemia, which he describes as the land drained by the Moldau and the Elbe, Purg. vii. 98–9. [**Molta.**]

Albuino della Scala, Alboino, second son of Alberto della Scala, who was lord of Verona, 1277–1301; he succeeded his elder brother, Bartolommeo, in 1304, and held the lordship until his death on Nov. 29, 1311. D. mentions A. slightingly in comparison with Guido da Castello, Conv. iv. 16⁷¹⁻²; he is alluded to, according to some, as *il gran Lombardo*, Par. xvii. 71 [Lombardo¹].

Albumassar, Albumazar (*Abú Mashar*), Arabian astronomer, born at Balkh in Turkestan A.D. 805, died 885. Three of his works are extant in Latin translations, viz. *Introductorium in astronomiam, Liber de magnis conjunctionibus*, and *Tractatus florum astronomiae*.

D. quotes (at second hand, from the *De Meteoris*, i. 4, of Albertus Magnus) his opinion that meteors, as being under the domination of the planet Mars, portend political catastrophes, such as the death of kings, Conv. ii. 14¹⁷⁰⁻⁴.

Alcamo, Ciullo d'. [Ciullo d' Alcamo.]

Alchimisti], Alchemists, placed among the Falsifiers in Bolgia 10 of Circle VIII of Hell (Malebolge), Inf. xxix. 67–139; their punishment is to be afflicted with paralysis and leprosy (*vv.* 71–84) [Falsatori].

Alcide, Alcides. [Ercole.]

Alcimus, the high-priest appointed by Demetrius I, King of Syria, in opposition to Judas Maccabaeus (1 *Maccab.* vii–ix); coupled with Demetrius as typifying respectively Clement V and Philip the Fair of France, Epist. viii. 4⁶⁵. [Demetrius.]

Alcithoë], one of the daughters of Minyas of Boeotia; she and her sisters, Arcippe and Leucippe, re-

fused to join in the worship of Bacchus during his festival, and spent the time in weaving instead, whereupon they were changed into bats, and their work into a vine. Ovid's account of their metamorphosis (*Metam*. iv. 1–35, 389–415) is referred to by D., who speaks of them as ' tres sorores contemtrices numinis in semine Semeles ', Epist. iv. 4⁴⁴⁻⁵. [Semele.]

Alderotto, Taddeo di. [Taddeo.]

Aldighiero. [Alighieri.]

Aldobrandeschi, ancient and powerful Ghibelline family, Counts of Santafiora in the Sienese Maremma, where they had been settled since Cent. ix.

D. mentions Santafiora, whence the counts took their title, Purg. vi. 111 [Santafiora]; and names two of the counts, viz. Guglielmo Aldobrandesco, Purg. xi. 59; and his son, Omberto, Purg. xi. 67 [Guglielmo Aldobrandesco: Omberto].

Aldobrandi, Tegghiaio, Florentine Guelf of the powerful Adimari family, Podestà of Arezzo in 1256, died before 1267 [Adimari]; he is mentioned (as *il Tegghiaio*) together with Farinata degli Uberti (with whom he is coupled), and Jacopo Rusticucci, Arrigo, and Mosca de' Lamberti, Inf. vi. 79; he is one of those *ch' a ben far poser gl' ingegni* (*v.* 81) of whom D. asks Ciacco for news, the reply being *ei son tra le anime più nere* (*v.* 85) [Ciacco]. Tegghiaio is one of the three Florentines (the other two being Guido Guerra and Jacopo Rusticucci) seen by D. afterwards among the Sodomites in Round 3 of Circle VII of

Hell, Inf. xvi. 41; *ombra, v.* 4; *l'altro, v.* 40 [**Sodomiti**]; his spirit is pointed out to D. by Jacopo Rusticucci, who alludes (*vv.* 41–2) to the fact of his having attempted to dissuade the Florentines from undertaking the disastrous expedition against Siena in 1260, which resulted in the crushing defeat at Montaperti, and the ruin of the Guelf party in Florence. [**Montaperti**.] Tegghiaio's house in Florence (in San Michele in Palchetto), and that of his neighbour, Jacopo Rusticucci, were among those destroyed by the victorious Ghibellines between 1260 and 1266.

Aldobrandino de' Mezzabati. [**Ildebrandinus Paduanus**.]

Alepri], one of the Florentine families which received knighthood from the Marquis Hugh of Brandenburg, 'il gran barone,' Par. xvi. 128. [**Ugo di Brandimborgo**.]

Alessandria, Alessandria della Paglia, town on the Tanaro, in the ancient duchy of Milan; mentioned in connexion with the war waged against it by the sons of William, Marquis of Montferrat, to avenge his capture and imprisonment, Purg. vii. 135 [**Guglielmo**[3]]; coupled with Trent and Turin as being near the frontier and consequently incapable of preserving a pure dialect owing to the introduction of foreign elements, *Alexandria,* V. E. i. 15[61–4].

Alessandro[1]. [**Alessandro da Romena**[1].]

Alessandro[2], Alexander the Great, of Macedon, born at Pella in Macedonia, B. C. 356. A. ascended the throne B. C. 336, on the murder of his father Philip; conquered Egypt (where he founded the city of Alexandria at the mouth of the Nile, B. C. 331), Syria, Media, Persia, and India; died at Babylon, B. C. 323, at the age of 32, after a reign of nearly thirteen years. D. speaks of him simply as *Alessandro,* Inf. xii. 107; xiv. 31; Conv. iv. 11[124]; *Alexander,* V. E. ii. 6[14]; Mon.ii. 9[61]; *rex Macedo,* Mon. ii. 9[62]; his place among the Tyrants in Round 1 of Circle VII of Hell, Inf. xii. 107; his marvellous experiences in India, Inf. xiv. 31; his munificence (of which he was the proverbial type in the Middle Ages), Conv.iv. 11[123–5]; contemporary with Aristotle, V. E. ii. 6[13–14]; more nearly attained universal monarchy than any other sovereign, Mon. ii. 9[61–7]. In this last passage D. says that A. sent ambassadors to Rome to demand submission, but died in Egypt before the reply of the Romans reached him, 'ut Livius narrat'. The circumstance is not mentioned by Livy, who on the contrary states his belief that the Romans never so much as heard of Alexander—'ne fama quidem illis notum arbitror fuisse' (ix. 18). The story is probably of Greek origin, but it is not known whence D. got it.

D.'s statement that A. died in Egypt and was buried there, in proof of which he quotes Lucan (*Phars.* viii. 692–4), Mon. ii. 9[65–74], is perhaps due to a confusion on his part between Babylon on the Euphrates and Babylon (Old Cairo) on the Nile, a confusion into which he appears to have fallen elsewhere also [**Babilonia**].

The majority of modern editors, contrary to the opinion of the old commentators, hold that the Alexander who is placed, together with Dionysius of Syracuse, among the Tyrants in Round 1 of Circle VII of Hell (Inf. xii. 107) is not Alexander the Great, but the Thessalian tyrant, Alexander of Pherae [**Alessandro Fereo: Dionisio**[1] **: Violenti**]. But it is not in accordance with D.'s principle as enunciated by Cacciaguida, ' ti son mostrate . . . nella valle dolorosa, Pur l' anime che son di fama note ' (Par. xvii. 136–8), that the individual mentioned here simply as ' Alessandro ', without any further description, should be the comparatively obscure tyrant of Pherae.

The view that the person intended is Alexander the Great is strongly supported by the fact that Orosius, whose *Historia adversum Paganos* was one of D.'s chief authorities in matters of ancient history, repeatedly brands the Macedonian conqueror as a cruel and bloodthirsty monster, and concludes his account of him with a long apostrophe on the ruin and misery which he had inflicted upon the whole world. Lucan also, another of D.'s historical authorities, denounces Alexander of Macedon as a robber and a bane of the world (*Phars.* x. 20 ff.). The fact that Alexander the Great does not appear among the great heroes of antiquity in Limbo is also in favour of the view that he is the Alexander referred to by D. in this passage.

D.'s allusion (Inf. xiv. 31–6) to the incident which happened to A. and his army in India was derived, directly or indirectly, from the apocryphal *Epistola Alexandri Regis ad*

Aristotilem praeceptorem suum de Mirabilibus Indiae ; there is, however, a notable discrepancy between the two accounts, for D. says that A. bade his soldiers trample the *flames*, whereas in the *Epistola* it is the *snow* they are bidden to trample. It has been assumed that D.'s version was due to a confused recollection of the details of the story as given in the *Epistola*; the immediate source of his account, however, was almost undoubtedly a passage in the *De Meteoris* (i. 4) of Albertus Magnus (a book with which D. was well acquainted), in which, owing to a misquotation of the *Epistola*, precisely the same confusion occurs, as to the trampling of the flames, as was made by D.

Alessandro IV], Pope Alexander IV (Rainaldo, of the family of the Counts of Segni and Anagni, Cardinal Bishop of Ostia, nephew of Pope Gregory IX; elected Pope at Naples, Dec. 12, 1254 ; died at Viterbo, May 25, 1261), thought by some to be included among the Popes referred to, Inf. xix. 73–4 [**Niccolò**[2]].

Alessandro degli Alberti. [**Alberti.**]

Alessandro da Romena[1]], Alexander (I), Count of Romena (d. prob. bef. July, 1304) ; he married a daughter of Ugolino de' Fantolini (Purg. xiv. 121), and was captain-general of the exiled Bianchi with whom D. was associated (Par. xvii. 61) ; with his brothers Guido and Aghinolfo he induced Maestro Adamo to counterfeit the Florentine gold florin, Inf. xxx. 77 [**Adamo, Maestro: Guidi, Conti**], he is supposed to be the Alexander mentioned in the titles of Epist. I, Epist. II.

Alessandro da Romena [2], Alexander (II), Count of Romena, according to some the nephew of the above, and identical with the Alexander mentioned in the titles of Epist. I, Epist. II. [Guidi, Conti.]

Alessandro Fereo], Alexander tyrant of Pherae, B. C. 368–359; defeated at Cynoscephalae by Pelopidas the Theban general, B. C. 364; killed by his own wife, B. C. 359. He was famed for his cruelty, one of his amusements being to dress up men in the skins of wild beasts, and to set dogs to worry them. Some think he is the Alexander placed along with Dionysius of Syracuse among the Tyrants in Round 1 of Circle VII of Hell, Inf. xii. 107; but it is more probable that the person meant by D. was Alexander the Great. [Alessandro [2].]

Alessandro Magno. [Alessandro [2].]

Alessandro Novello], native of Treviso, who was Bishop of Feltre from 1298 to 1320; alluded to by Cunizza (in the Heaven of Venus), in connexion with his treacherous surrender of certain refugees who had sought his protection, as *l'empio pastor di Feltro*, Par. ix. 52–3; *prete cortese*, *v.* 58. [Feltro [1].]

Alessio Interminei, native of Lucca, with whom D. appears to have been acquainted, at any rate by sight, and whom he places among the Flatterers in Bolgia 2 of Circle VIII of Hell (Malebolge), Inf. xviii. 122; *un*, *v.* 116; *quei*, *v.* 118; *lui*, *v.* 120; *egli*, *v.* 124 [Adulatori].

Of Alessio but little is known beyond the fact that he lived in the latter half of Cent. xiii; it appears from a document dated 1295 that he was alive in that year, and he must have died not long after.

Aletto, Alecto, one of the three Furies; she is stationed with Megaera and Tisiphone to guard the entrance to the City of Dis, Inf. x. 45–8 [Dite [2]].

Alexander. [Alessandro [2]: Alessandro da Romena.]

Alexandria. [Alessandria.]

[**Alexis**], name (borrowed from Virgil, *Ecl.* ii. 1, 6, 19, &c.) of a character in G. del Virgilio's Eclogue addressed to D., supposed to represent a servant of the writer, Ecl. R., 8. 56.

Alfa, Alpha, first letter of the Greek alphabet; mentioned (in allusion to *Rev.* i. 8), Par. xxvi. 17; *Alpha*, Epist. x. 33[625].

Alfarabio, Alfarabius (*Al-Farabi*), so called from Farab, his birthplace, in Transoxiana, one of the earliest of the Arabian philosophers; he practised as a physician at Damascus, where he died in 950. Latin translations of several of his *opuscula* are extant.

D. quotes A. (according to one reading) in support of the theory that every effect partakes of the nature of its cause, Conv. iii. 2[37] (where, however, the correct reading is almost certainly not *Alfarabio*, but *Alpetragio*, i.e. Alpetraus or Alpetragius) [Alpetragio].

Alfergano, Alfraganus (*Al-Farghani*), so called from his birthplace Fergana in Sogdiana (now Samarcand), celebrated Arabian astronomer, who flourished at the beginning of

Cent. ix, during the Caliphate of Ma'mún (d. 833). He wrote in Arabic (besides treatises on sundials and on the astrolabe) a work on the elements of astronomy, consisting of thirty chapters, which is based upon the principles of Ptolemy, whom A. frequently quotes. This work was translated from Arabic into Latin in Cent. xii by Gerardus Cremonensis (c. 1114–1187); and again (about the year 1242, as is supposed), by Johannes Hispalensis, under the title of *Alfragani Elementa Astronomica*, for which the alternative title *Liber de Aggregatione Scientiae Stellarum* (or *de Aggregationibus Stellarum*) is sometimes substituted. This latter version, the popularity of which is attested by the number of MSS. still in existence, is the one which was in common use in the Middle Ages.

D. was evidently familiar with the *Elementa Astronomica* of Alfraganus, and studied it closely, for he was largely indebted to it for astronomical and other *data*, though only on two occasions does he acknowledge his obligations; he mentions Alfraganus himself as his authority for the dimensions of the Earth and of the planet Mercury, Conv. ii. 14^{95} [**Mercurio**^{2} : **Terra**^{2}]; and refers to his *Elementa*, under the title of *Libro dell' Aggregazione delle Stelle* (but without mentioning the name of the author), for the demonstration of the threefold motion of the Heaven of Venus, Conv. ii. 6^{134} [**Venere, Cielo di**]; he was also indebted to Alfraganus for his information as to the projection of the shadow of the Earth as far as the sphere of

Venus, Par. ix. 118–19 [**Terra**^{2}]; the Syrian calendar and the Arabian usage in reckoning the commencement of the day from sunset, V. N. § 30^{1-6} [**Arabia : Tisrin primo**]; the poles and equators of the various heavens, Conv. ii. 4^{47-68}, iii. 5^{63-79} ; and the motion of the Heaven of the Fixed Stars from W. to E. 1° in 100 years, Conv. ii. 6^{141-3}, 15^{12-14}; V. N. §2^{10-12} [**Cielo Stellato**]; the distance of Venus from the Earth, Conv. ii. 7^{104-8} [**Terra**^{2} : **Venere**^{2}]; the diameter of the Earth, Conv. ii. 7^{106-8}, 14^{97-8}; iv. 8^{59-60} [**Terra**^{2}]; the diameter of the planet Mercury, Conv. ii. 14^{92-8} [**Mercurio** ^{2}]; the number of the Fixed Stars, Conv. ii. 15^{18-22} [**Stelle Fisse**]; the periods of the revolutions of the planets, Conv. ii. 15^{132-57} [**Cielo Cristallino**]; the circumference of the Earth, Conv. iii. 5^{80-107} [**Terra** ^{2}]; the difference between 'equal' and 'temporal' hours, Conv. iii. 6^{13-32} ; the diameter of the Sun, Conv. iv. 8^{56-8} [**Sole**].

Alfonso^1], Alphonso III, King of Aragon, 1285–1291, eldest son of Peter III, whom he succeeded in Aragon. D. places him in the valley of flowers in Ante-purgatory, among the princes who neglected to repent, and represents him as seated behind his father, referring to him, on account of his having died before he was thirty, as *lo giovinetto*, Purg. vii. 116 [**Antipurgatorio**]. D. implies that he was superior to his brothers, James (who succeeded him in Aragon as James II), and Frederick (who became King of Sicily as Frederick II, 1296–1337) [**Pietro**^{3}]. A. is perhaps referred to as *l' onor di Cicilia e d' Aragona*, Purg. iii. 115 [**Aragona. Table B**].

Alfonso²], Alphonso VIII, King of Castile, 1158–1214, one of the great patrons of the troubadours; most probably the King of Castile mentioned, together with the Marquis of Montferrat and the Count of Toulouse, on account of his liberality, as *il buon Re di Castella*, Conv. iv. 11¹²⁵⁻⁸. [**Castella.**]

Alfonso³], Alphonso X, El Sabio, King of Castile and Leon, 1252–1284, the most learned prince of his age, under whose auspices were compiled the celebrated astronomical tables known as the 'Alphonsine Tables'; thought by some to be alluded to by the Eagle in the Heaven of Jupiter as *quel di Spagna*, Par. xix. 125; but the reference is more probably to his grandson, Fernando IV (1295–1312) [**Castella : Ferdinando**]; some suppose also that he is the King of Castile commended for his munificence as *il buon Re di Castella*, Conv. iv. 11¹²⁵⁻⁶; but the reference in this case is almost certainly to his great-grandfather, Alphonso VIII, King of Castile, 1158–1214 [**Alfonso²: Table D**].

Alfragano. [**Alfergano.**]

Algazel, Algazali (*Al-Ghazzali*), Arabian philosopher and theologian (1058–1111). He wrote a treatise, which is extant, called *Destructio Philosophorum*, against the accepted Aristotelianism of the day. The work published under the title *Logica et Philosophia Algazelis Arabis*, contains neither the logic nor the philosophy of Algazali. It is a mere abstract of the Peripatetic systems, and was made preliminary to the *Destructio* mentioned above.

D. quotes the opinion of Algazali (*Logic. et Philos.* i. 4), which he shared with Plato and Avicenna, that substantial generation is effected by the motive powers of the Heavens, Conv. ii. 14³¹⁻²; the theory, held by him (*Logic. et Philos.* ii. 5) and Avicenna, that souls are noble or ignoble of themselves from the beginning, Conv. iv. 21¹⁵⁻¹⁷.

Ali, Ali ibn Abu Taleb, fourth in order of the Caliphs or successors of Mahomet, born at Mecca c. 597; his father was uncle of the prophet, by whom A. himself was adopted and educated; as a youth he was the first to declare his adhesion to the cause of Mahomet, who in return made him his vicegerent, and later rewarded him with the hand of his daughter Fatima. When Mahomet died (in 632) without male issue, A. did not press his legitimate claims to succeed him, but allowed three other companions of the prophet successively to become Caliph, viz. Abu-Bekr (632–634), Omar (634–644), and Othman (644–656); it was not until after the murder of Othman in 656 that he assumed the caliphate, which he held until his assassination at Kufa in 661. The question of Ali's right to succeed to the caliphate divided the Mahometans into two great sects, viz. the Sunnites (represented by the modern Turks), who deny his right, and the Shiites or Fatimites (represented by the Persians), who affirm it, and who venerate A. as second only to Mahomet himself.

D. places Ali, together with Mahomet, among the Schismatics in Bolgia 9 of Circle VIII of Hell (Malebolge), Inf. xxviii. 32; he is represented as 'cloven in the face from the chin to the forelock', while Mahomet is cloven 'from his chin to his fundament' (*vv.* 24, 33) [**Scismatici**].

Alichino, one of the ten demons in Bolgia 5 of Circle VIII of Hell (Malebolge) deputed by Malacoda to escort D. and Virgil, Inf. xxi. 118; xxii. 112; *quei, vv.* 125, 129; *compagno, v.* 137; *l' altro, v.* 139; he and his companions are placed as guardians of the Barrators, whom they rend with their iron prongs whenever the latter venture to appear above the surface of the boiling pitch in which they are immersed [**Barattieri : Malebranche**].

Alighieri [1]], Dante's family name, referred to by Cacciaguida, D.'s great-great-grandfather (in the Heaven of Mars), as *tua cognazione*, Par. xv. 92; *il tuo soprannome, v.* 138. Cacciaguida, who is said to have belonged to the Elisei, one of the ancient families of Florence who boasted their descent from the Romans, married one of the Aldighieri or Alighieri, probably of Ferrara, from whom he says D.'s surname was derived, 'Mia donna venne a me di val di Pado, E quindi il soprannome tuo si feo,' Par. xv. 137–8. [**Cacciaguida : Dante**.]

There has been much discussion as to the correct form of D.'s surname, which, as might be expected, is spelt in many various ways in MSS. The most recent investigations tend to show that in the Latin form the name was probably originally *Alagherius*, and in the Italian *Alighieri*. The name in its Latin form (spelt variously by different editors) occurs, Epist. ii. *tit.*; v. *tit.*; vi. *tit.*; vii. *tit.*; viii. *tit.*; ix. 3; x. *tit.*, 10; A. T. §§ 1 [2], 24 [4]; Ecl. i. *tit.*; Ecl. ii. *tit.*

Alighieri [2]. [**Alighiero** [2].]
Alighieri, Bello degli. [**Bello.**]
Alighieri, Dante. [**Dante.**]
Alighieri, Durante. [**Durante.**]
Alighieri, Francesco. [**Francesco** [3].]
Alighieri, Gaetana. [**Tana.**]
Alighieri, Tana. [**Tana.**]

Alighiero [1]], son of Cacciaguida, great-grandfather of Dante, whose father, Alighiero II, was the eldest son of Bellincione, the eldest son of Alighiero I; the second son of the last was Bello, father of Geri del Bello (Inf. xxix. 27) [**Table A**].

Cacciaguida (in the Heaven of Mars) refers to Alighiero as his own son, and D.'s great-grandfather, and as being the ancestor from whom the poet derived his surname Alighieri, Par. xv. 91–2, 94 [**Alighieri : Dante**]. This Alighiero is mentioned, together with his brother Preitenitto, in a document dated Dec. 9, 1189; and is proved by another document to have been alive on Aug. 14, 1201; it is evident that D. was ignorant of the exact date of his death, for he makes Cacciaguida say (in 1300) that his son had been 'a hundred years and more' among the Proud in Circle I of Purgatory (Par. xv. 92–3) [**Cacciaguida : Superbi**].

Alighiero [2]] (grandson of the preceding), father of D., alluded to, with his mother Bella, as *i miei generanti*,

Conv. i. 13[31]; he is mentioned by Forese Donati in his *tenzone* with D., *Alaghier*, Son. lii.* 8; *Alighier*, Son. liii.* 14; *Allaghieri*, Son. liv.* 1.

Alighiero II, D.'s father, lived in the quarter of San Martino del Vescovo; he was the son of Bellincione degli Alighieri, and was descended, as is supposed, from the ancient and noble family of the Elisei, who lived in the Sesto di Porta san Piero in Florence. Several names occur among D.'s ancestry which are common among the Elisei, and one of his ancestors, who is mentioned in the *D. C.* (Par. xv. 136), actually bore the name of Eliseo [**Eliseo**]. Alighiero, who was a notary, was twice married, and died when his son was about eighteen. His first wife, D.'s mother, was Bella, the daughter, as there are good grounds for believing, of Durante, son of Scolaio degli Abati. She died in or before 1278, and D. was her only child. By his second wife, Lapa, daughter of Chiarissimo Cialuffi, Alighiero had three children, a son Francesco (who survived his half-brother D. more than twenty years), a daughter Tana (i. e. Gaetana), and another daughter, name unknown, who married one Leon Poggi [**Francesco**[3] : **Tana**]. A son of this Leon Poggi, called Andrea, was an intimate friend of Boccaccio, who says that he bore a marked resemblance to his uncle D. both in face and figure. From Andrea Poggi Boccaccio learned many details about D.'s habits and manner of life. [**Table A.**]

D.'s father can hardly have been a person of much consequence in Florence; otherwise, as a Guelf, he would have shared the exile of his party after the disastrous defeat of the Florentine Guelfs at Montaperti (4 Sept. 1260), which, from the fact that D. was born in Florence in 1265, it would appear that he did not do. If he did leave Florence on that occasion he must have returned before the rest of his party, since the restoration of the Guelfs did not take place until Jan. 1267. The only contemporary references to Alighiero (other than in legal documents) occur in the not very edifying *tenzone*, or poetical correspondence (mentioned above), between D. and his friend Forese Donati, from whose expressions it would appear that D.'s father was either a personal coward, or of little moral worth. [**Forese.**]

Aliotti], noble Florentine family, said to have been a branch of the Visdomini, who, as some think, are alluded to by Cacciaguida (in the Heaven of Mars) as being patrons of the bishopric of Florence, the revenues of which they enjoyed during the vacancy of the See, Par. xvi. 112–14. [**Tosinghi: Visdomini.**]

Allagherius. [**Alighieri.**]
Allaghieri. [**Alighiero**[2].]
Allighieri. [**Alighieri.**]

Almeone, Alcmaeon, son of Amphiaräus the seer and Eriphyle. Amphiaräus, foreseeing that the expedition against Thebes would prove fatal to him, concealed himself in order to avoid joining it; but his wife Eriphyle, bribed by Polynices with the necklace of Harmonia, revealed his hiding-place, so that he went, and met his death [**Armonia**]. Before he died, however, he en-

joined Alcmaeon to slay Eriphyle to
avenge her betrayal of him; accordingly on his return from Thebes
Alcmaeon put his mother to death
[**Anfiarao: Erifile**]. The incident
of A. slaying Eriphyle is represented
among the graven pictures on the
ground in Circle I of Purgatory, where
E. figures as an example of defeated
pride, Purg. xii. 49–51 [**Superbi**];
A. is mentioned again in the same
connexion, Par. iv. 103–5.

Alpe[1], Alps, Inf. xiv. 30; xx. 62;
Purg. xvii. 1; xxxiii. 111; alluded
to as *alpestre rocce*, in connexion with
the source of the Po, Par. vi. 51
[**Po**]; the Tyrolese Alps are de-
scribed as *l'Alpe, che serra Lamagna
Sovra Tiralli*, Inf. xx. 62–3; the
Pennine Alps are perhaps referred to,
Inf. xx. 65 [**Pennino**].

Alpe[2], Apennines, Inf. xvi. 101;
Alpi, Canz. xi. 61. [**Apennino**[1]:
Benedetto, San.]

Alpetragio, Alpetragius or Alpetraus, an Arabian of Morocco, who
flourished about the middle of Cent.
xii. He has been identified with
a certain Nour-Eddin Alpetrongi, a
Christian of Seville, who became
a Mahometan, and wrote a treatise
on the Sphere, which was translated
in 1217 at Toledo by Michael Scot,
and which had an important influence
upon the astronomical studies of
Cent. xiii.

D. quotes A. in support of the
theory that every effect partakes of
the nature of its cause, Conv. iii. 2[37]
(where for *Alpetragio* some read
Alfarabio). [**Alfarabio.**]

Alpha. [**Alfa.**]

Alphesiboeus, name, borrowed
from Virgil (*Ecl.* v. 73; viii. 1),

under which D. is said to have concealed the identity of a friend at
Ravenna, a certain Maestro Fiducio
de' Milotti, a physician of Certaldo,
Ecl. ii. 7, 15, 44, 45, 49, 76.

Alpi. [**Alpe**[2].]

Altaforte, Hautefort, castle in the
Limousin in the bishopric of Périgord, some twenty miles NE. of
Perigueux (in the modern Department of Dordogne); it belonged to
the celebrated troubadour, Bertran
de Born, to whom D. refers as *colui
che già tenne Altaforte*, Inf. xxix. 29
[**Bertram dal Bornio**].

After the death of the 'Young
King' (June 11, 1183), eldest surviving son of Henry II of England,
Bertran was besieged in Hautefort
by Richard Cœur-de-Lion, and Alphonso II, King of Aragon, who
appeared with an army before its
walls on June 29 in that same year.
After holding out for a week, the
fortress fell, and was handed over
by Richard to Bertran's brother Constantine. In the end, however, it
was restored to Bertran, who held
it till his death.

[**Altafronte, Castel d'**], building
in Florence, subsequently known as
the Palazzo de' Castellani, which
still exists in the Piazza de' Giudici,
on the Lungarno della Borsa; mentioned by Forese Donati (the point of
whose allusion is unknown) in his
tenzone with D., Son. liii.* 7.

Alvernia[1], Auvergne, district in
S.-Central France, on the borders of
the old Languedoc, whence the troubadour Peire d'Alvernha took his
name, V. E. i. 10[24]. [**Petrus de
Alvernia.**]

Alvernia[2], La Verna, mountain in the Casentino E. of Florence, near Bibbiena, on the SW. slope of which St. Francis of Assisi founded a monastery (in 1218), the remains of which are still to be seen; it is here that St. Francis is said to have received the stigmata in 1224 after fasting for forty days. St. Thomas Aquinas (in the Heaven of the Sun), in connexion with this incident, refers to the mountain, which is situated between the sources of the Tiber and the Arno, as *il crudo sasso, intra Tevere ed Arno*, Par. xi. 106-7. [**Francesco** [2].]

Amalech, Amalek, the Amalekites; mentioned as typical of the Emperor Henry VII's opponents in Italy, Epist. vii. 5^{107-12} (where D. refers to the supposed meaning of the name, 'gens brutalis', which is given in the *Explanatio Nominum* in many MSS. of the Vulgate). [**Agag**.]

Amano], Haman, the chief minister of Ahasuerus, from whom he obtained a decree that all the Jews in the Persian empire should be put to death (*Esther* iii. 8-15); after the failure of this attempt to compass the destruction of the Jews, H., through the intervention of Esther and Mordecai, was hanged on the gallows which he had prepared for the latter (*Esther* vii. 7-10). [**Assuero: Ester: Mardocheo.**]

Haman figures among the examples of wrath seen by D. in Circle III of Purgatory, where he is represented as 'crucified', with Ahasuerus, Esther, and Mordecai grouped around him, Purg. xvii. 25-30 [**Iracondi**]. D.'s use of the term 'crocifisso', as applied to Haman, is explained by the Vulgate, where the

word rendered 'gallows' in A.V. is represented by Lat. *crux*.

Amanti, Spiriti. [**Spiriti Amanti.**]

Amata, wife of Latinus, King of Latium, and mother of Lavinia; she hanged herself rather than live to see her daughter married to Aeneas [**Lavinia**]. D. includes her among the examples of wrath in Circle III of Purgatory, Purg. xvii. 34-9, where in a vision he sees Lavinia weeping and reproaching her mother with her suicide, calling upon her as *regina* (*v.* 35), and *madre* (*v.* 39) [**Iracondi**]. In his letter to the Emperor Henry VII, D. compares the city of Florence to Amata, Epist. vii. 7^{148}.

The episode is narrated by Virgil (*Aen.* xii. 593-607), but D. supplies the words to which Virgil only alludes.

Ambrogio, Sant'. [**Ambrosius.**]

Ambrosius, St. Ambrose, celebrated Father of the Church (334-397). St. A. was educated at Rome, studied law, practised as a pleader at Milan, and in 369 was appointed governor of Liguria and Aemilia (N. Italy). In 374 he was nominated Bishop of Milan, though not yet baptized. He at first refused the dignity, but accepted it under persuasion. As Bishop he became the unswerving opponent of the Arian heresy [**Arrio**], which had the support of Justina, mother of Valentinian II, and, for a time, of the young Emperor himself. In 390, on account of the ruthless massacre at Thessalonica ordered by the Emperor Theodosius, St. A. refused him entrance into the church at Milan for eight months. St. Augustine was among those who received baptism at his hands [**Agostino**[2]]. St. A.'s exegetical works include an exposition of the Gospel of St. Luke, and commentaries on certain of the Psalms. He was also the author of many hymns, designed to combat the errors of Arianism, some of which have been adopted in the liturgies of the Western Church. The beginning of one of these, 'Te lucis ante,' is quoted by D., who represents the spirits in the valley of flowers in Ante-purgatory as chanting it, Purg. viii. 13–14.

D. reproaches the Italian cardinals with their neglect of the works of St. A., and of the other Fathers of the Church, Epist. viii. 7[114–17]. Some think that St. A. is alluded to as one of the four elders 'in humble guise' in the mystic Procession in the Terrestrial Paradise (the other three being St. Augustine, St. Gregory, and St. Jerome), Purg. xxix. 142. The reference, however, is more probably to the four writers of the canonical Epistles.

Several of the old commentators think St. A. is referred to as *Quel avvocato dei tempi Cristiani*, Par. x. 119; but there can be scarcely a doubt that Orosius is intended. [Orosio.]

Amfione. [**Anfione.**]

Amicitia, De, Cicero's treatise *On Friendship*, written in the form of a dialogue, the chief speaker being Laelius, to commemorate the friendship of the latter with Scipio Africanus the younger [**Lelio**]; quoted as *D'Amicizia*, Conv. i. 12[19]; *Del-*

l'Amistà, Conv. ii. 13[19]; one of the books with which D. consoled himself after the death of Beatrice, Conv. ii. 13[17–22]; Cicero's opinion (§§ 5, 9), in agreement with that of Aristotle, that love is begot by proximity and goodness, and increased by advantage, study, and habit, Conv. i. 12[18–25].

D. was indebted to the *De Amicitia* (§ 26) for the quotation (from the *Eunuchus* of Terence) which he puts into the mouth of Thais (the words attributed to her by D. being really those of Gnatho), Inf. xviii. 133–5 [**Taide**]. D. probably also got from the same work (§ 7) the story of Pylades and Orestes, alluded to, Purg. xiii. 32 [**Oreste**].

Amicizia, D'. [*Amicitia, De.*]

Amiclas. [**Amiclate.**]

Amiclate, Amyclas, a poor fisherman who 'Caesar and his fortune bare at once' in his boat from Epirus into Italy. Julius Caesar, being anxious to reach Italy, went secretly at night to the cottage of A., who, secure in his poverty, admitted him, and consented to convey him across the Adriatic.

A. is mentioned, in allusion to this incident, by St. Thomas Aquinas (in the Heaven of the Sun) in connexion with St. Francis, and his devotion to poverty, Par. xi. 67–9; Lucan's account of the incident quoted in a discussion as to the harmfulness of riches, Conv. iv. 13[110–21].

D. has closely followed Lucan's narrative (*Phars.* v. 515–31) of the episode (Par. xi. 67–9), the last four lines of which he translates in the *Convivio* (iv. 13[112–18]).

Amidei], noble Florentine family, whose murder of Buondelmonte, in revenge for a slight to a lady of their house, gave rise to the bloody factions of Guelfs and Ghibellines in Florence.

Cacciaguida, addressing D. (in the Heaven of Mars), refers to them as 'La casa di che nacque il vostro fleto' (i. e. the house which caused so much lamentation in Florence), and says that in his day they and their 'consorti' (i. e., according to the old commentators, the Uccellini and Gherardini) were held in high honour, Par. xvi. 136–9. [**Buondelmonte.**]

Amistà, Dell'. [**Amicitia, De.**]

Amore, Love, i.e. Cupid, the son of Venus, as is testified by Virgil (*Aen.* i. 664–5) and Ovid (*Metam.* v. 363), Conv. ii. 6[117–26]. [**Cupìdo.**]

Amore, Rimedio d'. [*Remedia Amoris.*]

Amos, Amoz, father of the prophet Isaiah, who is hence spoken of as *Amos filius,* Epist. vii. 2[28–9]. [**Isaia.**]

Amphitrite, daughter of Oceanus and wife of Neptune, goddess of the sea; mentioned to indicate the sea, Epist. vii. 3[58]; the ocean as distinct from inland seas, A.T. § 15[6].

Anacreonte, Anacreon, celebrated Greek lyric poet, born at Teos, an Ionian city in Asia Minor; he lived in Athens c. B.C. 522, and died c. 478 at the age of 85. According to the reading of some edd., A. is mentioned as being among the ancient poets in Limbo, Purg. xxii. 106 (where the correct reading is almost certainly *Antifonte*) [**Limbo**].

Anagna. [**Alagna.**]

Analytica Priora, *Prior Analytics,* logical treatise of Aristotle; quoted, as *Priora,* in illustration of the use of hypothesis in argument, A.T. § 19[19]; the first book, which deals with the form of the syllogism, is quoted (apparently) as *De Syllogismo,* to show that in a syllogism containing four terms the form of the syllogism is not kept, 'ut patet ex iis quae de Syllogismo simpliciter', Mon. iii. 7[15–20].

Anania[1], Ananias, 'the disciple at Damascus,' who healed St. Paul's blindness by laying his hands upon him (*Acts* ix. 10–18); the virtue of the glance of Beatrice compared to that of the hand of A., Par. xxvi. 12.

Anania[2], Ananias, husband of Sapphira; the two are included among the examples of lust of wealth proclaimed by the Avaricious in Circle V of Purgatory, *col marito Safira,* Purg. xx. 112. [**Avari: Safira.**]

Anassagora, Anaxagoras, celebrated Greek philosopher of the Ionian school; born at Clazomenae in Ionia, B.C. 500; died at the age of 72, at Lampsacus in Mysia, B.C. 428.

D. (whose knowledge of A. was probably derived from Cicero, *Acad.* i. 13; ii. 31, 37; *Tusc.* i. 43; iii. 13; v. 39; &c.), places him in Limbo among the great philosophers of antiquity, Inf. iv. 137 [**Limbo**]; his opinion as to the nature and origin of the Milky Way, Conv. ii. 15[55–9] [**Galassia**].

Anastagi, noble Ghibelline family of Ravenna, next in importance to the Polentani and Traversari

(Purg. xiv. 107), with the latter of whom, as well as with the Counts of Bagnacavallo (Purg. xiv. 115), they were in close alliance. Guido del Duca (in Circle II of Purgatory) mentions them among the ancient worthy families of Romagna, and speaks of them and of the Traversari as being without heirs, and consequently on the eve of extinction, Purg. xiv. 107–8. [**Traversara, Casa.**]

Anastagio. [**Anastasio.**]

Anastasio, Pope Anastasius II (496–498), placed by D. among the Heretics in Circle VI of Hell, where he is enclosed in a tomb bearing the inscription, 'I hold Pope Anastasius, who was drawn from the right way by Photinus', Inf. xi. 8–9 [**Eretici**]. D. appears to have confused Pope Anastasius II with his namesake and contemporary, the Emperor Anastasius I (491–518), who is said to have been led by Photinus, a deacon of Thessalonica, into the heresy of Acacius, bishop of Constantinople (d. 488), who denied the divine origin of Christ, holding that he was naturally begotten and conceived in the same way as the rest of mankind.

Anchise, Anchises, son of Capys and Themis, daughter of Ilus; he was beloved by Venus, by whom he became the father of Aeneas. On the capture of Troy by the Greeks Aeneas carried A. on his shoulders from the burning city. A. did not live to reach Italy; he died soon after the arrival of Aeneas in Sicily, where he was buried. When Aeneas descended to Hades he saw the shade of A., which conversed with

him and foretold the future greatness of Rome.

Aeneas referred to as *figliuol d' Anchise,* Inf. i. 74; Purg. xviii. 137; the meeting between D. and Cacciaguida in the Heaven of Mars compared to that of Aeneas and A. in Hades, Par. xv. 25–7; the death of A. in Sicily, Par. xix. 131–2; the fortitude of Aeneas in braving the terrors of Hades in order to seek the shade of A., as related by Virgil (*Aen.* vi. 236 ff.), Conv. iv. 26[70–6]; the prophecy of A. to Aeneas when they met in Hades (*Aen.* vi. 847–53), *Anchises,* Mon. ii. 7[67–77]. [**Enea.**]

Anchises. [**Anchise.**]

Anco, Ancus Marcius, fourth King of Rome, B. C. 640–616; he succeeded Tullus Hostilius, and was succeeded by Tarquinius Priscus, Conv. iv. 5[90]; he and the other six Kings of Rome are referred to, Par. vi. 41.

Anconitana, Marca. [**Marca Anconitana.**]

Anconitani, inhabitants of the March of Ancona, V. E. i. 10[66–7]; *incolae Anconitanae Marchiae,* V. E. i. 11[18]; *Marchiani,* V. E. i. 12[58]; coupled with the Trevisans as *utriusque Marchiae viri,* V. E. i. 19[19] [**Marca Anconitana**]; their dialect distinct from those of the inhabitants of Calabria and Romagna, V. E. i. 10[66–7]; the ugliest of the Italian dialects after that of the Romans, V. E. i. 11[18–20]; rejected by D., with those of the Romans and Spoletans, as unworthy to be the Italian vulgar tongue, V. E. i. 11[20–1]; the Apulian dialect infected by its barbarisms, and by those of the Roman dialect, V. E. i. 12[56–9]; their dialect abandoned by their most illustrious poets in favour of the Italian vulgar tongue, V. E. i. 19$^{16-19}$.

Andalò, Loderingo degli. [**Loderingo.**]

Andrea de' Mozzi], member of the noble Florentine family (who were Guelfs and Bianchi) of that name, Bishop of Florence, 1287–1295. In 1272 he was a canon of Florence, and in 1287 he was appointed bishop. In Sept. 1295, on account of his unseemly living, he was transferred by Boniface VIII to the see of Vicenza, where he died a few months later (Feb. 1296).

Andrea is referred to by Brunetto Latini as 'the one who was transferred by the Pope from Florence to Vicenza', and included by him among those who are with himself in Round 3 of Circle VII of Hell, where those guilty of unnatural offences are punished, Inf. xv. 112–14 [**Bacchiglione : Violenti**].

Andrea di Ungaria], Andrew III, King of Hungary, 1290–1301, the last of the line of St. Stephen; he seized the crown on the death of Ladislas III (IV), whose nephew, Charles Martel, was the rightful heir. [**Carlo Martello : Table L.**]

Andrew is referred to by the Eagle in the Heaven of Jupiter, who expresses the hope (perhaps ironically) that Hungary may no more be ill-treated at the hands of her kings, Par. xix. 142–3 [**Ungaria**].

Andrea, Jacomo da sant'. [**Jacomo**[3]].

Andromache, daughter of Eëtion, King of Thebes in Cilicia, and wife of Hector. On the capture of Troy she was taken prisoner by Neoptole-

mus, son of Achilles, who carried her to Epirus.

D. mentions A. in connexion with Virgil's account of her meeting with Aeneas at Buthrotum in Epirus, and her enquiry (*Aen.* iii. 339–40) after Ascanius, Mon. ii. 3$^{97-101}$ [**Ascanio**].

Anfiarao, Amphiaraus, son of Oicles and Hypermnestra, great prophet and hero of Argos. By his wife Eriphyle, sister of Adrastus, he was the father of Alcmaeon. He was one of the seven kings who joined in the expedition against Thebes (Inf. xiv. 68) [**Tebe**]; foreseeing that the issue would be fatal to himself, he concealed himself to avoid going to the war, but his hiding-place was revealed by his wife Eriphyle, who had been bribed by Polynices with the necklace of Harmonia (Purg. xii. 50–1) [**Armonia**]. A., as had been foreseen, met his death at Thebes, being swallowed up by the earth, but before he died he enjoined his son Alcmaeon to put Eriphyle to death on his return from Thebes, in punishment of her betrayal of him (Purg. xii. 50–1 ; Par. iv. 103–5). [**Almeone : Erifile.**]

D. places A. among the Soothsayers in Bolgia 4 of Circle VIII of Hell (Malebolge), and alludes to the manner of his death (the incident being borrowed from Statius, *Theb.* vii. 789–823 ; viii. 1 ff.), Inf. xx. 31–9 [**Indovini**].

Anfione, Amphion, son of Zeus and Antiope ; by the help of the Muses he built the walls of Thebes, the stones coming down from Mt. Cithaeron and placing themselves of their own accord, charmed by the magic skill with which he played on the lyre. D. mentions A. in connexion with the Muses and the assistance they gave him at Thebes, Inf. xxxii. 10–11 [Muse].

Angeli, Angels, the lowest Order in the Celestial Hierarchies, ranking last in the third Hierarchy, Conv. ii. 6^{44}; they preside over the Heaven of the Moon, Conv. ii. 6^{106-7} [Paradiso]; they are referred to by Beatrice (in the Crystalline Heaven) in her exposition of the Angelic Orders as *angelici ludi*, Par. xxviii. 126. [Gerarchia.]

Angelo, Castello Sant'. [Castello Sant' Angelo.]

Angiolello, Angiolello da Carignano, nobleman of Fano, who together with Guido del Cassero was invited by Malatestino, lord of Rimini, to a conference at La Cattolica on the Adriatic coast; as they were on their way to the rendezvous they were surprised in their boat, and thrown overboard and drowned off the promontory of Focara, by Malatestino's orders. The event took place soon after 1312, the year in which Malatestino succeeded his father as lord of Rimini.

This crime is foretold to D. by Pier da Medicina (in Bolgia 9 of Circle VIII of Hell), who bids him warn Angiolello and Guido of the fate which is in store for them, Inf. xxviii. 76–90. [Cattolica, La: Focara: Malatestino.]

Anglia. [Inghilterra.]

Anglici. [Inglesi.]

Anglicus. English; *Anglicum mare*, the English Channel, one of the limits of the *langue d'*oïl, V. E. i. 8^{61}. [*Lingua Oïl*.]

Anima, De, Aristotle's treatise *On Soul*, quoted as *Dell' Anima*, Conv. ii. 9^{64}, 10^{68}, 14^{241}; iii. 2^{83}, ^{125}, 6^{111}, 9^{54}; iv. 7^{111}, ^{139}, 13^{68}, 15^{116}, 20^{59}; *De Anima*, Mon. i. 3^{78}; iii. 16^{27}; A. T. § 5^{5-6}; the comment of Averroës on, Conv. iv. 13^{68}; Mon. i. 3^{77-8}; A. T. § 5^{5-6}; Aristotle's opinion that the soul is immortal, Conv. ii. 9^{63-4} (*An.* ii. 2); that the influence of the agent affects the passive nature disposed to receive it, Conv. ii. 10^{66-8} (*An.* ii. 2); that science is of high nobility because of the nobleness of its subject and its certainty, Conv. ii. 14^{240-3} (*An.* i. 1); that the principal faculties of the soul are three in number, viz. vegetative, sensitive, and intellectual, and that it is further endued with scientific, deliberative, inventive, and judicatory faculties, Conv. iii. 2^{82-6}, $^{122-31}$ (*An.* ii. 2; iii. 9); that the soul is the active principle of the body and hence its cause, Conv. iii. 6^{110-13} (*An.* ii. 1); that, strictly speaking, light and colour alone are visible, Conv. iii. 9^{51-4} (*An.* ii. 7); that life is the existence of the living, and that the several faculties of the soul stand one above the other, just as do the pentagon, quadrangle, and triangle, Conv. iv. 7^{110-12}, $^{139-45}$ (*An.* ii. 2; ii. 3); that the mind is healthy when it knows things as they are, Conv. iv. 15^{111-16} (*An.* iii. 3); that things should be adapted to the powers acting upon them, in order to receive their influence, Conv. iv. 30^{58-61} (*An.* ii. 2); that the soul, being eternal, is alone incorruptible, Mon. iii. 16^{25-9} (*An.* ii. 2). [Aristotile.]

Animae, De Quantitate, St. Augustine's treatise *On the Capacity of the Soul*; cited in support of the contention that memory is powerless to retain the most exalted impressions of the human intellect (cf. *De Quant.* Cap. 33), Epist. x. 28^{556-7}. [**Agostino**[2].]

Animalibus, De, Aristotle's books *On Animals*, quoted as *Degli Animali*, Conv. ii. 3^{14}, 9^{79}. Under this title D. apparently quotes two different works of Aristotle, viz. the *De Historia Animalium* (in ten books) and the *De Partibus Animalium* (in four books), since of the two passages referred to by him one comes from the former work and one from the latter; further, he speaks (Conv. ii. 9^{79}) of the *twelfth* book *On Animals*, from which it is evident that two or more of Aristotle's works on this subject were regarded in his time as forming one collection. In the Arabic versions, upon which the Latin translation of Michael Scot was based, the ten books of the *De Historia Animalium*, the four of the *De Partibus Animalium*, and the five of the *De Generatione Animalium*, were grouped together in a single collection of nineteen books. Since D. quotes the last of these works separately (A. T. § 13^{42}), and the passage he refers to as occurring in the twelfth book *On Animals* comes from the eighth book of the *De Historia Animalium*, it appears that the *De Animalibus*, as known to him, consisted of the four books *De Partibus Animalium* and the ten *De Historia Animalium*, in that order; this would satisfactorily account for his speaking of the

eighth book of the latter as 'il duodecimo degli Animali'.

D. quotes Aristotle's opinion that the pleasures of the intellect transcend those of the senses, Conv. ii. 3^{10-15} (*Part. Anim.* i. 5); that man is the most perfect of all animals, Conv. ii. 9^{78-80} (*Hist. Anim.* viii. 1). [**Aristotile**.]

Animalium, De Generatione, Aristotle's treatise *On the Generation of Animals*; his saying that God and Nature always work for the best, A. T. § 13^{39-42} (*Gen. Anim.* ii. 6). [**Aristotile**.]

Anna[1], St. Anne, mother of the Virgin Mary; placed in the Celestial Rose, where her seat is pointed out to D. by St. Bernard, Par. xxxii. 133–7 [**Rosa**]; mentioned as the mother of the Virgin and wife of Joachim, Conv. ii. 6^{13-14} [**Gioachino**[2]: **Maria Salome**].

Anna[2], Annas, father-in-law of Caiaphas the high-priest; he is referred to (by Catalano) as 'il suocero' of Caiaphas (in allusion to *John* xviii. 13), and represented as being crucified on the ground, together with the latter and the Pharisees who condemned Christ, among the Hypocrites in Bolgia 6 of Circle VIII of Hell (Malebolge), Inf. xxiii. 115–23. [**Ipocriti**.]

Annibale, Hannibal, the great Carthaginian general, son of Hamilcar Barca, born B. C. 247, died c. B. C. 183. After overrunning Spain, H. carried the war against the Romans into Italy, and in the course of the second Punic war defeated them at the Lacus Trasimenus B.C. 217, and at Cannae in the next year. After the defeat and death of his

brother Hasdrubal at the Metaurus
(B.C. 207) he crossed over to Africa,
where he was completely defeated
by Publius Scipio Africanus at Zama,
B.C. 202 [**Scipione** [1]].

D. mentions Hannibal in connexion with his defeat at Zama, Inf.
xxxi. 117 [**Zama**]; his passage of
the Alps and the victories of the
Roman Eagle, Par. vi. 50 [**Arabi**:
Po]; his victory over the Romans
at Cannae, Inf. xxviii. 11; Conv.
iv. 5[166] [**Canne**]; his threatened assault on Rome, *Hannibal*, Mon. ii.
4[58—64]; his final overthrow by Scipio,
Mon. ii. 11[59—61]; the condition of
Rome in D.'s day such as to merit
even the pity of Hannibal, Epist. viii.
10[142—3].

Ansalone. [**Absalone.**]

Anselmo, Anselm, Archbishop of
Canterbury; he was born at Aosta
in Piedmont in 1033, entered the
abbey of Bec in Normandy in 1060,
became Prior in 1063, Abbot in
1078; in 1093 he was appointed
Archbishop of Canterbury, where
he died in 1109. The most important of his theological works are
the *Monologion*, the *Proslogion* and
the *Cur Deus Homo*, a treatise on the
Atonement.

A. is placed among the doctors
of the Church (*Spiriti Sapienti*) in
the Heaven of the Sun, Par. xii. 137.
[**Sole, Cielo del.**]

Anselmuccio, grandson of Count
Ugolino della Gherardesca of Pisa,
whose imprisonment and death he
shared in 1288 in the Tower of
Famine at Pisa, Inf. xxxiii. 50; he and
his uncle Uguccione, and his elder brother Nino, are referred to as *li tre*, *v.*
71; and he and his uncle Gaddo as

gli altri due, *v.* 90 [**Ugolino,
Conte**]. A., who was about 15 at
the time of his death, was the
younger brother of Nino il Brigata
(*v.* 89), they being the sons of
Guelfo, eldest son of Ugolino, and
Elena, natural daughter of Enzio,
King of Sardinia, natural son of
Frederick II. [**Brigata, Il.**]

Antaeus. [**Anteo.**]

Antandro, Antandros, city of
Great Mysia, on the Adramyttian
Gulf, whence Aeneas sailed for Italy
after the fall of Troy (*Aen.* iii. 1—11).
The Emperor Justinian (in the
Heaven of Mercury) mentions it, together with the Simoïs (*Aen.* v. 634)
and the tomb of Hector (*Aen.* v.
371), to indicate the Troad, which
he says was revisited by the Roman
Eagle after the battle of Pharsalia
(the reference being probably to the
visit of Julius Caesar to Troy while
in pursuit of Pompey, which is recorded by Lucan, *Phars.* ix. 961 ff.),
Par. vi. 67.

Antenora, name (derived from
the Trojan Antenor, who was universally, in the Middle Ages, held
to have betrayed Troy to the Greeks)
given by D. to the second of the four
divisions of Circle IX of Hell, where
Traitors are punished, Inf. xxxii.
88 [**Inferno**]; here are placed those
who have been traitors to their country, their city, or their party, Inf.
xxxii. 70—xxxiii. 90 [**Traditori**].
Examples: Bocca degli Abati [**Bocca**]; Buoso da Duera [**Buoso** [3]];
Tesauro de' Beccheria [**Beccheria**];
Gianni de' Soldanieri; [**Gianni** [1]];
Tebaldello de' Zambrasi [**Tebaldello**]; Ganalon [**Ganellone**];
Ugolino della Gherardesca [**Ugo-**

lino, Conte]; Archbishop Ruggieri degli Ubaldini [**Ruggieri, Arcivescovo**].

Antenori, descendants of the Trojan Antenor, who is said to have betrayed Troy to the Greeks; name applied by Jacopo del Cassero (in Ante-purgatory) to the inhabitants of Padua, which is supposed to have been founded by Antenor, Purg. v. 75. [**Antenora.**]

Anteo, Antaeus, son of Neptune and Earth, mighty giant and wrestler of Libya, whose strength was invincible so long as he remained in contact with his mother earth. Hercules discovered the source of his strength, lifted him from the ground, and crushed him in the air.

A. is placed, along with Nimrod, Ephialtes, and Briareus, to keep ward at the mouth of Circle IX of Hell, Inf. xxxi. 100, 113, 139; *quegli, v.* 130; *il gigante,* xxxii. 17; at Virgil's request A. lifts him and D. down on to the ice of Cocytus (Inf. xxxi. 115–43) [**Giganti**]; D. describes the contest between Hercules and Antaeus, referring to Ovid (*Metam.* ix. 183–4) and Lucan as his authorities, Conv. iii. 3⁵⁰⁻⁶⁶; and refers to it as an instance of a single combat, *Antaeus,* Mon. ii. 878⁻⁸³, 10⁸⁷⁻⁹. [**Atalanta.**]

A., for details in his account of whom (Inf. xxxi. 115–121, 132) D. was indebted to Lucan (*Phars.* iv. 593–660), is represented as being unbound (Inf. xxxi. 101), since, unlike the other giants, who are in chains (*vv.* 87, 88, 104), he did not join in the war against the gods (*vv.* 119–121).

Antepraedicamenta, name by which D. quotes the first part of the *Praedicamenta* or *Categories* of Aristotle, which forms an introduction to the rest of the work, A. T. § 12⁵⁶.

The *Categories* are twice elsewhere quoted under the title of *Praedicamenta,* Mon. iii. 15⁵⁸; A. T. § 2⁶. [***Praedicamenta.***]

Antictona, Antichthon (Gk. ἀντίχθων), i.e. 'counter-Earth', name given by Pythagoras (according to Aristotle, *De Coelo,* ii. 13) to a supposed sphere, opposite to, and corresponding with, the Earth, Conv. iii. 5²⁹⁻³². [**Terra².**]

Antifonte, Antiphon, Greek tragic poet, mentioned by Aristotle (*Rhet.* ii. 2, 6, 23); Virgil names him, together with Simonides and Agathon, among the poets of antiquity who are with Homer and himself in Limbo, Purg. xxii. 106 (where for *Antifonte* some edd. read *Anacreonte*) [**Limbo**].

Antigone, daughter of Oedipus, King of Thebes, by his mother Jocasta, and sister of Ismene, Eteocles, and Polynices; when Oedipus had put out his eyes, and was compelled to leave Thebes, she accompanied him and remained with him until he died at Colonus; she then returned to Thebes, and, after her two brothers had killed each other, in defiance of Creon, King of Thebes, she buried the body of Polynices; Creon thereupon had her shut up in a cave, where she put an end to her life. [**Edipo : Eteocle.**]

Virgil, addressing Statius (in Purgatory), mentions A., together with Deiphyle, Argia, Ismene, Hypsipyle, Manto, and Thetis, and Deidamia and her sisters, as being 'delle genti tue' (i.e. mentioned in the *Thebaid* or *Achilleid*), among the great women of antiquity in Limbo, Purg. xxii. 109–14. [**Limbo.**]

Antinferno], Ante-hell, a division of Hell, outside the river of Acheron, where are the souls of those who did neither good nor evil, and were not qualified to enter Hell itself; these are naked and are tormented by gadflies and wasps, so that their faces stream with blood, Inf. iii. 1–69 [**Inferno**]; among them D. sees the shade of Pope Celestine V, *vv*. 58–60 [**Celestino: Vigliacchi**].

Antioco], Antiochus Epiphanes, King of Syria (d. B.C. 164), youngest son of Antiochus the Great. Together with the high-priest Jason he endeavoured to root out the Jewish religion and to introduce Greek customs and the worship of Greek divinities (2 *Maccab.* iv. 13–16). This attempt led to a rising of the Jewish people under Mattathias and his sons the Maccabees, which resulted in the preservation of the name and faith of Israel.

Pope Nicholas III (in Bolgia 3 of Circle VIII of Hell), speaking of Jason, alludes to A. as 'suo re', and, referring to the Book of Maccabees, draws a parallel between their machinations and those of Clement V and Philip the Fair of France, Inf. xix. 82–7 [**Clemente**[2] **: Filippo**[2] **: Jasone**[2]].

Antipurgatorio], Ante-purgatory, region outside the actual gate of Purgatory, answering somewhat to the Limbo of Hell; referred to by Forese Donati (in Circle VI of Purgatory) as *la costa ove s'aspetta*, Purg.

xxiii. 89 [**Purgatorio**]. Here are located the spirits of those who died without having availed themselves of the means of penitence offered by the Church. They are divided into four classes:—1. Those who died in contumacy of the Church, and only repented at the last moment; these have to remain in Ante-purgatory for a period thirtyfold that during which they had been contumacious, unless the period be shortened by the prayers of others on their behalf (Purg. iii. 136–41). *Example*: King Manfred [**Manfredi**].—2. Those who in indolence and indifference put off their repentance until just before their death; these are detained outside Purgatory for a period equal to that of their lives upon earth, unless it be shortened by prayers on their behalf (Purg. iv. 130–5). *Example*: Belacqua of Florence [**Belacqua**].—3. Those who died a violent death, without absolution, but repented at the last moment; these are detained under the same conditions as the last class; during their detention they move round and round, chanting the *Miserere* (Purg. v. 22–4, 52–7). *Examples*: Jacopo del Cassero [**Cassero, Jacopo del**]; Buonconte da Montefeltro [**Buonconte**]; La Pia of Siena [**Pia, La**]; Benincasa of Arezzo [**Benincasa**]; Cione de' Tarlati [**Cione**]; Federico Novello of Battifolle [**Federico Novello**]; Farinata degli Scornigiani [**Farinata**[2]]; Count Orso [**Orso, Conte**]; Pierre de la Brosse [**Broccia, Pier dalla**]; and Sordello, who is stationed apart (Purg. vi. 58) [**Sordello**].—4. Kings and princes who deferred their repentance owing to the pressure of temporal interests ; these are detained for the same period as the last two classes ; they are placed in a valley full of flowers, and are guarded at night by two angels against the attacks of a serpent (Purg. vii. 64–84 ; viii. 22–39). *Examples* : Emperor Rudolf [**Ridolfo**] ; Ottocar of Bohemia [**Ottachero**] ; Philip III of France [**Filippo**[1]] ; Henry I of Navarre [**Arrigo**[7]] ; Peter III of Aragon [**Pietro**[3]] ; Charles I of Naples [**Carlo**[1]] ; Alphonso III of Aragon [**Alfonso**[1]] ; Henry III of England [**Arrigo**[9]] ; William of Montferrat [**Guglielmo**[3]] ; Nino Visconti of Pisa [**Nino**[2]] ; and Conrad Malaspina the younger [**Malaspina, Currado**[2]].

Antonio, Sant', St. Anthony the Egyptian hermit (not to be confounded with his namesake of Padua), born at Coma in Upper Egypt in 251, died at the age of 105 in 356. His symbol is a hog, which is generally represented as lying at his feet. The monks of his order kept herds of swine, which were fattened at the public expense, and which were regarded by the common folk with superstitious reverence, a fact which the monks turned to account when collecting alms.

Beatrice (in the Crystalline Heaven) mentions St. A. and his hog in the course of her denunciation of the Preaching Friars, who practised upon the credulity of the common people, Par. xxix. 124–6.

Anubis, Egyptian divinity, which was identified by the Romans and by mediaeval writers with Mercury ; D. uses the name as a synonym for Mercury, whose address to Aeneas (*Aen.* iv. 272–6) he quotes, Epist. vii. 4[86] (where for *Anubis* some read *a nubibus*).

[**Aonides**], the Muses (so called from Aonia, part of Boeotia, in which were Mt. Helicon and the fountain Aganippe, sacred to them), Carm. 36. [**Muse.**]

Aonius, of Aonia (part of Boeotia) ; *montes Aonii,* the range of Mt. Helicon, Ecl. i. 28. [**Aonides : Elicona.**]

Apennino[1], Apennine range, which forms the backbone of Italy, branching off from the Alps at the head of the Gulf of Genoa ; mentioned in connexion with the source of the Acquaqueta, Inf. xvi. 96 [**Acquaqueta**], and of the Archiano, Purg. v. 96 [**Archiano**] ; one of the S. limits of the *langue d'oïl,* V. E. i. 8[62–3] ; taken by D. as the dividing line (from N. to S.) of Italy in his examination of the various local dialects, V. E. i. 10[41–7], 14[1–2] ; crossed by the Roman Eagle in company with the Emperor Henry VII, Epist. vii. 1[16] ; alluded to as *alpe,* Inf. xvi. 101 [**Benedetto, San**] ; *alpi,* Canz. xi. 61 ; *il giogo di che il Tever si disserra,* Inf. xxvii. 30 [**Tevere**] ; *il gran giogo,* Purg. v. 116 [**Casentino**] ; *l' alpestro monte,* Purg. xiv. 32 [**Peloro**] ; *il monte,* Purg. xiv. 92 [**Romagna**] ; *lo dosso d' Italia,* Purg. xxx. 86 ; *grave giogo,* Par. xi. 48 [**Gualdo**] ; *sassi,* the peaks of the Apennines being described as rising between the shores of the Adriatic and the Mediterranean, Par. xxi. 106 [**Catria**] ; *pater Apenninus,* Carm. 42.

Some think the Apennines are the mountains referred to as *Apennino*

(var. *Pennino*), Inf. xx. 65 ; the reference is more probably to the Pennine
Alps [Apennino [2] : Pennino].

Apennino [2], spur of the Rhaetian
Alps, situated above Gargnano,
NW. of the Lago di Garda ; thought
by some to be the *Apennino* (var.
Pennino) mentioned Inf. xx. 65
[Pennino : Val Camonica].
Apenninus. [Apennino [1].]

Apocalypsis], *Apocalypse* or *Revelation of St. John* ; quoted as *Johannis
Visio*, Epist. x. 33[626] (*Rev.* i. 8) ;
referred to, Inf. xix. 106-10 (ref. to
Rev. xvii. 1-3) ; Purg. xxix. 105
(ref. to *Rev.* iv. 8) ; Par. xxv. 94-6
(ref. to *Rev.* vii. 9) ; Par. xxvi.
17 (ref. to *Rev.* i. 8). The Apocalypse is supposed to be symbolized
by the solitary elder, who walks
sleeping with undimmed countenance
behind all the rest, in the mystical
Procession in the Terrestrial Paradise, Purg. xxix. 143-4. [Gio-
vanni [2].]

Apollo, son of Jupiter and Latona, who gave birth to him and his
twin-sister Diana on the island of
Delos [Delo : Diana : Latona].
A. was god of the Sun, Diana of the
Moon, hence D. speaks of them together as *li due occhi del cielo*, Purg.
xx. 132 ; and of the Sun and Moon
as *ambedue i figli di Latona*, Par.
xxix. 1 ; similarly he speaks of the
Sun as *Phoebae frater*, Mon. i. 11[35] ;
Phoebus, Mon. ii. 9[95] ; *Delius*, Epist.
vi. 2[55] [Sole].

D. invokes A. as god of music
and song, Par. i. 13 [Calliope :
Parnaso] ; Par. ii. 8 ; Epist. x.
18[315-16], 31[386, 389] ; calls him
Timbreo (from Thymbra, where he
had a celebrated temple), Purg. xii.

31 [Timbreo] ; *divina virtù*, Par.
i. 22 ; *la Delfica deità* (from his famous oracle at Delphi), Par. i. 32 ;
refers to his worship, Par. xiii. 25
[Peana] ; the prophecy of his oracle
that the two daughters of Adrastus
would marry a lion and a wild-boar,
Conv. iv. 25[66] [Adrasto] ; being
obliged to serve a mortal for a year,
for having slain the Cyclops, he
tended the flocks of Admetus, King
of Pherae in Thessaly, hence G. del
Virgilio speaks of him as *pastor
Apollo*, Ecl. R. 79.

Apostoli, the twelve Apostles ;
only three of them (St. Peter, St.
James, and St. John) present at the
Transfiguration, Conv. ii. 1[46-8] ;
Par. xxv. 33 ; the saying of Christ
to Peter (*Matt.* xvi. 19 ; *John* xx.
23) addressed equally to the rest of
the Apostles, Mon. iii. 8[1-8] ; all
present with Christ at the Last Supper, Mon. iii. 9[33-4] ; the Pope not
entitled to receive temporal goods,
save for the purpose of dispensing
them to the poor, as did the Apostles, Mon. iii. 10[128-32] ; the *Acts of
the Apostles*, Mon. ii. 8[70] ; iii. 13[42]
[Actus Apostolorum].

Apostolo. [Jacopo : Paolo.]
Apostolorum, Actus. [Actus
Apostolorum.]
Apostolus. [Apostolo.]
Aprilis, of April ; *Kalendae
Apriles*, the kalends of April (i.e.
April 1), Epist. vi. 6[197].

Apuli, Apulians ; their dialect
differs from those of the Romans
and Sicilians, V. E. i. 10[61-3] ; condemned as harsh, V. E. i. 12[56] ; rejected by some of their poets in favour
of the 'curial' language, V. E. i.
12[61-9] ; their best writers, like those

of Sicily, Tuscany, Romagna, Lombardy, and the two Marches, wrote in the Italian vulgar tongue, V. E. i. 19$^{15-19}$ [**Apulus.**]

Apulia. [**Puglia.**]

Apulus, Apulian ; *Apulum Vulgare,* the Apulian dialect, neither that nor the Sicilian the most beautiful in Italy, V. E. i. 12$^{71-3}$. [**Apuli : Pugliese.**]

Aqua et Terra, Quaestio de. [***Quaestio de Aqua et Terra.***]

Aquario, Aquarius ('the Waterbearer'), constellation and eleventh sign of the Zodiac, which the Sun enters about Jan. 20 (equivalent to Jan. 10 in D.'s day); D. speaks of the time of the young year 'when the Sun is tempering (i. e. warming) his rays beneath Aquarius', the period indicated being the latter half of January or the beginning of February, Inf. xxiv. 1–2. [**Zodiaco.**]

Aquila[1], the Imperial Eagle, the Roman standard, Purg. x. 80 ; Par. vi. 1 ; *l' uccel di Giove,* Purg. xxxii. 112 ; *l' uccel di Dio,* Par. vi. 4 ; *il sacrosanto segno,* Par. vi. 32 ; *il pubblico segno,* Par. vi. 100 ; *il segno Che fe' i Romani al mondo riverendi,* Par. xix. 101 ; *il segno del mondo,* Par. xx. 8 ; *lo benedetto segno,* Par. xx. 86 ; hence, as symbol of the Roman Emperors, Purg. xxxii. 125 ; xxxiii. 38 ; Mon. ii. 11^{25}, 13^{55} ; Epist. v. 4^{53} ; vi. 3^{81} ; *signa Tarpeia,* Epist. vii. 1^{17} ; *Jovis armiger,* Carm. 26 [**Jupiter**].

In the Heaven of Mercury the Emperor Justinian traces the course of the Imperial Eagle from the time when it was carried westward from Troy by Aeneas (the founder of the Roman Empire), down to the time when the Guelfs opposed it, and the Ghibellines made a party ensign of it, Par. vi. 1–111 (cf. Conv. iv. 5$^{88-176}$, and Mon. ii. 4$^{27-70}$, 11$^{8-63}$, where similar summaries of periods of Roman history are given).

Aquila[2], the Eagle in the Heaven of Jupiter; the spirits of the Just (*Spiriti Giudicanti*), having formed successively the letters of the

Figures illustrating the successive changes of the shape assumed by the Spirits of the Just, from M to the Florentine lily and Imperial Eagle.
(From the design of the Duke of Sermoneta.)

sentence 'Diligite justitiam qui judicatis terram' (Par. xviii. 79–93), remain for a time in the shape of M, the final letter (fig. *a*) (*vv.* 94–6) ; then gradually other spirits join them, and the M is by degrees metamorphosed, first into the lily of Florence or fleur-de-lys (fig. *b*), and then into the Imperial Eagle (fig. *c*) (*vv.* 97–114) ; *aquila,* Par. xviii. 107 ; *imprenta, v.* 114 ; *bella image,* Par. xix. 2, 21 ; *quel segno, v.* 37 ; *benedetta imagine, v.* 95 ; *il segno Che fe' i Romani al mondo riverendi, vv.* 101–2 ; *il segno del mondo,* Par. xx. 8 ; *aquila, v.* 26 ; *l' imago della imprenta Dell' eterno piacere, vv.* 76–7 ; *benedetto segno, v.* 86 ; *imagine divina, v.* 139. [**Aquila**[1] : **Giove, Cielo di.**]

After an apostrophe from D. on

Papal avarice (Par. xviii. 115, 136), the Eagle begins to speak, using the first person as representing the spirits of which it is composed (Par. xix. 10–13); having stated that it owes its place in Heaven to the righteousness of the spirits while on earth (vv. 13–18), it goes on to reprehend the evil deeds of certain princes, referring in particular to the invasion of Bohemia by Albert of Austria (vv. 115–17) [**Alberto**[2]: **Buemme**]; the debasement of his coinage by Philip IV of France, and his coming death (vv. 118–20) [**Filippo**[2]]; the wars between England and Scotland (vv. 121–3) [**Inghilese**]; the luxury and effeminacy of Ferdinand IV of Castile and of Wenceslas IV of Bohemia (vv. 124–6) [**Spagna: Buemme**]; the depravity of Charles II of Naples (vv. 127–9) [**Carlo**[2]]; the avarice and baseness of Frederick II of Sicily (vv. 130–5) [**Federico**[3]]; the 'filthy works' of Don Jaime of Majorca and of James II of Aragon (vv. 136–8) [**Jacomo**[1]: **Jacomo**[2]]; the misdoings of Dionysius of Portugal and Hakon Longshanks of Norway, and the false coining of Stephen Ouros of Rascia (vv. 139–41) [**Dionisio**[3]: **Acone**[2]: **Rascia**]; the misfortunes of Hungary, and the union of Navarre with France (vv. 142–4) [**Ungaria: Navarra**]; and finally the miseries of Cyprus under Henry II of Lusignan (vv. 145–8) [**Arrigo**[8]: **Cipri.**] After a pause the Eagle resumes, explaining to D. that the spirits which form its eye and eyebrow (the head being in profile, only one eye is visible—see engraving

below) are the most exalted (Par. xx. 31–6); it then proceeds to name these, pointing out that the pupil of the eye is formed by David (vv. 37–42), while the eyebrow, beginning

Eye and eyebrow of the Eagle formed by—1. David; 2. Trajan; 3. Hezekiah; 4. Constantine; 5. William of Sicily; 6. Rhipeus.

from the side nearest the beak, is formed by five others, viz. Trajan (vv. 43–8), Hezekiah (vv. 49–54), Constantine (vv. 56–60); William the Good of Sicily (vv. 61–6), and Rhipeus (vv. 67–72) [**David: Ezechia: Costantino: Guglielmo**[2]: **Rifeo: Traiano**].

Aquileienses, inhabitants of Aquileia, ancient city in the Venetian territory, at the head of the Adriatic; their dialect distinct from those of the Trevisans, Venetians, and Istrians, V. E. i. 10[69–70]; condemned, with that of the Istrians, as harsh and unpleasant, V. E. i. 11[76–8].

Aquilone, Aquilo, the N. wind, Purg. xxxii. 99 [**Austro**]; hence the N., Purg. iv. 60; Conv. iv. 20[76] [**Borea**].

Aquino, Rinaldo d'. [**Renaldus de Aquino.**]

Aquino, Tommaso d'. [**Tommaso**[2].]

Arabi, Arabs; term applied by an anachronism to the Carthaginians (whose territory in D.'s day was occupied by the Arabs), the reference being to their passage of the

Alps under Hannibal, and their subsequent defeat by Scipio, Par. vi. 49–51. [Cartaginesi.]

Arabia, Arabia; alluded to as *ciò che di sopra il mar rosso ee,* i.e. the country above the Red Sea (though some think that Egypt is intended), Inf. xxiv. 90; mentioned in connexion with the Arabian usage of reckoning the commencement of the day from sunset, instead of from sunrise, with reference to the death of Beatrice, which D. says took place 'secondo l'usanza d'Arabia, nella prima ora del nono giorno del mese' (i.e. not on June 9, as usually supposed, but on the evening of June 8, which according to the Arabian usage would be the beginning of June 9), V.N. § 30[1–3].

D.'s object in introducing the Arabian usage is plain. He wishes to bring in the number *nine* in connexion with the day, month, and year of B.'s death. The year, he says, was that in which the number ten had been nine times completed in Cent. xiii, i.e. 1290; the month, June, the sixth according to our usage, but the ninth according to the Syrian usage; and the day, the eighth according to our usage, but the ninth according to the Arabian usage. The information as to the Arabian and Syrian reckonings D. got from the *Elementa Astronomica* (Cap. i) of Alfraganus [Alfergano: Tisrin primo].

Aragne, Arachne (i.e. 'spider'), Lydian maiden, who excelled in the art of weaving, and, proud of her skill, challenged Minerva to compete with her. A. produced a piece of cloth in which the amours of the gods were woven; and Minerva, unable to find fault with it, tore it in pieces. In despair A. hanged herself, but the goddess loosened the rope and saved her life, the rope being changed into a cobweb, and A. herself into a spider. D. mentions A. (whose story is told by Ovid, *Metam.* vi. 1–145) on account of her skill in weaving, Inf. xvii. 18; and includes her amongst the examples of defeated pride in Circle I of Purgatory, Purg. xii. 43–45 [Superbi].

Aragona, Aragon, one of the old kingdoms of Spain, of which (with Catalonia) it forms the NE. corner; Manfred (in Ante-purgatory) mentions it in connexion with his daughter Constance, the wife of Peter III of Aragon, whom he speaks of as ' genitrice Dell' onor di Cicilia e d'Aragona ' (the allusion being probably to the second and third sons of Constance and Peter, viz. James, King of Aragon, and Frederick, King of Sicily), Purg. iii. 115–16 [Federico[3]: Jacomo[1]: Table B]; *montes Aragoniae,* i.e. the Pyrenees, one of the limits of the *langue d'*oïl, V. E. i. 8[26]. [Lingua Oïl: Pirenes.]

Aragones, inhabitants of Aragon, which is bounded on the E. by Catalonia, on the S. and W. by Castile, and on the NW. by Navarre; their king an instance of a prince whose jurisdiction is limited by the confines of the neighbouring kingdoms, while that of the Emperor is bounded by the ocean alone, Mon. i. 11[82–7].

Aragonia. [Aragona.]

Arbia, small stream of Tuscany, which rises a few miles S. of Siena and runs into the Ombrone at Buon-convento; on its left bank is the hill of Montaperti, where was fought (Sept. 4, 1260) the great battle be-tween the Ghibellines and Guelfs of Florence, referred to by D. as *Lo strazio e il grande scempio Che fece l'Arbia colorata in rosso*, Inf. x. 85–6. [**Montaperti.**]

Arca, Dell', ancient noble family of Florence (extinct in D.'s day); mentioned by Cacciaguida (in the Heaven of Mars) as having been of importance in his lifetime, Par. xvi. 92.

[**Arcades**], inhabitants of Arcadia, a pastoral people and lovers of music, Ecl. R. 21, 22.

Arcangeli, Archangels, the low-est Order but one in the Celestial Hierarchies, ranking next above the Angels, Conv. ii. 6$^{44-5}$; they pre-side over the Heaven of Mercury, Conv. ii. 6^{108} [**Gerarchia: Para-diso**]; Beatrice (in the Crystalline Heaven) mentions them as forming, together with Principalities and An-gels, the third Celestial Hierarchy, Par. xxviii. 124–6.

Archemoro, Archemorus or Opheltes, son of Lycurgus, King of Nemea; while under the charge of the captive Hypsipyle he was killed by the bite of a serpent, whereupon Lycurgus would have put H. to death had she not been rescued by her two sons. D. quotes from Statius (*Theb.* v. 609–10) the apo-strophe of Hypsipyle to A., Conv. iii. 11$^{165-9}$; the death of A. is referred to as *la tristizia di Licurgo*, Purg. xxvi. 94. [**Isifile: Licurgo**[1]**.**]

Archiano, now Archiana, tor-rent in Tuscany, which rises in the Apennines above Camaldoli and falls into the Arno just above Bibbiena in the Casentino, Purg. v. 95, 125.

Arcippe], daughter of Minyas of Boeotia; referred to, with her sisters Alcithoë and Leucippe, Epist. iv. 5$^{44-5}$. [**Alcithoë.**]

Ardinghi, ancient noble family of Florence (in low estate in D.'s day); mentioned by Cacciaguida (in the Heaven of Mars) among the great families existing in his time, Par. xvi. 93.

Aretini, Aretines, inhabitants of Arezzo, Inf. xxii. 5; in describing the course of the Arno, Guido del Duca (in Circle II of Purgatory) refers to the Aretines, who were in a state of almost constant feud with Florence, as *Botoli . . . Ringhiosi più che non chiede lor possa*, 'curs who snarl more than their power warrants', Purg. xiv. 46–7 [**Arno**]; their dialect distinct from that of the Sienese, V. E. i. 10$^{75-6}$; con-demned with the rest of the Tuscan dialects, a specimen of it being given, V. E. i. 13$^{27-8}$. [**Arezzo.**]

Aretino, inhabitant of Arezzo, Inf. xxx. 31 [**Griffolino**]; Purg. vi. 13 [**Benincasa**]; Purg. vi. 15 [**Cione**]; V. E. i. 13^7; ii. 6^{87} [**Guittone**].

Aretinus. [**Aretino.**]

Aretinus, Guitto. [**Guittone.**]

Aretusa, Arethusa, one of the Nereids, nymph of the fountain of Arethusa in the island of Ortygia near Syracuse; being pursued by the river-god Alpheus, she appealed to Artemis, who changed her into the fountain of the same name; Ovid's account (*Metam.* v. 587 ff.) of the metamorphosis is alluded to, Inf. xxv. 97–8.

Arezzo, city in SE. of Tuscany, about midway between Florence and Perugia; mentioned as his native place by the alchemist Griffolino (in Bolgia 10 of Circle VIII of Hell), Inf. xxix. 109 [**Griffolino**]; alluded to by Guido del Duca (in Circle II of Purgatory) in his description of the course of the Arno, which flows SE. through the Casentino to within four or five miles of the city, and then makes a great bend and flows NW. towards Florence, Purg. xiv. 46–8. [**Aretini: Arno.**]

Argenti, Filippo, member of a branch of the Adimari family of Florence, placed by D. among the Wrathful in Circle V of Hell, Inf. viii. 61; *un pien di fango, v.* 32; *persona orgogliosa, v.* 46; *il fiorentino spirito bizarro, v.* 62. [**Iracondi.**]

Argi, Argives; their hospitality abused by the Trojans (allusion to the rape of Helen from Sparta by Paris), Epist. v. 8[129]. In classical Latin *Argi* could only mean Argos, but by post-classical and mediaeval writers it was used also in the sense of Greeks.

Argía, daughter of Adrastus, King of Argos, sister of Deiphyle, and wife of Polynices of Thebes; Virgil, addressing Statius (in Purgatory), mentions her as being 'delle genti tue' (i. e. mentioned in the *Thebaid* or *Achilleid*) among the great women of antiquity in Limbo, Purg. xxii. 110 [**Antigone: Limbo**]; she and Deiphyle are mentioned as examples of modesty, Conv. iv. 25[78–88]. [**Adrasto.**]

Argivi, Argives; Adrastus, King of, Conv. iv. 25[62]. [**Adrasto.**]

Argo[1], ship Argo, built by Argus, son of Phrixus, in which the Argonauts sailed to Colchis in search of the golden fleece, Par. xxxiii. 96. [**Argonauti: Jasone**[1].]

Argo[2], Argus, son of Arestor, surnamed Panoptes ('all-seeing') because he had a hundred eyes. Juno, jealous of Jupiter's love for Io, set A. to watch over her after she had been metamorphosed into a cow; but Jupiter commanded Mercury to slay him. Mercury therefore descended to earth in the guise of a shepherd, and, having beguiled A. to sleep with the story of the metamorphosis of Syrinx, cut off his head. Juno thereupon transplanted his eyes into the tail of her favourite bird, the peacock.

A. is mentioned in connexion with his eyes, which are compared to those on the wings of the four beasts in the mystical Procession in the Terrestrial Paradise, Purg. xxix. 95–6; his being set to sleep by the story of Syrinx and his death (related by Ovid, *Metam.* i. 622 ff.) are referred to, Purg. xxxii. 64–6 [**Siringa**].

Argolico, belonging to Argolis or Argos; *gente Argolica,* i.e. the Greeks, mentioned by Pier da Medicina (in Bolgia 9 of Circle VIII of Hell), perhaps with an allusion to the Argonauts, Inf. xxviii. 84. [**Argonauti: Greci.**]

Argonauti], Argonauts, 'sailors of the Argo' who, under the leadership of Jason, sailed to Colchis in search of the golden fleece; D. speaks of them as *Quei gloriosi che passaro a Colco,* Par. ii. 16; and alludes to them (perhaps) as *gente*

Argolica, Inf. xxviii. 84; and to their expedition, Inf. xviii. 86–7. [**Argo**[1] : **Jasone**[1].]

Arianna], Ariadne, daughter of Minos and Pasiphaë, and sister of the Minotaur [**Minos : Pasife : Minotauro**]. She fell in love with Theseus when he came to Crete to bring the tribute of the Athenians to the Minotaur, and gave him the sword with which he slew the monster, and the clue of thread by means of which he found his way out of the Labyrinth [**Dedalo**]. Theseus in return promised to marry her, and took her away with him from Crete, but deserted her in Naxos; here she was found by Bacchus, who made her his wife and at her death placed among the stars, as the constellation of the Crown, the garland she had worn at her marriage (Par. xiii. 13–14) [**Bacco**].

Virgil (in Round 1 of Circle VII of Hell) refers to A. (whose story is told by Ovid, *Metam.* viii. 156 ff.) as the sister of the Minotaur, with an allusion to her love for Theseus, Inf. xii. 19–20 [**Teseo**]; she is referred to, in connexion with the constellation of the Crown, as *la figliuola di Minoi*, Par. xiii. 14 [**Corona**].

[**Aries**], the Ram; G. del Virgilio speaks of the river Montone as *Aries fluvialis*, Ecl. R. 15 [**Montone**[2]].

Ariéte, Aries ('the Ram'), constellation and the first of the twelve signs of the Zodiac, which the Sun enters at the vernal equinox (about March 21), Par. xxviii. 117; Conv. iii. 5[78, 134, 143, 178]; Canz. xv.

41; *il Montone*, Purg. viii. 134; Par. xxix. 2; alluded to as *quella luce Che raggia dietro alla celeste Lasca*, 'the light which beams behind the heavenly Carp' (since Aries comes next to Pisces in the zodiacal circle), Purg. xxxii. 53–4 [**Pesci**]; *migliore stella* (since, according to the old belief, the Sun was in Aries at the time of the Creation and of the Incarnation), Par. i. 40; hence, *quelle stelle*, Inf. i. 38, where D. indicates the time of the Creation, are also those of Aries.

The vernal equinox is described, Purg. viii. 133–5 [**Montone**[1]]; Canz. xv. 41; the rising of the Sun at the vernal equinox, Par. i. 37–41; *notturno Ariete*, 'the Ram seen by night' (i.e. when the Sun is in Libra, after the autumnal equinox), Par. xxviii. 117; *ambedue li figli di Latona Coperti del Montone e della Libra*, 'both the children of Latona brooded over by the Ram and the Scales' (i.e. the Sun and Moon opposite to each other at the equinox, the one being in Aries, the other in Libra), Par. xxix. 1–2 [**Libra**]; Aries and Libra opposite signs at opposite points of the zodiacal circle, being entered by the Sun at the vernal and autumnal equinoxes respectively, Conv. iii. 5[130–42] [**Zodiaco**].

Aristotele, Aristoteles. [**Aristotile.**]

Aristotile, Aristotle, the Greek philosopher, born at Stagira (whence he is sometimes called 'the Stagirite'), a town in Chalcidice in Macedonia, B.C. 384. In 367 he went to Athens, where he became the pupil of Plato. After the death of Plato he returned to Macedonia, where at the request of Philip of Macedon he became the instructor of his son Alexander (afterwards Alexander the Great). A. remained in Macedonia seven years, and then went back to Athens, where he founded the Peripatetic school of philosophy. He presided over his school for thirteen years (335–323), during which period he composed the greater part of his works. After the death of Alexander (323) he left Athens, and retired to Chalcis in Euboea, where he died in 322 at the age of sixty-three. His numerous works, which treated of almost all the subjects of human knowledge cultivated in his time, have always exercised a powerful influence upon learning, especially in the Middle Ages.

D. places A. in Limbo together with Plato, Socrates, and other great philosophers of antiquity, Inf. iv. 131 [Limbo].

In the *D.C.* he is mentioned by name once, *Aristotele*, Purg. iii. 43; referred to as *il maestro di color che sanno*, Inf. iv. 131; (by Charles Martel addressing D.), *il maestro vostro*, Par. viii. 120 (ref. to *Pol.* ii. 2); he is (probably) alluded to (by Statius addressing D.) as *più savio di te* (though some think the allusion is to Averroës), Purg. xxv. 63; it is probably to A. too (but possibly to Plato or Dionysius the Areopagite) that D. alludes as *Colui, che mi dimostra il primo amore*, Par. xxvi. 38.

In the *Vita Nuova* A. is referred to twice by the title of *il Filosofo*, the Philosopher (as he was commonly called *par excellence* in the Middle Ages), V. N. §§ 25^{15}, 42^{30}.

In the *Convivio* he is mentioned by name upwards of fifty times, *Aristotile*, Conv. i. 9; ii. 3, 4, 5, 9, 10, 14, 15; iii. 2, 5, 7, 9, 11, 14, 15; iv. 2, 6, 7, 8, 11, 13, 15, 17, 20, 21, 22, 23, 25, 27, 28; referred to as *il Filosofo* upwards of forty times, Conv. i. 1, 12; ii. 1, 3, 5, 10, 14, 15, 16; iii. 1, 2, 3, 4, 5, 6, 8, 9, 10, 11, 14, 15; iv. 3, 4, 8, 10, 12, 15, 16, 17, 19, 20, 22, 27; D. also speaks of him as *il mio maestro*, Conv. i. 9^{61}; *quello glorioso filosofo al quale la natura più aperse li suoi segreti*, Conv. iii. 5^{54-6}; *maestro della umana ragione*, Conv. iv. 2^{138}; *maestro e duca della gente umana, . . . il maestro e l'artefice che ne dimostra il fine della umana vita*, Conv. iv. 6^{66-72}; *maestro de' filosofi*, Conv. iv. 8^{141}; *maestro della nostra vita*, Conv. iv. 23^{81}; he alludes to A.'s surname 'the Stagirite', mentions him as the founder of the Peripatetic School, and describes his genius as 'quasi divino', his opinion as 'somma e altissima autoritade', and himself as 'degnissimo di fede e d'obbedienza', Conv. iv. 6^{50-152}.

In D.'s Latin works A. is mentioned by name four times, *Aristoteles*, V. E. ii. 6^{13}; Mon. i. 1^{21}, 11^{71}; A. T. § 12^{37}; referred to by the title of *Philosophus* forty times, Mon. i. 3, 5, 10, 11, 12, 13, 14, 15; ii. 2, 3, 6, 7, 8, 12; iii. 1, 4, 10, 16; Epist. viii. 5^{82}; x. 5^{91}, 16^{279}, 18^{296}, 27^{511}; A. T. §§ 2, 6, 12, 13, 21, 23; he is also referred to as *Magister*, Mon. iii. 7^{36}; *magister sapientum*, V. E. ii. 10^{8}; *prae-*

ceptor morum, Mon. iii. 1[17]; *praeceptor*, Epist. viii. 5[82].

With the exception of the Bible, Aristotle's works are quoted by D. more frequently than those of any other author, the direct quotations or references to them numbering about 150. The following are quoted by name:—*Prior Analytics*, [*Analytica Priora*]; *On Sophistical Refutations* [*Sophisticis Elenchis, De*]; *Categories* [*Praedicamenta*]; *Art of Rhetoric* [*Rhetorica*]; *Nicomachean Ethics* [*Ethica*]; *Politics* [*Politica*]; *Physics* or *Physical Discourse* [*Physica*]; *On the Heavens* [*Coelo, De*]; *On Generation and Corruption* [*Generatione et Corruptione, De*]; *Meteorologics* [*Meteora*[1]]; *History of Animals* and *On Parts of Animals* [*Animalibus, De*]; *On Soul* [*Anima, De*]; *On Sense and Sensible Things* [*Sensu et Sensibili, De*]; *On Youth and Old Age* [*Juventute et Senectute, De*]; *On Generation of Animals* [*Generatione Animalium, De*]; *First Philosophy* or *Metaphysics* [*Metaphysica*]; *On Causes* (pseudo-Aristotelian work) [*Causis, De*].

D. mentions two Latin translations of Aristotle, which he says differed materially in places, and which he calls respectively the 'New' and the 'Old', Conv. ii. 15[64-8]. The earliest Latin translations of Aristotle were made, not from the original Greek, but from Arabic versions. Subsequently St. Thomas Aquinas made or caused to be made a new translation, direct from the Greek, of several of the Aristotelian treatises. This Greek-Latin version probably answers to D.'s 'New' translation, the 'Old' being the representative of the earlier Arabic-Latin version [**Tommaso**[2]]. At a later date the Latin version of the *Ethics* was translated into Italian; but it was an untrustworthy rendering, and is spoken of by D. with contempt, Conv. i. 10[70-1]. [**Taddeo.**]

Arli, Arles, town in Provence, in the modern department of Bouches-du-Rhône, close to where the Rhone forms its delta before entering the Mediterranean [**Rodano**]. D. mentions Arles, *Arli, ove Rodano stagna*, in connexion with the famous cemetery (originally a Roman burying-ground) Aliscamps (*Elysios Campos*) and its great sarcophagus tombs, Inf. ix. 112, 115.

Armonia], Harmonia, daughter of Mars and Venus, wife of Cadmus, founder of Thebes. On his wedding-day Cadmus received a present of a necklace, which he gave to H., and which afterwards became fatal to whoever possessed it. D. refers to this necklace (the story of which is told by Statius, *Theb.* ii. 265 ff.) as *lo sventurato adornamento*, Purg. xii. 51 [**Almeone: Anfiarao: Erifile**]. By Cadmus H. became the mother of Autonoë, Ino, Semele, Agave, and Polydorus, and when C. was transformed into a serpent she shared his fate, an incident to which D. alludes, Inf. xxv. 97. [**Cadmo: Ino: Semele.**]

Arnaldo Daniello], Arnaut Daniel, famous Provençal poet (fl. 1180–1200); but little is known of his life beyond that he belonged to a noble family of Ribeyrac in Périgord, that he spent much of his time at the court of Richard Cœur-de-Lion, and that he visited Paris, where he attended the coronation of Philip Augustus, as well as Spain, and perhaps Italy. His works, such as they have been preserved, consist of eighteen lyrical poems, one satirical, the rest amatory.

He is placed by D. (who puts into his mouth eight lines of Provençal) among the Lustful in Circle VII of Purgatory, *Arnaut*, Purg. xxvi. 142; *questi, v.* 115; *spirto, v.* 116; *il mostrato, v.* 136; *ei, v.* 139 [**Lussuriosi**].

Arnaut is said to have been the originator of the *sestina*, a form of composition which D. imitated from him, as he himself states, V. E. ii. 10^{24-8}; D. regarded him pre-eminently as the poet of love, V. E. ii. 2^{80-1}; he is mentioned as having employed a stanza without refrain and without rime, wherein D. copied him, V. E. ii. 10^{24-8}, 13^{8-14}; the first lines of three of his poems are quoted, V. E. ii. 2^{87}, 6^{61}, 13^{12}.

Arnaldus Danielis, Arnaut. [**Arnaldo Daniello.**]

Arno, principal river of Tuscany, which, rising, like the Tiber, among the spurs of Falterona in the Apennines, flows SE. through the Casentino to within four or five miles of Arezzo, where it makes a sudden sweep away to the NW.; then with a more rapid descent it flows past Pontassieve, where it is joined by the Sieve, and turning W. flows through Florence; then, descending more gently, after passing through the deep gorge of Pietra Golfolina, it enters the plain of Empoli, whence it flows through Pisa into the Mediterranean, after a course of some 150 miles, its mouth being six or seven miles below the city of Pisa.

The Arno is mentioned, in connexion with the ancient statue of Mars on the Ponte Vecchio, Inf. xiii. 146 [**Marte**[1]: **Ponte Vecchio**]; the transference of Andrea de' Mozzi from Arno (i.e. Florence) to Bacchiglione (i. e. Vicenza), Inf. xv. 113 [**Andrea de' Mozzi : Bacchiglione**]; D. born and brought up at Florence on the Arno, Inf. xxiii. 95; Purg. xiv. 19; V. E. i. 6^{18-19}; Ecl. i. 44 [**Firenze**]; the streamlets by which it is fed from the hills in the Casentino, Inf. xxx. 65 [**Casentino**]; the islands of Caprara and Gorgona called upon by D. to choke its mouth and so drown Pisa, Inf. xxxiii. 82–4 [**Caprara : Gorgona : Pisa**]; its confluence with the Archiano, Purg. v. 125 [**Archiano**]; the situation of Alvernia between the Arno and the Tiber, Par. xi. 106 [**Alvernia**[2]]; D.'s description of it, Purg. xiv. 16–19; its course described by Guido del Duca, Purg. xiv. 29–54; its source, Purg. xiv. 17, 31; Epist. vi. 6^{198}; vii. 8^{191}; its course more than a hundred miles, Purg. xiv. 18; its mouth, Inf. xxxiii. 83; Purg. xiv. 34–5; alluded to, as *il bel fiume*, Inf. xxiii. 95; *lo fiume real* (so called as flowing direct into the sea), Purg. v. 122; *un fiumicel che nasce in Falterona E cento miglia di corso nol sazia*, Purg. xiv. 17–18; *quella riviera, v. 26*; *valle, v. 30*; *la maladetta e sventurata fossa, v. 51*; *il fiero fiume, v. 60*; *il fiume*, Canz. xi. 62; in the Latin works called *Sarnus*, V. E. i. 6^{19}; Ecl. i. 44; Epist. iii. 2^{13}; vi. 6^{198}; vii. 8^{191}; also by G. del Virgilio, Ecl. R. 37 [**Sarnus**].

Aronta, Aruns, Etruscan soothsayer, who, according to Lucan (*Phars.* i. 584–638) foretold the civil war, which was to end in the death of Pompey and the triumph of Caesar. D. places A. among the Soothsayers in Bolgia 4 of Circle VIII of Hell (Malebolge), Inf. xx. 46 [**Indovini**]; and describes him as having dwelt in a cave ' nei monti di Luni', i.e. in the Carrara hills (*v.* 47) [**Luni**].

Arpie, Harpies, foul monsters in the shape of birds, with long claws, with the heads of maidens, and faces pale with hunger. D. places them as tormentors of the Suicides in Round 2 of Circle VII of Hell (his account of them, and of how they drove the Trojans from the Strophades, being taken from Virgil, *Aen.* iii. 209 ff.), Inf. xiii. 10, 101 [**Violenti**].

Arrigo[1], Florentine, of whom nothing certain is known, mentioned together with Farinata degli Uberti, Tegghiaio Aldobrandi, Jacopo Rusticucci, and Mosca de' Lamberti, Inf. vi. 80; he is one of those *ch' a ben far poser gl' ingegni* (*v.* 81), of whom D. asks Ciacco for news, the reply being *ei son tra le anime più nere* (*v.* 85) [**Ciacco**]. All the others are referred to again subsequently, but no more is heard of A.

Arrigo[2], Henry VII of Luxemburg, Emperor, 1308–1313; *l' alto A.*, Par. xvii. 82 ; xxx. 137; *Henricus*, Epist. v. 2[27]; vi. 6 *fin.*; vii. *tit.*, *fin.*; the successor of Albert I, Purg. vi. 102 [**Alberto Tedesco**]; the other, *altri*, who was to heal the wounds of Italy neglected by Rudolf, Purg. vii. 96 [**Ridolfo**]; *Titan pacificus*, Epist. v. 1[10]; *alius Moyses*,

Epist. v. 1[19]; *Sponsus Italiae, mundi solatium, gloria plebis suae, clementissimus Henricus, Divus et Augustus et Caesar*, Epist. v. 2[25–8]; *novus agricola Romanorum*, Epist. v. 5[82]; *Hectoreus pastor*, Epist. v. 5[86]; *Rex Italiae*, Epist. v. 6[100]; *Romanus princeps, mundi rex, et Dei minister*, Epist. vi. 2[31–2]; *delirantis Hesperiae domitor*, Epist. vi. 3[87]; *Romanae rei bajulus, divus et triumphator Henricus*, Epist. vi. 6[180–1]; *sanctissimus triumphator et dominus singularis*, Epist. vii. *tit.*; *Sol noster*, Epist. vii. 2[25]; *praeses unicus mundi*, Epist. vii. 6[125–6]; *excellentissimus principum*, Epist. vii. 7[135]; *proles altera Isai*, Epist. vii. 8[176–7]; he is alluded to by G. del Virgilio (with reference to his death) as *Jovis armiger*, Carm. 26.

D. refers to the secret opposition encountered by Henry VII from the Gascon Pope, Clement V, who was ostensibly his supporter, Par. xvii. 82; xxx. 142–4 [**Guasco**]; Beatrice points out to D. the throne prepared for Henry in the Celestial Rose, and refers to him as the coming regenerator of Italy, Par. xxx. 137–9 [**Rosa**].

D. wrote three Letters with especial reference to the Emperor Henry VII—one addressed to the Princes and Peoples of Italy, exhorting them to receive him, Epist. v; the second to the rebellious Florentines who opposed his coming, Epist. vi; the third addressed to the Emperor himself, beseeching him to come into Tuscany and chastise Florence without delay, Epist. vii.

Henry, Count of Luxemburg,

was at the instance of Clement V unanimously elected Emperor (at the age of forty), Nov. 1308, in opposition to Charles of Valois, the candidate of the French king, Philip the Fair, and was crowned at Aix, Jan. 6, 130⅞. In the following May he sent ambassadors to Florence to announce that he was coming into Italy to receive the Imperial crown, a ceremony which had been neglected by his predecessors for the last sixty years. To this advent of Henry D. looked anxiously for a settlement of the affairs of Italy (Par. xxx. 137), and for a means to secure his own return to Florence. But his hopes were doomed to bitter disappointment. The Emperor crossed the Alps in the autumn of 1310, and at first was well received. But he soon had to encounter opposition. Tumults and revolts broke out in Lombardy; and at Rome, whither he went to be crowned, Henry found St. Peter's in the hands of the brother of King Robert of Naples, so that the coronation had to take place, shorn of its ceremony, in St. John Lateran, on the southern bank of the Tiber (June 29, 1312). The hostility of the Guelfic league, headed by the Florentines, with King Robert as their acknowledged leader, compelled the Emperor to hasten back to Tuscany, for the purpose of laying siege to Florence, which had persistently defied him. To counterbalance the opposition of the Guelfs, he was obliged to abandon his policy of impartiality, and to identify himself with the Ghibellines. Meanwhile Clement V, yielding to the menaces of the French king, had secretly withdrawn his support from the Emperor (Par. xvii. 82; xxx. 142–4). Henry arrived before Florence on September 19 (1312); but on October 31 he was obliged to raise the siege. On August 8 of the next year he set out from Pisa with the intention of reducing Naples. On his way south he was seized with illness, and on August 24, 1313, he expired at Buonconvento, near Siena. His somewhat sudden death, which was probably due to a malarious fever contracted at Rome, was currently ascribed to poison administered by a Dominican monk in the consecrated wafer. The Emperor's body was taken to Pisa and interred in the Cathedral, where a monument (removed in 1830 to the Campo Santo), ascribed to Giovanni Pisano, was erected to him.

Arrigo ³], Emperor Henry II, 1002–1024; referred to as *lo Imperadore*, how he was answered from the *Psalms* (c. 3) by a priest at whom he had scoffed on account of his ugliness, Conv. iii. 4⁷⁴⁻⁸⁰.

Arrigo ⁴], Prince Henry of England, second son of Henry II, born 1155, died 1183. Owing to the fact that he was twice crowned during his father's lifetime (at Westminster in 1170, and at Winchester in 1172) he was commonly known at home and abroad as the Young King. Shortly after his second coronation he went over with his brothers Geoffrey and Richard to the French court, and from there, backed by his mother Queen Eleanor, and by Louis VII (whose daughter Margaret he had married in 1170), he demanded from Henry II that either England or Normandy should be handed over to him. The refusal of this demand was made the occasion of open hostilities, which were carried on at intervals for nearly ten years, and were finally terminated by the death of Prince Henry of fever at Martel in Périgord, June 11, 1183.

D. mentions Henry by his title of the Young King in connexion with the troubadour Bertran de Born, who describes himself (in Bolgia 9 of Circle VIII of Hell) as 'quelli Che diedi al re giovane i mai conforti', Inf. xxviii. 134–5 [**Bertram dal Bornio**].

Little or nothing is known historically of the part played by Bertran in abetting the Young King in his rebellion against his father; nor do Bertran's own poems throw much light upon the subject. D's. authority for the statement which he puts into the mouth of Bertran ('Io feci il padre e il figlio in sè ribelli,' Inf. xxviii. 136) was the old Provençal biography of the troubadour, in which it is explicitly mentioned that B. set father and son at variance, until the strife was ended by the death of the latter.

Arrigo [5]], Emperor Henry VI (1190–1197), son of Frederick Barbarossa, referred to by Piccarda Donati (in the Heaven of the Moon) as *il secondo vento di Soave* (i.e. the second Emperor of the Swabian or Hohenstaufen line), Par. iii. 119. Henry VI was actually the third Emperor of his line, but his great-uncle Conrad III (1138–1152) was never crowned at Rome, and never assumed the title of Emperor. [**Hohenstaufen: Table H.**]

Henry is here mentioned in connexion with his wife Constance (whom he married in 1185, when he was 22, and she 32), the daughter of Roger of Sicily, in whose right their son Frederick, afterwards. Emperor as Frederick II, became King of Sicily. [**Cicilia: Costanza** [1]**: Federico** [2].]

Arrigo [6]], Prince Henry 'of Almain', son of Richard, Earl of Cornwall, King of the Romans, nephew of Henry III of England. He was stabbed in 1271 by his cousin Guy de Montfort (son of Simon de Montfort and Eleanor, sister of Henry III) in the church of San Silvestro at Viterbo, according to the popular belief, at the moment of the elevation of the Host. His body was brought to England and interred in the Cistercian Abbey at Hayles in Gloucestershire, which had been built by his father. The heart was enclosed in a gold casket and placed, according to some, on a pillar on London Bridge, according to others in the hand of a statue of the prince in Westminster Abbey.

D. alludes to the crime in connexion with the murderer, Inf. xii. 119–20. [**Guido di Monforte.**]

Arrigo [7]], Enrique I (Henry), surnamed the Fat, King of Navarre, 1270–1274; he was the son of Thibaut I, and younger brother of Thibaut II, whom he succeeded; his daughter Juana or Joan married Philip the Fair, son of Philip III of France, and their son, Louis X, was the first sovereign of the united kingdoms of France and Navarre. [**Navarra: Table M.**]

D. places Henry in the valley of flowers in Ante-purgatory, where he is represented as seated close to Philip III of France, with his face resting on his hand; Sordello points him out as *colui che ha sì benigno aspetto*, and refers to Philip and him as *padre e suocero del mal di Francia*, i.e. father and father-in-law of Philip the Fair, whose evil doings they are bewailing, Henry by sighing, Philip by beating his breast, Purg. vii. 103–11. [**Antipurgatorio: Filippo**[1]: **Filippo**[2].]

Arrigo[8], Henry II of Lusignan, King of Cyprus, 1285–1324; referred to by the Eagle in the Heaven of Jupiter, in allusion to his sensuality and misgovernment (with a reference also perhaps to the lion on his shield), as *la bestia di Nicosia e di Famagosta*, Par. xix. 146–7. [**Cipri: Famagosta: Table F.**]

D. here alludes to the sufferings of Cyprus under the unsettled rule of the house of Lusignan. Hugh III of Antioch, King of Cyprus and Jerusalem, who derived the Lusignan title from his mother, died in 1284, leaving several dissolute sons. The eldest of these, John, succeeded, but died within a year, his death being attributed to poison administered by his brother Henry. The latter, second son of Hugh, a prince of feeble character and constitution, assumed the government in 1285, under the title of Henry II. Six years later (1291), Acre, the last possession of the Christians in the Holy Land, having been captured by the Saracens (Inf. xxvii. 89), Henry collected a force with the object of attempting its reconquest, and gave the command of it to his younger brother Amalric or Amaury, Prince

of Tyre. The failure of this expedition, and the unpunished depredations of some Genoese galleys on the coast of Cyprus, gave Amalric a pretext for declaring his brother incapable of governing. Having got himself appointed governor of the island by the supreme council (1307), Amalric kept Henry virtually a prisoner and assumed all the power into his own hands. Before, however, he could finally make himself master of the kingdom, he was assassinated by one of his own adherents (1310). On his death, his younger brother, Cammerino, attempted to seize the throne; but Henry's following demanded the restoration of the rightful king, who resumed the government, and retained it until his death in 1324. [**Table F.**]

Arrigo[9], Henry II, King of England, 1154–1189; referred to by Bertran de Born (in Bolgia 9 of Circle VIII of Hell), in connexion with the rebellion of his son Henry ('the Young King'), as *il padre*, Inf. xxviii. 135. [**Arrigo**[4]: **Bertram dal Bornio.**]

Arrigo d'Inghilterra, Henry III, King of England, 1216–1272; succeeded his father John at the age of 10 and reigned for 56 years; he married Eleanor, second daughter of Raymond Berenger IV, Count of Provence, whose younger daughter, Sanzia, married Henry's brother, Richard of Cornwall. [**Berlinghieri: Table J.**]

D. places Henry in the valley of flowers in Ante-purgatory, among the princes who neglected to repent, Purg. vii. 130–2; he is represented as seated alone (*v.* 131), probably as being unconnected with the Empire (compare the similar positions in Hell of Guy de Montfort, Inf. xii. 118, and of Saladin, Inf. iv. 129) [Antipurgatorio]. D. speaks of him as 'il re della semplice vita' (v. 130); and says (v. 132) that he was more fortunate in his issue than were Peter III of Aragon or Charles I of Anjou, thus praising by implication his son, Edward I [Edoardo¹].

Arrigo Manardi, gentleman of Bertinoro, mentioned by Guido del Duca (in Circle II of Purgatory), along with Lizio da Valbona, among the worthies of Romagna, Purg. xiv. 97 [Lizio]. Little is known of Arrigo, beyond that he was a contemporary of Guido del Duca (d. c. 1250) and of Pier Traversaro (d. 1225), that he was taken prisoner with the latter by the Faentines in 1170, and that he was still alive in 1228. [Traversaro, Pier.]

Arrigucci, ancient noble family of Florence, mentioned by Cacciaguida (in the Heaven of Mars), together with the Sizii, as having held office in his day, Par. xvi. 108. These two families resided in the 'quartiere della porta del Duomo' (Vill. iv. 10), they were Guelfs (v. 39, vi. 33), and were among those who fled from Florence to Lucca after the great Ghibelline victory at Montaperti (vi. 79), and afterwards threw in their lot with the Bianchi (viii. 39).

Arrio, Arius, presbyter of Alexandria (d. 336), the originator of the Arian heresy that the Father and the Son were not 'one substance', a doctrine which the Athanasian creed was designed to controvert. St. Thomas Aquinas (in the Heaven

of the Sun) mentions A. together with Sabellius as conspicuous among those who sought to distort the Scriptures, Par. xiii. 127.

Ars Nova. [Arte Nuova.]

Ars Poëtica, Poetics or Art of Poetry of Horace, a poem in hexameters, the subject of which is a discussion of dramatic poetry; quoted by D. as Poëtria, V. N. § 25⁹² (A. P. 141–2); Conv. ii. 14⁸⁸ (A. P. 70–1); V. E. ii. 4³⁵ (A. P. 38–9); Poëtica, Epist. x. 10²¹³, ²²⁹ (A. P. 93–5).

Ars Vetus. [Arte Vecchia.]

Arte Nuova, Ars Nova, or Nova Logica, name given in the Middle Ages to certain dialectical treatises of Aristotle; coupled by D. with the Ars Vetus, Conv. ii. 14¹⁰⁶. [Arte Vecchia.]

Arte Vecchia, Ars Vetus, or Vetus Logica, name given in the Middle Ages to certain dialectical treatises of Aristotle; coupled with the Ars Nova, in these two being contained the whole science of Dialectics, Conv. ii. 14¹⁰³⁻⁶.

According to Lambert of Auxerre (c. 1250) the Vetus Logica consisted of the Praedicamenta and De Interpretatione; and the Nova Logica of the Analytica Priora, Analytica Posteriora, Topica, and Sophistici Elenchi.

Artù, Arthur, mythical King of Britain, hero of the romances of the Round Table; he was wedded to Guenever, and was slain by the hand of his nephew (or, according to later tradition, his son) Mordred.

A. is mentioned by Camicione de' Pazzi (in Caina), who says that Alessandro and Napoleone degli Alberti were even worse traitors than him 'who had his breast and shadow pierced with one self-same blow by the hand of Arthur', i.e. A.'s nephew (or son), the traitor, Sir Mordred, Inf. xxxii. 62 [**Alberti**]. The incident here alluded to by D. is related in the Old French prose romance, the *Morte d'Arthur* :— Sir Mordred, having been appointed regent during King Arthur's absence, gave out falsely that the king had been slain, and assumed the crown. King Arthur returning met Sir Mordred in single combat and smote him through the body with his lance, so that, when the lance was withdrawn, a ray of sunlight passed through the wound.

D. mentions A. again in connexion with the Arthurian romances, 'Arturi regis ambages pulcherrimae,' which he cites as examples of prose compositions in the *langue d'* oïl, V.E. i. 10$^{12-19}$. His own acquaintance with them is evident from the fact that, besides King Arthur and Mordred, he mentions Gallehault (Inf. v. 137), Guenever (Par. xvi. 15), Lancelot (Inf. v. 128; Conv. iv. 28^{59}), and Tristan (Inf. v. 67). [**Lingua** *Oïl.*]

Arturus. [**Artù.**]

Ascanio, Ascanius, son of Aeneas and Creusa; mentioned, as having been trained in arms in Sicily, Conv. iv. 26$^{96-9}$ (ref. to *Aen.* v. 545–603); as son of Creusa, *Ascanius*, Mon. ii. 3^{100} (where D. quotes *Aen.* iii. 339–40, with the interpolated hemistich : 'peperit fumante Creusa'); his personation by Cupid is alluded to, Par. viii. 9 [**Cupído**]; the Emperor Henry VII's son John, King of Bohemia, a second Ascanius, Epist. vii. 5^{96} [**Johannes** ^{2}].

Ascanius. [**Ascanio.**]

Ascesi, now Assisi, town of Central Italy, in NE. of Umbria, on the road between Perugia and Foligno, celebrated as the birthplace of St. Francis [**Francesco** ^{2}]; mentioned by St. Thomas Aquinas (in the Heaven of the Sun), who says it should be named, not *Ascesi* ('I rose'), but rather *Oriente*, as having been the birthplace of 'a Sun', i.e. St. Francis, Par. xi. 49–54.

The situation of A., which stands on the SW. slope of Monte Subasio, between the streams Tupino (on the E.) and Chiassi (on the W.), is described, Par. xi. 43–8 [**Chiassi** ^{2} : **Subasio**].

Asciano, small town in Tuscany, on the Ombrone, about 15 miles SE. of Siena ; Caccia d'Asciano is mentioned by Capocchio (in Bolgia 10 of Circle VIII of Hell) among the spendthrifts of Siena, Inf. xxix. 131. [**Brigata Spendereccia : Caccia d'Asciano.**]

Ascoli, town of Central Italy, on the Tronto, in the S. of the Marches close to the border of the Abruzzo; thought by some to be the place mentioned under the name of *Casciòli* in the dialectal poem quoted, V.E. i. 11^{28}. [**Casciòli.**]

Asdente, Maestro Benvenuto, nicknamed Asdente (i.e. toothless), a shoemaker of Parma who was famed as a prophet and soothsayer during the latter half of Cent. xiii.

A. is placed, together with Guido Bonatti, among the soothsayers in Bolgia 4 of Circle VIII of Hell (Malebolge), Inf. xx. 118 [**Indovini**]; referred to, as 'il calzolaio di Parma ', as an instance of an indi-

vidual who would be noble, if noto-
riety constituted nobility, Conv. iv.
16⁶⁵⁻⁷¹.

Aser], Asher, son of Jacob by Zilpah, Leah's maid; he is among those
referred to by Virgil as having been released by Christ from Limbo, *Israel
co' suoi nati*, Inf. iv. 59. [**Limbo**.]

Asia, connexion of Aeneas
with Asia by descent and marriage,
Mon. ii. 3⁶¹⁻⁶, ⁹³⁻⁵ (ref. to *Aen*. iii.
1–2) [**Enea**]; subjected by Ninus,
King of Assyria, Mon. ii. 9²³⁻⁸
[**Nino¹**]; overrun by Vesoges, King
of Egypt, Mon. ii. 9³⁵⁻⁸ [**Vesoges**];
separated from Europe by the Hellespont, Mon. ii. 9⁵²⁻⁴ [**Ellesponto**]; partly occupied by Greeks,
V. E. i. 8¹⁹⁻²¹ [**Greci**].

Asiani, Asiatics; their rejection
of the proposition that the imperial
authority is derived from the Church,
Mon. iii. 14⁵⁹.

Asopo, Asopus, river in Boeotia,
in the neighbourhood of Thebes;
mentioned, together with the Ismenus,
in reference to the crowds of Thebans
who used to throng their banks at
night to invoke the aid of Bacchus,
when they needed rain for their vine-
yards (a reminiscence probably of Statius, *Theb*. ix. 434 ff.), Purg. xviii. 91.

Assalone. [**Absalone**.]

Assaracus, King of Troy, son
of Tros, father of Capys, grandfather
of Anchises, and great-grandfather
of Aeneas; mentioned to prove the
connexion of Aeneas with Asia,
Mon. ii. 3⁶² [**Enea**].

Assiri, Assyrians; their flight
from Bethulia after the death of
Holofernes (*Judith* xv. 1–3), Purg.
xii. 59 [**Oloferne**]; included among
the examples of defeated pride por-

trayed on the ground in Circle I of
Purgatory, Purg. xii. 58–60 [**Su-
perbi**]; mentioned in connexion with
Ninus, *Assyrii*, Mon. ii. 9²³ [**Nino¹**].

Assisi. [**Ascesi**.]

Assuero, Ahasuerus, King of
Persia; D., in a vision, sees him, together with Esther and Mordecai,
witnessing the death of Haman, Purg.
xvii. 25–30 [**Amano**.]

Assyrii. [**Assiri**.]

Astraea, daughter of Zeus and
Themis; she was goddess of justice,
and during the Golden Age lived
among mankind, but when the wickedness of the world increased she
withdrew to heaven and took her
place among the stars as the constellation *Virgo*. She is mentioned,
Mon. i. 11⁸; Epist. viii. 7¹¹⁰; alluded to as *giustizia* (in a translation
of Virgil, *Ecl*. iv. 6–7), Purg. xxii.
71–2; as *Virgo*, Epist. vii. 1²³.

Atalanta, Boeotian maiden, celebrated for her swiftness of foot;
being unwilling to marry, she declared
she would accept no suitor who failed
to outstrip her in running. Hippomenes succeeded by the assistance
of Venus, who gave him three
golden apples which he dropped in
the course of the race; A. stopped
to pick them up, and thus enabled
Hippomenes to pass her and win her
as his wife. This race, for the account of which D. refers to Ovid
(*Metam*. x. 560–680), is mentioned
as an example of a contest for a
prize, as distinguished from a contest or duel between two antagonists,
such as that between Hercules and
Antaeus, Mon. ii. 8⁸³⁻⁵. [**Anteo**.]

Atamante, Athamas, King of
Orchomenus in Boeotia, son of

Aeolus and Enarete, Inf. xxx. 4.
At the command of Juno, A. married
Nephele, but he was secretly in love
with the mortal Ino, daughter of
Cadmus, King of Thebes, by whom
he had two sons, Learchus and
Melicertes [Ino]. Having thus incurred the wrath both of Juno and
Nephele, he was seized with madness, and taking Ino and her two
sons for a lioness and cubs, he seized
Learchus and dashed him against a
rock. Ino (who had herself incurred
the wrath of Juno for having brought
up Bacchus, the son of Jupiter and
her sister Semele) thereupon threw
herself into the sea with Melicertes.
[Giunone: Semelè.] D. alludes
to the story (which he took from Ovid,
Metam. iv. 512–30), Inf. xxx. 1–12.

Atene, Athens, capital of Attica;
mentioned in connexion with the
slaying of the Minotaur by Theseus,
who (by an anachronism) is called
il duca d'A., Inf. xii. 17 [Arianna :
Minotauro : Teseo]; the laws of
Solon, Purg. vi. 139 [Solone]; the
flight of Hippolytus, Par. xvii. 46
[Fedra : Ippolito]; the Athenian
schools of philosophy, which are all
at one in *l'A. celestiale* (i.e. Heaven),
Conv. iii. 14$^{137-41}$; the war of
Cephalus with Crete, Conv. iv.
27$^{158-60}$ [Cefalo]; alluded to as *la
villa Del cui nome ne' Dei fu tanta
lite* (i. e. the town for the naming of
which Neptune and Minerva contested), Purg. xv. 97–8 [Minerva].

Atlante], giant Atlas; referred to
as *gigante*, Conv. iv. 29^{49}. [Atlas^1].

Atlantico], Atlantic Ocean, alluded to as *il mar*, Inf. xxvi. 142 ;
*l'onde Dietro alle quali . . . Lo sol
tal volta ad ogni uom si nasconde*,

i. e. the waters behind which the sun
sinks during the summer solstice, the
reference being more precisely to the
Gulf of Gascony, Par. xii. 49–51
[Guascogna, Golfo di]; *il varco
Folle d'Ulisse*, 'the mad track of
Ulysses,' i. e. over the Atlantic beyond the Pillars of Hercules, Par.
xxvii. 82–3 [Ulisse].

Atlantis, Electra, daughter of
Atlas and Pleione, and mother of
Dardanus, his father being Jupiter ;
Virgil's mention of her (*Aen.* viii.
134–7) as ancestress of Aeneas,
Mon. ii. 3$^{69-76}$. [Elettra : Enea.]

Atlas^1, son of Iapetus and Clymene ; he made war with the other
Titans upon Jupiter, and being conquered was condemned to bear the
heavens upon his head and hands.
He was the father of Electra, who
is hence called Atlantis, and grandfather of Dardanus, the ancestor of
Aeneas. He was of African origin,
the Atlas range in Africa being
named from him. D. mentions him,
quoting *Aen.* viii. 134–7, to prove the
connexion of Aeneas with Africa,
Mon. ii. 3$^{68-76}$ [Enea]; Juvenal's
saying: 'Nanum cujusdam Atlanta
vocamus' (*Sat.* viii. 32), translated,
Conv. iv. 29$^{48-9}$ [Giovenale].

Atlas^2, Atlas range in N. Africa;
Orosius quoted (*Hist.* i. 2. § 11)
to prove that it is in Africa, Mon.
ii. 3$^{85-91}$ [Atlas^1 : Orosio]; the
Imperial Eagle soars alike over the
Pyrenees, Caucasus, and Atlas,
Epist. vi. 3$^{82-3}$.

Atropòs, Atropos, one of the
three fates. At the birth of every
mortal, Clotho, the spinning fate,
was supposed to wind upon the distaff of Lachesis, the allotting fate,

a certain amount of yarn; the duration of the life of the individual being the length of time occupied in spinning the thread, which, when complete, was severed by Atropos, the inevitable fate [**Cloto: Lachesis**]. D. says that certain souls are consigned to Tolomea even before Atropos has given them movement, i.e. before death, Inf. xxxiii. 124–6 [**Tolomea**].

Attila, King of the Huns (A.D. 434–453), known, on account of the terror he inspired, as *Flagellum Dei*, 'the scourge of God'; in 452 he demanded in marriage the sister of the Emperor Valentinian III, with half the kingdom of Italy as her dowry, and on the refusal of this demand he invaded Italy, laid waste the plains of Lombardy, and marched upon Rome, but was persuaded by Pope Leo the Great to turn back and to evacuate Italy; he died in his own country in the next year.

D. places A. among the Tyrants in Round 1 of Circle VII of Hell, describing him, in allusion to his appellation of the 'scourge of God', as 'Attila che fu flagello in terra', Inf. xii. 134 [**Tiranni**]; he is mentioned in connexion with his (mythical) destruction of Florence, Inf. xiii. 149. The tradition accepted by D. in this latter passage arose doubtless from a confusion of Attila with Totila, King of the Ostrogoths (541–553), by whose forces Florence was besieged in 542. As a matter of fact there appears to be no truth in the tradition that Florence was destroyed, either by Attila or Totila, and rebuilt by Charlemagne, as D. believed (Inf. xiii. 148).

Auditu, De Naturali. [*Naturali Auditu, De.*]

Augusta, title of honour, borne by the mothers, wives, sisters, and daughters of the Roman Emperor; applied by D. to the Virgin Mary in the sense of Empress, Par. xxxii. 119 [**Maria**[1]].

Augustalis, Imperial; *solium Augustale*, 'the Imperial throne', during its vacancy the world goes astray, Epist. vi. 1[12].

Augustino, Augustinus. [**Agostino.**]

Augusto[1], Augustus, title of honour borne by the Roman Emperor; applied by D. to the Emperor Frederick II, Inf. xiii. 68 [**Cesare**[2]: **Federico**[2]]; the Emperor Henry VII, Epist. v. 2[27], 3[45–6]; vii. *tit.*, 4[76] [**Arrigo**[2]].

Augusto[2], Augustus, first Roman Emperor, born B.C. 63, died at Nola A.D. 14, at the age of 76. He was son of Caius Octavius by Atia, daughter of Julia, the sister of Julius Caesar. His original name was Caius Octavius, which, after his adoption by his great-uncle Julius Caesar, was changed to Caius Julius Caesar Octavianus. Augustus was a title of veneration conferred upon him by the Roman Senate and people, B.C. 27. After the murder of Julius Caesar at Rome (B.C. 44) he left his studies at Apollonia, hastened to Italy, defeated Antony at Mutina (B.C. 43) [**Modena**], Brutus and Cassius at Philippi (B.C. 42) [**Bruto**], took Perusia and defeated Lucius Antonius (B.C. 40) [**Perugia**], defeated Sextus Pompeius in Sicily (B.C. 36) [**Sesto**], and finally Antony and Cleopatra at Actium

(B. C. 31) [Cleopatra], thus putting
an end to the civil war. The further wars of A. were chiefly undertaken in defence of the frontiers of
the Roman dominions; Italy itself
remained at peace [Jano].

Augustus, contemporary of Virgil,
Inf. i. 71 ; removed V.'s body from
Brundusium to Naples, Purg. vii.
6 [Virgilio]; his victories in the
civil war and subsequent peace, Par.
vi. 73–81; his triumphs at Rome,
Purg. xxix. 116 ; Epist. v. 8¹³⁰;
universal peace under him at time
of Christ's birth, Par. vi. 80–1 ;
Conv. iv. 5⁶⁰⁻⁵ ; Mon. i. 16¹⁰⁻¹⁸ ;
his decree 'that all the world should
be taxed' (Luke ii. 1), Conv. iv.
5⁶⁵ ; Mon. ii. 9¹⁰⁰⁻³, 12⁴⁸⁻⁵⁴ ;
Epist. vii. 3⁶⁵ ; referred to as Octavian, Ottaviano, Purg. vii. 6 ; Octavianus, Epist. v. 8¹³⁰; bearer of the
Roman Eagle, baiulo, Par. vi. 73 ;
principe e comandatore del Roman
popolo, Conv. iv. 5⁶³⁻⁴ ; portent at
his death related by Seneca, Conv. ii.
14¹⁷⁴⁻⁶; Henry VII his successor,
Epist. vii. 1¹⁵.

Augustulo], Romulus Augustulus, last of the Roman Emperors
of the West, who, after reigning for
one year (475–6), was overthrown
and expelled by Odoacer; supposed
by some to be alluded to as Colui che
fece per viltate il gran rifiuto, Inf. iii.
59. [Celestino.]

Augustus. [Augusto.]

Aulide, Aulis, port in Boeotia,
where the Greek fleet assembled before sailing for Troy, and where it
was detained by Artemis until Agamemnon appeased her wrath, Inf.
xx. 111. [Agamemnone : Calcanta : Euripilo.]

Aurora, goddess of dawn, who
at the close of every night rose from
the couch of her spouse Tithonus,
and in a chariot drawn by swift
horses ascended up to heaven from
the river Oceanus to announce the
coming light of the Sun.

D. describes sunrise as the gradual deepening of the colour on A.'s
cheeks from white to vermilion,
which then passes into orange, Purg.
ii. 7–9; she is referred to as la chia-
rissima ancella del Sole, Par. xxx. 7 ;
and, perhaps (many thinking the Aurora of the Moon is intended), as concubina di Titone, Purg. ix. 1. [Titone.]

Ausonia, ancient name for the
part of Italy now known as Campania, hence used to indicate Italy itself. In describing the kingdom of
Naples, Charles Martel (in the
Heaven of Venus) speaks of it as
' that horn of Ausonia which has for
its limits the towns of Bari, Gaeta,
and Catona, from where the Tronto
and Verde disgorge into the sea' (Bari
on the Adriatic, Gaeta on the Mediterranean, and Catona at the extreme
S., roughly indicating the extent of
the Neapolitan territory, while the
Verde (or Garigliano) flowing into
the Mediterranean, and the Tronto
flowing into the Adriatic, represent
the frontier with the Papal States)
Par. viii. 61–3 [Italia : Napoli];
D. apostrophizes Italy as Ausonia,
Mon. ii. 13⁶⁶.

Auster. [Austro.]

Austericch, Austria, Inf. xxxii.
26.

Australe, southerly; austral
vento, ' S. wind', Purg. xxxi. 71
(where the better reading is nostral v.,
' wind of our land,' i.e. N. wind).

Austro, Auster, S. wind'; coupled with *Aquilone,* the two being mentioned as typically boisterous winds, Purg. xxxii. 99; its violence in Libya, Mon. ii. $4^{36, 40}$; hence, the S., 'Austri Regina' (*Matt.* xii. 42), i.e. the Queen of Sheba, Epist. x. 1^{10} [**Saba**].

Avari], the Avaricious, placed with Prodigals in Circle IV of Hell, Inf. vii. 22–66 [**Inferno**]. Their guardian is Pluto or Plutus, the accursed wolf (Inf. vii. 8; Purg. xx. 10) [**Pluto**]. They are compelled to roll about great weights, the Avaricious in one half of the Circle, the Prodigals in the other; when they meet they smite against and revile each other, and then turn back and meet again at the opposite end of the semicircle [**Cariddi**]. Among the Avaricious D. sees many 'clerks, popes, and cardinals', but names none of them as they are unrecognizable—'La sconoscente vita, che i fe' sozzi, Ad ogni conoscenza or li fa bruni' (*vv.* 53–4).

Those who expiate the sins of Avarice and Prodigality in Purgatory are placed in Circle V (***Beatitudini : Purgatorio***]; their punishment is to lie prostrate on the ground, bound hand and foot, their faces downward to remind them that on earth their thoughts were fixed on earthly things, while they murmur 'Adhaesit pavimento anima mea' (*Psalm* cxix. 25), Purg. xix. 70–5, 118–26. *Examples* : Pope Adrian V [**Adriano** [2]]; Hugh Capet [**Ciapetta**]; Statius [**Stazio**]. During the day the Avaricious proclaim instances of self-denial or liberality, viz. the Virgin Mary [**Maria** [1]], Fabricius [**Fabbrizio** [1]], and St. Nicholas [**Niccolao**]; during the night they inveigh against notorious instances of avarice or of the lust of wealth, viz. Pygmalion [**Pigmalione**], Midas [**Mida**], Achan [**Acan**], Ananias and Sapphira [**Anania** [2] : **Safira**], Heliodorus [**Eliodoro**], Polymestor [**Polinestor**], and Crassus [**Crasso**].

Avellana, Fonte], Benedictine monastery of Santa Croce di Fonte Avellana, situated in Umbria on the slopes of Monte Catria, one of the highest peaks of the Apennines, near Gubbio [**Catria**].

St. Peter Damian (in the Heaven of Saturn), who was Abbot c. 1043, describes its situation to D., Par. xxi. 106–10, speaking of it as *ermo, v.* 110; *quel chiostro, v.* 118; *quel loco, v.* 121. [**Damiano**.]

There is a tradition, based upon very slender foundations, that D. himself spent some time at Fonte Avellana after his departure from Verona in 1318.

Aventino, Mt. Aventine, one of the seven hills of Rome, where the giant Cacus had a cave, Inf. xxv. 26. [**Caco**.]

Averrois, Averroës (*Ibn-Roschd*), celebrated Arabian scholar, born at Cordova in Spain between 1120 and 1149, died in Morocco about 1200. His most famous work was a commentary upon Aristotle (whence he was commonly known as the Commentator *par excellence*), whose writings he knew through the medium of Arabic translations. A.'s works had a most important influence on the study of Aristotle, which up till his day had been almost neglected. A Latin translation of his great commentary, attributed to Michael Scot, was in existence before 1250 [**Michele Scotto**].

D. places A. among the great philosophers in Limbo, in a group with Hippocrates, Galen, and Avicenna, describing him as *A., che il gran comento feo*, Inf. iv. 144 [**Limbo**]. Some think he is alluded to as *più savio di te*, Purg. xxv. 63, but the reference is more probably to Aristotle [**Aristotle**].

D. mentions him, Mon. i. 3^{77}; and refers to him by the title of the Commentator, Conv. iv. 13^{68}; A. T. §§ 5^5, 18^{38}; his commentary on Aristotle's *De Anima*, Conv. iv. 13$^{68-9}$; Mon. i. 3$^{77-8}$; A. T. § 5$^{5-6}$ (where the passage quoted comes, not, as D. states, from A.'s commentary on *De Anima*, iii., but from that on *Physics*, viii.); his opinion, as recorded in his work *De Substantia Orbis* (according to D., but in fact in his commentary on *Metaphysics*, xii.), that all potential forms of matter are actually existent in the mind of the Creator, A. T. § 18$^{36-9}$.

Avicenna, Avicenna (*Ibn-Sina*), Arabian philosopher and physician of Ispahan in Persia, born near Bokhara A.D. 980, died 1037; he was a voluminous writer, among his works being commentaries upon Aristotle and Galen.

D. places A. among the great philosophers in Limbo, in a group with Hippocrates, Galen, and Averroës, Inf. iv. 143 [**Limbo**]; his opinion (*De Intelligentiis*, § 4), which he shared with Plato and Algazali, that 'substantial generation' is effected by the motive powers of the Heavens, Conv. ii. 14$^{27-32}$; that the Milky Way is made up of numbers of small stars, Conv. ii. 15$^{69-77}$ [**Galassia**]; that a distinction exists between 'light' and 'splendour' (*De Anima*, iii. § 3), Conv. iii. 14$^{38-41}$; his theory (*De Anima*, v. § 3), held also by Algazali, that souls are noble or ignoble of themselves from the beginning, Conv. iv. 21$^{15-17}$.

Azio], Actium, promontory of Acarnania, off which Octavianus defeated Antony and Cleopatra, B.C. 31; the victory is alluded to by the Emperor Justinian (in the Heaven of Mercury) in connexion with the triumphs of the Roman Eagle, Par. vi. 77. [**Cleopatra.**]

Azzo da Esti], Azzo VIII (III) of Este, son of Obizzo II, whom he succeeded in 1293 as Marquis of Este, and lord of Ferrara, Modena, and Reggio; married, as his second wife, in 1305, Beatrice, daughter of Charles II of Naples; died, without (legitimate) male issue, 1308. D. refers to him (or perhaps to his father) as *il Marchese*, Inf. xviii. 56; *quel da Esti*, Purg. v. 77; *Azzo Marchio*, V. E. i. 12$^{38-9}$; *Marchio Estensis*, V. E. ii. 6^{42}; the popular belief that he murdered his father by smothering him with a pillow is accepted by D., who speaks of him in this connexion as the 'stepson' (*figliastro*) of Obizzo, Inf. xii. 111–12 [**Obizzo da Esti**]; his intrigue (or, perhaps, that of his father) with Ghisolabella, sister of Caccianimico, and the vile conduct of the latter, Inf. xviii. 55–7 [**Caccianimico: Ghisolabella**]; his murder of Jacopo del Cassero of Fano, Purg. v. 77–8 [**Cassero**,

Jacopo del]; his marriage with Beatrice of Naples, Purg. xx. 79–81 [Beatrice³]; condemnation of him, together with Charles II of Naples (his father-in-law), Frederick II of Sicily, and John Marquis of Montferrat, for bloodthirstiness, treachery, and avarice, V. E. i. 12³⁶⁻⁴²; a passage in his praise quoted (ironically), V. E. ii. 6⁴²⁻⁴.

Azzo Marchio. [**Azzo da Esti.**]

Azzo, Ugolino d', native of Tuscany, domiciled at Faenza, who is mentioned by Guido del Duca (in Circle II of Purgatory), together with Guido da Prata, among the worthies of Romagna, Purg. xiv. 104–5.

The individual in question is probably Ugolino degli Ubaldini, son of Azzo degli Ubaldini da Senno, a member of the powerful Tuscan family of that name. Ugolino, who married a daughter of Provenzano Salvani of Siena, and died at an advanced age in 1293, is said to have been a nephew of Ubaldino dalla Pila (Purg. xxiv. 29), and of the famous Cardinal Ottaviano degli Ubaldini (Inf. x. 120), and first cousin of the Archbishop Ruggieri degli Ubaldini (Inf. xxxiii. 14). [**Ubaldini.**]

Azzolino¹, Ezzelino III da Romano, son of Ezzelino II and Adeleita degli Alberti di Mangona, son-in-law of the Emperor Frederick II, and chief of the Ghibellines of Upper Italy, born 1194, died 1259.

D. places him among the Tyrants in Round 1 of Circle VII of Hell, where he is pointed out by Nessus, who draws attention to his black hair, Inf. xii. 109–10 [**Tiranni**]; he is alluded to by his sister Cunizza (in the Heaven of Venus) as a firebrand (in allusion to the common belief that before his birth his mother dreamed she was delivered of a firebrand) which desolated the March of Treviso, and described as being from Romano and of the same 'root' as herself, Par. ix. 28–31 [**Cunizza: Romano⁴.**]

Ezzelino, whose lordship over the March of Treviso lasted for thirty-four years, was a ruthless and bloodthirsty tyrant, and was guilty of the most inhuman atrocities. In 1255 Pope Alexander IV proclaimed a crusade against him, and after a war of three years' duration, he was finally defeated (Sept. 16, 1259) by the Marquis of Este at Cassano, where he was desperately wounded and taken prisoner. He died a few days later in his prison at Soncino.

Azzolino²], Ezzelino II da Romano, father of Ezzelino III and Cunizza, by his third wife, Adeleita degli Alberti di Mangona; alluded to by his daughter Cunizza (in the Heaven of Venus) as the *radice* from which she and 'the firebrand' (her brother Ezzelino) were sprung, Par. ix. 29–31. [**Azzolino¹: Cunizza.**]

B

Babel, Tower of Babel; the word *Babel* means 'confusion', V. E. i. 6[52], 7[30]; up till the building of the Tower all Adam's descendants spoke the same language as he had spoken, V. E. i. 6[49−53] (an opinion recanted by D. in the *D. C.,* Par. xxvi. 124−6) [**Adamo**]; the Tower built at the instigation of Nimrod, V. E. i. 7[29−30]; the confusion of tongues the consequence of its building, V.E. i. 9[18−20]; the Tower alluded to as *il gran lavoro,* Purg. xii. 34; *l'ovra inconsumabile,* Par. xxvi. 125. [**Nembrotto.**]

Babilon, kingdom of Babylon; *l'esilio di B.,* i. e. life on earth as opposed to life in heaven, Par. xxiii. 135 (var. *Babilonia*); its destruction by Cyrus (B.C. 538) and transference of the kingdom to the Persians, *Babylon,* Mon. ii. 9[43−5]; the Florentine exiles compared to exiles in B., Epist. vii. 1[10], 8[187].

D., following St. Augustine, who interprets *Babylon,* like *Babel,* as meaning 'confusion' (*Civ. Dei,* xvi. 4), renders the expression 'super flumina Babylonis' (*Psalm* cxxxvii. 1) by 'super flumina confusionis', Epist. vii. 1[10]. [**Babel : Babilonia.**]

Babilonia, kingdom of Babylon or Babylonia, Par. xxiii. 135 (var. *Babilon*) [**Babilon**]. In speaking of the empire of Semiramis D. alludes to B. as *la terra che il Soldan corregge,* 'the land ruled by the Sultan,' Inf. v. 60 [**Soldano**]. He

has apparently confused the ancient kingdom of Babylonia (or Assyria) with Babylonia or Babylon (Old Cairo) in Egypt, which was the territory of the Sultan, a confusion which is perhaps responsible for D.'s statement (Mon. ii. 9[65−7]) that Alexander the Great died in Egypt [**Alessandro Magno**].

Babylon. [**Babilon.**]

Babylonii, Babylonians; the rebellious Florentines compared to, Epist. vi. 2[50].

Bacchiglione, river of N. Italy, which rises in the Alps above Vicenza, through which it passes, flowing in a SE. direction as far as Padua, where it divides into three streams, one of which, retaining the name of Bacchiglione, enters the Adriatic near Brondolo.

The river is mentioned by Brunetto Latini (in Circle VII of Hell), in connexion with Andrea de' Mozzi, to indicate Vicenza, Inf. xv. 113 [**Andrea**[1] : **Vicenza**]; it is referred to as *l'acqua che Vicenza bagna* by Cunizza (in the Heaven of Venus), who prophesies that the Paduans at the marsh 'will change the water' of the Bacchiglione, Par. ix. 46−7. This prophecy is usually understood to mean that the Paduans will stain with their blood the marsh formed by the river, the reference being to the war between Padua and Can Grande, Imperial Vicar in Vicenza, which resulted in the defeat of the former in 1314 [**Padova**]. It appears that when at war with Padua the Vicentines were in the habit of damming the B., so as to deprive the Paduans of the water needed for their mills, &c.; the consequent overflow of the river converted the low-lying land to the south of Vicenza, between the Monti Berici and the Monti Euganei, into a vast swamp, which is supposed to be the 'palude' alluded to in the text. According to another interpretation, *il Palude* is a proper name, and the allusion is to an incident which took place in 1314, when the Paduans, finding that the waters of the Bacchiglione had been cut off by the Vicentines, turned into the bed of the river the waters of the Brenta, thus defeating the object of the enemy. It appears that the district of Brusegana, where the Brentella flows into the Bacchiglione, was known by the name of *il Palude*.

Bacco, Bacchus, god of wine, son of Jupiter and Semele, the daughter of Cadmus, King of Thebes; mentioned in connexion with his worship by the Thebans, Purg. xviii. 93 [**Asopo**]; the invocation 'Evoe! Bacche!' alluded to, Par. xiii. 25; *la città di Baco* (in rime), i.e. Thebes, his birthplace, Inf. xx. 59. [**Semelè**.] One of the two peaks of Parnassus was sacred to B., hence some think there is an allusion to him, Par. i. 16–18 [**Parnaso**.] He is referred to as *semen Semeles*, Epist. iv. 4[44] [**Alcithoë**]; as *Bromius*, Ecl. ii. 53. [**Bromius: Mida**.]

Baco. [**Bacco**].

Badìa], ancient Benedictine monastery in Florence, known as the Badìa (opposite to the Bargello),

which was founded in 978 by the Countess Willa, mother of the Marquis Hugh of Tuscany (or of Brandenburg, as Villani calls him).

The church of the Badìa, and the old (Roman) wall of Florence on which it was situated, are referred to by Cacciaguida (in the Heaven of Mars), who says that from its chimes Florence took her time, 'la cerchia antica, Ond' ella toglie ancora e terza e nona,' Par. xv. 97–8. [**Fiorenza**.]

The Marquis Hugh was buried in the Badìa, where the anniversary of his death (1001) was solemnly commemorated every year on St. Thomas' day (Dec. 21), a custom to which Cacciaguida refers, Par. xvi. 128–9 [**Ugo di Brandimborgo**].

Bagnacaval, Bagnacavallo, town in the Emilia, between the rivers Senio and Lamone, midway between Imola and Ravenna. In D.'s time it was a stronghold belonging to the Ghibelline Malavicini, who thence took their title of Counts of Bagnacavallo. One daughter of this house was the wife of Aghinolfo da Romena (Inf. xxx. 77), while another married Guido da Polenta, D.'s host at Ravenna.

B. is mentioned by Guido del Duca (in Circle II of Purgatory), who implies that its Counts were becoming extinct, Purg. xiv. 115.

Bagnoregio, now Bagnorea, village in Italy, perched on the top of a hill, on the borders of Latium and Umbria, near the Lago di Bolsena, about 8 miles due S. of Orvieto; mentioned by St. Bonaventura (in the Heaven of the Sun) as the place of his birth, Par. xii. 127–8. [**Bonaventura**.]

Balaam, son of Beor, whose ass spake and saved him from destruction by the angel of God (*Numb.* xxii. 28–30); not she that spake, but the angel of God within her, V. E. i. 2⁴⁵⁻⁶; Epist. viii. 8¹²⁹⁻³¹.

Baldo d'Aguglione. [**Aguglione.**]

Barattieri], Barrators (those who sell justice, office, or employment), placed among the Fraudulent in Bolgia 5 of Circle VIII of Hell (Malebolge), Inf. xxi, xxii [**Frodolenti**]; their punishment is to be immersed in a lake of boiling pitch, and to be rent by devils armed with prongs whenever they appear above the surface, Inf. xxi. 16–57; xxii. 34–42, 55–75, 112–29. *Examples*: an 'Ancient' of Santa Zita [**Zita, Santa**]; Bonturo Dati [**Bonturo**]; Ciampolo di Navarra [**Ciampolo**]; Frate Gomita di Gallura [**Gomita**]; Michael Zanche [**Michel**].

Barbagia, mountainous district in S. of Sardinia, the inhabitants of which are said to have been originally called Barbaricini, and to have descended from a settlement of prisoners planted by the Vandals. They were proverbial in the Middle Ages, according to the old commentators, for the laxity of their morals and their loose living. In D.'s time they formed a semi-savage independent tribe, and refused to acknowledge the Pisan government. [**Sardigna.**]

Forese Donati (in Circle VI of Purgatory) refers to Florence as a second Barbagia, and compares the morals of the Florentine women unfavourably with those of the Sardinian savages, Purg. xxiii. 94–6 [**Fiorentine**].

Barbare, Barbarian women (or, according to some, women of Barbary); the Florentine women compared unfavourably with, Purg. xxiii. 103 [**Fiorentine**].

Barbari, Barbarians; mentioned by D. in connexion with the effect produced by the sight of Rome and its wonders upon visitors from outlandish parts, Par. xxxi. 31–6 (where the reference is probably, as in *vv.* 103–4, to the Jubilee of 1300). [**Giubbileo.**]

Barbariccia, name of the leader of the ten demons selected by Malacoda to escort D. and Virgil through Bolgia 5 of Circle VIII of Hell (Malebolge), where the Barrators are punished, Inf. xxi. 120; xxii. 29, 59, 145; hence spoken of as *duca*, Inf. xxi. 138; *decurio*, xxii. 74; *gran proposto*, v. 94. [**Alichino**: **Malebranche.**]

Barbarossa, 'Redbeard,' the Italian surname of the Emperor Frederick I (1152–1190); referred to by the Abbot of San Zeno (in Circle IV of Purgatory), in connexion with his destruction of Milan (March, 1162), as *lo buon B.*, Purg. xviii. 119. [**Federico¹: Milano.**]

Bardi], wealthy Guelf family of Florence, founders of the great Florentine banking house. Some think they are alluded to, Par. xvi. 94–8; but the reference is almost certainly to the Cerchi, and perhaps the Donati also [**Cerchi**].

It was to a member of this family, Simone de' Bardi, that Beatrice Portinari was married [**Beatrice¹**].

Bari, town of S. Italy in Apulia on the Adriatic coast; mentioned by Charles Martel (in the Heaven of

Venus) as one of the extreme points of the Kingdom of Naples, Par. viii. 62. [**Ausonia.**]

Barone, Il gran. [**Ugo di Bran- dimborgo.**]

Bartolommeo della Scala], eldest son of Alberto della Scala, whom he succeeded as lord of Verona, Sept. 10, 1301–March 7, 130¾; he is referred to (probably) as 'il gran Lombardo', Par. xvii. 71. [**Lombardo, Gran.**]

Barucci, ancient noble family of Florence (extinct in D.'s time), mentioned by Cacciaguida (in the Heaven of Mars) as having been of importance in his day, Par. xvi. 104.

Battifolle, Gherardesca da], Gherardesca di Donoratico, wife of Count Guido di Simone da Battifolle, said to be the Countess of Battifolle who in 1310 or 1311 addressed to the Empress, Margaret of Brabant, wife of Henry VII, three letters (printed by Torri and Giuliani) which are supposed by Witte and others to have been written by Dante. [*Epistole Dantesche.*]

Battista, Il, St. John the Baptist, Inf. xiii. 143; xxx. 74; Purg. xxii. 152; Par. xvi. 47; he was the patron saint of Florence, which in pagan times had been under the protection of Mars, hence Florence is spoken of as 'la città che nel Battista Mutò il primo patrone', Inf. xiii. 143–4; 'l'ovil di san Giovanni,' Par. xvi. 25; the Florentine florin, which was stamped on one side with the lily ('fiore', whence *fiorino*), and on the other with the image of the Baptist, referred to as 'la lega suggellata del Battista', Inf. xxx. 74 (cf. Par. xviii. 133–5); the Bap-

tistery of Florence, which was dedicated to the Baptist, referred to by D. as 'il mio bel san Giovanni', Inf. xix. 17; and as 'il Battista', the phrase 'tra Marte e il Battista' (i.e. between the Ponte Vecchio, on which the ancient statue of Mars used to stand, and the Baptistery) being used to indicate approximately the N. and S. limits of the city of Florence in the days of Cacciaguida, Par. xvi. 47 [**Battisteo: Fiorenza: Marte**[1]].

St. John the Baptist is mentioned (in allusion to *Matt.* iii. 4), as an example of temperance in the Circle of the Gluttonous in Purgatory, Purg. xxii. 151–4 [**Golosi**]; he is referred to as *Giovanni*, Inf. xix. 17; Par. iv. 29; xvi. 25; *il gran Giovanni*, Par. xxxii. 31; *quel Giovanni, lo quale precedette la verace luce*, V. N. § 24[36–7] (ref. to *Matt.* iii. 3); *Praecursor*, Epist. vii. 2[30] (ref. to *Matt.* xi. 2–3); *colui che volle viver solo, E che per salti fu tratto a martiro*, Par. xviii. 134–5 (ref. to *Matt.* iii. 1; xiv. 1–12); the forerunner of Christ, V. N. § 24[36–7]; Epist. vii. 2[30]; his life in the wilderness, Par. xviii. 134; xxxii. 32; his execution by Herod at the instance of the daughter of Herodias, Par. xviii. 135; xxxii. 32; his two years in Limbo (i. e. from his own death to that of Christ), Par. xxxii. 33; his place in the Celestial Rose (opposite to the Virgin Mary), Par. xxxii. 31–3 [**Rosa**]; the patron saint of Florence, Inf. xiii. 143; xix. 17; xxx. 74; Par. xvi. 25, 47 [**Giovanni**[1]].

Battisteo, Baptistery of San Giovanni at Florence; Cacciaguida (in the Heaven of Mars) tells D. that he was baptized, 'nell' antico vostro Battisteo', Par. xv. 134; it is referred to elsewhere (by D.) as 'il mio bel san Giovanni', Inf. xix. 17; (by Cacciaguida) as 'il Battista', Par. xvi. 47 [**Battista, Il**: **Giovanni**[1]].

In connexion with the Baptistery D. refers (Inf. xix. 16–21) to the fact that he once broke one of the 'pozzetti' of the font in order to rescue a child (said to have been one of the Cavicciuli, a branch of the Adimari family) who had fallen in and could not get out again. The 'pozzetti' were circular holes in the thickness of the outer wall of the font (such as may still be seen in that at Pisa), in which the officiating priest used to stand to escape the pressure of the crowd, and which apparently were also used on occasion as baptismal basins.

The present Baptistery, which is octagonal in form, was in D.'s time the Cathedral of Florence, that of Santa Maria del Fiore, which was begun by Arnolfo in 1298, not having been completed until the middle of Cent. xv. The structure dates back at least as early as Cent. vi, and was erected on the site of, or perhaps converted from, an ancient temple of Mars, the tutelary deity of Florence (Inf. xiii. 144). The existing exterior of black and white marble was erected (1288–1293) by Arnolfo. The font to which D. alludes is said to have been removed in 1576 by the Grand Duke, Francesco I de' Medici, on the occasion of the baptism of his son Philip.

Be, first syllable of the name *Bea-*

trice; D. speaks of his reverence for even the syllables of B.'s name, *Be* and *Ice*, Par. vii. 14. Some editors, reading *B*, think there is an allusion to the pet name *Bice*. [**Beatrice**[1] : **Bice** : **Ice**.]

Beatitudini], Beatitudes, the promises of blessing made by our Lord in the Sermon on the Mount (*Matt.* v. 3–12). In each Circle of Purgatory D. represents an Angel singing one of the Beatitudes to comfort those who are purging themselves of their sins. In Circle I, where the sin of Pride is purged, the Angel of Humility sings *Beati pauperes spiritu*, 'Blessed are the poor in spirit,' Purg. xii. 110. [**Superbi**.] In Circle II, where the sin of Envy is purged, the Angel of Charity sings *Beati misericordes*, 'Blessed are the merciful', Purg. xv. 38. [**Invidiosi**.] In Circle III, where the sin of Wrath is purged, the Angel of Peace sings *Beati pacifici*, 'Blessed are the peacemakers', Purg. xvii. 68. [**Iracondi**.] In Circle IV, where the sin of Sloth is purged, the Angel of the Love of God sings *Beati qui lugent*, 'Blessed are they that mourn', Purg. xix. 50. [**Accidiosi**.] In Circle V, where the sin of Avarice is purged, the Angel of Justice sings *Beati qui sitiunt justitiam*, 'Blessed are they who thirst after justice', Purg. xxii. 5. [**Avari**.] In Circle VI, where the sin of Gluttony is purged, the Angel of Abstinence sings *Beati qui esuriunt justitiam*, 'Blessed are they who hunger after justice', Purg. xxiv. 151. [**Golosi**.] In Circle VII, where the sin of Lust is purged, the Angel of Purity sings *Beati mundo corde*, 'Blessed are the pure in heart', Purg. xxvii. 8. [**Lus-suriosi.**] In the Terrestrial Paradise, as D. and Virgil enter, Matilda sings (from *Psalm* xxxii. 1), *Beati quorum tecta sunt peccata*, 'Blessed are they whose sins are covered', Purg. xxix. 3. [**Purgatorio.**]

Beatrice [1], Beatrice, the central figure of the *Vita Nuova* and of the *Divina Commedia*, commonly identified with Beatrice Portinari, daughter of Folco Portinari of Florence. [**Portinari, Folco.**] She was born in 1266, probably in June (Purg. xxx. 124); married Simone de' Bardi c. 1285; died June 8, 1290 (V.N. § 30[1-13]; Purg. xxxi. 2), at the age of 24 (Purg. xxx. 124). [**Arabia: Tisrin primo**].

The assumption that D.'s Beatrice was the daughter of Folco Portinari rests mainly upon a statement of Boccaccio which he makes in his *Vita di Dante*, and more explicitly in his *Comento* (on Inf. ii. 70); and on the evidence of the poet's own son, Pietro di Dante, in his comment on Inf. ii. 70 (in a passage which occurs in the Ashburnham MS. of the *Comento*, but is omitted from the printed version).

The function of Beatrice in the *D.C.* is to conduct D. from the Terrestrial to the Celestial Paradise. She appears to Virgil (having been moved by St. Lucy, at the bidding of the Virgin Mary), and sends him to the help of D. (Inf. ii. 52-118). Subsequently, when Virgil has left D., she appears to D. himself, standing on a mystic car, and clad in white, green, and red (the colours of the three theological virtues, faith, hope, and love) (Purg. xxx. 31-3); ad-dressing him by name (*v.* 55), she calls him to account for the error of his ways (Purg. xxx. 103-xxxi. 69); then, after having revealed to him the destiny of the Church, she accompanies him on his pilgrimage through heaven as his guide and interpreter, and finally leaves him (after a solemn denunciation of Boniface VIII and Clement V) to resume her seat among the elect, at the side of Rachel, in the Celestial Rose, sending St. Bernard to take her place with D. (Par. xxxi. 59). [**Bernardo: Rosa: Virgilio.**]

Allegorically, Beatrice represents Theology, the divine science, which leads man to the contemplation of God, and to the attainment of celestial happiness.

Speaking to Virgil, Beatrice refers to D. as *l'amico mio*, Inf. ii. 61; D. himself she addresses once only by name, *Dante* being her first word to him, Purg. xxx. 55; on other occasions she addresses him as *frate*, Purg. xxxiii. 23; Par. iii. 70; iv. 100; vii. 58, 130.

Beatrice is mentioned by name sixty-three times in the *D.C.*, but on no occasion does D. address her by name; the name occurs twice only in the *Inferno*, Inf. ii. 70, 103; seventeen times in the *Purgatorio*, Purg. vi. 46; xv. 77; xviii. 48, 73; xxiii. 128; xxvii. 36, 53; xxx. 73; xxxi. 80, 107, 114, 133; xxxii. 36, 85, 106; xxxiii. 4, 124; forty-four times in the *Paradiso*, Par. i. 46, 64; ii. 22; iii. 127; iv. 13, 139; v. 16, 85, 122; vii. 16; ix. 16; x. 37, 52, 60; xi. 11; xiv. 8, 79; xv. 70; xvi. 13; xvii. 5, 30; xviii. 17, 53; xxi. 63; xxii.

125; xxiii. 19, 34, 76; xxiv. 10, 22, 55; xxv. 28, 137; xxvi. 77; xxvii. 34, 102; xxix. 8; xxx. 14, 128; xxxi. 59, 66, 76; xxxii. 9; xxxiii. 38.

D. speaks of B. as *donna beata e bella*, Inf. ii. 53; *donna di virtù*, Inf. ii. 76; *loda di Dio vera*, Inf. ii. 103; *quella, il cui bel occhio tutto vede*, Inf. x. 131; *donna che saprà*, Inf. xv. 90; *quella che lume fia tra il vero e l'intelletto*, Purg. vi. 44; *la donna*, Purg. xxx. 64; *la donna mia*, Purg. xxxii. 122; Par. v. 94; vii. 11; viii. 15; &c.; *madonna*, Par. ii. 46; *quel sol, che pria d'amor mi scaldò il petto*, Par. iii. 1; *la dolce guida*, Par. iii. 23; *amanza del primo amante*, Par. iv. 118; *diva*, Par. iv. 118; *bella donna*, Par. x. 93; *colei ch' all' alto volo mi vestì le piume*, Par. xv. 54; *quella donna ch'a Dio mi menava*, Par. xviii. 4; *il mio conforto*, Par. xviii. 8; *quel miracolo*, Par. xviii. 63; *la mia celeste scorta*, Par. xxi. 23; *quella, ond' io aspetto il come e'l quando Del dire e del tacer*, Par. xxi. 46–7; *la mia guida*, Par. xxii. 1; *dolce guida e cara*, Par. xxiii. 34; *la dolce donna*, Par. xxii. 100; *quella pia, che guidò le penne Delle mie ali a così alto volo*, Par. xxv. 49–50; *quella che imparadisa la mia mente*, Par. xxviii. 3; *quella che vedea i pensier dubi Nella mia mente*, Par. xxviii. 97–8; *il sol degli occhi miei*, Par. xxx. 75; he refers (perhaps) to her familiar name *Bice*, Par. vii. 14. [**Bice**.]

In the *Vita Nuova* Beatrice is mentioned by name twenty-three times: V. N. §§ 2^7, $5^{17,\ 32}$, 12^{46}, 14^{34}, $22^{6,\ 23}$, $23^{18,\ 101,\ 102}$, $24^{25,\ 32,\ 42}$, 29^{11}, $32^{19,\ 27,\ 55,\ 95}$, 40^4, ^{16}, 41^{66}, 42^{59}, 43^{15}; D. refers to her as *la gloriosa donna della mia mente*, § 2^5; *la gentilissima B.*, §§ $5^{17,\ 32}$, 14^{34}, 23^{18}, 40^{16}; *la mia donna*, §§ $6^{9,\ 16}$, 18^{60}, 24^8, 41^6, &c.; *la gentilissima donna*, §§ 9^{14}, 11^{18}, 14^{37}, 26^1, 31^1, 41^9; *quella gentilissima, la quale fu distruggitrice di tutti i vizi e regina delle virtù*, § 10^{11-13}; *la donna della cortesia*, § 12^{10}; *la mirabile donna*, §§ 14^{42}, 23^{48}; *questa gentilissima*, §§ 14^2, 18^{63}, 21^3, 22^{25}, 23^{122}, 29^7; *questa donna*, §§ 14^{48}, 15^{62}, 16^{13}, 17^2, 18^{33}, 19^{112}, 21^{24}, $22^{13,\ 44}$, 35^2; *la mia gentilissima donna*, § 18^{14}; *madonna*, § 19^{48}; *tanta meraviglia*, § 22^4; *questa nobilissima B.*, § 22^5; *donna gentile*, § 22^{72}; *la mirabile B.*, § 24^{24}; *Bice*, § 24^{58}; *questa B. beata*, § 29^{10}; *la mia nobilissima donna*, § 37^5; *questa gloriosa B.*, § 40^4; *questa benedetta*, § 43^4; *quella benedetta B.*, § 43^{15}.

In the *Convivio* she is mentioned by name four times: Conv. ii. $2^{6,\ 31}$, 7^{80}, 9^{53}; D. speaks of her as *quella B. beata*, Conv. ii. 2^6; *quella gloriosa B.*, Conv. ii. 2^{31}, 7^{80}; *quella viva B. beata*, Conv. ii. 9^{53}; *quella gloriosa donna*, Conv. ii. 9^{134}; *il primo diletto della mia anima*, Conv. ii. 13^5.

Beatrice [2], Beatrice, youngest daughter of Raymond Berenger IV, Count of Provence; married (in 1246) to Charles of Anjou, who subsequently (in 1266) became King of Sicily and Naples as Charles I; by this marriage Provence became united to the French crown (Purg. xx. 61) [**Provenza**]. Beatrice, who died in 1267, and Margaret of Burgundy, Charles' second wife, are mentioned together by Sordello (in Antepurgatory) in connexion with their husband, who he says was as inferior to Peter III of Aragon, as Charles II of Anjou was to his father, Charles I, Purg. vii. 127–9 [Carlo¹: Carlo²: Margherita²].

B. is referred to by the Emperor Justinian (in the Heaven of Mercury) as one of the four daughters of Raymond Berenger IV, each of whom became a Queen, Par. vi. 133–4. [Beringhieri, Ramondo.]

Beatrice³], Beatrice, youngest daughter of Charles II of Naples; married (in 1305) to Azzo VIII, Marquis of Este, in consideration, it was said, of a large sum of money. This transaction, which D. compares to the selling of female slaves by corsairs, is alluded to by Hugh Capet (in Circle V of Purgatory), Purg. xx. 79–81. [Azzo da Esti: Carlo².]

Beatrice⁴], daughter of Obizzo II of Este, and sister of Azzo VIII; she was married first to Nino Visconti of Pisa, by whom she had a daughter Joan, and afterwards (at Modena in June, 1300) to Galeazzo Visconti of Milan, where she died in 1334. Nino Visconti (in Ante-purgatory) refers to Beatrice as the mother of his daughter Joan, and reproaches her with her second marriage, saying that the Milanese viper will not become her tomb so well as the cock of Gallura, Purg. viii. 73–81 [Giovanna²: Nino²: Galeazzo].

Beccheria, Tesauro de' Beccheria of Pavia, Abbot of Vallombrosa, and Legate in Florence of Alexander IV. After the expulsion of the Ghibellines from Florence in July, 1258, he was seized by the Florentines on a charge of intriguing with them, put to the torture, and beheaded in the Piazza di sant' Apollinare in September of the same year. For this act of sacrilege the Florentines were excommunicated by the Pope. From Villani (vi. 65) it appears that in spite of his confession, extracted by torture, many people thought him innocent; D., however, did not believe in his innocence, for he places him in Antenora among those who were traitors to their country, referring to him as *quel di Beccheria*, Inf. xxxii. 118–20. [Antenora.]

Beda, Venerable Bede, Anglo-Saxon monk, the father of English history, and most eminent writer of his age, was born c. 673, near Wearmouth in NE. of Durham; he was educated at the monastery at Wearmouth, whence he removed to the neighbouring monastery at Jarrow, where he spent the whole of his life in study and writing, and where he died in 735. His most important work is his Ecclesiastical History of England (*Historia Ecclesiastica Nostrae Insulae ac Gentis*) in five books, which he brought down to 731, within four years of his death.

D. places Bede, together with Isidore of Seville and Richard of St. Victor, among the great doctors (*Spiriti Sapienti*) in the Heaven of the Sun, where his spirit is pointed out by St. Thomas Aquinas, Par. x. 131 [Sole, Cielo del]; the Italian Cardinals reproached with their neglect of his works, Epist. viii. 7[117].

Belacqua, Florentine, contemporary of D., said by the old commentators to have been a musical instrument-maker; modern research has suggested his identification with one Duccio di Bonavia detto Belacqua, a notary; he is placed by D. in

Ante-purgatory among those who neglected their repentance until just before death, Purg. iv. 123 ; *un, v.* 106 ; *colui, v.* 110 ; *lui, v.* 117 ; *ei, v.* 127 [**Antipurgatorio**].

Belinoi. [Belnui.]

Bella], D.'s mother, his father's first wife (d. bef. 1278), conjectured to have been the daughter of Durante di Scolaio degli Abati ; alluded to as *colei che in te s'incinse,* Inf. viii. 45 ; and, with his father Alighiero, as *i miei generanti,* Conv. i. 13³¹. [**Alighiero** ² : **Table A.**]

Bella, Della], one of the Florentine families which received knighthood from the Marquis Hugh of Brandenburg, 'il gran barone', Par. xvi. 128 ; alluded to by Cacciaguida (in the Heaven of Mars) as having the same arms as the Marquis, but with a border of gold (*vv.* 131–2) (where some think there is a special reference to the famous Giano della Bella, the great law-maker and champion of the commons of Florence). [**Giano della Bella : Ugo di Brandimborgo.**]

Bellincion, Berti, Florentine (fl. c. 1175) of the ancient Ravignani family, father of 'la buona Gualdrada' (Inf. xvi. 37), through whose marriage with Guido Guerra IV, the Conti Guidi traced their descent from the Ravignani.

Cacciaguida (in the Heaven of Mars) quotes B. as an example of the simplicity of the Florentines of his day, describing how he was content to be girt with 'leather and bone', Par. xv. 112–13 ; he speaks of him as 'l'alto Bellincion' in connexion with the Ravignani, and their descendants the Conti Guidi, Par. xvi. 97–9 [**Gualdrada : Guidi, Conti : Ra-**

vignani]; and refers to the marriages of his two other daughters, one to Ubertino Donati, and the other to a member of the Adimari family (*vv.* 115–20). [**Adimari : Donato, Ubertin.**]

Bellisar, Belisarius, the famous general of the Emperor Justinian, born on the borderland between Thrace and Illyricum c. A.D. 505, died at Constantinople, March, 565. His great achievements were the overthrow of the Vandal kingdom in Africa, the reconquest of Italy from the Goths, and the foundation of the exarchate of Ravenna upon the ruins of the Gothic dominions.

Belisarius is mentioned by the Emperor Justinian (in the Heaven of Mercury), who says that he entrusted him with the conduct of his wars, while he himself was occupied with his great work on the Roman law, Par. vi. 23–7. [**Giustiniano.**]

Bello, Bello degli Alighieri, son of Alighiero I, and brother of Bellincione, D.'s grandfather ; he is described in documents as 'dominus' (in Italian 'messere'), which implies that he was either a judge or a knight ; he was one of the council of the Anziani in 1255, and must have been among those who had to fly from Florence after the Ghibelline victory at Montaperti in 1260, he and his branch of the family having been Guelfs ; he was dead in 1268, in which year his son Geri was granted compensation for a house which had been destroyed by the Ghibellines after his exile in 1260.

Bello is mentioned by Virgil (in Circle VIII of Hell) in connexion with his son Geri, Inf. xxix. 27. [**Bello, Geri del : Table A.**]

Bello, Geri del, Geri (i. e. Ruggieri) del Bello degli Alighieri, son of the preceding, and first cousin of D.'s father, Alighiero II ; his name appears as 'Geri quondam Dom. Belli Alaghieri' in a document dated 1269, containing a list of the compensations granted to Guelf families in Florence for the losses inflicted by the Ghibellines after the battle of Montaperti in 1260; he had three brothers, viz. Gualfreduccio, who in 1237 was enrolled in the Arte di Calimala, Cenni (i. e. Bencivenni), who died in 1277, and Cione (i. e. Uguccione), who was a knight of the golden spur ('cavaliere a spron d'oro'). [Table A.]

D. places Geri (who is said to have sown discord among the Sacchetti, and to have been killed in retaliation by one of that family) among the 'seminator di scandalo e di scisma' in Bolgia 9 of Circle VIII of Hell (Malebolge), Inf. xxix. 27; *un spirto del mio sangue, v.* 20; *ello, v.* 23 ; *ei, v.* 24; *lui, v.* 25 ; *gli, v.* 32; *lui, v.* 34 ; *ei, v.* 34; *sè, v.* 36. [Scismatici.] Virgil, having noticed that D. was gazing earnestly into the ninth Bolgia, asks him the reason, to which D. replies that he was looking for a spirit of his own race who should have been there, Inf. xxix. 3–21 ; V. then tells D. that he had seen this spirit, whose name was Geri del Bello, point threateningly at D., and then, as D. was intent upon Bertran de Born and did not notice him, go his way in silence (*vv.* 22–30); D. explains that Geri had died a violent death, and had not yet been avenged by any of his kin, and that that was doubtless the reason why he was indignant with himself and did not stop to speak, wherefore he felt all the more pity for him (*vv.* 31–6).

Geri's murder appears to have been avenged, thirty years later, by his nephews, the sons of Cione, who killed one of the Sacchetti in his own house. The existence of a blood-feud between the Alighieri and the Sacchetti is attested not only by Pietro di Dante in his commentary (according to the Ashburnham MS.), but also by the fact that in 1342 an act of reconciliation was entered into between these two families at the instance of the Duke of Athens, the guarantor on the part of the Alighieri being Dante's half-brother, Francesco, who appeared on behalf of himself and his two nephews, the poet's sons, Pietro and Jacopo, and the rest of the family.

[**Belluzzo**], relative of D., who has been identified with Bellino, nephew of Geri di Bello [Table A]; mentioned by Forese Donati in his *tenzone* with D., Son. liii.* 11.

Belnui, Namericus de. [Namericus[1].]

Belo Belus, King of Tyre, father of Dido (*Aen.* i. 625); the troubadour Folquet (in the Heaven of Venus), referring to Dido as 'la figlia di Belo', compares his love for Adalagia with hers for Aeneas, Par. ix. 97–9. [Adalagia: Dido: Folco.]

Beltramo dal Bornio. [Bertram dal Bornio.]

Belzebù, Beelzebub, 'prince of the devils' (*Matt.* xii. 24), name by which D. refers to Satan (whom he usually calls Lucifer), Inf. xxxiv. 127. [Lucifero.]

[**Benacius**], of Benacus, Ecl. R. 28. [Benaco.]

Benaco, the Roman Lacus Benacus, the modern Lago di Garda, lake
in N. of Italy, at the foot of the
Tyrolese Alps; its E. shore is in
Venetia, the W. in Lombardy.

Virgil mentions it, in his account
of the founding of Mantua, in connexion with the Mincio, which flows
out of the S. extremity of the lake,
Inf. xx. 63, 74, 77; *laco, v.* 61;
lago, v. 66; and describes its situation, *vv.* 61–3 [**Mantua: Mincio:
Tiralli**]. The southernmost point
of the lake is indicated by the mention of Peschiera (*vv.* 70–2) [**Peschiera**]; the northernmost, roughly,
by the mention of a spot where the
Bishops of Trent, Brescia, and Verona could all give their blessing (*vv.*
67–9), i.e. since a Bishop can only
give his episcopal blessing within the
limits of his own diocese, a place
where the three dioceses of Trent,
Brescia, and Verona meet. Attempts
have been made to identify the exact
locality indicated. According to
some it is the mouth of the river
Tignalga, near Campione, on the W.
shore of the lake. Others think it
is the little island off the point of
Manerba on the same shore.

Benedetto[1], St. Benedict, founder
of the Benedictine order, the first religious order of the West, was born
of a noble family at Nursia (now
Norcia) in the E. of Umbria, c. 480.
He was sent to school in Rome, but
ran away and lived in solitude for
some years among the mountains near
Subiaco on the borders of the Abruzzi. About the year 529 he founded
his famous monastery of Monte Cassino on the site of an ancient temple
of Apollo, where he died c. 543.

His rule, first introduced in this
monastery, eventually became the
rule of all the western monks. [**Cassino.**]

D. places St. Benedict among the
contemplative spirits (*Spiriti Contemplanti*) in the Heaven of Saturn,
la maggiore e la più luculenta (*margherita*), Par. xxii. 28; *lei, v.* 31;
lui, v. 52; *padre, v.* 58; *egli, v.*
61 [**Saturno, Cielo di**]; his place
in the Celestial Rose is pointed out
to D. by St. Bernard, Par. xxxii. 35
[**Rosa**]; D.'s statement that a man
may lead a religious life without assuming the habit of St. Benedict, or
St. Augustine, or St. Francis, or St.
Dominic, Conv. iv. 28[68–74].

In his account of the founding of
the monastery of Monte Cassino
(Par. xxii. 37–45), D. has closely
followed that of St. Gregory in his
Dialogues (ii. 2).

Benedetto[2]], Benedict XI (Niccolò Boccasini), son of a notary of
Treviso, was born in 1240, and became a Dominican in 1257; in 1296
he was elected General of the Order,
and two years later he was created
Cardinal Bishop of Ostia by Boniface
VIII; he was elected Pope at Rome,
Oct. 22, 1303, in succession to Boniface, and died at Perugia after a reign
of a little more than eight months,
July 7, 1304.

In his letter to the Italian Car-
dinals, urging them to elect an Italian
Pope as successor to Benedict XI,
D. refers to the latter as ' defunctus
Antistes', Epist. viii. 10[166–7].

Benedetto[3]. [**Benedictus[1]**.]

Benedetto, San[1], mountain in
the Etruscan Apennines, on the
slopes of which, above Forlì, is situ-

ated a monastery of St. Benedict, known as San Benedetto in Alpe. D. mentions it in connexion with the Acquacheta or Montone, the falls of which are close by, Inf. xvi. 100 [Acquacheta : Montone].

Benedetto,San[2]. [Benedetto[1].]

Benedictus[1], Pope Benedict V, 964; during the absence of the Emperor Otto I from Rome, the Romans rose against his nominee Leo VIII, drove him from the city, and set up as Pope John XII, whom Otto had deposed ; on the death of John soon after, they elected Benedict V in his place ; as soon, however, as Otto returned to Rome he deposed Benedict, whom he sent into exile to Germany, and restored Leo VIII. D., referring to these incidents, says that from this action of Otto it might be argued that the Church was dependent upon the Empire, Mon. iii. 11[16-21]. [Leo: Otto.]

Benedictus[2]. [Benedetto[2].]

Benevento, town in Campania, on the Calore, about 30 miles NE. of Naples. On the plain of Grandella, near Benevento, was fought (Feb. 26, 126$\frac{5}{6}$) the great battle between Charles of Anjou and Manfred, King of Sicily, which resulted in the total defeat and death of the latter.

D. mentions Benevento in connexion with the burial of Manfred's body at the head of the bridge over the Calore, close to the town, where it was laid under a great pile of stones cast upon it one by one by the soldiers of Charles' army, 'Sotto la guardia della grave mora,' Purg. iii. 128-9 ; subsequently the body was removed thence by the Archbishop

of Cosenza, at the bidding, it is said, of Clement IV, and cast unburied upon the banks of the Verde, outside the kingdom of Naples (*vv.* 130-2). [Manfredi.]

Beni, Di Fine de'. [*Finibus, De.*]

Beniamino], Benjamin, son of Jacob and Rachel; he is among those referred to by Virgil as having been released by Christ from Limbo, *Israel co' suoi nati*, Inf. iv. 59 [Limbo].

Benincasa d'Arezzo], Benincasa of Laterina (in the upper Val d'Arno), a judge of Arezzo; according to the old commentators, while acting as assessor for the Podestà of Siena, he sentenced to death a brother (or uncle) of Ghino di Tacco, a famous robber and highwayman of Siena ; in revenge Ghino stabbed him while he was sitting in the papal audit office at Rome, whither he had got himself transferred from Siena, at the expiry of his term there, in order to be out of Ghino's reach.

D. places B. in Ante-purgatory, among those who died a violent death, without absolution, but repented at the last moment, referring to him as 'l'Aretin, che dalle braccia Fiere di Ghin di Tacco ebbe la morte', Purg. vi. 13-14. [Antipurgatorio: Ghin di Tacco.]

Bergamaschi, inhabitants of Bergamo, town in Lombardy about 30 miles NE. of Milan ; Peschiera well placed to hold them and the Brescians in check, Inf. xx. 70-1 [Peschiera] ; their dialect and that of the Milanese condemned, V. E. i. 11[30-5]. [Bergamo.]

Bergamo. [Pergamum.]
Bergomates. [Pergamei.]

Beringhieri, Ramondo, Raymond Berenger IV, last Count of Provence (1209–1245); mentioned by the Emperor Justinian (in the Heaven of Mercury), who says he had four daughters, each of them a Queen, an honour which he owed to his faithful minister Romeo (i. e. Romieu of Villeneuve), Par. vi. 133–5. [**Romeo.**]

The Count's four daughters were: Margaret, married in 1234 to Louis IX, King of France [**Margherita**[1]]; Eleanor, married in 1236 to Henry III, King of England [**Eleonora**]; Sancha or Sanzia, married in 1244 to Henry's brother, Richard, Earl of Cornwall, afterwards (in 1257) King of the Romans [**Sanzia**]; and Beatrice, married in 1246 (the year after her father's death) to Charles of Anjou, brother of Louis IX, afterwards (in 1266) King of Sicily and Naples [**Beatrice**[2]]. As Beatrice was her father's heiress, and at the time of her marriage was Countess of Provence, her union with Charles of Anjou brought Provence into the possession of the royal house of France; this result is alluded to by Hugh Capet (in Circle V of Purgatory), Purg. xx. 61; and by Charles Martel (in the Heaven of Venus) son of Charles II of Anjou and Naples, who says that if he had lived he would have been Count of Provence (in right of his grandmother Beatrice), Par. viii. 58–60. [**Carlo**[3]: **Provenza.**]

The story of Romeo and Count Raymond, which D. adopted, is told by Villani (vi. 90).

Berlinghieri. [**Beringhieri.**]

Bernardin di Fosco, Bernardo, son of Fosco, of Faenza, said by the old commentators to have been of humble origin, but to have so distinguished himself as to be received on terms of equality by the nobles of his native city. He was Podestà of Siena in 1249, and played a prominent part in the defence of Faenza against the Emperor Frederick II in 1240, during the podestàship of Michele Morosini of Venice, a defence which lasted nearly a year, and was famous enough to be commemorated in a sirventese by Ugo di san Circ, who makes special mention of 'Miguel Moresi' and 'Bernart de Fosc'.

Guido del Duca (in Circle II of Purgatory), who speaks of him as 'verga gentil di picciola gramigna', mentions him among the worthies of Romagna, as an instance of a person who from base beginnings raised himself to a high position in virtue of his noble qualities, Purg. xiv. 101–2.

Bernardo[1], Bernard of Quintavalle, a wealthy merchant of Assisi, who was the first follower of St. Francis of Assisi. At first, though attracted by St. Francis, he distrusted him; but having convinced himself of his sincerity, he submitted himself to his direction, sold all his possessions for the benefit of the poor, and embraced the rule of poverty.

St. Thomas Aquinas (in the Heaven of the Sun) mentions B. as having been the first to follow St. F., and refers to his great eagerness to become his disciple, Par. xi. 79–81.

Bernardo[2], St. Bernard, the great Abbot of Clairvaux, and preacher of the disastrous second Crusade, was born of noble parents in the village of Fontaines, near Dijon, in Burgundy, in 1091. After studying in Paris, in 1113, at the age of twenty-two, he joined the newly-founded Benedictine monastery of Citeaux, not far from his own home. Two years later, in 1115, he was selected to be the head of one of the branches, which the increasing fame of Citeaux made it necessary to establish, and he set out with a small band of devoted followers, journeying N. until he came to a spot in the diocese of Langres in Champagne, known as the 'valley of wormwood', where he made a clearing and founded his famous abbey of Clairvaux. His influence soon spread beyond the limits of his monastery, and from this time until his death he is one of the most prominent figures in the history of his time. The news of the capture of Edessa by the infidels in 1144 led St. B., with the approval of the Pope, to preach a new Crusade, which resulted in the disastrous expedition of Louis VII and Conrad III (1147–9). The failure of the Crusade was a crushing blow to St. B., from which he never recovered, and though he continued to take an active part in public affairs, he gradually sank, and died, at the age of sixty-two, Aug. 20, 1153. He was canonized a few years after his death by Pope Alexander III. His numerous writings consist of epistles, sermons, and theological treatises, which are conspicuous for his devotion to the Virgin Mary. His most important work is the *De Considera-tione* (quoted by D., Epist. x. 28), written in the last years of his life, and addressed to his disciple, Pope

Eugenius III, which is largely a protest against the excessive centralization of the authority of the Church at Rome. [*Consideratione, De.*]

In the *D. C.*, St. Bernard acts as D.'s guide, when Beatrice leaves him, and remains with him until the end of the vision ; he is regarded as the symbol of contemplation (Par. xxxi. 110–11; xxxii. 1), whereby man attains the vision of the Deity.

St. B. is mentioned by name, Par. xxxi. 102, 139; xxxiii. 49; *Bernardus*, Epist. x. 28^{555}; he is referred to as *un Sene Vestito con le genti gloriose*, Par. xxxi. 59–60; *il santo Sene, v.* 94; *colui, che in questo mondo, Contemplando, gustò di quella pace, vv.* 110–11; *quel contemplante*, Par. xxxii. 1 ; *santo Padre, v.* 100; *colui, ch' abbelliva di Maria, v.* 107; *l'orator*, Par. xxxiii. 41. After Beatrice has departed, St. B. bids D. look steadfastly upon the Celestial Rose, and so prepare himself for the divine vision, which he says will be vouchsafed them at the instance of the Virgin Mary, whose faithful servant he declares himself to be (Par. xxxi. 70–102); D. then, by St. B.'s direction, looks to where the Virgin is seated amid countless angels, and St. B., seeing D.'s eyes fixed upon her, turns his own gaze towards her with deep devotion (*vv.* 103–42); having explained to D. the arrangement of the seats of the Elect in the Rose, and having solved his doubt as to the salvation of infants (xxxii. 1–138), St. B. offers up a prayer to the Virgin that she may help D. to attain the vision of the highest bliss, and may henceforth have him in her keeping, so that he slide not back into his evil affections (xxxii. 139–xxxiii. 39). [Maria[1] : Rosa.]

D. several times alludes to St. B.'s well-known devotion to the Virgin, which is apparent in all his works, and especially in his Homilies on the Annunciation, and on the Praises of the Virgin (Par. xxxi. 100–2, 139–42 ; xxxii. 40–2).

Bernardone, Pietro, wealthy wool-merchant of Assisi, father of St. Francis ; he strongly opposed his son's wish to devote himself to a life of asceticism, and even prosecuted him before the Bishop of Assisi for squandering his money in charity. St. Francis thereupon, in the presence of the Bishop and of his father, renounced all worldly possessions, stripping off even his clothes, so that the Bishop had to cover him with his mantle.

St. Thomas Aquinas (in the Heaven of the Sun), in his account of the life of St. F., alludes to Bernardone's opposition to his son, and to the incident of St. F.'s renunciation before the Bishop, Par. xi. 58–62 ; and refers to the fact that St. F. in his humility, to remind himself of his origin, used to call himself 'fi' di Pietro Bernardone' (vv. 88–90). [Francesco [2].]

Bernardus. [Bernardo [2].]

Berneil, Guiraut de. [Gerardus de Bornello.]

Berta, Bertha, imaginary personage, V. E. ii. 6[34] ; any gossip or simpleton, Par. xiii. 139.

Berti, Bellincion. [Bellincion Berti.]

Bertinoro. [Brettinoro.]

Bertram dal Bornio, Bertran de

Born, lord of Hautefort near Périgueux, one of the earliest and most famous of the troubadours ; he was born of a noble Limousin family about 1140, and died at the age of about 75 (probably in 1215), as a monk in the Cistercian monastery of Dalon, near Hautefort, which he had entered some twenty years before, and to which he and his family had made numerous donations.

Bertran is placed among the sowers of discord in Bolgia 9 of Circle VIII of Hell (Malebolge), Inf. xxviii. 134; un busto senza capo, v. 119 ; quel, v. 123; colui che già tenne Altaforte, Inf. xxix. 29 [Altaforte: Arrigo [4]: Scismatici].

D. mentions him as an example of munificence, Beltramo dal Bornio, Conv. iv. 11[128] ; and as the poet of arms par excellence, quoting the first line of one of his sirventes, Bertramus de Bornio, V. E. ii. 2[79–85].

More than forty of Bertran's poems have been preserved, the majority of them being of a warlike tone ; the most famous is his lament for the death of the Young King, i. e. Prince Henry, son of Henry II of England. Of the part played by Bertran in the rebellion of the Young King against his father, for which D. places him in Hell, little or nothing is known historically ; and not much is to be gathered from Bertran's own poems. The sources of D.'s information upon the subject were the old Provençal biographies of the troubadour and the razos or arguments to his poems.

Bertramus de Bornio. [Bertram dal Bornio.]

Bestemmiatori], Blasphemers ;

placed among the Violent in Round 3 of Circle VII of Hell, Inf. xiv. 43–72; *gente, vv.* 22, 26–7 [**Violenti**]; their punishment is to lie prone on the ground in a desert of burning sand, while flakes of fire fall upon them from above, Inf. xiv. 13–30. *Example*: Capaneus [**Capaneo**].

Betlemme], Bethlehem; alluded to as the birthplace of Christ, Purg. xx. 23. [**Maria**[1].]

Bianca, Blanche, pseudonym of a lady (called also *Giovanna* and *Cortese*) mentioned in one of D.'s poems, Canz. x. 153.

Bianchi], 'Whites', one of the divisions of the Guelf party in Florence, who eventually identified themselves with the Ghibellines, while their opponents, the Neri or 'Blacks', remained staunch Guelfs.

Ciacco (in Circle III of Hell) refers to the Bianchi as *la parte selvaggia*, and after adverting to the bloody strife between the two parties, foretells their expulsion of the Neri (in 1301), their own downfall (in 1302), and the triumph of their rivals with the help of an ally (Boniface VIII), adding that the latter will keep the upper hand for a long period, during which they will grievously oppress the Bianchi, Inf. vi. 64–72 [**Cerchi: Ciacco**]; Vanni Fucci (in Bolgia 7 of Circle VIII of Hell) foretells the expulsion of the Neri from Pistoja (in 1301), and the expulsion of the Bianchi from Florence (1301–2), and the defeat of the latter at 'Campo Piceno', and the operations (1302–6) against Pistoja of the Neri of Florence and the Lucchese under Moroello Malaspina,

Inf. xxiv. 143–50 [**Fucci, Vanni**]; Cacciaguida (in the Heaven of Mars) refers to the exiled Bianchi (from whom D. held aloof after 1303) as *la compagnia malvagia e scempia*, Par. xvii. 62. [**Dante**.]

The parties of the Bianchi and Neri had their origin towards the end of Cent. xiii in Pistoja, in a feud between two branches of the Cancellieri, a Guelf family of that city, who were descended from the same sire, one Ser Cancelliere, but by different mothers. These two branches adopted distinctive names, the one being known as the Cancellieri Bianchi, as being descended from Cancelliere's wife Bianca, the other as the Cancellieri Neri.

A strong feeling of rivalry existed between these two branches, which at last broke out into actual hostilities. The immediate occasion appears to have been two atrocious murders on the part of one of the Cancellieri Bianchi, named Focaccia, which led to reprisals, and in a short time put the whole city in a ferment. One half the citizens sided with the Neri, the other half with the Bianchi, so that Pistoja was reduced to a state of civil war. To put an end to this state of things the Florentines intervened. In the hopes of extinguishing the feud they secured the leaders of both factions, and imprisoned them in Florence. Unhappily this measure only led to the introduction of the feud among themselves. In Florence also there happened to be two rival families, the Donati, who were ancient but poor, and the Cerchi, who were rich upstarts. The former, headed by Corso Donati, took the part of the Cancellieri Neri, while the Cerchi, headed by Viero de' Cerchi, took the part of the Cancellieri Bianchi. So it came about that, through the private enmities of two Pistojan and of two Florentine houses, Florence, which was ostensibly Guelf at the time, became divided into Black Guelfs and White Guelfs. These two divisions, which had originally been wholly unpolitical, by degrees became respectively pure Guelfs and disaffected Guelfs, the latter, the White Guelfs, finally throwing in their lot with the Ghibellines. [Cancellieri : Cerchi : Donati : Focaccia.]

The commencement of actual hostilities in Florence between the Bianchi and Neri was due to a brawl one evening in the spring of the year 1300 (May 1) between some of the Cerchi and Donati on the occasion of a dance in the Piazza di santa Trinità, which led to serious fighting. The peace having once been broken, the conflict was carried on without intermission, until at last in 1302 the Neri, with the aid of Charles of Valois, finally expelled the Bianchi from Florence, D. being included in the decree of banishment.

Bianco, one of the Bianchi, or disaffected Guelfs of Florence, Inf. xxiv. 150. [Bianchi.]

Biante, Bias of Priene in Ionia (c. B.C. 550); mentioned as one of the Seven Sages of Greece, who were the predecessors of the philosophers (apparently on the authority of St. Augustine, *Civ. Dei* xviii. 25), Conv. iii. 11[34-41].

Bibbia, La, the Bible; mentioned in connexion with St. Jerome's preface to his Latin translation of the Bible (the Vulgate), Conv. iv. 5[143-4] [**Jeronimo**]; usually referred to as *la Scrittura*, Par. iv. 43 ; xii. 125 ; xix. 83 ; xxix. 90 ; xxxii. 68 ; Conv. iv. 12[86] ; *Scriptura*, V. E. i. 4[10] ; Mon. iii. 3[95], 4[6] ; *le Scritture,* Par. xiii. 128 ; *le vecchie e le nuove cuoia,* Par. xxiv. 93 ; *l'antica e la novella Proposizion,* Par. xxiv. 97–8; *le nuove e le Scritture antiche,* Par. xxv. 88 ; *il vecchio e il nuovo Testamento,* Par. v. 76 ; *vetus et novum Testamentum,* Mon. iii. 3[75-6] ; *duo Testamenta,* Mon. iii. 14[28]. [*Evangelio.*]

D. quotes the Bible upwards of 200 times :—

Inf. xi. 106–8 (*Gen.* i. 28; ii. 15; iii. 19); Purg. ii. 46 (*Psalm* cxiv. 1); Purg. v. 24 (*Psalm* li. 1); Purg. x. 40 (*Luke* i. 28) ; Purg. x. 44 (*Luke* i. 38) ; Purg. xii. 110 (*Matt.* v. 3); Purg. xiii. 29 (*John* ii. 3); Purg. xiii. 36 (*Matt.* v. 44); Purg. xiv. 133 (*Gen.* iv. 14) ; Purg. xv. 38 (*Matt.* v. 7); Purg. xvi. 19 (*John* i. 29); Purg. xvii. 68–9 (*Matt.* v. 9); Purg. xviii. 100 (*Luke* i. 39) ; Purg. xix. 50 (*Matt.* v. 4); Purg. xix. 73 (*Psalm* cxix. 25); Purg. xix. 137 (*Matt.* xxii. 30); Purg. xx. 136 (*Luke* ii. 14) ; Purg. xxii. 4–6 (*Matt.* v. 6) ; Purg. xxiii. 11 (*Psalm* li. 15); Purg. xxiii. 74 (*Matt.* xxvii. 46); Purg. xxiv. 151–4 (*Matt.* v. 6); Purg. xxv. 128 (*Luke* i. 34); Purg. xxvii. 8 (*Matt.* v. 8); Purg. xxvii. 58 (*Matt.* xxv. 34); Purg. xxviii. 80 (*Psalm* xcii. 4); Purg. xxix. 3 (*Psalm* xxxii. 1); Purg. xxix. 51 (*Matt.* xxi. 9); Purg. xxix. 85–7 (*Luke* i. 42);

Purg. xxx. 11 (*Cant.* iv. 8); Purg. xxx. 19 (*Matt.* xxi. 9); Purg. xxx. 83–4 (*Psalm* xxxi. 1–8); Purg. xxxi. 98 (*Psalm* li. 7); Purg. xxxiii. 1 (*Psalm* lxxix. 1); Purg. xxxiii. 10–12 (*John* xvi. 16); Par. iii. 121–2 (*Luke* i. 28); Par. viii. 29 (*Matt.* xxi. 9); Par. xiii. 93 (1 *Kings* iii. 5); Par. xvi. 34 (*Luke* i. 28); Par. xviii. 91–3 (*Wisd.* i. 1); Par. xx. 94 (*Matt.* xi. 12); Par. xxiv. 64–5 (*Heb.* xi. 1); Par. xxv. 38 (*Psalm* cxxi. 1); Par. xxv. 91 (*Isaiah* lxi. 7, 10); Par. xxv. 73–4, 98 (*Psalm* ix. 10); Par. xxvi. 42 (*Exod.* xxxiii. 19); Par. xxxii. 12 (*Psalm* li. 1); Par. xxxii. 67–70 (*Gen.* xxv. 22–5); Par. xxxii. 95 (*Luke* i. 28).

V. N. § 7$^{41-3}$ (*Lament.* i. 12); V. N. § 23$^{55-6}$ (*Mark* xi. 10); V. N. § 24$^{38-9}$ (*Matt.* iii. 3); V. N. §§ 29$^{1-3}$, 31$^{8-9}$ (*Lament.* i. 1); Conv. i. 4$^{81-2}$ (*Matt.* xiii. 57); Conv. i. 11$^{31-3}$ (*Matt.* xv. 14); Conv. ii. 1$^{46-8}$ (*Matt.* xvii. 1); Conv. ii. 1$^{58-60}$ (*Psalm* cxiv. 1); Conv. ii. 4$^{42-3}$ (*Psalm* viii. 1); Conv. ii. 6$^{5-7}$ (*Heb.* i. 1); Conv. ii. 6$^{16-18}$ (*John* i. 5); Conv. ii. 6$^{23-5}$ (*Luke* i. 26–7); Conv. ii. 6$^{26-8}$ (*Matt.* xxvi. 53); Conv. ii. 6$^{29-31}$ (*Matt.* iv. 6, 11); Conv. ii. 6$^{34-7}$ (*Cant.* viii. 5); Conv. ii. 6$^{103-5}$ (*Psalm* xix. 1); Conv. ii. 9$^{115-16}$ (*John* xiv. 6); Conv. ii. 11$^{82-5}$ (*Eccles.* v. 13); Conv. ii. 15$^{171-2}$ (*John* xiv. 27); Conv. ii. 15$^{175-8}$ (*Cant.* vi. 8–9); Conv. iii. 4$^{76-7}$ (*Psalm* c. 3); Conv. iii. 8$^{14-20}$ (*Ecclus.* i. 3; iii. 21–3); Conv. iii. 11$^{128-9}$ (*Prov.* viii. 17); Conv. iii. 14$^{58-60}$ (*Ecclus.* xxiv. 9); Conv. iii. 14^{62} (*Prov.* viii. 23); Conv. iii. 14^{63}

(*John* i. 1–2); Conv. iii. 15$^{45-6}$ (*Wisd.* iii. 11); Conv. iii. 15$^{53-5}$ (*Wisd.* vii. 26); Conv. iii. 15$^{161-2}$ (*Wisd.* ix. 9); Conv. iii. 15$^{166-77}$ (*Prov.* viii. 27–30); Conv. iii. 15$^{190-2}$ (*Prov.* iv. 18); Conv. iv. 2$^{74-5}$ (*Eccles.* iii. 7); Conv. iv. 2$^{83-7}$ (*James* v. 7); Conv. iv. 5$^{14-15}$ (*Prov.* viii. 6); Conv. iv. 5$^{43-4}$ (*Isaiah* xi. 1); Conv. iv. 5$^{64-5}$ (*Luke* ii. 1); Conv. iv. 6$^{164-6}$ (*Wisd.* vi. 23 in *Vulg.*, omitted from A.V.); Conv. iv. 6$^{174-9}$ (*Eccles.* x. 16, 17); Conv. iv. 7$^{95-7}$ (*Prov.* xxii. 28); Conv. iv. 7$^{98-102}$ (*Prov.* iv. 18–19); Conv. iv. 7$^{130-3}$ (*Prov.* v. 23); Conv. iv. 11$^{112-13}$ (*Luke* xvi. 9); Conv. iv. 12$^{143-4}$ (*Gen.* i. 26); Conv. iv. 13$^{81-2}$ (*Rom.* xii. 3); Conv. iv. 15$^{69-71}$ (*Eccles.* iii. 21); Conv. iv. 15$^{137-9}$ (*Prov.* xxix. 20); Conv. iv. 16$^{1-4}$ (*Psalm* lxiii. 11); Conv. iv. 16$^{8-10}$ (*Wisd.* vi. 23 in *Vulg.*); Conv. iv. 16$^{49-54}$ (*Eccles.* x. 16–17); Conv. iv. 16$^{110-12}$ (*Matt.* vii. 15–16); Conv. iv. 17$^{94-101}$ (*Luke* x. 41–2); Conv. iv. 19$^{60-8}$ (*Psalm* viii. 1, 4–6); Conv. iv. 20$^{28-9}$ (*Acts* x. 34); Conv. iv. 20$^{51-3}$ (*James* i. 17); Conv. iv. 21^{56} (*Rom.* xi. 33); Conv. iv. 21$^{110-12}$ (*Isaiah* xi. 2); Conv. iv. 22$^{56-8}$ (1 *Cor.* ix. 24); Conv. iv. 22$^{149-59}$ (*Mark* xvi. 1–7); Conv. iv. 22$^{169-74}$ (*Matt.* xxviii. 2–3); Conv. iv. 23$^{79-80}$ (*Psalm* civ. 9); Conv. iv. 23$^{105-6}$ (*Luke* xxiii. 44); Conv. iv. 24$^{142-7}$ (*Prov.* i. 8, 10); Conv. iv. 24$^{163-5}$ (*Prov.* xv. 31); Conv. iv. 24$^{172-3}$ (*Coloss.* iii. 20); Conv. iv. 25$^{17-18}$ (*Prov.* iii. 34); Conv. iv. 25$^{19-20}$ (*Prov.* iv. 24); Conv. iv. 27$^{60-3}$ (1 *Kings* iii. 9); Conv. iv. 27$^{75-6}$ (*Matt.* x. 8); Conv. iv. 28$^{75-81}$

(*Rom.* ii. 28–9) ; Conv. iv. 30³⁷⁻⁸
(*Matt.* vii. 6).

V. E. i. 2⁴⁵ (*Numb.* xxii. 28);
V. E. i. 4¹³⁻¹⁸ (*Gen.* iii. 2–3); V.E.
i. 12³⁵ (*Matt.* v. 22); Mon. i. 1¹⁰⁻¹²
(*Psalm* i. 3) ; Mon. i. 1³⁸⁻⁹ (*James*
i. 5); Mon. i. 4¹⁴ (*Psalm* viii. 5);
Mon. i. 4²³⁻⁵ (*Luke* ii. 13–14);
Mon. i. 4²⁵ (*Luke* xxiv. 36); Mon.
i. 5⁶⁰⁻¹ (*Matt.* xii. 25); Mon. i.
8¹⁰⁻¹¹ (*Gen.* i. 26); Mon. i. 8²³⁻⁴
(*Deut.* vi. 4); Mon. i. 13³⁰ (*Psalm*
l. 16); Mon. i. 13⁶¹⁻³ (*Psalm* lxxii.
1); Mon. i. 14⁶⁶⁻⁷³ (*Exod.* xviii.
17–26); Mon. i. 15²²⁻⁴ (*Psalm* iv.
7); Mon. i. 16¹⁸ (*Gal.* iv. 4); Mon.
i. 16³⁶⁻⁸ (*Psalm* cxxxiii. 1); Mon. ii.
1¹⁻⁶ (*Psalm* ii. 1–3); Mon. ii. 2⁴²
(*John* i. 3–4); Mon. ii. 2⁷²⁻³ (*Rom.* i.
20); Mon. ii. 3²⁴⁻⁶ (*Luke* vi. 38); Mon.
ii. 4¹¹⁻¹⁴ (*Exod.* viii. 18–19); Mon.
ii. 8³⁶ (*Heb.* xi. 6); Mon. ii. 8³⁷⁻⁴²
(*Levit.* xvii. 3–4); Mon. ii. 8⁵⁷⁻⁹
(*Exod.* vii. 9); Mon. ii. 8⁶¹⁻⁴ (2 *Chron.*
xx. 12); Mon. ii. 8⁷⁰ (*Acts* i. 23–6);
Mon. ii. 9⁷⁵ (*Rom.* xi. 33); Mon. ii.
9¹⁰¹⁻³ (*Luke* ii. 1); Mon. ii. 10¹⁰
(*Psalm* xi. 7); Mon. ii. 11⁶⁹ (2 *Tim.* iv.
8); Mon. ii. 13⁸⁻¹¹ (*Rom.* v. 12);
Mon. ii. 13¹⁶⁻²⁵ (*Ephes.* i. 5–8);
Mon. ii. 13²⁶⁻⁷ (*John* xix. 30); Mon.
ii. 13³⁶⁻⁷ (*Exod.* ii. 14); Mon. ii.
13⁴⁴⁻⁵ (*Isaiah* liii. 4); Mon. ii.
1¹⁻³ (*Dan.* vi. 22); Mon. iii. 1¹³⁻¹⁶
(*Prov.* viii. 7); Mon. iii. 1²²
(*Ephes.* vi. 14); Mon. iii. 1²⁴⁻⁵
(*Isaiah* vi. 6–7); Mon. iii. 1²⁷
(*Coloss.* i. 13–14); Mon. iii. 1³¹⁻³
(*Psalm* cxii. 6–7); Mon. iii. 3⁷⁶
(*Psalm* cxi. 9); Mon. iii. 3⁷⁹ (*Cant.*
i. 3); Mon. iii. 3⁸⁴⁻⁶ (*Matt.* xxviii.
20); Mon. iii. 3⁹⁹⁻¹⁰⁴ (*Matt.* xv.
2–3); Mon. iii. 4¹⁰⁻¹³ (*Gen.* i. 16);
Mon. iii. 5⁸⁻¹⁰ (*Gen.* xxix. 34–5);

Mon. iii. 6⁴⁻⁵ (1 *Sam.* xv. 16, 23,
28); Mon. iii. 7¹⁻³ (*Matt.* ii. 11);
Mon. iii. 8²⁻⁵, ⁴¹ (*Matt.* xvi. 19);
Mon. iii. 9² (*Luke* xxii. 38); Mon.
iii. 9²⁵ (*Luke* xxii. 7); Mon. iii.
9³³⁻⁴² (*Luke* xxii. 14, 35–6); Mon.
iii. 9⁶⁰ (*Luke* xxii. 38); Mon. iii.
9⁷⁰⁻⁸⁰ (*Matt.* xvi. 15–16, 21–3);
Mon. iii. 9⁸⁴⁻⁶ (*Matt.* xvii. 4);
Mon. iii. 9⁹⁰ (*Matt.* xiv. 28); Mon.
iii. 9⁹⁴⁻⁷ (*Matt.* xxvi. 33, 35;
Mark xiv. 29); Mon. iii. 9⁹⁸⁻¹⁰²
(*Luke* xxii. 33); Mon. iii. 9¹⁰³⁻⁷
(*John* xiii. 6, 8); Mon. iii. 9¹⁰⁸⁻⁹
(*John* xviii. 10); Mon. iii. 9¹¹¹⁻¹⁴
(*John* xx. 5–6); Mon. iii. 9¹¹⁵⁻¹⁹
(*John* xxi. 7); Mon. iii. 9¹²⁰⁻²
(*John* xxi. 21); Mon. iii. 9¹³²⁻⁵
(*Matt.* x. 34–5); Mon. iii. 9¹³⁷⁻⁹
(*Acts* i. 1); Mon. iii. 10⁴⁴⁻⁶ (*John*
xix. 23–4, 34); Mon. iii. 10⁵⁰⁻³
(1 *Cor.* iii. 11); Mon. iii. 10⁵³
(*Matt.* xvi. 18); Mon. iii. 10⁵⁹⁻⁶¹
(*Cant.* viii. 5); Mon. iii. 10¹⁰⁹⁻¹¹
(*Matt.* x. 9); Mon. iii. 13⁴³⁻⁵ (*Acts*
xxv. 10); Mon. iii. 13⁴⁶⁻⁷ (*Acts*
xxvii. 24); Mon. iii. 13⁴⁹⁻⁵³ (*Acts*
xxviii. 19); Mon. iii. 13⁵⁷⁻⁸ (*Phil.*
i. 23); Mon. iii. 13⁶⁶⁻⁷⁶ (*Levit.*
ii. 11; xi. 43); Mon. iii. 14²²⁻³
(*Matt.* xvi. 18); Mon. iii. 14²³⁻⁵
(*John* xvii. 4); Mon. iii. 14³³⁻⁵
(*Numb.* xviii. 20); Mon. iii. 15²⁰⁻³
(*John* xiii. 15); Mon. iii. 15²⁴⁻⁶
(*John* xxi. 19); Mon. iii. 15²⁸⁻³⁴
(*John* xviii. 36); Mon. iii. 15³⁶⁻⁹
(*Psalm* xcv. 5); Mon. iii. 16⁷⁴
(*Psalm* xxxii. 9).

Epist. iv. 5⁵⁶⁻⁷ (*John* xv. 19);
Epist. v. 4⁶²⁻⁸ (*Psalm* xcv. 2; *Rom.*
xiii. 2 ; *Acts* ix. 5); Epist. v. 5⁷⁰⁻¹
(*Luke* xxi. 8); Epist. v. 7¹¹⁴⁻¹⁶
(*Psalm* xcv. 5); Epist. v. 8¹²⁰⁻²
(*Rom.* i. 20); Epist. v. 9¹⁵³ (*Matt.*

xxii. 2 1) ; Epist. v. 10^{160-5} (*Ephes.*
iv. 17 ; 1 *Pet.* ii. 17) ; Epist. vi.
1^{22-3} (*Deut.* xxxii. 35) ; Epist. vi.
5^{154} (*Rom.* vii. 23) ; Epist. vi. 6^{187-9}
(*Isaiah* liii. 4) ; Epist. vii. $2^{25-8,}$
$31-2,\ 45-6$ (*Josh.* x. 12–13 ; *Luke*
vii. 19 ; *John* i. 29) ; Epist. vii.
$3^{63-4, 73}$ (*Luke* ii. 1 ; *Matt.* iii. 15);
Epist. vii. 5^{102-7}(1 *Sam.* xv. 17–18);
Epist. viii. 1^{1-3} (*Lament.* i. 1);
Epist. viii. 2^{20-2}(*John* xxi. 15–17);
Epist. viii. 3^{35-6}(*Psalm* lxxix. 10);
Epist. viii. 4^{53-4} (*Ezek.* viii. 16) ;
Epist. viii. $5^{74-6,\ 90-1}$ (1 *Cor.* xv.
10; *Psalm* lxix. 9; *Matt.* viii.
24–6); Epist. viii. 8^{129-30} (*Numb.*
xxii. 28); Epist. x. 2^{40-2} (*Wisd.*
vii. 14); Epist. x. 7^{142-5} (*Psalm*
cxiv. 1); Epist. x. 22^{414-23} (*Jerem.*
xxiii. 24; *Psalm* cxxxix. 7–9 ;
Wisd. i. 7 ; *Ecclus.* xlii. 16); Epist.
x. 27^{517-23} (*Ephes.* iv. 10 ; *Ezek.*
xxviii. 12–13) ; Epist. x. 28^{540-64}
(2 *Cor.* xii. 3–4 ; *Matt.* xvii. 6 ;
Ezek. i. 28 ; *Dan.* ii. 3 ; *Matt.* v.
45); Epist. x. $33^{615-16, 625-6}$ (*John*
xvii. 3 ; *Rev.* i. 8); A. T. § 21^{69}
(*Gen.* i. 9); A. T. § 22^{6-8}(*Job* xi.
7); A. T. § 22^{9-11} (*Psalm* cxxxix.
6); A. T. § 22^{11-13} (*Isaiah* lv.
9); A. T. § 22^{15-18} (*Rom.* xi. 33);
A. T. § 22^{20} (*John* viii. 21).

The above references are to the
Authorized Version (A.V.) ; the
Vulgate references, where they differ
from these (as in the *Psalms*), are
given under the headings of the
several books quoted by D.

St. Jerome, in his preface to the
Latin translation of the Bible (*Prologus Galeatus*), reckons the canonical
books of the O. T. at twenty-four ;
he divides them into three groups
—the first of which comprises the five

books of Moses, viz. Genesis, Exodus, Leviticus, Numbers, and Deuteronomy ; the second comprises
eight prophetical books, viz. Joshua,
Judges, Samuel, Kings, Isaiah, Jeremiah, Ezekiel, and the twelve minor
prophets (counting as one book);
the third comprises nine hagio-
graphical books, viz. Job, Psalms,
Proverbs, Ecclesiastes, Canticles, Daniel, Chronicles, Esdras, and Esther;
to which he adds Ruth and Lamentations, making twenty-four in all.

The twenty-four books of the
O. T., according to this reckoning
of St. Jerome, are supposed to be
symbolized by the four-and-twenty
elders in the mystical Procession in
the Terrestrial Paradise, Purg. xxix.
83–4; the O. T. itself being symbolized by the left wheel of the car,
and the N. T. by the right wheel
(*v.* 107). [Carro [2].]

Bibbia, Proemio della. [*Proemio della Bibbia.*]

Bicci, Bicci Novello. [Forese.]

Bice, familiar abbreviation of Beatrice ; coupled with *Vanna*, the
familiar name of Giovanna, the lady-
love of Guido Cavalcanti, Son. xiv.
9 (V. N. § 24^{58}) [Giovanna [4]];
alluded to (perhaps), Par. vii. 14,
where, however, D. probably merely
means to express his reverence for
every part of the name of B. [Bea-
trice [1].]

Bilacqua. [Belacqua.]

Billi], name of a Florentine family, supposed by some to be alluded
to by the arms *la colonna del vaio*,
Par. xvi. 103 (where the reference is
more probably to the Pigli). [Pigli.]

Bindi, people of the name of
Bindo, popular abbreviation of Aldo-

brando; mentioned together with Lapo, as being among the commonest names in Florence, Par. xxix. 103. [**Lapi.**]

Bisdomini. [**Visdomini.**]

Bisenzio, stream in Tuscany, which flows close to Prato and Campi, and falls into the Arno opposite Lastra, about 10 miles below Florence; mentioned by Camicione dei Pazzi (in Caina) in connexion with the Conti Alberti, whose castles of Vernia and Cerbaia were situated in the Val di Bisenzio, Inf. xxxii. 56. [**Alberti.**]

Bismantova, village in the Emilia on a steep hill of the same name about 20 miles S. of Reggio; mentioned by D. in connexion with the precipitous ascent to it, Purg. iv. 26. In the Middle Ages it was strongly fortified and was a place of some importance. Nothing now remains but a huge sheer semicircular rock, known as 'La Pietra di Bismantova'. For *su B. in cacume* there is a variant *su B. e in Cacume*, the last word being taken for the name of another mountain. [**Cacume.**]

Bocca, Bocca degli Abati, one of the Ghibellines who remained in Florence after the expulsion of the rest of the party in 1258, and who, while ostensibly fighting on the side of the Florentine Guelfs at the battle of Montaperti, at the moment when the latter were hard pressed by Manfred's German cavalry, treacherously cut off the hand of the Florentine standard-bearer, thus creating a panic, which ended in the disastrous defeat of the Guelfs. [**Arbia: Montaperti.**]

Bocca is placed in Antenora, the second division of Circle IX of Hell, among those who have betrayed their country, Inf. xxxii. 106; *una (testa)*, *v.* 78; *colui che bestemmiava*, *v.* 85; *malvagio traditor*, *v.* 110 [**Antenora**].

Boemia. [**Buemme.**]

Boëtius. [**Boezio.**]

Boezio, Boëthius (Anicius Manlius Torquatus Severinus Boëthius), Roman statesman and philosopher, born at Rome c. A.D. 475, died at Pavia (Ticinum) 525. His father, Flavius Manlius Boëthius, was consul in 487, and died soon after. As a wealthy orphan Boëthius inherited the patrimony and honours of the Anician family, and was educated under the care of the chief men at Rome. He also studied at Athens, and translated or commented on 'the geometry of Euclid, the music of Pythagoras, the arithmetic of Nicomachus, the mechanics of Archimedes, the astronomy of Ptolemy, the theology of Plato, and the logic of Aristotle, with the commentary of Porphyry'. To his works was due to a great extent the knowledge of Aristotle in the Middle Ages. From Theodoric, King of the Ostrogoths, who was then master of Italy, he received the title of patrician while still a youth, and in 510 he was made consul. But his good fortune did not last; he was accused by his enemies of plotting against Theodoric, and the king, believing him guilty, threw him into prison at Pavia, while the senate without a trial passed a sentence against him of confiscation and death. After he had spent some time in prison he was put to death by torture. He was

buried in the church (now dese-
crated) called St. Peter's of the
Golden Ceiling (S. Pietro in Cielo
d'Oro. It was during his imprisonment at Pavia that Boëthius wrote
his most celebrated work, the *De
Consolatione Philosophiae* [**Consolatione Philosophiae, De**].

D. places B. among the great doctors (*Spiriti Sapienti*) in the Heaven
of the Sun, Par. x. 121–9 [**Sole,
Cielo del**]; his spirit is pointed out
by St. Thomas Aquinas, who speaks
of him as *l'ottava* (*luce*) (*v.* 123);
*l'anima santa, che il mondo fallace Fa
manifesto* (*vv.* 125–6), and alludes to
his exile and torture, and to his burial
at Pavia (*vv.* 127–9) [**Cieldauro**].

B. is frequently mentioned by D.
in his prose works, in connexion with
the *De Consolatione*, Conv. i. 2[96],
11[56]; ii. 8[27], 11[18], 13[15], 16[4];
iii. 1[78], 2[142]; iv. 12[35, 74], 13[130],
139; *Boëtius*, Mon. i. 9[25]; ii. 9[91];
Epist. x. 33[616]; he is spoken of as
il Savio, Conv. iv. 13[108]; and is alluded to (as some think, though the
reference is most probably to Virgil)
by Francesca da Rimini (addressing
D. in Circle II of Hell) as *il tuo
dottore*, Inf. v. 123 [**Virgilio**]; B.
obliged, by the nature of his book,
to speak of himself in the *De Consolatione*, Conv. i. 2[95–101]; his contempt for popular glory, Conv. i.
11[56–8]; his book one of those wherein D. sought consolation after the
death of Beatrice, Conv. ii. 13[14–16],
16[4–8].

Bologna, city of N. Italy, capital of the Emilia (in the old Romagna), situated on a plain between
the Apennines and the Po, with the
two rivers Savena and Reno about

two miles distant on the E. and W.
respectively. It was the seat of one
of the most famous mediaeval universities (founded in 1119), at which
D. is said to have studied. Among
the buildings in existence in D.'s
day were the two great towers, the
Asinelli (1109) and the Carisenda
(1110). The Bolognese for a long
time remained neutral in the contest
between the Guelfs and Ghibellines,
but eventually sided with the former.

Bologna is mentioned in connexion with Catalano and Loderingo,
two Bolognese Frati Gaudenti, Inf.
xxiii. 142 [**Catalano**]; Fabbro of
Bologna, one of the worthies of Romagna, Purg. xiv. 100 [**Fabbro**];
the dialect of B. rejected by the
chief Bolognese poets, *Bononia*, V. E.
i. 15[41–54] [**Bolognesi**]; Caccianimico, a native of B. (in Bolgia 1 of
Malebolge), alludes to the situation
of the city between the Savena and
the Reno, Inf. xviii. 61 [**Reno** [2] :
Savena]; he refers to the Bolognese use of *sipa* for *sia,* and declares
that there are more pandars in Hell
from B. than would equal the whole
population of the city at that time
(*vv.* 59–61) [**Caccianimico : Seduttori**]; D. mentions the Salse, a
ravine near B., where the bodies of
criminals were thrown, Inf. xviii. 51
[**Salse**]; and the Carisenda tower,
Inf. xxxi. 136 [**Carisenda**]; the
university is referred to, Inf. xxiii.
142 ; Bologna itself is referred to as
antrum Cyclopis, Ecl. ii. 47 [**Cyclops**]; and alluded to under the
guise of a nymph of the Reno, Ecl.
ii. 85 [**Naias**].

Bolognese, native of Bologna;
of Venedico Caccianimico, Inf. xviii.

58 [Caccianimico]; of the two Frati Gaudenti, Catalano dei Catalani and Loderingo degli Andalò, Inf. xxiii. 103 [Catalano : Loderingo].

Bolognese, Franco, Franco of Bologna, an illuminator mentioned by Oderisi (in Circle I of Purgatory) as being a better artist than himself, Purg. xi. 82–4. Little is known of Franco; Vasari, who possessed some of his drawings, says (in his *Vita di Giotto*) that he was employed, together with Oderisi (whose pupil he is said to have been), by Boniface VIII in the Vatican library, where he illuminated many of the MSS. He appears to have been still living in 1310. [Oderisi.]

Bolognesi, Bolognese ; the B. of the Borgo san Felice and those of the Strada Maggiore instances of inhabitants of the same city speaking different dialects, V. E. i. 9^{42-4} ; their dialect discussed at length and pronounced to be the best of the Italian dialects (a superiority due to importations from neighbouring dialects), but at the same time not worthy to rank as the language of Italy, as is evident from the fact that the chief Bolognese poets did not employ it, V. E. i. 15^{3-53}; two Bolognese poets, Guido dei Ghisilieri and Fabruzzo dei Lambertazzi, writing in the 'tragic' style began with a line of seven syllables, V. E. ii. 12^{38-41}; two Bolognese Frati Gaudenti, Inf. xxiii. 103 [Catalano : Loderingo]; D. (by the mouth of Caccianimico in Bolgia 1 of Malebolge) reproaches the B. with being pandars and avaricious, Inf. xviii. 58–63.

Bolsena, Lake of Bolsena, in the extreme N. of Latium, one of the largest lakes in Central Italy ; famous for its eels. Forese Donati (in Circle VI of Purgatory) mentions the lake and its eels in connexion with Pope Martin IV, who was in the habit of gorging himself on eels stewed in wine, Purg. xxiv. 22–4 [Martino [2]].

Bonaccorsi, Pinamonte de'. [Pinamonte.]

Bonagiunta, Bonagiunta Orbicciani degli Overardi, son of Riccomo di Bonagiunta of Lucca, notary and poet of the latter half of Cent. xiii; he was alive on Dec. 6, 1296, on which date he is mentioned in a document as having been engaged in superintending the works of the church of San Michele at Lucca. A considerable number of his poems has been preserved ; they show little originality of either thought or expression, and are imitated for the most part from Provençal models.

D. places B. among the Gluttonous in Circle VI of Purgatory, Purg. xxiv. 19, 20; *questi, v.* 19; *quel da Lucca, v.* 35 [Golosi]; B., who is pointed out to D. by Forese Donati (Purg. xxiv. 19–20), shows a desire to speak to the former, and mutters something about 'Gentucca', which D. overhears (*vv.* 34–9); being invited by D. to speak, he foretells to him that he will become enamoured of a certain lady of Lucca, who is not yet married (*vv.* 40–8) [Gentucca]; he then asks D. if he is the author of the 'new rimes' beginning 'Donne, ch'avete intelletto d'Amore' (being the first *canzone* in the *V. N.*) (*vv.* 49–51); D. replies that he writes as Love dictates (*vv.* 52–4); B. acknowledges in this the secret of the 'dolce stil nuovo', and of D.'s superiority over Jacopo da Lentino, Guittone d'Arezzo and himself; he then relapses into silence and D. moves on (*vv.* 55–63) [Guittone: Notaro, Il]; D. blames Bonagiunta, together with Guittone d'Arezzo, Brunetto Latini, and other Tuscan poets, for having written in their local dialects, to the exclusion of the 'curial vulgar tongue', V. E. i. 13⁷⁻¹³.

Bonatti, Guido, famous astrologer and soothsayer of Forlì, placed by D. among the Soothsayers, along with Asdente, in Bolgia 4 of Circle VIII of Hell (Malebolge), Inf. xx. 118 [Indovini]. B., who was a tiler by trade, seems to have acted as domestic astrologer to Guido da Montefeltro; it is said to have been by his aid that the latter won his decisive victory over the French papal forces at Forlì, May 1, 1282 [Forlì]. B. wrote (c. 1270) a work on astrology (*Decem Tractatus Astrologiae*), which was printed at Augsburg in 1491.

Bonaventura, St. Bonaventura, otherwise Giovanni Fidanza, was born at Bagnoregio (now Bagnorea), near Orvieto, in 1221, the year of St. Dominic's death. As a child he was attacked by a dangerous disease, which was miraculously cured by St. Francis of Assisi. When the latter heard that the child had recovered he is said to have exclaimed 'buona ventura' (happy chance), whereupon the boy's mother changed his name to Bonaventura. In 1243 he entered the Franciscan Order. After studying at Paris under Alex-

ander of Hales, he became successively professor of philosophy and theology, and in 1255 was made doctor. Having risen to be General of the Franciscan Order (in 1256), he was offered the Archbishopric of York by Clement IV, which he declined. He was afterwards (1274) created Cardinal Bishop of Albano by Gregory X, whom he accompanied to the second Council of Lyons, where he died, July 15, 1274. St. B. was canonized in 1482 by Sixtus IV, and placed among the doctors of the Church, with the title of 'Doctor Seraphicus', by Sixtus V. He was a voluminous writer, one of his works being a life of St. Francis, which was utilized by D. in the account of that saint which he puts into the mouth of St. Thomas Aquinas (Par. xi. 40–117).

D. places St. B. among the doctors of the Church (*Spiriti Sapienti*) in the Heaven of the Sun, Par. xii. 127; luce, v. 28 [Sole, Cielo del]. When St. Thomas Aquinas has finished his account of the life of St. Francis, St. B. proceeds to relate that of St. Dominic (Par. xii. 31–105); after bewailing the degeneracy of the Franciscan Order (*vv.* 106–26), he names himself (*vv.* 127–29) and eleven others who are with him (*vv.* 130–45 [Domenico: Francesco ²].

Bonconte. [Buonconte.]
Bondelmonti. [Buondelmonti.]
Bonifazio¹, Boniface VIII (Benedetto Gaetani or Guatani), born at Anagni c. 1217; created Cardinal by Martin IV in 1281; elected Pope at Naples, in succession to Celestine V, Dec. 24, 1294;

crowned at Rome, Jan. 23, 1295;
died at Rome, Oct. 11, 1303.

Boniface is spoken of (by Nicholas III in Bolgia 3 of Malebolge) as
Bonifazio, Inf. xix. 53; (by Guido
da Montefeltro in Bolgia 8 of Malebolge) as *il gran Prete*, Inf. xxvii.
70; and *lo Principe dei nuovi Farisei*, Inf. xxvii. 85; (by Hugh Capet
in Circle V of Purgatory) as *il
Vicario di Cristo*, Purg. xx. 87;
(by St. Bonaventura in the Heaven
of the Sun) as *colui che siede, che traligna*, Par xii. 90; (by St. Peter in
the Heaven of the Fixed Stars) as
Quegli ch' usurpa in terra il luogo mio,
Par. xxvii. 22; (by Beatrice in the
Empyrean) as *quel d'Alagna*, Par.
xxx. 148.

D. assigns to Boniface, by anticipation (he not having died until
three years after the assumed date
of the Vision), his place among the
Simoniacs in Bolgia 3 of Circle VIII
of Hell (Malebolge), by the artifice
of making Nicholas III mistake D.
himself for Boniface, Inf. xix. 52–7
[Niccolò [2]: Simoniaci]; the dealings of B. with Guido da Montefeltro are referred to, Inf. xxvii.
70–111 [Guido Montefeltrano];
his war with the Colonna family,
Inf. xxvii. 85–7 [Colonnesi:
Laterano]; his imprisonment at
Anagni, Purg. xx.86–90[Alagna];
his evil reign, Par. xii. 90; xxvii.
25–7; his usurpation of the Papal
See (his election not being valid so
long as his predecessor Celestine V
was alive), Par. xxvii. 22–4 [Celestino]; his place among the Simoniacs between Nicholas III and
Clement V, Par. xxx. 146–8 (cf.
Inf. xix. 52–4).

Boniface VIII is referred to by
Ciacco (in Circle III of Hell) (in
allusion to his double-dealing in ostensibly attempting to mediate between the Bianchi and Neri in
Florence, while he was in reality
favouring the latter, the ultra Guelfs,
whose ultimate triumph was thus
assured) as *tal che testè piaggia*, Inf.
vi. 69; B. is probably also alluded
to (though the reference may be to
the devil, or to the Pope in general,
or to the Emperor, or to both) as *il
capo reo*, Purg. viii. 131; and as *la
puttana sciolta*, Purg. xxxii. 149, and
consequently *la fuia*, Purg. xxxiii.
44 (the harlot of the mystic Procession in the Terrestrial Paradise,
who represents the Church, but with
especial reference to Boniface VIII
and Clement V); the part he played
in the expulsion of the Bianchi, D.
among them, from Florence is supposed to be alluded to by Cacciaguida (in the Heaven of Mars), Par.
xvii. 49–51; there is perhaps a
further reference to him in the expression of Marco Lombardo (in
Circle III of Purgatory), 'è giunta
la spada Col pasturale,' Purg. xvi.
109–10, the allusion to the union of
the sword with the crook, of the
temporal power with the spiritual,
being, as some think, to the action
of B. after the victory of Albert of
Hapsburg over Adolf of Nassau in
1298, when he not only refused to
crown the victor, but placed the
crown on his own head, and seizing
a sword, cried: 'I am Caesar, I am
Emperor, I will defend the rights of
the Empire' [Alberto Tedesco].
Some see an allusion to the death of
Boniface (but the reference is more

probably to the removal of the Papal court to Avignon in 1305) in the prophecy of Folquet of Marseilles (in the Heaven of Venus), Par. ix 139-42.

Boniface VIII, after procuring the abdication of the incapable Celestine V, secured his own election through the influence of Charles II of Naples, whose support he gained by promising to help him in his war for the recovery of Sicily. It was at the invitation of Boniface that Charles of Valois, brother of Philip IV of France, went to Florence in Nov. 1301, ostensibly to make peace between the Bianchi and Neri, his intervention resulting in the expulsion of the former and the exile of D. [Carlo⁴]. Boniface was thus the ultimate cause of D.'s lifelong banishment, and the poet in consequence indulges towards him a fierce hatred, assigning him, as is noted above, his place of torment in Hell while he was yet alive. It is noteworthy, however, that notwithstanding his personal hatred for Boniface D. refuses in any way to condone the enormity of the offence committed by Philip IV in laying hands on the Vicar of Christ, when the long struggle between them, and the bitter contest with the Colonna family, finally culminated in the tragedy of Anagni [Alagna].

Apart from his having prostituted the influence of the Church in the furtherance of the designs of Charles II of Naples, Boniface was repeatedly guilty of simony in advancing his own family and adherents to ecclesiastical dignities, as is recorded by Villani (viii. 64).

Bonifazio², Bishop (identified by modern commentators with Bonifazio dei Fieschi of Genoa, Archbishop of Ravenna, 1274-1295), whom D. places among the Gluttonous in Circle VI of Purgatory, describing him (in allusion to his extensive see) as 'Bonifazio Che pasturò col rocco molte genti', Purg. xxiv. 29-30 [Golosi].

The ancient pastoral staff of the Archbishops of Ravenna, which is still preserved, bears at the top an ornament shaped like a chess 'rook', hence the term *rocco* used by D.

Bonifazio dei Fieschi, who was a nephew of Innocent IV, was appointed Archbishop of Ravenna by Gregory X in 1274, during the second Council of Lyons ; he was sent to France by Honorius IV in 1285 to help Edward I of England in his efforts to bring about a reconciliation between Alphonso III of Aragon and Philip the Fair, and to negotiate for the release of Charles II of Naples; he died Feb. 1, 129⅘. He is known to have been immensely wealthy, but there is no record of his having been addicted to gluttony.

Bonifazio³], Fazio or Bonifazio de' Mori Ubaldini of Signa, a lawyer who was Gonfaloniere di Giustizia in Florence in 1316, and several times Prior. He and Baldo d'Aguglione were renegade Bianchi, and took an active part in helping the Neri to expel their old allies from Florence in 1301. He was sent as ambassador to Clement V in 1310 for the purpose of organizing the opposition to the Emperor Henry VII when he came into Italy; and his name figures in consequence on the list of those con-

demned by the Emperor in 1313.
He is probably the individual referred
to as *quel da Signa*, whom Cacciaguida (in the Heaven of Mars)
couples with Baldo d'Aguglione, Par.
xvi. 56. [Aguglione.]

Bonifazio di Monferrato.
[Monferrato.]

Bononia. [Bologna.]

Bononienses. [Bolognesi.]

Bononiensis, Bolognese; *vulgare Bononiense*, the Bolognese dialect, V. E. i. 15[38]. [Bolognesi.]

Bonorum, De Fine. [*Finibus,
De.*]

Bonsignori, Niccolò de'. [Nic-
colò [1].]

Bonturo, Bonturo Dati, head of
the popular party in Lucca at the
beginning of Cent. xiv; mentioned
ironically by one of the devils in
Bolgia 5 of Malebolge as being the
only man in Lucca who was not a
barrator (he having been in reality
an 'archbarrator'), Inf. xxi. 41.
[Barattieri.]

B. appears to have carried on his
nefarious traffic on so large a scale
that nearly all the offices in Lucca
were manipulated by him. It is said
that once, when he was on a mission
to Boniface VIII, the Pope, by way
of remonstrance at some piece of
double-dealing, shook him by the
arm, whereupon B. exclaimed :
'Holy Father, you have shaken the
half of Lucca.'

In 1314 his insolent reply to the
demand of the Pisans for the restitution of the castle of Asciano led
to a fierce war between Pisa and
Lucca, which terminated disastrously
for the latter. The Lucchese in consequence expelled Bonturo from

Lucca, and he was obliged to take
refuge in Florence, where he died.

Boote], Boötes (or Arcas), son
of Helice (or Callisto) by Jupiter.
Juno having in jealousy metamorphosed Callisto into a she-bear, she
was one day pursued by her son
Arcas while hunting ; when he was
on the point of killing her Jupiter
transformed them both into Constellations, Callisto becoming the
Great Bear, Arcas the Little Bear
or Boötes. D., referring to Boötes
as *il figlio d'Elice*, speaks of the
North as the region which is covered
every day by Helice and her son, i. e.
by the Great and Little Bear, Par.
xxxi. 31-3 [Elice]; the two
Bears are spoken of as *l'Orse*, Purg.
iv. 65; Par. ii. 9 [Orsa]; the
Little Bear is alluded to, Par. xiii.
10 [Corno].

Borea, Boreas, the N. wind, Par.
xxviii. 81 ; D. here speaks of it as
blowing 'from that cheek whence it
is most gentle', and clearing away
the fog, by which, as is evident from
what Brunetto Latini says in his
Trésor (i. 107), he means the NE.
wind ; Lucan's mention of Boreas
(*Phars.* ix. 480), quoted, Mon. ii.
4[41].

Borgo, Borgo sant' Apostolo, one
of the ancient quarters of Florence,
situated close to the Arno, between
the Ponte Vecchio and the Ponte S.
Trinità ; mentioned by Cacciaguida
(in the Heaven of Mars), who says
that in his day the Gualterotti
and Importuni lived there, and that
the quarter would have been more
peaceful had they not had new neighbours, Par. xvi. 133-5. The 'nuovi
vicini' were the Buondelmonti, who

came into Florence in 1135, and subsequently (in 1215) gave rise to the feuds which led to the introduction of the Guelf and Ghibelline factions into Florence. [Buondelmonti : Fiorenza.]

Borgo san Felice. [Burgum S. Felicis.]

Borneil, Gerardus de. [Gerardus de Borneil.]

Bornio, Born, name of a forest, on the borders of the Limousin and Périgord, in the midst of which, on the shore of a small lake, not far from the village of Bellegarde, was situated the castle where the famous troubadour, Bertran de Born, was born, Inf. xxviii. 134.

Bornio, Bertram dal. [Bertram dal Bornio.]

Borsiere, Guglielmo, a Florentine, said to have been a pursemaker, placed by D. in Round 3 of Circle VII of Hell among those guilty of unnatural offences ; he is mentioned by Jacopo Rusticucci, who asks D. for news of Florence, saying that Guglielmo, who had but recently joined them (i.e. had died shortly before 1300), gave them a grievous report of it, Inf. xvi. 67–72. [Sodomiti.]

A quip of Guglielmo's is the subject of one of the tales of the *Decameron* (i. 8).

Boso. [Buoso.]

Bostichi, ancient noble Florentine family, mentioned by Cacciaguida (in the Heaven of Mars) as having been of importance in his day, Par. xvi. 93. They lived near the Mercato Nuovo (Vill. iv. 13) and were Guelfs (v. 39; vi. 33); they fled from Florence with the rest of the party in 1260 after the Ghibelline victory

at Montaperti (vi. 79), and subsequently sided, some with the Bianchi, some with the Neri (viii. 39).

Bottaio, Martino], magistrate of Lucca, said by some to be the person referred to by D. as 'un degli anzian di Santa Zita', who is placed among the Barrators, Inf. xxi. 38 [Barattieri : Zita, Santa].

Brabante, Brabant, ancient duchy, now one of the provinces of Belgium ; mentioned in connexion with the second wife of Philip III of France, whom D. calls *la donna di Brabante*, Purg. vi. 23. Mary, daughter of Henry III, Duke of Brabant, married Philip III as his second wife in 1274. [Filippo[1].] She is said to have accused Pierre de la Brosse, Philip's chamberlain, of an attempt upon her chastity, in consequence of which he was put to death. D. appears to have believed that Pierre was innocent, and he urges Mary to repent of having caused his death, while she yet had time (*vv.* 22–4). Mary died, Jan. 12, 1321, in the same year as D., and may not improbably have read this warning. [Broccia.]

Brabante, Donna di. [Brabante.]

Brabante, Margherita di], Margaret of Brabant, daughter of John I, Duke of Brabant; married (1292) Henry, Count of Luxemburg, afterwards Emperor Henry VII ; died at Genoa, Dec. 1311. Three letters (printed by Torri and Giuliani) addressed to her in 1310 or 1311 by the Countess of Battifolle, are said to have been written by Dante. [*Epistole Dantesche.*]

Branca d'Oria, member of the famous Ghibelline house of Doria at

Genoa, who, with the aid of his nephew, treacherously murdered (c. 1290) his father-in-law, Michael Zanche, governor of Logodoro in Sardinia, at a banquet to which he had invited him.

D. places his soul in Tolomea, the third division of Circle IX of Hell, among the Traitors, although he was not yet dead, Inf. xxxiii. 137, 140 ; *un tal*, v. 155. [**Michel Zanche: Tolomea.**]

Branda, Fonte, spring near the castle of Romena, in the Casentino, supposed to be that referred to by Maestro Adamo (in Bolgia 10 of Malebolge), Inf. xxx. 78. All the old commentators take the reference to be to the famous Fonte Branda at Siena (at the foot of the hill on which the church of San Domenico stands) ; but it seems more probable that D. had in mind the spring in the Casentino, which was close to the scene of Maestro Adamo's crime and punishment. [**Adamo, Maestro : Romena.**]

Brandimborgo, Ugo di. [**Ugo di Brandimborgo.**]

Brandino Padovano. [**Ildebrandinus Paduanus.**]

Brandizio, Brundusium (Brindisi), town on the Adriatic in Apulia (the Roman Calabria), the termination of the Via Appia, and the usual port of embarkation in ancient times for Greece and the East ; Virgil died here on his return from Greece, Sept. 26, B.C. 19.

Addressing D. (in Ante-purgatory), Virgil says of his own body, ' Napoli l'ha, e da Brandizio è tolto,' Purg. iii. 27 ; the allusion is to the transference of V.'s body from Brundusium to Naples by order of Augustus, and to the old epitaph recorded by Suetonius :—

' Mantua me genuit, Calabri rapuere, tenet nunc
Parthenope ; cecini pascua, rura, duces '—

(i. e. I was born at Mantua, died at Calabrian Brundusium, and was buried at Naples ; I wrote the *Eclogues*, the *Georgics*, and the *Aeneid*) [**Augusto [2] : Virgilio.**]

Brenno, Brennus, leader of the Senonian Gauls, who in B.C. 390 crossed the Apennines, defeated the Romans at the Allia, and took Rome ; after besieging the Capitol for six months he quitted the city upon receiving 1,000 pounds of gold as a ransom for the Capitol, and returned safe home with his booty. According to later tradition (followed by Livy, v. 48–9), at the moment when the gold was being weighed, and Brennus, declaring the Roman weights to be false, had thrown his sword into the scale, Camillus and a Roman army appeared, fell upon the Gauls and slaughtered them.

The Emperor Justinian (in the Heaven of Mercury) mentions the defeat of Brennus among the exploits of the Roman Eagle, Par. vi. 44 ; the story of the attack of the Gauls on the Capitol, and their repulse by Manlius, is referred to, Conv. iv. 5[160–4] ; and told on the authority of Livy (v. 47) and Virgil (*Aen.* viii. 652–6), *Brennus*, Mon. ii. 4[42–57] [**Camillo : Galli [2] : Manlius**].

Brennus. [**Brenno.**]

Brenta, river of Upper Italy, which rises in the Tyrolese Alps above Trent, flows SE. and then S. past Bassano, and after being joined by the Bacchiglione just below Padua, falls into the Venetian lagoons by two mouths (the southernmost, near Brondolo, being now the outlet of the Brenta canal).

D. mentions the B. in connexion with the embankments built by the Paduans as a protection against its floods, Inf. xv. 7–9 [**Chiarentana**]; Cunizza (in the Heaven of Venus) mentions it as one of the boundaries of the March of Treviso, Par. ix. 27 [**Marca Trivisiana**].

Brescia, town in Lombardy about 16 miles W. of the Lago di Garda ; mentioned by Virgil, in his account of the founding of Mantua, in connexion with a place on the lake where the three dioceses of Trent, Brescia, and Verona meet, Inf. xx. 68 [**Benaco**]; a neighbour of Mantua, Cremona, and Verona (from which it is distant about 38, 30, and 40 miles respectively), *Brixia*, V. E. i. 15⁹⁻¹¹ ; one of the Guelfic cities which opposed the Emperor Henry VII, Epist. vii. 6¹²⁸.

Bresciani, inhabitants of Brescia, Inf. xx. 71 ; *Brixiani*, V. E. i. 14³¹; *Brixienses*, V. E. i. 14²⁶ ; Peschiera well placed to hold them and the Bergamasks in check, Inf. xx. 70–1 [**Peschiera**]; their dialect, together with those of the Veronese, Vicentines, Paduans, and Trevisans, condemned as harsh, especially in a woman's mouth, one of their peculiarities being a fondness for consonantal endings in *f*, V. E. i. 14²⁰⁻³⁵.

Brettinoro, now Bertinoro, small town in the Emilia, between Forlì and Cesena ; it was the native place of Guido del Duca (Purg. xiv. 81) and Arrigo Mainardi (Purg. xiv. 97). Guido del Duca (in Circle II of Purgatory) mentions it in allusion to the expulsion of the Ghibellines in 1295, probably with especial reference to the Mainardi family (though some think the allusion is to the extinction of the Cavalcaconti family), Purg. xiv. 112–14. After being for a time under the lordship of the Malatesti of Rimini, the town passed towards the end of Cent. xiii into the hands of the Ordelaffi of Forlì, in whose possession it was at the date of the Vision.

Briareo, Briareus, son of Uranus and Gaea, one of the giants who warred against Olympus. He was slain by Jupiter with a thunderbolt and buried under Mt. Aetna. D. calls him *lo ismisurato B.* (a reminiscence of the 'immensus Briareus' of Statius, *Theb.* ii. 596), and places him with Antaeus, Ephialtes and Nimrod, as one of the warders at the mouth of Circle IX of Hell, Inf. xxxi. 98 [**Giganti**]; he is represented, transfixed by the bolt of Jupiter, among the examples of defeated pride in Circle I of Purgatory, Purg. xii. 28–30. [**Superbi.**]

Brigata, Il, Nino il Brigata, grandson of Count Ugolino della Gherardesca of Pisa, whose imprisonment and death he shared in 1288 in the Tower of Famine at Pisa, Inf. xxxiii. 89; he and his uncle Uguccione, and his younger brother Anselmuccio, referred to by Ugolino (in Antenora) as *li tre, v.* 71 [**Anselmuccio: Ugolino, Conte**]. Nino was the son of Guelfo, eldest son of Ugolino, and Elena, daughter of Enzio, King of Sardinia, the natural son of Frederick II. D. represents both the two sons of Ugolino, and his two grandsons, as being of tender age ('età novella', *v.* 88), a phrase used by him in the *Convivio* (iv. 19$^{81-2}$) as the equivalent of 'gioventute', which he elsewhere (iv. 24$^{11-37}$) defines as the period between twenty-five and forty-five. Nino cannot have been very young, for he is said to have been married, and not long before his death the Ghibellines had wished to associate him with his grandfather in the government of Pisa.

Brigata Spendereccia], 'Spendthrift Brigade' of Siena, a company of twelve wealthy young men, who vied with each other in squandering their means; the 'brigade', which flourished for a short time during the second half of Cent. xiii, was celebrated in a series of twelve sonnets, one for each month of the year, by Folgore da San Gemignano; Capocchio (in Bolgia 10 of Malebolge) alludes to it as *la brigata*, Inf. xxix. 130; and mentions four of its most conspicuous members by name, viz. Stricca, *v.* 125; Niccolò, *v.* 127; Caccia d'Asciano, *v.* 131; and 'l'Abbagliato', *v.* 132; a fifth member, Lano, is mentioned, Inf. xiii. 120. [Abbagliato: Caccia d' Asciano: Lano: Niccolò [1]: Stricca.]

Brisso, Bryson, ancient Greek philosopher, mentioned by Aristotle (*Soph. Elench.* i. 10; *Anal. Post.* i. 8) as having attempted to square the circle, a problem which apparently he tried to solve dishonestly by non-geometrical methods.

St. Thomas Aquinas (in the Heaven of the Sun) mentions B., together with Parmenides and Melissus, as examples of bad reasoners, Par. xiii. 125.

Brixia. [Brescia.]

Brixiani, Brixienses. [Bresciani.]

Broccia, Pier dalla, Pierre de la Brosse, favourite and chamberlain of Philip III of France. On the sudden death in 1276 of the heir to the throne, Louis, Philip's son by his first wife, Isabella of Aragon, an accusation was brought against the Queen, Mary of Brabant, of having poisoned Louis, in order to secure the succession of her own son, among her accusers being Pierre de la Brosse.

Not long afterwards Pierre was suddenly arrested and imprisoned by order of the King. After being tried at Paris before an assembly of the nobles, he was hanged by the common hangman, June 30, 1278. The suddenness and ignominy of his execution appear to have caused great wonder and consternation, especially as the charge on which he was condemned was not made known. According to the popular account he had been accused by the Queen of an attempt upon her chastity. The truth seems to be that he was hanged upon a charge of treasonable correspondence with Alphonso X, King of Castile, with whom Philip was at war, the intercepted letters on which the charge was based having, it is alleged, been forged at the instance of the Queen.

D., who evidently regarded him as the innocent victim of the Queen, places Pierre de la Brosse in Ante-purgatory among those who put off repentance, Purg. vi. 22 [**Antipurgatorio : Brabante**].

Bromius, surname of Bacchus; mentioned, in connexion with King Midas, Ecl. ii. 53. [**Bacco: Mida.**]

Bruggia, Bruges, capital of Western Flanders, about 25 miles NW. of Ghent, and about ten from the coast; mentioned, together with Wissant, in connexion with the embankments built by the Flemings to keep back the sea, B. roughly indicating the eastern limit of the Flemish seaboard, Wissant the western, Inf. xv. 4 [**Guizzante**]; coupled by Hugh Capet (in Circle V of Purgatory) with Douay, Ghent, and Lille, to indicate Flanders (in reference to the dealings of Philip IV of France with Flanders between 1297 and 1304, in which those towns played a conspicuous part), Purg. xx. 46. [**Fiandra.**]

Brunelleschi, Agnello. [**Agnèl.**]

Brunetto Latini, Florentine Guelf, son of Buonaccorso Latino, born in Florence, c. 1210, died 1294; he was a notary (whence the title of ' Ser ' given him by D., Inf. xv. 30, 101), and is commonly supposed (from a misunderstanding of Inf. xv. 82–5) to have been D.'s master, which in the ordinary sense of the word he cannot have been, since he was about fifty-five when D. was born. It is uncertain at what period he began to take part in public affairs in Florence; he held an official position in 1253, and in the next year he attested, in his capacity of notary, two public documents (April 20 and Aug. 25), which are still preserved, and one of which is drawn up in his own hand-

writing. In 1260 he was sent on an embassy to Alphonso X of Castile (one of the candidates for the imperial crown) in order to induce him to assist the Guelfs against Manfred and the Ghibellines. While he was on his way back, he learnt from a student, who had come from Bologna, the news of the decisive victory of the Ghibellines over the Florentine Guelfs at Montaperti (Sept. 4, 1260), and the consequent expulsion of the latter from his native city (*Tesoretto*, ii. 11–50). On the receipt of this disastrous news he abandoned his intention of returning to Italy, and took refuge in France. He appears first to have gone to Montpellier (*Tesoretto*, xxi. 3); he was in Paris in Sept. 1263, and at Bar-sur-Aube in April, 1264, as we know from notarial documents in his handwriting under those dates. While in France he compiled his encyclopaedic work, the *Livre dou Tresor*, as he himself records (i. 99).

After Manfred's defeat and death at the battle of Benevento (Feb. 26, 126$\frac{5}{6}$), and the consequent discomfiture of the Ghibellines of Tuscany, Brunetto returned to Florence and resumed his share in public affairs; in 1273 he was secretary to the Florentine government, and in 1275 he was president of the notarial guild; in 1287 (Aug. 15 to Oct. 15) he served the office of prior; and in 1289 he was appointed one of the public orators of Florence; he died in Florence, aged over eighty, in 1294. His influence and authority with the Florentines are attested by the fact that his name appears in no less than thirty-five public documents (between

Oct. 21, 1282, and July 22, 1292) as having been consulted by the government on various important matters, and for the most part it is recorded that his advice was followed.

Brunetto was buried in the church of Santa Maria Maggiore at Florence. His portrait, according to Vasari (in his *Vita di Giotto*), is one of those associated with that of D. in the fresco attributed to Giotto in the Bargello.

Brunetto's two best known works are the *Livre dou Tresor*, a sort of encyclopaedia of history, natural science, ethics, rhetoric, and politics, in French prose (written between 1262 and 1266); and the *Tesoretto*, a didactic poem, written (in 1262 or 1263) in a popular style in Italian heptasyllabic couplets.

D. places Brunetto Latini in Round 3 of Circle VII of Hell, among those guilty of unnatural offences, *ser Brunetto*, Inf. xv. 30, 101; *Brunetto Latini*, v. 32; *un*, v. 23; *quegli*, v. 31 [**Sodomiti**]; in the course of conversation with D., Brunetto predicts that D. will become famous, and that he will be persecuted by the Florentines (*vv.* 46–69); on taking leave of D. he recommends to him his *Trésor* (*vv.* 115–24). [**Tesoro.**]

In his estimate of the Tuscans and their dialects, D. blames Brunetto, together with Bonagiunta of Lucca, Gallo of Pisa, and Mino Mocato of Siena, for having written in their own local dialect, *Brunetus Florentinus*, V. E. i. 13[8–13].

Brunetus Florentinus. [**Brunetto.**]

Bruto[1], Lucius Junius Brutus,

son of Marcus Junius and of Tarquinia, sister of Tarquinius Superbus. His elder brother was murdered by Tarquinius, and Lucius only escaped his brother's fate by feigning idiotcy, whence he was surnamed Brutus. After the rape of Lucretia by Sextus Tarquinius, and her consequent suicide, B. roused the Romans to expel the Tarquins; and upon their banishment he was elected first consul with Tarquinius Collatinus. While consul he proved his unflinching patriotism by putting to death his two sons, who had attempted to restore the Tarquins. He fell in battle shortly after, fighting against Aruns, son of Tarquinius.

D. places B. in Limbo among the great heroes of antiquity, describing him as *quel Bruto che cacciò Tarquino*, Inf. iv. 127 [**Limbo: Lucrezia**]; he is mentioned, as first Consul and founder of the Roman Republic, Conv. iv. 5[99–100]; as having sacrificed his sons on the altar of duty, Conv. iv. 5[121–2]; D. refers to Livy's account (ii. 4) of the latter incident, and quotes *Aen.* vi. 821–2, Mon. ii. 5[112–20].

Bruto[2], Marcus Junius Brutus, the so-called tyrannicide. When the civil war broke out (B.C. 49) he joined Pompey. After the battle of Pharsalia (B.C 48) he was pardoned by Caesar, and was admitted by him into confidence and favour; but in spite of all his obligations to Caesar, he was persuaded by Cassius to murder him under the delusive idea of again establishing the republic. After Caesar's death, B. took possession of the province of Macedonia, where he was joined by Cassius, and their

united forces were opposed to Octavian (afterwards Augustus) and
Antony. Two battles were fought
in the neighbourhood of Philippi (B.C.
42), in the former of which B. was
victorious, though Cassius was defeated; but in the latter B. also was
defeated, whereupon he put an end to
his own life. [Cassio.]

D. places Brutus, with Cassius and
Judas Iscariot, in Giudecca, the last
division of Circle IX of Hell, the
nethermost pit, in the jaws of Lucifer,
Inf. xxxiv. 65. [Giudecca: Luci-
fero]; the Emperor Justinian (in
the Heaven of Mercury) mentions
him in connexion with his defeat by
Augustus at Philippi, Par. vi. 74.

Brutus. [Bruto [1].]

Bucciola, Tommaso. [Faenza,
Tommaso da.]

Bucciola, Ugolino, Ugolino
Bucciola or Buzzola, poet of Faenza,
son of Frate Alberigo (Inf. xxxiii.
118), of the Guelf Manfredi family
of Faenza; he was born probably
between 1240 and 1250, was Podestà
of Bagnacavallo in 1282, and died at
Ravenna, Jan. 8, 1301.

His contemporary, Francesco da
Barberino (1264–1348), who knew
him personally, speaks of him in his
Documenti d'Amore as having written
a didactic poem in the Faentine dialect, and quotes him in his *Reggimento
e Costumi di Donna* (I. iii. § 2); two
sonnets of his (one addressed to
Onesto Bolognese) have been preserved.

D. mentions Ugolino, together
with Tommaso da Faenza (who, according to some, was his brother), as
having rejected the local dialect in
their poems, V. E. i. 14[18-20].

Bucolica, the Bucolics or Ec-
logues of Virgil; referred to as *i
Bucolici Carmi*, Purg. xxii. 57;
Bucolica, Mon. i. 11[5]; D. quotes
and comments on *Ecl.* iv. 6, Mon.
i. 11[5-10]; three lines from the same
Eclogue (iv. 5–7) are translated,
Purg. xxii. 70–2; and referred to,
Epist. vii. 1[22-4] [Astraea]; Vir-
gil, as the author of the Eclogues,
is called 'il Cantor de' Bucolici
Carmi', Purg. xxii. 57. [Virgilio.]

Bucolici Carmi. [Bucolica.]

Buemme, Bohemia, in the Middle
Ages an independent kingdom, under
the Premysl dynasty from 1197 to
1310, and then under the Luxemburg
dynasty (founded by John of Luxemburg, son of the Emperor Henry
VII) till 1437. [Table C.]

Wenceslas IV is referred to by
the Eagle in the Heaven of Jupiter
as *quel di Buemme*, Par. xix. 125
[Vincislao]; Bohemia itself is alluded to by the Eagle (in reference
to the cruel invasion of the country
in 1304 by Albert of Hapsburg, who
attempted to force Wenceslas IV to
submit to the exclusion of his own
son, Wenceslas, from the throne of
Hungary in favour of Charles Martel's son, Charles Robert) as *il regno
di Praga*, Par. xix. 117 [Alberto
Tedesco: Praga]; and by Sordello (in Ante-purgatory), in connexion with Ottocar II, as *la terra dove
l'acqua nasce, Che Multa in Albia, e
Albia in mar ne porta* (i.e. the country drained by the Moldau and the
Elbe), Purg. vii. 98–9. [Albia:
Multa: Ottachero.]

Buggea, Bougia or Bougie, town
in N. Africa, in Algeria, on the gulf
of the same name. In the Middle

Ages it was a very important commercial port, its chief article of export being wax and wax-candles, whence the latter came to be known as *bougies*.

Bougie is situated about 100 miles E. of Algiers, and is on almost exactly the same meridian as Marseilles; hence the troubadour Folquet of Marseilles (in the Heaven of Venus), wishing to indicate his birthplace, says it is a place where the sun rises and sets at almost the same hour as it does at Bougie, Par. ix. 91–3. [**Folco : Marsilia.**]

Buiamonte, Giovanni], Florentine of the Bicchi family, who was Gonfaloniere di Giustizia in 1292, said by the old commentators to be the individual referred to (by Rinaldo degli Scrovigni) as 'il cavalier sovrano Che recherà la tasca con tre becchi' (i.e. three eagles' beaks), Inf. xvii. 72–3 ; Rinaldo informs D. that the advent of Buiamonte is eagerly awaited by the Florentine usurers who are with himself in Round 3 of Circle VII of Hell (*vv.* 71–3) [**Rinaldo : Usurai**]. D. condemns B. and Vitaliano of Padua to Hell by anticipation, they both having been alive at the date of the Vision (1300).

Bulgari], Ghibelline family of Bertinoro, thought by some to be alluded to, Purg. xiv. 113.

Bulicame, hot sulphurous spring near Viterbo, to the stream of which D. compares Phlegethon, one of the rivers of Hell, Inf. xiv. 79 [**Flegetonta**]. Like similar establishments in all times, the hot-spring of Bulicame was the resort of prostitutes ('le peccatrici', *v.* 80), who being compelled to reside in a special quar-

ter had the water supplied to baths in their houses by means of conduits leading from the spring.

The use of the word *bulicame*, Inf. xii. 117, 128, was doubtless suggested to D. by the association of Viterbo, a reference to which occurs in the same passage (*vv.* 118–20). [**Viterbo.**]

Buona— [Bona—]

Buonconte, Buonconte da Montefeltro, son of the famous Ghibelline captain, Guido da Montefeltro. In June 1287 Buonconte helped the Ghibellines to expel the Guelfs from Arezzo, an event which was the beginning of the war between Florence and Arezzo (Vill. vii. 115); in 1288 he was in command of the Aretines when they defeated the Sienese at Pieve del Toppo (Vill. vii. 120) [**Toppo, Il**] ; and in 1289 he was appointed captain of the Aretines and led them against the Guelfs of Florence, by whom they were totally defeated (June 11) at Campaldino, among the slain being Buonconte himself, whose body, however, was never discovered on the field of battle (Vill. vii. 131). [**Campaldino.**]

Buonconte is placed by D. in Ante-purgatory among those who delayed their repentance to the last, Purg. v. 88 ; *un altro, v.* 85 ; *il secondo (spirito), v.* 132. [**Antipurgatorio**] ; being questioned by D. as to what became of his body, he relates how it was washed by the floods into the Archiano, and carried down by that stream into the Arno, *vv.* 94–129. [**Archiano.**]

Buondelmonte, Buondelmonte de' Buondelmonti of Florence, whose breach of faith with a lady of the

Amidei family, whom he had promised to marry, led to his murder by the outraged Amidei at the foot of the statue of Mars on the Ponte Vecchio in 1215; Cacciaguida (in the Heaven of Mars) apostrophizes B., and reproaches him with his breach of troth, and with its fatal consequences, Par. xvi. 140–1. [Buondelmonti.]

Buondelmonti, leaders of the Guelf party in Florence, whose family left the country and took up their residence in Florence (where other members of the family had settled a century before) in 1135, on account of the destruction of their castle of Montebuono in the Valdigreve close to Florence, in the process of the expansion of the city.

Cacciaguida (in the Heaven of Mars) laments the extension of Florence, which brought the Buondelmonti, amongst others, into the city, Par. xvi. 66 [Valdigreve]; and says that the Borgo sant' Apostolo, the quarter of Florence in which they dwelt, would have been more peaceful had they never entered it (vv. 134–5) [Borgo]; he then apostrophizes Buondelmonte, one of the family, whose murder by the Amidei gave rise to the Guelf and Ghibelline factions in Florence, and laments that he had not rather been drowned in the Ema when the family originally came into the city (vv. 140–4) [Ema]; he adds, however, that it was meet that the statue of Mars, at the foot of which B. was killed, should claim its victim (vv. 145–7). [Buondelmonte: Marte[1].]

Buondelmonte de' Buondelmonti (Par. xvi. 140–7) was murdered by the Amidei in 1215 at the instigation of Mosca de' Lamberti, in revenge for an insult to their family, Buondelmonte having, it appears, promised to marry a lady of the Amidei, and having capriciously thrown her over for one of the Donati. In consequence of this murder a bitter feud arose between the partisans of the Buondelmonti and those of the Uberti (a member of whose family had been implicated in the murder), which resulted in the introduction into Florence of the Guelf and Ghibelline factions, the former being headed by the Buondelmonti, the latter by the Uberti. [Amidei: Ghibellini: Mosca: Uberti.]

Buoso, one of five Florentines (Inf. xxvi. 4–5) placed by D. among the Robbers in Bolgia 7 of Circle VIII of Hell (Malebolge), Inf. xxv. 140 [Ladri]. Nothing is known of B., the commentators not being agreed even as to his name, some calling him Buoso degli Abati, while others identify him with Buoso Donati, who is mentioned, Inf. xxx. 44 [Buoso Donati]. B. is one of three spirits seen by D. to undergo transformation (Inf. xxv. 35–141); B., who is originally in human shape (v. 86), exchanges forms with another robber, Francesco de' Cavalcanti (vv. 103–41), who appears, to begin with, in the shape of a serpent (v. 83).

Buoso Donati, one of the Donati family of Florence (mentioned in the 'estimo' of 1269, a document containing a list of the compensations granted to Guelf families in Florence for damage done by the Ghibellines in 1260 after the battle of Montaperti, and in the peace proposals of

Cardinal Latino in 1280), supposed by some to be the Buoso who is placed among the Robbers in Malebolge, Inf. xxv. 140 [**Buoso: Donati**]; he is mentioned by his full name in connexion with the fraud of the mimic Gianni Schicchi de' Cavalcanti, who, after his death, in collusion with his son Simone, personated him on his supposed death-bed, and dictated a will in favour of Simone; Gianni took care, however, to insert several clauses containing bequests to himself, by way of commission on the transaction, amongst others being that of a favourite and very handsome mare (or she-mule) of Buoso's, to which D. alludes as *la donna della torma* (i.e. the leader of the team), Inf. xxx. 42-5.

It appears that before his death Buoso had expressed a desire to make amends to some of the persons he had robbed; Simone, in alarm lest his father should have given effect to this resolve in his will, consulted Gianni Schicchi, who hit upon the above-mentioned device for securing the property to Simone [**Gianni Schicchi**].

Buoso da Duera], Ghibelline of Cremona, where he and the Marquis Pallavicino were heads of the party; he was expelled from Cremona in 1267, and in spite of repeated attempts did not succeed in re-establishing himself there until 1282.

When Charles of Anjou entered Italy in 1265 on his way to encounter Manfred and take possession of the kingdom of Naples, the French troops under Guy de Montfort, accompanied by Charles' wife, Beatrice of Provence, advanced through Lombardy, and made their way into Parma, unmolested by the force of Cremonese and other Ghibellines of Lombardy, with which the Marquis Pallavicino had been ordered by Manfred to block their passage. This neglect of Manfred's instructions was due to some act of treachery, not clearly specified, on the part of the Cremonese leader, Buoso da Duera, who was believed to have been bribed by the French.

D. places Buoso in Antenora, the second division of Circle IX of Hell, among those who were traitors to their country, *quel da Duera*, Inf. xxxii. 116; *un altro, v.* 106; *quei, v.* 114; and says that he is there bewailing the money of the French, *v.* 115 [**Antenora**].

Burella, name of a prison in Florence (in the ancient amphitheatre, which stood close to the W. extremity of the present Piazza di Santa Croce); hence D. refers to the cranny in which he finds himself on his way out of Hell as 'natural burella', Inf. xxxiv. 98.

Burgum S. Felicis, Borgo san Felice, quarter of Bologna; its dialect different from that of the Strada Maggiore in the same city, V. E. i. 9^{41-4}. [**Bolognesi.**]

Buzzola. [**Bucciola.**]

C

Caccia d' Asciano, Caccia dei Cacciaconti, whose family was a branch of the Scialenghi, a member of the 'Spendthrift Brigade' of Siena, supposed by some to be identical with Caccia da Siena, a Sienese poet; mentioned by Capocchio (in Bolgia 10 of Circle VIII of Hell) among other Sienese spendthrifts as having recklessly squandered his means, Inf. xxix. 131. [**Asciano: Brigata Spendereccia.**]

Cacciaguida, great-great-grandfather of D., of whose life nothing is known beyond what D. himself tells us; viz. that he was born in Florence (Par. xv. 130–3) in the Sesto di Porta san Piero (Par. xvi. 40–2) about the year 1090 (*vv.* 34–9); that he belonged (possibly) to the Elisei, one of the old Florentine families which boasted Roman descent (Par. xv. 136; xvi. 40); that he was baptized in the Baptistery of San Giovanni in Florence (Par. xv. 134–5); that he had two brothers, Moronto and Eliseo (*v.* 136); that his wife came from the valley of the Po, and that from her, through his son, D. got his surname of Alighieri (*vv.* 91–4, 137–8); that he followed the Emperor Conrad III on the Second Crusade, and was knighted by him (*vv.* 139–44); and finally that he fell fighting against the infidel about the year 1147 (*vv.* 145–8). His existence is attested by the mention of his name in two documents (still preserved in Florence), dated respectively April 28, 1131, and Dec. 9, 1189; in the former he is described as 'Cacciaguida filius Adami', in the latter his two sons are mentioned ('Preitenittus et Alaghieri fratres, filii olim Cacciaguide'). [**Table A.**]

D. places Cacciaguida in the Heaven of Mars among those who fought for the faith (*Spiriti Militanti*), Par. xv. 135; his spirit is spoken of as *astro, v.* 20; *gemma, v.* 22; *lume, vv.* 31, 52; *spirto, v.* 38; *luce,* Par. xvi. 30; xvii. 28, 121; *santa lampa,* Par. xvii. 5; *anima santa, v.* 101; *specchio beato,* Par. xviii. 2; *fulgor santo, v.* 25; *alma, v.* 50; he is addressed by D. as *vivo topazio,* Par. xv. 85; *voi,* Par. xvi. 16, 17, 18; *padre mio,* Par. xvi. 16; xvii. 106; *cara mia primizia,* Par. xvi. 22; *cara piota mia,* Par. xvii. 13; and referred to by him as *amor paterno,* Par. xvii. 35; *il mio tesoro, v.* 121; he addresses D. as *sanguis meus,* Par. xv. 28: *figlio,* Par. xv. 52; xvii. 94; *fronda mia,* Par. xv. 88, speaking of himself as *la tua radice, v.* 89; and refers to him as *il mio seme,* Par. xv. 48; C. addresses D., and after giving details as to his family and his life (xv. 91–148), and indicating the date of his birth (c. 1090), and the situation of his house in Florence (xvi. 34–45), he foretells D.'s exile, and his association at first with the exiled Bianchi and Ghibellines, and his subsequent withdrawal from them, and refuge with one of the Scaligers (xvii. 46–99).

Cacciaguida indicates (Par. xvi. 40–2) the situation of the house in which he and his ancestors lived in Florence, as being ' in the place where the last sextary is first attained by him who runs in the yearly horse-race ', i.e. on the boundary of the district known later as the Sesto di Porta san Piero. The house of the Elisei (Vill. iv. 11) stood not far from the junction of the Mercato Vecchio and the Corso, apparently just at the angle formed on the N. side of the present Via degli Speziali by its intersection with the Via de' Calzaioli. The Sesto di Porta san Piero appears to have been the last of the city divisions to be traversed by the competitors in the ' annual gioco ', who entered the city probably at the Porta san Pancrazio, close to where the Palazzo Strozzi now stands, crossed the Mercato Vecchio, and finished in the Corso which was thence so called. [**Fiorenza.**]

Caccianimico, Venedico, Venetico Caccianemici dell' Orso, of Bologna, son of Alberto de' Caccianemici, who was head of the Geremei or Guelf party of Bologna from 1260 till 1297. Venetico, who was a man of blood, as appears from the fact that in 1268 he murdered his cousin, was Capitano del Popolo at Modena, 1273–4, and successively Podestà of Imola (1264), Milan (1275), and Pistoja (1283); in 1267, though an active opponent of the Lambertazzi or Ghibelline party of Bologna, he co-operated with the Frati Gaudenti, Loderingo and Catalano, in an attempt to reconcile the two parties. He was a staunch ally of the Marquis of Este, and his support of the policy of the latter with regard to Bologna appears to have led to his

expulsion from his native city in 1289.

D., who appears to have been personally acquainted with C. (perhaps at Pistoja), places him among the Pandars and Seducers in Bolgia 1 of Circle VIII of Hell (Malebolge), for having handed over his sister, Ghisolabella, to the evil passions of the Marquis of Este, Inf. xviii. 50; *uno* (*peccatore*) *v.* 40; *costui, v.* 42; *quel frustato, v.* 46; *egli, v.* 52; *il, v.* 64; *ruffian, v.* 66 [**Ghisolabella : Seduttori**].

Caco, Cacus, son of Vulcan, a firebreathing monster who lived in a cave on Mt. Aventine, and preyed upon the inhabitants of the district. He stole from Hercules, while he was asleep, some of the cattle which the latter had taken from Geryon in Spain, and, to prevent their being tracked, dragged them into his cave by their tails; but their whereabouts being discovered by their bellowing as the rest of the herd passed by the cave, Hercules attacked Cacus and, according to Virgil (*Aen.* viii. 193–267), strangled him, but according to Livy (i. 7), whom D. here follows, slew him with his club.

D., who, in common with other mediaeval writers, represents Cacus as a Centaur, places him among the Robbers in Bolgia 7 of Circle VIII of Hell (Malebolge), Inf. xxv. 25; *un Centauro, v.* 17; *egli, v.* 20; *ei, v.* 34 [**Ladri**]; and explains (*vv.* 28–30) that he is not placed in Circle VII with the other Centaurs, because, unlike them, he employed fraud in his theft [**Centauri**].

Cacume, peak of the Monti Lepini, near Frosinone, in the Province of Rome ; supposed to be the peak referred to, Purg. iv. 26 (according to the reading *su Bismantova e in Cacume*, for which most modern edd. read *su B. in cacume*). [Bismantova.]

Cadmo, Cadmus, founder of Thebes, son of Agenor, King of Phoenicia, and brother of Europa [Europa[2]]. He married Harmonia, daughter of Mars and Venus [Armonia], by whom he became the father of Autonoë, Agave, Semele, Ino, and Polydorus [Ino : Semelè]. As a penalty for having slain a dragon sacred to Mars, C. was transformed into a serpent, Harmonia, at her own request, sharing his fate.

D. alludes to this transformation, Inf. xxv. 97–8; and refers to Ovid's account of it (*Metam.* iv. 575 ff.; v. 453 ff.), from which several touches in his own description are borrowed (*vv.* 103–38).

Caelo, De. [Coelo, De.]

Caesar[1], Julius Caesar, Mon. ii. 5[161]; Epist. vii. 1[15], 4[82] [Cesare[1]]; Augustus, Mon. ii. 9[102], 12[49] [Augusto[2]] ; Tiberius, Mon. ii. 13[47]; Epist. v. 10[159] [Tiberio]; Nero, Mon. iii. 13[44–53] [Nerone].

Caesar[2], appellative of the Roman Emperors, hence of the sovereigns of the Holy Roman Empire; of Frederick II, V. E. i. 12[21]; Epist. vi. 5[131]; of Henry VII, Epist. v. 2[28], 3[38]; vi. *fin.*; of the Emperor in general, Mon. iii. 16[135]; Epist. v. 5[91], 9[152]. [Cesare[2].]

Caesareus, pertaining to the Holy Roman Empire, imperial, Epist. x. *tit.*

Caetani, inhabitants of Gaeta ;

their dialect distinct from that of the Neapolitans, V. E. i. 9[39–41]. [Gaeta.]

Cagioni, Libro delle. [*Causis, De.*]

Cagnano, small river of Upper Italy in Venetia, now known as the Botteniga, which unites with the Sile at Treviso ; Cunizza (in the Heaven of Venus) alludes to Treviso as the place *dove Sile e Cagnan s'accompagna*, Par. ix. 49; the two rivers are mentioned together to indicate Treviso, Conv. iv. 14[116–17]. [Gherardo da Cammino : Trevigi.]

Cagnazzo, one of the ten demons in Bolgia 5 of Circle VIII of Hell (Malebolge) deputed by Malacoda to escort D. and Virgil, Inf. xxi. 119; xxii. 106; *quei, v.* 120. [Alichino : Malebranche.]

Caiaphas. [Caifas.]

Caifas], Caiaphas, the high-priest, placed, together with his father-in-law Annas, among the Hypocrites in Bolgia 6 of Circle VIII of Hell (Malebolge), *un crocifisso in terra,* Inf. xxiii. 111; *quel confitto, v.* 115; *ei, v.* 119; *colui ch'era disteso in croce, v.* 125 [Anna[2]: Ipocriti]; he is mentioned with Pilate in connexion with the judgement of Christ, *Caiphas,* Mon. ii. 13[51]. [Pilato.]

Caina, name given by D. to the first of the four divisions of Circle IX of Hell, where Traitors are punished, Inf. v. 107 (var. *Cain*); xxxii. 58 [Inferno]. In this division, which is named after Cain, the murderer of his brother, are placed those who have been traitors to their own kindred, Inf. xxxii. 16–69 [Traditori]. *Examples :* Alessandro and Napoleone degli Alberti [Alberti]; Mordred [Mordarette];

Focaccia dei Cancellieri [**Focac-cia**]; Sassolo Mascheroni [**Mas-cheroni**]; Camicione dei Pazzi (and Carlino dei Pazzi) [**Camicione : Carlino**].

Caino, Cain, eldest son of Adam and Eve, the murderer of his brother Abel ; mentioned in connexion with the old popular belief that the ' man in the Moon' was Cain with a bun-dle of thorns (probably with reference to his unacceptable offering), *Caino e le spine* (i. e. the Moon), Inf. xx. 126 ; the spots on the Moon which gave rise to this popular superstition about Cain, Par. ii. 49–51. [**Luna.**]

Cain is introduced as an example of Envy in Circle II of Purgatory, where his voice is heard crying *Anciderammi qualunque m'apprende*, 'Every one that findeth me shall slay me' (*Gen.* iv. 14), Purg. xiv. 133. [**Invidiosi.**]

Some MSS. read *Cain* or *Caino* (which seems preferable) instead of *Caina*, Inf. v. 107. [**Caina.**]

Caiphas. [**Caiaphas.**]

Calabrese, inhabitant of Calabria (the province which forms the ' toe' of Italy), Calabrian ; *il Calabrese abate*, i.e. the abbot Joachim, Par. xii. 140. [**Gioacchino**[1].]

Calabri, Calabrians ; distinction between their dialect and that of the inhabitants of Ancona, V. E. i. 10[66].

Calaroga. [**Callaroga.**]

Calboli, name of an illustrious Guelf family of Forlì ; mentioned by Guido del Duca (in Circle II of Purgatory), Purg. xiv. 89; he refers to two members of this house, viz. Rinieri da Calboli (*vv.* 89–90) [**Ri-nier**[1]], and his grandson, Fulcieri (*vv.* 58–66) [**Fulcieri**]. The castle

of Calboli (destroyed by Guido da Montefeltro in 1277), whence the family derived their name, was situ-ated in the upper valley of the Mon-tone, near Rocca S. Casciano.

Calboli, Fulcieri da. [**Ful-cieri.**]

Calboli, Rinieri da. [**Rinier**[1].]

Calcabrina, one of the ten de-mons in Bolgia 5 of Circle VIII of Hell (Malebolge) deputed by Mala-coda to escort D. and Virgil, Inf. xxi. 118; xxii. 133. [**Alichino : Malebranche.**]

Calcanta, Calchas, son of Thes-tor, the soothsayer who accompanied the Greeks to Troy ; D. associates him with Eurypylus as having fore-told the time of the sailing of the Greek fleet from Aulis, where it was detained by Artemis, and refers to Virgil's account (*Aen.* ii. 114–24, where, however, no mention occurs of the circumstance here referred to), Inf. xx. 110–14 [**Aulide : Euri-pilo**].

Calcidonio, native of Chalcedon, a Greek city of Bithynia, on the coast of the Propontis, at the en-trance of the Bosphorus, nearly op-posite to Byzantium ; epithet applied to Xenocrates, Conv. iv. 6[132]. [**Se-nocrate.**]

Calfucci, ancient noble family at Florence (extinct in D.'s time), mentioned by Cacciaguida (in the Heaven of Mars) as being descended from the Donati, who are hence described as *Lo ceppo di che nacquero i Calfucci*, Par. xvi. 106 [**Donati**].

Calisto, Calixtus I, Bishop of Rome, 217–222 ; D. follows the tradition that he was martyred, and includes him among those of his immediate successors mentioned by St. Peter (in the Heaven of Fixed Stars) as having, like himself, shed their blood for the Church, Par. xxvii. 44.

Callaroga, ancient Calagurris, now Calahorra, city in Old Castile, between Logroño and Tudela, two miles from the Ebro; mentioned by St. Bonaventura (in the Heaven of the Sun) as the birthplace of St. Dominic, whence he calls it *la fortunata Callaroga*, Par. xii. 52; he describes it as being in the kingdom of Castile and Leon, a country not far from the Atlantic (*vv.* 49–54). [Atlantico : Castiglia.]

Calliopè, Calliope, Muse of Epic Poetry; invoked by D. at the commencement of the *Purgatorio*, Purg. i. 9 (var. *Calliopea*). At the commencement of the *Inferno* he invoked the Muses in general (Inf. ii. 7); at the commencement of the *Paradiso* he invokes Apollo (Par. i. 13) [Parnaso], and claims to be under the inspiration of Minerva and the nine Muses as well (Par. ii. 8–9). [Muse.]

Calliopea. [Calliopè.]

Calliopeus, of Calliope; *C. sermo*, a poetical composition in a lofty style, Epist. iv. 2[18].

Callisto, nymph Callisto, otherwise known as Helice, the mother of Boötes; she was transformed into the constellation of the Great Bear, her son becoming the Little Bear, Purg. xxv. 131; Par. xxxi. 32. [Boote : Elice.]

Calpe], Mt. Calpe, the modern Gibraltar; alluded to by Ulysses (in Bolgia 8 of Circle VIII of Hell) as one of the Pillars of Hercules, Inf. xxvi. 108. [Colonne di Ercole.]

Camaldoli], monastery perched high among the mountains, in a thick pine forest, in the Casentino, about 30 miles from Florence, founded in 1012 by St. Romualdus for his Order of Reformed Benedictines; alluded to by Buonconte da Montefeltro (in Ante-purgatory) as *l' Ermo*, Purg. v. 96. [Romoaldo.]

Camicion de' Pazzi, Alberto (or Uberto) Camicione, one of the Pazzi of Valdarno, of whom nothing is known save that he treacherously killed his kinsman Ubertino [Pazzi]; he is placed in Caina, the first division of Circle IX of Hell, among those who have been traitors to their own kindred, Inf. xxxii. 68; *un, v.* 52 [Caina]; he addresses D., and after naming several of those who are with him, tells his own name, adding that he awaits the arrival of his kinsman Carlino de' Pazzi, the heinousness of whose crime will make his own appear trivial in comparison (*vv.* 54–69) [Carlino de' Pazzi].

Camilla. [Cammilla.]

Camillo, M. Furius Camillus, one of the great heroes of the Roman republic; he was six times consular tribune and five times dictator. During his first dictatorship (396) he gained an important victory over the Faliscans and Fidenates, took Veii, and entered Rome in triumph. Five years later (391), however, he was accused of having made an unfair distribution of the plunder from Veii, and went into voluntary exile at Ardea; but in the next year (390), the Gauls having taken Rome and besieged the Capitol, the Romans recalled C., who having been made dictator in his absence, hastily collected an army, attacked the Gauls, and completely defeated them. He died of the pestilence in 365.

The story of C.'s liberation of Rome from the Gauls, and his voluntary return into exile after his victory, is referred to, Conv. iv. 5$^{134-9}$; and given on the authority of Livy (v. 46) and Virgil (*Aen.* vi. 825), *Camillus*, Mon. ii. 5$^{100-11}$. [Brenno: Galli ^{2}.]

Camillus. [Camillo.]
Camino. [Cammino.]
Cammilla, Camilla, daughter of King Metabus of the Volscian town of Privernum; she assisted Turnus, King of the Rutulians, against Aeneas, and after slaying a number of the Trojans, was at length killed by Aruns (*Aen.* xi. 768-831).

D. mentions her, with Turnus, Nisus, and Euryalus, as having died for Italy, Inf. i. 107; and places her in Limbo, among the heroes of antiquity, in company with Penthesilea (*Aen.* xi. 662), Latinus, and Livinia, Inf. iv. 124-6. [Limbo.]

Cammino, Gherardo da, gentleman of Treviso, of which he was lord, under the title of Captain-General, from 1283 until his death in 1306, when he was succeeded by his son Riccardo (Par. ix. 50-1); he is mentioned by Marco Lombardo (in Circle III of Purgatory), who, in speaking of the degenerate state into which Lombardy had fallen after the wars between Frederick II and the Church, says that there yet survive three old men whose lives are a reproach to the younger generation, viz. Currado da Palazzo, Guido da Castello, and 'il buon Gherardo', Purg. xvi. 121-6; D.

then asks of what Gherardo Marco is speaking (*vv.* 133-5); whereupon Marco expresses astonishment that D. should never have heard of G., whose name must have been well known throughout Tuscany (*vv.* 136-8), and adds that he knows him by no other name than that of 'il buon Gherardo', unless it be as the father of Gaia (*vv.* 139-40) [Federico ^{2}: Gaia]; in the *Convivio* D. singles out Gherardo as an illustrious instance of true nobility, Conv. iv. 14$^{114-23}$.

Cammino, Riccardo da], son of the preceding, whom he succeeded in the lordship of Treviso in 1306; he married (in 1308) Giovanna, daughter of Nino Visconti of Pisa, and was murdered in 1312 while playing at chess in his own palace with Altiniero degli Azzoni, a gentleman of Treviso, who had planned the assassination in order to avenge the honour of his wife whom Riccardo had seduced. Riccardo's assassination is foreshadowed by Cunizza (in the Heaven of Venus), who says of him 'Tal signoreggia e va con la testa alta, Che già per lui carpir si fa la ragna', Par. ix. 50-1. [Cunizza: Giovanna ^{2}.]

Camonica, Val. [Valcamonica.]

Campagnatico, village and castle, belonging to the Ghibelline Counts Aldobrandeschi, situated on a hill in the valley of the Ombrone, not far from Grosseto in the Sienese Maremma; it was in the possession of the Aldobrandeschi from Cent. x until the end of Cent. xiii, when it passed into the hands of the Sienese. Omberto Aldobrandeschi (in

Circle I of Purgatory) refers to it as
the place where he was murdered (in
1259) by the Sienese, Purg. xi. 65–
6. [Aldobrandeschi: Omberto.]

Campaldino, small plain in the
Casentino, in the Upper Valdarno,
between Romena and Poppi, the
scene of the battle, fought June 11,
1289, between the Florentine Guelfs
and the Ghibellines of Arezzo, in
which the latter were totally defeated, Buonconte da Montefeltro,
one of their leaders, being slain on
the field.

In his interview with Buonconte
(in Ante-purgatory) D. questions him
as to what became of his body, which
was never discovered on the battle-
field of Campaldino, Purg. v. 91–3.
[Buonconte.]

D. himself is said to have been
present at this battle, fighting on the
side of the Guelfs.   Leonardo Bruni
in his *Vita di Dante* quotes a fragment of a letter alleged to have been
written by D. in which he describes
his experiences on the occasion, con-
fessing that at first he was greatly
afraid, but at the end felt the greatest
elation, according to the varying fortunes of the day.   The opening lines
of Inf. xxii, and Purg. xxiv. 94–6,
are probably reminiscences of this
event, among other of D.'s military
experiences.

Campi, village in Tuscany, on
the Bisenzio, about nine miles NW.
of Florence, under whose jurisdiction
it passed from that of Siena in 1176;
mentioned, together with Certaldo
and Figline, by Cacciaguida (in the
Heaven of Mars), who laments that,
owing to the immigration into Florence of the inhabitants of these places,

the character of the Florentines had
become debased, Par. xvi. 49–51.

Campidoglio, modern name of
the Capitol of Rome ; applied by an
anachronism by D. to the ancient
Capitol, in connexion with the siege
by the Gauls under Brennus in
390, Conv. iv. 5[162]. [Capitolium :
Galli [2].]

Campo di Siena, principal piazza
in Siena, formerly known as the
Campo or the Piazza del Campo,
now called the Piazza Vittorio Ema-
nuele ; mentioned by Oderisi (in
Circle I of Purgatory) in connexion
with Provenzano Salvani, Purg. xi.
134. [Provenzan Salvani : Siena.]

Campo Piceno, name applied to
the territory in the immediate neighbourhood of Pistoja, to the siege
and capture of which by the Florentine Neri and the Lucchese under
Moroello Malaspina in 1306, Vanni
Fucci (in Bolgia 7 of Circle VIII of
Hell) refers, when he prophesies the
defeat of the Bianchi, ' sopra Campo
Piceno,' Inf. xxiv. 148. [Bianchi :
Malaspina, Moroello.]

The ancient Picenum, or ager
Picenus, was a district on the Adriatic
coast.   The transference of the name
by mediaeval chroniclers (the mistake
was long anterior to D.) to the territory of Pistoja is supposed to have
been due to a misunderstanding of
a passage in Sallust, in whose account
of the defeat of Catiline it is stated that
when Metellus Celer, who was commanding ' in agro Piceno', heard of
Catiline's move ' in agrum Pistorien-
sem', he succeeded by rapid marches
in blocking the mountain route from
Pistoja into Gaul (*Catil.* § 57).

Can Grande della Scala, third son of Alberto della Scala (lord of Verona, 1277–1301), was born on March 9, 129$\frac{9}{1}$; he married Joan, daughter of Conrad of Antioch; and died at Treviso, July 22, 1329, and was buried at Verona, where his sarcophagus and equestrian statue are still to be seen among the tombs of the Scaligers. In 1308 he was associated with his brother Alboino in the lordship of Verona, and was made joint Vicar Imperial with him by the Emperor Henry VII; on the death of Alboino (Nov. 1311) he became sole lord of Verona, a position which he maintained until his death.

Cacciaguida (in the Heaven of Mars) foretells to D. that he shall see Can Grande at the court of 'il gran Lombardo' (i.e., according to the most probable interpretation, Bartolommeo, Cane's eldest brother), Par. xvii. 70–6; after referring to the fact that Cane was born under the influence of the planet Mars, which gave promise of his future warlike character (vv. 76–8), and stating that he was at that time (i.e. in 1300, the assumed date of the Vision) unknown, owing to his being only nine years old (vv. 79–81), C. forecasts his future greatness and magnificence, and his signal services to the Emperor Henry VII and the Ghibelline cause, and bids D. repose his hopes in him (vv. 82–8); he then, in conclusion, makes a vague reference to Cane's future achievements, and suddenly breaks off (vv. 89–93). [Lombardo[1].]

Can Grande is identified by many with the 'Veltro' of Inf. i. 101; and the 'Cinquecento diece e cinque' of Purg. xxxiii. 43 [Veltro: DXV]; he is mentioned at the close of the treatise De Aqua et Terra (which is dated from Verona in 1320, a year before D.'s death, at a time when Cane was Imperial Vicar), A. T. § 24[3]; he is alluded to by G. del Virgilio as Molossus, Carm. 28.

Of Cane's character D. speaks in terms of high praise in the D. C., mentioning his warlike exploits ('notabili fien l'opere sue,' Par. xvii. 78), his indifference to money or to toil ('sua virtute In non curar d'argento nè d'affanni,' vv. 83–4), and his magnificent bounty ('Le sue magnificenze conosciute Saranno,' vv. 85–6). To him he dedicated the Paradiso, in a lengthy letter addressed, 'Magnifico atque victorioso domino, domino Kani Grandi de Scala, sacratissimi Caesarei Principatus in urbe Verona et civitate Vicentia Vicario Generali,' in which the title and subject of the Divina Commedia are discussed. The letter opens with a eulogy of Can Grande's magnificence and bounty, of which D. says he himself partook, and which he acknowledges to have surpassed even the extravagant reports he had heard of it, Epist. x. 1[1–16].

Can Grande, who had been present when Henry VII received the iron crown at Milan (Jan. 6, 1311), was on the point of embarking at Genoa to assist at the coronation in Rome, when the news of Alboino's death reached him (Dec.), and he returned at once to Verona to assume the lordship. One of his first acts was to rescue Brescia, which had submitted to the Emperor a few months before, from the hands of the Guelfs; and thenceforward until his death he played the leading part in the affairs of Lombardy.

The following is a summary of the most important events in his career :—

1308–1311. Joint lord of Verona with Alboino.—1311. Vicar Imperial in Verona ; (Oct.) Sole lord of Verona ; (Dec.) Rescues Brescia from the Guelfs ; helps to take Vicenza from the Paduans.—1312. Vicar Imperial in Vicenza.—1314. (Sept.) Repels Paduan attack on Vicenza ; (Oct.) makes peace with Padua and is confirmed in lordship of Vicenza.—1315. Attacks Cremona, Parma, and Reggio, in alliance with Passerino de' Bonaccorsi, lord of Mantua and Modena.—1316. Dante perhaps at Verona.—1317. (May) With help of Uguccione della Faggiuola repels fresh attack of Paduans on Vicenza ; (Dec.) appointed Vicar Imperial in Verona and Vicenza by Frederick of Austria ; besieges Padua.—1318. (April) Takes Cremona ; (Dec. 16) elected Captain General of Ghibelline league in Lombardy at Soncino.—1319. (Aug.) Besieges Padua.—1320. (Aug. 25) Repulsed by Paduans, Uguccione della Faggiuola being killed.—1322. (Sept.) Takes part with Passerino de' Bonaccorsi in siege of Reggio.—1324. (June) Attacked in Padua by German forces of Otho of Austria, whom he repels.—1327. Besieges Padua.—1328. Captures Mantua ; (Sept. 28) at invitation of Paduan Ghibellines becomes lord of Padua.—1329. (July 18) Takes Treviso, where he dies (July 22) ; buried at Verona.

Canavese, district of Upper Italy, which lies between the Dora Riparia and the Dora Baltea, and stretches from the slopes of the Pennine and Graian Alps down to the Po ; it formed part of the ancient marquisate of Montferrat, together with which it is mentioned by Sordello (in Antepurgatory), in connexion with William

Longsword, Marquis of Montferrat and Canavese (1254–1292), Purg. vii. 136. [**Guglielmo**[3] : **Monferrato.**]

Cancellieri], Guelf family of Pistoja, which, owing to a feud between two branches, known as the Cancellieri Bianchi and the Cancellieri Neri, gave rise to the factions of the Bianchi and Neri, first in Pistoja and later in Florence. Focaccia, a member of this family, who was one of those principally concerned in the original strife, is mentioned by Camicione de' Pazzi (in Caina) as a typical traitor, Inf. xxxii. 63. [**Bianchi : Focaccia.**]

Cancro, Cancer ('the Crab'), constellation and fourth sign of the Zodiac, which the Sun enters at the summer solstice (about June 21) [**Zodiaco**]. Speaking of the brightness of the spirit of St. John, D. says that if a luminary of that brilliance were to shine in Cancer, it would be as light as day during a whole winter month, Par. xxv. 100–2. During the middle month of winter, when the Sun is in Capricorn, Cancer, being then exactly opposite the Sun, is up throughout the night, which, in the case D. supposes, would thus be turned into day, so that daylight would be continuous throughout the month. D.'s meaning is that the spirit of St. John shone with a brilliancy equal to that of the Sun [**Giovanni**[2]].

Cancer and Capricorn each of them distant somewhat more than 23 degrees (actually 23° 28′) from the Equator, Conv. iii. 5[137–42].

Cane della Scala. [**Can Grande.**]

Canne], Cannae, village in Apulia,

famous as the scene of the defeat of the Romans by Hannibal during the Second Punic War, B.C. 216. D. alludes to the battle of Cannae and to the heap of gold rings taken from the bodies of the dead Romans and produced in the senate-house at Carthage by Hannibal's envoy as proof of his victory, Inf. xxviii. 10–12; Conv. iv. 5^{164–8}; in the former passage (*v.* 12) D. mentions Livy as his authority, but from the context of the second passage it appears that he was indebted rather to Orosius (*Hist.* iv. 16, §§ 5, 6) than to Livy (xxiii. 11–12). [Livio : Orosio : Scipione[1].]

Canticum Canticorum,Canticles or the Song of Songs (in A. V. the Song of Solomon), Mon. iii. 10^{58}; quoted, Purg. xxx. 11 (*Cant.* iv. 8); Conv. ii. 6^{34–7} (*Cant.* viii. 5); Conv. ii. 15^{175–8} (*Cant.* vi. 8–9 : *Vulg.* vi. 7–8); Mon. iii. 3^{79} (*Cant.* i. 3); Mon. iii. 10^{59–61} (*Cant.* viii. 5). [*Bibbia.*]

Canzoniere], collection of D.'s lyrical poems, consisting of sonnets, *canzoni, ballate,* and *sestine.* A large proportion of these belong to the *Vita Nuova,* and a few to the *Convivio;* the rest appear to be independent pieces, though some think that the 'canzoni pietrose' (viz. Canz. xii, Sest. ii, Canz. xv, and Sest. i), so called from the frequent recurrence in them of the word *pietra* (supposed, like the *selvaggia* of Cino da Pistoja and the *lauro* of Petrarca, to be a lady's name), form a special group.

The *Vita Nuova* contains twenty-five sonnets (Son. i–xxv) two of which (Son. ii, iv) are irregular, while one (Son. xviii) has two ver-

sions of the first quatrain (V. N. §§ 3, 7, 8, 9, 13, 14, 15, 16, 20, 21, 22, 24, 26, 27, 33, 35, 36, 37, 38, 39, 40, 41, 42); five *canzoni* (Canz. i–v), of which two (Canz. iii, v) are imperfect (V. N. §§ 19, 23, 28, 32, 34); and one *ballata* (Ball. i, V. N. § 12). [*Vita Nuova.*]

The *Convivio* contains three *canzoni* (Canz. vi–viii) with an accompanying commentary, out of fourteen which it was intended to contain. [*Convivio.*]

In the *De Vulgari Eloquentia* D. quotes the first lines of nine of his poems, all of which are extant, except one, beginning 'Traggemi della mente Amor la stiva' (V. E. ii. 11^{22}), which is not included in the existing collections, and so far has not been discovered in MSS.; of the eight others, two are given at length in the *Vita Nuova* (Canz. i, ii), and one in the *Convivio* (Canz. vii); the references to these eight poems occur as follows, V. E. ii. 2^{94} (Canz. x); V. E. ii. 5^{50}, 11^{38} (Canz. ix); V. E. ii. 6^{73}; Conv. iii; Purg. ii. 112 (Canz. vii); V. E. ii. 8^{73}, 12^{19}; V. N. § 19 (Canz. i); V. E. ii. 10^{28}, 13^{14} (Sest. i); V. E. ii. 11^{41}; V. N. § 23 (Canz. ii); V. E. ii. 12^{65} (Canz. xix); V. E. ii. 13^{96} (Sest. ii).

In the *Epistolae,* a *canzone* (Canz. xi) is appended to the letter addressed to Moroello Malaspina (Epist. iii); and either a sonnet (Son. xxxvi) or a *canzone* (Canz. vi) was probably appended to the letter addressed to Cino da Pistoja (Epist. iv).

This gives a total, so far, of twenty-six sonnets, i. e. twenty-five (V. N.) and one (Epist. iv); thirteen *canzoni*, i. e. five (V. N.), three (Conv.), four

(V. E.), and one (Epist. iii); two *sestine* (V. E.); and one *ballata* (V. N.).

In addition to these, a considerable number of other lyrical poems is attributed to D., many of which are of doubtful authenticity. In the several editions of the *Canzoniere* the number varies according to the taste or caprice of the various editors, there being as yet no accepted critical test. In the Oxford Dante are printed fifty-four sonnets (including the *tenzone*, or poetical correspondence, between D. and Forese Donati, which consists of six sonnets, three addressed by D. to Forese, and three of Forese's in reply), twenty-one *canzoni*, ten *ballate*, and four *sestine*, eighty-nine poems in all, some of which, it is now recognized, are certainly not by D.

Among those to whom D. addressed poems were his friends Guido Cavalcanti (Son. xxxii), Cino da Pistoja (Son. xxxiv, xlvi), and Forese Donati (Son. lii, liii, liv) [**Cavalcanti, Guido: Cino: Forese**].

Caorsa, Cahors, town in S. of France, on the river Lot, capital of the ancient Province of Quercy in Guyenne, chief town of mod. Department of Lot; famous in the Middle Ages as a great centre of usurers, whence the term *Caorsinus* became a common synonym for 'usurer'.

D. uses the terms Sodom and Cahors, to indicate Sodomites and Usurers, who are punished in Round 3 of Circle VII of Hell, among the Violent, Inf. xi. 49–51 [**Sodomiti: Usurai**].

Caorsino, inhabitant of Cahors; St. Peter, in his denunciation (in the Heaven of Fixed Stars) of his successors in the See of Rome, referring to the extortions and avarice of John XXII (who was a native of Cahors), and of his predecessor, the Gascon Clement V, says 'Del sangue nostro Caorsini e Guaschi S'apparecchian di bere', Par. xxvii. 58–9 [**Caorsa : Clemente[2]: Giovanni XXII**].

Caos, Chaos, the vacant and infinite space, which, according to the ancient cosmogonies, existed previous to the creation of the world, and out of which the gods, men, and all things came into being; mentioned by D. in connexion with the theory of Empedocles, that the alternate supremacy of hate and love was the cause of periodic destruction and construction in the scheme of the universe, Inf. xii. 41–3 [**Empedocles**].

Caosse. [**Caos**.]

Capaneo, Capaneus, son of Hipponoüs, one of the seven kings who besieged Thebes; he was struck by Zeus with a thunderbolt as he was scaling the walls of the city, because he had dared to defy the god.

D. places C. (whose story he got from Statius, *Theb.* x. 897 ff.) among the Blasphemers in Round 3 of Circle VII of Hell, and represents him as defying the gods even in Hell, Inf. xiv. 63; *quel grande, v.* 46; *quel medesmo, v.* 49; *l'un de' sette regi Ch' assiser Tebe, vv.* 68–9 [**Bestemmiatori**]; he is referred to (in connexion with Vanni Fucci, than whom D. says he saw no spirit in all Hell more rebellious against God, not even Capaneus) as *quel che cadde a Tebe giù da' muri,* Inf. xxv. 15.

Capeti], Capets, the third race of French kings; alluded to by Hugh

Capet (in Circle V of Purgatory) as 'the evil plant which overshadows all Christendom', Purg. xx. 43–4.

In the year 1300 (the assumed date of the Vision) a Capet was on the throne of France (viz. Philip IV, who was also King-consort of Navarre), and another on the throne of Naples (viz. Charles II of Anjou, whose grandson, Charles Robert, was heir to the Hungarian throne). The first of the Capets known in history was Robert the Strong, who was Count of Paris in 861, Count of Anjou in 864, and Duke of France in 866, in which year he died ; his great-grandson, Hugh Capet (Duke of France, 960), son of Hugh the Great (Duke of France, d. 956), was elected King of France in 987, and thus supplanted the Carlovingian dynasty. In the Capetian dynasty the French crown descended from father to son (from Hugh Capet down to Louis X, who was succeeded by his two brothers) for more than three hundred years. [Cia-petta, Ugo: Table K.]

Capitolium, Capitol of Rome ; besieged by the Gauls (under Brennus in 390) and saved by M. Manlius, who was aroused from sleep by the cackling of the sacred geese, Mon. ii. 4$^{42-9}$; referred to, by an anachronism, in connexion with the same incident, as *Campidoglio*, Conv. iv. 5$^{160-4}$ [Campidoglio: Galli^2: Manlius].

Capocchio, 'Blockhead', name (or nickname) of a Florentine (or, according to some, a Sienese) who was burnt alive at Siena in 1293 as an alchemist; placed by D. (who implies that he had been acquainted

with him) among the Falsifiers in Bolgia 10 of Circle VIII of Hell (Malebolge), Inf. xxix. 136 ; xxx. 28 ; *l'altro lebbroso*, xxix. 124 [Fal-satori].

Caponsacchi. [Caponsacco, Il.]

Caponsacco, Il, one of the Caponsacchi, ancient noble family of Florence (to which the mother of Beatrice Portinari belonged), who originally (in 1125) came from Fiesole. Cacciaguida (in the Heaven of Mars) alludes to this fact and says that they were already settled in the Mercato Vecchio in his day, Par. xvi. 121–2. The Caponsacchi were one of the original Ghibelline families in Florence (Vill. v. 39); they took part in the expulsion of the Florentine Guelfs in 1244 (vi. 33), and were among the Ghibellines who were expelled in 1258 (vi. 65).

Cappelletti, party nickname ('shockheads') of the Guelfs ('Pars Capellatorum') at Cremona (not a family name as usually supposed), their Ghibelline opponents being known as Barbarasi ('shavers') or Troncaciuffi ('cropheads'); mentioned by D., together with the Montecchi (the Ghibelline leaders in Verona), in his appeal to the Emperor, Albert of Austria, to come into Italy to look after the interests of his adherents, Purg. vi. 106. [Montec-chi.]

Capra. [Capricorno.]

Capraia. [Caprara.]

Caprara, Capraia, small island in the Mediterranean, about 20 miles E. of the N.-most point of Corsica; D. calls upon it and Gorgona, another island further N. (both of which belonged to Pisa at that time), to come and block up the mouth of the Arno, in order that Pisa and its inhabitants may be annihilated, Inf. xxxiii. 82–4 [Gorgona].

Capricorno, Capricorn, constellation and tenth sign of the Zodiac, which the Sun enters at the winter solstice (about Dec. 22) [Zodiaco]. D. speaks of the Sun driving Capricorn from mid-heaven, meaning that C. had passed the meridian, the time indicated being about 6 a.m., Purg. ii. 56–7 ; the sign is referred to as 'il corno della Capra del ciel' (the season indicated being mid-winter), Par. xxvii. 68–9 ; Cancer and Capricorn each of them distant rather more than 23 degrees (actually 23° 28′) from the Equator, Conv. iii. 5[137–42].

Caprona, castle in the territory of Pisa, about 5 miles from that city, on a hill close to the Arno. In August, 1289, shortly after the death of Count Ugolino and the expulsion of the Guelfs from Pisa, the Tuscan Guelfs, headed by the Lucchese and Florentines, invaded the Pisan territory, and captured several forts, including that of Caprona.

D. mentions Caprona, with reference to the capitulation of the Pisan garrison, and their issue from the fort through the midst of the besieging force under a safe-conduct, an incident which he says he himself witnessed (doubtless as a member of the Florentine force), Inf. xxi. 94–6.

Cardinale, Il, Cardinal Ottaviano degli Ubaldini, member of a powerful Tuscan Ghibelline family, known to his contemporaries as 'the Cardinal' par excellence, was brother

of Ubaldino della Pila (Purg. xxiv. 29) and uncle of the Archbishop Ruggieri (Inf. xxxiii. 14) ; he was made Bishop of Bologna in 1240, when he was under thirty, by special dispensation of Pope Gregory IX, and in 1244 he was created Cardinal by Innocent IV at the Council of Lyons ; he was papal legate in Lombardy, and died in 1272 [Ubaldini]. The Cardinal, who was suspected of favouring the imperial party, and who is credited with a saying : 'If I have a soul, I have lost it a thousand times over for the Ghibellines,' is placed by D. among the Heretics in Circle VI of Hell, Inf. x. 120. [Eretici.]

Cariddi, Charybdis, eddy or whirlpool in the Straits of Messina, which was regarded as peculiarly dangerous by ancient navigators, because in the endeavour to avoid it they risked being wrecked upon Scylla, a rock opposite to it.

D. compares the jostling of the Misers and the Prodigals in Circle IV of Hell, to the tumbling and breaking of the waves in the whirlpool, as the opposing currents from the Ionian aud Tyrrhenian Seas meet together, Inf. vii. 22–4.   [Avari.]

Carignano, Angiolello da. [Angiolello.]

Carisenda, one of the leaning towers (163 ft. high and 10 ft. out of the perpendicular) at Bologna, built in 1110 by Filippo and Oddo dei Garisendi.   At its side stands the Asinelli tower (320 ft. high and 4 ft. out of the perpendicular), which was erected in 1109 by Gherardo degli Asinelli.

These two towers stand in a small

piazza at the E. end of what is now the Via Rizzoli, in the quarter formerly known as the Porta Ravignana, nearly in the centre of the town. The Carisenda (which is now also known as 'la torre mozza') was considerably higher at the time D. wrote, a great part of it having been thrown down by Giovanni di Oleggio, one of the Visconti of Milan, during his 'tyranny' (1351–1360) at Bologna.

D. compares the stooping giant Antaeus to the Carisenda tower as it appears to a spectator when the clouds are sailing over it from behind him, Inf. xxxi. 136–8. [Anteo.]

Carlino, Carlino de' Pazzi of Valdarno, who, while the Neri of Florence and the Lucchese were besieging Pistoja in 1302, held the castle of Piantravigne in the Valdarno for the Bianchi of Florence, but treacherously for a bribe delivered it into the hands of the Neri.

Carlino's act of treachery not having yet taken place at the assumed date of the Vision (1300), D. assigns him his place in Caina by anticipation, making his kinsman Camicione, who had himself been guilty of the treacherous murder of a relative, say that he awaited Carlino's coming to excuse him (meaning that his own crime would appear trivial beside that of Carlino), Inf. xxxii. 69. [Camicione : Pazzi.]

Carlo[1], Charles I, King of Naples and Sicily, Count of Anjou and Provence, younger son of Louis VIII of France and Blanche of Castile, and brother of St. Louis; he was born in 1220; in 1246 he married Beatrice, youngest daughter of Count Raymond Berenger IV of Provence, in whose right he became Count of Provence; and in 1266, after the defeat of Manfred at Benevento, he became King of Naples and Sicily; in 1268 (Beatrice having died in the previous year) he married Margaret, Countess of Tonnerre, daughter of Eudes of Burgundy, who survived him more than twenty years; he died Jan. 7, 128$\frac{4}{5}$. [Berlinghieri, Ramondo : Provenza : Table E.]

D. places Charles in the valley of flowers in Ante-purgatory among the princes who neglected to repent, where he is seated beside Peter III of Aragon; Sordello, who points him out, refers to him as *colui del maschio naso*, Purg. vii. 113; *il nasuto*, v. 124; *il seme*, v. 127 [Antipurgatorio]; and says that he ('il seme') is as superior to his son, Charles II ('la pianta'), as Peter III of Aragon is to him (Charles I) (vv. 127–9) [Beatrice[2] : Carlo[2] : Margherita[2] : Pietro[3]]; he is mentioned in connexion with Pope Nicholas III, who was his enemy, Inf. xix. 99 [Niccolò[2]]; Oderisi (in Circle I of Purgatory) mentions him in connexion with Provenzano Salvani, whose friend (taken prisoner at Tagliacozzo) he held to ransom, Purg. xi. 136–7 [Provenzano Salvani]; Hugh Capet (in Circle V of Purgatory) speaks of his coming into Italy, and charges him with the murder of Conradin and of Thomas Aquinas, Purg. xx. 67–9 (Curradino : Tommaso[2]]; his grandson Charles Martel (in the Heaven of Venus) speaks of him (or, as some think, of his son, C. M.'s father, Charles II) as the ancestor in whose right his own descendants ought to have been on the throne of Sicily, Par. viii. 67–72 [Carlo³].

Charles of Anjou, 'the greatest champion the Guelf cause ever had,' having been invited (in 1263) by Urban IV to assume the crown of Naples, of which Manfred was in possession, in response to the entreaties of the new Pope, Clement IV, came into Italy in the spring of 1265, and in little more than three years, by his defeat of Manfred at Benevento (Feb. 26, 126⅚), and of Conradin at Tagliacozzo (Aug. 23, 1268), completely and finally crushed the power of the Hohenstaufen in Italy.

Charles arrived in Rome in May, 1265, and was forthwith elected Senator. On Jan. 6, 126⅚, he was crowned King of Sicily and Apulia, and immediately after he set out to invade Manfred's dominions. Meeting the proposal of the latter for negotiations with the defiance, 'I will send him to Hell, or he shall send me to Paradise,' Charles engaged him on Feb. 26 at Benevento, the pass at Ceperano having been treacherously left open, and totally defeated him, Manfred himself being among the slain [**Benevento : Ceperano: Manfredi**]. Charles thus became master of the kingdom ; but in less than two years the insupportable tyranny of the French led to an invitation to the young Conradin, son of the Emperor Conrad IV, to come and assert his hereditary rights and deliver the country from the foreign yoke. In response to this appeal Conradin entered Italy, and, during the absence of Charles in Tuscany, made his way to Rome, where he was received with enthusiasm, notwithstanding his having been excommunicated by the Pope. After collecting men and treasure at Rome, he set out on Aug. 10, 1268, to make good the Hohenstaufen claim to the kingdom of Naples. Charles, on hearing of his advance, hastened to oppose him, and a fortnight later (Aug. 23) the two armies met at Tagliacozzo in the Abruzzi. Though inferior in numbers Charles gained a complete victory, owing

to the superior strategy of the veteran captain Erard de Valéry, who had offered his services to the brother of his sovereign. Conradin fled from the field and attempted to escape into Sicily, but he was betrayed into the hands of Charles, who, after a mock trial, had him beheaded like a felon in the market-place at Naples (Oct. 29) [**Alardo: Curradino: Tagliacozzo**].

Thus confirmed in the possession of the two Sicilies, Charles gradually extended his influence in Italy, until he became one of the most powerful princes in Europe. The people of Sicily, however, rendered desperate by the tyranny and exactions of their conquerors, determined to throw off the French yoke, and at length in 1282 an insurrection, which had been carefully fostered for some time previously by John of Procida, a devoted adherent of the Hohenstaufen, with the connivance and help (as was commonly believed) of Pope Nicholas III and the Greek Emperor Palaeologus, suddenly broke out. The immediate occasion of the rising was a tumult provoked by a French soldier during the Easter festival at Palermo, which led to the frightful massacre of the French, known as the 'Sicilian Vespers', and to the termination of their rule in the island. After the expulsion of the Angevins the crown of Sicily was offered to and accepted by Peter III of Aragon, who had a claim to it in right of his wife, Constance, the daughter of Manfred [**Costanza²**]. Charles made several unsuccessful attempts to regain possession of the island, and finally died at Foggia in Apulia, in the midst of preparations for a fresh invasion. In his description of Charles' person, Villani (vii. 1) mentions his large nose, a characteristic to which D. refers (Purg. vii. 113, 124).

Carlo², Charles II, King of Naples, Count of Anjou and Provence, son of the preceding by Beatrice of Provence ; he was born in 1248, before his father became King of Naples, after which he bore the title of Prince of Salerno ; he married (c. 1271) Mary, daughter of Stephen V of Hungary, by whom he had nine sons and five daughters; on his father's death (in 1285) he became King of Naples, but being at the time a prisoner in Spain, where he was detained till 1288, he was not crowned until May 29, 1289; he died May 6, 1309. His two eldest sons, Charles Martel, titular King of Hungary (d. 1295), and Louis (d. 1297), having predeceased him, he was succeeded in Naples by his third son, Robert, Duke of Calabria [Carlo³: Luigi³: Roberto²: Table E]. Of his daughters, the eldest, Margaret, married (1290) Charles of Valois [Carlo⁴]; the second, Blanche, married (1295) James II of Aragon [Jacomo¹]; the third, Eleanor, married (1302) Frederick II of Sicily [Federico³]; the fourth, Mary, married Sancho, King of Majorca; and the youngest, Beatrice, married (1305) Azzo VIII of Este [Azzo].

Charles is mentioned by Jacopo del Cassero (in Ante-purgatory) in connexion with the kingdom of Apulia, which the latter refers to as *quel di Carlo*, Purg. v. 69 [Puglia]; the Emperor Justinian (in the Heaven of Mercury) warns him, as the leader of the Guelfs, not to oppose the Imperial Eagle, referring to him (to distinguish him from his father) as *Carlo novello*, Par. vi. 106–7 [Guelfi]; his son Charles Marte' (in the Heaven of Venus) speaks of him (or, as some think, of Charles I) as the ancestor in whose right his own descendants ought to have been on the throne of Sicily, Par. viii. 67–72 [Carlo³: Ridolfo¹]; and

contrasts his 'larga natura' with the niggardliness of his son (C. M.'s brother) Robert (*vv.* 82–3) [Roberto²]; the Eagle in the Heaven of Jupiter refers to him as *il Ciotto di Gerusalemme*, he being lame, and the title of Jerusalem being attached to the crown of Naples (since the abandonment of her claim by Mary of Antioch to Charles I), and says that his good qualities might be indicated by I (one), his bad ones by M (thousand), Par. xix. 127–9 [Gerusalemme, Il Ciotto di]; the Eagle mentions him again in connexion with the sufferings of Sicily during his war with Frederick of Aragon, Par. xx. 62–3 [Cicilia]; Sordello (in Ante-purgatory), alluding to him as *la pianta*, refers to his inferiority to his father (*il seme*), Purg. vii. 127–9 [Carlo¹]; Hugh Capet (in Circle V of Purgatory) rebukes him for having married his youngest daughter Beatrice, from mercenary motives, to Azzo VIII, the old Marquis of Este, referring to him (in allusion to his capture on board ship in 1284 by Ruggieri di Loria) as *l'altro* (*Carlo*), *che già uscì preso di nave*, Purg. xx. 79–81 [Azzo: Beatrice³]; D. denounces him and his adversary Frederick of Aragon for their evil doings, both in the *Convivio* (iv. 6¹⁸²⁻³) and the *De Vulgari Eloquentia* (i. 12³⁶⁻⁸).

After the 'Sicilian Vespers' (in 1282), Charles, who was then Prince of Salerno, set out from Provence to join his father in his attempt to recover the island of Sicily, and was entrusted by him with the command of the fleet at Naples, but with strict injunctions not to engage the enemy. Incensed, however, by the taunts of the Sicilian admiral, Ruggieri di Loria, who was in command of the fleet of Peter III of Aragon, Charles came out and attacked him, but was totally defeated (June, 1284) and himself taken prisoner on board his ship (Purg. xx. 79), and conveyed to Sicily. The Sicilians, having got the Prince of Salerno into their hands, were for beheading him, as his father had beheaded Conradin ; but by the advice of Manfred's daughter Constance, wife of Peter of Aragon, his life was spared, and he was sent a prisoner into Spain. In the following year (1285) Charles I of Naples and Peter III of Aragon both died. The latter was succeeded in Aragon by his eldest son, Alphonso, while James, his second son, was crowned King of Sicily. The Prince of Salerno being still a captive in the hands of the Aragonese in Catalonia, his eldest son, Charles Martel, assumed the government of the kingdom of Naples. In 1288, through the intervention of Edward I of England, Charles was liberated by Alphonso of Aragon, on the understanding that Sicily should remain in the possession of Alphonso's brother, James, while Charles was to retain the kingdom of Naples ; the latter, further, undertook to induce Charles of Valois to abandon his claim to the crown of Aragon, which had been bestowed upon him by Martin IV on the excommunication of Peter III. [**Carlo⁴.**] Leaving his three sons, Louis, Robert, and John, as hostages, and pledging himself to return to captivity if the conditions were not fulfilled within a specified period, Charles hastened into Italy to the Papal court. On May 29, 1289, in defiance of his pledges, he was crowned King of Sicily and Naples by Nicholas IV, who granted him a large subsidy in aid of his operations against Sicily. Meanwhile Charles of Valois, with the support of Sancho IV of Castile, invaded Aragon, and compelled Alphonso to withdraw the troops he had sent to the assistance of his brother James in Sicily. In 1291, on the sudden death of Alphonso, James assumed the crown of Aragon, leaving the government of Sicily in the hands of his brother Frederick. A few years later, however, through the mediation of Boniface VIII, a treaty was made between Charles II

and James, whereby the latter, ignoring the claims of his brother, Frederick, agreed to abandon Sicily to Charles, and to support him with his troops in the event of resistance on the part of the Sicilians, and at the same time to release his three sons from captivity ; in consideration of which Charles bestowed (in 1295) on him his daughter Blanche with a large dowry, while the Pope granted him the sovereignty of Corsica and Sardinia, which of right belonged to the Pisans and Genoese. When the news of this treaty reached the Sicilians, they at once renounced their allegiance to James, and elected his brother Frederick king in his stead (1296). Charles thereupon declared war on Frederick, and with the aid of James of Aragon and Ruggieri di Loria, who had abandoned Frederick's cause, had all but reduced Sicily, when in 1299, after Frederick had been defeated (July 4) in a naval battle off Cape Orlando, James suddenly withdrew, declaring that he would not be the instrument of his brother's overthrow. Shortly after, Frederick defeated the French troops of Charles and took prisoner his son Philip, Prince of Tarentum. In April, 1302, Charles of Valois, who as pacificator in Tuscany had been engaged in crushing the Bianchi and Ghibellines in Florence, made a descent upon Sicily, in company with Robert, Duke of Calabria, Charles II's eldest surviving son. But the expedition was a failure, and he was forced to conclude an ignominious peace with Frederick, who was confirmed in the sovereignty of Sicily with the title of King of Trinacria, and received in marriage (May, 1302) Eleanor, third daughter of Charles II. The latter, having been foiled in every attempt to regain possession of the kingdom of Sicily, died on May 3, 1309, and was succeeded in the kingdom of Naples by his son Robert.

Carlo³, Charles Martel, eldest son of Charles II of Naples and Anjou (the preceding), and of Mary, daughter of Stephen IV (V) of Hungary ; he was born in 1271 ; and in 1291 he married Clemence of Hapsburg, daughter of the Emperor Rudolf I, by whom he had three children, Charles Robert (Carobert) (afterwards King of Hungary), Clemence (married Louis X of France), and Beatrice[Carlo[6]]; he died at Naples in 1295, at the age of twenty-four.

D. places C. M. (with whom he had been personally acquainted) in the Heaven of Venus among the spirits of lovers (*Spiriti Amanti*), Par. ix. 1 ; *un lume*, Par. viii. 31 ; *luce*, *v.* 43 ; *signor*, *v.* 86 ; *lume santo*, Par. ix. 7 [Venere, Cielo di] ; the spirit of C. M. addresses D., and after quoting the first line of one of his *canzoni* (Canz. vi. 1), refers to their acquaintance during his lifetime, and to D.'s love for him (Par. viii. 31–57) ; he goes on to say that if he had lived he would have been Count of Provence (*vv.* 58–60) [Provenza], King of Apulia (*vv.* 61–3) [Puglia], and King of Hungary (*vv.* 64–6) [Ungaria] ; and adds that had it not been for the misgovernment which led to the 'Sicilian Vespers' and the expulsion of the French from Sicily, the descendants through himself of Charles I of Anjou and of the Emperor Rudolf (whose son-in-law he was) would have ruled in 'Trinacria' (i.e. the island of Sicily) (*vv.* 67–75) [Cicilia : Trinacria] ; he then proceeds to reproach his brother Robert (afterwards King of Naples) for his avarice and for the greed of his Catalan followers, contrasting his niggardliness with the openhandedness of his father (*vv.* 76–84) [Catalogna] ; in reply to a question of D. he explains how, if Nature be thwarted, a good seed may produce

evil fruit (*vv.* 85–135), men's natural dispositions being influenced by circumstances (*vv.* 136–48), as in the case of his own brothers, Louis, who, being a king's son, became a monk (*vv.* 145–6), and Robert, who became a king, when he had better have been a monk (*v.* 147) [Luigi[3]: Roberto[2]]; when C. M. has ceased speaking, D. apostrophizes his daughter Clemence, and tells her how her father had foretold the future wrongs of his line (with special allusion probably to the exclusion of Charles Robert from the throne of Naples by his uncle Robert), but had bidden him not to reveal them (Par. ix. 1–6 [Carlo[6]: Clemenza].

On the death of his grandfather in 1285, Charles Martel, who was then only fourteen, assumed the government of the kingdom of Naples (his father being then a prisoner in Catalonia), under the guardianship of his cousin, Robert of Artois. In 1290, on the death (July 19) without issue of his mother's brother, Ladislas III (IV), he became titular King of Hungary, and on Sept. 8 was crowned with great pomp at Naples ; but he never reigned in Hungary, the kingdom being seized by Andrew III (1290–1301), who was first cousin to Stephen IV (V) his maternal grandfather [Ungaria : Table L]. In the spring of 129¾ he visited Florence (as is proved by the record of expenditure in his honour, still preserved in the Florentine archives), where he remained more than three weeks, awaiting the arrival of his father from France ; he became very popular with the Florentines, and it was on this occasion doubtless that Dante made his acquaintance (Par. viii. 55–7).

In 1295, on the departure of Charles II for the court of Aragon, with his daughter Blanche, the destined bride of James II, Charles Martel was appointed by his father Vicar-General in the kingdom of Naples, but he died at Naples in August of that same year, his wife dying within a few weeks of him, both of the plague.

Carlo[4], Charles, Count of Alençon and Valois (1285), and of Anjou (1290), commonly known as Charles of Valois, third son of Philip III of France (by his first wife, Isabella of Aragon), brother of Philip IV, and father of Philip VI; he was born in 1270; in 1284, when he was only fourteen, he was nominated by Pope Martin IV to the crown of Aragon, which the latter had declared vacant upon the excommunication of Peter III in the previous year, and some years later he made an unsuccessful attempt to take possession of the kingdom, in spite of the undertaking which had been given by Charles II of Naples to Alphonso, son and successor of Peter III, that his claims should be abandoned [Carlo[2]: Pietro[3]]; he married (in 1290) Margaret of Anjou, eldest daughter of Charles II, in whose right he became Count of Anjou, and by whom he had two sons (the elder of whom was subsequently King of France as Philip VI), and four daughters; he died Dec. 16, 1325.

Charles is mentioned by Hugh Capet (in Circle V of Purgatory), who refers to him as *un altro Carlo* (to distinguish him from Charles I of Anjou, previously mentioned), and foretells his coming into Italy without an army, but armed only with 'the lance of treachery', wherewith he would 'burst the paunch of Florence', and gain for himself not land (in allusion to his nickname 'Sanzaterra'), but disgrace and remorse, Purg. xx. 70–8; he is alluded to by D., under the title of *Totila*, with reference to his expulsion of the Bianchi from Florence, and his fruitless expedition to Sicily in 1302, V. E. ii. 6[46–8].

In the year 1300 Charles of Valois was summoned to Italy by Boniface VIII, for the twofold purpose of helping Charles II of Naples in his war against Frederick II of Aragon in Sicily, and of making peace between the contending factions of the Bianchi and Neri in Tuscany, the Pope promising in return to secure his election as Emperor. He arrived in Florence on All Saints' Day, 1301, having been allowed to enter the city unopposed, on the faith of his promise to hold the balance between the two parties, and to maintain peace. No sooner, however, had he obtained command of the city, than he treacherously espoused the cause of the Neri, armed his followers, and threw the whole of Florence into confusion. In the midst of the panic Corso Donati, the exiled leader of the Neri, made his way into the city, broke open the prisons and released the prisoners, who, together with his own adherents, attacked and pillaged the houses of the Bianchi during five days, Charles of Valois meanwhile, in spite of his promises, making no attempt to interfere. Finally, in the following April, the Bianchi were expelled from Florence, D. being among those who were condemned to be exiled.

The secret object of his mission to Florence having thus been fulfilled, in accordance with the designs of Boniface VIII, Charles of Valois left Tuscany (April, 1302), and proceeded to Naples to make preparations for a campaign against Sicily. Accompanied by Robert, Duke of Calabria, eldest surviving son of Charles II, he landed in Sicily with a large force; but the guerilla warfare carried on by Frederick II, and the ravages of the climate, soon reduced him to such extremities that he was forced to conclude an ignominious peace. Without the knowledge of Charles II he agreed that Frederick should marry Eleanor, the second daughter of the former, and should be confirmed in the possession of Sicily [**Federico**³]. In November of the same year he returned to France, the barren result of his expedition having earned him the nickname in Italy of *Carlo Sanzaterra* ('Lackland').

Charles died at Nogent in 1325, leaving a son, Philip, who afterwards (in 1328) became King of France as Philip VI, being the first of the Valois line. His countrymen remarked of Charles that he was 'fils de roi, frère de roi, oncle de trois rois, père de roi, et jamais roi'; he having unsuccessfully aspired to no less than four crowns, viz. those of Aragon, of Sicily, of Constantinople (through his second wife, Catherine, daughter of Philip Courtenay, titular Emperor of Constantinople), and of the Empire.

Carlo⁵], Charles, Duke of Lorraine, fourth son of Louis IV of France (936–954), and brother of Lothair (954–986). On the death, without issue, of Louis V (986–987), eldest son of Lothair, the rightful successor to the throne was his uncle, Charles, who was the last remaining representative of the Carlovingian line; but owing to the fact that, as Duke of Lorraine, he was a vassal of the German Emperor, the French would not accept him as king. The throne was thereupon seized by Hugh Capet, who besieged Charles in Laon, took him prisoner, and kept him in captivity until his death in 992.

Charles of Lorraine is alluded to by Hugh Capet (whom D. appears to have confounded with his father, Hugh the Great), who (in Circle V of Purgatory) says that when the 'ancient kings' had come to an end 'fuor ch' un renduto in panni bigi' (i. e. with the exception of one who became a monk), he was so powerful that his own son (if Hugh Capet is the speaker, this must be Robert II, who was crowned in 980—if Hugh the Great, the son, of course, is Hugh Capet) was promoted to the vacant throne, and thus commenced the Capetian line of kings, Purg. xx. 53–60 [**Capeti: Ciapetta: Table K**].

The difficulty here is that Charles of Lorraine, who is undoubtedly the person intended, did not become a monk. There can hardly be a question, however, that D. has confused him, the last of the Carlovingians, with Childeric III, the last of the Merovingians, who, after his deposition by Pepin le Bref in 752, was confined in the monastery of Sithieu, where he died in 755. [**Childerico.**]

Carlo⁶], Charles Robert (Carobert), King of Hungary, 1308–1342; he was the son (born 1292) of Charles Martel (eldest son of Charles II of Naples) and Clemence of Hapsburg; on the death of Otho of Bavaria (in 1308) he succeeded to the throne of Hungary, of which his father had been titular king (1290–1295), and on the death (in 1309) of his grandfather, Charles II, he claimed the throne of Naples also; his claim, however, was disputed by his uncle Robert, eldest surviving son of Charles II, who appealed in person to Pope Clement V, and obtaining a decision in his favour, was crowned King of Naples at Avignon, June, 1309, his nephew being at the same time recognized by Clement as King of Hungary [**Ungaria: Table L**].

Charles Martel (in the Heaven of Venus) alludes to his son with reference to the fact that, had it not been for the misgovernment of the French, the descendants through himself of Charles of Anjou and of Rudolf of Hapsburg (whose son-in-law he was) would have reigned in Sicily (in which case the contending factions of Italy would have found a common chief in the person of Charles Robert), Par. viii. 67–75; the supersession of Charles Robert in the kingdom of Naples is referred to (probably), Par. ix. 6 [Carlo ³: Roberto ²].

Carlo Magno, Charlemagne (Charles the Great), restorer of the Empire of the West, eldest son (born at Salzburg in 742) of Pepin le Bref, King of the Franks (752–768); on his father's death he became joint king with his brother Carloman, and on the death of the latter (in 771) he became sole king of the Frankish Empire; in 774, after his defeat of Desiderius, he assumed the title of King of Lombardy; and on Christmas Day, 800, he was crowned Emperor of the West, at Rome, by Pope Leo III; he died on Jan. 28, 814, and was buried at Aix-la-Chapelle; he was canonized in 1165.

D. places Charlemagne, together with Roland, in the Heaven of Mars, among those who fought for the faith (*Spiriti Militanti*), Par. xviii. 43 [Marte, Cielo di]; he is mentioned in connexion with the destruction of his rearguard under Roland at Roncesvalles, Inf. xxxi. 17 [Roncisvalle]; and (by the Emperor Justinian in the Heaven of Mercury) in connexion with his defence of the Church against Desiderius and the Lombards, Par. vi. 96 [Desiderius]; his defeat of

Desiderius, and his coronation at Rome by the Pope as Emperor of the West, are referred to, *Carolus Magnus*, Mon. iii. 11¹–¹³, where D. combats the theory that the latter incident implies the dependence of the Empire upon the Church. D. here states that C. was crowned by Pope Adrian I, while the Emperor Michael was on the throne of Constantinople; whereas he was crowned by Pope Leo III (795–816) during the reign of the Empress Irene (797–802) [Constantinopolis].

Carlo Martello. [Carlo³.]

Carlovingi], Carlovingian line of French kings (752–987), the second dynasty, which supplanted that of the Merovingians (448–752); there were twelve kings of this line, the first being Pepin le Bref (752–768), and the last Louis V (986–987), on whose death the crown was seized by Hugh Capet, the first king of the Capetian line. [Capeti.]

Hugh Capet (in Circle V of Purgatory) refers to the Carlovingians as ' li regi antichi' (though, perhaps, owing to D.'s having confused the last of that line with the last of the Merovingians, it is the latter who are meant, the designation of ' ancient kings' being more appropriate to them than to the comparatively recent Carlovingians), Purg. xx. 53. [Carlo⁵.]

Carnali Peccatori. [Lussuriosi.]

Carnaro. [Quarnaro.]

Carolus Magnus. [Carlo Magno.]

Carolus Secundus. [Carlo².]

Caron, Charon, son of Erebus, the boatman who ferried the shades of the dead across the rivers of the lower world; introduced by D. (whose description of him is borrowed from *Aen.* vi. 298–301) as ferryman on the river of Acheron in Hell, across which he conveys in his boat the souls of those who have died in the wrath of God, Inf. iii. 94, 109, 128; *un vecchio, bianco per antico pelo, v.* 83; *il nocchier della livida palude, v.* 98; *dimonio, con occhi di bragia, v.* 109 [**Acheronte**].

Carpigna, now Carpegna, town in Romagna (in the present province of the Marches) in the district of Montefeltro, about 15 miles NW. of Urbino, between the sources of the Marecchia and the Foglia.

Guido di Carpegna, who belonged to a branch of the Counts of Montefeltro, is mentioned by Guido del Duca (in Circle II of Purgatory), together with Pier Traversaro, among the worthies of Romagna, Purg. xiv. 98.

Two members of the Carpegna family, grandfather and grandson, bore the name of Guido; the elder (who died before 1221) had a son, Rinieri, whose eldest son, Guido di Carpegna the younger, is probably the person alluded to by D. This Guido, who was Podestà of Ravenna in 1251, died before 1289.

Carpigna, Guido di. [**Carpigna.**]

Carrarese, inhabitant of Carrara, a town in the NW. corner of Tuscany, at the foot of the Carrara hills, famous for their quarries of white marble; mentioned by Virgil (in Bolgia 4 of Circle VIII of Hell) in connexion with the soothsayer Aruns, Inf. xx. 48 [**Aronta**].

Carro, Il [1], 'the Wain', constellation otherwise known as *Ursa Major*, 'the Great Bear'; described as lying *tutto sopra il Coro*, i.e. right upon the NW. line (the time indicated being between 4 a.m. and 5 a.m.), Inf. xi. 114 [**Coro**]; no longer visible to D. by the time he was well advanced into the S. hemisphere, Purg. i. 30; never invisible from the N. hemisphere in the course of its revolution round the Pole, Par. xiii. 7–9 (cf. Canz. xv. 28–9); this constellation is referred to elsewhere as *Orsa*, Purg. iv. 65; Par. ii. 9 [**Orsa**]; *settentrione*, Purg. xxx. 1; *Elice*, Par. xxxi. 32 [**Elice**]; *sette stelle gelide*, Canz. xv. 29; and (in a quotation from Boëthius) *septem gelidi triones*, Mon. ii. 9[96] [**Settentrione** [1]].

Carro, Il [2], the two-wheeled Car in the mystic Procession in the Terrestrial Paradise (usually understood to be symbolical of the Church, its two wheels representing the Old and New Testaments), Purg. xxix. 107, 151; xxx. 9, 61, 101; xxxii. 24, 104, 115, 126, 132; *divina basterna*, Purg. xxx. 16; *benedetto carco*, Purg. xxxii. 26; *trionfal veiculo*, Purg. xxxii. 119; *dificio santo*, Purg. xxxii. 142; *vaso*, Purg. xxxiii. 34.

Cartagine, Carthage, situated in the recess of a large bay in the northernmost extremity of N. Africa; founded, according to the mythical account adopted in the *Aeneid*, by Dido.

D. mentions Carthage in connexion with the imprisonment and death of Regulus in the first Punic war, Conv. iv. 5[124–9] [**Regolo**]; its capture and destruction by Scipio, *Carthago*, Epist. viii. 10[169] [**Scipione**[2]]; referred to by G. del Virgilio as the kingdom of Dido, *regnum Elissae*, Carm. 32 [**Elissa**].

Cartaginesi, Carthaginians; their negotiations with the Romans through Regulus for an exchange of prisoners in the first Punic war, Conv. iv. 5[124—7] [**Regolo**]; Dido their queen, *Carthaginenses*, Mon. ii. 3[102—3] [**Dido**]; their meditated attack upon Rome under Hannibal in the second Punic war frustrated by a sudden storm of hail, as is recorded by Livy (xxvi. 11), Mon. ii. 4[58—64] [**Annibale**]; defeated by the Romans in the great struggle for empire, Mon. ii. 11[59—63] [**Romani**[1]]; alluded to in connexion with the second Punic war, and their defeat of the Romans at Cannae, Inf. xxviii. 10 [**Canne**]; described (by an anachronism) as Arabs, Par. vi. 49 [**Arabi**]; the Punic race, Mon. ii. 4[61], 11[53] [**Poeni**]; Africans, Mon. ii. 11[60—1] [**Afri : Africani**].

Carthaginenses. [**Cartaginesi.**]

Carthago. [**Cartagine.**]

Casale, town of N. Italy in Piedmont, on the right bank of the Po, about 30 miles E. of Turin; mentioned by St. Bonaventura (in the Heaven of the Sun) together with Acquasparta (in allusion to Ubertino da Casale and Matteo d'Acquasparta, the leaders of the two sects which arose within the Franciscan Order soon after the death of St. Francis), Par. xii. 124 [**Matteo d'Acquasparta : Ubertino da Casale**].

Casalodi, castle near Brescia, whence the Guelf Counts of Casalodi, who in 1272 made themselves masters of Mantua, took their title; it is mentioned by Virgil (in Bolgia 4 of Circle VIII of Hell) in reference to the expulsion of Alberto da Casalodi from Mantua by the stratagem of Pinamonte de' Buonaccorsi, and the consequent slaughter of a large number of the inhabitants, Inf. xx. 95. [**Pinamonte.**]

Cascìòli, name of a place (identified by some with Casoli, in the Abruzzo, on a branch of the Sangro, about 20 miles SE. of Chieti; by others with Ascoli, in the Marches, on the Tronto, close to the border of the Abruzzo) mentioned in a poem attributed by D. to Castra of Florence and quoted, V. E. i. 11[28]. [**Castra.**]

Cascoli. [**Cascìòli.**]

Casella, musician of Florence (or, according to some, of Pistoja), and friend of D., who recognizes him in Ante-purgatory among those who have just arrived, and addresses him as *Casella mio*, Purg. ii. 91; *una (anima)*, v. 76; *l'ombra, v.* 83 [**Antipurgatorio**]; after they had attempted to embrace one another, and had conversed together awhile (*vv.* 76–105), D. begs Casella to sing, whereupon he begins to chant one of D.'s *canzoni* (Canz. vii) (*vv.* 106–14).

C., who has been identified with one Casella or Scarsella de Florentia, mentioned in a Sienese document dated July 13, 1282, as having been fined for perambulating the streets at night, is said to have set to music some of D.'s verses. In the Vatican Library is a poem by Lemmo da Pistoja, who lived towards the end of Cent. xiii, with the inscription

Casella diede il sono, i.e. set to music by Casella.

Casentinenses, inhabitants of the Casentino; their dialect, like that of the people of Prato, harsh and discordant owing to their exaggerated accentuation, V.E.i. 11^{40-2}; alluded to as *brutti porci*, Purg. xiv. 43. [**Casentino**.]

Casentino, district in Tuscany, comprising the upper valley of the Arno and the slopes of the Etruscan Apennines; mentioned by Maestro Adamo (in Bolgia 10 of Circle VIII of Hell) in connexion with the numerous streams which descend thence into the Arno, Inf. xxx. 65; Buonconte (in Ante-purgatory) mentions it in connexion with the Archiano (which falls into the Arno just above Bibbiena), Purg. v. 94 [**Archiano**]; and alludes to it as *la valle . . . Da Pratomagno al gran giogo*, i.e. the valley between the ridge of Pratomagno (on the W. side), and the main ridge of the Apennines (on the E.), Purg. v. 115–16 [**Pratomagno**]; in tracing the course of the Arno, Guido del Duca (in Circle II of Purgatory) speaks of the inhabitants as *brutti porci* (with especial reference probably to the Conti Guidi, lords of Romena and Porciano in the Casentino, there being perhaps an allusion to the latter name), Purg. xiv. 43. [**Arno**.]

Casino. [**Cassino**.]

Casoli. [**Casciòli**.]

Cassentinenses. [**Casentinenses**.]

Cassero, Guido del], nobleman of Fano, who, together with Angiolello da Carignano, was murdered (c. 1312) by order of Malatestino of Rimini, Inf. xxviii. 77. [**Angiolello**.]

Cassero, Jacopo del], member of a powerful Guelf family of Fano (probably a relative of the preceding), was the son of Uguccione del Cassero, and nephew of Martino del Cassero, professor of law at Arezzo in 1255. He was among the Guelf leaders who joined the Florentines in their expedition against Arezzo in 1288. He incurred the enmity of Azzo VIII of Este by his opposition to the designs of the latter upon Bologna, of which city Jacopo was Podestà in 1296. In revenge Azzo had him assassinated at Oriaco, between Venice and Padua, while he was on his way (in 1298) to assume the office of Podestà at Milan at the invitation of Maffeo Visconti. He appears to have gone by sea from Fano to Venice, and thence to have proceeded towards Milan by way of Padua; but while he was still among the lagoons, only about eight miles from Venice, he was waylaid and stabbed. After his assassination his body was conveyed to Fano, where it was buried in the Church of San Domenico, with a long inscription which is still legible.

D. places Jacopo (who relates to him the circumstances of his murder) in Ante-purgatory among those who put off their repentance to the last, Purg. v. 64–84; *uno (peccatore)*, v. 64 [**Antipurgatorio**].

Cassino, monastery of Monte Cassino, 'the parent of all the greatest Benedictine monasteries in the world,' founded by St. Benedict of Nursia in 529, and the scene of his death in 543. It is situated on a spur of Monte Cairo, a few miles from Aquino in the N. of Campania, almost exactly halfway between Rome and Naples. When St. Benedict first came to the spot, it was still the centre of pagan worship, the summit of the hill being crowned by a temple of Apollo, and a grove sacred to Venus, both of which were destroyed by him.

Cassino is mentioned by St. Benedict (in the Heaven of Saturn) in his account of the foundation of the monastery, Par. xxii. 37; *badia*, v. 76. [**Benedetto** [1].]

Cassio, Caius Cassius Longinus, partisan of Pompey, and one of the murderers of Julius Caesar. After the defeat of Pompey at Pharsalia in B.C. 48, C. surrendered to Caesar, who pardoned him; but he did not cease to regard Caesar as his enemy, and it was he who formed the conspiracy against the life of the dictator, and gained over Marcus Brutus to take part in it. After the murder of Caesar (March 15, 44), he and Brutus crossed over to Greece in order to oppose Octavian and Antony. The opposing forces met at Philippi (42), where C. was defeated by Antony, while Brutus, who commanded the other wing of the army, drove Octavian off the field. C., ignorant of the success of Brutus, would not survive his defeat, and put an end to his life. In a second battle, shortly after, Brutus also was defeated, whereupon he too killed himself.

D. places Cassius (whom, apparently by a confusion with Lucius Cassius, whose corpulence is men-tioned by Cicero, he describes as *membruto*) with Brutus and Judas Iscariot in the jaws of Lucifer in Giudecca, the last division of Circle IX, the nethermost pit of Hell, Inf. xxxiv. 67 [**Bruto** [2]: **Giudecca**: **Lucifero**]; he is mentioned with Brutus by the Emperor Justinian (in the Heaven of Mercury) in connexion with the victories of the Roman Eagle under Augustus, the reference being to the battle of Philippi, Par. vi. 74 [**Filippi** [3]].

Castalia], celebrated fountain on Mt. Parnassus, sacred to Apollo and the Muses; referred to as *la cisterna di Parnaso*, Purg. xxxi. 141 (cf. Purg. xxii. 65). [**Parnaso**.]

Castalius, Castalian; *Castaliae sorores*, i.e. the Muses, Ecl. i. 54; Carm. 22. [**Castalia**: **Muse**.]

Castel, Guido da, gentleman of Reggio, mentioned by Marco Lombardo (in Circle III of Purgatory) as one of three old men (the other two being Currado da Palazzo and Gherardo da Cammino) who yet survive as a reproach to the younger generation in Lombardy, Purg. xvi. 125; Marco adds that Guido is better named, in the French fashion, the simple Lombard, 'il semplice Lombardo' (v. 126), apparently by way of contrast to the usual association of the name of 'Lombard' with usurers.

D. mentions Guido, who was his contemporary, and is said to have been his fellow-guest at the court of Can Grande della Scala at Verona, as a type of nobility, Conv. iv. 16[72-3].

Castella, Castile, one of the old kingdoms of Spain, comprising the modern provinces of Old and New Castile. The kingdom of Castile was united to that of Leon from 1037 till the death of Alphonso VII in 1157, when the two were separated, Alphonso's eldest son, Sancho III, succeeding to the throne of Castile, the second son, Fernando II, to that of Leon. The two kingdoms were reunited in 1230, in which year Fernando III, who had succeeded to the throne of Castile in 1217, on the death of his maternal uncle, Enrique I, became also King of Leon, in succession to his father, Alphonso IX. [Table D.]

The kingdom of Castile and Leon is alluded to by St. Bonaventura (in the Heaven of the Sun), who describes it as the country in the W. of Europe, not far from the Atlantic, in which is situated Callaroga, the birthplace of St. Dominic, which he says 'lies under the protection of the great shield, in which the lion is subject and subjugates', the arms of Castile and Leon consisting of two castles and two lions, the lion being above the castle on one half of the shield, and below it on the other, Par. xii. 46-54 [Callaroga]; Fernando IV, King of Castile and Leon (1295-1312), is alluded to (probably) by the Eagle in the Heaven of Jupiter as *quel di Spagna*, Par. xix. 125 [Spagna]; Castile is mentioned, in connexion with its king, *il buon re di Castella* (i. e. probably Alphonso VIII, King of Castile, 1158-1214), Conv. iv. 11[125-6] [Alfonso 2]; and as being a neighbour of Aragon, Mon. i. 11[86-7] [Aragona].

Castellana Civitas, either Città

di Castello, on the Tiber, in extreme N. of Umbria, or Civita Castellana, in the Province of Rome, about 15 miles due N. of Rome; its dialect, as well as those of Perugia, Orvieto, and Viterbo, not discussed by D. as being closely connected with the Roman and Spoletan dialects, V. E. i. 13[29-32].

Castello, Città di. [Castellana Civitas.]

Castello, Guido da. [Castel, Guido da.]

Castello Sant' Angelo], Castle of St. Angelo on the right bank of the Tiber at Rome, originally the Moles Hadriani, the mausoleum erected by Hadrian for himself and his successors. In 537, when Rome was besieged by the Goths, it was converted into a fortress. It owes its modern name to the tradition that Gregory the Great(590-604), while leading a procession to pray for the cessation of the plague, beheld the Archangel Michael sheathing his sword above the Castle, in commemoration of which the chapel of S. Angelo inter Nubes was subsequently erected at the summit of the building by Boniface IV (608-614). The great bronze pine-cone (referred to, Inf. xxxi. 59) is said at one time to have been placed on the pinnacle of the Castle.

D. refers to it, in connexion with the crowds of pilgrims who swarmed across the bridge of St. Angelo during the Jubilee of 1300, as *il castello*, Inf. xviii. 32. [Giubbileo.]

Castiglia. [Castella.]

Castore, Castor, twin-brother of Pollux; Leda, having been visited by Jupiter in the form of a swan, brought forth two eggs, from one of which issued Helen, and from the other Castor and Pollux. At their death Jupiter placed the twins among the stars as the constellation Gemini. [Leda.]

Virgil(in Ante-purgatory)mentions Castor and Pollux to indicate the sign Gemini, and intimates to D. that if it were the month of June, when the Sun is in Gemini, that part of the Zodiac in which the Sun would then be, would lie nearer the N. (Gemini being to the N. of Aries, in which the Sun was at the time of the Vision), Purg. iv. 61–6. [Gemelli : Zodiaco.]

Castra, Florentine, to whom D. attributes the authorship of a *canzone* (the first two lines of which he quotes) in ridicule of the dialect of the men of Ancona, Rome, and Spoleto, V. E. i. 11²¹⁻⁹. The poem in question has been preserved in one MS. only (*Cod. Vat.* 3793), where it appears with the name 'Messer Osmano' prefixed to it, which may be either a pseudonym of the author, or the name of the person to whom the poem is addressed.

Castrocaro, formerly a strong castle, now a village, in Romagna, in the valley of the Montone, a few miles from Forlì, which in Cent. xiii belonged to the Counts of Castrocaro, who were Ghibellines, but submitted (in 1282) to the Church. About the year 1300 the castle passed into the hands of the Ordelaffi of Forlì; subsequently it appears to have been purchased by the Florentines. It was for some years one of the principal Guelf strongholds in Romagna.

Guido del Duca (in Circle II of Purgatory) includes its Counts among the degenerate families of Romagna, and laments that they had not died out, Purg. xiv. 116–17.

Catalano, member of the Guelf Catalani family of Bologna, where he was born c. 1210; he was Podestà of Milan in 1243, of Parma in 1250, of Piacenza in 1260; in 1249 he commanded a division of the Bolognese infantry at the battle of Fossalta, in which King Enzio was defeated and taken prisoner; in 1261 he was associated with Loderingo degli Andalò of Bologna in founding the Order of the Knights of Our Lady (subsequently known as the 'Frati Gaudenti'); in 1265 and 1267 he and Loderingo shared the office of Podestà in Bologna, and in 1266 in Florence; shortly after his last term of office he retired to the monastery of the Frati Gaudenti at Ronzano near Bologna, where he died and was buried in 1285.

After the defeat and death of Manfred at Benevento (Feb. 26, 126⅚), the Florentine commons (for the most part Guelf) began to murmur against the government of Guido Novello and the Ghibelline nobles, who, as a conciliatory measure, arranged that the office of Podestà should be held jointly by a Guelf and a Ghibelline, instead of by a single individual as heretofore ; and they selected for the purpose the two Bolognese, Frati Gaudenti, Catalano de' Catalani, a Guelf, and Loderingo degli Andalò, a Ghibelline, in the expectation that they would administer the office impartially. Their establishment, however, of the 'Council of Thirty-six', which was selected from nobles and commons of both parties, gave offence to Guido

Novello and the Ghibelline nobles, who attempted to suppress it ; but the commons rose upon them, and they were forced to leave the city, the houses of many of the Ghibellines (that of the Uberti, in the quarter known as the Gardingo, among them) being wrecked by the populace. Catalano and Loderingo thereupon quitted Florence, not without a suspicion on the part of the Florentines (which D. regarded as well founded) that ' under cover of false hypocrisy', as Villani (vii. 13) puts it, they had combined together for their own advantage rather than for that of the state. [Frati Gaudenti : Gardingo.]

D. places Catalano, together with Loderingo, among the Hypocrites in Bolgia 6 of Circle VIII of Hell (Malebolge), Inf. xxiii. 104, *due, v.* 82 ; *frati, v.* 109 ; Catalano, *l'un, v.* 100 ; *il frate Catalan, v.* 114 ; *il frate, vv.* 127, 142 [Ipocriti].

Catalogna, Catalonia(Cataluña), province in NE. corner of Spain, which in D.'s time formed part of the kingdom of Aragon ; mentioned by Charles Martel (in the Heaven of Venus), who, in allusion, as is supposed, to the greed of the needy Catalan retainers, whom his brother Robert is said to have brought back with him from his seven years' captivity in Spain, speaks of *l'avara povertà di Catalogna,* Par. viii. 77. [Carlo³ : Roberto².]

Catania, Golfo di], Gulf of Catania, on the E. of Sicily ; alluded to by Charles Martel (in the Heaven of Venus) as *il golfo Che riceve da Euro maggior briga,* i.e. the gulf which is most exposed to the SE. wind, it being open to the E., Par. viii. 68–9 ; he also refers to the circumstance that owing to the proximity of Mt. Aetna, the gulf, which

lies ' tra Pachino e Peloro ' (*v.* 68), i.e. between Cape Passaro and Cape Faro, is often covered with a dense pall of smoke. [Aetna.]

Catellini, ancient noble family of Florence (extinct in D.'s day), mentioned by Cacciaguida (in the Heaven of Mars) as having been already in their decline in his time, Par. xvi. 88.

Catilina, Lucius Sergius Catilina, the famous Roman conspirator ; born c. B.C. 108, praetor 68, died 62. C. was a candidate for the consulship in 66, but was disqualified, and in revenge formed a plot to murder the two consuls who had been elected. This plot having failed he engaged in a more extensive conspiracy, which came to a head during the consulship of Cicero (B.C. 63), by whose vigilance C.'s plans were baffled, and he himself was forced to leave Rome. Cicero having obtained legal evidence against the rest of the conspirators, they were put to death. A force was then dispatched against C., who was defeated and killed in the neighbourhood of Florence, B.C. 62 (on which occasion, according to tradition, the town of Fiesole was destroyed by the Romans).

D. alludes to the conspiracy of C. and its frustration by Cicero, Conv. iv. 5¹⁷²⁻⁶. [Cicerone : Fiesole.]

Cato, Marcus. [Catone².]

Catona, small town of S. Italy, in Calabria, a few miles N. of Reggio, almost exactly opposite Messina ; mentioned by Charles Martel (in the Heaven of Venus) to indicate the southernmost limit of the kingdom of Naples, Par. viii. 62 (where

some read *Crotona*) [**Ausonia** :
Crotona : Napoli].

Catone [1], Marcus Porcius Cato,
the Censor, commonly called Cato
Major (i. e. the Elder), to distinguish
him from his great-grandson, Cato
of Utica [**Catone** [2]]; born B.C. 234,
elected Censor in 184, died at the
age of 85 in 149.

D. refers to him as *Catone*, Conv.
iv. 21[82]; *Catone Vecchio*, Conv. iv.
27[151], 28[45]; his opinion (as put into
his mouth by Cicero) as to the divinity of the soul (*Senect.* § 21),
Conv. iv. 21[80—6]; his increased
delight in conversation as he grew
older (*Senect.* § 14), Conv. iv. 27[151—4];
his eagerness to see (after death) the
great Romans who had gone before
him (*Senect.* § 23), Conv. iv. 28[44—8].
[***Senectute, De.***]

Catone [2], Marcus Porcius Cato
Uticensis, great-grandson of Cato
the Censor, born B.C. 95 ; brought
up as a devoted adherent of the Stoic
school, he became conspicuous for
his rigid morality.   On the outbreak
of the civil war in 49 he sided with
Pompey; after the battle of Pharsalia
he joined Metellus Scipio in Africa ;
when the latter was defeated at
Thapsus, and all Africa, with the exception of Utica, submitted to Caesar,
he resolved to die rather than fall
into Caesar's hands; he therefore put
an end to his own life, after spending
the greater part of the night in reading
Plato's *Phaedo* on the immortality
of the soul, B.C. 46.

Cato is mentioned in connexion
with his march through the desert
of Libya shortly before his death
(*Phars.* x. 411 ff.), Inf. xiv. 15 ;
he is placed by D. (whose description of his personal appearance,
with long white hair and beard, is
borrowed from Lucan, *Phars.* ii.
372–6) as warder at the entrance to
Purgatory, *un veglio solo*, Purg. i. 31 ;
altrui, *v.* 133 (where some think the
reference is to God); *il veglio onesto*,
Purg. ii. 119 ; on their arrival on
the island from which rises the Mt.
of Purgatory, D. and Virgil meet
Cato, who asks them who they are,
taking them for damned spirits (Purg.
i. 31–48); V., after making D. do
reverence, replies that through the
intervention of Beatrice D. is come
to see the spirits under his guardianship, and is seeking freedom, for
the sake of which Cato himself had
died at Utica (*vv.* 49–75); after
explaining that D. is yet alive, and
that he himself was come from Limbo, where Cato's wife Marcia was,
V. implores him for the latter's sake
to grant them admittance (*vv.* 76–
84); Cato replies that Marcia can
no longer move him now, but that
for Beatrice's sake he will grant their
request (*vv.* 85–93); then having
bidden V. gird D. with a rush and wash
his face, he disappears (*vv.* 94–109);
he appears once more to chide the
loitering spirits who were listening
to Casella's singing (after which he
is not seen again), Purg. ii. 119–23.

Cato's escape from Julius Caesar
into Africa, Conv. iii. 5[121—3] [**Cesare** [1]]; his greatness not to be
measured by words, Conv. iv. 5[140—2];
belonged to the Stoic sect of philosophers, Conv. iv. 6[93—6]; his belief
that he was born not for himself,
but for his country and the whole
world (from Lucan, *Phars.* ii. 383),
Conv. iv. 27[31—3]; the return of his

wife Marcia to him, as described by Lucan (*Phars.* ii. 326–47), symbolical of the return of the noble soul to God, Conv. iv. 28[97–123] [**Marzia**]; the most staunch champion of liberty, choosing death as a free man, rather than life without liberty, Mon. ii. 5[132–40]; Cicero's estimate of his character in the *De Officiis* (i. 31) quoted (freely), *Marcus Cato*, Mon. ii. 5[158–70].

As a suicide and a pagan, and as the bitter opponent of Caesar, the founder of the Roman Empire, we should expect to find Cato in Hell, with Pier delle Vigne, or with Brutus and Cassius, instead of being admitted to Purgatory and destined eventually to a place in Paradise (Purg. i. 75). D., however, regards him, not in his relation to the Roman Empire, but as the devoted lover of liberty, the representative of the soul made free by the annihilation of the body. The employment of Cato as warder of Purgatory was probably suggested to D. by Virgil, who, instead of placing him among the suicides in Tartarus (*Aen.* vi. 434–9), represents him as a lawgiver among the righteous dead in Elysium (*Aen.* viii. 670). In his estimate of Cato, for which he was mainly indebted to Lucan (*Phars.* ii. 380–91; ix. 554–5, 601–4), and Cicero (*Off.* i. 31), D. has probably not distinguished very clearly between Cato the Censor and his great-grandson.

Catria, Monte Catria, one of the highest peaks of the Apennines, on the borders of Umbria and the Marches, between Gubbio and Pergola.

St. Peter Damian (in the Heaven of Saturn) describes it as a 'boss' formed by the lofty Apennines which rise between the shores of the Adriatic and of the Mediterranean, and refers to the fact that on its slopes was situated the monastery of Fonte Avellana, of which he was at one time Abbot, Par. xxi. 106–14. [**Apennino**[1]: **Avellana.**]

Cattolica, La, small town on the Adriatic, between Rimini and Pesaro, at the point where the Emilia and the Marches meet; mentioned by Pier da Medicina (in Bolgia 9 of Circle VIII of Hell) in connexion with the murder of Guido del Cassero and Angiolello da Carignano by order of Malatestino of Rimini, Inf. xxviii. 80. [**Angiolello.**]

Caucasus, Mt. Caucasus; the Florentines threatened with the Imperial Eagle, which soars alike over the Pyrenees, Caucasus, and Atlas, Epist. vi. 3[82]; the haunt of Hyrcanian tigers, Ecl. ii. 22.

Caudinae Furcae, the 'Caudine Forks', narrow passes in the mountains near Caudium, a town in Samnium on the road from Capua to Beneventum, where the Roman army surrendered to the Samnites, B.C. 321; Lucan quoted (*Phars.* ii. 135–8) to show how nearly the Empire in Italy was transferred from the Romans to the Samnites, Mon. ii. 11[43–51]. [**Sanniti.**]

Causis, De, pseudo-Aristotelian treatise of unknown authorship, on which commentaries were written by Albertus Magnus, St. Thomas Aquinas, and Aegidius Romanus. The treatise, which was translated from Arabic into Latin between 1167 and 1187 by Gerardus Cremonensis, was regarded as of great weight and authority in the Middle Ages. Albertus Magnus was the first to suspect that it was a compilation from Aristotle and the Arabian philosophers. St. Thomas Aquinas identified portions of it as extracts from the *Elevatio Theologica* of Proclus, upon whose work it was probably based.

D., who makes no reference to the authorship of the work, quotes from the *De Causis* (the references being to the thirty-two *Propositiones* into which the Latin work is divided) the theory that every 'substantial form' proceeds from its First Cause, which is God, Conv. iii. 2^{24-7} (*Prop.* xx); that the Divine Goodness and its gifts become diverse by the concurrence of that which receives them, Conv. iii. 2^{31-4} (*Prop.* xx); that the first of all things is 'being', Conv. iii. 2^{52-4} (*Prop.* iv *init.*); that every Intelligence on high knows what is above itself and what below, Conv. iii. 6^{39-42} (*Prop.* viii *init.*); that every cause informs its effect with the goodness it has received from its own cause, which is God, Conv. iii. 6^{113-18} (*Prop.* i); that the Primal Goodness dispenses its bounty 'with a single affluence', Conv. iii. 7^{17-19} (*Prop.* xx); that every noble soul has three methods of operation, the animal, the intellectual, and the divine, Conv. iv. 21^{89-91} (*Prop.* iii *init.*); that the difference between causes is one of degree, Mon. i. 11^{129-33} (*Prop.* i); that every primary cause has greater influence upon the object affected than a universal secondary cause, Epist. x. 20^{380-3} (*Prop.* i *init.*); that every intelligence is full of forms, Epist. x. 21^{407-8} (*Prop.* x *init.*).

Cavalcaconti], Counts of Bertinoro, who became extinct at the end of Cent. xii; thought by some to be alluded to by Guido del Duca (in Circle II of Purgatory) as 'la famiglia di Brettinoro', Purg. xiv. 113. [**Brettinoro.**]

Cavalcante Cavalcanti. [**Cavalcanti, Cavalcante.**]

Cavalcanti, Cavalcante], Florentine Guelf, father of D.'s friend, the poet Guido Cavalcanti; he was Podestà of Gubbio in 1257, and died before 1280. The Cavalcanti, whom Villani describes as being very wealthy and powerful (viii. 39, 71), were originally Guelfs (v. 39; vi. 33); on the outbreak of the Bianchi and Neri feuds in Florence they for the most part sided with the Cerchi, the leaders of the Bianchi faction, of which they were subsequently some of the most prominent supporters.

Cavalcante, who is said to have been an Epicurean and to have disbelieved in the immortality of the soul, is placed among the Heretics in Circle VI of Hell, but is not mentioned by name; *ombra*, Inf. x. 53; *costui*, *v.* 65; *quel caduto*, *v.* 110; he addresses D. while the latter is conversing with Farinata degli Uberti, and inquires as to the fate of his son, Guido (*vv.* 52–69) [**Eretici: Cavalcanti, Guido**].

Cavalcanti, Guido, famous Florentine poet, son of the preceding, his mother being (probably) a lady of the house of the Conti Guidi; he was born probably between 1250 and 1255, but in any case not later than 1259; while still a youth (in 1267) he was betrothed by his father to Beatrice degli Uberti, daughter of the famous Farinata, at the time when an attempt was made to conciliate the feuds in Florence by means of matrimonial alliances between members of the opposing factions; the date of the marriage, by which Guido had two children, is unknown. In 1280 Guido acted as one of the sureties of the peace arranged by the Cardinal Latino. From 1283 dates his friendship with D. (V. N. § 3$^{102-3}$). In 1284 he was a member, together with Brunetto Latini and Dino Compagni, of the Grand Council. He was an ardent Guelf, and when the Guelf party in Florence split up into Bianchi and Neri, headed respectively by the Cerchi and the Donati, he threw in his lot with the former and distinguished himself by the violence of his opposition to the Donati, and especially to Corso Donati. Between 1292 and 1296 Guido set out on a pilgrimage to Compostela in Galicia, but he got no further on his way than Toulouse, whence he appears to have turned back to Nîmes. While he was on this journey Corso Donati made an attempt to assassinate him, in retaliation for which Guido on his return attacked Corso in the streets of Florence, receiving a wound in the affray. In the summer of 1300, during D.'s priorate (June 15–Aug. 15), it was decided (June 24), in order to put an end to the disturbances caused by the continued hostilities between the two factions, to banish the leaders of both sides, the Neri being sent to Castel della Pieve, the Bianchi (Guido being among them) to Sarzana in Lunigiana, among those who approved this decision being Dante, in his capacity as Prior. It thus came about that D. was instrumental in sending his own friend into exile, and, as it proved, to his death ; for though the exiles were recalled very shortly after

the expiry of D.'s term of office (Aug. 15), so that Guido only spent a few weeks at Sarzana, he never recovered from the effects of the malarious climate of the place, and died in Florence at the end of August in that same year ; he was buried in the cemetery of Santa Reparata on Aug. 29, as is attested by an entry in the official records still preserved in Florence.

Of Guido's poems, which consist of canzoni, sonnets, and ballate, some didactic, some purely lyrical, a large number has been preserved ; the most famous of the didactic poems is the canzone on the nature of love, which is twice quoted by D. (V. E. ii. 12$^{17, 63}$), and was the subject of numerous commentaries ; the sonnets are for the most part amatory, five of them being addressed to Dante. Guido Cavalcanti belongs with Dante to the school of 'il dolce stil nuovo', which superseded that of Guido Guinizelli—the Guido whom his namesake eclipsed as a poet in the vulgar tongue, according to D.'s estimate (Purg. xi. 97–8).

In the D. C., Guido is mentioned in the conversation between D. and Cavalcante in Circle VI of Hell, where the latter refers to him as 'mio figlio' and asks why he is not with D., Inf. x. 60 ; D. in his reply refers to him as 'Guido vostro', and, indicating Virgil, hints that Guido 'held him in disdain' (vv. 61–3) ; D. having used the past tense, Cavalcante assumes that his son is dead, and asks D., 'non viv' egli ancora?' (vv. 67–9) ; D. does not reply, but subsequently bids Farinata tell Cavalcante that Guido is still alive (*vv.* 109–14) [Caval-cante]; he is mentioned again (by Oderisi in Circle I of Purgatory) as 'l'uno Guido' whose fame as an Italian poet should eclipse that of 'l'altro Guido' (i. e. Guido Guini-zelli), and who in his turn should perhaps be eclipsed by another con-temporary poet (i. e. according to some, by D. himself), Purg. xi. 97–9. [Guido [4].]

In the *Vita Nuova*, which is dedicated to Guido Cavalcanti (§ 31[22–3]), D. several times refers to him as his most intimate friend, 'quegli, cui io chiamo primo de' miei amici,' V. N. § 3[98–9]; 'mio primo amico,' §§ 24[19], 25[111–12], 31[22], 33[3–4]; he includes him among the famous poets of the day, and mentions that G. was one of those to whom he sent his sonnet 'A ciascun' alma presa e gentil core', to which G. re-plied, and which D. says was the beginning of their friendship, V. N. § 3[96–104].

To him D. addressed a sonnet referring to G.'s love for a lady of the name of Giovanna, Son. xxxii.

In the *De Vulgari Eloquentia* Guido is referred to as *Guido Floren-tinus*, V. E. i. 13[36]; ii. 12[61]; *Guido Cavalcantis*, V. E. ii. 6[68]; *Guido de Florentia*, V. E. ii. 12[16]; his poems quoted, V. E. ii. 6[69], 12[17, 63]; he, like D. himself and Lapo, rejected the Florentine dialect in his poems, V. E. i. 13[32–7]; com-posed *canzoni* in the most illustrious style, V. E. ii. 6[68]; wrote stanzas of eleven-syllabled lines, V. E. ii. 12[14–16]; employed three-syllabled lines in his *canzone* on the nature of love, V. E. ii. 12[62–3].

The meaning of D.'s expression with regard to Guido that 'haply he held Virgil in disdain' (Inf. x. 63) has not been satisfactorily explained; some suppose D. intended to imply that Guido preferred philosophy to poetry; others think the reason was political, and that Guido, who was a Guelf, was in antagonism with Virgil as the poet of the Roman Empire; others again think it was because of his desire to see the Latin language give place in poetry and literature to Italian, a desire to which D. alludes in the *Vita Nuova*, where he says that Guido wished him to write to him in the vulgar tongue only (§ 31[21–4]).

Cavalcanti, Francesco de'], member of the Cavalcanti family of Florence (nicknamed Guercio, 'squint-eyed'), who was murdered by the inhabitants of Gaville, a village in the Upper Valdarno; his death was speedily avenged by the Caval-canti, who in their fury are said to have almost dispeopled Gaville. He is one of five Florentines (Inf. xxvi. 4–5) whom D. places among the Robbers in Bolgia 7 of Circle VIII of Hell (Malebolge), alluding to him as *quel, che tu, Gaville, piagni*, Inf. xxv. 151. [Ladri.] Francesco is one of three spirits seen by D. to undergo transformation; he is a ser-pent to begin with (*un serpentello acceso*, v. 83), and gradually ex-changes forms with another robber, who is at first in human shape (*vv.* 103–41).

Cavalcanti, Gianni Schicchi de'. [Gianni Schicchi.]

Caÿster, river of Asia Minor, which rises in Mt. Tmolus, and flows through Lydia and Ionia into the Aegean Sea a few miles above Ephesus; it was famous for its swans, in which connexion (in imitation of *Georg.* i. 384) D. mentions it, Ecl. ii. 18.

Cecilio, Caecilius Statius, a native of Milan, originally a slave, Roman comic poet, contemporary of Ennius, and immediate predecessor of Terence; died B.C. 168; he is mentioned, together with Terence, Plautus, and Varro (or Varius) by Statius (in Purgatory), who asks Virgil for news of them, and is told that they and Persius and many others are with Homer and V. himself in Limbo, Purg. xxii. 98. [**Limbo.**]

Cécina, river of Tuscany, which flows into the Mediterranean about 20 miles S. of Leghorn; mentioned together with Corneto, which is situated on the Marta, about 10 miles N. of Civitavecchia, these two rivers indicating roughly the N. and S. limits of the Maremma or marshy seaboard of Tuscany, Inf. xiii. 9 [**Maremma**].

Cefalo, Cephalus, King of Athens; mentioned in connexion with Ovid's account of how C., being at war with Crete, sought assistance from Aeacus, King of Aegina (*Metam.* vii. 501–5), of how Aeacus complied (*vv.* 506–11, a passage which D. translates from a corrupt text), and of how he related to C. the history of the pestilence that destroyed the people of Aegina and of the repopulation of the island (*vv.* 523–657), Conv. iv. 27[155–87] [**Eaco**].

Celestino V], Celestine V (Pietro da Morrone), elected Pope at the

age of nearly 80, at Perugia, July 5, 1294; abdicated at Naples, Dec. 13 of the same year; died 1296. After the death of Nicholas IV in 1292, the Cardinals, who had been in conclave for nearly two years without coming to a decision, agreed to elect the venerable hermit, Pietro da Morrone, whom they summoned from his cell in the remote Abruzzi to assume the papal crown. Pietro, who was of humble birth, had scarcely ascended the pontifical throne, ere, weary of his dignity, he began to cast about for some way of vacating his office, which he resigned after a reign of little more than five months. According to the current belief, which was shared by D. (Inf. xix. 56), Celestine's abdication was brought about by the crafty Benedetto Gaetani, who a few days after, through the interest of Charles II of Naples, secured his own election, and became Pope as Boniface VIII. In order to secure himself from any attempt at opposition on the part of Celestine, Boniface put him in prison, where he remained until his death. He was canonized a few years later (in 1313) by Clement V. [**Bonifazio**[1].]

Celestine is alluded to as the predecessor of Boniface VIII, in connexion with his abdication, Inf. xxvii. 105; and according to the most general opinion (dating from the earliest commentators) he is the person indicated by D. as 'colui Che fece per viltate il gran rifiuto', whose shade he saw among the souls of those 'Che visser senza infamia e senza lodo', and who were not worthy to enter Hell, Inf. iii. 36, 59–60.

Centauri, Centaurs, mythical

race, half horses and half men, said to have been the offspring of Ixion, King of the Lapithae, and a cloud in the shape of Hera ; D., who hence refers to them as 'i maladetti Nei nuvoli formati', introduces them as examples of gluttony in Circle VI of Purgatory, in allusion to their fight with the Lapithae and Theseus at the wedding-feast of Pirithoüs, their half-brother, and Hippodame (the story of which he got from Ovid, *Metam.* xii. 210 ff.), Purg. xxiv. 121-3 [Golosi : Teseo].

The Centaurs, who are elsewhere referred to as the brothers of Cacus, Inf. xxv. 28 [Caco], and who, with their semi-bestial form, typify the sins of bestiality (Inf. xi. 83), are placed as guardians of the Tyrants and Murderers in Round I of Circle VII of Hell, Inf. xii. 56 ; *fiere snelle, v.* 76 ; they are armed with bows and arrows (*vv.* 56, 60), and shoot any of the spirits who attempt to evade their punishment (*vv.* 73-5); three of them, Chiron, Nessus, and Pholus, advance from the troop (*vv.* 59-60); Nessus threatens D. and Virgil (*vv.* 61-3), but is rebuked by the latter (*vv.* 64-6), who explains to D. who they are (*vv.* 67-72), and requests Chiron to give them an escort (*vv.* 91-6); Chiron sends Nessus with them, who points out the different sinners to them as they go along (*vv.* 97-139) [Chirone : Folo : Nesso : Violenti].

Centauro, Centaur ; of Nessus, Inf. xii. 61, 104, 115, 129 [Nesso]; of Cacus (who was not properly speaking a Centaur), Inf. xxv. 17 [Caco].

Ceperano, town in Latium on the banks of the Liris (branch of the Garigliano), which there forms part of the frontier between the Papal States and the kingdom of Naples.

D. mentions C. in allusion to the betrayal of Manfred by the Apulians just before the fatal battle of Benevento (Feb. 26, 126$\frac{5}{8}$), Inf. xxviii. 16-7.

Hearing of the approach of Charles of Anjou, Manfred directed all his energies to the defence of the passes into his kingdom. At the point called the bridge of Ceperano, where the road crosses the Liris, he posted the Count Giordano, and his relative, the Count of Caserta ; the latter, however, turned traitor, and abandoned the pass, leaving Charles to advance unopposed. D. implies that there was a battle at Ceperano, but as a matter of fact no engagement took place at the bridge ; he has perhaps confused what happened there with the action at San Germano a few days later (Vill. vii. 6) ; or possibly, since the context seems to point to an engagement in which there was great loss of life, his words (taken somewhat loosely) refer to the decisive battle at Benevento itself, during which, at a critical moment, the greater part of the Apulian barons deserted Manfred and fled from the field (Vill. vii. 9). [Benevento : Manfredi.]

Cephas (Syriac word, answering to the Greek Peter, and signifying a rock), name given by Christ to Simon (*John.* i. 42).

St. Peter Damian (in the Heaven of Saturn) contrasts the simplicity of St. Peter (whom he calls by the name of Cephas) and St. Paul with the luxury of the prelates of his day, Par. xxi. 127–8 [Pietro[1]].

Cerbero, Cerberus, huge dog-like monster, with three heads, who guarded the entrance to the infernal regions; the last and most difficult of the twelve labours of Hercules was to bring Cerberus into the upper world, which he accomplished by putting the monster in a chain and carrying him off.

D., taking C. as the type of gluttony, places him as guardian of Circle III of Hell, where the Gluttonous are punished, Inf. vi. 13; *fiera crudele e diversa, v.* 13; *il gran vermo, v.* 22; *demonio, v.* 32; he is described as a cruel and uncouth brute, with three heads, scarlet eyes, a greasy black beard, a huge belly, and paws armed with nails, with which he claws and rends the spirits under his charge (*vv.* 13–18), while he deafens them with his barking (*vv.* 32–3) [Golosi]; when he catches sight of D. and Virgil, he shows his tusks at them, but V. appeases him by throwing handfuls of earth down his throats (*vv.* 22–31) (an incident which is imitated from *Aen.* vi. 417–23).

The heavenly messenger at the gate of Dis mentions C. as having had ' his chin and throat peeled', in allusion to his having been chained and carried off to the upper world by Hercules, Inf. ix. 98–9 (cf. *Aen.* vi. 395–6).

Cerchi, wealthy Florentine family of low origin, who originally came from Acone, a small village in the neighbourhood of Florence; in 1215, when Florence was divided into Guelfs and Ghibellines, they espoused the cause of the former, and were already at that date rising into prominence; subsequently, when the Florentine Guelfs split up into Bianchi and Neri, by which time they were wealthy merchants, and very powerful in the commercial world, they became the leaders of the former, while the Donati, who were of noble origin, headed the Neri [Bianchi]. Villani, whose father was a partner in the house of Cerchi, and who acted as their agent in England, speaks of them as a wealthy and powerful family, located in the Porta san Piero, who had raised themselves in a short space of time to a great position by trade (v. 39; viii. 39).

The Cerchi are mentioned by Cacciaguida (in the Heaven of Mars), who laments the extension of the city of Florence, which brought them within its walls from their original home at Acone, Par. xvi. 65 [Acone[1]]; he alludes to their residence in the Porta san Piero, where the Ravignani, the ancestors of the Conti Guidi (whose palace the Cerchi bought in 1280), dwelt in his time, and refers to their upstart origin, and to the ruin which the Bianchi and Neri feuds were destined to bring upon the city (*vv.* 94–8) [Guidi, Conti: Ravignani].

After their purchase of the palace of the Conti Guidi (Vill. iv. 11) the Cerchi became the near neighbours of the more ancient but less wealthy Donati, and in consequence great jealousy, ending in a deadly feud, arose between the two houses, which led to constant breaches of the peace in Florence.

Cerere, Ceres, daughter of Saturn and Rhea, and sister of Jupiter, by whom she became the mother of Proserpine. Jupiter, without her knowledge, had promised her daughter to Pluto, the god of the lower world, and while Proserpine was gathering flowers near Enna in Sicily, she 'herself, a fairer flower, by gloomy Dis was gathered', and carried off to the lower regions. After wandering many days in search of her daughter C. learnt from the Sun that Pluto had carried her off; whereupon she quitted Olympus in anger and came to dwell on earth among men, becoming the protectress of agriculture.

D. mentions her as goddess of Corn, Conv. ii. 5$^{43-4}$; and alludes to her as the mother of Proserpine, to whom he compares Matilda, as she appeared to him gathering flowers upon the banks of the river Lethe, Purg. xxviii. 49–51 [Matelda : Proserpina].

Certaldo, village in Tuscany, in the Val d'Elsa, about seven miles from Poggibonsi on the road between Florence (under whose jurisdiction it passed in 1198) and Siena; mentioned, together with Campi and Figline, by Cacciaguida (in the Heaven of Mars), who laments the immigration into Florence of inhabitants from these places, and the consequent debasement of the Florentine character, Par. xvi. 50.

Cervia, small town in the Emilia (in the old Romagna) on the Adriatic, about twelve miles S. of Ravenna, a place of some importance in the Middle Ages, as enjoying a salt monopoly.

In answer to an inquiry from Guido da Montefeltro (in Bolgia 8 of Circle VIII of Hell) as to the condition of Romagna, D. informs him that the Polenta family, who had long been lords of Ravenna (since 1270), were at that time (in 1300) also lords of Cervia, Inf. xxvii. 40–2. [Polenta].

Cesare[1], Caius Julius Caesar (born B.C. 100), according to D.'s theory, the first of the Roman Emperors; he was Consul in 59, conquered Gaul and invaded Britain between 58 and 49 (in which year he passed the Rubicon and marched on Rome), and subsequently defeated Pompey's lieutenants in Spain; in 48 he crossed over to Greece and defeated Pompey at Pharsalia, and pursuing him into Egypt, after his death, made war upon Ptolemy in 47; in 46 he defeated Scipio and Juba in Africa at Thapsus, and in the next year crossed over to Spain and defeated Pompey's sons at Munda; in the autumn of 45 he returned in triumph to Rome, where in the following spring (March 15, 44) he was assassinated by Brutus and Cassius.

D. places Caesar, whom he represents as armed and as having the eyes of a hawk, among the great heroes of antiquity in Limbo, in company with the Trojan warriors Hector and Aeneas (the mythical founder of the Roman Empire), Inf. iv. 122–3 [Limbo]; he is mentioned in connexion with his hesitation to advance on Rome after crossing the Rubicon, Inf. xxviii. 98; Epist. vii. 4^{82} [Curio[2] : Rubicon]; his campaign in Spain against

Pompey's lieutenants, Afranius and Petreius, Purg. xviii. 101 [Ilerda]; the belief that he had been guilty of sodomy, Purg. xxvi. 77; his victories in Gaul, Spain, Greece, and Egypt, Par. vi. 57-72; his victory at Thapsus, Conv. iii. 5^{123}; Mon. ii. 5^{161} [Catone^2]; his office as 'first supreme prince' (i. e. Emperor of Rome), Conv. iv. 5^{100}; called *Julius* by Virgil, Inf. i. 70 [Julius]; alluded to (by St. Thomas Aquinas in the Heaven of the Sun), in connexion with the story of the fisherman Amyclas, as *Colui ch' a tutto il mondo fe' paura*, Par. xi. 69; and mentioned in the same connexion, Conv. iv. 13$^{118-19}$ [Amiclate].

D. consistently regards Julius Caesar as the first of the Roman Emperors, hence he addresses Henry VII of Luxemburg as 'Caesaris successor', Epist. vii. 1^{15}; and it is as traitors to Caesar, the representative of the highest civil authority ('primo principe sommo,' Conv. iv. 5^{100}), that he condemns Brutus and Cassius to the lowest pit of Hell, along with Judas, the betrayer of the representative of the highest spiritual authority. [Bruto^2.]

Cesare^2, Caesar, appellative of the Roman Emperors, applied by D. to the sovereigns of the Holy Roman Empire as well [Caesar]; of Frederick II, Inf. xiii. 65; V. E. i. 12^{21}; Epist. vi. 5^{131} [Federico^2]; of Albert I, Purg. vi. 92, 114 [Alberto Tedesco]; of Henry VII, Epist. v. 2^{28}, 3^{38}; vi. *fin.* [Arrigo^2]; of the Roman Emperor in general, Par. i. 29; xvi. 59; Mon. iii. 16^{135}; Epist. v. 5^{91}, 9^{152}; of Justinian,

Par. vi. 10 [Giustiniano]; of Tiberius, who, as having succeeded Julius Caesar and Augustus, is called *il terzo Cesare*, Par. vi. 86; Mon. ii. 13^{47}; Epist. v. 10^{159} [Tiberio]; of Julius Caesar, Mon. ii. 5^{161}; Epist. vii. 1^{15}, 4^{82} [Cesare^1]; of Augustus, Mon. ii. 9^{102}, 12^{49} [Augusto^2]; of Nero, Mon. iii. 13$^{44-53}$ [Nerone].

Cesena], town of N. Italy in the Emilia (in the old Romagna), on the Savio, midway between Forlì and Rimini, at the foot of the hills belonging to the Etruscan Apennine range.

In answer to an inquiry from Guido da Montefeltro (in Bolgia 8 of Circle VIII of Hell) as to the condition of Romagna, D. refers to Cesena as the city 'a cui il Savio bagna il fianco', and remarks that, just as it is placed between hill and plain, so it has alternate experience of tyranny and freedom, Inf. xxvii. 52-4.

Cesena, about the time of which D. is speaking (1300) appears to have been to a certain extent independent. Galasso da Montefeltro (cousin of Guido) was Captain and Podestà in 1289, and Podestà again in 1299; on his death in 1300 Ciapettino degli Ubertini became Podestà, while Uguccione della Faggiuola and Federigo da Montefeltro (Guido's son) were Captains, but they were driven out in the following year. In 1314 the lordship of the town was assumed by Malatestino, lord of Rimini.

Chermontesi. [Chiaramontesi.]

Cherubi. [Cherubini.]

Cherubini, Cherubim; Guido da

Montefeltro says that on his death St. Francis claimed him, but that he was carried off to Hell by a devil, one of the black Cherubim, and thrust into Bolgia 8 of Circle VIII (Malebolge), Inf. xxvii. 112-14.

Beatrice (in the Crystalline Heaven) mentions the Cherubim, in her exposition of the arrangement of the Angelic Hierarchies, as ranking second in the first Hierarchy, the Seraphim ranking first of all, *Cherubi*, Par. xxviii. 98-9 (cf. Conv. ii. 6⁵⁴⁻⁵) [**Gerarchia**]; they contemplate the second Person of the Trinity, Conv. ii. 6⁸¹⁻⁴; they preside over the Heaven of the Fixed Stars, the eighth (hence the fallen Cherubim are appropriately placed in charge of the eighth Circle of Hell, Inf. xxvii. 113) [**Paradiso** ¹].

The Cherubim were said to excel in knowledge, the Seraphim in ardour; as these were respectively the characteristics of the two orders of St. Dominic and St. Francis, the Dominicans being more especially distinguished by their attention to doctrine, the Franciscans by their good works, a parallel was established between the two angelic and the two monastic orders, to which allusion is made, Par. xi. 37-9 [**Domenicani**].

Chiana, river in Tuscany, noted in D.'s time for the sluggishness of its stream, the silting up of whose bed turned the whole Valdichiana (the district between Arezzo, Cortona, Montepulciano, and Chiusi) into a malarious swamp, which was a byword for its unhealthiness.

D., referring to its sluggishness, says that the dancing of the two

garlands of stars in the Heaven of the Sun as greatly surpassed such dancing as we are accustomed to, as the motion of the Primum Mobile, the most swiftly revolving of the Heavens, surpasses that of the Chiana, Par. xiii. 22-4 [**Mobile Primo**]; he mentions the Valdichiana in allusion to the crowded state of its hospitals in the month of August on account of its unhealthiness, coupling it with the malarious Maremma of Tuscany and the lowlands of Sardinia, Inf. xxix. 46-8.

Chiara, Santa], St. Clara, foundress of the Franciscan nuns; she was born of a noble family of Assisi in 1194; founded in 1212, under the direction of St. Francis, the order of nuns which bears her name; died in 1253, and was canonized, by Alexander IV, in 1255. The rule of her order, which was confirmed in 1247, and again in 1253, two days before her death, by Pope Innocent IV, was characterized by extreme austerity.

St. C. is alluded to by Piccarda Donati (addressing D. in the Heaven of the Moon), who had been a nun of the order, as *Donna . . . alla cui norma Nel vostro mondo giù si veste e vela*, Par. iii. 98-9. [**Piccarda.**]

Chiaramontesi], ancient noble family of Florence, alluded to by Cacciaguida (in the Heaven of Mars) as having been among the great families of his day; he speaks of them, in reference to a fraud of a member of the house (one Durante de' Chiaramontesi, who, about the year 1299, when overseer of the salt customs in Florence, used to receive the salt in a measure of the legal capacity, but distributed it in a measure from which a stave had been withdrawn, and thus made a large profit on the difference), as *Quei ch' arrossan per lo staio*, 'those who blush for the bushel,' Par. xvi. 105; this same fraud is alluded to again, together with that of Niccola Acciaiuoli, in connexion with the ascent to the church of San Miniato, the steps of which D. says were made in the days 'when the ledger and the stave were safe' in Florence, Purg. xii. 103–5 [Acciaiuoli, Niccola].

The Chiaramontesi lived in the Porta san Piero (Vill. iv. 11), and were Guelfs (v. 39).

Chiarentana, Carinthia, mountainous province of Illyria, which lies between Styria and the Tyrol, and is separated from Venetia by the Carnic Alps. D. mentions C. (which in his day included the headwaters of the Brenta) in connexion with the Brenta, the floods of which he says are caused by the melting of the snows in that district during the summer, Inf. xv. 7–9. [Brenta.]

Chiascio. [Chiassi².]

Chiassi¹, Roman Classis, the ancient harbour of Ravenna, which under Augustus was an important naval station. The name of Chiassi, which was destroyed by the Lombards in 728, is preserved in that of the church of Sant' Apollinare in Classe, which stands on the site of part of the old town. D. mentions it in connexion with the 'Pineta' or pine-forest, which extends along the shore of the Adriatic for several miles N. and S. of Ravenna, Purg. xxviii. 20. [Pineta.]

Chiassi²], Chiassi or Chiascio, stream in N. of Umbria, which rises in the hill near Gubbio, on which St. Ubaldo lived as a hermit before he was made Bishop of Gubbio, and enters a branch of the Tiber a few miles SE. of Perugia. St. Thomas Aquinas (in the Heaven of the Sun), in his description of the situation of Assisi, which stands on the SW. slope of Monte Subasio, between the streams of Tupino (on the E.) and Chiassi (on the W.), alludes to it as *l'acqua che discende Del colle eletto dal beato Ubaldo*, Par. xi. 43–4 [Ascesi].

Chiaveri, now Chiavari, town in Liguria, on the Riviera di Levante, some 20 miles E. of Genoa; mentioned by Pope Adrian V (in Circle V of Purgatory) in connexion with the Lavagna, which runs into the sea between that town and Sestri Levante, Purg. xix. 100 [Lavagna].

Chiesa, the Church, Par. v. 77; vi. 22; xxii. 82; Conv. iii. 6²¹; iv. 23¹⁴²; *Ecclesia*, Mon. ii. 13⁶⁰; iii. 3⁴²⁻¹³³, 6¹¹, 10⁵⁻¹³⁰, 13¹³⁻⁷⁶, 14¹⁻⁵⁰, 15⁷⁻⁶²; *Mater Ecclesia*, Mon. iii. 3⁴²; Epist. viii. 6¹⁰¹; *santa Chiesa*, Purg. iii. 137; xxiv. 22; Par. iv. 46; v. 35; vi. 95; x. 108; xxxii. 125; Conv. ii. 4³¹, 6³⁴; *Chiesa militante*, Par. xxv. 52; *Ecclesia militans*, Epist. viii. 4⁴²; *l'esercito di Cristo*, Par. xii. 37; *Sposa di Dio*, Par. x. 140; *Sposa di Cristo*, Par. xi. 32; xii. 43; xxvii. 40; xxxi. 3; xxxii. 128; *Sposa e Secretaria di Cristo*, Conv. ii. 6³³⁻⁴; *Sponsa Christi*, Epist. viii. 7¹⁰⁸, 11¹⁷⁹⁻⁸⁰; *Crucifixi Sponsa*, Epist. viii. 4⁴⁴,⁵¹; *bella Donna*, Inf.

xix. 57; *Vigna*, Par. xviii. 132; *Orto di Cristo*, Par. xii. 72, 104; xxvi. 64; *Barca di Pietro*, Par. xi. 119; *Navicella*, Purg. xxxii. 129; *Navicula Petri*, Epist. vi. 1[13-14]; *la Sedia che fu benigna . . . ai poveri giusti*, Par. xii. 88-9; *Apostolica Sedes*, Epist. viii. 2[26], 11[175]; *Chiesa di Roma*, Purg. xvi. 127; spoken of by St. Peter (in the Heaven of Fixed Stars) as *il loco mio*, Par. xxvii. 22; and by St. James (in the same) as *nostra Basilica*, Par. xxv. 30.

In the mystic Procession in the Terrestrial Paradise the Church is represented as a two-wheeled Car, *Carro*, Purg. xxix. 107, 151; xxx. 9, 61, 101; xxxii. 24, 104, 115, 126, 132; *divina basterna*, Purg. xxx. 16; *benedetto carco*, Purg. xxxii. 26; *trionfal veiculo*, Purg. xxxii. 119; *dificio santo*, Purg. xxxii. 142; *vaso*, Purg. xxxiii. 34. [Carro, Il [2].]

Childerico], Childeric III, last of the Merovingian Kings of France, surnamed 'Le Fainéant'; he was born c. 734, succeeded to the throne in 742, and was deposed by Pepin le Bref in March, 752. After his deposition he was compelled by Pepin to become a monk, and was shut up in the convent of Sithieu at St. Omer, where he died in 755. D. has apparently confused Charles, Duke of Lorraine, the last of the Carlovingian line, with Childeric, the last of the Merovingians, Purg. xx. 53-60. [Carlo [5].]

Chilon, of Lacedaemon (c. B.C. 590); one of the Seven Sages of Greece, Conv. iii. 11[38]. [Biante.]

Chirone, Chiron, the Centaur, son of Saturn and Philyra, daughter of Oceanus. Saturn, being enamoured of Philyra, and fearing the jealousy of his wife Rhea, changed himself into a horse, and in this shape begat Chiron, who hence had the form of a Centaur. C. educated Achilles, Aesculapius, Hercules, and many other famous Greeks.

D. places C., along with Nessus and Pholus, as leader of the Centaurs, who act as guardians of the Violent in Round 1 of Circle VII of Hell, Inf. xii. 65, 71, 77, 97 [Centauri]; Virgil, being questioned by Nessus as to his errand, replies that he will give his answer to Chiron, whereupon N. points out the latter to D., describing him as 'il gran Chirone, il qual nudrì Achille' (*vv.* 61-71); V. then approaches C., and asks him for an escort, which C. grants, bidding Nessus accompany them (*vv.* 83-99) [Nesso]; C. is mentioned again as the tutor of Achilles in connexion with the fact that Thetis took her son away from him and hid him in Scyros for fear he should be sent to the Trojan War, Purg. ix. 37; spoken of by G. del Virgilio as *Achilleus Chiron*, Ecl. R. 79. [Achille: Schiro.]

Chiusi, ancient Clusium, situated in the Valdichiana, close to the lake of the same name, on the borders of Tuscany and Umbria, midway between Florence and Rome.

Cacciaguida (in the Heaven of Mars) mentions Chiusi, together with Sinigaglia, and says that these two once-powerful cities were rapidly falling into decay, as Luni and Urbisaglia had already done, Par.

xvi. 73–8. Chiusi doubtless owed its decay to the malaria prevalent in the district. [Chiana.]

Chremes, imaginary personage, typical father in a comedy; introduced by Horace in the *Ars Poëtica*, in a passage (*vv.* 93–5) which D. quotes in illustration of his argument that the language of comedy is more lowly than that of tragedy, Epist. x. 10^{216}.

Christiana, De Doctrina. [*Doctrina Christiana, De.*]

Christiani. [**Cristiani.**]

Christianus, Christian; *fides Christiana*, Mon. ii. 12^3; *Christiana religio*, Mon. iii. 3^{132}. [**Cristiano.**]

Christus. [**Cristo.**]

Chrysippus, celebrated Stoic philosopher, born at Soli in Cilicia, B.C. 280; died B.C. 207. D. quotes from Cicero's *De Officiis* (iii. 10) the dictum of C. that a man who runs in a race should do his best to win, but should in no wise try to trip up his rival, Mon. ii. 8^{94-101}. [**Eurialo.**]

Ciacco, Florentine, contemporary and apparently acquaintance of D. (who has been identified with the poet Ciacco dell' Anguillaia), placed among the Gluttons in Circle III of Hell, Inf. vi. 52, 58; *una (ombra)*, *v.* 38; *anima trista*, *v.* 55; *quegli*, *v.* 85 [**Golosi**]; in conversation with D., C. foretells the future of the Bianchi and Neri parties in Florence (*vv.* 64–72) [**Bianchi**]; D. then inquires for news of five Florentines, Farinata degli Uberti (Inf. x. 32), Tegghiaio Aldobrandi (Inf. xvi. 41), Jacopo Rusticucci (Inf. xvi. 44), a certain Arrigo, and

Mosca de' Lamberti (Inf. xxviii. 106), whether they are in Heaven or Hell (*vv.* 77–84); C. replies that they are among the blackest souls, and that if D. goes far enough down into Hell he will see them (*vv.* 85–7).

Ciacco is the hero of one of the tales of the *Decameron* (ix. 8), in which he figures in company with two other Dantesque personages, Corso Donati and Filippo Argenti.

Ciampolo], name given by the commentators to a native of Navarre, who is placed by D. among the Barrators in Bolgia 5 of Circle VIII of Hell (Malebolge), and who describes himself as a retainer of King Thibaut II of Navarre, in whose service he practised jobbery for which he is now undergoing punishment, Inf. xxii. 48–54; *uno (peccatore)*, *v.* 32; *lo sciagurato*, *v.* 44; *quei*, *v.* 47; *il sorco*, *v.* 58; *lo spaurato*, *v.* 98; *lo Navarrese*, *v.* 121; *quegli*, *v.* 128; *quei*, *v.* 135; *il barattier*, *v.* 136 [**Barattieri: Tebaldo**[2]].

Cianfa, according to the old commentators, a member of the Donati family of Florence (supposed to be identical with a 'Dominus Cianfa de Donatis', mentioned in the will of Corso Donati, who in 1280 was one of the Guelf sureties in the peace of the Cardinal Latino, and who in 1282 was a member of the 'Consiglio del Capitano per il Sesto di Porta san Piero'); one of five Florentines (Inf. xxvi. 4–5) placed by D. among the Robbers in Bolgia 7 of Circle VIII of Hell (Malebolge), Inf. xxv. 43 [**Ladri**]; C. appears in the form of a serpent with six feet, which fastens on to one of the robbers in human shape, until gradually the two forms, of serpent and man, are blended together and become indistinguishable (*vv.* 52–78).

Cianghella, Florentine lady of ill repute, contemporary of D. ; said to have been the daughter of Arrigo della Tosa of Florence, and wife of Lito degli Alidosi of Imola, and to have died c. 1330 ; she is mentioned by Cacciaguida (in the Heaven of Mars), who, speaking of the degenerate state of Florence, says that in his day such a person as she would have been as great a marvel in that city as Cornelia would be now, Par. xv. 128 [**Corniglia**].

Cianghella is mentioned by Boccaccio in the *Corbaccio* as the type of a dissolute woman, and as having given her name to 'la setta Cianghellina', who followed her way of life. Benvenuto da Imola records instances of her disreputable conduct, which he had heard from his father, a neighbour of hers in Imola.

Ciapetta, Ugo, Hugh Capet, King of France, 987–996, the first king of the Capetian line ; placed by D. among the Avaricious in Circle V of Purgatory, Purg. xx. 49 ; *quello spirto, v.* 30 ; *esso, v.* 31 ; *anima, v.* 34 ; *egli, v.* 40 ; *esso, v.* 124 [**Avari**] ; after giving an account of the origin of the Capetian dynasty, Hugh Capet foretells the misdeeds of his descendants, from the annexation of Provence to the French crown, to the destruction of the Templars by Philip the Fair (*vv.* 40–93). [**Capeti : Carlo** [5] **: Table K.**]

The statements put by D. into the mouth of Hugh Capet as to the origin of the Capetian dynasty are in several respects at variance with the historical facts, and can only be explained on the supposition that D. has confused Hugh Capet with his father, Hugh the Great, some of them being applicable to the one, some to the other. The facts are as follows : Hugh the Great died in 956 ; Louis V, the last of the Carlovingians, died in 987, in which year Hugh Capet became king ; on his death in 996, he was succeeded by his son Robert, who had previously been crowned in 988. D. makes Hugh Capet say :—firstly, that he was the son of a butcher of Paris (*v.* 52), whereas common tradition assigned this origin not to Hugh Capet, but to his father Hugh the Great ; secondly, that when the Carlovingians came to an end he was so powerful that he was able to make his son king (*vv.* 53–60), whereas on the failure of the Carlovingian line Hugh Capet himself became king (987) ; and thirdly, that with his son the Capetian line began (*vv.* 59–60), whereas in fact it began with himself.

Cicero, Marcus Tullius Cicero, the celebrated Roman writer, philosopher, and statesman ; born B. C. 106, died B. C. 43. He was elected Consul, B. C. 63, and during his consulship crushed the famous Catiline conspiracy. D. alludes to this incident in his career, with especial reference to the fact that he was a 'novus homo' (probably from Sallust, *Catilin.* § 23, 6), Conv. iv. 5[172–6]. [**Catilina.**]

C. is placed among the great men of antiquity in Limbo, Inf. iv. 141 [**Limbo**] ; D. usually speaks of him as Tully, *Tullio,* Inf. iv. 141 ; Conv. i. 11[94], 12[19] ; ii. 9[66], 13[17], 16[4] ; iv. 5[174], 6[109], 8[9, 17], 12[55, 71], 15[123], 21[81], 22[15], 24[62, 93, 100], 25[95], 27[18], 111, 134, 151, 28[14, 44], 29[73] ; *Tullius,* Mon. ii. 5[16, 141, 142], 8[95], 10[22, 37] ; Epist. x. 19[320] ; *Cicero,* Mon. i. 1[23] ; ii. 5[54, 67, 84].

D. quotes Cicero's works up- wards of thirty times ; the following are quoted by name :—

De Officiis [**Officiis, De**]; *De Finibus* [**Finibus, De**] ; *De Amicitia* [**Amicitia, De**] ; *De Senectute* [**Senectute, De**] ; *De Inventione Rhetorica* (commonly known as *De Inventione*) [**Inventione, De**] ; *Paradoxa* [**Paradoxa**]; besides which D. made use of the *Academicae Quaestiones* [**Academicae Quaestiones**].

The saying ascribed by D. to Cicero, that 'the son of a worthy man ought to strive to bear good witness to his father', Conv. iv. 29$^{72-5}$, which has not been identified in any of Cicero's works, he probably got at secondhand from some collection of adages.

Cicilia, island of Sicily, Inf. xii. 108; Purg. iii. 116; *Sicilia*, Conv. iv. 26^{95}, ^{138}; V. E. i. 8^{57}, 10^{57}, 12^{31}; *Trinacria*, Par. viii. 67; V. E. i. 12^{15}; ii. 6^{48}; Ecl. ii. 71; alluded to as *l'isola del fuoco*, Par. xix. 131; *quella terra*, Par. xx. 62; the sufferings of the island under Dionysius, tyrant of Syracuse, Inf. xii. 107–8 [**Dionisio**[1]] ; Manfred (in Ante-purgatory) speaks of his daughter Constance, wife of Peter III of Aragon and Sicily, as *genitrice Dell' onor di Cicilia e d'Aragona*, Purg. iii. 115–6 [**Aragona**]; Charles Martel (in the Heaven of Venus) speaks of the island as *la bella Trinacria* (there being probably a special significance in his use of this particular name), and refers to the smoke from Aetna which overhangs its E. coast, Par. viii. 67–70 [**Catania : Trinacria**]; and adds

that his descendants would have been ruling in Sicily if the misgovernment of his grandfather, Charles I of Anjou, had not brought about the massacre of the French at the ' Sicilian Vespers' (*vv.* 71–5) [**Carlo**[1] : **Carlo**[3]]; the Eagle in the Heaven of Jupiter refers to the island as *l'isola del fuoco* (on account of the eruptions of Aetna), in connexion with Frederick II of Aragon (King of Sicily, 1296–1337), and alludes to the fact that Anchises died there, Par. xix. 130–2 [**Anchise** : **Federico**[3]]; the Eagle refers to it again, in allusion to its sufferings during the war between Frederick of Aragon and Charles II of Naples, as ' quella terra Che piange Carlo e Federico vivo', Par. xx. 62–3 [**Carlo**[2]]; Aeneas leaves there his aged followers in the care of Acestes, Conv. iv. 26$^{92-6}$ [**Aceste**]; trains Ascanius to arms there, Conv. iv. 26$^{96-9}$ [**Ascanio**]; and institutes games in memory of Anchises, Conv. iv. 26$^{137-8}$ [**Enea**]; Sicily one of the S. limits of the Italian language, V. E. i. 8$^{53-7}$; to be reckoned with Sardinia as on the right side of Italy, if the Apennines be taken as the dividing line (from N. to S.), V. E. i. 10$^{56-9}$; its dialect distinct from that of Apulia, V. E. i. 10$^{61-2}$; the seat of the Court (in the time of the Emperor Frederick II), whence the name Sicilian applied to Italian poetry, V. E. i. 12$^{30-5}$; the Sicilian dialect the most famous of all the Italian dialects, both because all poems written in Italian were called Sicilian, and because many important poems were written by Sicilians, V. E. i. 12$^{6-11}$; this fame a reproach to the princes of Italy, who neglected letters, V. E. i. 12$^{15-19}$; the common Sicilian dialect unworthy of preference, that spoken by the nobles worthy of commendation, but neither the Sicilian nor the Apulian to be reckoned the most beautiful dialect of Italy, V. E. i. 12$^{43-74}$; the Italian vulgar tongue employed by Sicilian poets, V. E. i. 19$^{15-17}$; the fruitless expedition of Charles of Valois against Sicily, V. E. ii. 6^{48} [**Carlo**^{4}]; Aetna the most rich in pasture of all the Sicilian mountains, Ecl. ii. 71–2. [**Aetna.**]

The name Sicily is sometimes loosely applied to the kingdom of the Two Sicilies, comprising Naples (Apulia and Calabria) and Sicily proper. This kingdom was ruled successively by Norman (1129-1194), Swabian (1194-1266), and Angevin (1266-1282) sovereigns [**Napoli: Puglia**]. In 1282 the Sicilians rose against the house of Anjou, and expelled the French, after the massacre known as the 'Sicilian Vespers' [**Vespro Siciliano**]. This revolt led to the separation of the two kingdoms, Sicily passing to the house of Aragon, while Naples remained in the hands of the Angevins [**Tables B, E.**]

Ciciliano, Sicilian, Inf. xxvii. 7; *Sicilianus*, V. E. i. 12$^{5, 6, 8, 33,}$ ^{44}; *Siculus*, V. E. i. 12^{71}; Ecl. ii. 72; *il bue Cicilian*, i. e. the brazen bull made by Perillus for Phalaris, tyrant of Agrigentum in Sicily, in which human beings were tortured by being roasted alive, and which was so constructed that the shrieks of the victims sounded like the bellowing of the bull, Inf. xxvii. 7–12 [**Perillo**]; the name Sicilian applied to Italian poetry from the fact that

the seat of the Court (in the time of Frederick II) was in Sicily, V. E. i. 12$^{8-9, \ 30-5}$; the Sicilian dialect, *vulgare Sicilianum*, V. E. i. 12$^{5, 6, 44}$; *Siculum vulgare*, V. E. i. 12^{71}; the mountains of Sicily, Ecl. ii. 72. [**Cicilia : Siculi.**]

Ciclope, Ciclopi. [**Cyclops : Cyclopes.**]

Cieldauro, church of San Pietro in Ciel d'Oro ('Golden Ceiling') at Pavia; mentioned by St. Thomas Aquinas (in the Heaven of the Sun) in connexion with Boëthius, who was buried there, Par. x. 128 [**Boezio**].

Cielo e Mondo, Di. [*Coelo, De.*]

Cielo Cristallino, Crystalline Heaven, Conv. ii. 4$^{11-12}$; 15^{122}; origin of the name, Conv. ii. 4$^{12-13}$; the ninth Heaven, Conv. ii. 4$^{9-13}$, 14^{62}; A. T. § 21$^{3-4}$; otherwise called the *Primum Mobile*, or First Movement, Par. xxx. 107; Conv. ii. 3$^{41-2}$, 4^{20}, 6^{149}, 15^{122}; Mon. i. 9^{11}; A. T. § 21^3; the origin of the motion of all the other Heavens, Conv. ii. 15$^{132-5}$; Inf. ix. 29; Par. xxvii. 106–8; xxviii. 70–1; its existence first conceived by Ptolemy to account for the complex motion of the Heaven of the Fixed Stars, Conv. ii. 3$^{36-45}$; its revolution accomplished in something under 24 hours, Conv. ii. 3$^{45-8}$; imperceptible to sense save for its motion, Conv. ii. 4$^{9-10}$; its almost inconceivable velocity caused by its longing to be united with the Empyrean, Conv. ii. 4$^{20-7}$; has its two poles 'firm, fixed, and immutable' as regards all things else, those of the lower Heavens being fixed only as regards themselves, Conv. ii. 4$^{48-51}$; like the other Heavens, has an equator or circle equidistant from each pole, where the motion is most rapid, Conv. ii. 4^{52-68}; resembles Moral Philosophy, inasmuch as it directs by its motion the daily revolutions of all the other Heavens, Conv. ii. 14^{62-3}, 15^{122-38}; if its motion were to cease a third part of the Heavens would be invisible to every part of the Earth, while there would be neither life nor measure of time on the latter, and the whole Universe would be in disorder, Conv. ii. 15^{139-57}; the largest of the corporeal Heavens (the Empyrean being incorporeal), Par. xxvii. 68; xxx. 39; is encircled by the Empyrean, and itself encircles all the other Heavens, Son. xxv. 1; Par. i. 122-3; ii. 113-14; xxiii. 112; xxvii. 112-13; the most rapid of the Heavens, Conv. ii. 4^{20}; Purg. xxxiii. 90; Par. i. 123; xiii. 24; xxvii. 99; its motion not measured by that of any of the other Heavens, but their motion measured by it, hence it is the origin of time, Par. xxvii. 115-19 (cf. Conv. ii. 15^{154-5}); 'has no other where than the mind of God,' Par. xxvii. 109-10; is perfectly uniform throughout, Par. xxvii. 100-1; A. T. § 21^{3-6}.

D. refers to the Crystalline Heaven as *la spera che più larga gira*, Son. xxv. 1; *il ciel che tutto gira*, Inf. ix. 29; *il cielo che più alto festina*, Purg. xxxiii. 90; *il ciel che ha maggior fretta*, Par. i. 123; *corpo nella cui virtute L'esser di tutto suo contento giace*, Par. ii. 113-14; *il ciel che tutti gli altri avanza*, Par. xiii. 24; *Lo real manto di tutti i volumi Del mondo*, Par. xxiii. 112-

13; *testo*, Par. xxvii. 118; *il maggior corpo*, Par. xxvii. 68; xxx. 39; *ciel velocissimo*, Par. xxvii. 99; *volume*, Par. xxviii. 14; *il ciel che tutto quanto rape L'altro universo seco*, Par. xxviii. 70-1.

The Crystalline Heaven is the ninth in D.'s conception of the Universe, Conv. ii. 4^9, 14^{62}; A. T. § 21^4 [**Paradiso**[1]: Universo]; resembles Moral Philosophy, Conv. ii. 14^{62-3}, 15^{122-64}; it is presided over by the Seraphim, Par. xxviii. 71-2 [**Serafini**].

Cielo decimo. [Cielo Empireo.]

Cielo del Sole. [Sole, Cielo del.]

Cielo della Luna. [Luna, Cielo della.]

Cielo delle Stelle Fisse. [Cielo Stellato.]

Cielo di Giove. [Giove, Cielo di.]

Cielo di Marte. [Marte, Cielo di.]

Cielo di Mercurio. [Mercurio, Cielo di.]

Cielo di Saturno. [Saturno, Cielo di.]

Cielo di Venere. [Venere, Cielo di.]

Cielo Empireo, Empyrean, the highest Heaven, the abode of the Deity, Inf. ii. 21; Conv. ii. 4^{14}, 15^{165}; Epist. x. 24^{448}, 26^{509}; meaning of the name, Conv. ii. 4^{15-16}; Epist. x. 24^{448-50}; the tenth or last Heaven, Conv. ii. $4^{13-15, 25}$, 6^{101}, 14^{63}; Purg. xv. 52; Par. xxii. 62; xxiii. 108; Epist. x. 24^{443}; or, regarded from the opposite point of view, the first, Purg. xxx. 1; Par. iv. 34; Epist.

x. 25^{462}, $26^{482, \; 491}$; in it is contained the *Primum Mobile*, Par. i. 122–3; ii. 113–14; xxvii. 112–14 [Cielo Cristallino]; contains all bodies and is contained by none, Conv. ii. 4^{35-7}; Purg. xxvi. 63; Epist. x. 24^{443-5}, 25^{455}; within it all bodies move, Epist. x. 24^{455}; but itself remains motionless in eternal peace, Conv. ii. $4^{17-19, 25, 28}$, 15^{165-7}; Par. i. 122; ii. 112; Epist. x. 24^{446}; immaterial, Par. xxx. 39; Epist. x. $24^{447, 451}$; composed purely of light, Par. xxiii. 102; xxx. 39; of which it receives more than any other of the Heavens, Par. i. 4; Epist. x. 25^{469-70}, 26^{492}; does not exist in space, but in the divine Mind, Conv. ii. 4^{37-9}; the abode of Angels and of the Blessed, Conv. ii. 4^{30-2}; Par. xxx. 43–xxxi. 27; and of the Deity, Conv. ii. 4^{28-9}; Par. xxxiii. 52–141; hence replete with love, Purg. xxvi. 63; Epist. x. 24^{452}; resembles the divine science of Theology, inasmuch as it is full of peace, Conv. ii. 14^{63-4}, 15^{165-7}; whereas the other Heavens are presided over by the several Angelic Orders or Intelligences, God Himself is the Intelligence of the Highest Heaven, Conv. ii. 6^{99-102}; Par. xxvii. 112; xxxiii. 124–6.

D. refers to the Empyrean as *cielo divinissimo e quieto*, Conv. ii. 4^{25}; *luogo quieto e pacifico*, Conv. ii. 4^{28}; *cielo quieto*, Conv. ii. 14^{63}; *il sovrano edificio del mondo*, Conv. ii. 4^{35}; *spera suprema*, Purg. xv. 52; Par. xxiii. 108; *primo cielo*, Purg. xxx. 1; *primo giro*, Par. iv. 34; *primum coelum*, Epist. x. 25^{462}, $26^{482,491}$; *ultima spera*, Par. xxii. 62; *coelum supremum*, Epist. x. 24^{443}; *decimo cielo*, Conv.

ii. 4^{25}, 6^{101}, 14^{63}; *ampio loco*, Inf. ii. 84; *il ciel . . . Ch' è pien d'amore e più ampio si spazia*, Purg. xxvi. 62–3; *il ciel che più della luce prende*, Par. i. 4; *il ciel sempre quieto, Nel qual si volge quel ch' ha maggior fretta*, Par. i. 122–3; *il ciel della divina pace*, Par. ii. 112; *il ciel più chiaro*, Par. xxiii. 102; *il ciel ch' è pura luce*, Par. xxx. 39.

The Heaven of the Empyrean is the tenth in D.'s conception of the Universe, Purg. xv. 52; Par. xxii. 62; xxiii. 108; Conv. ii. 4^{25}, 6^{101}, 14^{63}; Epist. x. 24^{443} [Paradiso¹]; resembles Theology, Conv. ii. 14^{63-4}, 15^{165-7}; it is presided over by the Deity, Conv. ii. 6^{99-102}.

In the Celestial Rose in the Empyrean are the seats of the Blessed, the arrangement of which is explained to D. by St. Bernard, Par. xxxi. 115–17; xxxii. 1–36 [Rosa].

Cielo nono. [Cielo Cristallino.]

Cielo ottavo. [Cielo Stellato.]

Cielo primo. [Luna, Cielo della.]

Cielo quarto. [Sole, Cielo del.]

Cielo quinto. [Marte, Cielo di.]

Cielo secondo. [Mercurio, Cielo di.]

Cielo sesto. [Giove, Cielo di.]

Cielo settimo. [Saturno, Cielo di.]

Cielo Stellato, Starry Heaven, or Heaven of the Fixed Stars, V.N. § 2^{10}; Conv. ii. 3^{43}, 4^{75}, 15^{18}; *coelum stellatum*, A.T. § 21^{9}; *cielo delle Stelle Fisse*, Conv. ii. 3^{23}, 4^{8}; *la spera stellata*, Conv. ii. 14^{59}; *l'ottava spera*, Conv. ii. 3^{24}, 14^{59}; Par. ii. 64; *octava sphaera*, A.T. § 21^{9-10}; *l'ottavo cielo*, Conv. ii. 4^{8};

lo ciel . . . che ha tante vedute, Par. ii. 115; *il ciel, cui tanti lumi fanno bello,* Par. ii. 130; *il cerchio che più tardi in cielo è torto,* Purg. xi. 108 (cf. Conv. ii. 15); erroneously believed by Aristotle, who held that there were only eight Heavens, to be the outermost and last of the Heavens, Conv. ii. 3$^{19-25}$; Ptolemy, noticing its complex motion, conceived that there must be another Heaven beyond, viz. the *Primum Mobile,* Conv. ii. 3$^{36-45}$; the Heaven of the Fixed Stars the eighth in order of position, Conv. ii. 3$^{23-5}$, 4$^{8-9}$; A. T. § 21^{9}; those of its stars which are nearest to its equator possessed of the greatest virtue, Conv. ii. 4$^{75-7}$; resembles Physics and Metaphysics, Conv. ii. 14$^{59-62}$, 15$^{4-121}$; reasons for this resemblance, Conv. ii. 15$^{18-121}$; the number of its stars estimated by the wise men of Egypt at 1,022, Conv. ii. 15$^{18-22}$ [**Stelle Fisse**]; its Galaxy, Conv. ii. 15$^{44-86}$ [**Galassia**]; one of its poles visible, the other invisible, Conv. ii. 15$^{10-11}$, $^{87-94}$; its double motion, one from E. to W. (i. e. the daily motion of the heavens), and another hardly perceptible from W. to E. (i. e. the precession of the equinoxes), this latter being so slow that it only advances one degree in a hundred years, and hence the revolution will never be completed, the world being already in its last age, and only a little more than a sixth part of its revolution having been accomplished since the beginning of the world, Conv. ii. 15 $^{12-14, 95-118}$; if the motion of the *Primum Mobile* were to be suspended, and only this motion of the Starry Heaven to remain, a third part of

the Heavens would not yet have been seen from the Earth, and the Sun and planets would be hidden for half their revolutions, Conv. ii. 15$^{139-52}$ [**Cielo Cristallino**]; the Starry Heaven had moved one-twelfth part of a degree towards the E. since the birth of Beatrice (which took place therefore about eight years and four months before), V. N. § 2$^{9-12}$ [**Beatrice**].

The Heaven of the Fixed Stars is the eighth in D.'s conception of Paradise, Par. ii. 64; Conv. ii. 3^{24}, 4^{8}, 14^{50}; A. T. § 21$^{9-10}$ [**Paradiso**[1]]; resembles Physics in three respects and Metaphysics also in three respects, Conv. ii. 15$^{4-121}$; it is presided over by the Cherubim [**Cherubini**]. Inside of the Empyrean revolves the *Primum Mobile,* in which originate the influences which are distributed by the Starry Heaven to the various spheres which make up the Universe, Par. i. 122–3; ii. 112–17.

Cielo terzo. [Venere, Cielo di.]

Cielo d'Alcamo. [Ciullo d'Alcamo.]

Cimabue, Giovanni Cimabue, the great Florentine artist, and master of Giotto, commonly regarded as the regenerator of painting in Italy; he was born c. 1240, and died in or after 1302, in which year, as is proved by documentary evidence, he was painting in Pisa; he was buried in Santa Maria del Fiore at Florence. His portrait, according to Vasari, was introduced by Simone da Siena in one of his frescoes in the Spanish Chapel of Santa Maria Novella at Florence.

Oderisi (in Circle I of Purgatory)

mentions him in illustration of the brief endurance of fame, that of C. having been speedily eclipsed by the fame of Giotto, Purg. xi. 94–6.

Cincinnato, Lucius Quintius Cincinnatus, one of the heroes of the old Roman republic, the Roman model of frugality and integrity; he lived on his farm, which he cultivated himself. In B. C. 458 he was called from the plough to assume the dictatorship, in order to deliver the Roman army from the Aequians; having accomplished this task, and defeated the enemy, he returned to his farm, after holding the dictatorship only sixteen days. In 439 he was a second time appointed dictator, at the age of eighty.

The Emperor Justinian (in the Heaven of Mercury) mentions him in connexion with the exploits of the Roman Eagle, referring to him (in allusion to his surname Cincinnatus, i. e. 'shaggy-haired') as *Quinzio che dal cirro Negletto fu nomato,* Par. vi. 46–7; he is mentioned again (as *Cincinnato*) by Cacciaguida (in the Heaven of Mars), who, speaking of the degenerate state of Florence, says that in his day such a person as Lapo Salterello would have been as great a marvel in that city as Cincinnatus would be now, Par. xv. 127–9 [**Lapo [2]**]; his laying down of the dictatorship and voluntary return to the plough is referred to, Conv. iv. 5^{130-4}; and, with a reference to Livy (iii. 28) (though D. was more probably thinking of the account of Orosius, ii. 12, §§ 7, 8), and to Cicero (*Fin.* ii. 4), *Cincinnatus,* Mon. ii. 5^{76-89}.

Cincinnatus.   [Cincinnato.]

Cino, Cino (i. e. Guittoncino) di ser Francesco de' Sinibuldi of Pistoja, commonly known as Cino da Pistoja, the friend of D., and one of the principal poets of the new lyric school in Italy (which comprised, among others, Lapo Gianni, Guido Cavalcanti, and Dante), was born at Pistoja c. 1270; he was a lawyer by profession, and was the author of several legal works, the most important of which is the *Lectura in Codicem,* a commentary on the first nine books of the Code of Justinian; after studying at Pistoja (whence he appears to have been exiled with the Neri from 1301 to 1306) and Bologna, he received his doctorate at Bologna (1314), and lectured on law successively at Siena (1321), Florence (1324), Perugia (1326), where he had among his pupils the famous Bartolo da Sassoferrato, and Naples (1330). Towards the close of his life he returned to Pistoja, which he had revisited at various intervals, and held several official posts in his native town, where he died at the end of 1336 or the beginning of 1337. He was buried in the Cathedral of San Jacopo at Pistoja, where a monument to him by Cellino di Nese of Siena is still to be seen; on it is a bas-relief representing Cino lecturing to nine pupils, among them Francesco Petrarca, who afterwards composed a sonnet on his death. Among Cino's friends, besides D., who in the *De Vulgari Eloquentia* usually speaks of himself as 'amicus Cini' (V. E. i. 10^{30}, 17^{25}; ii. 2^{93}, 5^{49}, 6^{73}), were Onesto da Bologna, Cecco d'Ascoli, Bosone da Gubbio, and his pupil Petrarca.

Cino is said to have been one of those who replied to D.'s sonnet, 'A ciascun' alma presa, e gentil core' (V. N. § 3[77]); among numerous poems of his which have been preserved, several of them addressed to D., is a *canzone* on the death of Beatrice, one on the death of the Emperor Henry VII, and another on the death of D. himself. His love-poems are said to have been inspired by his passion for Selvaggia, daughter of Filippo Vergiolesi of Pitecchio, who afterwards married Focaccia de' Cancellieri of Pistoja.

D. addressed two sonnets to Cino, Son. xxxiv, xlvi; and a letter ('Exulanti Pistoriensi Florentinus exul immeritus'), Epist. iv; Cino is named, Son. xxxiv. 2; xlvi. 12; *Cinus Pistoriensis*, V. E. i. 10[30], 13[38], 17[24-5]; ii. 2[82], 5[47]; *Cinus*, V. E. ii. 2[91]; *Cinus de Pistorio*, V. E. ii. 6[70]; he is addressed by D. as *carissime*, Epist. iv. 1[3]; *frater carissime*, Epist. iv. 5[50]; his poems are quoted, V. E. ii. 2[92], 5[48], 6[71]; D. couples C. with himself as having written poems in the vulgar tongue, V. E. i. 10[28-31]; and with Guido Cavalcanti, Lapo Gianni, and himself, as having rejected the Tuscan dialect, C. being mentioned last on account of D.'s hatred to Pistoja, V. E. i. 13[33-9]; the excellence of the vulgar tongue exemplified in the *canzoni* of C. and D., V. E. i. 17[18-26]; C. the poet of love, D. the poet of rectitude, V. E. ii. 2[82-3]; he and D. both made use of eleven-syllabled verses, V. E. ii. 5[39-50]; and both employed the most excellent form of *canzone*, V. E. ii. 6[70-3].

Cinus Pistoriensis. [Cino.]

Cinyras, King of Cyprus, son of Apollo, and father of Adonis by his own daughter Myrrha, who deceived him by disguising herself as another woman; D. alludes to the incest of C., Inf. xxx. 38–41; and compares Florence to Myrrha, Epist. vii. 7[146-7]. [Mirra.]

Ciolus, Ciolo, said to be the name of one of the Florentine exiles who submitted to the degrading terms imposed upon those who were desirous of returning to Florence. D. says in his letter to a Florentine friend, in which he scornfully rejects any such terms for himself, that it would ill become a man who was familiar with philosophy so far to humiliate himself as to submit to be treated after the manner of Ciolo and other infamous wretches, 'more cujusdam Cioli et aliorum infamium', Epist. ix. 3[32-6].

This Ciolo has been identified with the Ciolo degli Abati, who, alone of his house, was expressly excepted by name from the decree known as the 'Riforma di messer Baldo d'Aguglione' issued in 1311 (Sept. 2) against the contumacious exiles, D. being one of them.

Cione de' Tarlati. [Guccio de' Tarlati.]

Ciotto di Gerusalemme. [Gerusalemme.]

Cipri, Cyprus, the most easterly island in the Mediterranean; mentioned by Pier da Medicina (in Bolgia 9 of Circle VIII of Hell) together with Majorca, one of the most westerly, to indicate the whole length of the Mediterranean Sea, Inf. xxviii. 82; it is alluded to by the Eagle in the Heaven of Jupiter by the mention of two of its chief cities, Famagosta and Nicosia, with reference to the sufferings of the island under the misgovernment of Henry II of Lusignan, Par. xix. 145–7. [Arrigo⁸.]

Ciprigna, Cypriote, name applied by D. to the planet Venus, Cyprus having been regarded as the birthplace of the goddess, Par. viii. 2 [Venere¹].

Circe, the enchantress Circe, daughter of Helios (the Sun) and Perse, who dwelt in the island of Aeaea, upon which Ulysses was cast, and had the power of transforming men into beasts; she is mentioned by Ulysses (in Bolgia 8 of Circle VIII of Hell), who describes how he stayed more than a year with her in the neighbourhood of Gaeta, before Aeneas had so named it (*Aen.* vii. 1–4, 10), Inf. xxvi. 91–3 [Ulisse]; Guido del Duca (in Circle II of Purgatory) compares the inhabitants of the Valdarno to the men transformed by her into beasts (*Aen.* vii. 15, 17–20), Purg. xiv. 40–2.

Ciriatto, one of the ten demons in Bolgia 5 of Circle VIII of Hell (Malebolge), deputed by Malacoda to escort D. and Virgil, Inf. xxi. 122; xxii. 55; he is represented as being tusked like a boar ('sannuto'), Inf. xxi. 122; and with one of his tusks he rips up the barrator Ciampolo, Inf. xxii. 55–7 [Alichino : Ciampolo : Malebranche].

Ciro, Cyrus the elder, founder of the Persian Empire, son of Cambyses, a Persian noble, and of a daughter of Astyages, King of Media; he led the Persians against Astyages, defeated him and took him prisoner, and became King of the Medes, B. C. 559; conquered the kingdom of Lydia and took Croesus prisoner, B. C. 546; conquered Babylon, B. C. 538; was defeated and slain in a battle against the Massagetae, a Scythian people, B. C. 529.

D. includes him among the examples of defeated pride in Circle I of Purgatory, and refers to the story (which he got from Orosius, *Hist.* ii. 7, § 6) of the vengeance of Tomyris, Queen of the Massagetae, whose son he had slain, how after his defeat and death she had his head cut off and thrown into a vessel filled with human gore, and mocked it, saying, 'For blood thou hast thirsted, drink thy fill', Purg. xii. 56 [Superbi]; his conquest of Babylon, and dream of universal empire, and his subsequent defeat and death at the hands of Tomyris, are referred to, *Cyrus*, Mon. ii. 9⁴³⁻⁸ [Tamiri].

Cirra, Cirrha, town in Phocis, on the Crissaean Gulf, about fifteen miles SW. of Delphi, the seat of the oracle of Apollo, whence Cirrha was sometimes used as a synonym of Delphi; D. mentions it in connexion with Apollo, Par. i. 35–6.

Citerea, Cytherea, name of Venus, who was so called from Cythera (now Cerigo), an island off the SE. point of Laconia, near which she is said to have risen from the foam of the sea; D. applies the name to the planet Venus, the time indicated being the early morning before dawn, Purg. xxvii. 95. [Venere².]

Città di Castello. [Castellana Civitas.]

Ciuffagni], one of the Florentine

families which received knighthood from the Marquis Hugh of Brandenburg, 'il gran barone', Par. xvi. 128. [**Ugo di Brandimborgo.**]

Ciullo d'Alcamo], author (called by some Cielo d'Alcamo or Cielo dal Camo) of the poem (written between 1231 and 1250), the third line of which is quoted by D. as an example of the Sicilian dialect as spoken by the lower classes, V. E. i. 12^{50}.

Alcamo is a town in the NW. of Sicily, about twenty-five miles SW. of Palermo. Ciullo is said to be an abbreviation of Vincenciullo, the diminutive of Vincenzio.

Civita Castellana. [**Castellana Civitas.**]

Civitate Dei, De, St. Augustine's work (in twenty-two books) *On the City of God,* an apologetic treatise (written between 413 and 426) in vindication of Christianity and the Christian Church; his comparison (*Civ. Dei* xvi. 2) of the significant and insignificant parts of a narrative to the share and other parts of a plough, Mon. iii. 4$^{51-9}$ [**Agostino**^{2}]. D. was also indebted to this work for information as to Pythagoras and the Seven Sages of Greece [**Biante : Pittagora**].

Clemens. [**Clemente**^{2}.]

Clemente^1; Clement IV (Guy Foulquois), a native of Languedoc; created Cardinal (by Urban IV, whom he succeeded), 1261; elected Pope at Perugia, Oct. 8, 1264; died at Viterbo, Nov. 29, 1268.

Manfred (in Ante-purgatory) mentions him in connexion with the Bishop of Cosenza, who by his orders disinterred M.'s body from its grave

beneath the heap of stones at the bridge of Benevento, and had it cast outside the limits of the kingdom of Naples, Purg. iii. 124–9 [**Benevento : Manfredi**]. Some think Clement IV is included among the Popes mentioned by Nicholas III (in Bolgia 3 of Circle VIII of Hell), Inf. xix. 73–4 [**Niccolò**^{2}].

Clemente^2], Clement V (Bertrand de Goth), a native of Gascony; appointed Archbishop of Bordeaux by Boniface VIII, 1299; elected Pope (in his absence) at Perugia, June 5, 1305, in succession to Benedict XI; crowned at Lyons, Nov. 14 of the same year; died at Roquemaure, near Avignon, April 20, 1314. It was during the pontificate of Clement V, who appears never to have entered Italy, that the Papal See was removed to Avignon, where it remained in what Italian writers call the 'Babylonian Captivity' for over seventy years.

Clement owed his election to the influence of Philip the Fair, and was in consequence little more than the creature of the French king, whose behests he was forced to execute one after another. When in 1308, on the assassination of the Emperor Albert of Austria, the Imperial crown became vacant, Clement was pressed by Philip to support the candidature of his brother, Charles of Valois. Ostensibly the Pope complied, but, dreading any further extension of the formidable power of France, he secretly exerted all his influence against Charles, and favoured the claims of his rival, Henry of Luxemburg, who was elected as Henry VII. When the new Emperor descended into Italy to assert his imperial rights Clement for a time loyally co-operated with him; but, yielding to the menaces of the French king, he gradually withdrew his support, leaving Henry to carry out his task alone, unaided, if not actually opposed, by the Papal influence. Clement survived the Emperor he had betrayed less than a year.

D. assigns to Clement, who is not mentioned by name in the *D. C.*, a place among the simoniacal Popes in Bolgia 3 of Circle VIII of Hell (Maleboge), Inf. xix. 82–7 [Simo· niaci]; Nicholas III, who is already in Hell, foretells his coming there next after Boniface VIII (the intervening Pope, Benedict XI, having by his uprightness escaped condemnation), speaking of him as ' a lawless pastor from the Westward ' (i. e. from Gascony) ' of fouler works' than Boniface (*vv.* 82–4); and alludes to his dealings with Philip the Fair in the matter of his election to the Papacy, comparing him to Jason, ' who laboured underhand to to be high-priest' (*Macc.* iv. 7) by bribing King Antiochus (*vv.* 85–7) [Antioco : Jasone²: Niccolò²]; his dealings with Philip are alluded to again (by Hugh Capet in Circle V of Purgatory) with especial reference to the destruction of the Templars, Purg. xx. 91–3 [Templari]; and also in the mystical Procession in the Terrestrial Paradise, in which the Church, with especial reference to Boniface VIII and Clement V, is figured as a whore ('puttana sciolta', ' fuia'), who dallies with a giant (Philip IV), Purg. xxxii. 148–56; the removal of the Papal See to Avignon being alluded to, *vv.* 157– 60 [Filippo²]; Cacciaguida (in the Heaven of Mars) refers to his betrayal of the Emperor Henry VII, and in allusion to his nationality speaks of him as *il Guasco*, Par. xvii. 82 [Arrigo²]; St. Peter (in the Heaven of Fixed Stars), in reference to the simony and extortions of him and John XXII (a native of Cahors), says ' Del sangue nostro Caorsini e Guaschi S'apparecchian di bere', Par. xxvii. 58–9 [Caorsino: Guasco]; finally, Beatrice (in the Empyrean) denounces C.'s treachery to Henry VII (these being her last words in the poem), foretelling that his death (April 20, 1314) shall follow hard upon that of the Emperor (Aug. 24, 1313), and that for his simony he shall be thrust into Hell, making Boniface VIII go lower down, Par. xxx. 142–8 [Bonifazio¹].

D. mentions Clement in his letter to the Princes of Italy, in connexion with his support of Henry VII in Italy, *Clemens*, Epist. v. 10¹⁶⁷ ; and, in his letter to the Italian Cardinals at Carpentras, refers to his death, and to his removal of the Papal See to Avignon, Epist. viii. 10¹⁴³⁻⁵, 11¹⁷⁷⁻⁸ ; in the same letter he and Philip the Fair are typified as Alcimus and Demetrius, Epist. viii. 4⁶⁵ [Alcimus].

Clemenza, Clemence of Hungary, daughter of Charles Martel, titular King of Hungary, by his wife, Clemence of Hapsburg, daughter of the Emperor Rudolf I; she was married in 1315 (as his second wife) to Louis X of France, and died in 1328 ; D. apostrophizes her (after

his interview with her father in the
Heaven of Venus) as *bella Clemenza*
(she being at that time, i. e. in 1300,
the assumed date of the Vision,
seven or eight years old), Par. ix. 1
[Carlo [3]].

Cleobulo, Cleobulus, of Lindus
in Rhodes (c. B. C. 580); one of the
Seven Sages of Greece, Conv. iii.
11 [40]. [Biante.]

Cleopa], Cleophas, one of the
two disciples to whom Christ appeared on the road to Emmaus after
His resurrection (*Luke* xxiv. 13–
35); alluded to, Purg. xxi. 8.

Cleopatra, Queen of Egypt,
daughter of Ptolemy Auletes, celebrated for her beauty. At the death
of her father (B. C. 51) she became
joint sovereign with her brother
Ptolemy, but was expelled from the
throne by the guardians of the latter.
She was replaced upon the throne
by Julius Caesar, by whom she had
a son, Caesarion. After Caesar's
death she became the mistress of
Mark Antony, and was present with
him at the battle of Actium, where
he was defeated by Octavianus.
She then fled to Alexandria, and,
Antony having stabbed himself, tried
to gain the love of Augustus; but
failing in this, and seeing that he was
determined to carry her captive to
Rome, she put an end to her life with
the poison of an asp (B. C. 30).

D. places C. among the Lustful
in Circle II of Hell, speaking of her
as *Cleopatras lussuriosa*, Inf. v. 63
[Lussuriosi]; the Emperor Justinian (in the Heaven of Mercury)
mentions her in connexion with the
victories of the Roman Eagle, and
refers to her flight from Actium

and to her death, *la trista Cleopatra*,
Par. vi. 76–8.

Cleopatras. [Cleopatra.]

Cleto, Cletus (or Anacletus),
Bishop of Rome from 76 (or 78)
to 88 (or 90), successor of Linus,
who is held to have been the immediate successor of St. Peter. C., who
was martyred under Domitian, is mentioned by St. Peter (in the Heaven
of Fixed Stars), together with Linus,
in connexion with their martyrdom
and his own, Par. xxvii. 41 [Lino [1]].

Climenè, Clymene, mother of
Phaëthon by Phoebus. Phaëthon's
comrade, Epaphus, having insinuated
that he was not the son of Phoëbus,
C. swore to him by Phoebus himself
that he was truly the son of the god,
and urged him to go and ask Phoebus in person. The result was that
Phaëthon induced his father to let
him drive his chariot, an enterprise
that proved fatal to him (Ovid,
Metam. i. 750 ff.) [Fetonte]. D.
compares himself, in his uncertainty
as to what Cacciaguida (in the Heaven of Mars) was going to prophesy
about his fate, to Phaëthon, when he
went to his mother Clymene to
learn if he were really the son of
Phoebus, Par. xvii. 1–6.

Cliò, Clio, muse of History;
mentioned by Virgil, addressing
Statius (in Purgatory), in reference to
the fact that the latter had invoked
her at the beginning of the *Thebaid*
(i. 41; cf. x. 630), thus proving that
he was a pagan, Purg. xxii. 58.

Cloelia, Roman maiden, one of
the hostages given to Porsena, King
of Clusium, who made her escape
and swam across the Tiber to Rome,
but was sent back by the Romans.

Porsena was so struck with her exploit that he set her at liberty, together with some of the other hostages.

D. refers to the incident of her escape (his account being borrowed from Orosius, *Hist.* ii. 5, § 3), Mon. ii. 4⁶⁵⁻⁷⁰.

Cloto, Clotho, the spinning fate, the youngest of the three fates, who at the birth of every mortal was supposed to wind on the distaff of Lachesis, the allotting fate, a certain amount of yarn, the duration of the individual's life being determined by the length of time it took to spin. [**Atropòs.**]

Clotho and Lachesis are mentioned by Virgil, who explains to Statius (in Purgatory) that D.'s life has not yet run its course, Purg. xxi. 25–7. [**Lachesìs.**]

Clugnì, Cluny, town in France, about ten miles NW. of Macon, the site of a famous Benedictine abbey, founded in 910; some modern edd. read *Clugnì*, instead of *Cologna*, Inf. xxiii. 63. [**Cologna.**]

Cocito, Cocytus, river of Hell, whose waters are frozen and form a vast sheet of ice in the nethermost pit, in which, immersed to various depths, and in various postures, are placed the four classes of Traitors, Inf. xiv. 119; xxxi. 123; xxxiii. 156; xxxiv. 52; *stagno,* Inf. xiv. 119 (cf. *Aen.* vi. 323); *lago,* Inf. xxxii. 23; *la ghiaccia,* Inf. xxxii. 35; xxxiv. 29; *la gelatina,* Inf. xxxii. 60; *i gelati guazzi, v.* 72; *là dove i peccatori stanno freschi, v.* 117; *la gelata,* Inf. xxxiii. 91; *la fredda crosta, v.* 109; *le gelate croste,* Inf. xxxiv. 75. [**Traditori.**]

Like Acheron, Styx, and Phle-

gethon, C. owes its origin to the tears of the 'gran veglio di Creta' (Inf. xiv. 112–19) [**Creta**]; these unite in a stream which under various names flows down to the bottom of Hell, where it forms Cocytus, the waters of which are collected into a lake, and frozen by the wind generated by the wings of Lucifer (Inf. xxxiv. 46–52) [**Fiumi Infernali : Lucifero**].

Coelesti Hierarchia, De, treatise *On the Celestial Hierarchy*, reputed to be the work of Dionysius the Areopagite; his doctrine that every essence and virtue proceeds from the First Cause, and is reflected, as it were, from the higher to the lower Intelligences, Epist. x. 21⁴⁰⁰⁻⁶ [**Dionisio ²**].

Coelo, De ¹, Aristotle's treatise *On the Heavens*; quoted by D. under two titles, *Di Cielo e Mondo*, Conv. ii. 3²⁹, ⁶¹, 4³⁴, 5¹³; iii. 5⁵⁴, 9¹¹¹; iv. 9²⁶; *De Coelo et Mundo*, A.T. §§ 12⁴⁴, 13⁴¹; and *De Coelo*, Epist. x. 27⁵¹¹⁻¹²; A.T. § 21⁵⁶. It may be noted that D. appears at times to be quoting rather from the *De Coelo et Mundo* of Albertus Magnus (which is a commentary on Aristotle's treatise) than from the *De Coelo* itself, which however was usually quoted by the title *De Coelo et Mundo* in the Middle Ages.

D. quotes from it Aristotle's erroneous opinion that there were only eight Heavens, the eighth and outer one being that of the Fixed Stars, also that the Heaven of the Sun was next to that of the Moon, Conv. ii. 3¹⁹⁻³⁰ (*Coel.* ii. 10, 12); his observation of the occultation of Mars by the Moon, Conv. ii. 3⁵⁹⁻⁶⁵ (*Coel.* ii. 12); his opinion that the Empyrean is the abode of blessed spirits, Conv. ii. 4^{30-4} (*Coel.* i. 3, 9); that the celestial Intelligences equal in number the celestial revolutions, Conv. ii. 5^{12-17} (*Coel.* i. 8); his rejection of the Platonic theory that the Earth revolves on its own axis, Conv. iii. 5^{53-8} (*Coel.* ii. 8, 12, 14); his opinion that the stars have no change save that of local motion, Conv. iii. 9^{109-11} (*Coel.* ii. 8); that the jurisdiction of Nature has fixed limits, Conv. iv. 9^{21-7} (*Coel.* i. 2, 7); that the material of the Heavens increases in perfection with its remoteness from the Earth, Epist. x.27^{511-15} (*Coel.* i. 2); that bodies are 'heavy' or 'light' in respect of motion, A. T. § 12^{42-4} (*Coel.* iv. 1); that God and Nature always work for the best, A. T. § 13^{39-41} (*Coel.* i. 4); that to inquire into the reasons for God's laws is presumptuous and foolish, they being beyond our understanding, A. T. § 21^{56} (*Coel.* ii. 5). [**Aristotile**.]

D. was also indebted to the *De Coelo* (ii. 13) for the Pythagorean theory as to the constitution of the universe, with the central place occupied by fire, round which revolve the Earth and a 'counter-Earth' (*antictona*), Conv. iii. 5^{29-41}. [**Antictona : Pittagora**.]

Coelo, De[2]], treatise of Albertus Magnus, otherwise known as *De Coelo et Mundo*, a commentary upon the Aristotelian treatise of the same name [*Coelo, De*[1]]; from here (ii. 3) D. got the opinions of Aristotle and Ptolemy as to the number and order of the several heavens, Conv. ii. 3^{36-45}. [**Alberto**[1].]

Coelo et Mundo, De. [*Coelo, De.*]

Coelum Empyreum. [Cielo Empireo.]

Coelum Stellatum. [Cielo Stellato.]

Colchi, Colchians, inhabitants of Colchis; mentioned by Virgil, in connexion with the expedition of Jason and the Argonauts in search of the golden fleece, Inf. xviii. 87. [Colco : Jasone[1].]

Colchus, Colchian; *vellera colcha*, 'the golden fleece', Ecl. ii. 1. [Colco.]

Colco, Colchis, country of Asia, bounded on the W. by the Euxine, on the N. by the Caucasus, on the E. by Asian Iberia; famous as the land to which Jason and the Argonauts sailed in search of the golden fleece.

D. mentions it in connexion with the Argonauts, whom he speaks of as *Quei gloriosi che passaro a Colco*, Par. ii. 16 [**Argonauti**].

Colle, town in Tuscany, in the Valdelsa, situated on a hill about ten miles NW. of Siena. It was the scene of a battle (June, 1269) in which the Sienese Ghibellines, with a mixed force of Germans and Spaniards, under Provenzano Salvani (who was taken prisoner) and Count Guido Novello, were defeated by the Florentine Guelfs with the help of some of the French troops of Charles of Anjou—a victory whereby the Florentines avenged the disastrous defeat of Montaperti nine years before. Colle is mentioned by Sapía (in Circle II of Purgatory) in connexion with this engagement, Purg. xiii. 115. [Sapía : Provenzano Salvani.]

Collina Porta, Colline gate, the most N. of the gates of ancient

Rome; Lucan's mention of it (*Phars.* ii. 135), in connexion with the battle between the Samnites and the Romans under Sulla (B. C. 82), quoted, Mon. ii. 11⁴⁸. [Sanniti.]

Cologna, Cologne on the Rhine; mentioned by D. in his description of the Hypocrites, who, he says, had 'cowls with hoods down in front of their eyes shaped like those worn by the monks of Cologne', Inf. xxiii. 61–3 (where for *Cologna* some modern edd. read *Clugnì*). [Ipocriti.]

Cologna, Alberto di. [Alberto¹.]

Colonia. [Cologna.]

Colonna, Egidio. [Egidio².]

Colonna, Jacopo], one of the Colonna cardinals deprived by Boniface VIII; he and his brother Pietro are alluded to as the colleagues of Napoleone Orsini, 'collegae Ursi', Epist. viii. 10¹⁵⁹⁻⁶⁰. [Colonnesi: Orsini, Napoleone.]

Colonna, Pietro], one of the Colonna cardinals deprived by Boniface VIII; he and his brother Jacopo are alluded to as the colleagues of Napoleone Orsini, 'collegae Ursi', Epist. viii. 10¹⁵⁹⁻⁶⁰. [Colonnesi: Orsini, Napoleone.]

Colonna, Sciarra], nephew of the two preceding, one of the leaders in the attack upon Boniface VIII at Anagni; he and William of Nogaret are alluded to by Hugh Capet (in Circle V of Purgatory) as 'vivi ladroni', Purg. xx. 90. [Alagna : Bonifazio¹: Colonnesi : Guglielmo di Nogaret.]

Colonne, Guido delle, judge of Messina in Sicily, who belonged to the Sicilian school of poetry which flourished under the Emperor Frede-

rick II and his son Manfred. Besides poems Guido also wrote a romance of Troy in Latin prose, the *Historia Trojana*, which was widely popular in the Middle Ages. Guido, who accompanied Edward I to England when the latter was on his way home from the Crusade after the death of Henry III, was well known in England; he is mentioned by Chaucer in the *Hous of Fame* (iii. 379), while his *Historia Trojana* was translated into English under the name of the 'Geste Hystoriale' of the Destruction of Troy. In 1276 (or perhaps earlier) Guido was made Judge of Messina, whence he is commonly known as Guido delle Colonne, Giudice di Messina. According to an English chronicler he was still alive during the pontificate of Nicholas IV (1288–1292). A small number of Guido's poems has been preserved, including two which are quoted by D.

D. (who makes no reference to the *Historia Trojana*) quotes, but without mentioning the author's name, the first lines of two of Guido's *canzoni* as examples of the lofty style of Sicilian poetry, V. E. i. 12¹², ¹⁴; one of the lines is quoted again as an instance of the use of the eleven-syllabled line, the author's name being given as *Judex de Columnis de Messana*, V. E. ii. 5⁴³⁻⁴.

Colonne di Ercole], Pillars of Hercules, i.e. Mt. Abyla in N. Africa and Mt. Calpe (Gibraltar) in Spain, supposed to mark the W. limit of the habitable world, so called from the tradition that they were originally one mountain, which was torn asunder by Hercules; they are referred to by Ulysses (in Bolgia 8 of Circle

VIII of Hell) in connexion with the Strait of Gibraltar, which he describes as 'quella foce stretta Ov' Ercole segnò li suoi riguardi', Inf. xxvi. 107–8; spoken of as the W. limit of the habitable world, 'termini occidentales ab Hercule positi', A. T. § 19$^{41-2}$; Carm. 30. [**Abile:** **Calpe.**]

Colonnesi], Colonna family of Rome; their war with Boniface VIII, who proclaimed a crusade against them, is alluded to by Guido da Montefeltro (in Bolgia 8 of Circle VIII of Hell), Inf. xxvii. 85–7, 96–111 [**Laterano: Penestrino**]; the Colonna cardinals, Jacopo and Pietro, are referred to by D. in his letter to the Italian cardinals as the colleagues of Napoleone Orsini, 'collegae Ursi', Epist. viii. 10$^{159-60}$ [**Orsini, Napoleone**].

The feud between the Colonnesi and Boniface, which existed throughout his reign, came to a head in 1297, in which year it appears that Sciarra Colonna robbed part of the Papal treasure. The Pope in consequence deprived his two uncles, Jacopo and Pietro, of their rank as Cardinals, excommunicated them and the rest of their house, and razed to the ground their palaces in Rome. The Colonnesi thereupon left Rome and openly defied Boniface from their strongholds of Palestrina and Nepi. The latter was captured, but Palestrina held out, and was at last surrendered on promise of an amnesty from the Pope, who, however, as soon as he got it into his hands, had it destroyed [**Penestrino**]; the Colonnesi, who had received absolution on their submission, furious at this

piece of treachery, again defied the Pope, and were again excommunicated. During the remainder of Boniface's reign they remained in exile. They had their revenge when Sciarra Colonna, as agent of Philip the Fair, captured Boniface at Anagni. [**Alagna.**]

Colossenses, Epistola ad. [**Colossensi.**]

Colossensi, Colossians; Epistle of St. Paul to, quoted, Conv. iv. 24$^{172-3}$ (*Coloss*. iii. 20).

Columnis, Judex de. [**Colonne, Guido delle.**]

Comentatore, Il. [**Averrois.**]

Comestore, Pietro. [**Pietro Mangiadore.**]

Commedia, Comedy, title given by D. to his poem, Inf. xvi. 128; xxi. 2; *Comoedia*, Epist. x. 3^{71}, 10$^{1,\ 218}$, 13$^{255-7}$; his reasons for so calling it, Epist. x. 10$^{188-225}$.

The title *Divina Commedia*, which is subsequent to D., perhaps had its origin in D.'s own description of the poem as 'lo sacrato poema', Par. xxiii. 62; 'il poema sacro', Par. xxv. 1. In the earliest printed editions the title is simply 'La Comedia di D. A.'

The form of the poem is triple, the three divisions corresponding with the three kingdoms of the next world, Hell, Purgatory, Paradise. Each division or Cantica contains thirty-three cantos (with an introductory one to the first Cantica); the whole poem thus contains 100 cantos, the square of the perfect number ten (V. N. § 30$^{9-10}$; Conv. ii. 15$^{30-6}$). These contain in all 14,233 lines, viz. 4,720 in the *Inferno*, 4,755 in the *Purgatorio*, and

4,758 in the *Paradiso*. The average length of each canto is 142·33 lines; the longest being Purg. xxxii, with 160 lines, the shortest, Inf. vi, with 115 lines. D. himself applies the term *canzone* (Inf. xx. 3) or *cantica* (Purg. xxxiii. 140) to the three main divisions of the poem, and *canto* (Inf. xx. 2; Par. v. 139) to the subdivisions.

D. places the date of the action of the poem in the Jubilee year 1300. Thus he describes the Vision as having taken place 'Nel mezzo del cammin di nostra vita' (Inf. i. 1), i. e. in his thirty-fifth year, the days of our life, according to the Psalmist, being 'three-score years and ten' (*Psalm* xc. 10), and D. having been born in 1265. Further, he says (Inf. xxi. 112) that Christ's descent into Hell took place 1266 years ago, which, with the addition of the thirty-four years from Christ's Incarnation, gives the date 1300.

As regards the duration of the action of the poem there is much difference of opinion. The most probable estimate, on the whole, seems to be that which puts it at seven days, viz. from the morning of Good Friday, April 8, until (and including) Thursday, April 14. In this case the chronology of the poem would be briefly as follows: *Good Friday* (April 8), Inf. i–vii. 99; *Saturday* (April 9), Inf. xi. 113–xxxiv. 96; *Easter Sunday* (April 10), Purg. i. 19–ix. 9; *Monday* (April 11), Purg. ix. 13–xviii. 76; *Tuesday* (April 12), Purg. xix. 1–xxvii. 89; *Wednesday* (April 13), Purg. xxvii. 94–xxxiii. 103; *Thursday* (April 14), Par. i–xxxiii).

Commentator. [Averrois.] *Comoedia.* [*Commedía.*] *Confessioni, Le,* *Confessions* of St. Augustine, an autobiographical account (in thirteen books), written c. 397, of the reformation of his life; mentioned as the kind of work in which it is allowable for the author to speak of himself, Conv. i. 2[104]. [Agostino[2].]

Conio, castle in Romagna, not far from Imola, now destroyed; its Counts, who appear to have been for the most part Guelfs, are mentioned among the degenerate families of Romagna, together with those of Castrocaro, by Guido del Duca (in Circle II of Purgatory), who laments that they had not died out, Purg. xiv. 116.

Consideratione, De, treatise of St. Bernard (in five books) *On Consideration*; cited in support of the contention that the memory is powerless to retain the most exalted impressions of the human intellect (*De Consid.* v. 14), Epist. x. 28[555] [Bernardo[2]].

Consiglieri Frodolenti], Counsellors of evil, placed among the Fraudulent in Bolgia 8 of Circle VIII of Hell (Malebolge); their punishment is to be tormented within a flame, in which they are enveloped and concealed from view, thus symbolizing the hidden ways by which they worked evil during their lifetime, Inf. xxvi. 31–xxvii. 132 [Frodolenti]. *Examples*: Ulysses and Diomed (enveloped in one and the same flame) [Ulisse : Diomede]; Guido da Montefeltro [Guido Montefeltrano].

Consolatione Philosophiae, De,

work of Boëthius (in five books), *On the Consolation of Philosophy*, in the form of a dialogue, in prose and verse, between the author and his visitant, Philosophy, composed during his imprisonment at Pavia; quoted by D. as *De Consolatione*, Epist. x. 33^{617}; *Di Consolazione*, Conv. ii. 11^{18}; iv. 12^{35}, 13^{131}; referred to as *quello, non conosciuto da molti, libro di Boezio*, Conv. ii. 13^{14-15}.

D., who was intimately acquainted with the work, relates that it and the *De Amicitia* of Cicero were the two books which he read in order to get consolation after the death of Beatrice, Conv. ii. 13^{17-22}. He quotes from it as follows, but these direct quotations only represent a fraction of his indebtedness to the work: Inf. v. 121–3 (*Cons.* ii. *pr.* 4); Conv. i. 2^{96-100} (*Cons.* i. *pr.* 4); Conv. i. 11^{56-8} (*Cons.* iii. *pr.* 6); Conv. ii. 8^{24-7} (*Cons.* iv. *pr.* 3); Conv. ii. 11^{18-20} (*Cons.* ii. *pr.* 1); Conv. iii. 1^{78-82} (*Cons.* ii. *pr.* 1); Conv. iii. 2^{142-9} (*Cons.* i. *pr.* 4; *Cons.* iii. *met.* 9); Conv. iv. 12^{35-9} (*Cons.* ii. *met.* 5); Conv. iv. 12^{74-8} (*Cons.* ii. *met.* 2); Conv. iv. $13^{108-10, 130-2, 140-2}$ (*Cons.* ii. *pr.* 5); Mon. i. 9^{25-8} (*Cons.* ii. *met.* 8); Mon. ii. 9^{91-8} (*Cons.* ii. *met.* 6); Epist. x. 33^{617} (*Cons.* iii. *met.* 9).

Consolazione, Di. [*Consolatione Philosophiae, De.*]

Constantino. [Costantino.]

Constantinopolis, Constantinople, capital of the Eastern Empire, founded by Constantine the Great (A.D. 330), on the site of the ancient Byzantium; alluded to by the Emperor Justinian (in the Heaven of Mercury), in connexion with the transference of the seat of the Roman Empire to Byzantium, as *lo stremo d'Europa*,Par.vi. 5. [Giustiniano.] D. states that Charlemagne received the Imperial dignity from the Pope, notwithstanding that Michael was Emperor at Constantinople, Mon. iii. 11^{5-7}. As a matter of fact the Empress Irene (797–802) was on the throne of Constantinople at the time of Charlemagne's coronation. Michael I did not become Emperor until 811. [Carlo Magno: Michael.]

Constantinus. [Costantino.]

Constanza. [Costanza.]

Contemplanti, Spiriti. [Spiriti Contemplanti.]

Contemplatione, De, treatise (otherwise known as *Benjamin major*) of Richard of St. Victor *On Contemplation*; cited in support of the contention that the memory is powerless to retain the most exalted impressions of the human intellect (*De Contempl.* iv. 23), Epist. x. 28^{554}. [Riccardo.]

Conti, I. [Guidi, Conti.]

Contra Gentiles. [*Gentiles, Summa Contra.*]

Convito. [*Convivio.*]

Convivio, *Banquet* of D., a treatise in Italian, in four books (not completed), written in prose, consisting of a philosophical commentary on three of his *canzoni*, viz. 'Voi che intendendo il terzo ciel movete' (Canz. vi); 'Amor che nella mente mi ragiona' (Canz. vii); 'Le dolci rime d'amor ch' io solia' (Canz. viii). The *Convivio* was originally intended to be a commentary on fourteen canzoni (Conv. i. 1^{102-5}), and, if completed, would have consisted of fifteen books, the first being introductory. Of the projected books, the seventh is referred to, Conv. iv. 26^{66-7}; the fourteenth, Conv. i. 12^{87-8}; ii. 1^{35-6}; iv. 27^{101-2}; and the fifteenth, Conv. i. 8^{131-2}; iii. 15^{144}. The division of the books into chapters (Bk. i containing thirteen chapters; Bk. ii, sixteen; Bk. iii, fifteen; and Bk. iv, thirty) was due to D. himself (cf. Conv. i. 4^4; ii. 7^1; iii. 6^1; iv. 2^{77}, &c.).

The title *Convivio* was given to the work by D. himself, Conv. i. 1^{111-12}; iv. 22^7; he explains the meaning of the title, the aim of the work, and the difference between it and the *Vita Nuova*, Conv. i. 1; D. as the author represents the servants at an actual banquet, Conv. i. 2^{1-8}; the book is of the nature of a commentary, Conv. i. 3^{10}, 4^{105}, 5^{36}, 7^{70}, 9^{49}, $10^{27, 80, 97}$; it is written in a lofty style in order to give it an air of gravity and authority, and so to counterbalance the objection of its being in Italian, Conv. i. 4^{94-105}; reasons for its being written in the vulgar tongue instead of in Latin, Conv. i. 5; the commentary stands in the same relation to the *canzoni* as a servant does to his master, Conv. i. 5^{35-41}, 7^{68-70}; unlike other commentaries as being written, not in Latin, but in the vulgar tongue, Conv. i. 9^{65-75}; in it is set forth the great excellence of the Italian language, Conv. i. 10^{80-109}.

Cordelliero. [Cordigliero.]

Cordigliero, Cordelier, Franciscan monk, so called from the rough cord worn by members of the Order, in imitation of St. Francis, their founder, who bound his body with a cord, regarding it as a beast which required to be controlled by a halter [Francescani]; Guido da Montefeltro, who in his old age became a Franciscan monk, speaks of himself (in Bolgia 8 of Circle VIII of Hell) as having been a Cordelier, Inf. xxvii. 67. [Guido Montefeltrano.]

Coreggiero, wearer of the thong, Dominican monk, so called from the leathern girdle (*coreggia*) worn by members of the Order [Domenicani]; St. Thomas Aquinas (in the Heaven of the Sun) applies the term to himself, Par. xi. 138. [Tommaso ².]

Coribanti], Corybantes (or Curetes), priests of Cybele or Rhea, who celebrated her worship with dances and music. At the birth of the infant Jupiter Rhea caused them to raise shouts so as to drown his cries and thus conceal his existence from his father Saturn. Virgil alludes to this incident in connexion with Mt. Ida, Inf. xiv. 100-2. [Ida ¹ : Rea.]

Corinthios, Epistola ad, St. Paul's Epistle to the Corinthians, Mon. iii. 10^{50}; Epist. x. 28^{539}; quoted, Conv. iv. 22^{56-8} (1 *Cor.* ix. 24); Mon. iii. 10^{50-3} (1 *Cor.* iii. 11); Epist. viii. 5^{74-5} (1 *Cor.* xv. 10); Epist. x. 28^{539-44} (2 *Cor.* xii. 3-4).

Corneto, town in the Campagna of Rome, on the river Marta, about five miles from the coast; mentioned in connexion with the highwayrobber, Rinier da Corneto, Inf. xii. 137; and again, to indicate roughly the S. limit of the Tuscan Maremma, Inf. xiii. 9. [Cecina : Maremma.]

Corneto, Rinier da, famous highway-robber in D.'s day, of whom little is known, beyond that he was a sort of bandit chief, who frequented the roads leading into Rome; placed, together with Rinier Pazzo, among the violent Robbers in Round 1 of Circle VII of Hell, Inf. xii. 137. [Predoni.]

Corniglia, Cornelia, daughter of Scipio Africanus Major, and wife of Tiberius Sempronius Gracchus, by whom she became 'the mother of the Gracchi', viz. the tribunes Tiberius and Caius. On being condoled with on the death of her sons, who were both slain during her lifetime, she is said to have exclaimed that she who had borne them could never deem herself unhappy.

D. places her, along with Lucretia, Julia, and Marcia, among the noble spirits of antiquity in Limbo, Inf. iv. 128 [Limbo]; she is mentioned by Cacciaguida (in the Heaven of Mars), by way of contrast to the dissolute Florentine Cianghella, Par. xv. 129. [Cianghella.]

Corno, 'the Horn', i.e. the constellation of the Little Bear, which is conceived as a horn, the mouth ('bocca', v. 10) being formed by the two stars furthest from the pole-star, which forms the pointed end of the horn, Par. xiii. 10. [Boote.]

Corno della Capra. [Capricorno.]

Coro, Caurus, the NW. wind; mentioned to indicate the quarter whence it blows, Inf. xi. 114.

Corona], constellation of the Crown, i.e. the marriage-garland of Ariadne, which Bacchus placed among the stars after her death; alluded to, Par. xiii. 13–15. [Arianna.]

Corradino. [Curradino.]
Corrado. [Currado.]
Corruptione, De Generatione et. [Generatione, De.]

Corsi, inhabitants of Corsica; mentioned to indicate the island itself, the period when the Sun sets W. by S. (i.e. about the end of November) being described as the time when to the inhabitants of Rome it appears to set between Corsica and Sardinia, Purg. xviii. 79–81.

Corso], the present Via del Corso in Florence; alluded to by Cacciaguida (in the Heaven of Mars) in his description of the situation of the house in which he and his ancestors lived in Florence, Par. xvi. 40–2. [Cacciaguida.]

Corso Donati], head of the Donati family and leader of the Neri faction in Florence, the brother of Forese (Purg. xxiii. 48, 76; xxiv. 74) and Piccarda (Purg. xxiv. 10; Par. iii. 49; iv. 97, 112). He was Podestà of Bologna in 1283 and 1288, of Pistoja in 1289 (in which year, as Captain of Pistoja, he took part in the battle of Campaldino, and by his gallantry largely contributed to the victory of the Florentines), and of Treviso in 1308. In the summer of 1300 the Priors of Florence, of whom D. was one, in order to put an end to the disturbances occasioned by the Bianchi and Neri feud, decided to exile the heads of both parties. Corso, counting on the sympathies of Boniface VIII, repaired to Rome and urged the Pope to send Charles of Valois to Florence to pacify the city in his name. Charles entered Florence, Nov. 1, 1301, and was followed not long after by Corso Donati and a band of exiled Neri, who forced their way into the city, broke open the prisons, and at the head of the rabble attacked the houses of the Bianchi, pillaging, burning, and murdering for five days and nights, without any attempt being made by Charles to check them. After the departure of the latter the Neri were left in possession of Florence, and Corso now attempted to get the supreme power into his own hands. But his pretensions soon rendered him an object of detestation and suspicion, and at length he was formally charged by the Priors with conspiring against the liberties of the commonwealth in concert with his father-in-law, the Ghibelline captain Uguccione della Faggiuola, and was summoned to appear before the Podestà. On his refusal to comply he was condemned to death as a traitor, besieged in his own house, and eventually slain while attempting to escape, Oct. 6, 1308.

Corso Donati is not mentioned by name in the *D. C.*; he is referred to by his brother Forese (in Circle VI of Purgatory), in conversation with D., as the chief cause of the unhappy condition of Florence, *quei che più n' ha colpa*, Purg. xxiv. 82 ; and his death is foretold (*vv.* 83–4) [**Forese**]; he and his associates are spoken of by Piccarda (in the Heaven of the Moon), in reference to their forcible removal of her from a convent in order to make her marry, as *uomini a mal più ch' a bene usi*, Par. iii. 106. [**Donati : Piccarda.**]

According to Vasari (in his *Vita di Giotto*), Corso's portrait is one of those associated with that of D. in the fresco painted by Giotto in the Palazzo del Podestà (the present Bargello) at Florence.

Cortese, 'Courteous', pseudonym of a lady (called also *Bianca* and *Giovanna*) mentioned in one of D.'s poems, Canz. x. 153.

Cortigiani], Florentine family, thought by some to be alluded to by Cacciaguida (in the Heaven of Mars) as one of the families who were patrons of the bishopric of Florence, the revenues of which they enjoyed during the vacancy of the See, Par. xvi. 112.

Cortonese, of Cortona, town in Tuscany, about eighteen miles S. of Arezzo, situated some 2,000 ft. above the sea ; D. uses the term *copertoio cortonese*, to signify a warm covering, such as hill-folk use, in his *tenzone* with Forese Donati, whose wife, he insinuates (in allusion to Forese's irregular habits), requires something more to keep her warm in bed than a thick blanket, Son. lii. 8. [**Forese.**]

[**Corydon**], name (borrowed from Virgil, *Ecl.* ii. 1, 56, 65, &c.) of a character in the Eclogues addressed to D. by G. del Virgilio, supposed to represent a friend of the writer, Ecl. R. 57.

Cosenza, town in Upper Calabria, on a branch of the Crati, about twelve miles inland from the Tyrrhenian Sea. Cardinal Bartolommeo Pignatelli, Archbishop of Cosenza, 1254–1266 (or, according to some, his successor, Tommaso d'Agni), who by command of Clement IV caused the body of King Manfred to be disinterred from its resting-place by the bridge of Benevento, is referred to (by Manfred in Ante-purgatory) as *il pastor di Cosenza,* Purg. iii. 124. [**Benevento: Man-fredi: Pignatelli.**]

Costantino, Constantine the Great, Roman Emperor, A.D. 306–337, eldest son of the Emperor Constantius Chlorus, born A.D. 272. On the death of his father at York in 306, C. laid claim to a share of the Empire, and was acknowledged as sovereign of the countries beyond the Alps. In 308 he received the title of Augustus. During his campaign against Maxentius in 312, whom he defeated near Rome, he is said to have been converted to Christianity by the appearance in the sky during his march to Rome of a luminous cross, with the inscription 'in hoc signo vinces'. After his defeat of Licinius, who had made himself master of the whole of the East, C. became sole sovereign of the Empire, the seat of which he transferred from Rome to Byzantium, changing the name of that city to Constantinopolis, 'the city of Constantine'. The remainder of his reign he spent in peace; he died in May, 337, having been baptized by Eusebius shortly before.

According to the legend, which was universally accepted in the Middle Ages, Constantine before he migrated to Byzantium abandoned to the Church the whole temporal power of the West. This so-called 'Donatio Constantini' is said to have been made by the Emperor in return for his having been cured of leprosy by Pope Sylvester.

D., though he deplores the con-sequences of the Donation of Constantine (Inf. xix. 115–17; Purg. xxxii. 124–9; Par. xx. 58–60; Mon. ii. 12^{15-18}, 13^{66-9}), yet considered that it was bestowed with a good motive (Par. xx. 55–7; Mon. ii. 12^{15-18}, 13^{66-9}). He refers to it repeatedly in the *De Monarchia* (ii. 12^{15-18}, 13^{66-9}; iii. 10^{1-6}, 105^{-7}, 13^{60-4}), where he combats the theory that in consequence the Empire is dependent upon the Church, inasmuch as the dignity of the Empire is what Constantine could not alienate, nor the Church receive. The Emperor, in so far as he is Emperor, cannot alter the Empire. Besides, even if Constantine had been able to grant the temporal power to the Church, the Church was disqualified from receiving it by the express command of Christ (*Matt.* x. 9); therefore it is manifest that neither could the Church receive in the way of possession, nor Constantine bestow in the way of alienation (Mon. iii. 10).

Constantine is mentioned, in connexion with the 'Donatio', Inf. xix. 115; Mon. iii. $10^{1, 23, 27, 41, 117}$, 13^{60}; *infirmator Imperii,* Mon. ii. 13^{67-8}; in allusion to the legend that he was healed of leprosy by Pope Sylvester, Inf. xxvii. 94; Mon. iii. 10^1 [**Silvestro¹**]; and in reference to his transference of the seat of Empire to Byzantium, Par. vi. 1 (cf. Par. xx. 57). [**Greco ¹**.]

D. places Constantine among the spirits of those who loved and exercised justice (*Spiriti Giudicanti*) in the Heaven of Jupiter, where the Eagle, in allusion to his migration to Byzantium, refers to him as *L'altro che . . . Per cedere al pastor, si fece Greco*, Par. xx. 55–7, and alludes to the 'Donatio' (*vv.* 56–9). [**Aquila**[2]: **Giove, Cielo di.**]

Costanza [1], Constance, daughter of Roger, King of Sicily, wife of the Emperor Henry VI, and mother of the Emperor Frederick II; William II, Roger's grandson, having no issue, his aunt Constance became presumptive heiress to the throne, which the Emperor Frederick Barbarossa desired to acquire for his own house. To effect his object he projected an alliance between Constance and his son Henry Duke of Swabia, afterwards Emperor as Henry VI. The marriage took place in 1185, when Constance was about thirty-two and Henry twenty-two, but their son, Frederick of Palermo, the heir to the Sicilian throne, was not born until nine years later (Dec. 1194), only four years before the death of his mother (Nov. 1198). According to the current tradition (accepted by D.), Constance had been a nun, and had been taken from the convent by the Archbishop of Palermo, and married to the son of the Emperor, against her will.

D. places her in the Heaven of the Moon, among those who failed to observe their vows of religion (*Spiriti Votivi Mancanti*), Par. iii. 118; *quest' alto splendor, v.* 109; *sorella, v.* 113; *luce, v.* 118 [**Luna, Cielo della**]; Manfred (in Ante-purgatory), who describes himself as her grandson, speaks of her as *Costanza Imperadrice*, Purg. iii. 113 [**Manfredi**]; Piccarda (in the Heaven of the Moon) refers to her as *la gran Costanza, Che del secondo vento di Soave Generò il terzo* (i. e. the wife of Henry VI and mother of Frederick II), Par. iii. 118–20; and alludes to the story of her having been forcibly taken from the convent in order to be married, so that in her heart she had remained faithful to her conventual vow (*vv.* 112–17); Beatrice mentions her in the same connexion, Par. iv. 98 [**Arrigo** [5]].

Costanza [2], Constance, daughter of Manfred of Sicily and Beatrice of Savoy; married (1262) Peter III of Aragon, by whom she had three sons, Alphonso (King of Aragon, 1285–1291), James (King of Sicily, 1285–1296; King of Aragon, 1291–1327), and Frederick (King of Sicily, 1296–1337). It was through his marriage with Constance that Peter III claimed the crown of Sicily, which he assumed in 1282 after the 'Sicilian Vespers'. Constance died at Barcelona in 1302, having outlived both her husband and her eldest son. [**Alfonso** [1]: **Federico** [3]: **Jacomo** [1]: **Pietro** [3].]

Manfred (in Ante-purgatory) speaks of his daughter as *la mia buona Costanza*, Purg. iii. 143; and refers to her as *mia bella figlia, genitrice Dell' onor di Cicilia e d' Aragona* (*vv.* 115–16) [**Aragona: Cicilia**]; Sordello (in Ante-purgatory) names her as the wife of Peter III, and implies that her husband was as superior to Charles I of Naples (husband of Beatrice of Provence and Margaret of Burgundy) as Charles I was to his own son Charles II, Purg. vii. 127–9. [**Carlo** [1]: **Beatrice** [2]: **Margherita** [2].]

Crasso, Marcus Licinius Crassus, triumvir with Caesar and Pompey, B.C. 60; his ruling passion was the love of money, which he set himself to accumulate by every possible means; in 55 he was consul for the second time and received the province of Syria, where he looked to greatly increase his wealth, but in that same year he was defeated and killed by the Parthians, who cut off his head, and, having filled the mouth with molten gold in mockery of his passion for money, sent it, together with his right hand, to Orodes the Parthian king, in token of their victory.

D. (who apparently got the story from Florus, iii. 11) includes C. (with an allusion to his mouth having been filled with gold) among the instances of avarice recalled by the Avaricious in Circle V of Purgatory, Purg. xx. 116–17. [Avari.]

Cremona, town in S. of Lombardy, on the Po, about midway between Pavia and Mantua; its vicinity to Mantua, V. E. i. 15$^{9-10}$; has a dialect of its own, V. E. i. 19$^{5-6}$; one of the Guelfic towns which opposed the Emperor Henry VII, Epist. vii. 6^{127}.

Cremonensis, of Cremona; *Vulgare Cremonense*, the Cremonese dialect, V. E. i. 19$^{12-13}$. [Cremona.]

Creta (elsewhere *Creti*, Inf. xii. 12; Conv. iv. 27^{160}), island of Crete in the Mediterranean, in which is situated Mt. Ida [Creti]; mentioned by Virgil (in his description of the rivers of Hell), who describes it as a waste land, situated in mid-sea, and refers to the reign of its king (Saturn) as the Golden Age, Inf. xiv. 94–6 [Saturno [1]]; he then mentions Mt. Ida as the place chosen by Rhea for the birthplace of Jupiter (*vv.* 97–

102) [Ida : Rea]; and proceeds to describe how within the mountain stands the image of a great elder, who turns his back upon Damietta, and looks towards Rome (*vv.* 103–105) [Damiata]; his head is of gold, his arms and breast of silver, his trunk of brass (*vv.* 106–8); from the fork downwards he is of iron, save that the right foot, upon which he rests more than on the other, is of baked earth (*vv.* 109–111); in every part of him, except the gold, is a fissure from which tears issue and flow out of the mountain (*vv.* 112–14), forming in their course the infernal rivers Acheron, Styx, Phlegethon, and Cocytus (*vv.* 115–20). [Fiumi Infernali.]

This image of 'il veglio di Creta' (the idea of which is borrowed from *Dan.* ii. 32–3) typifies the history of the human race. It is placed in Crete (at the point where the boundaries of Europe, Asia, and Africa meet, i. e. at the centre of the world as known at that time), on Mt. Ida, in accordance probably with the Virgilian theory that here was the cradle of the Trojan, and hence of the Roman, race (*Aen.* iii. 104–6). The division into metals, representing the Golden, Silver, Bronze, and Iron Ages, follows the commonplace of the poets, Ovid's description of the four ages (*Metam.* i. 89–131) having been probably in D.'s mind, as well as the passage in Daniel. D. differs from Daniel in making the brass terminate with the trunk, in order no doubt to emphasize his theory of the dual organization of Church and Empire; the right leg with the foot of baked earth, on which the image rests

most, being the symbol of the ecclesiastical power, corrupted and weakened by the acquisition of the temporal power from Constantine, but
at the same time that to which mankind chiefly looked for support and
guidance. The image stands with
its back to Damietta (i. e. the East,
representing the old monarchies), and
looks towards Rome, the centre of
the imperial monarchy of the West.
The tears flowing from the fissure
in every part save the gold signify
that all ages except the Golden were
subject to sin and sorrow.

Creti, island of Crete; *l'infamia
di C.,* i.e. the Minotaur, Inf. xii. 12
[**Minotauro**]; the war of Athens
with, Conv. iv. 27$^{159-60}$ [**Cefalo :
Creta.**]

Creusa, daughter of Priam and
Hecuba, wife of Aeneas, and mother
of Ascanius; she perished on the
night of the fall of Troy, having
been separated from Aeneas in the
confusion.

The troubadour Folquet (in the
Heaven of Venus), speaking of the
love of Dido for Aeneas, says she
thereby wronged both her own husband Sichaeus, and Aeneas' wife
Creusa, Par. ix. 98 [**Dido**]; C. is
spoken of as Aeneas' first wife (D.
regarding Dido as his second), and
the mother of Ascanius, to prove the
connexion of Aeneas with Asia by
marriage (*Aen.* iii. 339–40 being
quoted with the interpolated hemistich ' peperit fumante Creusa '),
Mon. ii. 3$^{93-101}$. [**Enea.**]

Crisostomo, St. John Chrysostom (' Golden-mouth '), celebrated
Greek Father of the Church, born
at Antioch c. 344; he was ordained

deacon in 381, and presbyter in 386,
in which capacity he so distinguished
himself by his preaching that the
Emperor Arcadius appointed him (in
397) patriarch of Constantinople.
His zeal for reform made him an
object of hatred to the clergy, and
led to his deposition at the instance
of Theophilus, patriarch of Alexandria, and the Empress Eudoxia,
whose excesses he had publicly rebuked. Sentence of exile was pronounced against him, but the people,
to whom he had endeared himself
by his preaching, rose in revolt, and
he was reinstated in his office.
Shortly after he was again banished,
and he finally died in exile (407) at
Comana in Pontus.

St. Bonaventura names C. among
the great Doctors (*Spiriti Sapienti*)
who are with himself in the Heaven
of the Sun, speaking of him as *il
Metropolitano,* and coupling him with
the prophet Nathan (both having been
distinguished for their boldness in
rebuking the sins of kings), Par. xii.
136–7. [**Sole, Cielo del.**]

Cristallino, Cielo. [**Cielo
Cristallino.**]

Cristiani, Christians, Purg. x.
121; Par. xix. 109; V. N. § 30^{12};
Canz. viii. 73; *Christiani,* Mon. iii.
3^{40}; as opposed to pagans, Par. v.
73; Conv. iv. 15^{90}; of Rhipeus
and Trajan, Par. xx. 104 [**Rifeo :
Traiano**]; alluded to as *l'esercito
di Cristo,* Par. xii. 37; *la milizia
di Dio,* Par. xii. 41; *popol cristiano,*
Par. xxvii. 48; *i battezzati,* Par.
xxvii. 51; *la cristiana prole,* Son.
xxxvii. 10; *omnes Christianam re-
ligionem profitentes,* Mon. iii. 3^{132};
Statius (in Purgatory) calls the early

Christians *i nuovi predicanti*, Purg. xxii. 80.

Cristiano, Christian, Par. xxvii. 48; V. N. § 30[17]; Conv. iv. 15[92]; as opposed to Jews and Gentiles, Conv. ii. 5[62]; as opposed to Saracens and Jews, Inf. xxvii. 88; of Statius, Purg. xxii. 73, 90; of Cacciaguida, in allusion to his 'christening', Par. xv. 135; St. Peter addresses D. as *buon cristiano*, Par. xxiv. 52.

Cristo, Christ; mentioned by name thirty-nine times in the *D. C.*, Purg. xx. 87; xxi. 8; xxiii. 74; xxvi. 129; xxxii. 102; Par. vi. 14; ix. 120; xi. 72, 102, 107; xii. 37, 71, 73, 75; xiv. 104, 106, 108; xvii. 51; xix. 72, 104, 106, 108; xx. 47; xxiii. 20, 72; xxv. 15; xxvi. 53; xxvii. 40; xxix. 98, 109; xxxi. 3, 107; xxxii. 20, 24, 27, 83, 85, 87, 125; five times in the *Purgatorio*, and thirty-four in the *Paradiso*, but not once in the *Inferno*, being there referred to by means of a periphrasis. Whenever the name *Cristo* occurs at the end of a line D. does not rime with it, but repeats the name itself, Par. xii. 71, 73, 75; xiv. 104, 106, 108; xix. 104, 106, 108; xxxii. 83, 85, 87. Christ is mentioned elsewhere, *Cristo*, Son. liv. 11; V. N. § 41[4]; Conv. ii. 1[47], 6[12], 9[115]; iv. 16[110], 17[94, 103], 23[96, 109], 24[64]; *Christus*, Mon. i. 16[16]; ii. 1[4, 35], 8[32, 42], 9[100], 12[5-70], 13[2-61]; iii. 3[37-130], 7[2, 6], 8[2, 56], 9[2-143], 10[45, 49, 52, 130], 13[40-58], 14[36], 15[15, 27, 35], 16[69]; Epist. v. 10[156]; vi. 6[185]; viii. 2[23], 7[108], 11[179]; x. 7[149], 27[517]; A. T. § 24[15]; *Gesù Cristo*, Par. xxxi. 107; V. N. § 41[4]; *Jesus Christus*, Mon. ii. 13[18];

iii. 3[37], 10[53], 16[69]; Epist. viii. 5[71]; A. T. § 24[14]; *Gesù*, Par. xxv. 33; *Jesus*, Mon. iii. 9[70, 115, 121, 138].

Christ is referred to as the Son of God, Par. x. 1; V. N. § 30[35]; Conv. ii. 6[67, 82, 90]; Mon. i. 16[4]; ii. 12[45], 13[21]; iii. 1[31], 3[64], 9[73], 16[69]; Epist. v. 9[148]; vii. 3[69]; viii. 2[71]; *l'alto Filio Di Dio e di Maria*, Par. xxiii. 136-7; *Figliuolo del sovrano Iddio e Figliuolo di Maria Vergine*, Conv. ii. 6[12-13]; *Figliuol di Dio*, Par. vii. 119; xxvii. 24; xxxii. 113; Conv. iv. 5[22, 39]; — the Son of Mary, *Figliuol (di Maria)*, Purg. xv. 89; Par. xxiii. 137; Conv. ii. 6[13]; *il portato santo (di Maria)*, Purg. xx. 24; *la semenza della coronata fiamma*, Par. xxiii. 120; — the Lamb of God, *Agnel di Dio*, Purg. xvi. 18; Par. xvii. 33; *benedetto Agnello*, Par. xxiv. 2; *Agnus Dei*, Purg. xvi. 19; Epist. vii. 2[45]; — our Lord, *nostro Signore*, Inf. xix. 91; Purg. xx. 94; Par. xxiv. 35; xxxi. 107; V. N. § 26[18]; Conv. iv. 11[111], 17[108], 19[60], 27[75], 30[37]; *nostro Imperadore*, Par. xxv. 41; *Imperadore dell' Universo*, Conv. ii. 6[11]; *Imperadore del Cielo*, Conv. iii. 12[116]; — our Saviour, *nostro Salvatore*, Conv. ii. 6[26]; iv. 23[96]; *il Salvatore*, Conv. iii. 11[26]; iv. 17[106], 22[151, 154, 164]; *Redemptor noster*, V. E. i. 6[56]; *summus Salvator*, Mon. i. 4[27]; *Salvator noster*, Mon. ii. 12[22]; A. T. § 24[17]; *Salus hominum*, Mon. i. 4[26]; — the Crucified One, *Crucifixus*, Epist. viii. 4[44]; *Colui che fu crocifisso*, Conv. iii. 7[164]; *Sommo Giove, Che fu in terra crocifisso*, Purg. vi. 118-19; *il glorioso Sire, lo quale non negò la morte a sè*, V. N. § 22[2-3]; *Quel che, forato dalla lancia, . . . d'ogni colpa vince la bilancia*, Par. xiii. 40-2;

Colui che il morso in sè punío, Purg. xxxiii. 63 ; *lo Diletto . . . ch' ad alte grida Disposò* (*la Chiesa*) *col sangue benedetto*, Par. xi. 31–3 ; *Colui che la gran preda Levò a Dite*, Inf. xii. 38–9 ; — the Spouse of the Church, *Sponsus Ecclesiae*, Mon. ii. 13[61] ; iii. 3[79] ; *quello Sposo ch' ogni voto accetta*, Par. iii. 101 ; xi. 31–3 ; — the ' Word made flesh ', *Verbo di Dio*, Par. vii. 30 ; *Verbo divino*, Par. xxiii. 73 ; Epist. v. 7[118] ; — ' Wisdom ', *Sapienza*, Par. xxiii. 37 ; *somma S.*, Inf. iii. 6 ; — ' Power ', *Possanza*, Par. xxiii. 37; *suprema P.*, Par. xxvii. 36 ; — ' Light ', *la verace Luce*, V. N. § 24[37] ; *viva Luce*, Par. xiii. 55 ; xxiii. 31 ; *Luce intelletta*, Par. xxxiii. 125 ; *Lume*, Par. xxxiii. 119 ; *Luce che allumina noi nelle tenebre*, Conv. ii. 6[16–17] ; *Via, Verità, Luce*, Conv. ii. 9[115–16] ; *Lux nostra*, Epist. v .10[158] ; — ' Truth ', *infallibilis Veritas*, Mon. i. 5[60] ; iii. 1[13] ; *Dio verace*, Par. xxxi. 107 ; *Verità*, Conv. ii. 9[115] ; *Colui che in terra addusse La verità*, Par. xxii. 41–2.

In the *Inferno* Christ is never mentioned by name, but is referred to as *somma Sapienza*, Inf. iii. 6 ; *un Possente Con segno di vittoria incoronato*, Inf. iv. 53–4 ; *la nimica Podésta*, Inf. vi. 96 ; *Colui che la gran preda Levò a Dite*, Inf. xii. 38–9 ; *nostro Signore*, Inf. xix. 91 ; *l'Uom che nacque e visse senza pecca*, Inf. xxxiv. 115.

Christ is also referred to as *Abate* (' il chiostro ' being Paradise), Purg. xxvi. 129 ; *il Maestro*, Purg. xxxii. 81 ; Conv. iv. 4[135] ; *Romano* (' Roma ' being Paradise), Purg. xxxii. 102 ; *il nostro Diletto*, Par. xiii. 111 ; *Colui ch' ogni torto disgrava*, Par.

xviii. 6 ; *Lui che poteva aiutar*, Par. xx. 114 ; *Sol*, Par. xxiii. 29, 72 ; *il nostro Disiro*, Par. xxiii. 105 ; *il nostro Pellicano*, Par. xxv. 113 ; *Ortolano eterno*, Par. xxvi. 65 ; *nostra Beatitudine somma*, Conv. iv. 22[196] ; *Quelli che la nostra immortalità vede e misura*, Conv. ii. 9[122–4] ; *Ostium Conclavis aeterni*, Mon. ii. 8[43].

Christ, as Second Person of the Trinity, is referred to as *somma Sapienza*, Inf. iii. 6 ; Conv. ii. 6[66] ; iii. 12[97] ; *Verbo di Dio*, Par. vii. 30 ; *Figlio*, Par. x. 1 (cf. Par. vii. 119 ; x. 51 ; xxiii. 136–7 ; xxvii. 24 ; xxxii. 113 ; V. N. § 30[35] ; Conv. ii. 6[12, 67, 82, 90] ; Mon. i. 16[4] ; iii. 1[31], 3[64]) ; *Natura divina ed umana*, Par. xiii. 26–7 ; *viva Luce*, Par. xiii. 55 ; *Lume riflesso*, Par. xxxiii. 119 ; *Luce intelletta*, Par. xxxiii. 125. [Trinità.]

His twofold nature as God and Man is referred to, Par. ii. 41–2 ; vi. 13–21 ; vii. 35–6 ; xiii. 26–7 ; xxiii. 136 ; xxxiii. 4–6 ; Conv. ii. 6[12–13] (also as represented by the Griffin in the Terrestrial Paradise), Purg. xxxi. 80–81, 122 ; xxxii. 47, 96.

D. alludes to the following incidents connected with the life and death of Christ :—His birth, Purg. xx. 24 (*Luke* ii. 7) ; Conv. iv. 5[24] ; Mon. i. 16[4–5] ; iii. 13[41] ; the offering of the wise men, Mon. iii. 7[2–3] (*Matt.* ii. 11) ; His teaching in the Temple, Purg. xv. 88–92 (*Luke* ii. 41–9) ; the miracle at Cana, Purg. xiii. 29 (*John* ii. 1–10) ; His Transfiguration, Purg. xxxii. 73–81 (*Matt.* xvii. 1–8) ; Conv. ii. 1[45–8] ; Mon. iii. 9[81–6] ; Epist. x. 28[548–50] ; His instruction to the young man to sell his goods and give to the poor, Par. xii. 75 (*Matt.* xix. 21); His walking on the water, Mon. iii. 9$^{87-91}$ (*Matt.* xiv. 25-8); His questioning of the disciples as to who He was, Mon. iii. 9$^{70-3}$ (*Matt.* xvi. 15-23); His charge to Peter, Mon. iii. 8$^{1-8}$ (*Matt.* xvi. 19); the raising of Lazarus, and of the widow's son of Nain, Purg. xxxii. 78 (*John* xi; *Luke* vii. 11-15); His washing of the disciples' feet, Mon. iii. 9$^{103-7}$ (*John* xiii); the Last Supper, Mon. iii. 9$^{24-34}$ (*Luke* xxii. 7-14); His capture, Purg. xx. 87 (*Matt.* xxvi. 47-57); His trial before Pilate, Purg. xx. 91 (*Matt.* xxvii); Mon. ii. 13$^{50-4}$; iii. 15$^{27-33}$; Epist. v. 10$^{156-7}$; His selection of St. John to take care of the Virgin Mary, Par. xxv. 114 (*John* xix. 26-7); the Crucifixion, Inf. xxiii. 117; xxxiv. 114-15; Purg. vi. 119; xx. 88-90; xxiii. 74; xxxiii. 6, 63; Par. vi. 90; vii. 20, 47-48, 57; xi. 32, 72; xii. 37-8; xiii. 41; xiv. 104-8; xix. 105; xxv. 114; xxvi. 59; xxvii. 36; xxix. 98; xxxi. 3; V. N. § 22$^{2-3}$; Conv. iii. 7^{164}; iv. 24^{64}; Epist. viii. 4^{44}; the earthquake at His death, Inf. xxi. 112-14; Par. vii. 48; and eclipse, Par. xxvii. 35-6; xxix. 97-9; His descent into Hell, Inf. iv. 53; xii. 38; xxi. 114; His Resurrection, Purg. xxi. 9 (*Luke* xxiv. 15-16); Par. xxiv. 126 (*John* xx. 1-8); Conv. iv. 22$^{149-59}$; Mon. iii. 9$^{115-16}$ (*John* xxi. 7); the three Maries at His sepulchre, Conv. iv. 22$^{149-59}$ (*Luke* xxiv); the visit of St. Peter and St. John to the sepulchre, Par. xxiv. 125-6 (*John* xx. 3-6); Mon. iii. 9$^{115-16}$; His appearance to the two disciples

on the way to Emmaus, Purg. xxi. 7-9 (*Luke* xxiv. 13-16); His appearance to St. Peter and the other disciples at the Sea of Tiberias, Mon. iii. 9$^{87-91}$ (*John* xxi); His mission of the disciples to baptize and teach all nations, Mon. iii. 3$^{80-7}$ (*Matt.* xxviii. 20).

Christ's Transfiguration teaches us, in the moral sense, that in most secret things we should have few companions, Conv. ii. 1$^{46-51}$; the existence of angels attested by Christ himself, Conv. ii. 6$^{26-31}$; His teaching that man is both mortal and immortal, Conv. ii. 9$^{114-32}$; the miracles performed by Christ and His saints the foundation of our faith, Conv. iii. 7$^{161-4}$; His teaching that the contemplative life is best, though the active life is good, Conv. iv. 17$^{94-111}$; Christ died in the thirty-fourth year of His age, since it was not fitting that Divinity should suffer decline, the thirty-fifth year being the age of perfection; similarly He died at the sixth hour, i. e. at the culmination of the day, Conv. iv. 23$^{95-110}$; had Christ lived out the natural term of His life, He would have died in His eighty-first year, Conv. iv. 24$^{63-8}$; Christ born during the reign of Augustus, at a time when the whole world was at peace, Conv. iv. 5$^{24-66}$; Mon. i. 16$^{1-12}$; He willed to be born subject to the edict of Augustus in order that the Son of God made man might be counted as a man in the Roman census, Mon. ii. 12$^{41-7}$; Epist. vii. 3$^{67-72}$; being under the jurisdiction of the Roman Empire He was rightly judged before a Roman tribunal, which Herod and Caiaphas brought about by sending

Him to Pilate, Mon. ii. 13^{45-54}; by His birth and death under the Roman Empire Christ gave His sanction to the Empire, Mon. ii. 12^{41-9}; Epist. viii. 2^{22-3}; His acceptance of frankincense and gold from the wise men symbolical of His lordship over things spiritual and things temporal, Mon. iii. 7^{1-5}.

Croazia, Croatia, country (forming, with Slavonia, a province of the present Empire of Austria-Hungary) which lies to the SW. of Hungary, between the river Save and the Adriatic; mentioned by St. Bernard (in the Empyrean), who pictures pilgrims coming thence to see the 'Veronica' at Rome, Par. xxxi. 103. [Giubbileo: Veronica.]

Crociata], Crusade; the disastrous Second Crusade (1147–9) preached by St. Bernard, and undertaken by the Emperor Conrad III and Louis VII of France, is alluded to by Cacciaguida (in the Heaven of Mars), who says that he followed the Emperor Conrad and met his death among the Mahometans, Par. xv. 139–48. [Cacciaguida: Currado[1].]

Crotona, now Crotone, city of Calabria in the old kingdom of Naples, a few miles NW. of Cape Colonne at the mouth of the Gulf of Taranto; reading adopted by some edd. for *Catona*, Par. viii. 62. [Catona.]

Cunizza, sister of the Ghibelline, Ezzelino III da Romano, youngest daughter of Ezzelino II and Adeleita dei Conti di Mangona; she was born c. 1198, and in 1221 or 1222 was married, for political reasons, to the Guelf captain, Count Ricciardo di San Bonifazio of Verona. Shortly after her marriage she became enamoured of the troubadour Sordello, by whom (c. 1226), with the connivance of her brother, she was abducted from Verona and conveyed back to Ezzelino's court [Azzolino[1]: Sordello]. Her intrigue with Sordello (which, however, appears to have been renewed later on at Treviso) did not last long, and she then went to the court of her brother Alberico at Treviso, where she abandoned herself to a knight named Bonio, with whom she wandered about the world, leading a life of pleasure. After the death of Bonio, who was slain while defending Treviso on behalf of Alberico against his brother Ezzelino, Cunizza was married by the latter to Aimerio, Count of Breganze; after his death, he having fallen a victim to a quarrel with Ezzelino, she married a gentleman of Verona; and subsequently she married a fourth husband in the person of Salione Buzzacarini of Padua, Ezzelino's astrologer. In or about 1260, both Ezzelino and Alberico being dead, and the fortunes of her house being at a low ebb, Cunizza went to reside in Florence, where in 1265, in the house of Cavalcante Cavalcanti, the father of D.'s friend Guido, she executed a deed granting their freedom to her father's and brothers' slaves, with the exception of those who had been concerned in the betrayal of Alberico. In 1279, being then upwards of eighty, she made her will, at the castle of La Cerbaia, whereby she bequeathed her possessions to the sons of Count Alessandro degli Alberti of Mangona, her mother's family. The date of her death is unknown.

D. (mindful perhaps of *Luke* vii. 47 and 1 *Peter* iv. 8) condones the dissoluteness of Cunizza's life in consideration of her merciful acts, and places her in Paradise, in the Heaven of Venus, among the spirits of those who were lovers upon earth (*Spiriti Amanti*), Par. ix. 32 ; *un altro* (*splendore*), *v.* 13 ; *beato spirito*, *v.* 20 ; *luce nuova*, *v.* 22 [**Venere, Cielo di**].

Cupído, Cupid, son of Venus, Par. viii. 7 ; D. says he was worshipped as well as his mother, and Dione, her mother, as being endowed with the power of inspiring love (*vv.* 7–8) [**Ciprigna**] ; and alludes to Virgil's account (*Aen.* i. 657 ff.) of how Cupid in the form of Ascanius sat in Dido's lap and inspired her fatal passion for Aeneas (*v.* 9).

D. refers to Cupid as *figlio* (*di Venere*), in allusion to the unintentional wounding of Venus by him while she was kissing him (Ovid, *Metam.* x. 525–6), Purg. xxviii. 65–6 ; and speaks of him as *Amore*, quoting Virgil (*Aen.* i. 665) and Ovid (*Metam.* v. 365), to prove that he was regarded by the ancients as the son of Venus (and Jupiter), Conv. ii. 6[117–26] [**Venere** [1]] ; Cupid (or love) is referred to elsewhere as *colui al quale ogni arma è leggiera* (his bow, *arco*, being mentioned in the same connexion), Conv. ii. 10[48].

Curiatii, celebrated Alban family, three brothers of which fought with the three Roman Horatii in the reign of Tullus Hostilius, to determine whether Rome or Alba was to be mistress. The fight was long doubt-

ful ; two of the Horatii fell, but the third, who was unhurt, seeing that the three Curiatii were severely wounded, feigned to fly, and, managing to engage his opponents singly, succeeded in killing them one after another (*Livy*, i. 25).

The fight of 'i tre ai tre' is alluded to by the Emperor Justinian (in the Heaven of Mercury) in connexion with the fortunes of the Roman Eagle, which he says remained in Alba for 300 years, i.e. up till the time of the defeat of the Curiatii by the Horatii, Par. vi. 37–9. D. mentions the Curiatii, in connexion with the combat, referring to Livy (i. 24, 25) and Orosius (ii. 4) as his authorities, Mon. ii. 11[22–38]. [**Alba : Horatii.**]

Curiazii. [**Curiatii.**]

Curio[1], Marcus Curius Dentatus, favourite hero of the Roman republic, celebrated in later times as an example of Roman frugality and virtue. He was twice Consul, B.C. 290 and 275 ; and Censor, 272. In his first consulship he successfully held the Samnites in check ; and in the second he completely defeated Pyrrhus, King of Epirus, and forced him to leave Italy. On this and on other occasions he declined to share in the large booty which he gained. At the close of his military career he retired to his small farm in the country of the Sabines, which he cultivated with his own hands. He rejected costly presents offered him by the Samnites with the remark that he preferred ruling over those who possessed gold, to possessing it himself, an incident to which D. refers (his authority probably being

Cicero, *Senect.* § 16), Conv. iv.
5[110-15]. [*Senectute, De.*]

Curio[2], Caius Scribonius Curio,
originally an adherent of the Pompeian party, by whose influence he
was made tribune of the plebs, B.C.
50. He was afterwards bought over
by Caesar, and employed his power
as tribune against his former friends.
When Caesar was proclaimed by the
Senate an enemy of the Republic, C.
fled from Rome and joined the
former, who sent him to Sicily with
the title of propraetor. After ex-
pelling Cato from Sicily he crossed
over to Africa, where he was defeated
and slain by Juba.

D. places C. among the Sowers
of discord in Bolgia 9 of Circle VIII
of Hell (Malebolge), Inf. xxviii.
102; *tal*, *v.* 86; *colui*, *v.* 93; *compagno*, *v.* 95; *questi*, *vv.* 96, 97
[**Scismatici**]; C. is pointed out to
D. by Pier da Medicina, who describes him (in words mainly borrowed from Lucan, *Phars.* i. 269 ff.),
as the man who urged Caesar to
advance on Rome after crossing the
Rubicon (*vv.* 97–102); in his letter
to the Emperor Henry VII D. mentions Curio again and quotes Lucan
(*Phars.* i. 280–2) in the same connexion, Epist. vii. 2[82-5] [**Cesare**[1]].

Curradino, Conradin, son of the
Emperor Conrad IV, the last legitimate representative of the Swabian
line, the last scion of the Hohenstaufen. On the sudden death of
his father in 1254, C., who was
barely three years old, was the rightful claimant to the crowns of Sicily
and Naples. But his uncle, Manfred, assuming first the regency in
C.'s name, on a report of his death

accepted the crown at the invitation
of the great nobles (1258). He
met the protests of C.'s mother by
saying it was not for the interests of
the realm that Naples should be ruled
by a woman and an infant, and
declared that, C. being his only
relative, he should preserve the
kingdom for him, and should appoint
him his successor. After Manfred's
defeat and death at Benevento (Feb.
26, 126$\frac{5}{6}$), the Sicilies, impatient of
the French yoke, and the Ghibellines
throughout Italy, called upon Conradin to assert his hereditary rights.
In response to this appeal C. descended into Italy in the next year
with an army in order to wrest his
kingdom from Charles of Anjou.
But the attempt resulted in a disastrous failure. C. was defeated by
Charles at Tagliacozzo (Aug. 23,
1268), and having been betrayed
into his hands was executed (Oct.
29) at Naples, where his body was
buried, Charles not allowing it to be
laid in consecrated ground. [**Carlo**[1]:
Tagliacozzo.]

The murder of C. by Charles of
Anjou is referred to by Hugh Capet
(in Circle V of Purgatory), who
says that Charles came into Italy
and 'for amends made a victim
of Conradin', Purg. xx. 68.

Currado[1], Conrad III of Swabia,
Emperor 1138–1152, the first of
the Hohenstaufen line [**Table H**].
In 1147, at the instigation of St.
Bernard, he undertook the disastrous
Second Crusade, in company with
Louis VII of France. He returned
to Germany in 1149, and died at
Bamberg three years after.

He is mentioned by Cacciaguida

(in the Heaven of Mars), who says he followed the Emperor, and was knighted by him, and afterwards met his death in his train while fighting against the Mahometans, Par. xv. 139–48. [Cacciaguida.]

Currado [2]. [Malaspina, Currado.]

Currado da Palazzo, Guelf of Brescia, who was Vicar of Charles of Anjou in Florence in 1276, captain of the Brescians in their war against Trent in 1279, and Podestà of Piacenza in 1288; he is mentioned by Marco Lombardo (in Circle III of Purgatory), who, speaking of the degenerate state into which Lombardy had fallen after the wars between Frederick II and the Church, says there yet remain three old men whose lives are a reproach to the young generation, the other two being Gherardo da Cammino and Guido da Castello, Purg. xvi. 121–6.

Currado Malaspina. [Malaspina, Currado.]

Curzii, Curtii; reading adopted by some edd. for Drusi (which is almost certainly the right reading), Conv. iv. 5[123] [Drusi]. The reference would be to M. Curtius, who, according to the tradition, when (in B.C. 362) the earth in the Roman forum gave way, and a great chasm appeared, which the soothsayers declared could only be filled up by throwing into it Rome's greatest treasure, mounted his steed in full armour, and leapt into the abyss, exclaiming that Rome possessed no greater treasure than a brave citizen (Livy, vii. 6; Oros., iii. 5, § 3).

Cyclopes, one-eyed giants, the assistants of Vulcan, who forged the thunderbolts of Jupiter. D. alludes to them as gli altri (fabbri di Giove), and represents them at work in the 'black smithy' of Mt. Aetna (volcanoes being regarded as the workshops of Vulcan), Inf. xiv. 55–6; their abode beneath Mt. Aetna, Ecl. ii. 27. [Vulcano.]

Cyclops, the Cyclops Polyphemus; antrum Cyclopis, 'the cave of Polyphemus', i.e. (according to the old commentator) Bologna, P. himself representing King Robert of Naples, Ecl. ii. 47. [Polyphemus: Roberto [2].]

Cyrus. [Ciro.]

D

D, first letter of the word Diligite, formed by the spirits of the Just in the Heaven of Jupiter, Par. xxviii. 78. [Aquila [2]: Giove, Cielo di.]

Dafne [1], Daphne, daughter of the Thessalian river-god Peneus; she was pursued by Apollo, who was enamoured of her, and when on the point of being overtaken by him she prayed for help and was transformed into a laurel, which in consequence became the favourite tree of Apollo. In allusion to the metamorphosis of Daphne, the laurel is

spoken of as *fronda Peneia,* Par. i.
32–3; *frondes versa Peneide cretae,*
Ecl. i. 33; and (by G. del Virgilio)
as *Penea serta,* Carm. 38 [**Peneio**].

Dafne [2]], Daphne, a daughter of
the soothsayer Tiresias, supposed
by some to be referred to, Purg.
xxii. 113; the reference, however,
is almost certainly to T.'s better-
known daughter Manto, the prophetess. [**Manto: Tiresia.**]

Damascenus, Johannes Damascenus, John of Damascus, eminent
Father of the early Greek Church
(c. 680–756); he was the author
of the first system of Christian theology in the Eastern Church, and
famed for his exposition of the ortho-
dox faith. His most important work
was translated into Latin in Cent.
xii under the title *De Fide Orthodoxa;*
it thus became familiar to Peter
Lombard and St. Thomas Aquinas,
through whom it exercised considerable influence upon the scholastic
theology of the West.

In his Letter to the Italian Cardinals D. reproaches them with
neglecting the works of Damascenus
and other Fathers of the Church,
Epist. viii. 7[114–17] (where for
Damascenus some edd. read *Damianus*).

Damiano, Pier, St. Peter Damian, a Father of the Church, born
at Ravenna c. 1007. After a youth
spent in hardship and privation, he
became a teacher, and acquired some
celebrity. At the age of about 30,
however, he entered the Benedictine
monastery of Santa Croce di Fonte
Avellana on the slopes of Monte
Catria, of which he became Abbot
c. 1043 [**Avellana**]. In 1058,

much against his will, he was created
Cardinal and Bishop of Ostia, but
was allowed to resign his bishopric
in 1067. He was zealous in his
efforts to reform Church discipline,
and made journeys into France and
Germany with that object. After
fulfilling several important missions
under Nicholas II and Alexander II,
he died at Faenza in 1072.

D. places St. P. D. among the
contemplative spirits (*Spiriti Contemplanti*), in the Heaven of Saturn,
Par. xxi. 43–139; and represents
him as inveighing against the luxury
of the prelates of his day (*vv.*
127–35). [**Saturno, Cielo di.**]

The three lines (*vv.* 121–3) in
which St. Peter Damian names
himself to D. have been the subject
of much discussion. Some (reading
fui in *v.* 122) take the meaning to
be: 'I was known as Pietro Damiano in the monastery of Fonte
Avellana, but called myself Pietro
Peccatore in the monastery of Santa
Maria in Porto fuori at Ravenna'.
According to others (who read *fu*),
D. intended to correct a confusion
between Peter Damian and Pietro
degli Onesti of Ravenna, who was
also known as Pietro Peccatore:
'I, Pietro Damiano, was at Fonte
Avellana, but Pietro Peccatore (i.e.
Pietro degli Onesti) was at Santa
Maria in Ravenna'. Others, again,
identifying 'la casa di Nostra Donna
in sul lito Adriano' with the monastery of Santa Maria in Pomposa,
situated on a small island at the
mouth of the Po, near Comacchio
(where Peter Damian is known to
have resided for two years), interpret
(reading *fui* in *v.* 122): 'At Fonte

Avellana was I, Pietro Damiano, known as Pietro Peccatore; I resided also at the monastery of Santa Maria in Pomposa on the Adriatic coast'. Of these interpretations, none of which is free from objection, the first is perhaps the most generally accepted. [**Pietro degli Onesti**.]

Some edd. read *Damianus* for *Damascenus*, Epist. viii. 7$^{114-17}$ [**Damascenus**].

Damianus. [**Damiano**.]

Damiata, old town of Damietta in Egypt (the name of which was familiar in western Europe during Cent. xiii, owing to its having been taken by the Crusaders in 1218, and again in 1249), situated at the mouth of the easternmost of the two principal branches formed by the Nile at its delta; mentioned, in connexion with 'il veglio di Creta', to indicate the East (as representing the ancient monarchies), while Rome indicates the West, Inf. xiv. 103–5. [**Creta**.]

Dan], Dan, son of Jacob by Bilhah, Rachel's maid; he is among those referred to by Virgil as having been released by Christ from Limbo, *Israel co' suoi nati*, Inf. iv. 59 [**Limbo**].

Daniel. [**Daniello**.]

Daniel, Arnaut. [**Arnaldo Daniello**.]

Danielis, Prophetia], Book of Daniel; quoted, Mon. iii. 1$^{1-3}$ (*Dan.* vi. 22); referred to, Purg. xxii. 146–7 (ref. to *Dan.* i. 3–20); Par. iv. 13 (ref. to *Dan.* ii. 12, 24); Par. xxix. 134, Conv. ii. 6$^{34-9}$ (ref. to *Dan.* vii. 10); Epist. x. 28^{560} (ref. to *Dan.* ii. 3). [***Bibbia***.]

Daniello, prophet Daniel; mentioned as an example of temperance in Circle VI of Purgatory, where the sin of Gluttony is purged, Purg. xxii. 146–7 (ref. to *Dan.* i. 3–20) [**Golosi**]; Beatrice, who divined and solved D.'s doubts, is compared to Daniel, who told Nebuchadnezzar his dream and interpreted it to him, thereby appeasing his wrath, and saving the lives of the wise men of Babylon, whom he had commanded to be slain for not being able to interpret the dream (*Dan.* ii. 12, 24), Par. iv. 13–15; Daniel's estimate of the number of the angels (*Dan.* vii. 10), Par. xxix. 134; Conv. ii. 6$^{34-9}$; his answer to Darius from the lions' den (*Dan.* vi. 22), *Daniel*, Mon. iii. 1$^{1-3, 19}$; his account of Nebuchadnezzar's dream (*Dan.* ii. 3), Epist. x. 28$^{559-62}$.

Daniello, Arnaldo. [**Arnaldo Daniello**.]

Danoia. [**Danubio**.]

Dante, the poet's Christian name, said to be a contraction of Durante; mentioned once only in the *D. C.*, it being the first word addressed to D. by Beatrice, Purg. xxx. 55; *il nome mio, v.* 62. Many MSS. and some edd. read *Dante* for *Da te* in the passage where D. is addressed by Adam, Par. xxvi. 104; but there can be little doubt, in view of D.'s own precept as recorded in the *Convivio* (i. 2$^{8-17}$; cf. Purg. xxx. 62–3), that the latter is the correct reading.

D. does not name himself in the *Vita Nuova, Convivio, De Monarchia*, or *De Vulgari Eloquentia*; in the last treatise he usually refers to himself as the friend of Cino da Pistoja,

amicus Cini, V. E. i. 10^{30}, 17^{25};
ii. 2$^{83, 93}$, 5^{49}, 6^{72}; *alius Florentinus*,
V. E. i. 13^{36}; *nos*, V. E. ii. 8^{71},
10^{26}, 12^{18}, 13^{13}; in his Letters he
names himself, *Dantes*, Epist. ix.
4^{42}; x. 13^{258}; *Dantes Alagherius*,
Epist. ix. 3^{28}; x. 10^{189}; also
A. T. § 24^4; *Dantes Alagherii*,
A. T. § 1^2; his name is prefixed to
the following Letters, *Dantes*,
Epist. iii; *Dantes Alagherius*, Epist.
ii, v, vi, vii, viii, x. [**Alighieri.**]
In his *tenzone* with D. Forese Donati speaks of him as *Dante*, Son.
lii*. 12; in his poetical correspondence with G. del Virgilio D. figures
under the name of *Tityrus*, Ecl. i.
6, 24, &c. [**Tityrus.**]

D. is spoken of by the Virgin
Mary (to St. Lucy) as *il tuo fedele*,
Inf. ii. 98; by Beatrice (to Virgil)
as *l'amico mio*, Inf. ii. 61; B. addresses him once by name, Purg.
xxv. 55; otherwise as *frate*, Purg.
xxxiii. 23; Par. iii. 70; iv. 100;
vii. 58, 130; he is also addressed
as *frate* by Belacqua, Purg. iv. 127;
by Oderisi, Purg. xi. 82; by Sapia,
Purg. xiii. 94; by Marco Lombardo,
Purg. xvi. 65; by Adrian V, Purg.
xix. 133; by Statius, Purg. xxi.
13; by Forese Donati, Purg. xxiii.
97, 112; by Bonagiunta, Purg.
xxiv. 55; by Guido Guinicelli,
Purg. xxvi. 115; by Matilda, Purg.
xxix. 15; by St. Benedict, Par.
xxii. 61; he is addressed by Virgil
as *figlio*, Inf. vii. 115; Purg. xxvii.
35, 128; *dolce figlio*, Purg. iii. 66;
figliuol, Inf. vii. 61; (*figliuolo*), viii.
67; Purg. i. 112; viii. 88; (*fi-
gliuole*), xvii. 92; xxiii. 4; *figliuol
mio*, Inf. iii. 121; xi. 16; Purg. iv.
46; xxvii. 20; by Brunetto Latini,

as *figliuol mio*, Inf. xv. 31; *figliuol*,
xv. 37; by Statius, as *frate*, Purg.
xxi. 13; *figlio*, xxv. 35; by Cacciaguida, as *figlio*, Par. xv. 52; xvii.
94; by Adam, as *figliuol mio*, Par.
xxvi. 115; by St. Peter, as *buon
cristiano*, Par. xxiv. 52; *figliuol*,
Par. xxvii. 64; by St. Bernard, as
figliuol di grazia, Par. xxxi. 112.

D. is escorted through Hell and
Purgatory by Virgil (Inf. i. 61—
Purg. xxx. 48), who, after taking
formal leave of him on the threshold
of the Terrestrial Paradise (Purg.
xxvii. 124–42), accompanies him
for a short time longer, and then
finally departs (Purg. xxx. 49),
leaving him to the charge of Beatrice; by her he is conducted from
the Terrestrial to the Celestial Paradise, and through the successive
Heavens of the latter, until they
reach the Celestial Rose, where she
quits him, sending St. Bernard to
take her place (Par. xxxi. 59); with
him D. remains until the termination
of the Vision (Par. xxxiii. 145).

In the light of the fourfold interpretation of the *Commedia* indicated
in his Letter to Can Grande (Epist.
x. 7), D., as he appears in the poem,
represents in the literal sense the
Florentine Dante Alighieri; in the
allegorical, Man on his earthly pilgrimage; in the moral, Man turning
from vice to virtue; in the anagogical,
the Soul passing from a state of sin
to that of glory.

D. supplies, directly or indirectly,
the following information about himself in his various works:—that he
was a native of Florence (Inf. xxiii.
94–5; cf. Inf. x. 25–7; xvi. 9;
xxxiii. 11; Purg. xiv. 19; xxiv.

79; Par. vi. 53–4; xxv. 5; xxxi. 39; Conv. i. 3²²⁻⁵; V. E. i. 6¹⁹, 13³⁶; A. T. § 1²; Ecl. i. 43–4; and the titles of several of his Letters); that his family were Guelfs (Inf. x. 42–51); that he was born in 1265 (Inf. i. 1; xxi. 113; cf. Conv. i. 3²²⁻⁵), under the Constellation of Gemini (Par. xxii. 112–17; cf. Inf. xv. 55); that he was baptized in the Baptistery of San Giovanni (Par. xxv. 8–9; cf. Inf. xix. 17), the font of which he once broke in order to rescue a boy from suffocation (Inf. xix. 17–21); that his Christian name was Dante (Purg. xxx. 55; cf. Epist. ix. 3, 4; x. 13; A. T. § 1²); that his surname was derived from the wife of his great-great-grandfather, Cacciaguida (Par. xv. 91–2, 137–8); (apparently) that he was of noble descent (Par. xvi. 40–5; cf. Inf. xv. 74–8); that he taught himself the art of versifying (V. N. § 3⁶⁹⁻⁷¹); that he could ride (V. N. § 9⁴⁰, ⁴⁴) and draw (V. N. § 35⁵); that he loved music (Purg. ii. 106–23); that he suffered from a weakness of the eyes, caused by excessive weeping (V.N.§40³⁰⁻⁴), and too much reading (Conv. iii. 9¹⁴⁷⁻⁵⁷); (possibly) that he was present at the battle of Campaldino (Purg. v. 92), and at the capitulation of Caprona (Inf. xxi. 94–6); that (after 1291) he frequented the schools of philosophy (Conv. ii. 13⁴⁵⁻⁹); that he was exiled from Florence as a member of the Bianchi faction (Par. xvii. 46–93; xxv. 4–5; cf. Inf. vi. 67–9; x. 81; Purg. xi. 140–1; Canz. xi. 77–9; Canz. xvi. 5; Conv. i. 3²²⁻³; V. E. i. 6¹⁷⁻²³; ii. 6³⁶⁻⁹,

46–7; Epist. ii. 1; ix; and the titles of Epist. iv, v, vi, vii); that he took refuge first with one of the Scaligers at Verona (Par. xvii. 70), then with the Malaspini in Lunigiana (Purg. viii. 133–9); that he formed an attachment for a Lucchese lady named Gentucca (Purg. xxiv. 37–48); and that he spent some time as the guest of Can Grande at his court at Verona (Par. xvii. 88). The history of his love for Beatrice, whom he first saw at the age of nine, is told in the *Vita Nuova*. Among his friends were Guido Cavalcanti (Son. xxxii; V. N. § 3⁹⁸⁻⁹), his friendship with whom dated from 1283 (V.N. § 3¹⁰²⁻³), Cino da Pistoja (Son. xxxiv, xlvi; V. E. i. 10³⁰, 17²⁵; ii. 2⁸³, ⁹³), Lapo Gianni (Son. xxxii. 1), Forese Donati (Son. lii, liii, liv), the musician Casella (Purg. ii. 76–117), Giovanni Quirini of Venice (Son. xxxvii), and (as is commonly supposed) the artist Giotto (Purg. xi. 95); while he revered as a master Brunetto Latini (Inf. xv. 82–5).

Biography. Dante Alighieri was born in Florence in 1265 (probably in the latter part of May), in the quarter of San Martino al Vescovo, as appears from documentary evidence. Judging from his allusions in the *D. C.* (Par. xvi. 40–5; cf. Inf. xv. 74–8), and from the position of their house in the heart of the city, the Alighieri would seem to have been a noble family. They were descended, as is supposed, from the ancient family of the Elisei, who lived in the Porta san Piero in Florence. They belonged to the Guelf party (Inf. x. 42–51); D.'s father, however, inasmuch as the poet was born in Florence, was apparently not among the Guelfs who were exiled from Florence in 1260, after the battle of Montaperti. D.'s ancestry has been traced back as far as his great-great-great-grandfather, one Adamo, whose son, Cacciaguida, was knighted by the Emperor Conrad III, as he himself relates (Par. xv. 139–41) [Cacciaguida]. D.'s father and great-grandfather were both named Alighiero, this name being derived from Cacciaguida's wife, Aldighiera degli Aldighieri [Alighieri]. His father, who appears to have been a notary, married twice, D. being the son of his first wife, Bella; by his second wife, Lapa, he had another son, Francesco, and a daughter, Tana. [Alighiero[2] : Bella : Francesco[3] : Tana.] The family of D.'s mother is not known; it has been conjectured that she was the daughter of Durante di Scolaio degli Abati, in which case D.'s Christian name was probably derived from his maternal grandfather. D. himself married (not later than 1298) Gemma di Manetto Donati, by whom he had four children, Pietro, Jacopo, Antonia, and Beatrice. [Table A.] When D. was exiled from Florence, Gemma and his children did not accompany him, and it is probable that he never saw his wife again. He makes no mention of her in any of his works. There is no evidence to support the conjectures that he lived on bad terms with Gemma while they were together.

Little is known of D.'s early years, beyond the episode of his love, at the age of nine, for Beatrice, commonly supposed to be Beatrice Portinari (d. 1290), the story of which is told in the *Vita Nuova* [Beatrice[1]]. The statements of the old biographers that D.'s 'master' (in the ordinary sense of the word) was Brunetto Latini (who was well over fifty when D. was born), and that he studied before the year 1300 at Bologna and Padua, have little or no evidence to support them. His name appears in a document dated 1283 (in which year he was 18, and, both his father and mother being dead, according to Florentine usage was of age) as representative of the Alighieri family in a matter of business which had been left unsettled at the death of his father. He is said, on the authority of Leonardo Bruni, to have fought on the Guelf side at the battle of Campaldino (June 11, 1289) [Campaldino]. He himself records (Inf. xxi. 94–6) that he was present at the capitulation of the Pisan garrison of Caprona two months later [Caprona].

As no one could participate in the higher offices of the government of Florence without belonging to one of the ' Arti ' or Guilds, D. enrolled himself (probably in 1295 or 1296) in the Guild of Physicians and Apothecaries (' Arte dei Medici e Speziali '). A few details of his public life have been preserved in various documents. On July 6, 1295, he gave his opinion as to certain proposed modifications of the ' Ordinamenti di Giustizia ' [Giano della Bella]; on Dec. 14 of the same year he took part in the bi-monthly election of Priors; and on June 5, 1296, he spoke in the

'Consiglio dei Cento'. In the spring of 1300 he went as envoy to San Gemignano, where he delivered a speech in discharge of his office on May 8. In the same year he was elected to serve as one of the Priors, for the two months from June 15 to Aug. 15, this being the highest office in the Republic of Florence. During his priorate it was decided to banish from Florence the leaders of the Neri and Bianchi factions, among the latter being D.'s friend, Guido Cavalcanti [**Cavalcanti, Guido**]. In this year (1300), the year of the great Jubilee, it would appear from D.'s own reference to the event (Inf. xviii. 28–33) that he paid a visit to Rome [**Giubbileo**]. Meanwhile the city of Florence was in a state of ferment owing to the feuds between these two factions, the former of whom, the Neri, were the partisans of Boniface VIII, and were clamouring for Charles of Valois as his representative, while the Bianchi, to which faction D. belonged, were bitterly opposed both to Boniface and to Charles. In the midst of these troubles we find D. (who had voted, April 13, 1301, in the 'Consiglio delle Capitudini delle Dodici Arti Maggiori') entrusted with the charge (April 28, 1301) of superintending the works on the street of San Procolo, which were intended to facilitate the introduction of forces from the outside districts. On June 19 in this year he voted in the 'Consiglio dei Cento' against the proposal to supply a contingent of a hundred soldiers to serve with the Papal forces, on the requisition of Pope Boniface VIII; and he re-

corded his vote on various matters several times in one or other of the Councils during the month of September, the last of which mention is preserved being on Sept. 28. In the following October, with a view to counteract the influence of the Neri with the Pope, and if possible to avert the coming of Charles of Valois, the Bianchi sent an embassy to Rome, of which, according to Dino Compagni (ii. 25), D. was a member. During their absence, however, Charles of Valois entered Florence (Nov. 1, 1301); and, soon after, the Podestà, Cante de' Gabrielli of Gubbio, pronounced a sentence, under date Jan. 27, $130\frac{1}{2}$, against D. and sundry others, who had been summoned and had failed to appear, on a charge of pecuniary malversation in office and of having conspired against the Pope, and the admission into the city of his representative, Charles of Valois, and against the peace of the city of Florence, and of the Guelf party, the penalty being a fine of 5,000 florins and restitution of the monies illegally exacted, payment to be made within three days of the promulgation of the sentence, in default of which all their goods to be forfeited and destroyed; in addition to the fine the delinquents are sentenced to banishment from Tuscany for two years, and to perpetual deprivation from office in the Commonwealth of Florence, their names to that end being recorded in the book of the Statutes of the People, as peculators and malversators in office. This sentence having been disregarded, on March 10 in the same year (1302) a second, severer sentence was pronounced against D. and fourteen others, condemning them to be burned alive should they at any time fall into the hands of the Republic.

Of D.'s movements from this time onwards little is known for certain. He appears at first to have joined the rest of the exiles, who assembled at Gargonza, a castle of the Ubertini between Arezzo and Siena, and decided to make common cause with the Ghibellines of Tuscany and Romagna, fixing their headquarters at Arezzo, where they remained until 1304. He was, at any rate, present at a meeting of the exiles, held on June 8, 1302, in the Church of San Godenzo, in the Tuscan Apennines, about twenty miles from Florence, when a convention was entered into with the Ubaldini, the ancient enemies of Florence. In July 1304, having been disappointed in their hopes of a peaceable return to Florence, through the mediation of the Cardinal Niccolò da Prato, the legate of Benedict XI, the exiles made an abortive attempt from Lastra (to which D. perhaps alludes, Par. xvii. 65-6), in concert with the Pistojans, to effect an entry into the city, an attempt from which D. seems to have held aloof. There is evidence of his having been at Forlì in 1303, and it was doubtless about this time that, dissatisfied with the proceedings of his companions in exile, 'la compagnia malvagia e scempia' (Par. xvii. 62), he separated himself from them, and took refuge at Verona, with one of the Scaligers (probably Bartolommeo della Scala). [**Lombardo** [1].]

It is impossible to follow D.'s wanderings, which, as he records in a passage in the *Convivio* (i. 3[28-30]), led him nearly all over Italy. It has been presumed (but the fact is very doubtful) from a legal document still existing that he was at Padua on Aug. 27, 1306; and it is known from others that he was shortly after (Oct. 6, 1306) at Sarzana in Lunigiana as agent for the Malaspini, his host on this occasion being Franceschino Malaspina [**Malaspina**]. How long he remained in Lunigiana (probably not beyond the summer of 1307), and whether, as some of the biographers maintain, he went thence to the Casentino and again to Forlì, and returned once more to Lunigiana on his way to Paris, it is difficult to decide. That he visited Paris during his exile is stated both by Boccaccio and by Villani (ix. 136), but at what precise period this visit took place remains a matter of conjecture.

From a phrase of Boccaccio in a Latin poem addressed to Petrarca, in which he mentions that D. visited 'Pariseos dudum serusque Britannos', it has been assumed that D. came to England; and Giovanni Serravalle, in a commentary on the *D.C.* written at the beginning of Cent. xv, goes the length of stating that he studied at Oxford. In the absence, however, of more trustworthy evidence, the fact of this alleged visit to England must be regarded as extremely doubtful.

It seems certain that he was in Italy between September 1310 and January 13$\frac{10}{11}$, when he wrote his letter to the Princes and Peoples of

Italy (Epist. v) on the advent of the Emperor Henry VII into Italy; and he was undoubtedly in Tuscany (probably as the guest of Guido Novello of Battifolle at Poppi) when his terrible letter to the Florentines (Epist. vi), dated 'from the springs of the Arno', March 31, 1311, was written, as well as that dated from the same place, April 17, 1311, and addressed to the Emperor himself (Epist. vii), who was at the time besieging Cremona, urging him to crush first the viper Florence, as the root of all the evils of Italy.

In this same year (1311), under date Sept. 2, was issued a proclamation, known as the 'Riforma di Messer Baldo d'Aguglione', granting pardon to a portion of the Florentine exiles, but expressly excepting certain others, D. among them, by name; his exclusion being doubtless due to the above letters and to his active sympathy with the Imperial cause [**Aguglione**]. From this time until nearly a year after the death of Henry VII at Buonconvento (Aug. 24, 1313), nothing whatever is known of D's movements. After the death of Clement V (April 20, 1314) he addressed a letter (Epist. viii) to the Italian Cardinals in conclave at Carpentras, calling upon them to elect an Italian Pope who should restore the Papal See to Rome. Some time after June 14, 1314, when the city of Lucca fell into the hands of the Ghibelline captain, Uguccione della Faggiuola, D. appears to have been there; and it may have been at this time that he formed an attachment for a certain Lucchese lady named Gentucca, but

what was the nature of his relations with her we have no means of knowing [**Gentucca**]. The supposition that he subsequently stayed at Gubbio, Fonte Avellana, and Udine, has little evidence to support it.

On May 19, 1315, a general offer of pardon was made to the exiles, in which D. was implicitly included, on condition that they should pay a fine and formally undergo the humiliating ceremony of 'oblation' in San Giovanni as released prisoners. These terms, the acceptance of which would necessarily have implied a confession of guilt on the part of those pardoned, were scornfully rejected by D. in a letter (Epist. ix) addressed to a friend in Florence (probably his brother-in-law, Teruccio Donati), by whom they had been communicated to D., though many of the exiles appear to have submitted to them.

After the success of the Ghibellines at Monte Catini (August 29, 1315), when under the leadership of Uguccione della Faggiuola they completely defeated the Florentines and Tuscan Guelfs, a last sentence was pronounced against D., his sons being included with him this time. By this decree, which is dated Nov. 6, 1315, he and those named with him are branded as Ghibellines and rebels, and condemned, if captured, to be beheaded on the place of public execution.

Not long after this, on June 2, 1316, the Florentine chief magistrate, Lando da Gubbio, proclaimed a fresh amnesty to certain of the exiles, from which, however, all those who had been originally condemned by the

Podestà, Cante de' Gabrielli, in 1302, were expressly excluded, D. among them.

After paying a second visit to Verona, where he was the guest of Can Grande (at what particular time it is impossible to decide), D., on the invitation of Guido Novello da Polenta, went to Ravenna (probably in 1317 or 1318), where his sons Pietro and Jacopo and his daughter Beatrice lived with him. While he was at Ravenna, after the *Inferno* and *Purgatorio* had been completed and made public, D. was invited by a poet and professor of Bologna, Giovanni del Virgilio, in a Latin poem, to come and receive the laurel crown at Bologna, an invitation which D. declined in a Latin eclogue (Ecl. i.), on the ground that the laurel had no attraction for him unless conferred by his own fellow-citizens in the baptistery where he had received his name [*Egloghe*[2]].

At the end of 1319 or beginning of 1320 D. appears to have paid a visit to Mantua, on which occasion a discussion was started as to the relative levels of land and water on the surface of the globe. D. subsequently wrote a treatise on the subject, which was delivered as a public dissertation at Verona on Jan. 20, 1320 [*Quaestio de Aqua et Terra*]. From the mention of D.'s name in a document lately discovered in the Vatican, from which it appears that he had the reputation of a sorcerer in his own lifetime, it has been inferred that he was at Piacenza some time in 1319 or 1320. In the summer of 1321 Guido da Polenta sent him on an embassy to Venice, where he appears to have fallen ill; on his return to Ravenna he grew worse, and died on September 14 of that year, aged 56 years 4 months. At Ravenna he was buried, and there ' by the upbraiding shore' his remains still rest, every effort on the part of the Florentines to secure 'the metaphorical ashes of the man of whom she had threatened to make literal cinders if she could catch him alive' having been in vain.

D.'s remains were placed in an ancient stone sarcophagus by Guido da Polenta, whose intention to erect a monument worthy of the poet was frustrated by his own expulsion from Ravenna and death not long after at Bologna. The tomb was repaired in 1483 by Bernardo Bembo, and again in 1692 by Cardinal Corsi, and a third time in 1780 by Cardinal Gonzaga, who erected the mausoleum, surmounted by a dome, which remains to the present day. In 1865, when preparations were being made for the celebration of the sixth centenary of D.'s birth, his bones were accidentally discovered in a wooden chest (bearing the date 1677) in a cavity of the wall adjoining the tomb. It appears that they had been secretly transferred from the sarcophagus at the beginning of Cent. xvi, to prevent their being forcibly removed by the Florentines, who had obtained permission for their translation to Florence from Leo X. After they had been publicly exhibited for three days, the remains were consigned once more to the original sarcophagus in which they had been placed by Guido da Polenta. The

well-known inscription on the sarcophagus ('Jura Monarchiae, &c.')
was composed, not by D. himself,
as was formerly supposed, but by one
Bernardo Canaccio, who is believed
to have been an acquaintance of D.
at Ravenna.

Numerous elegies were written on
the occasion of D.'s death by poets
in various parts of Italy, among them
being poems by Cino da Pistoja and
Giovanni Quirini of Venice, with both
of whom D. had exchanged sonnets
in his lifetime. A contemporary
account of D. has been left by his
fellow-citizen and friend, Giovanni
Villani, who describes him in his
Cronica (ix. 136) as 'a great
scholar, and poet and philosopher,
and a fine speaker, somewhat haughty
and reserved, and scornful in his
manner to his inferiors in learning'.
Boccaccio, who derived his information from some of those who had
frequented D.'s society at Ravenna,
records that the poet was 'of middle
height and, as an elderly man, walked
with a stoop; his gait was grave and
sedate. His face was long, his
nose aquiline, his eyes rather large
than small, and his jaws heavy, with
the under lip projecting beyond the
upper. His complexion was dark,
and his hair and beard thick, black,
and crisp; and his countenance
always sad and thoughtful.'

Sundry portraits of D. exist, but
only one which has any claim to
have been executed in the lifetime of
the poet. This is the portrait which
Vasari (in his *Vita di Giotto*) records
as having been painted by D.'s contemporary and friend Giotto, together
with those of Brunetto Latini and

Corso Donati, in the Palace of the
Podestà (the present Bargello) at
Florence. This work, which had
been whitewashed over some time
after 1550, was rediscovered in
1840, and a careful tracing of the
portrait, by Seymour Kirkup, taken
before it was ruined by 'restoration',
has preserved to us the lineaments
of D. as a young man, from the
hand of one who had known him in
the flesh. The authenticity of the
work has been questioned, but it is
commonly accepted as a genuine work
of Giotto. Of other representations
of D. the most interesting are the
alleged death-mask and the bronze
bust (modelled to all appearance from
the mask) which is preserved in the
National Museum at Naples.

Works. Besides the *Divina
Commedia* [**Commedia**], D. wrote
in Italian the *Vita Nuova*, containing the history of his love for
Beatrice [**Vita Nuova**]; the *Convivio* (incomplete), a philosophical
commentary in four books on three
of his *canzoni* [**Convivio**]; and a
number of lyrical poems, which have
been collected together under the
title of *Canzoniere* or *Rime* [**Canzoniere**].

In Latin he wrote the *De Vulgari
Eloquentia* (incomplete), a treatise in
two books on Italian as a literary
language [**Eloquentia, De Vulgari**];
the *De Monarchia*, 'the creed of his
Ghibellinism', a treatise in three
books on the nature and necessity of
a universal temporal monarchy, coexistent with the spiritual sovereignty
of the Pope [**Monarchia, De**]; sundry *Epistles*, chiefly political [**Epistole Dantesche**]; two *Eclogues*

[*Egloghe*[2]]; and the scientific dissertation known as the *Quaestio de Aqua et Terra* [**Quaestio de Aqua et Terra**].

In addition to the above works D. has been credited with the authorship of a translation in *terza rima* of the seven Penitential Psalms, and of a poem in the same metre, of eighty-three *terzine*, known as his *Professione di Fede*, which consists of a paraphrase of the Apostles' Creed, the ten Commandments, the *Pater Noster*, and the *Ave Maria*, together with reflections on the seven Sacraments and the seven Deadly Sins.

Dante, Fratello di. [**Francesco**[3].]

Dante, Madre di. [**Bella.**]

Dante, Padre di. [**Alighiero**[2].]

Dante, Sorella di. [**Tana.**]

Danubio, river Danube; Charles Martel (in the Heaven of Venus) describes Hungary as *quella terra che il D. riga Poi che le ripe tedesche abbandona*, Par. viii. 65–6 [**Carlo**[3]: **Ungaria**]; its mouths the E. limit of the original universal European language, *Danubius*, V. E. i. 8[25]; the ice of Cocytus compared to its frozen surface in winter, *Danoia*, Inf. xxxii. 26; mentioned by G. del Virgilio to indicate the N., *Ister*, Carm. 31.

Danubius. [**Danubio.**]

Dardanidae, Trojans, so called by Virgil (*Aen.* iii. 94) as being descended from Dardanus, V. N. § 25[84]. [**Dardano.**]

Dardano, Dardanus, son of Zeus and Electra, mythical ancestor of the Trojans, and through them of the Romans; discussion as to his nobility and mythical parentage, Conv.

iv. 14[134–48] [**Laomedonte**]; the male founder of Aeneas' race, and of European origin as testified by Virgil (*Aen.* viii. 134–7; iii. 163–7), *Dardanus*, Mon. ii. 3[67–84] [**Enea**].

Dardanus. [**Dardano.**]

Darius, King of Persia, B.C. 521–485; the most memorable event of his reign was the commencement of the great war between Persia and Greece, which was continued after his death by his son Xerxes, Mon. ii. 9[49]. [**Serse.**]

Dati, Bonturo. [**Bonturo.**]

David, King David; one of those released by Christ from Limbo, Inf. iv. 58 [**Limbo**]; rebellion of his son Absalom, Inf. xxviii. 138 [**Absalone**]; the son of Jesse, forefather of the Virgin Mary, Conv. iv. 5[39–45]; his birth contemporary with the arrival of Aeneas in Italy, and the foundation of the Roman Empire, Conv. iv. 5[46–9]; the father of Solomon, his invective against riches, Conv. iv. 12[81]; testified to the nobility of man, Conv. iv. 19[57–70]; God's rebuke to (*Psalm* l. 16), and his prayer to God (*Psalm* lxxii. 1), Mon. i. 13[29–31, 59–63]; his victory over Goliath, Mon. ii. 10[86]; his declaration that the righteous 'shall not be afraid of evil tidings' (*Psalm* cxii. 6–7) a comfort to D., Mon. iii. 1[30–3]; the mouthpiece of the Holy Spirit, Mon. iii. 1[31], 4[85]; Jerusalem his city, Epist. viii. 1[7].

D. places David among the Spirits of the Just (*Spiriti Giudicanti*) in the Heaven of Jupiter, where he is represented as forming the pupil of the eye of the Imperial Eagle, into the shape of which the blessed spirits group themselves, Par. xx. 37–42 [Aquila[2]: Giove, Cielo di]. He figures among the examples of humility sculptured on the wall of Circle I of Purgatory, where the sin of Pride is purged, being represented in the act of dancing before the Ark when it was brought back to Jerusalem from Kirjathjearim (2 *Sam.* vi. 14), Purg. x. 64–6 [Micol: Superbi].

He is referred to as *l'umile Salmista*, Purg. x. 65; *Salmista*, Conv. ii. 4[41], 6[103]; iv. 19[59], 23[79]; *Psalmista*, Mon. i. 15[22]; iii. 15[36]; A. T. § 22[8]; *Profeta*, Conv. ii. 1[58]; iii. 4[78]; *Propheta*, Mon. ii. 1[44]; iii. 3[76]; *il cantor dello Spirito Santo* (where D. alludes to his removal of the Ark, 2 *Sam.* vi), Par. xx. 38; *sommo cantor del sommo duce* (i. e. the Psalmist of God), Par. xxv. 72; *il cantor che, per doglia Del fallo, disse Miserere mei* (where D. alludes to his adultery with Bathsheba and his compassing the death of Uriah, 2 *Sam.* xi, and describes him as the great-grandson of Ruth), Par. xxxii. 11–12 [Rut]; *rex sanctissimus*, Mon. i. 13[59]; *padre di Salomone*, Conv. iv. 12[87]; quoted, Conv. ii. 1[58] (*Psalm* cxiv. 1); Conv. ii. 4[42] (*Psalm* viii. 1); Conv. ii. 6[103] (*Psalm* xix. 1); Conv. iii. 4[76] (*Psalm* c. 3); Conv. iv. 19[64] (*Psalm* viii. 1, 4–6); Conv. iv. 23[79] (*Psalm* civ. 9); Mon. i. 13[30, 61] (*Psalm* l. 16; lxxii. 1); Mon. i. 15[22] (*Psalm* iv. 7); Mon. ii. 1[1–6] (*Psalm* ii. 1–3); Mon. ii. 10[10] (*Psalm* xi. 7); Mon. iii. 1[31] (*Psalm* cxii. 6–7); Mon. iii. 3[77] (*Psalm* cxi. 9); Mon. iii. 15[37] (*Psalm* xcv. 5); Epist. x. 22[416–19] (*Psalm* cxxxix. 7–9); A. T.

§ 22[8–11] (*Psalm* cxxxix. 6) [*Psaltero*].

[Davus], character in the *Andria* of Terence; mentioned by G. del Virgilio in allusion to his saying, 'Davus sum, non Oedipus (i. e. I am no solver of riddles), Carm. 9.

De Anima; De Coelo; &c. [*Anima, De; Coelo, De; &c.*]

Deci, the Decii, famous Roman family, three members of which, father, son, and grandson, all bearing the same name, Publius Decius Mus, sacrificed their lives for their country. The first, who was Consul B.C. 340 with Titus Manlius Torquatus, lost his life in the war with the Latins, into whose ranks he flung himself, in obedience to a vision, when the Roman soldiers under his command began to waver (*Liv.* viii. 9). The second, who was four times Consul, followed his father's example in the battle with the Gauls and Samnites at Sentinum, B.C. 295 (*Liv.* x. 27–8). The third, who was Consul B.C. 279, lost his life in the campaign against Pyrrhus, King of Epirus.

The Emperor Justinian (in the Heaven of Mercury) mentions the Decii in connexion with the exploits of the Roman Eagle, Par. vi. 47; they are coupled with the Drusi, and their heroic deaths are referred to, Conv. iv. 5[122–3] [Drusi]; Livy's mention of them, and Cicero's account of them in the *De Finibus* (ii. 19), Mon. ii. 5[128–32, 140–58].

Decii. [Deci.]

Decimo Cielo. [Cielo Empireo.]

Decius, Publius, the first of the

three Decii who sacrificed their lives for their country ; Cicero's mention of him and his son and grandson, Mon. ii. 5$^{143-58}$. [Deci.]

Decretales. [*Decretali.*]

Decretali, Decretals, i.e. the Papal decrees, which form the groundwork of a large part of the Roman ecclesiastical law. A compilation of them, with additions of his own, was issued by Pope Gregory IX in 1234. Previously, about 1140, Gratian of Bologna had published his *Decretum*, a general collection of canons, Papal epistles, and sentences of Fathers, in imitation of the Pandects ; this work appears to have been the chief authority on the canon law in the Middle Ages [Graziano].

D. complains that the study of the Gospel and of the Fathers was abandoned, attention being paid to the Decretals alone, 'as appears from their margins' (i.e. either because they were well-thumbed, or were covered with annotations), Par. ix. 133–5 ; the Decretals, though worthy of veneration, not to be regarded as of higher authority than Holy Scripture, *Decretales*, Mon. iii. 3$^{55-6}$, $^{93-6}$; ought not to be studied to the neglect of the Fathers, Epist. viii. 7 (cf. Par. ix. 133–5) [Decretalistae]; the canon law is referred to as *Ragione Canonica*, Conv. iv. 12$^{100, 103}$ [*Ragione*].

Decretalistae, the Decretalists, commentators on the Decretals ; utterly without knowledge of theology and philosophy, Mon. iii. 3$^{53-5}$; D. mentions the famous decretalists, Henry of Susa, Cardinal of Ostia, Par. xii. 83 ; Epist. viii. 7^{119}; and

Pope Innocent IV, Epist. viii. 7^{118}; and refers to the *Speculum Juris* of Durandus, Epist. viii. 7^{118} [Enrico di Susa: Innocenzio ^{2}: *Speculum*]; the decretalists are alluded to, Par. ix. 134 [*Decretali*].

Dedalo, Daedalus, the father of Icarus ; he made the wooden cow for Pasiphaë, and when she gave birth to the Minotaur he constructed the Labyrinth in Crete, in which the monster was kept, and where the latter was afterwards slain by Theseus with the aid of Ariadne [Arianna]. In order to escape from the wrath of Minos, who had seized all the ships on the coast of Crete, D. procured wings for himself and his son Icarus, and fastened them on with wax. D. reached Italy in safety, but, Icarus having, contrary to his father's bidding, flown too high, the sun melted the wax, and he fell into the sea. (Ovid, *Metam.* viii. 183 ff.)

D. is mentioned by Griffolino (in Bolgia 10 of Circle VIII of Hell), who says that Albero da Siena had him burned ' because he did not make him a Daedalus ', i.e. did not teach him to fly as he had promised, Inf. xxix. 116–17 [Griffolino]; he is alluded to as the father of Icarus, *il padre*, Inf. xvii. 111 ; and (by Charles Martel in the Heaven of Venus) as *quello Che volando per l' aere il figlio perse*, Par. viii. 125–6 [Icaro].

Dei, De Civitate. [*Civitate Dei, De.*]

Deianira, daughter of Althaea and Oeneus, King of Calydon in Aetolia, and sister of Meleager [Meleagro]; she was the wife of

Hercules, whose death she unwittingly caused. The Centaur Nessus, having attempted to violate her, was shot by Hercules, but before he died he gave to D. a robe dipped in his blood, telling her it would act as a charm to preserve her husband's love. When D., jealous of his love for Iole, gave it to Hercules, the poison from the blood of Nessus maddened him ; he attempted to tear off the garment, but the flesh came with it, and at last, to put an end to his agony, he burned himself on a funeral pile, and D., in remorse, hanged herself [Ercole : Iole].

D. is mentioned in connexion with Nessus, who ' died for her, and himself avenged his own death ' (the story of which D. got from Ovid, *Metam.* ix. 127 ff.), Inf. xii. 67–9 [Nesso].

Deidamia, daughter of Lycomedes, King of Scyros, with whom Thetis left her son Achilles, disguised in woman's clothes, in order that he might not take part in the expedition against Troy. After D. had become the mother of Pyrrhus (or Neoptolemus) by Achilles, the latter, yielding to the persuasions of Ulysses, who had penetrated his disguise, abandoned her and sailed to Troy, in consequence of which she died of grief. [Schiro.]

D. is mentioned in connexion with Ulysses, whose craft was the means of her death (Statius, *Achill.* i. 536 ff.), Inf. xxvi. 62 [Ulisse]; Virgil (addressing Statius in Purgatory) mentions her, among the women named in the *Thebaid* and *Achilleid*, as being with her sisters in Limbo, Purg. xxii. 114 [Antigone : Limbo].

Deifile, Deiphyle, daughter of Adrastus, King of Argos, sister of Argia, wife of Tydeus, mother of Diomed [Argía: Diomede: Tideo]; mentioned by Virgil (addressing Statius in Purgatory) among the women named in the *Thebaid* and *Achilleid*, as being in Limbo, Purg. xxii. 10 [Antigone: Limbo]; she and her sister Argia quoted as examples of modesty, Conv. iv. 25[80–8] [Adrasto].

Delfico, Delphic; *la Delfica deità*, i. e. Apollo, who had an oracle at Delphi, Par. i. 32. [Apollo.]

Delia, surname of Diana, as having been born on the island of Delos [Delo]; goddess of the Moon, hence the Moon, *il cinto di D.*, the lunar halo, Purg. xxix. 78 ; *Delius et Delia*, Apollo and Diana, i.e. the Sun and Moon, Epist. vi. 2[54–5] [Apollo: Diana].

Delius, surname of Apollo, as having been born on the island of Delos [Delo]; god of the Sun, hence the Sun, Epist. vi. 2[55] [Apollo].

Delo, island of Delos, the smallest of the Cyclades ; it was said to have been raised from the deep by Neptune in order that Latona might have a refuge from the wrath of Juno, but was a floating island until Jupiter fixed it with adamantine chains to the bottom of the sea. Here Latona gave birth to Apollo and Diana (hence sometimes spoken of as Delius and Delia), her offspring by Jupiter. D. mentions it in this connexion, and refers to its shaking (Ovid, *Metam.* vi. 186–92), Purg. xx. 130 [Latona].

Demetrius, Demetrius I, King

of Syria, B.C. 162–150. When he came to the throne, Alcimus, who was captain of 'all the wicked and ungodly men of Israel', wishing to be appointed high-priest, accused Judas Maccabaeus of being hostile to the king, who sent a force against Judas, and made Alcimus high-priest (1 *Macc.* vii. 9). [Alcimus.]

D. mentions Demetrius and Alcimus together as typifying respectively Philip the Fair and Clement V, in their dealings with regard to the election of the latter to the Papal See, Epist. viii. 4[65]. [Clemente[2].]

Democrito, Democritus, celebrated Greek philosopher, born at Abdera, in Thrace, c. B. c. 460, died B.C. 361; he was the originator of the 'atomic theory', believing that the world was formed by the haphazard aggregation of atoms.

D. places him in Limbo among the ancient philosophers, describing him, in allusion to his theory of the creation (for which he was probably indebted to Cicero, *Nat. Deor.* i. 24), as 'D. che il mondo a caso pone', Inf. iv. 136 [Limbo]; his theory that the Milky Way is caused by the reflected light of the Sun, Conv. ii. 15[56] [Galassia]; his devotion to philosophy proved by his neglect of his person (D.'s description of which is probably a confused recollection of Horace, *Ars Poët.* 296 ff.), Conv. iii. 14[74–6].

Demofoonte, Demophoön, son of Theseus and Phaedra; he accompanied the Greeks against Troy, and on his return gained the love of Phyllis, daughter of Sithon, King of Thrace, and promised to marry her after he had been home to Athens.

As he stayed away longer than Phyllis expected, she thought him faithless, and put an end to her life.

Folquet of Marseilles (in the Heaven of Venus) compares his own love-torments to those of Phyllis after she had been deceived by D., Par. ix. 100–1. [Folco: Rodopeia.]

Demonio, Il, 'the Demon', nickname applied by Guido del Duca (in Circle II of Purgatory) to Maghinardo or Mainardo Pagano da Susinana, Purg. xiv. 118. [Mainardo Pagano.]

Dente, Vitaliano del. [Vitaliano.]

Deo. [Dio.]

Derivazioni, the *Magnae Derivationes* of Uguccione da Pisa; quoted as D.'s authority for the derivation of *autore* from the Greek word *autentin*, Conv. iv. 6[38–41]. [Uguccione[2].]

Desiderius, King of the Longobards (or Lombards), 757–74; his attack on the Papal territory repelled by Charlemagne (773–4) at the instance of Pope Adrian I, Mon. iii. 11[1–4]; C.'s defence of the Church against the Lombards one of the exploits of the Roman Eagle (an anachronism, inasmuch as Charlemagne did not receive the Imperial crown until twenty-seven years later, 800), Par. vi. 94–6. [Carlo Magno: Longobardi.]

Deus. [Dio.]

Deuteronomium], Book of Deuteronomy; quoted, Mon. i. 8[23–4] (*Deut.* vi. 4); Epist. vi. 1[22–3] (*Deut.* xxxii. 35); referred to, Mon. i. 14[65–73] (ref. to *Deut.* i. 10–18). [Bibbia.]

Diabolus. [Lucifero.]

Diana[1], daughter of Jupiter and Latona, who gave birth to her and her twin brother Apollo on the island of Delos [**Delo**]; she was goddess of hunting, in which capacity she is mentioned, in connexion with Helice, one of her nymphs, Purg. xxv. 131 [**Elice**].

As Apollo was identified with the Sun, so was Diana with the Moon; hence D. refers to them as *li due occhi del cielo*, Purg. xx. 132; *ambedue i figli di Latona*, Par. xxix. 1 [**Latona**], similarly he speaks of the Moon as *la donna che qui regge*, i.e. Hecate (who was identified with Diana), Inf. x. 80; *Delia*, Purg. xxix. 78; Epist. vi. 2[54]; *la figlia di Latona*, Par. x. 67; xxii. 139 (cf. Par. xxix. 1); *Phoebe*, Mon. i. 11[35]; *Trivia tra le ninfe eterne*, Diana and her nymphs (i.e. the Moon and Stars), Par. xxiii. 26 [**Delia: Ecate: Luna: Phoebe: Trivia**].

Diana[2], name of a river, which the Sienese believed to exist beneath their city, and in the unsuccessful search for which they spent large sums of money; their disappointment is referred to by Sapía (in Circle II of Purgatory) in connexion with their recent (1303) purchase of the seaport of Talamone, which she says will cause them still greater disappointment, Purg. xiii. 151–3. [**Talamone.**]

Diavolo. [Lucifero.]

Dido, also called Elissa, daughter of Belus, King of Tyre, and sister of Pygmalion; she married her uncle Sichaeus, who was murdered by Pygmalion for the sake of his wealth, whereupon she fled from Tyre and landed in Africa, where she founded Carthage (B. C. 853) [**Cartagine: Pigmalione**]. Virgil makes her a contemporary of Aeneas, with whom she falls in love on his arrival in Africa, and on his leaving her to go to Italy she in despair slays herself on a funeral pile.

D. mentions her, Inf. v. 85; Par. viii. 9; Canz. xii. 36; Conv. iv. 26[65]; Mon. ii. 3[102–6]; and alludes to her as *colei che s' ancise amorosa*, Inf. v. 61; *la figlia di Belo*, Par. ix. 97; she is placed in Circle II of Hell, among those who met their death through love, Inf. v. 61, 85 [**Lussuriosi**]; her suicide and faithlessness to Sichaeus, Inf. v. 61–2; her deception by Cupid in the person of Ascanius, Par. viii. 9 [**Cupído**]; her love for Aeneas an injury both to his wife Creusa and to her own husband Sichaeus, Par. ix. 97–8 [**Creusa: Sicheo**]; her death through love, Canz. xii. 36 (cf. Inf. v. 61); her welcome of Aeneas to Carthage, his love for, and desertion of, her, Conv. iv. 26[64–70]; Aeneas' connexion with Africa through her, she being 'regina et mater Carthaginensium in Africa', and his second wife, as testified by Virgil (*Aen.* iv. 171–2), Mon. ii. 3[102–6] [**Enea**]; G. del Virgilio speaks of her as *Elissa*, Carm. 32 [**Elissa**].

Digesta. [*Digesto.*]

Digesto, Digest of the Roman law, the body of the Roman laws arranged under proper titles, originally drawn up by order of the Emperor Justinian [**Giustiniano**]. At a later period the Digest consisted of three parts, known as *Digestum Vetus, Infortiatum*, and *Digestum Novum*, which comprised the whole *Corpus Juris*.

D. quotes the Digest as *Digesta*, Mon. ii. 5[7]; *Vecchio Digesto*, Conv. iv. 9[87]; *Inforziato*, Conv. iv. 15[175]; *Jura*, Par. xi. 4; *Legge*, Conv. iv. 24[158]; *Ragione*, Conv. i. 10[14] ; iv. 19[24], 24[19] ; *Ragione civile*, Conv. iv. 12[100, 103] ; *Ragione scritta*, Conv. iv. 9[82, 85, 87] ; the law holds that innovations should be justified by reasons which are plainly manifest, Conv. i. 10[15-19]; the *Digestum Vetus* defines the written law as the art of right-doing and of equity, Conv. iv. 9[87-8] ; the canon and civil law designed to provide a remedy against the cupidity which is generated by the heaping-up of riches, Conv. iv. 12[100-2]; it is laid down in the *Infortiatum* that a testator must be of sound mind, but not necessarily of sound body, Conv. iv. 15[175-8] ; it is held a rule of law that things which are self-evident require no proof, Conv. iv. 19[24-6] ; the law forbids a man to do certain things before the age of 25, Conv. iv. 24[19-21] ; it is ordained by the law that sons should regard their father's person as sacred, Conv. iv. 24[158-60]; the definition of *jus* in the Digests does not give the essence of right, but merely describes it for practical purposes, Mon. ii. 5[6-9].

Digesto Vecchio. [*Digesto.*]
Dino Perini. [Perini.]
Dio, God; the name of the Deity, *Dio* or *Iddio*, occurs 130 times in the *D. C.*, 26 times in the *Inferno*, 41 in the *Purgatorio*, 63 in the *Paradiso*; for the first time, Inf. i. 131 ; for the last, Par. xxxiii. 40. Once only it is used specially of Christ,

who is called *Dio verace*, Par. xxxi. 107 ; and once it is used in the sense of Holy Scripture, the Word of God, Purg. iii. 126. The form *Deo* for *Dio* occurs once (in rime), Purg. xvi. 108; *Iddio* occurs, Inf. iii. 103 ; as variant of *Dio*, Inf. i. 131 ; xxv. 3 ; Purg. xiii. 117 ; Par. xx. 138 ; xxiv. 130; the Latin form *Deus* is used, Purg. ix. 140; x. 44; xvi. 19; xx. 136; xxv. 121; xxxiii. 1 ; Par. vii. 1 ; xii. 93 ; xv. 29.

Other names for God used in the *D. C.* are *Alfa ed Omega*, Par. xxvi. 17; so Epist. x. 33[625]; *El*, Par. xxvi. 136; so V. E. i. 4[29]; *Elì*, Purg. xxiii. 74; *Eliòs*, Par. xiv. 96; *I*, Par. xxvi. 134; *Giove*, Purg. vi. 118.

God is spoken of by periphrasis as *Avversario d'ogni male*, Inf. ii. 16; *Tal*, Inf. viii. 105; *Colui che tutto muove*, Par. i. 1; *Quei che puote*, Par. i. 62 ; *Quei che vede e puote*, Par. iv. 123 ; *Colui che cerne i Beati*, Par. iii. 75; *Colui che a tanto ben sortì* (*San Francesco*), Par. xi. 109; *Quel ch' è primo*, Par. xv. 56; *Colui ch' ogni torto disgrava*, Par. xviii. 6; *Colui che volse il sesto All' estremo del mondo*, Par. xix. 40; *Colui per cui tutte le cose vivono*, V. N. § 43[8-9]; *Colui ch' è Sire della cortesia*, V. N. § 43[12-13]; *Colui qui est per omnia saecula benedictus*, V. N. § 43[16-17] ; *Colui che da nulla è limitato*, Conv. iv. 9[31].

D. frequently indicates the Deity by a personification of the divine attributes or functions; hence God is spoken of as *Agente, primo A.*, Conv. iii. 14[32] ; *Altissimo*, V. N. § 41[43] ; *Amante, primo A.*, Par. iv. 118 ; *Amore, A. che il ciel governa*, Par. i.

74; *caldo A.*, Par. xiii. 79; *eterno A.*, Par. xxix. 18; *primo A.*, Par. x. 3; xxvi. 38; xxxii. 142; *l'A. che queta l'Empireo*, Par. xxx. 52; *l'A. che muove il sole e l'altre stelle*, Par. xxxiii. 145; *Autore, verace A.*, Par. xxvi. 40; *Bene*, Purg. xxxi. 23; Par. viii. 97; xxvi. 16; *infinito ed ineffabil B.*, Purg. xv. 67; *sommo B.*, Purg. xxviii. 91; Par. iii. 90; vii. 80; xiv. 47; xix. 87; xxvi. 134; Conv. iv. 12^{154}; *quel B. Che non ha fine, e sè con sè misura*, Par. xix. 50–1; *Benefattore, universalissimo B.*, Conv. i. 8^{17}; *Beninanza, somma B.*, Par. vii. 143; *Bontà, B. infinita*, Purg. iii. 122; *divina B.*, Inf. xi. 96; Par. vii. 64, 109; Conv. iii. 7^{11-12}; iv. 5^{16}; *prima B.*, Conv. iii. 7^{18}; iv. 9^{32}; *Cagione, prima C.*, Conv. ii. 6^{80}; *universalissima C. di tutte le cose*, Conv. iii. 6^{46}; *causa omnium*, Epist. x. 20^{362}; *prima C.*, Epist. x. 21^{398}, 25^{467}; *Creatore*, Purg. xvii. 91; Par. xxx. 101; Son. xxxvii. 7; *Deità*, Conv. iv. 21^{96}; *somma D.*, Conv. iv. 21^{101}; *la somma D. che sè sola compiutamente vede*, Conv. ii. 4^{29}; *Dictator, unicus D. divini eloquii*, Mon. iii. 4^{88-9}; *Dispensatore dell' Universo*, Conv. i. 3^{15-16}; *Dispensator*, A. T. § 21^{63}; *Duce, sommo D.*, Inf. x. 102; Par. xxv. 72; *Egualità, prima E.*, Par. xv. 74; *Essenza*, Par. xxiv. 140; xxvi. 31; Conv. iii. 12^{93}; *buona E., d'ogni ben frutto e radice*, Purg. xvii. 134; *divina E.*, Conv. iii. 12^{103}; *somma E.*, Par. xxi. 87; *prima Essentia*, Epist. x. 21^{385}; *Faber*, V. E. i. 5^{10}; *Factor*, V. E. i. 7^{33}; Epist. viii. 8^{128}; *Fattore*, Par. vii. 31, 35; xxvi. 83; xxxiii. 5; *alto F.*, Inf. iii. 4; *maggior F.*,

Conv. iv. 9^{65}, 12^{142}; *F. dei miracoli*, V. N. § 30^{34}; *Giudice*, Purg. viii. 109; xxxi. 39; *Giustizia, viva G.*, Par. vi. 88, 121; *divina G.*, Par. xix. 29; *Gubernator, omnium spiritualium et temporalium G.*, Mon. iii. 16^{139-40}; *Imperadore, quello I. che lassù regna*, Inf. i. 124; *lo I. che sempre regna*, Par. xii. 40; *lo nostro I.*, Par. xxv. 41; *I. del Cielo*, Conv. iii. 12^{116}; *I. dell' Universo*, Conv. ii. 6^{11}, 16^{101-2}; *Intelligibile, sommo I.*, Conv. iv. 22^{142}; *Mente, la M. ch' è da sè perfetta*, Par. viii. 101; *prima M.*, Conv. ii. 4^{38-9}; *Motore, primo M.*, Purg. xxv. 70; *unicus Motor*, Mon. i. 9^{12}; *primus M.*, Mon. ii. 2^{16}; Epist. x. 20^{349}; *Naturans*, V. E. i. 7^{28}; *Ortolano eterno* ('l'orto' being Paradise), Par. xxvi. 65; *Padre*, Par. xxvii. 1; *P. nostro*, Purg. xi. 1; *alto P.*, Par. x. 50; *pio P.*, Par. xviii. 129; Conv. ii. 6^{27-85}; *P. de' lumi*, Conv. iv. 20^{53}; *Pater*, Mon. ii. 13^{16}; iii. 1^{30}; Epist. viii. 2^{16}; *Potestate, divina P.*, Inf. iii. 5; *Princeps et Monarcha universi*, Mon. i. 7^{14-15}; *Princeps universi*, Mon. iii. 16^{13}; *Principio, P. delle nostre anime*, Conv. iv. 12^{141}; *Principium*, Epist. x. 20^{357}, ^{623}, *Provvidenza*, Par. i. 121; *alta P.*, Inf. xxiii. 55; Par. xxvii. 61; *la P. che governa il mondo*, Par. xi. 28; *divina P.*, Conv. iv. 4^{113}, 5^{2}, ^{153}, 25^{147}; *Punto*, Par. xxviii. 41, 95; *il P. A cui tutti li tempi son presenti*, Par. xvii. 17–18; *Re*, Par. iii. 84; Son. xxxvii. 1; *R. dell' universo*, Inf. v. 91; *santo Re celestiale*, Conv. ii. 6^{25}; iv. 5^{34}; *Rege, lo R. per cui l'Empireo pausa*, Par. xxxii. 61; *R. eterno*, Purg. xix. 63; *sommo R.*, Purg. xxi. 83;

Rex aeternus, Epist. vi. 1[1]; *Salute, ultima S.,* Par. xxii. 124; xxxiii. 27; *Sapienza, somma S.,* Inf. xix. 10; *Seminante, altissimo e gloriosissimo S.,* Conv. iv. 23[29–30]; *Signore,* Inf. ii. 73; Purg. xxi. 72; *altissimo S.,* Son. xviii. 3; *S. degli angeli,* V. N. § 82[2–3]; *S. della giustizia,* V. N. § 296[6–7]; *Sire,* Par. xxix. 28; *alto S.,* Inf. xxix. 56; Purg. xv. 112; *giusto S.,* Purg. xix. 125; *altissimo S.,* V. N. § 6[10]; *eterno S.,* Canz. iv. 23; *S. della cortesia,* V. N. § 43[12]; *Valore,* Par. ix. 105; xiii. 45; *eterno V.,* Purg. xv. 72; Par. i. 107; *primo ed ineffabile V.,* Par. x. 3; *V. infinito,* Par. xxxiii. 81; *Vero,* Par. iv. 125; *primo V.,* Par. iv. 96; *Virtù,* Purg. iii. 32; *V. divina,* Inf. v. 36; *prima V.,* Par. xiii. 80; xxvi. 84; *Volontà, prima V.,* Par. xix. 86.

D. speaks of God metaphorically as *Fonte, F. ond' ogni ver deriva,* Par. iv. 116; *F. di pensieri,* Par. xxiv. 9; *Luce, verace L.,* Par. iii. 32; *L. eterna,* Par. v. 8; xi. 20; xxxiii. 83, 124; *prima L.,* Par. xxix. 136; *trina L.,* Par. xxxi. 28; *somma L.,* Par. xxxiii. 67; *Lume, alto L.,* Purg. xiii. 86; Par. xxxiii. 116; *eterno L.,* Par. xxxiii. 43; *Lucente,* Par. xiii. 56; *Mare, quel M. al qual tutto si muove,* Par. iii. 86; *Porto, quello P. onde l'anima si partio,* Conv. iv. 288[8–9]; *Sereno,* ' clear sky', *il S. che non si turba mai,* Par. xix. 64–5; *Sol,* Par. ix 8; xviii. 105; xxv. 54; *alto S.,* Purg. vii. 26; *S. degli angeli,* Par. x. 53; *il S. che sempre verna,* Par. xxx. 126; *Speglio,* Par. xv. 62; *verace S.,* Par. xxvi. 106; *Stella,* Par. xxxi. 28.

The Deity being the Origin of all things, D. frequently applies to God the epithet *primo*; hence he speaks of God as *il Primo,* Par. viii. 111; *Primum,* Epist. x. 20, 26; *primo Agente,* Conv. iii. 14[34]; *primo Amante,* Par. iv. 118; *primo Amore,* Par. xxvi. 38; xxxii. 142; *prima Bontà,* Conv. iv. 9[32]; *prima Cagione,* Conv. ii. 6[80]; *prima Causa,* Epist. x. 21, 25; *prima Egualità,* Par. xv. 74; *prima Essentia,* Epist. x. 21; *prima Luce,* Par. xxix. 136; *prima Mente,* Conv. ii. 4[38–9]; *primo Motore,* Purg. xxv. 70; *primo Valore,* Par. x. 3; *primo Vero,* Par. iv. 96; *prima Virtù,* Par. xiii. 80; *prima Volontà,* Par. xix. 86.

God in three Persons, the Holy Trinity, is referred to, *una Sustanzia in tre Persone,* Purg. iii. 36; Conv. ii. 6[59–60]; *tre Persone in divina natura,* Par. xiii. 26; *tre Persone eterne,* Par. xxiv. 139; *trina Luce in unica Stella,* Par. xxxi. 28; *tre Giri Di tre colori e d'una Continenza,* Par. xxxiii. 115–19; *Padre, Figliuolo e Spirito Santo, li quali sono Tre ed Uno,* V. N. § 30[35–6]; *altissimo e congiuntissimo Concistoro,* Conv. iv. 5[21]; also, Inf. iii. 5–6; Par. vii. 30–3; x. 1–3, 50–1; xiv. 28–30; xxxiii. 124–6. [**Trinità.**]

God, as God the Father, *divina Potestate,* Inf. iii. 5; *Fattore,* Par. vii. 31; *primo ed ineffabile Amore,* Par. x. 3; *Lucente,* Par. xiii. 56; *uno Dio solo ed eterno,* Par. xxiv. 130–1; *alto Lume,* Par. xxxiii. 116; *Luce eterna,* Par. xxxiii. 124; *somma Potenza,* Conv. ii. 6[62]; *sommo Atto,* Conv. iii. 12[97–8].

God, as God the Son, *somma Sapienza,* Inf. iii. 6; Conv. ii. 6[66]; iii. 12[97]; *Verbo di Dio,* Par. vii.

30 ; *Figlio*, Par. x. 1 ; *Figliuolo*, V. N. § 30³⁵ ; *viva Luce*, Par. xiii. 55 ; *Natura divina ed umana*, Par. xiii. 26–7 ; *Lume riflesso*, Par.xxxiii. 119 ; *Luce intelletta*, Par. xxxiii. 125. [Cristo.]

God, as God the Holy Ghost, *primo Amore*, Inf. iii. 6 ; *eterno Amore*, Par. vii. 33 ; *Amore*, Par. x. 1 ; xiii. 57 ; *Fuoco*, Par. xxxiii. 119 ; *Luce amante ed arridente*, Par. xxxiii. 126 ; *somma Carità*, Conv. ii. 6⁶⁹ ; *sommo Amore*, Conv. iii. 12⁹⁷. [Spirito Santo.]

Diogenes, Diogenes, the celebrated Cynic philosopher, born at Sinope in Pontus c. B.C. 412 ; died at Corinth at the age of nearly 93, B.C. 323 ; placed by D. in Limbo among the ancient philosophers, Inf. iv. 137. [Limbo.]

Diomede, Diomed, son of Tydeus and Deiphyle, King of Argos, one of the Greek heroes who fought against Troy; together with Ulysses he planned the stratagem of the wooden horse, and carried off the Palladium [Palladio], the secret of which was betrayed to them by the Trojan Antenor, who delivered it into their hands ; he was also concerned with Ulysses in the abduction of Achilles from Scyros. [Deidamia.]

D. places Diomed and Ulysses together among the Counsellors of evil in Bolgia 8 of Circle VIII of Hell (Malebolge), Inf. xxvi. 56 ; *Greci*, *v*. 75 ; *due dentro ad un foco*, *v*. 79 ; they are enveloped in a single flame, which is divided at the top, *foco diviso di sopra*, *vv*. 52–3 ; *fiamma cornuta*, *v*. 68 ; *fiamma*, *v*. 76 ; xxvii. 1 ; *foco*, *v*. 79 ; *fiamma antica*, *v*. 85. [Consiglieri Frodolenti : Ulisse.]

Dione, daughter of Oceanus and Thetis, and mother of Venus by Jupiter, whence Venus is sometimes called Dionaea or even Dione. D. says that Dione and Cupid were worshipped by the ancients as the mother and son of Venus, Par. viii. 7–8 [Ciprigna] ; the planets of Venus and Mercury are called by the names of their respective mothers, viz. Dione and Maia, Par. xxii. 144 [Venere : Maia : Mercurio ²].

Dionisio ¹, Dionysius the Elder, tyrant of Syracuse, B.C. 405–367 ; placed, together with Alexander the Great, among the Tyrants in Round 1 of Circle VII of Hell, Inf. xii. 107 ; D. describes him (in allusion to his long tyranny of 38 years, during which his subjects were made to suffer from his lust of power and cruelty) as *Dionisio fero, Che fe' Cicilia aver dolorosi anni* (*vv*. 107–8) [Tiranni].

Dionisio ², Dionysius the Areopagite, an eminent Athenian, whose conversion to Christianity by the preaching of St. Paul is mentioned in the *Acts* (xvii. 34). He is said to have been the first Bishop of Athens, and to have been martyred there about the year 95. In the Middle Ages he was universally credited with the authorship of works on the Names of God, on Symbolical and Mystic Theology, and on the Celestial Hierarchy, all of which are now admitted to be the productions of Neo-Platonists of the fifth or sixth century. The work on the Celestial Hierarchy was translated into Latin in the ninth century by Johannes Erigena, and became the mediaeval text-book of angelic lore. Another translation of this work, as well as of the *De Divinis Nominibus* (to both of which D. was indebted), was made in the latter half of the twelfth century.

Dionysius is placed among the great Theologians (*Spiriti Sapienti*) in the Heaven of the Sun, where his spirit is pointed out by St. Thomas Aquinas, who speaks of him, in reference to his reputed work on the Celestial Hierarchy, as *quel cero Che, giuso in carne, più addentro vide L'angelica natura e il ministero*, ' that taper which, below in the flesh, saw most deeply into the nature of angels and their office', Par. x. 115–17 [Sole, Cielo del]; *Dionisio*, Par. xxviii. 130; *Dionisio Accademico* (so called, probably, on the ground that he was an Athenian and a Platonist), Conv. ii. 14$^{34-5}$; *Dionysius*, Epist. viii. 7^{117}; x. 21^{405}; his arrangement of the Angelic Orders in the Celestial Hierarchy identical with that adopted by D., but different from that of St. Gregory, Par. xxviii. 130–5; Dionysius right, inasmuch as he was instructed by St. Paul, who had himself been 'caught up into heaven', *vv.* 136–9 [Gerarchia]; his opinion that material generation is the effect of stellar influence, Conv. ii. 14$^{32-5}$; his works and those of the Fathers neglected for the Decretalists, Epist. viii. 7^{117} [Ambrogio]; his *De Coelesti Hierarchia* quoted for the opinion that the Celestial Intelligences receive their light from God and transmit it to those below them, Epist. x. 21^{405}.

Dionisio [3], Dionysius Agricola (Diniz), King of Portugal, 1279–1325; son of Alphonso (Affonso)

III, whom he succeeded, and Beatrice, daughter of Alphonso X of Castile; married Isabella, daughter of Pedro III of Aragon. [Table G.]

The Eagle in the Heaven of Jupiter includes him among the princes whose misdoings he denounces, referring to him as *quel di Portogallo*, Par. xix. 139. [Aquila [2].]

Dionisio Accademico. [Dionisio [2].]

Dionisio Areopagita. [Dionisio [2].]

Dionysius. [Dionisio [2].]

Dioscoride, Dioscorides of Anazarba in Cilicia, Greek physician of the first century A.D. He was the author of a work on *materia medica*, treating of plants and their medicinal qualities, which had a great reputation and was translated into Arabic.

D. places him in Limbo, among the great philosophers of antiquity, speaking of him, in reference to his book, as *il buono accoglitor del quale*, ' the skilful assembler of qualities,' Inf. iv. 139–40. [Limbo.]

Dite, Dis, name given by the Romans to Pluto, King of the Infernal Regions, used by D. (as a synonym of *Lucifero*) in the sense of Satan, Inf. xi. 65; xii. 39; xxxiv. 20. [Lucifero.]

D. also uses the name *Dite* for one of the divisions of Hell, within which, beginning with Circle VI, is the lower Hell ('basso inferno', Inf. viii. 75), where are punished sins of malice and bestiality (those of incontinence being punished outside), *città che ha nome Dite*, Inf. viii. 68; *terra sconsolata, v.* 77; *terra, v.* 130; ix. 104; x. 2; *città del foco, x.* 22; *città roggia, xi.* 73.

The city of Dis, which begins at Circle VI, is fiery-red owing to the eternal fire burning within it (Inf. viii. 70–5), and is fortified with moats, and towers, and walls of iron (*vv.* 76–8) (a description which is borrowed from *Aen.* vi. 548 ff.).

It appears not to be any lower than Circle V, the descent hitherto having been very gradual, the only changes of level mentioned being between the first and second Circles (Inf. v. 1), and between the third and fourth (Inf. vi. 114). It is not until the brink of Hell proper is reached that the descent becomes steep (Inf. x. 135–6; xi. 1–5; xx. 1–10). [Inferno: Porta di Dite.]

Dite, Porta di. [Porta [6].]

Doagio, Douay, town in NE. corner of France, on the Scarpe, about twenty miles S. of Lille, in the modern Département du Nord, which in D.'s day formed part of Flanders.

Hugh Capet (in Circle V of Purgatory) mentions it, together with Ghent, Lille, and Bruges, to indicate Flanders, Purg. xx. 46. [Bruggia: Fiandra.]

Doctrina, Christiana, De, St. Augustine's work (in four books) *On Christian Doctrine*; his comparison of those who wrongfully interpret the Scriptures to a man who abandons the direct path and arrives at his destination by a circuitous route, Mon. iii. 4[60–8] (*Doct. Christ.* i. 36, § 41). [Agostino [2].]

Dolcino, Fra, Dolcino de' Tornielli of Novara, said to have been the natural son of a priest, born in the latter half of Cent. xii near Romagnano in the Val di Sesia, about 20 miles N. of Novara in Piedmont.

He was known as 'Fra' Dolcino because of his connexion with the sect of the Apostolic Brothers, founded in 1260 by Gherardo Segalelli of Parma, with the object of bringing back the Church to the simplicity of the Apostolic times. After the death of Segalelli, who was burned alive at Parma in 1300, Fra Dolcino became the acknowledged head of the sect. Preaching the community of goods and of women, he soon attracted a large number of proselytes. In 1305, on the promulgation of a Bull of Clement V for the total extirpation of his sect, he with some thousands of followers withdrew to the hills between Novara and Vercelli, where he defied for more than a year the repeated attacks of the Church authorities, aided by 'Crusaders' from the neighbourhood, and from distant parts as well. Finally they were reduced by starvation— large numbers were massacred on the mountains, others were burned, and Fra Dolcino and his companion, the beautiful Margaret of Trent, who was asserted to be his mistress, were taken prisoners, and burned alive at Vercelli (June, 1307).

D. assigns, by implication, to Fra Dolcino, who was still alive at the assumed date of the Vision, a place among the Schismatics and Sowers of Discord in Bolgia 9 of Circle VIII of Hell (Malebolge), Inf. xxviii. 55. [Scismatici.]

Domenicani], Dominicans or Preaching Friars, called also Black Friars from the habit of the Order; founded by St. Dominic at Toulouse in 1215. They were originally a Medicant Order like their rivals the

Franciscans, whose Order had been founded by St. Francis of Assisi a short time before; but in both cases the rule of poverty was gradually relaxed, until finally the two Orders became wealthy and powerful institutions.

The Dominicans are referred to by St. Thomas Aquinas (in the Heaven of the Sun), himself a Dominican, as *la santa greggia, Che Domenico mena per cammino*, Par. x. 94–5; *il suo peculio*, Par. xi. 124; *le sue pecore*, vv. 127, 130; he alludes to the distinctive characteristics of the Franciscan and Dominican Orders, vv. 37–9 [Cherubini]; and reproves the degeneracy of the latter, vv. 124–39, referring to himself (v. 138) as *il coreggier* (i. e. the wearer of the leathern girdle characteristic of the Dominicans) [Coreggiero]; the Franciscan St. Bonaventura (in the Heaven of the Sun) (who alludes, Par. xii. 58–60, to the dream of St. Dominic's mother that she had given birth to a dog bearing a lighted torch in its mouth, whence arose the punning appellation of the *Dominicani* as *Domini canes*) refers to them as *rivi Onde l' orto cattolico si riga*, Par. xii. 103–4.

Domenico, St. Dominic, born 1170, twelve years before St. Francis of Assisi, in the village of Calahorra, in Old Castile; he is supposed to have belonged to the noble family of Guzman, his father's name being Felix, his mother's Joanna. At the age of fifteen he went to the University of Palencia, where he studied theology for ten years. He was early noted for his self-denial and charity, it being told of him that during a famine he sold his books and furniture to feed the poor, and that, in order to ransom a captive, he offered to sell himself as a slave to the Moors. In 1195 he joined the Chapter of the Cathedral of Osma. In 1202 he accompanied his bishop on a diplomatic mission to Denmark and thence to Rome. On his way back two years later he spent some time in Languedoc, where he took an active part in the Albigensian Crusade, preaching, and, according to some accounts, even fighting, against the heretics. In 1215 he accompanied Folquet, Bishop of Toulouse, to the Lateran Council; and in the same year, on his return to Toulouse, he founded his Order of Preaching Friars, which was formally recognized by Honorius III in 1217. By the latter he was appointed Master of the Sacred Palace at Rome, where he henceforth resided. He died in August, 1221, at Bologna, where the centre of his Order had been established in 1219; and here h was buried, his remains being preserved in the marble tomb by Niccolò Pisano in the Church of San Domenico. He was canonized in 1234 by Gregory IX.

St. D. is mentioned by name by St. Thomas Aquinas (in the Heaven of the Sun), Par. x. 95; by St. Bonaventura, Par. xii. 70; by the former, who was a Dominican, and as such laments the degeneracy of his Order, he is spoken of as *principe*, Par. xi. 35; *l' altro* (as distinguished from St. Francis), v. 38; *splendore di cherubica luce*, v. 39;

colui, che degno Collega fu a mantener la barca Di Pietro (i. e. the worthy colleague of St. F.), *vv.* 118–20; *nostro patriarca, v.* 121; *pastor, v.* 131; by St. Bonaventura, a Franciscan, he is referred to as *l'altro duca* (as distinguished from St. F.), Par. xii. 32 (so *l'altro, v.* 34); *campione, v.* 44; *l'amoroso drudo Della fede cristiana, vv.* 55–6; *il santo atleta, Benigno ai suoi, ed ai nemici crudo, vv.* 56–7; *l'agricola, che Cristo Elesse all' orto suo per aiutarlo, vv.* 71–2; *messo e famigliar di Cristo, v.* 73; *gran dottor, v.* 85; *torrente ch' alta vena preme, v.* 99; *l'una rota della biga, In che la santa Chiesa si difese* (St. F. being the other), *vv.* 106–7; *cotanto paladino, v.* 142; St. D. and St. F. are referred to together, by St. T. A., as *due principi (della Chiesa)*, Par. xi. 35; by St. B., as *due campioni (della Chiesa)*, Par. xii. 44; *l'una e l'altra rota della biga (di santa Chiesa), vv.* 106–7.

St. Bonaventura (in the Heaven of the Sun) relates the life of St. Dominic, Par. xii. 31–105; after describing the situation of Calahorra, St. D.'s birthplace (*vv.* 46–57) [Callaroga], he alludes to the dream of St. D.'s mother before he was born (*vv.* 58–60) [Domenicani], and to that of his godmother at his baptism (namely, that she saw him with a star on his forehead which illuminated the whole world) (*vv.* 61–6); he then explains the name *Dominicus* as being the possessive of *Dominus*, 'the Lord', whose he wholly was (*vv.* 67–70), and adds that verily, too, were his father and mother well named (*vv.* 78–81)

[Felice: Giovanna [3]]; St. B. then, after drawing a parallel between St. Dominic and St. Francis, concludes with a lamentation over the backslidings of the Franciscan Order (*vv.* 106–26) [Francescani].

St. D. is mentioned, together with St. Benedict, St. Augustine, and St. Francis, in connexion with the statement that a man may lead a religious life without belonging to a religious order, Conv. iv. 28[68–71].

Dominazioni, Dominions, mentioned by Beatrice (in the Crystalline Heaven), in her exposition of the arrangement of the Angelic Hierarchies, as ranking first in the second Hierarchy, Virtues and Powers ranking next, Par. xxviii. 122–3; in the *Convivio* D. says that the second Hierarchy consists of Principalities, Virtues, and Dominions, in that order, Conv. ii. 6[50–3] [Gerarchia]. The Dominions preside over the Heaven of Jupiter [Paradiso[1]].

Dominico. [Domenico.]

Domiziano, Domitian (Titus Flavius Domitianus Augustus), Roman Emperor, younger son of Vespasian, and successor of his brother, Titus; he was born at Rome A. D. 51, became Emperor in 81, and was murdered in 96. Among the many crimes traditionally imputed to him was a relentless persecution of the Christians, which is mentioned by Orosius (*Hist.* vii. 10, § 1), who was doubtless D.'s authority; this persecution is referred to by Statius (in Purgatory), Purg. xxii. 82–4 [Stazio].

Donati], ancient noble family of Florence (with which D. was connected by marriage, his wife Gemma having been the daughter of Manetto Donati), who were Guelfs and lived in the Porta san Piero (Vill. iv. 11; v. 39). In 1300, when the Bianchi and Neri feuds were introduced into Florence from Pistoja, the Donati took the side of the latter party, of which they became the head, while their near neighbours the Cerchi sided with the Bianchi [**Bianchi**]. This partisanship led to the outbreak into actual hostilities of a long-standing rivalry between these two houses, the Donati, who were proud of their noble descent but poor, being bitterly jealous of the upstart and wealthy Cerchi [**Cerchi**].

Cacciaguida (in the Heaven of Mars) refers to the Donati as *lo ceppo di che nacquero i Calfucci*, Par. xvi. 106 [**Calfucci**]; the family, and Corso Donati in particular, are alluded to (probably with a reference to their nickname *Malefami*) by Piccarda Donati (in the Heaven of the Moon) in connexion with their forcible removal of her from the convent of St. Clara, as *uomini a mal più ch' a bene usi*, Par. iii. 106. [**Corso : Piccarda.**]

Donati, Buoso. [Buoso Donati.]
Donati, Cianfa. [Cianfa.]
Donati, Corso. [Corso Donati.]
Donati, Forese. [Forese.]
Donati, Gemma. [Gemma Donati.]
Donati, Niccolò. [Niccolò Donati.]
Donati, Piccarda. [Piccarda.]
Donati, Simone. [Simone Donati.]

Donati, Teruccio. [Teruccio Donati.]
Donati, Tessa. [Tessa.]
Donati, Ubertino. [Donato, Ubertin.]

Donatio Constantini], the so-called 'Donation of Constantine', the pretended grant by the Emperor Constantine to Pope Sylvester and his successors of the sovereignty of Italy and of the whole West; spoken of by D. as *quella dote che da Costantin prese il primo ricco patre*, Inf. xix. 115-17; and alluded to, Purg. xxxii. 124-9; Par. xx. 55-60; Mon. ii. 12$^{15-18}$, 13$^{66-9}$; iii. 10$^{1-6}$, 105-7, 13$^{60-4}$. [**Costantino.**]

Donato, Aelius Donatus, celebrated Roman grammarian of Cent. iv, said to have been the preceptor of St. Jerome; his most famous work was an elementary Latin grammar, *De octo partibus Orationis*, which has formed the groundwork of most similar treatises down to the present day.

D. places Donatus in the Heaven of the Sun, where he is named by St. Bonaventura among the great Doctors (*Spiriti Sapienti*) who are with himself, as *quel Donato Ch' alla prim' arte degnò poner mano* (i. e. D. the grammarian), Par. xii. 137-8. [**Sole, Cielo del.**]

Donato, Ubertin, one of the Donati of Florence, who married a daughter of Bellincione Berti of the house of Ravignani; mentioned by Cacciaguida (in the Heaven of Mars), who refers to the displeasure of Ubertino at the marriage of his wife's sister to one of the Adimari, a family of inferior rank, Par. xvi. 119-20. [**Adimari : Bellincion Berti : Donati.**]

Doria, Branca. [Branca d' Oria.]

Draghignazzo, one of the ten demons in Bolgia 5 of Circle VIII of Hell (Malebolge), deputed by Malacoda to escort D. and Virgil, Inf. xxi. 121; he joins in the attack on the Barrator Ciampolo, Inf. xxii. 73 [Alichino : Ciam-polo : Malebranche].

Drusi, distinguished Roman fa-mily of the Livia gens ; mentioned with the Decii (cf. *Aen.* vi. 824) as having laid down their lives for their country, Conv. iv. 5$^{122-4}$.

Dryades, Dryads, nymphs of the trees, who were believed to die with the trees which had been their abode, and with which they had come into existence, Ecl. ii. 56.

Duca, Guido del. [Guido del Duca.]

Ducatus, Duchy of Spoleto, dis-trict of central Italy, corresponding roughly to the modern province of Umbria ; described as being on the right side of Italy if the Apennines be taken as the dividing line (from N. to S.), V. E. i. 10^{50}. [Spole-tum : Spoletani.]

Duera, Buoso da. [Buoso da Duera.]

Durante Alighieri], son of D.'s half-brother Francesco, and of Piera di Donato Brunacci ; thought by some to be the nephew of D. re-ferred to, Epist. ix. 2$^{13-14}$; the reference is more probably to one of the Donati, a nephew of D.'s wife [Donati, Niccolò.]

Durazzo, Dyrrachium, the an-cient Epidamnus, town in Greek Illyria (the modern Albania) on a peninsula in the Adriatic sea. Caesar was here repulsed by the Pompeian troops in B. C. 48, and forced to re-treat, with considerable loss, towards Thessaly, where on Aug. 9 he com-pletely defeated Pompey at the battle of Pharsalia.

Durazzo is mentioned by the Emperor Justinian (in the Heaven of Mercury), together with Pharsalia, in connexion with the exploits of the Roman Eagle, Par. vi. 65.

DXV, ' Five hundred ten and five ', the mystic number ' sent from God ', *un cinquecento diece e cinque Messo da Dio* (usually understood to indicate a ' leader ', DVX, and identified by the majority of com-mentators with the *Veltro* of Inf. i. 101), which Beatrice foretells is to slay the ' harlot ' and the ' giant ' of the Procession in the Terrestrial Para-dise, Purg. xxxiii. 43–4. [Veltro.]

E

Eaco, Aeacus, King of Aegina, son of Jupiter and the nymph Aegina, after whom the island was named. D. mentions him as an instance of prudence, justice, liberality, and affability, referring to Ovid's account (*Metam.* vii. 476–657, six lines of which D. translates, but evidently from a corrupt text) of how he helped Cephalus in the war between Athens and Crete, how the population of Aegina was destroyed by a plague, how in answer to his prayer Jupiter repopulated the island by changing the ants into men, who were hence called Myrmidons, and how he was the father of Telamon, Peleus, and Phocus, and grandfather of Ajax and Achilles, Conv. iv. 27$^{155-95}$. [**Aeacidae: Cefalo: Egina: Mirmidoni.**]

Eber. [**Heber.**]

Ebree, Hebrew women; their place in the Celestial Rose pointed out by St. Bernard, who specially indicates Rachel, Sarah, Rebekah, Judith, and Ruth, the last (who was only a Hebrew by marriage) being referred to as the great-grandmother of David, Par. xxxii. 7–18. [**Rosa.**]

Ebrei, Hebrews, the inhabitants of Jerusalem, Purg. iv. 83 (where the meaning is that Jerusalem in the N. and the Mt. of Purgatory in the S. hemisphere are equidistant from the Equator, being antipodes) [**Gerusalemme**]; the Hebrews of Gideon's army, ' who showed them-

selves weak at the drinking,' i.e. ' bowed down on their knees to drink ' (*Judges* vii. 6), introduced as an example of gluttony in Circle VI of Purgatory, Purg. xxiv. 124 [**Gedeone: Golosi**]; the Hebrews obliged by the Mosaic law on vows to make the offering, but permitted to commute it (*Lev.* xxvii), Par. v. 49; they are referred to as *la gente a cui il mar s'aperse* (i.e. the people that crossed the Red Sea), being introduced, in allusion to their murmuring in the desert (*Deut.* i. 26–8), as an example of sloth in Circle IV of Purgatory, Purg. xviii. 134 [**Accidiosi**]; and spoken of, in allusion to the capture of Jerusalem by Titus, as *la gente che perdè Gerusalemme*, Purg. xxiii. 29; and, in allusion to their murmuring against Moses in the wilderness, as *la gente ingrata, mobile e ritrosa,* Par. xxxii. 132; called Hebrews after Heber, from whom they inherited the Hebrew tongue, *Hebraei,* V. E. i. 6$^{54-5}$ [**Heber**]; the children of Israel, Purg. ii. 46; Conv. ii. 1^{59}, 6^4; V. E. i. 7^{68}; Mon. i. 8^{23}, 14^{68}; ii. 8^{59}; Epist. vii. 8^{183}; x. 7^{142} [**Giudei: Israel**].

Ebreo, Hebrew tongue; the Psalter translated from Hebrew into Greek, and from Greek into Latin, Conv. i. 7$^{99-102}$; the language spoken by Adam (an opinion which D. retracts, Par. xxvi. 124–6), and transmitted by Heber to the Hebrews, who alone retained it after the confusion of tongues at Babel, in order that Christ 'might use not the language of confusion but that of grace,' *hebraicum idioma*, V. E. i. 6⁴⁹⁻⁶¹ [**Adamo : Babel : Heber**].

Ebro, river Ebro in Spain, which rises in the Cantabrian Mts. and flows SE. through Navarre, Aragon, and Catalonia, entering the Mediterranean some eighty miles SW. of Barcelona; the troubadour Folquet (in the Heaven of Venus) indicates his birthplace Marseilles as lying between the Ebro and the Macra, Par. ix. 89 [**Folco : Macra**]; mentioned to indicate the W. limit of the habitable globe, the Ganges indicating the E. limit, *Ibéro*, Purg. xxvii. 3–4 [**Gange**].

Ecate], Hecate, deity of the lower world, identified with the Moon in heaven, Diana on earth, and Proserpine in the infernal regions; alluded to by Farinata in Circle VI of Hell as *la donna che qui regge,* i. e. the Moon, Inf. x. 80. [**Luna.**]

Ecclesia. [**Chiesa.**]

Ecclesiaste, Book of Ecclesiastes of Solomon, Conv. ii. 11⁸²; iv. 2⁷⁴, 6¹⁷⁴, 16⁴⁹; quoted, Conv. ii. 11⁸²⁻⁵ (*Eccles.* v. 13 : *Vulg.* v. 12); Conv. iv. 2⁷⁴⁻⁵ (*Eccles.* iii. 7); Conv. iv. 6¹⁷⁴⁻⁹ (*Eccles.* x. 16–17); Conv. iv. 15⁶⁹⁻⁷¹ (*Eccles.* iii. 21); Conv. iv. 16⁴⁹⁻⁵⁵ (*Eccles.* x. 16–17). [*Bibbia.*]

Ecclesiastes. [*Ecclesiaste.*]

Ecclesiastico, apocryphal Book of Ecclesiasticus, Conv. iii. 8¹⁴; Epist. x. 22⁴²¹; quoted, Conv. iii. 8¹⁴⁻¹⁶ (*Ecclus.* i. 3); Conv. iii. 8¹⁶⁻²⁰ (*Ecclus.* iii. 21–3 : *Vulg.* iii. 22); Conv. iii. 14⁵⁸⁻⁶⁰ (*Ecclus.*

xxiv. 9 : *Vulg.* xxiv. 14); Epist. x. 22⁴²¹ (*Ecclus.* xlii. 16).

Ecclesiasticus. [*Ecclesiastico.*]

Eco], nymph Echo, who used to keep Juno engaged by incessantly talking to her, while Jupiter sported with the nymphs. Juno, on finding this out, punished Echo by changing her into an echo. In this state the nymph fell in love with Narcissus, but, her love not being returned, she pined away in grief, so that nothing remained of her but her voice.

D., comparing the double rainbow to a voice and its echo, refers to Echo (whose story he got from Ovid, *Metam.* iii. 356–401) as *quella vaga Ch' amor consunse come sol vapori,* Par. xii. 14–15. [**Narcisso.**]

Ecuba, Hecuba, wife of Priam, King of Troy, and mother of Hector, Paris, Polydorus, Polyxena, and several other children. After the fall of Troy she was carried away as a slave by the Greeks. On the way to Greece, Polyxena was torn from her and sacrificed on the tomb of Achilles; at the same time the lifeless body of her son Polydorus, who had been murdered by Polymestor, was washed up on the shore. Mad with grief, she went out of her mind and was changed into a dog, in which state she leapt into the sea at a place hence called Cynosema, 'tomb of the dog'.

D. mentions her in connexion with her madness, alluding to the deaths of Polyxena and Polydorus, and to her barking like a dog (his account being taken from Ovid, *Metam.* xiii. 404–575), Inf. xxxv. 13–21 [**Polissena : Polidoro**].

Edipo, Oedipus, son of Laius,

King of Thebes, and of Jocasta. Laius, having learned from an oracle that he was doomed to be slain by his own son, exposed Oedipus on Mt. Cithaeron, with his feet pierced and tied together. The child was found by a shepherd and brought up by Polybus, King of Corinth, whom Oedipus supposed to be his father. Having in his turn learned from an oracle that he was destined to slay his father and commit incest with his mother, he departed from Corinth in order to avoid his fate. As he journeyed he met Laius, whom he slew in a quarrel, not knowing him to be his father. In the neighbourhood of Thebes he encountered the Sphinx, which, seated on a rock, put a riddle to every Theban that passed by, and slew whoever failed to solve it. In order to get rid of the monster, the Thebans proclaimed that they would bestow the kingdom of Thebes and the hand of Jocasta on the person who should solve the riddle. This Oedipus succeeded in doing, whereupon the Sphinx flung herself down from the rock [**Sfinge**]. He now became King of Thebes, and unwittingly married his mother Jocasta, by whom he became the father of Eteocles, Polynices, Antigone, and Ismene. In consequence of this incestuous marriage the country of Thebes was visited with a plague. The oracle, on being consulted, declared that the murderer of Laius must be expelled. Being told by the seer Tiresias that he himself was the guilty man, Oedipus in horror put out his eyes and left Thebes, Jocasta having hanged herself [**Jocasta**].

D. mentions Oedipus as having blinded himself in order to hide his shame, and translates a line from Statius (*Thebaid* i. 47) referring to the fact, Conv. iii. 8$^{91-5}$; the reluctance of his son Polynices to reveal to Adrastus his father's name on account of his shame for the crimes of Oedipus, Conv. iv. 25$^{105-15}$. [**Adrasto : Polinice.**]

The solving of the riddle of the Sphinx by Oedipus is alluded to, Purg. xxxiii. 49, where, following a corrupt reading of a passage in Ovid (*Metam.* vii. 759–60), D. implies that the riddle was solved by the Naiads, instead of by Laiades, i. e. Oedipus, son of Laius. [**Naiade.**]

Edoardo], Edward I, King of England, 1272–1307, son of Henry III and Eleanor of Provence; alluded to by Sordello (in Ante-purgatory) as *migliore uscita*, 'the better issue' of *il re della semplice vita* (i.e. Henry III), Purg. vii. 132 [**Arrigo d'Inghilterra: Table J**]; the long war between England and Scotland during his reign is alluded to (by the Eagle in the Heaven of Jupiter), Par. xix. 122 [**Inghilese**].

Egidio[1], Giles of Assisi, one of the three earliest followers of St. Francis; died at Perugia in 1262. St. Thomas Aquinas (in the Heaven of the Sun) mentions him, together with Sylvester, in connexion with St. Francis, Par. xi. 83. [**Francesco**[2].]

Egidio[2], Egidio Colonna Romano, commonly called Aegidius Romanus Eremita, Roman monk of the Augustinian Order of Eremites, was born c. 1245; he studied under

St. Thomas Aquinas at Paris, and while there was appointed tutor to Philip (afterwards Philip IV), the son of Philip III, for whose instruction his best known work, the *De Regimine Principum*, was composed; in 1292 he was appointed General of his Order, and in 1295 he was made Archbishop of Bourges by Boniface VIII, at whose instance a few years later (c. 1298) he wrote a work, *De Renunciatione Papae*, in support of the validity of Celestine's abdication; in 1302 Boniface made him a Cardinal; he died at Avignon, Dec. 22, 1316, and was buried at Paris. Besides the *De Regimine Principum* he was the author of numerous works, including several astronomical treatises and commentaries upon Aristotle, Peter Lombard, and Aquinas; he also wrote in Italian a commentary on the famous *canzone* of Guido Cavalcanti on the nature of love ('Donna mi prega'). D. mentions E. in connexion with the *De Regimine Principum*, speaking of him as *Egidio Eremita*, Conv. iv. 24⁹⁷⁻⁹. [*Regimine Principum, De.*]

Egidio Eremita. [Egidio².]

Egina, island of Aegina, in the Saronic Gulf, between Argolis and Attica; said to have been named from the nymph Aegina, daughter of the river-god Asopus, who here became the mother of Aeacus, by Jupiter. As the island had been depopulated by a pestilence sent by Juno, Jupiter, in answer to the prayers of Aeacus, restored the population by changing ants into men, who were hence called Myrmidons, an incident to which D. (who got the

story from Ovid, *Metam.* vii. 523–657) refers, Inf. xxix. 58–64. [Eaco: Mirmidoni.]

Egitto, Egypt; wise men of, their computation of the stars, Conv. ii. 15¹⁹⁻²² [Savi¹]; Alexander the Great died there while waiting for the return of his embassy to the Romans, and was buried there, Mon. ii. 9⁶¹⁻⁷⁴ [Alessandro²]; Vesoges and Ptolemy, Kings of, Mon. ii. 9³⁵, ⁷⁰ [Vesoges : Tolommeo²]; alluded to as *ciò che di sopra il mar rosso èe*, i.e. the country bordering the Red Sea (though some think Arabia is intended), Inf. xxiv. 90 ; *terra di Soldano*, Inf. xxvii. 90 [Soldano]; in Ante-purgatory D. hears the Spirits chanting the words : ' In exitu Israel de Aegypto' (from *Psalm* cxiv. 1), Purg. ii. 46; this passage is quoted again and commented on, Conv. ii. 1⁵⁹⁻⁶⁵ ; Epist. x. 7¹⁴²⁻⁵⁵ ; D. uses *Egitto* in the allegorical sense of life upon earth, as opposed to that in *Gerusalemme*, the heavenly Jerusalem, Par. xxv. 55 ; G. del Virgilio indicates Egypt by the mention of Pharos, Carm. 32. [Pharos.]

Egiziani. [Aegyptii.]

*Egloghe*¹], Eclogues of Virgil; referred to as *Bucolici Carmi*, Purg. xxii. 57 ; *Bucolica*, Mon. i. 11⁵. [*Bucolica.*]

*Egloghe*²], Latin Eclogues of D., addressed between 1319 and 1321 to Giovanni del Virgilio, a professor at Bologna. Giovanni in 1319 had addressed to D. a Latin poem urging him to write poetical compositions in Latin. D. replied in a Latin eclogue (Ecl. I), in which he himself figures under the name of Tityrus, Giovanni under that of Mopsus, and a friend (said to be Dino Perini) under that of Meliboeus. Giovanni sent an eclogue in response inviting D. to Bologna, to which D. replied in a second eclogue (Ecl. II), written between Sept. 1319 and Sept. 1321, declining the invitation. [**Virgilio, Giovanni del.**]

There exists an anonymous Latin commentary upon the Eclogues, by a contemporary writer, whom some suppose to be Boccaccio.

El, appellation of God; Adam (in the Heaven of Fixed Stars) says that during his lifetime God was called on earth *I* (or *J*) (i.e. 'Jah' or 'Jehovah'), but afterwards He was called *El* (i.e. 'Elohim', God Almighty), Par. xxvi. 133–6 (where some edd. read *Elì*). [**I³.**]

D. (who was probably thinking of *Exod.* vi. 3) here retracts the opinion expressed in the *De Vulgari Eloquentia*, where he says the first word spoken by Adam was doubtless *El*, the name of God, V. E. i. 4²⁶⁻³¹.

Electra. [**Elettra.**]

Elementorum, De Proprietatibus. [*Proprietatibus Elementorum, De.*]

Elena[1], Helen, daughter of Jupiter and Leda, wife of Menelaus, King of Sparta, whose abduction by Paris led to the long Trojan war; placed in Circle II of Hell among the Lustful, Inf. v. 64 [**Lussuriosi**]. The rape of Helen is alluded to, Epist. v. 8¹²⁹ [**Argi**].

Elena[2]. [**Helena.**]

Elena, Sant'. [**Santelena.**]

Elenchis, De Sophisticis. [*Sophisticis Elenchis, De.*]

Eleonora], Eleanor, second daughter of Raymond Berenger IV of Provence; married in 1236 to Henry III of England, died 1291; she is referred to by the Emperor Justinian (in the Heaven of Mercury) as one of the four daughters of Raymond, each of whom became a Queen, Par. vi. 133–4. [**Beringhieri, Ramondo.**]

Elettra, Electra, daughter of Atlas, and mother of Dardanus, the founder of Troy (*Aen.* viii. 134 ff.); placed in Limbo together with Hector and Aeneas, Inf. iv. 121 [**Limbo**]; mentioned as ancestress of Aeneas, *Electra*, Mon. ii. 3⁶⁹⁻⁷⁶ [**Atlantis**].

Elì, Hebrew word meaning 'my God', Purg. xxiii. 74 (ref. to *Matt.* xxvii. 46); as variant of *El*, Par xxvi. 136. [**El.**]

Elia, prophet Elijah; his assumption into Heaven in a fiery chariot, Inf. xxvi. 35 (ref. to 2 *Kings* ii. 9–12); his appearance with Moses at the Transfiguration, Purg. xxxii. 80 (ref. to *Matt.* xvii. 8); *Elias*, Mon. iii. 9⁸¹⁻³ (ref. to *Matt.* xvii. 4).

Elias. [**Elia.**]

Elice, Helice or Callisto, daughter of Lycaon, King of Arcadia; she was one of Diana's nymphs, but was dismissed when the latter discovered that she had been seduced by Jupiter, by whom she became the mother of Arcas. Juno in jealousy turned her into a bear, in which shape she was pursued by her son, who was on the point of slaying her when Jupiter transformed them both into constellations, Callisto becoming the Great Bear, and Arcas the Little Bear or Boötes (Ovid, *Metam.* ii. 401–530). Her dismissal by Diana is alluded to, Purg. xxv. 130–2; she and her son are mentioned as constellations, Par. xxxi. 32–3. [Boote: Carro, Il¹: Corno: Orsa.]

Elicona, Helicon, celebrated range of mountains in Boeotia, sacred to Apollo and the Muses, in which rose the famous fountains of the Muses, Aganippe and Hippocrene. D. (perhaps through a misunderstanding of *Aen.* vii. 641; x. 163) speaks of Helicon itself as a fountain, Purg. xxix. 40; *Helicon*, V. E. ii. 4⁶⁷; he mentions the visit of Pallas Athene to H. to assure herself of its wonders (told by Ovid, *Metam.* v. 250–72), as a parallel to his own visit to the court of Can Grande at Verona, Epist. x. 1¹¹ [Saba]; referred to as *montes Aonii*, Ecl. i. 28 [Aonius].

Eliodoro, Heliodorus, treasurer of Seleucus, King of Syria, by whom he was commissioned to remove the treasures from the Temple at Jerusalem; as he was about to lay hands on them 'there appeared an horse with a terrible rider upon him, and he ran fiercely, and smote at Heliodorus with his forefeet' (2 *Maccab.* iii. 25). H. is included among the instances of Avarice in Circle V of Purgatory, where this incident is alluded to, Purg. xx. 113. [Avari.]

Eliòs, name (Greek for 'Sun') used by D. for God, Par. xiv. 96.

Elisabetta], Elisabeth, wife of Zacharias, mother of John the Baptist, and 'cousin' (*Luke* i. 36) of the Virgin Mary; the visit of the latter to her is alluded to by the Slothful in Circle IV of Purgatory, who cry, *Maria corse con fretta alla montagna* (ref. to *Luke* i. 39–40), Purg. xviii. 100 [Accidiosi]; her salutation of the Virgin (*Luke* i. 42)

is chanted by the four-and-twenty elders in the Terrestrial Paradise, Purg. xxix. 85–7.

Eliseo¹, brother of D.'s great-great-grandfather, Cacciaguida, Par. xv. 136. [Cacciaguida: Dante.]

Eliseo²], prophet Elisha; referred to (in connexion with his having witnessed the assumption of Elijah into Heaven in a fiery chariot) as *colui che si vengiò con gli orsi*, Inf. xxvi. 34 (ref. to 2 *Kings* ii. 9–12, 23–4).

Elisio, Elysium, abode of the Blessed in the lower world; mentioned in connexion with the meeting of Aeneas with the shade of Anchises in the Elysian Fields, Par. xv. 27 (ref. to *Aen.* vi. 684–91). [Anchise.]

[Elissa], another name of Dido; G. del Virgilio speaks of *regnum Elissae*, the kingdom of Dido, i.e. Carthage, to indicate Africa, hence the South, Carm. 32.

Ellesponto, Hellespont, the present Straits of the Dardanelles, across the narrowest part of which, between Abydos and Sestos, Xerxes built his famous bridge of boats, Purg. xxviii. 71; Mon. ii. 9⁵²⁻⁸ (where D. quotes Lucan, *Phars.* ii. 672–3) [Serse]; at the same place Leander used to swim across nightly from Abydos to visit Hero at Sestos, in connexion with which incident D. compares the Strait to the stream of Lethe, which separated him from Matilda, Purg. xxviii. 73–4 [Leandro].

Eloquentia, De Vulgari, D.'s treatise *On the Vulgar Tongue*, a dissertation in Latin on the Italian language as a literary tongue, with an examination of the fourteen dialects of Italy, and a consideration of the metre of the *canzone*, the latter portion of the work forming a fragmentary 'art of poetry'. The work (to the projected composition of which reference is made in the *Convivio*, i. 5^{67-9}) was originally planned to consist of at least four books, as appears from the fact that D. twice reserves points for consideration in the fourth book, 'in quarto hujus operis' (V. E. ii. 4^{13}, 8^{83}). In its unfinished state it consists of two books only; the first, which is introductory, is divided into nineteen chapters; the second, into fourteen, the last of which is incomplete, the work breaking off abruptly in the middle of the inquiry as to the structure of the stanza. The division into chapters is due to D. himself, as is evident from the fact that on one occasion he refers back to a previous chapter, 'in tertio hujus libri capitulo' (V. E. ii. 8^{61-2}).

Eloquio, De Vulgari. [*Eloquentia, De Vulgari.*]

Elsa, river of Tuscany, which rises in the hills to the W. of Siena, and, flowing NW., joins the Arno a few miles below Empoli. In certain parts of the river its water has the property of 'petrifying' objects immersed in it, being charged with carbonic acid and sub-carbonate of lime. This peculiarity is referred to by Beatrice, who likens the worldly thoughts that obscure D.'s mental vision to the incrustations formed by the Elsa water, Purg. xxxiii. 67–8.

Ema, small stream in Tuscany, which rises in the hills S. of Florence and falls into the Greve a few miles from the city. It is crossed near Galluzzo by the road from the Valdigreve to Florence.

Cacciaguida (in the Heaven of Mars) laments that the first Buondelmonte who came to Florence had not been drowned in the Ema on his way from his castle of Montebuono in the Valdigreve, Par. xvi. 143. [**Buondelmonti.**]

Emilia. [**Aemilis.**]

Emmaus], village about eight miles from Jerusalem, on the road to which Christ appeared to Cleopas and his companion after His resurrection (*Luke* xxiv. 13–35); alluded to, Purg. xxi. 7–9.

Empedocles, philosopher of Agrigentum in Sicily, c. B.C. 450; he is said to have thrown himself down the crater of Mt. Aetna, that by his sudden disappearance he might be taken to be a god; but the volcano revealed the manner of his death by throwing up one of his sandals.

D., whose knowledge of E. was probably derived from Cicero (*Acad.* i. 5; *N. D.* i. 12), places him in Limbo among the great philosophers of antiquity, Inf. iv. 138 [**Limbo**]; and alludes to his theory of periodic destruction and construction in the scheme of the universe, Inf. xii. 42–3 [**Caos**].

Empireo, Cielo. [**Cielo Empireo.**]

Empyreum, Coelum. [**Cielo Empireo.**]

Enea, Aeneas, son of Anchises and Venus, one of the great champions of Troy against the Greeks in the Trojan war. After the fall of Troy he crossed over to Europe, and finally settled at Latium in Italy, where he became the ancestral hero of the Romans. The *Aeneid* of Virgil contains an account of his wanderings before he reached Latium. Here he founded Lavinium, so called after his wife Lavinia, the daughter of Latinus. Turnus, to whom Lavinia had been betrothed, made war against Latinus and Aeneas, in the course of which the former was slain. Aeneas afterwards slew Turnus, and was eventually himself slain in battle with the Rutulians. [**Lavinia: Latino** [1]**: Turno.**]

Aeneas, whom D. consistently regards as the founder of the Roman Empire, is placed in Limbo in company with his ancestress Electra, Hector, and Julius Caesar, Inf. iv. 122 [**Limbo**]; *Enea*, Inf. ii. 32; iv. 122; xxvi. 93; Conv. ii. 11[38]; iii. 11[159]; iv. 5[48], 26[61]; *Aeneas*, Mon. ii. 3[30-113], 4[51], 7[69, 80], 11[9, 16]; Epist. vii. 4[87]; *figliuol d'Anchise*, Inf. i. 74; Purg. xviii. 137; Par. xv. 27; *parente di Silvio*, Inf. ii. 13; *l'antico che Lavinia tolse* (i.e. the ancient hero who wedded Lavinia), Par. vi. 3; *primus pater Romani populi*, Mon. ii. 3[30], 11[9]; *invictissimus atque piissimus pater*, Mon. ii. 3[36].

His departure from Troy, Inf. i. 73-5; his arrival in Italy contemporary with the birth of David, Conv. iv. 5[47-8]; his sojourn in Africa with Dido, and laudable self-restraint in quitting her, Conv. iv. 26[64-70]; his departure from Africa commanded by Jupiter (*Aen.* iv. 272-6), Epist. vii. 4[86-92]; his stay with Acestes in Sicily (*Aen.* v. 35 ff.), his training of Ascanius to arms (*Aen.* v. 545 ff.), his institution of games in memory of Anchises (*Aen.* v. 45 ff.), his consideration for his aged followers (*Aen.* v. 715-18), his honourable burial of Misenus (*Aen.*

vi. 162-84), Conv. iv. 26[93-142]; his naming of Gaëta after his nurse Caieta (*Aen.* vii. 1-4), Inf. xxvi. 92-3; his descent to the infernal regions and interview with Anchises (*Aen.* vi. 98 ff.), Inf. ii. 13-15, 32; Par. xv. 25-7; Conv. iv. 26[70-6]; Mon. ii. 7[68-70] [**Anchise**]; his marriage with Lavinia (*Aen.* vi. 764; xii. 194), Par. vi. 3; his combat with Turnus, whom he would have spared but for the belt of Pallas (*Aen.* xii. 887-952), Mon. ii. 11[6-21]; his shield (*Aen.* viii. 652-6), Mon. ii. 4[50-1]; his son Silvius, Inf. ii. 13 [**Silvio**]; the predestined founder of the Roman Empire, Inf. ii. 20-1; the father of the Roman people as testified by Virgil throughout the *Aeneid*, Mon. ii. 3[30, 120], 7[69]; his justice and piety, Inf. i. 73; Mon. ii. 3[46-7]; called 'pius' by Virgil, Conv. ii. 11[38-9]; 'the light and hope of the Trojans', Conv. iii. 11[159-60] (where D. appears to have written *Enea* by a slip for *Ettore*, the latter being the person referred to by Virgil in the passage quoted, *Aen.* ii. 281); compared to Hector, Mon. ii. 3[53-4]; his nobility both by descent and marriage in respect of all three continents,—of Asia, by descent from Assaracus and by marriage with Creusa,—of Europe, by descent from Dardanus and by marriage with Lavinia,—of Africa, by descent from Electra and by marriage with Dido, Mon. ii. 3[58-117] [**Assaraco: Creusa: Dardano: Lavinia: Elettra: Dido.**]

Some think Aeneas is *il messo del cielo*, who is sent to open the gates of the city of Dis for D. and Virgil, Inf. ix. 85.

Eneida. [*Aeneis.*]

Enrico. [*Arrigo.*]

Enrico di Susa], Henry of Susa (Enrico Bartolomei), the Decretalist, born c. 1200, died 1271 ; after lecturing on canon law at Bologna and Paris, and spending some time in England, where he was in high favour with Henry III (Purg. vii. 130), he was created successively Bishop of Sisteron (1241), Archbishop of Embrun (1250), and Cardinal-Bishop of Ostia (1261) ; his most famous work was the *Summa super titulis Decretalium*, otherwise known as *Summa Ostiensis* ; from the name of his see at Ostia he was commonly styled Ostiensis, by which 'title' D. refers to him, Par. xii. 83 ; Epist. viii. 7[118]. [*Decretalistae : Ostiense.*]

Ente, De Simpliciter, Aristotle's treatise *On Simple Being*, more commonly called the *Metaphysics.* [*Metaphysica.*]

Eolo, Aeolus, god of the winds, which he was supposed to keep shut up in a mountain and to let out at will, Purg. xxviii. 21 ; Juno's speech to (*Aen.* i. 65), *Aeolus*, V. N. § 25[77].

Eoo, Eous, one of the four horses which drew the chariot of the Sun, Conv. iv. 23[136] (where D. refers to Ovid, *Metam.* ii. 153–5); *Eous*, Ecl. ii. 1.

Eous. [*Eoo.*]

Ephesios, Epistola ad, St. Paul's Epistle to the Ephesians, Mon. ii. 13[16]; Epist. x. 27[516]; quoted, Mon. ii. 13[16–25] (*Ephes.* i. 5–8); Mon. iii. 1[22] (*Ephes.* vi. 14); Epist. v. 10[160–2] (*Ephes.* iv. 17); Epist. x. 27[516–18] (*Ephes.* iv. 10).

Epicurei, Epicureans; so called from Epicurus, Conv. iv. 6[111]; the E., the Stoics, and the Peripatetics, the three great philosophical schools at Athens, Conv. iii. 14[138–9] ; the three sects of the active life, symbolized by the three Maries at the sepulchre of our Lord, Conv. iv. 22[159–62] ; Torquatus an Epicurean, Conv. iv. 6[110–12] [**Torquato**[2]]; *i seguaci di Epicuro* (a term of wide signification in the Middle Ages, which covered many forms of heresy), placed among the Heretics in Circle VI of Hell, Inf. x. 14 [**Epicuro**].

Epicuro, Epicurus, celebrated Greek philosopher, B.C. 342–270 ; he started at Athens the philosophical school called after him, which taught that the *summum bonum*, or highest good, is happiness—not sensual enjoyment, but peace of mind, as the result of the cultivation of the virtues. He held that virtue was to be practised because it led to happiness, whereas the Stoics held that virtue should be cultivated for its own sake.

D. places E. and his followers in Circle VI of Hell among the Heretics, as having denied the immortality of the soul, Inf. x. 14 (cf. Conv. ii. 9[55–8]) [**Epicurei : Eretici**]; he gives a summary of the philosophy of Epicurus, Conv. iv. 6[100–10] ; dismisses as false the opinions of E. and the Stoic Zeno as to the real end of life, that of Aristotle being the true one, Conv. iv. 22[27–31] ; quotes Cicero's arguments against E. in the *De Finibus* (ii. 4, 19), Mon. ii. 5[83–9].

Epicurus. [*Epicuro.*]

Epistola Jacobi, Judae, etc. [*Jacobi, Judae, etc., Epistola.*]

Epistola ad Colossenses, ad Corinthios, etc. [*Colossenses, Corinthios, etc., Epistola ad.*]

Epistolae Canonicae], canonical Epistles of St. James, St. Peter, St. John, and St. Jude; supposed to be symbolized by the four elders in humble guise, crowned with roses and other crimson flowers (as emblems of love), in the mystical Procession in the Terrestrial Paradise ('quattro in umile paruta'), Purg. xxix. 142, 145–8.

Epistolae Paulinae], Pauline Epistles, supposed to be symbolized by the elder with a sword in the mystical Procession in the Terrestrial Paradise, Purg. xxix. 134, 139–41, 145–8.

Epistole Dantesche], D.'s Letters; of the thirteen Latin letters which have been attributed to D., ten are commonly accepted as genuine; these ten are addressed as follows:—Epist. i. To Niccolò da Prato, Cardinal-Bishop of Ostia (written probably after July, 1304);—Epist. ii. To Oberto and Guido, Counts of Romena, nephews of Alessandro da Romena (written c. 1304);—Epist. iii. To the Marquis Moroello Malaspina (written c. 1307);—Epist. iv. To a Pistojan exile, commonly supposed to be Cino da Pistoja (written probably between 1302 and 1306);—Epist. v. To the Princes and Peoples of Italy, on the advent of the Emperor Henry VII into Italy (written in 1310);—Epist. vi. To the People of Florence (dated March 31, 1311) (probably the letter threatening the Florentines with the vengeance of the Emperor referred to by Bruni in his *Vita di Dante*);—Epist. vii. To the Emperor Henry VII (dated April 17, 1311) (mentioned by Villani, ix. 136);—Epist.

viii. To the Italian Cardinals in conclave at Carpentras after the death of Clement V (written in 1314, after April 20) (mentioned by Villani, ix. 136);—Epist. ix. To a Florentine friend (written in 1315);—Epist. x. To Can Grande della Scala (written not later than 1318) (an introduction to the interpretation of the *D. C.*; it formed the subject of the opening lecture on the *D.C.* delivered by Filippo Villani in Florence in 1391).—There are also three short letters written (between 1310 and 1311) by the Countess of Battifolle to Margaret of Brabant, wife of the Emperor Henry VII, which are supposed on plausible grounds to have been composed by D.—Besides the above there exists an Italian letter, purporting to have been written from Venice (on March 30, 1314) to Guido Novello da Polenta at Venice, which is undoubtedly spurious.

D. is recorded to have written several other letters which have not been preserved. Of three mentioned by Villani (ix. 136) only two (Epist. vii, viii) are extant; the third, a complaint addressed to the Florentines on the subject of his undeserved exile, is probably identical with the letter referred to by Bruni as beginning 'Popule mee, quid feci tibi?' Other letters are mentioned by Bruni, among them one giving an account of the battle of Campaldino, and another referring to his Priorate as the origin of all his misfortunes. D. himself in the *Vita Nuova* (§ 31$^{5-9}$) refers to a letter he composed, beginning 'Quomodo sedet sola civitas'.

The identity of the Florentine friend to whom Epist. ix was

addressed has not been established. Since D. speaks of his correspondent's nephew as being also his own nephew (ll. 13–14), it has been conjectured either that he was a member of the Brunacci family, whose sister, Piera di Donato Brunacci, married D.'s half-brother, Francesco, and had a son, Durante, who would be the nephew in question; or, more probably, that he was D.'s brother-in-law, Teruccio, son of Manetto Donati, and brother of Gemma, who was a member of a religious order and bachelor of divinity, and had a nephew, Niccolò, son of Foresino (or Forese) di Manetto Donati, who would be also D.'s nephew (by marriage).

Era, river of France, the Araris of the Romans, now known as the Saône, which rises in the Vosges Mts. and flows into the Rhone at Lyon; mentioned by the Emperor Justinian (in the Heaven of Mercury), together with the Var, Rhine, Isère, Seine, and Rhone, in connexion with Caesar's victories in Gaul, Par. vi. 59.

The name *Era* being used by Petrarch and Matteo Villani for the Loire, some think that this river is the one referred to by D.; but there can hardly be a doubt that the reference is to the Saône, since D. is here evidently following Lucan, by whom all these rivers are mentioned together in the same passage and who makes the Araris fall into the Rhone (*Phars*. i. 371 ff.).

Eraclito, Heraclitus, Greek philosopher of Ephesus, c. B.C. 510, who held fire to be the primary form of all matter; D., whose knowledge of H. was probably derived from

Cicero (*Fin*. ii. 5; *N. D.* iii. 14), places him among the great philosophers of antiquity in Limbo, Inf. iv. 138. [**Limbo.**]

Ercole, Hercules, great hero of antiquity, son of Zeus and Alcmene, grandson of Alcaeus, whence he is often called Alcides; referred to as *Ercole*, Inf. xxv. 32; xxvi. 108; xxxi. 132; Conv. iii. 3$^{51-60}$; *Hercules*, Mon. ii. 8^{80}, 10^{89}; A. T. § 19^{42}; *Alcide*, Par. ix. 101; *Alcides*, Epist. vii. 6^{116}; Carm. 30; his slaughter of Cacus, Inf. xxv. 32 [**Caco**]; the 'Pillars of Hercules', Inf. xxvi. 108; A. T. § 19$^{41-2}$; Carm. 30 [**Colonne d'Ercole**]; his combat with Antaeus, Inf. xxxi. 132; Conv. iii. 3$^{50-65}$; Mon. ii. 8$^{78-83}$, 10$^{87-9}$ [**Anteo**]; his love for Iole, Par. ix. 101 [**Iole**]; his encounter with the Lernaean Hydra, Epist. vii. 6^{116} [**Hydra**]; his contest with Cerberus referred to, Inf. ix. 98–9 [**Cerbero**]; and his death at the hands of Deianira, Inf. xii. 68 [**Deianira**].

Eresiarche, Heresiarchs; placed with other Heretics in Circle VI of Hell, Inf. ix. 127. [**Eretici.**]

Eresitone, Erysichthon, son of the Thessalian King Triopas, who, having cut down trees in a grove sacred to Ceres, was afflicted by the goddess with a fearful hunger, which drove him to devour his own flesh.

D. (who got the story from Ovid, *Metam*. viii. 738–878) compares him, as an instance of extreme emaciation, with the Spirits who expiate the sin of Gluttony in Circle VI of Purgatory, Purg. xxiii. 26. [**Golosi.**]

Eretici, Heretics, placed in Circle

VI of Hell, Inf. ix. 112–xi. 9;
they are confined, 'like with like',
in tombs set in the midst of flames,
whereby they are heated 'some more,
some less' (ix. 130–1); their tombs
are open, but after the Day of Judgement will be closed down for ever
(x. 8–12); they have no knowledge
of the present, but can to some extent foresee the future, as far as
affairs on earth are concerned (x.
97–108). *Examples*: Farinata degli
Uberti [**Farinata**]; Cavalcante
Cavalcanti [**Cavalcante**]; Emperor
Frederick II [**Federico**²]; Cardinal
Ottaviano degli Ubaldini [**Cardinale, Il**]; Pope Anastasius II [**Anastasio**]. With these are included Epicurus and his followers [**Epicuro**].

Eridanus. [**Po.**]

Erifile], Eriphyle, wife of Amphiaraus, whom she betrayed for the
sake of the necklace of Harmonia,
in consequence of which she was put
to death by her son Alcmaeon;
alluded to as the mother of the latter,
Purg. xii. 50; Par. iv. 104 [**Almeone: Anfiarao**]; she figures
among the examples of defeated pride
in Circle I of Purgatory, Purg. xii.
49–51 [**Superbi**].

Erine, the three Erinyes or Furies,
Alecto, Megaera, and Tisiphone,
who dwelt in the depths of Hell
and punished men both in this world
and after death. D., who describes
them (after Statius, *Theb.* i. 103 ff.)
as being of the hue of blood, with
the limbs and shapes of women, girt
with green water-snakes, and with
snakes for hair, places them on a lofty
tower as guardians of the entrance to
the City of Dis (cf. *Aen.* vi. 554–
5), Inf. ix. 36–42 [**Dite**]; *tre furie*

infernali, v. 38; *le meschine Della
regina dell' eterno pianto* (i. e. the
minions of Proserpine), *vv.* 43–4
[**Proserpina**]; *le feroci Erine, v.*
45; *cacciati del ciel, gente dispetta, v.*
91; as D. approaches with Virgil,
the Furies threaten him, but they are
quelled by a messenger from Heaven
(probably an angel, but thought by
some to be Mercury, by others Aeneas), who opens the gate of Dis
with a wand and admits D. and V.
(*vv.* 50 ff.). [**Porta di Dite.**]

Erisiton. [**Eresitone.**]

Eriton, Erichtho, Thessalian
sorceress, who, according to Lucan
(*Phars.* vi. 508–830), was employed
by Pompey's son Sextus to conjure
up the spirit of one of his dead
soldiers on the eve of the battle of
Pharsalia, that he might learn what
was to be the issue of the campaign.
D. makes Virgil say (on what authority is not known) that, shortly after
his death, he himself had been
summoned by E. to fetch a spirit
from Giudecca, the nethermost pit
of Hell, Inf. ix. 22–7.

Ermafrodito, Hermaphroditus,
son of Hermes and Aphrodite.
Having inherited the beauty of both
his parents, he excited the love of
the nymph of the fountain of Salma-
cis, near Halicarnassus, who tried
in vain to win his affections. One
day as he was bathing in the fountain she embraced him, and prayed
to the gods that she might be united
with him for ever. The gods granted
the request, and the bodies of the
two became united together, but retained the characteristics of each sex
(Ovid, *Metam.* iv. 288–388).

D. uses the name to indicate the

nature of the sin (common to both sexes), as distinct from sodomy, expiated by certain of the Lustful in Circle VII of Purgatory, Purg. xxvi. 82 [Lussuriosi].

Ermo, L', the Hermitage, i.e. the monastery of Camaldoli in the Casentino, Purg. v. 96 [Camaldoli]; the monastery of Santa Croce di Fonte Avellana in Umbria, Par. xxi. 110 [Avellana].

Ero], Hero, priestess of Venus at Sestos, to visit whom Leander used to swim nightly across the Hellespont from Abydos, Purg. xxviii. 74. [Leandro.]

Erode], Herod the tetrarch; divine import of his action in sending Christ to be judged before Pilate, *Herodes*, Mon. ii. 13[45-54] (ref. to *Luke* xxiii. 11); his execution of John the Baptist in compliance with the request of Herodias' daughter, Par. xviii. 135 (ref. to *Mark* vi. 27). [Battista.]

Esaù, Esau, eldest son of Isaac and Rebekah, twin-brother of Jacob; mentioned with the latter by Charles Martel (in the Heaven of Venus), in reference to the different dispositions of the two brothers in spite of the identity of their begetting, Par. viii. 130; the two are alluded to by St. Bernard (in the Empyrean), in connexion with the doctrine of predestination (with a reference also to the colour of Esau's hair), as *quei gemelli, Che nella madre ebber l'ira commota*, Par. xxxii. 68-70 (ref. to *Gen.* xxv. 22, 25; *Rom.* ix. 10-13); some think Esau, who sold his birthright for a mess of pottage (*Gen.* xxv. 29-34), is the person alluded to as *colui Che fece ber vil-tate il gran rifiuto*, Inf. iii. 59-60. [Celestino.]

Esopo, Aesop the fabulist (c. B.C. 570), the reputed author of the collection of fables which goes by his name, none of which probably were actually written by him; D. mentions him in connexion with the fable of the Mouse and the Frog, Inf. xxiii. 4-6; and speaks of him as 'Esopo poeta' in connexion with 'la prima favola', that of the Cock and the Pearl, Conv. iv. 30[40-4].

Esperia, -ero. [Hesperia,-erus.]

Este. [Esti.]

Estensis, of Este; *Marchio Estensis*, 'the Marquis of Este', i.e. Azzo VIII of Este, V. E. ii. 6[42]. [Azzo.]

Ester, Esther the Jewess, wife of Ahasuerus, King of Persia; D. in a vision sees E. with Ahasuerus and Mordecai witnessing the death of Haman, Purg. xvii. 29 (*Esth.* v. 14; vii. 10). [Amano.]

Esti, now Este, small town of N. Italy in Venetia, at the S. base of the Euganean Hills, whence the Este family took their name; *Quel da Esti*, i.e. Azzo VIII, Purg. v. 77 [Azzo].

Esti, Azzo da. [Azzo.]

Esti, Beatrice da. [Beatrice[4].]

Esti, Obizzo da. [Obizzo.]

Eteócle, Eteocles, son of Oedipus, King of Thebes, and Jocasta, and twin-brother of Polynices. The brothers having compelled Oedipus to abdicate and leave Thebes, he prayed the gods that they might be eternally at enmity with each other. E. and Polynices agreed to reign in Thebes alternately year by year, but when E.'s term had expired he refused to resign the throne to his brother. The latter consequently invoked the aid of Adrastus, King of Argos, and thus originated the famous war of the Seven against Thebes (Inf. xiv. 68–9) [**Adrasto**]. The prayer of Oedipus was now answered, for in the course of the war Polynices and E. killed each other in single combat. Their bodies were burned on the same funeral pile, but so intense was the hatred between them, even after death, that the flame from the pyre divided in two as it ascended. [**Polinice**.]

D. mentions E. and his brother, and compares this divided flame (the account of which he got from Statius, *Theb.* xii. 429 ff.) to that in which Ulysses and Diomed are enveloped, Inf. xxvi. 52–4 [**Diomede**]; the two brothers are referred to, in allusion to their fratricidal strife, as *la doppia tristizia di Jocasta*, Purg. xxii. 56. [**Jocasta**.]

Ethica, *Nicomachean Ethics* (in ten books) of Aristotle, so called after his son, Nicomachus, to whom he addressed the work; quoted as *Etica*, Inf. xi. 80; Conv. i. 9^{62}, 10^{71}, $12^{21, \, 76}$; ii. 5^{91}, 14^{43}, 15^{126}, ^{128}; iii. 1^{57}, 3^{90}, 4^{54}, 7^{89}, 8^{169}, $11^{75, \, 92, \, 144}$, 15^{130}; iv. $8^{4, \, 142}$, 12^{127}, $13^{70, \, 74}$, 15^{147}, 16^{59}, $17^{9, \, 11, \, 18, \, 75, \, 94}$, 19^{83}, 20^{37}, 21^{127}, 22^{15}, 25^{8}, $27^{47, \, 110}$; Canz. viii. 85; *Ethica*, A. T. §§ 18^{68}, 20^{18}; *Ad Nicomachum*, Mon. i. 3^{4}, 11^{72}, 13^{26}, 14^{37}, 15^{72}, ii. 2^{63}, 3^{56}, 8^{17}, 12^{40}; iii. 10^{101}, 12^{67}; A. T. § 11^{14}; referred to by Virgil, addressing D., as *la tua scienza*, Inf. vi. 106.

D.'s opinion of the Italian translation of the (Latin) *Ethics*, Conv. i.

10^{70-2} [**Taddeo: Aristotile**]; the commentary of St. Thomas Aquinas on the *Ethics*, his opinion that the study of Moral Philosophy is a preparation for all the other sciences, Conv. ii. 15^{125-7}; the prologue of St. Thomas to the *Ethics*, his saying that to understand the relation of one thing to another is the special act of reason, Conv. iv. 8^{3-6}; D.'s opinion that the science of Ethics is secondary to Metaphysics, which he calls the 'First Philosophy', Conv. iii. 11^{176} [*Metafisica*].

D. quotes from the *Ethics* upwards of fifty times :—in proportion as a thing is more perfect, it is more conscious of good, and so of suffering, Inf. vi. 106–8 (*Eth.* x. 4, 7); three forms of things to be avoided in morals, viz. incontinence, malice, bestiality, Inf. xi. 80 (*Eth.* vii. 1); one swallow does not make the spring, Conv. i. 9^{62} (*Eth.* i. 7); proximity and goodness the causes which beget love, Conv. i. 12^{21} (*Eth.* viii. 3); justice so lovable that even her enemies love her, Conv. i. 12^{76} (D. refers to *Eth.* v., but the quotation comes from Cicero, *De Officiis*, ii. 11); the energy of the Deity, as it surpasses all others in blessedness, must be contemplative, Conv. ii. 5^{91} (*Eth.* x. 8); truth the good of the intellect, Conv. ii. 14^{43} (*Eth.* vi. 2); legal (as distinct from universal) justice enjoins the study of the sciences, Conv. ii. 15^{128-9} (*Eth.* v. 2); some mutual relation necessary for the preservation of friendship between persons of unequal station, Conv. iii. 1^{56-62} (*Eth.* ix. 1); Epist. x. 3^{61-3}; the friendship of the good, and of those who are alike in virtue, perfect, Conv. iii.

3^{84-90} (*Eth.* viii. 3); a man deserving of praise or blame only in so far as he is a free agent, Conv. iii. 4^{54-7} (*Eth.* iii. 1); there is a sort of heroic and divine virtue, which is above human nature, Conv. iii. 7^{84-92} (*Eth.* vii. 1); virtue becomes spontaneous through force of habit, Conv. iii. 8^{164-9} (*Eth.* ii. 1, 3); three kinds of friendship, arising from advantage, pleasure, or disinterestedness, Conv. iii. 11^{74-89} (*Eth.* viii. 3); friendship arising from advantage or pleasure not true friendship, Conv. iii. 11^{89-92} (*Eth.* viii. 3); the end of true friendship the virtuous delight derived from natural human intercourse, Conv. iii. 11^{139-44} (*Eth.* ix. 9); by association with wisdom man gains happiness and content, Conv. iii. 15^{47-50} (*Eth.* x. 7); happiness a certain energy of the soul according to perfect virtue, Conv. iii. 15^{129-31}; iv. 17^{75-7} (*Eth.* i. 9); happiness the end of all human actions, Conv. iv. 4^{3-4} (*Eth.* i. 7); the opinion of the majority not likely to be altogether wrong, Conv. iv. 8^{42-4} (*Eth.* i. 8); truth to be preferred to friendship, Conv. iv. 8^{142-4} (*Eth.* i. 6); Mon. iii. 1^{17-18}; Epist. viii. 5^{82-5}; perfect knowledge free from doubt, Conv. iv. 12^{127-8} (*Eth.* vi. 3); man should bring himself as near as possible to divine things, Conv. iv. 13^{71-2} (*Eth.* x. 7); the educated man demands certainty of knowledge, where certainty is attainable, Conv. iv. 13^{74-7} (*Eth.* i. 3); Mon. ii. 2^{64-6}; A. T. § 20^{15-18}; such as do not reason, nor listen to reason, incapable of benefiting by moral philosophy, Conv. iv. 15^{146-8} (*Eth.* i. 4); a man may be a child by

reason not only of years, but also of ill habits and faulty life, Conv. iv. 16^{56-9} (*Eth.* i. 3); moral virtue is an 'elective habit', Conv. iv. 17^{7-9} (*Eth.* ii. 6); Canz. viii. 85; Aristotle's definitions of the eleven virtues, Conv. iv. 17^{28-64} (viz. fortitude, *Eth.* iii. 6; temperance, *Eth.* iii. 10; liberality, *Eth.* iv. 1; magnificence, *Eth.* iv. 2; magnanimity, *Eth.* iv. 3; desire of honour, *Eth.* iv. 4; meekness, *Eth.* iv. 5; affability, *Eth.* iv. 6; truthfulness, *Eth.* iv. 7; graceful wit, *Eth.* iv. 8; justice, *Eth.* v. 1); prudence one of the intellectual virtues, Conv. iv. 17^{78-80} (*Eth.* i. 13; x. 8); the contemplative life conducive to the highest happiness, Conv. iv. 17^{90-4} (*Eth.* x. 7); shame commendable in the young but blameworthy in the old, Conv. iv. 19^{83-5} (*Eth.* iv. 9); some men almost divine, as proved by Homer, Conv. iv. 20^{36-7} (*Iliad* xxiv. 258; *Eth.* vii. 1); man should accustom himself to do good and to curb his passions to the end that he may be happy, Conv. iv. 21^{125-7} (*Eth.* ii. 1); definite aim desirable in pursuit of right, Conv. iv. 22^{15-17} (*Eth.* i. 2); perfect life impossible without friends, Conv. iv. 25^{7-8} (*Eth.* viii. 1); man naturally a social being, Conv. iv. 27^{29} (*Eth.* i. 7); wisdom impossible without virtue, Conv. iv. 27^{47-8} (*Eth.* vi. 13); liberality must be tempered by prudence and justice, Conv. iv. 27^{109-15} (*Eth.* iv. 1); the answer to the question, what is the end of all human actions, disposes of half the whole question of Ethics, Mon. i. 3^{1-5} (*Eth.* i. 7); justice more admirable than the evening or morning star, Mon. i. 11^{32-4} (*Eth.*

v. 1); appetite the strongest opponent of justice, Mon. i. 11$^{69-72}$ (*Eth.* v. 2); arguments less convincing than facts in matters of feeling and action, Mon. i. 13$^{25-8}$; ii. 12$^{38-40}$ (*Eth.* x. 1); laws not infallible as dealing with human institutions, hence the need of ἐπιεικεία, i.e. equity, Mon. i. 14$^{34-8}$ (*Eth.* v. 10); the wills of men need direction on account of their passions, Mon. i. 15$^{69-73}$ (*Eth.* x. 9); Hector praised by Homer (*Iliad* xxiv. 258) above all men, Mon. ii. 3$^{54-7}$ (*Eth.* vii. 1); in discussing εὐβουλία A. admits the possibility of arriving at a right result by false syllogism, Mon. ii. 6$^{43-9}$ (*Eth.* vi. 9); to discover the good of an individual is satisfactory, but to discover that of a state or nation is more noble and divine, Mon. ii. 8$^{17-19}$ (*Eth.* i. 2); the Egyptians do not concern themselves with the political system of the Scythians, Mon. iii. 3$^{12-15}$ (altered from *Eth.* iii. 3); Agathon's saying that even God cannot make what has been, not to have been, Mon. iii. 6$^{50-4}$ (*Eth.* vi. 2); earth cannot be made by nature to go upwards, nor fire to go downwards, Mon. iii. 7$^{30-2}$ (*Eth.* ii. 1); the giver and receiver of a gift in the relation of agent and patient, each of whom must be properly qualified before a gift can be properly bestowed, Mon. iii. 10$^{98-105}$ (*Eth.* iv. 1); the best man the measure and ideal of all mankind, Mon. iii. 12$^{62-8}$ (*Eth.* x. 5); friendships for the sake of utility found as a rule between persons of unequal station, Epist. x. 2$^{25-8}$ (*Eth.* viii. 8); moral philosophy deals with practice, not speculation, Epist. x.

16$^{273-5}$ (*Eth.* i. 3); some principles perceived by induction, others by sensation, A.T. § 11$^{11-14}$ (*Eth.* i. 7); man naturally prone to indulge his passions, yet restrains them in obedience to reason, A.T. § 18$^{66-8}$ (*Eth.* i. 13).

Etica[1]], moral philosophy or Ethics; *Ethica*, Epist. x. 16^{273}, *scienza morale*, Conv. ii. 14^{63}; iii. 11^{176}; *morale filosofia*, Conv. ii. 15$^{124, 158}$; the ninth or Crystalline Heaven likened to, Conv. ii. 14$^{63-4}$, 15$^{122-4}$ [**Cielo Cristallino**]; the study of, according to St. Thomas Aquinas, a preparation for all the other sciences, Conv. ii. 15$^{124-7}$; together with Physics and Metaphysics makes up the whole body of philosophy, Conv. iii. 11$^{173-6}$; deals with practice, not speculation, Epist. x. 16$^{273-5}$ [***Ethica***].

Etica[2]. [***Ethica***.]

Etiópe, Ethiopian; in sense of 'heathen', Par. xix. 109; inhabits a thirsty land, *Etiópo*, Purg. xxvi. 21; Ethiopians alluded to with reference to their swarthy complexion, Inf. xxxiv. 44-5.

Etiopia, Ethiopia, district of Africa S. of Egypt, comprising modern Nubia, Kordofan, Sennaar, and Abyssinia; its venomous serpents, Inf. xxiv. 89; its hot winds, which reach Europe laden with vapour, Canz. xv. 14; *là onde il Nilo s'avvalla*, Inf. xxxiv. 45.

Etiópo. [**Etiope.**]

Etna. [**Aetna.**]

Eton, Aethon, one of the four horses that drew the chariot of the Sun, Conv. iv. 23^{136}. [**Eoo.**]

Ettore, Hector, eldest son of Priam, King of Troy, and Hecuba, husband of Andromache. During the siege of Troy, H., who was the chief hero of the Trojans, was slain by Achilles, who dragged his dead body behind his chariot into the Greek camp; subsequently it was restored to Priam and buried in Troy.

D. places H. in Limbo among the heroes of antiquity, together with Aeneas and Julius Caesar, Inf. iv. 122 [Limbo]; his tomb at Troy, Par. vi. 68 (*Aen.* v. 371) [Antandro]; called by Virgil 'the light and hope of the Trojans' (*Aen.* ii. 281), Conv. iii. 11$^{158-60}$ (where D. by a slip has written *Enea* for *Ettore*); his trumpeter Misenus, Conv. iv. 26$^{113-14}$ [Miseno]; praised above all men by Homer (*Iliad* xxiv. 258), as quoted by Aristotle (*Ethics* vii. 1); Aeneas compared to him by Virgil (*Aen.* vi. 170), Mon. ii. 3$^{48-57}$; the epithet *Hectoreus*, in the sense of Trojan (and hence Roman), applied to the Emperor Henry VII, *Hectoreus pastor*, Epist. v. 5^{86}.

Euclide, Euclid, celebrated Greek mathematician, who lived at Alexandria c. B.C. 300, author of the famous Elements of Geometry; placed together with Ptolemy the astronomer among the philosophers of antiquity in Limbo, Inf. iv. 142 [Limbo]; his opinion that the point is the starting-point of Geometry, and the circle the most perfect figure, Conv. ii. 14$^{209-12}$; a waste of labour to demonstrate any theorem afresh after him, Mon. i. 1$^{19-21}$.

Euclides. [Euclide.]

Eufrates, Euphrates, river of Asia, which rises in the mountains of Armenia, and flows into the Per-

sian Gulf, after being joined by the Tigris. D., who shared the common belief (cf. Lucan, *Phars.* iii. 256–8; Boëthius, *Cons. Phil.* v. met. 1) that the two rivers issued from the same source, mentions them together in connexion with the rivers Lethe and Eunoë in the Terrestrial Paradise, which, he says, like them spring from one fount, Purg. xxxiii. 112–13. [Eunoè.]

Euneo], Euneos, son of Jason and Hypsipyle, brother of Thoas; he and his brother are referred to as *due figli*, in connexion with the episode of their recognition and rescue of their mother from the wrath of Lycurgus, King of Nemea, whose son, Archemorus, had met his death while under her charge, Purg. xxvi. 94–5. [Archemoro: Isifile.]

Eunoè (from Gk. εὔνοος, 'well-minded'), name of one of the rivers of the Terrestrial Paradise, the other being Lethe, Purg. xxviii. 131; xxxiii. 127; *acqua*, v. 116; *santissima onda*, v. 142; both streams issue from one source, which is of divine, not natural, origin, the waters returning whence they came (Purg. xxviii. 121–6); the waters of one branch, named Lethe, have the power of taking away from man the memory of sin (*vv.* 127–8); those of the other branch, Eunoë, that of restoring to him the recollection of his good actions (*v.* 129); to produce these effects the waters, whose savour is sovereign, must in each case be tasted (*vv.* 131–3). After being drawn by Matilda through the waters of Lethe to the opposite bank, and having swallowed some in the process (Purg. xxxi. 91–105), D. is taken by her at Beatrice's bidding (with Statius) to drink of the waters of Eunoë, the 'sweet draught' of which makes him fit to ascend to Heaven (Purg. xxxiii. 127–145). [Letè.]

Eurialo, Euryalus, Trojan youth, who with his friend Nisus accompanied Aeneas to Italy, where they perished together in a night attack on the Rutulian camp (*Aen.* ix. 176–449); E. and N. are mentioned, together with Camilla and Turnus, as having died for Italy, Inf. i. 108; E. is mentioned also in allusion to *Aen.* v. 334–8, where Virgil makes Aeneas award him the prize in a foot-race, though it was unfairly gained, as his rival was tripped up by N., D. being of the opinion of Chrysippus, as quoted by Cicero (*Off.* iii. 10), that athletes ought not to hinder one another in their contests, *Euryalus*, Mon. ii. 8[86–101]. [Chrysippus.]

Euripide, Euripides, Greek tragic poet, born at Salamis, on the day of the battle of Salamis, B. C. 480; died in Macedonia, 406. Virgil (addressing Statius in Purgatory) mentions E. as being with himself and the other great poets of antiquity in Limbo, Purg. xxii. 106. [Limbo.]

Euripilo, Eurypylus, augur sent by the Greeks to consult the oracle of Apollo as to their departure from Troy; he brought back the reply that, as their departure from Greece had cost them a bloody sacrifice in the death of Iphigenia, so by blood must they purchase their return (*Aen.* ii. 114–19). D., who describes E. as having a long beard, places him among the Soothsayers in Bolgia 4 of Circle VIII of Hell (Malebolge), Inf. xx, 112 [Indovini]; he makes Virgil say (*vv.* 110–13) that E. was associated with Calchas in foretelling the time of the sailing of the Greek fleet from Aulis; but there is no mention of this fact in the *Aeneid*. [Calcanta.]

Euro, Eurus, name given by the ancients to the E. or SE. wind; mentioned by Charles Martel (in the Heaven of Venus) in connexion with the Gulf of Catania in Sicily, where the prevailing wind is the stormy SE. or Scirocco, Par. viii. 69; G. del Virgilio mentions it, *Eurus*, Ecl. R. 17.

Europa [1], daughter of Agenor, King of Phoenicia, sister of Cadmus. Jupiter, being enamoured of her, assumed the form of a bull, and, having induced her to mount on his back, swam with her to Crete, where she became the mother of Minos, Rhadamanthus, and Sarpedon (Ovid, *Metam.* ii. 833–75). D. speaks of Phoenicia as *il lito Nel qual si fece Europa dolce carco*, Par. xxvii. 83–4.

Europa [2], continent of Europe, one of three divisions of the world according to the geography of D.'s time; in the sense of the civilized world, Purg. viii. 123; *lo stremo d'E.*, i.e. Constantinople, Par. vi. 5; the W. shores of E., i.e. Spain, Par. xii. 48; the region which never loses the Great Bear, Canz. xv. 28 [Orsa]; *questo emispero*, *v.* 19; populated by immigrants from the East, perhaps originally of European stock, who brought a threefold language with them, and settled, some in N., some in S., and some (the Greeks) partly in Europe, partly in

Asia, V. E. i. 8[5-21]; distribution of languages in, V. E. i. 8[21-64]; connexion of Aeneas with, by descent and marriage, Mon. ii. 3[67-117] [**Enea**]; Italy its noblest region, Mon. ii. 3[116-17]; separated from Asia by the Hellespont, Mon. ii. 9[52-4]; the majority of its inhabitants repudiate the claim of the Church to the disposal of the Imperial authority, Mon. iii. 14[60]; the Imperial power not limited by the shores of *Europa tricornis* (the shape of the continent being represented roughly as a triangle by the ancient geographers), Epist. vii. 3[55].

Eurus. [**Euro.**]

Euryalus. [**Eurialo.**]

Eva, Eve, the first woman, Purg. viii. 99; xii. 71; xxiv. 116; xxix. 24; V. E. i. 4[12]; *l'antica madre*, Purg. xxx. 52; *quella ch'al serpente crese*, Purg. xxxii. 32; *la bella guancia, Il cui palato a tutto il mondo costa*, Par. xiii. 37 (cf. Par. xxxii. 122); *colei che aperse la piaga che Maria richiuse*, Par. xxxii. 4-6 [**Maria**[1]]; *prima mulier*, V. E. i. 2[44]; Adam and Eve, *la prima gente*, Purg. i. 24; *l'umana radice*, Purg. xxviii. 142; *li primi parenti*, Par. vii. 148; *primi parentes*, Mon. i. 16[7] [**Adamo**]; creation of Eve from Adam's rib, Par. xiii. 37-9; her temptation by the Serpent, Purg. viii. 99; xxxii. 32; V. E. i. 2[43-4], 4[12-13]; her tasting of the forbidden fruit, Purg. viii. 99; xxiv. 116; xxix. 24; Par. xiii. 37; V. E. i. 4[12-18]; according to the Scriptural account (*Gen.* iii. 2), the first of the human race who spoke, V. E. i. 4[10-11]; her place in the Celestial Rose pointed out to D. by St. Bernard,

Par. xxxii. 3-5 [**Rosa**]; she is described (probably with reference to *Gen.* iii. 5-6) as *praesumptuosissima*, V. E. i. 4[12] (cf. Purg. xxix. 24); hence the Proud in Circle I of Purgatory are called *figliuoli d'Eva*, Purg. xii. 71 (cf. Purg. xxix. 86).

Evander, Arcadian settler in Italy before the Trojan war, founder and King of Pallanteum, city on the banks of the Tiber; Aeneas addresses him on their common ancestry (*Aen.* viii. 134-7), Mon. ii. 3[71-6]; his son Pallas is mentioned, Par. vi. 36; Mon. ii. 11[17]. [**Pallante.**]

Evangelio, the Gospel, Purg. xxii. 154; Par. ix. 133; xxiv. 137; xxix. 114; Conv. iv. 22[148]; *Vangelo*, Conv. ii. 1[46]; iii. 14[63]; iv. 16[109], 17[95]; *Evangelium*, Mon. ii. 10[47]; *evangelico suono*, Purg. xix. 136; *evangelica doctrina*, Par. xxiv. 144; *tuba evangelica*, Mon. ii. 10[55]; the Gospel of St. Matthew, Conv. iv. 16[109] [**Matteo**]; of St. Mark, Conv. iv. 22[148] [**Marco**]; of St. Luke, Conv. iv. 17[95] [**Luca**[1]]; of St. John, Conv. iii. 14[63] [**Giovanni**[2]]. D. quotes from the Gospels upwards of eighty times [**Bibbia.**] The four Gospels are supposed to be typified by the *quattro animali*, Purg. xxix. 92 [**Evangelisti**].

Evangelisti], Evangelists; *scribae Christi*, Mon. iii. 9[68]; *Giovanni Evangelista*, Conv. ii. 6[18] [**Giovanni**[2]]; *Luca Evangelista*, Conv. iv. 5[65] [**Luca**[1]]. Some think the four Evangelists are typified by the *quattro animali*, Purg. xxix. 92, in accordance with *Rev.* iv. 7, where the beast with the face as a man is taken to represent St. Matthew, that like a lion St. Mark, that like a calf St. Luke, that like a flying eagle St. John ; others interpret D.'s four beasts as typifying the Gospels themselves.

Evangelium. [*Evangelio.*]

Evangelium secundum Joannem, Lucam, Marcum, Matthaeum. [Giovanni[2]: Luca[1]: Marco: Matteo.]

Exodus], Book of Exodus; quoted, Par. xxvi. 42 (*Exod.* xxxiii. 19); Mon. ii. 4[11-14] (*Exod.* viii. 18–19); Mon. ii. 13[36-7] (*Exod.* ii. 14); referred to, Par. xxxii. 131–2 (ref. to *Exod.* xvi. 14–21); Mon. i. 14[66-73] (ref. to *Exod.* xviii. 17–26); Mon. ii. 8[57-9] (ref. to *Exod.* iv. 21; vii. 9). [*Bibbia.*]

Ezechia], Hezekiah, King of Judah ; placed among the spirits of those who loved justice (*Spiriti Giudicanti*) in the Heaven of Jupiter, where he is one of the five that form the eyebrow of the Eagle, being referred to as *quel che . . . Morte indugiò per vera penitenza* (in allusion to 2 *Kings* xx. 1–6), Par. xx. 49–51. [Aquila[2]: Giove, Cielo di.]

Ezechiel, prophet Ezekiel, Purg. xxix. 100 ; Epist. x. 27[520], 28[551]; *Propheta*, Epist. viii. 4[53] ; the four Cherubim in his vision (*Ezek.* i. 4–14) compared to the four animals seen by D. in the mystical Procession in the Terrestrial Paradise, which, however, instead of four wings (*Ezek.* i. 6), had six, like those described by St. John (*Rev.* iv. 8), Purg. xxix. 100–5 ; his prophecy quoted, Epist. x. 27[520-3] (*Ezek.* xxviii. 12–13) ; Epist. x. 28[551-2] (*Ezek.*i. 28 : *Vulg.* ii. 1) ; referred to, Epist. viii. 4[53] (*Ezek.* viii. 16). [*Bibbia.*]

Ezzolino. [Azzolino.]

F

Fabbrizio, Caius Fabricius, famous Roman hero, Consul B.C. 282, 278, Censor 275. During the invasion of Italy by Pyrrhus, King of Epirus, he was sent to the latter to negotiate an exchange of prisoners. Pyrrhus used every effort to gain him over, but F. refused all his offers. On a later occasion he sent back to Pyrrhus the traitor who had offered to poison him, after which he succeeded in arranging terms for the evacuation of Italy by the former. He and his contemporary Curius Dentatus are lauded by Roman writers for their frugality, and probity in in refusing the bribes of the enemy [Curio[1]].

F.'s preference of virtuous poverty to ill-gotten riches is proclaimed by Hugh Capet as an example to the Avaricious in Circle V of Purgatory, Purg. xx. 25–7 [Avari] ; his refusal to betray his country for gold, Conv. iv. 5[107-10]; Virgil's allusion to this when he speaks of ' parvoque potentem Fabricium'(*Aen.* vi. 844), *Fabricius*, Mon. ii. 5[90-9] ;

his discomfiture of Pyrrhus, Mon.
ii. 11[55-7] [Pirro[2]].

Fabbro, Fabbro de' Lambertazzi,
leader of the Ghibellines of Bologna
who adopted the name of the Lambertazzi family as their party designation,
while the Guelfs assumed that of the
Geremei. Fabbro's great renown
and authority are attested by the fact
that he was invited to fill the office
of Podestà at Faenza in 1230, 1235,
and 1239; at Brescia in 1240 and
1252; at Viterbo in 1244–5; at
Pistoja in 1251; at Pisa in 1252–3
and 1256; at Modena in 1254–5;
and finally at Forlì in 1258. He
died in 1259, leaving several sons,
who shortly after his death were involved in a deadly conflict with the
Geremei, which led to the ruin of the
Lambertazzi and to the downfall of
the Ghibelline party in Bologna.
Fabbro is mentioned among the
former worthies of Romagna by
Guido del Duca (in Circle II of
Purgatory), who, after lamenting
the degeneration of the Romagnole
families, asks when a second Fabbro
will arise in Bologna, Purg. xiv.
99–100.

Fabi, the Fabii, ancient patrician
family at Rome, celebrated as having
furnished a long line of distinguished
men, among whom the most famous
were Q. Fabius Vibulanus, three
times Consul, B.C. 484–479; Q.
Fabius Maximus Rullianus, six times
Consul, B.C. 322–296, the most
eminent of the Roman generals in
the second Samnite war; Q. Fabius
Maximus Gurges, three times Consul,
B.C. 292–265; and Q. Fabius Maximus Cunctator, five times Consul,
B.C. 233–209.

The Emperor Justinian (in the
Heaven of Mercury) mentions the
Fabii, together with the Decii, in
connexion with the exploits of the
Roman Eagle, Par. vi. 47.

Fabricius. [**Fabbrizio: Fa-
brut us.**]

Fabritius. [**Fabricius.**]

Fabrutius, Fabruzzo de' Lambertazzi, Bolognese poet of the school
of Guido Guinizelli, said to have been
the nephew of the Fabbro mentioned
by Guido del Duca (Purg. xiv. 100).
He was expelled from Bologna with
the rest of his family in 1274, at the
same time as Guido Guinizelli. He
was still alive in 1298, in which year
he is mentioned as one of the leaders
of the exiled party. One poem of
his, a sonnet, has been preserved. D.,
who speaks of him simply as ' Fabrutius Bononiae', couples him with
Guido Guinizelli, Guido Ghisilieri,
and Onesto Bolognese, and quotes
his rejection of the Bolognese dialect as a proof of its inferiority, V. E.
i. 15[41-4]; his use of the seven-syllabled line at the beginning of poems
in the lofty style, V. E. ii. 12[38-41];
three of his lines quoted, V. E.
ii. 12[42-6]; and one of the same,
V.E. i. 15[49-50]. [**Guido Guinizelli.**]

Fabruzzo de' Lambertazzi.
[**Fabrutius.**]

Faentini. [**Faventini.**]

Faenza, town in the Emilia, on
the Lamone, between Forlì and
Imola, on the road to Bologna; mentioned by Bocca degli Abati (in
Antenora) in connexion with the
treachery of Tebaldello, Inf. xxxii.
123 [**Tebaldello**]; the degeneracy
of its inhabitants since the days of

Bernardin di Fosco, referred to by Guido del Duca (in Circle II of Purgatory), Purg. xiv. 101 [Bernardin]; D. alludes to it as *la città di Lamone*, and informs Guido da Montefeltro, in answer to his inquiry as to the condition of Romagna, that both it and *la città di Santerno* (i.e. Imola) are under the lordship of Mainardo Pagani, Inf. xxvii. 49–51 [Mainardo].

Faenza, Tommaso da], Tommaso Bucciola or Buzzola, poet of Faenza, several of whose sonnets and *canzoni* have been preserved ; he was a judge, and flourished c. 1280 ; D. mentions him as *Thomas Faventinus*, with Ugolino Bucciola (who was perhaps his brother), as having rejected the Faentine dialect, V. E. i. 14$^{18-20}$ [Bucciola, Ugolino].

Faggiuola], castle in the N. of the Marches, between San Leo Feltrio and Macerata Feltria, birthplace of the Ghibelline leader Uguccione della Faggiuola ; supposed by some to be the place indicated, Inf. i. 105. [Feltro ^{2} : Uguccione ^{3}.]

Falaride], Phalaris, tyrant of Agrigentum, c. B.C. 570 ; alluded to in connexion with the brazen bull made for him by Perillus, Inf. xxvii. 7–12. [Perillo.]

Falsatori, Falsifiers, Inf. xxix. 57 ; placed among the Fraudulent in Bolgia 10 of Circle VIII of Hell (Malebolge), Inf. xxix. 40–xxx. 148 [Frodolenti]. They are divided into four classes—1. Falsifiers of metals, Alchemists ; punished with paralysis (xxix. 71–2) and leprosy (*vv.* 72–84). *Examples*: Griffolino of Arezzo; Capocchio [Griffolino: Capocchio].—2. Falsifiers of

the person, Personators ; punished with madness (xxx. 25–33, 46). *Examples* : Gianni Schicchi de' Cavalcanti ; Myrrha [Gianni Schicchi : Mirra].—3. Falsifiers of coins, Coiners ; punished with dropsy and burning thirst (xxx. 49–69). *Examples*: Maestro Adamo: Aghinolfo da Romena [Adamo^2: Aghinolfo].—4. Falsifiers of their word, Liars ; punished with reeking and sharp fever (xxx. 91–9). *Examples* : 'La falsa che accusò Giuseppo' (i. e. Potiphar's wife); Sinon [Giuseppo^1: Sinone].

Falterona, one of the central peaks of the Tuscan Apennines, lying NE. of Florence; mentioned in connexion with the Arno, which rises high up on the S. side, Purg. xiv. 17 ; the discovery of a hoard of coin by a peasant while digging on its slopes, Conv. iv. 11$^{77-80}$.

Famagosta, Famagusta, seaport on E. coast of Cyprus, of considerable importance in the Middle Ages, now in decay ; mentioned by the Eagle in the Heaven of Jupiter, together with Nicosia, to indicate the kingdom of Cyprus, the reference being to Henry II of Lusignan, Par. xix. 146. [Arrigo^8 : Cipri.]

Fano, town in the Marches on the Adriatic coast between Pesaro and Ancona, a few miles N. of the mouth of the Metauro, subject in D.'s time to the Malatesta of Rimini ; it is mentioned by Pier da Medicina (in Bolgia 9 of Circle VIII of Hell), who refers to Guido del Cassero and Angiolello da Carignano as 'i due miglior di Fano', Inf. xxviii. 76 [Angiolello] ; and by Jacopo del Cassero (in Ante-purgatory) as his native place, Purg. v. 71 [Cassero].

Fantolini, Ugolino de', gentle-man of Cerfugnano, near Faenza, who was born at the beginning of Cent. xiii ; he belonged to the Guelf party, and was several times (1253, 1257, 1259) Podestà of Faenza ; he died in 1278, leaving two sons, Ottaviano, who was killed at Forlì in 1282, on the occasion of the re-pulse of the Guelfs and the French troops of Martin IV by Guido da Montefeltro (Inf. xxvii. 43–4), and Fantolino, who died before 1291. Ugolino is mentioned among the former worthies of Romagna by Guido del Duca (in Circle II of Purgatory), who says he is fortu-nate in that he has no descendants left alive to sully his name, Purg. xiv. 121–3.

Faraone. [Pharao.]

Farfarello, one of the ten demons in Bolgia 5 of Circle VIII of Hell (Malebolge) deputed by Malacoda to escort D. and Virgil, Inf. xxi. 123; xxii. 94. [Alichino: Male-branche.]

Farinata, Manente, called Far-inata, son of Jacopo degli Uberti, the 'Saviour of Florence', was born in Florence at the beginning of Cent. xiii ; while still a boy he witnessed the introduction into the city of the Guelf and Ghibelline factions, of the latter of which his family became the leaders; in 1239 he became the head of his house, and in 1248 he took a prominent part in the expulsion of the Guelfs, who however returned in 1251, and a few years later (in 1258) expelled the Ghibellines in their turn, Farinata among them ; the latter, who was now the acknow-ledged head of his party, took refuge with the rest of the Ghibelline ex-iles in Siena, where he organized the measures which led to the crushing defeat of the Florentine Guelfs and their allies at Montaperti, and left the Ghibellines masters of Tuscany (Sept. 4, 1260) [Arbia]. After their victory the Ghibellines held a council at Empoli, about twenty miles from Florence, at which it was pro-posed, in order to put an end once for all to the power of the Floren-tines, that the city of Florence should be razed to the ground. To this proposal, which was generally ap-proved, Farinata offered the most determined opposition, declaring that he would defend his native city with his own sword as long as he had breath in his body, even though he should have to do it single-handed. In consequence of this protest the proposal was abandoned and Florence was saved from destruction. The Florentines subsequently showed little gratitude to Farinata for his patriotic intervention, for they always expressly included the Uberti with the other Ghibelline families who were excepted from the terms offered to the other exiles.

After Montaperti Farinata returned to Florence, where he died in or about 1264, the year before D.'s birth. A few years later (Jan. 126⅚), at a time when an attempt was made to reconcile the Guelf and Ghibelline factions in Florence by means of matrimonial alliances, a daughter of Farinata was betrothed to the Guelf Guido Cavalcanti, and the marriage was subsequently carried into effect. [Cavalcanti, Guido.]

Farinata, whose place in Hell

' tra le anime più nere ', had been in-dicated by Ciacco (in Circle III of Hell), in response to D.'s inquiry as to the fate of him and Tegghiaio, ' che fur sì degni' (Inf. vi. 79–87), is placed by D., who accepted the common belief that Farinata was a freethinker, among the Heretics in Circle VI, where he is pointed out by Virgil, Inf. x. 32 ; *quell' altro magnanimo*, v. 73 ; *lo spirto, v.* 116 [**Epicurei : Eretici**] ; F., in con-versation with D., recalls the fact that the Guelfs had twice been scattered by himself (in 1248 and in 1260) (*vv.* 43–8); D. retorts that after each occasion they had contrived to return (in 1251 and in 1266), which was ' an art he and his had not well learned' (the Uberti having been expressly excluded from the paci-fication of 1280) (*vv.* 49–51); F. then foretells that before fifty months (i. e. before the spring of 1304) D. himself would find how hard it was to learn ' the art of returning ' (*vv.* 79–81); F. next asks D. why the Florentines were so pitiless towards his house in all their decrees, to which D. replies that it was in revenge for the defeat of Montaperti (*vv.* 82–7); F. thereupon retorts that others be-side himself were concerned there, and reminds D. that it was he who single-handed prevented the proposed destruction of Florence (*vv.* 88–93).

Farinata degli Scornigiani], the name by which some of the old commentators identify the individual referred to as ' quel da Pisa' (whose real name appears to have been Gano), Purg. vi. 17.   [**Gano : Marzucco.**]

Farinata degli Uberti. [**Fari-nata.**]

Farisei, Pharisees ; counselled by Caiaphas that it was expedient one man should die for the people (*John* xi. 50 ; xviii. 14), Inf. xxiii. 116 ; their avarice the cause of the de-struction of Jerusalem, Epist. viii. 1³⁻⁸ ; suppressors and distorters of the truth, Epist. viii. 5⁷⁹⁻⁸¹ ; Bon-iface VIII referred to by Guido da Montefeltro (in Bolgia 8 of Circle VIII of Hell) as ' lo principe dei nuovi Farisei ' (the ' modern Phar-isees' being the Cardinals and dig-nitaries of the Court of Rome), Inf. xxvii. 85 [**Bonifazio** [1]].

Farsaglia [1], Pharsalia in Thessaly, territory in which Pharsalus is situated, the scene of the decisive battle between Pompey and Julius Caesar, which made the latter master of the Roman world, B.C. 48 ; mentioned by the Emperor Justinian (in the Heaven of Mercury) in connexion with the vic-tories of the Roman Eagle, and the sub-sequent murder of Pompey in Egypt, Par. vi. 65–6 [**Nilo**].   In his Letter to the Princes and Peoples of Italy D. indicates Tuscany under the name of Thessaly, and by implication points to Florence as a second Pharsalia, Epist. v. 3⁴⁶⁻⁹ [**Thessalia**].

Farsaglia [2], *Pharsalia* or *De Bello Civili* of Lucan, heroic hexa-meter poem in ten books (unfinished), describing the civil war between Caesar and Pompey [**Lucano**] ; the work is mentioned, *Farsaglia,* Conv. iv. 28⁹⁹ ; *Pharsalia,* Mon. ii. 4³⁵, 8⁸¹, 9⁵⁵ ; quoted, V. N. § 25⁸⁷ (*Phars.* i. 44); Conv. iv. 11²⁸⁻³¹ (*Phars.* iii. 119–21); Conv. iv. 13¹¹²⁻¹⁸ (*Phars.* v. 527–31); Conv. iv. 28¹⁰⁰⁻⁵³ (*Phars.* ii. 326–47); Mon. ii. 4³⁷⁻⁴¹ (*Phars.* ix. 477–80); Mon. ii. 9⁵⁷⁻⁸ (*Phars.*

ii. 672 ff. ; viii. 692–4 ; i. 109–11) ; Mon. ii. 11[48–51] (*Phars.* ii. 135–8, where D. reads *superavit* for *speravit*); Epist. vii. 4[83–5] (*Phars.* i. 280–2); Epist. x. 22[425–6] (*Phars.* ix. 580) ; referred to, Inf. xxv. 94–5 (ref. to *Phars.* ix. 763–804); Conv. iii. 3[52] (ref. to *Phars.* iv. 642 ff.) ; Conv. iii. 5[116] (ref. to *Phars.* ix. 438–45, 531–2); Conv. iv. 27[31–3] (ref. to *Phars.* ii. 383) ; Conv. iv. 28[142–3] (ref. to *Phars.* ii. 338–45) ; V. E. i. 10[46] (ref. to *Phars.* ii. 396–438) ; Mon. ii. 8[81] (ref. to *Phars.* iv. 609 ff.).

D. was also indebted to Lucan for details about the following :—Erichtho, Inf. ix. 23–4 (*Phars.* vi. 507 ff.) [**Eriton**] ; Cato in the Libyan desert, Inf. xiv. 13–15 (*Phars.* ix. 371 ff.) [**Catone**[2]] ; Aruns, Inf. xx. 46–7 (*Phars.* i. 586) [**Aronta**] ; the snakes in the Libyan desert, Inf. xxiv. 85–7 (*Phars.* ix. 710 ff.) [**Libia**] ; Sabellus and Nasidius, Inf. xxv. 94–5 (*Phars.* ix. 763 ff.) [**Nassidio : Sabello**] ; Curio, Inf. xxviii. 97–9 (*Phars.* i. 280–2); Inf. xxviii. 101–2 (*Phars.* i. 269) [**Curio**[2]] ; Hercules and Antaeus, Inf. xxxi. 115 ff. ; Mon. ii. 8[80] (*Phars.* iv. 587 ff.) [**Anteo : Ercole**] ; Typhoeus and Tityus, Inf. xxxi. 124 (*Phars.* iv. 595–6) [**Tifeo: Tizio**]; Cato, Purg. i. 24–6 (*Phars.* ii. 374–6) ; Purg. i. 80 ; Conv. iv. 5[140–1] (*Phars.* ix. 561) [**Catone**[2]] ; Cato and Marcia, Purg. i. 79 ff. ; Conv. iv. 28[100–53] (*Phars.* ii. 338 ff.) [**Marzia**] ; Marcellus, Purg. vi. 125 (*Phars.* i. 313) [**Marcello**] ; Metellus, Purg. ix. 136–8 (*Phars.* iii. 153 ff.) [**Metello**]; Pelorus, Purg. xiv. 32 (*Phars.* ii. 438) [**Peloro**] ; the Hellespont,

Purg. xxviii. 71–2 ; Mon. ii. 9[55–8] (*Phars.* ii. 672 ff.) [**Ellesponto**] ; Caesar's siege of Marseilles, Par. ix. 93 (*Phars.* iii. 572 ff.) [**Marsilia**]; Caesar and Amyclas, Par. xi. 67–9 ; Conv. iv. 13[110–21] (*Phars.* v. 527 ff.) [**Amiclate**].

Farsalia. [**Farsaglia.**]

[**Fauni**], Fauns, sylvan deities, half men, half goats, with horns, supposed to haunt the mountains of Arcadia, Ecl. R. 25.

Faventini, inhabitants of Faenza; their dialect, different from that of their neighbours of Ravenna, V. E. i. 9[41]; rejected by their own poets, V. E. i. 14[17–20]. [**Bucciola : Faenza.**]

Faventinus, Thomas. [**Faenza, Tommaso da.**]

Fazio da Signa. [**Bonifazio**[3].]

Februarius, of February ; *Kalendae Februariae*, the Kalends of February (i. e. Feb. 1), A. T. § 24[21].

Federico[1], Emperor Frederick I, second Emperor of the Hohenstaufen line, better known by his Italian surname Barbarossa; he was the son (born in 1121) of Frederick, Duke of Swabia, and succeeded his uncle, Conrad III, in 1152. For twenty-five years of his reign (from 1158 to 1183) Frederick was engaged in a stubborn contest with the cities of Italy, which formed the celebrated Lombard League in defence of their liberties. He made, in all, four great expeditions, during which he took Rome, Milan, and many other important cities. In 1176 he was defeated by the League at Legnano, and seven years later (in 1183) he was forced to accept the articles of the Peace of Constance, by which the independence of the Italian Republics was recognized. In 1189 he joined Richard Cœur-de-Lion and Philip Augustus in the third Crusade, which had been undertaken on the receipt of the disastrous news of the capture of Jerusalem by Saladin two years before ; and he was drowned while crossing the river Calicadnus in Cilicia, June 10, 1190. [**Hohenstaufen : Table H.**]

Frederick is mentioned by the Abbot of San Zeno at Verona (in Circle IV of Purgatory), who refers to him, in connexion with his destruction of Milan in 1162, as *lo buon Barbarossa*, Purg. xviii. 119–20; in his letter to the Florentines, in which he warns them, in reference to their opposition to the Emperor Henry VII, of the fate of Milan and Spoleto under Frederick, D. speaks of the latter as *Federicus prior*, Epist. vi. 5[135–6]. [**Milano: Spoletum.**]

Federico[2], Emperor Frederick II, grandson of Frederick Barbarossa, son of the Emperor Henry VI and Constance of Sicily ; he was born at Jesi, near Ancona, Dec. 26, 1194 ; was elected King of the Romans in 1196 ; succeeded his father as King (Frederick I) of Sicily and Naples in 1197 ; was elected Emperor in 1212; crowned himself King of Jerusalem in 1229 ; died Dec. 13, 1250. He married :—1. (in 1209) Constance (d. 1222), sister of Peter II of Aragon, and widow of Emeric, King of Hungary, by whom he had a son Henry (d. 1242).—2.(in 1225) Iolanthe (Yolande) of Brienne (d. 1228), who brought him the title of King of Jerusalem, and by whom he had a son Conrad (afterwards Emperor as Conrad IV).—3. (in 1235)

Isabella, sister of Henry III of England. Besides Henry and Conrad he had two natural sons, Manfred (afterwards King of Sicily and Naples) and Enzio (afterwards King of Sardinia). [**Arrigo**[5]: **Costanza**[1]: **Hohenstaufen : Table E : Table H.**]

Frederick Barbarossa had been succeeded by his son Henry VI (1190–1197), on whose death the succession to the Empire was disputed by Henry's brother, Philip, Duke of Swabia, and Otho, son of Henry the Lion, Duke of Saxony and Bavaria. The war between the rival Emperors lasted till 1208, when Philip was assassinated, and Otho IV, the Guelf, became sole Emperor. In 1211 Otho, having quarrelled with Pope Innocent III, was excommunicated and deposed by him. On the invitation of the partisans of the Hohenstaufen, Frederick of Palermo, the young King of Sicily, son of Henry VI, crossed the Alps into Germany, and was elected Emperor as Frederick II (1212), being crowned at Rome, Nov. 22, 1220. Though he entered the field as champion of the Holy See against the excommunicated Otho, Frederick soon himself became its enemy, and finally its victim. The imperial crown and that of the Two Sicilies could not be in the possession of one sovereign, least of all of a Hohenstaufen, without endangering the independence of the Papacy, and before he had been Emperor many years Frederick was plunged into a deadly struggle with the Church. After having been repeatedly placed under the ban of the Holy See (in 1227, 1238, and 1243), he was at last (in

1245) formally deposed by Innocent IV at the Council of Lyons; he, however, defied the Pope, who vainly attempted to raise Germany against him, and maintained the struggle until it was put an end to by his death at Firenzuola in 1250. Himself an accomplished poet (several of his *canzoni* have been preserved), Frederick was a liberal patron of men of letters, as well as of all who in any way excelled in the arts to which he was devoted.

Frederick II is referred to by D. as *lo secondo Federico*, Inf. x. 119; *Federico*, Inf. xiii. 59; xxiii. 66; Purg. xvi. 117; *Federico di Soave*, Conv. iv. 3[38]; *Federicus Caesar*, V. E. i. 12[20]; *Caesar*, Epist. vi. 5[131]; *Cesare*, Inf. xiii. 65; *Augusto*, Inf. xiii. 68; *il terzo vento di Soave*, Par. iii. 120; *lo Imperadore*, Conv. iv. 3[32], 10[26, 31] (cf. Canz. viii. 21; Conv. iv. 2[9], 10[44]).

D., accepting the contemporary estimate of Frederick's religious opinions, places him among the Heretics in Circle VI of Hell, where he is named by Farinata as being with himself and the Cardinal Ottaviano degli Ubaldini and 'more than a thousand others', Inf. x. 118–19 [**Epicurei : Eretici**]; his secretary, Pier delle Vigne (in Round 2 of Circle VII of Hell), mentions him in connexion with his own disgrace and suicide, Inf. xiii. 58–69 [**Pier delle Vigne**]; his punishment of traitors in copes of lead, Inf. xxiii. 66; Marco Lombardo (in Circle III of Purgatory) refers to his wars with the Church in Lombardy and Romagna (though some think the reference is to the wars between Barba-

rossa and the Lombard League), Purg. xvi. 117 [**Federico** [1]]; Piccarda (in the Heaven of the Moon) refers to him, in connexion with his mother Constance, as the third Emperor of the Swabian or Hohenstaufen line (he was actually the fourth, but Barbarossa's uncle and predecessor, Conrad III, was never crowned at Rome, and consequently never assumed the title of Emperor), and the last powerful Emperor, Par. iii. 120 (cf. Conv. iv. 3[38—43]); his definition of nobility quoted, Canz. viii. 21–4; and discussed, Conv. iv. 3[30—45], 10[24—35]; the last of the Roman Emperors, Conv. iv. 3[38—9]; his court and that of his son Manfred the focus of Italian letters, whence vernacular Italian poetry was commonly known as Sicilian, V. E. i. 12[20—35] [**Sicilianus**]; his siege of Parma and building of the fort of Victoria, Epist. vi. 5[127—34] [**Victoria**].

Federico [3], Frederick II, King of Sicily, 1296–1337; third son (born 1272) of Peter III of Aragon and Constance, daughter of Manfred. On the death of Peter III, King of Aragon and Sicily, in 1285, his eldest son Alphonso became King of Aragon, while James, the second son, succeeded to the crown of Sicily. When Alphonso died in 1291 James succeeded him in Aragon, leaving the government of Sicily in the hands of his younger brother, Frederick. A few years later, however, at the instigation of Boniface VIII, James, ignoring the claims of his brother, agreed to cede Sicily to the Angevin claimant, Charles II of Naples. The Sicilians, on hearing of this agreement, renounced their allegiance to

James, and proclaimed his brother Frederick king in his stead (1296). Charles and James thereupon made war upon Frederick, but in 1299 James withdrew his troops, and in 1302, on the failure of a fresh expedition against him, under Charles of Valois and Robert, Duke of Calabria, Frederick was confirmed in possession of the kingdom of Sicily under the title of King of Trinacria, receiving in marriage at the same time Charles II's third daughter Eleanor. He died in 1337, after a reign of 41 years, leaving three sons, of whom the eldest succeeded him as Peter II. [Carlo [2]: Cicilia: Jacomo [1]: Table B.]

F. (of whom D. never speaks save with reproach) is named, together with his brother James, by Sordello (in Ante-purgatory), who says they possess their father's kingdoms, but not his virtues, Purg. vii. 119–20 [Piero [2]]; the Eagle in the Heaven of Jupiter couples him with Charles II of Naples, and says that Sicily laments their being still living, Par. xx. 63 [Aquila [2]: Carlo [2]]; he and Charles are denounced for their evil doings in the *Convivio* (iv. 6[180–90]), and again in the *De Vulgari Eloquentia*, where F. is spoken of as *novissimus Federicus* (i. 12[35–42]); F. is alluded to (probably) by his grandfather Manfred (in Ante-purgatory) as *l'onor di Cicilia*, Purg. iii. 116 [Aragona: Cicilia]; the Eagle in the Heaven of Jupiter reproaches him for his 'avarice and baseness', referring to him as *quel che guarda l'isola del fuoco* (i. e. the ruler of Sicily), Par. xix. 130–4; there is perhaps a reference to his title 'King

of Trinacria' in the mention by Charles Martel (in the Heaven of Venus) of the island of Sicily by the name of Trinacria, Par. viii. 67 [Trinacria].

Federico Novello, one of the Conti Guidi, son of Guido Novello of Bagno (who was King Manfred's vicar in Florence from 1260 to 1266), and of a daughter of the Emperor Frederick II (sister of Manfred); he was killed on Sept. 27, 1291, at Giazzolo (now Raggiolo), about five miles from Poppi, in the Casentino, in a skirmish against some of his Guelf relations, his slayer having been apparently Fumaiolo di Alberto de' Bostoli of Arezzo.

D. places him in Ante-purgatory among those who put off their repentance, Purg. vi. 17. [Antipurgatorio : Guidi, Conti.]

Federico Tignoso, noble of Rimini, who lived probably in the first half of Cent. xiii; the family of the Tignosi were of some importance in Rimini and the neighbourhood from Cent. xi to the middle of Cent. xiv, but of Federico personally nothing is known; he is mentioned by Guido del Duca (in Circle II of Purgatory) among the former worthies of Romagna, Purg. xiv. 106.

Federicus Caesar. [Federico [2].]

Federicus Novissimus. [Federico [3].]

Federicus Prior. [Federico [1].]

Federigo. [Federico.]

Fedra], Phaedra, daughter of Minos, and Pasiphaë, wife of Theseus; she falsely accused her stepson Hippolytus of having tried to seduce her, in consequence of which he was banished from Athens. [**Ip-polito.**]

Cacciaguida (in the Heaven of Mars) refers to her as *la spietata e perfida noverca* (i. e. the heartless and treacherous step-mother of Hippolytus), and foretells to D. that as Hippolytus had to leave Athens, so he will have to leave Florence, Par. xvii. 46–8.

Felice, Don Felix Guzman, father of St. Dominic; mentioned by St. Bonaventura (in the Heaven of the Sun) with a play on the name, Par. xii. 79. [**Domenico.**]

Feltro [1], Feltre, town of N. Italy in Venetia, midway on the road between Bassano and Belluno, which in D.'s day was under the lordship of its own Bishops; mentioned by Cunizza (in the Heaven of Venus) in connexion with 'the crime of its unholy pastor, who for party purposes shed so much Ferrarese blood', Par. ix. 52–60.

The main facts of the incident referred to appear to be as follows:— In 1314, while Alessandro Novello of Treviso was Bishop of Feltre (1298–1320), certain Ferrarese Ghibellines of the house of Fontana, having failed in a conspiracy against Pino della Tosa, King Robert's Vicar in Ferrara, took refuge in Feltre and placed themselves under the protection of the Bishop. The latter, however, on the requisition of Pino, delivered them up, and they were taken back to Ferrara, and publicly executed with their confederates to the number of thirty in all.

Feltro [2], name of the two places between which, according to Virgil's prophecy, the 'Veltro', the future deliverer of Italy, was to be born, Inf. i. 105.

The identification of these places differs of course with the identification of the 'Veltro' himself. Those who take the latter to be Can Grande identify them with Feltre in Venetia, and Montefeltro in Romagna, thus indicating roughly the country in which Verona is situated, and which was the scene of the greater part of Cane's operations in the Imperial cause [**Can Grande: Feltro** [1]: **Montefeltro**]. If Uguccione della Faggiuola be meant, the places would be San Leo Feltrio and Macerata Feltria in the N. of the Marches, between which was situated the castle of Faggiuola, Uguccione's birthplace [**Uguccione** [3]].

Some hold that *feltro* is the name, not of a place, but of a material ('felt'), and that D. means to indicate that the 'Veltro' would be of humble birth; but as *feltro* was likewise used of rich material, the indications might equally point to a deliverer who should be well born.

Fenicia], Phoenicia, narrow strip of coastland in the N. of Syria; alluded to as *il lito Nel quale si fece Europa dolce carco*, Par. xxvii. 83–4. [**Europa** [1].]

Ferdinando], Fernando IV, King of Castile and Leon, 1295–1312; alluded to by the Eagle in the Heaven of Jupiter, who blames him for his luxury and effeminacy, as 'quel di Spagna', Par. xix. 125. [**Table D.**]

Ferrara], city of old Lombardy, in NE. of the Emilia, a few miles from the S. bank of the Po; alluded to (probably) by Cacciaguida (in the Heaven of Mars) as the place in the valley of the Po whence his wife came, Par. xv. 137. [**Cacciaguida.**]

Ferrarese, Ferrarese ; Cunizza (in the Heaven of Venus) alludes to the betrayal of certain Ghibellines of Ferrara by the Bishop of Feltre, Par. ix. 56. [**Feltro**[1].]

Ferrarienses, inhabitants of Ferrara ; their dialect distinct from that of Piacenza, though both belong to Lombardy, V. E. i. 10[76—7] ; the Bolognese dialect modified by that of Ferrara and Modena, whence it gets a certain shrillness characteristic of the Lombard dialects, V. E. i. 15[3—8, 14—18] ; this characteristic the reason why there have been no Ferrarese poets, V. E. i. 15[20—5]. [**Lombardia.**]

Festus, Porcius Festus, Procurator of Judaea, A. D. 60–62 ; St. Paul's speech to him, claiming to be tried as a Roman citizen (*Acts* xxv. 10), Mon. iii. 13[42—3]. [**Paolo.**]

Fesulani, inhabitants of Fiesole ; the Florentines, in reference to their reputed descent from Fiesolan stock, addressed as *miserrima Fesulanorum propago*, Epist. vi. 6[168]. [**Fiesolano : Fiorentini.**]

Fetòn. [**Fetonte.**]

Fetonte, Phaëthon, son of Phoebus Apollo and Clymene ; having been told by Epaphus, son of Jupiter and Io, that Apollo was not his father, he begged Apollo to let him prove his parentage by driving the chariot of the Sun for one day ; Apollo granted the request, but, P. being too weak to hold the horses, they rushed out of the usual track

and approached so near to the Earth as almost to set it on fire ; Jupiter, thereupon, in answer to the prayer of Earth, killed P. with a thunderbolt and hurled him down into the river Eridanus.

D., who makes frequent allusion to the story of Phaëthon (which he got from Ovid, *Metam.* ii. 1–324), refers to him as *Fetòn*, Inf. xvii. 107 ; Purg. iv. 72 ; *Fetonte*, Par. xxxi. 125 ; Conv. ii. 15[53] ; *falsus auriga Phaëthon*, Epist. viii. 4[45—6] ; *Quei ch' ancor fa i padri ai figli scarsi* (i. e. the one who makes fathers chary of granting their sons' requests), Par. xvii. 3 [**Climenè**] ; the Pythagorean theory that the Milky Way was caused by the scorching of the Heavens on the occasion of P.'s mishap, Inf. xvii. 107–8 ; Conv. ii. 15[47—55] [**Galassia**] ; 'la strada Che mal non seppe carreggiar F.' (i. e. the path of the Sun, the Ecliptic), Purg. iv. 71–2 ; 'il temo Che mal guidò F.' (i. e. the pole of the chariot of the Sun) (*Metam.* ii. 316), Par. xxxi. 124–5 ; the misguidance of the Church by the Italian Cardinals compared to that of Apollo's chariot by P., Epist. viii. 4[43—6] ; the prayer of Earth to Jupiter (*Metam.* ii. 272–300), and the splendour of the chariot of the Sun (*Metam.* ii. 107–10), Purg. xxix. 118–20 [**Sole : Terra**[1]].

Fialte, Ephialtes the Giant, son of Neptune and Iphimedia ; at the age of nine, being endued with marvellous strength, he, with his brother Otus, made war upon the Olympian gods, but they were slain by Apollo, during their attempt to pile Ossa on Olympus, and Pelion on Ossa.

D. places Ephialtes, together with Antaeus, Briareus, and Nimrod, to keep ward at the mouth of Circle IX of Hell, Inf. xxxi. 94, 108; *l'altro* (*gigante*), *v.* 84; *questo superbo, v.* 91; *questo* (*gigante*), *v.* 104; he is described as being fiercer-looking and bigger than Nimrod (*v.* 84), but of less ferocious aspect than Briareus (*v.* 105); he is bound with a chain which encircles him five times from the neck downward, fastening his left arm in front of him, and his right behind his back (*vv.* 85–90). [Giganti.]

Fiamminghi, Flemings, inhabitants of Flanders; mentioned in connexion with the dykes built by them to keep out the sea, Inf. xv. 4. [Bruggia : Guizzante.]

Fiandra], Flanders, district of modern Belgium consisting of East and West Flanders, of which Ghent and Bruges are the respective capitals; in D.'s time it comprised also part of modern Zealand, as well as French Flanders (modern Département du Nord) and part of Artois (modern Pas de Calais).

The Flemish sea-board is indicated roughly by the mention of Wissant and Bruges, Inf. xv. 4; the country itself is indicated by Hugh Capet (in Circle V of Purgatory) by the mention of Douay, Ghent, Lille, and Bruges, four of its principal cities, the reference being to the dealings of Philip IV of France with Flanders between 1297 and 1304, Purg. xx. 46.

In 1297 Guy, Count of Flanders, having by his dealings with Edward I of England excited the suspicions of Philip IV of France, was forced by the latter to swear to renounce all communication with Edward; but he broke his oath, whereupon Philip sent his brother, Charles of Valois, into Flanders to reduce the country. Guy, being abandoned by Edward, was compelled to come to terms and sue for pardon ; Philip, however, treacherously imprisoned him, and proceeded to take possession of Flanders. But the cruelty of his Governor soon drove the people to rise, and they formed an army which totally defeated the French at Courtrai, March 21, 130½. In this battle, in which they lost the flower of their nobility, the French met with the vengeance to which D. alludes, Purg. xx. 47. After this defeat Philip made peace with Flanders, the N. portion of which was surrendered to Guy's eldest son, while the S. portion was annexed to France.

Fidanza, Giovanni. [Bonaventura.]

Fiducio de' Milotti. [Milotti.]

Fieschi, Alagia de'. [Alagia.]

Fieschi, Bonifazio de'. [Bonifazio [2].]

Fieschi, Ottobuono de'. [Adriano [2].]

Fieschi, Sinibaldo de'. [Innocenzio [2].]

Fiesolano, belonging to Fiesole ; *bestie fiesolane,* 'beasts from Fiesole', term by which Brunetto Latini (in Round 3 of Circle VII of Hell) refers to those of the Florentines who were descended from the old inhabitants of Fiesole, Inf. xv. 73 (cf. *vv.* 61–2); Brunetto also speaks of them as *lazzi sorbi,* 'sour crab-apples', as opposed to the *dolce fico,* which represents the Florentines of the old Roman stock (the Florentine tradition being that their nobility was descended from Romans, while the commons were originally immigrants from Fiesole) (*vv.* 65–6) ; in his letter to the Florentines D. addresses them as *miserrima Fesulanorum propago*, 'most wretched offshoot of Fiesole', Epist. vi. 6[168]. [Fiesole : Fiorentini.]

Fiesole, Roman Faesulae, city of Tuscany, situated on a hill about three miles NE. of Florence, commanding a view of the latter and of the valley of the Arno ; it was anciently one of the twelve Etruscan towns, and considerable remains of Cyclopean walls are still visible, as well as the ruins of a Roman theatre.

According to the Florentine tradition, Fiesole, after being besieged by Julius Caesar for nearly nine years, was destroyed by the Romans, who then founded Florence, which was peopled with a mixture of Romans and Fiesolans.

Brunetto Latini (in Round 3 of Circle VII of Hell) mentions Fiesole in connexion with the tradition that Florence was originally partly peopled by immigrants from there, Inf. xv. 61–2 ; he alludes to its situation on a hill, and to the fact that the city of Florence was largely built of stone ('macigno') from the quarries of Fiesole (*v.* 63) ; Cacciaguida (in the Heaven of Mars) couples it with Troy and Rome in allusion to the same tradition, Par. xv. 126 ; he mentions that the Caponsacchi were of Fiesolan stock, Par. xvi. 121–2 [Caponsacchi : Fieso-

lano] ; the site of the city is alluded to by Brunetto as *il monte*, Inf. xv. 63 ; and by the Emperor Justinian (addressing D. in the Heaven of Mercury), in connexion with the destruction of Fiesole by the Romans after the defeat of Catiline, as *quel colle Sotto 'l qual tu nascesti*, Par. vi. 53–4. [Catilina.]

Fifanti, ancient noble family of Florence, mentioned by Cacciaguida (in the Heaven of Mars) as having been of importance in his day, Par. xvi. 104. They were among the early inhabitants of Florence (Vill. iv. 13); were Ghibellines (v. 39), and as such were expelled from Florence in 1258 (vi. 65).

Fighine, now Figline, town in the Valdarno, about fifteen miles SE. of Florence, under whose jurisdiction it passed in 1198; mentioned, together with Campi and Certaldo, by Cacciaguida (in the Heaven of Mars), who laments the immigration thence into Florence, and the consequent debasement of the Florentine character, Par. xvi. 49–51.

Filattiera, Gherardino da], member of the Malaspina family, of the Spino Fiorito branch, Bishop of Luni, 1312–1321. He was an ardent Guelf, and in consequence of his refusal to submit to the Emperor Henry VII, and to assist at his coronation at Milan, Gherardino was deprived of his temporal power ; which, however, after Henry's death he partially regained by the aid of Castruccio Castracani, whom he nominated viscount of the Bishopric of Luni, July 4, 1314.

D., in his letter to the Italian Cardinals, refers to Gherardino as

'Lunensis pontifex', and excepts him (ironically) from his condemnation of the Italian Church dignitaries, Epist. viii. 7[112–13]. [**Lunensis.**]

Filippeschi, leading Ghibelline family of Orvieto, mentioned by D., together with the Monaldi (the leaders of the Guelfs in the same city), in his appeal to the Emperor, Albert of Austria, to come into Italy to look after the interests of his adherents, Purg. vi. 107.

Filippi[1], ancient noble family of Florence (extinct in D.'s time), mentioned by Cacciaguida (in the Heaven of Mars) as having been already in their decline in his day, Par. xvi. 89.

Filippi[2], kings of France of the Capetian line who bore the name of Philip; mentioned by Hugh Capet (in Circle V of Purgatory), who says that from him were descended the kings of the name of Philip and Louis of the reigning dynasty of France, Purg. xx. 50–1. [**Capeti.**]

From Hugh Capet down to the year 1300, the assumed date of the Vision, there were four kings of each name in the Capetian line, viz. Philip I (1060–1108), Louis VI (1108–1137), Louis VII (1137–1180), Philip Augustus (1180–1223), Louis VIII (1223–1226), Louis IX (1226–1270), Philip III (1270–1285), and Philip IV (1285–1314). [**Table K.**]

Filippi[3], Philippi in Macedonia, the scene of the decisive victory of Octavianus (Augustus) and Antony over Brutus and Cassius, B. C. 42; alluded to by the Emperor Justinian (in the Heaven of Mercury) in connexion with the victories of the Roman Eagle, Par. vi. 73–4.

Filippo[1], Philip III, the Bold, King of France, 1270–1285; he was the second son (born in 1245) of Louis IX and of Margaret of Provence; in 1262 he married Isabella, daughter of James I of Aragon, by whom he had four sons, of whom the second, Philip, succeeded him, and the third, Charles, became Count of Valois; in 1274, Isabella having died in 1271, he married Mary, daughter of Henry, Duke of Brabant, by whom he had a son (Louis, Count of Evreux) and two daughters (Margaret, wife of Edward I of England, and Blanche, wife of Rudolf of Austria); he accompanied St. Louis on his second expedition to the East, and on the death of his father before Tunis was proclaimed king and returned to France (1270). [**Carlo**[4]: **Filippo**[2]: **Luigi**[2]: **Table K.**]

After the 'Sicilian Vespers' in 1282 and the loss of Sicily by his uncle, Charles of Anjou, Philip, with the assistance of Don Jaime, King of the Balearic Isles, made war upon Peter III of Aragon, whose crown had been offered him by Pope Martin IV. After a long siege he captured Gerona, but, his fleet having been destroyed in the Gulf of Rosas by Roger di Loria, Peter III's admiral, and his supplies being thus cut off, he was forced to retreat. Sick with fever and vexation at this reverse, he was carried in a litter as far as Perpignan, where he died on Oct. 5, 1285. A few days later Gerona was recaptured by Peter of Aragon, who himself died before the close of the year. [**Pietro** [3].]

D. places Philip in the valley of flowers in Ante-purgatory, where he is represented as seated close to Henry I of Navarre; Sordello points him out as *quel nasetto*, 'the small-nosed man', describing him as having died 'flying and deflowering the lily', and refers to him and Henry as *padre e suocero del mal di Francia* (i.e. father and father-in-law of Philip the Fair, whose evil doings they are bewailing, Philip by beating his breast, Henry by sighing), Purg. vii. 103–11 [**Antipurgatorio**: **Arrigo** [7]]; Philip's second wife, Mary of Brabant, is referred to as 'la donna di Brabante', Purg. vi. 23 [**Brabante**].

Filippo [2]], Philip IV, the Fair, King of France, 1285–1314; he was second son (born in 1268) of Philip III, whom he succeeded (his elder brother Louis having died in youth), and brother of Charles of Valois; he married in 1284 Juana, daughter of Henry I of Navarre, by whom he became the father of three Kings of France and Navarre, viz. Louis X, Philip V, and Charles IV. [**Arrigo** [7]: **Carlo** [4]: **Filippo** [1]: **Navarra**: **Table K.**]

The reign of Philip the Fair is famous for his bitter quarrel with Boniface VIII. The origin of the quarrel was the taxation of the clergy by Philip, which led to the issue of the famous Bull *Clericis Laicos*, in which Boniface declared the property of the Church to be severed from all secular obligations, and himself as Pope to be the one exclusive trustee of all possessions held throughout Christendom by the clergy, on which no aid nor subsidy could be raised without his consent. Philip replied that if the clergy might not be taxed for the exigencies of France, nor be in any way tributary to the king, France would cease to be tributary to the Pope; and he issued an edict by which the Pope was deprived of all supplies from France. After a lull the quarrel culminated in the excommunication of the French king by Boniface, to which Philip replied by seizing the Pope's person at Anagni, an outrage which resulted in the death of Boniface soon after. After the brief pontificate of Benedict XI, a Frenchman, Bertrand de Goth, Archbishop of Bordeaux, was elected Pope as Clement V by the influence of Philip, in whose hands he became little more than a tool. During his pontificate the Papal See was transferred to Avignon, and the Order of the Templars at the instigation of Philip was cruelly persecuted, and finally suppressed, the Grand Master, Du Molay, being burned (1313). In the following year Philip himself died from the effects of a fall from his horse, which was overthrown by the charge of a wild boar.

Philip is not mentioned by name in the *D.C.*; he is referred to by Pope Nicholas III (in Bolgia 3 of Circle VIII of Hell) as *chi Francia regge*, Inf. xix. 87; by Sordello (in Ante-purgatory) as *il mal di Francia*, Purg. vii. 109; by Hugh Capet (in Circle V of Purgatory) as *il nuovo Pilato*, Purg. xx. 91 [**Pilato**]; by the Eagle in the Heaven of Jupiter as *Quei che morrà di colpo di cotenna*, Par. xix. 120; his relations with the Papal See, and with Clement V in particular, are typified by the dealings of the Giant (*gigante*, Purg. xxxii. 152; xxxiii. 45 ; *feroce drudo*, xxxii. 155) with the Harlot in the Procession in the Terrestrial Paradise, Purg. xxxii. 148–60; xxxiii. 44–5; he himself is typified by Demetrius, King of Syria, Clement V being typified by Alcimus, the high-priest, Epist. viii. 4[65] [**Alcimus**]; his intrigues with Clement V, Inf. xix. 87 ; Purg. xxxii. 148–60; xxxiii. 44–5 ; Epist. viii. 4[65] [**Clemente**[2]] ; the son of Philip III and son-in-law of Henry I of Navarre, Purg. vii. 109 [**Arrigo**[7]]; his seizure of Ponthieu and Gascony, Purg. xx. 66 [**Pontì**] ; his imprisonment of Boniface VIII at Anagni, Purg. xx. 91 [**Alagna : Bonifazio**[1]]; his persecution of the Templars, Purg. xx. 92–3 [**Templari**]; his debasement of the French coinage, Par. xix. 118–19 ; his death, Par. xix. 120 [**Aquila**[2]].

Filippo Argenti. [**Argenti, Filippo.**]

Filistei. [**Philistei.**]

Filli. [**Rodopeia.**]

Filomela], Philomela, daughter of Pandion, King of Athens, and sister of Procne, the wife of Tereus, King of Thrace. The story as told by Ovid (*Metam.* vi. 412–676), whose version D. adopts, is as follows :—Procne, having been married to Tereus, to whom she bore a son Itys, was desirous of seeing her sister Philomela, from whom she was parted. At her request, therefore, Tereus set out for Athens to fetch Philomela. On the way back to Thrace he ravished her, and, to prevent her revealing what had happened,

cut out her tongue, and abandoned her, informing Procne on his return that her sister was dead. Philomela, however, contrived to weave her story into a piece of cloth and thus conveyed the truth to Procne. The latter in fury killed her son Itys and served up his flesh to his father Tereus, who partook of it, unconscious that he was feeding on his own child. Learning from Procne what she had done, Tereus pursued her and Philomela with an axe, and was about to slay them, when in answer to the prayers of the two sisters all three of them were metamorphosed into birds, Procne becoming a nightingale, Philomela a swallow, and Tereus a hoopoo (or, according to some, Procne became a swallow, Philomela a nightingale, and Tereus a hawk).

D. alludes to the transformation of Philomela into a swallow, Purg. ix. 14–15 ; the slaying of Itys by Procne, who is introduced as an example of wrath (cf. *Metam.* vi. 609–10, 623, 627) in Circle III of Purgatory, and her transformation into a nightingale, Purg. xvii. 19–21 [**Iracondi**].

Filosofia, Prima. [**Metaphysica.**]

Filosofo, Il. [**Philosophus.**]

Fine Bonorum, De. [**Finibus, De.**]

Fine de' Bene, Di. [**Finibus, De.**]

Finibus, De, Cicero's treatise (in five books) *De Finibus Bonorum et Malorum* ; quoted as *Di Fine de' Beni*, Conv. i. 11[95] ; iv. 6[110] ; *Del Fine de' Beni*, Conv. iv. 22[16]; *De Fine Bonorum*, Mon. ii, 5[85, 141].

D. quotes the *De Finibus* some half-dozen times:—some of Cicero's contemporaries disparaged their own language and extolled Greek, Conv. i. 11[93–8] (*Fin.* i. 1); pleasure is the absence of pain, Conv. iv. 6[108–10] (*Fin.* i. 11); Torquatus, one of the Epicureans, Conv. iv. 6[110–14] (*Fin.* i. 5); the appetite of the mind called ' hormen ' in Greek, Conv. iv. 21[122], 22[35] (*Fin.* iii. 7); he aims badly who does not see his mark, Conv. iv. 22[15–17] (quoted freely from *Fin.* iii. 6); Cincinnatus taken from the plough to be dictator, Mon. ii. 5[83–9] (*Fin.* ii. 4); Cicero's account of the patriotism of the Decii (quoted loosely or from corrupt text), Mon. ii. 5[140–58] (*Fin.* ii. 19).

Fiorensa. [Fiorenza.]

Fiorentine, Florentine women; Forese Donati (in Circle VI of Purgatory) inveighs against them for their immodesty, comparing them unfavourably with the women of Barbagia in Sardinia, and with barbarian and Saracen women, and calling them *sfacciate donne Fiorentine*, and *svergognate*, Purg. xxiii. 94–105; and threatens them with vengeance swiftly to come (*vv.* 106–11) [Barbagia : Barbare : Saracine]; Cacciaguida (in the Heaven of Mars) contrasts the simplicity and modesty of the Florentine women of his day with the luxury and wantonness of D.'s contemporaries, Par. xv. 97–126; and mentions by name one notoriously immoral lady, to wit Cianghella, who he says would have been as great a marvel in Florence in those days as a Cornelia would now (*vv.* 127–9) [Cianghella : Corniglia].

Fiorentini, Florentines, Inf.

xvii. 70; Par. xvi. 86; *Florentini*, V. E. i. 9[39], 13[17, 37]; *populus florentinus, gens florentina*, Epist. i. 3[34, 41]; referred to by Brunetto Latini (in Round 3 of Circle VII of Hell) as *quel ingrato popolo maligno, Che discese di Fiesole ab antico*, Inf. xv. 61–2; *gente avara, invidiosa e superba*, v. 68; *bestie fiesolane*, v. 73; the upstart families of Florence, probably with special reference to the Cerchi and their feud with the Donati, spoken of by D. as *la genta nuova*, Inf. xvi. 73 [Cerchi]; the Florentine Guelfs referred to by Oderisi (in Circle I of Purgatory), in connexion with their defeat at Montaperti, as *la rabbia fiorentina*, Purg. xi. 113 [Arbia]; and by Guido del Duca (in Circle II of Purgatory) as *lupi*, Purg. xiv. 50, 59 (cf. Par. xxv. 6) [Guelfi]; addressed by D. as *Tuscorum vanissimi*, Epist. vi. 5[141]; *miserrima Fesulanorum propago*, Epist. vi. 6[168].

The descent of the Florentines from Fiesolan stock, Inf. xv. 61–2, 73; Epist. vi. 6[168] [Fiesolano]; and from the ancient Romans, Inf. xv. 76–8 (cf. Conv. i. 3[21–2]; Epist. vii. 7[144, 153]) [Romani[1]]; their malignity and ingratitude, Inf. xv. 61; their avarice and arrogance, Inf. xv. 68; Epist. vi. 2, 3, 5; their proverbial blindness, Inf. xv. 67; their instability and restlessness, Purg. vi. 128–51; their injustice and wickedness, Par. xxxi. 37; compared to the Babylonians, Epist. vi. 2[50]; the most vainglorious of the Tuscans, Epist. vi. 5[141]; their dialect distinct from that of the Romans, V. E. i. 9[35–9]; a barbarous and degraded form of speech, yet employed, strange to say, by Brunetto Latini, V. E. i.

$13^{4-10, 17-20}$; but rejected by certain other Florentines (viz. Guido Cavalcanti, Lapo Gianni, and D. himself), V. E. i. 13^{32-7}.

There are two traditions as to the proverbial blindness of the Florentines (Inf. xv. 67). Villani says (ii. 1) they were called blind because they allowed themselves to be beguiled by their foe Totila into admitting him within their gates, whereby they brought about the destruction of their own city.

According to another account, the proverb arose from a trick played upon the Florentines by the Pisans, who, to recompense the former for protecting Pisa while they themselves were engaged in the conquest of Majorca (in 1117), gave them their choice from among the spoils between some bronze gates and a pair of porphyry columns; the Florentines chose the columns, which were draped with scarlet cloth, but on getting them home found they had been spoiled by the Pisans (Vill. iv. 31). When Pisa was taken by the Florentines in 1406, two wide-open eyes were painted on these columns (which now flank the E. door of the Florentine Baptistery), with the inscription, *Occhi traditi son ralluminati ; Però ringratia Dio tu che gli guati.*

Cacciaguida (in the Heaven of Mars) contrasts the simplicity and peaceableness of the Florentines of his day with the luxury and unrest of D.'s contemporaries, Par. xv. 97–133; and mentions some forty of the ancient noble Florentine families who were contemporary with himself, Par. xvi. 86–154.

Fiorentino [1], Florentine, *la rabbia fiorentina*, i.e. the Florentine Guelfs, Purg. xi. 113 [Fiorentini]; *le sfacciate donne Fiorentine*, i.e. the shameless Florentine women of D.'s day, Purg. xxiii. 101 [Fiorentine].

Fiorentino [2], citizen of Florence; *il f. spirito bizzarro*, i.e. Filippo

Argenti, Inf. viii. 62 [Argenti, Filippo]; D. recognized from his speech as a Florentine (as he had been by his fellow-citizen Farinata, Inf. x. 25–7; and, from his dress, by Guido Guerra and his companions, Inf. xvi. 8–9) by the Pisan Ugolino, Inf. xxxiii. 11; an unidentified Florentine from Semifonte, Par. xvi. 61 [Simifonti]; Florentine poets, Castra, V.E. i. 11^{25-6} [Castra]; Guido Cavalcanti, V. E. i. 13^{36}, ii. 12^{62} [Cavalcanti, Guido]; Brunetto Latini, V. E. i. 13^{10-11} [Brunetto]; Lapo Gianni, V. E. i. 13^{36} [Lapo [1]]; D. describes himself as a Florentine, V. E. i. 13^{36}; and in the titles of his letters, Epist. iv–vii, x [Dante].

Fiorenza, Florence, on the Arno, the capital of Tuscany, Inf. x. 92; xvi. 75; xxiv. 144; xxvi. 1; xxxii. 120; Purg. vi. 127; xx. 75; Par. xv. 97; xvi. 84, 111, 146, 149; xvii. 48; xxix. 103; xxxi. 39; Canz. xi. 77; Conv. i. 3^{22}; ii. 14^{176}; *Firenze*, Conv. iv. 20^{39}; *Fiorensa*, V. E. i. 13^{22}; *Florentia*, V. E. i. $6^{25, 35}$; ii. 6^{47}, 12^{16}; Epist. i. *tit.*, 4; vii. 7^{142}; viii. *tit.*; ix. 2^{16}, 4^{45-6}; A.T. §1^2; *Florentina civitas*, Epist. ix. 4^{51}; referred to by Ciacco (in Circle III of Hell) as *città piena d'invidia*, Inf. vi. 49; by D., as *la città partita*, Inf. vi. 61; by Farinata (in Circle VI of Hell), as *nobil patria*, Inf. x. 26; by Lotto degli Agli (in Round 2 of Circle VII of Hell), as *la città che nel Battista Mutò il primo patrone* (i.e. the city which changed its ancient patron Mars for John the Baptist), Inf. xiii. 143–4; by Brunetto Latini (in Round 3 of Circle VII of Hell), as *nido di malizia*, Inf. xv. 78 ; by Guido Guerra and his companions (in Round 3 of Circle VII of Hell), as *terra prava*, Inf. xvi. 9; by D., as *la gran villa Sovra il bel fiume d'Arno*, Inf. xxiii. 95 ; *la ben guidata sopra Rubaconte*, Purg. xii. 102 ; by Guido del Duca (in Circle II of Purgatory), as *la trista selva*, Purg. xiv. 64 (the Florentines being ' lupi', *v.* 59) ; by Forese Donati (in Circle VI of Purgatory), as *la Barbagia*, Purg. xxiii. 96 ; by D., as *il luogo u' fui a viver posto*, Purg. xxiv. 79 ; by the troubadour Folquet (in the Heaven of Venus), as *la città, che di colui è pianta Che pria volse le spalle al suo Fattore* (i. e. the city planted by Satan, as having had the pagan god Mars for its patron), Par. ix. 127–8; by Cacciaguida (in the Heaven of Mars), as *dolce ostello*, Par. xv. 132 ; by D., as *l'ovil di san Giovanni*, Par. xvi. 25 ; *il bello ovile ov' io dormii agnello*, Par. xxv. 5 ; it is indicated by Brunetto Latini, by the mention of the Arno, Inf. xv. 113 ; by the Emperor Justinian (in the Heaven of Mercury), by that of the hill of Fiesole, Par. vi. 53–4 ; by Cacciaguida, by that of Uccella- toio, Par. xv. 110.

In the *Vita Nuova* D. speaks of Florence as *la cittade ove la mia donna fu posta dall' altissimo Sire*, V. N. § 6^{8-10} (7^{3-4}, 8^{5-6}, 9^3, 19^{15-16}, 31^{2-3}); *questa desolata cittade*, V. N. § 31^5 ; *la cittade ove nacque, vivette, e morío la gentilissima donna*, V. N. § 41^{8-9} ; *la dolorosa cittade*, V. N. § 41^{22} ; *la città dolente*, V. N. § 41^{60} (Son. xxiv. 6) ; in the *Convivio* he refers to it as *la bellissima e famosis- sima figlia di Roma*, Conv. i. 3^{21-2}; and apostrophizes it as *misera, misera*

patria mia! Conv. iv. 27^{96-7} ; in his letter to the Emperor Henry VII, he reviles it as ' a stinking vixen', 'a viper', 'a sick sheep that contaminates the whole flock', ' the rebellious daughter of Rome', 'a mad woman', ' a second Myrrha', ' a second Amata', Epist. vii. 7 [**Amata : Mirra**].

Florence, the birthplace of D., Inf. x. 26 ; xxiii. 94–6 ; Purg. xxiv. 79; Par. vi. 53 ; ix. 127 ; xv. 130; xxv. 5 ; Conv. i. 3^{21-5} ; iv. 27^{96-7} ; V. E. i. 6^{19}, 13^{36} ; of Beatrice, V. N. §§6^{8-10}, 41^{8-9} ; of Cacciaguida, Par. xv. 130–5 ; of Farinata, Inf. x. 26 ; the pleasantest spot on earth, V. E. i. 6^{25-6} ; D.'s exile from, referred to by Ciacco, Inf. vi. 67–8 ; by Farinata, Inf. x. 81 ; by Oderisi (in Circle I of Purgatory), Purg. xi. 140–1 ; by Cacciaguida, Par. xvii. 46–69; by D. himself, Par. xxv. 4–6; Canz. xi. 77–9; Conv. i. 3^{20-33}; V. E. i. 6^{20-1}; Epist. ii. 1^{24} ; iv. *tit.* ; v. *tit.* ; vi. *tit.*; vii. *tit.* ; [**Dante**] ; her situation on the banks of the Arno, Inf. xv. 113 ; xxiii. 95 ; Purg. xiv. 50; V. E. i. 6^{19-20}; at the foot of the hills of San Mi- niato, Purg. xii. 100–2 ; and of Fiesole, Par. vi. 53–4 ; the daughter of Rome, Inf. xv. 76–8 ; Conv. i. 3^{21-2}; Epist. vii. $7^{144, 153}$; com- pared with Rome, Par. xv. 109–11 [**Montemalo : Uccellatoio**]; John the Baptist her patron saint, she having been originally under the protection of Mars, Inf. xiii. 143–4; xix. 17 ; xxx. 74; Par. xvi. 25, 47, 145–6 [**Battista : Marte** [1]], her gold florin, Inf. xxx. 74 [**Adamo, Maes- tro**] ; Par. xviii. 133–5 [**Giovanni XXII**]; her population (in first half of Cent. xii), Par. xvi. 46–8 ; saved from destruction by Farinata degli Uberti, Inf. x. 91–3 [**Farinata**] ; her sacrilege in executing Tesauro de' Beccheria, the papal legate, Inf. xxxii. 119–20 [**Beccheria**] ; her betrayal by Charles of Valois, Purg. xx. 71–5 ; Conv. ii. 14$^{176-7}$ [**Carlo** [4]] ; denounced as the city of envy, Inf. vi. 49 ; xv. 68 ; discord, Inf. vi. 61 ; pride, Inf. xv. 68 ; xvi. 74 ; avarice, Inf. xv. 68 ; excess, Inf. xvi. 74 ; immodesty, Purg. xxiii. 96 ; Par. xv. 127–9 ; and of every sort of iniquity, Inf. xv. 78 ; xvi. 9 ; xxvi. 1–6 ; Purg. xiv. 64 ; Par. xxxi. 37–9 ; Epist. vii. 7 ; her want of stability, Inf. xxiv. 144 ; Purg. vi. 128–51 ; her degeneracy from her primitive simplicity and peacefulness, Par. xv. 97–132 ; xvi. 49–154 ; the child of the devil, Par. ix. 127–8 ; a second Barbagia, Purg. xxiii. 96 [**Barbagia**] ; a second Babylon, Epist. vi. 2^{50} [**Fiorentini**].

In response to D.'s inquiry as to the population of Florence in the days of Cacciaguida (Par. xvi. 2 5–6), the latter states that the number of those fit to bear arms was a fifth of those then alive (in 1300, the assumed date of the Vision), Par. xvi. 46–8. It has been reckoned that in 1300 the population of Florence was about 70,000, of whom 30,000 were fit to bear arms ; consequently in Cacciaguida's day (c. 1090–1147) the number of those fit to bear arms would have been about 6,000, and the total population about 14,000.

In the *Convivio* (ii. 14$^{176-80}$) D. alludes to the appearance of a fiery cross in the sky (a phenomenon which is recorded also by Dino Compagni, ii. 9, and Villani, viii. 48, and has been identified with Halley's comet) over the city of Florence 'nel principio della sua distruzione', i. e. at the time of the entry of Charles of Valois into the city, Nov. 1301.

The following public buildings and places in Florence are mentioned or alluded to by D. : Baptistery, *san Giovanni*, Inf. xix. 17 ; *l'antico Battisteo*, Par. xv. 134 ; *il Battista*, Par. xvi. 47 [**Battisteo**] ; Church of San Miniato, Purg. xii. 101–2 [**Miniato, San**] ; the old Roman wall and Badia, Par. xv. 97–8 [**Badia**] ; Ponte Vecchio, *il passo d'Arno*, Inf. xiii. 146 ; *Marte*, Par. xvi. 47 ; *il ponte*, Par. xvi. 146 [**Ponte Vecchio**] ; Ponte di Rubaconte, Purg. xii. 102 [**Rubaconte**] ; Gardingo, Inf. xxiii. 108 [**Gardingo**] ; Porta san Piero, Par. xvi. 40, 94 [**Porta san Piero**] ; Porta Peruzza, Par. xvi. 126 [**Porta Peruzza**] ; Corso, Par. xvi. 40–2 [**Corso**] ; Mercato Vecchio, Par. xvi. 121 [**Mercato**] ; Borgo sant' Apostolo, Par. xvi. 134 [**Borgo**].

The city of Florence, which is situated in a plain in the valley of the Arno, in the heart of Tuscany, sprang originally from Fiesole, having, according to tradition, been founded by the Romans after their destruction of the latter, the population of the new town consisting partly of Fiesolan, partly of Roman stock (Vill. i. 38). The old Roman city was popularly supposed to have been destroyed in Cent. vi by Totila, King of the Goths, and the new city to have been founded some 300

years later by Charlemagne (Vill. ii.
1; iii. 1).

Firenze. [**Fiorenza.**]

Fisica[1], natural science or Physics, Conv. ii. 14[60], 15[5-120]; iv. 15[167]; *scienza naturale*, Conv. ii. 14[60]; iii. 11[175]; the eighth or Starry Heaven likened to, Conv. ii. 14[59-61], 15[4-120] [**Cielo Stellato**]; treats of material and corruptible matters, Conv. ii. 15[88-102]; together with Ethics and Metaphysics makes up the whole body of philosophy, Conv. iii. 11[172-81]; one of the subjects discussed by idiots who scarcely so much as know the alphabet, Conv. iv. 15[164-7].

Fisica[2]. [*Physica.*]

Fiumi Infernali], rivers of Hell, Acheron, Styx, Phlegethon, and Cocytus, which originate in the tears of the 'gran veglio di Creta', Inf. xiv. 115-20. [**Creta.**]

These rivers appear in reality to be one and the same stream, which assumes different names and different aspects on its course through Hell. At first it bears the name of Acheron, and forms the boundary of Hell proper (Inf. iii. 78) [**Acheronte**]; after being lost for a time it reappears in Circle IV in the shape of a boiling black spring, the waters of which form the filthy marsh of Styx (Inf. vii. 101-7) [**Stige**]; again disappearing, it emerges from the wood of Suicides as the blood-red stream of Phlegethon (Inf. xiv. 76-8) [**Flegetonte**]; and finally flows down to the bottom of Hell, where it forms the frozen lake of Cocytus (Inf. xiv. 118-20) [**Cocito**].

Fiumi del Purgatorio], rivers of Purgatory, Eunoë and Lethe,

Purg. xxviii. 121-7. [**Eunoè:** Letè.]

Flaccus. [**Orazio.**]

Flegetonta. [**Flegetonte.**]

Flegetonte, Phlegethon, one of the rivers of Hell, Inf. xiv. 131; *Flegetonta, v.* 116; *la riviera di sangue*, Inf. xii. 47; *il sangue, vv.* 75, 125; *il bollor vermiglio, v.* 101; *bulicame, vv.* 117, 128; *il rio, v.* 121; *un picciol fiumicello, Lo cui rossore ancor mi raccapriccia*, Inf. xiv. 77-8; *il fosso tristo, v.* 11; *quello (ruscello), v.* 81; *lo presente rio, v.* 89; *il presente rigagno, v.* 121; *l'altro, v.* 132; *l'acqua rossa, v.* 134; *il ruscel*, Inf. xv. 2; *l'acqua tinta*, Inf. xvi. 104; *gorgo*, Inf. xvii. 118. [**Fiumi Infernali.**]

The river of Phlegethon, whose waters are of blood and boiling-hot, issues from the wood of Suicides [**Suicidi**], flows down through the burning sand of the third Round of Circle VII, and finally disappears over a precipice, Inf. xvi. 103-5; xvii. 118; its bed and margins are of stone, Inf. xiv. 76-84; the steam rising from it quenches the surrounding flames, so that D. and Virgil are able to walk alongside of it unharmed by them, Inf. xiv. 89-90, 142; xv. 1-3; in it are immersed to various depths those who have been guilty of violence towards their neighbours, Inf. xii. 47-8 [**Violenti**].

Flegias, Phlegyas, son of Mars, and King of Orchomenos in Boeotia, father of Ixion and Coronis; the latter having been violated by Apollo, by whom she became the mother of Aesculapius, Phlegyas in fury set fire to the temple of Apollo at

Delphi, for which sacrilege he was slain by the god and condemned to eternal punishment in the lower world.

D. places P. as ferryman on the Styx where the Wrathful are punished, Inf. viii. 19, 24; *galeoto*, *v.* 17; *nocchier*, *v.* 80 [Iracondi: Stige]; he conveys D. and Virgil across the marsh and lands them under the walls of the City of Dis, Inf. viii. 10–81 [Dite].

Flegon, Phlegon, one of the four horses which drew the chariot of the Sun, Conv. iv. 23[137]. [Eoo.]

Flegra, Phlegra, valley in Thrace, where Jupiter defeated and slew the Giants who attempted to storm Olympus; the contest is referred to by Capaneus (in Round 3 of Circle VII of Hell) as *la pugna di Flegra* (the phrase being a translation of the ' proelia Phlegrae ' of Statius, *Theb.* x. 909; xi. 7), Inf. xiv. 58. [Capaneo : Giganti.]

Florentia. [Fiorenza.]

Florentia, Guido de. [Cavalcanti, Guido.]

Florentini. [Fiorentini.]

Florentinus, Florentine ; *Florentina civilitas*, Epist. vi. 2[52] ; *Florentina civitas*, Epist. ix. 4[51] ; native of Florence, V. E. i. 11[25], 13[11, 36]; ii. 12[62]; Epist. iv–vii, ix–x. *tit.* [Fiorentino : *Epistole Dantesche*.]

Focaccia, one of the Cancellieri of Pistoja, mentioned by Camicione de' Pazzi (in Circle IX of Hell) as a traitor worthy of a place in Caina, Inf. xxxii. 63. [Caina.]

This Focaccia appears to have been the chief occasion of the outbreak of the bloody hostilities between the two branches of the Cancellieri family in Pistoja, which led ultimately to the introduction of the Bianchi and Neri factions into Florence [Bianchi].

The story as told in the Pistojan chronicle is briefly as follows. Focaccia, one of the Cancellieri Bianchi, being a notorious brawler and man of blood, the Cancellieri Neri determined to make an end of him. Accordingly three youths, one of whom was the notorious Vanni Fucci, were told off to engage him and bring him to account. F., however, managed to evade them, excusing himself to his friends for his cautious tactics by saying it was better the Neri should boast of Focaccia's flight than of his death. Failing in their object of making away with F., the Cancellieri Neri struck terror into the Bianchi by killing M. Bertino de' Vergiolesi, one of the most prominent members of their party. F., whose wife was a relative of the murdered man, avenged his death by treacherously slaying one of the leaders of the Neri. These vindictive murders led to reprisals, and at length the city of Pistoja was reduced to such a state of disorder that the Podestà, finding himself powerless, threw up his office and quitted the city. Taking advantage of the confusion, F. proceeded to further avenge the death of Bertino by treacherously killing one of his actual murderers, who had been also one of the three deputed to put himself out of the way. This fresh outrage was the signal for a general uprising on both sides, and at last, in despair, the Pistojan authorities called in the aid of the Florentines with the well-known disastrous result to the latter that the blood-feud was imported with all its terrible consequences into the city of Florence.

Focara, lofty headland on the Adriatic, between La Cattolica and Fano in the Marches, dreaded by sailors on account of the violent squalls which swept down from it. It was the custom to offer vows for a safe passage round the point, whence arose a proverbial saying, 'God preserve you from the wind of Focara!' Pier da Medicina (in Bolgia 9 of Circle VIII of Hell), prophesying the drowning of Guido del Cassero and Angiolello da Carignano off this headland by order of Malatestino of Rimini, says they will have no need to make vows or prayers on account of 'il vento di Focara', Inf. xxviii. 89–90 [Angiolello].

Foco, Phocus, son of Aeacus, King of Aegina, and brother of Telamon and Peleus, Conv. iv. 27[192-3]. [Eaco.]

Folco, Folquet of Marseilles, famous troubadour, who flourished as a poet from 1180 to 1195; he was made Bishop of Toulouse in 1205, and died in 1231. According to the old Provençal biography, he was the son of a rich merchant of Genoa, who bequeathed him a large fortune. Devoting himself to a life of pleasure, Folquet became a frequenter of courts, his special patrons being Richard Cœur-de-Lion, Alphonso VIII of Castile, Raymond V, Count of Toulouse, and Barral, Viscount of Marseilles. He attached himself to Adelais, the wife of the last, to whom he paid court, composing songs in her honour, but she appears to have rejected his addresses. After the death of Adelais and of the princes whose favour he had enjoyed, Folquet retired from the world and entered a Cistercian monastery. Subsequently (in 1201) he became Abbot of Torronet in the diocese of Toulon, and in 1205 he was appointed Bishop of Toulouse, in

which capacity he was deeply implicated in the sanguinary persecution of the Albigensian heretics (1208–1229).

D. places Folquet in the Heaven of Venus among those who had been lovers upon earth (*Spiriti Amanti*), Par. ix. 94; *luculenta e cara gioia*, v. 37; *l' altra letizia*, v. 67; *beato spirto*, v. 74; in reply to a question from D., F., after describing the situation of Marseilles, his birthplace, names himself, and then, having confessed that he lived on earth under the influence of love, compares his passion with that of Dido for Aeneas, that of Phyllis for Demophoön, and that of Alcides for Iole (the three instances being introduced doubtless in allusion to the fact, stated in the Provençal biography, that he had been in love at different times with three different women) (*vv.* 82–102) [Venere, Cielo di]; the first line of one of his poems quoted as an example of a *canzone* in the illustrious style, *Folquetus de Marsilia*, V. E. ii. 6[58-9].

Folco Portinari. [Portinari, Folco.]

Folo, Pholus, one of the Centaurs, placed with Chiron and Nessus to guard the Violent in Round 1 of Circle VII of Hell, Inf. xii. 72. [Centauri.]

Folquetus de Marsilia. [Folco.]

Fonte Avellana. [Avellana, Fonte.]

Fonte Branda. [Branda, Fonte.]

Foraboschi], ancient Florentine family, supposed by some to be referred to by Cacciaguida (in the Heaven of Mars) as the family whose arms were the 'balls of gold' (the reference being, however, more probably to the Lamberti), Par. xvi. 110. [**Lamberti.**]

Forese, Forese Donati, son of Simone, and brother of Corso and Piccarda, of the ancient noble Donati family of Florence, to which D.'s wife Gemma also belonged. [**Donati.**]

Forese, who was nicknamed Bicci Novello, was a contemporary and friend of D.; he died on July 28 (a few days after his father Simone), 1296; his friendship with D. is attested not only by the references to their intimacy in the *D. C.*, but also by the fact that they engaged in a poetical correspondence or *tenzone* (written c. 1290), consisting of six sonnets (three addressed by D. to Forese, and three of his in reply), in which they both indulged in personalities. In two of these sonnets D. makes allusion to Forese's gluttonous propensities; in another he commiserates Forese's wife on account of her spouse's irregular habits. Forese retorted by making reflections upon D.'s father, and implying, apparently, that the latter was a coward.

D. places Forese among the Gluttonous in Circle VI of Purgatory, Purg. xxiii. 48, 76; xxiv. 74; *un' ombra*, xxiii. 41; *lo, v.* 43; *lui, vv.* 57, 76, 115; *egli, vv.* 61, 85; *lui,* xxiv. 76; *ei, v.* 82; F. converses with D. and informs him that his sister Piccarda is already in Paradise, and that his brother Corso, who was most to blame for

the miserable state of Florence, will soon meet his death (*vv.* 40–93) [**Golosi**]; in his *tenzone* with Forese D. speaks of him by his nickname, *Bicci,* Son. lii. 2; liv. 12; *Bicci Novello,* Son. liii. 2; *Bicci Novel,* Son. liv. 1; and refers to his mother, *Tessa,* Son. liv. 2; and (perhaps) to his father, *Simone,* Son. liii. 5 [**Simone Donati : Tessa**].

Forlì, town in the Emilia, headquarters of the Ghibelline party in Romagna, on a plain between the rivers Montone and Ronco, about twenty miles SW. of Ravenna; mentioned in connexion with the Acquacheta, which on reaching there receives the name of Montone, Inf. xvi. 99 [**Acquacheta**]; the winebibber, messer Marchese of Forlì, Purg. xxiv. 32 [**Marchese**]; D. speaks of it as being under the lordship of the Ordelaffi, and alludes to it as *La terra che fe' già la lunga prova, E dei Franceschi sanguinoso mucchio* (the reference being to the attack on Forlì in 1282 by the French troops of Martin IV under John of Appia, Count of Romagna, which was repulsed with heavy loss to the besiegers by Guido da Montefeltro), Inf. xxvii. 43–4 [**Ordelaffi**]; Forlì, the central town of Romagna, V. E. i. 14^13–15. [**Forlivenses.**]

Forlivenses, inhabitants of Forlì; their dialect, like those of the other peoples of Romagna, peculiar for its softness, V. E. i. 14^7–13; their use of *deusci* as sign of affirmation, and of *oclo meo, corada mea,* as terms of endearment, V. E. i. 14^15–17. [**Romandioli.**]

Fortuitorum Remedia, the *Liber*

ad Galionem de Remediis Fortuitorum of Martinus Dumiensis, Archbishop of Braga (d. c. 580), commonly attributed in the Middle Ages, and as late as Cent. xvi, to Seneca; referred to by D. as the work of Seneca, Epist. iv. 5⁵³⁻⁴. [**Martinus Dumiensis: Seneca.**]

Fortunatae Insulae. [**Insulae Fortunatae.**]

Forum Julii, Friuli, formerly an independent duchy, of which Udine was the capital, at the head of the Adriatic; it now forms part of the E. extremity of the province of Venetia. D. couples it with Istria as being on the left side of Italy, if the Apennines be taken as the dividing line (from N. to S.), V. E. i. 10⁵⁴⁻⁶.

Fosco, Bernardin di. [**Bernardin di Fosco.**]

Fotino, Photinus, deacon of Thessalonica of Cent. v, who is said to have led Pope Anastasius II into heresy, Inf. xi. 9. [**Anastasio.**]

Fra Dolcino. [**Dolcino, Fra.**]
Fra Tommaso. [**Tommaso²**]

Francesca, Francesca da Rimini, daughter of Guido Vecchio da Polenta, lord of Ravenna (d. 1310), and aunt of Guido Novello, D.'s host at Ravenna; she married (c. 1275) Gianciotto, eldest son of Malatesta da Verrucchio, lord of Rimini. [**Malatesta : Polenta.**]

According to the accepted story, Francesca, having been betrothed to Gianciotto, fell in love with his younger brother Paolo, who had acted as his proxy at the betrothal, and shortly after the marriage was surprised with him by Gianciotto, who killed them both on the spot. As a matter of fact at the time of their tragic death (which took place probably c. 1283) Francesca had a daughter nine years old, and Paolo, who was about 36 and had been married some fourteen years, was the father of two children. [**Malatesta, Paolo.**]

D. places Francesca, together with Paolo, among the Lustful in Circle II of Hell, Inf. v. 116; *l'uno spirto, v.* 139; she and Paolo, *que' due, v.* 74; *quei, v.* 78; *anime affannate, v.* 80; *quelle anime offense, v.* 109; *costoro, v.* 114; *loro, v.* 115 [**Lussuriosi**]; in response to D.'s request, F. relates the story of how she and Paolo fell in love, and of how they met their end (*vv.* 82–138). [**Galeotto.**]

Francescani], Franciscans, i.e. monks of the order of St. Francis of Assisi (founded in 1210); called also Minor Friars and Cordeliers [**Cordiglieri: Frati Minori**]; they are referred to as *frati minori,* Inf. xxiii. 3; Guido da Montefeltro (in Bolgia 8 of Circle VIII of Hell) speaks of himself after he had joined the order as *cordigliero,* Inf. xxvii. 67; and of the members of the order as those who were 'girt with the halter', *cinti del capestro* (*vv.* 92–3); St. Thomas Aquinas (in the Heaven of the Sun) refers to them as *quella famiglia Che già legava l'umile capestro,* Par. xi. 86–7; and, in allusion to their vow of poverty, as *la gente poverella,* Par. xi. 94; St. Bonaventura (in the Heaven of the Sun) refers to them as *la famiglia di Francesco,* Par. xii. 115; and *gli scalzi poverelli, Che nel capestro* *a Dio si fero amici* (*vv.* 131–2); and reproves their backslidings (*vv.* 112–26); St. Thomas alludes to the distinctive characteristics of the Franciscan and Dominican orders, Par. xi. 37–9 [**Domenicani**].

Franceschi, Frenchmen; the defeat of the French papal troops under John of Appia in their attack on Forlì (in 1282), Inf. xxvii. 44 [**Forlì**]; the betrayal of Manfred by Buoso da Duera for French gold, Inf. xxxii. 115 [**Buoso**³]; referred to as *la gente francesca*, D. declaring them to be less foolish than the Sienese, Inf. xxix. 123; the Gauls spoken of by an anachronism as *Franceschi*, Conv. iv. 5¹⁶¹ [**Arabi**: **Galli**²]; their country one of the W. boundaries of Europe, *Franci*, V. E. i. 8²⁵⁻⁹ [**Europa**²]; their use of *oïl* as the sign of affirmation, V. E. i. 8⁴²⁻⁴.

Francesco¹, French; *la gente francesca*, Inf. xxix. 123. [**Franceschi**.]

Francesco², St. Francis of Assisi, son of Pietro Bernardone, a wool-merchant of Assisi; born 1182, died 1226. In his youth he was given up to a life of pleasure and prodigality, but was always open-handed to the poor. When he was about 25 he was seized with a severe illness, which gave his thoughts a serious turn; and after a second illness at Spoleto (in 1206), while he was on his way to join a military expedition into Apulia, he determined to devote himself to a religious life. Vowing himself to poverty, which he spoke of as his bride, he renounced every sort of worldly goods, including even his clothes, which he stripped off in the market-place in the sight of the Bishop to whom his enraged father had appealed for the protection of his property. Two or three years after this, hearing one day in church the injunction of Christ to His Apostles: 'Provide neither gold nor silver nor brass in your purse, nor scrip for your journey, neither two coats, neither shoes nor yet staves', he cast aside shoes, staff, and girdle, and girt himself with a cord, which subsequently became the distinguishing mark of his Order, hence known as the Cordeliers. He soon began to gather followers around him, whom he sent forth to preach, and in 1210 he drew up the rules of his Order, the members of which were called Frati Minori in token of humility, and which received the verbal sanction of Innocent III. In 1212 he was presented by the Benedictines of Monte Subasio with the little church of the Portiuncula (Santa Maria degli Angeli) in the vicinity of Assisi, which became the home of his Order, and in the same year the Order of Franciscan nuns was founded by St. Clara under his direction. [**Chiara, Santa.**] Two years later (1214) his Order received formal sanction from Innocent III. In 1219 he went to Egypt with the object of converting the Sultan, and preached to him in his camp before Damietta, but without success. On his return he founded (in 1221) his Tertiary Order of penitents of both sexes; and in 1223 his Order was solemnly confirmed by a bull of Honorius III. In September 1224 in the solitude

of the convent of La Verna in the
Apennines he received in a vision
the 'Stigmata', or marks of our
Lord's Crucifixion, in his hands
and feet and side [Alvernia[2]];
and after two years of great bodily
suffering he died at Assisi, at the
age of forty-four, Oct. 4, 1226.
His body was laid first in the
Cathedral of Assisi, but was claimed
four years later by the brethren of
his Order and removed to their
church outside the walls. He was
canonized in 1228 by Gregory IX.

St. Francis is mentioned by name
by the Franciscan Guido da Montefeltro (in Bolgia 8 of Circle VIII
of Hell), Inf. xxvii. 112 [Guido
Montefeltrano]; by the Dominican
St. Thomas Aquinas (in the Heaven
of the Sun), Par. xi. 74; by St.
Benedict (in the Heaven of Saturn),
Par. xxii. 90; and by St. Bernard
(in the Empyrean), who points out
to D. his place in the Celestial Rose,
Par. xxxii. 35 [Rosa]; he is mentioned, together with St. Benedict,
St. Augustine, and St. Dominic, in
connexion with the statement that a
man may lead a religious life without
belonging to a religious order, Conv.
iv. 28[68-71]; he is spoken of by St.
T. A. as *principe*, Par. xi. 35; *tutto
serafico in ardore*, v. 37; *l'un* (as distinguished from St. Dominic), v. 40;
un sole, v. 50; *giovinetto*, v. 58;
costui, vv. 66, 95; *sposo* (i. e. the
bridegroom of poverty), v. 84;
padre e maestro, v. 85; *fi' di Pietro
Bernardone*, v. 89; by St. Bonaventura, as *l'un duca* (as distinguished
from St. Dominic), Par. xii. 34;
campione, v. 44; *l'altra rota della
biga* (*di santa Chiesa*), v. 110; by

D., as *il poverel di Dio*, Par. xiii.
33; St. F. and St. D. are referred
to together by St. T. A. as *due
principi* (*della Chiesa*), Par. xi. 35;
by St. B., as *due campioni* (*della
Chiesa*), Par. xii. 44; *l'una e l'altra
rota della biga* (*di santa Chiesa*), Par.
xii. 106-7 [Domenicani: Fran-
cescani].

St. Thomas Aquinas (in the
Heaven of the Sun) relates the life
of St. F. (Par. xi. 40-117); after
describing the situation of Assisi,
the birthplace of St. F. (*vv.* 43-54),
he relates how, while yet a youth,
St. F. incurred his father's wrath
for the sake of his bride, Poverty
(*vv.* 55-60), and how he was united
to her in the presence of the Bishop
and of his father (*vv.* 61-3) [Ber-
nardone]; henceforth Poverty (who
for 1100 years and more, since the
death of her first spouse, Christ,
had languished in neglect) and St.
F. became lovers (*vv.* 64-75);
inspired by them, Bernard, Egidius,
and Sylvester follow the example
of St. F., whose Order now is
founded in all humility (*vv.* 76-87);
it is sanctioned first by Innocent III,
and afterwards confirmed by Honorius III (*vv.* 88-99); after preaching to the Sultan in Egypt without
success, St. F. returns to Italy (*vv.*
100-5) [Soldano], and two years
before his death receives the 'Stigmata', the final sanction of his work,
on Monte Alvernia (*vv.* 106-8);
on his death-bed he commends his
bride, Poverty, to his followers (*vv.*
109-14), and on her bosom (having
been laid naked on the bare ground)
he dies (*vv.* 115-17); subsequently
St. Bonaventura, having related the

life of St. D. (Par. xii. 31–105), draws a parallel between him and St. F., and concludes with a lamentation over the backslidings of the Franciscan Order (*vv.* 106–26) [Bonaventura: Domenico].

[Francesco [3]], half-brother of Dante (born before 1279, died c. 1348), son of Alighiero and his second wife, Lapa Cialuffi; he married Piera di Donato Brunacci, by whom he had a son, Durante, whom some identify with the nephew of D. referred to, Epist. ix. 2[13–14]. Francesco is mentioned by Forese Donati in his *tenzone* with D. as *il Francesco*, Son. liii.* 10. [Alighiero [2]: Dante: Durante: Table A.]

Francesco d'Accorso. [Accorso, Francesco d'.]

Francesco de' Cavalcanti. [Cavalcanti, Francesco de'.]

Franci. [Franceschi.]

Francia, France; Philip the Fair referred to by Pope Nicholas III (in Bolgia 3 of Circle VIII of Hell) as *lui chi Francia regge*, Inf. xix. 87; and by Sordello (in Antepurgatory) as *il mal di Francia*, Purg. vii. 109 [Filippo [2]]; the Kings of France of the Capetian line who bore the name of Philip or Louis, Purg. xx. 50–1 [Capeti: Table K]; Charles of Valois leaves France for Italy, Purg. xx. 71 [Carlo [4]]; the women of Florence deserted by their husbands, who went to seek their fortunes in France, Par. xv. 120; one of the W. boundaries of Europe, *fines Francorum*, V. E. i. 8[27–8].

Franco Bolognese. [Bolognese, Franco.]

Frate Alberigo. [Alberigo, Frate.]

Frate Catalano. [Catalano.]

Frate Gomita. [Gomita, Frate.]

Frate Loderingo. [Loderingo.]

Fratenses, inhabitants of Fratta, i. e. probably Fratta di Valle Tiberina, the modern Umbertide, in Umbria, about twelve miles SW. of Gubbio; mentioned (according to one reading, there being a variant, *Pratenses*) in connexion with their harsh dialect, V. E. i. 11[40–2] [Pratenses].

Frati Gaudenti, 'Jovial Friars', popular name of the knights of a military and conventual order, called the Knights of Our Lady (' Ordo militiae beatae Mariae '), which was founded in 1261 by certain citizens of Bologna under the sanction of Urban IV. The object of the order was to make peace between the contending factions in the different cities of Italy, and to reconcile family feuds, and to protect the weak against their oppressors. The nickname ' Frati Gaudenti' is supposed to have been bestowed upon the knights on account of the laxity of their rules, which permitted them to marry and to live in their own homes, and merely required them to abstain from the use of gold and silver trappings, from attending at secular banquets, and from encouraging actors; while they bound themselves not to take up arms, save in defence of widows and orphans, and of the Catholic faith, or for the purpose of making peace between man and man.

D. mentions the Frati Gaudenti in connexion with two members of the order, Catalano de' Catalani and Loderingo degli Andalò (one of the founders), who together served the office of Podestà in Florence, Inf. xxiii. 103 [Catalano: Loderingo]. Another member of the order mentioned by D. was the poet Guittone d'Arezzo [Guittone].

Frati Minori, ' Minor Friars ', name borne by the Franciscans in token of their humility. [Franciscani.]

D. compares Virgil and himself, as they walked along in silence, one behind the other, to two Franciscans going along a road (the usual custom of the order being to journey two together in single file), Inf. xxiii. 1–3.

Frigi. [Phryges.]

Frigia. [Phrygia.]

Frisoni, Frisians, natives of Friesland, one of the northernmost provinces of Holland.

The Frieslanders were famous for their great stature, hence, to give an idea of the size of the giant Nimrod, D. says it would take three of them, one on the top of the other, to reach from his middle to his neck (whence it has been calculated that N.'s stature must have been nearly 70 ft.), Inf. xxxi. 64 [Nembrotto].

Friuli. [Forum Julii.]

Frodolenti, the Fraudulent; these are divided into two classes, inasmuch as a man may practise fraud upon those who trust him, in which case he is a traitor, or upon those who do not trust him, in which case he is merely a deceiver, Inf. xi. 52–4; these two classes are subdivided, the former into four divisions, which are punished in Circle IX of Hell [Traditori]; the latter into ten divisions, which are punished in Circle VIII of Hell (Malebolge). This Circle is divided into ten compartments or *bolge*, and in each *bolgia* is punished a different kind of fraud [Malebolge]. In Bolgia 1 are Seducers and Pandars, Inf. xviii. 22–99 [Seduttori]; in Bolgia 2 are Flatterers, Inf. xviii. 100–36 [Adulatori]; in Bolgia 3 are Simoniacs, Inf. xix. [Simoniaci]; in Bolgia 4 are Soothsayers, Inf. xx [Indovini]; in Bolgia 5 are Barrators, Inf. xxi–xxii [Barattieri]; in Bolgia 6 are Hypocrites, Inf. xxiii. [Ipocriti]; in Bolgia 7 are Thieves and Robbers, Inf. xxiv–xxv [Ladri]; in Bolgia 8 are Evil Counsellors, Inf. xxvi–xxvii [Consiglieri Frodolenti]; in Bolgia 9 are Schismatics, Inf. xxviii–xxix. 1–36 [Scismatici]; in Bolgia 10 are Falsifiers, divided into four classes, Inf. xxix. 40–xxx [Falsatori].

Frontinus, Sextus Julius Frontinus, governor of Britain A. D. 75–78 ; he was appointed ' curator aquarum', superintendent of aqueducts, in 97 ; and died in 106.

F., who was the author of two extant treatises, one on the Art of War, the other on Roman Aqueducts, is mentioned, with Livy, Pliny, and Orosius, as having written excellent prose, V. E. ii. 6[83–4].

Fucci, Vanni, natural son of one of the Lazzari, a noble family of Pistoja; he was a violent partisan of the Neri, and was one of the three members of that party told off to make away with Focaccia, the champion of the Bianchi [Focaccia]. In January, 1293, certain unknown thieves burst the doors of the church of San Zeno, and made an unsuccessful attempt to rob the treasure of the chapel of San Jacopo, their special object being to carry off two tablets of silver, with the images of the Virgin and the Apostles, which had been placed there six years before. The authors of the outrage were not discovered till the following year (1294), when, during the podestàship, at Pistoja, of the famous Giano della Bella, one of the thieves, Vanni della Monna, confessed to the crime, naming as one of his accomplices Vanni Fucci. Among those who had been suspected of the crime was Rampino Rannuccio, who had been arrested and kept in custody, and was only set at liberty in March, 1295, when the real culprits were condemned.

D. places Vanni (i. e. Giovanni) Fucci (whom he had known, at any rate by sight, Inf. xxiv. 129) among the Robbers in Bolgia 7 of Circle VIII of Hell (Malebolge), Inf. xxiv. 125; *un* (*ladro*), *v.* 97; *peccator*, *vv.* 118, 130; *mulo* (i. e. bastard), *v.* 125; *bestia*, *v.* 126; *uomo di sangue e di crucci*, *v.* 129; *ladro*, Inf. xxv. 1; *quei*, *v.* 16; *l'acerbo*, *v.* 18 [**Ladri**]; in reply to Virgil F. states that he had but lately come thither from Tuscany, that while in the flesh he had led the life of a beast, like the bastard he was, and that his name was Vanni Fucci, the beast, for whom Pistoja was a fit den (*vv.* 121–6); D. then begs V. to ask him what crime had brought him there, as he had known him for a man of blood in his lifetime (*vv.* 127–9); F. explains that he is being punished for his sacrilegious robbery of the treasury of San Jacopo, the blame of which had been wrongfully laid on another (*vv.* 136–9); he then, lest D. should exult over him, hastens to predict the downfall of the Bianchi, foretelling how, after they had helped to expel the Neri from Pistoja (May, 1301), they would themselves be driven out of Florence (at the coming of Charles of Valois, Nov. 1301), and would, finally, be defeated by Moroello Malaspina at Campo Piceno (*vv.* 140–51) [**Bianchi: Campo Piceno**]; having finished his speech, Vanni makes a blasphemous remark, accompanied by an insulting gesture at the Deity, whereupon D. observes that he is the most presumptuous against God of all the spirits he has seen in Hell, not even excepting Capaneus (Inf. xxv. 1–18) [**Capaneo**].

Fulcieri da Calboli], member of the illustrious Guelf family of that name at Forlì; he was Podestà of Florence in 130⅔, after the return of the Neri through the influence of Charles of Valois, and proved himself a bitter foe of the Bianchi. Guido del Duca (in Circle II of Purgatory) addressing Rinieri da Calboli, refers to F. as his degenerate grandson, and foretells his ferocious doings against the Bianchi as Podestà of Florence, Purg. xiv. 55–66 [**Calboli: Rinier** [1]].

Furie. [**Erine.**]

G

Gabriello, archangel Gabriel, the angel of the Annunciation (*Luke* i. 21) ; represented by the Church in human likeness, as are the other archangels, Par. iv. 47 [**Michele** : **Raffaele**]; *Là dove G. aperse l' ali,* i. e. Nazareth, the scene of the Annunciation (*Luke* i. 26), Par. ix. 138 ; alluded to, in connexion with the Annunciation (the scene of which D. sees sculptured on the walls of the Circle of the Proud in Purgatory), as *L' Angel che venne in terra col decreto Della molt' anni lagrimata pace,* Purg. x. 34–5 [**Superbi**]; *l' Angelo,* Par. xiv. 36 ; *facella,* Par. xxiii. 94; *amore angelico,* v. 103 ; *l' amor che . . . discese, Cantando : Ave Maria,* Par. xxxii. 94–5 ; *Angelo, vv.* 103, 110; *quegli che portò la palma Giù a Maria, vv.* 112–13 ; *quel sì grande legato, che venne a Maria . . . da parte del Santo Re celestiale,* Conv. ii. 6²³⁻⁵. D. sees the archangel Gabriel circling round the Virgin Mary in the form of a garland of flame in the Heaven of the Fixed Stars, Par. xxiii. 94–108 ; and again in the Empyrean, where he is stationed with his wings spread out in front of her, Par. xxxii. 94–114 [**Maria**¹].

Gad], Gad, son of Jacob by Zilpah, Leah's maid; he is among those referred to by Virgil as having been released by Christ from Limbo, *Israel co' suoi nati,* Inf. iv. 59. [**Limbo.**]

Gaddo, name of one of the sons of Count Ugolino della Gherardesca of Pisa, whose imprisonment and death he shared in 1288 in the Tower of Famine at Pisa, Inf. xxxiii. 68 ; he and his brother Uguccione are referred to as *figliuoi* (*vv.* 48, 87); he and his nephew Anselmuccio, as *gli altri due* (*v.* 90) ; he was the first of the captives to die (*vv.* 67–70). D. represents the sons and grandsons of Ugolino who died with him as being of 'tender age' (*v.* 88); as a matter of fact, all except Anselmuccio were grown men. [**Brigata, Il : Ugolino, Conte.**]

Gade, Gades, mod. Cadiz, seaport on SW. coast of Spain, a few miles S. of the mouth of the Guadalquivir ; mentioned in connexion with the voyage of Ulysses beyond the Pillars of Hercules, Par. xxvii. 82 [**Ercole : Ulisse**]; the W. limit of the habitable globe, the mouth of the Ganges being the E. limit, *Gades,* A. T. § 19³⁸⁻⁴³; mentioned by G. del Virgilio to indicate the W., Carm. 30 [**Gange: Gerusalemme**].

Gades. [**Gade.**]

Gaeta, town of S. Italy in the N. of Campania, situated on a promontory at the head of the Gulf of Gaeta ; mentioned by Ulysses (in Bolgia 8 of Circle VIII of Hell), who refers to the tradition that it was named after Caieta, the nurse of Aeneas (*Aen.* vii. 1–4), in connexion with his detention by Circe, Inf. xxvi. 91–3 [**Circe**]; named by Charles Martel (in the Heaven of Venus) as one of the limits of the kingdom of Naples, Par. viii. 62 [**Ausonia**]; its dialect distinct from that of Naples, V. E. i. 9⁴⁰⁻¹ [**Caetani**].

Gaetana Alighieri. [**Tana.**]

Gaetani, Francesco], said to be the Cardinal addressed by D. as 'Transtiberinae sectator factionis', Epist. viii. 10¹⁶⁵⁻⁶. [**Transtiberinus.**]

Gaia, daughter of Gherardo da Cammino of Treviso, by his second wife, Chiara della Torre of Milan, and sister of Riccardo (Par. ix. 50); she married a relative, Tolberto da Cammino, died Aug. 16, 1311, and was buried at Treviso.

Marco Lombardo (in Circle III of Purgatory) having mentioned ' il buon Gherardo' as one of the worthies of the past generation, D. asks who Gherardo was, Purg. xvi. 124–35 ; to which Marco replies that he knows nothing of him beyond his good report, except it were the reputation of his daughter Gaia (*vv.* 136–40). [**Cammino, Gherardo da.**]

The old commentators differ as to what was the nature of Gaia's reputation ; some state that she was famed for her beauty and virtue ; others (among them Benvenuto da Imola, who writes as if he were well acquainted with her history) that she was notorious on account of her loose conduct.

In spite of the arguments of recent commentators, there can be little doubt that D. meant to imply that Gaia's reputation was a bad one, and that he mentions her ironically by way of contrast to her father.

[**Gal, San**], the 'Spedale di Santa Maria a San Gallo', ancient foundling hospital in Florence (demolished in 1529); mentioned by Forese Donati in his *tenzone* with D., Son. liii.* 1.

Galassia, Galaxy or Milky Way ; D. describes it as ' gleaming white with greater and lesser lights between the poles of the world', and refers to the doubts of the philosophers as to its origin, Par. xiv. 97–9 ; the Pythagorean theory that it was caused by the scorching of the sky on the occasion of Phaëthon's mishap with the chariot of the Sun, alluded to, Inf. xvii. 107–8 [**Fetonte**] ; spoken of as ' quello bianco cerchio, che il vulgo chiama la Via di santo Jacopo', the popular belief in Italy being that the Milky Way was a sign by night for those who were on a pilgrimage to the shrine of St. James at Compostela in Galicia, Conv. ii. 15⁸⁻¹⁰ [**Galizia**]; D. says it forms part of the Heaven of Fixed Stars, and discusses the various theories as to its origin (which he got from the *De Meteoris*, i. 2, of Albertus Magnus), Conv. ii. 15⁴⁵⁻⁸⁶.

Galasso da Montefeltro, first cousin of Guido da Montefeltro, and, like him, a staunch Ghibelline ; he was Podestà of Cesena, 1289, 1299; of Arezzo, 1290, 1297 ; of Pisa, 1294 ; died, 1300. D. mentions him, together with Bertran de Born and five others, as an example of munificence (on what ground is unknown), Conv. iv. 11¹²⁹.

Galatas, Epistola ad], St. Paul's Epistle to the Galatians ; quoted, Mon. i. 16¹⁸ (*Gal.* iv. 4).

Galatea, one of the Nereids, daughter of Nereus and Doris ; she was wooed by the Cyclops Polyphemus, but she rejected his addresses, as she loved the youth Acis, whom the Cyclops thereupon in jealousy crushed under a rock, whence his blood gushed forth and was changed by Galatea into the stream Acis (or Acinius) at the foot of Mt. Aetna.

D. mentions G. (whose story is told by Ovid, *Metam.* xiii. 740–897) in connexion with the death of Acis, Ecl. ii. 78. [**Acis : Polyphemus.**]

Galeazzo], son of Matteo Visconti of Milan, who brought about his marriage (in 1300) with Beatrice of Este, daughter of Obizzo II, and widow of Nino Visconti of Pisa, although she had already been promised to Alberto Scotto of Piacenza. In revenge, the latter helped to expel Matteo and his son from Milan in 1302. After the death of his father, who had returned to Milan in 1310, Galeazzo assumed the lordship of the city (June, 1322); he was expelled, however, within a few months, but returned before the end of the year, and remained in possession until 1327, when he was deposed by Lewis of Bavaria. He died in the following year.

From a curious record recently brought to light it appears that Matteo and Galeazzo Visconti in 1320 (the year before D.'s death) were involved in a process before the Papal Court at Avignon for an attempt upon the life of Pope John XXII by means of sorcery, in connexion with which D.'s name was mentioned as that of a reputed sorcerer.

Galeazzo is referred to by Nino Visconti (in Ante-purgatory), who, speaking of his wife Beatrice and her second marriage, says that 'the viper under which the Milanese take the field' (i. e. the arms of the Visconti) will not look so well on her tomb as his own arms, the cock of Gallura, Purg. viii. 79–81 [**Beatrice** [4] : **Gallura** : **Nino** [2]].

Galeno, -us. [**Galieno.**]

Galeotto, Gallehault (not to be confounded with Galahad), one of the characters in the O. F. Romance of 'Lancelot du Lac'; he was 'Roy d'outre les marches', and made war upon King Arthur, but by the intervention of Lancelot was induced to come to terms. During his residence at King Arthur's court a warm friendship sprang up between him and Lancelot, who confided to him his love for Queen Guenever. The latter, who secretly loved Lancelot, was easily persuaded by Gallehault to meet the Knight privately. In the course of the interview Gallehault urged the Queen to give Lancelot a kiss, which was the beginning of their guilty love.

From the part he played on this occasion, the name of Gallehault came to be used, like that of 'Sir Pandarus of Troy', as a synonym for a pandar; hence D. makes Francesca da Rimini (in Circle II of Hell) say of the Romance of Lancelot, which she and Paolo were reading, *Galeotto fu il libro e chi lo scrisse* (i. e. a pandar was the book, and a pandar he who wrote it), Inf. v. 137. [**Francesca.**]

The first meeting between Lancelot and Guenever is referred to again by D., who alludes to the cough (mentioned in the MSS., but not in the printed versions of the romance) given by the Lady of Malehaut, one of the Queen's companions, on perceiving the familiarity between them (she herself being in love with Lancelot, who was aware of the fact, and was in great anxiety lest it should injure him with the Queen), Par. xvi. 13–15. [Ginevra: Lancilotto.]

Galieno, Galen (Claudius Galenus), celebrated physician, born at Pergamum in Asia A.D. 130, died c. 200. After practising in his native city he went to Rome, where he acquired great celebrity, and numbered the Emperors Marcus Aurelius and Lucius Verus among his patients. Next to Hippocrates he was the most celebrated physician of antiquity, and his authority in medicine remained supreme down to the middle of Cent. xvi. There are still extant eighty-three treatises which are acknowledged to be his, besides many that are spurious or doubtful. Among his works was a commentary on the 'Aphorisms' of Hippocrates; this and his Τέχνη ἰατρική (*Methodus Medendi*) were translated into Latin from Arabic versions early in Cent. xi, and were in constant use in the Middle Ages, especially in the Universities of Paris and Bologna [*Aforismi : Tegni*].

D. places Galen, together with Hippocrates, among the philosophers of antiquity in Limbo, Inf. iv. 143 [**Limbo**]; his *Tegni* (i.e. the *Methodus Medendi*), Conv. i. 8[33]; his saying (in the *De Cognosc. Animi Morbis*) that those who have to unlearn a wrong method 'require double time to acquire knowledge', Mon. i. 13[45–7].

Galigaio, Galigaio de' Galigai, member of an ancient noble family of Florence; mentioned, as representing the family, by Cacciaguida (in the Heaven of Mars), who says that in his day 'he had the gilded hilt and pommel in his house' (i.e. the symbols of knightly rank), Par. xvi. 101–2.

The Galigai lived in the Porta san Piero (Vill. iv. 11); they were Ghibellines (v. 39), and as such were expelled from Florence in 1285 (vi. 65). To this family belonged Puccio Sciancato (Inf. xxv. 148).

Galilea, Galilee, northernmost of the three provinces into which the Holy Land was divided in the time of our Lord; mentioned in connexion with the message of the Angel at the holy sepulchre to Peter and the disciples that Christ had departed into Galilee (*Mark* xvi. 6–7), which word signifies 'whiteness' (according to the etymology of Uguccione da Pisa, followed by D.), and is hence symbolical of contemplation, Conv. iv. 22[157–8, 180–91].

Galizia, Galicia, province in NW. corner of Spain; mentioned in connexion with the pilgrimages to the shrine of St. James the Great at Santiago de Compostela, a town in that province, Par. xxv. 18; V. N. § 41[47] [**Jacopo** 1]; D., distinguishing between the several classes of pilgrims, states that those who visited the tomb of St. James were known *par excellence* as 'peregrini', V. N. § 41[34–50] [**Peregrini**]; the Milky Way, popularly known in Italy as 'la Via di santo Jacopo', according to the common belief that the Galaxy was a sign by night for pilgrims to Galicia, Conv. ii. 15^{8-10} [**Galassia**].

Galli[1], ancient noble family of Florence, mentioned by Cacciaguida (in the Heaven of Mars) as having been of importance in his day, Par. xvi. 105.

They were Ghibellines (Vill. v. 39), and lived in the Mercato Nuovo, and in D.'s time had become of no account (iv. 13).

Galli[2], Gauls; their occupation of Rome under Brennus, and assault upon the Capitol, which was foiled through the awakening of Marcus Manlius by the cackling of a goose, as is recorded by Livy (v. 47) and Virgil (*Aen.* viii. 652–6), Mon. ii. 4^{42-57}; spoken of by an anachronism, in reference to the same incident, as *Franceschi*, Conv. iv. 5^{160-4}. [**Brenno : Campidoglio : Franceschi : Manlius.**]

Gallo, San. [**Gal, San.**]

Gallura, name of one of the four *Giudicati*, or Judicial Districts, into which Sardinia was divided by the Pisans, to whom the island belonged in D.'s time ; it comprised the NE. portion of the island, and is said to have taken its name from the cock borne by the Pisan Visconti, who were Giudici or governors of that division [**Sardigna.**]

Ciampolo (in Bolgia 5 of Circle VIII of Hell) refers to Frate Gomita as *quel di Gallura*, Inf. xxii. 82 [**Gomita, Frate**]; Nino Visconti of Pisa (in Ante-purgatory) refers to the arms of his family as *il gallo di Gallura*, Purg. viii. 81 [**Nino**[2] **: Visconti**[2]].

Gallus Pisanus, Gallo or Galletto of Pisa, poet of the school of

Guittone d'Arezzo (c. 1250–1300), two of whose *canzoni* in the Pisan dialect have been preserved ; mentioned, together with Bonagiunta of Lucca and Brunetto Latini, as having written in his own local dialect, V. E. i. 13^{8-13}.

Galluzzo, ancient village of Tuscany, to the S. of Florence, about two miles from the Porta Romana on the road to Siena, a little to the N. of the confluence of the Ema with the Greve ; Cacciaguida (in the Heaven of Mars), laments that it and Trespiano were included within the Florentine territory, Par. xvi. 53–4.

Ganellone, Ganelon, the traitor who brought about the destruction of Charlemagne's rearguard at Roncesvalles, where Roland, Oliver, and the rest of the twelve peers were slain. His name, like that of Antenor, the betrayer of Troy, became a byword for treachery in the Middle Ages. D. places him in Antenora, the second division of Circle IX of Hell, among those who betrayed their country, Inf. xxxii. 122. [**Antenora.**]

Ganelon (who probably represents an historical personage, Wenilo or Wenelon, Archbishop of Sens, accused of treason towards Charles the Bald in 859), was the stepfather of Roland, and at his suggestion was sent by Charlemagne to the Saracen King Marsiccius, with the demand that he should either receive baptism or pay tribute. Marsiccius, however, bought over G., who persuaded Charlemagne to cross the Pyrenees, saying that Marsiccius would follow and make his submission in person in France. The

Emperor consequently returned over the mountains, leaving only his nephew Roland and the rear-guard in Spain. Marsiccius thereupon laid an ambush for Roland, and a fierce battle ensued, during which the latter, being hard pressed, sounded his 'dread horn' to summon Charlemagne to his aid. The Emperor, hearing it, was for turning back to help him, but was dissuaded by G., who said that Roland often sounded his horn merely for amusement while hunting. Roland, meanwhile, after a desperate resistance, was overpowered by the Saracens at Roncesvalles and slain, together with all his company. When G.'s treachery was discovered, he was tried by Charlemagne, and being found guilty was condemned to be drawn asunder by four horses. [Orlando.]

The legendary destruction by the Saracens of Charlemagne's rearguard at Roncesvalles (for which D. was doubtless indebted to the *Historia Karoli Magni* attributed to Archbishop Turpin, and to the O.F. *Chanson de Roland*) is based upon the historical fact, related by Eginhard in his *Vita Karoli* (Cap. ix), that the rear-guard of the Frankish king's army was overwhelmed and plundered by swarms of Gascon mountaineers during his retreat from Spain in 778. [Roncisvalle.]

Gangalandi], one of the Florentine families which received knighthood from the Marquis Hugh of Brandenburg, 'il gran barone', Par. xvi. 128. [Ugo di Brandimborgo.]

Gange, river Ganges in India, the mouth of which, according to D.'s cosmography, was the E. limit of the habitable globe, Cadiz in Spain being the W. limit, *Ganges*, A. T. § 19$^{40-3}$; hence *Gange* is used to indicate the E. horizon where the Sun rises, Purg. ii. 5; xxvii. 4 (where the meaning is that it was sunrise at Jerusalem, midnight in Spain, noon in India, and therefore sunset in Purgatory); Par. xi. 51. [Gerusalemme.]

Ganges. [Gange.]

Ganimede, Ganymede, son of Tros and Callirrhoë; he was the most beautiful of mortals, and was carried off by an eagle while hunting with his companions on Mt. Ida in Mysia, that he might take his place among the immortals as the cupbearer of Zeus (*Aen.* v. 252–7); D. hence alludes to Mt. Ida as 'là dove foro Abbandonati i suoi da Ganimede, Quando fu ratto al sommo concistoro', Purg. ix. 22–4. [Ida².]

Gano degli Scornigiani], son of Marzucco degli Scornigiani of Pisa, who was killed in 1287 by Baccio da Caprona (as is believed), at the instigation of Nino il Brigata, grandson of Count Ugolino della Gherardesca. D. places him in Ante-purgatory, and refers to him as *quel da Pisa, Che fe' parer lo buon Marzucco forte* (in allusion, as is supposed, to Marzucco's fortitude in forgiving, instead of avenging, the murder of his son), Purg. vi. 17–18. [Marzucco.]

Garamantes. [Garamanti.]

Garamanti, Garamantes, according to the ancients the S.-most inhabitants of N. Africa; they occupied the district of the interior of Africa S. of Tripoli, now known as

Fezzan, their name being derived from their chief town, Garama (the modern Germa).

D. mentions the G. as being among the inhabitants of the first 'climate' or terrestrial zone, and refers to their nakedness, and to their having been visited by Cato and his army in their flight from Caesar, Conv. iii. 5$^{119-23}$ (cf. Lucan, *Phars.* iv. 334; ix. 369, 511 ff.); contrasted with the Scythians, who live beyond the seventh 'climate', and suffer almost unbearable cold owing to the inequality of their days and nights, while the G. live in an equinoctial country, where they wear hardly any clothes owing to the excessive heat, *Garamantes*, Mon. i. 14$^{42-51}$.

By *climates* the ancients understood belts of the earth's surface, divided by lines parallel to the equator, those lines being determined according to the different lengths of the day (the longest day being the standard) at different places—an imperfect development of the more complete system of parallels of latitude. Ptolemy (from whom Alfraganus, D.'s authority, derived his account) divided the habitable globe, i.e. the N. hemisphere, into seven climates, the first being nearest the equator.

Garda, town in Venetia on the E. shore of the Lago di Garda, about fifteen miles NW. of Verona; mentioned by Virgil in his account of the founding of Mantua, Inf. xx. 65. [Benaco.]

Gardingo, name of part of Florence in the neighbourhood of the Palazzo Vecchio, on the site of the present Piazza di San Firenze, so called from an ancient Lombard watch-tower ('torre a guardia della città') which stood there; for a long time the site appears to have been covered with ruins, until the Uberti, the heads of the Ghibelline party in Florence, built their palace there, which was wrecked by the populace during a rising against the Ghibellines while Catalano and Loderingo jointly held the office of Podestà.

Catalano (in Bolgia 6 of Circle VIII of Hell) mentions the Gardingo in connexion with this incident, Inf. xxiii. 108. [Catalano.]

Gaudenti, Frati. [Frati Gaudenti.]

Gaville, village belonging to the Ubertini in the upper Valdarno, not far from Figline, which was almost dispeopled by the Cavalcanti in revenge for the murder of a member of their family, Inf. xxv. 151. [Cavalcanti, Francesco de'.]

Gedeon, Gideon, son of Joash the Abiezrite, one of the Judges of Israel who was chosen by God to deliver the children of Israel from the Midianites. He collected an army of thirty-two thousand men, which by God's directions was reduced to three hundred, that being the number of those who 'lapped, putting their hand to their mouth', all the rest, who 'bowed down upon their knees to drink water', being rejected (*Judges* vii. 1-7).

D. mentions Gideon in connexion with this incident, Purg. xxiv. 125. [Ebrei: Madian.]

Gelboè, Gilboa, mountain range in NE. corner of Samaria, rising over the city of Jezreel; the scene of Saul's death (1 *Sam.* xxxi), in consequence of which it was cursed by David (2 *Sam*. i), 'and thereafter felt not rain nor dew', Purg. xii. 41 [**Saul**]; the rebellious Florentines compared to the summits of, Epist. vi. 3[68].

Gemelli, Gemini ('the Twins'), constellation and third sign of the Zodiac, so named from its two brightest stars, Castor and Pollux. The Sun is in Gemini from about May 21–June 21 [**Zodiaco**]. D. speaks of the constellation as *gli eterni Gemelli*, Par. xxii. 152; *il segno Che segue il Tauro*, vv. 110–11 [**Tauro**]; *gloriose stelle, v.* 112; *Castore e Polluce*, Purg. iv. 61 [**Castore**]; *il bel nido di Leda*, Par. xxvii. 98 [**Leda**]; some think it is also alluded to as *tua stella*, Inf. xv. 55; *stella buona*, Inf. xxvi. 23; the sky in which Gemini is rising as the Sun sets (i.e. in winter) is spoken of as *il geminato cielo*, Canz. xv. 3.

The passage, Par. xxii. 112–23, where D. apostrophizes the constellation, and states that he was born when the Sun was in Gemini (*vv.* 115–17), is important as fixing approximately the date of D.'s birthday. It has been calculated that in 1265 the Sun entered Gemini on May 18 and left it on June 17, so that the day was between those two dates. D. enters the sign of Gemini in company with Beatrice in the Heaven of the Fixed Stars, Par. xxii. 110–54.

Gemma Donati], D.'s wife, daughter of Manetto and Maria Donati, married to D. probably between 1291, the year after the death of Beatrice, and 1296, she having borne at least four children to D. before his exile from Florence in 1301. She was still living in 1332,

eleven years after D.'s death; but was dead before Jan. 8, 1343. D. makes no direct reference to her in his works, but some think she is identical with the 'donna pietosa' of the *Vita Nuova* (§§ 36–9) and *Convivio* (ii. 2, 7, &c.); she has also been identified with the 'Pietra' of Canz. xii, Sest. ii, Canz. xv, and Sest. i [**Pietra**]; and some suppose that she is the *Phyllis* of the poetical correspondence between D. and G. del Virgilio, Ecl. R. 45 [**Phyllis**].

Generatione et Corruptione, De, Aristotle's treatise *On Generation and Corruption*, quoted as *Di Generazione*, Conv. iii. 10[16]; iv. 10[91]; A.'s statement that the more closely agent and patient are united the stronger the passion, Conv. iii. 10[13–17] (*De Gen*. i. 6); that everything which suffers change is of necessity united with the changing principle, Conv. iv. 10[88–91] (*De Gen*. i. 2). [**Aristotile.**]

Generatione Animalium, De. [***Animalium, De Generatione.***]

Generazione, Di. [*Generatione et Corruptione, De.*]

Genesi. [***Genesis.***]

Genesis, Book of Genesis, referred to as *Genesi*, Inf. xi. 107 (ref. to *Gen*. i. 28; ii. 15; iii. 19); *Genesis*, V. E. i. 4[9] (ref. to *Gen*. iii 2–3); Mon. iii. 4[11] (ref. to *Gen*. i. 16); quoted, Purg. xiv. 133 (*Gen*. iv. 14); Par. xxxii. 67–70 (*Gen*. xxv. 22–5); Conv. iv. 12[143–4] (*Gen*. i. 26); V. E. i. 4[13–18] (*Gen*. iii. 2–3); Mon. i. 8[10–11] (*Gen*. i. 26); Mon. iii. 5[8–10] (*Gen*. xxix. 34–5); A. T. § 21[69] (*Gen*. i. 9). [***Bibbia.***]

Gennaio, January; Beatrice (in

the Crystalline Heaven) prophesies the coming of a saviour of the world, *prima che Gennaio tutto si sverni*, 'before that January is wholly out of winter', Par. xxvii. 142.

The allusion is to the error in the Julian Calendar, which put the length of the year at $365\frac{1}{4}$ days, and made every fourth year a leap-year. This was, however, too long by somewhat less than the hundredth part of a day ('la centesma negletta', Par. xxvii. 143), so that in Dante's time the error was above eight days, and January had been advanced by this amount nearer to the end of winter. This error was not corrected until 1582, by which time it amounted to ten days, when Gregory XIII introduced the reformed or Gregorian Calendar (not adopted in England until 1752), which provided that ten days should be dropped, and that three out of every four hundredth years should be ordinary years, instead of every hundredth year being a leap year as under the old calendar. In this way began the new style (N.S.) as opposed to the old style (O. S.). The Greek Church testifies its independence of Rome by keeping to the latter, which now differs twelve days from the new.

Januariae idus, the Ides of January (i. e. Jan. 13), A. T. § 24[20].

Genovese, Genoese; *lo Genovese*, inhabitant of Genoese territory, divided from the Tuscans by the river Magra, Par. ix. 90 [**Macra**]; *Januensis Marchia*, 'the Genoese March', on the right side of Italy if the Apennines be taken as the dividing line (from N. to S.), V. E. i. 10[49-51]

Genovesi, the Genoese; apostrophized as barbarians, Inf. xxxiii. 151-3; *Januenses*, their march the E. limit of the 'Lingua Oc', the W. limit of Italian, V. E. i. 8[50-5]; their dialect distinct from those of the Tuscans and Sardinians, V. E. i. 10[64-5]; its distinctive characteristic the prevalence of *z*, whence its harshness, V. E. i. 13[44-52].

Gentile, Gentile; as distinct from Jew or Christian, Conv. ii. 5[62].

Gentiles. [**Gentili.**]

Gentiles, Summa Contra, treatise of St. Thomas Aquinas on the Catholic Faith *Against the Heathen*, in which he shows that a Christian theology is the sum and crown of all science; quoted as *Contra Gentili*, Conv. iv. 15[125], 30[29]; *Contra Gentiles*, Mon. ii. 4[6]; his condemnation of those who think they can measure all things with their intellect, Conv. iv. 15[125-30] (*Summ.* I. v. § 2); the title of D.'s *canzone* 'Contra gli erranti' (Canz. viii. 141) borrowed from that of St. Thomas's work, which was written for the confusion of such as stray from the faith, Conv. iv. 30[24-30]; his definition of a miracle, Mon. ii. 4[6-8] (*Summ.* III. ci. § 1).

From this treatise (I. v. § 3) is also taken the quotation attributed by D. to Aristotle in the *Ethics*, 'contra Simonide poeta parlando', Conv. iv. 13[70-2]. [**Simonide.**]

Gentili, Gentiles; as opposed to Christians, Par. xx. 104; Conv. iv. 15[51-91]; *gentes*, Epist. v. 10[161]; viii. 2[25]; Pagans, *la gente folle*(ref. to *Rom.* i. 22), their belief in oracles, Par. xvii. 31; their gods and goddesses, Conv. ii. 5[34-44]; their sacrificial rites, Conv. ii. 5[45-8]; Mon. ii. 4[32]; believed in the immortality of the soul, Conv. ii. 9[67-9]; held that mankind had one beginning, not several, as testified by Ovid (*Metam.* i. 78-83), Conv. iv. 15[50-84]; represented the chariot of the Sun with four horses, Conv. iv. 23[134-5]; believed in the manifestation of the divine judgement by trial of combat, *Gentiles*, Mon. ii. 8[79], 10[87].

Gentucca, name (according to the most probable interpretation) of a Lucchese lady mentioned by Bonagiunta (in Circle VI of Purgatory), who speaks of her as being as yet (i.e. in 1300) unmarried, and tells D. that her charms will cause him to modify his opinion of Lucca, Purg. xxiv. 37, 43-5. [**Bonagiunta.**]

The lady in question has been identified with some probability as a certain Gentucca Morla, wife of Buonaccorso (commonly called Coscio or Cosciorino) di Lazzaro di Fondora of Lucca, in whose will (dated Dec. 15, 1317) she is several times mentioned.

Gerarchia, hierarchy, term used to indicate the several divisions of the Angelic orders, Par. xxviii. 121; Conv. ii. 6[39-100]; in the Crystalline Heaven D. sees the nine Angelic Hierarchies (which preside over the various Heavens), the order of which Beatrice expounds to him, Par. xxviii. 40-139. [**Paradiso**[1].]

The mediaeval doctrine on the subject of the Angelic Hierarchies was based mainly on the work (*De Coelesti Hierarchia*) ascribed to Dionysius the Areopagite, and on a sermon of St. Gregory the Great (*Hom.* xxxiv. § 7).

D. in the *D. C.* follows the arrangement of Dionysius (Par. xxviii. 130-2), and refers to the fact that St. Gregory departed from it (*vv.* 133-5). He himself in the *Convivio* adopts yet another (which is that of St. Gregory in the *Moralia,* whence it was borrowed by Brunetto Latini in the *Trésor*, i. 12, which was probably D.'s authority), Conv. ii. 6[39-55].

The three different arrangements are as under:—

Dionysius and D.(*D. C.*).	St. Gregory (*Homiliae*).	St. Gregory (*Moralia*) and D. (*Conv.*).
First Hierarchy.		
Seraphim.	Seraphim.	Seraphim.
Cherubim.	Cherubim.	Cherubim.
Thrones.	Thrones.	Powers.
Second Hierarchy.		
Dominions.	Dominions.	Principalities.
Virtues.	Principalities.	Virtues.
Powers.	Powers.	Dominions.
Third Hierarchy.		
Principalities.	Virtues.	Thrones.
Archangels.	Archangels.	Archangels.
Angels.	Angels.	Angels.

Gerardus de Borneil, Giraut de Borneil, one of the most famous troubadours of his century, born at Essidueil, near Limoges, c. 1175, died c. 1220. He introduced a more popular style of lyric poetry and was distinguished for his facility and versatility as a poet. A number of his poems have been preserved.

Guido Guinizelli (in Circle VII of Purgatory), who says that they are fools who consider Giraut superior to Arnaut Daniel, refers to him as *quel di Lemosì,* Purg. xxvi. 120 [**Arnaldo Daniello**]; he is referred to as *il Provenzale,* and four lines of his canzone, *Los Apleitz,* are translated, Conv. iv. 11[92-5]; in the *De Vulgari Eloquentia* D. refers to him

as *Gerardus de Borneil*, V. E. i. 9²³;
Gerardus de Bornello, V. E. ii. 2⁸¹,
5²⁵; *Gerardus*, V. E. ii. 2⁸⁸, 6⁵⁴;
he is quoted as having used the
Provençal word *amor*, V.E. i. 9²³⁻⁵;
he was the singer of rectitude (as
Arnaut Daniel was of love, and
Bertran de Born of arms), V. E. ii.
2⁷⁹⁻⁸²; quoted as such, V. E. ii.
2⁸⁸⁻⁹⁰; employed the decasyllabic
line, an example being quoted, V. E.
ii. 5²⁵⁻⁶; wrote *canzoni* in the most
illustrious style, the first line of one
of them being quoted, V. E. ii. 6⁵⁴⁻⁵.

Gerardus de Bornello. [Gerar-
dus de Borneil.]

Geremia, prophet Jeremiah, V. N.
§§ 7⁴⁰, 31⁸; *Jeremias*, Epist. viii.
2²⁸; *Hieremias*, Epist. x. 22⁴¹⁴;
quoted, V. N. § 7⁴⁰⁻³ (*Lament.* i.
12); V. N. § 29¹⁻³ (*Lament.* i. 1);
V. N. § 31⁸⁻⁹ (*Lament.* i. 1); Epist.
viii. 1¹⁻³ (*Lament.* i. 1); Epist. x.
22⁴¹⁴⁻¹⁵ (*Jerem.* xxiii. 24). [**Bibbia.**]

Geri del Bello. [Bello, Geri del.]

Gerico], city of Jericho, its capture
by Joshua (*Josh.* vi. 1–27) alluded
to by the troubadour Folquet (in the
Heaven of Venus), in connexion
with Rahab, as *la prima gloria Di
Josuè in su la Terra Santa*, Par. ix.
124–5. [**Josuè: Raab.**]

Gerion, Geryon, according to
classical mythology, a monster with
three bodies united together (*Aen.*
viii. 202), who was a king in Spain,
and was slain by Hercules for the
sake of his oxen.

D. makes him the symbol of
fraud and places him as guardian of
Circle VIII of Hell (Malebolge)
where the Fraudulent are punished,
representing him as a kind of dragon,

Inf. xvii. 1–27; he has the face of
a righteous man (*v.* 10), two hairy
arms (*v.* 13), and the body of a serpent (*v.* 12), with a pointed tail
(*v.* 1), forked at the extremity like
that of a scorpion (*vv.* 25–7), its
back, breast, and sides being 'painted
with knots and little rings' (*vv.* 14–
15); he is named, Inf. xvii. 97,
133; xviii. 20; Purg. xxvii. 23;
referred to as *figura maravigliosa*,
Inf. xvi. 131–2; *la fiera con la coda
aguzza*, Inf. xvii. 1; *colei che tutto
il mondo appuzza*, *v.* 3; *la sozza
imagine di froda*, *v.* 7; *fiera pessima*,
v. 23; *bestia malvagia*, *v.* 30. On
leaving the last division of Circle
VII of Hell D. and Virgil arrive at
the brink of a deep ravine, into which
the river Phlegethon falls in a roaring
cascade (Inf. xvi. 91–105); V. casts
into the abyss the cord with which
D. was girt, as a signal to Geryon
(*vv.* 106–26), who comes swimming
up through the air from below (*vv.*
127–36); V. having explained to
D. the nature of the monster, they
approach him (xvii. 1–34), and V.
mounts on his back, bidding D. do
the same (*vv.* 79–96); Geryon then,
having received the word from V.,
descending in wide circles, carries
them down to the bottom, and, after
depositing them in Malebolge, van-
ishes out of sight (*vv.* 97–136);
the descent of V. and D. on the back
of Geryon is referred to by V.,
Purg. xxvii. 16–24.

Germania. [Lamagna.]

Germanico Mare. [Mare Germanico.]

Geronimo. [Jeronimo.]

Gerusalem. [Gerusalemme.]

Gerusalemme, Jerusalem, Purg.

xxiii. 29 ; Par. xix. 127 ; xxv. 56 ; *Gerusalem*, Purg. ii. 3 ; *Jerusalem*, Epist. ii. 2³⁵ ; vii. 8¹⁸⁷ ; viii. 1¹³ ; *Hierusalem*, Mon. iii. 9⁷⁵ ; Epist. x. 1¹⁰ ; *civitas David*, Epist. viii. 1⁷ ; *Civitas*, V. N. § 29¹, 31⁹ ; *il colmo della gran secca* (i. e. the highest point of the N. hemisphere), Inf. xxxiv. 114 ; *Sion*, Purg. iv. 68 ; *Là dove il suo fattore il sangue sparse*, Purg. xxvii. 2 ; Jerusalem, the antipodes of Purgatory, Purg. ii. 3 ; iv. 68 ; xxvii. 2 [**Gange**] ; *la gente che perdè G.*, i. e. the Jews, Purg. xxiii. 29 [**Giudei**] ; *il Ciotto di G.*, i. e. Charles II of Naples, Par. xix. 127 ; the scene of the Crucifixion, Inf. xxxiv. 113–15 ; Purg. xxvii. 2 ; Christ's saying that He must go to J. and suffer many things (*Matt.* xvi. 21), Mon. iii. 9⁷⁴⁻⁶ ; the Florentine exiles yearn for Florence as did the Babylonian exiles for J., Epist. vii. 8¹⁸⁶⁻⁸ ; lament of Jeremiah over (*Lament.* i. 1), V. N. §§ 29¹, 31⁹ ; Epist. viii. 1¹⁻³ ; visit of the Queen of Sheba to (1 *Kings* x. 1–13), Epist, x. 1¹⁰⁻¹¹; the heavenly Jerusalem as opposed to *Egitto* (i. e. life upon earth), Par. xxv. 56 ; Epist. ii. 2³⁵.

The zenith, or vertical point of the heavens, above Jerusalem is alluded to as *la plaga, Sotto la quale il sol mostra men fretta* (the Sun seeming to travel slower when near the zenith, because the shadows change less in a given time than they do when it is lower in the sky), Par. xxiii. 11–12 (cf. Purg. xxxiii. 103–4).

In D.'s conception of the universe Jerusalem is the central point of the N. hemisphere (cf. *Ezek.* v. 5), and the exact antipodes of the Mt.

of Purgatory, the latter being consequently the central point of the S. hemisphere. Since they are antipodes, Jerusalem and Purgatory have a common horizon (Purg. iv. 70–1), which is terminated in the E. by the Ganges in India, and in the W. by Cadiz in Spain. D. speaks of the N. hemisphere as 'la gran secca' (Inf. xxxiv. 113), in accordance with the geography of the time, which imagined the inhabited hemisphere to contain all the dry land of the globe, the S. hemisphere, ' il mondo senza gente ' (Inf. xxvi. 117), consisting wholly of water (with the exception, in D.'s view, of the Mt. of Purgatory).

Gerusalemme, Il Ciotto di, ' the Cripple of Jerusalem ', title by which the Eagle in the Heaven of Jupiter refers to Charles II of Naples, who was lame, Par. xix. 127. [**Carlo².**]

Charles derived the title of Jerusalem from his father, Charles of Anjou, King of Naples and Sicily, who claimed to have acquired the right to it by purchase from Mary of Antioch in 1272 ; he further claimed it in his own right, as one of the forfeited Hohenstaufen dignities, with which he had been invested by the Pope. The title had come to the Hohenstaufen through the marriage of Frederick II to Iolanthe (his second wife), daughter of John of Brienne and Mary of Montferrat, who was eldest daughter of Isabella of Jerusalem and Conrad of Montferrat.

Gesù. [**Cristo.**]

Gherardesca, Anselmuccio della. [**Anselmuccio.**]

Gherardesca, Brigata della. [**Brigata, Il.**]

Gherardesca, Gaddo della. [Gaddo.]

Gherardesca, Nino della. [Brigata, Il.]

Gherardesca, Ugolino della. [Ugolino, Conte.]

Gherardesca, Uguccione della. [Uguccione [1].]

Gherardino da Filattiera. [Filattiera, Gherardino da.]

Gherardo. [Zeno, San.]

Gherardo da Cammino. [Cammino, Gherardo da.]

Ghibellini, Ghibellines, supporters of the Empire, as opposed to the Guelfs, the supporters of the Church; mentioned by name once only in the *D. C.*, viz. by the Emperor Justinian (in the Heaven of Mercury), who reproaches them for converting the Imperial Eagle into a party standard, Par. vi. 100–3; Farinata degli Uberti (in Circle VI of Hell) refers to them as *mia parte*, and alludes to their discomfiture of the Guelfs in 1248 and 1260, Inf. x. 47–8; D., addressing Farinata, calls them *i vostri*, and reminds him that after each occasion the Guelfs contrived to regain the upper hand (viz. in 1251 and 1266), Inf. x. 49–51 [Farinata]; Oderisi (in Circle I of Purgatory) refers to the Ghibelline victory over the Florentine Guelfs at Montaperti (Sept. 4, 1260), Purg. xi. 112–13 [Montaperti]; Cacciaguida (in the Heaven of Mars) alludes to the party strife between the Guelfs and Ghibellines, Par. xvi. 154; as does St. Peter (in the Heaven of Fixed Stars), Par. xxvii. 46–8 [Guelfi].

The terms *Guelfo* and *Ghibellino* are Italianized forms of the two German names *Welf* and *Weiblingen*. Of these the former was the name of an illustrious family, several members of which had successively been Dukes of Bavaria in the tenth and eleventh centuries. The heiress of the last of these intermarried with a younger son of the house of Este; and from them sprang a second line of Guelfs, from whom the royal house of Brunswick is descended. Weiblingen was the name of a castle in Franconia, whence Conrad the Salic (Emp. 1024–1039) came, the progenitor, through the female line, of the Swabian Emperors. At the election of Lothair in 1125 in succession to Henry V (Emp. 1106–1125) the Swabian family were disappointed of what they regarded almost as an hereditary possession; and at this time a hostility appears to have commenced between them and the house of Welf, who were nearly related to Lothair. In 1071 Henry IV (Emp. 1056–1106) had conferred the Duchy of Bavaria on the Welfs; and in 1080 the Duchy of Swabia had been conferred upon the Counts of Hohenstaufen, who represented the Franconian line. The accession of Conrad III of Swabia (Emp. 1138–1152) to the Imperial throne, and the rebellion of Henry the Proud, the Welf Duke of Bavaria, gave rise to a bloody struggle between the two houses; and at the battle of Weinsberg (Dec. 21, 1140) the names *Welf* and *Weiblingen* were for the first time adopted as war cries, which were subsequently naturalized in Italy as *Guelfo* and *Ghibellino*, and became the distinctive appellations of the opposing factions of the Pope and the Emperor.

The names of Guelf and Ghibelline are said to have been introduced into Florence in 1215, on the occasion of the quarrel which arose out of the murder of Buondelmonte de' Buondelmonti by the Amidei on Easter Sunday in that year [Buondelmonti].

The struggle between the two parties in Florence continued, with varying fortune to either side, for sixty-three years, from 1215 to 1278, when the Guelfs finally remained masters of the situation. In 1248 the Emperor Frederick II, wishing to retaliate upon the papacy for the unjust sentence pronounced against him at the Council of Lyons, and to weaken the Church Party, made offers to the Uberti, the leaders of the Florentine Ghibellines, to help them to expel from their city his enemies and their own ; and, his offer being accepted, the Guelfs were driven out of Florence (Inf. x. 48). On the death of Frederick (Dec. 13, 1250) the Guelfs were allowed to return (Inf. x. 49), and the first pacification between the two parties took place. In 1258 the Ghibellines in their turn were expelled in consequence of their having entered into a conspiracy, at the head of which were the Uberti, with the aid of King Manfred, to break up the popular government of Florence, which was essentially Guelf. The majority of the banished Ghibellines took refuge in Siena, and not long after, with the help of troops supplied by Manfred, they gained under the leadership of Farinata degli Uberti the decisive victory at Montaperti (Sept. 4, 1260) over the Florentine Guelfs, who precipitately fled from Florence and took refuge in Lucca (Inf. x. 85–93) [**Montaperti : Farinata**]. The whole of Tuscany was now in the hands of the Ghibellines. In a few years, however, the tide once more turned against them. Manfred, their champion and protector, was defeated and slain at Benevento (Feb. 26, 126⅚) by Charles of Anjou with the aid of the Tuscan

Guelfs; and this reverse was followed by a rising in Florence against the Ghibellines, the most prominent of whom were expelled (Nov. 1266). Shortly after this a second attempt was made to effect a reconciliation between the opposing parties, by means of matrimonial alliances—it was at this time that the daughter of Farinata degli Uberti was married to the Guelf Guido Cavalcanti. In the next year (1267), however, the Guelfs expelled the remaining Ghibellines from Florence, and offered the lordship of the city to Charles of Anjou for ten years. After this the Ghibellines never regained their influence in Florence ; and, though a partial pacification was effected in 1278 by Cardinal Latino at the instance of Pope Nicholas III, the government still remained in the hands of the Guelfs. In 1289 the exiled Ghibellines made an attempt to enter Florence by force of arms, and supported by the Aretines, who were in alliance with Pisa against the Tuscan league, they risked a battle at Campaldino (June 11, 1289), where they were totally defeated [**Campaldino**]. The capitulation of Caprona in the same year completed their discomfiture [**Caprona**]. Twenty years later the hopes of the Ghibellines were once more raised by the advent of the Emperor Henry VII into Italy, only to be finally dashed by his sudden death at Buonconvento, near Siena, Aug. 24, 1313.

Ghin di Tacco, famous highwayman (said to have been the son of Tacco Monaceschi de' Pecorai da Turita, a noble of Siena), who in revenge for the condemnation to death of one of his relatives (a brother or uncle) stabbed the judge, one Benincasa da Laterina of Arezzo, who had sentenced him, while he was sitting as Papal assessor at Rome.

D. mentions Ghino in connexion with his victim, whom he sees in Ante-purgatory among those who died a violent death, Purg. vi. 13–14. [Benincasa.]

Anecdotes of Ghino are told by Francesco da Barberino in the Commentary on his *Documenti d' Amore*, and by Boccaccio in the *Decameron* (x. 2), where he is described as 'per la sua fierezza e per le sue ruberie uomo assai famoso'.

Ghisileriis, Guido de. [Ghisilerius, Guido.]

Ghisilerius, Guido, Guido Ghisilieri (1244–1278), Bolognese poet of the school of Guido Guinizelli (his cousin), with whom he is coupled by D., together with Fabruzzo dei Lambertazzi and Onesto Bolognese ; none of his poems appear to have been preserved ; *Guido Ghisilerius*, V. E. i. 15⁴²; *Guido de Ghisileriis*, V. E. ii. 12⁴⁰; his rejection of the Bolognese dialect a proof of its inferiority, V. E. i. 15⁴⁰⁻⁶; his use of the seven-syllabled line at the beginning of poems in the lofty style, V. E. ii. 12³⁸⁻⁴⁰.

Ghisilieri, Guido. [Ghisilerius, Guido.]

Ghisolabella, daughter of Alberto de' Caccianemici of Bologna, and sister of Venetico Caccianemici (or, as D. calls him, Venedico Caccianimico), who is said to have handed her over to the evil passions of the Marquis of Este (either Obizzo II, 1264–1293, or his son Azzo VIII, 1293–1308), in order to curry favour with him ; she married, in or before 1270, Niccolò da Fontana of Ferrara, so that it was most likely previous to that date that the outrage took place. The old commentators and editors write the name 'Ghisola bella', in two words, and assume that she was so called on account of her beauty ; but her actual name was Ghisolabella, or Ghislabella, as is proved by her will (dated Sept. 1, 1281), in which she is described as 'D. Ghislabella filia quondam domini Alberti de Cazanimitis, et uxor domini Nichollay de Fontana'.

G. is mentioned by Caccianimico (in Bolgia 1 of Circle VIII of Hell), who informs D. that he was the intermediary between her and the Marquis, Inf. xviii. 55–6. [Caccianimico, Venedico.]

Giacobbe. [Jacob.]

Giacomo. [Jacomo.]

Giacopo. [Jacopo.]

Giampolo. [Ciampolo.]

Gianciotto Malatesta. [Malatesta, Gianciotto.]

Giandonati], one of the Florentine families which received knighthood from the Marquis Hugh of Brandenburg, 'il gran barone', Par. xvi. 128. [Ugo di Brandimborgo.]

Gianfigliazzi], Florentine family, alluded to by the mention of their arms (on a field or a lion azure), one of whom D. sees among the Usurers in Round 3 of Circle VII of Hell, Inf. xvii. 59–60. [Usurai.]

They lived in the Sesto di Borgo and were Guelfs (Vill. v. 39), and as such were exiled from Florence in 1248 (vi. 33), and in 1260 after the battle of Montaperti (vi. 79); subsequently, when the Guelf party split up into Bianchi and Neri, they sided with the latter (viii. 39); they were still prominent in Florence in Cent. xiv (xii. 3).

Gianicolo, Monte], Mons Janiculus at Rome, on the right bank of the Tiber; supposed by some to be the hill referred to by D. as *il monte*, in his description of the pilgrims crossing the Tiber as they leave St. Peter's during the Jubilee, Inf. xviii. 33. [Giordano, Monte: Giubbileo.]

The Janiculus, though on the same side of the river as St. Peter's and the Castello Sant' Angelo, is, owing to a bend, almost exactly in face of any one crossing the river on the way back to the city.

Gianni de' Soldanier, Florentine Ghibelline (d. after 1285), placed by D. among those who were traitors to their party, in Antenora, the second division of Circle IX of Hell, Inf. xxxii. 121. [Antenora: Soldanieri.]

After the defeat and death of Manfred at Benevento (Feb. 26, 126⅚), the Florentine commons, who were for the most part Guelf, became restive, and began to murmur against the government of Guido Novello and the Ghibelline nobles ; and, in spite of the conciliatory measures of the latter, finally rose against them and drove them from Florence. On this occasion Gianni de' Soldanieri, though a Ghibelline, placed himself at the head of the populace in opposition to his own party.

Gianni Schicchi, Florentine, of the Cavalcanti family, noted for his powers of mimicry, which he utilized in order to perpetrate a fraud in collusion with Simone Donati, by personating Buoso, the father of the latter; D. places him among the Falsifiers in Bolgia 10 of Circle VIII of Hell (Malebolge), Inf. xxx. 32; *ombra, v.* 25 ; *folletto, v.* 32 ; *l'altro, v.* 42 ; *rabbioso, v.* 46. [Falsatori.]

Gianni, Lapo. [Lapo Gianni.]

Giano. [Jano.]

Giano della Bella], the famous Florentine tribune, who, though a noble by birth, espoused the cause of the commons, and as Prior in 1293 enforced the severe *Ordinamenti di Giustizia* against the nobles of Florence ; he is commonly supposed to be alluded to by Cacciaguida (in the Heaven of Mars), who, referring to the arms of the Marquis Hugh of Brandenburg ('il gran barone'), which were borne by the families which received knighthood from him, says that 'he who binds them with a fringe is to-day united with the commons ', Par. xvi. 131–2. [Ugo di Brandimborgo.]

Giapeto, Iapetus, one of the Titans, son of Uranus (Heaven) and Ge (Earth), and father of Atlas, Prometheus, and Epimetheus ; mentioned as the father of Prometheus in the translation of a passage from the *Metamorphoses* (i. 78–83) of Ovid, Conv. iv. 15[82] [Prometeo].

Giason. [Jason.]

Gibilterra, Stretto di], Strait of Gibraltar ; alluded to by Ulysses (in Bolgia 8 of Circle VIII of Hell) as *quella foce stretta Ov' Ercole segnò li suoi riguardi*, Inf. xxvi. 107–8. [Colonne di Ercole.]

Gigante[1]. [Anteo.]

Gigante[2], Giant in the mystical Procession in the Terrestrial Paradise, whose dealings with the Harlot are commonly understood to typify the relations of Philip IV of France with the Papal See, Purg. xxxii. 152; xxxiii. 45; *feroce drudo*, Purg. xxxii. 155. [**Filippo** [2].]

Giganti, Giants of mythology, who were said to have sprung from the blood that fell from Uranus (Heaven) upon the earth, whence Ge (Earth) was regarded as their mother. They made an attack upon Olympus, the abode of the gods, but the latter, with the aid of Hercules, destroyed them all, and buried them under Aetna and other volcanoes.

D. mentions them in connexion with their war upon the gods, Inf. xxxi. 95; Purg. xii. 33; *i figli della terra*, Inf. xxxi. 121; they figure among the examples of defeated pride in Circle I of Purgatory, where Jupiter, Apollo, Minerva, and Mars are represented as surveying their strewn limbs after their discomfiture by the gods, Purg. xii. 31–3 (where there is a reminiscence of Statius, *Theb.* ii. 597–9, and of Ovid, *Metam.* x. 150–1) [**Superbi**].

D. places four Giants, Antaeus, Briareus, Ephialtes, and Nimrod, as warders at the mouth of Circle IX of Hell, Inf. xxxi. 31, 44; xxxiv. 31; and implies that the two Titans, Tityus and Typhon, acted in the same capacity, Inf. xxxi. 124 [**Tifo : Tizio**].

As D. and Virgil approach the brink of the last descent in Hell, D. sees what he takes to be lofty towers in front of him (Inf. xxxi. 19–21); V. informs him that they are not towers but Giants, who stand immersed in the icy pit from

the navel downwards (*vv.* 22–45); the first they come to is Nimrod (*vv.* 46–81) [**Nembrotto**]; they next see Ephialtes (*vv.* 84–96) [**Fialte**]; and then come to Antaeus (*vv.* 112–45) [**Anteo**]; Briareus, who is the farthest off of all, they do not see close (*vv.* 103–5) [**Briareo**].

Gigas. [**Nembrotto.**]

Gilbertus Porretanus], Gilbert de la Porrée, scholastic logician and theologian, born at Poitiers, 1075; he was a pupil of Bernard of Chartres and of Anselm of Laon, and after being Chancellor of the Cathedral at Chartres for about twenty years he went to Paris, where he lectured on dialectics and theology; he was made Bishop of Poitiers in 1141, and died in 1154. His chief logical work, the treatise *De Sex Principiis*, whence he was styled 'Magister Sex Principiorum', consists of an elaborate criticism of the ten Aristotelian categories.

D., who refers to Gilbert by his title of 'Magister Sex Principiorum', quotes his statement (*Sex Princip.* § 1) to the effect that certain forms belong to things compounded, and exist in a simple and unchanging essence, Mon. i. 11[20–3].

Ginevra, Guenever, the wife of King Arthur, in the Romance of 'Lancelot du Lac'. She secretly loved Lancelot, and at an interview between them, brought about by Gallehault, she, at the instigation of the latter, gave Lancelot a kiss, which was the beginning of their guilty love.

D. refers to the incident in connexion with the cough given by the Lady of Malehaut, one of the

Queen's companions, on perceiving the familiarity between Lancelot and her mistress, Par. xvi. 13–15; the love of Guenever and Lancelot is alluded to, Inf. v. 128, 133–4. [Galeotto : Malehaut, Dama di.]

Gioacchino¹, the Calabrian Abbot Joachim, born c. 1130 at Celico, about four miles NE. of Cosenza in Calabria. He made a pilgrimage to the Holy Land, and on his return to Italy became a monk, entering (c. 1158) the Cistercian monastery of Sambucina. In 1176 he was made Abbot of Corazzo in Calabria. In 1185 Pope Urban III appointed a deputy Abbot in order that he might have leisure to devote himself to his writings. In 1189 Joachim founded a community at Flora (now San Giovanni in Fiore) in the forest of Silla among the mountains of Calabria, whence he was named 'de Floris'. From this institution, the rule of which was sanctioned by Celestine III in 1196, ultimately sprang the so-called 'Ordo Florensis'. Joachim died in 1202. He wrote a commentary upon the Apocalypse (*Expositio in Apocalypsin*), a Harmony of the Old and New Testaments (*Concordia utriusque Testamenti*), besides the *Psalterium decem chordarum*, and other works. He was credited with the authorship of a Book of the Popes, in which the persons and names of all the future Popes were described. In 1254, more than fifty years after his death, there appeared at Paris a work entitled *Liber Introductorius ad Evangelium Eternum*, an introduction to the works of Joachim, written by a Franciscan, Gherardo da Borgo San Donnino, in which it was maintained that the Old and New Testaments were superseded by the writings of Joachim, three of which, the *Concordia*, the *Expositio*, and the *Psalterium*, constituted the Everlasting Gospel, which was to take the place of the Scriptures. This work was denounced by the University of Paris to Pope Innocent IV, by whose successor, Alexander IV, it was formally condemned in 1256, a condemnation which in 1260 was extended to Joachim's own writings.

D. was undoubtedly influenced by the Joachist doctrines, and it is significant that, in spite of the official condemnation, he places Joachim among the Doctors of the Church (*Spiriti Sapienti*) in the Heaven of the Sun, where his spirit is pointed out by St. Bonaventura, who describes him as endowed with the gift of prophecy, Par. xii. 140–1 [Sole, Cielo del].

Gioacchino ², Joachim, the first husband of St. Anne, by whom he was the father of the Virgin Mary ; he and St. Anne are mentioned together as the parents of the Virgin in proof of the human nature of the latter, though she was the mother of our Lord, Conv.ii.6¹²⁻¹⁴. [Anna¹: Maria ¹.]

Giobbe. [Job.]

Giocasta. [Jocasta.]

Giordan. [Jordan.]

Giordano, Monte], hill in Rome, near the Tiber; supposed by some to be *il monte* referred to by D. in his description of the pilgrims crossing the Tiber as they leave St. Peter's during the Jubilee, Inf. xviii. 33 [Gianicolo, Monte : Giubbileo].

Giosaffàt. [Josaffàt.]
Gioseppo. [Giuseppo.]
Giosuè. [Josuè.]
Giotto, the great Florentine artist, disciple of Cimabue, born in 1266 (the year after the birth of D., whose intimate friend he is said to have been), at the village of Colle, near Vespignano, about fourteen miles from Florence; died in Florence, Jan. 8, 133⁶⁄₇.

Oderisi (in Circle I of Purgatory) mentions him as having eclipsed the fame of Cimabue, Purg. xi. 95. [Cimabue.]

According to Vasari, Giotto painted the portraits of Dante, Brunetto Latini, and Corso Donati in what is now the Bargello at Florence. [Dante.]

Giovacchino. [Gioacchino.]
Giovane, Il Re. [Arrigo⁴.]
Giovanezza e di Vecchiezza, Di. [*Juventute et Senectute, De.*]

Giovanna¹, Joan, wife of Buonconte da Montefeltro; the latter (in Ante-purgatory) complains to D. that neither she nor his other relatives showed any concern for him after his death, Purg. v. 89. [Buonconte.]

Giovanna², Joan, daughter (born c. 1291) of Nino Visconti of Pisa and Beatrice of Este; in 1296, while still an infant, she was entrusted by Boniface VIII to the guardianship of the town of Volterra, as the daughter of a Guelf who had deserved well of the Church, but she was deprived of all her property by the Ghibellines, and, after living with her mother at Ferrara and Milan, was married (in 1308) to Riccardo da Cammino, lord of Treviso; after the death of

her husband in 1312 she seems to have been reduced to poverty; in 1323 she was living in Florence, where a grant of money was made her in consideration of the services of her father; the date of her death is uncertain, but she was almost certainly dead in 1339.

Nino Visconti (in Ante-purgatory) begs D. to ask his daughter Joan to pray for him, and laments that her mother, who had married again, no longer cares for him, Purg. viii. 70-3. [Beatrice⁴: Cammino, Riccardo da: Nino².]

Giovanna³, Joan, mother of St. Dominic; St. Bonaventura (in the Heaven of the Sun), with a play upon the meaning of the name (John, of which it is the feminine, signifying in Hebrew 'the grace of God'), says of her in reference to St. D., 'O madre sua veramente Giovanna', Par. xii. 80. [Domenico.]

Giovanna⁴, Joan, name of a lady-love of Guido Cavalcanti; D. speaks of seeing her in company with Beatrice, and says of her, 'era di famosa beltade, e fu già molto donna di questo mio primo amico'; he adds that she was also called *Primavera* (a name applied to her by Guido Cavalcanti in one of his *ballate*), which he interprets 'the forerunner' ('cioè prima verrà'), and explains that this is also the meaning of *Giovanna*, which is the feminine of *Giovanni*, i. e. John the Baptist, the forerunner of Christ, V.N. §24¹⁶⁻³⁷; elsewhere he speaks of her familiarly as *monna Vanna*, Son. xiv. 9 (V. N. §24); Son. xxxii. 9. [Primavera: Vanna.]

Giovanna⁵, Joan, pseudonym of

a lady (called also *Bianca* and *Cortese*) mentioned by D. in one of his *canzoni*, Canz. x. 153.

Giovanna[6]], Juana I, daughter of Enrique I, King of Navarre, by whose marriage (in 1284) with Philip the Fair the kingdom of Navarre became annexed to the crown of France ; the union of the two kingdoms through this marriage is alluded to by the Eagle in the Heaven of Jupiter, Par. xix. 143–4. [**Navarra : Table M.**]

Giovanni[1], St. John the Baptist, Inf. xix. 17 ; Par. iv. 29 (where the reference applies equally to St. John the Evangelist); xvi. 25 ; (*il gran Giovanni*) xxxii. 31 ; V.N. § 24[36]. [**Battista.**]

Giovanni[2], St. John the Apostle and Evangelist, son of the fisherman Zebedee and Salome, and younger brother of St. James the Apostle ; commonly regarded as the author of the Book of Revelation, as well as of the Gospel which bears his name.

St. John is mentioned, *Giovanni*, Purg. xxix. 105 ; xxxii. 76 ; Par. iv. 29 (where the reference applies equally to St. John the Baptist); Conv. iii. 14[63] ; *Giovanni Evangelista*, Conv. ii. 6[18] ; *Vangelista*, Inf. xix. 106 ; *Johannes*, Mon. ii. 13[26] ; iii. 8[8], 9[103, 111, 121], 15[20] ; Epist. x. 33[614, 626] ; *filius Zebedaei*, Mon. iii. 9[83] ; alluded to (according to one interpretation), as one of *i quattro animali* in the mystical Procession in the Terrestrial Paradise, Purg. xxix. 92 [**Evangelisti**] ; *un veglio solo*, Purg. xxix. 143 [**Apocalypsis**] ; *i più giovani piedi*, i.e. the feet of St. John, who outran St. Peter in their race to the sepulchre

of our Lord, though St. Peter was the first to enter (*John* xx. 6), Par. xxiv. 126 ; the representative of Love, as St. James was of Hope, and St. Peter of Faith, on the occasions when the three Apostles were present alone with Christ, i. e. at the raising of Jairus's daughter (*Luke* viii. 51), at the Transfiguration (*Matt.* xvii. 1 ; *Mark* ix. 2 ; *Luke* ix. 28), and in the garden of Gethsemane (*Matt.* xxvi. 37 ; *Mark* xiv. 33), the three being referred to by Beatrice as *i tre* (*ai quali*) *Gesù fe' più chiarezza*, Par. xxv. 33 ; D. speaking to St. James (in the Heaven of Fixed Stars) calls St. John *il tuo fratello*, Par. xxv. 94 ; he is described as *un lume*, Par. xxv. 100 ; *splendore*, Par. xxv. 106 ; *fuoco*, Par. xxv. 121 ; *fiamma*, Par. xxvi. 2 ; *colui che giacque sopra il petto Del nostro Pellicano, e . . fue D'in su la croce al grande uficio eletto*, Par. xxv. 112–14 (ref. to *John* xiii. 23 ; xix. 26–7); *aguglia di Cristo*, Par. xxvi. 53 ; *quei che vide tutti i tempi gravi, Pria che morisse, della bella sposa* (i. e. of the Church), Par. xxxii. 127–8.

D. refers to St. John as the author of the *Gospel*, Inf. xix. 106 ; Purg. xxix. 92 ; Conv. ii. 6[18] ; iii. 14[63] ; Mon. ii. 13[26] ; iii. 8[8], 9[103, 111], 15[20] ; Epist. x. 33[614] ; as the author of the *Apocalypse*, Inf. xix. 106–8 ; Purg. xxix. 105 [**Ezechiel**] ; Purg. xxix. 143–4 ; Par. xxv. 94–6 ; xxxii. 127 ; Epist. x. 33[626] ; his presence at the Transfiguration with St. Peter and St. James, Purg. xxxii. 76 ; Par. xxv. 33 ; Conv. ii. 1[48] ; Mon. iii. 9[83] ; at the raising of Jairus's daughter, Par. xxv. 33; in the garden of Gethsemane, Par. xxv. 33; the disciple who leaned on Jesus's bosom, Par. xxv. 112–13; the Virgin Mary committed to his charge, Par. xxv. 113–14; his visit with St. Peter to the tomb of Christ, Par. xxiv. 126; Mon. iii. 9$^{111-14}$; St. Peter's question concerning him, ' Lord, what shall this man do?' (*John* xxi. 21), Mon. iii. 9$^{120-2}$.

In the Heaven of Fixed Stars D. sees a light of dazzling brilliancy equal to that of the Sun, which Beatrice explains is the spirit of St. John (Par. xxv. 100–17); D. gazes at St. J. in the expectation of seeing his earthly body (*vv.* 118–21), but the latter reproves him, reminding him that his body is earth on earth, the only two who ascended to Heaven with their earthly bodies being Christ and the Virgin Mary (*vv.* 122–9); he then proceeds to examine D. concerning love (Par. xxvi. 1–66) (as St. Peter had examined him concerning faith, Par. xxiv. 19–147, and St. James concerning hope, Par. xxv. 25–99). While adopting the legend as to the dazzling brilliance of the transfigured body of St. John (Par. xxv. 100–2, 118–21, 138; xxvi. 1–2 [Cancro]), D. rejects the common belief (based on *John* xxi. 22–3) as to his assumption (Par. xxv. 118–29).

In the Celestial Rose D. assigns to St. John the seat on the right of St. Peter, Par. xxxii. 124–30. [Rosa.]

In the mystical Procession in the Terrestrial Paradise St. John is represented by his writings, his *Gospel* appearing (according to the most probable interpretation) as one of the four beasts (*quattro animali*), Purg. xxix. 92; his *Epistles* as one of the four elders in humble guise (*quattro in umile paruta*), Purg. xxix. 142, 145–8; while his *Book of Revelation* appears under the guise of a solitary elder asleep (*un veglio solo dormendo*), who comes last of all (*diretro da tutti*), the Apocalypse being the last book in the Bible (*vv.* 143–4).

The *Gospel of St. John* is quoted, Purg. xiii. 29 (*John* ii. 3); Purg. xvi. 19 (*John* i. 29); Purg. xxxiii. 10–12 (*John* xvi. 16); Conv. ii. 6$^{16-17}$ (*John* i. 5); Conv. ii. 9$^{115-16}$ (*John* xiv. 6); Conv. ii. 15$^{171-2}$ (*John* xiv. 27); Mon. ii. 2$^{42-3}$ (*John* i. 3–4); Mon. ii. 13^{27} (*John* xix. 30); Mon. iii. 9$^{103-7, 111-22}$ (*John* xiii. 6, 8; xx. 5–6; xxi. 7, 21); Mon. iii. 14$^{23-5}$ (*John* xvii. 4); Mon. iii. 15$^{20-33}$ (*John* xiii. 15; xxi. 22; xviii. 36); Epist. iv. 5$^{56-7}$ (*John* xv. 19); Epist. vii. 2$^{45-6}$ (*John* i. 29); Epist. viii. 2$^{21-2}$ (*John* xxi. 17); Epist. x. 33$^{615-16}$ (*John* xvii. 3); A. T. § 22$^{20-1}$ (*John* viii. 21); referred to, Par. xxiv. 126; Mon. iii. 9$^{111-14}$ (ref. to *John* xx. 6); Par. xxv. 112–13 (ref. to *John* xiii. 23); Par. xxv. 113–14 (ref. to *John* xix. 26–7); Conv. iii. 14$^{63-4}$ (ref. to *John* i. 1); Mon. iii. 8$^{2-8}$ (ref. to *John* xx. 23).

The *Revelation of St. John* is quoted, Epist. x. 33$^{625-6}$ (*Rev.* i. 8); referred to, Inf. xix. 106–10 (ref. to *Rev.* xvii. 1–3); Purg. xxix. 105 (ref. to *Rev.* iv. 8);

Par. xxv. 94–6 (ref. to *Rev.* vii. 9);
Par. xxvi. 17 (ref. to *Rev.* i. 8).

Giovanni[3], John, imaginary personage, Conv. i. 8[94]; iii. 11[67].

Giovanni, Il gran. [Giovanni[1].]

Giovanni, Il Re. [Arrigo[4].]

Giovanni Buiamonte. [Buiamonte, Giovanni.]

Giovanni del Virgilio. [Virgilio, Giovanni del.]

Giovanni XXI. [Ispano, Pietro.]

Giovanni XXII], John XXII
(Jacques d'Euse or Duèse), born
at Cahors in Guienne c. 1244;
elected Pope in succession to Clement V (after a vacancy of more
than two years) at Lyons, Aug. 7,
1316; died at Avignon, at the age
of over ninety, Dec. 4, 1344. In
his youth he went as a student to
Naples, where he afterwards became
tutor in the family of Charles II.
He was subsequently appointed
successively Bishop of Fréjus (c.
1300), Chancellor in Naples, Archbishop of Avignon (1310), and
finally, in recognition of his services
to Clement V at the Council of
Vienne, Cardinal-Bishop of Oporto.
He appears to have owed his election
as Pope, partly to the dissensions
between the Gascon and Italian
Cardinals, and partly to the influence
of King Robert of Naples. At his
death, he left a treasure of more than
18 millions of gold florins (Vill. xi.
20).

St. Peter (in the Heaven of Fixed
Stars)alludes to John XXII and
Clement V, with reference to their
avarice and extortions, when he
says, *Del sangue nostro Caorsini e*

Guaschi S'apparecchian di bere, Par.
xxvii. 58–9. [Caorsino : Clemente[2].]

There is a further reference to
John XXII in the passage (Par.
xviii. 128–36) in which D. denounces the venality and avarice of
the Pope, which led to the trafficking in interdicts and excommunications (*v.* 130). D. here taunts him
with his 'devotion to John the Baptist' (*vv.* 133–5), i. e. to the Florentine gold florin, on one side of
which was represented the Baptist
(the patron saint of Florence), imitations of which were struck by the
Pope at Avignon (Vill. ix. 171).

Giove[1], Jove, name applied to
God by D., who doubtless thought
it identical with Jehovah, Purg. vi.
118. [Dio.]

Giove[2], Jove or Jupiter, chief of
the Roman gods, son of Saturn and
Rhea, and father of Apollo, Mars,
Minerva, &c.; *il fabbro di Giove*
(i. e. Vulcan), Inf. xiv. 52 [Capaneo : Vulcano]; the attack of the
Giants on Jove, Inf. xxxi. 45, 92
(cf. Purg. xii. 32); slays Phaëthon
with a thunderbolt, Purg. xxix. 120
[Fetonte]; *l'uccel di Giove* (i.e. the
Eagle), Purg. xxxii. 112; so *Jovis
armiger* (after Ovid, *Metam.* xv. 386),
with especial reference to the Emperor Henry VII, Carm. 26 [Aquila]; the Pagan worship of Jove,
Mercury, and Mars, Par. iv. 62;
Jove the son of Saturn and father of
Mars, Par. xxii. 145–6; Dardanus,
the mythical ancestor of the Trojans,
the son of Jove, Conv. iv. 14[146–7]
[Dardano]; speech of Jove to Mercury concerning Aeneas, Mon. ii.
7[79–80] [*Aeneis*]; alluded to, as the

son of Rhea, in connexion with Mt.
Ida, Inf. xiv. 101 [**Rea**]; as the
father of Apollo, Minerva, and Mars,
in connexion with the attack of the
Giants on Olympus, Purg. xii. 32
(cf. Inf. xxxi. 45, 92) [**Giganti**];
as the father of Cupid, *il sommo Padre*,
Conv. ii. 6¹²² [**Cupido**].

Giove³, planet Jupiter, Par. xviii.
95; xxii. 145; xxvii. 14; Conv.
ii. 4⁷, 14¹⁹⁴, 15¹⁴⁴; *la temprata
stella Sesta*, Par. xviii. 68–9; *la
giovial facella*, Par. xviii. 70; *dolce
stella*, Par. xviii. 115; *il sesto lume*,
Par. xx. 17; *quella luce che . . .
regge tra Saturno e Marte*, Son.
xxviii. 1–3; Jupiter the sixth in
order of the planets, its position
being between Mars and Saturn, Par.
xviii. 68–9; xx. 17; xxii. 145–6;
Son. xxviii. 1–3; Conv. ii. 4⁷,
14¹⁹⁶⁻²⁰²; of a silvery colour compared to the other stars, Par. xviii.
68, 96; Conv. ii. 14²⁰²⁻⁴; a star
of temperate complexion, as opposed
to the heat of Mars and the frigidity
of Saturn, according to the opinion
of Ptolemy, Conv. ii. 14¹⁹⁹⁻²⁰² (cf.
Par. xviii. 68, 115; xxii. 145); the
period of its revolution twelve years,
for half of which it would be concealed from the Earth if the motion
of the *Primum Mobile* were suspended, Conv. ii. 15¹⁴⁴⁻⁵.

Giove, Cielo di, Heaven of Jupiter; the sixth in D.'s conception of
Paradise, Conv. ii. 4⁶⁻⁷[**Paradiso**];
resembles Geometry in two respects,
Conv. ii. 14¹⁹⁴⁻²²³; it is presided
over by the Dominions [**Dominazioni**].

In the Heaven of Jupiter D. places
the spirits of those who loved and
exercised justice (*Spiriti Giudicanti*),

among whom he names David [**David**]; Trajan [**Traiano**]; Hezekiah [**Ezechia**]; Constantine [**Costantino**]; William II of Sicily
[**Guglielmo** ²]; and Ripheus [**Rifeo**]. These six are arranged in
the shape of the eye and eyebrow of
an Eagle, the Eagle itself being
formed by the rest of the spirits in
this Heaven. David forms the pupil
of the eye, while the other five form
a semicircle round him in the shape
of the eyebrow, Par. xx. 37–9, 43
[**Aquila**²].

Giovenale, Juvenal (Decimus
Junius Juvenalis), Roman satirist,
born at Aquinum, probably in the
reign of Nero (A. D. 54–68), died at
the age of over eighty in the reign
of Antoninus Pius (A.D. 138–161);
his extant works consist of sixteen
satires.

Virgil (addressing Statius in Purgatory) mentions Juvenal among
those who are with himself in
Limbo, and says that it was from
him that he learned of the affection
of Statius for himself, Purg. xxii.
14–15 (where D. erroneously assumes that Statius outlived Juvenal)
[**Limbo**].

Juvenal's denunciation of riches
(*Sat.* x. 1–27; xiv. 139), Conv.
iv. 12⁸³; his lines upon hereditary
nobility (*Sat.* viii. 1–32, 54–5)
paraphrased and discussed, Conv.
iv. 29³⁷⁻⁶⁴; his saying that virtue is
the only true nobility (misquoted from
Sat. viii. 20), *Juvenalis*, Mon. ii. 3¹⁸;
one of his lines (*Sat.* x. 22) quoted
from Boëthius (*Cons. Phil.* ii. *pr.* 5),
Conv. iv. 13¹⁰⁸⁻¹⁰. [**Boezio.**]

Gioventute e Senettute, Di.
[**Juventute et Senectute, De.**]

Gioviale facella, the torch of Jove, i. e. the planet Jupiter, Par. xviii. 70. [Giove[3].]

Giovinetto, Lo. [Alfonso[1].]

Giraut de Borneil. [Gerardus de Borneil.]

Girolamo. [Jeronimo.]

Giuba. [Juba.]

Giubbileo, the first Jubilee of the Roman Church, instituted by Boniface VIII in the year 1300.

D. compares the sinners passing along one of the bridges of Malebolge in opposite directions, to the throngs of pilgrims crossing the bridge of Castello Sant' Angelo on their way to and from St. Peter's at Rome during the Jubilee (when measures were taken to keep the two streams of traffic distinct in order to prevent accidents), Inf. xviii. 28–33.

The Jubilee is alluded to by Casella (in Ante-purgatory), who tells D. that he had been admitted into Purgatory since its commencement, three months before, Purg. ii. 98–9 [Casella] ; there is doubtless also a reference to the Jubilee in D.'s allusion to the 'barbarians' coming to see the wonders of Rome, Par. xxxi. 31–6 [Barbari] ; and to the pilgrims from Croatia coming to see the Veronica, which was exhibited during the Jubilee, Par. xxxi. 103–4 [Croazia.]

Giuda[1], Judas Iscariot, the betrayer of Christ, *Giuda*, Inf. ix. 27 ; xxxi. 143 ; Purg. xx. 74 ; xxi. 84 ; *Giuda Scariotto*, Inf. xxxiv. 62 ; alluded to as *l'anima ria*, Inf. xix. 96 ; *peccatore*, Inf. xxxiv. 56 ; *quel dinanzi*, *v.* 58 ; *anima*, *v.* 61 ; his place with Lucifer in the nethermost pit of Hell, hence called *il cerchio di Giuda*, Inf. ix. 27 ; xxxi. 143 ; xxxiv. 62 ; Matthias elected to fill his place as Apostle, Inf. xix. 94– 6 ; *la lancia Con la qual giostrò Giuda* (i. e. fraud and treachery), Purg. xx. 73–4 ; his betrayal of Christ avenged by Titus, Purg. xxi. 82–4. [Tito.]

D. places Judas, with Brutus and Cassius, in the jaws of Lucifer in the lowest division of Hell, which is named *Giudecca* after him ; his head is inside Lucifer's mouth, who gnaws it, while his legs project outside, and his back is flayed by Lucifer's claws, Inf. xxxiv. 55–63 [Giudecca : Lucifero.]

Giuda[2], name of an ancient Florentine, mentioned, as representing the Giudi family, by Cacciaguida (in the Heaven of Mars), who speaks of him as having been a good citizen in his day, Par. xvi. 123.

The Giudi, who are not mentioned by Villani, appear to have held consular office in Florence in Cent. xii ; according to the old commentators they lived in San Piero Scheraggio, and, having joined the Ghibellines, eventually threw in their lot with the Bianchi ; in D.'s day they are said to have fallen into low estate.

Giuda[3]], St. Jude the Apostle, son of Alpheus and Mary (the sister of the Virgin Mary), and brother of James the Less, author of the Epistle which bears his name ; thought by some to be symbolized by one of the four elders in humble guise in the mystical Procession in the Terrestrial Paradise, Purg. xxix. 142. According to a better interpretation the four elders represent, not the authors of the four canonical Epistles, but the Epistles themselves personified.

Giuda [4]. [**Judas.**]

Giuda Maccabeo. [**Maccabeo.**]

Giudea, the land of Judaea, mentioned in connexion with *Psalm* cxiv. 1–2, Conv. ii. 1[60]; *Judaea*, Epist. x. 7[144]. [*Psalmi.*]

Giudecca, name given by D. to the last of the four divisions of Circle IX of Hell, where Traitors are punished, Inf. xxxiv. 117; *cerchio di Giuda*, Inf. ix. 27; *il più basso loco e il più oscuro, E il più lontan dal ciel che tutto gira*, vv. 28–9 [**Inferno**]. In this division, which is named after Judas, who betrayed his Master, are placed those who have been traitors to their benefactors, Inf. xxxiv. 1–69 [**Traditori**]. *Examples*: Lucifer and Judas, who represent the betrayers of the highest spiritual authority [**Giuda**[1]: **Lucifero**]; Brutus and Cassius, representative of the betrayers of the highest civil authority [**Bruto**[2]: **Cassio**].

Giudei, the Jews, Inf. xxiii. 123; xxvii. 87; Par. vii. 47; xxix. 102; Conv. ii. 9[70]; *Giudeo*, Par. v. 81; Conv. ii. 5[62]; iv. 28[75–8]; *Judaei*, Mon. iii. 13[48–9], 15[32]; Epist. viii. 3[33]; their council of the chief priests and Pharisees, at which it was determined to put Christ to death (*John* xi. 47), Inf. xxiii. 122–3; coupled with the Saracens as unbelievers, Inf. xxvii. 87; Conv. ii. 9[70]; Epist. viii. 3[33]; though having only the Old Testament to guide them, yet they know what is right in the matter of vows, and do it, Par. v. 81; both God and they willed the

death of Christ, but from different motives, Par. vii. 47; the eclipse of the Sun at the Crucifixion visible equally to the Jews at Jerusalem, and to the inhabitants of Spain and India (i. e. to the whole inhabited world), Par. xxix. 101–2 [**Gerusalemme**]; the Jews share the universal belief in angels, Conv. ii. 5[62]; and in the immortal somewhat in man, Conv. ii. 9[70]; St. Paul's saying that outward conformance does not make a man a Jew (*Rom.* ii. 28–9), Conv. iv. 28[75–81]; the release of St. Paul opposed by the Jews (*Acts* xxviii. 19), Mon. iii. 13[48–50]; Christ did not seek to be delivered from them, His kingdom not being of this world (*John* xviii. 36), Mon. iii. 15[27–33] [**Ebrei**].

Giudeo. [**Giudei.**]

Giudicanti, Spiriti. [**Spiriti Giudicanti.**]

Giudice, Il. [**Nino**[2].]

Giudice delle Colonne. [**Guido delle Colonne.**]

Giuditta. [**Judit.**]

Giulia. [**Julia.**]

Giuliano, Monte San], mountain in Tuscany, between Lucca and Pisa, 'that hill whose intervening brow Screens Lucca from the Pisan's envious eye'; alluded to by Ugolino (in Circle IX of Hell) as *il monte Per che i Pisan veder Lucca non ponno*, Inf. xxxiii. 29–30.

Giulio. [**Julius.**]

Giuno, Juno, daughter of Saturn and Rhea, and wife and sister of Jupiter; *Giuno*, V. N. § 25[74]; Conv. ii. 5[39]; *Junone*, Inf. xxx. 1; Par. xii. 12; *Juno*, Par. xxviii. 32; her jealousy of Semele and wrath against the Thebans, Inf. xxx. 1–3

[**Semelè**]; Iris (the rainbow), her handmaiden, *ancella di Junone*, Par. xii. 12; and messenger, *messo di Juno*, Par. xxviii. 32 [**Iri**]; her hostility to the Trojans (owing to the judgement of Paris), and speech to Aeolus (*Aen.* i. 65 ff.), V. N. § 25[74-7] [**Eolo : Paris**]; regarded by the Pagans as the goddess of might, Conv. ii. 5[39-40].

Giunone. [**Giuno.**]

Giuochi, ancient noble family of Florence, mentioned by Cacciaguida (in the Heaven of Mars) as having been of importance in his day, Par. xvi. 104.

They were Ghibellines (Vill. v. 39; vi. 33), and lived in the Porta san Piero ; though originally noble, they had fallen into decay in D.'s time (iv. 11).

Giuseppe. [**Giuseppo.**]

Giuseppo [1], Joseph, son of Jacob and Rachel ; mentioned in connexion with the false accusation brought against him by Potiphar's wife, whom Maestro Adamo (in Bolgia 10 of Circle VIII of Hell) speaks of as *la falsa che accusò G.*, Inf. xxx. 97 [**Falsatori**]; he is among those referred to by Virgil as having been released by Christ from Limbo, *Israel co' suoi nati*, Inf. iv. 59 [**Limbo**].

Giuseppo [2], Joseph, son of Heli, the husband of the Virgin Mary, and reputed father of Christ ; mentioned, Son. liv. 11 ; alluded to in connexion with Mary's reproach to Christ, when He tarried behind to teach in the Temple at Jerusalem, 'Behold, thy father and I have sought thee sorrowing' (*Luke* ii 48), Purg. xv. 91. [**Maria** [1].]

Giuseppo della Scala], illegitimate son of Alberto della Scala, by whom he was made (1291) Abbot of San Zeno at Verona, a post which he held until his death in 1314 ; he is alluded to as Alberto's son by the Abbot of San Zeno (in Circle IV of Purgatory), who says he was deformed in person, and still more deformed in mind, besides having been basely born, Purg. xviii. 124–6. [**Alberto della Scala : Zeno, San.**]

Giustiniano, Justinian, surnamed the Great, Emperor of Constantinople, A. D. 527–565. During his reign the great general Belisarius overthrew the Vandal kingdom in Africa and the Gothic kingdom in Italy. Justinian, who is best known not by his conquests but by his legislation, appointed a commission of jurists to draw up a complete body of law, which resulted in the compilation of two great works ;—one, called *Digesta* or *Pandectae*, in fifty books, contained all that was valuable in the works of preceding jurists ; the other, called *Justinianeus Codex*, consisted of a collection of the Imperial constitutions. To these two works was subsequently added an elementary treatise in four books, under the title of *Institutiones* ; and at a later period Justinian published various new constitutions, to which he gave the name of *Novellae Constitutiones*. These four works, under the general name of *Corpus Juris Civilis*, form the Roman law as received in Europe. [**Digesto.**]

D. mentions Justinian in his apostrophe to Italy, with special allusion to his great legislative work, Purg. vi. 89; he is placed among the spirits of those who sought honour in the active life (*Spiriti Operanti*), in the Heaven of Mercury, Par. vi. 10; *un (spirto)*, Par. v. 121; *anima degna*, v. 128; *lumiera*, v. 130; *figura santa*, v. 137; *sustanza*, Par. vii. 5; in reply to D., Justinian gives a brief sketch of his own life (Par. vi. 1–27), in which he refers to his codification of the Roman law (*vv.* 12, 22–4), to his conversion by Agapetus (*vv.* 13–21) [Agabito], and to the victories of his general Belisarius (*vv.* 25–7) [Bellisar]; he then goes on to trace the career of the Imperial Eagle from the time when it was carried westward from Troy by Aeneas, down to the time when the Guelfs opposed it, and the Ghibellines made a party ensign of it (*vv.* 1–9, 28–111) [Aquila¹]; and finally tells D. who the spirits are in the Heaven of Mercury (*vv.* 112–42), giving a special account of Romieu of Ville-neuve (*vv.* 127–42) [Romeo: Mercurio, Cielo di.]

Giuvenale. [Giovenale.]

Glauco, Glaucus, fisherman of Anthedon in Boeotia, who became a sea-god by eating of the divine herb which Saturn had sown.

D. compares the change wrought in himself, while gazing upon Bea-trice, to the transformation under-gone by G. (whose story D. got from Ovid, *Metam.* xiii. 920 ff.), when he had partaken of the divine herb, Par. i. 67–9.

Godenti, Frati. [Frati Gau-denti.]

Golias, Goliath, the giant of Gath, who fought for the Philis-tines against Israel, and was slain by David with a stone from his sling (1 *Sam.* xvii); D. appeals to the Emperor Henry VII, as a second David, to overthrow King Robert of Naples, the modern Go-liath, Epist. vii. 8¹⁷⁸ [Arrigo²: Filistei: Roberto²].

Golosi], the Gluttonous, placed in Circle III of Hell, Inf. vi. 7–109 [Inferno]; their guardian is Cerberus, the emblem of gluttony, who claws and rends them (*vv.* 13–21) [Cerbero]; they lie prone in the mud, to remind them of their base life upon earth, while they are continually pelted with showers of rain, hail, and snow (*vv.* 7–12, 34–7). *Example*: Ciacco [Ciacco].

Those who expiate the sin of Gluttony in Purgatory are placed in Circle VI [*Beatitudini*: Purga-torio]; their punishment is, in a state of emaciation, to pass and re-pass before an apple-tree laden with fruit and watered by a fountain, without being able to satisfy their hunger and thirst, Purg. xxii. 130–8; xxiii. 19–27, 61–75. *Examples*: Forese Donati [Forese]; Bona-giunta da Lucca [Bonagiunta]; Pope Martin IV [Martino²]; Ubaldino dalla Pila [Ubaldin dalla Pila]; Bonifazio de' Fieschi [Bo-nifazio²]; and Messer Marchese da Forlì [Marchese³]. From the leaves of the tree issues a voice which proclaims examples of tem-perance, Purg. xxii. 139–54; viz. the Virgin Mary at the feast of Cana in Galilee (*vv.* 142–4) [Ma-ria¹]; the Roman women of old (*vv.* 145–6) [Romane]; Daniel (*vv.* 146–7) [Daniello]; those who lived in the Golden Age (*vv.* 148–50); and St. John the Baptist (*vv.* 151–4) [Battista]. The voice of one of the sinners is heard chanting 'Labia mea, Domine' (*Psalm* li. 15), Purg. xxiii. 10–11. From among the branches of a second apple-tree a voice proclaims examples of gluttony, Purg. xxiv. 118–26; viz. the Centaurs (*vv.* 121–2) [Centauri]; and the Hebrews rejected by Gideon (*vv.* 124–6) [Ebrei: Gedeon].

Gomita, Frate, Sardinian friar, who having been appointed chancellor or deputy of Nino Visconti of Pisa, judge of Gallura, abused his position to traffic in the sale of public offices. Nino turned a deaf ear to all complaints against him until he discovered that the friar had connived at the escape of certain prisoners who were in his keeping, whereupon Nino had him hanged forthwith. [Nino [2].]

D. places the friar, along with Ciampolo and Michael Zanche, among the Barrators in Bolgia 5 of Circle VIII of Hell (Malebolge), Inf. xxii. 81; *un* (*barattiere*), *v.* 67; *quel di Gallura*, *v.* 82; *vasel d'ogni froda*, *v.* 82; *barattier sovrano*, *v.* 87. [Barattieri.]

Gomorra, Gomorrah, ancient city of Palestine, destroyed by fire from heaven on account of the abominable wickedness of its inhabitants (*Gen.* xix. 4–8, 23–9); mentioned, together with Sodom, among the instances of lust proclaimed by the Lustful in Circle VII of Purgatory, Purg. xxvi. 40. [Lussuriosi: Sodomiti.]

Gorgon, Gorgon Medusa; she alone of the three Gorgons was mortal, and was at first a beautiful maiden, but, in consequence of her having given birth to two children by Poseidon in one of Athena's temples, the latter changed her hair into serpents, which gave her head such a fearful appearance that every one who looked upon it was changed into stone.

The three Furies stationed at the entrance to the City of Dis invoke Medusa (usually regarded here as symbolical of despair) to come and turn D. to stone in order to prevent his ingress, *Medusa*, Inf. ix. 52; *Gorgon*, *v.* 56. [Erine.]

Gorgona, small island in the Mediterranean, about twenty miles SW. of Leghorn; D. calls upon it and Capraia, another island further S., to come and block up the mouth of the Arno, in order that Pisa and its inhabitants may be annihilated, Inf. xxxiii. 82–4. [Caprara.]

Gostantino. [Costantino.]
Gostanza. [Costanza.]
Gottifredi, Duca, Duke Godfrey, i. e. Godfrey of Bouillon, Duke of Lorraine, the great Crusader, son of Count Eustace II of Bouillon in the Ardennes, born at Baisy (near Genappe in Belgium), c. 1060. He was one of the foremost leaders in the First Crusade, and was among the first to enter Jerusalem when that city was captured, after a siege of five weeks, in 1099. On the foundation of a Christian kingdom of Jerusalem, he was unanimously elected sovereign; but he refused to accept the kingly title, and adopted instead the humbler designation of Defender and Baron of the Holy Sepulchre.

During the single year of his rule he successfully repelled the Saracens, and drew up from the various feudal statutes of Europe the elaborate system of mediaeval jurisprudence known as the *Assizes of Jerusalem*. He died in 1100, and was buried in the Church of the Holy Sepulchre.

D. places Godfrey among those who had fought for the faith (*Spiriti Militanti*), in the Heaven of Mars, where his spirit is pointed out by Cacciaguida, Par. xviii. 47. [**Marte, Cielo di.**]

Gottus Mantuanus, Gotto of Mantua, poet of whom nothing certain appears to be known beyond that he was a contemporary of D., who was personally acquainted with him.

D. mentions him as having introduced into his stanza an unrimed line, which he called the key, and states that Gotto had recited to him many good *canzoni* of his own composition, V. E. ii. 13$^{26-30}$.

Governo, now Governolo, town in Lombardy, about twelve miles from Mantua, on the right bank of the Mincio, close to where it falls into the Po; mentioned by Virgil in connexion with the founding of Mantua by Manto, Inf. xx. 78. [**Mantova: Mincio.**]

Graeci. [**Greci**[1]**.**]

Graffiacane, one of the ten demons in Bolgia 5 of Circle VIII of Hell (Malebolge), deputed by Malacoda to escort D. and Virgil, Inf. xxi. 122; *Graffiacan*, Inf. xxii. 34. [**Alichino: Malebranche.**]

Graii, Graius. [**Greci**[1]**.**]

Graziano, Gratian (Franciscus Gratianus), founder of the science of canon law; born in Italy, c. 1090.

In early life he appears to have become a Benedictine monk, and to have entered the Camaldulian monastery of Classe near Ravenna, whence he afterwards removed to that of San Felice at Bologna. Here he spent many years in the preparation of his great work, the celebrated *Concordia discordantium Canonum*, better known as the *Decretum Gratiani*, which was published between 1140 and 1150. In this work, which forms the first part of the *Corpus Juris Canonici*, and which he compiled from the Holy Scriptures, the Canons of the Apostles and of the Councils, the Decretals of the Popes, and the writings of the Fathers, Gratian brought into agreement the laws of the ecclesiastical and secular courts. [*Decretali:* **Decretalistae.**]

D. places Gratian among the Doctors of the Church (*Spiriti Sapienti*), in the Heaven of the Sun, where his spirit is pointed out by St. Thomas Aquinas, who says of him, in allusion to his work on the canon and civil law, *l'uno e l'altro foro Aiutò*, Par. x. 104–5. [**Sole, Cielo di.**]

Greci[1], Greeks, Inf. xxvi. 75; Purg. ix. 39; xxii. 88, 108; Par. v. 69; Conv. ii. 4^{39}; iv. 22^{35}; *Graeci*, Canz. xxi. 4; V. E. i. 8^{20}; Mon. ii. 11$^{53,\ 57}$; *Graii*, Mon. ii. 3^{80}, 7^{82} [**Greco**]; of Ulysses and Diomed, Inf. xxvi. 75; Purg. ix. 39 [**Diomede: Ulisse**]; the account of the siege of Thebes by the Greeks in the *Thebaid*, Purg. xxii. 88–9 [**Stazio: Tebe**]; the Greek poets in Limbo, Purg. xxii. 106–8 [**Limbo**]; *lo gran duca dei Greci*, i. e. Agamemnon, Par. v. 69 [**Agamemnone**]; the term *Protonoë* applied by the Greeks to the divine Intelligence, Conv. ii. 4^{38-9}; their term *hormen* (ὁρμὴν) for the blind animal instinct (taken by D. from Cicero, *Acad. Quaest.* iv. 8; *De Fin.* iii. 7), Conv. iv. 21^{120}, 22^{35}; the Greeks dwell partly in Europe, partly in Asia, V. E. i. 8^{20-1}; called *Graii* by Virgil (*Aen.* viii. 135; iii. 163), Mon. ii. 3^{80}; (*Aen.* iv. 228), Mon. ii. 7^{82}; the struggle for supremacy between them and the Romans, under the leadership respectively of Pyrrhus and Fabricius, terminated in favour of the Romans, Mon. ii. 11^{53-9} [**Fabbrizio : Pirro**].

Greci [2], ancient noble family of Florence (extinct in D.'s day), mentioned by Cacciaguida (in the Heaven of Mars) as having been already in their decline in his time, Par. xvi. 89.

The Borgo de' Greci in Florence (which at the present time leads from the Piazza di San Firenze to the Piazza di Santa Croce) was named from them.

Grecia, Greece; Virgil (addressing D.) refers to the Trojan war as the time 'quando Grecia fu di maschi vota' (all the men having departed to take part in the siege of Troy), Inf. xx. 108; in ancient Greece love was treated of in poetry, not by writers of the common tongue, but by men of letters, V. N. § 25^{29-31}.

Greco [1], a Greek; Sinon, the Greek who persuaded the Trojans to admit the wooden horse within their walls, *Sinon Greco*, Inf. xxx. 98; *il Greco, v.* 122 [**Sinone : Troia**]; the Greek poet most beloved by the Muses, i.e. Homer, Purg. xxii. 101-2 [**Omero**]; Constantine the

Great, who transferred the seat of the Empire from Italy to Greece, Par. xx. 57 [**Costantino**].

Greco [2], the Greek language; Homer's poems, if translated from Greek into Latin, would lose their harmony and melody, just as the Psalter has done, which was translated from Hebrew into Greek, and thence into Latin, Conv. i. 7^{91-103}; *filos* in Greek the same as *amatore* in Italian, Conv. iii. 11^{47-51}; the animal instinct in man termed *hormen* (ὁρμὴν) in Greek, Conv. iv. 21^{120-2} (cf. iv. 22^{35}). [**Greci** [1].]

Greco [3], Greek; Cicero's blame of the Romans (*De Fin.* i. 1) for praising 'Greek grammar' (i. e. Greek literature), at the expense of their own, Conv. i. 11^{93-8} [***Finibus, De***]; the Greek proverb, that friends ought to have all things in common (from Cicero, *De Off.* i. 16), Conv. iv. 1^{16-18}; the Greek word *autentin*, according to Uguccione, the origin of the Italian *autore*, Conv. iv. 6^{38-41} [**Uguccione** [2]].

Gregorio, Pope Gregory I, the Great, born at Rome, of a noble family, c. 540. He was educated for the law, and when about 30 was elected prefect of Rome, which office he held for three years. On the death of his father he retired from public life, and gave up his whole fortune to public uses, founding monasteries and charitable institutions. In a monastery which he built in Rome he embraced the Benedictine rule, and spent his time in works of charity and devout exercises. About 579 he was appointed abbot, and also one of the seven deacons of the Roman Church.

In 582 Pope Pelagius II sent him on a diplomatic mission to Constantinople, where he remained for more than three years. In 590, on the death of Pelagius, he was unanimously chosen as his successor, and, in spite of his reluctance, was crowned Pope in September of that year. During his pontificate of 14 years he checked the aggressions of the Lombards, and restored order and tranquillity to Rome ; in Italy and France he enforced stricter ecclesiastical discipline, and in England, Spain, and Africa he waged an effectual war against paganism and heresy. He died at Rome, March 12, 604. The chief of his writings are the *Moralia*, an exposition of the book of Job in 35 books, his *Homilies* on Ezekiel, and on the Gospels, and his *Dialogues* in four books on the lives and miracles of the Italian saints.

St. Gregory is mentioned in connexion with the legend (alluded to again, Par. xx. 106–17) that by his prayers he delivered the soul of the Emperor Trajan from hell, Purg. x. 75 [Traiano]; Beatrice (in the Crystalline Heaven) mentions him in connexion with the difference between his arrangement of the angelic orders and that of Dionysius, Par. xxviii. 133 [Dionisio [2]: Gerarchia]; D. reproaches the Italian Cardinals with the neglect of his writings and of those of other Fathers of the Church, *Gregorius*, Epist. viii. 7[114].

Some think St. Gregory is alluded to as one of the four elders, 'in humble guise', in the mystical Procession in the Terrestrial Paradise (the other three being St. Ambrose, St. Augustine, and St. Jerome),

Purg. xxix. 142. The reference is more probably to the four writers of the canonical Epistles.

The legend, alluded to by D. (Purg. x. 75 ; Par. xx. 106–17), that the Emperor Trajan was recalled to life from hell, through the intercession of Gregory the Great, in order that he might have room for repentance, was widely believed in the Middle Ages, and is repeatedly recounted by mediaeval writers.

Gregorius. [Gregorio.]

Greve, Val di. [Valdigreve.]

Griffolino], alchemist of Arezzo (still living in 1259), placed by D. among the Falsifiers in Bolgia 10 of Circle VIII of Hell (Malebo1ge); he is not named, but is alluded to as *l'uno* (*lebbroso*), Inf. xxix. 86, 92, 110; *l'Aretin*, Inf. xxx. 31 ; in reply to D., G. states that he belonged to Arezzo, and was burnt at the instance of Albero of Siena, because in jest he had offered to teach him to fly, and had not done so ; he adds, however, that it was not on that account that he was in Hell, but because he had been an alchemist (Inf. xxix. 109–20) [Albero: Falsatori].

Grifone, the Griffin in the mystical Procession in the Terrestrial Paradise (commonly understood to be symbolical of Christ, its twofold nature, half lion, half eagle, representing the twofold nature of Christ, human and divine), Purg. xxix. 108 ; xxx. 8 ; xxxi. 113, 120; xxxii. 26, 43, 89 ; *la fiera, Ch' è sola una persona in due nature*, Purg. xxxi. 80 ; *doppia fiera*, Purg. xxxi. 122 ; *animal binato*, Purg. xxxii. 47 ; *biforme fiera*, Purg. xxxii. 96.

Gualandi, noble Ghibelline family of Pisa, mentioned by Count Ugolino (in Circle IX of Hell), with the Sismondi and Lanfranchi, as having been foremost among those whom the Archbishop Ruggieri incited to work his destruction, Inf. xxxiii. 32.

The tower in which Ugolino and his sons and grandsons were starved to death (hence named 'Torre della Fame'), which stood in the Piazza degli Anziani, nearly on the spot where the modern clock-tower in the Piazza dei Cavalieri now stands, was called after this family 'la torre de' Gualandi alle Sette Vie'. [**Ruggieri, Arcivescovo : Ugolino, Conte.**]

Gualdo, village of Gualdo Tadino in Umbria, on the slopes of the Apennines, about 20 miles NE. of Perugia, and 8 miles N. of Nocera; mentioned by St. Thomas Aquinas (in the Heaven of the Sun) in his description of the situation of Assisi, where he says that Gualdo and Nocera (not to be confounded with Nocera in Apulia), which are in the upper valley of the Tupino, on the E. side of the ridge of Monte Subasio (on the SW. slope of which stands Assisi), lament behind it (the ridge) 'per grave giogo' (i. e. on account of the overshadowing Apennine range, several peaks of which rise to the height of nearly 5,000 feet, a few miles to the E. of those two places), Par. xi. 47–8.

Gualdrada, daughter of Bellincion Berti de' Ravignani of Florence; through her marriage (c. 1180) with Guido Guerra IV, the Conti Guidi traced their descent from the Ravignani [**Bellincion Berti**]. Jacopo Rusticucci mentions her as the grandmother of the Guido Guerra who is with him in Round 3 of Circle VII of Hell, calling her *la buona Gualdrada*, Inf. xvi. 37 [**Guidi, Conti : Guido Guerra**].

According to the old accounts (which are at variance with history) Guido Guerra IV, otherwise known as Guido Vecchio (d. 1213), married Gualdrada at the instigation of the Emperor Otto IV. The story was that the Emperor, being in Florence, was struck with the beauty of the maiden and asked who she was. Bellincione replied that she was the daughter of a man who would be proud to let the Emperor kiss her; whereupon Gualdrada exclaimed that no man alive should kiss her save he who was to be her husband. The Emperor, delighted with her spirit, urged Guido, who was present, to ask her in marriage, and, the match having been made, dowered the couple with lands in the Casentino.

As a matter of fact, as appears from documentary evidence, Gualdrada was married to Guido Guerra about 1180, some twenty years before Otto IV was chosen Emperor. She was Guido's second wife, he having previously married Agnese, daughter of Guglielmo il Vecchio, Marquis of Monferrato.

Gualterotti, ancient noble family of Florence, mentioned by Cacciaguida (in the Heaven of Mars), together with the Importuni, as having been of importance in his day, and as having had the Buondelmonti as their neighbours in the Borgo sant' Apostolo, Par. xvi. 133–5.

Both families, who were Guelfs (Vill. v. 39), had fallen into decay in D.'s time.

Guanto, Ghent, on the Scheldt, the capital of East Flanders ; mentioned by Hugh Capet (in Circle V of Purgatory), together with Douay, Lille, and Bruges, to indicate Flanders, Purg. xx. 46. [**Bruggia : Fiandra.**]

Guaschi, Gascons ; St. Peter (in the Heaven of Fixed Stars), alluding to the simony of Clement V, who was a native of Gascony, and to the avarice of John XXII, who was a native of Cahors, says *Del sangue nostro Caorsini e Guaschi S'apparecchian di bere*, Par. xxvii. 58–9 [**Caorsino : Giovanni XXII**]; Cacciaguida (in the Heaven of Mars), alluding to Clement V's betrayal of the Emperor Henry VII, refers to him as *il Guasco*, Par. xvii. 82 [**Arrigo** [2]] ; D. refers to Clement and his following as *Vascones*, Epist. viii. 11[186] [**Clemente** [2]].

Guasco, Gascon ; *il Guasco*, i. e. Clement V, Par. xvii. 82. [**Guaschi.**]

Guascogna, Gascony, province in SW. corner of France, which for many years was held by the Kings of England, the French crown claiming homage from them in consideration of their tenure of it.

Hugh Capet (in Circle V of Purgatory) refers to the taking of Gascony and Ponthieu from Edward I of England in 1294 by Philip the Fair, Purg. xx. 66 [**Ponti**]; the province is alluded to by Nicholas III (in Bolgia 3 of Circle VIII of Hell) in connexion with the Gascon

Pope Clement **V**, Inf. xix. 83 [**Clemente** [2]].

Guascogna, Golfo di], Gulf of Gascony, or Bay of Biscay ; alluded to by St. Bonaventura (in the Heaven of the Sun) in his description of the situation of Calahorra, the birthplace of St. Dominic, as *l'onde Dietro alle quali . . . Lo sol talvolta ad ogni uom si nasconde* (i. e. the waters behind which the sun sinks during the summer solstice), Par. xii. 49–51. [**Callaroga.**]

Guccio de' Tarlati], one of the Tarlati of Pietramala in the territory of Arezzo, in which city they were the chiefs of the Ghibelline party ; he is said to have been uncle of the celebrated Guido Tarlati, Bishop of Arezzo, and to have been drowned in the Arno while in pursuit of some of the Bostoli, Guelf exiles from Arezzo, who had taken refuge in Castel di Rondine in the Valdarno ; the old commentators (some of whom call him Cione) identify him with the person alluded to by D. as *l'altro (Aretino) che annegò correndo in caccia*, whom he saw in Antepurgatory among those who died a violent death without absolution, but repented at the last moment, Purg. vi. 15. [**Antipurgatorio.**]

Guelfi, Guelfs, supporters of the Church, as opposed to the Ghibellines or supporters of the Empire ; mentioned by name once only in the *D. C.*, viz. by the Emperor Justinian (in the Heaven of Mercury), who refers to their alliance with Charles II of Naples, Par. vi. 107 [**Carlo** [2]]; and reproaches them with opposing the golden *fleurs-de-lys* of France to the Imperial Eagle (*vv.* 100–1)

[**Aquila** [1]]; Farinata degli Uberti (in Circle VI of Hell) refers to their discomfiture in 1248 and 1260, Inf. x. 46-8; D., addressing Farinata, reminds him that after each occasion the Guelfs contrived to regain the upper hand (viz. in 1251 and 1266), Inf. x. 49-50 [**Farinata**]; Oderisi (in Circle I of Purgatory), referring to the defeat of the Florentine Guelfs by the Ghibellines at Montaperti (Sept. 4, 1260), speaks of the former as *la rabbia fiorentina*, Purg. xi. 112-14 [**Montaperti**]; St. Peter (in the Heaven of Fixed Stars) alludes to the strife between the Guelfs and Ghibellines, Par. xxvii. 46-8 [**Ghibellini**].

Throughout the *D. C.* the *wolf* is symbolical of the Guelf party (doubtless from the association of the name), and, further, of the sin of avarice, and, as connected with these, of the Papal power and pretensions of the Church.

The Guelf party generally is alluded to as *lupa*, Inf. i. 49; Purg. xx. 10; *lupi*, Par. xxvii. 55; the Florentine Guelfs are alluded to as *lupi*, Purg. xiv. 50, 59; Par. xxv. 6; *lupo*, Par. ix. 132; the Pisan Guelfs (Ugolino and his sons) as *il lupo e i lupicini*, Inf. xxxiii. 29. [**Ugolino, Conte.**]

Guercio Cavalcanti. [**Cavalcanti, Francesco de'.**]

Guerra, Guido. [**Guido Guerra.**]

Guglielmo [1], William, Count of Orange, who, under the name of Guillaume Fierebrace or Guillaume au Court-Nez, was the central figure of the twenty-four Old French *Chansons de Geste*, known as the *Geste de Guillaume*, in which his exploits against the Saracens in defence of Christendom are celebrated.

D. places William, together with his fellow-champion Renouard, another hero of the same *Geste*, among those who fought for the faith (*Spiriti Militanti*), in the Heaven of Mars, where their spirits are pointed out by Cacciaguida, Par. xviii. 46. [**Marte, Cielo di : Rinoardo.**]

In the *Chansons de Geste* William is represented as one of the twelve children of Count Aimeri of Narbonne. After a series of adventures, in one of which he had his nose cut off (whence his sobriquet 'au Court-Nez'), he married Orable, daughter of Desramé, the Saracen King of Cordova, after she had been baptized by the name of Guibourc. Subsequently William was disastrously defeated by his father-in-law at the battle of Aliscans, in the neighbourhood of Arles. This defeat was afterwards avenged in a second great battle of Aliscans, where the victory of William's army was mainly due to the prowess of Renouard. The latter, a sort of giant, half comic, half terrible, commonly known as 'Rainouart au tinel', from the immense club which was his favourite weapon, was a son of Desramé and brother of Orable. He had been sold into slavery in France, and served for some time as scullion in the kitchen of Louis the Pious, until William, observing his immense strength, enrolled him in his army and made him his companion in arms. After the second battle of Aliscans, in which Renouard engaged eleven of the Saracen chiefs successively in single combat, and by his prowess saved the Frankish host from another disastrous defeat, he was baptized, and married Aélis, the daughter of the Emperor. Finally both William and Renouard entered a monastery, where the former received the title of saint. The most important poem in the *Geste de Guillaume* is that entitled *Aliscans* which is the chief authority for the (legendary) exploits both of William and Renouard. The author of this poem, which was written probably c. 1170 by Jendeu de Brie in Sicily, anticipates D. in placing the Count of Orange in Paradise:—

'Si est sains; Diex l'a fait beneïr
En paradis celestre.'
                              (vv. 641–2.)

Historically speaking, William, Count of Orange, was of Northern French origin; he was born towards the middle of Cent. viii, his parents being probably of royal descent. William in his youth was attached to the court of Charlemagne, and became one of the most trusted councillors and warriors of the Frankish king. Nothing precise is known of him until the year 790, when he was appointed Duke of Septimanie (or of Toulouse or Aquitaine) by Charlemagne. His most glorious achievement belongs to the year 793, when Hescham, the Caliph of Cordova (788–796), having proclaimed the *Jehad* or holy war, invaded France with an army of 50,000 men and penetrated as far as Narbonne. William went to meet the invaders, encountered them at Villedaigne, near the river Orbieu, and gave them battle. Though defeated, his heroic efforts checked the Saracen advance and compelled them to return to Spain. By William's valour on this occasion France was once more saved from the Saracens, as she had been saved sixty years before (Oct. 732) by Charles Martel at Poitiers. In 801 (or 803) William took a chief part in the capture of Barcelona from the Saracens by the forces of Louis, King of Aquitaine. In 804 he founded the monastery of Gellone (St. Guillem du Désert) near Montpellier in the diocese of Lodève, into which he retired, June 29, 806. Here he died in the odour of sanctity, May 28, 812, two years before Charlemagne. He was afterwards canonized as St. William of Gellone. The dates of William's career fall entirely within the reign of Charlemagne, but romance has assigned his chief actions to the reign of Louis le Débonnaire (814–843).

Guglielmo [2], William II, the Good, King of Sicily and Naples in the Norman line, 1166–1189; he was son (born 1154) of William I, the Bad (1153–1166) (so called on account of his cruelty towards his rebellious barons), and married (in 1177) Joan, youngest daughter of Henry II of England, by whom he had no issue. On his death, at the age of 35, the crown of Sicily passed to his cousin Tancred, whose son and successor, William III, was dispossessed by the Emperor Henry VI, who, as Duke of Swabia, had married Constance, the aunt of William II, and heiress presumptive to the throne. The kingdom of the two Sicilies thus passed to the Hohenstaufen line, in the person of Frederick I (afterwards Emperor as Frederick II), the son of Henry VI and Constance. [Cicilia: Costanza [1]: Arrigo [5]: Table E.]

William II is placed in the Heaven of Jupiter among the spirits of those who loved and exercised justice (*Spiriti Giudicanti*), Par. xx. 62; *quel, v.* 61; *il giusto rege, v.* 65 [Giove, Cielo di]; the Eagle, who points out his spirit to D., and speaks of him as 'the just king', says that Sicily deplores William's death, and laments that Charles II of Anjou and Frederick II of Aragon are still alive (*vv.* 62–3) [Aquila [2]: Carlo [2]: Federico [3]].

Guglielmo [3], William VII (or V), surnamed Spadalunga ('Longsword'), Marquis of Montferrat and Canavese, 1254–1292. D. places him among the Negligent Princes, but in an inferior position as being of lower rank, in the valley of flowers in Ante-purgatory, Purg. vii. 133–6 [**Antipurgatorio**]; some think that he is 'il buono Marchese di Monferrato', who is commended for his liberality, Conv. iv. 11[126–7], but the reference is almost certainly to his ancestor, Boniface II [**Monferrato**].

William, who was the son of Boniface III, Marquis of Montferrat and titular King of Salonica (1225–1254), was twice married—first, in 1257, to Isabella, daughter of Richard Earl of Gloucester; secondly, in 1271, to Beatrice, daughter of Alphonso X of Castile, by whom he had a son John, who succeeded him (1292–1305) [**Johannes**[3]].

Shortly after his accession to power William took advantage of internal dissensions in several of the independent Lombard cities to reduce them to subjection. In 1264 he made an alliance with Charles I of Anjou and aided him in his descent into Italy, but he vigorously opposed him later, when Charles, after the defeat of Manfred and the conquest of Naples, attempted the subjugation of Lombardy. In 1281 William was at the head of a powerful Ghibelline league, several members of which, however, seceded in the following year and joined the Guelfs. In 1290, after having reduced the rebellious members of the league, he marched against Alessandria to quell a rising which had been fostered by the people of Asti, but he was taken prisoner by the Alessandrians, and placed in an iron cage, in which he died (Feb. 6, 1292), after having been exhibited like a wild beast for seventeen months. In order to avenge his death, his son and successor, John I, declared war against the Alessandrians, who replied by invading Montferrat—operations to which D. alludes, Purg. vii. 135–6 [**Alessandria**].

Guglielmo Aldobrandesco, Count of Santafiora in the Sienese Maremma [**Santafiora**]; mentioned by his son Omberto (in Circle I of Purgatory), Purg. xi. 59; *un gran Tosco*, v. 58.

Guglielmo, who belonged to one of the most powerful families in Tuscany, in 1221 submitted to the Sienese, but shortly after took up arms against them, and being taken prisoner was kept in confinement in Siena for six months. After his release he continued hostilities, having in the meanwhile allied himself with the Florentines, the hereditary foes of the Sienese, until 1237, when he came to terms with the latter. He died between 1253 and 1256, leaving two sons, the younger of whom, Omberto, became lord of Campagnatico, where he was murdered by the Sienese in 1259. [**Aldobrandeschi : Omberto.**]

Guglielmo Borsiere. [**Borsiere, Guglielmo.**]

Guglielmo Marchese. [**Guglielmo**[3].]

Guglielmo di Monferrato. [**Guglielmo**[3].]

Guglielmo di Nogaret], William of Nogaret, a French knight, minister of Philip the Fair, who, with Sciarra Colonna, led the attack upon Boniface VIII at Anagni; he and Sciarra are referred to by

Hugh Capet (in Circle V of Purgatory), in connexion with the death of Boniface, as *vivi ladroni*, Purg. xx. 90. [**Alagna.**]

Guidi, Conti, powerful family of Lombard origin, whose possessions lay chiefly in Tuscany and Romagna, frequently referred to in the *D. C.*; Cacciaguida (in the Heaven of Mars) speaks of them as *i Conti*, 'the Counts' *par excellence*, in connexion with their sale of the castle of Montemurlo to the Florentines, Par. xvi. 64 [**Montemurlo**]; and refers to the whole family under the name of an individual Count, *il Conte Guido*, in connexion with their descent from the Ravignani, Par. xvi. 98 [**Ravignani**]; Guido del Duca (in Circle II of Purgatory), in tracing the course of the Arno, alludes to the men of Casentino as *brutti porci*, with especial reference doubtless to the Conti Guidi, who were lords of Porciano, Purg. xiv. 43 [**Arno**]; individual members of the family referred to are Guido Guerra, Inf. xvi. 34–9 [**Guido Guerra**]; Aghinolfo da Romena, Inf. xxx. 77 [**Aghinolfo**]; Alessandro da Romena, Inf. xxx. 77 [**Alessandro**[1]]; Guido da Romena, Inf. xxx. 77 [**Guido**[3]]; Federico Novello da Battifolle, Purg. vi. 17 [**Federico Novello**]; Uberto and Guido da Romena, Epist. ii. *tit.* [**Guido da Romena**].

From Cent. xi to Cent. xiii the Guidi were one of the richest and most powerful families of Italy. They gradually extended their influence in every direction from their original possessions in the higher valleys of the Apennines, until they

were lords of nearly the whole of Romagna (Vill. iv. 1). In the Casentino they established their principal seats, in the castles of Poppi, Romena, and Porciano ; while other members of the family settled on the other side of the mountains, in the strongholds of Bagno and Montegranelli. They also possessed strong castles in the country of Dovadola and Modigliana. Their many castles and strongholds were of imposing size and solid in construction, as the numerous ruins still to be seen in the Casentino, the Val di Sieve, and Romagna testify.

In Cent. xiii the Guidi are found occupying important positions, such as podestà, captain of the people, imperial or papal vicar, and sometimes as Church dignitaries, not only in Romagna but also in the Tuscan towns of Pistoja, Arezzo, Pisa, and Florence.

Like almost all the Italian nobles of that time, who were principally of Lombard or German origin, the Guidi were for a long time loyal adherents of the Empire. As early as the latter part of the eleventh century, however, we find them closely allied with the great Countess Matilda of Tuscany, and hence siding with Gregory VII against Henry IV ; and in the thirteenth century we find them, especially the Romena branch of the family, constantly shifting from side to side, now Guelf, now Ghibelline.

The Conti Guidi traced their descent from Tegrimo, a Lombard, who was Count Palatine of Tuscany in Cent. x. A descendant of Tegrimo's in the eighth generation,

Guido Guerra IV, married (c. 1180) 'the good Gualdrada' (Inf. xvi. 37), daughter of Bellincion Berti de' Ravignani, from whom were descended the Conti Guidi of D.'s day [Bellincion Berti : Gualdrada]. This descent, which is referred to by Cacciaguida (Par. xvi. 97-9), was as follows :—Guido Guerra had five sons, one of whom, Ruggero, died in 1225 ; from the other four, Tegrimo, Aghinolfo, Guido, and Marcovaldo, descended the four different branches of the Guido family, which are distinguished by the names of their respective estates. From Tegrimo descended the Counts of Modigliana and Porciano, known as the Porciano line ; from Aghinolfo, the Counts of Romena ; from Guido, those of Bagno and Battifolle, known as the Bagno line ; and from Marcovaldo, those of Dovadola.

Guido [1]. [Cavalcanti, Guido.]
Guido [2]. [Cassero, Guido del.]
Guido [3], Guido da Romena, one of the Conti Guidi, who with his brothers, Alessandro and Aghinolfo, induced Maestro Adamo to counterfeit the Florentine gold florin, Inf. xxx. 77. [Adamo[2]: Guidi, Conti.]

Guido [4], name of two Italian poets, of whom Oderisi (in Circle I of Purgatory) says that one has eclipsed the fame of the other, *ha tolto l' uno all' altro Guido La gloria della lingua* (meaning, according to the most generally accepted interpretation, that Guido Cavalcanti, the Florentine poet, surpassed Guido Guinizelli, the Bolognese poet), Purg. xi. 97-8. [Cavalcanti, Guido: Guinizelli, Guido.]

Oderisi goes on to say that pos-sibly one (usually understood to be D. himself, though some think the reference to be indeterminate) was already born who would eclipse the fame of both the Guidi (*vv.* 98-9).

Guido Aretinus. [Guittone.]
Guido Bonatti. [Bonatti, Guido.]
Guido Cavalcanti. [Cavalcanti, Guido.]
Guido, Conte, one of the Conti Guidi, the singular being used for the plural to indicate the whole family, Par. xvi. 98; Son. lii. 14. [Guidi, Conti.]
Guido da Castel,-ello. [Castel, Guido da.]
Guido da Montefeltro. [Guido Montefeltrano.]
Guido da Polenta. [Polenta.]
Guido da Prata, native of Romagna, mentioned by Guido del Duca (in Circle II of Purgatory), together with Ugolino d'Azzo, among the former worthies of Romagna, Purg. xiv. 104.

Guido, who took his name from Prata (now Prada), a village in Romagna, between Forlì, Faenza, and Ravenna, about two miles S. of Russi, is mentioned in documents in the years 1184, 1222, 1225, and 1228, in which last year he was present with Arrigo Mainardi (Purg. xiv. 97) at a council in Ravenna ; he appears to have been a person of some importance in Ravenna, and to have been possessed of considerable landed property in the neighbourhood of that city; he died probably between 1235 and 1245.

Guido da Romena, one of the Conti Guidi of the Romena branch, to whom, and his elder brother

Uberto, D. addressed a letter on the death of their uncle Alessandro, Epist. ii. *tit.*

Uberto and Guido were the sons of Aghinolfo da Romena, who with his brothers Alessandro and Guido was implicated in the crime of forging the Florentine florin, for which Maestro Adamo suffered death (Inf. xxx. 46–90). [Adamo, Maestro: Guidi, Conti.]

Guido de Florentia. [Cavalcanti, Guido.]

Guido de Ghisileriis. [Ghisilerius, Guido.]

Guido del Cassero. [Cassero, Guido del.]

Guido del Duca, gentleman of Bertinoro, near Forlì, in Romagna, son of Giovanni del Duca of the Onesti family of Ravenna. The earliest mention of Guido occurs in a document dated May 4, 1199, in which he is described as holding the office of judge to the Podestà of Rimini. In 1202, and again in 1204, he is mentioned as playing an important part in the affairs of Romagna, both times in connexion with Pier Traversaro (Purg. xiv. 98), whose adherent he appears to have been. In 1218, Pier Traversaro, with the help of his Ghibelline friends, and especially of the Mainardi of Bertinoro, made himself master of Ravenna, and expelled the Guelfs from the city. The latter, in revenge, seized Bertinoro, destroyed the houses belonging to the Mainardi, and drove out all Piero's adherents; among them was Guido del Duca, who at this time apparently, together with his family, betook himself to Ravenna, his father's native place,

and resided there under the protection of Pier Traversaro. Some ten years later (in 1229) Guido's name appears as witness to a deed at Ravenna; he was still alive in 1249, in which year he is mentioned in a deed as holding land of the Traversari (at that time Guelfs).

D. places Guido (whom he represents as lamenting over the degeneracy of the men of Romagna, many of whose families he mentions by name), together with Rinieri da Calboli, among the Envious in Circle II of Purgatory, Purg. xiv. 81; *l'uno* (*spirto*), *vv.* 7, 10; *quei, v.* 24; *l'ombra, v.* 28; *l'una* (*anima*), *v.* 73; *lo spirto, v.* 76; *anima cara, v.* 127; *lo spirto di Romagna*, Purg. xv. 44 [Invidiosi].

Guido delle Colonne. [Colonne, Guido delle.]

Guido di Carpigna. [Carpigna, Guido di.]

Guido di Monforte], Guy de Montfort, son of Simon de Montfort, Earl of Leicester (who was killed at the battle of Evesham, Aug. 4, 1265), and Eleanor, daughter of King John of England. In revenge for his father's death, and for the indignities offered to his corpse, in 1271 Guy, at that time Vicar of Charles of Anjou in Tuscany, murdered his first cousin, Prince Henry 'of Almain', son of Richard, Earl of Cornwall, and King of the Romans, in the church of San Silvestro at Viterbo. For this atrocious crime, which is popularly believed to have been committed at the moment of the elevation of the Host, when Henry was on his knees, Guy was (1273) excommunicated and imprisoned by the Pope; he was subsequently (1283) pardoned and appointed captain-general of the Papal forces in Romagna; in 1287, while in the service of Charles of Anjou, he was captured by the Aragonese admiral, Ruggieri di Loria, and imprisoned in Sicily, where he died shortly after.

D. places Guy among the Murderers in Round I of Circle VII of Hell, where his shade is pointed out by Nessus, who, in allusion to his crime, says of him, *Colui fesse in grembo a Dio Lo cor che in sul Tamigi ancor si cola*, Inf. xii. 118–20. [Arrigo [6]: Omicide.]

Guido Florentinus. [Cavalcanti, Guido.]

Guido Ghisilerius. [Ghisilerius, Guido.]

Guido Guerra, one of the Conti Guidi of the Dovadola line, eldest son of Marcovaldo, the fourth son of Guido Guerra IV and of Gualdrada de' Ravignani. [Guidi, Conti.] Guido is one of the Florentines (the other two being Jacopo Rusticucci and Tegghiaio Aldobrandi) seen by D. among the Sodomites in Round 3 of Circle VII of Hell, Inf. xvi. 4 [Sodomiti]; he is named to D. by Jacopo Rusticucci, who describes him as the grandson of the good Gualdrada, and praises both his wisdom and his valour, *vv*. 34–9 [Gualdrada].

This Guido Guerra was a zealous Guelf, although his family before him appear to have belonged to the Imperial party. He was one of those who attempted to dissuade the Florentine Guelfs from undertaking the disastrous expedition against Siena in 1260, which resulted in the defeat at Montaperti, and the ruin of the Guelf party in Florence [Aldobrandi, Tegghiaio]. In consequence of this reverse the Guelfs fled from Florence and took refuge in Romagna, where Guido acted as their leader. At the battle of Benevento (1266⅚) his troop of Florentine and Tuscan Guelfs did good service on behalf of Charles of Anjou, and materially contributed to the defeat of Manfred. After the restoration of the Guelfs to Florence, Guido held various offices in that city; he died in 1272 at Montevarchi in the Valdarno.

Guido Guinizelli, the most illustrious of the Italian poets prior to D., belonged to the family of the Principi of Bologna, in which city he was born c. 1230. In 1270 he was Podestà of Castelfranco; in 1274, when the Ghibelline Lambertazzi were expelled from Bologna, Guido with the rest of the Principi, who belonged to the same party, was forced to leave his native city; he is said to have died in exile at Verona in 1276.

Guido Guinizelli, who at first was a great admirer of Guittone d'Arezzo, but afterwards condemned him (cf. Purg. xxvi. 124–6), belonged to the school of Bolognese poets, which included Fabruzzo de' Lambertazzi, Guido Ghisilieri, and Onesto Bolognese; and from him sprang subsequently the illustrious school of the 'dolce stil nuovo' (Purg. xxiv. 57), the school of Lapo Gianni, Guido Cavalcanti, Cino da Pistoja, and of Dante himself, who acknowledges Guido as his father, Purg. xxvi. 97–9.

The extant poems of Guido Guinizelli, several of which are quoted by D., consist of *canzoni*, sonnets, and *ballate*, dealing for the most part with love, some being of a satiric turn.

D. places Guido among the Lustful in Circle VII of Purgatory, Purg. xxvi. 92 ; *un* (*spirito*), *v.* 25 ; *colei* (*anima*), *v.* 74 ; *il padre mio*, *v.* 97 [**Lussuriosi**] ; in conversation with D. Guido names himself, whereupon D. expresses his grief at finding him there, and calls him his father, and after gazing at him fondly offers to serve him as he can (*vv.* 94–105) ; Guido, touched by D.'s affectionate expressions, asks the reason of his love for himself (*vv.* 106–11) ; D., in reply, refers to his admiration for Guido's poems (*vv.* 112–14) ; Guido rejoins that Arnaut Daniel was a better poet than himself, and adds that the reputation of Giraut de Borneil was exaggerated, as had been that of Guittone d'Arezzo (*vv.* 115–26) [**Arnaut Daniel : Gerardus de Borneil : Guittone**].

Guido is several times mentioned in D.'s other works ; he is spoken of as *quel nobile Guido Guinizelli*, Conv. iv. 20[67] ; *dominus Guido Guinizelli*, V. E. i. 9[28] ; *maximus G. G.*, V. E. i. 15[41–2] ; *maximus Guido*, V. E. i. 15[47] ; and simply named, V. E. ii. 5[41], 6[66] ; he is referred to as *il Saggio*, Son. x. 2 (V. N. § 20[14]) ; and, according to the most general interpretation, as *l'altro Guido*, Purg. xi. 97 [**Guido**[4]] ; ranked by D. below Arnaut Daniel, Purg. xxvi.

115–17 ; his saying that ' love and the gentle heart are one ', Son. x. 1–2 (V. N. § 20[13–14]) ; that an imperfect gem cannot receive the celestial virtue, Conv. iv. 20[64–7] ; coupled with Guido Ghisilieri, Fabruzzo de' Lambertazzi, and Onesto Bolognese, as having rejected the Bolognese dialect, V. E. i. 15[41–52] ; his employment of the endecasyllabic line, an example being quoted, V. E. ii. 5[41–2] ; his *canzoni* written in the most illustrious style, the first line of one of them being quoted, V. E. ii. 6[66–7] ; his *canzone*, ' Al cor gentil ripara sempre Amore ', quoted, Conv. iv. 20[64–9] ; V. E. i. 9[28–30] ; ii. 5[42] ; and alluded to, Son. x. 1–2 (V. N. § 20[13–14]) ; Inf. v. 100 ; his *canzone* (now lost), ' Madonna, il fermo core ', V. E. i. 15[48] ; his *canzone*, ' Tegno di folle impresa allo ver dire ', V. E. ii. 6[67].

Guido Maximus. [**Guido Guinizelli.**]

Guido Montefeltrano, Guido, Count of Montefeltro, the great Ghibelline captain, called by Villani ' il più sagace e il più sottile uomo di guerra ch' al suo tempo fosse in Italia ' (vii. 80), was born c. 1220. In 1268 he was Conradin's vicar in Rome; in 1274 he was captain of Forlì, and in the next year was appointed captain-general of the Ghibellines of Romagna. In June 1275 at the head of the combined forces of the Ghibellines of Romagna and the exiled Ghibellines of Bologna and Florence he won a decisive victory at Ponte san Procolo, between Faenza and Imola, over the Guelfs with the Geremei of Bologna under Malatesta da Rimini. In September of the same year he again defeated the Guelfs at Reversano near Cesena, and took possession of the latter town, whence he expelled Malatesta, and of Cervia. In 1276 he besieged and took Bagnacavallo. In 1282 he held Forlì against the French troops of Martin IV, on whom he inflicted severe loss (Inf. xxvii. 44) [**Forlì**]; but in the following year he was driven out by the inhabitants, who had come to terms with the Pope, and nearly the whole of Romagna submitted to the Church. In 1286 Guido himself made his submission to the Pope (Honorius IV), and was reconciled to the Church, but was banished to Piedmont. About three years later, however, having been elected captain of the Pisan Ghibellines, he returned from exile and went to Pisa, where his arrival was followed by the murder of Count Ugolino; for this act of disobedience the Pope excommunicated him and his family, and laid Pisa under an interdict. Under his leadership the Pisans gained some successes against the Florentines, including the capture of Pontadera in 1291. In 1292 he made himself master of Urbino, which he held and defended against Malatestino of Rimini, at that time Podestà of Cesena. In 1294 he was once more reconciled to the Church, and received absolution from Celestine V; and in 1296 he joined the Franciscan order (Inf. xxvii. 67). In the following year he was induced by Boniface VIII to leave his retirement in order to give him advice as to the reduction of the stronghold of Palestrina, which the Colonna family was hold-

ing against him, the advice being, 'lunga promessa con l'attender corto' i. e. promise freely, but perform little (Inf. xxvii. 110), by which means the fortress was taken [**Colonnesi**].

Guido (whose son Buonconte was killed at the battle of Campaldino in 1289, while fighting on the Ghibelline side) died in September, 1298, at the age of 75, in the Franciscan monastery at Assisi, where he was buried.

D. places Guido, on account of his wicked advice to Pope Boniface, among the Counsellors of evil in Bolgia 8 of Circle VIII of Hell (Malebolge), Inf. xxvii. 4–132; *un' altra* (*fiamma*), *v.* 4; *fuoco, v.* 14; *questi, v.* 33; *anima, v.* 36; *fuoco, v.* 58; *fiamma, vv.* 63, 131; *questi, v.* 127; in response to D.'s request, Guido gives a brief account of his life upon earth, and relates how he became a Franciscan monk in the hope of making amends for his past crimes, and how he was led once more into sin by Boniface VIII, to whom he gave the treacherous advice as to the capture of Palestrina (*vv.* 58–111); he concludes by describing how after his death St. Francis came for his soul, which was claimed and carried off to Hell by one of the 'black cherubim' (*vv.* 112–23) [**Consiglieri Frodolenti**]; he is coupled with Lancelot, as having, like him, devoted himself to religion at the end of his days, *Guido Montefeltrano*, Conv. iv. 28[59–65] [**Lancilotto**].

The incident of Guido's interview with Boniface VIII, and his advice as to how the Pope might get Palestrina into his hands, described by D.

(Inf. xxvii. 85–111), is related also by contemporary chroniclers—by Villani, who follows D. (viii. 23), and by Pipino, who, writing in 1314, and apparently independently of D., gives Guido's advice as 'plurima eis pollicemini, pauca observate'.

Guido Novello da Polenta. [Polenta.]

Guido Vecchio da Polenta. [Polenta.]

Guidoguerra. [Guido Guerra.]
Guiglielmo. [Guglielmo.]
Guinicelli. [Guinizelli.]
Guinizelli, Guido. [Guido Guinizelli.]

Guiscardo, Roberto, Robert Guiscard, Duke of Apulia and Calabria, was born at Hauteville, near Coutances in Normandy, c. 1015. While still a youth he left his father's castle and went to Apulia, where he gradually won his way with his sword. On the death of his brother Humphrey in 1057, Robert, who had earned the nickname of Guiscard (i.e. Cunning), succeeded to the chief command of the Norman troops. In 1059 he was confirmed by Pope Nicholas II in the title of Duke of Apulia and Calabria, and was at the same time appointed Gonfalonier of the Church. For the next 21 years he was continually engaged in warlike operations against the Greeks and Saracens in the S. of Italy and in Sicily. In 1084, Pope Gregory VII, his suzerain, being besieged in Rome by the Emperor Henry IV, Robert captured the city and rescued the Pope. He died in the following year of pestilence in the island of Cephalonia (July 17, 1085).

D. mentions Robert Guiscard in connexion with his conquest of Apulia, Inf. xxviii. 14 [Puglia]; he is placed, together with Godfrey of Bouillon, among the Christian warriors who have fought for the faith (*Spiriti Militanti*), in the Heaven of Mars, Par. xviii. 48 [Marte, Cielo di].

Guitto Aretinus. [Guittone.]

Guittone, Guittone del Viva, more commonly known as Fra Guittone d'Arezzo, one of the earliest Italian poets, was born c. 1240 at Santa Firmina, about two miles from Arezzo. But little is known of the details of his life, a great part of which was spent in Florence, where D. may have known him. About the year 1266 Guittone, who was married and had a family, entered the Order of the Frati Gaudenti [Frati Gaudenti]. In 1293 he helped to found the monastery of Sta. Maria degli Angeli at Florence, in which city he appears to have died in the following year.

Guittone was the head of an influential school of poetry, which numbered adherents in Florence, Siena, Lucca, and Pisa; among the last being the Gallo of Pisa mentioned by D. (V. E. i. 13[9]) [Gallus Pisanus]. In his earlier days the celebrated Bolognese poet, Guido Guinizelli, was an admirer of Guittone, but he subsequently severely condemned his poetical methods. Guittone's style is obscure and artificial, and reveals unmistakeable traces of Provençal influence. He is usually credited with having first brought the Italian sonnet to the perfect form which it has since preserved. His letters, one of which is addressed to Marzucco degli Scornigiani of Pisa (Purg. vi. 18), to whom he also addressed a *canzone* [**Marzucco**], are among the earliest examples of literary Italian prose.

D. speaks disparagingly of Guittone each time he mentions him; *Guittone*, Purg. xxiv. 56; xxvi. 124; *Guitto Aretinus*, V. E. i. 13[7]; *Guido Aretinus*, V. E. ii. 6[86-7]; Bonagiunta of Lucca is represented (in Circle VI of Purgatory) as condemning G., together with himself and Jacopo da Lentino, for the artificiality of their style, as compared with that of the school to which D. belonged, Purg. xxiv. 55-60 [**Bonagiunta**]; Guido Guinizelli (in Circle VII of Purgatory) refuses to admit G.'s claim to the first place among Italian poets which his contemporaries had assigned to him, Purg. xxvi. 124-6 [**Guido Guinizelli**]; he is blamed, together with Bonagiunta, Brunetto Latini, and other Tuscan poets, for having written in the local dialect, to the exclusion of the 'curial vulgar tongue', V. E. i. 13[7-13]; his style condemned as being plebeian in vocabulary and construction, V. E. ii. 6[85-9]; it is probably to him in particular that D. alludes in the *Vita Nuova*, where he speaks of 'quelli che così rimano stoltamente', § 25[113].

Guizzante, mediaeval port of Wissant, between Calais and Cape Grisnez, in what was formerly part of Flanders. It was a place of great importance in the Middle Ages, as being the port through which passed the bulk of the traffic between England and the Continent.

D. compares the embankment on the borders of the river Phlegethon in Hell to the dykes built by the Flemings along the sea-coast between Wissant and Bruges (these two points indicating respectively the W. and E. limits of the Flemish coast, according to the then boundaries of Flanders), Inf. xv. 4-6. [**Bruggia.**]

H

Hadrianus. [**Adrianus.**]

Hamericus, mistake for *Namericus* of the MSS., representing the Provençal *Naimerics* (i.e. *En Aimerics*), V. E. ii. 6[62, 64], 12[22]. [**Namericus.**]

Hannibal. [**Annibale.**]

Harnaldus Daniel. [**Arnaut.**]

Heber, patriarch Heber (called Eber in A. V.) great-grandson of Shem (*Gen.* x. 21-4; xi. 11-14); the Hebrews named from him, and from him got the Hebrew language, which they alone retained after the confusion of tongues (a statement for which D. appears to have been indebted to Vincent of Beauvais, *Spec. Hist.* i. 62), V. E. i. 6[53-6] [**Ebrei : Ebreo**].

Hebraei. [**Ebrei.**]

Hebraeos, Epistola ad, St. Paul's Epistle to the Hebrews, Mon. ii.

8^{36}; quoted, Par. xxiv. 64–5 (*Heb.* xi. 1); Conv. ii. 6^6 (*Heb.* i. 1); Mon. ii. 8^{35-7} (*Heb.* xi. 6).

Hebraicus. [Ebreo.]

Hector. [Ettore.]

Hectoreus, pertaining to Hector; epithet applied by D. in sense of Trojan (and hence, in his view, Roman) to the Emperor Henry VII, *Hectoreus pastor*, Epist. v. 5^{86} [Ettore].

Helena, St. Helena, wife of Constantius Chlorus, by whom she had one son, Constantine the Great. When her son was converted to Christianity, she followed his example. Shortly before her death she made a pilgrimage to Jerusalem, where she is said to have discovered the true Cross, in honour of which she founded the Church of the Holy Sepulchre. She died at the age of 80, c. 328, and, having been a zealous patron and protector of the Christian religion, was reverenced as a saint and subsequently canonized.

In the chapel dedicated to St. Helena at Verona, D. is said to have made public the treatise ascribed to him under the title of *Quaestio de Aqua et Terra*, A. T. § 24^6. [Quaestio.]

It is probably after St. Helena that the coins denominated *Santeléne* (Conv. iv. 11^{80}) were named. [Santeléna.]

Helias. [Elia.]

Helicon. [Elicona.]

Hellespontus. [Ellesponto.]

Henricus. [Arrigo ^{2}.]

Henricus de Segusia. [Ostiensis.]

Hercules. [Ercole.]

Herodes. [Erode.]

Hesperia, Western land, name given by the Greeks to Italy because

it lay W. of Greece; Virgil's use of the name (*Aen.* iii. 163) quoted, Mon. ii. 3^{80}; the Emperor Henry VII spoken of as 'delirantis Hesperiae domitor', Epist. vi. 3^{87}. [Italia.]

Hesperus, the evening star; Aristotle's saying (*Eth.* v. 1), that neither the evening nor the morning star is so admirable as justice, quoted, Mon. i. 11^{31-4}.

Hieremias. [Geremia.]

Hierusalem. [Gerusalemme.]

Hippomenes, son of Megareus, and great-grandson of Neptune, who by the assistance of Venus managed to outstrip Atalanta in a race and so won her hand; this contest is referred to, Mon. ii. 8^{84}. [Atalanta.]

Hispani. [Ispani.]

Hohenstaufen], the house of Hohenstaufen or Swabia, so called from their hereditary family seat, the Castle of Staufen or Hohenstaufen at the outlet of the Swabian Alps. There were five Emperors of this line— Conrad III (1138–1152) [Currado ^{1}]; Frederick I, Barbarossa (1152–1190) [Federico ^{1}]; Henry VI (1190–1197) [Arrigo ^{5}]; Frederick II (1212–1250) [Federico ^{2}]; and Conrad IV (1250–1254) [Soave: Table H].

Homerus. [Omero.]

Honestus Bononiensis, Onesto Bolognese (Onesto di Bonacosa degli Onesti), Bolognese poet of the school of Guido Guinizelli; he was a native of Bologna, where he became a doctor of laws, and was living as late as September, 1301. He appears to have been a friend of Cino da Pistoja, with whom he carried on a poetical correspondence. A few of his poems are extant. D., who speaks of him simply as 'Honestus Bononiae', couples him with Guido Guinizelli, Guido Ghisilieri, and Fabruzzo de' Lambertazzi, as having rejected the Bolognese dialect in his writings, in proof of which he quotes a line of one of his *canzoni* (now lost), V. E. i. 15^{51} [Guido Guinizelli].

Horatii, one of the most ancient patrician families at Rome, three brothers of which fought with the three Alban Curiatii, in the reign of Tullus Hostilius, to determine whether Rome or Alba was to be mistress. After a long and doubtful fight victory finally rested with the champions of Rome.

The fight of 'i tre ai tre' is alluded to by the Emperor Justinian (in the Heaven of Mercury), Par. vi. 39; the victory of the Horatii is mentioned, Mon. ii. 11^{30} [Curiatii].

Horatius. [Orazio.]

Hostilius, Tullus Hostilius, third King of Rome; during his reign the struggle for supremacy between Rome and Alba was finally decided in favour of the former, her cham-pions, the three Horatii, having been victorious in the combat with the three Alban Curiatii. D. mentions him as the third of the Roman kings, calling him *Tullo,* Conv. iv. 5^{90}; the defeat of Alba and final triumph of Rome in his reign, *Hostilius,* Mon. ii. 11$^{35-6}$. [Alba : Curiatii.]

Hydra, the Lernaean Hydra, a monster which ravaged the country of Lerna, near Argos; it had nine heads, of which the central one was immortal. Hercules cut off its heads, but for every head he cut off, two fresh ones sprang up; finally he destroyed the heads with fire, and buried the immortal one under a rock.

D. calls upon the Emperor Henry VII to come and crush his opponents in Italy, as Hercules did the Hydra, by striking at the 'seat of life' (i.e. Florence), Epist. vii. 6$^{113-21}$. [Arrigo^2.]

Hyperion. [Iperione.]

Hyrcanus, of Hyrcania, a province of the ancient Persian Empire, on the S. and SE. shores of the Caspian or Hyrcanian Sea; *Hyrcanae tigres,* Ecl. ii. 22.

I

I^1, letter I; D. says neither O nor I was ever written in such a short time as it took for Vanni Fucci to be turned into ashes after being stung by a serpent (in Bolgia 7 of Malebolge), Inf. xxiv. 100; the second letter of the word *Diligite* formed by the spirits of the Just in the Heaven of Jupiter, Par. xviii. 78 [Aquila ^{2}: Giove, Cielo di].

I^2, number I; the Eagle, speaking in the Heaven of Jupiter, says that the good qualities of Charles II of Anjou might be indicated by an I (one), his bad ones by an M (thousand), Par. xix. 127-9. [Carlo^2.]

I^3 (or *J*), appellation of God, Par. xxvi. 134 (where many MSS. and edd., taking *I* to be the numeral, read *Un*). [El.]

Ia-. [Ja-.]

Iarba, Iarbas, son of Jupiter Ammon by a Libyan nymph, King of the Gaetulians in N. Africa at the time that Dido founded Carthage; hence D. speaks of Africa (or, as some think, Numidia) as *la terra di Iarba*, Purg. xxxi. 72. [**Affrica**: **Numidia**.]

Ibéro. [**Ebro**.]

Icaro, Icarus, son of Daedalus, who, while attempting to fly by means of the wings provided him by his father, approached too near the sun; the heat having melted the wax with which his wings were fastened, he fell into the sea and was drowned. Icarus (whose story D. got from Ovid, *Metam.* viii. 200 ff.) is mentioned in connexion with this incident, Inf. xvii. 109; he is alluded to as the son of Daedalus, *il figlio*, Par. viii. 126. [**Dedalo**.]

Ice, the last syllables of the name *Beatrice*, Par. vii. 14. [**Be**.]

Ida[1], Mt. Ida in Crete, on which Rhea is said to have given birth to Jupiter, Inf. xiv. 98; *montagna*, v. 98; *il monte*, v. 103; D. refers to the birth of Jupiter, and to the artifice by which Rhea saved his life (*vv.* 100-2) [**Rea**]; he then describes how within the mountain stands the image of a great elder, 'il veglio di Creta' (*vv.*103-5) [**Creta**].

Ida[2], mountain range in Mysia, in Asia Minor, celebrated in mythology as the scene of the rape of Ganymede (*Aen.* v. 254-5), in which connexion D. refers to it, Purg. ix. 22-4. [**Ganimede**.]

Iddio. [**Dio**.]

Idra. [**Hydra**.]

Ie-. [**Je-**.]

Ifigénia, Iphigenia, daughter of Agamemnon and Clytaemnestra. In consequence of A.'s having killed a hart in the sacred grove of Artemis, the goddess in anger sent a pestilence on the Greek army, and caused a calm which prevented the Greek fleet in Aulis from sailing against Troy. On the advice of Calchas the seer, A. proceeded to sacrifice Iphigenia, in order to appease the wrath of the goddess (*Aen.* ii. 116-19). D. adopts the version according to which A. vowed to the goddess the fairest thing born in his realm during the year, which turned out to be his own daughter, Iphigenia. She is mentioned in connexion with the vow of Agamemnon, Par. v. 67-72 (cf. Cicero, *De Officiis*, iii. 25) [**Agamemnone**: **Calcanta**].

Ildebrandino de' Mezzabati. [**Ildebrandinus Paduanus**.]

Ildebrandinus Paduanus, Ildebrandino or Aldobrandino de' Mezzabati, jurist and judge of Padua, of whom notices exist in records ranging from 1275 to 1297; Aldobrandino, who was Capitano del Popolo in Florence from May 1291 to May 1292, wrote (probably during his year of office in Florence) a sonnet in reply to D.'s sonnet, 'Per quella via' (Son. xliv), in which a certain Lisetta (whom A. defends) is represented as seeking to win D.'s love, and as being dismissed with shame [**Lisetta**]. Besides this sonnet (which has been preserved in two MSS.), two *ballate* in a Vatican MS. have been attributed to Aldobrandino. D., who calls him *Ildebrandinus Paduanus*, says that he alone of the writers of Venetia attempted to write in the ' curial vulgar tongue', instead of in his own local dialect, V. E. i. 14[43].

Ilerda, now Lerida, on the Serge, capital of the province of the same name, in Catalonia in NE. corner of Spain. Caesar here defeated (B. C. 49) Pompey's lieutenants, Afranius and Petreius. On his way to Lerida he besieged Marseilles, leaving there part of his army under Brutus to complete the task. Lucan, who was D.'s authority for this campaign (*Phars.* iii–iv), likens Caesar to a thunderbolt (*Phars.* i. 151–4). [**Cesare**[1].]

The Slothful in Circle IV of Purgatory proclaim Caesar's haste to subdue Lerida as an example of alacrity, Purg. xviii. 101–2. [**Accidiosi.**]

Iliacus, Trojan; the expression *Iliaca urbs* (i.e. Troy), quoted from Virgil (*Aen.* viii. 134), Mon. ii. 3[73]. [**Troia.**]

Iliade], Homer's *Iliad*; quoted by D. at second-hand from Aristotle, V. N. § 2[51-2] (*Il.* xxiv. 258–9); Conv. iv. 20[37] (*Il.* xxiv. 258–9); Mon. i. 10[29-31] (*Il.* ii. 204); Mon. ii. 3[55] (*Il.* xxiv. 258–9). [**Omero.**]

Ilion, Ilium, one of the names of the city of Troy, from its founder, Ilus, son of Tros and great-grandson of Dardanus; it being called Troy (*Troja*) after Tros, father of the founder.

D., in imitation of Virgil (*Aen.* iii. 2–3), speaks of Troy as *il superbo Ilion,* Inf. i. 75 [**Troia**]; fallen Ilium figures among the examples of defeated pride represented in Circle I of Purgatory, Purg. xii. 62 [**Superbi**].

Ilioneus, one of the Trojans who accompanied Aeneas when he left Troy for Italy. During the storm raised by Aeolus at the request of Juno, he and some of his companions get separated from Aeneas, and reaching land arrive at Carthage without him. Ilioneus, as the senior, acts as spokesman and begs for Dido's protection (*Aen.* i. 76–560).

D. quotes his description of Aeneas (*Aen.* i. 544–5) as a proof of the nobility of the latter, Mon. ii. 3[44-7]. [**Enea.**]

Illuminato, Illuminato da Rieti, lord of Rocca Accarina, between Spoleto and Rieti, one of the earliest followers of St. Francis of Assisi, whom he accompanied into Egypt. He was appointed Bishop of Assisi in 1273, and died before March 1282.

D. places him, together with the Franciscan Augustine, among the Spirits who loved wisdom (*Spiriti Sapienti*), in the Heaven of the Sun, where they are named by St. Bonaventura, Par. xii. 130. [**Sole, Cielo del.**]

Imola], town in the Emilia (in the old Romagna), on the Santerno, about midway on the road between Bologna and Forlì; D. alludes to it as *la città di Santerno,* and informs Guido da Montefeltro, in answer to his inquiry as to the condition of Romagna, that both it and *la città di Lamone* (i.e. Faenza) are under the lordship of Mainardo Pagano, Inf. xxvii. 49–51 [**Mainardo**].

Imolenses, inhabitants of Imola; influence of their dialect on that of Bologna, which derived thence its smoothness and softness, V. E. i. 15[5, 15].

Imolesi. [**Imolenses.**]
Imperadore. [**Imperatore.**]

Imperatore[1], Emperor of the Roman Empire, Purg. x. 76; Conv. iv. 4[74]; *Cesare*, Par. vi. 86; *Caesar*, Mon. ii. 13[47]; iii. 13[44, 47, 50, 53]; Epist. v. 10[159]; *Comandatore del Roman Popolo*, Conv. iv. 5[64]; *Monarcha*, Mon. i. 16[11]; *Romano Principato*, Purg. x. 74; *Princeps Romanorum*, Mon. ii. 9[92]; *Principe del Roman Popolo*, Conv. iv. 5[63]. [**Imperatori**[1].]

Imperatore[2], Emperor of Constantinople, Par. xx. 57; Mon. iii. 11[6]; *Cesare*, Par. vi. 10. [**Imperatori**[2].]

Imperatore[3], Emperor of the Holy Roman Empire, Purg. vii. 94; Par. xv. 139; Conv. iv. 3[32, 39], 9[3], 91, 101, 154, 10[44]; *Imperator*, Mon. iii. 10[35, 40, 79—90, 124], 11[9, 18], 12[10—102]; *Imperator Romanorum*, Mon. iii. 11[9]; *Monarcha Romanus*, Mon. iii. 1[38]; *Augusto*, Inf. xiii. 68; *Augustus*, Epist. v. 2[27], 3[45—6]; vii. *tit.*, 4[76]; *Cesare*, Inf. xiii. 65; Purg. vi. 92, 114; Par. i. 29; vi. 10; xvi. 59; *Caesar*, V. E. i. 12[21]; Mon. iii. 16[135]; Epist. v. 2[28], 3[38], 5[91], 9[152]; vi. 5[131], *fin.*; vii. 1[15], 4[82]; *Curator Orbis*, Mon. iii. 16[88]; *Duce del mondo*, Par. xx. 8; *Nocchiere (della nave della umana compagnia)*, Conv. iv. 4[65]; *Principe*, Conv. iv. 4[36], 5[29], 100, 8[25]; *Romano Principe*, Conv. iv. 4[85]; *Romanus Princeps*, Mon. ii. 1[27], 9[91—2]; iii. 1[37], 14[2], 16[89]; Epist. v. 7[116—17]; vi. 2[31]. [**Imperatori**[3].]

Imperatori[1], Emperors of the Roman Empire [**Table Q i**]; the following are mentioned or alluded to by D :—Julius Caesar (regarded by D. as the first Roman Emperor) [**Cesare**[1]]; Augustus (B.C. 27—A.D. 14)

[**Augusto**[2]]; Tiberius (A. D. 14—37) [**Tiberio**]; Nero (A.D. 54—68) [**Nerone**]; Titus (A.D. 79—81) [**Tito**]; Domitian (A.D. 81—96) [**Domiziano**]; Trajan (A. D. 98—117) [**Traiano**]; Constantine (A. D. 306—337) [**Costantino**].

Imperatori[2], Emperors of Constantinople [**Table Q ii, iv**]; the following are mentioned or alluded to by D. :—Constantine (removed the seat of Empire to Byzantium, A. D. 330) [**Costantino: Greco**[1]]; Justinian (A.D. 527—565) [**Giustiniano**]; Michael I (A. D. 811—813) [**Michael**].

Imperatori[3], Emperors of the West (after 1155 of the Holy Roman Empire) [**Table Q iii**]; the following are mentioned or alluded to by D. :— Charlemagne (800—814) [**Carlo Magno**]; Otto I (962—973) [**Otto**]; Henry II (1002—1024) [**Arrigo**[3]]; Conrad III (1138—1152) [**Currado**[1]]; Frederick I (1152—1190) [**Federico**[1]]; Henry VI (1190—1198) [**Arrigo**[5]]; Frederick II (1212—1250) [**Federico**[2]]; Rudolf I (1272—1292) [**Ridolfo**[1]]; Adolf (1292—1298) [**Adolfo**]; Albert I (1298—1308) [**Alberto**[2]]; Henry VII (1308—1314) [**Arrigo**[2]].

Imperio Romano, the Roman Empire, Conv. iv. 4[126], 5[52, 154]; *Romanum Imperium*, Mon. ii. 1[53], 4[23, 27], 5[41], 11[5], 13[1, 48]; *Romana res*, Mon. ii. 4[60], 11[62]; Epist. vi. 6[180].

From Augustus to Constantine (B.C. 27—A.D. 323) the seat of Empire was at Rome. In the year 330 Constantine transferred it to Byzantium, thenceforward called after him Constantinople, which remained as the seat of the whole Empire for the next sixty-five years. On the death of Theodosius I in 395 the Empire was divided, his eldest son Arcadius becoming Emperor of the East (395–408), while his second son Honorius became Emperor of the West (395–423). The Western Line came to an end with Romulus Augustulus in 476 ; from which time, down to the coronation of Charlemagne by Pope Leo III at Rome in 800, the Emperors reigned at Constantinople. With Charlemagne (Charles I) began the new Western Line of the Roman Empire (which under Frederick I, Barbarossa, began to be known as the Holy Roman Empire); and thenceforward the Roman Empire in the West and the Byzantine Empire in the East remained independent of each other. [**Romani**[1]: **Romani**[2].]

Importuni, ancient noble family of Florence, mentioned by Cacciaguida (in the Heaven of Mars), together with the Gualterotti, as having been of importance in his day, and as having had the Buondelmonti as their neighbours in the Borgo sant' Apostolo, Par. xvi. 133–5. Both families, who were Guelfs (Vill. v. 39), had fallen into decay in D.'s time.

Indi, inhabitants of India; inhabit a thirsty land, Purg. xxvi. 21 [**Indo**[1]]; would have marvelled at the height of the mystic tree in the Terrestrial Paradise (cf. *Georg.* ii. 122–4), Purg. xxxii. 41–2 ; the eclipse of the Sun at the Crucifixion visible equally to them, and to the inhabitants of Spain, and to the Jews at Jerusalem (i. e. to the whole inhabited world), Par. xxix. 101–2 [**Gerusalemme**].

India, India; mentioned in connexion with the marvellous rain of fire which fell on Alexander the Great and his host during their Indian campaign, Inf. xiv. 32. [**Alessandro**[2].]

Indico, Indian; in describing the various colours of the flowers in the flowery valley in Ante-purgatory, D. mentions *Indico legno lucido e sereno*, Purg. vii. 74 ; the precise meaning of *indico legno* is doubtful, but most commentators are agreed that some shade of blue is indicated.

Indo[1], inhabitant of India; his longing for cold water on account of the heat of his native land, Purg. xxvi. 21. [**Indi**.]

Indo[2], river Indus; mentioned by D. to indicate India itself, as the extreme E. limit of the habitable world, Par. xix. 71 [**Gerusalemme**].

Indovini], Soothsayers, placed among the Fraudulent in Bolgia 4 of Circle VIII of Hell (Malebolge), Inf. xx [**Frodolenti**]; their punishment is to go slowly round and round in silence and weeping, walking backwards because their heads are twisted so that they cannot see in front of them, Inf. xx. 7–15 ; since in their lifetime they tried to see too far in advance, now they have to look and walk backwards (*vv.* 37–9). *Examples* : Amphiaraus [**Anfiarao**]; Tiresias [**Tiresia**]; Aruns [**Aronta**]; Manto [**Manto**]; Eurypylus [**Euripilo**]; Michael Scot [**Michele Scotto**]; Guido Bonatti [**Bonatti**]; Asdente [**Asdente**].

Infangato, name of an ancient Florentine, mentioned, as representing the Infangati family, by Cacciaguida (in the Heaven of Mars), who speaks of him as having been a good citizen in his day, Par. xvi. 123.

The Infangati lived in San Piero Scheraggio, and were Ghibellines, and as such were expelled from Florence in 1258 (Vill. v. 39; vi. 65).

Infernali Fiumi. [**Fiumi Infernali.**]

Inferno [1], Hell, the abode of the damned, Inf. i. 110; iii. 41; v. 10; vi. 40, 84; viii. 75; x. 36; xii. 35; xvi. 33; xviii. 1; xxv. 13; xxvi. 3; xxviii. 50; xxix. 96; xxxiv. 1, 81; Purg. i. 129; v. 104; vii. 21; xv. 1; xxi. 32; xxii. 14; Par. vi. 74; xx. 106; xxxi. 81; xxxii. 33; Canz. i. 27; Conv. iv. 26[73]; *Infernus*, Inf. xxxiv. 1; Epist. x. 10[221]; alluded to as *luogo eterno*, Inf. i. 114; *città dolente*, Inf. iii. 1; *valle d'abisso dolorosa*, Inf. iv. 8; *mondo cieco*, Inf. iv. 13; xxvii. 25; *abisso*, Inf. iv. 24; xi. 5; xxxiv. 100; Purg. i. 46; *doloroso ospizio*, Inf. v. 16; *il cupo*, Inf. vii. 10; *terra sconsolata*, Inf. viii. 77; *regno della morta gente*, Inf. viii. 85, 90; *buia contrada*, Inf. viii. 93; *mondo basso*, Inf. viii. 108; *trista conca*, Inf. ix. 16; *cieco carcere*, Inf. x. 59; Purg. xxii. 103; *baratro*, Inf. xi. 69; *valle buia*, Inf. xii. 86; *luoghi bui*, Inf. xvi. 82; xxiv. 141; *mal mondo*, Inf. xix. 11; *eterno esilio*, Inf. xxiii. 126; Purg. xxi. 18; *gola fera*, Inf. xxiv. 123; *mondo gramo*, Inf. xxx. 59; *fondo d'ogni reo*, Inf. xxxi. 102; *doloroso regno*, Inf. xxxiv. 28; *mare crudele*, Purg. i. 3; *prigione eterna*, Purg. i. 41; *profonda notte*, Purg. i. 44; xxiii. 122; *valle inferna*, Purg. i. 45; *dolente regno*, Purg. vii. 22; *luoghi tristi*, Purg. viii. 58; *ambascia infernale*, Purg. xvi. 39; Par. xxvi. 133; *valle ove mai non si scolpa*, Purg. xxiv. 84; *mondo defunto*, Par. xvii. 21; *mondo amaro*, Par. xvii. 112; *valle dolorosa*, Par. xvii. 137; (*vita amara*), Par. xx. 48; *infima lacuna Dell' universo*, Par. xxxiii. 22.

The Hell of Dante consists of nine concentric Circles (*cerchi*, Inf. iv. 24; v. 1; vi. 7; vii. 31, 35, 44, 100; viii. 129; ix. 27; xi. 28, 57, 64; xii. 39; xiv. 127; xvii. 44; xxv. 13; Purg. i. 78; vii. 22; *cerchie*, Inf. xviii. 3, 72; xxiii. 134; *cerchietti*, Inf. xi. 17; *cinghi*, Inf. xviii. 7; Purg. xxii. 103; *giri*, Inf. x. 4; xvi. 2; xxviii. 50; *gironi*, Inf. xi. 30, 39, 42, 49; xiii. 17; xvii. 38), of which the first and uppermost is co-extensive with the hemisphere of the Earth, which forms, as it were, a cover to it. The remaining Circles successively diminish in circumference, forming an immense inverted cone (*conca*, Inf. ix. 16), the lowest point of which is the centre of the Earth (Inf. xxxii. 73–4; xxxiv. 110–11), and of the Universe; at this point is placed Lucifer (Inf. xi. 64–5) [**Universo**]. Each of these nine Circles is presided over by one or more demons or evil spirits—Circle I by Charon [**Caronte**]; Circle II by Minos [**Minos**]; Circle III by Cerberus [**Cerbero**]; Circle IV by Plutus [**Pluto**]; Circle V by Phlegyas [**Flegias**]; Circle VI by the Furies [**Furie**]; Circle VII by the Minotaur [**Minotauro**]; Circle VIII by Geryon [**Gerione**]; Circle IX by the Giants [**Giganti**]. In each Circle a distinct class of sinners is punished. Hell as a whole may be divided into two main parts, which comprise four regions. Of these two parts, the first, in which sins of incontinence (Inf. xi. 82–90) are punished, forming a sort of Upper Hell, lies outside the City of Dis [Dite]; the other, or Lower Hell, in which sins of malice (Inf. xi. 82) are punished, is situated within the City of Dis. Upper Hell consists of the first five Circles, which are contiguous; these are arranged as follows :—On the upper confines of the abyss, above the first Circle, is a region, which forms, as it were, an Ante-hell, where are the souls of those who did neither good nor evil, the neutrals, who were not worthy to enter Hell proper [Antinferno : Vigliacchi]. In Circle I are placed unbaptized infants, and the good men and women of antiquity ; these are free from torture [Limbo]. At the entrance to Circle II is stationed Minos, the judge ; here begin the torments of Hell. Circles II–V are appropriated to the punishment of sins of incontinence. Then come the walls of the City of Dis, which form the division between Upper and Lower Hell. Within these walls lies Circle VI, where heretics are punished. After Circle VI comes a steep descent (*burrato*, Inf. xii. 10), and the second region is reached. This contains the three Rounds of Circle VII. After a still more pre-cipitous descent (*alto burrato*, Inf. xvi. 114) comes the third region, comprising the ten Pits of Circle VIII (*Malebolge*, Inf. xviii. 1). These Pits lie one below the other on a slope, like the rows of an am-phitheatre, and are divided from each other by banks, crossed at right angles by radial bridges of rock, resembling the transverse gangways of a theatre [Malebolge]. Below Malebolge is a third abyss (*pozzo*, Inf. xxxi. 32, 42; xxxii. 16), at the bottom of which lies the fourth or frozen region, comprising the four divisions of Circle IX, named respectively after Cain [Caina], Antenor of Troy [An-tenora], Ptolemy of Jericho [To-lomea], and Judas Iscariot [Giu-decca]; in the last of these, in the nethermost pit of Hell, is fixed Lucifer (Inf. xxxiv. 20) [Lucifero]. Down through Hell, from end to end, flows the infernal stream, under the various names of Acheron, Styx, Phlegethon, and Cocytus [Fiumi Infernali].

The time occupied by D.'s jour-ney through Hell is estimated at 24 or 25 hours, viz. from nightfall on the evening of Good Friday, April 8 (Inf. ii. 1), until shortly after sunset on Easter-eve, Saturday, April 9, 1300 (Inf. xxxiv. 96) [*Comme-dia*].

Inferno[2], first Cantica (consisting of 34 Cantos, comprising 4,720 lines) of the *D. C.*, Epist. x. 10[221]; referred to as *la prima canzone*, Inf. xx. 3. [*Commedia*.]

Inferno, Porta dell'. [Porta[3].]

Inforziato, Infortiatum, one of the three parts of the Digest of the Roman Law ; quoted, Conv. iv. 15[175–8]. [*Digesto*.]

Inghilese, Englishman; the Eagle, in the Heaven of Jupiter, in his survey of the Princes of Europe, condemns the pride and greed of the English and Scotch, who, in their eagerness for conquest, cannot remain peaceably within their own borders (the reference being to the prolonged border warfare between the English and Scotch in the reign of Edward I), Par. xix. 121–3.

Inghilterra, England; *Arrigo d'Inghilterra,* i.e. Henry III of England, Purg. vii. 131 [**Arrigo**[9]]; England one of the W. boundaries of Europe, *Anglia,* V. E. i. 8[27].

Inglesi, the English; coupled with the Germans, as foreigners to whom the commentary on the *Convivio* would have been intelligible if written in Latin, Conv. i. 7[84—7]; their tongue one of several into which the original language of Europe was split up, *Anglici,* V. E. i. 8[29–32].

Innocentius. [**Innocenzio**[2].]

Innocenzio[1], Innocent III (Lotario de' Conti di Segni ed Anagni), born at Anagni, 1161; elected Pope (in succession to Celestine III) in 1198, at the age of 37; died at Perugia, July 16, 1216.

St. Thomas Aquinas (in the Heaven of the Sun) mentions Innocent III in connexion with his formal sanction (in 1214) of the Order of St. Francis, Par. xi. 92 [**Francesco**[2]]. Some think he, and not Innocent IV, he having been famed as a canonist, is the *Innocentius* mentioned among the Decretalists, Epist. viii. 7[118] [**Decretalistae**].

Innocenzio[2], Innocent IV (Sinibaldo de' Fieschi of Genoa), elected Pope at Anagni (in succession to Honorius III) in 1243; died at Naples, Dec. 7, 1254. He was originally professor of law at Bologna, and was one of the most learned canonists of his time. It is probably

to him that D. refers as one of the Decretalists in his Letter to the Italian Cardinals, *Innocentius,* Epist. viii. 7[118] [**Decretalistae**]. Some think he is one of the simoniacal Popes referred to by Nicholas III, Inf. xix. 73 [**Niccolò**[2]].

Ino], daughter of Cadmus of Thebes and Harmonia, and wife of Athamas, King of Orchomenus in Boeotia, by whom she had two sons, Learchus and Melicertes [**Cadmo : Armonia**]. Athamas, having been driven mad by Juno, mistook Ino and his two sons for a lioness and cubs; he pursued them and killed Learchus, but Ino and Melicertes escaped, and, throwing themselves into the sea, were changed into marine deities.

D. (who got the story from Ovid, *Metam.* iv. 512–30) refers to Ino and her sons as *la moglie con due figli,* Inf. xxx. 5; *la leoncessa e i leoncini, v.* 8 [**Atamante**]; Ino herself had incurred the wrath of Juno for having brought up Bacchus, the son of Jupiter and her sister Semele (*vv.* 1–2) [**Semelè**].

Insulae Fortunatae, Fortunate Isles, or Isles of the Blessed, according to the old belief, the abode of the blessed, who passed thither without dying. The poets, and after them the geographers, placed them beyond the Pillars of Hercules; hence, when certain islands (usually identified with Madeira and the Canaries) were discovered in the Ocean, off the W. coast of Africa, the name of Fortunatae Insulae was applied to them.

D. quotes Orosius (*Hist.* i. 2, § 11) to prove that they and Mt.

Atlas were at the extremity of Africa, Mon. ii. 3[85—91].

Intellectu, De, treatise of Albertus Magnus *On the Understanding;* quoted (as *il libro dell' Intelletto*) for Albertus' opinion as to the distribution of the Sun's light (*Intell.* i. 3), Conv. iii. 7[27—43].

Interminei, Alessio. [Alessio Interminei.]

Inventione, De, *De Inventione Rhetorica* (in two books) of Cicero, quoted by D. under the title of *Prima Rhetorica,* Mon. ii. 5[16]; *Nova Rhetorica,* Epist. x. 19[320]; Cicero's saying that laws ought to be interpreted for the advantage of the State, Mon. ii. 5[15—18] (*Inv.* i. 38); his precept that three things are requisite to a good exordium, viz. to render the hearer well-disposed, attentive, and patient, Epist. x. 19[319—24] (*Inv.* i. 15).

Invidiosi], the Envious, placed, according to some, with the Wrathful and Slothful, in the Stygian marsh in Circle V of Hell, Inf. vii. 106—30 [Iracondi: Accidiosi].

Those who expiate the sin of Envy in Purgatory are placed in Circle II, Purg. xiii–xiv [*Beatitudini:* Purgatorio]; their punishment is to sit, clothed in hair-cloth, leaning on and supporting each other, to remind them of the precept they had neglected during life, 'Bear ye one another's burdens' (*Gal.* vi. 2); over the hair-cloth they wear cloaks of a livid colour, to recall to them the cloak of charity with which they ought to have covered the nakedness of their neighbours upon earth; and, as they could not keep their eyes from the goods of others, here they

are doomed to blindness (in accordance with the mediaeval etymology of *invidia*), their eyelids being sewn up with wire (Purg. xiii. 47–72). As D. and V. pass along they hear the voices of unseen spirits proclaiming examples of love, viz. Mary at the feast of Cana in Galilee (*John* ii. 3) (*vv.* 28–30) [Maria[1]]; the love of Orestes and Pylades (*vv.* 31–3) [Oreste]; and the precept of Christ (*Matt.* v. 44), 'Love your enemies' (*vv.* 34–6). Further on instances of envy are proclaimed; they hear the voice of Cain who envied his brother Abel (Purg. xiv. 130–5) [Caino]; and of Aglauros who envied her sister Herse (*vv.* 136–9) [Aglauro.] *Examples:* Sapia of Siena [Sapia]; Guido del Duca of Bertinoro [Guido del Duca]; Rinier da Calboli of Forlì [Rinier da Calboli].

Iò, Lingua. [Jò, Lingua.]
Io-. [Jo-.]

Iolas, name of a shepherd in Virgil's Eclogues (*Ecl.* ii. 57; iii. 76, 79), supposed to represent Guido Novello da Polenta, D.'s host at Ravenna, in D.'s poetical correspondence with G. del Virgilio, Ecl. ii. 95; Ecl. R. 80. [*Egloghe*[2]: Polenta, Guido Novello da.]

Iole, daughter of Eurytus, King of Oechalia in Thessaly, whom Hercules killed, carrying off Iole as his prisoner; he afterwards fell in love with her, and thereby aroused the jealousy of his wife Deianira; the latter, to win back his love, sent to Hercules a garment steeped in the blood of the Centaur Nessus, which poisoned him and maddened him with pain ; Deianira, seeing what she had unwittingly done, hanged herself. [Deianira: Nesso.]

The troubadour Folquet of Marseilles (in the Heaven of Venus) compares his passion for Adelais to that of Hercules for Iole (the story of Deianira's jealousy of whom is told by Ovid, *Metam.* ix. 136 ff.), Par. ix. 101–2 [Folco].

Iperione, Hyperion, one of the Titans, represented as the son of Heaven and Earth, and father of the Sun, Moon, and Aurora ; D., in imitation of Ovid (*Metam.* iv. 192), speaks of the Sun as *nato d' Iperione*, Par. xxii. 142 ; *Hyperione natus*, Epist. iv. 4⁴⁹. [Leucothoë: Sole.]

Ipocriti, Hypocrites, placed among the Fraudulent in Bolgia 6 of Circle VIII of Hell (Malebolge), Inf. xxiii. 92 [Frodolenti]; their punishment is to go round and round slowly, with painted faces (*Matt.* xxiii. 27), weeping bitterly, and crushed beneath the weight of hooded cloaks, which cover their eyes, and which outside are glittering with gold (in accordance with the mediaeval etymology of hypocrite, viz. 'gilded outside'), but inside are of heaviest lead, the weight causing them to creak as the sinners move (*vv.* 58–67, 100–2); certain of them (Caiaphas, Annas, and the rest of the Council of the Chief Priests and Pharisees) are doomed to special torment, being crucified naked on the ground, and so placed that all the others pass over their prostrate bodies in their mournful procession (*vv.* 110–23). *Examples*: Catalano de' Catalani [Catalano]; Loderingo degli Andalò

[Loderingo]; Caiaphas and Annas [Caifas: Anna²].

Ipolito. [Ippolito.]

Ippocrate, Hippocrates, the most famous physician of antiquity, the father of medicine; born in the island of Cos, c. B.C. 460, died at Larissa in Thessaly, at the age of 104, c. B.C. 357. His writings, which were held in high esteem at an early date, became the nucleus of a collection of medical treatises by various authors, which were long attributed to him, and still bear his name.

D. places H., together with Avicenna and Galen, among the philosophers of antiquity in Limbo, Inf. iv. 143 [Limbo]; St. Luke the Evangelist appears in the mystical Procession in the Terrestrial Paradise in the guise of 'one of the familiars of Hippocrates' (i.e. of a physician), Purg. xxix. 136–8 [Luca¹]; H. is mentioned in connexion with his 'Aphorisms', Conv. i. 8³³; they are referred to, Par. xi. 4 [*Aforismi*].

Ippolito, Hippolytus, son of Theseus by Hippolyte, Queen of the Amazons. Theseus afterwards married Phaedra, who fell in love with her step-son, Hippolytus, and on his rejecting her shameful proposals she accused him to his father of having attempted her dishonour. Theseus thereupon cursed his son, who was obliged to flee from Athens, and subsequently met his death in fulfilment of his father's curse.

Hippolytus (whose story D. got from Ovid, *Metam.* xv. 497 ff.) is mentioned by Cacciaguida (in the

Heaven of Mars), who foretells to D. that he will have to leave Florence, just as H. was forced to leave Athens, Par. xvii. 46–8. [Fedra.]

Iracondi], the Wrathful, placed in Circle V of Hell (as some think, in company with the Envious and Slothful), under the guardianship of Phlegyas, Inf. vii. 100–viii. 63 [Accidiosi: Invidiosi: Flegias]; their punishment is to be immersed naked in the mud of the Stygian marsh, where they pound, and rend, and bite each other (Inf. vii. 110–14); some of them are completely hidden beneath the surface, their presence being betrayed solely by the bubbles in the mud produced by their sighs (vv. 115–20); those who are visible proclaim their crime and punishment by means of a doleful gurgling chant (vv. 121–6.) Example: Filippo Argenti of Florence [Argenti, Filippo].

Those who expiate the sin of Wrath in Purgatory are placed in Circle III, Purg. xv. 85–xvii. 39 [Beatitudini: Purgatorio]; their punishment is to be enveloped in a dense pungent smoke, which blinds them as they had been, blinded on earth by their angry passions (Purg. xv. 142–xvi. 7); in a series of visions are exhibited examples of meekness, viz. the Virgin Mary seeking Christ in the Temple (Purg. xv. 85–92) [Maria [1]]; Pisistratus forgiving the young man who insulted his daughter (vv. 92–105) [Pisistrato]; Stephen forgiving his persecutors (vv. 106–14) [Stefano]; the voices of the spirits are heard praying to the Lamb of God for peace and mercy (Purg. xvi. 16–24);

in a second series of visions are exhibited instances of wrath and its punishment, viz. the slaying of Itys by Procne and her transformation into a nightingale (Purg. xvii. 19–21) [Filomela: Progne]; the hanging of Haman for his persecution of the Jews (vv. 25–30) [Mardocheo]; the wrathful disappointment and suicide of Amata after the death of Turnus (vv. 34–9) [Amata: Lavinia]. Example: Marco Lombardo of Venice [Marco [2]].

Iri, Iris, daughter of Thaumas and Electra; she was originally the personification of the rainbow, which was regarded as the swift messenger of the gods, and of Juno in particular.

D. mentions Iris, in the sense of the rainbow, Par. xxxiii. 118; alludes to her as figlia di Taumante, Purg. xxi. 50 (Ovid, Metam. xiv. 845); ancella di Junone, Par. xii. 12; messo di Juno, Par. xxviii. 32 (Ovid, Metam. i. 270); the rainbow itself is referred to as l'arco del Sole, Purg. xxix. 78; the double rainbow, Par. xii. 10–12; xxxiii. 118; the whole circle of the rainbow, Par. xxviii. 32–3.

Isaac], son of the patriarch Abraham and Sarah, and father by Rebekah of Esau and Jacob (otherwise called Israel); he is mentioned by Virgil, who refers to him as lo padre d'Israel, among those whom Christ liberated from Limbo, Inf. iv. 59. [Limbo.]

Isacco. [Isaac.]

Isai. [Jesse.]

Isaia, prophet Isaiah, son of Amoz, Par. xxv. 91 (ref. to Isaiah lxi. 7, 10); Conv. iv. 5[43], 21[110];

Isaias, Mon. iii. 1²⁵ (ref. to *Isaiah* vi. 6); Epist. vi. 6¹⁸⁶; A. T. § 22¹¹; *Amos filius*, Epist. vii. 2²⁸⁻⁹ (ref. to 2 *Kings* xx. 1–11); *Propheta*, Mon. ii. 13⁴⁴; Isaiah is quoted, Conv. iv. 5⁴³⁻⁴ (*Isaiah* xi. 1); Conv. iv. 21¹¹⁰⁻¹² (*Isaiah* xi. 2); Mon. ii. 13⁴³⁻⁵ (*Isaiah* liii. 4); Epist. vi. 6¹⁸⁶⁻⁹ (*Isaiah* liii. 4); A. T. § 22¹¹⁻¹³ (*Isaiah* lv. 9). [*Bibbia.*]

Isaiae, Prophetia. [Isaia.]
Isaias. [Isaia.]

Isara, Isère, river of France, which rises in the Graian Alps in Savoy, flows through the departments of Savoie and Isère, and enters the Rhone about ten miles N. of Valence; mentioned by the Emperor Justinian (in the Heaven of Mercury), together with the Var, Rhine, Saône, Seine, and Rhone, in connexion with Caesar's victories in Gaul, Par. vi. 59. [**Era.**]

Isidoro, Isidorus Hispalensis, St. Isidore of Seville, a learned Spaniard, one of the most influential writers of the early Middle Ages; he was born at Cartagena c. 560; in 599 he was appointed Bishop of Seville, where he died in 636. He wrote many works, the most important of which were the *Origines* or *Etymologiarum Libri XX*, a sort of encyclopaedia of the scientific knowledge of the age.

D. places St. Isidore among the great doctors of the Church (*Spiriti Sapienti*), in the Heaven of the Sun, where his spirit, in company with those of Bede and Richard of St. Victor, is pointed out by St. Thomas Aquinas, Par. x. 131. [**Sole, Cielo del.**]

Isifile, Hypsipyle, daughter of Thoas, King of Lemnos, whose life she saved when the Lemnian women killed all the men in the island. When the Argonauts landed in Lemnos she was seduced and abandoned by Jason, by whom she had twin sons, Thoas and Euneos. When it was discovered that her father Thoas was alive, H. was forced to fly from Lemnos; on her flight she was captured by pirates and sold to Lycurgus, King of Nemea, who entrusted her with the charge of his son Archemorus. One day as she was seated in a wood near Nemea with the child, the seven heroes who were warring against Thebes passed by, and, being thirsty, asked her to show them a fountain. Hypsipyle thereupon put down the child upon the grass, and led the warriors to the fountain of Langia. When she returned she found Archemorus dead from the bite of a serpent. Enraged at the death of his child, Lycurgus determined to put her to death, and was proceeding to put his resolve into execution when Thoas and Euneos, Hypsipyle's two sons, opportunely arrived and saved her.

Hypsipyle (whose story D. got from Statius) is mentioned in connexion with the rescue of her father from the Lemnian women (*Theb.* v. 240 ff.; vi. 142), and her seduction and desertion by Jason (*Theb.* v. 404–85), Inf. xviii. 92 [**Jason**¹]; her charge of Archemorus (*Theb.* iv. 785–92; v. 499 ff.), Conv. iii. 11¹⁶⁶ [**Archemoro**]; she is alluded to as *quella che mostrò Langía* (*Theb.* iv. 717–84), Purg. xxii. 112 [**Langía**]; her rescue from Lycurgus by her sons after the death of Archemorus, *la madre* (*Theb.* v. 541 ff.), Purg. xxvi. 95 [**Licurgo**].

Virgil, addressing Statius (in Purgatory), mentions H. as being 'delle genti tue' (i. e. mentioned in the *Thebaid* or *Achilleïd*) among the great women of antiquity in Limbo, Purg. xxii. 112. [**Antigone: Limbo.**]

Ismene, Ismene, daughter of Oedipus by his incestuous marriage with his mother Jocasta, and sister of Antigone, Eteocles, and Polynices.

Virgil, addressing Statius (in Purgatory), mentions her as being 'delle genti tue' (i. e. mentioned in the *Thebaid* or *Achilleid*) among the great women of antiquity in Limbo, Purg. xxii. 111 [**Antigone: Limbo**]; she is spoken of as appearing 'sì trista come fue' on account of the terrible tragedies she witnessed, viz. the violent death of her betrothed, the blinding of her father Oedipus by his own hand, the suicide of her mother Jocasta, the deaths at each other's hands of her brothers Eteocles and Polynices, and the total ruin and downfall of her father's kingdom [**Edipo: Eteocle: Jocasta**].

Ismeno, Ismenus, small river in Boeotia, which rises in Mt. Cithaeron and flows through Thebes; mentioned, together with the Asopus, Purg. xviii. 91. [**Asopo.**]

Isopo. [**Esopo.**]

Ispagna, Spain; the W. limit of the habitable world, Inf. xxvi. 103 [**Gerusalemme: Ispani**]; Caesar's expedition into, against Pompey's lieutenants, Afranius and Petreius, whom he defeated at Le-

rida, Purg. xviii. 102; Par. vi. 64 [**Ilerda**]; *quel di Spagna*, i. e. Fernando IV, King of Castile and Leon (1295–1312), Par. xix. 125 [**Ferdinando**]; Spain is alluded to as the country whence Zephyrus (the W. wind) springs, as being in the extreme W., Par. xii. 46 [**Zeffiro**].

As an alternative to Spain, to indicate the W. limit of the habitable world, D. uses Gades (Cadiz) [**Gade**], the Ebro [**Ibero**], Seville [**Sibilia**], or Morocco [**Morrocco**].

Ispani, Spaniards; the eclipse of the Sun at the Crucifixion visible equally to them (at the W. limit of the habitable world), and to the inhabitants of India (at the E. limit), and to the Jews at Jerusalem (in the centre), i. e. to the whole inhabited world, Par. xxix. 101–2 [**Gerusalemme: Ispagna**]; D. classes as 'Spaniards' those who spoke or wrote in the *langue d'*oc, i. e. Provençal, *Hispani*, V. E. i. 8⁴⁴; ii. 12²⁰ [*Oc*, **Lingua**].

Ispano, Pietro. [**Pietro Ispano.**]

Israel[1], Israel, name given to the patriarch Jacob after his wrestling with the angel at Peniel (*Gen.* xxxii. 28); by this name Virgil refers to Jacob, who is mentioned together with his father Isaac, his wife Rachel, and his sons, among those released by Christ from Limbo, Inf. iv. 59–60. [**Jacob: Limbo.**]

Israel[2], Israel, the children of Israel (*Exod.* i. 1), the national name of the twelve Hebrew tribes; *Israel*, Purg. ii. 46; Conv. ii. 6⁴; V. E. i. 7⁶⁸; Mon. i. 8²³, 14⁶⁸; ii. 8³⁸, ⁵⁹; Epist. vii. 8¹⁸³; x. 7¹⁴², ¹⁴⁷; *Israele*, Conv. ii. 1⁵⁹; *domus Jacob*, Epist.

x. 7[143] [**Ebrei**]; their exodus from Egypt (ref. to *Psalm* cxiv. 1), Purg. ii. 46; Conv. ii. 1[59]; Epist. x. 7[142-8] [**Egitto**]; their prophets taught them in part the truth concerning spiritual beings, Conv. ii. 6[4-5]; their descent from Shem, and their use of the Hebrew tongue, V. E. i. 7[68-70] [**Sem : Ebreo**]; the Lord their God one Lord (*Deut.* vi. 4), Mon. i. 8[23]; their elders entrusted by Moses with the lesser judgements, the more important being reserved to himself (*Exod.* xviii. 17-26; *Deut.* i. 10-18), Mon. i. 14[66-73] [**Moisè**]; the obligation upon them to make an offering at the door of the tabernacle on killing an ox, or lamb, or goat (*Levit.* xvii. 3-4), Mon. ii. 8[37-42]; God's judgement touching their liberation from Egypt revealed to Pharaoh by a sign (*Exod.* iv. 21), Mon. ii. 8[57-9]; their delivery from the Philistines by the death of Goliath at the hand of David (1 *Sam.* xvii) typical of the delivery of the oppressed Ghibellines from the Neri, Epist. vii. 8[183] [**Philistei**].

Israele. [**Israel.**]

Issacar], Issachar, son of Jacob and Leah; he is among those referred to by Virgil as having been released by Christ from Limbo, *Israel co' suoi nati*, Inf. iv. 59. [**Limbo.**]

[**Ister**], classical name for the Danube, Carm. 31. [**Danubio.**]

Istria, peninsula which projects into the NE. corner of the Adriatic, formerly an independent Italian duchy, now a part of the Austro-Hungarian dominions, its chief towns being Trieste and Pola. It owes its name to the old belief that a branch of the Danube (Ister) flowed through this province into the Adriatic.

D. couples Istria with Friuli (Forum Julii) as being on the left side of Italy, if the Apennines be taken as the dividing line (from N. to S.), V. E. i. 10[55]; it is alluded to, Inf. ix. 113-14. [**Pola : Quarnaro.**]

Istriani, inhabitants of Istria; their dialect distinct from that of the people of Aquileia, V. E. i. 10[70]; condemned, with that of the Aquileians, as harsh, V. E. i. 11[36].

Itali[1], inhabitants of ancient Italy, term applied by D. to the Romans; in their wars against Greece and Carthage, Fabricius won the day for them over Pyrrhus, and Scipio over Hannibal, Mon. ii. 11[52-61]. [**Latini**[2] : **Romani**[1].]

Itali[2], inhabitants of modern Italy, Italians, V. E. i. 8[27], 10[11], 11[13], 12[2, 8, 17], 18[19, 41, 43, 53]; Epist. ii. 1[12]; vi. 1[18]; viii. 10[151, 155]; called also *Latii*, V. E. ii. 5[12]; *Latini*, Inf. xxix. 91; V. E. i. 6[38], 8[44], 10[26, 71], 11[42-3], 12[29], 15[35], 16[35, 40], 17[19]; ii. 2[95]; Epist. viii. 11[188]; *sanguis Longobardorum*, Epist. v. 4[50]; alluded to, in the apostrophe to the Emperor Albert, as *i tuoi gentili*, Purg. vi. 110; elsewhere as *italica erba*, Par. xi. 105; the affirmative particle *sì* characteristic of their language, Inf. xxxiii. 80; V. N. § 25[38, 42]; Conv. i. 10[81]; V. E. i. 8[43], 9[13], 10[11]; their employment of the affirmative *sì*, the Latin *sic*, an indication that Italian is of earlier date than the 'lingua *oïl*' or the 'lingua *oc*' (i. e. French and Provençal), to which it is superior for two reasons, V. E. i. 10$^{9-11}$, 25^{-34}; many languages more agreeable and serviceable than theirs, V.E. i. 6$^{36-8}$; their frontier one of the W. confines of Europe, V. E. i. 8^{27}; the Sardinians not to be reckoned as Italians, though they have affinities with them, V. E. i. 11$^{42-4}$ (cf. Inf. xxii. 65-7); reason why poems written by Italians are called Sicilian, a term which remains as a reproach to the princes of Italy, V. E. i. 12$^{5-19}$; the Roman dialect the ugliest of all their dialects, V.E. i. 11$^{12-14}$, while that of the Bolognese is the best, V. E. i. 15$^{3-5}$, 27^{-33}; their manners, customs, and language to be judged by a national, not a provincial, standard, V. E. i. 16$^{35-43}$; their language susceptible of improvement by training and authority, V. E. i. 17$^{15-18}$; their court (aula) if they had one would be an Imperial one, but though they lack a court (curia) yet the members of such a court are not wanting, V. E. i. 18$^{18-20,\ 46-9}$; their poets employ lines of five, seven, and eleven syllables more frequently than any other metre, V. E. ii. 5$^{10-15}$; none of them so far had sung of arms, V. E. ii. 2$^{95-6}$; the fame of their heroes surpassed by that of Alessandro da Romena, Epist. ii. 1^{12}; their reputed descent from the Trojans and Romans, Epist. v. 4$^{50-2}$; their misfortunes too great for description, Epist. vi. 1^{18}; viii. 10^{155}; Rome ought to be the object of their affections, Epist. viii. 10^{151}; the Gascons eager to usurp their glory, Epist. viii. 11^{188}.

Italia, Italy, Inf. i. 106; ix. 114; xx. 61; Purg. vi. 76, 124; vii. 95; xiii. 96; xx. 67; xxx.

86; Par. xxi. 106; xxx. 137; V. N. § 30^{2}; Conv. i. 5^{56}, 6^{54}, 11^{2,147}; ii. 11^{67}; iii. 11^{22}; iv. 5^{48}, 6^{181}, 9^{106}; V. E. i. 8^{56}, 9^{34}, 10$^{55-8}$, 73, 81, 11^{3}, 12^{72}, 14^{2}, 15$^{55,\ 63}$, 16^{42}, 18^{48}, 19$^{10,\ 12}$; Mon. ii. 3^{116}, 7^{85}, 11^{23}; iii. 13^{49}; Epist. v. 2^{23}, 6^{100}; vi. 1^{14}; vii. 3^{54}; viii. 11^{180}; *Ausonia,* Par. viii. 61; Mon. ii. 13^{66} [**Ausonia**]; *Hesperia,* Mon. ii. 3^{80}; Epist. vi. 3^{87} [**Hesperia**]; *Latium,* V. E. i. 10^{39}, 14^{5}, 16^{59}; Epist. vii. 1^{20} [**Latium**]; *terra Latina,* Inf. xxvii. 27; xxviii. 71; *terra Italica,* Par. ix. 25; *Scipionum patria,* Epist. viii. 10^{170}; *bel paese dove il* sì *suona,* Inf. xxxiii. 80; the land for which Camilla, Turnus, Nisus, and Euryalus died, Inf. i. 106; the fatherland of the Scipios, Epist. viii. 10^{170}; the garden of the Empire, Purg. vi. 105; the noblest region of Europe, Mon. ii. 3$^{116-17}$; her cities full of tyrants, Purg. vi. 124; neglected by the Emperors Albert and Rudolf, Purg. vi. 97-9, vii. 94-5, she shall find a saviour in Henry VII, Purg. vii. 96; Par. xxx. 137; her backbone formed by the Apennines, Purg. xxx. 86; V. E. i. 10$^{39-59}$; changes in the vocabulary of her cities within the space of fifty years, Conv. i. 5$^{56-9}$; infamy of those of her sons who commend foreign tongues to the disparagement of their own native Italian, Conv. i. 11$^{1-4,\ 146-53}$; 'courtesy', if derived from 'courts' such as hers, would be the equivalent of 'baseness', Conv. ii. 11$^{65-8}$; Pythagoras an inhabitant of, about the time of Numa Pompilius, Conv. iii. 11$^{22-30}$; arrival of Aeneas in, coincident with the birth of David, so that the advent of Christ was prepared long beforehand at the same hour both in Syria and in Italy, Conv. iv. 5^{46-72}; denunciation of the wicked princes who have wrongfully possessed themselves of her kingdoms, Conv. iv. 6^{180-90}; the speech of the provinces on her right side different from that of the provinces on her left, V. E. i. 2^{31-5}; if the Apennines be taken as the dividing line (from N. to S.) Friuli and Istria must be reckoned among the provinces on her left side, and Sicily and Sardinia among those on her right, V. E. i. 10^{54-9}; though she numbers no less than fourteen dialects, V. E. i. 10^{72-4}, yet she possesses one tongue common to all her peoples, viz. the Italian vulgar tongue, V. E. i. 16^{57-63}, 19^{1-4}; the noblest actions of her sons peculiar to no one town, but common to them all, V. E. i. 16^{39-43}; Italy the cradle of two nations descended from the Trojans, viz. the Romans and the Albans, Mon. ii. 11^{22-4}; happy for her if Constantine, whose 'donation' so weakened the Empire, had never been born, Mon. ii. 13^{66-9}; her condition such as to be pitied even by the Saracens, Epist. v. 2^{23-4}; appeal to her sons to support the Emperor Henry VII, Epist. v. 6^{100}; with the advent of Henry VII dawned a more hopeful era for her, Epist. vii. 1^{20}; the power of the Empire not confined within the limits of her shores, Epist. vii. 3^{54}; appeal to the Italian Cardinals on her behalf, Epist. viii. 11^{180}; she is compared to—a slave, Purg. vi. 76; a hostel of woe, Purg. vi. 76; a storm-tost ship without a pilot, Purg. vi. 77;

Epist. vi. 1^{14}; a brothel, Purg. vi. 78; a riderless and unmanageable horse, Purg. vi. 89, 94, 98; Conv. iv. 9^{103-8}; a raving maniac, Epist. vi. 3^{87}.

Italica Lingua, Italian language, Conv. i. 9^{9-10}; *volgare Italico*, Conv. i. 6^{56}; *vulgare Latinum*, V. E. i. 10^{36}, 11^{1-2}, $19^{4, 15}$; ii. 1^{3-4}; *Latinorum vulgare*, V. E. i. 15^{35}; *vulgare Italum*, V. E. i. 12^{2}; *vulgare Italiae*, V. E. i. 10^{81}; *Italica loquela*, Conv. i. 10^{106}; *Italiae loquela*, V. E. i. 11^{3}; *parlare Italico*, Conv. i. 11^{99}; *volgare di* sì, Conv. i. 10^{81}; *lingua di* sì, V. N. § 25^{38}, ^{42}; Inf. xxxiii. 80; V. E. i. 8^{43}, 9^{13}, 10^{11}; the affirmative particle *sì* its distinguishing characteristic, V. N. § $25^{38, 42}$; Inf. xxxii. 80; Conv. i. 10^{81}; V. E. i. 8^{43}, 9^{13}, 10^{11}; presumably of earlier date than the 'lingua *oil*' and the 'lingua *oc*', to both of which it is superior, V. E. i. $10^{9-11, 25-34}$; not so agreeable nor so serviceable as many others, V. E. i. 6^{36-8}; susceptible of improvement by training and authority, V. E. i. 17^{15-18}; changes in its vocabulary during fifty years, Conv. i. 5^{56-9}; numbers no less than fourteen dialects, V. E. i. 10^{72-4}, of which the Roman is the ugliest, V. E. i. 11^{12-14}, and the Bolognese the best, V. E. i. 15^{3-5}, $^{27-33}$; if all the subordinate variations were reckoned they would amount to considerably over a thousand, V. E. i. 10^{80-5}; superior to the local dialects in that it is common to all the peoples of Italy, V. E. i. 16^{57-63}, 19^{1-4}; D.'s reasons for using it as the vehicle of the commentary on his *canzoni*, Conv. i. 6, 9, 10; its employment as a literary tongue dates back not more than 150 years before D.'s time, V. N. § 25³⁶⁻⁴⁰; its pre-eminence over French and Provençal due to the superiority of its poets, such as Cino da Pistoja and D. himself, and to its closer dependence upon 'grammar' (i. e. Latin), V. E. i. 10²⁵⁻³⁴; explanation of the term Sicilian as applied to the earliest Italian writings, V. E. i. 12⁶⁻³⁵; the ideal Italian tongue ought fitly to be described as illustrious, cardinal, courtly, and curial, V. E. i. 16⁵⁷⁻⁶⁰, 17¹⁻³, 19¹⁻⁴.

Italico, Italian, Par. ix. 26; xi. 105; Conv. i. 6⁵⁶, 9¹⁰, 10¹⁰⁶, 11⁹⁹; *Italicus*, V. E. i. 15¹, 18¹²; *Italus*, V. E. i. 12², ¹⁷; Epist. v. *tit.*; *Latialis*, Epist. viii. 10¹⁵⁰; *Latino*, Inf. xxii. 65; xxvii. 27, 33; xxviii. 71; xxix. 88, 91; Purg. xi. 58; xiii. 92; Conv. iv. 28⁶¹; *Latinus*, V. E. i. 10²⁶, ³⁶, ⁷¹, 11⁴²⁻³, 15³⁵, ⁶⁷⁻⁸, 16³⁵⁻⁴⁰, 17¹⁹, 19⁴, ¹⁵; ii. 1³, 2⁸⁵. [**Latino²**.]

Italicus. [**Italico.**]

Italus. [**Itali : Italico.**]

Iu-. [**Ju-.**]

J

J. [1³.]

Jacob, patriarch Jacob, younger son of Isaac and Rebekah, twin-brother of Esau, whose birthright he bought, and whom he deprived of his father's blessing by practising a deceit upon Isaac, at the instigation of his mother; after his wrestling with the angel at Peniel (*Gen.* xxxii. 28) he received the name of Israel. His first wife was Leah, eldest daughter of Laban, who bore him six sons, Reuben, Simeon, Levi, Judah, Issachar, Zebulun; his second wife was Leah's younger sister, Rachel, who bore him two sons, Joseph and Benjamin. Besides these he had two sons, Dan and Naphtali, by Bilhah, Rachel's maid; and two others, Gad and Asher, by Leah's maid, Zilpah.

Virgil mentions Jacob and his sons among those released by Christ from Limbo, referring to him by his name of Israel, Inf. iv. 59 [**Israel¹**];

Charles Martel (in the Heaven of Venus) mentions him, together with Esau, in reference to the different dispositions of the two brothers in spite of the identity of their begetting, Par. viii. 131; the two are alluded to by St. Bernard (in the Empyrean), in connexion with the doctrine of predestination, as *quei gemelli, Che nella madre ebber l'ira commota*, Par. xxxii. 68-9 [**Esaù**]; D. compares the celestial ladder in the Heaven of Saturn to the ladder seen by Jacob in his vision at Bethel, Par. xxii. 70-2 (ref. to *Gen.* xxviii. 12); his deception of his father Isaac, who believed the false evidence of his disguised hands rather than the true testimony of his natural voice, Mon. i. 13²²⁻⁵ (ref. to *Gen.* xxvii. 22); his sons Levi and Judah by his wife Leah, Mon. iii. 5²⁻⁴, ¹³⁻¹⁴ (ref. to *Gen.* xxix. 34-5); the children of Israel referred to as 'the house of Jacob', Epist. x. 7¹⁴³ (ref. to *Psalm* cxiv. 1) [**Egitto**: Israel [2]].

Jacobbe, -obo. [**Jacob.**]

Jacobi, Epistola, Epistle General of St. James, written, according to the accepted opinion, by St. James the Less, son of Alphaeus, but regarded by D. as the work of St. James the Great [**Jacobus: Jacopo** [1]]; referred to, Par. xxv. 29-30 (ref. to *James* i. 5, 17); Par. xxv. 77; Conv. iv. 2[83-4]; quoted, Conv. iv. 2[84-7] (*James* v. 7); Conv. iv. 20[51-3] (*James* i. 17); Mon. i. 1[38-9] (*James* i. 5); it is supposed to be symbolized by one of the four elders in humble guise, who form part of the mystical Procession in the Terrestrial Paradise, Purg. xxix. 142, 145-8 [**Epistolae Canonicae**].

Jacobi, Maria, 'Mary of James,' i. e. Mary, the husband of Alphaeus, otherwise called Clopas (in A.V. Cleophas), and mother of James the Less, Joses, Jude, and Simon; she was probably the elder sister of the Virgin Mary, being identical with Mary the wife of Clopas mentioned by St. John (xix. 25).

D. refers to St. Mark's record of her visit to the tomb of our Lord in company with Mary Magdalene and Salome, Conv. iv. 22[149-59] (ref. to *Mark* xvi. 1). [**Maddalena, Maria.**]

Jacobus, St. James the Less, son of Alphaeus (otherwise called Clopas or Cleophas), and Mary, the sister of the Virgin Mary, and brother of Joses, Jude, and Simon, he and Jude being among the Apostles; he is generally regarded as the author of the Epistle of St. James, the authorship of which, however, D. attributes to St. James the Great [**Jacopo** [1]].

D. mentions him in connexion with his mother, Conv. iv. 22[150] [**Jacobi, Maria**]; his Epistle is referred to, Par. xxv. 29-30, 77; Conv. iv. 2[83-4], 20[51-3]; Mon. i. 1[38-9] [**Jacobi, Epistola**].

Jacomo [1], James II, King of Sicily, 1285-1296, King of Aragon, 1291-1327; second son of Peter III of Aragon and Constance daughter of Manfred. On the death of Peter III, King of Aragon and Sicily, in 1285, James succeeded to the crown of Sicily, his elder brother, Alphonso, becoming King of Aragon. In 1291, on the death of Alphonso, James succeeded him in Aragon, and appointed his younger brother, Frederick, governor of Sicily. A few years later, ignoring the claims of Frederick, James proposed to cede Sicily to Charles II of Naples, whose daughter Blanche he had married; whereupon the Sicilians proclaimed Frederick king (1296), a title in which he was eventually (1302) confirmed, after Charles and James had vainly attempted to oust him. James, who by his own subjects was surnamed the Just, died at Barcelona, Nov. 2, 1327. [**Carlo** [2]: **Federico** [3]: **Cicilia**: **Table B.**]

James is named, together with his brother Frederick, by Sordello (in Ante-purgatory), who says they possess their father's kingdoms, but not his virtues, Purg. vii. 119 [**Piero** [2]]; the Eagle in the Heaven of Jupiter alludes to him as the brother of Frederick, and reproaches him and his uncle, the King of the Balearic Isles, with having dishonoured their respective crowns, Par. xix. 137 [Jacomo [2]]; he is alluded to (probably) by his grandfather Manfred (in Ante-purgatory) as *l'onor d'Aragona*, Purg. iii. 116 [Aragona : Cicilia].

Jacomo [2]], James, youngest son of James I of Aragon, and brother of Peter III. On the death of his father in 1276 he entered into possession of the kingdom of the Balearic Isles, which had been wrested from the Moors by James I in 1232, and of which he had been assigned the sovereignty in 1262. He also claimed Valencia under his father's will, and in order to enforce his claim he joined Philip III of France in his luckless expedition against Peter III of Aragon in 1284 [Filippo [1]]. The campaign proved a disastrous failure, and James was deprived of his kingdom; in 1295, however, he was reinstated in accordance with an agreement between his nephew, James II of Aragon, and Philip IV of France and Charles II of Naples. He died in 1311.

James is alluded to by the Eagle in the Heaven of Jupiter as the uncle of Frederick, King of Sicily, he and his nephew James of Aragon being reproached with having dishonoured their respective crowns, Par. xix. 137. [Jacomo [1] : Federico [3].]

Jacomo da sant' Andrea, Jacomo della Cappella di sant' Andrea of Padua, the son of Odorico Fontana da Monselice and Speronella Delesmanini, a very wealthy lady,

whose fortune Jacomo inherited, and squandered in the most senseless acts of prodigality. He is supposed to have been put to death by order of Ezzelino da Romano in 1239.

D. places him, together with Lano of Siena, among those who have squandered their substance, in Round 2 of Circle VII of Hell, where they are pursued and torn to pieces by black hounds, Inf. xiii. 133; (he and Lano) *duo* (*peccatori*), v. 115; *l'altro*, v. 119; *quel*, vv. 127, 128 [Scialacquatori].

Jacopo [1], St. James the Apostle, son of the fisherman Zebedee and of Salome, and brother of St. John the Apostle and Evangelist; he was put to death by Herod Agrippa shortly before the day of the Passover in 44 (*Acts* xii. 2). According to tradition St. James preached the Gospel in Spain; and after his martyrdom at Jerusalem his body was transferred to Compostela in Galicia. In the Middle Ages the shrine which contained his relics was one of the most famous in Europe, and attracted pilgrims to Santiago de Compostela from all parts of Christendom. [Galizia.]

St. James is mentioned, *Jacopo*, Purg. xxxii. 76; *santo Jacopo*, V. N. § 41[41, 48]; Conv. ii. 15[10]; *Jacopo Apostolo*, Conv. iv. 2[83]; *Apostolo*, Conv. iv. 20[51]; *filius Zebedaei*, Mon. iii. 9[83]; alluded to as *il Barone, Per cui laggiù si visita Galizia*, Par. xxv. 17–18; *grande Principe glorioso*, Par. xxv. 22–3; the representative of Hope, as St. John was of Love, and St. Peter of Faith, on the occasions when the

three Apostles were present alone
with Christ, i. e. at the raising of
Jairus's daughter (*Luke* viii. 51) at
the Transfiguration (*Matt.* xvii. 1 ;
Mark ix. 2 ; *Luke* ix. 28), and in
the garden of Gethsemane (*Matt.*
xxvi. 37 ; *Mark* xiv. 33), the three
being referred to by Beatrice as *i tre*
(*ai quali*) *Gesù fe' più chiarezza*, Par.
xxv. 33 ; he is described as *un lume*,
Par. xxv. 13 ; *inclita vita*, v. 29 ;
fuoco secondo, v. 37 ; *secondo lume*, v.
48; *incendio*, v. 80; *splendore*, v. 107.

D. refers to St. James as the
author of the *Epistle of St. James*
(which is generally supposed to have
been written by St. James the Less),
Par. xxv. 29–30 (ref. to *James* i.
5, 17); Par. xxv. 77 ; Conv. iv.
2⁸³ (*James* v. 7); Conv. iv. 20⁵¹
(*James* i. 17) [*Jacobi Epistola*]; his
presence at the Transfiguration with
St. Peter and St. John, Purg. xxxii.
76; Par. xxv. 33 ; Conv. ii. 1⁴⁵⁻⁸;
Mon. iii. 9⁸¹⁻³ ; at the raising of
Jairus's daughter, Par. xxv. 33 ; in
the garden of Gethsemane, Par. xxv.
33 ; his shrine at Compostela in
Galizia, Par. xxv. 17–18 ; V. N.
§ 41⁴¹, ⁴⁸ ; Conv. ii. 15¹⁰ ; the
pilgrims thereto termed *peregrini*,
because of its distance from St.
James's native land, V. N. § 41⁴⁶⁻⁵⁰
[Galizia] ; the Galaxy, or Milky
Way, popularly termed *la Via di santo
Jacopo*, Conv. ii. 15¹⁰ [Galassia].

After D. has been examined by
St. Peter concerning faith in the
Heaven of the Fixed Stars (Par.
xxiv. 52–xxv. 12), St. James examines him concerning hope (Par.
xxv. 25–99), as subsequently St.
John does concerning love (Par.
xxvi. 1–66).

Jacopo ²], St. James the Less,
Conv. iv. 22¹⁵⁰. [Jacobus.]

Jacopo da Lentino], commonly
called ' il Notajo ' (the Notary) of
Lentino (now Lentini) in Sicily ;
Jacopo, who was a notary in the
chancellery of the Emperor Frederick II, belonged to the Sicilian
school of poetry which flourished
under Frederick and his son Manfred; he is believed to have studied
at Bologna and afterwards to have
lived in Tuscany, where his reputation was such that he was regarded
as the chief of the lyric poets anterior
to Guittone d'Arezzo (c. 1230–
1294) [Guittone]. A great many
of his *canzoni* and sonnets, which
exhibit marked traces of Provençal
influence, have been preserved, including a poetical correspondence or
tenzone in sonnets with Pier delle
Vigne (minister of Frederick II).
He died c. 1250.

The first line of one of his *canzoni*
(which is still extant), is quoted by
D. as an example of polished diction,
though the author's name is not
given, V. E. i. 12⁶⁷ ; in the *D. C.*
Bonagiunta of Lucca (in Circle VI
of Purgatory) is represented as condemning Jacopo (whom he speaks
of as *il Notaro*), together with Guittone d'Arezzo and himself, for the
artificiality of their style as compared with that of the school to
which D. belonged, Purg. xxiv. 56.
[Bonagiunta.]

Jacopo da sant' Andrea. [Ja-
como.]

Jacopo del Cassero. [Cas-
sero, Jacopo del.]

Jacopo Rusticucci, Florentine
Guelf, mentioned together with

Farinata degli Uberti, Tegghiaio Aldobrandi, Arrigo, and Mosca de' Lamberti, Inf. vi. 80; he is one of those *ch' a ben far poser gl' ingegni* (*v.* 81) of whom D. asks Ciacco (in Circle III of Hell) for news, the reply being *ei son tra le anime più nere* (*v.* 85) [Ciacco]. Jacopo is one of the three Florentines (the other two being Guido Guerra and Tegghiaio Aldobrandi) seen by D. afterwards among the Sodomites in Round 3 of Circle VII of Hell, Inf. xvi. 44; *ombra, v.* 4; *uno, v.* 30; *quegli, v.* 65; Jacopo addresses D. and, after naming himself and his two companions, states that he owes his place in Hell to the savage temper of his wife, which drove him to evil courses (*vv.* 28–45) [Sodomiti].

Jacopo Rusticucci, whose name occurs several times as witness to the acts of the Podestà of Florence in 1236–7, was in 1254 one of two procurators specially appointed to represent Florence in negotiations with the other cities of Tuscany. His house (in San Michele in Palchetto) and that of his neighbour in Florence (and in Hell), Tegghiaio Aldobrandi, were among those destroyed after the battle of Montaperti by the victorious Ghibellines between Sept. 1260 and Nov. 1266, at which latter date Jacopo was still alive.

Jacopo tra' Fossi, Sa'. [Sa' Jacopo tra' Fossi.]

Janicolo. [Gianicolo.]

Jano, Janus, ancient Roman deity, whose temple was opened in times of war and closed in times of peace.

The Emperor Justinian (in the Heaven of Mercury) refers to the closing of the temple of Janus during the reign of Augustus after he had put an end to the civil war, Par. vi. 81. [Augusto [1].]

Januarius. [Gennaio.]

Januensis,-es. [Genovese,-esi.]

Japeto. [Giapeto.]

Jason [1], Jason, leader of the Argonauts on their celebrated expedition to Colchis in quest of the golden fleece. His father Aeson, the rightful King of Iolcus in Thessaly, was deprived of his throne by his half-brother Pelias, who also attempted to kill the infant Jason. The latter, however, was saved from his uncle, and when he had grown up, demanded his father's kingdom from Pelias, who promised to give it up to him on condition he brought the golden fleece from Colchis, where it was guarded by a dragon. Jason consented to the terms and set sail for Colchis in the ship Argo, accompanied by the chief heroes of Greece. After many adventures, in the course of which they visited Lemnos, where Jason seduced and abandoned Hypsipyle, the Argonauts at length arrived at the mouth of the river Phasis. Aeëtes, the Colchian king, undertook to deliver up the golden fleece if Jason would yoke to a plough two fire-breathing oxen, and sow the dragon's teeth. Medea, the daughter of Aeëtes, having fallen in love with Jason, who promised to marry her, enabled him to secure the fleece, with which he and his companions sailed away, taking Medea with them, whom Jason married but afterwards deserted.

D. places Jason in Bolgia 1 of

Circle VIII of Hell (Malebolge) among the Seducers, Inf. xviii. 86; *quel grande*, v. 83; *quelli, v.* 86 [**Seduttori**]; Virgil points out to D. one of the sinners among the crowd of Seducers, who wears the aspect of a king, and explains that it is Jason, who fetched the golden fleece from Colchis, and that he here expiates his seduction and desertion of Hypsipyle, and his faithlessness to Medea (*vv.* 82–96) [**Colchi: Isi-file: Medea**].

D. compares the wonder his readers will feel at the contents of the *Paradiso* with the surprise of the Argonauts when they saw Jason 'turn ploughman', Par. ii. 16–18. [**Argonauti: Colco.**]

The several episodes referred to in connexion with Jason are taken from Statius and Ovid—the seduction of Hypsipyle is from *Theb.* v. 404–85 (cf. *Heroid.* vi); the betrayal of Medea is from *Heroid.* xii; the scene of Jason ploughing is from *Metam.* vii. 104–22.

Jason[2], Jason, second son of the high-priest Simon II, and brother of the high-priest Onias III. He succeeded by means of bribes in obtaining the office of high-priest from Antiochus Epiphanes (c. B.C. 175) to the exclusion of his elder brother (2 *Maccab.* iv. 7–8).

Pope Nicholas III (in Bolgia 3 of Circle VIII of Hell) compares the relations of Jason with Antiochus to those of Clement V (whom he speaks of as *nuovo Jason*) with Philip the Fair, and refers to the account in *Maccabees*, Inf. xix. 85–6. [**Antioco: Clemente**[2]**: Filippo**[2]**.**]

Jeptè, Jephthah, the Gileadite, Judge of Israel, who sacrificed his daughter in fulfilment of his vow that if the children of Ammon were delivered into his hands he would offer as a burnt-offering whatsoever first came out of his house to meet him (*Judges* xi. 30, 34).

Beatrice (in the Heaven of the Moon) mentions Jephthah in connexion with his vow, which she says he ought not to have kept, Par. v. 66.

Jeremiae, Prophetia. [**Geremia.**]

Jeremias. [**Geremia.**]

Jerico. [**Gerico.**]

Jeronimo, St. Jerome, celebrated Father of the Latin Church, born in Dalmatia c. 340; he was baptized in Rome, and went in 373 to Antioch in Syria, where he was ordained presbyter. After studying under Gregory of Nazianzen at Constantinople, in 382 he returned to Rome, where his exposition of the Scriptures gained many adherents; among these was St. Paula, who in 386 accompanied him to Bethlehem, where she founded four convents, in one of which St. Jerome remained until his death (Sept. 30, 420). While at Bethlehem St. Jerome completed his Latin version of the Old Testament from the Hebrew, which was the foundation of the Vulgate edition.

St. Jerome is mentioned by Beatrice (in the Crystalline Heaven) in connexion with his opinion (stated in his comment on *Titus* i. 2) as to the creation of angels before the rest of the world was made, Par. xxix. 37.

D. quotes St. Jerome's remark about St. Paul in his Preface to the Bible (i. e. *Hieronymus Paulino*), that it is better to be silent than to say too little, Conv. iv. 5[143−5]; and was apparently indebted to his *Prologus Galeatus* for the word *Malachoth*, Par. vii. 3. [*Malachoth*.]

Some think that St. Jerome is alluded to as one of the four elders 'in humble guise' in the mystical Procession in the Terrestrial Paradise (the other three being St. Ambrose, St. Augustine, and St. Gregory), Purg. xxix. 142. The reference is more probably to the four writers of the canonical Epistles.

Jerusalem, -emme. [**Gerusalemme.**]

Jerusalemme, Ciotto di. [**Carlo** [2].]

Jesse, Jesse, son of Obed, grandson of Boaz and Ruth, and father of David; D. mentions him as the ancestor of the Virgin Mary, quoting *Isaiah* xi. 1, Conv. iv. 5[42−5]; the Emperor Henry VII is addressed as a second son of Jesse, *proles altera Isai*, Epist. vii. 8[176−7] [**Arrigo** [2]].

Jesù, -us. [**Gesù.**]

Jò, Lingua. [*Lingua Jò.*]

Joannes. [**Johannes.**]

Job, patriarch Job, regarded by D. as the author of the Book of Job, and hence as the mouthpiece of the Holy Spirit, Mon. iii. 4[85]; the words of Job's friend, Zophar the Naamathite, quoted (*Job* xi. 7), A. T. § 22[6−8].

Job, Liber], Book of Job; quoted, A.T. § 22[6−8] (*Job* xi. 7). [**Bibbia.**]

Jocasta, Jocasta, wife of Laius, King of Thebes, and mother of Oedipus, whom she afterwards married, becoming by him the mother of Eteocles, Polynices, Antigone, and Ismene.

Virgil, addressing Statius (in Purgatory), speaks of the fratricidal strife between Eteocles and Polynices, of which he had sung in the *Thebaid*, as *la doppia tristizia di Jocasta*, Purg. xxii. 56 [**Eteocle**]; Jocasta is referred to as the mother of Polynices, Conv. iv. 25[116] [**Polinice**].

Johannem, Evangelium secundum. [**Giovanni** [2].]

Johannes [1]. [**Giovanni** [2].]

Johannes [2], John of Luxemburg, eldest son of the Emperor Henry VII, born 1295, killed at the battle of Crecy, 1346. He married Elizabeth, daughter of Wenceslas IV, and sister of Wenceslas V of Bohemia, and was King of Bohemia from 1310 till his death. Having lost both his eyes, he was commonly known as the 'Blind King of Bohemia'. [**Table C.**]

D. in his letter to the Emperor Henry VII (written in 1311) speaks of King John, then in his sixteenth year, as 'a second Ascanius', who, following in the footsteps of his father, should rage like a lion against 'the followers of Turnus' (i. e. the opponents of the Empire) on all occasions, Epist. vii. 5[93−9]. [**Ascanio.**]

Johannes [3], John I, surnamed the Just, Marquis of Montferrat, 1292–1305, son of William VII (or V) of Montferrat and of his second wife Beatrice, daughter of Alphonso X of Castile; born in 1276, succeeded his father in 1292, married in 1296 Margaret, daughter of

Amadeus V, Count of Savoy; died without issue in 1305. [Guglielmo³: Monferrato.]

D. condemns John, together with Frederick II of Sicily, Charles II of Naples, and Azzo of Este, as bloodthirsty, treacherous, and avaricious, *Johannes Marchio*, V. E. i. 12³⁸.

Johannes Marchio. [Johannes³.]

Johannis, Epistolae], Epistles of St. John; supposed to be symbolized by one of the four elders in humble guise, who form part of the mystical Procession in the Terrestrial Paradise, Purg. xxix. 142, 145–8. [*Epistolae Canonicae.*]

Johannis Visio. [*Apocalypsis.*]

Jordan, river Jordan in Palestine, which rises in Anti-Lebanon and flows due S. into the Dead Sea; mentioned to indicate Palestine or the Promised Land, Purg. xviii. 135 [Accidiosi]; St. Benedict (in the Heaven of Saturn) says that the reformation of the monastic orders would be a miracle not more impossible to God than the driving back of Jordan or the fleeing of the sea (in allusion to *Psalm* cxiv. 3), Par. xxii. 94.

Josaffàt, valley of Jehoshaphat, the name given to the deep ravine which separates Jerusalem from the Mount of Olives, where, according to a tradition common both to Jews and Moslems (based on *Joel* iii. 2, 12), the Last Judgement is to take place; D. mentions it in connexion with this belief, Inf. x. 11.

Joseppo. [Giuseppo.]

Josue. [Josuè.]

Josuè, Joshua, the son of Nun, the successor of Moses and conqueror of the land of Canaan; his wrath at the sin of Achan, Purg. xx. 111 [Acan]; his taking of the city of Jericho, Par. ix. 125 [Gerico]; Cacciaguida points out his spirit to D. among those of the warriors who had fought for the faith (*Spiriti Militanti*), in the Heaven of Mars, Par. xviii. 38 [Marte, Cielo di]; the Emperor Henry VII's delay to come into Tuscany compared to the standing still of the sun at Joshua's bidding, *Josue*, Epist. vii. 2²⁵⁻⁹ (ref. to *Josh.* x. 13).

Josue, Liber], Book of Joshua; referred to, Purg. xx. 109–11 (*Josh.* vii. 18–25); Par. ix. 116–25 (*Josh.* ii. 1 – vi. 27); Epist. vii. 2²⁵⁻⁹ (*Josh.* x. 13). [*Bibbia.*]

Jove. [Giove.]

Juba, son of Hiempsal, King of Numidia; he supported Pompey against Caesar, whose legate Curio he defeated, B.C. 49. After the death of Pompey, he joined Metellus Scipio, whose defeat by Caesar at Thapsus he shared, B.C. 46.

Juba is mentioned by the Emperor Justinian (in the Heaven of Mercury) in connexion with the victories of the Roman Eagle, Par. vi. 70.

Jubileo. [Giubbileo.]

Judae, Epistola], Epistle General of St. Jude; supposed to be symbolized by one of the four elders in humble guise, who form part of the mystical Procession in the Terrestrial Paradise, Purg. xxix. 142, 145–8. [*Epistolae Canonicae.*]

Judaea. [Giudea.]

Judaei. [Giudei.]

Judas, Judah, son of Jacob and Leah; discussion of the argument as to the precedence of the Church over the Empire, which are typified respectively by Levi and Judah, Mon. iii. 5$^{1-23}$; 'the strong lion of the tribe of Judah ', Epist. v. 1$^{17-18}$; he is among those referred to by Virgil as having been released by Christ from Limbo, *Israel co' suoi nati*, Inf. iv. 59 [Limbo].

Judex de Columnis. [Guido delle Colonne.]

Judicum Liber], Book of Judges; referred to, Purg. xxiv. 124–6 (*Judges* vii. 7–9); Par. v. 66 (*Judges* xi. 31). [*Bibbia.*]

Judit, Judith, daughter of Meraris, heroine of the apocryphal book which bears her name, and in which she is represented as the ideal type of piety, of beauty, and of courage and chastity. When Holofernes, one of Nebuchadnezzar's captains, was besieging Bethulia, Judith, having by means of her beauty gained access to his tent, one night cut off his head with his own sword while he was asleep. The Assyrians, struck with panic at the death of their captain, took to flight, and were pursued with great slaughter by the Jews, who hailed Judith as their deliverer. (*Jud.* x–xv.)

Judith is placed in the Celestial Rose, where her seat is pointed out to D. by St. Bernard, Par. xxxii. 10 [Rosa]; the flight of the Assyrians after she had slain Holofernes is included among the examples of defeated pride depicted in Circle I of Purgatory, Purg. xii. 58–60 [Assiri: Oloferne].

Julia, generally supposed to be the daughter of Julius Caesar, and wife (B.C. 59) of Pompey; she is placed, together with Lucretia, Marcia, and Cornelia, among the great women of antiquity in Limbo, Inf. iv. 128 [Limbo].

Julii, Forum. [Forum Julii.]

Julius, Julius Caesar, thus referred to by Virgil, who says to D., ' Nacqui *sub Julio* ancorchè fosse tardi', Inf. i. 70. As a matter of fact Virgil was born B. C. 70 in the consulate of Pompey and Crassus, when Caesar was as yet by no means the chief man in the state, and was only 30 years old. D., however, regards Caesar as the first of the divinely ordained Emperors of Rome, and speaks of him throughout as such [Cesare[1]]. Virgil says 'though late', perhaps because he was too young at the time of Caesar's death (B. C. 44) to have had much opportunity of distinguishing himself, and of attracting Caesar's notice. Another suggestion is that D. is here referring to the error of three months in the calendar (before it was reformed in B. C. 46 by Julius Caesar, in whose honour the name of the month *Quintilis*—the fifth month, since the Roman year began in March—was then changed to *Julius*), whereby the nominal month of October actually corresponded to July; so that the date of Virgil's birth, according to tradition, Oct. 15, was actually July 15. In this case the ' lateness ' would refer not to the birth of Virgil, but to the month —' I was born *sub Julio* (though *Julius* was belated).'

Juno, -one. [Giuno, -one.]

Jupiter. [Giove[2].]

Jura. [*Digesto.*]

Juvenalis. [Giovenale.]

Juventute et Senectute, De[1],
Aristotle's treatise *On Youth and Old Age*; quoted as, *Di Giovanezza e di Vecchiezza*, his definition of youth as an increase of life, Conv. iv. 23[86-8] (*De Juv. et Senect.* xiv); *Di Gioventute e Senettute*, his statement that death in old age is without 'sadness', Conv. iv. 28[31-4] (*De Juv. et Senect.* xiv).

Juventute et Senectute, De[2],
Albertus Magnus' treatise *On Youth and Old Age*; quoted (though D. refers to the *De Meteoris*) in illustration of the various 'qualities' inherent in the composition of man, Conv. iv. 23[118-26] (*De Juv. et Senect.* i. 2) [**Alberto di Cologna: Meteora[2]**].

K

Kanis Grandis de Scala.   [Can Grande.]

L

L, third letter of the word *Diligite*, formed by the spirits of the Just in the Heaven of Jupiter, Par. xviii. 78. [**Aquila[2]: Giove, Cielo di.**]

Lacedemone, Lacedaemon or Sparta, the capital of Laconia and chief city of the Peloponnesus; D. alludes to the legislation of Lycurgus at Sparta and of Solon at Athens, with which he contrasts the constant changes in Florence, Purg. vi. 139. [**Licurgo[2]: Solone.**]

Lachesìs, Lachesis, the allotting fate, on to whose distaff Clotho, the spinning fate, was supposed to wind a certain quantity of yarn at the birth of every mortal, the length of time it took to spin being the duration of the individual's life; hence D. speaks of the death of the human body as taking place 'when Lachesis has no more thread', Purg. xxv. 79; Virgil, explaining to Statius (in Purgatory) that D.'s life has not yet run its course, alludes to Lachesis as *lei che dì e notte fila*, Purg. xxi. 25. [**Cloto.**]

Ladri], Thieves and Robbers, placed among the Fraudulent in Bolgia 7 of Circle VIII of Hell (Malebolge), *genti nude e spaventate*, Inf. xxiv. 92; *la settima zavorra*, Inf. xxv. 142 [**Frodolenti**]; their punishment is to be tormented by serpents (*serpenti*, Inf. xxiv. 83; *serpi*, xxiv. 94; *bisce*, xxv. 20), which fasten upon their naked bodies; in some cases they are turned to ashes and thence retransformed into their previous shapes (Inf. xxiv. 82-118); in others they are gradually transformed into serpents, which in turn assume the forms of the tormented spirits (Inf. xxv. 49-143). *Examples*: Vanni Fucci [**Fucci**]; Cacus [**Caco**]; Cianfa Donati [**Cianfa**];

Agnello Brunelleschi [**Agnèl**]; Francesco de' Cavalcanti [**Cavalcanti⁴**]; Buoso Donati (or degli Abati) [**Buoso**]; Puccio Sciancato [**Puccio**].

Laerte], Laertes, King of Ithaca, father of Ulysses; he was still alive when the latter returned home after the fall of Troy. Ulysses (in Bolgia 8 of Circle VIII of Hell) relates how his desire to travel and see the world was stronger than his love for his son or for *il vecchio padre*, Inf. xxvi. 94–9. [**Ulisse.**]

Lageus, Lagaean; term applied by Lucan to Ptolemy I, King of Egypt, the son of Lagus, whose descendant, Ptolemy XII, he denounces in a passage (*Phars.* viii. 692–4) quoted by D., Mon. ii. 9⁷²⁻⁴ [**Tolommeo²**].

Lagia, name of a lady-love of Lapo Gianni, Son. xxxii. 9. [**Lapo¹**.]

Lago di Garda. [**Benaco.**]

Lamagna, Germany, Inf. xx. 62; *la Magna*, Conv. iii. 5¹¹³; *Alamania*, V. E. i. 18⁴⁷; divided from Italy by the Tyrolese Alps, at the foot of which lies the Lago di Garda, Inf. xx. 62 [**Benaco: Tiralli**]; the native country of Albertus Magnus, Conv. iii. 5¹¹³ [**Alberto¹**]; the imperial court of the 'King of Germany', V. E. i. 18⁴⁷⁻⁸; the banks of the Danube on its course through Germany, *le ripe tedesche*, Par. viii. 66 [**Danubio**].

Lambertazzi, Fabbro de'. [**Fabbro.**]

Lambertazzi, Fabruzzo de'. [**Fabricius².**]

Lamberti], ancient noble family of Florence, referred to by Caccia-

guida (in the Heaven of Mars) as having been of importance in his day (they being not named but indicated by the mention of their arms, *le palle dell' oro*), Par. xvi. 110. Cacciaguida couples them with the Uberti, who like them are said to have been of German origin and to have come to Florence in Cent. x with the Emperor Otto I (Vill. iv. 1).

The Lamberti, who lived in the Porta di san Brancazio (Vill. iv. 12), were Ghibellines (v. 39), and as such were expelled from Florence in 1258 (vi. 33).

It appears from an expression of D.'s (Inf. xxviii. 109) that this family (to which belonged the notorious Mosca, who instigated the murder of Buondelmonte) became extinct before the end of Cent. xiii [**Mosca**].

Lamberti, Mosca de'. [**Mosca.**]

Lamentationes Jeremiae], Lamentations of Jeremiah; quoted, V. N. § 7⁴⁰⁻³ (*Lament.* i. 12); V.N. § 29¹⁻³ (*Lament.* i. 1); V. N. § 31⁸⁻⁹ (*Lament.* i. 1); Epist. viii. 1¹⁻³ (*Lament.* i. 1). [**Bibbia.**]

Lamone, small river of N. Italy, which rises in the Etruscan Apennines, flows through the S. of the Emilia, past Faenza, and enters the Adriatic about ten miles N. of Ravenna. In D.'s day it had no direct outlet to the sea, but flowed into the Po di Primaro. [**Acquacheta.**]

D. speaks of Faenza, which is on its banks, as *la città di Lamone*, Inf. xxvii. 49. [**Faenza.**]

Lancelotto, Lancelot of the Lake, hero of the Romance of 'Lancelot du Lac', the most famous of the Knights of the Round Table, son of Ban, King of Benoic (or Brittany); he was brought up by Merlin the Enchanter, and Vivien, the Lady of the Lake. At the court of King Arthur he became enamoured of Queen Guenever, and in consequence of his guilty love for her he failed in the quest for the Holy Grail. After the death of Arthur he retired into a monastery.

The first meeting between Lancelot and Guenever, which was contrived by Gallehault, is referred to by Francesca da Rimini (in Circle II of Hell), Inf. v. 127–37; it is alluded to again, Par. xvi. 14–15 [Galeotto : Ginevra]; D. couples 'il cavaliere Lancilotto' with Guido da Montefeltro, as having, like him, devoted himself to religion at the close of his life, Conv. iv. 28⁵⁹⁻⁶⁵ [Guido Montefeltrano].

Lancilotto. [Lancelotto.]

Lanfranchi, noble Ghibelline family of Pisa, mentioned by Count Ugolino (in Circle IX of Hell) together with the Gualandi and Sismondi, as having been foremost among those whom the Archbishop Ruggieri incited to work his destruction, Inf. xxxiii. 32. [Ugolino, Conte.]

Langía, name of a fountain near Nemea in the Peloponnesus, to which Hypsipyle conducted Adrastus and his companions; hence Virgil, addressing Statius (in Purgatory), refers to her as *quella che mostrò Langía*, Purg. xxii. 112. [Isifile.]

Lano, gentleman of Siena, placed by D., together with Jacomo da sant' Andrea, among those who have squandered their substance in Round 2 of Circle VII of Hell, Inf. xiii. 120; *duo* (*peccatori*), *v.* 115; *quel dinanzi, v.* 118 [Scialacquatori]; in the wood of the Suicides, D. sees two spirits (those of Lano and Jacomo), naked and bleeding, come flying through the bushes, pursued by black hounds (*vv.* 109–26); the one in front (Lano) calls upon death to release him, whereupon the other reminds him that he had not run so quickly when he was 'at the jousts of Il Toppo' (*vv.* 118–21) [Jacomo da sant' Andrea].

Lano is said to have been a member of the 'Spendthrift Brigade' of Siena, and to have squandered all his property in riotous living. He took part in an expedition of the Florentines and Sienese against Arezzo in 1288, which ended in the Sienese force falling into an ambush and being cut to pieces by the Aretines under Buonconte da Montefeltro at a spot near Arezzo, called the ford of the Pieve al Toppo. Lano, being ruined and desperate, chose to fight and be killed, rather than run away and make his escape; hence the allusion of Jacomo in the text. [Brigata Spendereccia : Toppo, Il.] Two sonnets have been preserved addressed to Lano by his fellow citizen, Cecco Angiolieri.

Laomedonte, Laomedon, King of Troy, great-great-grandson of Dardanus, the mythical founder of the Trojan race, son of Ilus, and father of Priam; he and his ancestor Dardanus are mentioned in a discussion as to the nature of nobility, Conv. iv. 14¹³⁴⁻⁴⁸. [Dardano.]

Lapi, people of the name of Lapo (popular abbreviation of Jacopo); mentioned, together with Bindo, as being among the commonest names in Florence, Par. xxix. 103. [Bindi.]

Lapo[1], Lapo Gianni, Florentine notary and accomplished lyric poet, intimate friend of Dante and Guido Cavalcanti; little further is known of him save that he belonged to the Ricevuti family and was still living in May, 1328, so that he survived both D. and Guido. A number of his poems have been preserved, besides the register of his notarial acts for thirty years, from May 24, 1298, to May 24, 1328.

D. mentions Lapo in a sonnet addressed to Guido Cavalcanti, in which he expresses the wish that they all three might be wafted in a boat on the sea with their respective mistresses and discourse of love, Son. xxxii. 1; he is coupled with Guido Cavalcanti, Cino da Pistoja, and D. himself, as having recognized the excellence of the vulgar tongue, *Lapus Florentinus*, V. E. i. 13³⁴⁻⁷.

Lapo[2], Lapo Salterello, Florentine lawyer and judge, a relative and adherent of the Cerchi, the leaders of the Bianchi faction in Florence. He belonged to the same party as D., and was included in the same decree of banishment (March 10, 1302). He was a prominent and active politician, and his name recurs continually in contemporary documents as having been concerned in most of the important public acts in Florence during the twenty years

between the institution of the priorate (1282) and the banishment of the Bianchi (1302). In 1300 he served the office of Prior during the two months (April 15–June 15) preceding D.'s priorate. After the outbreak in Florence of the Bianchi and Neri feuds, and the triumph of the latter, he attempted to conceal himself, but was discovered, and proscribed with most of the other members of his party. He appears to have been very corrupt, and was specifically accused of having taken bribes to pervert the course of justice. He is said to have died in exile in great poverty.

Cacciaguida (in the Heaven of Mars), speaking of the degenerate state of Florence, says that in his day such a person as Lapo would have been as great a marvel in that city as Cincinnatus would be now (i. e. in 1300), Par. xv. 128. [Cincinnato.]

Lapo Salterello. [Lapo[2].]
Lapus Florentinus. [Lapo[1].]
Lasca celeste. [Pesci.]
Laterano, Lateran palace at Rome, which in D.'s time was the usual residence of the Pope.

Guido da Montefeltro (in Bolgia 8 of Circle VIII of Hell) mentions the Lateran in connexion with the contest between Boniface VIII and the Colonna family, who lived near the palace, Inf. xxvii. 86 [Colonnesi]; it is mentioned again, probably with special reference to the Jubilee of 1300, Par. xxxi. 35 [Barbari: Giubbileo].

Latiale caput. [Roma[2].]
Latii. [Itali[2].]
Latina gente. [Romani[1].]

Latina terra. [Italia.]

Latini [1], inhabitants of Latium, Latins as distinguished from the Romans; Cicero's reference to the heroism of Publius Decius in the Latin war quoted, Mon. ii. 5[142-54] (*Fin.* ii. 19) [Decius]; the followers of Latinus, King of Latium, as opposed to *Turni*, the followers of Turnus, King of the Rutuli, the two standing respectively for the supporters and opponents of the Empire, Epist. vii. 5[99] [Johannes[2]: **Latino** [3] : Turno].

Latini [2], Latins, i. e. the ancient Romans; Sordello (in Ante-purgatory) addresses Virgil as *gloria de' Latin*, i. e. of the whole Latin race, Romans and Italians, Purg. vii. 16; the progenitors of the Italian people, Epist. v. 4[52]; *gente Latina*, Conv. iv. 4[101]. [Romani [1].]

Latini [3], Italians, Inf. xxix. 91; V. E. i. 6[38], 8[44], 10[26, 71], 11[42-3], 12[29], 15[35], 16[35, 40], 17[19]; ii. 2[95]; Epist. viii. 11[188]. [Itali [2] : Latino [2].]

Latini, Brunetto. [Brunetto Latini.]

Latino [1], Latin, the Latin language; of the *Historiae adversum Paganos* of Orosius, Par. x. 120 [Orosio]; the rival merits of Latin and Italian discussed, V. N. § 25; Conv. i. 5, 6, 7, 8, 9, 10, 11, 13; Latin interpretation of the Greek words *filosofia*, Conv. iii. 11[47-51]; and *autentin*, Conv. iv. 6[38-43]; *Latina lingua*, use of by writers of love-poems, V. N. § 25[26-7]; *Latino Romano*, classical Latin, Cicero's complaint (*Fin.* i. 1) of the neglect of it in favour of Greek, Conv. i. 11[95].

From its original meaning of Latin, the word *latino* came to be transferred to that of language in general, often with especial reference to the language natural to the speaker; and as every man's mother-tongue is easy to him, the word came to be used in the secondary sense of easy, clear, intelligible. D. uses it in this sense, Par. iii. 63; and similarly *latinamente*, Conv. ii. 3[1]; it is used in the sense of speech, language, of St. Thomas Aquinas, Par. xii. 144; of Cacciaguida, Par. xvii. 35.

Latino [2], Italian, inhabitant of Italy, Inf. xxii. 65; xxvii. 33; xxix. 88, 91; Purg. xi. 58; xiii. 92; Conv. iv. 28[61]; *Latinus*, V. E. i. 10[26,36,71], 11[42-3], 12[29], 15[35,67-8], 16[35, 40], 17[19]; ii. 2[95]; Epist. viii. 11[188]; hence Italy is called *terra Latina*, Inf. xxvii. 27; xxviii. 71; and the language, *vulgare Latinum*, V. E. i. 10[36], 11[1-2], 15[35], 19[4, 15]; ii. 1[3-4]; affinity between Italian and Sardinian, which are distinct, though nearly related, Inf. xxii. 65, 67; V. E. i. 11[42-4]. [Italico : Latini [3] : Sardi.]

Latino [3], Latinus, King of Latium, husband of Amata and father of Lavinia, whom he bestowed on Aeneas, though she had been previously promised to Turnus; the latter in consequence made war upon Aeneas, by whose hand he was finally slain. D. places Latinus with Lavinia (*Aen.* vii. 72) among the heroes of antiquity in Limbo, Inf. iv. 125 [Limbo]; he is mentioned in connexion with Lavinia, his daughter and heiress, who became the third wife of Aeneas,

Latinus, Mon. ii. 3^{108–10} [**Enea** : **Lavinia**.]

Latino Romano. [**Latino** [1].]
Latinus. [**Latino.**]
Latium. [**Italia.**]

Latius, variant for *Latinus*, in the sense of Italian, in many places where the latter occurs in V. E. [**Latinus : Semilatius.**]

Latona, mother of Apollo and Diana by Jupiter. Being persecuted by Juno, who was jealous of Jupiter's love for her, Latona wandered from place to place till she came to the island of Delos, which had previously been a floating island, but was fixed by Jupiter with adamantine chains to the bottom of the sea ; here she gave birth to Apollo and Diana.

D. compares the shaking of the Mt. of Purgatory to the tossing of Delos before Latona gave birth to her offspring there, Purg. xx. 130–2 [**Delo**] ; Apollo and Diana, being identified respectively with the Sun and Moon, are spoken of as *li due occhi del cielo*, Purg. xx. 132 ; conversely the Sun and Moon are spoken of as *i figli di Latona*, Par. xxix. 1 ; and the Moon alone as *la figlia di Latona*, Par. x. 67 ; xxii. 139 [**Apollo : Diana** [1]].

Lavagna], small river of Liguria, which falls into the Gulf of Genoa between Chiavari and Sestri Levante ; Pope Adrian V (Ottobuono de' Fieschi) (in Circle V of Purgatory) alludes to it in reference to the fact that from it the Fieschi family took their title of Counts of Lavagna, Purg. xix. 100–2. [**Adriano** [2].]

Lavina. [**Lavinia.**]
Lavinia, daughter of Latinus,

King of Latium, and of Amata ; she had been betrothed to Turnus, King of the Rutuli, but Latinus gave her in marriage to Aeneas, upon whom Turnus consequently made war ; when eventually Turnus was slain in battle with Aeneas, Amata, who had strongly opposed the marriage of her daughter with the latter, in despair hanged herself.

D. places Lavinia with Latinus (*Aen.* vii. 72) among the heroes of antiquity in Limbo, Inf. iv. 126 [**Limbo**] ; she is introduced in Circle III of Purgatory in a vision where she is represented as weeping bitterly and reproaching her mother for her wrath against Aeneas and for her suicide after the death of Turnus, Purg. xvii. 34–9 ; *Lavina*, *v.* 37 ; *fanciulla*, *v.* 34 [**Amata** : **Iracondi**] ; she is mentioned in connexion with her marriage to Aeneas, whose third wife she was, Par. vi. 3 ; and as co-founder with him of the Roman race, Mon. ii. 3^{108–9} [**Enea**].

Lazaro], Lazarus of Bethany, brother of Mary and Martha, who was raised from the dead by Christ, after he had been dead four days (*John* xi. 1–44) ; referred to as *colui che quattro dì è stato nel sepolcro*, Conv. iv. 7^{41–2}.

Leandro, Leander, youth of Abydos, who used to swim every night across the Hellespont to visit Hero, the priestess of Venus at Sestos. One night, as he was attempting the passage, he was drowned, and his dead body was washed ashore at Sestos ; Hero thereupon in despair threw herself into the sea and perished also.

D. mentions Leander in connexion with the Hellespont, which he says was not more odious to L., as the barrier between him and Hero (cf. Ovid, *Heroid.* xix. 139–40), than was the stream of Lethe to himself, which separated him from Matilda in the Terrestrial Paradise, Purg. xxviii. 73–5 [Abido: Ellesponto].

Learco, Learchus, son of Athamas, King of Orchomenus in Boeotia, and Ino, daughter of Cadmus, King of Thebes. Athamas, having been seized with madness, took Ino and her two sons, Learchus and Melicertes, for a lioness and cubs, and pursuing them caught up L. and hurled him against a rock.

This incident (which D. got from Ovid, *Metam.* iv. 512 ff., whom he has closely followed) is referred to, Inf. xxx. 10–11. [Atamante: Ino.]

Leda, wife of Tyndareus, King of Sparta, and mother by Jupiter of Castor and Pollux and Helen. According to the story, Jupiter visited Leda in the form of a swan, and she brought forth two eggs, from one of which issued Helen, and from the other the twin-brothers Castor and Pollux. At their death Jupiter placed the twins among the stars as the constellation Gemini; hence D. alludes to this constellation as *il bel nido di Leda*, Par. xxvii. 98. [Castore: Gemelli.]

Legge. [Digesto.]

Lelio, Caius Laelius Sapiens, born c. B.C. 186, Consul 140; he was celebrated for his love of literature and philosophy, and for his intimate friendship with Scipio Africanus Minor, which is immortalized in Cicero's treatise *Laelius sive de Amicitia*, in which Laelius is introduced as the principal interlocutor.

D. mentions him in connexion with the *De Amicitia*, Conv. ii. 13²⁰. [Amicitia, De.]

Lemosì, Limoges, town of W. France, on the Vienne, formerly capital of the Province of Limousin, now capital of the Department of Haute-Vienne; it is mentioned by Guido Guinizelli (in Circle VII of Purgatory) in connexion with the troubadour Giraut de Borneil, who was born near there, and is hence spoken of as *quel di Lemosì*, Purg. xxvi. 120. [Gerardus de Borneil.]

Lenno, Lemnos, island in the Aegaean Sea, nearly midway between Mt. Athos and the Hellespont. When Jason and the Argonauts landed there they found it inhabited only by women, all the males having been killed by them, with the exception of Thoas, the King of Lemnos, whose life was saved by his daughter Hypsipyle. During his stay on the island Jason seduced the latter, and subsequently abandoned her when the Argonauts set out again on their voyage to Colchis.

Lemnos is mentioned in connexion with these incidents, Inf. xviii. 88–94. [Isifile: Jason¹.]

Lentino, Jacopo da. [Jacopo da Lentino.]

Leo, Leo VIII, Pope 963–965; at the instance of the Emperor Otto I, he was elected Pope by the Roman synod which deposed John XII on Dec. 4, 963, and when in Feb. 964 the Emperor withdrew from Rome, Leo found it necessary to seek safety in flight, whereupon he was deposed by a synod presided over by John XII. On the sudden death of the latter, the populace elected Benedict V as his successor; but the Emperor returning to Rome laid siege to the city, deposed Benedict, and compelled the Romans to accept Leo as Pope. Leo died in the spring of 965, little more than a year after his election.

D. mentions the deposition of Benedict V by the Emperor Otto I, and his restoration of Leo VIII, as facts from which it might be argued that the Church was dependent upon the Empire, Mon. iii. 11[16-21]. [**Benedetto**[3] : **Otto**.]

Leo, San. [**Sanleo.**]

Leone, Leo ('the Lion'), constellation and fifth sign of the Zodiac, which the Sun enters about July 22, leaving it about Aug. 22. [**Zodiaco.**]

The constellation of the Lion is mentioned by Cacciaguida (in the Heaven of Mars), who says that from the Incarnation of Christ down to the day of his own birth the planet Mars had returned *al suo Leone* 580 times (i.e. had made that number of revolutions in its orbit), Par. xvi. 34–9. [**Cacciaguida : Marte**[2].]

Beatrice describes the Heaven of Saturn, in which she and D. had just arrived, as shining *sotto il petto del Leone ardente* (the planet Saturn having been in that constellation in the spring of 1300, the date of the Vision), Par. xxi. 14. [**Saturno.**]

Lerici, town in Liguria on the E. shore of the Gulf of Spezia.

D. compares the abruptness of

the rocks at the foot of the Mt. of Purgatory to the rugged and broken ground between Lerici and Turbia (representing the coast-line of the province of Liguria), Purg. iii. 49. [**Turbia.**]

Letè (from Gk. λήθη, 'oblivion'), Lethe, name of one of the rivers of the Terrestrial Paradise, the other being Eunoë, Inf. xiv. 131, 136; Purg. xxvi. 108; xxviii. 130; xxx. 143; xxxiii. 96, 123; *ruscelletto*, Inf. xxxiv. 130; *cieco fiume*, Purg. i. 40; *rio*, xxviii. 25; *fiumicel*, xxviii. 35; *riviera*, xxviii. 47; *bel fiume*, xxviii. 62; *fiume*, xxviii. 70; *acqua*, xxviii. 85, 121; *fiume*, xxix. 7; *acqua*, xxix. 67; *fiume*, xxix. 71; *chiaro fonte*, xxx. 76; *fiume sacro*, xxxi. 1; *acqua*, xxxi. 12; *riviera*, xxxi. 82; *fiume*, xxxi. 94; *acqua*, xxxi. 96, 102; *fiume*, xxxii. 84; *fontana*, xxxiii. 113; *Lethe*, Carm. 5.

Virgil having named the rivers of Hell without mentioning Lethe (Inf. xiv. 116), D. asks where it is to be found (*vv.* 130-1); V. replies that D. shall see it, not in Hell, but in Purgatory (*vv.* 136-8). Guido Guinizelli (in Circle VII of Purgatory) declares that he is so touched by D.'s kindly bearing toward him that not even the waters of Lethe will be able to make him forget it, Purg. xxvi. 106–8. Eventually D. sees the stream of Lethe in the Terrestrial Paradise, where it appears as a rivulet, purer than any earthly stream, flowing from S. to N. through a wood, which perpetually shades it from the sun and moon, Purg. xxviii. 25–33; on the further bank he sees a solitary lady (Matilda) gathering flowers and singing as she goes, whom he prays to come near to the stream that he may hear what she sings (*vv.* 34–51); she approaches the opposite bank and smiles upon him across the stream, which is but three paces wide, yet forms as effectual a barrier betwixt her and D. as did the Hellespont between Hero and Leander (*vv.* 52–75); she addresses D. and explains to him the origin and properties of the two rivers, Eunoë and Lethe (*vv.* 121–33); subsequently, after D. has made confession to Beatrice, he is drawn through the stream of Lethe to the opposite bank by Matilda, who plunges him under the water and causes him to swallow some of it (Purg. xxxi. 1–90, 91–102); afterwards she takes him to drink also of the waters of Eunoë (Purg. xxxiii. 127–45) [Eunoè].

Lethe. [Letè.]

Leucippe], daughter of Minyas of Boeotia ; she and her sisters Alcithoë and Arcippe are referred to, Epist. iv. 4⁴⁴⁻⁵. [Alcithoë.]

Leucothoë, daughter of the Babylonian King Orchamus and his wife Eurynome ; being beloved by Apollo she was buried alive by her father, whereupon the god metamorphosed her into a fragrant shrub.

D. refers to Ovid's account (*Metam.* iv. 192 ff.), where Apollo (as the Sun) is taunted with having deserted all the other nymphs whom he had loved, and with being enslaved by Leucothoë alone, Epist. iv. 4⁴⁰⁻⁹.

Levante. [Oriente.]

Levì, Levi, son of Jacob and Leah ; *li figli di Levì,* i. e. the Levites, Purg. xvi. 132 [Levitae]; discussion of the argument as to the precedence of the Church over the Empire, which are typified respectively by Levi and Judah, Mon. iii. 5¹⁻²³ ; Levi is among those referred to by Virgil as having been released by Christ from Limbo, *Israel co' suoi nati,* Inf. iv. 59 [Limbo].

Levitae, Levites, members of the tribe of Levi, who served as subordinate ministers of the Temple; D. quotes the command to the Levites that they should abstain from creeping things (*Levit.* xi. 43), Mon. iii. 13⁷¹⁻⁶; they are referred to as *li figli di Levì* in connexion with their exclusion from the inheritance of Israel (*Numb.* xviii. 23), Purg. xvi. 132.

Leviticus, Book of Leviticus, Mon. ii. 8³⁷; iii. 13⁶⁶; quoted, Mon. ii. 8³⁷⁻⁴² (*Levit.* xvii. 3–4); Mon. iii. 13⁶⁶⁻⁷⁶ (*Levit.* ii. 11; xi. 43). [Bibbia.]

Lia, Leah, daughter of Laban, first wife of Jacob, elder sister of Rachel, his second wife. In the Middle Ages Leah and Rachel were universally regarded by theologians as the types respectively of the active and contemplative life in the O. T. (as Martha and Mary were in the N. T.—see Conv. iv. 17⁹⁴⁻¹¹¹), and D. represents them as such in the *D. C.,* in which their secular counterparts are Matilda and Beatrice.

At the foot of the ascent to the Terrestrial Paradise D. has a dream, in which he sees a lady, young and fair, going through a plain singing and gathering flowers, *giovane e bella*

Donna, Purg. xxvii. 97–8 ; as she sings she names herself as Leah (*v.* 101), and describes her own occupation and that of her sister Rachel (*vv.* 101–8). [**Matelda : Rachele.**]

Libanus, Mt. Lebanon, name given in the Bible to the two parallel ranges of mountains which run from SW. to NE. in the N. of Palestine.

The voice of one of the four-and-twenty elders in the mystical Procession in the Terrestrial Paradise is heard chanting ' Veni, sponsa, de Libano' (*Cant.* iv. 8), Purg. xxx. 11. [*Bibbia.*]

Liber Alfragani de Aggregatione Scientiae Stellarum. [**Alfergano.**]

Liber Sententiarum. [*Sententiarum, Liber.*]

Liber Ugutionis de Derivationibus Verborum. [**Uguccione [2].**]

Libia, Libya, Roman province of N. Africa, hence Africa in general.

D. says that the Libyan desert could not produce such deadly snakes (cf. Lucan, *Phars.* ix. 711 ff.) as those which tormented the Robbers in Bolgia 7 of Circle VIII of Hell (Malebolge), Inf. xxiv. 85–7 [**Ladri**] ; Lucan's account (*Phars.* ix. 477–80) of the violence of the S. wind in Libya quoted, *Libya*, Mon. ii. 4[34–42]. [**Austro.**]

Libicocco, one of the ten demons in Bolgia 5 of Circle VIII of Hell (Malebolge), deputed by Malacoda to escort D. and Virgil, Inf. xxi. 121. [**Alichino: Malebranche.**]

Libra, ' the Balance ', constellation and seventh sign of the Zodiac, which the Sun enters at the autumnal equinox (about Sept. 23), Purg. xxvii. 3 ; Par. xxix. 2 ; Conv. iii. 5[79, 135, 182] ; *le bilance*, Purg. ii. 5. [**Ariete : Zodiaco.**]

Libri Regum. [*Regum, Libri.*]

Libro dell' Aggregazione delle Stelle. [*Liber Alfragani.*]

Libro delli Regi. [*Regum, Libri.*]

Libya. [**Libia.**]

Libyus, Libyan ; *Libyus coluber,* i. e. the serpents which infest the Libyan desert, Ecl. ii. 23. [**Libia.**]

Licio. [**Lizio.**]

Licurgo [1], Lycurgus, King of Nemea, whose son Archemorus, while under the charge of Hypsipyle, was killed by a snake-bite ; the death of A. is referred to as *la tristizia di Licurgo*, Purg. xxvi. 94. [**Archemoro : Isifile.**]

Licurgo [2], Lycurgus (c. B. C. 825), the famous law-giver of Sparta, the whole constitution of which, military and civil, was remodelled by him. D. alludes to the laws of Solon at Athens, and to those of Lycurgus at Sparta, Purg. vi. 139. [**Lacedemone.**]

Ligures, inhabitants of Liguria ; D. reproaches the Emperor Henry VII with neglecting Tuscany, as though he believed that the Imperial interests in Italy ceased at the Ligurian frontier, Epist. vii. 3[51–2] ; G. del Virgilio speaks of the Ligurian Apennines as *Ligurum montes,* Carm. 29. [**Liguria.**]

Liguria, maritime province of Italy, of which the capital is Genoa ; in D.'s time the whole extent of coast, from Sarzana at the E. extremity to where Ventimiglia now stands at the W. extremity, was in the possession of the Genoese.

D. roughly indicates the coast-line of Liguria by describing it as the country between Lerici and Turbia, Purg. iii. 49 [Lerici]; the river Macra is mentioned by the troubadour Folquet (in the Heaven of Venus) as the dividing line between the Genoese territory and Tuscany, Par. ix. 90 [Genovese].

Lilla, Lille, formerly capital of the old province of Flanders, now capital of the French Département du Nord; mentioned by Hugh Capet (in Circle V of Purgatory), together with Douay, Ghent, and Bruges, to indicate Flanders, Purg. xx. 46. [Bruggia: Fiandra.]

Limbo, 'the Border', name given by D. to Circle I of Hell, Inf. iv. 45; *limbo del inferno*, Purg. xxii. 14; alluded to as *il primo cerchio che l'abisso cigne*, Inf. iv. 24; *il cerchio superno*, Inf. xii. 39; *loco laggiù*, Purg. vii. 28; *l'ampia gola d'inferno*, Purg. xxi. 31–2; *il primo cinghio del carcere cieco*, Purg. xxii. 103; *l'uscio dei morti*, Purg. xxx. 139; *laggiù*, Par. xxxii. 84. Virgil explains to D. that here are placed the spirits of those who, having lived before Christianity, did not worship God aright, and of those who, living after Christ, died unbaptized, he himself being among the former, Inf. iv. 33–9; he adds that the only pain they suffer is that they live with the longing, but without the hope, of seeing God (*vv.* 40–2). He describes Limbo as ' a place, not sad with torments, but with gloom only', Purg. vii. 28–9; the sighs of the spirits cause the everlasting air

to tremble, but there is no audible lamentation among them, Inf. iv. 25–7; Purg. vii. 29–30. D. having inquired if any souls had ever been released from there, V. replies that soon after his own arrival there a Mighty One (i. e. Christ) came and delivered many thence (cf. Inf. xii. 38–9), among whom he mentions Adam, Abel, Noah, Moses, Abraham, David, Jacob and his twelve sons, and Rachel (Inf. iv. 43–63). In the light of a fire are certain 'honourable folk', who are thus distinguished on account of their honoured reputation in the world, among whom are Homer, Horace, Ovid, and Lucan (Inf. iv. 67–90); on the farther side of a noble castle, encircled with seven walls and a rivulet, is a green meadow where are stationed various great personages of antiquity connected with Troy and Rome, viz. Electra, the mother of Dardanus who founded Troy, Hector the defender of Troy, Aeneas the founder of the Roman Empire, and Julius Caesar the first Emperor (according to D.'s theory); then Camilla who died in defence of Latium, Penthesilea who died in defence of Troy, and Latinus, King of Latium, with his daughter Lavinia, the wife of Aeneas; then Lucius Junius Brutus, who delivered Rome from the Tarquins, with Lucretia, Julia, Marcia, and Cornelia, as representatives of the virtues to which Rome owed her greatness; then sitting apart from the rest, as being of a different faith and race and having no connexion with the Roman Empire, Saladin; in another group D. sees great philosophers and men of science, viz. Aristotle, with So-crates and Plato close to him, sur-rounded by Democritus, Diogenes, Anaxagoras, and Thales, Empe-docles, Heraclitus, and Zeno; and Dioscorides, Orpheus, Tully, Linus, and Seneca the moralist; Euclid and Ptolemy, Hippocrates, Avicen-na, Galen, and Averroës (*vv.* 106–44).

Besides the great spirits above named, we learn from Virgil's con-versation with Statius later on (Purg. xxii. 10–114) that with himself and Homer in Limbo were Juvenal (*v.* 14), Terence, Caecilius, Plau-tus, and Varro (or Varius) (*vv.* 97–8), and Persius (*v.* 100); to-gether with Euripides, Antiphon, Simonides, Agathon, and other Greek poets (*vv.* 106–8); and Antigone, Deiphyle, Argia, Ismene, and Hypsipyle; the daughter of Tiresias (supposed to be Manto), Thetis, and Deidamia with her sisters (*vv.* 109–14).

Lin. [Lino [1].]

Lingua di *sì*. [*Italica Lingua.*]
Lingua d'*oco*. [*Lingua Oc.*]

Lingua *Jò*, general term under which are included the various tongues spoken by the Slavonians, Hungarians, Teutons, Saxons, and English, in all of which, according to D., *jò* is the common sign of affirmation, V. E. i. 8[29–35].

Lingua *Oc*, the *langue d'*oc or Provençal tongue, so called from the affirmative particle *oc*, V. E. i. 8[42, 51], 9[13], 10[21]; *lingua d'*oco, V. N. § 25[37]; Conv. i. 10[77]; *il Provenzale*, Conv. i. 6[56]; *lo parlare di Provenza*, Conv. i. 11[100]; *vulgare* oc, V. E. ii. 12[21]; its domain in SW. of Europe,

the Genoese boundary being its E. limit, V. E. i. 8[50–3]; the term em-ployed by D. to include the language spoken by the Spaniards (' alii *oc*, alii *oil*, alii *sì*, affirmando loquuntur, ut puta Hispani, Franci, et Latini'), V. E. i. 8[42–4]; ('dico Hispanos qui poetati sunt in vulgari *oc* '), V. E. ii. 12[20–1]; the affirmative particle *oc* the distinguishing characteristic of this tongue, V. E. i. 8[42, 51], 9[13], 10[21]; its employment as a literary tongue dates back not more than 150 years before D.'s time, V. N. § 25[35–40]; a German unable to distin-guish it from Italian, Cònv. i. 6[55–6]; its claim of priority over Italian and French as a vehicle for poetry in the vulgar tongue, owing to its being a more perfect and sweeter language, V. E. i. 10[20–4]; the superiority claimed for it over Italian, on the score of its greater beauty, not ad-mitted by D., Conv. i. 10[75–9]; just as the Romans of Cicero's day decried Latin and eulogized Greek, so in D.'s day it was the fashion to depreciate Italian and cry up Pro-vençal, Conv. i. 11[93–100] [Pro-venza].

Lingua *Oil*, the *langue d'*oïl or French tongue, so called from the affirmative particle *oïl* (mod. *oui*), V. E. i. 8[42, 57], 9[13], 10[13]; its domain bounded on the E. and N. by Germany, on the W. by the English sea and the mountains of Aragon, and on the S. by Provence and the Apennines, V. E. i. 8[57–64]; its claim to be regarded as the special vehicle for prose in the vulgar tongue, owing to its being an easy and pleasant language, justified by the fact that the Trojan and

Roman *gestes* and the Arthurian romances were written in French, V. E. i. 10[12-20].

D.'s acquaintance with the French prose Arthurian romances is evidenced by his references to the *Lancelot du Lac* (Inf. v. 127–37; Par. xvi. 14–15), to the *Tristan* (Inf. v. 67), and to the *Morte d'Arthur* (Inf. xxxii. 61–2). The Troy romance referred to by D. is doubtless the abridged French prose version (Cent. xiii) of the celebrated verse *Roman de Troie* of Benoît de Sainte-More (written c. 1160); while that of Rome may be some version of the verse *Roman d'Énéas* (written, probably by the same author, somewhat earlier), which was widely popular in the Middle Ages.

Lino[1], Linus, a native of Volterra, known to St. Paul and Timothy (2 *Tim.* iv. 21), according to tradition, the immediate successor of St. Peter as Bishop of Rome. He is said to have been beheaded in 76 or 78.

Linus, who is reckoned among the martyrs by the Romish Church, is mentioned by St. Peter (in the Heaven of Fixed Stars), together with Cletus (the successor of L.), in connexion with their martyrdom and his own, Par. xxvii. 41 [**Cleto**].

Lino[2], Linus, mythical Greek poet, supposed to be the son of Apollo and one of the Muses; D. mentions him, together with Orpheus (cf. Virg. *Ecl.* iv. 55–7; vi. 67), Cicero, and Seneca, among those whom he saw in Limbo, Inf. iv. 141 (where for *Lino* some edd. read *Livio*) [**Limbo**].

Lisetta, name of a lady mentioned by D. as having attempted to gain

his love, and as being dismissed with shame, Son. xliv. 3, 12. A sonnet in reply to this sonnet of D.'s (which was probably composed during 1291 or 1292, not long after the death of Beatrice) was written, in defence of Lisetta, by Aldobrandino de' Mezzabati (V. E. i. 14[43]). [**Ildebrandinus Paduanus**.] Lisetta, who has been identified by some with the 'donna gentile' of the *Vita Nuova* (§§ 36–9), is mentioned among the ladies of whom D. had been enamoured by the author of the *Ottimo Comento* (on Purg. xxxi. 58–60).

Livio, Livy (Titus Livius), the Roman historian, born at Patavium (Padua) B.C. 59, died A.D. 17. Of his great work, the History of Rome, which begins with the landing of Aeneas in Italy and closes with the death of Drusus (B.C. 9), only 35 books (i–x, xx–xlv), out of 142; are now extant, two (xli and xliii) being incomplete.

D.'s first-hand knowledge of Livy was evidently slight; for some of the information quoted on the authority of Livy he was certainly indebted to Orosius, other data were probably derived from Florus or some other epitome. [**Orosio**.]

Livy is mentioned, *Livio*, Inf. xxviii. 12; *Tito Livio*, Conv. iii. 11[31]; iv. 5[94]; *Livius*, Mon. ii. 4[33, 48, 63], 5[79, 103, 114, 126, 130], 9[66], 11[37, 43, 62]; *Titus Livius*, Mon. ii. 3[32]; V. E. ii. 6[83]; he is described as 'Livio, che non erra', Inf. xxviii. 12; and as 'gestorum Romanorum scriba egregius', Mon. ii. 3[33]; and is included with Pliny, Frontinus, and Orosius, among the masters of

lofty prose, V. E. ii. 6⁸²⁻⁴. Some
editors read *Livio* (which is almost
certainly wrong) for *Lino*, Inf. iv.
141 [Lino²].

D. refers to Livy's account (xxiii.
11–12—his actual authority being
rather Orosius, *Hist.* iv. 16. §§ 5, 6)
of the defeat of the Romans by
Hannibal at Cannae during the Second
Punic War, and of the three bushels
of gold rings taken from the bodies
of the dead Romans and produced
in the senate-house at Carthage by
Hannibal's envoy as proof of his
victory, Inf. xxviii. 10–12 ; Conv.
iv. 5¹⁶⁵⁻⁸ [Canne] ; the statement
(carelessly attributed by D. to Livy)
that Pythagoras came to Italy in the
time of Numa Pompilius, Conv. iii.
11²⁷⁻³³ [Pittagora] ; Livy's history testifies to the diverse natures
of the seven kings of Rome, Conv.
iv. 5⁸⁹⁻⁹⁷ ; his confirmation (i. 1)
of Virgil's testimony that Aeneas
was the father of the Roman people,
Mon. ii. 3³⁰⁻⁵ ; his mention (i. 20)
of the falling from heaven of the
sacred shield in the time of Numa,
Mon. ii. 4³⁰⁻⁴ ; his account (v. 47)
of the preservation of the Capitol at
Rome from the Gauls owing to the
awakening of Marcus Manlius by
the sacred geese, Mon. ii. 4⁴²⁻⁹ (cf.
Conv. iv. 5¹⁶⁰⁻⁴) [Manlius] ; his
account (xxvi. 11) of how the Carthaginians under Hannibal were only
prevented from taking Rome by
a sudden storm of hail, which drove
them back to their camp, Mon. ii.
4⁵⁸⁻⁶⁴ [Annibale] ; Cloelia's feat
of swimming across the Tiber, Mon.
ii. 4⁶⁵⁻⁷⁰ (where D. follows Orosius,
ii. 5, rather than Livy, ii. 13)
[Cloelia] ; the call of Cincinnatus

to the dictatorship from the plough,
to which he returned when his task
was performed, Mon. ii. 5⁷⁶⁻⁸⁰
(where D. refers to Livy, but had
apparently the account of Orosius,
ii. 12, in mind) [Cincinnato] ;
Livy's account (v. 46) of the liberation of Rome from the Gauls by
Camillus, and of his voluntary return
to exile after his victory, Mon. ii.
5¹⁰⁰⁻⁸ (cf. Conv. iv. 5¹³³⁻⁹) [Ca-
millo] ; his account (ii. 4) of the
patriotism of Lucius Junius Brutus,
who, as consul, put to death his own
sons for conspiring to restore the
Tarquins, Mon. ii. 5¹¹²⁻¹⁶ (cf. Conv.
iv. 5¹¹⁸⁻²²) [Bruto¹] ; his account
(ii. 12) of the heroism of Caius
Mucius, who, having failed to
assassinate Porsena, thrust his hand
into the fire and held it there without flinching, Mon. ii. 5¹²¹⁻⁷ (cf.
Par. iv. 84 ; Conv. iv. 5¹¹⁵⁻¹⁸)
[Muzio] ; his accounts (viii. 9
x. 27–8) of the heroic deaths of the
Decii, Mon. ii. 5¹²⁸⁻³² (cf. Par. vi.
47 ; Conv. iv. 5¹²²⁻⁴) [Deci] ; the
statement (wrongfully attributed by
D. to Livy) that Alexander the
Great died in Egypt while awaiting
the reply of the Romans to his embassy demanding their submission,
Mon. ii. 9⁶¹⁻⁷ [Alessandro²] ;
Livy's account (i. 23–5) of the war
with Alba, and of the combat be-
tween the Horatii and the Curiatii,
Mon. ii. 11²⁸⁻³⁷ (cf. Par. vi. 39)
[Curiazii] ; his accounts of the
Sabine (i. 30, 36–7) and Samnite
(vii. 29 ff.) wars of the Romans,
Mon. ii. 11³⁹⁻⁴³ (cf. Conv. iv. 5¹¹¹)
[Sabini : Sanniti] ; his account
(xxx. 33–5) of the defeat of Hanni-
bal by Scipio at the battle of Zama,

Livius 332 Lombardi

Mon. ii. 11^{59-63} (cf. Inf. xxxi. 115; Conv. iv. 5^{169-71} [Zama].
Livius. [Livio.]

Lizio, Lizio of Valbona (castle in the upper valley of the Savio, near Bagno), noble of Romagna, mentioned by Guido del Duca (in Circle II of Purgatory), who calls him 'il buon Lizio', together with Arrigo Mainardi, among the departed worthies of Romagna, Purg. xiv. 97.

Lizio, who was born in the first half of Cent. xiii, was a contemporary and adherent of Rinieri da Calboli (Purg. xiv. 88). In 1260, though a Guelf, he was in the service of Guido Novello, the Ghibelline Podestà of Florence after the battle of Montaperti, and in this capacity he acted as witness to the treaty of alliance concluded on Nov. 22 of that year between the Ghibellines of Florence and the Sienese. In 1276 he joined with Rinieri da Calboli and other Guelfs in an attempt upon Forlì, which was defeated by Guido da Montefeltro. The last mention of Lizio occurs in 1279. The date of his death, which must have occurred before 1300, is unknown.

Locorum, De Natura, treatise of Albertus Magnus *On the Nature of Places*; D. says that so far as he can gather from this work (perhaps i. 6), which he quotes as *il Libro della Natura de' Luoghi*, the equatorial circle divides the hemisphere of the land from that of the sea almost entirely at the extremity of the first climate, in that region which is inhabited by the Garamantes, Conv. iii. 5^{113-20}. [Garamanti.]

Loderingo, Loderingo degli Andalò, Ghibelline of Bologna, founder in 1261 of the Order known subsequently as the 'Frati Gaudenti'. He was Podestà of Modena in 1251, and, jointly with the Guelf Catalano de' Catalani, of Bologna in 1265 and 1267, and of Florence in 1266. He retired shortly after to the monastery of the Frati Gaudenti at Ronzano, near Bologna, where he died in 1293. Guittone d'Arezzo (Purg. xxvi. 124), a member of the same Order, addressed to him a *canzone*, which has been preserved. [Catalano: Frati Gaudenti.]

D. places Loderingo, together with Catalano, among the Hypocrites in Bolgia 6 of Circle VIII of Hell (Malebolge), Inf. xxiii. 104 [Ipocriti].

Logicales, Summulae. [Summulae Logicales.]

Logodoro, name of the largest of the four *Giudicati*, or Judicial Districts, into which Sardinia was divided by the Pisans, to whom the island belonged in D.'s time; it comprised the NW. portion of the island. [Sardigna.]

Ciampolo (in Bolgia 5 of Circle VIII of Hell) mentions Logodoro in connexion with Michael Zanche, who was governor of that district, Inf. xxii. 89. [Michel Zanche.]

Lombardi, Lombards, inhabitants of Lombardy; D., by an anachronism, makes Virgil speak of his parents as Lombards, Inf. i. 68; Ciampolo offers to show D. and V. either Tuscans or Lombards (probably as a sort of ironical compliment to their respective native lands) among the Barrators who are with himself in Bolgia 5 of Circle VIII of Hell (Malebolge), Inf. xxii. 99; the dialect of the Lombards distinct from that of the inhabitants of Romagna, as well as from those of the Trevisans and Venetians, V. E. i. 10^67–9; it is characterized by a certain shrillness, which is supposed to be a legacy from the old Longobard invaders, V. E. i. 15^17–20 [**Longobardi**]; the best Lombard writers, like those of Sicily, Apulia, Tuscany, Romagna, and the two Marches, wrote in the Italian vulgar tongue, V. E. i. 19^15–19; their race a mixture of the old Longobards with a strain of Trojan and Roman blood, Epist. v. 4^50–2; their supposed Scandinavian origin, Epist. v. 4^56–7 (cf. Paulus Diaconus, *Hist. Langobard.*, i. 1; and Vincent of Beauvais, *Spec. Hist.*, xvi. 10).

Lombardia, Lombardy, which at the beginning of Cent. xiv comprised the immense plain which commences at Vercelli, a town halfway between Milan and Turin in the present Piedmont, and stretches as far as the Adriatic, at the mouth of the Po di Volano, about thirty miles W. of Ravenna. Old Lombardy was bounded on the N. by the Alps, on the W. by the Dora Baltea and the Po, on the S. by the Apennines and the Adriatic, and on the E. by the Mincio and the Lago di Garda. Modern Lombardy lies between the Ticino, the Mincio, the Po, and the Alps.

Pier da Medicina (in Bolgia 9 of Circle VIII of Hell) describes Lombardy as *lo dolce piano Che da Vercelli a Marcabò dichina*, Inf. xxviii. 74–5 [**Marcabò: Vercelli**]; Marco

Lombardo (in Circle III of Purgatory) refers to it, together with Romagna and the March of Treviso, as *il paese ch' Adice e Po riga*, Purg. xvi. 115 [**Adice**]; it lies on the left side of Italy, if the Apennines be taken as the dividing line (from N. to S.), V. E. i. 10^51–4, 19^9–10; though there is a vulgar tongue proper to Lombardy, V. E. i. 19^5–13, yet none the less there are distinctions of dialect within its boundaries, as for instance between the inhabitants of Ferrara and those of Piacenza, V. E. i. 10^76–7.

Lombardo[1], inhabitant of Lombardy; of Marco Lombardo, Purg. xvi. 46 [**Marco Lombardo**]; *il semplice Lombardo*, i. e. Guido da Castello, Purg. xvi. 126 [**Castel, Guido da**]; *il gran Lombardo*, i. e. (probably) Bartolommeo della Scala, Par. xvii. 71.

In this last passage, Cacciaguida (in the Heaven of Mars), foretelling D.'s exile, tells him that his first refuge shall be with the great Lombard ' who bears as his arms the Imperial Eagle over the Ladder ', i. e. some member of the Della Scala family. Nearly all the commentators take the reference to be to Bartolommeo della Scala (d. March 130¾), eldest son of Alberto della Scala, lord of Verona, 1277–1301, whom he succeeded. Some think the reference is to Alboino, who succeeded his elder brother Bartolommeo, and died in Oct. 1311; but he appears to be excluded by the fact that D. elsewhere (Conv. iv. 16^59–74) speaks of him with contempt [**Albuino della Scala**]. The third son, Cangrande, is excluded by the fact that he is expressly alluded to independently in the same passage (*vv.* 76–81) as one whom D. shall see with the ' gran Lombardo', while special mention is made of his tender years (' la novella età ', *v.* 80), he being at that time only nine years old.

Lombardo [2], belonging to Lombardy; D. apostrophizes Sordello as *anima Lombarda*, Purg. vi. 61 [**Sordello**];—the Lombard dialect, Inf. xxvii. 20; *Lombardum vulgare*, V. E. i. 19$^{5-13}$ [**Lombardi: Lombardia**].

Lombardo, Il gran. [**Lombardo** [1].]

Lombardo, Il semplice. [**Castel, Guido da.**]

Lombardo, Marco. [**Marco Lombardo.**]

Lombardo, Pietro. [**Pietro** [2].]

Lombardus. [**Lombardo** [2].]

Lombardus, Petrus. [**Pietro** [2]].

Londra, London; referred to by the mention of the Thames, the precise reference being to Westminster Abbey, Inf. xii. 120. [**Arrigo** [6]: **Tamigi**.]

Longobardi, Longobards (afterwards called Lombards), Teutonic tribe, which in Cent. vi descended into Italy by the great plain at the head of the Adriatic, and with the help of the Saxons and other barbarian tribes conquered the N. part of the country, which hence received the name of Lombardy. The most noteworthy of their kings were Rothari (636–652), the Lombard legislator; and Liutprand (712–744), who extended his sway, at least temporarily, over nearly the whole of Italy. At the invitation of Pope Stephen II, Pepin, son of Charles Martel, crossed into Italy and defeated (754–6) King Aistulf, who had threatened Rome; and the Lombard kingdom was finally destroyed by Pepin's son, Charlemagne, who, likewise in answer to the appeal of the Pope (Adrian I), descended into Italy, captured Pavia, the Lombard capital, after a siege of six months, and took prisoner Desiderius, the last Lombard king (774).

The defeat of Desiderius and the Lombards by Charlemagne is referred to (by an anachronism) as one of the exploits of the Imperial Eagle, Par. vi. 94–6; and again, Mon. iii. 11$^{1-4}$ [**Desiderius**]; the shrillness of the Lombard dialect supposed to be a relic of the old Longobard speech, V. E. i. 15$^{17-20}$; the Lombards addressed as *sanguis Longobardorum* and *Scandinaviae soboles*, in allusion to their barbarian origin, Epist. v. 4$^{50,\ 56-7}$ [**Lombardi**].

Longobardo, Longobard or Lombard; *il dente Longobardo*, i. e. the Lombard attacks on the Church, which were finally put an end to by Charlemagne, Par. vi. 94. [**Longobardi.**]

Lorenzo, St. Lawrence, deacon of the Church of Rome, said to have been a native of Huesca in Spain, who suffered martyrdom under the Emperor Valerian, Aug. 10, 258. Having been commanded by the Prefect of Rome to deliver up the treasures of the Church, which had been entrusted to his charge by Pope Sixtus II, he refused; whereupon he was tortured, and finally was stretched on an iron frame with bars, like a gridiron, beneath which a fire was kindled so that his body was gradually consumed. In the midst of his agony he is said to have remained steadfast, and to have mocked his executioners, bidding them to turn his body that it might be equally roasted on both sides.

Beatrice (in the Heaven of the Moon) mentions St. Lawrence as an instance of fortitude, coupling him with Mucius Scaevola, Par. iv. 83–4. [Muzio.]

Lotto degli Agli. [Agli, Lotto degli.]

Luca, St. Luke the Evangelist, author of the Gospel which bears his name, and of the Acts of the Apostles, was born at Antioch in Syria, was educated as a physician (*Coloss.* iv. 14), and died (probably as a martyr) between A.D. 75 and 100; he is mentioned, *Luca*, Purg. xxi. 7; Conv. iv. 17⁹⁵, 23¹⁰⁵; *Luca Evangelista*, Conv. iv. 5⁶⁵; *Lucas*, Mon. ii. 9¹⁰⁰, 12⁴², 13⁵³; iii. 9¹, ²⁴, ³³, ⁹⁸, ¹³⁷, 10¹¹²; *scriba Christi*, Mon. i. 16¹⁶; ii. 9⁹⁹, 12⁴²; in allusion to the fact that he was symbolized by an ox (*Ezek.* i. 10; *Rev.* iv. 7), D. speaks of him as *Bos evangelizans*, Epist. vii. 3⁶⁵⁻⁶; in the mystical Procession in the Terrestrial Paradise St. Luke is represented by his writings, his *Gospel* appearing (according to the most probable interpretation) as one of the four beasts (*quattro animali*), Purg. xxix. 92; while the *Acts of the Apostles* appears under the guise of an elder in the habit of a physician (in allusion to *Coloss.* iv. 14), *vv.* 134, 136–8, 145–8.

The *Gospel of St. Luke* is quoted, Purg. x. 40 (*Luke* i. 28); Purg. x. 44 (*Luke* i. 38); Purg. xviii. 100 (*Luke* i. 39); Purg. xx. 136 (*Luke* ii. 14); Purg. xxv. 128 (*Luke* i. 34); Purg. xxix. 85–7 (*Luke* i. 42); Par. iii. 121–2 (*Luke* i. 28); Par. xvi. 34 (*Luke* i. 28); Par.

xxxii. 95 (*Luke* i. 28); Conv. iv. 11¹¹²⁻¹³ (*Luke* xvi. 9); Conv. iv. 17⁹⁴⁻¹⁰¹ (*Luke* x. 41; x. 42); Conv. iv. 23¹⁰⁵⁻⁶ (*Luke* xxiii. 44); Mon. i. 4²³⁻⁶ (*Luke* ii. 14; xxiv. 36); Mon. ii. 3²⁴⁻⁶ (*Luke* vi. 38); Mon. ii. 9¹⁰¹⁻³ (*Luke* ii. 1); Mon. iii. 9²⁻⁶⁰, ⁹⁸⁻¹⁰² (*Luke* xxii. 38; xxii. 7; xxii. 14; xxii. 35–6; xxii. 38; xxii. 33); Epist. vii. 2³¹⁻² (*Luke* vii. 19); referred to, Purg. xxi. 7 (ref. to *Luke* xxiv. 13–32); Conv. iv. 5⁶⁵ (ref. to *Luke* ii. 1); Mon. i. 16¹⁶ (ref. to *Luke* ii. 1, 14); Mon. ii. 12⁴² (ref. to *Luke* ii. 1–5); Mon. ii. 13⁵⁰⁻³ (ref. to *Luke* xxiii. 1, 11); Mon. iii. 10¹¹² (ref. to *Luke* ix. 3; x. 4); Epist. vii. 3⁶⁴⁻⁷ (ref. to *Luke* ii. 1).

The *Acts of the Apostles* is quoted, Conv. iv. 20²⁹ (*Acts* x. 34); Mon. iii. 9¹³⁸⁻⁹ (*Acts* i. 1); Mon. iii. 13⁴³⁻⁵³ (*Acts* xxv. 10; xxvii. 24; xxviii. 19); Epist. v. 4⁶⁸ (*Acts* ix. 5); referred to, Mon. ii. 8⁷⁰ (ref. to *Acts* i. 26).

Lucam, Evangelium secundum. [Luca.]

Lucano, Lucan (Marcus Annaeus Lucanus), the Roman poet, born at Corduba in Spain, A.D. 39. Having incurred the enmity of Nero, he joined the conspiracy of Piso against the life of the Emperor, and upon the discovery of the plot put an end to his own life by opening his veins, in his twenty-sixth year, A.D. 65. He left an unfinished poem in ten books (the last of which is incomplete) entitled *Pharsalia* or *De Bello Civili*, in which a detailed account is given of the civil war between Caesar and Pompey.

D. places Lucan in Limbo together with Homer, Horace, and Ovid, Inf. iv. 90; these poets, with Virgil, make up 'la bella scuola Di quei signor dell' altissimo canto' (*vv.* 94–5) [**Limbo**]; he is named, together with Virgil, Ovid (as far as the *Metamorphoses* are concerned), and Statius, as one of the 'regulati poetae', V. E. ii. 6$^{80-1}$; and is mentioned in connexion with his poem, Inf. xxv. 94; V. N. § 25^{85}; Conv. iii. 3^{52}, 5^{116}; iv. 11^{27}, 13^{111}, 119, 28^{99}; *Lucanus,* V. E. i. 10^{46}; Mon. ii. 4^{34}, 8^{81}, 9$^{55,\ 68,\ 87}$, 11^{46}; Epist. x. 22^{425}; he is alluded to by G. del Virgilio (with reference to Inf. iv. 88–90, 101–2), Carm. 17. [*Farsaglia*^{2}.]

    Lucanus.   [**Lucano.**]
    Lucas.   [**Luca.**]

    Lucca, town in Tuscany, on a plain in the valley of the Serchio, about fifteen miles NE. of Pisa, V. E. i. 13^{24}; native place of Alessio Interminei, Inf. xviii. 122 [**Alessio**]; hidden from Pisa by Monte San Giuliano, Inf. xxxiii. 30 [**Giuliano, Monte San**]; native place of Bonagiunta degli Urbiciani, Purg. xxiv. 20, who is referred to as *quel di Lucca* (*v.* 35), and speaks of Lucca as *la mia città* (*v.* 45) [**Bonagiunta**]; referred to under the name of Santa Zita, the patron saint of Lucca, Inf. xxi. 38 [**Zita, Santa**]; alluded to as *quella terra,* in connexion with Bonturo Dati and the other barrators with whom, D. says, the place abounds, Inf. xxi. 40 [**Bonturo**]; indicated by the mention of the Serchio, which flows close to its walls, Inf. xxi. 49 [**Serchio**].

    The *Santo Volto* ('Holy Face')

of Lucca, an ancient crucifix in cedar-wood of great sanctity (said to have been carved by Nicodemus, and still preserved in the Cathedral of San Martino), is mentioned, Inf. xxi. 48.

    D. was in Lucca probably in 1314, and while there formed a connexion with a certain Lucchese lady of the name of Gentucca, who is referred to by Bonagiunta (in Circle VI of Purgatory), Purg. xxiv. 37–48. [**Dante: Gentucca.**]

    Lucenses, inhabitants of Lucca; their dialect condemned, together with the rest of the Tuscan dialects, V. E. i. 13$^{23-4}$.

    Lucensis, Lucchese; of Bonagiunta, who was a native of Lucca, V. E. i. 13$^{8-9}$. [**Bonagiunta.**]

    Lucia^1, St. Lucy, noble Christian virgin of Syracuse, who was martyred in the time of Diocletian (Emp. 284–305). She is regarded as the special patroness of those who suffer from disease of the eyes.

    In the *D. C.* St. Lucy (whom the old commentators regard as the symbol of illuminating grace) appears as one of the three heavenly ladies who are interested in D.'s salvation, as is explained to him by Virgil, Inf. ii. 49–126; the latter says that he was moved to come to D.'s help by Beatrice (*vv.* 52–93), who in her turn had been warned of D.'s plight by St. Lucy, who again had been sent to Beatrice by the Virgin Mary (*vv.* 94–108); the three heavenly ladies are referred to as *tre donne benedette,* Inf. ii. 124; the Virgin speaks to St. Lucy of D. as 'il tuo fedele' (*v.* 98), perhaps in allusion to the fact that D. was in a special sense under her protection, as being a sufferer from weak eyes (V. N. § 40[27–34]; Conv. iii. 9[147–57]) [Dante].

While D. is asleep during his first night in Purgatory he is conveyed in the early dawn from the Valley of Kings to the gate of Purgatory proper by St. Lucy, as is explained to him by Virgil on his awaking, Purg. ix. 49–63.

St. Bernard points out to D. St. Lucy's place in the Celestial Rose, and reminds him that it was she who moved Beatrice to come to his aid (Inf. ii. 100–8) at the commencement of his journey through Hell, Par. xxxii. 136–8. [Rosa.]

Lucia [2], name given by D. to an imaginary city, which he places at the S. Pole of the Earth, exactly at the antipodes of another, called *Maria*, at the N. Pole, Conv. iii. 5[80–184]. [Terra [2].]

Lucifer [1]. [Lucifero.]

Lucifer [2], the morning star; Aristotle's saying (*Eth.* v. 1) that neither the evening nor the morning star is so admirable as justice, quoted, Mon. i. 11[33–4].

Lucifero, Lucifer, name given by D. (following St. Jerome on *Isaiah* xiv. 12) to Satan, the Evil One, whom in the *D. C.* he represents as the King of Hell, Inf. xxxi. 143; xxxiv. 89; called also *Dite*, Inf. xi. 65; xii. 39; xxxiv. 20 [Dite]; *Belzebù*, Inf. xxxiv. 127 [Belzebù]; *nimica podesta*, Inf. vi. 96; *superbo strupo*, Inf. vii. 12; *il mal dell' universo*, Inf. vii. 18; *Rex inferni*, Inf. xxxiv. 1; *la creatura ch' ebbe il bel sembiante*, Inf. xxxiv. 18; *lo imperador del doloroso regno*, Inf. xxxiv.

28; *il vermo reo che il mondo fora*, Inf. xxxiv. 108; *colui che fu nobil creato Più ch' altra creatura*, Purg. xii. 25–6; *colui . . . Che pria volse le spalle al suo fattore*, Par. ix. 127–8; *il primo superbo*, Par. xix. 46; *la somma d'ogni creatura*, Par. xix. 47; *il perverso*, Par. xxvii. 26; *colui che tu (Dante) vedesti Da tutti i pesi del mondo costretto*, Par. xxix. 56–7; the Evil One is also spoken of as *Satan*, Inf. vii. 1; *Satanas*, Mon. iii. 9[80]; *Diavolo*, Inf. xxiii. 143; *Diabolus*, V. E. i. 2[47], 4[13]; Mon. iii. 3[47]; *Lucifer*, Epist. x. 27[520].

Lucifer, the King of Hell, Inf. xxxiv. 1, 28; cast out from Heaven by the archangel Michael, Inf. vii. 11–12; before his fall was the fairest and noblest of created things, Inf. xxxiv. 18, 34; Purg. xii. 25–6; Par. xix. 47; the cause of his fall was pride, Inf. vii. 12; xxxiv. 35; Purg. xii. 25–7; Par. ix. 127–8; xix. 46; xxvii. 26; xxix. 55–6; he is now as foul as he was fair before, Inf. xxxiv. 34; his place is in the nethermost pit of Hell, in the centre of the Earth, and hence the centre of the Universe, Inf. xi. 64–5; xxxi. 142–3; xxxiv. 107–8; Par. xxix. 56–7 [Universo]; he fell from Heaven on the side of the Earth opposite to our hemisphere, to which the land which was previously in the other hemisphere retired, its place being taken by the sea, Inf. xxxiv. 121–4; at the place where he fell was opened the abyss of Hell, the earth retreating from him, and thus forming the island and Mt. of Purgatory, the only dry land in the opposite hemisphere, Inf. xxxiv.

124-6; he is a liar and the father of lies, Inf. xxiii. 143-4; Mon. iii. 3⁴⁷; and the origin of all woe, Inf. vii. 18; xxxiv. 36; it was he who spake to Eve in the shape of the serpent, V. E. i. 2⁴⁷, 4¹³; Christ's rebuke to St. Peter, 'get thee behind me, Satan' (*Matt.* xvi. 23), Mon. iii. 9⁷⁹⁻⁸⁰; Ezekiel's reproach to Lucifer (in the person of the prince of Tyrus, *Ezek.* xxviii. 12-13), Epist. x. 27⁵²⁰⁻³.

Lucifer figures among the examples of defeated pride in Circle I of Purgatory, where he is portrayed (in allusion to *Luke* x. 18) as falling like lightning from heaven, Purg. xii. 25-7. [Superbi.]

As D. and Virgil enter Giudecca, the fourth division of Circle IX of Hell, V. warns D. that they are approaching Lucifer, and tells him to look if he can see him in the distance (Inf. xxxiv. 1-3); D. dimly sees something resembling a windmill (being Lucifer's six huge whirling wings), and then feeling a great wind he shrinks behind V. for shelter (*vv.* 4-9); when they have advanced somewhat further, V. suddenly stepping aside from before D. makes him halt, and points to Lucifer just in front of them (*vv.* 16-21); D., half dead with terror, sees before him a gigantic monster, emerging as far as the middle of his breast from the ice (*vv.* 22-9); his enormous bulk is such that D. says he himself more nearly compares with a giant in size than does a giant with Lucifer's arm (whence L.'s stature has been estimated at 840 yards) (*vv.* 30-3); the monster has three faces, the one in front being crimson,

that on the right yellowish-white, and that on the left black (*vv.* 37-45); beneath each face is a pair of huge wings, not feathered, but like those of a bat (*vv.* 46-50); with the flapping of these wings are generated three winds, the blast of which causes the waters of Cocytus to freeze (*vv.* 50-2); from his six eyes flow tears, which, mingled with bloody foam from his mouths, drip down over his three chins (*vv.* 53-4); in each mouth he crunches a sinner, in the front one Judas Iscariot, whose back is at the same time flayed by Lucifer's claws, in the right one Cassius, and in the left one Brutus (*vv.* 55-67); D. having gazed on this terrible sight, V. tells him that he has seen all, and that now they must be gone from Hell (*vv.* 68-9); V. then, with D. on his back, climbs down Lucifer's shaggy sides into the icy chasm (*vv.* 70-5); when he has reached the monster's middle, V. with a great effort turns himself so that his head is where his legs had been before, and then commences to climb up (Lucifer being so situated that the upper part of his body, from head to middle, is in the N. hemisphere, while the lower part, from middle to feet, is in the S. hemisphere, to the surface of which D. and V. are now ascending, their descent having ceased at Lucifer's middle, which coincides with the centre of the Earth), so that D. thinks they are returning to Hell (*vv.* 76-84); at last they issue forth through a perforated rock, and D. to his amazement sees that Lucifer is holding his legs upwards, instead of downwards as he had seen them previously (*vv.* 85–93); before they proceed on their way he asks V. for an explanation of this marvel, and learns that they are now in the S. hemisphere (*vv.* 100–17).

Lucillo, mistake of D. (or of the copyists) for *Lucilio*, Lucilius, a friend and correspondent of Lucius Annaeus Seneca, and procurator of Sicily.

D. refers to the invectives of Seneca (*Epist.* cxix. § 9) against riches, 'massimamente a Lucillo scrivendo', Conv. iv. 12[82–3]. [**Seneca.**]

Lucrezia, Lucretia, wife of Lucius Tarquinius Collatinus, who, having been outraged by her husband's cousin, Sextus Tarquinius, son of Lucius Tarquinius Superbus, the King of Rome, stabbed herself, after calling upon Collatinus to avenge her dishonour. This 'deed of shame' led to the dethronement and banishment of Tarquinius Superbus, and the establishment of the republic at Rome, B.C. 510 (Livy, i. 57–60).

D. sees Lucretia, together with Julia, Marcia, and Cornelia, among the great women of antiquity in Limbo, Inf. iv. 128 [**Limbo**]; the period during which Rome was governed by kings began and ended with a deed of shame, viz. the rape of the Sabine women and the dishonour of Lucretia, Par. vi. 40–1.

Luglio, month of July; D. refers to the crowded state of the hospitals of Valdichiana, owing to the malaria generated by its swamps, during the month of August, *tra il luglio e il settembre*, Inf. xxix. 47. [**Chiana.**]

Luigi[1], Kings of France of the Capetian line who bore the name of Louis; mentioned by Hugh Capet (in Circle V of Purgatory), who says that from him were descended the kings of the name of Philip and Louis of the reigning dynasty of France, Purg. xx. 50–1. [**Capeti.**]

From Hugh Capet down to the year 1300, the date of the Vision, there were four kings of each name in the Capetian line. [**Filippi**[2]: **Table K.**]

Luigi[2]], Louis IX, St. Louis, King of France, 1226–1270; he was the son (born in 1215) of Louis VIII and Blanche of Castile, and succeeded his father in 1226; he married in 1234 Margaret, eldest daughter of Raymond Berenger IV, Count of Provence; in 1248 he sailed to the East on a crusade, and in 1249 took Damietta, but, being himself taken prisoner by the Saracens shortly after, was obliged to surrender the city as a condition of his release; in 1254 he returned to France, but in 1270 he undertook a second crusade, and sailed against Tunis, the citadel of which he took; during the siege, however, a plague broke out, to which Louis and a large part of his army fell victims, Aug. 1270. During his reign he devoted himself to the welfare of his people, and by his wise administration greatly promoted the prosperity of his kingdom. Owing to the saintliness of his character Louis IX was in 1297 canonized by Boniface VIII. [**Table K.**]

D., who nowhere mentions St. Louis by name, is supposed by some to refer to him disparagingly, together with his brother, Charles of Anjou, in connexion with their respective wives, Margaret and Beatrice of Provence, whose husbands, he says (by the mouth of Sordello in Ante-purgatory), were as inferior to Peter III of Aragon as Charles II of Naples was to his father, Charles I, Purg. vii. 127–9 [**Beatrice**[2]: **Margherita**[1]]; the Margaret there mentioned, however, is more probably Margaret of Burgundy, second wife of Charles I [**Margherita**[2]].

Luigi[3], Louis of Sicily, second son of Charles II of Anjou and Naples, and of Mary of Hungary, and younger brother of Charles Martel; he was one of the three sons who were left as hostages in the hands of Alphonso, King of Aragon, when their father was released from his captivity in Catalonia in 1288 [**Carlo**[2]]. He and his brothers Robert and John remained in captivity until 1295; almost immediately after his release Louis renounced all his hereditary rights and became a monk. He was appointed Bishop of Tou-louse by Boniface VIII, Dec. 29, 1296, and died the next year; he was canonized in 1311.

It is probably to Louis that Charles Martel (his elder brother) refers, when he says (in the Heaven of Venus) that such an one is 'wrested to religion', who was born to wear a sword, Par. viii. 145–6 [**Carlo**[3]].

Luna, Moon, Inf. vii. 64; xv. 19; xx. 127; xxvi. 131; xxix. 10; xxxiii. 26; Purg. x. 14; xviii. 76; xix. 2; xxviii. 33; xxix. 53; Par. i. 115; xvi. 82; xxvii. 132; xxviii. 20; xxix. 97; Conv. ii. 3[27, 58, 61, 65], 4[3], 6[107], 14[67, 69], 15[150]; iii. 3[12]; iv. 16[92]; Mon. iii.

4[130–58]; Epist. x. 26[474, 481]; A.T. §§ 7[2–6], 19[48], 20[59–69], 23[50]; as a measure of time, Inf. x. 79–80; xxxiii. 26; Par. xxvii. 132; Diana being goddess of the Moon, D. also speaks of the Moon as *Delia*, Purg. xxix. 78; Epist. vi. 2[54]; *Phoebe*, Mon. i. 11[35]; *Trivia*, Par. xxiii. 26; *figlia di Latona*, Par. x. 67; xxii. 139; xxix. 1; *suora del Sole*, Purg. xxiii. 120 [**Diana**[1]]; it is referred to as *occhio del cielo*, Purg. xx. 132; *luminare minus*, Mon. iii. 1[35], 4[13]; Epist. v. 10[170]; *prima stella*, Par. ii. 30; *eterna margherita*, Par. ii. 34; *stella margherita*, Son. xxvi. 14; *la donna che qui regge*, i.e. the Queen of Hell, Hecate, Inf. x. 80 [**Ecate**]; and, in allusion to the legend of Cain and the bundle of thorns, *Caino e le spine*, Inf. xx. 126; *lo corpo, che laggiuso in terra, Fa di Cain favoleggiare altrui*, Par. ii. 50–1 [**Caino.**]

The Moon is referred to as the sister of the Sun, Purg. xxiii. 120; Mon. i. 11[35] [**Phoebe**]; the daugh-ter of Latona, Purg. xx. 131–2; Par. x. 67; xxii. 139; xxix. 1 [**Latona**]; the Heaven of the Moon being the first in D.'s conception of the Universe, he refers to the Moon itself as *la prima stella*, Par. ii. 30 [**Luna, Cielo della**].

The halo round the Moon, men-tioned, Par. xxviii. 23; referred to, *il cinto di Delia*, Purg. xxix. 78; *la zona della figlia di Latona*, Par. x. 67–9.

The eclipse of the Moon, Mon. iii. 4[141]; A. T. § 19[47–8].

The spots on the Moon are re-ferred to as *Caino e le spine*, Inf. xx. 126; Par. ii. 50–1; *segni bui della Luna*, Par. ii. 49-50; *ombra nella Luna*, Par. xxii. 140; Conv. ii. 14[72]. In the *Convivio* D. ascribes the phenomenon, which he calls 'the shadow in the Moon', to the rarity of the lunar substance in certain parts of its sphere, which allows the light of the Sun to pass through, instead of being reflected, as it is by the denser parts, Conv. ii. 14[69-76]; this theory (which was doubtless derived from the *De Substantia Orbis* of Averroës) is specifically rejected in the *D. C.* in favour of another, viz. that the phenomenon is due to the diverse effects of the diverse 'intelligences' which govern the heavenly bodies, Par. ii. 139-48.

The new Moon, Inf. xv. 19; Conv. ii. 3[62]; full Moon, Inf. xx. 127; Purg. xxiii. 119-20; xxix. 53; Par. xxiii. 25-6; xxix. 97; Mon. i. 11[35-6]; gibbous Moon, Purg. xviii. 76-8; Conv. iv. 16[92]; half Moon, Conv. ii. 3[62] (according to some edd.); waning Moon, Inf. xxix. 10; Purg. x. 14; xviii. 76-8; rising Moon, Purg. ix. 1-3; xviii. 76; setting Moon, Inf. xx. 125-6; Purg. x. 14-15; Par. xxix. 1.

D. refers to the influence of the Moon on the tides, Par. xvi. 82-3; A. T. § 7[1-3]; the theory that fire mounts upwards towards the Moon, Purg. xviii. 28; Par. i. 115; Conv. iii. 3[11-13]; the supposition of some that the darkening of the Sun at the time of the Crucifixion was caused by a miraculous eclipse of it by the Moon, Par. xxix. 97-9; occultation of Mars by the Moon witnessed by Aristotle, Conv. ii. 3[59-65]; the Moon lower in the heavens than the

Sun, Conv. ii. 3[58]; variation in the illumination of the Moon according as the Sun shines on it from one side or the other, Conv. ii. 14[76-9]; the suspension of the movement of the *Primum Mobile* would cause the Moon to be hidden from the Earth during half its course, viz. 14½ days, Conv. ii. 15[139-51]; the Moon, while it receives the greater portion of its light from the Sun, yet possesses light of its own, as is manifest during an eclipse, and is otherwise independent of the Sun, viz. as regards its being, its power, and its working, Mon. iii. 4[130-45].

In a figurative sense the Moon represents the temporal power of the Emperor, as does the Sun the ecclesiastical power of the Pope, Mon. iii. 1[35-7], 4[10-21, 156-9]; Epist. v. 10[170].

Luna, Cielo della, the Heaven of the Moon; the first in D.'s conception of Paradise, Conv. ii. 4[2-3]; Son. xxviii. 11 [**Paradiso**[1]]; resembles Grammar in two respects, Conv. ii. 14[67-79]; it is presided over by the Angels, Conv. ii. 6[105-7] [**Angeli**]; Aristotle erroneously believed that immediately above it was the Heaven of the Sun, which would thus be next but one to the Earth, Conv. ii. 3[25-7]; the theory that fire mounts upwards to the Heaven of the Moon, Conv. iii. 3[11-13] (cf. Purg. xviii. 28; Par. i. 115); this Heaven not the cause of the elevation of the land, A. T. § 20[68-71]; like all the other Heavens it is moved on account of something which it has not, Epist. x. 26[474, 481]; it is referred to as *primo cielo*, Conv. ii. 4[2-3]; Son. xxviii. 11;

quel ciel che ha minor li cerchi sui, Inf. ii. 78; *la spera più tarda*, Par. iii. 51; and (according to some) *la prima volta*, Purg. xxviii. 104.

In the Heaven of the Moon D. places the spirits of those who took holy vows but failed to keep them (*Spiriti Votivi Mancanti*), Par. iii. 30, 56–7; among whom he names Piccarda, sister of Corso and Forese Donati [**Piccarda**]; and Constance, wife of the Emperor Henry VI, and mother of the Emperor Frederick II [**Costanza** [1]].

Lunensis, belonging to Luni; *Lunensis pontifex*, the Bishop of Luni (i. e. Gherardino da Filattiera), Epist. viii. 7[112–13] [**Filattiera** : **Luni** : **Malaspina**].

Luni, formerly Luna, ancient Etruscan town on the left bank of the Macra, not far from Sarzana, on the borders of Liguria and Tuscany, which fell into decay under the Roman Emperors, and was sacked by the Lombards in 630, and by the Saracens in 849 and again in 1016. The site of the ancient town is still marked by the ruins of an amphitheatre and circus.

D. mentions Luni in connexion with the Etruscan augur, Aruns, who he says (following Lucan) lived in a cavern in the midst of the white marble, *nei monti di Luni* (i. e. in the Carrara hills), Inf. xx. 47–9 [**Aronta**]; Cacciaguida (in the Heaven of Mars) mentions it, together with Urbisaglia, as instances of the decay and disappearance of once powerful cities, Par. xvi. 73.

Lunigiana], district in NW. corner of Tuscany, between the Apennines and the Ligurian border,

through which the Macra flows; its name is derived from the ancient city of Luni, which formerly was a flourishing port [**Luni**]. In D.'s time Lunigiana, together with Massa and Carrara, belonged to the Malaspina family, who received him there in Oct. 1306 [**Dante**]. D. speaks of it in conversation with Currado Malaspina (in Ante-purgatory) as *li vostri paesi*, Purg. viii. 121; *la contrada*, *v.* 125; it is referred to by Vanni Fucci (in Bolgia 7 of Circle VIII of Hell) as *Valdimagra*, Inf. xxiv. 145; and by Currado Malaspina (in Ante-purgatory) as *Valdimacra*, Purg. viii. 116 [**Macra** : **Malaspina**].

Luoghi, Della Natura de'. [*Locorum, De Natura.*]

Lussuriosi], the Lustful, placed in Circle II of Hell, Inf. v. 28–142 [**Inferno**]; their punishment is to be driven about incessantly in total darkness by a violent whirlwind (symbolical of the passions to which they were slaves on earth), which hurls them this side and that, and causes them to blaspheme God (*vv.* 28–36); at the entrance to the Circle stands Minos, the infernal judge (*vv.* 4–12) [**Minos**]. *Examples* : Semiramis [**Semiramis**]; Dido [**Dido**]; Cleopatra [**Cleopatras**]; Helen of Troy [**Elena**]; Achilles [**Achille**]; Paris [**Paris**]; Tristan [**Tristano**]; Paolo Malatesta [**Paolo** [2]]; Francesca da Polenta [**Francesca**].

Those who expiate the sin of Lust in Purgatory are placed in Circle VII, Purg. xxv. 109–xxvii. 57 [*Beatitudini* : **Purgatorio**]; their punishment is, to pass and repass through the midst of intensely hot flames, Purg. xxv. 112, 116, 122, 124, 137; xxvi. 8, 18, 28, 81, 102, 134, 149; as they go the spirits sing, commemorating examples of chastity, viz. the Virgin Mary's reply to the Angel (*Luke* i. 34), Purg. xxv. 128 [**Maria** [1]]; Diana's reprobation of Helice (*vv.* 130-2) [**Diana** [1]: **Elice**]; and chaste wives and husbands (*vv.* 133-5); other spirits, who are divided into two troops, which keep separate and move in opposite directions, proclaim instances of lust, Purg. xxvi. 13-

36, 43-8; those who have been guilty of unnatural offences recall the sins of Sodom and Gomorrah (*vv.* 37-40, 76-81) [**Gomorra: Sodoma: Sodomiti**]; while those who have indulged in excess of natural passion recall the bestiality of Pasiphaë (*vv.* 41-2, 82-7) [**Ermafrodito: Pasife**]. *Examples*: Guido Guinizelli [**Guido Guinizelli**]; and Arnaut Daniel [**Arnaldo Daniello**].

[**Lycaeus**], mountain in Arcadia, the birthplace of Pan, Ecl. R. 25.

M

M [1], last letter of the word *Terram*, formed by the spirits of the Just in the Heaven of Jupiter, Par. xviii. 94, 98. [**Aquila** [2]: **Giove, Cielo di.**]

M [2]], numerical cipher M; the Eagle in the Heaven of Jupiter says that the good qualities of Charles II of Anjou might be indicated by an I (one), his bad ones by an M (thousand), *un emme*, Par. xix. 127-9. [**Carlo** [2].]

Maccabei, apocryphal Books of the Maccabees; D. refers to the account (2 *Maccab.* iv. 7-8) of the underhand relations between Jason the high-priest, and Antiochus Epiphanes, which he compares to those of Clement V with Philip the Fair, Inf. xix. 85-6 [**Jason** [2]]; he also got from the Maccabees his accounts of Alcimus and Demetrius (1 *Maccab.* vii-ix), Epist. viii. 4[65] [**Alci-**

mus]; and of Heliodorus (2 *Maccab.* iii. 25), Purg. xx. 113 [**Eliodoro**].

Maccabeo, Judas Maccabaeus, the great Jewish warrior, who, first under the leadership of his father Mattathias, and, after his death (B.C. 166), as leader himself, carried on the war against Antiochus Epiphanes, King of Syria, and his successor Demetrius, and successfully resisted their attempts to destroy the Jewish religion. After having gained a series of victories over the generals of both kings, and having restored and purified the Temple at Jerusalem (B.C. 163), Judas was defeated and slain by the Syrians (B.C. 161).

D. places him among the great warriors (*Spiriti Militanti*), in the Heaven of Mars, calling him *l'alto Maccabeo*, Par. xviii. 40. [**Marte, Cielo di.**]

Maccario, St. Macarius, probably the Younger, of Alexandria (d. 405), who is credited with having established the monastic rule of the East, as St. Benedict did that of the West; placed by D. among the contemplative spirits (*Spiriti Contemplanti*), in the Heaven of Saturn, where his spirit is pointed out by St. Benedict, Par. xxii. 49. [**Saturno, Cielo di.**]

Macedo, Macedonian; *rex Macedo,* i.e. Alexander the Great, Mon. ii. 9⁶², ⁷⁴. [**Alessandro Magno.**]

Machabaeorum, Libri. [*Maccabei.*]

Macra, small river of Tuscany, which rises in the Apennines in the N. extremity of Lunigiana, and flows into the Mediterranean just E. of the Gulf of Spezia; in D.'s day it divided the Genoese territory from Tuscany (Par. ix. 90); the troubadour Folquet (in the Heaven of Venus) indicates his birthplace, Marseilles, as being on the Mediterranean, midway between the Ebro and the Macra, Par. ix. 88–90; the valley of the Macra is mentioned to indicate Lunigiana, *Valdimagra,* Inf. xxiv. 145; *Valdimacra,* Purg. viii. 116 [**Valdimacra**].

Maddalena, Maria, Mary Magdalene; D. quotes St. Mark's account (xvi. 1–7) of her visit, with Mary the mother of James, and Salome, to the tomb of our Lord, and takes the three women as types of the three sects of the active life, viz. the Epicureans, the Stoics, and the Peripatetics, Conv. iv. 22¹⁴⁹⁻⁶².

Madian, Midian, i. e. the Midianites, who were descended from Midian, the son of Abraham and Keturah (*Gen.* xxv. 2); D. refers to their defeat by Gideon, after they had oppressed Israel for seven years, Purg. xxiv. 124–6 [**Ebrei: Gedeon**].

Maenalus, mountain in Arcadia, celebrated as the favourite haunt of the god Pan; used by D. (as is supposed) to typify pastoral verse, Ecl. i. 11, 23 (his description of it as 'celator Solis', v. 12, being intended to indicate that in this kind of poetry the truth is concealed under the form of an allegory); *Maenala celsa,* Ecl. R. 18.

Maeotidus, belonging to the Maeotae, Scythian tribe who dwelt on the shores of the Sea of Azov, which from them was called by the Romans Maeotis Palus; *Maeotidae paludes,* i. e. the Sea of Azov, the E. limit of the original universal European language, V. E. i. 8²⁶.

Maggio, month of May; D. compares the soft fragrant breath from the wings of the Angel, which fans his forehead in Circle VI of Purgatory, to the breeze just before dawn on a May morning, fragrant of grass and flowers, Purg. xxiv. 145–50; *Kalendae Maiae,* the Kalends of May (i.e. May 1), Epist. vii. 8¹⁹².

Maghinardi. [**Mainardi.**]

Maghinardo Pagano. [**Mainardo Pagano.**]

Magi, the 'wise men from the East', who came to Jerusalem to worship Christ (*Matt.* ii. 1–2); Christ's acceptance of their offering of frankincense and gold, symbolical of His lordship over things spiritual and things temporal, Mon. iii. 7¹⁻⁵ (ref. to *Matt.* ii. 11).

Magi Pharaonis, the 'magicians' of Pharaoh ; their inability to perform the miracle of turning dust into lice, Mon. ii. 4$^{10-14}$ (ref. to Exod. viii. 16-19).

Magister Sapientum. [Aristotile.]

Magister Sententiarum. [Pietro ^{2}.]

Magister Sex Principiorum. [Gilbertus Porretanus.]

Magna, La. [Lamagna.]

Magna, Alberto della. [Alberto ^{1}.]

Mago, Simon. [Simon Mago.]

Magra. [Macra.]

Maia, daughter of Atlas and Pleione, one of the seven Pleiades ; she became by Jupiter the mother of Mercury (Aen. viii. 138-41).

D. speaks of the planets of Mercury and Venus by the names of their respective mothers, viz. Maia and Dione, Par. xxii. 144. [Mercurio ^{2}: Dione.]

Mainardi], family of Bertinoro, thought by some to be alluded to by Guido del Duca (in Circle II of Purgatory) as 'la famiglia di Brettinoro', Purg. xiv. 113. [Brettinoro.]

Mainardi, Arrigo. [Arrigo Mainardi.]

Mainardo Pagano], Maghinardo or Mainardo Pagano da Susinana, head of the Pagani family, lord of Faenza (1290), Forlì (1291), and Imola (1296) ; although a Ghibelline by birth, and a staunch supporter of the Ghibellines in Romagna, yet on the S. side of the Apennines he was equally devoted to the Florentine Guelfs, out of a feeling of gratitude to Florence for the care that had

been taken of him and his property by the Florentines after he had been placed under their protection as a minor by his father Piero. He appears to have fought on the side of the Guelfs at the battle of Campaldino (1289), when the Ghibellines of Arezzo were defeated (Vill. vii. 131) ; and in November of the next year he repelled the Guelfs from Faenza and made himself master of the city (Vill. vii. 144) ; from 1290 to 1294 he was in alliance with the Guelf Malatesta and Polenta families, but after the peace in 1294 he gave his services to the Counts of Romagna, while after the second peace in 1299 he helped Boniface VIII in his war with the Colonnesi ; and he accompanied Charles of Valois when he entered Florence, Nov. 1, 1301 ; he died at Imola in 1302.

D., addressing Guido da Montefeltro (in Bolgia 8 of Circle VIII of Hell), speaks of him, in allusion to his arms (on a field argent a lion azure), as il leoncel dal nido bianco, and informs Guido that both Faenza and Imola were at that time under his lordship ; he further speaks of him as changing sides between summer and winter, ' muta parte dalla state al verno', in allusion to his support of the Florentine Guelfs although he himself was a Ghibelline, Inf. xxvii. 49-51 ; Guido del Duca (in Circle II of Purgatory), apostrophizing the Pagani, speaks of Mainardo as il Demonio, Purg. xiv. 118. [Pagani.]

Maiolica, island of Majorca, largest of the Balearic Islands at the W. extremity of the Mediterranean ;

mentioned by Pier da Medicina (in Bolgia 9 of Circle VIII of Hell), together with Cyprus, the most easterly island in the Mediterranean, to indicate the whole extent of the Mediterranean Sea from E. to W., Inf. xxviii. 82.

Maius. [**Maggio.**]

Malachoth, corrupted form of a Hebrew word, used by D. (who probably got it from St. Jerome's Preface to the Vulgate) as the equivalent of Lat. *Regnorum*, Par. vii. 3.

Malacoda; 'Evil-tail', name of the chief devil in Bolgia 5 of Circle VIII of Hell (Malebolge), where the Barrators are punished, Inf. xxi. 76, 79; *un (demonio), v. 77*; *quel demonio, v.* 103; *colui che i peccator di là uncina*, Inf. xxiii. 141; he deputes ten of his underlings to escort D. and Virgil to the next Bolgia, Inf. xxi. 115–26. [**Malebranche.**]

Malacoth, -hoth. [*Malachoth.*]

Malaspina], noble and wealthy family of N. Italy, whose chief possessions lay in the Valdimacra in Lunigiana [**Lunigiana**]. At the beginning of Cent. xiii the family divided into two main branches, known as the 'Spino Secco' branch and the 'Spino Fiorito' branch, from their respective coats of arms. The earliest member of the family referred to by D. is Currado I, of the 'Spino Secco' branch, known as 'Currado l'Antico', Purg. viii. 119 [**Malaspina, Currado** [1]]; his grandson, Currado II da Villafranca, known as 'Currado il Giovane', is placed among the Negligent Princes in the valley of flowers in Ante-purgatory, Purg. viii. 65, 118 [**Malaspina, Currado** [2]]; another grand-

son, Moroello III da Giovagallo, is referred to as 'Vapor di Val di Magra', Inf. xxiv. 145, and is thought by some to be the individual to whom D. addressed one of his letters, Epist. iii [**Malaspina, Moroello**]; yet another member of the family is referred to by D., viz. Gherardino da Filattiera, of the 'Spino Fiorito' branch, who was Bishop of Luni, 1312–1321, and is spoken of as 'Lunensis Pontifex', Epist. viii. 7[112–13] [**Lunensis**].

The family in general is spoken of in very laudatory terms by D. in conversation with Currado II (in Ante-purgatory), *vostra casa*, Purg. viii. 124; *vostra gente onrata, v.* 128. [**Malaspina, Currado** [2].]

Malaspina, Currado [1]], Currado I, called 'l'Antico', member of the 'Spino Secco' or elder branch of the Malaspina family; he married Costanza, a natural daughter of the Emperor Frederick II, by whom he had four sons, of whom the eldest, Moroello II, was father of Franceschino, D.'s host in Lunigiana in 1306; the second, Federigo, was the father of Currado II, whom D. sees in the valley of flowers in Ante-purgatory; and the third, Manfredi, was father of Moroello III, who is alluded to as 'Vapor di Val di Magra', Inf. xxiv. 145, and to whom D. is supposed to have addressed one of his letters, Epist. iii.

Currado, who was a warm supporter of his father-in-law, the Emperor Frederick II, died about the year 1254; he is mentioned by his grandson, Currado II, who in conversation with D. (in Ante-purgatory) explains that though he was called

Currado Malaspina he was not 'l'Antico', but was descended from him, Purg. viii. 119. [Malaspina.]

Malaspina, Currado [2], Currado II, called 'il Giovane', son of Federigo of Villafranca (d. before 1266), and grandson of the preceding; he was first cousin of Franceschino, D.'s host in Lunigiana in 1306, and of Moroello of Giovagallo (Inf. xxiv. 145); he died c. 1294 [Malaspina]. D. places him among the Negligent Princes in the valley of flowers in Ante-purgatory, *Currado*, Purg. viii. 65; *Currado Malaspina*, v. 118; *un*, v. 64; *ombra*, v. 109; *ella*, v. 115; *egli*, v. 133 [Antipurgatorio]; he addresses D., and, naming himself, asks for news of Valdimacra, to which D. replies that he had never been in the Malaspina territory, but that the name of the family was well known to him by report, as it was throughout all Europe (*vv.* 112–26); he assures Currado that his house is still worthy of its great name, and alone holds the right course, amid the general wrong-doing (*vv.* 127–32); Currado then foretells to D. that before seven years he shall himself in person test the truth of the good opinion he bears of the Malaspina family (a prediction which was verified in 1306, when D. was the guest, at Sarzana, of Franceschino da Mulazzo, grandson of Currado I, and the speaker's first cousin) (*vv.* 133–39) [Dante: Lunigiana].

Malaspina, Moroello, Moroello III, son of Manfredi of Giovagallo (d. 1282) of the 'Spino Secco' branch of the Malaspina family; he was first cousin of Currado II (Purg. viii. 65, 118), and grandson of Currado I (Purg. viii. 119). Unlike most of the members of the Malaspina family, Moroello was a Guelf; in 1288 he appears to have acted as captain of the Florentines in their campaign against the Ghibellines of Arezzo; in 1297 the Guelfs of Bologna elected him captain-general in their war against Azzo of Este, and in the next year they appointed him Podestà of Bologna. In 1299 the Milanese appointed him captain of their forces during their operations against the Marquis of Montferrat. From 1301 to 1312 he was constantly in arms on behalf of the Neri of Tuscany, and during the campaigns of the latter against the Ghibellines of Pistoja he added greatly to his military fame. After the reduction of Pistoja by the Florentines and Lucchese in 1306 he was appointed captain of the people in that city, and in 1307 he was chosen captain of the Guelfic league in Tuscany. Moroello, who married Alagia de' Fieschi, niece of Pope Adrian V (Purg. xix. 142), died c. 1315.

Vanni Fucci (in Bolgia 7 of Circle VIII of Hell), in his prophecy to D. of the defeat of the Bianchi on the 'Campo Piceno', refers to Moroello Malaspina as *il vapor di Valdimagra*, Inf. xxiv. 145 [Campo Piceno: Macra]; he is supposed by some to be the Moroello to whom D. addressed a letter, with an accompanying *canzone* (Canz. xi), Epist. iii.

Boccaccio (in his *Vita di Dante*) states that D. was a friend and guest of Moroello Malaspina, and relates that it was while under his roof in Lunigiana that D. was induced to continue the *D. C.*, the composition of which had been interrupted by his exile from Florence. Boccaccio also states that D. dedicated the *Purgatorio* to Moroello.

Malatesta], powerful family of Romagna, who in Cent. xiii became lords of Rimini. Giovanni Malatesta, who had been Podestà of Rimini, died in 1247, leaving a son, Malatesta · da Verrucchio, 'il mastin vecchio' (Inf. xxvii. 46), who in 1275 was elected captain of the Guelfs of Rimini, but in 1288 was expelled by the Ghibellines. In 1289, however, he returned and once more established himself in the city. In 1295 Montagna de' Parcitati, head of the Ghibelline party in Rimini, was treacherously overpowered by Malatesta; his adherents were expelled, and he himself was made prisoner and handed over by Malatesta to the charge of his son, Malatestino, by whom he was murdered [**Montagna**]. Malatesta remained lord of Rimini till his death in 1312, when he was succeeded by his third son Malatestino, who was in his turn succeeded (1317) by his half-brother, Pandolfo (d. 1326).

Malatesta da Verrucchio], eldest son (born 1212) of Giovanni Malatesta (d. 1247); he was the first Malatesta lord of Rimini, of which he made himself master in 1295, after the overthrow of Montagna de' Parcitati and the Ghibellines; he retained the lordship until his death, at the age of 100, in 1312. Malatesta, who was twice married, had four sons—Giovanni (Gianciotto) (husband of Francesca da Polenta) (d. 1304), Paolo

(Francesca's lover) (d. c. 1283), Malatestino ('il mastin nuovo', Inf. xxvii. 46), who succeeded him in the lordship of Rimini (d. 1317), and (by his second wife) Pandolfo (d. 1326), who succeeded Malatestino. [**Malatesta.**]

D. refers to Malatesta and his son Malatestino, in connexion with their murder of Montagna de' Parcitati, as *il mastin vecchio e il nuovo da Verrucchio*, Inf. xxvii. 46. [**Malatestino: Montagna.**]

Malatesta, Gianciotto], Giovanni, nicknamed Gianciotto ('lame John'), eldest son of the preceding, and brother of Malatestino, 'il mastin nuovo' (Inf. xxvii. 46). He appears to have been a man of brutish exterior, but valiant and able. He married (probably in 1275) Francesca, daughter of Guido Vecchio da Polenta, by whom he had a daughter. Having surprised Francesca, some time after their marriage, with his younger brother Paolo, who had acted as his proxy at the betrothal, Gianciotto slew them both (c. 1283). He himself died in 1304, eight years before his father.

Francesca (in Circle II of Hell), in the course of her story of the death of her lover and herself, refers to Gianciotto as *chi vita ci spense*, and foretells his doom in the lowest pit of Hell, Inf. v. 107. [**Francesca.**]

Malatesta, Paolo], second son (born c. 1247) of Malatesta da Verrucchio, lord of Rimini, 'il mastin vecchio' (Inf. xxvii. 46), and younger brother of the preceding. He married in 1269 Orabile Beatrice, daughter of the Count of Ghiacciuolo, by whom he had a son and a daughter.

Paolo acted as proxy for his brother, Gianciotto, at the betrothal of the latter to Francesca, daughter of Guido Vecchio da Polenta (probably in 1275). Eight or nine years later, when he himself had been married some fourteen years and was the father of two children, and Francesca was the mother of a daughter nine years old, the two were surprised together by Gianciotto and slain on the spot.

Paolo, whose father had been Charles of Anjou's Vicar in Florence, was Capitano del Popolo in that city from March 1282 to Feb. 1283, at which time D., then in his eighteenth year, may have become acquainted with him, at any rate by sight.

D. places Paolo, whom he does not name (and who figures merely as a mute personage), together with Francesca, among the Lustful in Circle II of Hell, *costui*, Inf. v. 101, 104; *questi*, v. 135; *l'altro* (*spirto*), v. 139; Paolo and Francesca together, *que' due*, v. 74; *anime affannate*, v. 80; *anime offense*, v. 109; *costoro*, v. 114; *l'uno e l'altro spirto*, vv. 139, 140. [**Francesca: Lussuriosi.**]

Malatestino], lord of Rimini, 1312–1317, third son (born 1249) of Malatesta da Verrucchio, whom he succeeded, and younger brother of Gianciotto and Paolo Malatesta. When his father by treachery in 1295 overpowered Montagna de' Parcitati and the Ghibellines of Rimini, Montagna, who was taken prisoner, was entrusted to the charge of Malatestino, who, on a hint from his father, shortly after had him murdered in prison. [**Malatesta.**]

D. refers to Malatestino and his father, in connexion with their murder of Montagna, as *il mastin vecchio e il nuovo da Verrucchio*, Inf. xxvii. 46 [**Montagna**]; Pier da Medicina (in Bolgia 9 of Circle VIII of Hell) speaks of Malatestino (in connexion with his murder of Guido del Cassero and Angiolello da Carignano, two gentlemen of Fano) as *un tiranno fello*, and, in allusion to the fact that he had lost an eye, as *Quel traditor che vede pur con l'uno*, Inf. xxviii. 81, 85 [**Angiolello**].

Malavicini], Ghibelline Counts of Bagnacavallo in the Emilia; alluded to by Guido del Duca (in Circle II of Purgatory), who implies that they were becoming extinct, Purg. xiv. 115. [**Bagnacaval.**]

Malebolge, 'Evil-pouches', name given by D. to Circle VIII of Hell, so called from the ten *bolge* into which it is divided, Inf. xviii. 1; xxi. 5; xxiv. 37; xxix. 41; it consists of an immense inverted hollow cone, truncated at the apex (where Circle IX is placed), towards which the ground slopes gradually on all sides (Inf. xx. 37–8); it is intersected with ten concentric valleys or ravines (*valli*, Inf. xviii. 9; *tomba*, Inf. xix. 7; *vallon*, Inf. xix. 133; xx. 7; xxiii. 135; *fossi*, Inf. xviii. 17; *fosse*, Inf. xxiii. 56; *fessura*, Inf. xxi. 4; *bolge*, Inf. xviii. 24, 104; xix. 6; xxii. 17; xxiii. 32, 45; xxiv. 81; xxvi. 32; xxviii. 21; xxix. 7, 118), lying one below the other on the slope, after the arrangement of the rows of seats in an amphitheatre; these valleys, which are half a mile across at the bottom (Inf. xxx. 87), are divided from each other by an enormous thickness of solid ground, forming banks or ramparts between them (*argini*, Inf. xviii. 17, 101 ; xix. 40, 129 ; xxi. 136; *ripe*, Inf. xviii. 15, 69, 106 ; xix. 35, 68 ; xxi. 18 ; xxii. 116 ; xxiii. 43 ; xxiv. 80) ; connecting these banks, and crossing the valleys at right angles, run arched bridges of rock (*scoglio*, Inf. xviii. 16, 69, 111 ; xix. 8, 131 ; xx. 26 ; xxi. 30, 43, 107 ; xxiv. 61 ; xxvi. 17 ; xxvii. 134; xxviii. 43 ; xxix. 38, 53 ; *sasso*, Inf. xxiii. 134 ; *ponte*, Inf. xviii. 79 ; xxi. 1, 37, 47, 64, 89; xxiv. 19, 79; xxvi. 43 ; xxviii. 127; *ponticello*, Inf. xviii. 15 ; xxi. 70; xxix. 25 ; *arco*, Inf. xviii. 102, 111 ; xix. 128; xxi. 108; xxiv. 68; xxvii. 134), forming gangways, like the transverse passages in a theatre.

In Malebolge, of which D. gives a detailed description (Inf. xviii. 1–18), are punished the Fraudulent, who are divided into ten classes, each class being distinct and having a separate *bolgia* and distinctive punishment assigned to it [**Frodolenti**]. Their guardian is Geryon, the symbol of fraud. [**Gerione**.]

Malebranche, ' Evil-claws ', the name given by D. to the demons in Bolgia 5 of Circle VIII of Hell (Malebolge), where the Barrators are punished, Inf. xxi. 37 ; xxiii. 23 ; xxxiii. 142 ; *demoni*, Inf. xxi. 47 ; xxii. 13 ; *diavoli*, Inf. xxi. 92 ; *ministri della fossa quinta*, Inf. xxiii. 56 ; hence this Bolgia is spoken of by Frate Alberigo as 'il fosso di Malebranche ', Inf. xxxiii. 142.

The individual names given by D. to the ' Malebranche ' are Malacoda (Inf. xxi. 76, 79), Scarmiglione

(xxi. 105), Alichino (xxi. 118 ; xxii. 112), Calcabrina (xxi. 118 ; xxii. 133), Cagnazzo (xxi. 119 ; xxii. 106), Barbariccia (xxi. 120 ; xxii. 29, 59, 145), Libicocco (xxi. 121 ; xxii. 70), Draghignazzo (xxi. 121 ; xxii. 73), Ciriatto (xxi. 122 ; xxii. 55), Graffiacane (xxi. 122 ; xxii. 34), Farfarello (xxi. 123 ; xxii. 94), and Rubicante (xxi. 123 ; xxii. 40).

Malehaut, Dama di], the Lady of Malehaut, one of Queen Guenever's companions, who was in love with Lancelot, and during the first interview between him and the Queen, at which she was present, coughed on perceiving the familiarity between them ; D. alludes to her as *quella che tossìo Al primo fallo scritto di Ginevra*, Par. xvi. 14–15. [**Galeotto : Ginevra**.]

Malta, name of a prison in which ecclesiastical delinquents used to be confined ; mentioned by Cunizza (in the Heaven of Venus), Par. ix. 54.

There is some doubt as to the identity of the place in question, as there were several prisons of this name. The majority of commentators think the reference is to the fortress at the S. extremity of the Lake of Bolsena ; others, to La Malta, a prison in Viterbo ; others, again, to the stronghold of Citadella, between Vicenza and Treviso, which was built in 1251 by Ezzelino da Romano, brother of Cunizza, the speaker.

Manardi, -ardo. [**Mainardi, -ardo.**]

Manfredi, Manfred, natural son (born in Sicily c. 1231) of the Emperor Frederick II; he was grandson of the Emperor Henry VI and of Constance of Sicily (Purg. iii. 113), and father, by his wife Beatrice of Savoy, of Constance, who married Peter III of Aragon (Purg. iii. 115–16). At his father's death (1250) he was appointed regent of Sicily during the absence of his brother, Conrad IV. On the death of the latter in 1254, his son, Conradin, the rightful successor to the throne of Sicily, being only three years old, Manfred at the invitation of the Sicilian barons again assumed the regency. Having made himself master of the kingdom, nominally on behalf of Conradin, in 1258, on a rumour of the death of the latter, he was entreated to assume the crown, which he did at Palermo on Aug. 11 in that year. But the Pope could not tolerate a Ghibelline and infidel on the throne of Sicily; in 1259 Manfred was excommunicated by Alexander IV, and again in 1261 by Urban IV, by whom the forfeited crown of Sicily was offered, first to Louis IX of France, and, on his refusal, to his brother, Charles of Anjou. Urban's offer having been confirmed by his successor, Clement IV, Charles advanced into Italy with a large force in the autumn of 1265, and entered Rome, where, after being elected senator in opposition to Manfred, he was crowned King of Sicily, Jan. 6, 126⅚. Immediately afterwards he set out to take possession of his kingdom. Manfred was prepared to make a stout resistance, but he was surrounded by traitors; the passage of the Garigliano at Ceperano was betrayed to the enemy by his relative,

the Count of Caserta (Inf. xxviii. 6), and the French entered Campania, took the stronghold of San Germano (Feb. 10, 126⅚) and advanced towards Benevento, where Manfred and his army were stationed [**Ceperano.**] On Feb. 26, 126⅚, the two armies met on the plain of Grandella, near Benevento, where Manfred, deserted by the Apulian barons, was defeated and slain. His body was recovered, but as he had been excommunicated, Charles would not have him laid in consecrated ground, but caused him to be buried at the foot of the bridge of Benevento; upon his grave was made a great pile of stones, each one of the army throwing one upon it as he passed (Purg. iii. 128–9). Subsequently, it is said by command of Clement IV, the Archbishop of Cosenza caused the body to be disinterred from its resting-place in Church territory, and had it cast unburied upon the banks of the river Verde, outside the limits of the kingdom of Naples (Purg. iii. 124–31) [**Benevento: Verde.**] The defeat and death of Manfred was a crushing blow to the Ghibelline cause, which had constantly received powerful support from him, notably during the struggle against the Tuscan Guelfs, when he contributed largely to the great Ghibelline triumph at Montaperti (1260). The ascendency of the Guelfs was henceforth assured under the protection of the house of Anjou.

D. places Manfred in Antepurgatory among those who died excommunicate, but repented of their sins before death, *Manfredi*,

Purg. iii. 112 ; *uno, v.* 103 ; *quello spirto,* Purg. iv. 14 [**Antipurgatorio**] ; Manfred addresses D., who looking at him fixedly, sees that he is 'fair-haired and beautiful and of noble countenance', but he does not recognize him (Purg. iii. 103–10) ; M. then names himself, saying that he was grandson of the Empress Constance, and begs D., when he returns, to inform his daughter Constance how, after receiving two deadly wounds, he penitently turned to God, and how, though his sins were horrible, his repentance was accepted (*vv.* 110–23) [**Costanza** [1] : **Costanza** [2]].

Like his father, Manfred was a poet and musician, and patron of letters. D., in explaining in the *De Vulgari Eloquentia* how it was that the early Italian poets were always spoken of as 'Sicilian', pays a high tribute to 'the two illustrious heroes, the Emperor Frederick and his high-born son Manfred', for their love of letters, V. E. i. 12[20–35].

Manfredi da Vico, hereditary Prefect of Rome, who as such was entitled to assist at the coronation of the Emperor, and to receive the golden rose from the Pope on the fourth Sunday in Lent. Manfredi, who was a godson of King Manfred, and appears to have succeeded his elder brother Pietro as Prefect between 1303 and 1306, when he was already middle-aged, is mentioned by D., in his discussion as to the nature of nobility, as the type of those whose character belied the nobility of their descent (but it is not known on what ground), Conv. iv. 26[16–25].

Manfredi, Alberigo de'. [**Alberigo, Frate.**]

Manfredi, Tebaldello de'. [**Tebaldello.**]

Mangiadore, Pietro. [**Pietro Mangiadore.**]

Mangona, Conti di], the Alberti, Counts of Mangona, referred to, Inf. xxxii. 55–7. [**Alberti.**]

Manlius, Marcus Manlius Capitolinus, Consul B. C. 392 ; when Rome was taken by the Gauls under Brennus in 390, and the Romans were besieged in the Capitol, Manlius, aroused during a night attack by the cackling of the sacred geese, hastily collected a handful of men and drove back the enemy, who had just reached the summit of the hill ; for this heroic deed he received the surname of Capitolinus.

D. mentions this incident, referring to Livy (v. 47) and quoting Virgil (*Aen.* viii. 652–6), Mon. ii. 4[42–58] (cf. Conv. iv. 5[160–4]). [**Galli** [2].]

Manto, daughter of Tiresias, Theban prophetess, placed by D. among the Soothsayers in Bolgia 4 of Circle VIII of Hell (Malebolge), Inf. xx. 55 ; *quella, v.* 52 ; *questa, v.* 60 ; *vergine cruda, v.* 82 ; *colei, v.* 92 [**Indovini**] ; D. here puts into Virgil's mouth an account of the founding of Mantua by Manto, daughter of Tiresias, which is totally inconsistent with Virgil's own account as given in the *Aeneid* (x. 198–200), Inf. xx. 55–99 [**Mantova**]. By an oversight D. also includes *la figlia di Tiresia,* who can be none other than Manto, among the persons mentioned by Statius who Virgil says are together with himself in Limbo, Purg. xxii. 113 [**Limbo**].

Mantova, Mantua, town in SE. extremity of Lombardy, situated not many miles from the confluence of the Mincio with the Po. The ancient Mantua was celebrated on account of its connexion with Virgil, who claimed it as his birthplace, although he was actually born in the neighbouring village of Andes, which has been identified with the modern Pietola. [**Virgilio.**]

Mantua is mentioned as the birthplace of Virgil in connexion with the story of its foundation by Manto, after whom it was named, Inf. xx. 93; *là dove nacqu' io*, v. 56; *la città*, v. 91; *la mia terra*, v. 98 [**Manto**]; Virgil mentions it again as his birthplace, Purg. vi. 72 (cf. Inf. xx. 56); and it is referred to (perhaps) in the same connexion as *villa Mantovana*, Purg. xviii. 83 [**Pietola**]; it is mentioned also as the native land of Sordello (who was born at Goito near Mantua), *Mantua*, V. E. i. 15[9]; and as the scene of the discussion as to the relative heights of land and sea, which led to D.'s disputation *De Aqua et Terra*, A. T. § 1[2]. [**Quaestio.**]

Mantovano, Mantuan; Virgil, who claimed to be a Mantuan by birth, describes his parents as *Mantovani*, Inf. i. 69; Beatrice addresses V. as *anima cortese Mantovana*, Inf. ii. 58; Sordello addresses V. as *Mantovano*, Purg. vi. 74 [**Virgilio**]; D. speaks of Sordello (who was a native of Goito near Mantua) as *il Mantovan*, Purg. vii. 86 [**Sordello**]; Mantua (according to one interpretation) is spoken of as *villa Mantovana*, Purg. xviii. 83, where the meaning may be merely

'Mantuan village' [**Pietola**]; the poet Gotto of Mantua, *Gottus Mantuanus*, V. E. ii. 13[26—7] [.**Gottus**].

Mantua. [**Mantova.**]

Mantuanus. [**Mantovano.**]

Mantuanus, Gottus. [**Gottus.**]

Maomettani], Mahometans or Saracens; referred to by Cacciaguida (in the Heaven of Mars), in connexion with the Second Crusade (in which he lost his life), as *gente turpa*, Par. xv. 145; their religion, Islam, is referred to in connexion with their possession of the Holy Sepulchre, Par. xv. 142–4; they are spoken of as *Saracini*, Inf. xxvii. 87; Purg. xxiii. 103; Conv. ii. 9[70]; *Saraceni*, Epist. v. 2[24]; viii. 3[33]. [**Saracini.**]

Maometto, Mahomet, founder of the Mahometan religion; born at Mecca c. 570, proclaimed himself as prophet c. 610, fled from Mecca to Medina, July 16, 622 (this year of the flight, called the Hégira, being the first of the Mahometan era); in 630 he conquered Mecca, and was recognized as sovereign throughout the country between the Euphrates and the Red Sea; he died June 8, 632.

D. places Mahomet (who, according to mediaeval tradition, was originally a Christian, was ordained priest, and, having become a Cardinal, aspired to the Papacy), together with his son-in-law Ali, among the Schismatics in Bolgia 9 of Circle VIII of Hell (Malebolge), Inf. xxviii. 31, 62; *un*, v. 23. [**Alì: Scismatici.**]

Some think Mahomet is typified by the dragon, which fixes its tail into the bottom of the car in the mystical Procession in the Terrestrial Paradise, and draws part of it away, Purg. xxxii. 130–5.

Marca Anconitana, March of Ancona, former province of Italy, corresponding roughly with that now known as the Marches, bordering on the Adriatic, the N. limit of the coast-line being at Cattolica, the S. at the mouth of the river Tronto ; on the left side of Italy if the Apennines be taken as the dividing line (from N. to S.), V. E. i. 10^{52}; its dialect distinct from those of the inhabitants of Calabria and Romagna, V. E. i. 10^{66-7}; the ugliest of the Italian dialects after that of the Romans, V. E. i. 11^{18-20}; rejected by D., with those of the Romans and Spoletans, as unworthy to be the Italian vulgar tongue, V. E. i. 11^{20-1}; the Apulian dialect affected by its barbarisms, and by those of the Romans and Trevisans, V. E. i. 12^{56-9}; the inhabitants of the March of Ancona coupled with those of the March of Treviso as *utriusque Marchiae viri*, V. E. i. 19^{19}; the March of Ancona referred to (by Jacopo del Cassero in Ante-purgatory) as *quel paese Che siede tra Romagna e quel di Carlo* (i. e. the district between Romagna and the kingdom of Naples), Purg. v. 68–9. [**Anconitani.**]

Marca Trivisiana, March of Treviso, former province of Italy, comprising the greater part of the modern Venetia; it was bounded on the N. by the Tagliamento, on the S. by the Po, on the E. by the Gulf of Venice, and on the W. by the Adige; on the left side of Italy if the Apennines be taken as the dividing line (from N. to S.), V. E.

i. 10^{51-4}; its inhabitants coupled with those of the March of Ancona as *utriusque Marchiae viri*, V. E. i. 19^{19}; included in the jurisdiction of the Bishop of Ostia as papal legate, *Marchia Tervisina* (according to the correct reading), Epist. i. *tit.* The March of Treviso, together with Lombardy and Romagna, is referred to by Marco Lombardo (in Circle III of Purgatory) as *il paese ch'Adice e Po riga*, Purg. xvi. 115; Cunizza (in the Heaven of Venus) refers to the March itself (in a more confined sense) as *quella parte della terra prava Italica, che siede tra Rialto E le fontane di Brenta e di Piava* (i. e. the country which lies between the Piave on the N., the Brenta on the S., and Venice on the E.), Par. ix. 25–7 ; she refers to the peoples of the March (i. e. the inhabitants of Vicenza, Padua, Treviso, Feltro, and Belluno), as *la turba presente, Che Tagliamento e Adice richiude*, Par. ix. 43–4. [**Trivisiani.**]

Marcabò, castle in the territory of Ravenna near the mouths of the Po; mentioned by Pier da Medicina (in Bolgia 9 of Circle VIII of Hell) as the E. extremity of the old Lombardy, which he describes as *lo dolce piano Che da Vercelli a Marcabò dichina*, Inf. xxviii. 74–5. [**Lombardia : Vercelli.**]

Marcello, Marcellus, Roman Consul, and determined opponent of Julius Caesar (probably M. Claudius Marcellus, Consul B. C. 51); D. in his apostrophe to Italy says that the Italian cities are full of tyrants, and that every villager who takes part in politics thinks himself another Marcellus (i. e. opponent of the Empire), Purg. vi. 124–6.

> **Marchese** [1].   [Azzo da Esti.]
> **Marchese** [2].   [Guglielmo [3].]
> **Marchese** [3].   [Bonifazio di Monferrato.]

Marchese [4], Marchese (or Marchesino) degli Orgogliosi of Forlì, who was Podestà of Faenza in 1296. D., who refers to his having been an insatiable wine-bibber during his lifetime, places him among the Gluttonous in Circle VI of Purgatory, Purg. xxiv. 31–3. [Golosi.]

Marchese di Monferrato, Boniface II, Marquis of Montferrat (1192–1207), Conv. iv. 11[126–7]; William Longsword, Marquis of Montferrat (1254–1292), Purg. vii. 136; John I, Marquis of Montferrat (1292–1305), V. E. i. 12[38]. [Monferrato.]

Marchia Anconitana. [Marca Anconitana.]

Marchia, Januensis. [Genovese.]

Marchia Tervisina, Trivisiana. [Marca Trivisiana.]

Marchiani, inhabitants of the March of Ancona, V. E. i. 12[58]; their near vicinity to the Apulians perhaps accounts for the harshness of the dialect of the latter, V. E. i. 12[56–9]; coupled with the inhabitants of the March of Treviso as *utriusque Marchiae viri*, V. E. i. 19[19]; their best writers, like those of Sicily, Apulia, Tuscany, Romagna, and Lombardy, wrote in the Italian vulgar tongue, V. E. i. 19[16–19]. [Anconitani: Trivisiani.]

> **Marchio** [1].   [Azzo da Esti.]
> **Marchio** [2].   [Johannes [3].]

Marco, St. Mark the Evangelist, Conv. iv. 22[148–9]; *Marcus*, Mon. iii. 9[98]; his Gospel is quoted, V. N. § 23[55–6] (*Mark* xi. 10); Conv. iv. 22[148–59] (*Mark* xvi. 1; xvi. 6–7); referred to, Mon. iii. 9[97–8] (ref. to *Mark* xiv. 29).—In the mystical Procession in the Terrestrial Paradise the Gospel of St. Mark is represented (according to the most probable interpretation) by one of the four beasts (*quattro animali*), Purg. xxix. 92.

Marco Lombardo, Lombard (or Venetian) gentleman, placed by D. among the Wrathful in Circle III of Purgatory, Purg. xvi. 46; *Marco*, *v.* 130; *lui*, *v.* 52 [Iracondi].

The commentators differ as to the meaning of 'Lombardo' as applied to Marco. Some say that he was so called because he was a native of Lombardy or of Lombard extraction; others state that he was a frequent visitor to Paris, and was so termed 'in the French fashion', in which case the name would simply mean 'Marco the Italian'; while others assert that he belonged to the Lombardi of Venice, and that 'Lombardo' consequently was his family name. He figures as Marco Lombardo in the *Cento Novelle Antiche* (lxxii), as well as in Villani (vii. 121), who relates a story of how he foretold his coming misfortunes to Count Ugolino, then at the height of his power and prosperity.

Marcum, Evangelium secundum. [Marco [1].]

Marcus. [Marco.]

Mardocheo, Mordecai, the Jew, the 'nursing father' of Esther; D. in a vision sees him, together with

Esther and Ahasuerus, witnessing the death of Haman, Purg. xvii. 29. [**Amano.**]

Mare Adriano, Adriatic Sea, Conv. iv. 13[121]; *Adriaticum mare*, V. E. i. 8[56], 10[49]; *Adria*, Ecl. ii. 68 [**Adria**]; referred to as *la marina*, Inf. v. 98; Purg. xiv. 92; *il mare*, Par. viii. 63; the coast (near Ravenna), *lito Adriano*, Par. xxi. 123; *litus Adriacum*, Ecl. R. 11 [**Adriano**[1]]; receives the waters of the Po, Inf. v. 98 [**Po**]; and of the Tronto, Par. viii. 63 [**Tronto**]; the E. boundary of Romagna, Purg. xiv. 92 [**Romagna**]; crossed by Caesar in the boat of the fisherman Amyclas, Conv. iv. 13[119-21] [**Amiclas : Cesare**[1]]; its shores the E. limit of the Italian language, V. E. i. 8[53-7] [*Italica Lingua*]; receives the waters on the left side of Italy (if the Apennines be taken as the dividing line from N. to S.), V. E. i. 10[48-9].

Mare Adriaticum. [**Mare Adriano.**]

Mare Anglicum, English Channel; one of the limits of the *langue d'*oïl, V. E. i. 8[61]. [*Lingua Oil.*]

Mare Germanico], North Sea; referred to as *il mare*, in connexion with the embankments against its encroachments on the Flemish coast, Inf. xv. 6; receives the waters of the Elbe, Purg. vii. 99.

Mare Mediterraneo], Mediterranean Sea; referred to as *il mare*, Inf. xiv. 94; xxvi. 100, 105; xxx. 19; Par. viii. 63; *La maggior valle in che l'acqua si spanda . . . Fuor di quel mar che la terra inghirlanda* (i. e. the largest expanse of water with the exception of the great

Ocean), Par. ix. 82-4; its extent from E. to W. indicated as the domain of Neptune, *Tra l'isola di Cipri e di Maiolica*, Inf. xxviii. 82.

Mare Oceano. [**Oceano.**]

Mare Rosso, Red Sea; *ciò che di sopra il mar rosso ee*, i. e. Arabia, Inf. xxiv. 90 [**Arabia**]; referred to, in connexion with the passage of the Israelites, as *il mare*, Purg. xviii. 134; Par. xxii. 95 [**Ebrei**]; the coast (i. e. the furthest shores of Egypt), *il lito rubro*, Par. vi. 79 (*Aen.* viii. 686).

Mare Tyrrenum, the Tyrrhenian Sea, that part of the Mediterranean which adjoins the W. and SW. coast of Italy, lying between Corsica and Calabria; it receives the waters of the right side of Italy (if the Apennines be taken as the dividing line from N. to S.), V. E. i. 10[47-8]; the islands of (viz. Sicily and Sardinia), to be reckoned as belonging to the right side of Italy, V. E. i. 10[56-7]; mentioned by G. del Virgilio, *aequor Tirrhenum*, Carm. 43.

Mare di Tiberiade], Sea of Tiberias or Sea of Galilee (*John* vi. 1); referred to by Beatrice (in the Heaven of Fixed Stars) as *lo mare*, in connexion with Christ's walking on the water and St. Peter's attempt to join Him (*Matt.* xiv. 22-31), Par. xxiv. 39. [**Pietro**[1].]

Maremma, wild marshy district along the coast of Tuscany, which from its low situation and want of drainage was infested with malaria and notoriously unhealthy.

D. mentions it in connexion with the snakes which harboured there, Inf. xxv. 19; its unhealthiness, Inf. xxix. 48; the imprisonment and death of Pia in the Sienese Maremma, Purg. v. 134 [Pia]; the Tuscan Maremma, together with part of the Campagna of Rome, is alluded to as the district, *tra Cecina e Corneto*, Inf. xiii. 9 [Cecina].

Margherita [1], Margaret, eldest daughter of Raymond Berenger IV, Count of Provence; she was married (1234) to Louis IX (St. Louis), King of France, whose younger brother, Charles of Anjou, afterwards King of Sicily and Naples, married (1246) her youngest sister, Beatrice.

Margaret is referred to by the Emperor Justinian (in the Heaven of Mercury) as one of the four daughters of Raymond Berenger IV, each of whom became a Queen, Par. vi. 133-4 [Beringhieri, Ramondo]. Some think Margaret of Provence is the Margaret mentioned by Sordello, Purg. vii. 128; but the reference is more probably to Margaret of Burgundy, second wife of Charles I of Naples [Margherita [2]].

Margherita [2], Margaret of Burgundy, Countess of Tonnerre, second daughter of Eudes of Burgundy (d. 1269) and of Mahaud of Bourbon; she married, Oct. 12, 1268, as his second wife, Charles I of Anjou, King of Sicily and Naples, and died, Sept. 5, 1308, having survived her husband by more than twenty years. Charles's first wife, Beatrice of Provence, who died in 1267, and she are mentioned together by Sordello (in Ante-purgatory) in connexion with their husband, who, he says, was as inferior to Peter III of Aragon as

Charles II of Naples was to his father, Charles I, Purg. vii. 127-9 [Beatrice [2]: Carlo [1]: Carlo [2].]

Margherita di Brabante. [Brabante.]

Maria [1], Virgin Mary, mother of our Lord, Purg. iii. 39; v. 101; viii. 37; x. 50; xiii. 50; xviii. 100; xx. 19; xxii. 142; xxxiii. 6; Par. iii. 122; iv. 30; xi. 71; xiv. 36; xv. 133; xxiii. 111, 126, 137; xxxii. 4, 95, 107, 113; V. N. § 29[9]; Conv. ii. 6[13, 24]; iv. 5[42, 54]; Son. xviii. 4; *Maria Vergine*, Conv. ii. 6[13]; *Vergine*, Par. xiii. 84; *Vergine Madre*, Par. xxxiii. 1; *Virgo Mater*, Mon. ii. 12[44]; Epist. viii. 2[18]; *Augusta*, Par. xxxii. 119; *Regina*, Purg. vii. 82; Par. xxxi. 116; xxxii. 104; xxxiii. 34; *Regina coeli*, Par. xxiii. 128; *Regina del cielo*, Par. xxxi. 100; *Regina della gloria*, V. N. § 5[3]; *Reina benedetta*, V. N. § 29[8-9]; *Donna del cielo*, Par. xxiii. 106; xxxii. 29; *nostra Donna*, Par. xxi. 123; referred to also as *donna gentile*, Inf. ii. 94; *donna*, Purg. xv. 88; xxvi. 59; Par. xxxiii. 13; *Quella Che ad aprir l'alto amor volse la chiave*, Purg. x. 41-2; *unica sposa Dello Spirito Santo*, Purg. xx. 97-8; *la rosa in che il Verbo Divino Carne si fece*, Par. xxiii. 73-4; *il bel fior*. Par. xxiii. 88; *viva stella*, Par. xxiii. 92; *bel zaffiro*, Par. xxiii. 101; *il ventre Che fu albergo del nostro disiro*, Par. xxiii. 104-5; *coronata fiamma*, Par. xxiii. 119; *luce*, Par. xxv. 128; *pacifica oriafiamma*, Par. xxxi. 127; *bellezza*, Par. xxxi. 134; *la faccia che a Cristo Più si somiglia*, Par. xxxii. 85-6; *figlia (d'Anna)*, Par. xxxii. 134;

Conv. ii. 6[14]; *meridiana face Di caritate*, Par. xxxiii. 10–11; *di speranza fontana vivace*, Par. xxxiii. 12; *occhi da Dio diletti e venerati*, Par. xxxiii. 40; *figlia di Giovacchino e d'Anna*, Conv. ii. 6[14]; *giovinetta donzella*, Conv. ii. 6[24]; *la baldezza e l'onore dell' umana generazione*, Conv. iv. 5[41-2].

The Virgin Mary belonged to the house of David, Conv. iv. 5[40-2]; was the daughter of St. Anne, Par. xxxii. 134; Conv. ii. 6[14]; and of Joachim, Conv. ii. 6[14] [**Anna**[1]: **Gioacchino**[2]]; fourteen years old at the time of the Annunciation, Conv. ii. 6[24-5]; the bride of the Holy Spirit (*Matt.* i. 20), Purg. xx. 97–8; the mother of our Lord, Purg. iii. 39; xx. 19–24; Par. xxiii. 104–5, 136–7; xxxii. 4; xxxiii. 1; Conv. ii. 6[13]; iv. 5[54]; Mon. ii. 12[43-4]; man's intercessor with Christ, Purg. x. 41–2; Par. xxiii. 88; xxxii. 148; invoked by women in travail, Purg. xx. 19–21; Par. xv. 133; in *D. C.* she is symbolized by the rose, Par. xxiii. 73, 88; her place in Paradise, Purg. viii. 37; Par. iv. 30; xxiii. 73–119; xxv. 128; xxxi. 127, 134; xxxii. 85–120; Son. xviii. 4; invoked, by Buonconte at the moment of his death, Purg. v. 101; by the spirits in Ante-purgatory, Purg. vii. 82; by the spirits of the Envious, Purg. xiii. 50; by D. in his daily and nightly prayers, Par. xxiii. 88; by the spirits in the Heaven of Fixed Stars, Par. xxiii. 128; by St. Bernard in the Empyrean, Par. xxxii. 148; xxxiii. 1–39; the abode of the angels spoken of as *il grembo di Maria*, Purg. viii. 37.

The following incidents in the life of the Virgin Mary are referred to by D. :—the Annunciation, Purg. x. 41–50; xxv. 128; Par. iii. 122; xiv. 36; xxxii. 95, 112–14; Conv. ii. 6[23-5] [**Gabriello**]; her visit to her 'cousin' Elisabeth, the mother of John the Baptist (*Luke* i. 39), Purg. xviii. 100; Elisabeth's salutation of her (*Luke* i. 42), Purg. xxix. 85–7 [**Elisabetta**]; her journey with Joseph to Bethlehem 'to be taxed' (*Luke* ii. 4–7), Mon. ii. 12[41-6]; the Nativity of Christ, Purg. xx. 22–4; Mon. ii. 12[43-4]; her finding of Christ in the Temple (*Luke* ii. 46–9), Purg. xv. 88–92; her presence at the marriage-feast at Cana (*John* ii. 1–10), Purg. xiii. 29; xxii. 142–4; at the Crucifixion (*John* xix. 25–7), Purg. xxxiii. 6; Par. xi. 71–2; xxv. 113–14 [**Giovanni**[2]]; her Assumption into Heaven, Par. xxv. 128.

In the *Inferno* D. avoids the mention of the name of the Virgin, as he does that of Christ; in Virgil's account of how he was sent to D.'s aid it is related that the Virgin, who is referred to as 'donna gentil' (Inf. ii. 94), dispatched St. Lucy to Beatrice, who in her turn dispatched Virgil to rescue D. from his 'impedimento', Inf. ii. 52–120.

In the *Purgatorio* the Virgin plays an important part, an episode from her life being introduced in each of the seven Circles as an example to those who are purging the various deadly sins; thus in the Circle of the Proud she figures as an example of Humility, the scene of the Annunciation, with the Virgin represented as saying 'Ecce Ancilla Dei'

(*Luke* i. 38), being among the marble sculptures on the wall, Purg. x. 34–44 [Superbi]; in the Circle of the Envious she is introduced as an example of Love, her words 'Vinum non habent' (*John* ii. 3), recalling her loving care for the unprovided guests at the marriage-feast at Cana, being chanted by the voices of unseen spirits, Purg. xiii. 28–30 [Invidiosi]; in the Circle of the Wrathful she is introduced as an example of Meekness, the scene of her finding Christ in the Temple (*Luke* ii. 46–8) being shown to D. in a vision, Purg. xv. 85–92 [Iracondi]; in the Circle of the Slothful she is introduced as an example of Activity, her haste to visit her 'cousin' Elisabeth (*Luke* i. 39) being recalled by the spirits as they run to and fro, Purg. xviii. 99–100 [Accidiosi]; in the Circle of the Avaricious she is introduced as an example of Poverty, the nativity of Christ in a manger (*Luke* ii. 7) being recalled by one of the spirits, Purg. xx. 19–24 [Avari]; in the Circle of the Gluttonous she is introduced as an example of Temperance, her thought for the wants of others, and not for her own gratification, at the marriage-feast at Cana (*John* ii. 3) being recalled by a hidden voice, Purg. xxii. 140–4 [Golosi]; in the Circle of the Lustful she is introduced as an example of Chastity, her words to the angel Gabriel, 'Virum non cognosco' (*Luke* i. 34), being proclaimed by the spirits as they pass through the purging flames, Purg. xxv. 127–8 [Lussuriosi].

St. Bernard points out to D. the Virgin Mary's seat in the Celestial Rose, her place being on the highest tier, at the point where the light is most dazzling (Par. xxxi. 122–9) [Rosa]; around her hover more than a thousand angels of various orders (*vv.* 130–2); before her, with his wings outspread, stands the archangel Gabriel (Par. xxxii. 94–6) [Gabriello]; at her feet is seated Eve, who caused the wound which she healed (Par. xxxii. 4–6) [Eva]; on her left sit Adam and Moses, on her right St. Peter and St. John the Evangelist (*vv.* 121–32); opposite to her, on the same tier, sits St. John the Baptist (*vv.* 28–33), on his right, and opposite to St. Peter, being St. Anne, the mother of the Virgin, with her eyes steadfastly fixed upon her daughter (*vv.* 133–5) [Anna [1]].

In the Heaven of Fixed Stars Beatrice shows D. Christ in glory, surrounded by countless spirits in the form of lights of dazzling brilliancy (Par. xxiii. 19–33); among these appears a greater light, that of the Virgin Mary, around whom circles chanting the archangel Gabriel, in the form of a garland of flame (*vv.* 88–110); when the archangel has ceased, all the other spirits take up the chant, singing the name of Mary (*vv.* 110–11); the Virgin then mounts up to the Empyrean, following Christ (*vv.* 118–20), while the spirits remain below in adoration (*vv.* 121–9). [Cielo Stellato.]

In the Empyrean St. Bernard shows D. the Celestial Rose, and the Virgin seated in her place (Par. xxx. 97–xxxii. 150); he bids D.

look upon 'the face which most resembles Christ', viz. that of the Virgin (Par. xxxii. 85–6), to whom he then addresses a prayer for aid on behalf of D. (Par. xxxiii. 1–39). [**Bernardo** [2] : **Cielo Empireo.**]

Maria [2], Mary of Bethany, sister of Martha and Lazarus (*John* xi. 1); D. mentions her as a type of the contemplative life, and refers to St. Luke's account (**x.** 38–42) of the entertainment of Christ by her and her sister Martha, Conv. iv. 17[94—115]. [**Marta.**]

Maria [3], Mary, a Jewess, who (according to Josephus, whose account is reproduced by Vincent of Beauvais in the *Speculum Historiale*, x. 5) during the siege of Jerusalem by Titus was driven by famine to kill and eat her own infant son. D. mentions her in connexion with the capture of Jerusalem, of which he is reminded by the emaciated appearance of those who are being purged of gluttony in Circle VI of Purgatory, Purg. xxiii. 29–30. [**Golosi.**]

Maria [4], name given by D. to an imaginary city, which he places at the N. Pole of the Earth, exactly at the antipodes of another, called *Lucia*, at the S. Pole, Conv. iii. 5[80—184]. [**Terra** [2].]

Maria di Brabante. [**Brabante.**]

Maria Jacobi. [**Jacobi, Maria.**]

Maria Maddalena. [**Maddalena, Maria.**]

Maria Salome, name by which D. describes the woman mentioned by St. Mark (xvi. 1) as having accompanied Mary Magdalene and Mary the mother of James to the tomb of our Lord, Conv. iv. 22[150—1]. [**Maddalena, Maria.**]

By St. Mark (xv. 40; xvi. 1) the woman in question is called Salome; by St. Matthew (xxvii. 56) she is described as 'the mother of Zebedee's children'. According to Brunetto Latini (*Trésor*, i. 64), whom D. appears to have followed, Salome was the name of the third husband of Anne, the mother of the Virgin, by whom he had a daughter Mary, hence known as 'Maria Salome'.

Maro. [**Virgilio.**]

Marrocco. [**Morrocco.**]

Mars. [**Marte** [1].]

Marsia, Marsyas, satyr of Phrygia, who challenged Apollo to a musical contest, and, being beaten, was punished by Apollo for his presumption by being flayed alive.

D. mentions M. (whose story he got from Ovid, *Metam.* vi. 383 ff.) in connexion with this incident in his invocation to Apollo, whom he prays to inspire him to sing as sweetly as the god played when he vanquished the satyr, Par. i. 19–21.

Marsiglia. [**Marsilia.**]

Marsilia, Marseilles, city in S. of France on the Mediterranean, capital of the modern Department of Bouches-du-Rhône. In the civil war between Caesar and Pompey (B.C. 49) it espoused the cause of the latter, but after a protracted siege it was obliged to submit to Caesar, who commenced the operations against it, and then proceeded to Spain, leaving Brutus to complete its reduction.

D. mentions it in connexion with Caesar's campaign, Purg. xviii. 101–2

[Ilerda] ; it was the birthplace of the troubadour Folquet, who is hence called *Folquetus de Marsilia*, V.E.ii.6⁵⁸ ; Folquet (in the Heaven of Venus) describes the situation of Marseilles as being almost on the same meridian as Bougie in N. Africa, and alludes to the defeat of the Pompeians by Caesar's fleet under Brutus, Par. ix. 91–3 [Buggea : Folco].

Marsilia, Folquetus de. [Folco.]

Marta, Martha, sister of Mary of Bethany and of Lazarus ; mentioned as a type of the active life, in contrast to her sister, who represents the contemplative life, as may be seen from St. Luke's account of them (x. 38–42), Conv. iv. 17⁹⁴⁻¹¹⁵. [Maria².]

Marte¹, Mars, Roman god of war, son of Jupiter, and father, by Rhea Silvia, of Romulus (Quirinus), the founder of Rome ; he was the patron god of pagan Florence, where a statue was erected in his honour ; he is mentioned as the god of war, Inf. xxiv. 145 ; xxxi. 51 ; *Mars*, Carm. 43 ; the son of Jupiter, Purg. xii. 31 ; *figlio* (*di Giove*), Par. xxii. 146 [Giove²] ; portrayed in Circle I of Purgatory, together with Jupiter, Apollo, and Minerva, as surveying the discomfited Giants after the failure of their attack upon Olympus, Purg. xii. 31–3 [Giganti] ; worshipped by the pagans, together with Jupiter and Mercury, Par. iv. 63 ; the father of Romulus, Par. viii. 132 [Quirino] ; the tutelary deity of Florence, *primo padrone* (*di Firenze*), Inf. xiii. 144 ; his statue at Florence, Par. xvi. 47 ; *quella bietra*

scema Che guarda il ponte, Par. xvi. 145–6 (cf. Inf. xiii. 146–7) [Fiorenza].

The allusion in Inf. xiii. 146–7 ; Par. xvi. 47, 145–6, is to a statue, commonly believed to be that of Mars, which existed in Florence in D.'s day, and was held in great reverence by the Florentines as being the representation of the former patron of their city. Cacciaguida's phrase ' tra Marte e il Battista ' (Par. xvi. 47) means ' between the Ponte Vecchio (where the statue of Mars used to stand) and the Baptistery of San Giovanni ', i. e., approximately, between the S. and N. limits of the city of Florence as it then was.

Marte², planet Mars, Purg. ii. 14 ; Par. xiv. 101 ; xxvii. 14 ; Conv. ii. 3⁶²⁻³, 4⁶, 14¹⁵⁴⁻⁶², 174, 180, 198, 202, 15¹⁴⁵ ; Son. xxviii. 3 ; *la stella . . . roggia*, Par. xiv. 86–7 ; *questo foco*, Par. xvi. 38 ; *questa stella*, Par. xvii. 77 ; *quinta soglia*, Par. xviii. 28 ; *il figlio di Giove*, Par. xxii. 145–6 ; Mars the fifth in order of the planets, its position being between the Sun and Jupiter, Par. xviii. 28 ; xxii. 145–6 ; Son. xxviii. 3 ; Conv. ii. 4⁵⁻⁶, 14¹⁵⁹ ; of a red colour compared with the other stars, Purg. ii. 14 ; Par. xiv. 87 ; Conv. ii. 14¹⁶⁵ ; a star of fiery nature, as opposed to the temperateness of Jupiter and the cold of Saturn, Conv. ii. 14¹⁹⁷⁻²⁰² (cf. Par. xvi. 38) ; especially connected with the phenomenon of meteors, according to Albumazar, Conv. ii. 14¹⁷⁰⁻⁴ ; one of the 'lords' of the constellation Leo, Par. xvi. 37–9 ; the period of its revolution about two years, Par. xvi.

34–9; Conv. ii. 15[145]; for half of this period it would be concealed from the Earth if the motion of the *Primum Mobile* were suspended, Conv. ii. 15[145]; the star under which Can Grande was born, Par. xvii. 77; its occultation by the Moon witnessed by Aristotle, Conv. ii. 3[59–65].

Marte, Cielo di, Heaven of Mars; the fifth ˘ in D.'s conception of Paradise, Par. xviii. 28; Conv. ii. 4[5–6],14[159] [**Paradiso**]; the middle-most of the nine Heavens, Conv. ii. 14[159–60]; resembles Music in two respects, Conv. ii. 14[154–93]; it is presided over by the Virtues [**Virtudi**].

In the Heaven of Mars D. places the spirits of those who fought for the faith (*Spiriti Militanti*), Par. xviii. 31–3; among these he names Cacciaguida [**Cacciaguida**]; Joshua [**Josuè**]; Judas Maccabaeus [**Maccabeo**]; Charlemagne [**Carlo Magno**]; Roland [**Orlando**]; William, Count of Orange [**Guglielmo**[1]]; Renouard [**Rinoardo**]; Godfrey of Bouillon [**Gottifredi**]; and Robert Guiscard [**Guiscardo**].

Martello, Carlo. [**Carlo**[3].]

Martino[1], Martin, imaginary personage, Conv. i. 8[94–6]; iii. 11[67]; any gossip or simpleton, Par. xiii. 139.

Martino [2]], Martin IV (Simon de Brie), native of Champagne; he was treasurer of St. Martin of Tours, and was appointed chancellor of France by Louis IX in 1260; he was made a cardinal in 1262, and, on the death of Nicholas III (Aug. 22, 1280), after a vacancy of six months, was elected Pope through the influence of Charles of Anjou, Feb. 22, 128⁰⁄₁. He died at Perugia, March 28,

1285, after a reign of four years. The cause of his death is said to have been a surfeit of eels from the Lake of Bolsena, which he used to keep in milk and then stew in wine.

Martin IV is placed among the Gluttonous in Circle VI of Purgatory, where he is pointed out to D. by Forese Donati, who informs D. that he was of Tours and is there purging 'the eels of Bolsena and the sweet wine', Purg. xxiv. 20–4. [**Golosi.**]

It was in command of the troops of Martin IV that John of Appia made the attack on Forlì, which was repulsed by Guido da Montefeltro, to which D. refers, Inf. xxvii. 43–4. [**Forlì.**]

Martino Bottaio. [**Bottaio, Martino.**]

Martinus Dumiensis], St. Martin of Dumio in Portugal, born c. 510; he was successively Abbot of Dumio, Bishop of Tuy (567), and Archbishop of Braga in Portugal; he died c. 580. Among his writings were the *Formula Honestae Vitae* (otherwise called *De Quatuor Virtutibus Cardinalibus*), and the *De Remediis Fortuitorum*, both of which were for a long time ascribed to Seneca.

D. quotes the *De Quatuor Virtutibus Cardinalibus*, without naming the author, Conv. iii. 8[107–10]; it is quoted as the work of Seneca, Mon. ii. 5[24–6] [***Quatuor Virtutibus Cardinalibus, De***]; the *De Remediis Fortuitorum* is mentioned, as the work of Seneca, Epist. iv. 5[53] [***Fortuitorum Remedia*: Seneca**].

Marzia, Marcia, daughter of Lucius Marcius Philippus, and second wife of Cato of Utica. After she had borne Cato three children, he ceded her to his friend, Q. Hortensius, the orator, after whose death she returned to Cato, and was remarried to him at her own request. [**Catone** [2] : **Ortensio.**]

D. mentions her, together with Lucretia, Julia, and Cornelia, among the great women of antiquity whom he saw in Limbo, Inf. iv. 128 [**Limbo**]; Virgil, in his address to Cato, having begged him for Marcia's sake, who is with him in Limbo, to let D. and himself pass into Purgatory, Cato replies that, however much Marcia pleased him in life, now she can move him no more, Purg. i. 78–90.

In the *Convivio* D. allegorizes the story of Cato and Marcia, representing the latter as the symbol of the noble soul, and likening her return to Cato to the returning of the noble soul to God, and he refers to, and translates extracts from, Lucan's account of her coming to Cato after the death of Hortensius and begging to be received back (*Phars.* ii. 328 ff.), Conv. iv. 28[97–159].

Marzucco, Marzucco degli Scornigiani, judge of Pisa; he was a man of some note outside his own city, and is frequently mentioned in documents between 1249 and 1298. He acted as assessor of Arezzo in 1249, three times served as Pisan ambassador (1258, 1275, 1276), was procurator of the judge of Arborea in Sardinia (1266, 1272), and Podestà of Fabriano (1282). In 1286 he became a Franciscan, and is known to have been resident from 1291 to 1298 in the Franciscan monastery of Santa Croce at Florence, where he probably died (before the end of 1301). He was a friend of Guittone d'Arezzo (Purg. xxiv. 56), who addressed to him a letter and a *canzone*, which have been preserved. In 1287 his son Gano was killed at the instigation of Nino il Brigata (Inf. xxxiii. 89), grandson of Count Ugolino, whereupon, it is said, Marzucco, instead of seeking to avenge his death, displayed his magnanimity by forgiving the murderer.

D. mentions Marzucco in connexion with his son, whom he saw in Ante-purgatory, and whom he describes as *quel da Pisa, Che fe' parer lo buon Marzucco forte*, i.e. the Pisan who made the worthy M. show his fortitude, Purg. vi. 17–18. [**Gano degli Scornigiani.**]

Mascheroni, Sassol, Florentine of the Toschi family, who is said to have murdered a relative for the sake of his inheritance, and on the discovery of the crime to have been rolled through the streets of Florence in a cask full of nails, and afterwards beheaded.

D. places Sassol in Caina, the first division of Circle IX of Hell, among those who were traitors to their own kin, where Camicion de' Pazzi points him out to D., and says that if D. was a Tuscan he ought to know who S. was, Inf. xxxii. 63–6. [**Caina: Traditori.**]

MastinNuovo. [**Malatestino.**]

Mastin Vecchio. [**Malatesta da Verrucchio.**]

Matelda, Matilda, the lady who acts as D.'s guide through the Terrestrial Paradise, when Virgil is no longer competent to fill the office, and Beatrice has not yet appeared; she represents the active life to D.'s waking eyes as Leah had done in his vision, being the secular counterpart of Leah, as Beatrice is of Rachel, the representative of the contemplative life. [**Lia.**]

Matilda is named once only, viz. by Beatrice, who refers D. to her for the answer to an inquiry he had addressed to herself, Purg. xxxiii. 118 ; D. speaks of her as *una donna soletta*, Purg. xxviii. 40; *la bella donna*, Purg. xxviii. 43, 148 ; xxxi. 100 ; xxxii. 28 ; xxxiii. 121, 124; *la donna*, Purg. xxix. 14, 61 ; xxxiii. 15 ; *la donna ch' io avea trovata sola*, Purg. xxxi. 92 ; *quella pia . . . che conducitrice Fu dei miei passi lungo il fiume pria*, Purg. xxxii. 82–4 ; D. addresses her as *bella donna*, Purg. xxviii. 43 ; in response to D.'s request, M. explains to him the physical conditions of the Terrestrial Paradise, and the nature of its two streams, Lethe and Eunoë, (Purg. xxviii. 85–133); subsequently she draws him through Lethe, and makes him swallow some of its water (xxxi. 91–102) ; and finally she leads him to drink of the waters of Eunoë (xxxiii. 112–45).

The old commentators are almost unanimous in identifying Matilda with the great Countess Matilda of Tuscany (1046–1115), the friend and ally of Pope Gregory VII (to whom at her castle of Canossa in 1077 the Emperor Henry IV made his humiliating submission), and the benefactress of the Papal See by the bequest of her territories to the Church. Modern commentators are inclined to find the prototype of Matilda in one or other of two German nuns who lived and wrote in the second half of Cent. xiii, viz. Matilda of Magdeburg (c. 1220–c. 1290), and Matilda of Hackeborn (c. 1240–1298), by whose mystical writings it is alleged D. was more or less influenced in various passages of the *Divina Commedia*.

Matteo, St. Matthew the Evangelist, Conv. iv. 16^{110}, 22^{168-9}; *Matthaeus*, Mon. iii. $3^{86, \ 101}$, 4^{85}, $7^{1, \ 9}$, 8^7, $9^{70, \ 132}$, 10^{109} ; Epist. x. 28^{548} ; referred to as the mouthpiece of the Holy Spirit, Mon. iii. 4^{85-7} ; his Gospel is quoted, Purg. xii. 110 (*Matt.* v. 3) ; Purg. xiii. 36 (*Matt.* v. 44) ; Purg. xv. 38 (*Matt.* v. 7) ; Purg. xvii. 68–9 (*Matt.* v. 9) ; Purg. xix. 50 (*Matt.* v. 4 : *Vulg.* v. 5) ; Purg. xix. 137 (*Matt.* xxii. 30) ; Purg. xxii. 4–6 (*Matt.* v. 6) ; Purg. xxiii. 74 (*Matt.* xxvii. 46) ; Purg. xxiv. 151–4 (*Matt.* v. 6) ; Purg. xxvii. 8 (*Matt.* v. 8) ; Purg. xxvii. 58 (*Matt.* xxv. 34) ; Purg. xxix. 51 (*Matt.* xxi. 9) ; Purg. xxx. 19 (*Matt.* xxi. 9) ; Par. viii. 29 (*Matt.* xxi. 9) ; Par. xx. 94 (*Matt.* xi. 12) ; V. N. § 24^{38-9} (*Matt.* iii. 3) ; Conv. i. 4^{81-2} (*Matt.* xiii. 57) ; Conv. i. 11^{31-3} (*Matt.* xv. 14) ; Conv. ii. 6^{26-31} (*Matt.* xxvi. 53 ; iv. 6, 11) ; Conv. iv. 9^{167} (*Matt.* xxii. 21) ; Conv. iv. 16^{110-12} (*Matt.* vii. 15, 16) ; Conv. iv. 22^{170-4} (*Matt.* xxviii. 2–3) ; Conv. iv. 27^{75-6} (*Matt.* x. 8) ; Conv. iv. 30^{38} (*Matt.* vii. 6) ; V. E. i. 12^{35} (*Matt.* v. 22) ; Mon. i. 5^{60-1} (*Matt.* xii. 25) ; Mon. iii. $3^{84-6, \ 90-104}$ (*Matt.* xxviii. 20 ; xv. 2 ; xv. 3) ; Mon. iii. 8^{2-5} (*Matt.* xvi. 19) ; Mon. iii. 9^{70-96}, $^{132-5}$ (*Matt.* xvi. 15, 16, 21, 22, 23 ; xvii. 4 ; xiv. 28 ; xxvi. 33,

35; x. 34–5); Mon. iii. 10^{109–11}
(*Matt.* x. 9); Mon. iii. 14^{22–3}
(*Matt.* xvi. 18); Epist. v. 9¹⁵³
(*Matt.* xxii. 21); Epist. vii. 3⁷³
(*Matt.* iii. 15); Epist. viii. 5^{76–7}
(*Matt.* xxi. 16); Epist. x. 28^{563–4}
(*Matt.* v. 45); his Gospel is re-
ferred to, Conv. iv. 22^{168–74} (ref. to
Matt. xxviii. 2); Mon. iii. 7^{1–2}
(ref. to *Matt.* ii. 11); Epist. x.
28^{548–9} (ref. to *Matt.* xvii. 6).

In the mystical Procession in the
Terrestrial Paradise the Gospel of
St. Matthew is represented (according to the most probable interpretation) by one of the four beasts
(*quattro animali*), Purg. xxix. 92.

Matteo d'Acquasparta], Matteo
Bentivenga d'Acquasparta, monk of
the Franciscan Order, who was appointed General of the Order in 1287,
and created cardinal by Nicholas IV in
the next year. In 1300, and again in
1301, he was sent by Boniface VIII to
Florence to act as mediator between
the Bianchi and the Neri, but he was
unsuccessful on both occasions. He
died in 1302. As General he introduced relaxations in the discipline of the Franciscan Order, which
allowed abuses to creep in, and which
were vehemently opposed by the
ascetic Ubertino da Casale, the head
of the so-called Spiritualists.

Matteo and Ubertino are referred
to by St. Bonaventura (in the Heaven of the Sun) in allusion to their
different views as to the interpretation of the rule of St. Francis,
Par. xii. 124–6. [**Acquasparta** :
Ubertino da Casale.]

*Matthaeum, Evangelium se-
cundum.* [**Matteo.**]

Matthaeus. [**Matteo.**]

Matthias. [**Mattia.**]

Mattia, St. Matthias the Apostle,
who was elected to fill the place of
Judas Iscariot (*Acts* i. 15–26).

D., in his address to Nicholas III
(in Bolgia 3 of Circle VIII of Hell)
on the simony of the Popes, says
that St. Peter and the other Apostles
did not require silver and gold of
Matthias when he was elected to be
an Apostle, Inf. xix. 94–6; the
mode of his election is adduced as
a proof that the judgement of God
is sometimes revealed to man by
casting lots, *Matthias*, Mon. ii.
8^{68–71}.

Maximus Guido. [**Guido Guinizelli.**]

Medea, daughter of Aeëtes, King
of Colchis, by whose help Jason
secured the golden fleece. As the
condition of her assistance Jason
promised to marry her, and he took
her with him when he sailed from
Colchis, but afterwards abandoned
her for Creusa, daughter of Creon,
King of Corinth. In revenge Medea
poisoned Creusa, and murdered her
own two children by Jason.

D. mentions Medea in connexion
with Jason, whom he places among
the Seducers in Malebolge, Inf.
xviii. 96. [**Jason**¹.]

Medicina, Pier da, member of
a family who in Cent. xiii were
lords, with the title of 'cattani'
(i.e. captains) of Medicina, a small
town, formerly a strong independent
fortress, in the Emilia, about twenty
miles E. of Bologna.

D. places Pier da Medicina, who
claims to have seen him in his
native land, and whom the old commentators describe as an inveterate

mischief-maker, among the Sowers of discord in Bolgia 9 of Circle VIII of Hell (Malebolge), Inf. xxviii. 64–99. [Scismatici.]

Mediolanenses. [Milanesi.]

Mediolanum. [Milano.]

Mediterraneo. [Mare Mediterraneo.]

Medusa. [Gorgon.]

Megera, Megaera, one of the Furies; placed by D. with Alecto and Tisiphone to guard the entrance to the City of Dis, Inf. ix. 46. [Erine.]

Melan, -ano, -anesi. [Milan, -ano, -anesi.]

Melchisedech, Melchizedek, 'the priest of the most high God' and 'King of Salem' (*Gen.* xiv. 18); mentioned as type of a priest (or good king) by Charles Martel (in the Heaven of Venus), who says that one man is born to be a Solon (or lawgiver), another a Xerxes (or warrior), and a third a Melchizedek, Par. viii. 124–5.

Meleagro, Meleager, son of Oeneus, King of Calydon, leader of the heroes who slew the Calydonian boar, the skin of which he gave to Atalanta, whom he loved ; but his mother's brothers took it from her, whereupon M. in fury slew them. When he was seven days old the Fates had declared that his life would last as long as a brand which was burning on the hearth should remain unconsumed. His mother, Althaea, hearing this, extinguished the brand, and kept it carefully concealed ; but now, to avenge the death of her brothers, she threw it into the fire and it was consumed, whereupon M. expired.

The manner of Meleager's death (whose story is told by Ovid, *Metam.* viii. 445 ff.) is referred to by Virgil in answer to D.'s inquiry as to how hunger can be felt where there is no body (as in the case of those who are being purged of gluttony), Purg. xxv. 22–3. [Golosi.]

Meliboeus, name (borrowed from Virgil, *Ecl.* i. 6, 20, 43, &c.) of a character, supposed to represent Dino Perini, a notary of Florence and companion of D. at Ravenna, in D.'s poetical correspondence with G. del Virgilio, Ecl. i. 4, 28, 34, 36, 67; ii. 29; Ecl. R. 35, 61, 71. [*Egloghe*[2]: Perini, Dino.]

Melicerta], Melicertes, son of Athamas, King of Orchomenus in Boeotia, and of Ino, and brother of Learchus; he and his mother, to escape from Athamas, who in his madness mistook Ino and her two sons for a lioness and cubs, threw themselves into the sea.

Ino and her sons are referred to as *la moglie con due figli,* Inf. xxx. 5; *la leoncessa e i leoncini, v.* 8; Melicerta, *l'altro, v.* 12. [Atamante: Ino.]

Melisso, Melissus, of Samos (c. B.C. 450), a follower of Parmenides, the founder of the Eleatic school of philosophy.

St. Thomas Aquinas (in the Heaven of the Sun) mentions him, together with Parmenides and Bryson, as examples of bad reasoners, Par. xiii. 125; Melissus and Parmenides are coupled together again, as having been condemned by Aristotle (*Phys.* i. 3) for the same reason, *Melissus,* Mon. iii. 4[30–3].

Melissus. [Melisso.]

Menalippo, Menalippus, a Theban, who mortally wounded Tydeus in the war of the Seven against Thebes; Tydeus, however, succeeded in killing him, and in a fury of madness seized on his head and, fixing his teeth in it, gnawed through the skull and ate part of the brain.

D. (who borrowed the incident from Statius, *Theb.* viii. 739 ff.) represents Count Ugolino in Circle IX of Hell gnawing the head of the Archbishop Ruggieri in the same way as Tydeus did that of Menalippus, *Inf.* xxxii. 130–2. [Tideo : Ugolino, Conte.]

Mencio. [Mincio.]

Meotidus. [Maeotidus.]

Mercato, Il, the old market-place, 'Mercato Vecchio', at Florence, one of the oldest quarters of the town, and formerly considered as one of the best; mentioned by Cacciaguida (in the Heaven of Mars) in connexion with the Caponsacchi, who settled there on their immigration from Fiesole, *Par.* xvi. 121.

Mercurio[1], Mercury, Roman god, son of Jupiter and Maia; mentioned as being worshipped by the pagans, together with Jupiter and Mars, *Par.* iv. 63; Jupiter's speech to him concerning Aeneas (*Aen.* iv. 227–30) quoted, *Mon.* ii. 7⁷⁹⁻⁸⁵; referred to under the name of *Anubis*, *Epist.* vii. 4⁸⁶ [Anubis].

Mercurio[2], planet Mercury, *Conv.* ii. 4³, 6¹⁰⁸, 14⁹², 15¹⁴⁸; *Mercuro*, *Son.* xxviii. 9; *pianeta*, *Par.* v. 96; *stella*, *v.* 97; *la spera, Che si vela ai mortal con gli altrui raggi, vv.* 128–9; *questa picciola stella*, *Par.* vi. 112; *la presente margherita, v.* 127; the planet is alluded to by the name

of the mother of the god Mercury, *Maia*, *Par.* xxii. 144 [Maia : Mercurio[1]]; Mercury the second in order of the planets, its position being between the Moon and Venus, *Par.* v. 93; xxii. 144; *Son.* xxviii. 9; *Conv.* ii. 4²⁻⁴, 6¹⁰⁸, 14⁹⁰; the smallest of the planets, *Par.* vi. 112; *Conv.* ii. 14⁹²; its diameter not being more than 232 miles, according to Alfraganus, who puts it at $\frac{1}{28}$ of the diameter of the Earth, *Conv.* ii. 14⁹³⁻⁸ [Terra[2]]; owing to its proximity to the Sun it is mostly concealed from view by the brightness of the Sun's rays, *Par.* v. 128–9; *Conv.* ii. 14⁹⁸⁻¹⁰⁰; the period of its revolution, like that of Venus, about one year, for half of which it would be concealed from the Earth if the motion of the *Primum Mobile* were suspended, *Conv.* ii. 15¹⁴⁸⁻⁵⁰.

Mercurio, Cielo di, Heaven of Mercury; the second in D.'s conception of Paradise, *Par.* v. 93; *Conv.* ii. 4³, 14⁹⁰ [Paradiso]; referred to as *secondo regno*, *Par.* v. 93; *secondo cielo*, *Conv.* ii. 4³; and, according to some, as *quella parte, ove il mondo è più vivo*, *Par.* v. 87; resembles Dialectics in two respects, *Conv.* ii. 14⁹⁰⁻¹⁰⁹; it is presided over by the Archangels, *Conv.* ii. 6¹⁰⁸ [Arcangeli].

In the Heaven of Mercury D. places the spirits of those who, for the love of fame, wrought great deeds upon earth (*Spiriti Operanti*), *Par.* vi. 112–14; among these he names the Emperor Justinian [Giustiniano]; and Romieu of Villeneuve [Romeo].

Mercuro. [Mercurio[2].]

Meridies. [Mezzodì.]

Merovingi], Merovingian Kings of France (448–752), alluded to by D. (in mistake for the Carlovingians) as *regi antichi*, Purg. xx. 53. [Carlo [5]: Carlovingi: Childerico.]

Messana, Judex de Columnis de. [Guido delle Colonne.]

Messina. [Messana.]

Metafisica [1], first philosophy or Metaphysics, Conv. ii. 14^{62}, 15^{6-121}; iii. 11^{176}; *prima scienza*, Conv. ii. 14^{61}; *vera filosofia*, Conv. iii. 11^{182}; the eighth or Starry Heaven likened to, Conv. ii. 14^{59-62}, 15^{6-121} [Cielo Stellato]; treats of immaterial and incorruptible matters, Conv. ii. $15^{81-4, 91-2}$; together with Ethics and Physics makes up the whole body of philosophy, Conv. iii. 11^{172-81}.

Metafisica [2]. [*Metaphysica.*]

Metamorfoseos. [*Metamorphoseos.*]

Metamorphoseos, *Metamorphoses* of Ovid; quoted as *Metamorphoseos*, V. E. i. 2^{54}; ii. 6^{81}; *Metamorfoseos*, Conv. ii. 6^{124}, 15^{55}; iv. 15^{73}, 23^{138}, 27^{157}; *Ovidio Maggiore*, Conv. iii. 3^{51}; *De Rerum Transmutatione*, Mon. ii. $8^{82, 85}$; *De Rerum Transformatione*, Epist. iv. 4^{41}. [Ovidio.]

D. quotes from this work directly six times (the passages quoted in the *Convivio* being translated more or less freely), Conv. ii. 6^{123-6} (*Met.* v. 365) [Cupido: Venere [1]]; Conv. iv. 15^{72-84} (*Met.* i. 78–83) [Giapeto: Prometeo]; Conv. iv. 27^{173-80} (*Met.* vii. 507–11) [Cefalo]; Mon. ii. 9^{30-4} (*Met.* iv. 58, 88) [Nino [1]: Semiramis]; Epist. iv. 4^{41} (*Met.* iv. 192) [Hyperion].

D. was very largely indebted to the *Metamorphoses* for his mythology, his information about the following being in most cases primarily derived from this work:—Nessus and Deianira, Inf. xii. 66–9 (*Met.* ix. 101 ff.) [Deianira: Nesso]; Icarus and Daedalus, Inf. xvii. 109–11 (*Met.* viii. 225 ff.) [Dedalo: Icaro]; Tiresias, Inf. xx. 40–5 (*Met.* iii. 324 ff.) [Tiresia]; the Phoenix, Inf. xxiv. 108–10 (*Met.* xv. 393 ff.) [Fenice]; Cadmus, Inf. xxv. 97–8 (*Met.* iv. 570 ff.) [Cadmo]; Arethusa, Inf. xxv. 97–8 (*Met.* v. 572 ff.) [Aretusa]; Aegina and the Myrmidons, Inf. xxix. 58–66 (*Met.* vii. 528 ff.) [Egina: Mirmidoni]; Athamas and Ino, Inf. xxx. 4–12 (*Met.* iv. 511 ff.) [Atamante: Ino]; Hecuba, Inf. xxx. 15–21 (*Met.* xiii. 404 ff.) [Ecuba]; Myrrha and Cinyras, Inf. xxx. 37; Epist. vii. 7^{146} (*Met.* x. 298 ff.) [Cinyras: Mirra]; Narcissus, Inf. xxx. 128; Par. iii. 18 (*Met.* iii. 407 ff.) [Narcisso]; Pierides, Purg. i. 11; V. E. i. 2^{54} (*Met.* v. 298 ff.) [Pierides]; Niobe, Purg. xii. 37–9 (*Met.* vi. 182 ff., 301 ff.) [Niobè]; Arachne, Purg. xii. 43–5 (*Met.* vi. 140 ff.) [Aragne]; Aglauros, Purg. xiii. 139 (*Met.* ii. 708 ff.) [Aglauro]; Philomela and Procne, Purg. xvii. 19–20 (*Met.* vi. 609 ff.) [Filomela: Progne]; Midas, Purg. xx. 106–8 (*Met.* xi. 100 ff.) [Mida]; Polymestor and Polydorus, Purg. xx. 115 (*Met.* xiii. 429 ff.) [Polidoro: Polinestor]; Latona at Delos, Purg. xx. 130–2 (*Met.* vi. 185 ff.) [Delo: Latona]; Iris, Purg. xxi. 50 (*Met.* xiv. 845);

Par. xxviii. 32 (*Met.* i. 270) [Iri];
Erisichthon, Purg. xxiii. 22–7;
xxiv. 28 (*Met.* viii. 777 ff., 825 ff.)
[Eresitone]; Theseus and the
Centaurs, Purg. xxiv. 121–3 (*Met.*
xii. 210 ff.) [Centauri: Teseo];
Meleager, Purg. xxv. 22–4 (*Met.*
viii. 511 ff.) [Meleagro]; Callisto
and Diana, Purg. xxv. 130 (*Met.*
ii. 453 ff.) [Callisto: Diana¹];
Pasiphaë, Purg. xxvi. 41–2, 85–6
(*Met.* viii. 131–7) [Pasife]; Pyramus and Thisbe, Purg. xxvii. 37–9;
xxxiii. 69 (*Met.* iv. 55–166) [Pi-
ramo: Tisbe]; Proserpina, Purg.
xxviii. 50–1 (*Met.* v. 397 ff.)
[Proserpina]; Venus and Cupid,
Purg. xxviii. 65–6 (*Met.* x. 525 ff.)
[Cupido: Venere¹]; Argus, Purg.
xxix. 95–6 (*Met.* i. 625 ff.); Purg.
xxxii. 64–6 (*Met.* i. 682 ff.) [Ar-
go²]; Phaëthon, Purg. xxix.
118–19 (*Met.* ii. 107 ff., 227 ff.);
Par. xvii. 1–3 (*Met.* i. 755 ff.);
Conv. ii. 15⁵³⁻⁵ (*Met.* ii. 35 ff.)
[Fetonte]; Syrinx, Purg. xxxii.
64–6 (*Met.* i. 682 ff.) [Siringa];
Themis, Purg. xxxiii. 46–8 (*Met.*
i. 379 ff.) [Temi]; Oedipus, Purg.
xxxiii. 49–51 (*Met.* vii. 759 ff.)
[Edipo]; Marsyas, Par. i. 20
(*Met.* vi. 383 ff.) [Marsia]; Glaucus, Par. i. 68–9 (*Met.* xiii. 940 ff.)
[Glauco]; Jason, Par. ii. 18
(*Met.* vii. 118 ff.) [Jason¹]; Alcmaeon, Par. iv. 105 (*Met.* ix. 407 ff.)
[Almeone]; Typhoeus, Par. viii.
67–70 (*Met.* v. 346–53) [Ti-
feo]; Echo, Par. xii. 14–15 (*Met.*
iii. 356 ff.) [Eco]; Ariadne, Par.
xiii. 13–15 (*Met.* viii. 174 ff.)
[Arianna]; Hippolytus and Phaedra, Par. xvii. 46–7 (*Met.* xv.
493 ff.) [Fedra: Ippolito]; Se-

mele, Par. xxi. 6 (*Met.* iii. 308 ff.)
[Semelè]; Hyperion, Par. xxii.
142; Epist. iv. 4⁴¹ (*Met.* iv. 192,
241) [Iperione]; Europa, Par.
xxvii. 84 (*Met.* ii. 868 ff.) [Eu-
ropa¹]; Helice, Par. xxxi. 32–3
(*Met.* ii. 500 ff.) [Elice]; Orpheus,
Conv. ii. 1²⁵⁻⁷ (*Met.* xi. 1 ff.) [Or-
feo]; Venus and Cupid, Conv. ii.
6¹²³⁻⁶ (*Met.* v. 365) [Cupido:
Venere¹]; Hercules and Antaeus,
Conv. iii. 3⁵¹; Mon. ii. 8⁸⁰⁻² (*Met.*
ix. 183) [Anteo: Ercole]; Prometheus, Conv. iv. 15⁸³ (*Met.* i.
78–83) [Giapeto: Prometeo];
the Horses of the Sun, Conv. iv.
23¹³⁴⁻⁹ (*Met.* ii. 153 ff.) [Eoo];
Aeacus and Cephalus, Conv. iv.
27¹⁵⁵⁻⁹⁵ (*Met.* vii. 474 ff.) [Cefalo:
Eaco]; Atalanta and Hippomenes,
Mon. ii. 8⁸³⁻⁵ (*Met.* x. 560 ff.)
[Atalanta: Hippomenes]; Ninus
and Semiramis, Mon. ii. 9³⁰⁻⁴ (*Met.*
iv. 58, 88) [Nino¹: Semiramis];
Pallas and Helicon, Epist. x. 1¹¹
(*Met.* v. 250 ff.) [Elicona: Pal-
lade]; Pyreneus and the Muses,
Ecl. ii. 65–6 (*Met.* v. 273–93)
[Muse: Pyreneus]; Acis and
Galatea, Ecl. ii. 78–9 (*Met.* xiii.
740 ff.) [Acis: Galatea]; Achae-
menides and Polyphemus, Ecl. ii.
76–83 (*Met.* xiv. 160 ff.) [Achae-
menides: Polyphemus].

Metaphysica, *Metaphysics* or
First Philosophy of Aristotle; quoted
as *Prima Filosofia,* Conv. i. 1²;
Prima Philosophia, Mon. iii. 12³;
Metafisica, V. N. § 42³⁰; Conv. ii.
3³², 5¹³, ¹¹⁸, 14¹⁴⁵, 16⁹⁰; iii. 11¹²,
14⁹⁸; iv. 10⁸³; *Metaphysica,* Epist.
x. 5⁹², 16²⁷⁹, 20³⁷¹; *De Simpliciter
Ente,* Mon. i. 12⁵¹, 13¹⁵, 15¹², ¹⁹;
iii. 14⁴⁹.

D. quotes from the *Metaphysics* some twenty times:—man's understanding weak as is the eyesight before the sun, V. N. § 42^{28-30} (*Met.* ii. 1); Conv. ii. 5^{116-18}; all men by nature desirous of knowledge, Conv. i. 1^{1-4} (*Met.* i. 1); Conv. iii. 11^{61-3}; Aristotle's opinions on astronomical matters not his own but borrowed from others, Conv. ii. 3^{31-5} (*Met.* xii. 8); A. appears to have believed that there were only as many Intelligences as there were heavenly revolutions, Conv. ii. 5^{12-17} (*Met.* xii. 8); the excellence of the celestial Intelligences too great for human understanding, as is the brightness of the sun for human eyesight, Conv. ii. 5^{112-18} (*Met.* ii. 1); V. N. § 42^{28-30}; the Pythagorean theory as to the numerical origin of all things, Conv. ii. 14^{144-7} (*Met.* i. 5); the attraction of philosophy for mankind, Conv. ii. 16^{90-3} (*Met.* i. 1); a definition declares the essence of a thing, Conv. iii. 11^{11-14} (*Met.* vi. 4, 10, 12—the editions read 'nel quarto'); that thing is free which exists for itself and not for another, Conv. iii. 14^{97-100} (*Met.* i. 2); Mon. i. 12^{48-52}; when one thing is generated by another, it is generated by virtue of having been contained in the essence of the latter, Conv. iv. 10^{82-5} (*Met.* vi. 7); the theory of A. that one sole essence exists in all men, Conv. iv. 15^{51-5} (*Met.* xi. 8); the rule of many not a good thing, there should be but one ruler, Mon. i. 10^{29-31} (quoted by Aristotle, *Met.* xii. 10, from Homer, *Iliad* ii. 204, but without a reference to him, whence D. attributes the saying to A. himself);

everything which becomes actual from being potential, becomes so by means of something actual of the same kind, Mon. i. 13^{15-18} (*Met.* ix. 8); in every kind of things, that which is most one is best, Mon. i. 15^{10-13} (*Met.* i. 1); in the Pythagorean tables Unity is placed in the same column as Good, and Plurality in the same as Evil, Mon. i. 15^{16-19} (*Met.* i. 5); every agent must be such in its action as answers to its intention, Mon. iii. 14^{46-9} (*Met.* ix. 8); a thing has the same relation to truth as it has to existence, Epist. x. 5^{92} (*Met.* ii. 1); practical men sometimes indulge in speculation, Epist. x. 16^{279}(*Met.*ii. 1); the causes of being not infinite, but derived from some first principle, Epist. x. 20^{371} (*Met.* ii. 1). [**Aristotile: Metafisica**.]

Metello, Quintus Caecilius Metellus, the tribune, an adherent of Pompey, who attempted to defend the Roman treasury in the temple of Saturn on the Tarpeian hill when Caesar plundered it after his triumphal entry into Rome, B. C. 49.

D. (whose account is borrowed from Lucan, *Phars.* iii. 153 ff.) compares the grating of the gate of Purgatory as it opened, to that of the door of the Roman treasury after Metellus' vain attempt to protect it, Purg. ix. 133–8.

Meteora[1], *Book on Meteors* or *Meteorologics* of Aristotle; the sea the beginning of all waters, A. T. § 6^{10-12} (*Met.* i. 2); water at the summits of mountains generated in the form of vapour, A. T. § 23^{46-8} (*Met.* i. 9). [**Aristotile**.]

Meteora[2], *Book on Meteors* of

Albertus Magnus; quoted as *Della Meteora*, for Albertus's account of the spontaneous ignition of meteoric vapours (*Met.* i. 4), Conv. ii. 14[169]; A.'s account of the four ages of life and the 'qualities' appropriated to them (a mistaken reference, the passage in question being not in the *De Meteoris* but in A.'s *De Juv. et Senect.*, i. 2), Conv. iv. 23[125] [*Juventute et Senectute, De*[2]].

D. was also indebted to the *De Meteoris* of Albertus for the quotations from Albumazar and Seneca, Conv. ii. 14[170-6][Albumassar: Seneca]; for his account of the incident which happened to Alexander the Great and his army in India, Inf. xiv. 31-6 [Alessandro[2]]; and for the various opinions as to the origin of the Galaxy or Milky Way, Conv. ii. 15[44-77] [Galassia: Alberto[1]].

Meteoris, De. [*Meteora.*]

Mezzabati, Aldobrandino de'. [Ildebrandinus Paduanus.]

Mezzodì, mid-day, hence the South, Inf. xxiv. 3 [Aquario]; the first climate, inhabited by the Garamantes, situated in the S., Conv. iii. 5[118-21] [Garamanti]; *Mezzogiorno*, the imaginary city of *Lucia* at the S. Pole, distant 7,500 miles S. from Rome, Conv. iii. 5[96-101] [Lucia[2]]; the Tropic of Capricorn distant 23° and more S. from the Equator, Conv. iii. 5[135-42] [Capricorno]; *Meridies*, of the S. limits of the *langue d'*oïl, V. E. i. 8[62] [Lingua *Oïl*]; referred to as *la plaga Sotto la quale il Sol mostra men fretta*, Par. xxiii. 11-12.

Mezzogiorno. [Mezzodì.]

Michael, Michael I, Emperor of Constantinople, 811-813; having been defeated by the Bulgarians, he was deposed in 813, and compelled to become a monk, Leo the Armenian being appointed his successor.

D. states (mistakenly) that Michael was Emperor of Constantinople at the time that Charlemagne was crowned Emperor of the West, Mon. iii. 11[5-7]. [Carlo Magno: Constantinopolis.]

Michel Zanche, Michael Zanche, Governor of Logodoro in Sardinia; he appears to have acted as intendant for Enzio, natural son of the Emperor Frederick II, who received the title of King of Sardinia on his marriage with Adelasia di Torres, heiress of Logodoro and Gallura; after Adelasia's divorce from Enzio, Michael Zanche married her, and assumed the government of the Sardinian provinces, which he retained until c. 1290, when he was murdered by his son-in-law, Branca d'Oria of Genoa (Inf. xxxiii. 137) [Branca d'Oria].

Michael Zanche is placed, together with Ciampolo of Navarre and friar Gomita of Gallura, among the Barrators in Bolgia 5 of Circle VIII of Hell (Malebolge), Inf. xxii. 88; xxxiii. 144 [Barattieri: Ciampolo: Gomita, Frate].

Michele, archangel Michael; his overthrow of Satan (*Rev.* xii. 7-9) is referred to, Inf. vii. 11-12 [Lucifero]; he is invoked, together with St. Peter and all saints, by those who are purging the sin of Envy in Circle II of Purgatory, Purg. xiii. 51 [Invidiosi]; like the other archangels, he is represented by the Church in human likeness, Par. iv. 47-8 [Gabriello: Raffaele].

Michele Scotto, 'the wondrous Michael Scot, the wizard of such dreaded fame'; placed by D. among the Magicians and Soothsayers in Bolgia 4 of Circle VIII of Hell (Malebolge), Inf. xx. 116; *quell' altro, v.* 115. [**Indovini.**]

Michael Scot, who perhaps belonged to the family of the Scots of Balwearie in Fifeshire, was born c. 1175; after studying at Oxford and Paris, he spent some time at Toledo, where he acquired a knowledge of Arabic, and thus gained access to the Arabic versions of Aristotle, some of which he translated into Latin at the instigation of the Emperor Frederick II, at whose court at Palermo he resided for several years; he died before 1235. His own works, which deal almost exclusively with astrology, alchemy, and the occult sciences in general, are doubtless responsible for his popular reputation as a wizard. Many of his alleged prophecies are recorded by the commentators, and by Villani, Salimbene, and others.

Micol, Michal, younger daughter of Saul, King of Israel, and wife of David. When David brought the ark in triumph from Kirjath-jearim to Jerusalem, and himself danced in the procession, Michal, who was watching from her window, 'despised him in her heart' (2 *Sam.* vi. 12–16).

The incident of David dancing before the ark, while Michal watches him from her window, figures among the sculptures representing instances of humility in the Circle of the Proud in Purgatory, Purg. x. 55–72. [**David: Superbi.**]

Mida, Midas, King of Phrygia, who was allowed by Bacchus to make a request of him, which the god promised to grant. Midas, in his greed for wealth, desired that everything he touched should be turned to gold. Bacchus fulfilled his desire, but Midas, finding that even the food which he touched turned to gold, soon implored him to take his favour back. The god accordingly ordered him to bathe in the sources of the Pactolus near Mt. Tmolus, the sands of which thenceforth became rich in gold, while Midas was relieved from his fatal gift.

Midas (whose story D. got from Ovid, *Metam.* xi. 100 ff.), is included among the instances of the lust of wealth proclaimed by those who are being purged of the sin of Avarice in Circle V of Purgatory, Purg. xx. 106–8 [**Avari**]; he is referred to as the king, *Qui jussu Bromii Pactolida tinxit arenam,* Ecl. ii. 53.

Milan. [**Milano.**]

Milanesi, the Milanese; *la vipera che i Milanesi accampa,* the viper under which the Milanese take the field (i. e. the arms of the Visconti of Milan), Purg. viii. 80 [**Galeazzo**]; *Mediolanenses,* V. E. i. 9^{38}, 11^{30}; their dialect different from that of their near neighbours the Veronese, V. E. i. 9^{36-8}; condemned, with that of Bergamo and the neighbouring towns, V. E. i. 11^{30-1}.

Milano, Milan, capital of Lombardy, situated on the plain between the Ticino and the Adda; it was destroyed by the Emperor Frederick Barbarossa in 1162, but in 1169 the city was rebuilt and fortified by the Lombard League.

The Abbot of San Zeno at Verona (in Circle IV of Purgatory) mentions Milan in connexion with Barbarossa, and alludes to its destruction by him, Purg. xviii. 119–20 [Federico[1]]; the Visconti of Milan, Conv. iv. 20[39] [Visconti[1]]; D. reminds the rebellious Florentines of the fate of Milan and Spoleto, both of which were destroyed for their resistance to the Emperor, Epist. vi. 5[136–7] [Spoletum]; he urges the Emperor Henry VII to leave Milan, and to come and chastise Florence, Epist. vii. 6[113] [Arrigo[2]].

Milano, Visconti di. [Visconti[1].]

Militanti, Spiriti. [Spiriti Militanti.]

Militari, De Re. [*Re Militari, De.*]

Milotti, Fiducio de'], physician of Certaldo, and companion of D. at Ravenna, who figures, as is supposed, in D.'s poetical correspondence with G. del Virgilio under the name of *Alphesiboeus*, Ecl. ii. 7, 15, 44, 45, 49, 76. [*Egloghe*[2].]

Mincio, river which flows out of the Lago di Garda, close to Peschiera; just above Mantua it forms a lake, its waters being dammed for the purpose; it enters the Po close to Governolo, about twelve miles below Mantua.

Virgil mentions it and describes its course in his account of the founding of Mantua, Inf. xx. 76–81. [Benaco: Mantua.]

Minerva, Roman goddess, identified by them with the Greek Pallas Athene; she was the daughter of Jupiter and was worshipped as the goddess of wisdom. The Greek goddess was the tutelary deity of the city of Athens. She and Poseidon having contested for the possession of the city, the gods decreed that it should be awarded to the one who should confer the most useful gift on mankind; Poseidon thereupon produced the horse, while Athene planted an olive; the gods decided in favour of Athene, after whom consequently the city was named.

D. refers to her as *Minerva*, Purg. xxx. 68; Par. ii. 8; *Pallade*, Purg. xii. 31; *Pallade ovvero Minerva*, Conv. ii. 5[42]; *Pallas*, Epist. x. 1[11]; the daughter of Jupiter, Purg. xii. 31 [Giove[2]]; portrayed in Circle I of Purgatory, together with Jupiter, Apollo, and Mars, as surveying the discomfited Giants after the failure of their attack upon Olympus, Purg. xii. 31–3 [Giganti]; her contest with Poseidon for the city of Athens referred to, Purg. xv. 97 [Atene]; the olive sacred to her, hence called *fronde di Minerva*, Purg. xxx. 68; invoked as the goddess of wisdom, together with Apollo, at the opening of the description of Paradise, Par. ii. 8; called by the heathen the goddess of wisdom, Conv. ii. 5[42–3]; her visit to Helicon to assure herself of its wonders, Epist. x. 1[11] [Elicona].

Miniato, San], church of San Miniato al Monte, one of the oldest churches of Florence (dating mainly from Cent. xii), situated on a hill to the SE. of the city beyond the Arno, just above the Ponte alle Grazie (formerly the Rubaconte).

D. speaks of it as *la chiesa, che soggioga La ben guidata sopra Rubaconte* (i. e. the church which, above the bridge of Rubaconte, lords it over the well-ordered city of Florence), and refers to the steps leading up to the church (which were erected in Cent. xiii), Purg. xii. 101–4 [**Fiorenza: Rubaconte**].

Minoi, Minos, King of Crete and lawgiver, grandson of Minos the son of Zeus (with whom D., like Boccaccio and others, probably confounded him); he was the husband of Pasiphaë and father of Deucalion, Ariadne (Inf. xii. 20), and Phaedra (Par. xvii. 47). [**Minos.**]

D. speaks of Ariadne, in connexion with the constellation of the Crown, as *la figliuola di Minoi*, Par. xiii. 14. [**Arianna.**]

Minos, Minos, King of Crete and lawgiver, son of Zeus and Europa; he was grandfather of the preceding. [**Minoi.**]

D. assigns to Minos the office of judge in Hell, in imitation of Virgil (*Aen*. vi. 432–3).

He is stationed at the entrance of Hell proper, as guardian of Circle II, where the Lustful are punished, Inf. v. 4, 17; xiii. 96; xx. 36; xxvii. 124; xxix. 120; Purg. i. 77; *conoscitor delle peccata*, Inf. v. 9 [**Lussuriosi**]. When the souls of the sinners come before him, Minos (who symbolizes the evil conscience) examines into their sins, each soul making a full confession to him, and he assigns to each its place in Hell, indicating the number of the Circle to which it is condemned by the number of times he encircles himself with his tail, Inf. v. 4–15;

xxvii. 124–5. At the entrance of Circle II, Minos tries to hinder D. from passing, but is quelled by Virgil's reference to the will of heaven, Inf. v. 16–24; he condemns suicides to Circle VII, Inf. xiii. 94–6; Amphiaraüs, on being swallowed up by the earth, descends to Minos (i. e. to Hell), Inf. xx. 35–6 [**Anfiarao**]; Guido da Montefeltro is condemned by Minos to a place among the Fraudulent in Bolgia 8 of Circle VIII (Malebolge), Inf. xxvii. 124–7 [**Guido Montefeltrano**]; he condemns Griffolino of Arezzo, as an alchemist, to Bolgia 10 of Circle VIII, Inf. xxix. 118–20 [**Griffolino**]; Virgil informs Cato that he is not under the jurisdiction of Minos (Limbo being outside the limits of Hell proper), Purg. i. 77 [**Limbo**].

Minotauro, the Minotaur, a monster half man, half bull, the offspring of the intercourse of Pasiphaë, the wife of Minos, King of Crete, with a bull; it was kept in a labyrinth in Crete, which was constructed by Daedalus, and was supplied every year with seven youths and seven maidens from Athens, whom the Athenians were compelled by Minos to send as tribute. The monster was at length slain by Theseus, with the assistance of Ariadne, daughter of Minos, who supplied him with a clue to the labyrinth and a sword. [**Arianna: Dedalo: Minoi: Pasife.**]

D. places the Minotaur as guardian of Circle VII of Hell, where the Violent are punished, Inf. xii. 25; *l'infamia di Creti . . . Che fu concetta nella falsa vacca, vv.* 12–

13; *bestia*, v. 19; *ira bestial*, v. 33; its death at the hands of Theseus and Ariadne is referred to, *vv.* 16–20 [**Violenti**].

Minus Mocatus, Mino Mocato, poet of Siena, who is perhaps identical with Meo di Mocata de' Maconi, one of whose poems has been preserved in a Vatican MS.; he is coupled by D. with Bonagiunta of Lucca, Gallo of Pisa, and Brunetto Latini of Florence, as having, like them, written in his own local dialect, V. E. i. 13[10].

Mira, La, small town in Venetia, between Padua and Venice, about ten miles from the latter, on the banks of a canal of the Brenta; mentioned by Jacopo del Cassero (in Ante-purgatory) in connexion with his murder by Azzo of Este, Purg. v. 79–81. [**Cassero, Jacopo del.**]

Mirmidoni], Myrmidons, inhabitants of Aegina, so called from their having been transformed from ants (μύρμηκες) into men by Jupiter, to restore the population after the desolation of the island by pestilence; they are referred to by D., in connexion with the plague of Aegina, as *seme di formiche*, Inf. xxix. 64. [**Eaco : Egina.**]

Mirra, Myrrha, daughter of Cinyras, King of Cyprus; being seized with a fatal passion for her father, she contrived to introduce herself into his chamber in disguise during the absence of her mother; when Cinyras discovered the deception he attempted to slay Myrrha, but she escaped from him, and was transformed into a myrrh-tree.

D. places Myrrha (whose story he got from Ovid, *Metam.* x. 293 ff.), together with Gianni Schicchi, among the Falsifiers in Bolgia 10 of Circle VIII of Hell (Malebolge), Inf. xxx. 25–41 [**Falsatori : Gianni Schicchi**]; in his Letter to the Emperor Henry VII he compares Florence to her, *Myrrha*, Epist. vii. 7[146-8] [**Cinyras**].

Miseno, Misenus, trumpeter of Hector, and, after his death, of Aeneas; he was drowned off the promontory of Misenum in Campania, which received its name from him.

D. refers to the account given by Virgil (*Aen.* vi. 155–84) of how Aeneas himself helped to cut the wood for the funeral pyre of Misenus, which he instances as an example of courtesy, Conv. iv. 26[109-18]; Virgil, in recording the fact that Misenus passed from the service of Hector to that of Aeneas, says of him, ' non inferiora sequutus ' (*Aen.* vi. 170), thus showing that he considered Aeneas the equal of Hector, Mon. ii. 3[48-54]. [**Enea : Ettore.**]

Misenus. [**Miseno.**]

Mobile, Primo. [**Cielo Cristallino.**]

Mocatus, Minus. [**Minus Mocatus.**]

Modarette], Sir Mordred, the traitorous nephew (or, according to the later tradition, son) of King Arthur, whom he slew, and by whom he was slain; he is referred to by Camicione de' Pazzi (in Circle IX of Hell), in allusion to the manner of his death, as *quelli a cui fu rotto il petto e l'ombra Con esso un colpo per la man d'Artù*, Inf. xxxii. 61–2. [**Artù.**]

Modena, Roman Mutina, town of N. Italy, situated on the plain between the rivers Secchia and Panaro, in the centre of the Emilia, about midway between Parma and Bologna; it was the scene of the defeat (B. C. 43) of Marcus Antonius by Augustus and the consuls, Hirtius and Pansa.

The Emperor Justinian (in the Heaven of Mercury) mentions Modena in connexion with the victories of the Roman Eagle, Par. vi. 75.

Modenesi. [Mutinenses.]

Modona. [Modena.]

Moisè, Moses, lawgiver of the Hebrews, Inf. iv. 57 ; Purg. xxxii. 80 ; Par. iv. 29 ; xxiv. 136 ; xxvi. 41 ; *Moyses*, Mon. i. 14^{66} ; ii. 4^{10}, 13^{36} ; iii. 4$^{84, 123}$, 5^2, 9$^{82, 86}$, 14^{35}; Epist. v. 1^{19} ; x. 7^{148} ; *Quel Duca, sotto cui visse di manna La gente ingrata* (i. e. the leader under whom the Jews lived upon manna in the wilderness), Par. xxxii. 131–2.

Virgil mentions Moses, whom he describes as 'Moisè legista e ubbidiente', among those released by Christ from Limbo, Inf. iv. 57 [Limbo]; his appearance with Elias at the Transfiguration, Purg. xxxii. 80 ; Mon. iii. 9$^{81-6}$ (ref. to *Matt.* xvii. 3–4); coupled with Samuel (cf. *Jerem.* xv. 1) as among the holiest of the saints, Par. iv. 29 ; his place in Paradise, Par. xxxii. 130–2 ; his writings referred to by D. as establishing his faith in God, Par. xxiv. 136 ; the Israelites under his guidance fed with manna in the wilderness, Par. xxxii. 131–2 (ref. to *Exod.* xvi. 14–21); the words of God to him, 'I will make all my goodness pass before thee'

(*Exod.* xxxiii. 19), quoted, Par. xxvi. 41–2 ; the elders of Israel entrusted by him with the lesser judgements, the more important being reserved to himself, as is written in his law, Mon. i. 14$^{65-73}$ (ref. to *Exod.* xviii. 17–26; *Deut.* i. 10–18); his record of the inability of Pharaoh's magicians to turn dust into lice, a proof that God alone can work miracles, Mon. ii. 4$^{8-14}$ (ref. to *Exod.* viii. 16–19); his reproof of the Hebrew who strove with his fellow, and the questioning of his authority by the former, Mon. ii. 13$^{35-7}$ (ref. to *Exod.* ii. 13–14); his writings inspired by the Holy Spirit, of which he was the mouthpiece, Mon. iii. 4$^{84-7}$; his account of the birth of Levi and Judah, Mon. iii. 5$^{2-4}$ (ref. to *Gen.* xxix. 34–5); the express command of God to him that the Levites should be deprived of all inheritance in the land of the Israelites, Mon. iii. 14$^{33-5}$ (ref. to *Numb.* xviii. 20); the Emperor Henry VII, on his coming into Italy, compared to a second Moses, Epist. v. 1^{19} ; in its literal sense, 'When Israel went out of Egypt' (*Psalm* cxiv. 1) signifies the departure of the children of Israel from Egypt in the time of Moses, Epist. x. 7$^{145-8}$.

The place of Moses in the Celestial Rose is pointed out to D. by St. Bernard, Par. xxxii. 130–2. [Rosa.]

The five books of Moses, forming the Pentateuch, which is reckoned by St. Jerome as one book, are supposed to be symbolized by one of the four-and-twenty elders (representing the 24 books of the Old Testament), in the mystical Procession in the Terrestrial Paradise, Purg. xxix. 83–4. [*Bibbia.*]

Molta, river Moldau, which rises in SW. of Bohemia, and, after flowing SE. for some distance, turns N., and, passing by Prague, enters the Elbe about twenty miles N. of that city.

D. mentions it in connexion with Bohemia, which he describes as 'the land drained by the Moldau and the Elbe', Purg. vii. 98–9. [Albia.]

Monaldi, leading Guelf family of Orvieto, otherwise known as Monaldeschi; mentioned together with the Filippeschi, the Ghibelline leaders in the same city, Purg. vi. 107. [Filippeschi.]

Monarchia, De, D.'s treatise *On Monarchy*, written in Latin, the subject being the relations between the Empire and the Papacy, and a plea for the necessity of a universal temporal monarchy, coexistent with the spiritual sovereignty of the Pope. The work is divided into three books—in the first D. treats of the necessity of monarchy; in the second he discusses the question how far the Roman people were justified in assuming the functions of monarchy, or the imperial power; in the third he inquires to what extent the function of the monarchy, i. e. the Empire, depends immediately upon God.

The three books were divided into chapters by D. himself, as appears from several references in the course of the work (Mon. i. 6^{23}; ii. 8^{102-7}; iii. 16^1), but they are only vaguely indicated in the MSS. In the printed editions the number of chapters varies.

Monferrato, Montferrat, ancient marquisate of N. Italy, which corresponded roughly with the S. half of the modern province of Piedmont. Its princes, several of whom are mentioned by D., were among the most powerful Italian families of the Middle Ages.

Sordello (in Ante-purgatory) mentions Montferrat in connexion with William Longsword, Marquis of Montferrat and Canavese (1254–1292), Purg. vii. 136 [Canavese: Guglielmo^3]; his son John (1292–1305) is mentioned, V. E. i. 12^{38} [Johannes ^{3}]; a member of this family (probably the Marquis Boniface II, 1192–1207) is mentioned, together with the King of Castile and the Count of Toulouse, on account of his liberality, as *il buono Marchese di Monferrato*, Conv. iv. 11^{125-8}.

Monferrato, Giovanni di. [Johannes ^{3}.]

Monferrato, Guglielmo di. [Guglielmo ^{3}.]

Monforte, Guido di. [Guido di Monforte.]

Mongibello, modern name of Mt. Aetna, Inf. xiv. 56. [Aetna.]

Mont' Aperti. [Montaperti.]

Montagna, Montagna de' Parcitati, head of the Ghibelline party in Rimini, who was treacherously taken prisoner in 1295 by Malatesta da Verrucchio ('il mastin vecchio') and murdered in prison by Malatesta's son, Malatestino ('il mastin nuovo').

D. mentions Montagna in connexion with his murder by the Malatesta, Inf. xxvii. 47. [Malatesta: Malatestino.]

Montagne Rife, Rhipaean mountains, lofty range in N. part of the earth, used generally to express any cold northern region; mentioned by D. to indicate the N., Purg. xxvi. 43.

Montaperti, village in Tuscany, about five miles S. of Siena, on a hill near the left bank of the Arbia, a small river which flows into the Ombrone at Buonconvento; here took place the famous battle between the Ghibellines and the Guelfs of Florence (Sept. 4, 1260), resulting in the total defeat of the latter, to which D. refers, Inf. x. 85–6. [Arbia.]

Montaperti is mentioned in connexion with the traitor Bocca degli Abati (in Circle IX of Hell), who cut down the standard of the Florentines at a critical point of the battle, and thus caused the panic which led to the rout of the Guelfs, Inf. xxxii. 81. [Bocca.]

Monte Aventino. [Aventino.]

Monte Subasio], mountain in N. of Umbria, spur of the Central or Roman Apennines, on the SW. slope of which Assisi, the birthplace of St. Francis, is situated; this slope is referred to by St. Thomas Aquinas (in the Heaven of the Sun) in his description of the situation of Assisi, as *fertile costa d'alto monte*, Par. xi. 45, 49 [Ascesi]; he says that from this mountain Perugia on its SE. side feels the heat (in summer, from the refraction) and the cold (in winter, from the snows) (*vv.* 46–7) [Perugia].

Monte Veso, Monte Viso or Monviso, peak of the Cottian Alps in Piedmont, where the river Po rises.

D. mentions it in connexion with the Montone, which he says is the first river which, rising on the N. side of the Apennines, flows direct into the Adriatic without entering the Po, Inf. xvi. 94–6 [Acquacheta: Montone²].

Monte Viso (or perhaps the Alps in general) is referred to by the Emperor Justinian (in the Heaven of Mercury) as *L'alpestre rocce di che, Po, tu labi*, Par. vi. 51. [Po.]

[Montecatini], stronghold of the Florentines between Lucca and Pistoja, before which, on Aug. 29, 1315, the Ghibelline leader, Uguccione della Faggiuola, inflicted a disastrous defeat on the Florentine Guelfs and their Tuscan and Angevin allies, under the Prince of Tarento and the Duke of Gravina (brothers of King Robert of Naples), the latter of whom was killed; the event is alluded to by G. del Virgilio (who indicates the Florentines as *Flores*, the French as *Lilia*, and Uguccione as *Arator*), Carm. 27.

Montecchi, leaders of the Ghibelline party at Verona, who came originally from Montecchio near Vicenza; mentioned by D., together with the Cappelletti (the Guelf party in Cremona), in his appeal to the Emperor, Albert of Austria, to come into Italy, Purg. vi. 106 [Cappelletti]. The Montecchi, whose Guelf opponents were known as the 'Pars Comitorum', the party of the Counts of San Bonifazio, allied themselves with the notorious

Ezzelino da Romano, who through their means became lord of Verona (1236–1259). In D.'s day they appear to have sunk into comparative insignificance.

Montefeltrano, Guido. [Guido Montefeltrano.]

Montefeltro, small mountainous district situated in the extreme N. of the province of the Marches, at the foot of the Apennines; its chief town is San Leo (Purg. iv. 25), which was once called Montefeltro, the name being thence transferred to the whole district, which formed part of Romagna, and in D.'s time belonged to the Dukes of Urbino [Romagna]. Among the Counts of Montefeltro were the famous Guido da Montefeltro and his son, Buonconte.

Montefeltro is mentioned by Buonconte (in Ante-purgatory) as his native place, Purg. v. 88; it is referred to by Guido (in Bolgia 8 of Circle VIII of Hell) as the hill country between Urbino and the ridge of the Apennines where the Tiber rises, *i monti là intra Urbino E il giogo di che il Tever si disserra,* Inf. xxvii. 29–30 [Buonconte: Guido Montefeltrano]; it is generally supposed to be one of the places spoken of as *Feltro*, Inf. i. 105 [Feltro 2].

Montefeltro, Buonconte da. [Buonconte.]

Montefeltro, Galassoda. [Galasso.]

Montefeltro, Guido da. [Guido Montefeltrano.]

Montemalo, now Monte Mario, hill outside Rome, over which the road to Viterbo passes. It is from this point that a traveller from the N. first catches sight of the city of Rome.

Cacciaguida (in the Heaven of Mars), comparing Florence to Rome, says that in his day (in the middle of Cent. xii) the view of Rome from Montemalo was not yet surpassed by that of Florence from Uccellatoio, Par. xv. 109–10 [Uccellatoio].

Montemurlo, castle (the ruins of which are still visible) on a hill between Prato and Pistoja, belonging to the Conti Guidi, their rights over which they sold (in 1219, and again, after they had been resumed, in 1254) to the Florentines, as they themselves could not hold it against the Pistojans.

Cacciaguida (in the Heaven of Mars), deploring the troubled times, says that, if the Church had not by its hostility to the Emperor brought about a universal state of feud, among other things the castle of Montemurlo would still belong to the Conti Guidi, Par. xvi. 64.

Montereggioni, strongly fortified castle, built by the Sienese in 1213, on the road between Empoli and Siena, about eight miles NW. of the latter. It is situated on the crown of a low hill, and is surrounded with a massive wall surmounted by fourteen towers (now mostly levelled with the wall) placed at regular intervals throughout the whole circuit.

D. compares the Giants, who are placed as warders at the mouth of Circle IX of Hell, to the towers which surround the castle of Montereggioni, Inf. xxxi. 40–4. [Giganti.]

Montone[1], 'the Ram', i. e. Aries, constellation and the first of the twelve signs of the Zodiac, which the Sun enters at the vernal equinox (about March 21). [**Ariete.**]

D. describes the vernal equinox as 'the Sun betaking himself to the bed which the Ram bestrides with all four feet' (the meaning of the passage being that the vernal equinox shall not recur seven times, seven years shall not pass), Purg. viii. 133–5 ; the Sun and Moon opposite to each other at the equinox (the one being in Aries, the other in Libra), Par. xxix. 1–2. [**Libra.**]

Montone[2], ('Ram') river of N. Italy, which rises in the Etruscan Apennines, above the monastery of San Benedetto in Alpe, and flows past Forlì and Ravenna (where it is joined by the Ronco) into the Adriatic.

According to D., the river from its source as far as Forlì was known as the Acquacheta, and from Forlì to its mouth as the Montone, Inf. xvi. 94–9 ; G. del Virgilio speaks of it as *Aries fluvialis*, Ecl. R. 15. [**Acquacheta : Monte Veso.**]

Mopsus, name (borrowed from Virgil, *Ecl.* v. 1, 10 ; viii. 26, 30 ; &c.) under which Giovanni del Virgilio figures in the poetical correspondence between him and D., Ecl. i. 6, 7, 18, 24, 28, 37, 51, 56, 57, 64 ; ii. 25, 65, 74, 97 ; Ecl. R. 35, 39, 80, 87. [*Egloghe*[2].]

Mordarette. [**Modarette.**]

Moroello Malaspina. [**Malaspina, Moroello.**]

Moronto, brother of D.'s great-great-grandfather Cacciaguida, Par. xv. 136. [**Cacciaguida : Dante.**]

Morrocco, Morocco, most W. of the Barbary States, occupying the NW. corner of Africa ; mentioned by D. (as an alternative to Spain) to indicate the W. limit of the habitable globe, Inf. xxvi. 104 ; Purg. iv. 139. [**Gerusalemme.**]

Mosca, member of the Lamberti family of Florence, at whose instigation the Amidei in 1215 murdered Buondelmonte de' Buondelmonti, and thus led to the introduction of the Guelf and Ghibelline feuds into Florence. [**Buondelmonte.**]

Mosca de' Lamberti (whose name occurs several times in Florentine documents between 1202 and 1225) is one of the five Florentines about whom D. inquires of Ciacco (in Circle III of Hell), whether they are in Heaven or Hell, the answer being that they are among the blackest souls in Hell, Inf. vi. 79–85 [**Ciacco**] ; D. afterwards sees Mosca among the Sowers of discord in Bolgia 9 of Circle VIII of Hell (Malebolge), Inf. xxviii. 106 ; *un*, *v.* 103 [**Scismatici**] ; he is represented with both his hands cut off, and lifting his bleeding stumps in the air, while he calls upon D. to remember Mosca, who made use of the famous phrase 'cosa fatta capo ha', which led to the civil feuds in Florence, and, adds D., to the death of the Lamberti family (they having apparently totally died out before the end of Cent. xiii) (*vv.* 103–11) [**Lamberti**].

Moyses. [**Moisè.**]

Mozzi, Andrea de'. [**Andrea de' Mozzi.**]

Mucius. [**Muzio.**]

Multa. [**Molta.**]

Munda], town in Hispania Baetica, where Julius Caesar defeated Sextus and Cneius, the sons of Pompey, B.C. 45; the Emperor Justinian (in the Heaven of Mercury) alludes to the battle of Munda among the victories of the Roman Eagle, Par. vi. 71-2.

Muse, the nine Muses, who are represented as having been born in Pieria, at the foot of Mt. Olympus; their favourite haunt was Mt. Helicon in Boeotia, where were the sacred fountains of Aganippe and Hippocrene; Mt. Parnassus was also sacred to them, with the Castalian spring.

The Muses are mentioned, Inf. ii. 7; Purg. i. 8; xxii. 102; Par. ii. 9; xii. 7; xviii. 33; they are referred to, in connexion with the founding of Thebes by Amphion with their help, as *quelle Donne . . . Ch' aiutaro Anfion a chiuder Tebe*, Inf. xxxii. 10-11 [**Anfione**]; Virgil speaks of them as the 'nursing-mothers of the poets', *le nutrici nostre*, Purg. xxii. 105 (cf. *vv.* 101-2); they are also referred to as *sacrosante Vergini*, Purg. xxix. 37 (cf. Purg. i. 8); *Urania col suo coro*, Purg. xxix. 41; *Polinnia con le sue suore*, Par. xxiii. 56; *Castaliae sorores*, Ecl. i. 54; Carm. 22 [**Castalius**]; *illae Quae male gliscentem timidae fugere Pyreneum*, Ecl. ii. 65-6 [**Pyreneus**]; *Pierides*, Carm. 1 [**Pierides**[1]]; *Aonides*, Carm. 36 [**Aonides**]; the Muse in general is addressed (in allusion to the connexion of Pegasus with the Muses) as *diva Pegasea*, Par. xviii. 82 [**Pegaseus**].

D. invokes the aid of the Muses at the beginning of his description of Hell, Inf. ii. 7; before his account of Circle IX of Hell, Inf. xxxii. 10-11; at the beginning of his description of Purgatory, *sante Muse*, Purg. i. 8, where he alludes to the transformation of the daughters of Pierus into magpies (*vv.* 10-12) [**Pierides**[2]]; before his account of the mystical Procession in the Terrestrial Paradise, Purg. xxix. 37-42; he claims to be under their inspiration, and that of Minerva and Apollo, at the beginning of his description of Paradise, Par. ii. 8-9; and invokes them again before his account of the evolutions of the spirits in the Heaven of Jupiter, Par. xviii. 82.

The following Muses are specially mentioned by name, Calliope, Purg. i. 9 [**Calliopè**]; Clio, Purg. xxii. 58 [**Cliò**]; Polymnia, Par. xxiii. 55 [**Polinnia**]; Urania, Purg. xxix. 41 [**Urania**].

[**Muso**], Musone, small river in the Paduan territory, which flows past Mirano into the lagoons near Venice; in his poetical correspondence with D., G. del Virgilio refers to Albertino Mussato of Padua as *Muso Phrygius*, Ecl. R. 88. [*Egloghe*[2]: Mussato: Phrygius.]

[**Mussato, Albertino**], poet and historian of Padua, where he was born in 1261; he played a distinguished part as soldier and statesman in the affairs of his native city, and died in exile at Chioggia in 1329. His fame as a poet rests upon his Latin tragedy, *Ecerinis*, on the subject of the tyrant Ezzolino da Romano (Inf. xii. 109-10), which gained him the laurel crown. M. figures in the poetical correspondence between D. and G. del Virgilio as *Muso Phrygius*, Ecl. R. 88. [**Muso.**]

Mutinenses, inhabitants of Modena (the Roman Mutina); their dialect and that of Ferrara have contributed to the Bolognese dialect a certain shrillness, characteristic of the Lombard dialects; this characteristic the reason why there have been no Modenese poets, V. E. i. 15^{3-22}. [**Modena.**]

Mutius. [**Muzio.**]

Muzio, Caius Mucius Scaevola, Roman citizen, who, when Lars Porsena, King of Clusium, was besieging Rome, made his way into the enemy's camp with the intention of killing Porsena, but stabbed the king's secretary by mistake. Being seized, Mucius was ordered by the king to be burned alive, whereupon he thrust his right hand into the fire, and held it in the flames without flinching. Porsena, struck with admiration at his fortitude, ordered him to be set free. From the circumstance of the loss of his right hand Mucius was thenceforward known as Scaevola ('left-handed').

D. mentions Mucius in connexion with this incident, *Muzio*, Par. iv. 84; Conv. iv. 5^{115-18}; and, with a reference to Livy (ii. 12) as his authority, *Mucius*, Mon. ii. 5^{121-7}.

Myrrha. [**Mirra.**]

N

Nabuccodonosor, Nebuchadnezzar, King of Babylon, B.C. 604–561; mentioned in connexion with Daniel's interpretation of his dream, which he had forgotten, whereby the execution of the Babylonian wise men was stayed (*Dan.* ii. 1–30), Par. iv. 13–15; and again in the same connexion (with especial reference to *Dan.* ii. 3), *Nabuchodonosor*, Epist. x. 28^{560}. [**Daniello.**]

Nabuchodonosor. [**Nabuccodonosor.**]

Naiade, Naiads or fresh-water nymphs; D., following a corrupt reading of a passage in Ovid (*Metam.* vii. 759–760), implies that the riddle of the Sphinx was solved by the Naiads (instead of by Laiades, i. e. Oedipus, son of Laius), Purg. xxxiii.

49–51 [**Edipo: Sfinge: Temi**]; D. speaks of Bologna under the guise of a nymph of the river Reno, *Naias*, Ecl. ii. 85. [**Reno** ^{2}.]

Naias. [**Naiade.**]

Namericus de Belnui, Aimeric de Belenoi, a troubadour (fl. c. 1250), native of Lesparre in the Bordelais. He was a nephew of Peire de Corbiac, and was at first a cleric, but subsequently adopted the profession of troubadour. His poems were chiefly amatory. His chief patrons were Raymond VI, Count of Toulouse (1194–1222), and Nunyo Sanchez, Count of Roussillon, on whose death (in 1241) he wrote a touching 'Complaint'.

D. mentions A. twice, and quotes the first line of his poem, ' Nuls hom 'non pot complir adrechamen', firstly as an example of the illustrious style, V. E. ii. 6$^{62-3}$; secondly, as a specimen of the stanza of endecasyllabic lines, V. E. ii. 12$^{22-3}$; in the latter passage D. classes A. as a 'Spaniard', explaining that by this term he means those who wrote in the *langue d'*oc, i. e. Provençal [Ispani].

Namericus de Peculiano, Aimeric de Pegulhan, one of the most celebrated of the troubadours of the thirteenth century (1205–1270), son of a cloth-merchant of Toulouse.

He led a wandering life, spending his days at the courts of his various patrons, among whom were Alphonso VIII of Castile (1158–1214), Raymond VI, Count of Toulouse (1194–1222), Peter II of Aragon (1196–1213), the Emperor Frederick II (1212–1250), Azzo VI of Este (1196–1212), and Azzo VIII (1215–1264).

D. quotes the first line of his poem, 'Si cum l'arbres que per sobre carcar', as an example of the illustrious style, V. E. ii. 6^{65}.

Napoleone degli Alberti. [Alberti.]

Napoleone degli Orsini. [Orsini.]

Napoli, Naples, capital of the old kingdom of Naples (sometimes also called Apulia, from the province of that name, which, at one time independent, was afterwards united to Naples) [Puglia]; mentioned by Virgil in connexion with the tradition that his body was buried there, Purg. iii. 27 [Brandizio]; the Piscicelli family of Naples, Conv. iv. 29$^{27-8}$ [Piscicelli].

Charles Martel (in the Heaven

of Venus) roughly indicates the Neapolitan territory as the country lying between Bari, Gaeta, and Catona, Par. viii. 61–3 [Ausonia]; the kingdom itself is spoken of as *il Regno*, Purg. iii. 131; *quel di Carlo* (i. e. the kingdom of Charles II of Anjou), Purg. v. 69. [Carlo ^{2}.]

Until the 'Sicilian Vespers' in 1282, when the Sicilian crown was united to that of Aragon, Naples and Sicily formed one kingdom, commonly known as the kingdom of the Two Sicilies [Cicilia]. On the death of William II in 1189 without issue the crown passed first to his cousin Tancred (1189–1194), then to his cousin's son, William III (1194), and finally to the Emperor Henry VI (1194–1197), the husband of his aunt Constance, through whom it descended to the Emperor Frederick II (1197-1250), and his son Conrad IV (1250–1254). On Conrad's death Manfred, natural son of Frederick II, assumed the government, to the exclusion of his nephew Conradin. The Hohenstaufen line having been brought to an end by the defeat and death of Manfred at Benevento (126$\frac{5}{8}$) and of Conradin at Tagliacozzo (1268), Charles of Anjou assumed the crown of Naples and Sicily under the title of Charles I (1266–1282). After the 'Sicilian Vespers' (1282) Peter III of Aragon took possession of Sicily, which thus became annexed to the crown of Aragon, Naples alone remaining in the hands of the Angevins [Tables B, E].

Narcisso, Narcissus, beautiful Greek youth, of whom the nymph Echo became enamoured; but, finding him insensible to love, she pined away in grief, and was reduced to nothing but a voice. To punish Narcissus for his insensibility Nemesis caused him to see his own image reflected in a fountain, whereupon he became so enamoured of it that he too pined away gradually, until he was changed into the flower which bears his name (Ovid, *Metam.* iii. 407 ff.). [**Eco.**]

D. speaks of water as *lo specchio di Narcisso*, Inf. xxx. 128; his falling in love with his own reflected image is alluded to as *quel error ch' accese amor tra l'uomo e il fonte*, Par. iii. 18.

Nasetto, Il. [**Filippo**[1].]

Naso. [**Ovidio.**]

Nassidio, Nasidius, Roman soldier belonging to Cato's army in Africa, of whom Lucan relates that he was stung by a venomous serpent in the desert of Libya, the bite of which caused his body to swell up till his corselet burst and he died (*Phars.* ix. 790–7).

D. mentions N. in connexion with this incident, and refers to Lucan's account of it, Inf. xxv. 94–5.

Nasuto, Il. [**Carlo**[1].]

Natan, Nathan, the prophet, who was sent by God to reprove David for his sin in causing the death of Uriah the Hittite in order that he might take Bathsheba to wife (2 *Sam.* xii. 1–12).

St. Bonaventura names Nathan among the great Doctors (*Spiriti Sapienti*) who are with himself in the Heaven of the Sun, coupling him with St. Chrysostom (both having been outspoken in rebuking the sins of kings), Par. xii. 136–7. [**Sole, Cielo del.**]

Natura Locorum, De. [*Locorum, De Natura.*]

Naturali Auditu, De. [*Physica.*]

Navarra, Navarre, kingdom (independent until 1314, when it was united to the French crown in the person of Louis X) on both sides of the Pyrenees, consisting of French and Spanish Navarre, Inf. xxii. 48; Par. xix. 143; V. E. i. 9^{26}; ii. 5^{37}, 6^{56}. [**Table M.**]

One of the Barrators in Bolgia 5 of Circle VIII of Hell (Malebolge), a native of Navarre, Inf. xxii. 48 [**Ciampolo**]; the Eagle in the Heaven of Jupiter, alluding to the union of Navarre with France, laments that it is not surrounded with its own mountains (i.e. independent of France), Par. xix. 143–4; the poems of the King of Navarre (i.e. of Teobaldo I) quoted, V. E. i. 9^{26}; ii. 5^{37}, 6^{56} [**Tebaldo**[1]]; Teobaldo II of Navarre is mentioned, Inf. xxii. 52 [**Tebaldo**[2]]; Enrique I of Navarre is referred to, Purg. vii. 104, 109 [**Arrigo**[7]].

Navarrese, belonging to Navarre; *lo Navarrese*, i.e. the barrator, Ciampolo of Navarre, Inf. xxii. 121. [**Ciampolo.**]

Nazzarette, Nazareth, village of Galilee, about twenty miles W. of the S. extremity of the Sea of Tiberias; mentioned by the troubadour Folquet (in the Heaven of Venus) in connexion with the Annunciation (*Luke* i. 26), to indicate the Holy Land in general, Par. ix. 137–8. [**Gabriello.**]

Nazzaro, San, family of Pavia, mentioned by D. in his discussion as to the nature of nobility, together with the Piscicelli of Naples, as examples of Italian nobles, Conv. iv. 29^{27}.

Neapolitani, Neapolitans; their dialect different from that of their neighbours of Gaeta, V. E. i. 9^{40}. [**Napoli.**]

Neftali], Naphtali, son of Jacob by Bilhah, Rachel's maid; he is among those referred to by Virgil as having been released by Christ from Limbo, *Israel co' suoi nati*, Inf. iv. 59 [Limbo].

Negligenti a pentirsi], those who were negligent in repentance; placed in Ante-purgatory, Purg. i–vii. [Antipurgatorio.]

Negri, Neri or 'Blacks', one of the divisions of the Guelf party, who remained staunch Guelfs, in opposition to the Bianchi or 'Whites', who eventually identified themselves with the Ghibellines. [Bianchi.]

Vanni Fucci (in Bolgia 7 of Circle VIII of Hell) prophesies to D. the expulsion of the Neri from Pistoja (which came to pass in May, 1301), Inf. xxiv. 143 [Fucci, Vanni].

Nella, abbreviation (probably) of Giovanella, diminutive of Giovanna, name by which Forese Donati (in Circle III of Purgatory) speaks of his widow, Purg. xxiii. 87; *la vedovella mia*, v. 92; he dwells on her goodness and on his love for her, and contrasts her virtue with the shamelessness of the other women of Florence (*vv.* 91–6).

In the poetical correspondence between D. and Forese, D. commiserates the wife of the latter on account of her spouse's irregular life, speaking of her as *la mal fatata Moglie di Bicci vocato Forese*, Son. lii. 1–2. [Forese.]

Nello de' Pannocchieschi], husband (as is supposed) of Pia de' Tolomei, Purg. v. 135–6. [Pia.]

Nembrot. [Nembrotto.]

Nembrotto, Nimrod, the son of Cush, 'a mighty hunter before the Lord' (*Gen.* x. 8–9), commonly supposed to have been the builder of the Tower of Babel, on the plain of Shinar (the origin of the tradition being probably *Gen.* x. 10); he is mentioned, *Nembrotto*, Inf. xxxi. 77; *Nembrot*, Purg. xii. 34; Par. xxvi. 126; referred to as *Gigas*, V. E. i. 7[26].

D., who represents N. as a giant, places him as one of the warders at the mouth of Circle IX of Hell, together with Antaeus, Briareus, and Ephialtes, Inf. xxxi. 46–105; he describes his face as being as long and large as the great pine-cone of St. Peter's at Rome (i.e. about $7\frac{1}{2}$ ft. high), with the rest of his body in proportion, and adds that it would take three Frisians, one on the top of the other, to reach from his middle to his neck (which would give him a stature of about 70 English feet) (*vv.* 58–66); as D. and Virgil approach, N. begins to shout gibberish to them, whereupon V. informs D. that this is Nimrod, whose building of the Tower of Babel was the cause of the confusion of tongues (*vv.* 67–78). [Babel.]

There is nothing in the Bible to suggest that Nimrod was a giant, but both Orosius (*Hist.* ii. 6, § 7) and St. Augustine (*Civ. Dei*, xvi. 3, 4, 11), who probably were D.'s authorities, represent him as such.

Nimrod figures among the examples of defeated pride in Circle I of Purgatory, where he is represented as standing bewildered among the nations at the foot of the Tower of Babel on the plain of Shinar, Purg. xii. 34–6 [Superbi]; he is mentioned (by Adam in the Heaven of the Fixed Stars) in connexion with the Tower of Babel and the confusion of tongues, Par. xxvi. 124–6; and again, V. E. i. 7²⁴⁻³³. [Sennaar.]

Nereus, sea god, son of Pontus and Gaea, and father of the Nereids, Carm. 43; the sea spoken of by D. as *Nerei confinia*, Ecl. ii. 21.

Neri. [Negri.]

Nerli, ancient noble family of Florence, mentioned by Cacciaguida (in the Heaven of Mars), together with the Vecchietti, as examples of the simple life of the Florentines of his day as compared with their degenerate and luxurious descendants, Par. xv. 115–17.

The Nerli were one of the Florentine families which received knighthood from the Marquis Hugh of Brandenburg, 'il gran barone', Par. xvi. 128 [Ugo di Brandimborgo.] They were Guelfs (Vill. v. 39), and as such were expelled from Florence in 1248 (vi. 33), and went into exile in 1260 after the Ghibelline victory at Montaperti (vi. 79).

Nerone, Nero, Roman Emperor, A.D. 54–68; his definition of youth as beauty and bodily strength, Conv. iv. 9¹⁶⁹⁻⁷⁰; spoken of as *Caesar* in connexion with St. Paul's appeal to him (*Acts* xxv. 11), Mon. iii. 13⁴³⁻⁵³.

Nesso, Nessus, one of the Centaurs; placed with Chiron and Pholus as guardian of the Violent in Round I of Circle VII of Hell, Inf. xii. 67, 98; xiii. 1; *il Centauro*, Inf. xii. 115, 129; *il gran Centauro*, v. 104; *l'un* (*Centauro*), v. 61; *scorta fida*, v. 100; Virgil points out N. to D., describing him

as N. who died for Deianira, and wrought his own revenge (*vv.* 67–9) [Deianira]; subsequently N. is deputed by Chiron to escort V. and D., and to show them the ford across the river Phlegethon (doubtless in reminiscence of Ovid's epithet 'scitus vadorum' applied to N., *Metam.* ix. 108) (*vv.* 97–126). [Centauri: Violenti.]

Nettuno, Neptune, god of the sea (identified by the Romans with the Greek Poseidon), hence the sea itself; used by D. of the Mediterranean, Inf. xxviii. 83 [Mediterraneo]; of the track of the Argonauts, Par. xxxiii. 96 [Argonauti]; Neptune (Poseidon) is referred to in connexion with the contest between him and Minerva (Athene) for the possession of the city of Athens, Purg. xv. 97 [Atene: Minerva].

Niccola Acciaiuoli. [Acciaiuoli, Niccola.]

Niccolao, St. Nicholas, Bishop of Myra in Lycia, supposed to have lived in Cent. iv under Constantine and to have been present at the Council of Nice (325). In Cent. xi his remains were transported to Bari in Apulia, whence he is sometimes known as St. Nicholas of Bari.

St. Nicholas is proclaimed as an instance of liberality by Hugh Capet in the Circle of the Avaricious in Purgatory (in allusion to the legend that he saved three destitute maidens from prostitution by giving them each a dowry and so enabling them to marry), Purg. xx. 31–3 [Avari].

Niccolò¹, supposed to be a son of Giovanni de' Salimbeni of Siena, and brother of Stricca (Inf. xxix. 125), and like him a member of the 'Spendthrift Brigade' of Siena; he is mentioned by Capocchio (in Bolgia 10 of Circle VIII of Hell) ironically as an exception to the general empty-headedness of the Sienese, and described as the inventor of 'the rich fashion of the clove', Inf. xxix. 127–9. [**Brigata Spendereccia.**]

Niccolò [2], Nicholas III (Gian Gaetani degli Orsini), native of Rome; created cardinal-deacon of St. Nicholas in Carcere in 1244; elected Pope at Viterbo, Nov. 25, 1277, and crowned at Rome, Dec. 26, in succession to John XXI, after a vacancy of more than six months; died of apoplexy at his castle of Soriano, near Viterbo, Aug. 22, 1280.

D. places Nicholas III among the Simoniacs in Bolgia 3 of Circle VIII of Hell (Malebolge), speaking of him, in allusion to his simony and to the house of Orsini to which he belonged, as *figliuol dell' Orsa*, Inf. xix. 70; *colui*, v. 31; *quei*, v. 45; *anima trista*, v. 47; *lo spirto*, v. 64; [**Simoniaci**]; N. mistakes D. for Boniface VIII, and expresses surprise that he should have come down to Hell so soon (i. e. three years before he was due) (*vv.* 52–7); D. having undeceived him, N. reveals his own identity, and prophesies the coming to the same Bolgia of his successors, Boniface VIII and Clement V (*vv.* 58–84); D. then addresses to him a long invective against his simoniacal practices (*vv.* 88–117), making a special allusion to his having received money from the Emperor of Constantinople in

furtherance of the rising against Charles of Anjou in Sicily (*vv.* 97–9).

Villani (vii. 54) gives plentiful instances of the simony of Nicholas III, and refers to his relations with the Greek Emperor, Michael Palaeologus, who supplied the Pope with funds in aid of the intrigue against Charles of Anjou (Inf. xix. 97–9), which was being carried on in Sicily with the countenance and connivance of Nicholas, and which led up to the insurrection of the 'Sicilian Vespers', and the loss of Sicily to the house of Anjou [**Vespro Siciliano.**]

Niccolò Donati], son of Foresino (or Forese) di Manetto Donati, and nephew of Gemma Donati, D.'s wife; probably the nephew of D. referred to, Epist. ix. 2[13–14]; in which case his uncle, Teruccio Donati, D.'s brother-in-law, would be the correspondent to whom the letter was addressed. [**Teruccio Donati.**]

Niccolò da Prato. [**Nicholaus.**]

Nicholaus, Niccolò degli Alberti (or Albertini), of the family of the Counts of Prato in Tuscany, commonly called Niccolò da Prato, Bishop of Spoleto, Cardinal-Bishop of Ostia and Velletri, papal legate in France, England, and Sicily; created Cardinal by Benedict XI in 1303; died at Avignon, April 1, 1321.

In the spring of 1304 (March 10, 130¾) Niccolò arrived in Florence on a mission from Benedict XI to effect a pacification between the Guelfs and Ghibellines; but having failed in his mission, largely owing to the irreconcilable attitude of the

Neri, he left Florence on June 4, placing the city under an interdict, and excommunicating the inhabitants. Some see an allusion to this in D.'s mention of Prato, Inf. xxvi. 8–9 [Prato].

A letter, commonly supposed to have been written by D., was addressed to the Cardinal Niccolò da Prato (probably after his departure from Florence) in the name of the Florentine Bianchi, thanking him for his attempts to make peace in Florence and bring about the return of the exiles, and begging him to persevere in his efforts, and, further, promising in obedience to his wishes to abstain from hostilities against the Neri, Epist. 1.

Nicomachum, Ad. [*Ethica.*]

Nicosia, now Lefkosia, town in the centre of the island of Cyprus, of which it has been the capital since the time of the Lusignan kings; it is mentioned by the Eagle in the Heaven of Jupiter, together with Famagusta, to indicate the kingdom of Cyprus, the reference being to Henry II of Lusignan, Par. xix. 146. [**Arrigo** [8] : **Cipri**.]

Nilo, river Nile; Ethiopia described as *là onde il Nilo s'avvalla*, Inf. xxxiv. 45 [**Etiopia**]; cranes referred to as *gli augei che vernan lungo il Nilo*, Purg. xxiv. 64; the death of Pompey in Egypt and defeat of Ptolemy by Julius Caesar referred to, *Sì ch' al Nil caldo si sentì del duolo*, Par. vi. 66 [**Pompeio** [1] : **Tolommeo** [2]]; the Nile at its source a small stream, Canz. xx. 46.

Nin, Giudice. [**Nino** [2].]

Nino [1], Ninus, mythical founder

of the Assyrian empire of Nineveh; he was a great warrior and subdued the greater part of Asia.

D. mentions Ninus as the husband of Semiramis, who succeeded him, Inf. v. 59; he was the first who aspired to found a universal monarchy, but though he and Semiramis waged war for more than ninety years, as Orosius records (*Hist.* i. 4, § 5; ii. 3, § 1), yet in the end they failed of their object, *Ninus*, Mon. ii. 9[22–9] [**Semiramis**]; Ovid's mention of them both (*Metam.* iv. 58, 88) in the story of Pyramus and Thisbe, Mon. ii. 9[30–4]. [**Piramo**.]

Nino [2], Nino Visconti of Pisa, judge of the district of Gallura in Sardinia; he was grandson of Count Ugolino della Gherardesca, and in 1288 was chief of the Guelf party in Pisa; in that year he and the Guelfs were treacherously expelled from Pisa by Count Ugolino, whereupon he retired to Lucca, and in alliance with Genoa and the Lucchese and Florentine Guelfs made war upon Pisa, which he carried on at intervals for the next five years. In 1293, on the conclusion of peace between the Pisans and the Tuscan Guelfs, Nino betook himself to Genoa, and shortly after departed to his judgeship of Gallura in Sardinia. It was on this occasion, apparently, that he inflicted summary punishment upon his deputy, Frate Gomita, for his misdoings during Nino's absence [**Gomita, Frate**]. Nino died in Sardinia in 1296.

D. places Nino among the Negligent Rulers in the valley of flowers in Ante-purgatory, *Giudice Nin*, Purg. viii. 53; *il Giudice*, v. 109; *un*, *v.* 47; *l'altro, v.* 64 [**Antipurgatorio**]; D. having recognized Nino, the latter addresses him, and begs him, when he returns upon earth, to bid his daughter Joan to pray for him (*vv.* 49–72) [**Giovanna** [2]]; he adds that he fears her mother (Beatrice of Este) cares for him no more, since she has married again (her second husband having been Galeazzo Visconti of Milan), and concludes with the remark that the Milanese viper (the arms of the Visconti of Milan) will not grace her tomb so well as the cock of Gallura (the arms of the Visconti of Pisa) (*vv.* 79–81) [**Beatrice** [4] : **Galeazzo : Gallura**].

D., as appears from the text (*vv.* 46–55), was personally acquainted with Nino, whom he may have met in Florence, where Nino was present several times in 1290 in the interests of the Guelf league against Pisa.

Ninus. [**Nino** [1].]

Niobè, Niobe, daughter of Tantalus and wife of Amphion, King of Thebes ; being proud of the number of her children, she boasted herself superior to Latona, who had only two, viz. Apollo and Diana, whereupon the latter slew Niobe's seven sons and seven daughters with their arrows, Niobe herself being transformed by Jupiter into a stone, which during the summer always shed tears (Ovid, *Metam.* vi. 182 ff., 301 ff.).

Niobe, weeping over her dead children, figures among the examples of defeated pride represented in Circle I of Purgatory, Purg. xii. 37–9. [**Superbi.**]

[**Nisa**], name (borrowed from Virgil, *Ecl.* viii. 18, 26) of character in the Eclogue addressed by G. del Virgilio to D., supposed to represent the writer's wife or servant, Ecl. R. 8, 57, 63.

Niso, Nisus, Trojan youth, who with his friend Euryalus accompanied Aeneas to Italy, where they perished together in a night attack on the camp of the Rutulians (*Aen.* ix. 176–449); they are mentioned, together with Camilla and Turnus, as having died for Italy, Inf. i. 108. [**Eurialo**].

Noarese, inhabitant of Novara, town in NE. of Piedmont, on the plain between the Sesia and the Ticino, about thirty miles due W. of Milan. Mahomet (in Bolgia 9 of Circle VIII of Hell) speaks of *il Noarese* (sing. for plur.), meaning the Novarese, in connexion with Fra Dolcino, Inf. xxviii. 59. [**Dolcino, Fra.**]

Nocera, town in Umbria (not to be confounded with Nocera in Apulia), at the foot of the Apennines, about fifteen miles NE. of Assisi ; mentioned by St. Thomas Aquinas (in the Heaven of the Sun), together with Gualdo, in his description of the situation of Assisi, Par. xi. 48 [**Gualdo**].

Noè, patriarch Noah ; mentioned by Virgil among those whom Christ released from Limbo, Inf. iv. 56; God's covenant with him, signified by the rainbow, that there should never be another flood to destroy the earth (*Gen.* ix. 13–17), Par. xii. 17–18 ; the children of Israel descended from Shem, eldest (D. says third) son of Noah, *Noè,* V. E. i. 7[66–7] [**Sem**].

Noë. [**Noè.**]

Nogaret, Guglielmo di. [Guglielmo di Nogaret.]

Noli, town in Liguria on the Gulf of Genoa, about ten miles SW. of Savona on the Riviera di Ponente; mentioned by D. in connexion with the precipitous descent to it from the mountains behind, Purg. iv. 25.

Nono Cielo. [Cielo Cristallino.]

Normandia, Normandy, ancient duchy in N. of France, which was attached to the English crown from the Norman Conquest down to 1203, when it was taken from John by Philip Augustus.

Hugh Capet (in Circle V of Purgatory) refers to the taking of Normandy by his descendants, Purg. xx. 66. [Ciapetta, Ugo.]

Norvegia, kingdom of Norway; the Eagle in the Heaven of Jupiter bewails the backslidings of the King of Norway, who is referred to as *quel di Norvegia* (the reference being probably to Hakon V), Par. xix. 139 [Acone[2]: Table N].

Notaro, Il. [Jacopo da Lentino.]

Nova Rhetorica. [*Rhetorica Nova.*]

Novembre, month of November; the government of Florence so unstable that laws framed in October did not last till the middle of the next month, Purg. vi. 142–4.

Novum Testamentum. [*Bibbia.*]

Numa Pompilio, Numa Pompilius, second King of Rome, renowned for his piety and wisdom, which he was generally supposed to have derived from Pythagoras; D. speaks of him as *Numa*, Conv. iv. 5^{90}; Mon. ii. 4^{39}; *Numa Pompilio*, Conv. iii. 11^{27-8}; *Numa Pompilius*, V. E. i. 17^{15}; Mon. ii. 4^{30}; Livy's statement (misunderstood by D.) as to the coming of Pythagoras to Italy in his reign, Conv. iii. 11^{30-3} [Livio: Pittagora]; second in order of the Seven Kings of Rome, Conv. iv. 5^{90}; Mon. ii. 4^{30-1}; coupled with Seneca as having been well trained and in consequence a good guide to others, V. E. i. 17^{13-15}; the falling of the sacred shield from heaven in his reign, as testified by Livy (i. 20) and Lucan (*Phars.* ix. 477–80), Mon. ii. 4^{30-41}.

Numerorum, Liber], Book of Numbers; quoted, Mon. iii. 14^{33-5} (*Numb.* xviii. 20); referred to, Purg. xvi. 131–2 (*Numb.* xviii. 20); Purg. xviii. 133–5 (*Numb.* xiv. 22–3, 29–30); V. E. i. 2^{45} (*Numb.* xxii. 28); Epist. viii. 8^{129-30} (*Numb.* xxii. 28). [*Bibbia.*]

Numidia], ancient division of N. Africa; spoken of as *la terra di Iarba*, Purg. xxxi. 72 (where some think the reference is to Africa in general). [Iarba.]

Nuova, Arte. [*Arte Nuova.*]
Nuova, Vita. [*Vita Nuova.*]
Nuovo Testamento. [*Bibbia.*]

O

O, letter O, Inf. xxiv. 100 $[1^1]$; for Omega, last letter of the Greek alphabet, Par. xxvi. 17 [Omega].

Oberto da Romena, Uberto, one of the Conti Guidi of the Romena branch, to whom and his younger brother Guido D. addressed a letter on the death of their uncle Alessandro, *Obertus*, Epist. ii. *tit.* [Guido da Romena.]

Obizzo da Esti, Obizzo II of Este, Marquis of Ferrara and of the March of Ancona (1264–1293), grandson of Azzo VII (Azzo Novello) of Este, and son of Rinaldo and Adeleita da Romano. On the death of his grandfather in 1264 (his father having predeceased the latter in 1251) he was elected lord of Ferrara; in 1288 he received the lordship of Modena, and in the next year that of Reggio. Obizzo, who was an ardent Guelf, and supporter of Charles of Anjou in his operations against Manfred, is said to have wielded his power with pitiless cruelty. He was succeeded by his son, Azzo VIII, by whom he is commonly supposed to have been smothered, Feb. 13, 1293.

D. places him among the Tyrants in Round 1 of Circle VII of Hell, where he is pointed out by Nessus, who describes him as fair-haired, and states that he had been murdered by his 'figliastro' (meaning either his 'natural', or his unnatural, son), Inf. xii. 110–12. [Azzo da Esti: Tiranni.]

Some think Obizzo (and not his son Azzo) is 'il Marchese' referred to by Venetico Caccianimico (in Bolgia 1 of Circle VIII of Hell), in connexion with the seduction of his sister, Ghisolabella, Inf. xviii. 55–7. [Caccianimico, Venedico: Ghisolabella.]

Oc, Lingua. [Lingua *Oc.*]

Occidente, the West, Inf. xxvi. 113; Purg. xxvi. 5; xxvii. 63; Par. vi. 71 (where Justinian, Emperor of the East, speaks of the W. to D., as an Italian, as 'il vostro occidente'); of the movement of the Heavens from E. to W., Conv. ii. 3^{39-45}, 6^{145-7}; of the dual movement of the Heaven of the Fixed Stars, viz. the diurnal one from E. to W., and the almost imperceptible one of one degree in 100 years from W. to E., Conv. ii. 6^{141-7}, 15^{12-13} [Cielo Stellato]; of the oblique movement of the Heaven of the Sun from W. to E., Conv. iii. 5^{126-30} [Sole, Cielo del]; *Occidens*, of the W. limits of the *langue d'*oïl, V. E. i. 8^{61-2} [Lingua *Oïl*]; the quarter where the Sun sets, *Ponente*, Inf. xix. 83; Purg. ii. 15.

Oceano, the Ocean, the waters of which, according to the old belief, encircled the whole Earth, *Mare Oceano*, Conv. iii. $5^{82, \ 94, \ 118}$; alluded to as *quel mar che la terra inghirlanda*, Par. ix. 84; *Oceanus*, the limit of the Emperor's jurisdiction, Mon. i. 11^{83}; Epist. vii. 3^{58}; viii. 11^{183}.

Ochiover, Milanese form of *Ottobre*, V. E. i. 11[35]. [**Ottobre.**]

Octavianus. [**Augusto** [2].]

Oderisi, miniature-painter and illuminator of Gubbio in Umbria; placed by D. among the Proud in Circle I of Purgatory, Purg. xi. 79; *un, v.* 74; *egli, v.* 82; *anima carca,* Purg. xii. 2 [**Superbi**]; O. recognizes D. and addresses him, whereupon D. asks if he is not the famous illuminator of Gubbio; to which O. replies that Franco of Bologna is now the greatest master in that art, but that his pride would not have allowed him to make that admission while he was alive, Purg. xi. (76–87) [**Bolognese, Franco**].

Oderisi, who was the son of Guido d'Agobbio (Gubbio), was in residence at Bologna in 1268, 1269, and 1271; he is said to have gone to Rome in 1295, and to have died there in 1299. Vasari, who possessed some of his drawings, states that he was a friend of Giotto (Purg. xi. 95), and that he and Franco of Bologna (Purg. xi. 83) were employed by Boniface VIII to illuminate MSS. in the Papal library at Rome. It appears from the text (*vv.* 76–80) that D. and Oderisi were acquainted, or at least knew each other by sight.

Odissea], Homer's *Odyssey*; quoted by D. at second-hand from Horace and Aristotle, V. N. § 25[90–3] (*Od.* i. 1); Mon. i. 5[34–6] (*Od.* ix. 114). [**Omero.**]

Oenotrii, ancient inhabitants of the S. extremity of Italy; Virgil's mention of them (*Aen.* iii. 165) quoted, Mon. ii. 3[82].

Officii, Degli. [**Officiis, De.**]

Officiis, De, Cicero's work (in three books) *On Offices*, a treatise on moral obligations; quoted as *Degli Officii*, Conv. iv. 8[10], 15[124], 24[100], 25[95], 27[111, 134]; *Officia*, Mon. ii. 5[55, 158], 8[95], 10[24].

D. quotes from the *De Officiis* some dozen times:—the saying of Pythagoras that in friendship many are made one, Conv. iv. 1[5–6] (*Off.* i. 17); the Greek proverb that friends ought to have all things in common, Conv. iv. 1[15–18] (*Off.* i. 16); the necessity for reverence, and for a regard for the opinion of others, Conv. iv. 8[9–21] (*Off.* i. 28); arrogance and presumption detestable failings, Conv. iv. 15[123–4] (*Off.* i. 26); a man's obligations vary with his time of life, Conv. iv. 24[100] (*Off.* i. 34); there is no foul act which it would not be a foul thing to name, Conv. iv. 25[95–7] (misquot. from *Off.* i. 35); liberality must be exercised with caution lest it should be injurious instead of beneficial, Conv. iv. 27[111–14] (*Off.* i. 14); of the false ideas of liberality in some men, Conv. iv. 27[134–41] (*Off.* i. 14); Cicero's authority quoted with regard to the public bodies by which men are bound to the state, Mon. ii. 5[55–67] (*Off.* ii. 8); his estimate of the character of Cato of Utica (quoted carelessly or from a corrupt text), Mon. ii. 5[158–70] (*Off.* i. 31); his quotation of the opinion of Chrysippus that a man who runs in a race should do his best to win, but should in no wise attempt to hinder his rival, Mon. ii. 8[95–101] (*Off.* iii. 10); his opinion that war ought not to be declared until all peaceful means have been exhausted, Mon. ii. 10[18–24]

(*Off.* i. 11); wars which are waged for the crown of empire must be waged without bitterness, Mon. ii. 10^{37-40} (misquot. from *Off.* i. 12); Cicero's quotation from Ennius borrowed, Mon. ii. 10^{60-9} (*Off.* i. 12).

D. was also indebted to the *De Officiis* (i. 13) for his fundamental distinction of sins of violence and sins of fraud, Inf. xi, 22–66; for Guido da Montefeltro's description of his fraudulent doings, 'l'opere mie Non furon leonine, ma di volpe', Inf. xxvii. 74–5 (*Off.* i. 13 : 'fraus quasi vulpeculae, vis leonis videtur'); and for his account of the vow of Agamemnon, Par. v. 67–72 (*Off.* iii. 25).

Oil, Lingua. [*Lingua Oil.*]

Olimpo, Olympus, range of mountains separating Macedonia and Thessaly, in Greek mythology regarded as the abode of the gods; later the name came to be used as synonymous with heaven itself, hence D. speaks of Paradise as *l'alto Olimpo*, Purg. xxiv. 15.

Oloferne, Holofernes, 'the chief captain of Nabuchodonosor King of the Assyrians', who was slain by Judith [**Judit**]; the scene of the flight of the Assyrians after the death of Holofernes is portrayed on the ground in Circle I of Purgatory, where they figure as examples of defeated pride, Purg. xii. 58–60 [**Assiri : Superbi**].

Omberto, Omberto Aldobrandesco, second son of Guglielmo Aldobrandesco, Count of Santafiora in the Sienese Maremma, murdered by the Sienese at Campagnatico in 1259 [**Santafiora**]; placed by D.

among the Proud in Circle I of Purgatory, Purg. xi. 67 [**Superbi**]; he relates his history, how he belonged to a great Tuscan family, his father's name being Guglielmo Aldobrandesco; and how pride in the ancient blood and noble deeds of his ancestry was the cause of his death at the hands of the Sienese at Campagnatico (*vv.* 52–66) [**Guglielmo Aldobrandesco : Campagnatico**].

Omega, last letter of the Greek alphabet; mentioned (in allusion to *Rev.* i. 8), Par. xxvi. 17; Epist. x. 33^{625}.

Omero, poet Homer, Inf. iv. 88; V. N. §§ 2^{51}, 25^{92}; Conv. i. 7^{96}; iv. 20^{37}; *Homerus*, Mon. i. 5^{34}; ii. 3^{55}; he is referred to (according to some) as *quei* (var. *quel*) *signor dell' altissimo canto, Che sopra gli altri com' aquila vola,* Inf. iv. 95–6 (where others think Virgil is intended); Virgil (addressing Statius in Purgatory) speaks of him as *quel Greco Che le Muse lattar più ch' altro mai,* Purg. xxii. 101–2.

D. places Homer, together with Horace, Ovid, and Lucan, in Limbo, where he is represented, with a sword in his hand, at the head of the other three, Inf. iv. 86–8; these poets, with Virgil, make up ' la bella scuola Di quei signor dell' altissimo canto ' (*vv.* 94–5); he is mentioned by Virgil as being in Limbo along with himself and other poets of antiquity, Purg. xxii. 101–2 [**Limbo**]; he is alluded to by G. del Virgilio (with reference to Inf. iv. 88–90, 101–2), Carm. 17.

D., being ignorant of Greek, had no direct knowledge of Homer, of whose works no translation existed in his day; they were known to him only by means of quotations in various classical authors. D. himself refers to the fact that there was no Latin translation of Homer, alleging as the reason the impossibility of translating him, or any other poet, without entirely destroying all the sweetness and harmony of the poetic diction in the process, Conv. i. 7⁹⁵⁻¹⁰⁰. His quotations from Homer are borrowed (with or without acknowledgement) from Aristotle or Horace; thus the description of Hector as being more like the son of a god than of a man (*Iliad* xxiv. 258–9) is quoted as if from Homer direct, V. N. § 2⁵¹⁻² ; but the same passage is twice referred to elsewhere as occurring in the *Ethics* (vii. 1) of Aristotle, Conv. iv. 20³⁷ ; Mon. ii. 3⁵⁵ [*Ethica*]; the opening of the *Odyssey* is quoted from the *Ars Poëtica* (*vv.* 141–2) of Horace, V. N. § 25⁹⁰⁻³ [*Ars Poëtica*] ; Homer's definition of the duties of the head of a household (*Odyssey* ix. 114) is quoted (from Aristotle, *Polit.* i. 2), Mon. i. 5³⁴⁻⁶ [*Politica*]; a passage from Homer (*Iliad* ii. 204) is quoted as Aristotle's, it being introduced by the latter in the *Metaphysics* (xii. 10), but without a reference to Homer, Mon. i. 10²⁹⁻³¹ [*Metaphysica*].

Omicide, Murderers; placed, together with Tyrants and Robbers, among the Violent in Round 1 of Circle VII of Hell, Inf. xi. 37 ; xii. 103–39 ; their punishment is to be immersed up to their necks in Phlegethon, the boiling river of blood, Inf. xii. 116–17 (the Tyrants being immersed up to their eye-brows, *vv.* 103–5 ; and the Robbers up to their waists, *vv.* 121–2) [**Violenti**]. *Examples* : Guy de Montfort, who murdered his cousin, Prince Henry [**Guido di Monforte**]; and Pyrrhus, either the son of Achilles, or the King of Epirus [**Pirro**].

Onesti, Pietro degli. [**Pietro degli Onesti.**]

Onesto Bolognese. [**Honestus.**]

Onorio, Honorius III (Cencio Savelli), native of Rome, created Cardinal by Celestine III in 1193 ; elected Pope in succession to Innocent III at Perugia, July 18, 1216 ; died at Rome, March 18, 122⁶⁄₇. In 1223 he solemnly confirmed the Order of St. Francis, which had previously been sanctioned by Innocent III in 1214.

Honorius is mentioned by St. Thomas Aquinas (in his narrative of the life of St. Francis, in the Heaven of the Sun) in connexion with his confirmation of the Franciscan Order, Par. xi. 98 [**Francesco** ²].

Operanti, Spiriti. [**Spiriti Operanti.**]

Orazii. [**Horatii.**]

Orazio, poet Horace (Quintus Horatius Flaccus), born B.C. 65, died B.C. 8; his works consist of four books of Odes, one book of Epodes, two books of Satires, two of Epistles, and the 'Carmen Seculare' and 'Ars Poëtica'.

D. places Horace, together with Homer, Ovid, and Lucan, in Limbo, *Orazio satiro* (i. e. the moralist), Inf. iv. 89; these four poets, with Virgil, make up 'la bella scuola Di

quei signor dell' altissimo canto'
(*vv.* 94–5) [**Limbo**]; he is men-
tioned, in connexion with the 'Ars
Poëtica', *Orazio*, V. N. § 25⁹⁰;
Conv. ii. 14⁸⁷; *magister noster
Horatius*, V. E. ii. 4³³⁻⁴; *Horatius*,
Epist. x. 10²¹²; and coupled with
Seneca and Juvenal as having in-
veighed against riches, Conv. iv.
12⁸²⁻⁴; he is alluded to by G. del
Virgilio (with reference to Inf. iv.
88–90, 101–2), Carm. 17; and as
Flaccus, his horror of a bore, Carm.
13.

D. shows little or no acquaintance
with any of the works of Horace,
except the 'Ars Poëtica', which is
referred to four or five times [**Ars
Poëtica**]. One or two reminiscences
of the Epistles have been traced, and
a few vague resemblances to passages
in the Odes, which are probably
accidental.

Orbis, De Substantia. [**Substantia Orbis, De.**]

[**Orcus**], name of Pluto, god of
the nether world; hence hell,
Carm. 4.

Ordelaffi], family alluded to by
D. in conversation with Guido da
Montefeltro (in Bolgia 8 of Circle
VIII of Hell) as being (in the year
1300) rulers of Forlì, which he
says was under the dominion of
'the green claws', *le branche verdi*,
Inf. xxvii. 43–5 [**Forlì**]; the member of the family who was ruler
at the time was Scarpetta degli
Ordelaffi, who bore on his escutcheon
on a field or a lion rampant vert;
there is a tradition that D. acted for
a time during his exile as secretary
to Scarpetta, one of the most powerful members of the house, who was

in command of the combined Ghibelline and Bianchi forces against
Florence in 1302.

Oreste, Orestes, son of Agamemnon and Clytaemnestra; when his
father was murdered by Clytaemnestra and Aegisthus he was saved from
a similar fate by his sister Electra,
who had him secretly conveyed to
the court of the Phocian king Strophius, who had married the sister of
Agamemnon. Here Orestes formed
a close friendship with Pylades, the
king's son, with whom subsequently
he repaired in secret to Argos and
avenged his father's murder by
slaying both Clytaemnestra and
Aegisthus. Being pursued by the
Furies in consequence of this deed,
and seized with madness, he was
told by Apollo that he could only
recover after fetching the statue of
Artemis from the Tauric Chersonese.
On his arrival in that country he
was in danger of being slain by the
inhabitants, but Pylades, who had
accompanied him, in order to save
his friend's life, pretended that he
was Orestes; the latter, however,
would not allow Pylades to risk his
life for him, and persisted in declaring
who he was; ultimately they were
both saved through the instrumentality
of Iphigenia, the sister of Orestes,
who was priestess of Artemis.

The love of Pylades and Orestes
is introduced as an example to the
Envious in Circle II of Purgatory,
where a voice is heard proclaiming,
Io sono Oreste (representing probably
the assertion of Pylades that he was
Orestes, and the counter-assertion
of the latter as to his own identity,
the incident being taken perhaps from

Cicero's *De Amicitia*, § 7), Purg. xiii. 32 [**Invidiosi : Pilade**].

Orfeo, Orpheus, mythical Greek poet, who, according to the legend, played so divinely on the lyre given him by Apollo that he charmed not only wild beasts, but even the trees and rocks upon Olympus, so that they moved from their places and followed him.

D. mentions Orpheus, together with Linus, Cicero, and Seneca, among those whom he saw in Limbo, Inf. iv. 140 [**Limbo : Lino**[2]]; and refers to Ovid's account (*Metam.* xi. 1 ff.) of the magic influence of his music, Conv. ii. 1[25–7].

Orgogliosi, Marchese degli. [**Marchese**[4].]

Oria, Branca d'. [**Branca d'Oria.**]

Oriago, village in Venetia, between Padua and Venice, about nine miles from the latter, close to the lagoons ; mentioned by Jacopo del Cassero (in Ante-purgatory) as the place where he was overtaken by the assassins sent in pursuit of him by Azzo of Este, Purg. v. 80. [**Cassero, Jacopo del.**]

Oriente, the East, Purg. i. 20 ; viii. 11 ; ix. 2 ; xix. 5 ; xxvii. 94 ; Par. xi. 54 (where D. makes a play upon the word Assisi) [**Ascesi**] ; of the movement of the Heavens from E. to W., Conv. ii. 3[39–45], 6[145–7] ; of the dual movement of the Heaven of the Fixed Stars, viz. the diurnal one from E. to W., and the almost insensible one of one degree in 100 years from W. to E., Conv. ii. 6[141–7], 15[12–13] [**Cielo Stellato**] ; of the oblique movement of the Heaven of the Sun from W.

to E., Conv. iii. 5[126–30] [**Sole, Cielo del**] ; *Oriens*, of the E. limits of the *langue d'*oïl, V. E. i. 8[59] [**Lingua Oil**] ; the quarter where the Sun rises, *Levante*, Inf. xvi. 95 ; Purg. iv. 53 ; xxix. 12 ; Son. lii.* 11 ; referred to (according to some, but the reference is more probably to the Heaven of Mercury) as *quella parte, ove il mondo è più vivo*, Par. v. 87.

Oringa, Guglielmo di. [**Guglielmo**[1].]

Orlando, Roland, nephew of Charlemagne, one of the twelve peers (historically, the prefect of the Marches of Brittany), who, according to the poetical account, was slain at Roncesvalles by the Saracens in league with the traitor Ganelon. [**Ganellone : Roncisvalle.**]

D. mentions him in connexion with his famous horn, on which (according to the *Historia Karoli Magni* attributed to Archbishop Turpin, which, with the O. F. *Chanson de Roland*, was doubtless D.'s authority for the incident) during his last fight he blew a blast loud enough to be heard by Charlemagne eight miles away, and which D. compares to the horn sounded in Hell by the giant Nimrod, Inf. xxxi. 18 [**Nembrotto**] ; Roland is placed, together with Charlemagne, among the spirits of those who fought for the faith (*Spiriti Militanti*), in the Heaven of Mars, Par. xviii. 43 [**Marte, Cielo di**].

Ormanni, ancient noble family of Florence, mentioned by Cacciaguida (in the Heaven of Mars) as having been already in their decline in his time, Par. xvi. 89. They lived on the site of the Palazzo del

Popolo, and in D.'s day were represented by the Foraboschi (Vill. iv.
13).

Orosio, Paolo, Paulus Orosius,
the historian, born in Spain towards
the end of Cent. iv; he visited St.
Augustine at Hippo in 413 or 414,
and, after staying for a time in
Africa as his disciple, was sent by
him in 415 to St. Jerome in Palestine;
the date and place of his death are
unknown. His best known work
is the *Historiae adversum Paganos*
(in seven books), written at the suggestion of St. Augustine (to whose
De Civitate Dei it was intended to
be subsidiary) to prove by the evidence of history that the condition
of the world had not grown worse
since the introduction of Christianity,
as the pagans asserted.

Orosius, to whom D. was largely
indebted, not only for his geography
and ancient history, but also for many of
his favourite theories and arguments as
to the divine institution of the Roman
Empire, is mentioned by name, *Paolo
Orosio*, Conv. iii. 11²⁷; *Paulus Orosius*, V. E. ii. 6⁸⁴; *Orosius*, Mon. ii.
3⁸⁷, 9²⁶, ³⁸, 11³⁷; A. T. § 19⁴³;
he is included among the great
doctors of the Church (*Spiriti Sapienti*) who are placed in the Heaven
of the Sun, being referred to as
'Quell' avvocato dei tempi cristiani,
di cui latino Augustin si provvide'
(in allusion to his *Historiae*, in which
the phrase 'Christiana tempora'
occurs repeatedly), Par. x. 119–20
[Sole, Cielo del]; he is coupled
with Frontinus, Pliny, and Livy, as
a 'master of lofty prose', V. E. ii.
6⁸²⁻⁴; his authority is quoted for
the computation of the period between

the reign of Numa Pompilius and
the birth of Christ at about 650
years, Conv. iii. 11²²⁻⁸ (ref. to *Hist.*
iv. 12, § 9); his statement that Mt.
Atlas is in Africa, Mon. ii. 3⁸⁵⁻⁹¹
(*Hist.* i. 2, § 11); his account of
the reigns of Ninus and Semiramis
in Assyria, Mon. ii. 9²²⁻⁹ (*Hist.* i.
4, §§ 1–8; ii. 3, § 1); and of the
conquests of Vesoges, King of Egypt,
and of his repulse by the Scythians,
Mon. ii. 9³⁵⁻⁴² (*Hist.* i. 14, §§ 1–4);
Livy's account of the combat between
the Roman Horatii and the Alban
Curiatii, confirmed by that of Orosius,
Mon. ii. 11³⁶⁻⁸ (*Hist.* ii. 4, § 9);
O.'s description of the boundaries of
the habitable world, A. T. § 19³⁸⁻⁴³
(*Hist.* i. 2, §§ 7, 13).

Besides the passages in which D.
expressly names Orosius as his
authority, there are many others in
which he was indebted to him, in
several of which, however, he quotes
Livy as his authority [Livio].
O. was the chief source of D.'s
information about the following :—
Ninus and Semiramis, Inf. v. 54–60
(*Hist.* i. 4, § 4; ii. 3, § 1) [Nino¹:
Semiramis]; Alexander the Great,
Inf. xii. 107 (*Hist.* iii. 7, § 5; 18,
§ 10; 20, §§ 4, 5 ff.; 23, § 6)
[Alessandro²]; Cyrus and Tomyris, Purg. xii. 55–7; Mon. ii. 9
(*Hist.* ii. 6, § 12; 7, § 6) [Ciro:
Tamiri]; the persecution of the
Christians by Domitian, Purg. xxii.
83–4 (*Hist.* vii. 10, § 1) [Domi-
ziano]; the victories of Julius
Caesar in the civil war, Par. vi.
61–72 (*Hist.* vi. 15, §§ 2, 3, 6, 18,
22, 25, 28, 29; 16, §§ 3, 6, 7)
[Aquila¹: Cesare¹]; Sardana-
palus, Par. xv. 107–8 (*Hist.* i. 19,

§ 1) [Sardanapalo]; the defeat of the Romans at Cannae and the production of the heap of gold rings (taken from the bodies of the slain) by Hannibal's envoy in the senate-house at Carthage, Conv. iv. 5[164-8]; Inf. xxviii. 10–11 (*Hist.* iv. 16, §§ 5, 6) [Annibale: Canne: Scipione [1]].

D. was also evidently indebted to Orosius for his theories and arguments as to Titus, who destroyed Jerusalem, being the avenger of the crucifixion of Christ by the Jews, Purg. xxi. 82–4; Par. vi. 92–3 (*Hist.* vii. 3, § 8; 9, § 9) [Tito]; the universal peace under Augustus at the time of the birth of Christ, Par. vi. 80–1; Conv. iv. 5[60-7]; Mon. i. 16[10-19] (*Hist.* i. 1, § 6; iii. 8, §§ 3, 5, 7, 8; &c.) [Augusto[1]: Jano]; Christ's assertion of His human nature by being included in the census under Augustus, whereby He became a Roman citizen, Mon. ii. 9[99-105], 12[41-7]; Epist. vii. 3[64-72]; viii. 2[22-4] (*Hist.* vi. 22, §§ 6, 7, 8; vii. 3, § 4) [Augusto[1]: Cristo].

Orsa, 'She-Bear', term employed by D. of the constellations of the Great and Little Bear; he speaks of the two together (to indicate the Pole of the N. hemisphere) as *l' Orse*, Purg. iv. 65; Par. ii. 9. [Boote: Carro, Il[1]: Corno: Elice.]

Orsini], illustrious family of Rome, to which Pope Nicholas III (Inf. xix. 31–105) and the Cardinal Napoleone degli Orsini (Epist. viii. 10[159]) belonged; Nicholas (in Bolgia 3 of Circle VIII of Hell), in conversation with D., speaks of himself,

in allusion to his family name, as *figliuol dell' orsa*, Inf. xix. 70, and of his family as *gli orsatti*, *v.* 71. [Niccolò [2].]

Orsini, Napoleone], Napoleone degli Orsini del Monte, member of the illustrious Roman house of that name; created cardinal by Nicholas IV in 1288; died in 1342. On the death of Benedict XI, Napoleone took an active part in securing the election of the French Pope, Clement V. After the death of Clement in 1314, D. wrote a letter to the Italian Cardinals urging them to elect an Italian Pope in succession to the Gascon Clement, and he addressed himself in particular to Napoleone ('tu prae omnibus, Urse') reproaching him with his share in Clement's election, and with his lukewarmness in the matter of the restoration of his colleagues, the Colonna cardinals, Jacopo and Pietro, who had been deprived by Boniface VIII, Epist. viii. 10 [Bonifacio[1]: Colonnesi]. In the event, in spite of the efforts of the Italian cardinals, and of Napoleone in particular, another French Pope was chosen in the person of Jacques d'Euse, who took the title of John XXII [Giovanni XXII].

Orso, Cont', Orso degli Alberti della Cerbaia, son of Count Napoleone degli Alberti (Inf. xxxii. 55), and grandson of Count Alberto da Mangona (Inf. xxxii. 57); he was captain (in 1276) of the Lambertazzi after their exile from Bologna, and was killed in 1286 by his cousin Alberto, son of Count Alessandro degli Alberti (Inf. xxxii. 55); D. places him in Ante-purgatory among those who put off their repentance, Purg. vi. 19. [**Antipurgatorio.**] The murder of Count Orso (Purg. vi. 19–21) by his cousin Alberto was doubtless a continuance of the blood-feud which had existed between the fathers of the two cousins, Napoleone and Alessandro, who killed each other (Inf. xxxii. 55). [**Alberto** [3].]

Ortensio, Quintus Hortensius Hortalus, the orator, B.C. 114–50; mentioned in connexion with Marcia, the wife of Cato of Utica, who ceded her to Hortensius and, after his death, at her own request took her back as his wife, Conv. iv. 28[110–15]. [**Marzia.**]

Orvieto. [**Urbs Vetus.**]

Osteric, -icch, -icchi. [**Austericch.**]

Ostiense, belonging to Ostia, town in Latium, an episcopal see, about twenty miles SW. of Rome, and about four from the mouth of the Tiber; of Henry of Susa, the famous Decretalist, Cardinal-Bishop of Ostia (1261), Par. xii. 83; *Ostiensis*, Epist. viii. 7[118] [**Susa, Enrico di**]; of Niccolò da Prato, Cardinal-Bishop of Ostia (1303), Epist. i. *tit.* [**Nicholaus**].

Ostiensis. [**Ostiense.**]

Ottachero, Premysl Ottocar II, King of Bohemia, 1253–1278; he refused to recognize Rudolf as Emperor, and the latter in consequence made war upon him, and defeated him near Vienna, Ottocar being slain in the battle, Aug. 1278; he was succeeded by his son Wenceslas IV [**Buemme: Ridolfo** [1] : **Table C**].

D. places O. among the Negligent Princes in the valley of flowers in Ante-purgatory, where he is pointed out by Sordello, seated amicably in company with his former foe the Emperor Rudolf, Purg. vii. 97–100 [**Antipurgatorio**]; Sordello compares him with his son, Wenceslas, to the disparagement of the latter, saying that O. in his swaddling-clothes was better than W. when he was a bearded man (*vv.* 100–2) [**Vincislao.**]

Ottaviano. [**Augusto** [2].]

Ottaviano degli Ubaldini. [**Cardinale, Il.**]

Ottavo Cielo. [**Cielo Stellato.**]

Otto, Otto I, Duke of Saxony and King of Germany, 936; Emperor of the West, 962–973.

D. refers to his deposition of Benedict V, and restoration of Leo VIII, Mon. iii. 11[16–21]. [**Benedetto** [3] : **Leo.**]

Ottobre, month of October; the government of Florence so unstable that laws framed in October did not last till the middle of the next month, Purg. vi. 142–4; the month of October corresponds with the first month according to the Syrian reckoning, hence the month of June would, according to the Syrian usage, be the ninth, V. N. § 30[6] [**Tisrin primo**]; the name pronounced *Ochiover* in the Milanese dialect, V. E. i. 11[35].

Ovidio, poet Ovid (Publius Ovidius Naso), born B.C. 43, died A.D. 18; of his extant works the chief are the *Amores*, the *Heroides* and *Epistolae*, the *Ars Amatoria*, the *Remedia Amoris*, the *Metamorphoses*, the *Tristia*, the *Epistolae ex Ponto*, and the *Fasti*.

D. places Ovid, together with Homer, Horace, and Lucan, in Limbo, Inf. iv. 90 ; these four poets, with Virgil, made up ' la bella scuola Di quei signor dell' altissimo canto ' (*vv.* 94–5) [Limbo]; he is mentioned, as *Ovidio*, in connexion with his account of Arethusa (*Metam.* v. 572 ff.) and Cadmus (*Metam.* iv. 570 ff.), Inf. xxv. 97 [Aretusa: Cadmo]; as the author of the *Remedia Amoris*, V. N. § 25⁹⁴⁻⁷ ; in connexion with his account of Orpheus (*Metam.* xi. 1 ff.), Conv. ii. 1²⁵ [Orfeo] ; of Cupid and Venus (*Metam.* v. 365), Conv. ii. 6¹²³ [Cupido : Venere¹] ; of Prometheus, son of Iapetus (*Metam.* i. 78–83), Conv. iv. 15⁷² [Giapeto: Prometeo] ; of the Horses of the Sun (*Metam.* ii. 153 ff.), Conv. iv. 23¹³⁸ [Eoo] ; of Aeacus and Cephalus (*Metam.* vii. 474 ff.), Conv. iv. 27¹⁵⁶ [Cefalo : Eaco] ; as *Ovidius*, in connexion with his account of the Pierides (*Metam.* v. 298 ff.), V. E. i. 2⁵³ [Pierides²] ; as one of the ' regulati poetae ' (as far as the *Metamorphoses* are concerned), together with Virgil, Statius, and Lucan, V. E. ii. 6⁷⁹⁻⁸¹ ; in connexion with his account of Hercules and Antaeus (*Metam.* ix. 183), and of Atalanta and Hippomenes (*Metam.* x. 560 ff.), Mon. ii. 8⁸² [Anteo : Atalanta] ; of Ninus and Semiramis (*Metam.* iv. 58, 88), Mon. ii. 9³⁰ [Nino¹: Semiramis] ; as *Naso*, in connexion with his account of Hyperion (*Metam.* iv. 192, 241),

Epist. iv. 4⁴⁰ [Iperione] ; he is alluded to by G. del Virgilio (with reference to Inf. iv. 88–90, 101–2), Carm. 17.

Of Ovid's works D. quotes only the *Metamorphoses*, with which he was evidently familiar, and which was his chief authority for classical mythology [*Metamorphoseos*]; and the *Remedia Amoris* [Remedia Amoris] ; but he was probably also indebted to the *Heroides* and *Ars Amatoria* for details about various classical personages.

Ovidio Maggiore. [*Metamorphoseos.*]

Ovidius. [Ovidio.]

Oza, Uzzah, son of Abinadab, in whose house at Kirjath-jearim the ark rested for twenty years. Uzzah accompanied the ark when David undertook its removal to Jerusalem; on the way the oxen of the cart in which it was being borne stumbled, and Uzzah laid his hand upon it to prevent it from falling, whereupon for his presumption and profanation he was struck dead (2 *Sam.* vi. 3–7 ; 1 *Chron.* xiii. 6–10).

D. in his letter to the Italian Cardinals deprecates the comparison of himself with Uzzah, for his interference in the affairs of the Church, on the ground that the latter laid his hand upon the ark itself, while he only desires to admonish the oxen who are straying from the right path, Epist. viii. 5 ; Uzzah's presumption is referred to, Purg. x. 57.

P

P, first letter of the word *peccato*, 'sin'; at the entrance into Purgatory the guardian Angel inscribes upon D.'s brow with the point of his sword seven P's (Purg. ix. 112; xii. 121; *piaghe*, ix. 114; xv. 80; xxv. 139; *colpo*, xxii. 3) and bids him cleanse them away when he is within, Purg. ix. 112–14.

These seven P's are the symbols of the seven deadly sins, viz. Pride, Envy, Anger, Sloth, Avarice, Gluttony, and Lust, and are removed one by one as D. passes through the Circles where the traces of these sins are purged away. The first six are removed by the passage over D.'s face of the wings of the several Angels who are present in the several Circles; that of Pride is removed by the Angel of Humility (Purg. xii. 98), and at the same time all the others are lightened (*vv.* 118–26); that of Envy is removed by the Angel of Charity (Purg. xv. 34–9, 80); that of Anger is removed by the Angel of Peace (Purg. xvii. 67–9); that of Sloth is removed by the Angel of the Love of God (Purg. xix. 49–51); that of Avarice is removed by the Angel of Justice (Purg. xxii. 2–6); that of Gluttony is removed by the Angel of Abstinence (Purg. xxiv. 148–54); the seventh and last P (that of Lust) is only removed by D.'s passing through the fire (Purg. xxv. 139), as he learns from the Angel of Purity (Purg. xxvii. 6–11). [**Purgatorio.**]

Pachino, Pachynus, now Cape Passaro, promontory at the SE. extremity of Sicily; mentioned by Charles Martel (in the Heaven of Venus) together with Pelorus, the NE. extremity, to indicate the extent of the E. coast of Sicily, Par. viii. 68 (cf. Ovid, *Metam.* v. 350–1) [**Peloro**]; *Pachynus*, Ecl. ii. 59.

Pachynus. [**Pachino.**]

Pactolis, belonging to Pactolus, river of Lydia, which rises on Mt. Tmolus, and flows past Sardis into the Hermus; its golden sands, according to the story, were the consequence of King Midas bathing in the stream, at the bidding of Bacchus, in order to rid himself of his fatal gift of turning everything he touched into gold.

Midas is referred to in allusion to this incident, Ecl. ii. 53. [**Mida.**]

Pado. [**Po.**]

Padova, Padua, city of N. Italy, on the Bacchiglione (which joins the Brenta a few miles below), about 25 miles W. of Venice and 18 SE. of Vicenza. It claims to be the oldest city in Italy, and to have been founded by the Trojan Antenor [**Antenori**]. In 1237 Ezzelino da Romano, with the help of Frederick II and the Ghibellines, obtained possession of the city, but on the proclamation of the crusade against him by Pope Alexander IV in 1255 he was expelled by the Paduan Guelfs and the Venetians [**Azzolino**[1]]. After the death of Ezzelino in 1259 the Guelfs of Padua asserted their independence and conquered Vicenza (1265), whence, however, they were driven out in 1314 by the Vicentines under Can Grande della Scala, who was at that time Imperial Vicar in Vicenza.

Padua is mentioned by Cunizza (in the Heaven of Venus), who, prophesying the defeat of the Paduans by Can Grande in 1314, says (according to one interpretation) that ere long they will stain with their blood the swamp formed by the waters of the Bacchiglione, *tosto fia che Padova al palude Cangerà l'acqua che Vicenza bagna*, Par. ix. 46-7 [**Bacchiglione**].

Padovani, inhabitants of Padua, Inf. xv. 7; *Paduani*, V. E. i. 9³⁵, 14²⁸; referred to by Jacopo del Cassero (in Ante-purgatory), in allusion to the tradition that Padua was founded by the Trojan Antenor, as *Antenori*, Purg. v. 75 [**Antenori**]; their embankments along the Brenta to prevent its overflowing when in flood, Inf. xv. 7 [**Brenta**]; their speech quite distinct from that of the Pisans, who live on the opposite side of Italy, V. E. i. 9³⁵⁻⁶; their dialect, together with those of the Brescians, Veronese, Vicentines, and Trevisans, condemned as harsh, especially in a woman's mouth, one of its peculiarities being a fondness for consonantal endings in *f*, V. E. i. 14²⁰⁻³⁵; they are referred to by G. del Virgilio as *Phrygii damae*, Carm. 28 [**Phrygius**].

Padovano, Paduan, inhabitant of Padua, Inf. xvii. 70; *Paduanus*, V. E. i. 14⁴³; of a certain usurer of Padua, Inf. xvii. 70 [**Scrovigni**,

Rinaldo degli]; of the Paduan poet, Aldobrandino de' Mezzabati, V. E. i. 14⁴³ [**Ildebrandinus**].

Paduani, -anus. [**Padovani, -ano.**]

Padus. [**Po.**]

Pagani, noble Ghibelline family of Faenza, who at the end of Cent. xiii were lords of Faenza, Forlì, and Imola.

Guido del Duca (in Circle II of Purgatory) mentions them in connexion with the famous Mainardo Pagano da Susinana, and says that after his death (which took place in 1302) they will do well to become extinct, adding ironically that even so they will never clear the stain from their reputation, Purg. xiv. 118-20. [**Mainardo Pagano.**]

Pagano, Mainardo. [**Mainardo Pagano.**]

Palazzo, Currado da. [**Currado da Palazzo.**]

Palermo, capital of Sicily, situated on the Gulf of the same name in NW. of the island; mentioned by Charles Martel (in the Heaven of Venus) in connexion with the 'Sicilian Vespers', Par. viii. 75. [**Carlo³: Vespro Siciliano.**]

Palestina], Palestine; alluded to by the mention of the river Jordan, the reference being to God's punishment of the rebellious Israelites in the desert by depriving them of entering into the promised land (*Numb.* xiv. 26-35), Purg. xviii. 135 [**Jordan**]; referred to as *la terra santa*, in connexion with Rahab and Joshua, Par. ix. 125 [**Josuè: Raab**].

Pallade. [**Minerva.**]

Palladio, the Palladium, ancient image of Pallas Athene at Troy, on the preservation of which the safety of the city depended; it was stolen by Ulysses and Diomed and carried off to Greece (*Aen.* ii. 162–70).

The theft of the Palladium is mentioned as one of the crimes which Ulysses and Diomed are expiating in Hell, Inf. xxvi. 62. [**Diomede.**]

Pallante, Pallas, son of the Arcadian Evander, King of Pallanteum; he was slain by Turnus while fighting for Aeneas. His death led to that of Turnus, who appeared in battle wearing the belt of Pallas, and thus provoked Aeneas to slay him, whereby the latter became possessed of Lavinia and the kingdom of Latium. [**Evander.**]

Pallas is mentioned by the Emperor Justinian (in the Heaven of Mercury), who says that he died to give a kingdom to the Roman Eagle (*Aen.* x. 479 ff.), Par. vi. 36; the combat of Aeneas with Turnus, whom he would have spared but for the belt of Pallas, is mentioned, with a reference to Virgil's account of the incident (*Aen.* xii. 887–952), *Pallas*, Mon. ii. 11$^{8-21}$ [**Enea: Turno**].

Pallas. [**Pallade: Pallante.**]

Palmieri, Palmers, i.e. pilgrims who went overseas to the East and returned with a palm-branch; mentioned by D. in his explanation of the distinction between the several kinds of pilgrims, V. N. § 41$^{34-52}$ [**Peregrini**]; referred to, Purg. xxxiii. 78.

Palude, Il, i.e. the Marsh, at the junction of the Brentella with the Bacchiglione near Padua, Par. ix. 46. [**Bacchiglione.**]

Pannocchieschi, Nello de'. [**Nello.**]

Paolo, St. Paul the Apostle, born at Tarsus in Cilicia probably c. A.D. 3, beheaded at Rome (according to tradition) c. A.D. 68; mentioned, Inf. ii. 32; Par. xviii. 131; Conv. iv. 5^{144}, 13^{81}; *san Paolo*, Conv. iv. 28^{75}; *Polo*, Par. xviii. 136; *Paulus*, Mon. i. 4^{30}, 16^{17}; iii. 1^{22}, 4^{86}, 13$^{42-8}$; Epist. viii. 2^{25}; *Apostolo*, Conv. ii. 6^{7}; iv. 21^{56}, 22^{56}, 24^{172}; *Apostolus*, Mon. ii. 11^{68}, 13^{7}, 15; iii. 10^{50}; Epist. x. 27^{516}, 28^{539}; A. T. § 22^{15}; spoken of as *Vas d'elezione*, Inf. ii. 28; *gran Vasello dello Spirito Santo*, Par. xxi. 127; *il caro frate* of St. Peter, Par. xxiv. 62; *gentium praedicator*, Epist. viii. 2^{25}.

D. refers to the account given by St. Paul of his being 'caught up to the third heaven', Inf. ii. 28; Par. xxviii. 139 (ref. to 2 *Cor.* xii. 2–4); his calling to be 'a chosen vessel' and the Apostle to the Gentiles, Inf. ii. 28; Par xxi. 127; Epist. viii. 2^{25} (ref. to *Acts* ix. 15); his martyrdom for the Church of Christ, Par. xviii. 131; Epist. viii. 2$^{25-7}$; his teaching and example abandoned by the Church in its greed for wealth, Par. xviii. 133–6; St. Peter's reference to him as his beloved brother, Par. xxiv. 62 (ref. to 2 *Pet.* iii. 15); his supposed initiation of Dionysius the Areopagite into the mysteries of the celestial hierarchies, Par. xxviii. 138 [**Dionisio** ^{2}]; St. Jerome's mention of him in his Preface to the Bible, Conv. iv. 5^{144} [**Jeronimo**]; his brotherly salutation of peace, Mon. i. 4^{30} (ref. to *Rom.* i. 7; 1 *Cor.* i. 3; 2 *Cor.* i. 2; *Gal.* i. 3; *Ephes.* i. 2; *Coloss.* i. 2; &c.); his writings inspired by the Holy Spirit, of which he was the mouthpiece, Mon. iii.

4^{86}; his appeal to Caesar, Mon. iii. 13$^{42-59}$ (ref. to *Acts* xxv. 10; xxvii. 24; xxviii. 19).

D. quotes St. Paul some thirty times, either from his Epistles, or from his sayings as recorded in the Acts of the Apostles, viz. Conv. ii. 6$^{6-7}$ (*Heb.* i. 1); Conv. iv. 13$^{81-2}$ (*Rom.* xii. 3); Conv. iv. 21$^{56-8}$ (*Rom.* xi. 33); Conv. iv. 22$^{56-8}$ (1 *Cor.* ix. 24); Conv. iv. 24$^{172-4}$ (*Coloss.* iii. 20); Conv. iv. 28$^{75-81}$ (*Rom.* ii. 28-9); Mon. i. 16$^{17-18}$ (*Gal.* iv. 4); Mon. ii. 11$^{68-70}$ (2 *Tim.* iv. 8); Mon. ii. 13$^{7-11}$ (*Rom.* v. 12); Mon. ii. 13$^{15-25}$ (*Ephes.* i. 5-8); Mon. iii. 1^{22} (1 *Thess.* v. 8); Mon. iii. 10$^{50-3}$ (1 *Cor.* iii. 11); Mon. iii. 13$^{42-53}$ (*Acts* xxv. 10; xxvii. 24; xxviii. 19); Mon. iii. 13$^{56-7}$ (*Phil.* i. 23); Epist. x. 27$^{516-18}$ (*Ephes.* iv. 10); Epist. x. 28$^{539-44}$ (2 *Cor.* xii. 3-4); A. T. § 22$^{15-18}$ (*Rom.* xi. 33); also (without mention of St. Paul), Par. xxiv. 64-5 (*Heb.* xi. 1); Mon. ii. 2$^{72-3}$ (*Rom.* i. 20); Mon. ii. 8$^{36-7}$ (*Heb.* xi. 6); Mon. ii. 9$^{75-6}$ (*Rom.* xi. 33); Mon. iii. 1$^{26-7}$ (*Coloss.* i. 13-14); Epist. v. 4$^{64-5}$ (*Rom.* xiii. 2); Epist. v. 8$^{120-2}$ (*Rom.* i. 20); Epist. v. 10$^{160-2}$ (*Ephes.* iv. 17); Epist. vi. 5^{154} (*Rom.* vii. 23); Epist. viii. 5$^{74-5}$ (1 *Cor.* xv. 10).

The Pauline Epistles are supposed to be symbolized by the elder with a sword in the mystical Procession in the Terrestrial Paradise, Purg. xxix. 134, 139-41, 145-8.

Paolo Malatesta. [Malatesta, Paolo.]

Paolo Orosio. [Orosio, Paolo.]

Papa, the Pope, Inf. vii. 47; xi. 8; Par. ix. 126, 136; Mon. iii. 11^2, ^{19}, 12$^{12-101}$; *Antistes*, Epist. viii. 10^{167}; *Ecclesiae universalis Antistes*, Mon. iii. 6^{11}; *summus Antistes*, Mon. iii. 12^9; *Archimandrita*, Epist. viii. 6^{95}; *Claviger Regni Coelorum*, Mon. iii. 1$^{43-4}$ (cf. Inf. xix. 92, 101; xxvii. 104; Purg. ix. 117, 121; Par. xxiii. 139; xxiv. 35; xxvii. 49; xxxii. 125; Mon. iii. 8$^{56-8}$); *Culmen apostolicum*, Epist. viii. 10^{164}; *Marito (della Chiesa)*, Inf. xix. 111 (cf. Purg. xxiv. 22); *Nauclerus naviculae Petri*, Epist. vi. 1$^{12-13}$; *Ostiarius Regni Coelorum*, Mon. iii. 8$^{57-8}$; *Pastore*, Inf. xix. 83; Purg. xvi. 98; Par. xx. 57; *Pastor*, Mon. iii. 3^{131}; *Pastore della Chiesa*, Par. v. 77; *sommo Pastore*, Par. vi. 17; *Romano Pastore*, Purg. xix. 107; Conv. iv. 29^{23}; *Patre*, Inf. xix. 117; *Pater patrum*, Epist. vii. 7^{164}; *Petrus*, Mon. ii. 9^9; iii. 16^{135}; Epist. v. 5^{91}; *Pontifex Romanus*, Mon. iii. 1^{36}, 13^4, 16^{131}; *summus Pontifex*, Mon. iii. 3^{36}, 4^{152}, 7^{13}, 10^3, 16^4; Epist. vii. 7^{164}; *Prefetto nel foro divino*, Par. xxx. 142; *gran Prete*, Inf. xxvii. 70; *Servo de' servi*, Inf. xv. 112; *Successor del maggior Piero*, Inf. ii. 24; *Successor Petri*, Purg. xix. 99; Mon. iii. 1^{42}, 3^{37}, 6^{42}, 7^{28}, 8^9, ^{18}, ^{67}, 9^8; Epist. v. 10^{167}; *Vestito del gran manto*, Inf. xix. 69 (cf. Inf. ii. 27); *Vicario di Cristo*, Purg. xx. 87; Par. xxv. 15; *Christi Vicarius*, Mon. iii. 7^6; *Domini Nostri Jesu Vicarius*, Mon. iii. 3$^{36-7}$; *Dei Vicarius*, Mon. i. 2$^{14-15}$; iii. 1^{42}, 6^{10}, ^{39}, ^{42}, 7^{14}, ^{22}, 10^{128}; *Vicario di Pietro*, Purg. xxi. 54.

Pape Satan . . . [**Pluto.**]

Papi, Popes; the following are mentioned or alluded to by D. [**Table R**]:—Linus [**Lino** [1]]; Cletus or Anacletus [**Cleto**]; Sixtus I; [**Sisto**]; Pius I [**Pio**]; Calixtus I [**Calisto**]; Urban I [**Urbano** [1]]; Sylvester I [**Silvestro**]; Anastasius II [**Anastasio**]; Agapetus I [**Agabito**]; Gregory I [**Gregorio**]; Adrian I [**Adrianus**]; Leo VIII [**Leo**]; Benedict V [**Benedetto** [3]]; Innocent III [**Innocenzio** [1]]; Honorius III [**Onorio**]; Innocent IV [**Innocenzio** [2]]; Alexander IV [**Alessandro IV**]; Urban IV [**Urbano** [2]]; Clement IV [**Clemente** [1]]; Adrian V [**Adriano** [2]]; John XXI [**Ispano, Pietro**]; Nicholas III [**Niccolò** [2]]; Martin IV [**Martino** [2]]; Celestine V [**Celestino**]; Boniface VIII [**Bonifazio** [1]]; Benedict XI [**Benedetto** [2]]; Clement V [**Clemente** [2]]; John XXII [**Giovanni XXII**].

Papia. [**Pavia.**]

Papienses, inhabitants of Pavia; if the Pavians of former times could hold converse with their descendants in Pavia they would find them speaking quite a different tongue, V. E. i. 9[67–70]. [**Pavia.**]

Paradiso [1], Paradise, heaven, the abode of the blessed, Purg. i. 99; Par. iii. 89; x. 105; xiv. 38; xv. 36; xviii. 21; xxi. 59; xxiii. 61; xxvii. 2; xxx. 44; xxxi. 52; Canz. vii. 56; Conv. iii. 8[37, 45], 15[11, 20]; *Paradisus*, Mon. iii. 16[51]; Epist. x. 19[337], 24[440], 26[509], 27[523], 28[525, 543]; alluded to as *basilica* (*celeste*), Par. xxv. 30; *chiostro* (*celeste*), Purg. xv. 57; *chiostro nel quale è Cristo abate del*

collegio, Purg. xxvi. 128–9; *beato chiostro*, Par. xxv. 127; *beato concilio*, Purg. xxi. 16; *corte* (*celeste*), Purg. xvi. 41; xxxi. 41; Par. xxi. 74; xxv. 43; xxvi. 16; *corte del ciel*, Inf. ii. 125; Par. x. 70; *beata corte*, Par. xxxii. 98; *corte santa*, Par. xxiv. 112; *verace corte*, Purg. xxi. 17; *giardino* (*celeste*), Par. xxxi. 97; xxxii. 39; *bel giardino*, Par. xxiii. 71; *orto dell' ortolano eterno*, Par. xxvi. 64; *imperio giustissimo e pio*, Par. xxxii. 117; *imperium coeleste*, V. E. i. 7[34]; *mondo felice*, Par. xxv. 139; *mondo pulcro*, Inf. vii. 58; *secol* (*celeste*), Son. xvii. 36; *grande secol*, V. N. § 3[12]; *eterno palazzo*, Par. xxi. 8; *miro ed angelico templo*, Par. xxviii. 53; *regia sempiterna*, Epist. ii. 2[34]; *reame* (*celeste*), Par. xix. 28; xxxii. 52; *reame ove gli angeli hanno pace*, Canz. iv. 56; *region degli angeli*, Par. xx. 102; *dia region*, Par. xxvi. 11; *regno* (*celeste*), Purg. xi. 7; xxxii. 22; Par. iii. 83; viii. 97; xix. 103; xxiv. 43; xxxi. 117; xxxii. 61; *regnum coeleste*, Epist. x. 19[339, 345], 30[583]; *alto regno*, Canz. ii. 209; *beato regno*, Par. i. 23; *regno de' beati*, Conv. ii. 8[41]; *deiforme regno*, Par. ii. 20; *eterno regno*, Purg. xxii. 78; *regno santo*, Par. i. 10; *sicuro e gaudioso regno*, Par. xxxi. 25; *regno verace*, Par. xxx. 98; *Atene celestiale*, Conv. iii. 14[138]; *Jerusalemme* (*celeste*), Par. xxv. 56; *superna Jerusalem*, Epist. ii. 2[35]; *Roma onde Cristo è Romano*, Purg. xxxii. 102; *eterno dì*, Purg. xxx. 103; *esser giocondo*, Par. xxxi. 112; *primavera sempiterna*, Par. xxviii. 116; *dolce vita*, Par. xx. 48; *viver lieto*, Par. xxvii. 43.

According to D.'s conception, which is based upon the Ptolemaic system, the Universe consists of nine spheres or Heavens concentric with the Earth, round which they revolve, it being fixed at the centre (Conv. iii. 5^{57-8}; A. T. § 3^{6-7}). The Earth is surrounded by the spheres of air and fire, the latter being in immediate contact with that of the Moon (Purg. xviii. 28; Par. i. 115; Conv. iii. 3^{11-13}), which is the lowest of the nine Heavens [**Luna, Cielo della**]. Beyond the Heaven of the Moon come in order those of Mercury [**Mercurio, Cielo di**], Venus [**Venere, Cielo di**], the Sun [**Sole, Cielo del**], Mars [**Marte, Cielo di**], Jupiter [**Giove, Cielo di**], Saturn [**Saturno, Cielo di**], the Fixed Stars [**Cielo Stellato**], and last of all that of the *Primum Mobile* or First Movement. Each of these Heavens revolves with a velocity which increases in proportion to its distance from the Earth. Each of the planets revolves in the epicycle of its own Heaven, except the Sun, which revolves round the Earth. The *Primum Mobile* (or Crystalline Heaven) governs the general motion of the Heavens from E. to W., and by it all place and time are ultimately measured (Par. xxvii. 115–20; xxviii. 70–1; Conv. ii. 6^{145-7}, 15^{12-13}) [**Cielo Cristallino**]. Each of the Heavens is presided over by one of the Angelic Orders, and exercises its special influence on earthly affairs (Par. ii. 127–9; Conv. ii. 2^{62-3}, 5^{21-4}, 6^{105-16}; Mon. i. 9^{10-14}).

The three lowest Heavens are allotted to the souls of those whose life on Earth was rendered imperfect through their having yielded to the temptations of the world; the next four are tenanted by those whose actions were wholly directed by virtuous motives. The last two Heavens have no special occupants assigned to them, but serve apparently as common places of meeting, the one to the blessed spirits, the other to Angels. Finally, beyond and outside of all the other Heavens lies the Empyrean, an incorporeal and motionless Heaven, where there is neither time nor place, but light only (Par. xxvii. 106–20; xxx. 39); this is the special abode of the Deity and the resting-place of the Saints (Conv. ii. 4^{28-30}) [**Cielo Empireo**]. The latter, arranged in the form of the petals of a white Rose, gaze upon the beatific vision of the Deity, who is surrounded by the nine orders of the three Angelic Hierarchies [**Gerarchia: Rosa: Universo**].

Each of the first seven spheres or Heavens is representative of, and corresponds to, one of the seven Liberal Arts, the other three corresponding to Natural, Moral, and Divine Science (or Theology) respectively, Conv. ii. 14^{48-64}.

D. states his theory as to the form and order of the Heavens in various passages in the *Convivio* (cf. Conv. ii. 3^{49-56}, 4^{1-44}; iii. 5^{56-67}).

Paradiso [2], Terrestrial Paradise, formerly the Garden of Eden, Par. vii. 38, 87; *Paradisus*, V. E. i. 4^{14}, 5^{32}; *terrestris Paradisus*, Mon. iii. 16^{47}; *delitiarum patria*,

V. E. i. 7¹⁰⁻¹¹; referred to by
Virgil, as the place where his knowledge can no longer avail, *parte Ov'
io per me più oltre non discerno*, Purg.
xxvii. 128-9; by Matilda, as *questo
loco*, Purg. xxviii. 92; *la campagna
santa*, v. 118; *esto loco*, v. 141;
by Beatrice, as *qui*, Purg. xxx. 75;
xxxii. 100; *quassù*, v. 140; by
D., as *il loco Fatto per proprio dell'
umana spece*, Par. i. 56-7; *lo bel
cacume del monte*, Par. xvii. 113;
by Adam, as *l'eccelso giardino*, Par.
xxvi. 110; *il monte che si leva più
dall'onda*, v. 139.

D. represents the Terrestrial
Paradise as situated at the summit
of the Mt. of Purgatory (Purg.
xxvii. 125; xxviii. 101; Par.
xxvi. 110, 139); in it is a dense
forest ('divina foresta spessa e viva',
Purg. xxviii. 2; 'antica selva', v.
23; 'foresta', v. 85; 'selva folta',
v. 108; 'gran foresta', Purg. xxix.
17; 'alta selva', Purg. xxxii. 31;
'selva', v. 158), traversed by a
stream of pure water (Purg. xxviii.
25-30, 35, 47, 62, 70, 85, 121;
xxix. 7, 67, 71; &c.); it abounds
with grass (Purg. xxvii. 134;
xxviii. 27, 61; xxix. 88; xxx.
77), flowers (Purg. xxvii. 134;
xxviii. 36, 41-2, 55-6, 68; xxix.
88; xxx. 28; xxxii. 58, 114),
trees and shrubs (Purg. xxvii. 134;
xxviii. 10; xxix. 35; xxxii. 58-
60, 86-7, 113), all of which spring
up spontaneously (Purg. xxviii. 69,
116-17); sweet odours (Purg.
xxviii. 6) are wafted by a gentle
breeze, which stirs the leaves and
sways the branches of the trees
(*vv*. 7-15), among which birds are
carolling to the accompaniment of

the rustling foliage (*vv*. 16-18);
it is thus a land of eternal spring
and plenty, such as was figured of
the Golden Age by the poets of old
(Purg. xxviii. 139-44).

This place, where Adam remained but for six hours (Par. xxvi.
139-42), and which was lost to
mankind through the sin of Eve
(Purg. xxviii. 94; xxxii. 32; Par.
vii. 37-8, 86-7), is the symbol of
the blessedness of man's life upon
earth (Mon. iii. 16⁴⁵⁻⁷), and was
given to man by God 'for an earnest
to him of eternal peace' (Purg. xxviii.
91-3).

At the threshold of the Terrestrial Paradise Virgil tells D. that
his power to guide him is now at
an end, and that henceforth he must
act according to his own judgement
(Purg. xxvii. 127-42) [**Virgilio**];
they then pass in and meet Matilda, who explains the nature of
the vegetation and climate of the
place, and of the stream which
flows through it (Purg. xxviii. 1-
148), and acts as D.'s guide until the
office is assumed by Beatrice [**Matelda**].

Paradiso ³, third Cantica (consisting of 33 Cantos, comprising
4,758 lines) of the *D. C.*, Epist. x.
3⁷², 10²²², 13²⁵⁸, 17²⁸⁸. [*Commedia.*]

Paradiso Terrestre. [Para-
diso ².]

Paradisus. [Paradiso.]

Paradosso, Di. [*Paradoxa.*]

Paradoxa, *Paradoxes* of Cicero,
quoted by D. as *Di Paradosso*;
Cicero's declamation against wealth
and avarice, translated, Conv. iv.
12⁵⁵⁻⁷⁰ (*Parad.* § 1).

Paralipomenon (Libri), Books of Chronicles, so called in the Vulgate after the Septuagint, in which the title is Παραλειπόμενα, 'things omitted', meaning, as is supposed, that they are supplementary to the Books of Kings; quoted, Mon. ii. 8⁶¹⁻⁴ (2 *Chron.* xx. 12). [*Bibbia.*]

Parcitati,   Montagna   de'. [Montagna.]

Parigi, Paris, capital of France, on the Seine, Purg. xx. 52; *Parisi*, Purg. xi. 81; referred to, in connexion with Siger, by the mention of the Rue du Fouarre, *il vico degli strami*, Par. x. 137 [Sigieri]; in connexion with Philip IV's debasement of the coinage, by the mention of the Seine, Par. xix. 118.

There is a special significance in D.'s mention of Paris in connexion with the art of illuminating (Purg. xi. 80–1) (where the word *alluminare* is used, instead of the usual Italian *miniare*, in order to represent the French term), inasmuch as Paris in his day was the great centre for the production of illuminated MSS. of all kinds.

Paris, Paris of Troy, son of Priam and Hecuba; being appointed umpire to decide as to who was the fairest of the three goddesses, Juno, Minerva, or Venus, he gave his judgment in favour of Venus; she as a reward promised him the most beautiful woman in the world for his wife, and helped him to carry off Helen, the wife of Menelaus, King of Sparta, who, with the other Greek chiefs, sailed against Troy to recover her; hence arose the Trojan war, in which Paris re-ceived a wound from which he ultimately died, and in the course of which he killed the Greek hero Achilles by treachery. [**Achille.**]

D. places Paris, together with Tristan, in Circle II of Hell, among those who met their death through love, Inf. v. 67. [**Lussuriosi.**]

Parisi. [Parigi.]

Parma, town of N. Italy in the Emilia, on the river Parma, a small tributary of the Po, about thirty miles NW. of Modena, formerly a duchy; mentioned in connexion with the soothsayer Asdente, 'the cobbler of Parma', Conv. iv. 16⁶⁹⁻⁷⁰. [**Asdente.**]

Parmenide, Parmenides, Greek philosopher, born at Elea in Italy, c. B.C. 513, founder of the Eleatic school of philosophy; he is mentioned by St. Thomas Aquinas (in the Heaven of the Sun), together with Melissus and Bryson, as examples of bad reasoners, Par. xiii. 125; he and Melissus are coupled together again, as having been condemned by Aristotle (*Phys.* i. 3) for the same reason, *Parmenides*, Mon. iii. 4³⁰⁻³.

Parmenides. [Parmenide.]

Parmenses, inhabitants of Parma; roughness and ugliness of their dialect, in which *molto* is pronounced *monto*, V. E. i. 15²⁵⁻⁷; the Florentines warned not to be encouraged by the good fortune of the people of Parma, who (in 1248), during the siege of their town by Frederick II, made a sally while the Emperor was absent, and captured and destroyed the fortress of Vittoria, which had been erected opposite their walls

for the purposes of the siege, Epist.
vi. 5[127-35] [**Victoria**].

Parnaso, Parnassus, name of a
range of mountains in N. Greece,
more usually restricted to the loftiest
part, a few miles N. of Delphi,
consisting, as was supposed, of two
peaks, whence Parnassus is frequently spoken of by classical authors
as ' double-headed '. It is celebrated
as one of the chief seats of Apollo
and the Muses, and an inspiring
source of poetry and song. Just
above Delphi was the famous Castalian spring.

Statius (in Purgatory) tells Virgil
that it was he who first directed
him to Parnassus (i. e. inspired him
to become a poet), Purg. xxii. 64-5
[**Stazio**]; V. refers to Parnassus
as *il monte, Che sempre ha le nutrici
nostre seco* (i. e. the mountain which
is the abode of the Muses), Purg.
xxii. 104-5 ; the poets of old there
dreamed of the Golden Age, Purg.
xxviii. 141 ; the poet devoted to
his art described as growing pale
beneath the shadow of Parnassus,
and drinking of its fountain (i.e.
Castalia), Purg. xxxi. 141 ; both
peaks of Parnassus (implying the
need of a double portion of inspiration) invoked by D. at the beginning
of the *Paradiso*, one alone having
sufficed for the other portions of
the poem, Par. i. 16-18 ; *Parnassus,*
Epist. x. 31[597].

Parnassus. [**Parnaso.**]

[**Parrhasius**], of Parrhasia, district in S. of Arcadia ; hence Arcadian, Ecl. R. 68.

[**Parthenopaeus**], Neapolitan
(Parthenope being another name for
Naples) ; G. del Virgilio mentions

classes Parthenopaeas, the Neapolitan fleet, in allusion to the defeat
(in Feb. 1319) of the Ghibellines,
who were besieging Genoa, by the
sea and land forces of King Robert
of Naples, Carm. 29.

Pasife, Pasiphaë, daughter of
Helios (the Sun) and the nymph
Perseis ; she was the wife of Minos,
King of Crete, and mother of An-
drogeos, Ariadne, and Phaedra ; she
was also the mother of the mon-
strous Minotaur by her intercourse
with a bull, by means of a wooden
cow made for her by Daedalus, into
which she entered.

Pasiphaë (whose story is told by
Ovid, *Metam.* viii. 131-7) is named
among the instances of bestial lust
proclaimed by the Lustful in Circle
VII of Purgatory, Purg. xxvi.
41-2 ; she is referred to by Guido
Guinizelli, in the same connexion,
as *colei Che s'imbestiò nell' imbestiate
schegge, vv.* 85-6 [**Lussuriosi**];
the wooden cow, *la falsa vacca,* is
mentioned in connexion with the
Minotaur, Inf. xii. 13 [**Minotauro.**]

Paulinae Epistolae. [***Epistolae Paulinae.***]

Paulus. [**Paolo.**]

Pavia, town in Lombardy on the
Ticino, just above its confluence with
the Po, about twenty miles S. of
Milan ; the San Nazzaro family of
Pavia, Conv. iv. 29[27] [**Nazzaro,
San**] ; one of the Guelfic cities
which opposed the Emperor Henry
VII, *Papia,* Epist. vii. 6[128]. [**Pa-
pienses.**]

Pazzi, noble family of Tuscany
(not to be confounded with the
ancient Florentine family of that

name), whose possessions were in the upper Valdarno, between Florence and Arezzo; they appear to have been, some Guelfs, some Ghibellines, but subsequently attached themselves to the Bianchi. D. mentions three members of the family, viz. Camicione, and his kinsman, the infamous Carlino, Inf. xxxii. 68–9 [Camicion de' Pazzi : Carlino]; and the robber noble, Rinier Pazzo, Inf. xii. 137 [Pazzo, Rinier].

Pazzo, Rinier, famous highway robber, member of the noble family of the Pazzi of Valdarno [Pazzi]. In 1268 with a numerous following he attacked and robbed a company of ecclesiastics on their way through Tuscany to Rome, many of whom were slain in the conflict. For this crime he was excommunicated by Clement IV. He died before 1280.

Rinieri is placed, together with Rinieri da Corneto, among the violent Robbers in Round 1 of Circle VII of Hell, Inf. xii. 137 [Predoni].

Peana, a designation of Apollo (cf. Servius on *Aen.* x. 738), Par. xiii. 25. [Apollo.]

Peccatore, Pietro. [Damiano, Pier.]

Peculiano, Namericus de. [Namericus 2.]

Pegaseo, belonging to Pegasus, the horse of the Muses, who with the stroke of his hoof produced the celebrated fountain of Hippocrene ('fountain of the horse'), sacred to the Muses, on Mt. Helicon in Boeotia. D. invokes the Muse of song as 'goddess of the fountain', *diva Pegasea*, Par. xviii. 82 [Muse].

Pegulhan, Aimeric de. [Namericus 2.]

Peleus, son of Aeacus, and King of the Myrmidons of Phthia in Thessaly; by the Nereid Thetis, whom he married, he became the father of Achilles.

D. mentions him as the son of Aeacus, brother of Telamon and Phocus, and father of Achilles, Conv. iv. 27[193-4] [Eaco]; he is referred to, in connexion with the spear of Achilles, as the father of the latter, Inf. xxxi. 5 [Achille]. In this latter passage D. speaks of Achilles' spear as having formerly belonged to Peleus. This is the Homeric tradition (*Iliad* xvi. 143–4), but there does not appear to be any Latin authority from which D. could have learned it. There can be little doubt, however, that D.'s statement is due to a misinterpretation of the expression 'Pelias hasta' in Ovid's *Remedia Amoris* (l. 48), which D. took to mean the 'spear of Peleus', instead of 'the spear from Mt. Pelion' (the abode of the Centaur Chiron, who gave the spear to Peleus). This association of Peleus with the spear of Achilles, a wound from which could only be healed by another stroke from the same spear, was a commonplace in Provençal and Italian poetry anterior to D.

Pellicano, Pelican, term applied by Beatrice (in the Heaven of Fixed Stars) to Christ, of whom she speaks as *il nostro Pellicano*, Par. xxv. 113.

The pelican, according to the popular belief, nourished its young with its own blood, and hence in the Middle Ages was a favourite symbol of parental love, and especially of Christ.

Peloro, Pelorus, now Cape Faro, the promontory at the NE. extremity of Sicily; Guido del Duca (in Circle II of Purgatory) refers to the Apennine range, from which Pelorus is divided by the Strait of Messina, as *l'alpestro monte, ond' è tronco Peloro*, Purg. xiv. 32 (cf. Virgil, *Aen*. iii. 410-19; Lucan, *Phars*. ii. 437-8); Pelorus is mentioned by Charles Martel (in the Heaven of Venus), together with Pachynus, the SE. extremity of the island, to indicate the extent of the E. coast of Sicily, Par. viii. 68 (cf. Ovid, *Metam*. v. 350-1)[**Pachino**]; *Pelorus*, Ecl. ii. 46, 73.

Pelorus. [**Peloro.**]

Peneio, belonging to Peneus, Thessalian river-god, who was the son of Oceanus and Tethys, and father of Daphne; *fronda Peneia*, ' the leaf of Peneus' (i. e. the laurel, into which Daphne was metamorphosed when pursued by Apollo), Par. i. 32-3; spoken of also as *frondes versa Peneïde cretae*, ' the leaves which sprang from the transformed daughter of Peneus', Ecl. i. 33; *Penea serta*, Carm. 38 [**Dafne**[1]].

Peneis. [**Dafne**[1]: **Peneio.**]

Penelope, wife of Ulysses, and mother of Telemachus.

Ulysses (in Bolgia 8 of Circle VIII of Hell) relates how his desire to travel and see the world was stronger than his love for his son, or for his aged father, or for his wife Penelope, Inf. xxvi. 94-6. [**Ulisse.**]

Penestrino, the ancient Praeneste, now Palestrina, town in Latium situated on a steep and lofty hill about twenty-five miles E. of Rome.

During the feud between Boniface VIII and the house of Colonna, the fortress of Palestrina, which was a stronghold of the latter, held out against the papal forces, and was only surrendered (Sept. 1298) on a promise from the Pope of complete amnesty, a promise which was made by the advice of Guido da Montefeltro, and which was never intended to be kept (Inf. xxvii. 110); but no sooner did Boniface get possession of the fortress than he razed it to the ground.

Guido da Montefeltro (in Bolgia 8 of Circle VIII of Hell) relates how Boniface sought his advice as to the reduction of Palestrina, and of how he advised the Pope to beguile the Colonnesi with a false promise, Inf. xxvii. 101-11. [**Colonnesi: Guido Montefeltrano.**]

Peneus. [**Peneio.**]

Pennino, Pennine Alps (so called from Mons Penninus, the classical name of the Great St. Bernard), loftiest portion of the range of Alps, extending for sixty miles from Monte Rosa at the E. extremity to Mont Blanc at the W.

According to one reading, D. applies the name *Pennino* to the range between the town of Garda and the Valcamonica (the upper valley of the Oglio), from which, ' per mille fonti e più ', the Lago di Garda is fed, Inf. xx. 64-6,—a description which cannot apply to the Pennine Alps properly so called, which are more than 100 miles distant from the Valcamonica; but D. (if the reading is correct) was probably following Orosius (one of his chief geographical authorities), who locates the Pennine Alps to the SW. of Rhaetia (the Tyrol) (*Hist.* i. 2. § 60), the position indicated in the text. If *Apennino* be read, the name must be taken in the sense of mountain in general (cf. *alpe*, Inf. xvi. 101), or as referring to an alleged spur of that name in the Rhaetian Alps. [Apennino[2]: Val Camonica.]

Pentesilea, Penthesilea, daughter of Mars and Otrera, famed for her beauty, youth, and valour; she was Queen of the Amazons, and after the death of Hector came to the assistance of the Trojans, but was slain by Achilles.

D. places her, together with Camilla (*Aen.* xi. 662), among the heroes of antiquity in Limbo, Inf. iv. 124 [Limbo].

Pera, Della, ancient noble family of Florence (extinct in D.'s day), mentioned by Cacciaguida (in the Heaven of Mars) in his description of the Florence of his day, as having given their name to one of the city gates (the Porta Peruzza), Par. xvi. 124–6.

Peregrini, Pilgrims, term applied, properly speaking, to those on a pilgrimage in a foreign land, Purg. ii. 63; viii. 4; xxiii. 16; xxvii. 110; Par. i. 51; xxxi. 43; V. N. § 41[35]; Son. xxiv. 1; *nuovo peregrino*, i. e. one who is on his first pilgrimage, Purg. viii. 4.

In the *Vita Nuova* D. distinguishes three classes of pilgrims, viz. those who went to the shrine of St. James in Galicia, who were known as ' peregrini'*par excellence*; those who went to the East, known as ' Palmers'; and those who went to Rome, known as ' Romers', V. N. § 41[35–51] [Galizia: Palmieri: Romei].

Pergama, citadel of Troy, hence used of Troy itself. D. reminds the rebellious Florentines that the walls of their city are not like those of Troy (which stood a ten years' siege), Epist. vi. 4[104–5] [Troia].

Pergamei, inhabitants of Bergamo; their dialect condemned, with that of Milan and the neighbouring towns, V. E. i. 11[30] (where some edd. read *Bergomates*).

Pergamum, Bergamo, town in Lombardy, about thirty miles NE. of Milan; one of the Guelfic towns which opposed the Emperor Henry VII, Epist. vii. 6[131]. [Bergamaschi.]

Periandro, Periander, tyrant of Corinth, B.C. 625–585; one of the Seven Sages of Greece, Conv. iii. 11[40]. [Biante.]

Perillo], Perillus, inventor of the brazen bull in which Phalaris, tyrant of Agrigentum, is said to have roasted alive the victims of his cruelty, the contrivance being so fashioned as to cause the shrieks of those inside it to sound like the bellowing of a bull; according to the story Perillus was the first to perish by his own invention.

D. refers to the brazen bull as *il bue Cicilian*, and to Perillus as *colui che l'avea temperato con sua lima*, and alludes to the fact (which he probably derived from Valerius Maximus, ix. 2) that he was the first victim of his own contrivance, Inf. xxvii. 7–9 [Ciciliano: Falaride].

Perini, Dino], notary of Florence, and companion of D. at Ravenna, who figures, as is supposed, in D.'s poetical correspondence with G. del Virgilio under the name of *Meliboeus*, Ecl. i. 4, 28, 34, 36, 67; ii. 29; Ecl. R. 35, 61, 71. He is the same individual apparently who related to Boccaccio the story of the finding of the lost seven cantos of the *D. C.* after D.'s exile. [*Egloghe*[2]: **Meliboeus.**]

Peripatetici, Peripatetic or Aristotelian school of philosophers, so called from the circumstance that Aristotle delivered his lectures while walking up and down in the shady alleys of the Lyceum, and not sitting, according to the general practice of the philosophers; the opinion of Aristotle and the other Peripatetics as to the cause of material generation, Conv. ii. 14[37]; iv. 21[31]; the Stoics, the Peripatetics, and the Epicureans, the three great philosophical schools at Athens, Conv. iii. 14[138-9]; these three schools, the three sects of the active life, symbolized by the three Maries at the sepulchre of our Lord, Conv. iv. 22[159-62]; the origin of the Peripatetic school, which succeeded and supplanted that of the Academy, and explanation of the name, Conv. iv. 6[131-47]. [**Accademici.**]

Persae. [**Persi.**]

Persi, Persians; in sense of pagans in general, Par. xix. 112; Cyrus and Xerxes, Kings of the Persians, their dreams of universal empire, *Persae*, Mon. ii. 9[43-54]. [**Ciro: Xerse.**]

Persio, Persius (Aulus Persius Flaccus), Roman satirist, A.D. 34-

62; his extant works consist of six short satires.

D., who apparently was not familiar with the writings of Persius, includes him among the Roman poets mentioned by Virgil as being with himself in Limbo, Purg. xxii. 100. [**Limbo.**]

Perugia, town in N. of Umbria (the Roman Perusia), about fifteen miles E. of the Lago Trasimeno, and about the same distance NW. of Assisi; it was here that Lucius Antonius, brother of the triumvir, took refuge during the civil war, and was besieged by Octavianus (Augustus), B.C. 41-40, until forced to surrender through famine, when the city was burned to the ground.

The Emperor Justinian (in the Heaven of Mercury) mentions Perugia in connexion with the victories of the Roman Eagle, Par. vi. 74; St. Thomas Aquinas (in the Heaven of the Sun) mentions it in describing the situation of Assisi, and speaks of it as being made hot in summer and cold in winter, on the side towards Assisi (i. e. on the SE.) where the Porta Sole is, by Monte Subasio, a spur of the Apennines, Par. xi. 45-7 [**Assisi: Monte Subasio: Porta Sole**]; its dialect, as well as those of Orvieto, Viterbo, and Città di Castello, not discussed by D., as being closely connected with the Roman and Spoletan dialects, *Perusium*, V. E. i. 13[29-32].

Perusium. [**Perugia.**]

Peruzza, Porta. [**Porta Peruzza.**]

Pescatore, Il, the Fisherman, i. e. St. Peter (in allusion to *Matt.*

iv. 18–19, *Mark* i. 16–17), Purg. xxii. 63; Par. xviii. 136. [**Pietro**[1].]

Peschiera, town and fortress at the SE. extremity of the Lago di Garda, just at the outfall of the Mincio; it is in Venetian territory, close to the frontier of Lombardy, about twenty miles SE. of Brescia and fifty SE. of Bergamo.

Virgil describes its situation, in his account of the founding of Mantua, speaking of it as a strong fort well placed to hold the Brescians and Bergamasks in check, Inf. xx. 70–2.

Pesci, Pisces ('the Fishes'), constellation and the last of the twelve signs of the Zodiac, which the Sun enters about Feb. 19. Virgil tells D. as they leave Circle VI of Hell that 'the Fishes are quivering on the horizon', the time indicated being (since the Sun was in Aries, the next sign to Pisces) between 4 and 5 a.m. in the upper world, i. e. close upon sunrise, Inf. xi. 113; D. indicates the hour before sunrise by saying that Venus, the morning star, was 'veiling the Fishes that were in her escort' (she being in or near the constellation Pisces, and the Sun in the next following sign of Aries), Purg. i. 19–21; the constellation Aries is referred to as the light which beams behind 'the celestial Carp' (*la celeste Lasca*), Purg. xxxii. 53–4 [**Ariete : Zodiaco**]. Some think Pisces is referred to as *il freddo animale*, Purg. ix. 5, but the reference is almost certainly to Scorpio [**Scorpio**].

Petramala, Pietramala, village at the foot of the N. slopes of the Etruscan Apennines, on the borders of Tuscany and the Emilia, about twenty miles due S. of Bologna; spoken of by D. ironically as a place of importance with an immense population, V. E. i. 6[9–10].

Petrapiana. [**Pietrapana.**]

Petri, Epistolae], Epistles of St. Peter; referred to, Epist. v. 10[165–6] (ref. to 1 *Pet.* ii. 17); and also, perhaps, Purg. viii. 95 (ref. to 1 *Pet.* v. 8); Purg. xxxii. 74 (ref. to 1 *Pet.* i. 12); Par. xxiv. 49–51 (ref. to 1 *Pet.* iii. 15); Par. xxiv. 62 (ref. to 2 *Pet.* iii. 15); they are supposed to be symbolized by one of the four elders in humble guise, who form part of the mystical Procession in the Terrestrial Paradise, Purg. xxix. 142, 145–8. [*Epistolae Canonicae.*]

Petrus[1]. [**Papa: Pietro**[1].]

Petrus[2], Peter, imaginary personage, V. E. ii. 8[36]; coupled with *Berta*, V. E. ii. 6[34]. [**Berta.**]

Petrus Comestor. [**Pietro Mangiadore.**]

Petrus Lombardus. [**Pietro**[2].]

Petrus de Alvernia, Peire d'Alvernha, Peter of Auvergne, troubadour of the latter half of Cent. xii (1155–1215), who was a contemporary of Bernart de Ventadour and Peire Rogier at the court of Ermengarde of Narbonne (1143–1192). Peire, several of whose poems have been preserved, was regarded as the first and most excellent of the troubadours who preceded Giraut de Borneil.

D. mentions Peire as one of those who were the first to write poetry in the 'langue d'*oc*', V. E. i. 10[24].

Pettinagno, Pier, 'Peter the comb-seller', native of Campi in the

Chianti district NE. of Siena; he was a hermit of the Franciscan Order, and dwelt in Siena, where he was renowned for his piety and miracles. Ubertino da Casale (Par. xii. 124) in the prologue to his *Arbor Vitae Crucifixae Jesu* mentions that he had received spiritual instruction from him. Pier died on Dec. 5, 1289, and was buried at Siena, where he was long venerated as a saint, in a handsome tomb erected at the public expense.

Sapia (in Circle II of Purgatory), says that she owes it to the prayers of Pier Pettinagno (in return, it is said, for her alms) that she was admitted into Purgatory, Purg. xiii. 127-9. [Sapia.]

Phaëton. [Fetonte.]

Pharao, Pharaoh, King of Egypt; his magicians unable to perform the miracle of turning dust into lice (*Exod.* viii. 16-19), Mon. ii. 4^{10-14}; God's message to him that he should let the children of Israel go (*Exod.* iv. 21; vii. 9), Mon. ii. 8^{57-9}.

Pharisaei. [Farisei.]

[Pharos], small island off the Mediterranean coast of Egypt; mentioned by G. del Virgilio to indicate Egypt, and hence the E., Carm. 32.

Pharsalia. [Farsaglia.]

Philippenses, Epistola ad], St. Paul's Epistle to the Philippians; quoted, Mon. iii. 13^{57-8} (*Phil.* i. 23).

Philistei, Philistini, Philistines; typical of the Neri, Goliath, David, and Israel, typifying respectively King Robert of Naples, the Emperor Henry VII, and the oppressed Ghibellines, Epist. vii. 8^{176-83}.

Philosophia, Prima. [*Metaphysica.*]

Philosophus. [Aristotile.]

Phoebe, surname of Diana as goddess of the Moon, and sister of Phoebus (i. e. Apollo), the god of the Sun; used by D. to indicate the Moon, which, when low in the heavens at early dawn, he compares to Justice, Mon. i. 11^{35}. [Diana[1]: Luna: Phoebus.]

Phoebus, epithet of Apollo as god of the Sun; Boëthius' use of it to indicate the Sun quoted, Mon. ii. 9^{95}; referred to as *frater Phoebae*, Mon. i. 11^{35}. [Apollo: Sole: Phoebe.]

Phryges, Phrygians; term used by D., in imitation of Virgil (*Aen.* i. 472; ix. 134, &c.), to indicate the Trojans, Epist. v. 8^{129}. [Argi.]

Phrygia, Phrygia, country in Asia Minor, which at one time included the Troad; hence used by D., in imitation of Virgil (*Aen.* x. 582; &c.), to indicate the kingdom of Troy, Mon. ii. 3^{63}.

[Phrygius], Phrygian, hence Trojan [Phryges]; used by G. del Virgilio as the equivalent of Paduan, in allusion to the legendary foundation of Padua by Antenor of Troy [Antenori]; *Phrygii damae*, i. e. the Paduans (in allusion to the operations against Padua in 1314-18 of the 'molossus', Can Grande della Scala), Carm. 28; *Phrygius Muso*, i. e. the Paduan river Musone (as distinguished from the Musone in the Marches), Ecl. R. 88 [Muso].

[Phyllis], name (borrowed from Virgil, *Ecl.* vii. 63; x. 37, 41) of a character in the Eclogue addressed

by G. del Virgilio to D., supposed to represent either Florence, or D.'s wife, Gemma, Ecl. R. 45. [**Gemma Donati.**]
Physica, *Physics* or *Physical Discourse* of Aristotle; quoted as *Fisica*, Inf. xi. 101 ; Conv. ii. 1^{108} ; iii. 11^{10} ; iv. 2^{48}, 9^{26}, 10^{91}, 15^{162}, 16^{78} ; *Physica*, V. E. ii. 10^{9}; Epist. x. 25^{461}; A. T. §§ 11^{11}, 20^{23}; *De Naturali Auditu*, Mon. i. 9^{7}; ii. 7^{41}; iii. 15^{14}.

D. quotes from the *Physics* upwards of a dozen times:—art follows nature, Inf. xi. 101 (*Phys.* ii. 2); natural progress of knowledge from the well known to the less well known, Conv. ii. 1$^{107-12}$ (*Phys.* i. 1); A. T. § 20$^{20-3}$; three kinds of movements, of locality, of alteration, and of increase, Conv. ii. 15$^{40-2}$ (*Phys.* v. 1); to know a thing is to know it in its beginnings and in its elements, Conv. iii. 11$^{6-10}$ (*Phys.* i. 1); V. E. ii. 10$^{6-9}$; time a numeration of motion, Conv. iv. 2$^{48-9}$ (*Phys.* iv. 11); the jurisdiction of universal nature not unlimited, Conv. iv. 9$^{25-6}$ (*Phys.* iii. 1); everything which suffers change is of necessity united with the changing principle, Conv. iv. 10$^{88-91}$ (*Phys.* vii. 2); arguments out of place with those who deny first principles, Conv. iv. 15$^{162-4}$ (*Phys.* i. 2); Mon. iii. 3$^{122-4}$; A. T. § 11$^{8-11}$; a thing perfect when united with its own special quality, as a circle is perfect when a true circle, Conv. iv. 16$^{78-87}$ (*Phys.* vii. 3); man and the Sun produce man, Mon. i. 9$^{6-7}$ (*Phys.* ii. 2); nature always acts for the end, Mon. ii. 7$^{40-2}$ (*Phys.* ii. 2); the arguments of Parmenides and Melissus incorrect since they accepted what was false, Mon. iii. 4$^{30-3}$(*Phys.* i. 3); the term 'nature' used more properly of the form of a thing than of its matter, Mon. iii. 15$^{11-14}$ (*Phys.* ii. 1); the relation of form to matter similar to that of the mould to the plastic substance, Epist. x. 25$^{458-61}$ (*Phys.* iv. 4).

Pia, La, lady of Siena, probably a member of the Tolomei family; she is said to have been married to Nello or Paganello de' Pannocchieschi of Castello della Pietra in the Sienese Maremma, by whom she was put to death (c. 1295). The mode of her death is disputed, some saying that she was killed so secretly that no one knew how it was done, while others relate that she was by Nello's orders thrown out of a window of his castle in the Maremma. A tradition, still current in the neighbourhood, identifies the scene of the murder with a spot known as the ' Salto della Contessa'. Nello's motive for the crime is supposed to have been his desire to marry his neighbour, the Countess Margherita degli Aldobrandeschi, widow of Guy of Montfort (Inf. xii. 118–20). Nello, who was captain of the Tuscan Guelfs in 1284, and Podestà of Volterra (1279) and Lucca (1313), was still living in 1322.

D. places La Pia in Ante-purgatory among those who neglected to repent, Purg. v. 133 ; *terzo spirito*, *v.* 132 ; addressing D., she names herself, and states that she was born in Siena and died in the Maremma, the manner of her death being known to him who was her husband (*vv.* 133–6). [**Antipurgatorio.**]

Piacentini. [Placentini.]

Piava, Piave, river of N. Italy, which rises in the Carnic Alps, and falls into the Gulf of Venice some twenty miles above Venice; it is mentioned by Cunizza (in the Heaven of Venus) as one of the boundaries of the March of Treviso, Par. ix. 27. [**Marca Trivisiana.**]

Picae. [Pierides [2].]

Piccarda, daughter of Simone Donati, of the celebrated Florentine family of that name, and sister of Corso and Forese Donati [**Donati: Corso: Forese**]. Piccarda was a connexion by marriage of D., he having married Gemma, daughter of Manetto Donati [**Gemma Donati**].

At the close of his interview with Forese Donati (in Circle VI of Purgatory), D. asks for news of Piccarda, to which F., who says he knows not whether she were more beautiful or good, replies that she is already in Paradise, Purg. xxiv. 10, 13–15. Subsequently D. sees her in the Heaven of the Moon among those who failed to keep their religious vows, Par. iii. 49 ; iv. 97, 112 ; *ombra*, Par. iii. 34 ; in reply to D.'s inquiry as to her history, P. names herself and relates how as a girl she entered the convent of St. Clara and took the vows of the order, and how she was dragged thence against her will by her brother Corso, and compelled to resume the secular life, Par. iii. 42–108 [**Luna, Cielo della**]; afterwards Beatrice, in replying to D.'s doubts as to how merit can be diminished by acts done under compulsion, refers to what Piccarda had told him, Par. iv. 97–9, 112–14.

The commentators state that Piccarda was forced from her convent by her brother Corso, while he was Podestà of Bologna (i. e. in 1283 or 1288), in order to marry her to a Florentine, Rossellino della Tosa, and that she died soon after her marriage. Rossellino, who is described as an unscrupulous and violent man, was still alive at the date of the Vision (1300).

Piceno, Campo. [**Campo Piceno.**]

Piche, Le. [Pierides [2].]

Pier [1]. [Pietro [1].]

Pier [2]. [Pietro [3].]

Pier Damiano. [**Damiano, Pier.**]

Pier Pettinagno. [**Pettinagno, Pier.**]

Pier Traversaro. [**Traversaro, Pier.**]

Pier d'Aragona. [Pietro [3].]

Pier da Medicina. [**Medicina, Pier da.**]

Pier dalla Broccia. [**Broccia, Pier dalla.**]

Pier della Vigna], Petrus de Vinea, minister of the Emperor Frederick II, born at Capua c. 1190; after studying at Bologna, he received an appointment at the court of Frederick II as notary, and thenceforward he rapidly rose to distinction. He was made judge and protonotary, and for more than twenty years he was the trusted minister and confidant of the Emperor. He was at the height of his power in 1247, but two years later he was accused of treachery, and was thrown into prison and blinded ; and soon after he committed suicide (April, 1249). The cause of his fall is not accurately known; it was a general opinion, which D. shared, that he was the victim of calumnious accusations on the part of those who were jealous of his supreme influence with the Emperor. Like his Imperial master, Pier della Vigna was a poet; some of his poems have been preserved, besides a number of Latin letters.

D. places Pier della Vigna, whom he does not name, in Round 2 of Circle VII of Hell, among the Suicides, Inf. xiii. 31–108; in the wood of Suicides D., at Virgil's bidding, breaks a bough from one of the trees, whereupon the spirit in the tree cries out, and reveals itself as Pier della Vigna, who relates his story, and solemnly declares his innocence of any crime against the Emperor (vv. 31–78) [Suicidi].

[Pierides[1]], Pierides, the nine Muses, so called from Pieria, their birthplace, Carm. 1. [Muse: Pierius.]

Pierides[2]], Pierides, the nine daughters of Pierus, King of Emathia in Macedonia, to whom he gave the names of the nine Muses; they challenged the Muses to a musical contest, and being defeated were transformed into magpies; D. mentions them, as magpies, in connexion with their defeat by the Muses, Piche, Purg. i. 11; and again, as being endowed with human speech, according to the account given by Ovid in the Metamorphoses (v. 293 ff.), to which he refers, Picae, V. E. i. 2[53–4].

Pierius, Pierian, pertaining to the Muses, one of the earliest seats of their worship having been in Pieria,

a country on the SE. coast of Macedonia; Pierius sinus, i. e. the lap of the Muses, Ecl. i. 2.

Piero. [Pietro.]

Piero, Porta san. [Porta san Piero.]

Pietola, now Pietole, village about three miles SE. of Mantua, commonly identified with the ancient Andes, the birthplace of Virgil.

D. says that on Virgil's account Pietola is more renowned than any other Mantuan village (or, according to some, than Mantua itself), Purg. xviii. 82–3. [Mantovano.]

Pietra], name of lady of whom D. is said to have been enamoured, and who has been variously identified with one Pietra degli Scrovigni of Padua; with the Lisetta of Son. xliv. 3, 12; and with D.'s wife, Gemma Donati; and who is supposed to be the lady referred to by a play upon her name or disposition (pietra) in the so-called 'canzoni pietrose', Canz. xii, xv; Sest. i, ii.

Pietramala. [Petramala.]

Pietrapana, name of mountain mentioned by D. in connexion with the ice of Cocytus, which he says was so thick that it would not even crack if the mountain were to fall upon it, Inf. xxxii. 28–30. [Cocito.]

Pietrapana has been identified with one of the peaks (known as Pania) of the so-called Alpe Apuana (to which the Carrara mountains also belong), a group of lofty peaks in the NW. corner of Tuscany, which lie between Fivizzano and the upper valley of the Serchio.

Pietro[1]; St. Peter the Apostle, son of the fisherman Jonas, and

brother of St. Andrew the Apostle ;
according to tradition the first
Bishop of Rome, where he suffered
martyrdom by crucifixion in the
Neronian persecution, c. A.D. 68.

St. Peter is mentioned, Purg.
xiii. 51 ; xxi. 54 ; xxxii. 76 ;
Par. ix. 141 ; xi. 120 ; xviii. 131 ;
xxv. 12 ; xxxii. 133 ; Conv. iv.
22^{157}, 181^{-3} ; *san Pietro*, Inf. i.
134 ; xix. 91 ; xxxi. 59 ; Conv.
iv. 16^{68} ; *santo Pietro*, Inf. xviii.
32 ; *Pier*, Inf. xix. 94 ; Purg. ix.
127 ; Par. xxii. 88 ; *il maggior
Piero*, Inf. ii. 24 ; *Petrus*, Purg.
xix. 99 ; Mon. ii. 9^9 ; iii. 1^{42},
3$^{37-9}$, 6^{42}, 7^{28}, 8$^{2-69}$, 9$^{2-141}$,
15$^{24-6}$, 16^{135} ; Epist. v. 5^{91},
10$^{165, 167}$; vi. 1^{14} ; viii. 2$^{21, 25}$;
Cephas, Par. xxi. 127 ; he is referred
to as *il Pescatore*, Purg. xxii. 63 ;
Par. xviii. 136 ; *Archimandrita*,
Mon. iii. 9^{123} ; *Barone*, Par. xxiv.
115 ; *santo Padre*, Par. xxiv. 124 ;
Padre vetusto di santa Chiesa, Par.
xxxii. 124 ; *alto primipilo*, Par.
xxiv. 59 ; *primizia dei vicari di
Cristo*, Par. xxv. 14 ; *Dei vicarius*,
Epist. v. 10^{166} ; *gran viro*, Par.
xxiv. 34 ; *colui che tien le chiavi*,
Par. xxiii. 139 ; in the Heaven of
the Fixed Stars he appears as *un
fuoco felice*, Par. xxiv. 20 ; *fuoco
benedetto*, v. 31 ; *luce eterna*, v. 34 ;
luce, v. 54 ; *amore acceso*, v. 82 ;
luce profonda, v. 88 ; *apostolico lume*,
v. 153 ; *quella (face) che pria venne*,
Par. xxvii. 11 ; he was the representative of Faith, as St. James was
of Hope, and St. John of Love,
on the occasions when the three
Apostles were present alone with
Christ, i. e. at the raising of Jairus's
daughter, at the Transfiguration, and

in the Garden of Gethsemane, the
three being referred to by Beatrice
as *i tre (ai quali) Gesù fe' più chiarezza*, Par. xxv. 33.

D. refers to the following circumstances and incidents in the life of
St. Peter :—his occupation as a
fisherman (*Matt.* iv. 18–19 ; *Mark*
i. 16–17), Purg. xxii. 63 ; Par.
xviii. 136 ; called Cephas by Christ
(*John* i. 42), Par. xxi. 127 ; his
presence at the Transfiguration with
St. John and St. James (*Matt.* xvii.
1 ; *Mark* ix. 2 ; *Luke* ix. 28),
Purg. xxxii. 76 ; Par. xxv. 33 ;
Conv. ii. 1$^{47-8}$; Mon. iii. 9$^{81-6}$;
at the raising of Jairus's daughter
(*Luke* viii. 51), Par. xxv. 33 ; in
the garden of Gethsemane (*Matt.*
xxvi. 37 ; *Mark* xiv. 33), Par.
xxv. 33 ; his walking upon the
water to meet Christ (*Matt.* xiv.
28–30), Mon. iii. 9$^{87-91}$; his
recognition of Christ as the Son of
the living God (*Matt.* xvi. 16),
Mon. iii. 9$^{72-3}$; entrusted by Christ
with the keys of the kingdom of
heaven (*Matt.* xvi. 19), Inf. xix.
91–2, 101 ; xxvii. 104 ; Purg. ix.
117, 121, 127 ; Par. xxiv. 35 ;
xxvii. 49 ; xxxii. 125 ; Mon. iii.
1$^{42-4}$, 8$^{56-8}$; and with the power
of binding and loosing (*Matt.* xvi.
19), Mon. iii. 8$^{2-5}$; his rebuke of
Christ when He foretold His death
and resurrection, and Christ's rebuke
of him for his presumption (*Matt.*
xvi. 21–3), Mon. iii. 9$^{73-80}$; Christ
washes his feet (*John* xiii. 6–9),
Mon. iii. 9$^{103-7}$; his impulsive
character, Mon. iii. 9$^{63-119}$; his
declaration of his readiness to die
with Christ (*Matt.* xxvi. 35 ; *Luke*
xxii. 33), Mon. iii. 9$^{99-102}$; Christ

foretells his denial of Himself (*Matt.* xxvi. 33–5; *Mark* xiv. 29), Mon. iii. 9⁹²⁻⁷; the saying (attributed by D. to St. Peter) recorded by St. Luke (xxii. 38), 'here are two swords', Mon. iii. 9¹⁻³; his smiting of the high priest's servant with a sword (*John* xviii. 10), Mon. iii. 9¹⁰⁸⁻⁹; his visit with St. John to the tomb of Christ (*John* xx. 3–10), Par. xxiv. 126; Mon. iii. 9¹¹¹⁻¹⁴; the message of the angel to him and the disciples after the Resurrection that Christ would go before them into Galilee (*Mark* xvi. 7), Conv. iv. 22¹⁵⁶⁻⁹; Christ's appearance to him and the other disciples at the sea of Tiberias (*John* xxi. 1–7), Mon. iii. 7¹¹⁵⁻¹⁹; Christ's charge to him to feed His sheep and to follow Him (*John* xxi. 15–19), Mon. iii. 15²⁴⁻⁶; Epist. viii. 2²¹⁻²; his question concerning St. John, 'Lord, what shall this man do?' (*John* xxi. 21), Mon. iii. 9¹²⁰⁻²; his presence with the other Apostles at the election of Matthias to fill the place of Judas Iscariot (*Acts* i. 15–26), Inf. xix. 94; his saying, 'silver and gold have I none' (*Acts* iii. 6), Par. xxii. 18; his martyrdom for the Church of Christ, Par. ix. 141; xviii. 131.

D. speaks of the Pope as Peter, Mon. ii. 6⁹; iii. 16¹³⁵; Epist. v. 5⁹¹; and as his successor or vicar, Inf. ii. 24; Purg. xix. 99; xxi. 54; Mon. iii. 1⁴², 3³⁷, 6⁴², 7²⁸, 8⁹, ¹⁸, ⁶⁷, 9⁸; Epist. v. 10¹⁶⁷ [Papa] ; the Church is represented as the ship of St. Peter, Purg. xxxii. 129; Par. xi. 119–20; Epist. vi. 1¹³⁻¹⁴ [Chiesa]; the gate of St. Peter

(i. e. the gate of Purgatory, or, perhaps, of Paradise), Inf. i. 134 [Porta di san Pietro]; the church of St. Peter at Rome, Inf. xviii. 32; xxxi. 59; Conv. iv. 16⁶⁸ [Pietro, San ²].

St. Peter is invoked, together with St. Michael and all saints, by those who are purging the sin of Envy in Purgatory, Purg. xiii. 51 [Invidiosi]; his voice is heard during the progress of the pageant in the Terrestrial Paradise bewailing from heaven the acceptance by the Church of temporal power and possessions, Purg. xxxii. 128–9; his *Epistle* (1 *Pet.* ii. 17) referred to, Epist. v. 10¹⁶⁵⁻⁶ [*Petri, Epistolae*].

In the Heaven of the Fixed Stars St. Peter examines D. concerning the nature and matter of faith (Par. xxiv. 19–147); and finally commends him for his reply (*vv.* 148–54); D., having been approved by St. Peter as regards faith (Par. xxv. 10–12), is next examined by St. James concerning hope (*vv.* 25–99), and by St. John concerning love (Par. xxvi. 1–66), in the presence of St. Peter, who subsequently vehemently rebukes the wickedness of the Popes, contrasting their rapacity with the holy lives of his own immediate successors, and finally charges D. to make known on his return to earth what he has seen and heard above (Par. xxvii. 11–66).

In the Celestial Rose D. assigns to St. Peter the seat on the right of the Virgin Mary, on his right being St. John the Evangelist, and opposite to him Anna, the mother of the Virgin, Par. xxxii. 124–33. [Rosa.]

Pietro ², Peter Lombard, other-

wise known as 'Magister Sententiarum'(from the title of his work *Sententiarum Libri Quatuor*), born near
Novara, in what was formerly part
of Lombardy, c. 1100; he studied
first at Bologna, and then at Paris,
where he held a theological chair for
many years; in 1159 he was appointed Bishop of Paris, but died
shortly after, c. 1164. His best
known work, the *Libri Sententiarum*,
which attained immense popularity
and became the favourite text-book
in the theological schools, is, as its
name implies, primarily a collection
of the sentences of the Fathers.

D. places Peter among the great
doctors (*Spiriti Sapienti*) in the
Heaven of the Sun, where he is
pointed out by St. Thomas Aquinas
as *Quel Pietro, che con la poverella
Offerse a santa Chiesa il suo tesoro*
(the allusion being to a sentence in
the preface of his book, which he
presents, like the widow's mites, as
an humble offering to God), Par. x.
107–8 [**Sole, Cielo del**]; he is
referred to as *Magister* in connexion
with his opinion, as expressed in
the fourth book of the *Sententiae*
(iv. 5), that God can delegate the
power of baptism, Mon. iii. 7^{36-7};
his definition of hope (*Sent.* iii.
26) is literally translated, Par. xxv.
67–9.

Pietro [3]], Peter III, King of
Aragon, 1276–1285; he was the
son of James I of Aragon (1213–
1276), elder brother of James, King
of Majorca (1276–1311) [**Jacomo** [2]], and father of Alphonso III
(K. of Aragon, 1285–1291) [**Alfonso** [1]], James II (K. of Sicily,
1285–1296, K. of Aragon, 1291–

1327) [**Jacomo** [1]], Frederick II
(K. of Sicily, 1296–1337) [**Federico** [3]], and Isabella, wife of
Dionysius, King of Portugal [**Dionisio** [3]]; he married (1262) Constance, daughter of King Manfred
of Sicily, and thus had a claim on
the crown of Sicily, which he assumed after the massacre of the
'Sicilian Vespers' in 1282, and retained until his death in 1285, in
spite of all the efforts of Charles of
Anjou, backed by Pope Martin IV
(who excommunicated Peter in
1283), to regain his lost kingdom
[**Carlo** [1]: Tables B, E]. Peter
died, Nov. 8, 1285, at Villafranca,
near Barcelona, from the effects of
a wound received in a skirmish with
the French before Gerona, within
a few months of his two foes,
Charles of Anjou having died in the
previous January, in the midst of his
preparations for a fresh invasion of
Sicily, and Philip III of France the
month before (Oct. 6) at Perpignan,
after an unsuccessful campaign in
Catalonia for the conquest of Peter's
Spanish dominions, on behalf of his
brother Charles of Valois, on whom
they had been conferred by Martin
IV [**Carlo** [4]: **Filippo** [1]].

D. places Peter in the valley of
flowers in Ante-purgatory, among
the princes who neglected to repent,
Pier, Purg. vii. 125; *quel che par
sì membruto*, v. 112; *l'altro*, v. 125;
he is represented as seated beside
his ancient foe, Charles of Anjou,
and in front of his son and successor
in Aragon, Alphonso III (*vv.* 112–
13, 116, 125) [**Antipurgatorio**];
D. (by the mouth of Sordello)
speaks of Peter in highly laudatory

terms, saying of him 'D'ogni valor portò cinta la corda' (v. 114); he laments the short reign of his eldest son, Alphonso, who would have been a worthy successor to him, and deplores the degeneracy of his two younger sons, James and Frederick, to whom the crowns of Aragon and Sicily descended (vv. 115-20); and implies, by the mention of their respective wives, that Peter was as superior to Charles of Anjou as Charles was to his own son, Charles II (vv. 127-9) [Beatrice [2] : Costanza [2] : Margherita [2]].

Pietro Bernadone. [Bernadone, Pietro.]

Pietro Ispano, Petrus Hispanus (Pedro Juliani), native of Lisbon, where he at first followed his father's profession of medicine ; subsequently he was ordained and became Archbishop of Braga ; in 1274 he was created Cardinal Bishop of Tusculum (Frascati) by Gregory X ; on Sept. 8, 1276, he was elected Pope, under the title of John XXI, at Viterbo, in succession to Adrian V ; he died, after a reign of a little more than eight months, May 20, 1277. Besides several medical works of a more or less popular character, he wrote a manual of logic, in twelve parts, which, under the title of *Summulae Logicales*, attained a wide popularity in the Middle Ages.

D. places Petrus Hispanus among the doctors of the Church (*Spiriti Sapienti*), in the Heaven of the Sun, where he is named by St. Bonaventura, his *Summulae Logicales* being referred to as *dodici libelli*, Par. xii. 134-5. [Sole, Cielo del.]

Pietro Lombardo. [Pietro [2].]

Pietro Mangiadore, Petrus Comestor (i. e. 'Peter the Eater', so called because he was an insatiable devourer of books), priest, and afterwards dean, of the cathedral of Troyes in France, where he was born c. 1110 ; he became canon of St. Victor in 1164, and chancellor of the University of Paris, and died at St. Victor in 1179. His chief work was the *Historia Scholastica*, a history of the Church from the beginning of the world down to the times of the Apostles, which consists mainly of a compilation of the historical portions of the Bible, accompanied by a commentary and parallels from profane history, and was the great authority on the subject in the Middle Ages.

D. places Petrus Comestor among the doctors of the Church (*Spiriti Sapienti*) in the Heaven of the Sun, where he is named by St. Bonaventura, Par. xii. 134. [Sole, Cielo del.]

Pietro Peccatore. [Damiano, Pier.]

Pietro, San [1]. [Pietro [1].]

Pietro, San [2], Church of St. Peter at Rome ; mentioned in connexion with the crowds of pilgrims who flocked thither in the Jubilee year, Inf. xviii. 32 [Giubbileo] ; the face of the giant Nimrod compared for size to the huge bronze pine-cone, which used to stand in D.'s day in front of St. Peter's, Inf. xxxi. 59 [Nembrotto] ; the stone needle or obelisk of St. Peter's, Conv. iv. 16[68].

The Church of St. Peter (S. Pietro in Vaticano, is said to have been founded early in Cent. iv by the Emperor Constantine at the request of Pope Sylvester I. It was erected on the site of the circus of Nero, where, according to tradition, St. Peter suffered martyrdom; and in it was preserved the bronze sarcophagus containing the body of the Apostle. It was in this church that on Christmas Day, 800, Charlemagne was crowned Emperor of the West by Leo III; and it was subsequently the scene of the coronation of numerous Emperors and Popes. It is, of course, to this ancient structure that D. refers, the present building dating only from the beginning of Cent. xvi.

Pietro d'Aragona. [Pietro³.]

Pietro degli Onesti], Petrus de Honestis, monk of Ravenna, where he founded (1096) the monastery of Santa Maria in Porto fuori; died, 1119. Some think he is the 'Pietro peccator' mentioned by St. Peter Damian (who, however, is more probably St. Peter Damian himself), Par. xxi. 122 [**Damiano, Pier**].

Pigli], ancient noble family of Florence, referred to by Cacciaguida (in the Heaven of Mars) by the mention of their arms, 'la colonna del Vaio', as having been of importance in his day, Par. xvi. 103. They lived in the Porta di san Brancazio (Vill. iv. 12); they were for the most part Ghibellines (v. 39), and eventually joined the Bianchi (viii. 39).

Pigmalione, Pygmalion, son of Belus, King of Tyre, whom he succeeded, and brother of Dido, whose husband, Sychaeus, he murdered for the sake of his wealth. Dido, being made aware of the murder by the appearance of Sychaeus to her in a dream, secretly sailed from Tyre with the treasure, and landed in Africa, where she founded the city of Carthage (*Aen.* i. 340 ff.).

D. includes Pygmalion among the instances of the lust of wealth proclaimed by those who are being purged of the sin of Avarice in Circle V of Purgatory, speaking of him as 'traditore e ladro e patricida', inasmuch as he betrayed and robbed Sychaeus and Dido, and murdered the former, who was his uncle as well as his brother-in-law, Purg. xx. 103–5. [**Avari.**]

Pignatelli, Bartolommeo], Archbishop of Cosenza, 1254–1266, commonly supposed to be 'il pastor di Cosenza' (though some think it was his successor Tommaso d'Agni) mentioned by Manfred (in Antepurgatory) as having, at the bidding of Clement IV, disinterred his body from its resting-place by the bridge of Benevento, and cast it unburied on the banks of the river Verde, outside the boundaries of the kingdom of Naples, Purg. iii. 124–32. [**Cosenza.**]

Pila, Ubaldin dalla, Ubaldino degli Ubaldini of La Pila (castle in the Mugello, or upper valley of the Sieve, tributary of the Arno, N. of Florence), member of the powerful Ghibelline family of that name [**Ubaldini**]. Ubaldino, who was one of those who voted for the destruction of Florence (Inf. x. 92), and was a member of the Consiglio Generale, after the battle of Montaperti (Sept. 4, 1260), was brother of the famous Cardinal Ottaviano degli Ubaldini (Inf. x. 120), uncle of Ugolino d'Azzo (Purg. xiv. 105), and father of the Archbishop Ruggieri of Pisa (Inf. xxxiii. 14); he died in 1291.

D. places him among the Gluttonous in Circle VI of Purgatory, Purg. xxiv. 29 [Golosi].

Pilade], Pylades, son of Strophius, King of Phocis, and Anaxibia, sister of Agamemnon. After the murder of Agamemnon by Clytaemnestra his son Orestes was placed under the protection of Strophius, and thus originated the famous friendship between Pylades and Orestes. Pylades, after helping Orestes to avenge the death of Agamemnon, married his friend's sister Electra, and finally was instrumental in saving his life by pretending that he was Orestes.

D. alludes to this incident, putting into the mouth of Pylades the words, *Io sono Oreste*, Purg. xiii. 32. [Oreste.]

Pilato, Pontius Pilate, Roman procurator of Judaea (A. D. 26–37), by whom Christ was tried and condemned to be crucified; he is said to have died by his own hand, A. D. 40.

D. speaks of him as the vicar of Tiberius Caesar, in connexion with his trial of Christ, Mon. ii. 13[46–7]; Christ sent by Herod to be judged before him, as recorded by St. Luke (xxiii. 11), Mon. ii. 13[50–4] [Tiberius]; Christ's denial before him that His kingdom was of this world (*John* xviii. 36), Mon. iii. 15[27–33]; Epist. v. 10[156–7] [Cristo]; Hugh Capet (in Circle V of Purgatory) refers to Philip IV of France, in allusion to his seizure and imprisonment of Boniface VIII, the 'vicar of Christ', at Anagni, as *il nuovo Pilato*, Purg. xx. 91 [Alagna : Bonifazio[1] : Filippo[2]].

Some think Pilate is the person

referred to, Inf. iii. 59–60. [Celestino.]

Pilatus. [Pilato.]

Pinamonte, Pinamonte de' Buonaccorsi, Ghibelline lord of Mantua (1272–1291), through whose agency Count Alberto da Casalodi was expelled from Mantua. The Counts of Casalodi, a Guelf family of Brescia, having made themselves masters of Mantua, incurred the hostility of the people, who threatened them with expulsion. In order to avert this catastrophe Count Alberto da Casalodi in 1272, by the advice of Pinamonte, one of the 'rettori del popolo', who wished to get the government of Mantua into his own hands, expelled great numbers of the nobles, including his own adherents, who were obnoxious to the people. Whereupon Pinamonte, seeing that Alberto had thus left himself defenceless, suddenly, with the aid of the populace, compelled him to leave the city, confiscated all his possessions, and put to the sword or drove out nearly every family of note in Mantua.

To this incident, and the consequent depopulation of Mantua, Virgil refers in his account of the founding of Mantua by Manto, Inf. xx. 94–6. [Casalodi.]

Pineta, celebrated pine-forest of Ravenna; mentioned in connexion with the sough of the wind in the trees when the scirocco is blowing, Purg. xxviii. 20–1 [Chiassi[1]]. It has been suggested that D.'s description of the 'divina foresta' in the Terrestrial Paradise (Purg. xxviii. 2, 23) is a reminiscence of the 'Pineta' of Ravenna.

[Pinti, Spedale a], ancient hospital of San Paolo a Pinti, near Florence (suppressed in 1751); mentioned by Forese Donati in his *tenzone* with D., Son. liii.* 12.

Pio, Pius I, native of Aquileia in Venetia, Bishop of Rome, c. 140–155; D. follows the tradition that he was martyred, and includes him among those of his immediate successors mentioned by St. Peter (in the Heaven of Fixed Stars) as having, like himself, shed their blood for the Church, Par. xxvii. 44.

Piramo, Pyramus, the lover of Thisbe; the two on one occasion agreed to meet at the tomb of Ninus, and, while Thisbe, who arrived first, was waiting for Pyramus, she perceived a lioness which had just torn in pieces an ox; thereupon in terror she fled, dropping her garment in her flight, which the lioness soiled with blood. In the meantime Pyramus came to the tomb, and, finding Thisbe's garment covered with blood, supposed that she had been killed; in despair he stabbed himself at the foot of a mulberry tree, the fruit of which, from being white, thenceforth became crimson like blood. When Thisbe returned and discovered her lover, who was just able to recognize her before he died, she slew herself at his side (Ovid, *Metam.* iv. 55–166).

D. mentions Pyramus in connexion with the incident of his opening his eyes when he heard Thisbe calling him as he was on the point of death (cf. *Metam.* iv. 142–6), and refers to the change of colour in the mulberry, Purg. xxvii. 37–9; he is mentioned again in connexion with the latter incident, Purg. xxxiii. 69; the story of Pyramus and Thisbe is referred to again, in connexion with Ninus and Semiramis, the lines in Ovid's account (*vv.* 58, 88) being quoted in which the latter are mentioned, Mon. ii. 9³⁰⁻⁴.

[Nino ¹: Semiramis.]

Pireneo. [Pirenes.]

Pirenes, Pyrenees, mountain-range forming the dividing line between France and Spain; the Imperial Eagle soars alike over the Pyrenees, Caucasus, and Atlas, Epist. vi. 3⁸²⁻³; referred to as *il monte che fascia Navarra*, Par. xix. 144 [Navarra]; and, as one of the limits of the *langue d'*oïl, *montes Aragoniae*, V.E. i. 8⁶² [*Lingua Oil.*]

Piroi, Pyroeis, one of the four horses which drew the chariot of the Sun, Conv. iv. 23¹³⁶. [Eoo.]

Pirro¹, Pyrrhus or Neoptolemus, son of Achilles and Deidamia, the daughter of Lycomedes, King of Scyros. He was fetched from Scyros by Ulysses in order that he might take part in the Trojan war, it having been prophesied that Troy would not fall unless he were present. He was one of the Greeks who were concealed in the wooden horse, and after the capture of the city he killed the aged Priam before the altar of Jupiter, and his son Polites, and sacrificed his daughter Polyxena to the shade of Achilles. His violence and cruelty after the fall of Troy are recorded by Virgil (*Aen.* ii. 469 ff.).

Some think he is the Pyrrhus (whom others identify with the King of Epirus) placed by D. among the Violent in Round 1 of Circle VII of Hell, Inf. xii. 135 [Omicide : Pirro [2]].

Pirro [2], Pyrrhus, King of Epirus, born B.C. 318, died B. C. 272 ; he claimed descent from Pyrrhus, the son of Achilles and great-grandson of Aeacus. In 280 Pyrrhus crossed over into Italy at the invitation of the Tarentines to help them in their war against the Romans. In his first campaign he defeated the Romans, and advanced to within twenty-four miles of Rome ; but, being unable to compel them to accept terms of peace, he withdrew to Tarentum. In 279 he again defeated the Romans, under the consul P. Decius Mus (who was slain), but suffered such heavy losses that he retired from the war and crossed over into Sicily. In 276 he once more landed in Italy, but in 275 was defeated near Beneventum by the consul Curius Dentatus, and was compelled to return to Epirus. He was killed during the siege of Argos (B.C. 272) by a tile hurled by a woman from a house-top.

He is probably the Pyrrhus (whom some identify with the son of Achilles) placed by D. among the Violent in Round 1 of Circle VII of Hell, Inf. xii. 135 [Pirro [1] : Tiranni]; Pyrrhus is mentioned by the Emperor Justinian (in the Heaven of Mercury) in connexion with the exploits of the Roman Eagle, Par. vi. 44 ; Cicero's mention of him in his account (*Fin.* ii. 19) of the patriotism of the Decii, the third of whom lost his life while fighting against Pyrrhus, *Pyrrhus*, Mon. ii. 5[155] [Deci]; his descent from Aeacus, his speech to the Roman envoys as to the ransom of the Roman

prisoners (quoted from Ennius by Cicero, *Off.* i. 12, and thence, without acknowledgement, by D.), and his contempt for gold, Mon. ii. 10[57−83] [Aeacidae]; his discomfiture by Fabricius, Mon. ii. 11[52−8] [Fabbrizzio].

Pisa, city of Tuscany, on the Arno, in mediaeval times an important port, but now six or seven miles from the mouth of the river.

D. mentions Pisa in connexion with the cruel fate of Count Ugolino, speaking of it as 'the reproach of Italy', and 'a new Thebes', and calling upon the islands of Capraia and Gorgona to choke the Arno in order that all its inhabitants might be drowned, Inf. xxxiii. 79–89 [Capraia: Gorgona: Tebe: Ugolino, Conte]; *quel da Pisa*, i. e. Gano degli Scornigiani, Purg. vi. 17 [Gano: Marzucco]; it is mentioned in a quotation in the Pisan dialect, V. E. i. 13[22] [Pisani].

Pisani, Pisans ; prevented from seeing Lucca by the Monte San Giuliano, Inf. xxxiii. 30 [Giuliano, Monte San]; their dialect quite distinct from that of the Paduans, inasmuch as they live on opposite sides of Italy, V. E. i. 9[35−6]; specimen of their dialect, which is condemned with the rest of the Tuscan dialects, V. E. i. 13[21−2]; they are spoken of by Guido del Duca (in Circle II of Purgatory), in his description of the course of the Arno, as *volpi si piene di froda, Che non temono ingegno che le occupi* (i. e. foxes so false and cunning that they have no fear of being outwitted by any others), Purg. xiv. 53–4 [Arno].

Pisanus, Gallus. [Gallus Pisanus.]

Piscicelli, family of Naples, mentioned by D., in his discussion as to the nature of nobility, together with the San Nazzaro family of Pavia, as examples of Italian nobles, Conv. iv. 29[27-8].

Pisistrato, Pisistratus, tyrant of Athens (died B.C. 527); introduced as an example of meekness (he having forgiven a young man who publicly insulted his daughter) in Circle III of Purgatory, where the sin of wrath is expiated, Purg. xv. 97-105 [Iracondi].

Pistoia, town in Tuscany, about 20 miles NW. of Florence. It was near Pistoja (the ancient Pistorium) that Catiline was defeated by Petreius, B.C. 62, and there was a tradition that the town was founded by the survivors of Catiline's force (Vill. i. 32).

Pistoja is mentioned by Vanni Fucci (in Bolgia 7 of Circle VIII of Hell), who describes himself as a wild beast and Pistoja as his lair, Inf. xxiv. 126; he refers to it as the birthplace of the Bianchi and Neri factions, and prophesies the expulsion of the latter (which came to pass in May, 1301) (v. 143) [Bianchi: Negri]; D. apostrophizes Pistoja, with an allusion to the traditional descent of its inhabitants from Catiline's soldiers, Inf. xxv. 10-12; it is mentioned as the native place of the poet Cino, *Pistorium*, V. E. ii. 6[70] [Cino].

Pistoia, Cino da. [Cino.]
Pistoriensis, Cinus. [Cino.]
Pistorium. [Pistoia.]

Pittaco, Pittacus, of Mitylene in Lesbos, celebrated warrior, statesman, philosopher, and poet, B.C. 651-

569; one of the Seven Sages of Greece, Conv. iii. 11[41]. [Biante.]

Pittagora, Pythagoras, celebrated Greek philosopher, native of Samos, c. B.C. 582-506. His most famous doctrine was that of the transmigration of souls. The central thought of the Pythagorean philosophy is the idea of number, the recognition of the numerical and mathematical relations of things, number being regarded as the principle and essence of everything. Immediately connected with this theory is the Pythagorean theory of opposites; numbers are divided into odd and even, and from the combination of odd and even the numbers themselves (and therefore all things) seem to result. The odd number was identified with the limited, the even with the unlimited; and hence was developed a list of ten fundamental oppositions, known as the Pythagorean συστοιχία or parallel tables.

The Pythagoreans conceived the universe as a sphere, in the heart of which they placed the central Fire; around this move the ten heavenly bodies—furthest off the Heaven of the Fixed Stars, then the five Planets known to antiquity, then the Sun, the Moon, and the Earth, and lastly the counter-Earth (ἀντίχθων), revolving between the Earth and the central Fire, from which it continually shields the Earth.

D.'s knowledge of Pythagoras and his doctrines was derived mainly from Aristotle; but he was also indebted to Cicero and others.

The doctrine of Pythagoras as to 'the odd and even', and the numerical origin of all things (from Aristotle, *Metaphys.* i. 5; cf. Cicero, *Acad. Quaest.* iv. 37), Conv. ii. 14$^{144-7}$; Mon. i. 15$^{16-19}$; his invention of the term 'philosophy' (from Cicero, *Tusc. Quaest.* v. 3, or St. Augustine, *Civ. Dei*, viii. 2), Conv. ii. 16$^{102-3}$; iii. 11$^{41-53}$; his theory that the Earth was a star, and that there was a 'counter-Earth' (*Antictona*), and that both of them revolved, also that the central place in the universe was occupied by Fire (from Aristotle, *De Coelo*, ii. 13), Conv. iii. 5$^{29-44}$ [**Terra** [2]]; his residence in Italy at the time that Numa Pompilius was King of Rome (a misunderstanding of Livy, i. 18), and his claim to be reckoned, not a wise man, but a lover of wisdom or philosopher (from Cicero, *Tusc. Quaest.* v. 3, and St. Augustine, *Civ. Dei*, viii. 2), Conv. iii. 11$^{22-53}$; his saying that in friendship many are made one (from Cicero, *Off.* i. 17), Conv. iv. 1$^{5-6}$; his theory as to the equal nobility of all souls, whether of men, animals, plants, or minerals (apparently a general statement of the Pythagorean doctrine on the subject), Conv. iv. 21$^{20-5}$; his doctrine that number and the elements of number were the elements of all things, and his arrangement in his 'parallel-tables' of Unity and Good in one column, and of Plurality and Evil in the other (from Aristotle, *Metaphys.* i. 5), Mon. i. 15$^{13-19}$; referred to by G. del Virgilio as *Samius vates*, Ecl. R. 34.

Pittagorici, Pythagoreans, followers of Pythagoras; their theory as to the origin of the Galaxy or Milky Way, Conv. ii. 15$^{47-53}$. [**Galassia.**]

Placentini, inhabitants of Piacenza (Roman Placentia), town of Old Lombardy, in NW. corner of the Emilia, about half a mile from the S. bank of the Po; their dialect distinct from that of Ferrara, though both belong to Lombardy, V. E. i. 10$^{76-7}$. [**Lombardia.**]

Plato. [**Platone.**]

Platone, Plato, the Greek philosopher, born at Athens c. B.C. 428, died at the age of over eighty, B.C. 347. His family on the father's side claimed descent from Codrus, last King of Athens. In his youth Plato became a follower of Socrates and one of his most ardent admirers. After the death of Socrates in B.C. 399 he retired to Megara, and subsequently visited Egypt, Sicily, and the Greek cities in S. Italy in quest of knowledge. After his return (c. 389) he began to teach his philosophical system in the gymnasium of the Academy, whence his school was subsequently called the Academic [**Accademici**]. His extant writings consist of a large number of works on various philosophical subjects, in the form of dialogues. The most illustrious of Plato's pupils was Aristotle, the founder of the Peripatetic school [**Peripatetici**].

D.'s knowledge of Plato's works was practically confined to the *Timaeus*, which is the only one he quotes or mentions by name (Par. iv. 49; Conv. iii. 5^{46}) [**Timeo**]; he would be more or less familiar also with the numerous references to Plato which occur in the works of Aristotle and Albertus Magnus, as well as in the philosophical treatises of Cicero, the *De Civitate Dei* of St. Augustine, and the *Summa* of St. Thomas Aquinas.

D. mentions Plato by name some eighteen times, *Platone*, Inf. iv. 134; Par. iv. 24; Conv. iii. 5⁴⁵, 14⁷⁶, ⁸²; iv. 6¹¹⁶⁻²⁸, 24⁵⁷; *Plato*, Purg. iii. 43; Conv. ii. 5²¹, ³³, ³⁸, 14³², ³⁴; iii. 9¹⁰⁰; iv. 15⁵⁵, 21¹⁷; Epist. x. 29⁵⁷⁷.

Plato is placed with Socrates among the ancient philosophers who are grouped round Aristotle in Limbo, ranking next to the Master, Inf. iv. 134–5 [Limbo]; he is coupled with Aristotle as having failed to attain the ultimate *quia* or final cause, in spite of all their philosophical investigations, Purg. iii. 43; Plato's theory, as propounded in the *Timaeus* (41–2), that the souls of men abide in the stars, whence they descend to inhabit human bodies, and that after death they return again to their respective stars, Par. iv. 22–4, 49–50; Conv. ii. 14³³; iv. 21¹⁷⁻¹⁸ [Timeo]; his opinion that 'substantial generation' is effected by the motive powers of the Heavens, or by the stars, especially in the case of human souls, Conv. ii. 14²⁸⁻³⁵; his theory as to the number of the celestial intelligences, and his use of the term 'idea' for them (cf. Cicero, *Acad. Quaest.* i. 8; St. Augustine, *Civ. Dei*, vii. 28), Conv. ii. 5²¹⁻³⁴, 14³¹⁻⁴; iv. 15⁵⁵⁻⁸; cf. Par. xiii. 97–8; his theory, as propounded in the *Timaeus* (40), as to the position of the Earth in the centre of the universe, and as to its motions, which are axial but not orbital (cf. Aristotle, *De Coelo*, ii. 4; Cicero, *Acad. Quaest.* iv. 39),

Conv. iii. 5⁴⁵⁻⁵² [Terra²]; his theory that sight consists, not in the entering of the visible into the eye, but in the going forth of the visual power towards the visible object (*Tim.* 45; cf. Albertus Magnus, *De Sensu et Sensato*, i. 5), Conv. iii. 9⁹⁹⁻¹⁰³; his contempt for worldly goods, and for regal dignity, though of royal descent, Conv. iii. 14⁷⁶⁻⁹; Aristotle, though his best friend, yet did not scruple to differ from him, Conv. iii. 14⁷⁹⁻⁸²; the doctrine of the mean as applied to virtue held by him and his predecessor Socrates, Conv. iv. 6¹¹⁵⁻²⁵; the founder of the Academic school of philosophy, as the head of which he was succeeded by his nephew Speusippus, Conv. iv. 6¹²⁵⁻³⁰; his theory that souls differ in nobility according to the various degrees of nobility in the stars to which they belong, Conv. iv. 21¹⁷⁻¹⁹; Socrates' opinion of him, and Cicero's statement (*Senect.* § 5) that he died at the age of eighty-one, Conv. iv. 24⁵⁷⁻⁶³; his use of metaphors in order to convey to his readers what, for lack of suitable terms, could not otherwise be expressed, Epist. x. 29⁵⁷⁷; the Platonic theory as to the complex nature of the soul (*Tim.* 69; cf. Cicero, *Acad. Quaest.* iv. 39) qualified as an error, Purg. iv. 5–6; his attempt to solve (in the *Timaeus*) the secrets of the heavens, referred to by G. del Virgilio, Carm. 11.

Plauto, Plautus (Titus Maccius Plautus), celebrated Roman comic poet, native of Sarsina in Umbria, B. C. 254–184; mentioned, together with Terence, Caecilius, and Varro (or Varius), by Statius (in Purgatory), who asks Virgil for news of them, and is told that they and Persius and many others are with Homer and V. himself in Limbo, Purg. xxii. 98. [**Limbo**.]

Plinius, Pliny the Elder (Caius Plinius Secundus Major), Roman naturalist and historian, born at Comum in N. Italy A.D. 23, killed in the great eruption of Vesuvius, A.D. 79. His most important work is the *Historia Naturalis* in thirty-seven books, a storehouse of information on every branch of natural science as known to the ancient world.

D. mentions Pliny, together with Livy, Frontinus, and Orosius, as a 'master of lofty prose', V. E. ii. 6⁸³.

Pluto, either Pluto, the god of the nether world, or Plutus, the god of wealth, placed by D. as guardian of Circle IV of Hell, where the Avaricious and Prodigal are punished, Inf. vi. 115; viii. 2; *il gran nemico*, Inf. vi. 115; *egli*, vii. 5; *enfiata labbia*, *v.* 7; *maledetto lupo*, *v.* 8; *fiera crudele*, *v.* 15; as D. and Virgil approach he cries out to them some unintelligible words, with the intention of frightening them back, but being rebuked by V. he falls to the ground (Inf. vii. 1–15) [**Avari**].

Po, river Po (Roman Padus), principal river of Italy, which rises in Monte Viso, a peak of the Cottian Alps in Piedmont, and flows E. through Piedmont and the SW. extremity of Lombardy, after which it forms the N. boundary of the Emilia; about twenty miles from the sea it divides into two main branches, and enters the Adriatic by several mouths about midway between Venice and Ravenna, its total length being some 450 miles; its principal tributaries are the Ticino, the Adda, the Oglio, and the Mincio.

The Po is mentioned, *Po*, Inf. xx. 78; Purg. xvi. 115; Par. vi. 51; Conv. iv. 13¹²⁹; *il Po*, Inf. v. 98; Purg. xiv. 92; *Pado*, Par. xv. 137; *Padus*, Epist. vii. 7¹³⁹; Ecl. ii. 67; *Eridanus*, Epist. vii. 3⁴⁹; Carm. 47; Ravenna is described by Francesca (in Circle II of Hell) as being *Sulla marina dove il Po descende Per aver pace co' seguaci sui* (i. e. on the Adriatic coast near where the Po and its tributaries discharge into the sea), Inf. v. 98–9 [**Ravenna**]; the confluence of the Mincio and the Po near Governolo, Inf. xx. 77–8 [**Governo: Mincio**]; the plain of Old Lombardy (through which the Po flows) described by Pier da Medicina (in Bolgia 9 of Circle VIII of Hell) as *lo dolce piano Che da Vercelli a Marcabò dichina*, Inf. xxviii. 74–5 [**Marcabò : Vercelli**]; Romagna described by Guido del Duca (in Circle II of Purgatory) as being *tra il Po e il monte* (i. e. between the Po and the Apennines), Purg. xiv. 22 [**Romagna**]; the March of Treviso, together with Lombardy and Romagna, described by Marco Lombardo (in Circle III of Purgatory) as *il paese ch' Adice e Po riga*, Purg. xvi. 115 [**Marca Trivisiana**]; Monte Viso, in which the Po rises (or perhaps the Alps in general), referred to by the Emperor Justinian (in the Heaven of Mercury) as *L'alpestre rocce di che, Po, tu labi*, Par. vi. 51 [**Monte

Veso] ; Cacciaguida (in the Heaven of Mars) says that his wife came to him from the valley of the Po (i. e. probably from Ferrara), Par. xv. 137; the inhabitants of Upper Italy described as *i Latini dalla parte di Po*, as distinguished from those of Lower Italy, *dalla parte di Tevere*, Conv. iv. 13$^{129-30}$; D. urges the Emperor Henry VII to leave the valley of the Po, and to come and make an end of the noxious beast (i. e. Florence), which drinks not of Po, nor of Tiber, but of Arno, Epist. vii. 3$^{48-50}$, 7$^{138-41}$; Tityrus (i. e. D.) refers to Ravenna as being situated on the coast of the Emilia, between the right bank of the Po and the left of the Rubicon, Ecl. ii. 67–8 [**Ravenna : Rubicon**].

Podestadi, Powers, mentioned by Beatrice (in the Crystalline Heaven), in her exposition of the arrangement of the Angelic Hierarchies, as ranking last in the second Hierarchy, Dominions and Virtues ranking above them, Par. xxviii. 122–3; in the *Convivio* D. states that the second Hierarchy is composed of Principalities, Virtues, and Dominions, in that order, Powers (*Potestati*) coming last in the first Hierarchy, their function being to contemplate the third Person of the Trinity, Conv. ii. 6$^{53, 86-9}$ [**Gerarchia**]. They preside over the Heaven of the Sun [**Paradiso** [1]].

Poeni, Carthaginians (so called as being colonists from Phoenicia), Mon. ii. 4^{61}, 11^{53}. [**Cartaginesi.**]

Poëtica, Poëtria. [*Ars Poëtica.*]

Pola, sea-port near the S. extremity of the Istrian peninsula, on the Gulf of Quarnero [**Istria :**

Quarnaro] ; it is celebrated for its Roman remains, the most important of which is the unique amphitheatre, it being the only one now existing with the outer walls intact.

D. mentions Pola in connexion with the remains of old sepulchres which abound in the neighbourhood, Inf. ix. 113.

Polenta, castle near Bertinoro, in the Emilia, a few miles S. of Forlì, whence the Guelf Polenta family took their name.

In reply to an inquiry from Guido da Montefeltro (in Bolgia 8 of Circle VIII of Hell) as to the condition of affairs in Romagna, D. states that the 'eagle of Polenta' (in allusion to the arms of the family) still broods over Ravenna, as it had done for many years past (they having been lords of Ravenna since 1270), and that it now (1300) also covers Cervia with its wings, Inf. xxvii. 40–2 [**Cervia : Ravenna**]. The head of the house at the time of which D. is speaking was Guido Vecchio da Polenta (d. 1310), father of Francesca da Rimini, and grandfather of D.'s future host at Ravenna.

Polenta, Guido Novello da], lord of Ravenna (d. c. 1325), nephew of Francesca da Rimini, and grandson of the following; it was at his court at Ravenna that D. spent the last three or four years of his life (c. 1317–21), and it was he who gave the poet honourable burial, himself pronouncing the funeral oration; in the poetical correspondence between D. and G. del Virgilio he figures under the name of *Iolas*, Ecl. ii. 95 ; Ecl. R. 80. [**Iolas.**]

Polenta, Guido Vecchio da],

lord of Ravenna (d. 1310), father of Francesca da Rimini, and grandfather of the preceding; his lordship of Ravenna and Cervia is alluded to, Inf. xxvii. 40-2. [Polenta.]

Policreto, Polycletus, celebrated Greek sculptor (c. B.C. 452-412), contemporary of Phidias; mentioned in connexion with the sculptures in Circle I of Purgatory, which D. says would have shamed not only the Greek sculptor, but even Nature herself, Purg. x. 31-3.

Polidoro, Polydorus, son of Priam, King of Troy, and of Hecuba. Just before Troy fell into the hands of the Greeks, Priam entrusted Polydorus, together with a large sum of money, to Polymestor, King of the Thracian Chersonese; but after the destruction of Troy the latter killed Polydorus for the sake of the treasure, and cast his body into the sea. Subsequently the body was washed up on to the shore, and was found and recognized by Hecuba, who avenged her son's murder by putting out Polymestor's eyes, and killing his two children.

Polydorus (whose story is told by Ovid, *Metam.* xiii. 429-38) is mentioned in connexion with the finding of his corpse by Hecuba, Inf. xxx. 18 [Ecuba]; and again, in connexion with his murder by Polymestor, Purg. xx. 115 [Polinestor].

Polinestor, Polymestor, King of the Thracian Chersonese, who murdered his ward, Polydorus, son of Priam, for the sake of his treasure [Polidoro]. D. includes him among the instances of avarice proclaimed by the Avaricious in Circle V of Purgatory, Purg. xx. 115. [Avari.]

Polinice, Polynices, son of Oedipus, King of Thebes, and of Jocasta, and twin-brother of Eteocles. After the abdication of Oedipus, Polynices and Eteocles agreed to reign alternately in Thebes; but when E.'s term had expired he refused to admit P. to the throne, whereupon the latter appealed for aid to Adrastus, King of Argos. Out of this quarrel arose the celebrated war of the Seven against Thebes, in the course of which Polynices and Eteocles slew each other in single combat.

D. refers to Polynices as the brother of Eteocles, in connexion with the funeral pyre on which they were both laid, the hatred between them being perpetuated after death, as appeared from the fact that the flame from the pyre divided in two as it ascended, Inf. xxvi. 54 [Eteocle]; the two brothers are alluded to, in reference to their fratricidal strife, as *la doppia tristizia di Jocasta*, Purg. xxii. 56 [Jocasta].

Polynices is mentioned several times in connexion with the incidents related by Statius (in the *Thebaid*) as having occurred when he arrived at the court of Adrastus as a fugitive from Thebes, Conv. iv. 25[60-4], 78-88, 107-16. [Adrasto.]

Polinnia, Polymnia, Muse of the sublime Hymn; she and her sister Muses are mentioned together as the inspirers of poetic song, Par. xxiii. 56. [Muse.]

Polissena, Polyxena, daughter of Priam, King of Troy, and of Hecuba. Achilles, having become enamoured of her, and being tempted by the promise that she should be given him to wife if he would join the Trojans, went unarmed into the temple of Apollo at Thymbra, where he was treacherously assassinated by Paris [**Achilles**]. Subsequently, when the Greeks were on their voyage home, bearing Hecuba and Polyxena with them as captives, the shade of Achilles appeared to them on the coast of Thrace and demanded the sacrifice of Polyxena, who was thereupon torn from her mother and slain by Neoptolemus on the tomb of his father.

D. mentions Polyxena in connexion with the grief and rage of Hecuba at the sight of her dead body, Inf. xxx. 17 [**Ecuba**].

Politica, *Politics* of Aristotle; quoted as *Politica*, Conv. iv. 4^{46}; Mon. i. 3^{91}, 5^{15}, 12^{68}; ii. 3^{17}, 7^{56}, 8^{14}. D. quotes from the *Politics* upwards of a dozen times:—nature does nothing in vain, Par. viii. 113–14 (*Pol.* i. 2); Conv. iii. $15^{81, 91}$; Mon. ii. 7^{1-13}; man cannot attain his end unless he lives in society, Par. viii. 115–17 (*Pol.* i. 2); if man lives in society there must be diversity of functions, Par. viii. 118–20 (*Pol.* ii. 2); man is by nature a sociable animal, Conv. iv. 4^{9-10} (*Pol.* i. 2; iii. 6); Conv. iv. 27^{29}; where a number of things are ordained to one end, it behoves one of them to regulate or govern the others, and the others to submit, Conv. iv. 4^{46-50} (*Pol.* i. 5); Mon. i. 5^{15-19}; ii. 7^{51-9}; those who are strong in understanding the natural rulers of others, Mon. i. 3^{91-2} (*Pol.* i. 2); every house is ruled by the

oldest, Mon. i. 5^{33-4} (*Pol.* i. 2); man enjoys true liberty only under the rule of a monarch, Mon. i. 12^{55-63} (*Pol.* iii. 7); in a bad state the good man is a bad citizen, but in a good state the good man and the good citizen are one, Mon. i. 12^{67-71} (*Pol.* iii. 4); laws made to suit the state, not the state to suit the laws, Mon. i. 12^{77-83} (*Pol.* iv. 1); nobility consists in virtue and ancestral wealth, Mon. ii. 3^{15-17} (*Pol.* iv. 8); Par. viii. 113–14; Conv. iii. $15^{81, 91}$; a part should risk itself to save the whole, hence a man ought to risk himself for his country, Mon. ii. 8^{11-14} (*Pol.* i. 2). [**Aristotile**.]

Polluce, Pollux, son of Jupiter and Leda, and twin-brother of Castor. At their death Jupiter placed the twins among the stars as the constellation Gemini.

Castor and Pollux are mentioned together to indicate the sign Gemini, Purg. iv. 61. [**Castore: Gemelli**.]

Polo. [**Paolo**.]

Polyphemus, one of the Cyclopes in Sicily, gigantic monster who had but one eye in the centre of his forehead, and lived upon human flesh; his dwelling was a cave near Mt. Aetna. Having become enamoured of the nymph Galatea he wooed her, but was rejected in favour of the youth Acis, whom she loved; the Cyclops thereupon in jealousy crushed the latter under a rock. When Ulysses was driven upon Sicily, Polyphemus devoured some of his companions, and Ulysses would have shared their fate had he not blinded the monster and escaped. One of them, Achaemenides, who was left behind, was found there by the Trojans when they landed in Sicily, and related to them the horrible tale of how all his companions had been devoured by the Cyclops.

D. mentions Polyphemus (whom the old commentator identifies with King Robert of Naples, his cave representing Bologna) in connexion with the story of Acis and Galatea, Ecl. ii. 75, 76 [Acis : Galatea]; he is spoken of as *Cyclops*, Ecl. ii. 47 [Cyclops]; the story of Achaemenides is referred to (D. probably being indebted for it to Ovid, *Metam.* xiv. 160–222, from whom the words 'humano sanguine rictus' appear to be borrowed), Ecl. ii. 76–83 [Achaemenides].

Pompeiano, Pompeian; the Emperor Justinian (in the Heaven of Mercury) speaks of *la Pompeiana tuba,* 'the Pompeian trumpet' (i. e. the trumpet of Pompey's sons, Sextus and Cneius, who were defeated by Julius Caesar at Munda, B.C. 45), Par. vi. 72. [Munda.]

Pompeio, Pompey the Great (Cneius Pompeius Magnus), the triumvir, born B.C. 106, died B.C. 48; in his youth he distinguished himself as one of Sulla's most successful generals in the war against Marius and his party, and earned from Sulla the surname of Magnus on account of his victories in the African campaign against them; he was consul with Crassus in B.C. 70, and in B.C. 59 joined Julius Caesar and Crassus in the first triumvirate; at this time he married Caesar's daughter Julia; in B.C. 55 he was consul a second time with Crassus;

meanwhile Caesar's increasing power made a contest between them for supremacy inevitable, and in B.C. 49 the civil war broke out; in the next year Pompey was completely defeated by Caesar at the battle of Pharsalia, and fled to Egypt, where he was murdered by order of Ptolemy's ministers (Sept. 29, B.C. 48). [Cesare.]

The Emperor Justinian (in the Heaven of Mercury) mentions Pompey in connexion with his achievements in his youth under the Roman Eagle against Marius, Par. vi. 53.

Pompeio, Sesto. [Sesto [2].]
Pompeo. [Pompeio.]
Pompilio, Numa. [Numa Pompilio.]
Ponente. [Occidente.]
Ponte Rubaconte. [Rubaconte.]

Ponte Vecchio], bridge over the Arno at Florence; the ancient bridge which existed in D.'s time is said to have been of Roman origin; the present bridge was built by Taddeo Gaddi in 1362 to replace the one destroyed, together with the Ponte alla Carraja, by the great flood of 1333.

D. alludes to the Ponte Vecchio, in connexion with the ancient statue of Mars which used to stand upon the bridge, as *il passo d'Arno,* Inf. xiii. 146; *Marte,* Par. xvi. 46; *il ponte,* Par. xvi. 146. [Marte [1].]

Ponte di Castel Sant' Angelo], bridge over the Tiber at Rome, commonly known as the Ponte S. Angelo; it originally consisted of seven arches, and was built (A.D. 136) by the Emperor Hadrian to connect his tomb (the present Castello Sant' Angelo) with the city, being named Pons Aelius from his family name.

D. refers to it as *lo ponte*, in connexion with the arrangements made to divide the streams of pilgrims going to and from St. Peter's during the Jubilee in 1300, Inf. xviii. 21–33. [Giubbileo.]

Pontì, Ponthieu, former district of France, consisting of a ' county ', and comprising part of the province of Picardy; it is included in the modern department of Somme, and was situated at the mouth of the river of that name, with Abbeville for its capital. It belonged to the English crown, having been ceded to Edward I by Philip III in 1279; the succession to it was, however, disputed in 1290 between Prince Edward (afterwards Edward II) and the Comte d'Aumale, and it was held by the King of France until 1299, when Edward I recovered it as the dowry of his second wife, Margaret of France, daughter of Philip III.

Hugh Capet (in Circle V of Purgatory) mentions the seizure of Ponthieu, together with that of Normandy and Gascony, among the misdeeds of his descendants of the royal house of France, which he says began with the ' dowry of Provence' (i.e. the union of Provence to the French crown), Purg. xx. 61–6. [Guascogna: Normandia: Provenza.]

Porciano], stronghold of the Conti Guidi in the Casentino; alluded to by Guido del Duca in his description (in Circle II of Purgatory) of the course of the Arno, where he speaks of the inhabitants of the Casentino as *brutti porci*, Purg. xiv. 43. [Arno: Casentino.]

Porretanus, Gilbertus. [Gilbertus Porretanus.]

Porsena, Lars Porsena, King of the Etruscan town of Clusium, who marched against Rome at the head of a large army for the purpose of restoring Tarquinius Superbus to the throne. While he was besieging the city Mucius made an attempt to assassinate him, which led to Porsena's withdrawal from the siege.

D. mentions Porsena in connexion with the exploit of Cloelia, one of the Roman hostages, who escaped from the Etruscan camp and swam across the Tiber to Rome, Mon. ii. 4[65–8] [Cloelia]; and with the attempt made on his life by Mucius, Mon. ii. 5[121–6] [Muzio].

Porta Peruzza], one of the minor gates of the city of Florence, said to be the gate referred to by Cacciaguida (in the Heaven of Mars) as having been named after the Della Pera family, Par. xvi. 125–6. [Pera, Della.]

Porta Sole, one of the gates of Perugia, on the SE. side of the town, looking towards Assisi, Par. xi. 47. [Perugia.]

Porta dell' Inferno], gate of Hell; described, Inf. iii. 1–11; referred to, in contradistinction to the gate of Dis, as *men secreta porta*, Inf. viii. 125; and again, *la porta, Lo cui sogliare a nessuno è negato*, Inf. xiv. 86–7. [Porta di Dite.]

Porta del Paradiso], gate of Paradise; thought by some to be referred to as *la porta di san Pietro*, Inf. i. 134. [**Porta di san Pietro.**]

Porta del Purgatorio], gate of Purgatory; referred to as *la porta*, Purg. iv. 129; ix. 76, 90, 120; *la porta sacrata*, Purg. ix. 130; *l'entrata*, Purg. ix. 51, 62; *regge sacra*, Purg. ix. 134; *ove si serra*, Purg. xxviii. 102; and, perhaps, as *la porta di san Pietro*, Inf. i. 134. [**Porta di san Pietro.**]

The approach to the gate of Purgatory is by three steps of diverse colours ('tre gradi, di color diversi', Purg. ix. 76-7, 94-105; 'tre gradi', Purg. ix. 76, 106; xxi. 48, 53; 'scaletta dei tre gradi breve', Purg. xxi. 48); the first ('lo scaglion primaio') is of polished white marble (Purg. ix. 94-6); the second is of rock, almost black, rough and burnt as with fire, and cracked across its length and breadth, in the shape of a cross (*vv.* 97-9); the third and topmost is of porphyry of a bright blood-red colour (*vv.* 100-2); the threshold of the gate, upon which is seated the Angel of God, is of adamantine rock (*vv.* 103-5).

Porta di Dite], gate of the city of Dis; referred to as *l'entrata*, Inf. viii. 81; *la porta*, Inf. ix. 89; xiv. 45; *le porte*, Inf. viii. 82, 115 [**Dite**]; at the entrance is a lofty tower, which appears to be red-hot (Inf. ix. 36), upon which are stationed the three Furies as guardians of the approach, Inf. ix. 37-44 [**Erine**].

Porta di san Pietro, gate of St. Peter, Inf. i. 134; thought by some to be the entrance into Paradise, of which St. Peter held the keys, but usually understood of the gate of Purgatory, the keys of which were entrusted by St. Peter to the Angel Warder (Purg. ix. 127-9).

Porta san Piero], one of the gates of the ancient city of Florence; referred to by Cacciaguida (in the Heaven of Mars) as *la porta*, with especial allusion to the Cerchi, who lived in the quarter of the city which took its name from the gate, Par. xvi. 94. [**Cerchi.**]

The Porta san Piero was on the E. side of the city, and was approached by what is now the Via del Corso, the ancient Corso.

Portinari, Beatrice. [**Beatrice [1].**]

Portinari, Folco], father of Beatrice Portinari; he was one of the fourteen Buonomini instituted in 1281, and subsequently several times (in 1282, 1285, and 1287) held the office of Prior; he died Dec. 31, 1289, and was buried in the chapel of the Ospedale di Santa Maria Nuova (which he had founded in 1287), his funeral being attended by the Signoria of Florence in their official capacity. He married Cilia de' Caponsacchi of Florence, and had by her a number of children, besides his daughter Beatrice, who is specially mentioned (as the wife of Simone de' Bardi) in his will (dated Jan. 15, 128$\frac{7}{8}$). His death is recorded by D., who says that he was a man of great excellence and goodness, V. N. § 22[3-16]. [**Beatrice [1].**]

Portinari, Manetto], brother of Beatrice Portinari, to whom (or to his younger brother, Ricovero) D. is supposed to allude as his next best friend after Guido Cavalcanti, V. N. §§ 33^{2—7}, 34⁵.

Portinari, Ricovero], brother of Beatrice Portinari, who is perhaps alluded to, V. N. §§ 33^{2—7}, 34⁵. [**Portinari, Manetto.**]

Portogallo, Portugal ; *quel di Portogallo* (i. e. Dionysius Agricola, King of Portugal, 1279–1325), Par. xix. 139. [**Dionisio**³.]

Potestati. [**Podestadi.**]

Praedicamenta, *Categories* of Aristotle ; quoted as *Praedicamenta*, Mon. iii. 15⁵⁸ ; A. T. § 2⁵ ; and *Antepraedicamenta* (this being the title given by D. to the first part, which is introductory), A. T. § 12⁵⁶ [***Antepraedicamenta***] ; Aristotle's saying that truth and falsehood in speech arise from the being or the not-being of the thing, Mon. iii. 15^{56—9} (*Categ.* xii) ; form or shape the fourth kind of quality, according to Aristotle, A. T. § 2^{3—6} (*Categ.* viii) ; his definition of what is equivocal, A. T. § 12^{54—7} (*Categ.* i. *init.*) [**Aristotile**].

Praga, Prague on the Moldau, capital of Bohemia ; the Eagle in the Heaven of Jupiter speaks of Bohemia as *il regno di Praga*, and prophesies that it will be laid waste by the Emperor Albert I (in allusion to his invasion in 1304 of the dominions of his brother-in-law Wenceslas IV), Par. xix. 115–17 [**Alberto Tedesco : Buemme**].

Prata, Guido da. [**Guido da Prata.**]

Pratenses, inhabitants of Prato ; their dialect, like that of the people of the Casentino, harsh and discordant owing to their exaggerated accentuation, V. E. i. 11^{40—2} (where there is another reading, *Fratenses*, 'the people of Fratta') [**Fratenses**].

Prato, town in Tuscany, about ten miles NW. of Florence on the road to Pistoja.

D. mentions Prato in his apostrophe to Florence, where he says, ' thou wilt be aware within a little while of that which Prato, as well as others, is wishing thee', Inf. xxvi. 8–9. The allusion is not clear ; it is commonly supposed to refer to the Cardinal Niccolò da Prato, whose excommunication of Florence in 1304 was followed by several terrible calamities in the city (fires, &c.) in the same year, which were popularly attributed to this malediction (Vill. viii. 69–71) [**Nicholaus**].

Prato, Niccolò da. [**Nicholaus.**]

Pratomagno, mountain-ridge in Tuscany, which forms the W. barrier of the Casentino, the upper valley of the Arno, the main ridge of the Apennines on the opposite side forming the E. barrier.

Buonconte da Montefeltro (in Ante-purgatory) speaks of the Casentino as *la valle Da Pratomagno al gran giogo*, 'the valley between Pratomagno and the great ridge (of the Apennine)', Purg. v. 115–16. [**Casentino.**]

Predoni, Violent Robbers ; placed, together with Tyrants and Murderers, among the Violent in Round 1 of Circle VII of Hell, Inf. xi. 38 ; xii. 103–39 ; their punishment is to be immersed up to their waists in Phlegethon, the boiling river of blood, Inf. xii. 121–2 (the Tyrants being immersed up to their eyebrows, *vv.* 103–5, and the

Murderers up to their necks, *vv.*
116–17) [**Violenti**]. *Examples*:
Sextus Pompeius [**Sesto**[2]]; Rinieri da Corneto [**Corneto, Rinier
da**]; Rinieri de' Pazzi [**Pazzo,
Rinier**].

Prenestino [**Penestrino**].

Pressa, Della, ancient noble
family of Florence, mentioned by
Cacciaguida (in the Heaven of
Mars) as having been of importance
in his day, Par. xvi. 100. They
lived in the neighbourhood of the
Duomo (Vill. iv. 10); and were
among the Ghibelline families who
were expelled from Florence in 1258
(vi. 65).

Priamo. [**Priamus.**]

Priamus, Priam, son of Laomedon, King of Troy at the time of
the Trojan war. When the Greeks
landed he was already advanced in
years and took no active part in the
war. After the fall of Troy he
was slain by Pyrrhus, son of Achilles,
before the altar of Jupiter [**Pirro**[1]],
By his wife Hecuba he was the
father of Hector, Paris, Polydorus,
Polyxena, Creusa, and a large
number of other children.

D. quotes Virgil's description of
the Trojans as 'Priami gens'
(*Aen.* iii. 1), and mentions Priam as
the father of Creusa, the first wife
of Aeneas, Mon. ii. 3[65, 94] [**Creusa**]; he is referred to, in connexion
with the fall of Troy and his own
death, as *il re*, Inf. xxx. 15; his
inquiry of Sinon as to the origin and
purport of the wooden horse (*Aen.* ii.
148–51) is alluded to, Inf. xxx. 115
[**Sinone**].

Prima Philosophia. [**Philosophia Prima.**]

Prima Rhetorica. [**Rhetorica
Prima.**]

Primavera, 'Spring', name by
which Giovanna, the lady-love of
Guido Cavalcanti, was known on
account of her beauty, V. N.
§ 24[20–3]; Son. xiv. 15. [**Giovanna**[4].]

Primo Cielo. [**Luna, Cielo
della.**]

Primo Mobile. [**Cielo Cristallino.**]

Principati, Principalities, mentioned by Beatrice (in the Crystalline
Heaven) in her exposition of the
arrangement of the Angelic Hierarchies, as ranking first in the third
Hierarchy, Archangels and Angels
ranking below them, Par. xxviii.
124–6; *Principi celesti*, Par. viii.
34; in the *Convivio* D. ranks
Principalities first in the second
Hierarchy, above Virtues and Dominions, Conv. ii. 6[50–3] [**Gerarchia**]. They preside over the
Heaven of Venus [**Paradiso**[1]].

Principi Negligenti], Princes
who neglected repentance; placed
in a valley of flowers outside
Purgatory proper, Purg. vii–viii.
[**Antipurgatorio.**]

Principi, Reggimento de'.
[**Regimine Principum, De.**]

Principiorum, Magister Sex.
[**Magister**[3].]

Priora Analytica. [**Analytica
Priora.**]

Prisciano, Priscian (Priscianus
Caesariensis), celebrated Latin grammarian, born at Caesarea in Cappa-
docia, fl. c. A.D. 500. The work to
which he owes his fame is the *Institutiones Grammaticae*, a systematic

exposition of Latin grammar in eighteen books.

D. places Priscian (on what grounds is unknown), together with Brunetto Latini and Francesco d'Accorso, in Round 3 of Circle VII of Hell among those guilty of unnatural offences, Inf. xv. 109. [Sodomiti.]

Procne. [Progne.]

Prodighi], Prodigals; punished with the Avaricious in Circle IV of Hell, Inf. vii. 22–66; and in Circle V of Purgatory, Purg. xix. 70–5, 118–26 [Avari]; they are alluded to, Canz. xix. 20.

Proemio della Bibbia, St. Jerome's Preface to the Bible; quoted, Conv. iv. 5[143–4]. [Jeronimo.]

Proenza. [Provenza.]

Profeta. [Propheta.]

Progne], Procne, daughter of Pandion, King of Athens, wife of Tereus, and sister of Philomela; according to Ovid's version of the story (*Metam.* vi. 412–676), which D. follows, she was metamorphosed into a nightingale, her sister becoming a swallow, and Tereus a hawk.

D. introduces her as an example of wrath in Circle III of Purgatory, in connexion with her slaying of her son Itys, her crime being referred to as 'l'empiezza di lei, che mutò forma Nell' uccel che a cantar più si diletta', Purg. xvii. 19–20. [Filomela : Iracondi.]

Prometeo], Prometheus, son of the Titan Iapetus and Clymene; he is represented as the great benefactor of mankind, having furnished them with fire and a knowledge of all the useful arts; according to one tra-

dition he created man out of earth and water, and bestowed upon him a portion of all the qualities possessed by animals.

D. refers to him as *lo figlio di Giapeto*, quoting a passage from Ovid (*Metam.* i. 78–83) in allusion to his supposed creation of man, Conv. iv. 15[76–84]. [Giapeto.]

Propheta. [David : Ezechiel : Isaia.]

Proprietà degli Elementi, Delle. [*Proprietatibus Elementorum, De.*]

Proprietatibus Elementorum, De, treatise of Albertus Magnus *On the Properties of the Elements*; D. refers to this work (perhaps 1. i. 5), which he quotes as *il libro delle Proprietà degli Elementi*, and to the *De Natura Locorum*, for the opinion of Albertus as to the equatorial circle, Conv. iii. 5[111–15]. [Locorum, De Natura.]

Proserpina, Proserpine, daughter of Jupiter and Ceres; while she was gathering flowers in a meadow near Enna in Sicily, she 'herself, a fairer flower, was gathered' by Pluto, who suddenly appeared and carried her off to be the Queen of the lower world (Ovid, *Metam.* v. 385 ff.). [Cerere.]

D. says that Matilda in the Terrestrial Paradise reminded him of Proserpine 'nel tempo che perdette La madre lei, ed ella primavera' (i. e. either the 'perpetuum ver' of Enna mentioned by Ovid, or more probably, as in Par. xxx. 63, the spring flowers she had been gathering, 'collecti flores'), Purg. xxviii. 50–1; Proserpine is alluded to, in her capacity of Queen of the lower

world, as *la regina dell' eterno pianto*,
Inf. ix. 44; and (by Farinata in
Circle VI of Hell) as *la donna che
qui regge*, Inf. x. 80. [Ecate:
Luna.]

Provenza, Provence, former
province of France, at one time an
independent 'county', situated in the
extreme SE. on the Mediterranean,
and bounded on the W. by the
Rhone, on the E. by the maritime
Alps, and on the N. by the
Dauphiné. In 1246, through the
marriage of Charles of Anjou,
brother of Louis IX of France, with
Beatrice, heiress of Raymond Berenger IV (Count of Provence, 1209–
1245), Provence became a depen-
dency of the royal house of France
(Purg. xx. 61) [Provenzale].

Provence is mentioned, together
with Apulia, by Sordello (in Ante-
purgatory) in connexion with the
bad government of the Angevin
Charles II, who was King of Apulia and Count of Provence in succession to his father, Charles I,
Purg. vii. 126 [Puglia]; *lo parlare
di Provenza*, i.e. the Provençal
tongue, Conv. i. 11¹⁰⁰ [*Lingua Oc*];
it is referred to by Charles Martel
(in the Heaven of Venus), grandson
of Charles of Anjou and of Beatrice
of Provence (who would have been
Count of Provence if he had survived his father), as the country on
the left bank of the Rhone, below
its confluence with the Sorgue, Par.
viii. 58–9 [Carlo³: Sorga]; it is
indicated by the mention of its inhabitants as the S. limit of the
domain of the *langue d'oïl*, V. E. i.
8⁶³.

Provenzale, Provençal, per-

taining to Provence; *la gran dote
Provenzale* (i.e. the union of Provence with France through the
marriages of Louis IX and Charles
of Anjou with Margaret and Beatrice, daughters of Raymond Berenger IV, Count of Provence),
Purg. xx. 61 [Carlo¹: Pro-
venza]; the Provençal tongue,
Conv. i. 6⁵⁶ [*Lingua Oc*]; native of
Provence, *il Provenzale*, that is,
Giraut de Borneil, Conv. iv. 11⁹³
[Borneil, Gerardus de: Provenzali.]

Provenzali, inhabitants of
Provence; their sufferings under the
rule of Charles of Anjou a just
retribution for their ingratitude to
Romieu, the minister of Raymond
Berenger IV, Par. vi. 130–1
[Romeo]; *Provinciales*, their coun-
try forms the S. limit of the domain
of the *langue d'oïl*, V. E. i. 8⁶³
[Provenza: Provenzale].

Provenzan Salvani, Ghibelline
of Siena, where he was at the head
of affairs at the time of the great
victory over the Florentine Guelfs
at Montaperti, Sept. 4, 1260 [Mont-
aperti]; it was he who at the
Council of Empoli after the battle
advocated the destruction of the
city of Florence, which was averted
by the firmness and patriotism of
Farinata (Inf. x. 91) [Farinata];
he was Podestà of Montepulciano in
1261; he met his death in an
engagement with the Florentines at
Colle, in Valdelsa, June 11, 1269,
when he was taken prisoner and
beheaded [Colle].

D. places him among the Proud in
Circle I of Purgatory, Purg. xi. 121;
colui, v. 109 [Superbi]; he is

pointed out to D. by Oderisi, who mentions him as an instance of the hollowness of worldly renown, for at one time the whole of Tuscany resounded with his fame, whereas at the present his name is hardly mentioned even in Siena, where he was captain at the time of their great triumph over Florence (*vv.* 109–17); in response to D.'s inquiries O. explains who he was, and that he is now being punished for his presumption in trying to make himself all-powerful in Siena (*vv.* 118–26); O. further explains that Provenzano was admitted into Purgatory before his due time on account of his noble humility on one occasion during the height of his power, when he seated himself in the market-place at Siena and begged from the passers-by, until he had raised sufficient money to ransom a friend, who had been taken prisoner by Charles of Anjou (*vv.* 127–38).

Proverbi. [*Proverbiorum, Liber.*]

Proverbiorum, Liber, Book of the Proverbs of Solomon; quoted as *Proverbi*, Conv. iii. 11[128] (*Prov.* viii. 17); Conv. iii. 14[62] (*Prov.* viii. 23); Conv. iii. 15[167–77] (*Prov.* viii. 27–30); Conv. iii. 15[190] (*Prov.* iv. 18); Conv. iv. 5[14] (*Prov.* viii. 6); Conv. iv. 7[96] (*Prov.* xxii. 28); Conv. iv. 7[98–102] (*Prov.* iv. 18–19); Conv. iv. 7[131] (*Prov.* v. 23); Conv. iv. 15[137] (*Prov.* xxix. 20); Conv. iv. 24[142] (*Prov.* i. 8); Conv. iv. 24[145] (*Prov.* i. 10); Conv. iv. 24[163] (*Prov.* xv. 31, loosely quoted); Conv. iv. 25[17] (*Prov.* iii. 34); Conv. iv. 25[19] (*Prov.* iv. 24); *Proverbii*, Mon. iii. 1[15] (*Prov.*

viii. 7); indirectly, Purg. xxxi. 62–3 (*Prov.* i. 17); Epist. vi. 5[144] (*Prov.* i. 17); Epist. viii. 7[110] (*Prov.* xxx. 15). [*Bibbia.*]

Provinciales. [*Provenzali.*]

Provinzan Salvani. [*Provenzan Salvani.*]

Psalmi. [*Psalmorum, Liber.*]

Psalmista. [*David.*]

Psalmorum, Liber, Book of Psalms; quoted as *Salmi*, Inf. xxxi. 69; Purg. ii. 48; xxviii. 80; Par. xxiv. 136; Conv. iv. 19[59]; *Psalmi*, Mon. ii. 10[9]; Epist. x. 22[415]; *Psaltero*, Conv. i. 7[99]; *Salterio*, Conv. iii. 4[79]; *Teodía*, Par. xxv. 73; the lack of music and harmony in the Vulgate version of the Psalter due to the fact that it is a translation of a translation, being derived from the Hebrew through the Greek, Conv. i. 7[98–103].

D. quotes from the Psalms some forty times, besides frequently employing expressions which are evident reminiscences of the Psalmist's phraseology; the direct quotations are as follows (references being given to the Vulgate, from which, of course, D. quotes, as well as to the A.V., since the division of the Psalms does not always correspond in the two versions):—Purg. ii. 46 (*Ps.* cxiv. 1: *Vulg.* cxiii. 1); Purg. v. 24 (*Ps.* li. 1: *Vulg.* l. 3); Purg. xix. 73 (*Ps.* cxix. 25: *Vulg.* cxviii. 25); Purg. xxiii. 11 (*Ps.* li. 15: *Vulg.* l. 17); Purg. xxviii. 80 (*Ps.* xcii. 4: *Vulg.* xci. 5); Purg. xxix. 3 (*Ps.* xxxii. 1: *Vulg.* xxxi. 1); Purg. xxx. 83–4 (*Ps.* xxxi. 1–8: *Vulg.* xxx. 2–9); Purg. xxxi. 98 (*Ps.* li. 7: *Vulg.* l. 9); Purg. xxxiii. 1 (*Ps.* lxxix. 1: *Vulg.*

lxxviii. 1); Par. xxii. 94–5 (*Ps.* cxiv. 3, 5: *Vulg.* cxiii. 3, 5); Par. xxv. 38 (*Ps.* cxxi. 1: *Vulg.* cxx. 1); Par. xxv. 73–4, 98 (*Ps.* ix. 10: *Vulg.* ix. 11); Par. xxxii. 12 (*Ps.* li. 1: *Vulg.* l. 3); Conv. ii. 1⁵⁸ (*Ps.* cxiv. 1: *Vulg.* cxiii. 1); Conv. ii. 4⁴² (*Ps.* viii. 1: *Vulg.* viii. 2); Conv. ii. 6¹⁰³ (*Ps.* xix. 1: *Vulg.* xviii. 2); Conv. iii. 4⁷⁶ (*Ps.* c. 3: *Vulg.* xcix. 3); Conv. iv. 16¹ (*Ps.* lxiii. 11: *Vulg.* lxii. 12); Conv. iv. 19⁶⁰ (*Ps.* viii. 1: *Vulg.* viii. 2); Conv. iv. 19⁶⁴ (*Ps.* viii. 4–6: *Vulg.* viii. 5–7); Conv. iv. 23⁷⁹ (*Ps.* civ. 9: *Vulg.* ciii. 9); Mon. i. 1¹⁰ (*Ps.* i. 3); Mon. i. 4¹⁴ (*Ps.* viii. 5: *Vulg.* viii. 6); Mon. i. 13³⁰ (*Ps.* l. 16: *Vulg.* xlix. 16); Mon. i. 13⁶¹ (*Ps.* lxxii. 1: *Vulg.* lxxi. 1); Mon. i. 15²² (*Ps.* iv. 7: *Vulg.* iv. 8); Mon. i. 16³⁶ (*Ps.* cxxxiii. 1: *Vulg.* cxxxii. 1); Mon. ii. 1¹⁻⁶ (*Ps.* ii. 1–3); Mon. ii. 10¹⁰ (*Ps.* xi. 7: *Vulg.* x. 8); Mon. iii. 1³¹ (*Ps.* cxii. 6–7: *Vulg.* cxi. 7); Mon. iii. 3⁷⁶ (*Ps.* cxi. 9: *Vulg.* cx. 9); Mon. iii. 15³⁷ (*Ps.* xcv. 5: *Vulg.* xciv. 5); Mon. iii. 16⁷⁴ (*Ps.* xxxii. 9: *Vulg.* xxxi. 9); Epist. v. 4⁶²⁻⁴ (*Ps.* xcv. 2: *Vulg.* xciv. 2); Epist. v. 7¹¹⁴⁻¹⁶ (*Ps.* xcv. 5: *Vulg.* xciv. 5); Epist. viii. 3³⁵⁻⁶ (*Ps.* lxxix. 10: *Vulg.* lxxviii. 10); Epist. viii. 5⁷⁵⁻⁶ (*Ps.* lxix. 9: *Vulg.* lxviii. 10); Epist. x. 7¹⁴²⁻⁵ (*Ps.* cxiv. 1: *Vulg.* cxiii. 1); Epist. x. 22⁴¹⁶⁻¹⁹ (*Ps.* cxxxix. 7–9: *Vulg.* cxxxviii. 7–9); A. T. § 22⁸⁻¹¹ (*Ps.* cxxxix. 6: *Vulg.* cxxxviii. 6). [*Bibbia.*]

Psaltero. [*Psalmorum, Liber.*]

Ptolemaeus. [Tolommeo.]

Publius Decius. [Decius, Publius.]

Puccio Sciancato, 'lame Puccio', member of the Galigai family of Florence, one of five Florentines (Inf. xxvi. 4–5) placed by D. among the Robbers in Bolgia 7 of Circle VIII of Hell (Malebolge), Inf. xxv. 148; *l'altro, v.* 140; *quei, v.* 149 [Ladri]. Puccio and his sons were among the Ghibellines of Porta san Piero who were banished in 1268; his name appears in the list of those who in 1280 swore to maintain the peace made between Guelfs and Ghibellines by the Cardinal Latino.

Puglia, Apulia, strip of country in the SE. of Italy, which forms the 'heel' of the peninsula, and extends along the coast of the Adriatic as far N. as the river Fortore. In the Middle Ages the name was often used to indicate the kingdom of Naples, which included the whole of the SE. extremity of Italy, extending as far N. as the Tronto on the Adriatic, and the Garigliano on the Mediterranean. In the middle of Cent. xi Apulia was conquered by the Normans, and in 1127, on the death of Duke William II of Apulia, it was united to the Sicilian dominions of Roger of Sicily (King, 1129–1154), who subsequently added the principality of Capua, Naples, and the Abruzzi. Apulia and Naples thenceforward formed part of the kingdom of the Two Sicilies, until 1282, the year of the 'Sicilian Vespers', when the insurrection of the Sicilians against the house of Anjou led to the separation of the island of Sicily from the kingdom of Naples. [Cicilia: Napoli: Tables B, E.]

D. speaks of Apulia, in connexion with the slaughter in the long war

(B. C. 343–290) between the Romans and the Samnites (Livy, x. 15), as *la fortunata terra Di Puglia*, ' the fortune-tossed land ', Inf. xxviii. 8–9; it is mentioned by Sordello (in Ante-purgatory), together with Provence, as suffering under the misrule of Charles II of Anjou, Purg. vii. 126 [**Provenza**]; as indicating the kingdom of Naples, it is referred to (by Manfred in Ante-purgatory) as *il Regno*, Purg. iii. 131; (by Jacopo del Cassero in Ante-purgatory) as *quel di Carlo* (i. e. the dominion of Charles II of Anjou), Purg. v. 69; and spoken of as being divided in two by the Apennines, *Apulia*, V. E. i. 10$^{50-2}$; its limits described (by Charles Martel in the Heaven of Venus), Par. viii. 61–3 [**Ausonia**]; its conquest by Robert Guiscard, Inf. xxviii. 13–14 [**Guiscardo**]; the scene of the engagements at Ceperano and Tagliacozzo, Inf. xxviii. 16–18 [**Ceperano : Tagliacozzo**].

Pugliese, inhabitant of Apulia, and, in wider sense, of the kingdom of Naples; the treachery of the Apulian barons to Manfred at Ceperano, Inf. xxviii. 16–17 [**Ceperano**]; the Apulian dialect, *Apulum vulgare*, V. E. i. 10$^{61-3}$, 12$^{71-3}$, 19^{18} [**Apuli: Apulus**].

Pulci], one of the Florentine families which received knighthood from Marquis Hugh of Brandenburg, ' il gran barone', Par. xvi. 128 [**Ugo di Brandimborgo**].

Punicus, Punic, Carthaginian; *bellum Punicum*, the Second Punic War (B.C. 218–201), Mon. ii. 4^{64}; alluded to, Inf. xxviii. 10 [**Cartaginesi : Poeni**].

Purgatorio[1], Purgatory, the place of purgation and of preparation for the life of eternal blessedness, ' quel secondo regno, Ove l'umano spirito si purga, E di salire al ciel diventa degno', Purg. i. 4–6; vii. 39; ix. 49; alluded to as *il monte*, Purg. i. 108; ii. 60, 122; iii. 46; iv. 38, 69; vi. 48; vii. 4, 65; viii. 57; x. 18; xii. 24, 73; xiv. 1; xv. 8; xix. 117; xx. 114, 128; xxi. 35, 71; xxii. 123; xxv. 105; xxvii. 74; xxviii. 101; xxx. 74; Par. xv. 93; xvii. 113, 137; *il monte ove ragion ne fruga*, Purg. iii. 3; *l'alto monte*, Purg. v. 86; *lo monte che salendo altrui dismala*, Purg. xiii. 3; *il sacro monte*, Purg. xix. 38; *il santo monte*, Purg. xxviii. 12; *lo monte che l'anime cura*, Par. xvii. 20; *il monte che si leva più dall' onda*, Par. xxvi. 139; *la montagna*, Purg. iii. 6, 76; iv. 88; xxi. 42; xxiii. 125; *là ove vanno l'anime a lavarsi*, Inf. xiv. 137; *regno Ove l'umano spirito si purga*, Purg. i. 4–5; *mondo Dove poter peccar non è più nostro*, Purg. xxvi. 131–2.

According to D.'s conception, Purgatory consists of an island-mountain, formed by the earth which retreated before Lucifer as he fell from Heaven into the abyss of Hell (Inf. xxxiv. 122–6). This mountain, which has the form of an immense truncated cone, rises out of the ocean in the centre of the S. hemisphere, where, according to the Ptolemaic system of cosmography followed by D., there was nothing (except, of course, in D.'s view the mountain of Purgatory) but a vast expanse of water. It is the exact antipodes of Jerusalem (where Christ suffered for the sin of Adam committed in the Garden of Eden, i.e. the Terrestrial Paradise at the summit of the mountain) [**Gerusalemme**]. The lower part of the mountain is not part of Purgatory proper, but forms an Ante-purgatory, where souls have to wait until they have atoned for delay in repentance [**Antipurgatorio**]. Purgatory proper, which is entered by a gate guarded by an angel, consists of seven concentric terraces (*cerchi*, Purg. xvii. 137; xxii. 92; *cerchie*, Purg. xxii. 33; *cinghi*, Purg. xiii. 37; *cornici*, Purg. x. 27; xi. 29; xiii. 4, 80; xvii. 131; xxv. 113; Par. xv. 93; *giri*, Purg. xvii. 83; xix. 70; xxii. 2; xxiii. 90; *gironi*, Purg. xii. 107; xv. 83; xvii. 80; xviii. 94; xix. 38; *piani*, Purg. x. 20; xii. 117), each about seventeen feet wide (Purg. x. 22–4; xiii. 4–5), which rise in succession with diminished circuit (Purg. xiii. 4–6) as they approach the summit, where is situated the Terrestrial Paradise [**Paradiso**²]. These terraces are connected by steep and narrow stairways (*scale*, Purg. xi. 40; xiii. 1; xvii. 65, 77; xxv. 8; xxvii. 124; *scaglioni*, Purg. xii. 115; xxvii. 67; *scaleo*, Purg. xv. 36; *gradi*, Purg. xii. 92; xxvii. 125; *callaia*, Purg. xxv. 7; *foci*, Purg. xii. 112; xxii. 7; *passo*, Purg. xiii. 42; *pertugio*, Purg. xviii. 11; *porta*, Purg. xix. 36; *varco*, Purg. xi. 41; xvi. 44; xix. 43), the steps of which become successively less steep as each terrace is surmounted. Each of the seven terraces or circles corresponds to one of the seven deadly sins, from the traces of which the soul is there purged; thus Circle I is appropriated to Pride [**Superbi**], Circle II to Envy [**Invidiosi**], Circle III to Anger [**Iracondi**], Circle IV to Sloth [**Accidiosi**], Circle V to Avarice [**Avari**], Circle VI to Gluttony [**Golosi**], Circle VII to Lust [**Lussuriosi**]. The seven terraces, together with Ante-purgatory and the Terrestrial Paradise, form nine divisions, thus corresponding to the nine circles of Hell, and the nine spheres of Paradise. At the foot of the mountain is stationed Cato of Utica as guardian [**Catone**²]; at the entrance to Purgatory proper, and at the approach to each of the terraces, stands an Angel, who chants one of the Beatitudes to comfort those who are purging them of their sins [*Beatitudini*].

The system of purgation is explained to D. by Virgil (Purg. xvii–xviii):—love, he says, exists in every creature, and as, if rightly directed, it is the spring of every good action, so, if ill-directed, it is the spring of every evil action (xvii. 91–105); love may err through a bad object ('per malo obbietto', *v.* 95), thus giving birth to Pride, Envy, Anger—, through defect of vigour in pursuit of good ('per poco di vigore', *v.* 96), thus giving birth to Sloth—, through excess of vigour in the same ('per troppo vigore', *v.* 96), thus giving birth to Avarice, Gluttony, and Lust. The manner of purgation is threefold, consisting in (1) a material punishment intended to mortify the evil passions and incite to virtue; (2) a subject for meditation, bearing on the sin purged, and its opposite virtue, with examples of persons conspicuous for the one or the other drawn from sacred and profane history; (3) a prayer, whereby the soul is purified and strengthened in the grace of God.

In the Terrestrial Paradise are two streams, Lethe and Eunoë, the former of which washes away the remembrance of sin, while the latter strengthens the remembrance of good deeds. [**Eunoe : Letè.**]

The time occupied by D. in passing through Purgatory was four days :— one day (Easter Sunday, April 10) in Ante-purgatory (Purg. i. 19–ix. 9); two days in Purgatory proper, viz. Easter Monday (Purg. ix. 13– xviii. 76) and Easter Tuesday (Purg. xix. 1–xxvii. 89); and one day (Wednesday) in the Terrestrial Paradise (Purg. xxvii. 94–xxxiii. 103). [*Commedia.*]

Purgatorio[2]], second Cantica (consisting of 33 Cantos, comprising 4,755 lines) of the *D. C.*; referred to as *questa cantica seconda*, Purg. xxxiii. 140. [*Commedia.*]

Purgatorio, Porta del. [Porta[5].]

Putifar, Moglie di], Potiphar's wife; placed, together with Sinon, among the Falsifiers in Bolgia 10 of Circle VIII of Hell (Malebolge), where she is pointed out by Maestro Adamo as 'la falsa che accusò Giuseppo', Inf. xxx. 97; she and Sinon, *duo tapini, v.* 91. [**Falsatori : Giuseppo.**]

Pyramus. [**Piramo.**]

Pyreneus, King of Daulis in Phocis, who, when the Muses were caught in a storm on their way to Mt. Parnassus, gave them shelter in his palace, and then, having secured the doors, attempted to offer them violence. The Muses escaped in the shape of birds, and P., madly leaping after them from the top of a high tower, was dashed to pieces. D. (who got the story from Ovid, *Metam.* v. 273–93) mentions P. in connexion with the Muses, whom he refers to as those who fled in fear from the evil desires of P., Ecl. ii. 65–6. [**Muse.**]

Pyrrhus. [**Pirro**[2].]

Pythagoras. [**Pittagora.**]

Q

Quadrivio, *Quadrivium,* the four of the seven liberal arts (viz. music, arithmetic, geometry, and astronomy), which in the mediaeval system of academic studies constituted the second portion of the curriculum, being the graduates' course for the three years between the bachelor's and master's degree. The other three liberal arts (viz. grammar, logic, and rhetoric) were the subjects of the *Trivium,* the course followed during the four years of undergraduateship.

D. says that the seven sciences of the *Trivium* and *Quadrivium* correspond to the seven lowest Heavens, Conv. ii. 14[55–8]. [**Paradiso**[1].]

Quaestio de Aqua et Terra, title of a treatise attributed to D., which purports to be a scientific inquiry as to the relative levels of land and water on the surface of the globe. This treatise, of which no MS. is known, and which was first brought to light in 1508, until recently was regarded as an undoubted forgery, but it is now generally accepted as a genuine work of D.

The work, which is very brief, consisting of twenty-four short chapters, claims to be a report, written by D.'s own hand (A. T. § 1^{15-18}), of a public disputation held by him at Verona on Sunday, Jan. 20, 1320 (A. T. § 24^{1-21}), wherein he determined the question, which had previously been propounded in his presence at Mantua (A. T. § 1^{2-3}), in favour of the theory that the surface of the earth is everywhere higher than that of the water.

Quantitate Animae, De. [*Animae, De Quantitate.*]

Quarnaro, Gulf of Quarnero, at the head of the Adriatic, which separates Istria from Croatia.

D. mentions it in connexion with Pola, a town on the gulf near the S. extremity of the Istrian peninsula, and speaks of it as forming one of the boundaries of Italy (Istria in those days being an Italian duchy), Inf. ix. 113–14. [Istria: Pola.]

Quarto Cielo. [Sole, Cielo del.]

Quattro Virtù Cardinali, Delle. [*Quatuor Virtutibus Cardinalibus, De.*]

Quatuor Virtutibus Cardinalibus, De, treatise of Martinus Dumiensis *On the Four Cardinal Virtues*, otherwise known as the *Formula Honestae Vitae* ; this work, which was several times translated into Italian, was in the Middle Ages, and even as late as Cent. xvi, commonly ascribed to Seneca. D. quotes the treatise as *il Libro delle Quattro Virtù Cardinali*, Conv. iii. 8^{107-10} (§ *De Continentia*); and (as the work of Seneca) as *Liber de Quatuor Virtutibus*, Mon. ii. 5^{24-6} (§ *De Iustitia*) [**Martinus Dumiensis**].

Quinto Cielo. [Marte, Cielo di.]

Quinzio. [Cincinnato.]

Quirino, Quirinus, name given to Romulus after his death, when he had been raised to the rank of a divinity ; mentioned by D. in connexion with the fact (recorded by Livy, i. 4) that the vestal virgin, Rhea Silvia, claimed Mars as the father of her twin sons, Romulus and Remus, Par. viii. 131–2 [**Romolo**].

R

Raab, Rahab, harlot of Jericho, who received the two spies sent from Shittim by Joshua to spy the city (*Josh.* ii).

D. places her in the Heaven of Venus, among those who were lovers upon earth (*Spiriti Amanti*), Par. ix. 116 ; her spirit is pointed out to D. by the troubadour Folquet, who says she was the first soul, of those destined for that sphere, released by Christ from Limbo (*vv.* 118–20); and adds that it was fitting she should receive a place in Heaven, seeing that she contributed to Joshua's great victory at Jericho (*vv.* 121–

6). [Gerico: Josuè: Venere, Cielo di.]

Rabano, Hrabanus Maurus Magnentius, born at Mainz, c. 766; while quite a youth he entered the monastery at Fulda, where he received deacon's orders in 801. He was ordained priest in 814, and after a pilgrimage to the Holy Land returned to Fulda in 817, where he became abbot in 822. He held this office for twenty years until 842, when he retired in order to devote himself more completely to religion and literature. Five years later, however, he was appointed to the archbishopric of Mainz, which he held until his death in 856. Hrabanus, who was considered one of the most learned men of his time, wrote a voluminous commentary on the greater portion of the Bible, and was the author of numerous theological works.

He is placed among the spirits of those who loved wisdom (*Spiriti Sapienti*) in the Heaven of the Sun, Par. xii. 130. [**Sole, Cielo del.**]

Rachele, Rachel, younger daughter of Laban, second wife of Jacob, by whom she was the mother of Joseph and Benjamin.

Beatrice speaks of her as *l'antica Rachele* (as belonging to the times of old), Inf. ii. 102; Virgil mentions her among those released by Christ from Limbo, alluding to Jacob's seven years' service for her (*Gen.* xxix. 15–30), Inf. iv. 60 [**Limbo**]; in D.'s dream at the foot of the ascent to the Terrestrial Paradise, Leah describes herself as being fain of adorning herself with her hands, while Rachel is satisfied with gazing

at her own fair form (they being the types respectively of the active and contemplative life), Purg. xxvii. 100–8; St. Bernard points out to D. Rachel's place in the Celestial Rose in the Empyrean, Par. xxxii. 7–9 (cf. Inf. ii. 102) [**Rosa**].

Rachel and Leah in the *D. C.* represent respectively the contemplative and the active life, just as, according to the theologians, Mary and Martha do in the New Testament; and, as Leah is the type of the active life in D.'s dream, and Matilda the same to his waking eyes, so Rachel in the dream, and Beatrice in reality, are the types of the contemplative life. [**Lia: Matelda.**]

Raffaelle], archangel Raphael; referred to as being, like the other archangels, represented by the Church in human likeness, D. speaking of him as *l'altro che Tobia rifece sano*, Par. iv. 48. [**Tobia.**]

Ragione, the Law; usually with reference to the Digest of the Roman law, Conv. i. 10[14]; iv. 19[24], 24[19]; *Ragione civile,* Conv. iv. 12[100, 103]; *Ragione scritta,* Conv. iv. 9[82, 85, 87]; as distinguished from the canon law, *Ragione canonica,* Conv. iv. 12[100, 103] [**Decretali: Digesta**].

Ramondo Berlinghieri. [**Berlinghieri, Ramondo.**]

Ramondo di Tolosa. [**Tolosa.**]

Rampino Ranuccio], native of Pistoja, who was falsely accused of the robbery committed by Vanni Fucci in the church of San Zeno at Pistoja, and narrowly escaped being hanged for the crime; he is alluded to, Inf. xxiv. 139 [**Fucci, Vanni**].

Rascia, name by which the

kingdom of Servia was known in the Middle Ages, from the name of its capital, Rasça or Rasa, the modern Novi-Bazar; it comprised parts of the modern Servia, Bosnia, Croatia, and Dalmatia.

The Eagle in the Heaven of Jupiter denounces the King of Rascia for counterfeiting the Venetian coinage, referring to him as *quel di Rascia Che mal ha visto* (var. *aggiustò*) *il conio di Vinegia*, Par. xix. 140–1. [Aquila [2].]

The king in question is Stephen Ouros II, otherwise known as Milutin (1275–1321), who issued coins of debased metal in imitation of the Venetian *metapane* or *grosso*.

Ravenna, town in the Emilia on the Adriatic, between the mouths of the Lamone and Montone, originally only about a mile from the coast, now, owing to the retreat of the sea, about five miles inland. In D.'s day the lords of Ravenna were the Polenta family, one of whom, Guido Novello, was his host during the last three or four years of his life. At Ravenna D. died, and was buried.

D. mentions Ravenna in his response to the inquiries of Guido da Montefeltro (in Bolgia 8 of Circle VIII of Hell) as to the condition of Romagna, stating that it was still, as it had been for many years past (since 1270), under the lordship of the Polenta family, Inf. xxvii. 40–1 [Polenta]; it is mentioned by the Emperor Justinian (in the Heaven of Mercury), in his account of the victories of the Roman Eagle, in connexion with Caesar's departure thence to cross the Rubicon ,Par. vi. 61–2 [Rubicon]; it is

alluded to by Francesca da Rimini (in Circle II of Hell), who was daughter of Guido Vecchio da Polenta, as *la terra dove nata fui*, Inf. v. 97 [Francesca]; St. Peter Damian (in the Heaven of Saturn) alludes to it in connexion with his residence at the monastery of Santa Maria near Ravenna, *in sul lito Adriano*, Par. xxi. 122–3 [Damiano, Pier]; Tityrus (i. e. D.) refers to it as being situated on the coast of the Emilia, between the right bank of the Po and the left bank of the Rubicon, Ecl. ii. 67–8 [Po]; an Archbishop of Ravenna (said to be Bonifazio dei Fieschi, 1274–1295) and his pastoral staff ('il rocco') are referred to, Purg. xxiv. 29–30 [Bonifazio [2]]; the celebrated pineforest of Ravenna is mentioned, Purg. xxviii. 20 [Pineta].

Ravennates, inhabitants of Ravenna; their dialect different from that of their neighbours of Faenza, V. E. i. 9[41].

Ravignani, ancient noble family of Florence (extinct in D.'s day), mentioned by Cacciaguida (in the Heaven of Mars) as the ancestors of the famous house of the Conti Guidi, and of all who traced their descent from Bellincion Berti (among whom would be included members of the Donati and Adimari families, and, according to Pietro di Dante, also of the Alighieri), Par. xvi. 97–9 [Bellincion Berti: Guidi, Conti]; he says they lived over the Porta san Piero, where the Cerchi subsequently lived (*vv.* 94–6) [Cerchi].

Re Militari, De, treatise *On the Art of War* of Flavius Vegetius Renatus; D. quotes from it the opinion that war ought not to be resorted to until all peaceful means have been exhausted, Mon. ii. 10^{18-23}(*Re Milit.* iii. 9)[**Vegetius**].

Rea, Rhea, otherwise called Cybele, ancient goddess, who is represented as the daughter of Heaven (Uranus) and Earth (Ge), and the wife of Saturn. She was the mother of Vesta, Ceres, Juno, Pluto, Neptune, and Jupiter. Saturn, in order to avert the fulfilment of a prophecy that he would be dethroned by one of his children, devoured each one as soon as it was born, with the exception of Jupiter, who was saved by an artifice of his mother. When she was on the point of giving birth to Jupiter she retired to Mt. Ida in Crete, and when the infant was born she gave Saturn a stone wrapped up in swaddling clothes, which he swallowed, supposing it to be his child. To prevent Saturn from hearing the cries of the infant, she ordered her priests, the Curetes, to raise shouts, and clash their swords and shields. She thus succeeded in bringing up the child Jupiter without the knowledge of his father. Eventually in fulfilment of the prophecy Saturn was dethroned by Jupiter.

D. mentions Rhea (whose story he got from Ovid, *Fast.* iv. 197–214) in connexion with the birth of Jupiter on Mt. Ida, and her artifice in concealing him from Saturn, Inf. xiv. 100–2. [**Creta : Ida.**]

Rebecca, Rebekah, wife of Isaac, by whom she became the mother of Esau and Jacob.

St. Bernard points out to D. her place in the Celestial Rose, Par. xxxii. 10 [**Rosa**]; the struggling of her twin children in her womb (*Gen.* xxv. 22–3 ; *Rom.* ix. 10–13) referred to, Par. xxxii. 68–9 [**Esaù : Jacob**].

Reggiani. [**Regiani.**]

Reggimento de' Principi, Dello. [*Regimine Principum, De.*]

Reggio, town of N. Italy, in the centre of the Emilia, about midway on the high road between Parma and Modena ; mentioned as the native place of Guido da Castello, Conv. iv. 16^{73}. [**Castel, Guido da.**]

Regi, Libro delli. [*Libri Regum.*]

Regiani, inhabitants of Reggio ; the shrillness characteristic of their dialect, as of those of Ferrara and Modena, the reason why there have been no poets among them, V. E. i. 15^{20-2}.

Regimine Principum, De, work *On the Government of Princes* written (before 1285) by Egidio Romano for the instruction of his pupil, Philip (afterwards Philip IV), son of Philip III of France, to whom it is dedicated ; it was originally written in Latin, but was at an early date translated into French, one version having been made by Egidio himself for the benefit of Louis (afterwards Louis X), eldest son of Philip IV ; it was translated (from the French) into Italian before 1288.

D., who quotes it as *Dello Reggimento de' Principi*, refers to it for Egidio's account (i. i. 6 *ad fin.*) of the distinctive functions of youth and old age, Conv. iv. 24^{97-9} [**Egidio [2]**] ; and was perhaps indebted to it for his reference to Sardanapalus, Par. xv. 107–8 [**Sardanapalo**].

Regno, Il. [Puglia.]

Regolo, Marcus Atilius Regulus, favourite hero of Roman history; he was Consul B.C. 267 and 256; in the war with Carthage, after several times defeating the Carthaginians, he was himself totally defeated by them and taken prisoner (255). He remained in captivity for five years, till 250, when the Carthaginians sent an embassy to Rome to arrange for peace or at any rate an exchange of prisoners, and allowed Regulus to go with it on condition that he would return to Carthage if their proposals were declined. When he came before the senate at Rome Regulus dissuaded them from assenting to peace, or even to an exchange of prisoners, and, in spite of all the efforts of his friends to detain him, voluntarily returned to Carthage, where he was cruelly tortured and put to death.

Regulus is mentioned in connexion with his noble self-sacrifice, Conv. iv. 5$^{124-9}$.

Regum, Libri, Books of Kings, comprising, according to the arrangement of the Vulgate, which D. follows, the four books known in A. V. as First and Second of Samuel, and First and Second of Kings; mentioned, *terzo libro delli Regi*, Conv. iv. 27$^{60-3}$ (ref. to I *Kings* iii. 9); *primus liber Regum*, Mon. iii. 6$^{4-5}$ (ref. to I *Sam.* xv. 17, 23, 28); quoted, Par. xiii. 93 (I *Kings* iii. 5); referred to, Epist. vii. 5$^{102-7}$ (I *Sam.* xv. 17–18); Epist. vii. 2$^{25-9}$ (2 *Kings* xx. 1–11). [**Bibbia.**]

Remedia Amoris, Ovid's *Remedies of Love*; D., who refers to it as *il libro che ha nome Rimedio d'*

Amore, quotes the second line of it, V. N. § 25$^{96-7}$; he perhaps was indebted to it (*vv.* 47–8) for his statement as to the spear of Peleus and Achilles, Inf. xxxi. 5. [**Peleus : Ovidio.**]

Remedia Fortuitorum. [*Fortuitorum Remedia.*]

Renaldus de Aquino, Rinaldo d'Aquino, poet of the Sicilian school, of which the Emperor Frederick II was the head; he is probably identical with the Rinaldo d'Aquino who in 1257 was King Manfred's viceroy in the province of Otranto and Bari. About a dozen of his poems are extant.

D. quotes a line of one of his *canzoni* (which has been preserved) as an instance of the eleven-syllabled line, V. E. ii. 5$^{45-6}$; the same line is quoted (anonymously) as an instance of the use by an Apulian poet of the 'curial' language in place of his own harsh dialect, V. E. i. 12^{69}.

Reno [1], Rhine, which rises in the Grisons in Switzerland, and flows through the Lake of Constance, and thence through Germany and Holland into the North Sea.

It is mentioned by the Emperor Justinian (in the Heaven of Mercury), together with the Var, Isère, Saône, Seine, and Rhone, in connexion with Caesar's victories in Gaul, Par. vi. 58 [**Era**].

Reno [2], river of N. Italy, which rises in the Etruscan Apennines, and flows N. through the Emilia, leaving Bologna about two miles to the E.; it formerly held on its course and entered the Po N. of Ferrara, but it now flows E. through an artificial channel into the Po di Primaro.

Caccianimico (in Bolgia 1 of Circle VIII of Hell), a native of Bologna, refers to the situation of that city between the Savena and Reno, Inf. xviii. 61 [**Bologna**]; Guido del Duca (in Circle II of Purgatory) mentions it as one of the boundaries of Romagna, Purg. xiv. 92 [**Romagna**]; it is referred to by its classical name, *Rhenus*, Ecl. ii. 41, 85 ; Ecl. R. 1.

Rerum Transformatione, De. [*Metamorphoseos.*]

Rerum Transmutatione, De. [*Metamorphoseos.*]

Rettorica. [*Rhetorica.*]

Rhamnusia, name applied to Nemesis, the goddess of retributive justice (Ovid, *Metam.* iii. 406), from a celebrated temple in her honour at Rhamnus in Attica, Epist. iv. 5[51].

Rhenus. [**Reno**[2].]

Rhetorica, Aristotle's *Art of Rhetoric*; quoted as *Rettorica*, Conv. iii. 8[85]; *Rhetorica*, Epist. x. 18[297]; six passions, according to A., proper to the human soul, viz. grace, zeal, pity, envy, love, and shame, Conv. iii. 8[82–7] (*Rhet.* ii. 4, 6, 7, 8, 10, 11); his saying that nothing should be left to the judge if it can be decided by law, Mon. i. 11[74–6] (*Rhet.* i. 1); that the proem is the beginning in a rhetorical oration, as the prologue is in poetry, and the prelude in music, Epist. x. 18[297–300] (*Rhet.* iii. 14). [**Aristotile.**]

Rhetorica, Nova. [*Inventione, De.*]

Rhetorica, Prima. [*Inventione, De.*]

Rialto, one of the islands upon which the city of Venice was origin-ally built, and on which stand the Church of St. Mark and the Palazzo Ducale ; mentioned by Cunizza (in the Heaven of Venus) to indicate Venice itself, which she describes as the E. limit of the March of Treviso, Par. ix. 26. [**Marca Trivisiana : Vinegia.**]

Ricardus de Sancto Victore. [**Riccardo.**]

Riccardo, Richard of St. Victor, said to be a native of Scotland, celebrated scholastic philosopher and theologian, chief of the mystics of Cent. xii ; he studied at the University of Paris, where he became one of the canons-regular of the Augustinian monastery of St. Victor, of which he was appointed sub-prior in 1159, and prior in 1162. He was, with Peter Lombard, a pupil of the famous Hugh of St. Victor, and a friend of St. Bernard, to whom several of his works are dedicated ; he died at St. Victor in 1173. His writings (the influence of which on D. is perceptible in various passages of the *D. C.*) consist of commentaries on parts of the Old Testament, St. Paul's Epistles, and the Apocalypse, as well as of works on moral and dogmatic subjects, and on mystical contemplation, the last of which earned him the title of 'Magnus Contemplator'. [**Ugo da San Vittore.**]

D. places Richard of St. Victor, together with Bede and Isidore of Seville, among the great doctors of the Church (*Spiriti Sapienti*) in the Heaven of the Sun, where his spirit is pointed out by St. Thomas Aquinas, who speaks of him, probably in allusion to his title of 'Contemplator', as *Riccardo*, *Che a considerar fu più che viro*, Par. x. 131–2 [Sole, Cielo del]; he is mentioned as *Ricardus de Sancto Victore* in connexion with his treatise *De Contemplatione*, Epist. x. 28[553–4] [*Contemplatione, De*].

Riccardo da Cammino. [Cammino, Riccardo da.]

Riccardo da San Vittore. [Riccardo.]

Ridolfo[1], Rudolf I, Emperor from 1272 to 1292; he was born in 1218, and was the eldest son of Albert IV, Count of Hapsburg, and the founder of the imperial house of Austria. He first served under Ottocar, King of Bohemia, in his German wars, but in 1272, as he was encamped before the walls of Basle, he received the news that he had been elected Emperor, in preference to Ottocar and to Alphonso of Castile. Ottocar refused to acknowledge him as Emperor, but Rudolf, supported by powerful allies, made war upon him and compelled him to sue for peace, which was granted only upon condition that he should cede Austria, Styria, Carinthia, and Carniola. A few years later Ottocar again rebelled, and was finally defeated and slain near Vienna, Aug. 1278. Rudolf allowed Ottocar's son, Wenceslaus, to succeed to the throne of Bohemia, but Austria, Styria, and Carniola he granted to his own sons, Albert and Rudolf. [Ottacchero:Vincislao.]

The Emperor Rudolf is placed among the Negligent Princes in the valley of flowers in Ante-purgatory, where he is seated amicably in company with his former foe, Ottocar

of Bohemia, Purg. vii. 94 [Antipurgatorio]; D., by the mouth of Sordello, reproaches him with having neglected Italy, inasmuch as 'he might have healed the wounds which caused her death' (*vv.* 94–6); he is referred to as the father of the Emperor Albert I, and again reproached for his neglect of Italy, Purg. vi. 103 [Alberto Tedesco]; he is mentioned (in the Heaven of Venus) by Charles Martel of Hungary, who married his daughter Clemence, Par. viii. 72 [Clemenza: Carlo[3]]; D. mentions him, together with his successors Adolf and Albert I, among the successors of Frederick II, Conv. iv. 3[41–2] [Adolfo: Federico[2]].

Ridolfo[2]], Rudolf (or Arnould), natural son of Lothair, and brother of Louis V, the last of the Carlovingian Kings of France (986–7); he was Archbishop of Rheims in 988, and died in 1021.

Some think he is the person alluded to by Hugh Capet (in Circle V of Purgatory) as 'un renduto in panni bigi', Purg. xx. 54. The reference, however, is almost certainly to his uncle, Charles, Duke of Lorraine, son of Louis IV, and brother of Lothair. [Carlo[5].]

Rife, Montagne. [Montagne Rife.]

Rifeo, Rhipeus, Trojan hero, who was slain during the sack of Troy.

D., accepting Virgil's estimate of Rhipeus (*Aen.* ii. 426–7), places him, though a pagan, among the spirits of those who loved and exercised justice (*Spiriti Giudicanti*), in the Heaven of Jupiter, Par. xx.

68 ; *quinta luce, v.* 69 ; *quinta vita, v.* 100 ; *l'altra (anima), v.* 118; *luce, v.* 146 [**Giove, Cielo di**] ; the Eagle asks who would believe in the erring world below that Rhipeus was among the saved (*vv.* 67–9) ; and, in response to D.'s doubts, explains that the three virtues of faith, hope, and charity were to Rhipeus in the place of baptism, he having ' placed all his love below on righteousness' (*vv.* 118–29).

Rimedio d'Amore. [*Remedia Amoris.*]

Rimini], ancient Ariminum, town of N. Italy in the SE. corner of the Emilia ; it is situated on the Adriatic between the mouths of the Ausa and Marecchia. Rimini was made a Roman colony in B. C. 269, and formed the frontier-fortress of Italy in the direction of Cisalpine Gaul, and the termination of the Flaminian Way from Rome. In B. C. 82 the Italian frontier was moved about ten miles further N. as far as the Rubicon, near Cesena ; and it was at this point that Caesar crossed into Italy in B. C. 49, at the beginning of the civil war with Pompey, and entered Rimini, where he harangued his troops in the great square which still bears his name (Piazza Giulio Cesare).

During Cent. xiii Rimini was under the lordship of the powerful Malatesta family, who had originally (in 1216) been invited to lend their assistance against the neighbouring town of Cesena, and who availed themselves of this opportunity to acquire the permanent lordship of the city. [**Malatesta.**]

Rimini is referred to by Pier da Medicina (in Bolgia 9 of Circle VIII of Hell) in connexion with the tyrant Malatestino, and Curio, who urged Caesar to cross the Rubicon, Inf. xxviii. 86. [**Curio** [2] : **Malatestino.**]

Rimini, Francesca da. [**Francesca.**]

Rinaldo d'Aquino. [**Renaldus de Aquino.**]

Rinaldo degli Scrovigni], noted usurer of Padua, said by the old commentators to be the individual bearing ' a white satchel blazoned with a blue sow' (the arms of the Scrovigni of Padua being a sow azure on a field argent), whom D. places among the Usurers in Round 3 of Circle VII of Hell, Inf. xvii. 64–75. [**Usurai.**]

Rinier da Calboli, member of the illustrious Guelf family of that name at Forlì ; placed by D., with the Ghibelline Guido del Duca, among the Envious in Circle II of Purgatory, Purg. xiv. 88 ; *uno spirto, v.* 7 ; *l'altro, v.* 25 ; *l'altra anima, vv.* 70, 73 ; *il pregio e l'onore Della casa da Calboli, vv.* 88–9 [**Invidiosi**] ; as he passes on his way, D. overhears a conversation between Guido and Rinieri, in the course of which the former foretells the ferocious doings of R.'s grandson, Fulcieri da Calboli, as Podestà of Florence (*vv.* 55–66); then, addressing D., he eulogizes R., and contrasts him with his degenerate grandson (*vv.* 88–90)[**Fulcieri**].

Rinieri, who played an important part in the affairs of Romagna, was born probably at the beginning of Cent. xiii; he was Podestà of Faenza in 1247, of Parma in 1252, and of Ravenna in 1265 (the year of D.'s birth). In 1276 he made war upon Forlì, but was compelled to retire to his stronghold of Calboli, in the upper valley of the Montone, where he was besieged by Guido da Montefeltro (Inf. xxvii), at that time Captain of Forlì, who forced him to surrender, and destroyed the castle. In 1292, while for the second time Podestà of Faenza, of which Mainardo Pagano (Inf. xxvii. 50; Purg. xiv. 118) was Captain, R. captured Forlì, and expelled Aldobrandino da Romena, Count of Romagna, who held the city with his brothers Aghinolfo and Alexander (Inf. xxx. 77), the Counts of Mangona (Inf. xxxii. 55-7) and of Castrocaro (Purg. xiv. 116), Alberico de' Manfredi (Inf. xxxii. 122), and many other powerful Ghibellines. Two years later, however (in 1294), R. and his adherents were in turn expelled. In 1296 R. and the Guelfs once more made themselves masters of Forlì, but the Ghibellines, under Scarpetta degli Ordelaffi (Inf. xxvii. 45) and Galasso da Montefeltro (Conv. iv. 11[129]), quickly retook the city and killed many of the Guelfs, Rinieri among the number.

Rinier da Corneto. [Corneto, Rinier da.]

Rinier Pazzo. [Pazzo, Rinier.]

Rinoardo, Renouard, hero, with William of Orange, of the O. F. Chanson de Geste *Aliscans*. D. places the two together among those who fought for the faith (*Spiriti Militanti*), in the Heaven of Mars,

where their spirits are pointed out by Cacciaguida, Par. xviii. 46. [Guglielmo[1]: Marte, Cielo di.]

Roberto[1], Robert, King of France, 996-1031, son of Hugh Capet; he is referred to by Hugh Capet (in Circle V of Purgatory), in his account of the origin of the Capetian dynasty, as *mio figlio*, and spoken of, by a confusion, as the first king of that line, Purg. xx. 59-60. [Ciapetta, Ugo.]

Roberto[2], Robert, Duke of Calabria, afterwards King of Naples (1309-1343), third son of Charles II of Anjou and Naples, and of Mary of Hungary, and younger brother of Charles Martel, titular King of Hungary. He was one of the three sons who were left as hostages in the hands of Alphonso, King of Aragon, when their father was released from his captivity in Catalonia in 1288 [Carlo[2]]. An arrangement had been made for their liberation in 1291, but owing to the sudden death of Alphonso in that year it was not carried into effect. Consequently Robert, with his brothers Louis and John, remained in captivity until 1295, in which year they were set at liberty, in accordance with a treaty concluded, through the mediation of Boniface VIII, between their father and James II, Alphonso's successor in Aragon.

During his residence in Aragon Robert gathered around him a following of Catalan gentlemen, who are said to have accompanied him into Italy. It is to these needy Catalan retainers that Charles Martel (in the Heaven of Venus) refers, as is supposed, in his apostrophe to his

brother, Par. viii. 77 [Catalogna];
he goes on to refer (probably) to the
shipwreck of Robert and Ruggieri
di Loria (the famous admiral of
James II of Aragon) in the summer
of 1301, while on their way to pro-
vision Catania and other captured
fortresses of Sicily in the course of
the joint attack of Charles II of
Naples and James II of Aragon upon
Frederick, younger brother of the
latter, who had seized the crown of
Sicily when James succeeded (in
1291) to the throne of Aragon
(vv. 79–81) [Carlo ²: Jacomo ¹:
Federico ³]; Charles Martel then
speaks of Robert's character, describing him as the niggardly offspring
of a lavish father (vv. 82–3); and
alludes to him finally (according to
the most probable interpretation) as
the 'man of sermons' (v. 147)
[Carlo ³].

On the death of Charles II in
1309 the kingdom of Naples right-
fully fell to his grandson, Charles
Robert, the young King of Hungary, son of Charles Martel and
Clemence of Hapsburg. The right
of his nephew, however, was contested by Robert, who appealed to
the Pope in person in support of
his claim. Clement V decided in
his favour, and he was crowned
King of Naples at Avignon, June,
1309, and remained in possession
of the kingdom until his death in
1343. This exclusion of Charles
Robert from the throne of Naples
by his uncle Robert is alluded to
by D., Par. ix. 6. [Carlo ⁶:
Table E.]

The raising of the siege of Genoa,
and the defeat of the Ghibellines by

the sea and land forces of King
Robert, in Feb. 1319, are alluded
to by G. del Virgilio, Carm. 29
[Parthenopaeus.]

While he was King of Naples
Robert made vain attempts to recover Sicily from the house of
Aragon, into whose hands it had
passed after the 'Sicilian Vespers'
in 1282 [Cicilia]. As head of
the Guelfs Robert was the bitter
opponent of the Emperor Henry
VII, who proclaimed him under
the ban of the Empire as a rebellious vassal and sentenced him
to be deposed from his throne.
These fulminations, however, had
little effect upon Robert, who had
stronger support at his back than
any the Emperor could count on in
Italy [Arrigo ²].

King Robert is typified by Goliath, the second David being the
Emperor, Epist. vii. 8¹⁷⁸; and is
referred to in the poetical correspondence of D. with G. del Virgilio
as *Cyclops*, Ecl. ii. 47; and *Polyphemus*, Ecl. ii. 75, 76. [Cyclops:
Golias : Polyphemus.]

Roberto Guiscardo. [Guis-
cardo, Roberto.]

Roboam, Rehoboam, son of
Solomon; he succeeded his father
as King of Israel, but, owing to his
refusal of the demand of the people
for a remission of the heavy burdens
imposed by Solomon, ten of the
tribes revolted from him, and acknowledged Jeroboam as their king,
Judah and Benjamin alone remaining
faithful to Rehoboam, who fled to
Jerusalem.

Rehoboam figures among the examples of defeated pride portrayed

in Circle I of Purgatory, where D. sees graven on the ground a representation of him fleeing in a chariot, after the revolt of the ten tribes of Israel (1 *Kings* xii. 18), Purg. xii. 46-8. [Superbi.]

Rocco de' Mozzi. [Mozzi.]

Rodano, Rhone, river of France, which rises in the Alps, flows through the Lake of Geneva, past Lyons (where it is joined by the Saône), Avignon (a few miles above which it receives the waters of the Sorgue), and Arles, and enters the Mediterranean some miles W. of Marseilles.

D. mentions the Rhone in connexion with Arles, where he says it ' stagnates ' (*stagna*), it being at this point that the river begins to form its delta, Inf. ix. 112 [Arli]; it is mentioned by the Emperor Justinian (in the Heaven of Mercury), together with the Var, Rhine, Isère, Saône, and Seine, in connexion with Caesar's victories in Gaul, Par. vi. 60 [Era] ; Charles Martel (in the Heaven of Venus) refers to its confluence with the Sorgue, and speaks of it as being, below that point, one of the boundaries of Provence (of which he would have been Count had he survived his father), Par. viii. 58-60 [Provenza : Sorga].

Rodopea. [Rodopeia.]

Rodopeia, maid of Rhodope, i. e. Phyllis, daughter of Sithon, King of Thrace, who, having been abandoned (as she thought) by her lover Demophoön, killed herself (*Heroid.* ii. 147-8) ; called ' Rhodopeia Phyllis ' by Ovid (*Heroid.* ii. 1), from her home near Mt. Rhodope in Thrace.

She is mentioned by the troubadour Folquet (in the Heaven of Venus) in connexion with the supposed faithlessness of Demophoön, Par. ix. 100-1. [Demofoonte : Folco.]

Roma[1], Rome, on the Tiber, ancient Rome (B. C.), Inf. i. 71 ; ii. 20 ; Purg. xxi. 89 ; xxix. 115 ; Par. vi. 57 ; xv. 126 ; xvi. 10 ; xxvii. 62 ; V. N. § 25[87] ; Conv. i. 3[22], iii. 11[24] ; iv. 5[32, 47, 117, 125, 135, 160] ; Mon. ii. 5[105] ; iii. 10[4] ; *città Romana*, Conv. iv. 5[49] ; *santa città*, Conv. iv. 5[179] ; *urbs Deo electa*, Mon. ii. 4[32-3] ; *urbs*, Mon. ii. 4[61] ; *urbs sancta*, Mon. ii. 5[106].

Aeneas the predestined founder of, Inf. ii. 20 ; Conv. iv. 5[47-8] [Enea] ; the fore-ordained seat of Christ's Vicar upon earth, Inf. ii. 22-4 ; and of the Emperor, Conv. iv. 5[30-2] ; Mon. iii. 10[4] [Romani[1]] ; founded, according to Orosius (*Hist.* iv. 12, § 9), about 600 years before the birth of Christ, Conv. iii. 11[23-7] ; the foundation of, by Aeneas, contemporaneous with the birth of David, Conv. iv. 5[46-8] ; the seven Kings of, Par. vi. 41 ; Conv. iv. 5[85-91] ; Romulus first King of, Conv. iv. 5[83-5] [Romolo] ; Numa Pompilius second King of, Conv. iv. 5[90] ; Mon. ii. 4[30] [Numa] ; Lucius Junius Brutus first Consul of, Conv. iv. 5[99-100] [Bruto[1]] ; Julius Caesar first Emperor of, Conv. iv. 5[100] [Cesare[1]] ; besieged by Porsena, Mon. ii. 4[66-7], 5[122] (cf. Conv. iv. 5[115-18] ; Par. iv. 84) [Porsena] ; by Brennus, Par. vi. 44 (cf. Conv. iv. 5[160-4] ; Mon. ii. 4[42-57]) [Brenno] ; by Hannibal, Mon. ii. 4[58-63] [Annibale] ; heroic actions performed on her behalf by the Horatii, Conv. iv. 5[155–60] (cf. Par. vi. 39; Mon. ii. 11[22–36]) [**Horatii**]; by Mucius Scaevola, Conv. iv. 5[115–18]; Mon. ii. 5[121–6] (cf. Par. iv. 84) [**Muzio**]; by Cloelia, Mon. ii. 4[65–8] [**Cloelia**]; by Lucius Junius Brutus, Conv. iv. 5[121]; Mon. ii. 5[112–20] [**Bruto**[1]]; by Cincinnatus, Conv. iv. 5[130–3]; Mon. ii. 5[76–89] (cf. Par. vi. 46; xv. 129) [**Cincinnato**]; by Marcus Manlius, Mon. ii. 4[42–57] (cf. Conv. iv. 5[160–4]) [**Manlius**]; by Camillus, Conv. iv. 5[134–9]; Mon. ii. 5[100–111] [**Camillo**]; by Titus Manlius Torquatus, Conv. iv. 5[118–21] (cf. Par. vi. 46) [**Torquato**[1]]; by the Decii, Conv. iv. 5[122–4]; Mon. ii. 5[128–30] (cf. Par. vi. 47) [**Deci**]; by Fabricius, Conv. iv. 5[107–10]; Mon. ii. 5[90–9], 11[56] (cf. Purg. xx. 25) [**Fabbrizio**]; by Curius Dentatus, Conv. iv. 5[110–15] [**Curio**[1]]; by the Fabii, Par. vi. 47 [**Fabi**]; by Regulus, Conv. iv. 5[124–9] [**Regolo**]; by Scipio Africanus, Conv. iv. 5[169–71]; Mon. ii. 11[59] [**Scipione**[1]]; by the Drusi, Conv. iv. 5[123–4] [**Drusi**]; by Cato of Utica, Conv. iv. 5[140]; Mon. ii. 5[133–9] [**Catone**[2]]; by Cicero, Conv. iv. 5[172–6] [**Tullio**]; her fate dependent upon the life of a single Roman in the fight with the Albans, Conv. iv. 5[155–60] [**Albani**]; saved by the goose of the Capitol from capture by the Gauls under Brennus, Conv. iv. 5[160–4]; Mon. ii. 4[42–58] [**Galli**[2]]; and by a hailstorm from capture by Hannibal, Mon. ii. 4[58–63] [**Annibale**]; preserved from annihilation, under Providence, by the valour of Scipio Africanus, Par. xxvii. 61–2;

the scene of the triumphs of the latter and of Augustus, Purg. xxix. 115–16; confers the imperial authority upon Julius Caesar, Par. vi. 57; the first to make use of the consequential plural, Par. xvi. 10; the residence of Virgil under Augustus, Inf. i. 71; Lucan's address to (*Phars.* i. 44), V. N. § 25[85–7]; the winner of the crown of universal empire, Mon. ii. 7[59–66], 9[81]; her history one of the favourite themes of the Florentine women in the old days, Par. xv. 124–6; Florence the most beautiful and most famous of her daughters, Conv. i. 3[21–2] [**Fiorenza.**]

Roma[2], Rome, Christian Rome (A.D.), Inf. xiv. 105; xxxi. 59; Purg. vi. 112; xvi. 106, 127; xviii. 80; Par. ix. 140; xxiv. 63; xxxi. 34; V. N. § 41[51]; Conv. iii. 5[85, 96]; V. E. i. 10[50]; Mon. ii. 7[65]; Epist. vii. 7[154]; viii. 11[179]; *urbs Roma*, Epist. viii. 10[142]; *alma urbs*, Epist. v. *tit.*; *Latiale caput*, Epist. viii. 10[150]; *Imperii sedes*, Mon. iii. 10[4]; *sedes apostolica*, Epist. viii. 2[26], 11[175]; *sedes Sponsae Christi*, Epist. viii. 11[179]; *sacrosanctum ovile*, Epist. viii. 2[21]; *culmen apostolicum*, Epist. viii. 10[164]; *colei che siede sopra l'acque* (ref. to *Rev.* xvii. 1, 15), Inf. xix. 107–9; called by St. Peter *il mio cimiterio*, Par. xxvii. 25 (cf. Par. ix. 139–41); referred to by mention of the Lateran, Par. xxxi. 35; of the Tiber, Epist. vii. 7[139]; viii. 10[149].

Rome fore-ordained as the capital of the universal sovereignty, i.e. of the Roman Empire, Mon. ii. 7[59–66]; her fortunes the object of the special care of Providence, Conv. iv. 5[176–9];

converted to Christianity by St. Peter and St. Paul, Par. xxiv. 62–3; Epist. viii. 2²⁵; the scene of the martyrdom of St. Peter and of many of the saints, Par. ix. 139–41; xxvii. 25; the seat of the Church and of Christ's Vicar upon earth, Purg. xvi. 127; Epist. vii. 7¹⁵⁴; viii. 2²⁶, 10¹⁶⁴, 11¹⁷⁹ (cf. Inf. ii. 22–4; xix. 107–9); the seat of the Emperor, Conv. iv. 5³⁰⁻²; Mon. iii. 10⁴; Epist. viii. 10¹⁵⁰⁻²; her two Suns, the Pope and the Emperor, Purg. xvi. 106–7; Epist. viii. 10¹⁴³; herself compared to the Sun, Epist. viii. 10¹⁵⁸; deserving of the respect and love of all Italians, and especially of those who dwell within her walls, Epist. viii. 10¹⁴⁸⁻⁵²; the very stones of her walls, and the soil upon which she stands, worthy of the highest reverence, Conv. iv. 5¹⁸⁰⁻³; the scene of the coronation of Charlemagne as Emperor of the West, Mon. iii. 11²⁻⁵ [Carlo Magno]; her complaint that she is abandoned by the Emperor, Purg. vi. 112–14 (cf. Epist. viii. 4, 10); deprived of both her luminaries (cf. Purg. xvi. 106–7; Mon. iii. 1³⁶⁻⁷) through the deaths of the Emperor Henry VII (Aug. 1313) and Clement V (April, 1314), Epist. viii. 10¹⁴³ [Arrigo²: Clemente²]; her wretched condition such that even Hannibal would have felt compassion for her, Epist. viii. 10¹⁴³⁻⁴; the mother of Florence, who, like an undutiful daughter, rebels against her authority, Epist. vii. 7¹⁴³⁻⁵⁷ [Fiorenza]; on the right side of Italy if the Apennines be taken as the dividing line (from N. to S.),

V. E. i. 10⁵⁰; distant from the N. Pole 2,700 miles, from the S. Pole 7,500 miles, Conv. iii. 5⁸⁵⁻¹⁰⁰ [Lucia²]; to an observer at Rome about the end of November the sun sets between Sardinia and Corsica, Purg. xviii. 79–81; the 'ancient one of Crete' looks towards her as to his mirror, Inf. xiv. 105 [Creta]; view of the city from Montemalo, Par. xv. 109 [Montemalo]; the splendour of her buildings the admiration of foreigners, Par. xxxi. 31–6; the river Tiber, Inf. xxvii. 30; Purg. ii. 101; Par. xi. 106; Conv. iv. 13¹³⁰; Mon. ii. 4⁶⁸; Epist. vii. 7¹³⁹; viii. 10¹⁴⁹ [Tevero]; the Ponte Sant' Angelo, Inf. xviii. 29 [Ponte³]; the Church of St. Peter, Inf. xviii. 32; its pinecone, Inf. xxxi. 59; its obelisk, Conv. iv. 16⁶⁸ [Pietro, San²]; the Lateran, Inf. xxvii. 86; Par. xxxi. 35 [Laterano]; the Vatican, Par. ix. 139 [Vaticano]; the Janiculus, Inf. xviii. 33 [Gianicolo]; pilgrims and visitors to, Par. xxxi. 31–6, 103–8; V. N. § 41²⁻⁵, ⁵⁰⁻¹; the Veronica at, Par. xxxi. 104; V. N. § 41³⁻⁵ [Veronica]; the Jubilee of 1300, Inf. xviii. 29; Purg. ii. 98; Par. xxxi. 31, 103 [Giubbileo]; pilgrims to Rome known by the distinctive name of *Romei*, V. N. § 41⁵⁰⁻¹ [Peregrini].

Roma³, Rome, in the figurative sense; *quella Roma onde Christo è Romano*, 'that Rome of which Christ is a citizen', i. e. Heaven, Purg. xxxii. 102. [Paradiso¹.]

Romagna, former province of N. Italy, corresponding roughly to the E. portion of the modern

Emilia. According to D.'s definition (Inf. xxvii. 29–30; Purg.
xiv. 92), it extended from Bologna
to Rimini, and from the hills of
Montefeltro to the plain of Ravenna.

D., addressing Guido da Montefeltro (in Bolgia 8 of Circle VIII
of Hell), speaks of it as *Romagna
tua*, Inf. xxvii. 37; *il peggiore
spirto di R.*, i. e. Frate Alberigo of
Faenza, Inf. xxxiii. 154 [**Alberigo**];
*quel paese Che siede tra R. e quel di
Carlo*, i. e. the March of Ancona,
Purg. v. 68–9 [**Marca Anconi-
tana**]; *lo spirto di R.*, i. e. Guido
del Duca, Purg. xv. 44 [**Guido del
Duca**]; *Romandiola*, V. E. i. 10^{53}, 14^4;
Romaniola, Epist. i. *tit.*; Guido da
Montefeltro (in Bolgia 8 of Circle
VIII of Hell) speaks of his native
hill-country, which formed part of
Romagna, as *i monti là intra Urbino
E il giogo di che il Tever si disserra*,
Inf. xxvii. 29–30 [**Montefeltro**];
Guido del Duca (in Circle II of
Purgatory) describes Romagna as
lying between the Po, the Apennines,
the Adriatic, and the Reno, *Tra il
Po e il monte, e la marina e il Reno*,
Purg. xiv. 92 [**Reno** 2]; on the
left side of Italy, if the Apennines
be taken as the dividing line (from
N. to S.), V. E. i. 10^{51-3}, 14^{2-4};
its dialect, V. E. i. 10^{66-8}, $14^{7-12, 44}$
[**Romagnuoli**]; Forlì, the most
central town of the whole province,
V. E. i. 14^{13-5} [**Forlì**]; the province included in the jurisdiction of
the Bishop of Ostia as papal legate,
Epist. i. *tit.* [**Nicholaus**].

In response to the inquiry of
Guido da Montefeltro (Inf. xxvii.
28–30) as to the present state (i. e.
in 1300) of Romagna, whether it be
at peace or at war, D. says that
there is no open war at the moment,
but that there is, as there always
was, war in the hearts of its tyrants
(*vv.* 37–9); he then informs Guido
that Ravenna is still, as it has been
for years past, under the eagle of the
Polenta family, which now also
broods over Cervia (*vv.* 40–2)
[**Polenta**]; that Forlì is under the
claws of the green lion of the Ordelaffi (*vv.* 43–5) [**Ordelaffi**]; that
Rimini is under the Old and Young
Mastiffs (*vv.* 46–8) [**Malatesta**];
that Faenza and Imola are under the
lion-cub of Maghinardo Pagano (*vv.*
49–51) [**Mainardo**]; and that
Cesena alternates between a state of
tyranny and freedom (*vv.* 52–4)
[**Cesena**].

Guido del Duca, a native of
Bertinoro near Forlì, in conversation
with D. (in Circle II of Purgatory)
laments at length over the degeneracy
of the men of Romagna, charac-
terizing them as 'bastards', who
have fallen away from the noble
example of their illustrious fore-
fathers, many of whom he mentions
by name, Purg. xiv. 88–123.

Romagnuoli, inhabitants of Romagna; Guido da Montefeltro (in
Bolgia 8 of Circle VIII of Hell)
asks D. whether they are at peace
or war, Inf. xxvii. 28; Guido del
Duca (in Circle II of Purgatory)
reproaches them as 'bastards' on
account of their degeneracy, Purg.
xiv. 99 [**Romagna**]; *Romandioli*,
their dialect distinct from those of
Lombardy and of the March of
Ancona, V. E. i. 10^{66-8}; their
dialect so soft as to make a man's
voice sound like that of a woman,

especially at Forlì, the central town of the province, V. E. i. 14⁴⁻¹⁵; this dialect not worthy to rank as the vulgar tongue of Italy, V. E. i. 14⁴⁶⁻⁸; their most illustrious poets have abandoned their own dialect in favour of the Italian vulgar tongue, V. E. i. 19¹⁶⁻¹⁸.

Romandiola. [**Romagna.**]
Romandioli. [**Romagnuoli.**]
Romandiolus, belonging to Romagna; *Romandiolum vulgare*, the dialect of Romagna, V. E. i. 14⁴⁶. [**Romagnuoli.**]

Romane, Roman women, of ancient Rome; mentioned among the examples of temperance proclaimed in the Circle of the Gluttonous in Purgatory, as having been content to drink water, Purg. xxii. 145–6. [**Golosi.**]

Romani[1], Romans, of ancient Rome (B. C.), Inf. xv. 77; xxvi. 60; Par. vi. 44; xix. 102; Conv. iii. 11²⁸; iv. 4¹¹⁷, 5¹¹³, ¹⁵⁷; V. E. i. 10¹⁷; Mon. ii. 3¹⁰⁸, 4³¹, 5²⁹, 7⁶⁹, 9⁶⁴, ⁶⁵, ⁸⁴, ⁹¹, ¹⁰⁴, 10⁵⁹, 11³⁴, ⁵⁶, 12⁵²; *Romana gente*, Conv. iv. 4¹¹³; *Romano popolo*, Conv. iv. 5⁶³; *Romanus populus*, Mon. i. 2¹¹; ii. 1¹², ²⁷, ⁵⁶, 2⁵, 3², ⁷, ¹²⁰, 5³¹, ⁴⁹, 6⁴, ⁸, ¹¹, 7²³, ⁶⁶, ⁸⁶, ⁸⁸, 9¹², ¹⁹, ¹⁰⁷, 11¹, ²³, ⁷⁷, 13⁶⁴; iii. 16¹²⁵; *Latini*, Purg. vii. 16; Epist. v. 4⁵²; *gente Latina*, Conv. iv. 4¹⁰¹; *popolo santo*, Conv. iv. 4¹⁰³.

The ancient Romans the ancestors of the Florentines, Inf. xv. 76–8 (cf. Conv. i. 3²¹⁻²; Epist. vii. 7¹⁵⁴⁻⁷) [**Fiorentini**]; themselves descended from the Trojans, Inf. xxvi. 60; Conv. iv. 4¹⁰³⁻⁵ (cf. Conv. iv. 5⁴⁸⁻⁹; Mon. ii. 3³⁰⁻¹, 11²²⁻⁴); hence sometimes spoken of by D. as

Trojans, Inf. xxviii. 10 [**Troiani**]; Aeneas their father and founder, Inf. ii. 20; Conv. iv. 5⁴⁸⁻⁹; Mon. ii. 3³⁰, ¹²⁰; 7⁶⁹ [**Enea**]; Lavinia, third wife of Aeneas, their mother, Mon. ii. 3¹⁰⁸⁻⁹ [**Lavinia**]; their wars with the Albans, Par. vi. 37; Conv. iv. 5¹⁵⁷⁻⁸; Mon. ii. 11²²⁻³⁷ [**Albani**]; with Porsena, Mon. ii. 4⁶⁶⁻⁷, 5¹²² [**Porsena**]; with Brennus, Par. vi. 44 [**Brenno**]; with the Carthaginians, Par. vi. 49; Conv. iv. 5¹²⁵⁻⁷; Mon. ii. 4⁵⁸⁻⁶⁴, 11⁵²⁻⁶¹ [**Cartaginesi**]; with the Sabines, Mon. ii. 11⁴⁰ [**Sabini**]; with the Samnites, Conv. iv. 5¹¹¹; Mon. ii. 11⁴⁰ [**Sanniti**]; with Pyrrhus, Par. vi. 44; Mon. ii. 5¹⁵⁵, 10⁵⁷⁻⁸³, 11⁵²⁻⁸; the answer of Pyrrhus to their envoys who came to treat for the ransom of the Roman prisoners, Mon. ii. 10⁵⁷⁻⁶⁹ [**Pirro**]; Alexander's embassy demanding their submission, Mon. ii. 9⁶¹⁻⁵; his attempt to outstrip them in the race for universal empire, Mon. ii. 9⁷⁷⁻⁹ [**Alessandro**[2]]; their standard the Imperial Eagle, Par. xix. 101–2 [**Aquila**]; the foundation of their empire contemporaneous with the birth of David, Conv. iv. 5⁴⁶⁻⁵⁴ [**David**]; their history the subject of romances in the *langue d'*oïl, V. E. i. 10¹²⁻¹⁸ [**Lingua Oil**]; their chief chroniclers the illustrious historian Livy, Conv. iv. 5⁹⁴; Mon. ii. 3³², 4³³, ⁴⁸, ⁶³, 5⁷⁹, ¹⁰⁴, ¹¹⁴, ¹²⁶, ¹³⁰, 9⁶⁶, 11³⁷, ⁴³, ⁶² [**Livio**]; and Orosius, Mon. ii. 11³⁷ [**Orosio**]; the moderation of their women, who were content to drink water, Purg. xxii. 145–6 [**Romane**].

The ancient Romans in their relation to D.'s theory of the

Empire :—the power of the Roman
people not obtained by force, as
some might urge, but ordained, in
the first instance, by divine Providence, Conv. iv. 4[87-90], [111-14],
[124-6] (cf. Mon. ii. 1[19-20]); they
were endowed with boundless empire by God, as is testified by Virgil
(*Aen*.i. 278-9), Conv. iv. 4[115-19](cf.
Mon. ii. 9[81-111]; Epist. vii. 3[62-3]);
chosen by God for universal sovereignty on account of their being by
nature more gentle in governing, more
powerful in maintaining, and more
subtle in acquiring, than any other
nation, Conv. iv. 4[98-106] (cf. Mon.
ii. 7[23-4]); their employment of
force merely the instrumental, not
the motive, cause of their world-
wide dominion, Conv. iv. 4[119-24];
the world never so peaceful as when
under the governance of one sole
prince of the Roman people, Conv.
iv. 5[60-5] (cf. Mon. i. 16[10-12]);
their empire under divine guidance
from the time of Romulus to that
of Augustus, as has been made
manifest on numberless occasions,
Conv. iv. 5[80-179]; paramount
throughout the world, without any
to withstand them, Mon. ii. 1[12-13];
their pre-eminence due to the working
of divine Providence, Mon. ii. 1[19-20]
(cf. Conv. iv. 4[115-19]); the supreme
sovereignty vested in them by right,
not by usurpation, Mon. ii. 1[52-7],
2[5-6], 3[2-4], 4[25-6], 6[13-14], 13[64-5];
the noblest, and therefore the most
worthy, of all nations, Mon. ii.
3[7-9], [120-1]; their empire helped to
its perfection by miracles, as is
proved by the testimony of several
illustrious writers, Mon. ii. 4[23-9];
thus Livy (i. 20) and Lucan (*Phars.*

ix. 477-80) record the miraculous
descent from heaven of the sacred
shield in the days of Numa Pompilius, Mon. ii. 4[30-41]; Livy (v.
47), Virgil (*Aen*. viii. 652-6), and
others, relate how they were by a
miracle saved from destruction by
the Gauls, Mon. ii. 4[42-5]; Livy
(xxvi. 11), again, records their
miraculous deliverance from Hannibal, Mon. ii. 4[58-64]; and, again
(ii. 13), the marvellous escape of
Cloelia from the camp of Porsena
by swimming across the Tiber, Mon.
ii. 4[65-70]; in bringing the whole
world into subjection the Romans
aimed at the highest good, as their
deeds declare, for they renounced
their own private advantage in the
interests of the peace and welfare of
all mankind, Mon. ii. 5[31-9], 6[1-14],
7[88-90]; hence the justice of the
saying that the Roman Empire
' springs from the fountain of piety ',
Mon. ii. 5[40-2]; their good intentions
proved by their noble self-sacrifice,
both collectively and individually,
Mon. ii. 5[48-170]; their nation ordained for empire by nature, Mon.
ii. 7[23-4], [86-9] (cf. Conv. iv.
4[98-106]); they alone of all nations
attained to universal empire, Mon.
ii. 9[12-21]; all other attempts having
failed, such as those of Ninus,
King of Assyria, Vesoges, King of
Egypt, Cyrus and Xerxes, Kings
of Persia, and last, and greatest of
all, Alexander of Macedon, Mon.
ii. 9[22-80]; the attainment by the
Romans of this end testified by
Virgil (*Aen*. i. 234-6), Lucan
(*Phars.* i. 109-11), Boëthius (*Cons.
Phil.* ii. met. 6), and St. Luke (ii.
1), Mon. ii. 9[81-111]; their empire

gained by single combat between man and man, by which method all disputes concerning it were decided, Mon. ii. $11^{1-7, \ 77-9}$; as, for instance, between Aeneas and Turnus, the Horatii and the Curiatii, and in their fights with the Sabines and Samnites, and also between Fabricius and Pyrrhus, and Scipio and Hannibal, Mon. ii. 11^{39-61}; if the Roman Empire did not exist by right, Christ in being born under the edict of Augustus, and in submitting to the jurisdiction of Pilate, the deputy of Tiberius, sanctioned an unjust thing, Mon. ii. 12^{24}, 13^{49} (cf. Epist. vii. 3^{64-73}); and further, in that case, the sin of Adam was not punished in Christ, Mon. ii. 13^{1-3}; but these assumptions are false, for it has been sufficiently proved that the Roman Empire did exist by right, and Christ sanctioned it by His birth and by His death under it, Mon. ii. 13^{61-5}. [**Roma** ^{1}.]

Romani ^{2}, Romans, of Christian Rome (A.D.), Inf. xxviii. 28; Conv. iv. 3^{39}, 28^{75}; V. E. i. 9^{38}, 10^{63}, $11^{7, \ 12}$, 12^{58}, 13^{31}; Mon. iii. 11^8; Epist. v. 5^{82}; vi. 1^4; vii. *tit.*, 3^{53-4}; their arrangement for the regulation of the traffic on the Ponte Sant' Angelo during the Jubilee of 1300, Inf. xxviii. 28 [**Ponte** ^{3}]; Frederick II, the last real Emperor of the Romans, Conv. iv. 3^{39} [**Federico** ^{2}]; St. Paul's Epistle to the Romans, Conv. iv. 28^{75} [***Romanos, Epistola ad***]; the dialect of the Romans distinct from that of the Florentines, V. E. i. 9^{38}; different from that of the Apulians on the one hand, and from that of the Spoletans on the other, V. E. i. 10^{62-3};

their claim to take precedence of the rest of Italy, V.E. i. 11^{7-8}; their dialect, like their morals, the most degraded of all Italy, V. E. i. 11^{12-17}; the barbarisms of the Apulian dialect due in part to the vicinity of the Romans, V. E. i. 12^{56-9}; affinity of the dialects of Perugia, Orvieto, Viterbo, and Città di Castello (or Civita Castellana), with those of Rome and Spoleto, V. E. i. 13^{29-32}.

In their relation to D.'s theory of the Empire :—the opposition to the Roman Emperor chiefly on the part of those who profess most zeal for the faith of Christ, Mon. ii. 12^{1-4}; the two great lights for the guidance of mankind, the Roman Pontiff (who should lead them to eternal life, according to revelation), and the Roman Emperor (who should lead them to temporal happiness, according to the teaching of philosophy), Mon. iii. 1^{36-7}, 16^{75-82} (cf. Purg. xvi. 106-7; Epist. viii. 10); the question whether the authority of the Roman Emperor, who is by right Monarch of the world, depends immediately upon God, or on His Vicar, Mon. iii. 1^{37-42}; the authority of the Roman Emperor not derived from the Church, Mon. iii. 13^{1-4}, 14^{1-10}; but direct from God, Mon. iii. 16^{114-17}; seeing, however, that the Roman Emperor in certain matters is subject to the Roman Pontiff, it is meet that Caesar should show reverence to Peter, as a son to his father, Mon. iii. 16^{129-36}. [**Roma** ^{2}.]

Romani, Epistola alli. [***Romanos, Epistola ad.***]

Romaniola. [**Romagna.**]

Romano ^{1}, Roman, of ancient Rome (B.C.); *Latino Romano*, i. e.

classical Latin, Conv. i. 11[95] [**La- tino** [1]]; *Romano Principe*, i. e. the Roman Emperor, Conv. iv. 4[85]; *Romanorum Princeps*, Mon. ii. 9[91]; *Romano Imperio*, Conv. iv. 4[126], 5[52, 154]; *Romanum Imperium*, Mon. ii. 1[53], 4[23, 27], 5[41], 11[5], 12[24], 13[1, 48, 59]; *homo Romanus*, Mon. ii. 11[67]; *Romanum nomen*, Mon. ii. 4[45]; *Romani cittadini*, Conv. iv. 5[113–14]; *Romana potenza*, Conv. iv. 4[87]; *Romana auctoritas*, Mon. ii. 12[43]; *Romana gente*, Conv. iv. 4[112]; *città Romana*, Conv. iv. 5[49]; *Romana tellus*, Epist. vii. 4[91]; *Romana libertà*, Conv. iv. 5[175]; *Romana nobilitas*, Mon. ii. 4[58]; *Romana res*, Mon. ii. 4[60, 69], 11[62]; *Romana gesta*, Mon. ii. 3[33]; iii. 10[15]; *Romane*, Purg. xxii. 145; *Romane storie*, Conv. iv. 5[93]. [**Romani** [1].]

Romano [2], Roman, of Christian Rome (A.D.); *Romano Pastore*, i. e. the Pope, Purg. xix. 107; Conv. iv. 29[23]; *Romanus Pontifex*, Mon. iii. 1[36], 13[4], 16[131] [**Papa**]; *Romano Principato*, i. e. the Emperor, Purg. x. 74 [**Traiano**]; *Romanus Principatus*, Mon. ii. 12[2]; iii. 13[3]; *Romanus Princeps*, Mon. ii. 1[27]; iii. 1[37], 14[2], 16[89, 131]; Epist. v. 7[116–17]; vi. 2[31]; *Imperador de' Romani*, Conv. iv. 3[39]; *Romanorum Imperator*, Mon. iii. 11[8]; *Monarcha Romanus*, Mon. iii. 1[38]; *Romanorum Rex*, Epist. vii. *tit.* [**Imperatore** [3]]; *Romanum regimen*, Mon. iii. 10[20]; *Imperium sacrosanctum Romanum*, A. T. § 24[3–4]; *sacrosanctum Romanorum Imperium*, Epist. vi. 1[4]; *Romana res*, Epist. vi. 6[180]; *Romanorum potestas*, Epist. vii. 3[53–4]; *Romana civilitas*, Epist. vi. 2[52–3]; *Romana gloria*,

Epist. vii. 2[37–8]; *Romana aula*, Epist. ii. 2[33]; *Romanorum vulgare*, V. E. i. 11[12] [**Romani** [2]].

Romano [3], Roman, in figurative sense, Purg. xxxii. 102. [**Roma**[3].]

Romano [4]], village and castle in Venetia, a few miles NE. of Bassano, where the famous Ezzolino da Romano was born; alluded to by Cunizza (in the Heaven of Venus), Par. ix. 25–9 [**Azzolino** [1] : **Cunizza**]. The situation of Romano is here described as being placed on a low hill, ' between Rialto (Venice) and the streams of Brenta and Piave', i. e. in the March of Treviso [**Marca Trivisiana**].

Romanos, Epistola ad, St. Paul's Epistle to the Romans, Conv. iv. 28[75]; A. T. § 22[15]; quoted, Conv. iv. 13[81–2] (*Rom.* xii. 3); Conv. iv. 21[56–8] (*Rom.* xi. 33); Conv. iv. 28[75–81] (*Rom.* ii. 28–9); Mon. ii. 2[72–3] (*Rom.* i. 20); Mon. ii. 9[75–6] (*Rom.* xi. 33); Mon. ii. 13[8–11] (*Rom.* v. 12); Epist. v. 4[64–5] (*Rom.* xiii. 2); Epist. v. 8[120–2] (*Rom.* i. 20); Epist. vi. 5[154](*Rom.* vii. 23); A. T. § 22[15–18] (*Rom.* xi. 33).

Romei, ' Romers', i. e. pilgrims who went on a pilgrimage to Rome; mentioned by D. in his explanation of the distinction between the several kinds of pilgrims, V. N. § 41[34–52]. [**Peregrini**.]

Romena, village in the Casentino, on the road from Pratovecchio to Florence, the site in D.'s time of a castle belonging to the Conti Guidi; its situation is described by Maestro Adamo (in Bolgia 10 of Circle VIII of Hell), who says that it was there that he falsified the gold florin of

Florence, Inf. xxx. 73-4. [Adamo, Maestro : Guidi, Conti.]

Romena, Alessandro da. [Alessandro¹.]

Romena, Guido da. [Guido.]

Romena, Oberto da. [Oberto.]

Romeo, name of the seneschal of Raymond Berenger IV, Count of Provence ; he is placed by D. among those who for love of fame performed great deeds upon earth (*Spiriti Operanti*), in the Heaven of Mercury, where his spirit is pointed out by the Emperor Justinian, Par. vi. 127-42 [Mercurio, Cielo di] ; Justinian describes him as having been ' persona umile e peregrina' (evidently with a play upon his name, *romeo*, like *peregrino*, meaning ' pilgrim '), and recounts the great services he rendered to the Count, especially in the matter of the marriages of his four daughters, each of whom married a king (*vv.* 127-35) ; he then relates how, through the jealousy and ingratitude of the Provençal lords, Romeo fell into disgrace, and quitted the Count's service ' in poverty and old age' (*vv.* 136-42) [Provenzali].

The only foundation, apparently, for the story, adopted by D. (and Villani, vi. 90), of the 'pilgrim' who became the minister of the Provençal Count, is the fact that the name of Count Berenger's grand seneschal was Romieu (or Romée) of Villeneuve. This Romieu, who was a friend of Sordello (Purg. vi. 74), was born c. 1170, and died in 1250 (five years after his master), while still in charge of the affairs of Provence, the Count's youngest daughter, Beatrice, who subsequently married

Charles of Anjou, being under his guardianship. [Beringhieri, Ramondo.]

Romoaldo, St. Romualdus, founder of the Order of Camaldoli or Reformed Benedictines ; he belonged to the Onesti family of Ravenna, where he was born c. 960 ; he died c. 1027. D. places him among the Contemplative Spirits (*Spiriti Contemplanti*) in the Heaven of Saturn, where his spirit is pointed out by St. Benedict, Par. xxii. 49 [Saturno, Cielo di].

While he was quite a young man his father fought a duel in his presence and killed his adversary, the sight of which so affected him that he retired into a Benedictine convent near Ravenna, and became a monk. After many years, he succeeded in instituting his new Order of Reformed Benedictines, for whom he founded (in 1012) the famous monastery of Camaldoli, in the Casentino, about thirty miles from Florence [Camaldoli]. A purely contemplative life was enjoined on the members of the Order, which received the papal sanction from Alexander II in 1072.

Romolo, Romulus, mythical founder of the city of Rome, said to have been the son of Mars by Rhea Silvia ; referred to by D. as the first King of Rome, Conv. iv. 5[83, 90] ; mentioned, in connexion with his parentage, by his name Quirinus, Par. viii. 131 [Quirino].

Romuleus, belonging to Romulus ; the Virgilian expression, *Romuleus culmus*, i. e. the straw-built hut of Romulus on the Capitol (*Aen.* viii. 654), quoted, Mon. ii. 4[55].

Roncisvalle], Roncesvalles or Roncevaux, valley on the Spanish side of the Pyrenees, forming one of the passes into France; famous as the scene of the destruction of Charlemagne's rear-guard under Roland, to which D. refers as *la dolorosa rotta*, Inf. xxxi. 16 [Carlo Magno].

In the traditional account of the incident, preserved in the O.F. *Chanson de Roland* (Cent. xi), Roland and his force were annihilated by an army of Saracens, in accordance with a preconcerted plan agreed upon between the traitor Ganelon, Roland's step-father, and the Saracen King, Marsiccius. The historical basis for this tradition consists in the following facts:—In the year 777 Charlemagne, King of the Franks, made an expedition into Spain for the conquest of the country, which was only partially successful, as he failed to reduce the stronghold of Saragossa. As he was returning into France in the next year, after the main body of his army had passed through the defiles of the Pyrenees unmolested, the rear-guard, in which were his nephew Roland, ' the prefect of the Marches of Brittany ', and his chief nobles and captains, was suddenly attacked in the narrow pass of Roncesvalles by swarms of Gascon mountaineers (or Basques), attracted by the prospect of plunder, and was totally destroyed, not a soul being left alive (Aug. 15, 778). Before Charlemagne could send a force to chastise them, the mountaineers dispersed with their booty into the mountain forests beyond reach of his vengeance.

D. refers to a famous incident in this battle, viz. Roland's mighty blast upon his ivory horn, Inf. xxxi. 18 [Orlando]; the traitor Ganelon is mentioned, Inf. xxxii. 122 [Ganellone].

Rosa, the Celestial Rose in the Empyrean, in the petals of which are seated the Elect, Par. xxx. 117; xxxii. 15, 120; *rosa sempiterna*, Par. xxx. 124; *candida rosa*, Par. xxxi. 1; *circular figura*, Par. xxx. 103; *gran fior*, Par. xxxi. 10; *fior*, Par. xxxi. 16, 19; xxxii. 18, 22; *fior venusto*, Par. xxxii. 126; *città*, Par. xxx. 130; *sicuro e gaudioso regno*, Par. xxxi. 25; *regno*, Par. xxxii. 61; *reame*, Par. xxxii. 52.

According to D.'s description the Rose resembles a kind of amphitheatre, the centre (*il giallo*, Par. xxx. 124) being formed of a sea of light. After Beatrice has pointed out to D. the seat reserved for the Emperor Henry VII, 'l'alto Arrigo' (Par. xxx. 133–8), St. Bernard explains to him the arrangement of the seats of the Elect (Par. xxxi. 65–xxxii. 138). On the highest tier, at the point where the light is most dazzling, is seated the Virgin Mary, with more than a thousand Angels hovering around her (xxxi. 115–38). Next below Mary, who healed the wound inflicted upon Man at the Fall, sits Eve, who was the cause of the wound (xxxii. 4–6). Below Eve, on the third tier, sits Rachel, with Beatrice at her side (*vv.* 7–9). On successive tiers below them are Sarah, Rebekah, Judith, Ruth, and other Hebrew women (*vv.* 10–18). On the opposite side, facing Mary, on the same tier is seated St. John the Baptist (*vv.* 31–3). Below him on successive tiers are St. Francis, St. Benedict, St. Augustine, and others (*vv.* 34–6). These two lines (from Mary downwards on one side, and from the Baptist downwards on the other) form as it were a wall, which divides the Rose into two parts (*vv.* 20–1, 28–31). In one part are the seats (all filled) of those who believed in Christ to come, i. e. those who were under the Old Testament dispensation (*vv.* 22–4); in the other are the seats (only partially filled) of those who believed in Christ already come, i. e. those who were under the New Testament dispensation (*vv.* 25–7; cf. xxx. 131–2); these, when all the seats are filled, will be equal in number to those on the opposite side (*vv.* 38–9). The lowest tiers are filled by infants, who were saved, not by their own merits, but through baptism by the merit of Christ (*vv.* 40–8). On the left hand of Mary is seated Adam, the Father of the Old Covenant, and on her right is St. Peter, the Father of the New, these two being regarded as the ' roots', as it were, of the Rose (*vv.* 118–26). Next to St. Peter is seated St. John the Evangelist, next to Adam is Moses (*vv.* 127–32). Opposite to St. Peter, on the right of the Baptist, sits Anne, the type of the contemplative life, with her eyes fixed upon her daughter Mary (*vv.* 133–5). Opposite to Adam, on the left of the Baptist, sits Lucy, the type of the active life, who dispatched Beatrice to D.'s assistance (*vv.* 136–8).

Rubaconte, old name for the bridge at Florence now known as the Ponte alle Grazie ; it is the last stone bridge over the Arno up stream, and the road to San Miniato leads over it.

D. alludes to its position at the foot of the hill upon which the church of San Miniato stands, Purg. xii. 100–2. [**Miniato, San.**]

This bridge is the oldest stone bridge in Florence, and the only one still existing which was standing in D.'s lifetime. Villani records that it was built in 1237, and was named after the then Podestà (vi. 26).

Ruben], Reuben, eldest son of Jacob and Leah ; he is among those referred to by Virgil as having been released by Christ from Limbo, *Israel co' suoi nati*, Inf. iv. 59 [**Limbo**].

Rubicante, one of the ten demons in Bolgia 5 of Circle VIII of Hell (Malebolge), deputed by Malacoda to escort D. and Virgil, Inf. xxi. 123 ; xxii. 40. [**Alichino : Malebranche.**]

Rubicon, small river of N. Italy, which falls into the Adriatic, a few miles N. of Rimini ; during the period of the Roman Republic it formed the boundary between the province of Cisalpine Gaul and Italy proper. The stream is celebrated in history on account of Julius Caesar's passage across it at the head of his army in B.C. 49, by which act he declared war against the Republic.

The Emperor Justinian (in the Heaven of Mercury) mentions it, in connexion with this incident, in his account of the exploits of the Roman

Eagle, Par. vi. 61-2; Tityrus (i.e. D.) refers to Ravenna as being situated on the coast of the Emilia, between the right bank of the Po and the left bank of the Rubicon, Ecl. ii. 67-8 [Po : Ravenna].

Ruffiani, Pandars, punished with Seducers in Bolgia 1 of Circle VIII of Hell (Malebolge), Inf. xviii. 22-99 (cf. Inf. xi. 60). [Seduttori.]

Ruggieri, Arcivescovo, Ruggieri degli Ubaldini, Ghibelline Archbishop of Pisa (1278-1295), son of Ubaldino dalla Pila (Purg. xxiv. 29), nephew of the famous Ghibelline Cardinal Ottaviano degli Ubaldini (Inf. x. 120), and first cousin of Ugolino d'Azzo (Purg. xiv. 105) [Ubaldini]; it was through his double-dealing that the Guelf Count Ugolino della Gherardesca, with his sons and grandsons, was imprisoned and starved to death in the Tower of Famine at Pisa.

D. places Ruggieri, together with Ugolino, who is represented as gnawing his head, among the Traitors in Antenora, the second division of Circle IX of Hell, where those who have betrayed their country are punished, Ruggieri being below Ugolino, just on the confines of the next division, Tolomea, the place assigned to those who have betrayed their associates, Inf. xxxiii. 14; (R. and Ugolino) *duo*, Inf.

xxxii. 125; *l'altro*, vv. 126, 128; *colui*, v. 134; *il traditor*, xxxiii. 8; *questi*, vv. 14, 28 [Antenora : Tolomea : Traditori : Ugolino, Conte].

Rusticucci, Jacopo. [Jacopo Rusticucci.]

Rut], Ruth, Moabitish wife of Boaz, by whom she became the great-grandmother of David (*Matt.* i. 5-6).

St. Bernard points out her place in the Celestial Rose, referring to her as 'colei Che fu bisava al cantor che per doglia Del fallo disse, *Miserere mei*' (i.e. as the great-grandmother of the Psalmist), Par. xxxii. 10-12. [David : Rosa.]

Rutuli, Rutulians, ancient people of Italy, who inhabited a narrow slip of country on the coast of Latium, to the S. of the Tiber. They were subdued at an early period by the Romans. Virgil represents them as having been defeated by Aeneas, who slew Turnus their king with his own hand in single combat.

D. mentions the Rutulians in connexion with this duel, Mon. ii. 8[8-15] [Enea : Turno]; they are referred to, in connexion with John of Luxemburg, eldest son of the Emperor Henry VII, as *Turni*, 'the followers of Turnus' (i.e. the opponents of the Empire), Epist. vii. 5[98] [Johannes [2]].

S

[**Sa' Jacopo tra' Fossi**], quarter of Florence supposed to be alluded to by Forese Donati in his *tenzone* with D. by the phrase *tra le fosse*, Son. lii.* 8.

Saba, Regina], Queen of Sheba, referred to by D. as *Austri Regina*, 'the Queen of the South' (*Matt.* xii. 42); her visit to Jerusalem to satisfy herself as to the greatness of Solomon (1 *Kings* x. 1-7), Epist. x. 1[10].

Sabaoth, Greek form of the Hebrew *tsebâôth*, 'armies', adopted in the Vulgate (*Rom.* ix. 29; *James* v. 4); *Deus Sabaoth*, 'the Lord of Hosts', Par. vii. 1; Epist. vii. 8[178].

Sabellio, Sabellius, heresiarch of Cent. iii, born at Pentapolis in N. Africa, became presbyter of Ptolemaïs, died c. 265. He refused to accept the received doctrine of the Trinity, and held that the terms, Father, Son, and Holy Spirit, were merely different names for the One God.

Sabellius is mentioned by St. Thomas Aquinas (in the Heaven of the Sun), together with Arius, as conspicuous among those who sought to distort the Scriptures, Par. xiii. 127.

Sabello, Sabellus, Roman soldier belonging to Cato's army in Africa, of whom Lucan relates that he was stung by a venomous serpent in the desert of Libya, the bite of which caused his body to putrefy and fall to pieces in a mass of corruption (*Phars.* ix. 763-82).

D. mentions S. in connexion with this incident, and refers to Lucan's account of it, Inf. xxv. 94-5.

Sabine, Sabine women; *il mal delle Sabine*, i.e. the rape of the Sabines, Par. vi. 40. [**Sabini**.]

Sabini, Sabines, ancient people of Central Italy. Romulus, the founder of Rome, being in want of women for his new city, proclaimed that games were to be celebrated, and invited his neighbours, the Sabines. While the festival was in progress the Roman youths suddenly rushed upon their guests and carried off the virgins. This act gave rise to a war between the two peoples; but in the midst of a long and desperate battle the ravished Sabine women placed themselves between the armies, and prayed their husbands and fathers to be reconciled, whereupon peace was made, and the two peoples agreed to form one nation.

The rape of the Sabines (Livy, i. 9; Orosius, ii. 4, §§ 2-5) is referred to by the Emperor Justinian (in the Heaven of Mercury), in his account of the Roman Eagle, as *il mal delle Sabine*, Par. vi. 40; the war of the Romans with the Sabines of the nature of a duel, Mon. ii. 11[39-42].

Sacchetti, ancient noble family of Florence, mentioned by Cacciaguida (in the Heaven of Mars) as having been of importance in his day, Par. xvi. 104. They were Guelfs (Vill. v. 39), and were among those who fled from Florence to Lucca after the great Ghibelline victory at Montaperti (vi. 79).

Geri del Bello, the first cousin of D.'s father, is said to have been killed by a member of this family [Bello, Geri del].

Sadducei], Sadducees; Christ's answer to their question 'touching the resurrection of the dead' (*Matt.* xxii. 23-30) alluded to by Pope Adrian V (in Circle V. of Purgatory), Purg. xix. 136-7.

Safira, Sapphira, wife of Ananias, a disciple at Jerusalem; having sold their goods for the benefit of the Church, they kept back part of the price, bringing the remainder to the Apostles, as if it had been the whole; being rebuked by St. Peter for their hypocrisy they both fell down dead at his feet (*Acts* v. 1-11).

Sapphira, with her husband, is included among the examples of lust of wealth proclaimed by the Avaricious in Circle V of Purgatory, Purg. xx. 112. [Anania ^{2}: Avari.]

Saguntum, ancient town of Spain, on the river Palancia, on the E. coast, about twenty miles N. of Valencia, on the site of the present Murviedro. Saguntum was on friendly terms with the Romans, and its siege by Hannibal (B.C. 219-18), which lasted nine months, was the immediate cause of the Second Punic War.

In D.'s letter to the Florentines he tells them that, unless they submit themselves to the Emperor, Florence, for the sake of slavery, will have to undergo all the horrors that Saguntum did, in her faithfulness to Rome, for the sake of liberty, Epist. vi. 4$^{122-6}$.

Saladino, Il, Saladin (Salah-ed-din Yusuf), the great Sultan, born c. 1137. He early distinguished himself as a soldier, and on the death of the last of the Fatimite Caliphs in Egypt (1171) established himself as his successor; two years later he took possession of Damascus and S. Syria. In 1177 he was defeated by the Crusaders and compelled to retire to Egypt, but in 1182 he resumed the offensive, and in 1187, after inflicting a crushing defeat upon the crusading army in the battle of Tiberias (July 4), he besieged and captured Jerusalem (Oct. 2). Subsequently he was several times defeated by Richard Cœur-de-Lion, with whom he concluded a truce in 1192; he died at Damascus the next year.

D. places Saladin in Limbo, with the great heroes of Troy and Rome (but standing apart from them, probably as being unconnected with the Empire), Inf. iv. 129 [Limbo]; he is mentioned as an example of munificence (of which he was commonly regarded as the type in the Middle Ages), Conv. iv. 11^{126}.

Salamone. [Salomone.]

Salimbeni, Niccolò de'. [Niccolò ^{1}.]

Salmi. [*Psalmorum, Liber.*]

Salmista. [David.]

Salome. [Maria Salome.]

Salomon. [Salomone.]

Salomone, Solomon, King of Israel, son of David and Bathsheba; mentioned as the author of the Proverbs, Conv. iii. 11^{128}, 14^{61}, 15$^{166, 189}$; iv. 5^{12}, 7$^{93, 129}$, 15^{136}, 24$^{140, 162}$, 25^{16}; Mon. iii. 1^{13} [*Proverbiorum, Liber*]; as author of Ecclesiastes, Conv. ii. 11⁸²; iv. 2⁷⁴, 15⁶⁵, 16⁴⁹ [*Ecclesiastes*]; as author of the Song of Solomon, Conv. ii. 6³⁴, 15¹⁷⁵ [*Canticum Canticorum*]; *Salomon*, Mon. iii. 1¹³; alluded to as *il Re, che chiese senno*, Par. xiii. 95.

D. places Solomon among those who loved wisdom (*Spiriti Sapienti*), in the Heaven of the Sun, where his spirit is pointed out by St. Thomas Aquinas, it being the fifth light, *la quinta luce*, Par. x. 109; xiii. 48; and the brightest, in the lesser of the two rings in which the spirits revolve, *la luce più dia del minor cerchio*, Par. xiv. 34–5 [Sole, Cielo del]; St. T. A. refers to Solomon's authorship of the Canticles (Par. x. 110); to the controversy as to his ultimate salvation (Par. x. 110–11); to his great wisdom, which was such that there was no equal to him in that respect (Par. x. 112–14; xi. 26; xiii. 47), a statement which he afterwards qualifies by explaining that he meant that S., as a king, was wiser than all other kings (Par. xiii. 37–111); in response to a request of Beatrice, S. then solves certain doubts of D. with respect to the glorified body (Par. xiv. 1–60).

Solomon, like his father David, inveighed against the vanity of riches, Conv. iv. 12⁸¹; he asked God for the gift of wisdom that he might be a capable king, as is recorded in the Book of Kings (1 *Kings* iii. 5–14), Par. xiii. 93–6; Conv. iv. 27⁶⁰⁻³; visit of the Queen of Sheba to Jerusalem that she might judge of his greatness (1 *Kings* x. 1–7), Epist. x. 1¹⁰.

In the *tenzone* of D. and Forese Donati, Solomon is mentioned in connexion with a kind of knot in which both ends are concealed, popularly called *il nodo di Salamone*, Son. lii.* 10; liii. 1.

Salse, name of a ravine near Bologna, where the bodies of criminals used to be thrown; applied by D. (in conversation with a native of Bologna) to Bolgia 1 of Circle VIII of Hell (Malebolge), evidently with a play on the word *salsa*, 'pickle', Inf. xviii. 51.

Salterello, Lapo. [Lapo².]

Salterio. [*Psalmorum, Liber.*]

Salvani, Provenzan. [Provenzan Salvani.]

[**Samius**], of Samos, island in the Aegean Sea, the birthplace of Pythagoras, who is hence referred to as *Samius vates*, Ecl. R. 34. [Pittagora.]

Sammaritano, Samaritan; D. speaks of his thirst for knowledge as 'the natural thirst' (cf. Conv. i. 1²⁻¹¹), which is never sated save with the water for which Christ was asked by the 'woman of Samaria', *la femminetta Sammaritana*, Purg. xxi. 1–3 (ref. to *John* iv. 13–5).

Samnis, Samnites. [Sanniti.]

Samuel, Prophet, and last of the Judges of Israel; coupled with Moses (cf. *Jerem.* xv. 1), St. John the Evangelist, St. John the Baptist, and the Virgin Mary, as among the holiest of the saints, Par. iv. 29; the judgement of God against Saul, as revealed to Samuel (1 *Sam.* xv. 10–11), an instance of direct revelation, Mon. ii. 8⁵⁵⁻⁷; his deposition of Saul by God's command (1 *Sam.* xv. 23–8), Mon. iii. 6³⁻⁶, wherein he acted not as God's vicar, but as

His messenger, Mon. iii. 6[18–20], [38–9]; his rebuke of Saul for sparing Agag, King of Amalek (1 *Sam.* xv. 17–18), Epist. vii. 5[101–7].

Samuelis, Libri], First and Second Books of Samuel in A. V., called in the Vulgate the First and Second of Kings [**Regum, Libri**]; quoted, Mon. ii. 8[55–7] (1 *Sam.* xv. 10–11); Mon. iii. 6[3–6] (1 *Sam.* xv. 23–8); Epist. vii. 5[101–7] (1 *Sam.* xv. 17–18). [**Bibbia.**]

San Benedetto. [Benedetto, San.]

San Gallo. [Gal, San.]
San Giovanni. [Giovanni[1].]
San Leo. [Sanleo.]
San Miniato. [Miniato, San.]
San Nazzaro. [Nazzaro, San.]
San Pietro. [Pietro[1]: Pietro, San.]
San Simone. [Simone, San.]
San Vittore, Riccardo da. [Riccardo.]
San Vittore, Ugo da. [Ugo[2].]
San Zeno. [Zeno, San.]
Sancto Victore, Ricardus de. [Riccardo.]

Sanese, Sienese; *la gente sanese*, the Sienese people, more foolish than even the French, Inf. xxix. 121–3 (cf. Purg. xiii. 151); native of Siena, of Sapia, Purg. xiii. 106 [Sapia]; *Senensis*, of Minus Mocatus, V. E. i. 13[10] [Minus Mocatus].

Sanesi, the Sienese; Capocchio's abuse of, to D. (in Bolgia 10 of Circle VIII of Hell), Inf. xxix. 136 [Capocchio]; the murder of Omberto Aldobrandesco by, Purg. xi. 65 [Omberto]; referred to by D., in connexion with their foolishness, as *la gente sanese*, Inf. xxix. 122 [Sanese]; by Sapia (in Circle

II of Purgatory), in connexion with their defeat at Colle, as *i cittadin miei*, Purg. xiii. 115 [Colle]; and, in connexion with their harbour of Talamone, as *la gente vana* (cf. Inf. xxix. 121–3), Purg. xiii. 151 [Sapia: Talamone]; *Senenses*, their dialect distinct from that of the Aretines, V. E. i. 10[75–6]; condemned with the rest of the Tuscan dialects, a specimen of it being given, V. E. i. 13[25–6] [Siena].

Sanleo, San Leo, chief town of the mountainous district of Montefeltro (a name once borne by the town itself), in the ancient Duchy of Urbino, not far from San Marino, in the N. corner of the modern province of the Marches; it is situated on a steep and rugged hill, and is difficult of access.

D. mentions it in connexion with the precipitousness of the approach to it, Purg. iv. 25. [Montefeltro.]

Sannella, Della, ancient noble family of Florence, mentioned by Cacciaguida (in the Heaven of Mars) as having been of importance in his day, Par. xvi. 92. They lived near the Mercato Nuovo (Vill. iv. 13).

Sanniti, Samnites, inhabitants of Samnium, mountainous district in the N. extremity of Campania. The Romans, who were applied to by the Capuans for assistance against the Samnites, found them the most warlike and formidable foes they had yet encountered in Italy; and the war which thus originated (B.C. 343) was continued off and on for more than fifty years. At the battle of the 'Caudine Forks' (B.C. 321) the Roman army surrendered to the

Samnites, and were passed under the yoke. The latter, however, were eventually crushed by the Romans in the third Samnite war (B.C. 298–290). During the civil war between Marius and Sulla, the Samnites favoured the cause of the former in the hopes of recovering their independence; but they were totally defeated by Sulla at the Colline gate of Rome (B.C. 82).

D. mentions the Samnites in connexion with their embassy to Marcus Curius Dentatus and his rejection of their bribes, Conv. iv. 5^{110-15} [Curio[1]]; the war of the Romans with them of the nature of a duel, *Samnites*, Mon. ii. 11^{39-42}; Lucan's reference (*Phars.* ii. 135–8) to their victory over the Romans at the 'Caudine Forks', and to the immense slaughter on the occasion of their defeat at the Colline gate, when the Empire in Italy narrowly escaped being transferred from the Romans to them, Mon. ii. 11^{43-51} [Caudinae Furcae: Collina Porta].

Sant' Andrea, Jacomo da. [Jacomo[3].]

Sant' Antonio. [Antonio, Sant'.]

Santa Zita. [Zita, Santa.]

Santafiora, county in the Sienese Maremma, which from Cent. ix down to 1300 belonged to the powerful Ghibelline family of the Aldobrandeschi, who thence took their title of Counts of Santafiora. It was formerly an imperial fief, but at the time D. wrote it was in the hands of the Guelfs of Siena.

D. mentions it in his appeal to the Emperor Albert to come and visit Italy, Purg. vi. 111; he names two

of the Counts, Purg. xi. 59, 67. [Aldobrandeschi.]

Santelena, name of coin current in the Middle Ages in Italy; applied by D. to the silver coins composing a treasure discovered in his time by a peasant while digging on the slopes of Falterona in Tuscany, Conv. iv. 11^{76-82}.

Santerno, small river of N. Italy in the Emilia, which rises in the Etruscan Apennines, and flows NE., past Imola, into the Po di Primaro.

D. refers to Imola, which is situated on its N. bank, as *la città di Santerno*, Inf. xxvii. 49. [Imola.]

Santo Pietro. [Pietro, San[2].]

Santo Spirito. [Spirito Santo.]

Santo Volto, 'Holy Face', name of ancient wooden crucifix at Lucca, Inf. xxi. 48. [Lucca.]

Sanzia], Sancha, third daughter of Raymond Berenger IV of Provence; married in 1244 to Richard, Earl of Cornwall, afterwards (in 1257) King of the Romans, brother of Henry III of England; she is referred to by the Emperor Justinian (in the Heaven of Mercury) as one of the four daughters of Raymond, each of whom became a Queen, Par. vi. 133–4. [Beringhieri, Ramondo.]

Sapia, noble lady of Siena, placed by D. among the Envious in Circle II of Purgatory, Purg. xiii. 109; *ombra, v.* 100; *spirto, v.* 103; *spirito eletto, v.* 143 [Invidiosi]; in conversation with D. she relates how, when her countrymen were defeated at Colle, she rejoiced and blasphemously defied God (*vv.* 112–

123) [Colle]; and how towards the end of her life she repented, and was helped by the prayers of the hermit Pier Pettinagno, to which she owed it that she was already admitted to Purgatory (*vv.* 124-9) [Pettinagno, Pier.]

It is uncertain to what family Sapia belonged; she is believed to have married a certain Ghinibaldo Saracini, lord of Castglioncello, near Montereggioni, who died about 1269; she herself must have died before 1289, the date of Pier Pettinagno's death, as appears from Purg. xiii. 127-8.

Sapienti, Sette. [Savi, Sette.]
Sapienti, Spiriti. [Spiriti Sapienti.]

Sapientiae, Liber, apocryphal Book of Wisdom; referred to as *il libro di Sapienza,* Conv. iii. 15[45, 53]; iv. 6[164], 16[8]; *Sapientia,* Epist. x. 2[39], 22[420]; quoted, Par. xviii. 91, 93 (*Wisd.* i. 1); Conv. iii. 15[45-6] (*Wisd.* iii. 11); Conv. iii. 15[54-5] (*Wisd.* vii. 26); Conv. iii. 15[161-4] (*Wisd.* ix. 9); Conv. iv. 6[164-6], 16[8-10] (*Wisd.* vi. 23 in *Vulg.* ' Diligite lumen sapientiae omnes qui praeestis populis', a verse which is omitted from the Eng. version); Epist. x. 2[39-42] (*Wisd.* vii. 14); Epist. x. 22[420-1] (*Wisd.* i. 7).

Sapienza, Libro di. [*Sapientiae, Liber.*]

Sara, Sarah, wife of Abraham, and mother of Isaac; she is referred to in the New Testament as a type of conjugal obedience (1 *Pet.* iii. 6), and as one of the types of faith (*Heb.* xi. 11). St. Bernard points out to D. her place in the Celestial Rose, Par. xxxii. 10. [Rosa.]

Saraceni. [Saracini.]
Saracine, Saracen women; the Florentine women compared unfavourably with, Purg. xxiii. 103. [Barbare: Saracini.]

Saracini, Saracens, term used in the Middle Ages to designate the Arab and Mahometan races in Spain and N. Africa, Syria, and Palestine.

Guido da Montefeltro (in Bolgia 8 of Circle VIII of Hell) refers to the fact that Boniface VIII, instead of making war upon the infidels, was occupied in his quarrel with the house of Colonna, Inf. xxvii. 85-7; the Saracens, like the Jews and Tartars, believed in the immortality of the soul, Conv. ii. 9[70]; the condition of Italy such as to deserve even their compassion, *Saraceni,* Epist. v. 2[23-5]; their mockery of her in her misfortunes, Epist. viii. 3[33-6]; coupled with the Jews as unbelievers, Inf. xxvii. 87; Conv. ii. 9[70]; Epist. viii. 3[33]; their women more modest than the women of Florence, Purg. xxiii. 103 [Fiorentine]; their capture (in 1291) of Acre, Inf. xxvii. 89 [Acri]; their possession of the Holy Land, Par. xv. 142-5 [Maomettani.]

Sardanapalo, Sardanapalus, last King of the Assyrian empire of Ninus, noted for his luxury, licentiousness, and effeminacy. He spent his days in his palace, unseen by any of his subjects, dressed in female apparel, and surrounded by concubines. Being besieged in Nineveh by the satrap of Media, and unable to hold out, he burned himself and his concubines and treasures on a vast funeral pile.

Cacciaguida (in the Heaven of

Mars), in contrasting the simplicity
and innocence of Florence, as he
knew it, with the effeminacy and luxury
of the Florence of D.'s day, says,
'Non v'era giunto ancor Sardanapalo
A mostrar ciò che in camera si puote'
(a phrase apparently suggested by
a passage in the *De Regimine Principum* of Egidio Romano, 'omnes
collocutiones ejus erant in cameris ad
mulieres'), Par. xv. 107–8.

Sardi, inhabitants of Sardinia;
l'isola dei Sardi, i.e. Sardinia, mentioned (as an alternative to Spain)
to indicate the W. limit of the
habitable globe, Inf. xxvi. 104 [Ge-
rusalemme]; the island itself is
indicated by the mention of the
Sardinians, D. describing the period
when the Sun sets W. by S. (i.e.
about the end of November) as the
time when to the inhabitants of Rome
it appears to set between Corsica and
Sardinia, Purg. xviii. 79–81; their
dialect distinct from that of the
Genoese, V. E. i. 10⁶⁵; the Sardinians, who are not to be reckoned
as Italians, but are to be associated
with them (cf. Inf. xxii. 67), alone
among the Italian peoples have no
special dialect of their own, their
language being little more than an
imitation of Latin, V. E. i. 11⁴²⁻⁷;
Ciampolo (in Bolgia 5 of Circle VIII
of Hell), being asked if there are
any Italians among his fellow-sinners,
says there is one 'who was a neighbour to them', meaning a native of Sardinia, Inf. xxii. 64–7 [Sardigna].

Sardigna, island of Sardinia,
which in D.'s day belonged to the
Pisans; Ciampolo (in Bolgia 5 of Circle
VIII of Hell) says that friar Gomita
of Gallura, and Michael Zanche of

Logodoro, are never weary of talking
about Sardinia, Inf. xxii. 89 [Go-
mita, Frate: Michel Zanche];
mentioned, together with the Tuscan
Maremma, as being notoriously unhealthy, Inf. xxix. 48; the women
of Florence compared unfavourably
with those of Barbagia, a wild district in the S. of the island, Purg.
xxiii. 94–5 [Barbagia]; to be
reckoned, with Sicily, as being on
the right side of Italy, if the Apennines be taken as the dividing line
(from N. to S.), V. E. i. 10⁵⁶⁻⁹;
alluded to as *l'isola de' Sardi*, Inf.
xxvi. 104 [Sardi].

D. mentions two of the four
Giudicati, or Judicial Districts, into
which Sardinia was divided by the
Pisans, viz. Gallura, Inf. xxii. 82;
Purg. viii. 81; and Logodoro, Inf.
xxii. 89 [Gallura: Logodoro];
the other two were Cagliari and
Alborea.

Sardinia. [Sardigna.]

Sarnus, name by which D. speaks
of the Arno in his Latin works,
V. E. i. 6¹⁹; Epist. iii. 2¹³; vi.
6¹⁹⁸; vii. 8¹⁹¹; Ecl. i. 44; and so
G. del Virgilio, Ecl. R. 37. [Arno.]

Sarpina. [Savena.]

Sarra. [Sara.]

Sassol Mascheroni. [Mas-
cheroni, Sassol.]

Satan. [Lucifero.]

Saturnius, belonging to Saturn;
Saturnia regna, 'the reign of Saturn'
(i.e. the Golden Age), Virgil's mention of (*Ecl.* iv. 6), quoted, Mon. i.
11⁶, ⁸. [Saturno¹.]

Saturno¹, Saturn, mythical
King of Crete and afterwards of Italy,
regarded by the Romans as the father
(by Rhea) of Jupiter, Neptune, Pluto,

Juno, &c. [**Rea**]. Having been dethroned by his son Jupiter, he retired to Italy, where he became king, and introduced agriculture and civilization; hence his reign is looked upon as the Golden Age of Italy (*Aen.* viii. 319–25).

D. alludes to Saturn and the Golden Age in connexion with Crete, *Creta, Sotto il cui rege fu già il mondo casto*, Inf. xiv. 95–6 [**Creta**]; and speaks of him as *il chiaro duce, Sotto cui giacque ogni malizia morta*, Par. xxi. 26–7; the father of Jupiter and grandfather of Mars, Par. xxii. 145–6; his reign the Golden Age, *Saturnia regna*, Mon. i. 11⁶, ⁸.

Saturno ², planet Saturn, Purg. xix. 3; Conv. ii. 4⁸, 14¹⁹⁸, ²⁰¹, ²²⁴, 15¹⁴²; Son. xxviii. 3; *il settimo splendore*, Par. xxi. 13; *specchio*, Par. xxi. 18; *il cristallo che il vocabol porta, Cerchiando il mondo, del suo chiaro duce, Sotto cui giacque ogni malizia morta*, Par. xxi. 25–7; *il padre di Giove*, Par. xxii. 145–6; *quel pianeta, che conforta il gelo*, Canz. xv. 7; Saturn the seventh in order of the planets, its position being between Jupiter and the Fixed Stars, Par. xxi. 13; xxii. 145–6; Son. xxviii. 3; Conv. ii. 4⁷⁻⁸, 14¹⁹⁶⁻²⁰²; a star of cold nature (cf. *Georg.* i. 336), Purg. xix. 3; Canz. xv. 7; Conv. ii. 14²⁰¹; as opposed to the temperateness of Jupiter and the fieriness of Mars, Conv. ii. 14¹⁹⁴⁻²⁰²; in the spring of 1300 was in the constellation Leo, Par. xxi. 13–15; the highest in the Heavens of all the planets, Conv. ii. 14²³⁰⁻¹; and the slowest in its movement through the twelve signs of the Zodiac, Conv.

ii. 14²²⁶⁻⁷; the period of its revolution twenty-nine years and more, Conv. ii. 14²²⁷⁻³⁰, for half of which it would be concealed from the Earth, if the motion of the *Primum Mobile* were suspended, Conv. ii. 15¹⁴²⁻⁴.

Saturno, Cielo di, Heaven of Saturn, the seventh in D.'s conception of Paradise, Par. xxi. 13; Conv. ii. 4⁷⁻⁸, 14²³⁰⁻¹ [**Paradiso**]; resembles Astrology in two respects, Conv. ii. 14²²⁴⁻⁵³; it is presided over by the Thrones [**Troni**].

In the Heaven of Saturn D. places the spirits of those who led a contemplative life (*Spiriti Contemplanti*), Par. xxii. 46–8; among these he names St. Peter Damian [**Damiano, Pier**]; St. Benedict [**Benedetto**¹]; St. Macarius [**Maccario**]; and St. Romualdus [**Romoaldo**].

Saul, son of Kish of the tribe of Benjamin, first King of Israel; included among the examples of defeated pride represented in Circle I of Purgatory, where he is portrayed fallen upon his own sword on Mt. Gilboa (1 *Sam.* xxxi. 4; 2 *Sam.* i. 21), Purg. xii. 40–2 [**Superbi**]; the judgement of God against him, as revealed to Samuel (1 *Sam.* xv. 10–11), an instance of direct revelation, Mon. ii. 8⁵⁵⁻⁷; anointed king by Samuel (1 *Sam.* x. 1) and deposed by him (1 *Sam.* xv. 23–8), in obedience to the command of God, Mon. iii. 6¹⁻⁶; Samuel's rebuke of him for sparing Agag, King of Amalek (1 *Sam.* xv. 17–8), quoted, Epist. vii. 5¹⁰¹⁻⁷.

Savena, small river of N. Italy, which rises in the Etruscan Apennines near Pietramala, and flows N. through the Emilia, leaving Bologna about two miles to the W., soon after which it enters the Reno.

Caccianimico (in Bolgia 1 of Circle VIII of Hell), a native of Bologna, refers to the situation of that city between the Savena and the Reno, Inf. xviii. 61 [Bologna]; it is referred to by its Latin name, *Sarpina*, Ecl. ii. 41 ; Ecl. R. 1.

Savi d'Egitto, Wise Men of Egypt, i.e. Egyptian astronomers, with especial reference to the astronomer Ptolemy, who was a native of Egypt; their computation of the number of the Fixed Stars at 1022, Conv. ii. 15$^{18-22}$. [Stelle Fisse.]

Savi, Sette, Seven Sages of Greece, viz. Solon of Athens, Chilon of Lacedaemon, Periander of Corinth, Thales of Miletus, Cleobulus of Lindus, Bias of Priene, and Pittacus of Mitylene, Conv. iii. 11$^{35-41}$. [Biante.]

Savio, small river of N. Italy, which rises in the Etruscan Apennines, and flows N. past Cesena, falling into the Adriatic about eight miles S. of Ravenna ; Cesena is referred to as *quella (città) cui il Savio bagna il fianco*, Inf. xxvii. 52. [Cesena.]

Saxones, inhabitants of Saxony; their tongue one of several into which the original language of Europe was split up, V. E. i. 8$^{29-32}$.

Saxonia, Saxony, mediaeval duchy in N. Germany; Pope Benedict V carried into exile there by the Emperor Otto I (who was hereditary Duke of Saxony), Mon. iii. 11$^{18-21}$. [Benedetto [3].]

Scala, Della], the Della Scala (or Scaliger) family of Verona ; alluded to by their arms, a ladder surmounted by the imperial eagle, Par. xvii. 72 [Lombardo, Gran] ; the following members of the family are mentioned or referred to by D. :—Alberto, Purg. xviii. 121 [Alberto della Scala]; Alboino, Conv. iv. 16$^{71-2}$ [Albuino della Scala]; Bartolommeo, Par. xvii. 71 [Bartolommeo della Scala]; Can Grande, Epist. x. *tit.* ; A. T. § 24^3 [Can Grande della Scala]; Giuseppe, Purg. xviii. 124 [Giuseppo della Scala].

Scala, Alberto della. [Alberto della Scala.]

Scala, Albuino della. [Albuino della Scala.]

Scala, Bartolommeo della. [Bartolommeo della Scala.]

Scala, Can Grande della. [Can Grande della Scala.]

Scala, Giuseppo della. [Giuseppo della Scala.]

Scandalosi], Sowers of Scandal, placed with Schismatics in Bolgia 9 of Circle VIII of Hell (Malebolge), Inf. xxviii. 1-xxix. 36. [Scismatici.]

Scandinavia, ancient name for Norway, Sweden, and the adjacent islands ; *Scandinaviae soboles*, ' race of Scandinavia', i.e. the Lombards, who believed themselves to be of Scandinavian origin, Epist. v. 4$^{56-7}$. [Lombardi.]

Scariotto, Giuda. [Giuda [1].]

Scarmiglione, one of the demons in charge of the Barrators in Bolgia 5 of Circle VIII of Hell (Malebolge) ; he threatens D. with his prong, but is checked by Malacoda, who addresses him by name, Inf. xxi. 100-5. [Alichino : Malebranche.]

Schiavo, Slavonian, belonging to Slavonia, country (forming, with Croatia, a province of the present Empire of Austria-Hungary) lying to the SW. of Hungary, between the rivers Drave and Save ; *venti schiavi*, i. e. the cold NE. winds which reach Italy from Slavonia across the mountains of Dalmatia and the Adriatic, Purg. xxx. 87 ; *Sclavones*, Slavonians, their tongue one of several into which the original language of Europe was split up, V. E. i. 8²⁹⁻³².

Schicchi, Gianni. [Gianni Schicchi.]

Schiro, Scyros, island (one of the Sporades) E. of Euboea in the Aegaean Sea, whither Thetis conveyed her son Achilles in his sleep after she had withdrawn him from the custody of Chiron. Achilles remained hidden in Scyros, dressed like a woman, under the name of Pyrrha, among the daughters of Lycomedes, until Ulysses visited the island, disguised as a merchant, and offered women's dresses for sale, amongst which he had concealed some arms ; these were eagerly seized by Achilles, who, having thus disclosed his sex, was persuaded by Ulysses to accompany him to the Greek army, which was on its way to Troy.

D. compares his own surprise, on awaking from his vision and finding himself transported to the Gate of Purgatory, with that of Achilles on awaking and finding himself in Scyros (the incident being borrowed from Statius, *Achill.* i. 198 ff.), Purg. ix. 34–9 [Achille : Chirone.]

Scialacquatori], Spendthrifts ;

placed, together with Suicides, among the Violent, in Round 2 of Circle VII of Hell, Inf. xi. 40–1 ; xiii. 115–29; their punishment is to be torn limb from limb by fierce black hounds, Inf. xiii. 124–9 [Violenti]. *Examples* : Giacomo da Sant' Andrea [Jacomo ³] ; and Lano [Lano].

Sciancato, Puccio. [Puccio Sciancato.]

Scipio. [Scipione.]

Scipione ¹, Publius Cornelius Scipio Africanus Major, one of the greatest of the Romans, B. C. 234– c. 183; while quite a youth he fought against Hannibal at the battle of the Ticinus (218), where he saved his father's life by his valour, and at the battle of Cannae (216); it was by his courage and presence of mind after this latter disaster that the conspiracy of the Roman nobles to abandon Italy in despair was frustrated ; he was elected aedile in 212, and two years afterwards was appointed, at the age of 24, to the command of the army in Spain ; in 210 he captured Carthago Nova (Carthagena) and in the course of the next three years drove the Carthaginians altogether out of Spain ; he was elected consul in 205, and in the next year crossed over into Africa and at last brought to an end the long struggle between Rome and Hannibal by his decisive victory over the latter at the battle of Zama, Oct. 19, 202 ; he returned to Italy in 201, and entered Rome in triumph, receiving the surname of Africanus in commemoration of his brilliant services; he was elected censor in 199, and

consul, for the second time, in
194; he served under his brother
Lucius in the war against Antiochus
the Great in 190, and, being afterwards accused, with his brother, of
taking bribes from Antiochus, was
tried in Rome, on the anniversary
of the battle of Zama, in 185; the
prosecution was, however, dropped,
and Scipio left Rome, to which he
never returned; he died not long
after, probably in 183.

D. makes frequent mention of
Scipio, *Scipione*, Inf. xxxi. 116;
Par. vi. 53; *quello benedetto Scipione
giovane*, Conv. iv. 5$^{169-70}$; *Scipio*,
Par. xxvii. 61; Mon. ii. 11^{59};
Epist. viii. 10^{170}; *Affricano*, Purg.
xxix. 116; his defeat of Hannibal
at Zama, Inf. xxxi. 115-17; Conv.
iv. 5$^{170-1}$; Mon. ii. 11$^{59-61}$; his
heroic exploits under the Roman
Eagle as a young man, *giovinetto*,
Par. vi. 52-3; his frustration of
the design of the Roman nobles to
abandon Italy after the defeat at
Cannae, Conv. iv. 5$^{164-71}$; his
defeat of Hannibal at Zama, and
salvation, under Providence, of the
Roman Empire, Inf. xxxi. 115-17;
Par. xxvii. 61-2; Conv. iv.
15$^{170-1}$; Mon. ii. 11$^{59-61}$; his
triumphal entry into Rome, Purg.
xxix. 115-16; his great services
to Italy, Epist. viii. 10^{170}. [Sci-
piones.]

Scipione[2], Publius Cornelius
Scipio Aemilianus Africanus Minor,
c. B.C. 185-129; he was the son
of Lucius Aemilius Paulus, the
conqueror of Macedonia, and adopted
son of P. Cornelius Scipio, the son
of Scipio Africanus Major; on the
outbreak of the Third Punic War

(B.C. 149) he accompanied the
Roman army to Africa as tribune,
and three years later he took and
burned Carthage, for which he was
honoured with a triumph at Rome,
and the surname Africanus, which
he had already inherited by adoption
from the conqueror of Hannibal.
He was ardently devoted to literature, and was a friend of the poets
Lucilius and Terence; his intimate
friendship with Caius Laelius, whose
tastes and pursuits were similar to
his own, has been celebrated by
Cicero in his treatise *Laelius, sive de
Amicitia*.

D. mentions Scipio as the friend
of Laelius in connexion with the
De Amicitia, Conv. ii. 13$^{17-21}$
[**Amicitia, De** : **Lelio**]; his great
services to Italy, Epist. viii. 10^{170}
[Scipiones].

Scipiones, the Scipios, i.e.
Scipio Africanus Major, and his
grandson by adoption, Scipio Africanus Minor; Italy the land of the
illustrious Scipios, Epist. viii. 10^{170}.
[Scipione[1] : Scipione[2].]

Scirocco, Scirocco, oppressive
and relaxing SE. wind, which blows
across to Italy from the African
coast; mentioned in connexion with
the pine-forest of Ravenna, Purg.
xxviii. 21. [Pineta.]

Scismatici], Schismatics and
Scandalmongers (Inf. xxviii. 35),
placed among the Fraudulent in
Bolgia 9 of Circle VIII of Hell
(Malebolge), Inf. xxviii. 1-xxix.
36; *la molta gente*, Inf. xxix. 1
(cf. xxviii. 7-21) [**Frodolenti**];
their punishment is, to be continually
slashed and mutilated by the sword
of a demon (to remind them that in

their lifetime they caused dissensions and divisions), who, when they have completed the round of the Circle, reopens the wounds, which have healed up meanwhile, so that the torture is never-ending, Inf. xxviii. 19–21, 37–42. *Examples*: Mahomet and Ali [Alì : Maometto]; Fra Dolcino [Dolcino, Fra]; Pier da Medicina [Medicina, Pier da]; Mosca de' Lamberti [Mosca]; Bertran de Born [Bertram dal Bornio]; Gera del Bello [Bello, Geri del].

Sclavones. [Schiavo.]

Scornigiani, Gano degli. [Gano.]

Scornigiani, Marzucco degli. [Marzucco.]

Scorpio, 'the Scorpion,' constellation and eighth sign of the Zodiac, which the Sun enters about Oct. 22, after the autumnal equinox, Purg. xxv. 3 (where the time indicated is about 2 p.m.); Scorpio is alluded to as *il freddo animale, Che con la coda percuote la gente* (cf. Ovid, *Metam.* xv. 371), Purg. ix. 5–6 [Zodiaco].

Scotto, inhabitant of Scotland; mentioned by the Eagle in the Heaven of Jupiter, in connexion with the warfare between the English and Scotch in the reign of Edward I, Par. xix. 122. [Inghilese.]

Scotto, Michele. [Michele Scotto.]

Scriptura, Scrittura. [*Bibbia.*]

Scrovigni, Pietra degli. [Pietra.]

Scrovigni, Rinaldo degli. [Rinaldo degli Scrovigni:]

Scythae, Scythians, name applied to the nomad tribes who inhabited the regions to the N. of the Black Sea, and to the N. and E. of the Caspian ; the Romans under the Empire extended the use of the term so as to include the inhabitants of the whole region between the Volga and the frontiers of India.

The Scythians dwell beyond the seventh climate, where the inequality of the days and nights is very great, and the cold extreme, Mon. i. 14$^{43-6}$ [Garamanti]; Vesoges, King of Egypt, foiled by them in his attempt to attain universal empire, as is related by Orosius (i. 14), Mon. ii. 9$^{35-42}$ [Vesoges]; Cyrus, King of Persia, defeated and slain by the Scythian Queen, Tomyris, Mon. ii. 9$^{42-8}$ [Ciro : Tamiri]; their political system unknown to the Egyptians, who do not concern themselves with it, Mon. iii. 3$^{12-15}$ [Aegyptii.]

Secondo Cielo. [Mercurio, Cielo di.]

Seduttori], Seducers, placed with Pandars among the Fraudulent in Bolgia 1 of Circle VIII of Hell (Malebolge), Inf. xviii. 22–99 [Frodolenti]; their punishment is to be scourged on their naked bodies with great whips by horned demons, as they go round and round in two divisions, which pass and repass each other in opposite directions. *Examples*: Venedico Caccianimico [Caccianimico]; Jason the Argonaut [Jasone ^{1}].

Sem, Shem, eldest son of Noah, and 'father of all the children of Eber' (*Gen.* v. 32; x. 21); from his seed, who refrained from taking any part in the building of the Tower of Babel, was descended the people of Israel, who, of all the descendants of Noah, alone retained the use of the Hebrew tongue, V. E. i. 7^{61-70} (where D., by a slip, or perhaps misled by *Gen.* x. 2–22, speaks of Shem as the *third* son of Noah).

Semelè, Semele, daughter of Cadmus, King of Thebes, and Harmonia, and sister of Ino, Agave, and Autonoë; she was beloved by Jupiter, by whom she became the mother of Bacchus. Juno, in order to avenge herself upon Jupiter for his unfaithfulness to her, appeared to Semele in the disguise of her aged nurse Beroë, and induced her to ask Jupiter to show himself to her in the same splendour and majesty in which he appeared to Juno. Jupiter, after warning Semele of the danger, complied with her request, and appeared before her as the god of thunder, whereupon she was struck by lightning and consumed to ashes (Ovid, *Metam.* iii. 260–309). Juno, further, indulged her wrath against the Thebans on Semele's account, by driving mad her sister Ino's husband Athamas, who in his frenzy caused the deaths of his wife and two sons (*Metam.* iv. 512–30); and by causing her two other sisters, Agave and Autonoë, to tear in pieces Pentheus, the son of the former (*Metam.* iii. 511 ff.).

D. mentions Semele in connexion with Juno's wrath against Thebes on her account, Inf. xxx. 1–3 [**Ino**]; on arriving in the Heaven of Saturn Beatrice refrains from smiling upon D. lest he should be overcome by her beauty, as Semele was by the godhead of Jupiter, Par.

xxi. 4–6; Bacchus referred to as *semen Semeles*, in connexion with Alcithoë and her two sisters, Epist. iv. 4^{45} [**Alcithoë : Bacco**].

Semilatius, semi-Italian; *vulgare Semilatium*, name by which D. would distinguish the vernacular tongue of the left side of Italy, just as he speaks of that of the whole of Italy as *Latinum vulgare*, V. E. i. 19^{9-15}. [**Latius.**]

Semiramis, Semiramis, Queen of Assyria, wife of Ninus, mythical founder of the empire of Nineveh, whom she succeeded; she was slain by her son Ninus, 'quum concubitum eius petiisset' (Justin. *Hist.* i. 2).

S. is placed among the Lustful in Circle II of Hell, Inf. v. 58 [**Lussuriosi**]; D. (whose description of her is taken from Orosius, *Hist.* i. 4, §§ 4, 7, 8) speaks of her as having been *imperatrice di molte favelle*, 'empress of many tongues' (*v.* 54), perhaps with an allusion to the 'confusion of tongues', Babylon being included in the Assyrian empire; he goes on to refer to her licentiousness (*vv.* 55–7), and, after naming her as the spouse and successor of Ninus (*vv.* 58–9), states (by a confusion apparently between the ancient Kingdom of Babylonia or Assyria with Babylonia or Babylon in Egypt) that 'she held the land ruled by the Sultan', i. e. Egypt (*v.* 60) [**Babilon**].

D. mentions S. again together with Ninus, in connexion with their attempt to attain universal empire, an object for which they waged war for more than ninety years, as is recorded by Orosius (who puts the united reigns of the two at ninety-

four years, *Hist.* ii. 3, § 1), Mon. ii.
9^{22-9} [**Nino** [1]]; Ovid's mention of
them both (*Metam.* iv. 58, 88) in
the story of Pyramus and Thisbe,
Mon. ii. 9^{30-4}. [**Piramo.**]

Seneca, Lucius Annaeus Seneca,
Roman philosopher and tragedian,
born at Cordova, B.C. 4. He was
appointed tutor to the youthful
Domitius Nero, afterwards Emperor, under whom he amassed an enormous fortune, and was for a time
practically the administrator of the
Empire. He committed suicide by
command of Nero, who accused him
of complicity in the conspiracy of
Piso, A.D. 65. Seneca was a voluminous writer; his philosophical
works consist of formal treatises on
ethics, moral letters, and discussions
of natural philosophy from the point
of view of the Stoical system; his
Naturales Quaestiones was used as a
text-book of natural science in the
Middle Ages; his most important
philosophical work is the *De Bene-
ficiis*; he was also the author of
tragedies, written in imitation of the
Greek, nine of which are extant.
In the Middle Ages Seneca was
regarded as the author of two works
written (in Cent. vi) by Martin of
Braga, viz. the *De Quatuor Virtutibus Cardinalibus* (otherwise known
as *Formula Honestae Vitae*) and the
*Liber ad Galionem de Remediis For-
tuitorum*, both of which are quoted
by D. as Seneca's. [**Martinus
Dumiensis.**]

D. places Seneca, whom he qualifies as 'the moralist' (no doubt to
distinguish him from the author of
the tragedies, who in the Middle
Ages was held to be a different

person) among the great philosophers
of antiquity in Limbo, Inf. iv. 141
[**Limbo**]; his saying that nothing
costs so dear as that which is purchased with prayers, Conv. i. 8^{121-3}
(*De Ben.* ii. 1); his account of the
ball of fire which he saw in the sky
at the time of the death of the
Emperor Augustus, Conv.ii. 14^{174-6}
(*Nat. Quaest.* i. 1; quoted, not
from Seneca direct, but from Albertus Magnus (*Meteor.* i. 4), whence
the quotation from Albumazar in
the previous paragraph is also taken);
his contempt for life in comparison
with wisdom, Conv. iii. 14^{84-6};
his invective against riches, 'massimamente a Lucillo scrivendo', Conv.
iv. 12^{82-3} [**Lucillo**]; his saying
that even with one foot in the grave
he would still be desirous of learning,
Conv. iv. 12^{120-1} (apparently a mistaken attribution); Seneca coupled
with Numa Pompilius as having
been well trained, and in consequence a good guide to others, V. E.
i. 17^{14-15}; quoted as the author of
the *De Quatuor Virtutibus Cardinalibus*, Mon. ii. 5^{24-6} [*Quatuor
Virtutibus Cardinalibus, De*];
and of the *De Remediis Fortuitorum*,
Epist. iv. 5^{53-4} [*Fortuitorum
Remedia*]; Seneca the tragic poet,
Epist. x. 10^{202}.

Senectute, De, Cicero's treatise
On Old Age (in the form of a dialogue, the chief speaker being Cato
the Censor, otherwise known as
Cato Major); quoted as *Della Vecchiezza*, Conv. ii. 9^{67}; *Di Senettute*,
Conv. iv. 21^{81}, $24^{63, 93}$, $27^{18, 151}$,
28^{14}; Cicero agrees with other philosophers in believing the soul to be
immortal, Conv. ii. 9^{66-7} (*Senect.*

§ 21); Curius Dentatus, when the Samnites attempted to bribe him, declared that he did not care to possess gold, but to command those who possessed it, Conv. iv. 5$^{110-15}$ (*Senect.* § 16); the soul of celestial origin, its abiding place on earth opposed to its divine nature and to eternity, Conv. iv. 21$^{80-6}$ (*Senect.* § 21); Plato lived to be eighty-one, Conv. iv. 24$^{57-63}$ (*Senect.* § 5); the noble soul fits its actions to due times and seasons, which bring forth the fruit to which they were ordained, Conv. iv. 24$^{93-4}$ (*Senect.* § 2); the vine provided by nature with tendrils with which to support itself, Conv. iv. 24$^{108-12}$ (*Senect.* § 15); our life has a fixed course, and allotted seasons for certain things, Conv. iv. 27$^{17-22}$ (*Senect.* § 10); the *Senate* so called as being an assembly of elders, Conv. iv. 27$^{91-6}$ (*Senect.* § 6); Cato found his delight in conversation increase as he grew older, Conv. iv. 27$^{151-4}$ (*Senect.* § 14); natural death is as it were a haven of repose after a long voyage, Conv. iv. 28$^{13-16}$ (*Senect.* § 19); the soul quits the body in old age with as little violence as the ripe fruit falls from the tree, Conv. iv. 28$^{27-31}$ (*Senect.* § 19); Cato's eagerness to see (after death) the great Romans who had gone before him, Conv. iv. 28$^{44-8}$ (*Senect.* § 23); life on earth as it were a sojourn in a tavern, hence the soul returns to God as to its home, Conv. iv. 28$^{48-52}$ (*Senect.* § 23).

Senectute, De Juventute et. [*Juventute et Senectute, De.*]

Senensis. [Sanese.]

Senettute, Di. [*Senectute, De.*]

Senna, Seine, river of France, which rises about eighteen miles NW. of Dijon, and flows NW. through France, past Paris and Rouen, into the English Channel.

The Seine is mentioned by the Emperor Justinian (in the Heaven of Mercury), together with the Var, Rhine, Isère, Saône, and Rhone, in connexion with Caesar's victories in Gaul, Par. vi. 59 [Era]; and by the Eagle in the Heaven of Jupiter, to indicate Paris, in connexion with Philip IV's debasement of the coinage, Par. xix. 118 [Filippo ^{2}: Parigi].

Sennaar, Vulgate rendering of the name represented by Shinar in A. V., ancient name of the country known in later times as Chaldaea or Babylonia. It was upon 'a plain in the land of Shinar' that the Tower of Babel was built (*Gen.* xi. 2), and 'in the land of Shinar' was situated the kingdom of Nimrod (*Gen.* x. 10), who is commonly regarded as the builder of Babel.

D. mentions Shinar in connexion with Nimrod and the Tower of Babel, Purg. xii. 36; V. E. i. 7^{29}. [Babel: Nembrotto.]

Sennacherib, King of Assyria, B. C. 705–681; after a reign of twenty-four years, in the course of which he twice 'went up against' Hezekiah, King of Judah, and besieged Jerusalem (2 *Kings* xviii, xix), he was assassinated, while at worship, by his two sons (2 *Kings* xix. 37).

S. figures among the examples of defeated pride (cf. 2 *Kings* xix. 28, where the word translated by 'tumult' in A. V. is rendered in

Vulg. by *superbia*) portrayed in Circle I of Purgatory, where D. sees graven on the ground a representation of the scene of his murder by his two sons, Purg. xii. 52–4 [**Superbi**].

Senocrate, Xenocrates, the philosopher, native of Chalcedon, B.C. 396–314; he succeeded Plato's nephew Speusippus as president of the Academy, a post which he occupied for twenty-five years. Of his writings, which were chiefly metaphysical and ethical, nothing has been preserved but the titles.

D., in his account of the Academic and Peripatetic schools of philosophy (taken from Cicero, *Acad.* i. 4), couples Xenocrates with Aristotle as having brought moral philosophy to perfection, Conv. iv. 6¹³¹⁻⁸.

Senso e Sensato, Di. [**Sensu et Sensibili, De.**]

Sensu et Sensibili, De, Aristotle's treatise *On Sense and Sensible Things*; quoted as *Di Senso e Sensato*, Conv. iii. 9⁵⁴, ¹⁰⁵; A.'s opinion that, strictly speaking, light and colour alone are visible, Conv. iii. 9⁵¹⁻⁵ (*De Sens.*, Cap. 3); his refutation of the Platonic theory that sight consists, not in the entering of the visible into the eye, but in the going forth of the visual power towards the visible object, Conv. iii. 9⁹⁹⁻¹⁰⁵ (*De Sens.*, Cap. 2). [**Aristotile : Platone.**]

Sententiarum, Magister. [**Pietro²**.]

Septemtrio. [**Settentrione.**]
Serafi. [**Serafini.**]
Serafini, Seraphim, highest Order of Angels, they ranking before all others in the Celestial Hierarchy,

Par. iv. 28; viii. 27; xxi. 92; xxviii. 98–9; Conv. ii. 6⁵⁴; alluded to as *quei fuochi pii, Che di sei ale facean la cuculla,* 'the kindly fires which of six wings made their cowl', Par. ix. 77–8 (ref. to *Isaiah* vi. 2).

Beatrice (in the Crystalline Heaven) in her exposition of the arrangement of the Angelic Hierarchies states that the Seraphim rank first in the first Hierarchy, next below them being the Cherubim, *Serafi*, Par. xxviii. 98–9 (cf. Par. iv. 28; viii. 27; xxi. 92; Conv. ii. 6⁵⁴) [**Gerarchia**]; they contemplate the first Person of the Trinity, Conv. ii. 6⁷⁶⁻⁸¹, they preside over the Heaven of the *Primum Mobile* or Crystalline Heaven, Par. viii. 26–7; xxviii. 70–2 [**Paradiso¹**].

St. Thomas Aquinas (in the Heaven of the Sun) alludes to the 'seraphic ardour' of the Franciscan Order as distinguished from the 'cherubic light' of the Dominicans, Par. xi. 37–9. [**Cherubini.**]

Serchio, river of Tuscany, which rises in the Apennines of Lunigiana, flows S. towards Lucca, a few miles to the N. of which it turns SW., and runs into the Ligurian Sea between Viareggio and Pisa; it formerly joined the Arno a short distance from its mouth, but it now enters the sea by a separate channel.

The demons in Bolgia 5 of Circle VIII of Hell (Malebolge), where the Barrators are punished in a morass of boiling pitch, tauntingly observe to one of the latter, who is a native of Lucca, that the swimming there is not like that in the Serchio (doubtless in allusion to the fact, noted by the old commentators, that the river was a favourite bath-ing-resort of the Lucchese), Inf. xxi. 49.

Sergestus, one of the four Tro-jan captains who took part in the ship-race during the games in Sicily instituted by Aeneas in honour of his father's memory. Virgil de-scribes (*Aen.* v. 201–72) how Ser-gestus, who was in the rear at the start, in making a great effort to draw to the front, fouled the rock which they had to round, and came to grief, and how, after the race was over and the victors had received their prizes, Sergestus, having with difficulty got his ship off the rock, came in, rowing helplessly, amid the jeers of the spectators.

The jeering of Sergestus by the Sicilian onlookers after his mishap is referred to, Ecl. ii. 30–1.

Serse, Xerxes, son of Darius, King of Persia, B.C. 485–465 ; in the spring of B.C. 480 he set out from Sardis at the head of a count-less host on his memorable expedition against Greece, crossed the Helles-pont by a bridge of boats, and marched on Athens, after destroying Leonidas and his Spartans at Ther-mopylae ; on the defeat and dispersion of his fleet at the battle of Salamis, he retreated homewards, reaching Sardis again before the end of the same year. He was eventually assassinated by the captain of his body-guard, after a reign of twenty years.

D. mentions Xerxes in connexion with his passage of the Hellespont, Purg. xxviii. 71 [**Ellesponto**] ; he is introduced as the type of a warrior by Charles Martel (in the Heaven

of Venus), who says that one man is born to be a Solon (or lawgiver), another a Xerxes, and a third a Melchizedek (or good king), Par. viii. 124–5 ; his invasion of Greece with an immense army, with which he crossed the Hellespont from Abydos to Sestos, in his attempt to attain universal empire, and his miserable failure (cf. Orosius, *Hist.* ii. 9, § 2 ; 10, §§ 8–10), *Xerxes*, Mon. ii. 9^{49-60} [**Abido : Sesto** [1]].

Servio Tullio], Servius Tullius, sixth King of Rome ; included by D., in his list of the Kings of Rome, as one of *li re Tarquinii*, Conv. iv. 5^{91}. [**Tarquinii**.]

Sesto [1], Sestos, town in Thrace, on the narrowest part of the Helles-pont, opposite Abydos in Asia, from which it was rather more than a mile distant ; celebrated in fiction on account of the exploit of Leander, who used to swim nightly across from Abydos to visit Hero, Purg. xxviii. 74 [**Abido : Leandro**] ; and in history on account of the bridge of boats built by Xerxes across the Hellespont, *Sestos*, Mon. ii. 9^{53} [**Ellesponto : Serse**].

Sesto [2], Sextus Pompeius Mag-nus, younger son of Pompey the Great ; together with his brother Cneius he fought against Caesar at Munda, B.C. 45, where he was de-feated, and barely escaped with his life. After the murder of Caesar in the next year he put himself at the head of a fleet, and took posses-sion of Sicily, whence he ravaged the coasts of Italy, and cut off from the Romans their corn supplies from Egypt and Africa, so that Rome was threatened with famine (cf.

Lucan, *Phars.* vi. 420–3; Orosius, *Hist.* vi. 18, § 19). He was eventually (B.C. 36) defeated by the fleet of Augustus under Agrippa off the N. coast of Sicily, and shortly after was taken prisoner and put to death at Mitylene by an officer of Antony (B.C. 35).

D. places Sextus among the Robbers in Round 1 of Circle VII of Hell, Inf. xii. 135 [**Predoni**]; his defeat at Munda is alluded to, Par. vi. 71–2 [**Munda**].

Sesto Cielo. [**Giove, Cielo di.**]

Sestos. [**Sesto** [1].]

Setta, Ceuta, city in N. Africa, in Morocco, opposite to Gibraltar, situated on a peninsula which juts out from the mainland, and forms the E. extremity of the Strait of Gibraltar.

Ulysses (in Bolgia 8 of Circle VIII of Hell), in describing his voyage westwards, says he first passed Ceuta on his left hand, then Seville on his right, Inf. xxvi. 110–11.

Sette Regi [1], Seven Kings who warred against Thebes (viz. Adrastus, Polynices, Tydeus, Amphiaraus, Capaneus, Hippomedon, and Parthenopaeus); mentioned in connexion with Capaneus, Inf. xiv. 68–9. [**Capaneo : Tebe.**]

Sette Regi [2], Seven Kings of Rome (viz. Romulus, Numa Pompilius, Tullus Hostilius, Ancus Marcius, Tarquinius Priscus, Servius Tullius, and Tarquinius Superbus); mentioned by the Emperor Justinian (in the Heaven of Mercury) in connexion with the Roman Eagle, Par. vi. 41; their guardianship of

Rome during her infancy, their names being given as 'Romolo, Numa, Tullo, Anco, e li re Tarquinii', Conv. iv. 5[89–92] [**Tarquinii**].

Sette Savi. [**Savi, Sette.**]

Settembre, month of September; D. refers to the crowded state of the hospitals of Valdichiana, owing to the malaria generated by its swamps, during the month of August, *tra il luglio e il settembre,* Inf. xxix. 47. [**Chiana.**]

Settentrione [1], Constellation of 'the Plough' (Lat. *septem triones,* 'seven ploughing oxen'), otherwise known as 'the Wain' or 'the Great Bear'; figuratively, of the seven candlesticks of the mystical Procession in the Terrestrial Paradise, Purg. xxx. 1 (the constellation itself being referred to as *il più basso s., v.* 5); referred to as *sette stelle gelide,* Canz. xv. 29; and (in a quotation from Boëthius), *septem gelidi triones,* Mon. ii. 9[96] [**Carro, Il** [1]].

Settentrione [2], region of 'the Plough', i. e. the North; the mountain of Purgatory as far removed from the Equator towards the N. as Jerusalem is towards the S., Purg. iv. 79–84; the Tropic of Cancer distant 23° and more northwards from the Equator, Conv. iii. 5[135–42] [**Cancro**]; *Septemtrio,* of the N. limits of the *langue d'oïl,* V. E. i. 8[60] [**Lingua Oïl**]; *Tramontana,* the imaginary city of *Maria* at the N. Pole, distant 2,700 miles N. from Rome, Conv. iii. 5[85–91] [**Maria** [4]]; the region of intense cold, Sest. ii. 25–7; *Aquilone,* the region of the N. wind (Aquilo), Purg. iv. 60; xxxii. 99; Conv.

iv. 20[76] [**Aquilone**]; referred to as *settentrional vedovo sito*, 'widowed region of the N.,' as having been debarred from gazing upon the 'quattro stelle Non viste mai fuor che alla prima gente' (i. e., according to some, the Southern Cross), Purg. i. 23–7; described as *la plaga Che ciascun giorno d' Elice si cuopra, Rotante col suo figlio*, i. e. the region which is every day covered by the constellation of the Great Bear, Par. xxxi. 31–3 [**Boote : Elice**].

Settimo Cielo. [**Saturno, Cielo di.**]

Sfinge, Sphinx, she-monster, who appeared in the neighbourhood of Thebes, and, seated on a rock, put a riddle to every Theban that passed by, slaying all those who could not supply the answer. The riddle, which ran as follows—a creature with four feet has two feet and three feet, and only one voice, but its feet vary, and when it has most it is weakest—was solved by Oedipus, who replied that the creature was man ; in infancy he crawls upon all fours, in manhood he stands erect upon two feet, and in old age he supports his tottering steps with a staff. The Sphinx, on hearing the solution of the riddle, flung herself down from the rock and was killed.

D. mentions the Sphinx, together with Themis, in connexion with his mysterious prophecy of the DXV, Purg. xxxiii. 47. [**DXV : Edipo : Naiade : Temi**]; her riddle not to be solved by a Davus, *Sphinx*, Carm. 9 [**Davus**].

Sibilia, Seville, city of Spain in Andalusia, on the left bank of the Guadalquivir, about sixty miles NE. of Cadiz ; mentioned by D. to indicate the W. limit of the habitable world, in connexion with the setting of the Moon in the W. (the time in question being shortly after sunrise, about 6 a.m.), Inf. xx. 124–6 [**Ispagna**]; Ulysses (in Bolgia 8 of Circle VIII of Hell), in describing his voyage westwards, says he first passed Ceuta on his left hand, then Seville on his right, Inf. xxvi. 110–11 [**Ulisse**].

Sibilla, the Sibyl (of Cumae in Campania), who was consulted by Aeneas before he descended to the infernal regions, and accompanied him on his journey, as is related in *Aen.* vi.

D. compares the fading from his mind of the impression of the beatific vision, which he beheld in the Empyrean, to the whirling away by the wind of the leaves on which the oracles of the Sibyl were written (the incident being borrowed from *Aen.* iii. 441–52), Par. xxxiii. 61–6; the Sibyl is mentioned again in connexion with the courage of Aeneas in descending alone with her to the infernal regions (*Aen.* vi. 261–3), Conv. iv. 26[70–5].

Sicani, inhabitants of Sicania (Sicily) ; their jeers at Sergestus, after his mishap in the ship-race during the games in honour of the memory of Anchises in Sicily, Ecl. ii. 30–1 [**Sergestus**].

Sicheo, Sychaeus, wealthy Phoenician of Tyre, uncle and husband of Dido ; he was murdered for the sake of his wealth by his nephew, Dido's brother, Pygmalion, who kept his crime a secret, but the shade of Sychaeus appeared to Dido, and, revealing to her what had happened, urged her to fly from Tyre; she thereupon sailed across to Africa, where she founded the city of Carthage, and subsequently, forgetful of her vow to remain faithful to the memory of Sychaeus, became enamoured of Aeneas.

D. mentions S. in connexion with the unfaithfulness to him of Dido, whom he describes as *colei che . . . ruppe fede al cener di Sicheo* (an echo of *Aen.* iv. 552), Inf. v. 61–2; Dido's love for Aeneas referred to by the troubadour Folquet (in the Heaven of Venus) as an outrage to the memory both of his wife Creusa, and of her own husband Sychaeus, Par. ix. 97–8. [Dido.]

Sicilia. [Cicilia.]

Siciliano, Vespro. [Vespro Siciliano.]

Sicilianus. [Ciciliano.]

Siculi, inhabitants of Sicily; their dialect distinct from that of the Apulians, V. E. i. 12^{60-2}; that spoken by the Sicilian nobles the nearest approach of all the Italian dialects to the curial language, V. E. i. 12^{51-5}; the Italian vulgar tongue made use of by Sicilian poets, V. E. i. 19^{15-17}; *Sicani,* Ecl. ii. 31 [Cicilia : Ciciliano : Sicani.]

Siculus. [Ciciliano.]

Siena, city of N. Italy in the centre of Tuscany, situated on a hill about thirty miles due S. of Florence.

After the death (in 1115) of the Countess Matilda of Tuscany, Siena, like Pisa, Lucca, and Florence, succeeded in establishing its independence; as the result of a struggle between the nobles and the popular party the government fell into the hands of the former, and Siena became the chief stronghold of the Ghibelline party in Central Italy, as Florence was that of the Guelfs; during Cent. xii and xiii there was constant warfare between the two cities, which culminated in the great battle at Montaperti on Sept. 4, 1260, when the Florentine Guelfs were completely defeated by the Sienese, and Florence itself narrowly escaped destruction [**Montaperti**]. But with the triumph of the Guelf cause under the house of Anjou, and the fall of the Hohenstaufen, Siena fell from her high position, and her power as the Ghibelline stronghold was finally broken on the occasion of the defeat of the Sienese by the united forces of the Florentines and the Guelfs of Tuscany, aided by French troops of Charles of Anjou, at Colle in June 1269, when the Sienese leader, the powerful Provenzano Salvani, was killed [**Colle**].

Siena is mentioned by Griffolino of Arezzo (in Bolgia 10 of Circle VIII of Hell) as the native place of Albero, who caused him to be burned as an alchemist, Inf. xxix. 109 [**Albero : Griffolino**]; by La Pia (in Ante-purgatory) as her own native place, Purg. v. 134 [**Pia, La**]; and by Oderisi (in Circle I of Purgatory) in connexion with Provenzano Salvani, Purg. xi. 111, 123, 134 [**Provenzano Salvani**]; the name occurs in the specimen of the Sienese dialect, V. E. i. 13^{26} [**Sanese : Sanesi**];

the Campo, or public square, of Siena is mentioned by Oderisi, Purg. xi. 134 [**Campo di Siena**]; the Sienese Fonte Branda is supposed by some to be mentioned by Maestro Adamo (in Bolgia 10 of Circle VIII of Hell), Inf. xxx. 78 [**Branda, Fonte**].

Siestri, Sestri Levante, town in Liguria, on the Riviera di Levante, about twenty-five miles E. of Genoa; mentioned by Pope Adrian V (in Circle V of Purgatory) in connexion with the Lavagna, which runs into the sea between that town and Chiavari, Purg. xix. 100. [**Lavagna.**]

Sifanti, variant for *Fifanti*, Par. xvi. 104. [**Fifanti.**]

Sigieri, Siger of Brabant, doctor of philosophy and professor of the University of Paris in Cent. xiii; placed by D. among the great doctors (*Spiriti Sapienti*) in the Heaven of the Sun, Par. x. 136; *questi*, *v.* 133; *spirto*, *v.* 134; the 'eternal light' of Siger is pointed out by St. Thomas Aquinas, who says that 'in his weighty thoughts death seemed to come to him slowly' (*vv.* 134–6); he adds that Siger in his lectures in the Rue du Fouarre at Paris 'deduced truths which brought him envy' (*vv.* 137–8). [**Sole, Cielo del.**]

Siger took a prominent part in the violent disputes which arose between the lay members of the University of Paris and the friars of the mendicant orders concerning the liberty of teaching; in 1266 he and Guillaume de St. Amour were publicly refuted by St. Thomas Aquinas, the champion of the Dominicans. In 1275 the whole University was divided into two parties, the one being headed by a certain Albericus, the other by Siger. This schism was put an end to by the Papal legate in Paris, Simon de Brie (afterwards Pope Martin IV), who threatened the ringleaders in the disturbances with 'the sword of justice and of vengeance'. As a consequence, apparently, of this intervention of the Papal legate Siger quitted Paris, and retired to Liège; but in Nov. 1277 he was summoned to appear at Saint-Quentin before the Dominican Simon du Val, inspector-general of the faith for the province of France, on a charge of heresy, doubtless with reference to his teaching in Paris, and to the dangerous tendency of his writings, especially of the collection of controversial treatises entitled *Impossibilia*, in one of which the existence of the Deity is called in question.

The exact date of Siger's death is uncertain. It is known from a passage in an Italian imitation (in a series of sonnets) of the *Roman de la Rose*, written towards the end of Cent. xiii by one Durante (whom some would identify with D.), in which Siger is coupled with Guillaume de St. Amour, that he died 'by the sword' at the Court of Rome at Orvieto (*Son.* xcii. 9–14). From a record in the Brabantine continuation of the chronicle of Martin of Troppau it appears that he was stabbed at the Papal Court by a mad clerk. His death must have taken place some time between Nov. 1277, the date of his condemnation as a heretic, and Nov. 10, 1284, the date of a letter of

John Peckham, Archbishop of Canterbury, in which he is referred to as having died miserably ' in partibus transalpinis'.

A few fragments only of Siger's writings have been preserved; these consist of *Quaestiones Logicales*; *Quaestiones Naturales*, including a fragment 'De anima intellectiva'; and the collection of treatises entitled *Impossibilia*.

Signa, village of Tuscany, near the Arno, about ten miles W. of Florence; *quel da Signa*, i.e. probably Fazio (or Bonifazio) de' Mori Ubaldini of Signa, Par. xvi. 56. [**Bonifazio**[3].]

Sile, small river of Upper Italy in Venetia, which unites with the Cagnano at Treviso; hence D. alludes to Treviso as the place *dove Sile e Cagnan s'accompagna*, Par. ix. 49; the two rivers are mentioned together to indicate Treviso, Conv. iv. 14[116-17]. [**Cagnano : Trevigi.**]

Silvestro[1], Pope Sylvester I (314–335); mentioned, in connexion with the legend that he healed Constantine the Great of leprosy and converted him to Christianity, Inf. xxvii. 94; *Sylvester*, Mon. iii. 10[3]; referred to, in connexion with the so-called Donation of Constantine, as *il primo ricco patre*, Inf. xix. 117; *il pastore*, Par. xx. 57. [**Costantino.**]

According to the legend, Constantine, having been stricken with leprosy in punishment for his persecution of the Christians, was advised by the heathen priests to wash himself in a bath of infants' blood. Accordingly, three thousand

infants were collected for the purpose; but Constantine, touched by the lamentations and prayers of the bereaved mothers, ordered the babes to be restored to their parents, saying that it was better for him to die rather than that so many innocent lives should be sacrificed. That same night St. Peter and St. Paul appeared to him in a vision, and bade him send for Sylvester from his hiding-place in Mt. Soracte, who should cure him of his leprosy. Constantine did as he was bidden, and after receiving baptism at Sylvester's hands was immediately cured; he thereupon set himself to convert his mother Helena, and finally succeeded in bringing her and the whole of the Roman people to the true faith. In order still further to prove his gratitude, and to leave the Church completely at liberty, he bestowed upon Pope Sylvester the city of Rome, and the whole Empire of the West, and himself retired to Byzantium, which he rebuilt and named Constantinople after his own name.

Silvestro[2], Sylvester, one of the earliest followers of St. Francis of Assisi; mentioned by St. Thomas Aquinas (in the Heaven of the Sun), together with Giles of Assisi, in connexion with St. Francis, Par. xi. 83. [**Francesco**[2].]

Silvio, Silvius, posthumous son of Aeneas by Lavinia, daughter of Latinus, King of Latium; D. refers to Aeneas as *di Silvio lo parente*, Inf. ii. 13 (cf. *Aen.* vi. 763–6) [**Enea.**]

Simeone], Simeon, son of Jacob and Leah; he is among those referred to by Virgil as having been released by Christ from Limbo, *Israel co' suoi nati*, Inf. iv. 59 [Limbo].

Simifonti, Semifonte, strong fortress in the Valdelsa, SW. of Florence; in 1202 it was captured and destroyed by the Florentines, with whom it had long been carrying on hostilities.

Cacciaguida (in the Heaven of Mars) mentions it in connexion with some individual (who has not been identified), of whom he says that his grandfather was a beggar ('andava alla cerca') at Semifonte, while he (the descendant) had become a merchant and money-changer in Florence, Par. xvi. 61–3.

The reference may be to one of the Velluti family, who were well-known merchants and money-changers in Florence, and originally came from Semifonte; the special allusion being perhaps to Lippo del Velluto, who was a member of the government which expelled Giano della Bella in 1295.

Simoenta, Simoïs, one of the chief rivers of the Troad, celebrated in the accounts of the Trojan war (*Aen.* v. 634); it is mentioned by the Emperor Justinian (in the Heaven of Mercury), together with Antandros (*Aen.* iii. 6) and the tomb of Hector (*Aen.* v. 371), to indicate the Troad, Par. vi. 67. [Antandro.]

Simon Mago, Simon the sorcerer of Samaria (in Vulg. 'Simon magus'), who, after being baptized, offered money to the apostles for the gift of the Holy Ghost (*Acts* viii. 9–24); hence from his name

is derived the word *Simony*, as applied to all traffic in spiritual offices, those who are guilty of the offence being termed *Simoniacs*.

D. apostrophizes Simon and his followers at the entrance to Bolgia 3 of Circle VIII of Hell (Malebolge), where they are punished, Inf. xix. 1 [Simoniaci]; Beatrice (in the Empyrean) mentions him in her denunciation of Clement V, who, she says, shall be thrust down there where Simon is for his deserts, Par. xxx. 146–7 [Clemente [2]].

Simone Donati], father (d. 1296) of Forese Donati; supposed to be alluded to by the mention of *San Simone* in D.'s *tenzone* with Forese Donati, Son. liii. 5; his wife, Tessa, is mentioned, Son. liv. 2. [Forese: Simone, San: Tessa.]

Simone, San, ancient church and parish of Florence; mentioned by D. in his *tenzone* with Forese Donati, perhaps with an allusion to Forese's father, Simone, Son. liii. 5 [Simone Donati].

Simoniaci], Simoniacs, those guilty of simony; referred to as *miseri seguaci di Simon mago*, Inf. xix. 1; they are placed among the Fraudulent in Bolgia 3 of Circle VIII of Hell (Malebolge), Inf. xix. 1–123 [Frodolenti]; their punishment is to be thrust head-downwards into round holes in the rocky bottom of the Bolgia, with their legs as far as the calves projecting, and their feet on fire (*vv.* 13–5, 22–7); each one on the arrival of a fresh sinner is thrust further down below the rock (*vv.* 73–5). *Examples*: Simon Magus (Inf. xix. 1; Par. xxx. 147)

Simonide   491   Siratti

[**Simon Mago**]; Pope Nicholas III [**Niccolò**[2]]; and, by anticipation, Boniface VIII (Inf. xix. 52–7, 81; Par. xxx. 148) [**Bonifazio**[1]]; and Clement V (Inf. xix. 82–7; Par. xxx. 146–7) [**Clemente**[2]].

Simonide, Simonides, Greek lyric poet, born in the island of Ceos, c. B.C. 556; died at the court of Hiero at Syracuse, aged nearly ninety, B.C. 467; he is mentioned by Virgil (addressing Statius in Purgatory)as being among the Greek poets who are with Homer and himself in Limbo, Purg. xxii. 107 [**Limbo**]; Aristotle's opinion as expressed in the *Ethics*, 'contra Simonide poeta parlando', that man should bring himself as near as possible to divine things, Conv. iv. 13[70–2] (the actual source of D.'s quotation being, not the *Ethics*, but a passage in the *Summa Contra Gentiles* (I. v. § 3) of Aquinas in which Aristotle's opinion is cited).

Simpliciter Ente, De. [*Metaphysica.*]

Sinigaglia, now Senigallia, ancient Sena Gallica, situated on the Adriatic at the mouth of the Misa, about seventeen miles NW. of Ancona, in what was formerly the duchy of Urbino, but now forms part of the province of the Marches.

Cacciaguida (in the Heaven of Mars) mentions it and Chiusi as instances of once powerful cities which were rapidly falling into decay (the cause in each case being doubtless the unhealthiness of the climate), Par. xvi. 75 [**Chiusi**].

Sinone, Sinon, the treacherous Greek who during the siege of Troy allowed himself to be taken prisoner by the Trojans, and then by a lying tale persuaded them to admit within their walls a wooden horse, which the Greeks had constructed as a pretended atonement for the Palladium stolen from Troy by Ulysses and Diomed. The Trojans, taken in by his specious story, dragged the horse, which was full of armed Greeks, into the midst of the city; then, in the middle of the night Sinon let out his comrades, who fell suddenly upon the unsuspecting Trojans and thus made themselves masters of Troy (*Aen.* ii. 57 ff.).

D. places Sinon among the Falsifiers in Bolgia 10 of Circle VIII of Hell (Malebolge), *il falso Sinon greco da Troia*, Inf. xxx. 98; *Sinone*, v. 116; *il Greco*, v. 122; he and Potiphar's wife, *duo tapini*, v. 91; *l'altro*, v. 98; *l'un*, v. 100; *spergiuro*, v. 118; he and Maestro Adamo, *li*, v. 130 [**Falsatori**].

Sion, name of one of the two hills upon which the city of Jerusalem is situated, hence used as a synonym for the city itself (2 *Sam.* v. 7); Sion (i. e. Jerusalem), the antipodes of Purgatory, Purg. iv. 68. [**Gerusalemme**.]

Siratti, ancient Soracte, now known as Monte di S. Oreste, mountain near the Tiber about twenty-four miles N. of Rome; on its summit stands the church of San Silvestro.

D. mentions Soracte in connexion with Pope Sylvester I, who is said to have taken refuge in a cave on the mountain during the persecutions of Constantine, and to have been summoned thence by the Emperor just before his conversion to Christianity, Inf. xxvii. 94. [**Silvestro.**[1]]

Sirena, one of the Sirens; allegorical personage who appears to D. in a vision, commonly understood to denote the pleasures of the flesh, especially those which lead to the sins of avarice, gluttony, and lust, Purg. xix. 7–33; *femmina balba*, v. 7; *dolce Sirena*, v. 19; *l'altra*, v. 31; *antica strega*, v. 58.

In the hour before dawn, after leaving Circle IV of Purgatory, D. has a dream, in which there appears to him a woman with a stammering utterance, squinting eyes, crooked gait, deformed hands and pallid complexion (Purg. xix. 1–9); D. gazes upon her, and under his gaze her deformities disappear, her face assumes a rosy hue, and she begins to sing so sweetly that D. feels entranced (*vv.* 10–18); in her song she describes herself as the Siren who turned Ulysses from his path, as she does all those who come within hearing of her voice (*vv.* 19–24); scarcely has she ceased ere a holy lady (representative probably of reason) appears and calls to Virgil, who comes at her bidding (*vv.* 25–30); she then (or, according to some, Virgil) seizes the Siren, tears her open in front, and exposes her belly, from which issues such a stench as to awaken D. from his dream (*vv.* 31–3); later on V., noticing that D. is preoccupied, bids him bear in mind that if he has seen the 'ancient witch', and her allurements, he has also seen the way of escape from her (*vv.* 52–60). The statement of the Siren (*vv.* 22–3), that she turned Ulysses from his path by her singing, is not in accord with the Homeric account

[**Sirene**]. D., to whom Homer was not accessible, probably had in mind a passage in the *De Finibus* of Cicero (v. 18), in which he translates several lines from the Sirens' song in Homer, and in his comment implies that Ulysses was ensnared by them.

Sirene, Sirens, sea-nymphs who dwelt on an island near Sicily and by their singing lured to destruction all who sailed within hearing of them. When Ulysses approached their island he stopped the ears of his companions with wax and bound himself to the mast of his ship, whereby he escaped without being ensnared. The Sirens are said to have been three in number, and are commonly regarded as symbolical of the pleasures of the senses.

D. mentions the Sirens, as symbolical of sensual pleasures, Purg. xix. 19 [**Sirena**]; Purg. xxxi. 45; Epist. v. 4[60]; as typical sweet singers, Par. xii. 8.

Sirenes. [**Sirene**.]

Siria, Syria, modern name for the Holy Land; according to the Syrian usage Beatrice died in the ninth month of the year, V. N. § 30[4–5] [**Tisrin primo**]; the land of Christ's nativity, Conv. iv. 5[71].

Siringa, Syrinx, nymph of Arcadia, who, being pursued by Pan, took refuge in the river Ladon, where in answer to her prayers she was metamorphosed into a reed; out of this reed Pan made a flute, which was thus invented for the first time. It was with the tale of Syrinx that Mercury lulled to sleep the watchful Argus. D. mentions Syrinx (whose story is told by Ovid,

Metam. i. 622 ff.) in connexion with this incident, Purg. xxxii. 65. [Argo².]

Sismondi, noble Ghibelline family of Pisa, mentioned by Count Ugolino (in Circle IX of Hell), together with the Gualandi and Lanfranchi, as having been foremost among those whom the Archbishop Ruggieri incited to work his destruction, Inf. xxxiii. 32. [Ugolino, Conte.]

Sisto, Sixtus I, Bishop of Rome, c. 119-127; D. follows the tradition that he was martyred, and includes him among those of his immediate successors mentioned by St. Peter (in the Heaven of Fixed Stars) as having, like himself, shed their blood for the Church, Par. xxvii. 44.

Sizii, ancient noble family of Florence, mentioned by Cacciaguida (in the Heaven of Mars), together with the Arrigucci, as having held office in his day, Par. xvi. 108. [Arrigucci.]

Soave, Swabia, ancient duchy in SW. of Germany, which corresponded roughly to the modern Würtemberg, Baden, and Hohenzollern, together with a part of Bavaria. The dukedom was founded early in Cent. x, and was held for the most part by members of the Saxon and Franconian royal and imperial houses. In 1079 it passed to Frederick I of Hohenstaufen, the founder of the Hohenstaufen or Swabian line, in which there were five Emperors; and became extinct in 1268, at the death of Conradin, the last of the Hohenstaufen. [Hohenstaufen : Table H.]

Piccarda (in the Heaven of the Moon) refers to the Emperor Henry VI (1190–1197) as *il secondo vento di Soave*, and to his son, the Emperor Frederick II (1212–1250), as *il terzo vento*, Par. iii. 119–20; the latter is spoken of as *Federigo di Soave*, Conv. iv. 3³⁸⁻⁹. [Arrigo⁵ : Federico².]

Socrate, Socrates, famous Greek philosopher, born near Athens, c. B.C. 470; in his youth he followed the profession of his father, who was a sculptor, but he soon abandoned it in order to devote himself to teaching, his object being to promote the intellectual and moral improvement of his fellow-men; in 406 he was a member of the senate, but in 399 he was indicted as an offender against public morality, on the charges of denying the gods, and of corrupting the young; being found guilty, he was condemned to death, and after thirty days' imprisonment drank hemlock, and died in the seventieth year of his age. Socrates wrote nothing, and made no attempt to found a school or system of philosophy.

D. places S. with Plato among the ancient philosophers who are grouped around Aristotle in Limbo, ranking them next to the Master, Inf. iv. 134-5 [Limbo]; his opinion, which he shared with Plato and Dionysius, that 'substantial generation' is the effect of the stars, especially in the case of human souls, Conv. ii. 14²⁸⁻³⁵; his contempt for life in comparison with knowledge, Conv. iii. 14⁸⁴⁻⁵; the doctrine of the mean as applied to virtue held by him and by his successor Plato,

Conv. iv. 6^{115-25}; owing to the negative character of his philosophy no school was named after him, Conv. iv. 6^{128-30} (cf. Cicero, *Acad. Quaest.* i. 4); his favourable opinion of Plato on first seeing him, Conv. iv. 24^{59-61} [**Platone**].

Soddoma, Sodom, ancient city of Palestine, destroyed by fire from heaven on account of the abominable wickedness of its inhabitants (*Gen.* xix. 4–8, 23–9); mentioned together with Cahors to indicate the sins of sodomy and of usury, Inf. xi. 50 [**Caorsa**]; coupled with Gomorrah among the instances of lust proclaimed by the Lustful in Circle VII of Purgatory, Purg. xxvi. 40, 79 [**Lussuriosi: Sodomiti**].

Sodomiti], Sodomites, those who have been guilty of unnatural offences, placed among the Violent in Round 3 of Circle VII of Hell, Inf. xv. 16–xvi. 87 [**Violenti**]; their punishment is to be kept continually running, in two divisions, over a desert of burning sand, while flakes of fire fall upon them from above (Inf. xiv. 13–30); if any of them stop for as much as a moment they have to lie for a hundred years without being able to screen themselves from the falling fire (Inf. xv. 37–9). *Examples* (in the first division): Brunetto Latini [**Brunetto**]; Priscian [**Prisciano**]; Francesco d'Accorso [**Accorso, Francesco d'**]; Andrea de' Mozzi [**Andrea de' Mozzi**]; (in the second division): Guidoguerra [**Guido Guerra**]; Tegghiaio Aldobrandi [**Aldobrandi, Tegghiaio**]; Jacopo Rusticucci [**Jacopo Rusticucci**]; Guglielmo Borsiere [**Borsiere, Guglielmo**].

Those who expiate offences against nature in Purgatory are placed with the Lustful in Circle VII, their punishment being to pass and repass through intensely hot flames, while they proclaim aloud the names of Sodom and Gomorrah, Purg. xxvi. 28–81 [**Lussuriosi**]. No examples are named, but the charge brought against Julius Caesar of having been guilty of this offence is referred to, Purg. xxvi. 76–8 [**Cesare**[1]].

Soldan. [**Soldano.**]

Soldanier, Gianni de'. [**Gianni de' Soldanier.**]

Soldanieri, ancient noble family of Florence, mentioned by Cacciaguida (in the Heaven of Mars) as having been of importance in his day, Par. xvi. 93.

They lived in the Porta di san Brancazio (Vill. iv. 12), and were Ghibellines (v. 39; vi. 33), and as such were among the families expelled from Florence in 1258 (vi. 65).

A renegade member of this family, Gianni de' Soldanieri, who sided against his own party for the purposes of self-aggrandisement, is placed by D. among the traitors in Antenora, Inf. xxxii. 121. [**Gianni de' Soldanier.**]

Soldano, Sultan of Egypt, called also in D.'s time the Sultan of Babylon; the Sultan in 1300 (i. e. El-Melik En-Nâsir Muhammad, 1299-1309), Inf. v. 60; the Sultan in 1297 (i. e. El-Melik El-Mansoor Lágeen, 1296-1299), Inf. xxvii. 90; the Sultan in 1219 (i. e. El-Melik El-Kámil, 1218-1238), Par. xi. 101.

D. refers to Egypt as *terra di Soldano*, Inf. xxvii. 90; and, by a confusion, to the Empire of Semiramis (i. e. the kingdom of Babylon) as *la terra che il Soldan corregge*, Inf. v. 60. [**Babilon**.]

St. Thomas Aquinas (in the Heaven of the Sun) in his account of St. Francis of Assisi mentions the visit of the latter to the Sultan in Egypt, ' in his thirst for martyrdom ', for the purpose of preaching the Christian faith to him, Par. xi. 100–5 [**Francesco** [2]]. In 1219 (during the fifth Crusade) St. Francis joined the Crusaders' army before Damietta, and at the risk of his life making his way into the camp of the Sultan, El-Melik El-Kámil, summoned him to embrace Christianity. The Sultan received him courteously and listened to him, but remained unconvinced, and finally dismissed him in safety to the Crusaders' camp, whence he returned to Italy.

Saladin, the founder of the Ayubite dynasty of Sultans in Egypt, is mentioned Inf. iv. 129; Conv. iv. 11[126]. [**Saladino**.]

Sole, Sun, Inf. i. 38, 60; ii. 128; vi. 68; vii. 122; xi. 91; xxiv. 2; xxvi. 117; xxviii. 56; xxix. 105; xxxiii. 54; xxxiv. 96, 105; Purg. i. 39, 107; ii. 1, 56; iii. 16, 96; iv. 16, 56, 81, 119, 138; v. 39; vii. 26, 54, 85; viii. 133; ix. 44; xii. 74; xiii. 13, 67; xv. 5; xvi. 107; xvii. 6, 9, 52; xviii. 80, 110; xix. 10, 39; xxi. 101; xxii. 61; xxiii. 114, 121; xxv. 2, 77; xxvi. 4, 23, 45; xxvii. 5, 61, 66, 68, 79, 133; xxviii. 33; xxix. 6, 78, 117, 118; xxx. 25; xxxi. 121; xxxii.

11, 18, 56; xxxiii. 104; Par. i. 47, 54, 63, 80; ii. 33, 80; iii. 1; v. 133; viii. 12; ix. 8, 69, 85, 114; x. 41, 48, 53, 76; xi. 50; xii. 15, 51; xv. 76; xvii. 123; xviii. 105; xix. 5; xx. 31; xxii. 56; xxiii. 8, 12, 29, 79; xxv. 54, 119; xxvi. 120, 142; xxvii. 28, 69, 86; xxix. 99; xxx. 8, 25, 75, 105, 126; xxxi. 120; xxxii. 108; xxxiii. 64, 145; V. N. § 42[29]; Conv. i. 13[85, 88]; ii. 3[25, 57, 58], 4[5], 6[140], 14[123, 148], 15[48, 57, 146, 149], 16[46]; iii. 5[12, 18, 35, 78, 127, 132, 144, 156, 167, 175, 187, 199], 6[2, 8, 11], 7[23, 24, 30], 8[130], 12[43, 50, 51, 54, 59]; iv. 8[51, 56, 61], 23[135, 145]; Canz. ii. 50; vii. 19, 60; ix. 2, 42; xii. 57; xv. 2, 16; xix. 74, 117; Sest. ii. 20; Son. xxxvi. 2; xxxix. 9; *Sol*, Mon. i. 9[7]; iii. 4[19, 131, 133, 136, 144, 156]; Epist. iv. 4[46]; x. 2[44]; A. T. § 19[45], 24[16]; Apollo being god of the Sun, D. also speaks of the Sun as *Delius*, Epist. vi. 2[55]; *Phoebus*, Mon. ii. 9[95]; *Phoebae frater*, Mon. i. 11[35]; *figlio di Latona*, Par. xxix. 1 [**Apollo**]; it is otherwise referred to as *nato d' Iperione*, Par. xxii. 142; *Hyperione natus*, Epist. iv. 4[49]; *Titan*, Epist. v. 1[10]; vii. 1[19]; Ecl. ii. 2; *occhio del cielo*, Purg. xx. 132; *luminare majus*, Mon. iii. 1[35], 4[12]; *il pianeta Che mena dritto altrui per ogni calle*, Inf. i. 17–18; *quello specchio Che su e giù del suo lume conduce*, Purg. iv. 62–3; *dolce lume*, Inf. x. 69; Purg. xiii. 16; *gran luce*, Purg. xxxii. 53; *lucerna del mondo*, Par. i. 38; *carro della luce*, Purg. iv. 59; *ministro maggior della natura*, Par. x. 28; *padre d'ogni mortal vita*, Par. xxii. 116; *colui che il mondo schiara*, Inf. xxvi. 26;

colui che tutto il mondo alluma, Par.
xx. 1 ; *quei ch' apporta mane e lascia
sera*, Par. xxvii. 138; *quei che dal
ciel quarto non si parte*, Son. xxviii.
7 ; *il gran pianeta*, Canz. xix. 96 ;
colui, Purg. vi. 56; xxiii. 120;
quei, Purg. xi. 116.

The Sun is referred to as the
brother of the Moon, Purg. xxiii.
120 ; Mon. i. 11³⁵ [**Phoebe**]; the
son of Latona, Par. xxix. 1 [**Latona**]; the son of Hyperion, Par.
xxii. 142 ; Epist. iv. 4⁴⁹ [**Iperione**]; the Titan, Epist. v. 1¹⁰;
vii. 1¹⁹; Ecl. ii. 2 [**Titan**]; the
Heaven of the Sun being the fourth
in D.'s conception of the Universe,
he refers to the Sun itself as *Quei
che dal ciel quarto non si parte*, Son.
xxviii. 7 [**Sole, Cielo del**].

The Sun as a measure of time,
Purg. xii. 74 ; Par. x. 28–30 ; representing a year, Inf. vi. 68 ;
xxix. 105 ; Purg. xxi. 101 ; Par.
xxvi. 119–20 ; a day, Inf. xxxiii.
54; *dies Solis*, Sunday, A. T. § 24¹⁶.

In the *D. C.* indications of time
are frequently given by a reference
to the Sun—except during the
journey through Hell ('dove il Sol
tace', Inf. i. 60), when the hour is
indicated by a reference to the state
of the Moon [**Luna**];—the rising
Sun, morning, is indicated, Inf. i.
17, 38; xxxiv. 96, 105 ; Purg. i.
107, 122 ; ii. 1, 55; iii. 16; iv.
16, 56, 59; ix. 44; xix. 39; xxvii.
133 ; *il Sole a mezza terza riede*,
' the Sun is returning to mid tierce ',
i. e. to halfway between 6 a.m. and
9 a.m., viz. 7.30 a.m., Inf. xxxiv.
96 (cf. Conv. iv. 23¹⁵⁰⁻⁴); *cinquanta
gradi salito era Lo Sole*, i. e. the Sun
had been up three hours and twenty

minutes (since it passes through
fifteen degrees every hour), Purg.
iv. 15–16; midday, Purg. iv. 119,
138; xii. 74; xxxiii. 104; Par. i.
47, 54 ; afternoon, Purg. xiii. 13 ;
xv. 5; xxv. 2 ; setting Sun, evening, Purg. vii. 85 ; xvii. 9 ; xxvi.
4; xxvii. 5, 61, 66, 68 ; the Sun
mentioned in connexion with D.'s
journey, but without express indication of time, Purg. xxiii. 114,
121 ; xxvi. 23 ; Par. i. 80 ; x. 28;
xxii. 142 ; xxvii. 86.

The Sun in Aries, Inf. i. 38–40;
Purg. ii. 1–6, 56–7; viii. 133–5;
xxv. 2; xxxii. 53–4; Par. i. 37–40 ;
x. 8–9, 31 ; xxix. 1–2 ; Conv. iii.
5⁷⁸, ¹⁷⁸; in which sign it was at the
time of the Creation, and also at
the commencement of D.'s journey,
Inf. i. 38–40 ; when in Aries its
creative power is most active, Par.
i. 37–42 ; in Gemini at the time of
D.'s birth, Par. xxii. 112–17 (cf.
Inf. xv. 55 ; xxvi. 23) ; in Libra,
Conv. iii. 5⁷⁹, ¹⁸²; in Sagittarius,
Purg. xviii. 79–81 ; in Capricorn,
Par. xxv. 101–2 ; xxvii. 68–9 ; in
Aquarius, Inf. xxiv. 2.

The eclipse of the Sun, Par. ii.
80 ; xxv. 119; Conv. ii. 3⁵⁷;
A. T. § 20²⁶ ; at the time of the
Crucifixion, Par. xxvii. 35–6 ; the
darkening of the Sun on that occasion due either to a miraculous eclipse
of it by the Moon, or to a withdrawal of its light on the part of the
Sun, whence the phenomenon was
visible in every quarter of the habitable globe, Par. xxix. 99–102 ; the
Sun higher in the heavens than the
Moon, as is manifest during an
eclipse of the former, Conv. iii.
3⁵⁷⁻⁸ ; A. T. § 20²⁶⁻⁸.

The diameter of the Sun,—its apparent diameter one foot, Conv. iv. $8^{51-3,\ 60-2}$; Epist. x. 2^{44}; its actual diameter $5\frac{1}{2}$ times that of the Earth (i. e. $35,750 = 6,500 \times 5\frac{1}{2}$ miles), Conv. iv. 8^{56-64}. [Terra^2.]

The Sun illumines the world and all the other stars, Inf. xxvi. 26; Par. i. 38; xx. 1; Canz. xix. 117; Conv. ii. 14^{125-6}; iii. 12^{54-6}; hence most worthy to be an image of the Deity, Conv. iii. 12^{52-3}; its light too bright to be endured by the human eye, Purg. xvii. 52; xxxii. 11; Par. i. 54; x. 48; xxv. 118-20; Canz. vii. 60; Conv. ii. 14^{126-7}; iii. 8^{130}; affects the various bodies upon which it shines diversely according to the various substances of which they are composed, Conv. iii. 7^{24-45}; the Sun the source of heat, and hence of life and strength, Inf. ii. 127-9; Purg. xi. 116-17; xix. 10-11; xxv. 77-8; xxxii. 55-6; Par. xxii. 56, 116; Canz. xix. 96-101; Conv. iii. 12^{59-60}; Mon. i. 9^{6-7}; supplies the greater portion of the light of the Moon, Mon. iii. $4^{17-19,}$ $130-3,\ 143-5,\ 156$; but the latter is independent of it as regards its being, its power, and its working, Mon. iii. 4^{135-40}; motion of the Sun round the Earth, Canz. vii. 19; Son. xxxix. 9; Conv. iii. $5^{35,\ 78,\ 199}$, $6^{2,\ 8}$, 12^{43}; at midday its heat is at its greatest, and its motion at its slowest, Purg. xxxiii. 103-4; Par. xxiii. 11-12; if the movement of the *Primum Mobile* were to be suspended, it would be hidden from the Earth during half its course, viz. 182 days, 14 hours, Conv. ii. 15^{139-47}; according to the Pytha-

goreans the Sun once deviated from its path and scorched that part of the heavens through which it passed, thus causing what is known as the Milky Way, Conv. ii. 15^{47-52}; according to Anaxagoras and Democritus the latter is caused by the reflection of the light of the Sun, Conv. ii. 15^{55-8}. [Galassia.]

The chariot of the Sun, Purg. xxix. 117-18; Conv. iv. 23^{134-5}; the horses of the Sun, Purg. xxxii. 57; Conv. iv. 23^{134-9} [Eoo]; 'the brightest handmaid of the Sun', i. e. the dawn, Par. xxx. 7 [Aurora].

In a figurative sense the Sun represents the ecclesiastical power of the Pope, as does the Moon the temporal power of the Emperor, Mon. iii. 1^{35-7}, $4^{10-21,\ 156-9}$; Pope and Emperor represented as two Suns, Purg. xvi. 107-8; the Sun, used figuratively for God, Purg. vii. 26; Par. ix. 8; x. 53; xviii. 105; xxv. 54; xxx. 126; Conv. iii. 12^{51}; for the Blessed, Par. x. 76; for St. Francis, Par. xi. 50; for Virgil, Inf. xi. 91; for Beatrice, Par. iii. 1; xxx. 75; for the Emperor Henry VII, Epist. vii. 2^{25}.

Sole, Cielo del, Heaven of the Sun; the fourth in D.'s conception of Paradise, Par. x. 49; Conv. ii. 4^5; Son. xxviii. 7 [Paradiso^1]; resembles Arithmetic in two respects, Conv. ii. 14^{123-7}; it is presided over by the Powers [Podestadi]; Aristotle erroneously believed it to be immediately above the Heaven of the Moon, and thus next but one to the Earth, Conv. ii. 3^{25-7}; its movement corresponds with that of the Heaven of Venus, Conv. ii. 6^{138-40}; its movement from W. to

E., not directly contrary to the diurnal movement from E. to W., but obliquely contrary to it, Conv. iii. 5$^{126-30}$; it is referred to as *quarto cielo*, Conv. ii. 4^5; Son. xxviii. 7; *cielo della luce*, V. N. § 2^2.

In the Heaven of the Sun D. places the spirits of great theologians and others who loved wisdom (*Spiriti Sapienti*), Par. x. 49–51; these are arranged in three circles (*corona*, x. 65; *ghirlanda*, x. 92; xii. 20; *coro*, x. 106; xiv. 62; *gloriosa ruota*, x. 145; *santa mola*, xii. 3; *giro*, xii. 4; xiv. 74; *circonferenza*, xiv. 75) one outside the other (xii. 5; xiii. 16–21; xiv. 74–5), with Beatrice and D. in the centre (x. 65; xiii. 21); in the first circle are twelve spirits, who are named as follows :—St. Thomas Aquinas [**Tommaso**^{2}]; Albertus Magnus [**Alberto**^{1}]; Gratian [**Graziano**]; Peter Lombard [**Pietro**^{2}]; Solomon [**Salomone**]; Dionysius the Areopagite [**Dionisio**^{2}]; Orosius [**Orosio**]; Boëthius [**Boezio**]; Isidore of Seville [**Isidoro**]; Bede [**Beda**]; Richard of St. Victor [**Riccardo**]; Siger of Brabant [**Sigieri**]; in the second circle are twelve others, viz. St. Bonaventura [**Bonaventura**]; Illuminato of Rieti [**Illuminato**]; Augustine the Franciscan [**Agostino**^{1}]; Hugh of St. Victor [**Ugo**^{2}]; Petrus Comestor [**Pietro Mangiadore**]; Petrus Hispanus [**Pietro Ispano**]; the prophet Nathan [**Natan**]; St. Chrysostom [**Crisostomo**]; Anselm of Canterbury [**Anselmo**]; Donatus the grammarian [**Donato**]; Hrabanus Maurus [**Ra-**

bano]; the Abbot Joachim [**Gioacchino**^{1}]; of the spirits of which the third circle (xiv. 74–5) is composed none is named.

Sole, Porta. [**Porta Sole.**]

Solone, Solon, celebrated Athenian legislator, one of the Seven Sages of Greece, c. B.C. 638–558. He was archon in 594, and entirely remodelled the constitution of Athens, making a large number of special laws.

Solon is mentioned as type of a lawgiver by Charles Martel (in the Heaven of Venus), who says that one man is born to be a Solon, another a Xerxes (or warrior), and a third a Melchizedek (or priest), Par. viii. 124–5; one of the Seven Sages of Greece, Conv. iii. 11^{38} [**Biante**]; his laws at Athens and those of Lycurgus at Sparta are alluded to, Purg. vi. 139.

Sophisticis Elenchis, De, Aristotle's treatise *On Sophistical Refutations*; his statement that the overthrow of an argument is the pointing out of the mistake, Mon. iii. 4$^{25-6}$ (*Soph. Elench.* ii. 3). [**Aristotile.**]

Sordello, famous troubadour of Cent. xiii, placed by D. in Antepurgatory among those who were negligent in repentance, Purg. vi. 74; viii. 38, 43, 62, 94; *il buon Sordello*, Purg. vii. 52; *Sordel*, Purg. vii. 3; ix. 58; *il Mantovan*, Purg. vii. 86; *un anima posta Sola soletta*, vi. 58–9; *quella* (*anima*), vv. 60, 69; *anima Lombarda*, v. 61; *ella*, v. 64; *l'ombra*, v. 72; *l'un*, v. 75; *anima gentil*, v. 79; *quegli*, vii. 13; *quell' ombra*, v. 67; *l'uno*, viii. 64. S. having learned the identity of D.'s companion, he and Virgil embrace

(vi. 69–75; vii. 1–14); V. then asks him to direct them to the Gate of Purgatory, whereupon S. offers himself as their guide, and on the way points out to them many kings and princes who through pressure of temporal affairs had deferred their repentance (vii. 37–136) [Anti-purgatorio]; S. is mentioned as a native of Mantua, and as having abandoned his own native dialect, not only in poetry but in every other form of utterance, and also as having been distinguished for his eloquence, *Sordellus*, V. E. i. 15$^{9-14}$.

Sordello was born (c. 1200) at Goito, village on the Mincio, about ten miles NW. of Mantua; shortly after 1220 he was resident at the court of Count Ricciardo di San Bonifazio at Verona, who had married (c. 1222) Cunizza, daughter of Ezzelino II da Romano (Par. ix. 32). In or about 1226, Sordello, with the connivance of her brother, Ezzelino III (Inf. xii. 109–10), abducted Cunizza, and took her to Ezzelino's court [Cunizza]. Later he formed a liaison with her, and, to escape her brother's resentment, was forced to take refuge in Provence, where he made a lengthened stay at the court of Count Raymond Berenger IV (Par. vi. 134). There he became acquainted with the Count's seneschal, Romieu de Villeneuve (Par. vi. 128). While in Provence (c. 1240) Sordello wrote one of his most important poems, the lament for Blacatz, one of Count Raymond's Provençal barons, from which D. is commonly supposed to have taken the idea of assigning to Sordello the function of pointing out

the various princes in Ante-purgatory (Purg. vii. 49–136). After Count Raymond's death (1245) Sordello remained for some years at the court of his son-in-law, Charles of Anjou (Purg. vii. 113) [Carlo ^{1}]. When the latter in the spring of 1265 set out on his expedition to Italy to take possession of the kingdom of Sicily, Sordello followed him. Sordello's presence in Italy is attested by a brief of Clement IV addressed to Charles (Sept. 22, 1266), in which the Pope refers to the fact that Sordello was in prison at Novara, and urges Charles to procure his release, on the ground of his past services to him—an application which has been taken to indicate that Sordello had been present on the occasion of Charles's crushing defeat of Manfred at the battle of Benevento in the previous February. In any case Sordello was among those who shared in the distribution of Apulian fiefs made by Charles to his Provençal barons after his victories over the Hohenstaufen at Benevento and Tagliacozzo, to Sordello and his heirs being assigned several castles in the Abruzzi, under deeds dated March and June, 1269. No further record of Sordello has been preserved, and the date and place of his death are unknown; there is a tradition that he came to a violent end, which though otherwise unconfirmed is to a certain extent rendered probable by the place assigned to him by D. in Ante-purgatory.

Of Sordello's poems some forty have been preserved, of which the most important, besides the lament for Blacatz already mentioned, is a lengthy didactic poem, the *Ensenha-men*, or *Documentum Honoris*.

Sordellus. [**Sordello.**]

Sorga, Sorgue, small river of France, which rises from a spring in the ravine of Vaucluse (famous as the retreat of Petrarca); the river enters the Rhone a short distance above Avignon after a course of about twenty-five miles.

Charles Martel (in the Heaven of Venus) mentions the confluence of the Sorgue with the Rhone in connexion with Provence (of which he would have been Count had he survived his father Charles II of Naples), Par. viii. 59. [**Provenza: Rodano.**]

Spagna. [**Ispagna.**]

Speculum Juris (more correctly *Speculum Judiciale*), treatise on civil and canon law, written c. 1270 by Wilhelmus Durandus (1237–1296), afterwards (1286) Bishop of Mende in Languedoc.

D., who quotes the treatise simply as *Speculum*, in his Letter to the Italian Cardinals deplores the fact that the works of the Fathers are neglected for those of the canonists and decretalists, Epist. viii. 7[118].

Speusippo, Speusippus, Athenian philosopher, nephew of Plato, whom he succeeded as head of the Academy (B.C. 347–339); mentioned with Plato in connexion with the Academic school of philosophy, Conv. iv. 6[126]. [**Accademici.**]

Sphinx. [**Sfinge.**]

Spiriti Amanti], Spirits of those who were lovers upon earth; placed in the Heaven of Venus, Par. viii–ix. [**Venere, Cielo di.**]

Spiriti Contemplanti], Spirits of those who upon earth led a contemplative life; placed in the Heaven of Saturn, Par. xxi–xxii. 99. [**Saturno, Cielo di.**]

Spiriti Giudicanti], Spirits of those who upon earth loved and exercised justice; placed in the Heaven of Jupiter, Par. xviii. 52–xx. [**Giove, Cielo di.**]

Spiriti Militanti], Spirits of those who upon earth fought for the faith; placed in the Heaven of Mars, Par. xiv. 79–xviii. 51. [**Marte, Cielo di.**]

Spiriti Operanti], Spirits of those who for love of fame performed great deeds upon earth (Par. vi. 112–14); placed in the Heaven of Mercury, Par. v. 85–vii. [**Mercurio, Cielo di.**]

Spiriti Sapienti], Spirits of those who upon earth loved wisdom or were great theologians; placed in the Heaven of the Sun, Par. x–xiv. 78. [**Sole, Cielo del.**]

Spiriti Votivi Mancanti], Spirits of those who upon earth took holy vows but failed to keep them; placed in the Heaven of the Moon, Par. ii. 34–v. 84. [**Luna, Cielo della.**]

Spirito Santo, the Holy Spirit, Purg. xx. 98; Par. iii. 53; xix. 101; xx. 38; xxi. 128; xxiv. 92; xxvii. 1; xxix. 41; V. N. § 30[36]; Conv. ii. 6[69, 86, 90, 110]; iv. 21[107–9]; *Santo Spiro*, Par. xiv. 76; *Spiritus Sanctus*, Mon. i. 16[35]; iii. 3[88], 4[86], 16[67]; Epist. x. 22[413]; *ardente Spiro*, Par. xxiv. 138; *eterno Spiro*, Par. xi. 98; *Spiritus aeternus*, Mon. iii. 4[83]; *Spiritus Patri et Filio coaeternus*, Mon. iii.

1^{30-1}, 16^{67-9}; *Amore*, Par. x. 1; xiii. 57; *primo Amore*, Inf. iii. 6; Par. vi. 11; *eterno Amore*, Par. vii. 33; alluded to, Par. xxxiii. 119–20, 126.

David is referred to as *il cantor dello Spirito Santo*, Par. xx. 38 [**David**]; the Virgin Mary, as *l'unica Sposa Dello Spirito Santo*, Purg. xx. 97–8 [**Maria** [1]]; St. Paul, as *il gran vasello Dello Spirito Santo*, Par. xxi. 127–8 [**Paolo**]; Holy Scripture, as *La larga ploia Dello Spirito Santo*, Par. xxiv. 91–2; *tuba Sancti Spiritus*, Mon. i. 16^{35}; the writers of Holy Scripture, as *gli scrittor dello Spirito Santo*, Par. xxix. 41; the divine will, *il piacer dello Spirito Santo*, Par. iii. 53; the Spirits in the Heaven of the Sun, *vero isfavillar del Santo Spiro*, Par. xiv. 76; the Spirits in the Heaven of Jupiter, *quei lucenti incendi Dello Spirito Santo*, Par. xix. 100–1.

The Holy Spirit the third Person of the Trinity, Inf. iii. 6; Par. vi. 11; vii. 33; x. 1; xiii. 57; xxvii. 1; xxxiii. 119–20, 126; V. N. § 30^{36} [**Trinità**]; proceeding from the Father and the Son, Par. x. 1–3; xiii. 57; Conv. ii. $6^{86-8, 90}$; and co-eternal with them, Mon. iii. 1^{30-1}, 16^{67-9}; love the special attribute of the Holy Spirit, Inf. iii. 6; Par. vi. 11; vii. 33; x. 1; xiii. 57; xxxiii. 126; Conv. ii. $6^{69, 110}$; iv. 21^{106-7}; the seven gifts of the Spirit, according to Isaiah (xi. 2–4), Conv. iv. 21^{108-12}; the Holy Spirit speaks by the mouth of the Scriptures, Par. xx. 38; xxiv. 91–2, 138; xxix. 41; Mon. i. 16^{35}; iii. 4^{86-7}, 16^{67-8}; Epist. x. 22^{413-14}; of the Psalmist, Par. xx. 38; of the Prophets, Mon. iii.

16^{67}; Epist. x. 22^{414}; of the Apostles, Par. xxiv. 138; Mon. iii. 16^{70}; of the Pope, Par. xi. 98; of the Fathers, Mon. iii. 3^{87-9}.

In the celestial Hierarchy it is the function of the Powers to contemplate the Holy Spirit, Conv. ii. 6^{86-9} [**Podestadi**]; and the Thrones are informed with the love thereof, Conv. ii. 6^{109-10} [**Troni**].

Spiro, Santo. [**Spirito Santo.**]

Spoletani, inhabitants of Spoleto; their dialect distinct from those of the Romans and Tuscans, V. E. i. 10^{63-4}; rejected, with those of the Romans and of the inhabitants of the March of Ancona, as unworthy to be the Italian vulgar tongue, V. E. i. 11^{18-21}; has certain affinities with those of Perugia, Orvieto, Viterbo, Città di Castello (or Civita Castellana), and Rome, V. E. i. 13^{29-32}. [**Ducatus: Spoletum.**]

Spoletum, Spoleto, capital of the ancient duchy of that name, in the centre of the modern province of Umbria. [**Ducatus.**]

D. reminds the rebellious Florentines of the fate of Milan and Spoleto, both of which were chastised (the former in 1162, the latter in 1152) for their resistance to the Emperor Frederick Barbarossa, Epist. vi. 5^{135-7}.

Stagirita, native of Stagira, town of Macedonia, in Chalcidice, on the Strymonic Gulf, famous as the birthplace of Aristotle, who was hence surnamed the Stagirite. D., in reference to this fact, speaks of Aristotle as *Aristotile, che Stagirita ebbe soprannome*, Conv. iv. 6^{131-2}. [**Aristotile.**]

Stagno, name of unknown personage (probably Florentine), whose sons, 'i fi' di Stagno', had become a byword on account of their infamous practices (probably the same for which Brunetto Latini and his companions are condemned to Circle VII of Hell, Inf. xv. 101–14); mentioned by D. in his *tenzone* with Forese Donati, Son. liii. 14.

Statius. [**Stazio.**]

Stazio, Roman poet Statius (Publius Papinius Statius), the most eminent poet of the Silver Age, born at Naples, c. A. D. 61, died c. A. D. 96. His chief work is the *Thebaid,* an epic poem in hexameters on the expedition of the Seven against Thebes; he began another epic, the *Achilleid,* on the life of Achilles and the whole Trojan war, but only the first book and part of the second were completed; besides these he published a collection of miscellaneous and occasional poems under the title of *Silvae.* To the *Thebaid* and *Achilleid* D. was indebted for many details of classical mythology. [**Achilleide: Thebaidos.**]

By a poetical fiction, for which there does not appear to be any historical foundation, D. represents Statius as having secretly embraced Christianity before the completion of the *Thebaid,* the means of his conversion having been the famous passage in Virgil's fourth *Eclogue* (*vv.* 5–7), which was commonly regarded in the Middle Ages as prophetic of the coming of Christ (Purg. xxii. 67–91).

D. also, by an error common to mediaeval writers, describes Statius as a native of Toulouse (Purg. xxi. 89)—an error which arose apparently from a confusion by Lactantius (in his commentary on the *Thebaid*) of the poet Statius with a rhetorician of the same name, Lucius Statius, who was born at Toulouse c. A. D. 58.

Statius is placed among the Prodigals in Circle V of Purgatory (whence, having just obtained his release, he accompanies D. and Virgil through the remaining Circles, and into the Terrestrial Paradise, remaining with D. after V. has disappeared, and sharing with the former, as some think, the draught of the water of Eunoë to which Matilda leads them), Purg. xxi. 91; xxii. 25; xxiv. 119; xxv. 29, 32; xxvii. 47; xxxii. 29; xxxiii. 134; *ombra,* xxi. 10; *quello spirto, v.* 86; *ombra, v.* 110; *antico spirto, v.* 122; referred to as *poeta,* Purg. xxii. 115, 139; xxviii. 146; *savio,* Purg. xxiii. 8; xxxiii. 15; *scorta,* Purg. xxvii. 19; *saggio, v.* 69; *maestro, v.* 114; D. refers to V. and S. as *gli spiriti veloci,* Purg. xxii. 9; *li poeti, v.* 115; *li duo poeti, v.* 139; *i savi,* xxiii. 8; *le buone scorte,* xxvii. 19; *li miei saggi, v.* 69; *i gran maestri, v.* 114; *i miei poeti,* xxviii. 146; S., who attracts the attention of Virgil and D. by greeting them, at V.'s request explains the recent phenomenon of the shaking of the Mt. of Purgatory (xxi. 1–72); he then names himself, and relates his own history, how as a poet he drew inspiration from the *Aeneid,* and how he became a Christian under the influence of V.'s prophetic lines in *Eclogue* iv

(*vv.* 73–93; xxii. 64–93); as
they proceed, in answer to a question
of D., he expounds the theory of
generation, and of the development
of the soul, from its first origin in
the embryo to its life in the spiritual
body which it forms to itself after
the mortal body is dead (xxv. 1–
108); finally, after V. has disappeared, he accompanies D. to the
banks of Eunoë (xxxii. 28–xxxiii.
135).

The part played by Statius in the
allegory of the *D. C.* has not been
satisfactorily explained. It has been
suggested that, as Virgil represents
human reason and Beatrice revelation or theology, so Statius typifies
something intermediate, such as
human reason enlightened by Christianity. That D. had in view some
definite piece of symbolism is evident from the precision with which
he indicates the positions of Virgil
and Statius with regard to himself
on their way through Purgatory—
before the fire of purification (Purg.
xxvii. 10–12) is reached D. walks
behind V. and S. (Purg. xxii.
127–8); during the passage through
the fire he is between them, V. being
in front of him and S. behind (Purg.
xxvii. 46–8); but when they reach
the Terrestrial Paradise D. goes in
front, while V. and S. follow behind
(Purg. xxviii. 82, 145–6).

Statius is several times mentioned
in D.'s prose works:—as *Stazio*, in
connexion with his account of Oedipus (*Theb.* i. 47), Conv. iii. 8^{93}
[**Edipo**]; and of Hypsipyle and
Archemorus (*Theb.* v. 609–10),
Conv. iii. 11^{165} [**Archemoro : Isifile**]; as *Stazio il dolce poeta* (cf.

Purg. xxi. 88, and Juvenal, *Sat.* vii·
84–5), in connexion with his account
of Adrastus, Polynices, and Tydeus
(*Theb.* i. 397 ff., 671–81), Conv.
iv. 25^{60, 108} [**Adrasto : Polinice :
Tideo**]; and of Acaste, Argia, and
Deiphyle (*Theb.* i. 537–9), Conv.
iv. 25^{79} [**Aceste** ^2 **: Argia : Deifile**]; and, as *Statius*, as one of
the ʻregulati poetaeʼ, together with
Virgil, Ovid, and Lucan, V. E. ii.
6^{79–81}; Statius is alluded to by
G. del Virgilio, addressing D., as
ʻquem consequeris coeloʼ, Carm. 18.

Stefano, Santo], St. Stephen,
first Christian martyr, who was
stoned outside the gates of Jerusalem by the Hellenistic Jews on
a charge of blasphemy (*Acts* vi–
vii).

D. introduces him as an example
of meekness in Circle III of Purgatory, where the sin of wrath is
expiated, referring to him as *un
giovinetto* (St. Stephen being traditionally represented as a young
man in sacred art), Purg. xv. 106–
14. [**Iracondi.**]

Stefano Urosio], Stephen Ouros
II, King of Rascia (the mediaeval
kingdom of Servia), 1275–1321;
alluded to as *quel di Rascia*, Par.
xix. 140. [**Rascia.**]

Stellato, Cielo. [**Cielo Stellato.**]

Stelle Fisse, Fixed Stars; their
Heaven the eighth, Conv. ii. 3^{23–5},
4^{8–9} [**Cielo Stellato**]; their light
derived by reflection from that of
the Sun, Par. xx. 6; xxiii. 30;
Conv. ii. 14^{125}; iii. 12^{54–6}; their
number 1022, according to the
astronomers (cf. Alfraganus, cap.
19), Conv. ii. 15^{18–22}.

StelleFisse, Cielodelle. [**Cielo Stellato.**]

Stige, Styx, one of the rivers of Hell, Inf. vii. 106; ix. 81; xiv. 116; *fonte*, vii. 101; *palude*, *v.* 106; *tristo ruscel*, *v.* 107; *pantano*, *v.* 110; viii. 12; *acqua*, vii. 103, 118, 119; viii. 16, 30; *limo*, vii. 121; *belletta negra*, *v.* 124; *lorda pozza*, *v.* 127; *fango*, *v.* 129; *sucide onde*, viii. 10; *loto*, *v.* 21; *morta gora*, *v.* 31; *broda*, *v.* 53; *lago*, *v.* 54; *torbid' onde*, ix. 64.

Like the other rivers of Hell, Styx owes its origin to the tears of the 'gran veglio di Creta' (Inf. xiv. 112–19) [**Fiumi Infernali**]. D.'s description of it as 'tristo ruscel' (vii. 107) was no doubt due to the etymology of the name ('a tristitia Styx dicitur') given by Servius (on *Aen.* vi. 134). The idea of representing Styx as a marsh ('palude', vii. 106) was doubtless borrowed from Virgil, who more than once uses the expression 'Stygia palus' (*Aen.* vi. 323, 369).

Stoici, Stoic school of philosophers, so called from the porch (*Stoa*) at Athens where Zeno, the founder of the school, used to teach. Their chief doctrine was that virtue is the supreme end of life, or the highest good. [**Zenone.**]

The Stoics appear to have believed in the immortality of the soul, Conv. ii. 9[65]; Zeno the founder of the school, and Cato of Utica one of his followers, Conv. iv. 6[83–4], [94–5]; the Stoic doctrine that virtue is the sole end of human life, Conv. iv. 6[85–93]; the Stoics, the Peripatetics, and the Epicureans, the three great philosophical schools at Athens,

Conv. iii. 14[138–9]; these three schools the three sects of the active life, symbolized by the three Maries at the sepulchre of our Lord, Conv. iv. 22[159–62]. [*Academicae Quaestiones.*]

Storia di Tebe. [*Thebaidos.*]
Storia Thebana. [*Thebaidos.*]

Strami, Vico degli, Rue du Fouarre (Vicus Stramineus) at Paris, so called from the straw-strewn floors of the Schools; it was close to the river, in the region which is still known as the Quartier Latin, and was the centre of the Arts Schools at Paris.

St. Thomas Aquinas (in the Heaven of the Sun) mentions it in connexion with Siger of Brabant, who taught there, Par. x. 137. [**Sigieri.**]

Stretto di Gibilterra. [**Gibilterra, Stretto di.**]

Stricca, young man of Siena, said by the old commentators to have been a member of the 'Spendthrift Brigade' of Siena and to have dissipated his patrimony in riotous living; he is mentioned by Capocchio (in Bolgia 10 of Circle VIII of Hell) ironically as an exception to the general empty-headedness of the Sienese, and described as having known 'how to make his expenditure moderate', Inf. xxix. 125–6. [**Brigata Spendereccia.**]

Stricca has been identified with Stricca di Giovanni dei Salimbeni of Siena (brother of Niccolò, *v.* 127), who was Podestà of Bologna in 1276 and 1286. [**Niccolò**[1].]

Strofade, Strophades, two small islands in the Ionian Sea, off the coast of Messenia; mentioned in connexion with the Harpies, who drove the Trojans from the islands, Inf. xiii. 11. [Arpie.]

Subasio, Monte. [Monte Subasio.]

Substantia Orbis, De, treatise of Averroës *On the Substance of the World*; his opinion that all potential forms of matter are actually existent in the mind of the Creator, quoted as from this treatise (whereas in fact it occurs in his commentary on *Metaphysics* xii), A. T. § 18³⁶⁻⁹. [Averrois.]

Suicidi], Suicides; placed, together with Spendthrifts, among the Violent in Round 2 of Circle VII of Hell, Inf. xi. 40–1; xiii. 1–151; their punishment is to be transformed into trees, on the leaves of which the Harpies feed, thus causing them excruciating agony, Inf. xiii. 94–108 [Violenti]. *Examples*: Pier delle Vigne [Pier delle Vigne]; and Lotto degli Agli [Agli, Lotto degli].

Summulae Logicales], title of a manual of logic (in twelve parts) compiled by Petrus Hispanus (Pope John XXI); referred to by St. Bonaventura (in the Heaven of the Sun) as *dodici libelli*, Par. xii. 135. [Pietro Ispano.]

Superbi], the Proud; those who expiate the sin of Pride in Purgatory are placed in Circle I, Purg. x–xii. 72 [*Beatitudini*: Purgatorio]; their punishment is to go bowed down beneath heavy weights, Purg. x. 115–19, 130–9; sculptured on the wall of the terrace are instances of Humility, Purg. x. 28–99; viz. the scene of the Annunci-

ation, with the angel Gabriel and the Virgin Mary (*vv.* 34–50) [Gabriello: Maria [1]]; David dancing before the Ark and Michal looking on (*vv.* 52–72) [David: Micol]; the Emperor Trajan and the widow (*vv.* 73–93) [Traiano]; further on, portrayed upon the ground are instances of defeated Pride, Purg. xii. 16–69; viz. the fall of Lucifer (*vv.* 25–7) [Lucifero]; the slaying of Briareus (*vv.* 28–30) [Briareo]; the defeat of the Giants (*vv.* 31–3) [Giganti]; Nimrod at the foot of the Tower of Babel (*vv.* 34–6) [Nembrotto]; Niobe and her dead children (*vv.* 37–9) [Niobe]; Saul transfixed by his own sword on Mt. Gilboa (*vv.* 40–2) [Saul]; Arachne and her ruined web (*vv.* 43–5) [Aragne]; Rehoboam fleeing to Jerusalem after the revolt of the ten tribes (*vv.* 46–8) [Roboam]; the slaying of Eriphyle by her son Alcmaeon (*vv.* 49–51) [Almeone: Erifile]; the slaying of Sennacherib by his sons (*vv.* 52–4) [Sennacherib]; the vengeance of Tomyris upon Cyrus (*vv.* 55–7) [Ciro: Tamiri]; the rout of the Assyrians after the slaying of Holofernes by Judith (*vv.* 58–60) [Assiri: Judit: Oloferne]; the fall of Troy (*vv.* 61–3) [Troia]. *Examples*: Omberto Aldobrandesco [Omberto]; Oderisi of Gubbio [Oderisi]; Provenzano Salvani of Siena [Provenzan Salvani]; Alighiero, D.'s great-grandfather [Alighiero [1]].

Susa, Enrico di. [Enrico di Susa.]

Sylvester. [Silvestro[1].]

T

Tabernic, -icch, -icchi. [Tam-bernic.]

Tacco, Ghin di. [Ghin di Tacco.]

Taddeo, Taddeo d'Alderotto of Florence, celebrated physician, and reputed founder of the scientific school of medicine at the University of Bologna, born c. 1215, died 1295. He wrote commentaries on the works of Hippocrates and Galen, with philosophical illustrations, and owing to his eminence as a physician was surnamed 'Ippocratista'. He also made an Italian translation of the Latin version of Aristotle's *Ethics*.

He is coupled by St. Bonaventura (in the Heaven of the Sun) with Henry of Susa, the Decretalist, Par. xii. 83 (where the two represent the *iura ed aforismi* of Par. xi. 4). [*Aforismi*: Decretalistae]; D. speaks with contempt of his trans-lation (as is supposed) of the *Ethics*, Conv. i. 10⁷⁰⁻¹.

Tagliacozzo, village of Central Italy, in the Abruzzi, about twenty miles S. of Aquila, in the neighbour-hood of which Charles of Anjou, with the help of the veteran Erard de Valéry, by means of a stratagem, with inferior numbers, defeated Conradin, the last of the Hohen-staufen (Aug. 23, 1268), Inf. xxviii. 17. [Alardo: Curradino.]

Tagliamento, torrential river of N. Italy, which rises in the Carnic Alps above Tolmezzo, and flowing through the province of Udine in Venetia, falls into the upper Adriatic some forty miles NE. of Venice.

Cunizza (in the Heaven of Venus) mentions the Tagliamento as one of the boundaries of the March of Treviso, whose peoples she refers to as *la turba presente, Che Taglia-mento e Adice richiude*, Par. ix. 43–4. [Adice: Marca Trivisiana.]

Taide, Thais, name of courtesan introduced by Terence in his *Eunu-chus* (iii. 1).

D. places her (as if she were a real person and not merely a fictitious character in a play) among the Flat-terers in Bolgia 2 of Circle VIII of Hell (Malebolge), Inf. xviii. 133; *sozza e scapigliata fante, v.* 130 (cf. *Isaiah* iii. 16, 24) [Adulatori]; she is pointed out by Virgil, who says that she is the harlot who, when asked by her paramour, 'Have I great thanks with thee?' answered, 'Nay, marvellous' (*vv.* 133–5). This passage from the *Eunuchus* is here quoted by D., not direct from the play of Terence (with which he was probably not acquainted), but from the *De Amicitia* of Cicero (§ 98) where it is introduced in illustration of the habitual exaggeration indulged in by flatterers. D., through ignor-ance of the context of the play itself, has attributed to Thais (whom he describes as a harlot perhaps by confusion with the Athenian cour-tesan) the reply ('ingentes') put by

Terence into the mouth of the parasite Gnatho, to whom (and not to Thais, as D. supposes) Thraso's question is addressed. [**Terenzio.**]

Talamone, small sea-port on the Tyrrhenian Sea, situated on a promontory of the same name in the SW. extremity of the Sienese Maremma.

In 1303 the harbour of Talamone was purchased by the Sienese, who were eager for an outlet to the sea, but the enterprise was a failure on account of the expense entailed by the constant dredging operations to keep the entrance clear, and also because of the malaria with which it was infected.

The hopes of the Sienese with regard to Talamone are referred to mockingly by Sapia (in Circle II of Purgatory), who prophesies that her fellow-citizens will lose both money and lives in the project, and will in the end be more disappointed even than in their search for the stream Diana, Purg. xiii. 151–4. [**Diana**[2].]

Tale. [**Talete.**]

Talete, Thales, Ionic philosopher, and one of the Seven Sages, born at Miletus c. B.C. 636, died c. B.C. 546; placed among the great philosophers of antiquity in Limbo, *Tale*, Inf. iv. 137 [**Limbo**]; mentioned as one of the Seven Sages, *Talete*, Conv. iii. 11[39] [**Biante**].

Tamberlic. [**Tambernic.**]

Tambernic, name of mountain mentioned by D. in connexion with the ice of Cocytus, which he says was so thick that it would not even crack if Tambernic were to fall upon it, Inf. xxxii. 28–30. [**Cocito.**]

This mountain has not been identified. Some think the reference is to the Frushka Gora ridge, immediately S. of the Danube (some seventy miles above Belgrade), in the neighbourhood of Tovarnik in Syrmia at the E. extremity of Slavonia; others suggest the mountain of Javornik, near Adelsberg, in the neighbourhood of the lake of Zirknitz in Carniola; or a mountain named Tovarnich, in the district of Fotcha, on the frontiers of Bosnia, Herzegovina, and Montenegro.

Tamigi, river Thames; mentioned to indicate London (or, more precisely, Westminster Abbey), in connexion with the heart of Prince Henry 'of Almain', Inf. xii. 120 [**Arrigo**[6].]

Tamiri, Tomyris, Queen of the Massagetae, Scythian people, by whom Cyrus was defeated and slain, B. C. 529.

D. mentions T. in connexion with the story (which he got from Orosius, *Hist.* ii. 7, § 6) of her revenge for the treacherous slaughter of her son by Cyrus, how after his defeat and death she had his head cut off and thrown into a vessel full of human gore, and mocked it, Purg. xii. 55–7; the defeat of Cyrus and his death at the hands of Tomyris (whom D., following Orosius, calls 'Queen of the Scythians') in the midst of his dream of universal empire, *Tamiris*, Mon. ii. 9[43–8]. [**Ciro.**]

Tamiris. [**Tamiri.**]

[**Tana**], (i. e. Gaetana), half-sister of Dante, daughter of Alighiero and his second wife, Lapa Cialuffi; mentioned by Forese Donati in his *tenzone* with D. as *la Tana*, Son. liii.* 10 [Alighiero [2]: Dante: Table A].

Tanai, river Don (classical Tanais), which rises in the heart of Russia, and discharges into the NE. extremity of the Sea of Azov; mentioned as a typical instance of a river which is ice-bound during the winter, Inf. xxxii. 27.

Tarlati, Cione de'. [Cione de' Tarlati.]

Tarpeia, Tarpeian hill at Rome on which, in the temple of Saturn, was placed the Roman treasury; mentioned in connexion with the violation of the latter by Julius Caesar in B.C. 49, after the vain attempt of the tribune Metellus to defend it, Purg. ix. 137. [Metello.]

Tarpeius, Tarpeian, hence Roman; *signa Tarpeia*, the Roman Eagle, Epist. vii. 1[17]. [Aquila [1].]

Tarquinii, Tarquin kings of Rome, i. e. Lucius Tarquinius Priscus, the fifth king, who succeeded Ancus Marcius, and reigned thirty-eight years, and Lucius Tarquinius Superbus, the seventh and last king, who succeeded his father-in-law, Servius Tullius, and reigned twenty-four years, until his banishment, B.C. 510.

D. (following Virgil, *Aen.* vi. 818) uses the term to include not only the two Tarquin kings, but also Servius Tullius, since he enumerates the seven kings of Rome as *Romolo, Numa, Tullo, Anco, e li re* (var. *tre*) *Tarquinii*, Conv. iv. 5[89—91]. Tullius, though not actually a Tarquin, was closely connected with the Tarquin family. His mother having been a slave of Tanaquil, wife of

Tarquinius Priscus, he was born in the royal palace, and brought up as the king's son; further, his wife was the daughter of Tarquinius Priscus, while his own two daughters married the sons of Tarquinius.

Tarquino, Lucius Tarquinius Superbus, seventh and last king of Rome, the Tarquins having been expelled by the Romans, at the instigation of Lucius Junius Brutus, after the rape of Lucrece by Sextus Tarquinius; mentioned in connexion with Brutus, who is referred to as *quel Bruto che cacciò Tarquino*, Inf. iv. 127. [Bruto [1]: Lucrezia.]

[**Tartareus**], belonging to Tartarus, infernal; *Tartareum praeceps*, the abyss of Hell, Carm. 10.

Tartari, Tartars, name applied loosely in the Middle Ages to the inhabitants of Central Asia, from the Caspian eastwards.

D. mentions them, together with the Turks, in connexion with the brilliancy of the colouring and design of the cloths (famous in the Middle Ages) manufactured by them, Inf. xvii. 17; and couples them with the Jews and Saracens as believing in the immortality of the soul, Conv. ii. 9[70-1].

Taumante, Thaumas, son of Pontus and Ge, and father of Iris by the ocean-nymph Electra; hence Iris is referred to as *la figlia di Taumante*, Purg. xxi. 50 (cf. *Aen.* ix. 5; *Metam.* xiv. 845; and Cicero, *Nat. Deor.* iii. 20). [Iri.]

Taurinum, Turin, city of N. Italy, at the confluence of the Dora Riparia and the Po, in the centre of the modern Piedmont; coupled with Trent and Alessandria della

Paglia as being on the confines of Italy and consequently incapable of preserving a pure dialect owing to the introduction of foreign elements, V. E. i. 15[61-4].

Tauro, Taurus ('the Bull'), constellation and second sign of the Zodiac, which the Sun enters about April 20.

D. indicates, approximately, the hour of 2 p.m. by saying that 'the meridian circle had been left by the Sun to Taurus, and by Night to Scorpio' (the opposite sign), Purg. xxv. 2–3 [Scorpio]; Gemini, which is the third sign of the Zodiac, is referred to as *il segno Che segue il Tauro*, Par. xxii. 110–11 [Gemelli]; Taurus, as being the next sign after Aries, is referred to as *altra stella*, Purg. xxxii. 57. [Zodiaco.]

Tebaide. [*Thebaidos.*]

Tebaldello, called by some Tribaldello, member of the Zambrasi family of Faenza, who in order to avenge a private grudge (due, according to the popular belief, to a dispute about some pigs) against some of the Ghibelline Lambertazzi (who after their expulsion from Bologna in 1274 had taken refuge in Faenza), treacherously opened the gates of that city in the early morning of Nov. 13, 1280, to their Guelf opponents, the Geremei of Bologna, who, in the words of a contemporary chronicler, 'rushed like wild beasts upon their prey, killing and wounding and spoiling in every direction'. Tebaldello himself was killed two years later (1282) during the assault on Forlì under John of Appia. [Forlì.]

T. is placed among the Traitors in Antenora, the second division of Circle IX of Hell, where he is named by Bocca degli Abati, who refers to him as *Tebaldello, Ch'aprì Faenza quando si dormia*, Inf. xxxii. 122–3. [Antenora.]

Tebaldo [1]], Thibaut IV, Count of Champagne, 1201–1253; he succeeded his uncle, Sancho VII, as King of Navarre, under the title of Teobaldo I, in 1234; he died in 1253. Thibaut, who took part, with Louis VIII of France, in the Crusade against the Albigenses, is celebrated for his passion, real or feigned, for Blanche of Castile, grand-daughter of Henry II of England, wife of Louis VIII, and mother of St. Louis. As a song-writer he stands at the head of the lyric poets of N. France during Cent. xiii.

D. refers to him as *Rex Navarrae*, V. E. i. 9[26]; ii. 5[37], 6[56]; his line, *De fin* (correctly *fine*) *amor si vient sen et bonté*, quoted for an instance of the use of the French word *Amor*, V. E. i. 9[27]; and again, as an example of an endecasyllabic line, V. E. ii. 5[38].

The line *Ire d'amor qui en mon cor repaire*, adduced as an example of the illustrious style, and attributed to Thibaut, V. E. ii. 6[56-7], in reality belongs to another Champenois poet, Gaces Brulez, a contemporary and friend of Thibaut—a wrong attribution, which, as the passage now stands, may be due to the accidental omission in MSS. of a line of Thibaut's, and of the name of Gaces Brulez before the line here attributed to the former.

Thibaut's eldest son, Teobaldo II of Navarre, is mentioned, Inf. xxii. 52 [Tebaldo ²]; and his second son, Enrique I of Navarre, is referred to, Purg. vii. 104, 109 [Arrigo ⁷ : Navarra : Table M].

Tebaldo ², Thibaut V, Count of Champàgne, King of Navarre (as Teobaldo II), 1253–1270; he was the eldest son of Teobaldo I of Navarre, and elder brother of Enrique I, and son-in-law of Louis IX of France, whose daughter Isabelle he married in 1258 [Tebaldo ¹ : Table M]. He accompanied St. Louis on his disastrous expedition against Tunis in 1270, and died on his way home at Trapani in Sicily in the same year. Ciampolo, the Navarrese barrator (in Bolgia 5 of Circle VIII of Hell), refers to him as *il buon re Tebaldo*, Inf. xxii. 52. [Ciampolo.]

Tebana, Storia. [*Thebaidos.*]

Tebani, Thebans; mentioned in connexion with Amphiaraus, who was swallowed up by the earth during the siege of Thebes, Inf. xx. 32 [Anfiarao]; the Theban worshippers of Bacchus on the banks of the Asopus and Ismenus, Purg. xviii. 93 [Asopo]; referred to as *il sangue tebano*, in connexion with Juno's wrath against them on Semele's account, Inf. xxx. 2 [Semelè].

Tebano, Theban; *il sangue tebano*, i. e. the Theban race, Inf. xxx. 2 [Tebani]; *la Tebana Storia*, i. e. the *Thebaid*, Conv. iv. 25⁶¹ [*Thebaidos*].

Tebe, Thebes, capital of Boeotia, on the river Ismenus ; according to tradition it was founded by Cadmus,

and was the birthplace of Bacchus; the walls were said to have been built, with the help of the Muses, by Amphion, at the sound of whose lyre the stones moved into their places of their own accord. In consequence of the dispute as to the sovereignty between Eteocles and Polynices, sons of Oedipus, an expedition against the city on behalf of Polynices, known as the war of the Seven against Thebes, was undertaken by Adrastus, King of Argos, who was accompanied by Amphiaraus, Capaneus, Hippomedon, Parthenopaeus, Polynices, and Tydeus; but, as had been foretold by Amphiaraus, the expedition ended disastrously, Adrastus being the only one of the Seven who lived to return.

Thebes is mentioned in connexion with Capaneus and the expedition of Adrastus, Inf. xiv. 69; xxv. 15 [Adrasto : Capaneo]; the madness of Athamas, Inf. xxx. 22 [Atamante]; the building of its walls by Amphion, Inf. xxxii. 11 [Anfione]; Pisa, on account of its cruel treatment of Ugolino, referred to as a second Thebes, Inf. xxxiii. 89 [Pisa]; its history the subject of the *Thebaid* of Statius, Purg. xxi. 92 ; xxii. 89 ; Conv. iv. 25⁷²⁻⁸⁰ [Stazio : *Thebaidos*]; referred to, in connexion with the wanderings of Manto, daughter of Tiresias, after the fall of the city, as *la città di Baco*, Inf. xx. 59 [Bacco : Manto].

Tebe, Storia di. [*Thebaidos.*]

Tecni. [*Tegni.*]

Tedeschi, Germans, Inf. xvii. 21 ; Conv. i. 7⁸⁶ ; *Alamanni*, V.E.

i. 8[59]; *Teutonici*, V. E. i. 8[30]; their gluttonous habits, Inf. xvii. 21; coupled with the English, as foreigners to whom the commentary on the *Convivio* would have been intelligible if written in Latin, Conv. i. 7[84–7]; their tongue one of several into which the original language of Europe was divided, V. E. i. 8[29–32]; their country the boundary of the domain of the *langue d'*oïl on the N. and W., V. E. i. 8[59–60]. [*Lingua Oil.*]

Tedesco [1], German; *Alberto Tedesco*, i.e. the Emperor Albert I of Austria, Purg. vi. 97 [Alberto [2]]; *ripe tedesche*, i.e. the banks of the Danube on its course through Germany, Par. viii. 66; a German unable to distinguish Provençal from Italian, Conv. i. 6[55–6] [*Lingua Oc*].

Tedesco [2], the German language; a knowledge of Latin does not enable a man to distinguish German from other vernaculars, Conv. i. 6[53–5].

Tegghiaio. [Aldobrandi, Tegghiaio.]

Tegni, Li, i.e. τέχνη (ἰατρική), the *Methodus Medendi*, 'Art of Healing', otherwise known as *Ars Parva*, of Galen; coupled with the 'Aphorisms' of Hippocrates as inappropriate gifts from a physician to a knight, Conv. i. 8[31–3]. [Galieno.]

Telamon, mentioned as being the son of Aeacus, the brother of Peleus and Phocus, and the father of Ajax, Conv. iv. 27[192–4]. [Eaco.]

Telemaco], Telemachus, son of Ulysses and Penelope; he was still an infant when Ulysses went to Troy, and after his father had been absent for nearly twenty years he set out in quest of tidings of him; on his return home he found that Ulysses had come back.

Ulysses (in Bolgia 8 of Circle VIII of Hell) relates how his desire to travel and see the world was more powerful than his love for his old father or for his young son, Inf. xxvi. 94–9. [Ulisse.]

Temi, Themis, daughter of Uranus (Heaven) and Ge (Earth); she was regarded as a prophetic divinity, and was supposed to have been Apollo's predecessor at Delphi.

D. mentions Themis, together with the Sphinx, in connexion with his mysterious prophecy of the DXV, Purg. xxxiii. 47 [DXV : Sfinge]; he says the mystery shall be solved 'without scathe of herds or crops' (*v.* 51), an allusion to the account given by Ovid (*Metam.* vii. 762–5) of how, after the riddle of the Sphinx had been solved by Oedipus, Themis in anger sent a monster to ravage the flocks and fields of the Thebans.

Templari], Knights Templars; their destruction by Philip IV of France, alluded to by Hugh Capet (in Circle V of Purgatory), Purg. xx. 91–3. [Clemente [2] : Filippo [2].]

The Knights Templars were one of the three great military orders founded in Cent. xii for the defence of the Latin Kingdom of Jerusalem. After having existed as a powerful and wealthy order for nearly two centuries they were in 1307 accused by Philip the Fair of heresy, sacrilege, and other hideous offences, in consequence of which he ordered their arrest, and by means of diabolical tortures wrung from them confessions (for the most part undoubtedly false) of their alleged enormities. Five years later, at Philip's instigation, they were condemned by Clement V, and the order was suppressed by decree of the Council of Vienne (May, 1312); in the following year the Grand Master, Du Molay, was burned alive at Paris in the presence of the king. The French king's motive in aiming at the destruction of the Templars was, it can hardly be doubted, a desire to get possession of the immense wealth of the order, as is implied by D., and stated in so many words by Villani (viii. 92).

Terentius. [Terenzio.]

Terenzio, Terence (Publius Terentius Afer), celebrated Roman comic poet, born at Carthage, B.C. 195; died in Greece, B.C. 159; his extant works consist of six comedies.

T. is mentioned, together with Caecilius, Plautus, and Varro (or Varius), by Statius (in Purgatory), who asks Virgil for news of them, and is told that they and Persius and many others are with Homer and V. himself in Limbo, Purg. xxii. 97 [Limbo]; he is mentioned again, in connexion with his plays, which are referred to as justifying the definition of a comedy as a play with a happy ending, *Terentius*, Epist. x. 10²⁰³⁻⁶.

D. shows no direct acquaintance with the works of Terence; the quotation from the *Eunuchus* (Inf. xviii. 133–5), which some think argues a first-hand knowledge of the play, is undoubtedly taken at second-hand from Cicero's *De Amicitia* [Taide].

Terra ¹, Tellus (Greek Ge), personification of the Earth, the first being that sprang from Chaos; she gave birth to Uranus (Heaven) and Pontus (Sea), and by the former became the mother of the Titans or Giants.

The Giants referred to as her sons, *i figli della terra*, Inf. xxxi. 121 (cf. Conv. iii. 3⁵⁵⁻⁶³) [Giganti]; her prayer to Jupiter that he would slay Phaëthon for scorching the earth by driving the chariot of the Sun too close to it (*Metam*. ii. 272–300), Purg. xxix. 118–20 [Fetonte].

Terra ², Earth, the terrestrial globe, Purg. xix. 3; xxix. 119; Conv. ii. 7¹⁰⁷, 14⁹⁷, 15¹⁴², ¹⁴⁴; Conv. iii. 5²⁴⁻¹⁶⁰; iv. 8⁵⁷, ⁵⁹; A.T. §§ 3¹⁶, 12¹⁶, 13⁷, 22¹², 23¹⁰; referred to as *vostro mondo*, Par. ix. 119; *questo globo*, Par. xxii. 134; *l'aiuola che ci fa tanto feroci*, Par. xxii. 151; *questo mondo*, Conv. iii. 5²⁰⁻⁹, 6⁸; *questa palla*, Conv. iii. 5⁹⁵⁻²⁰⁰; its natural frigidity, Purg. xix. 3; nearly set on fire when Phaëthon was driving the chariot of the Sun, Purg. xxix. 119 [Fetonte: Terra ¹]; its shadow (Par. xxx. 3) extends as far as the sphere of Venus, where it comes to a point, Par. ix. 118–19; insignificant appearance of the Earth as seen from the Heaven of the Fixed Stars, whence it was visible 'from its hills to its rivermouths', Par. xxii. 134–5, 151–3; its diameter (6,500 miles), Conv. ii. 7¹⁰⁶⁻⁸, 14⁹⁷⁻⁸; iv. 8⁵⁹⁻⁶⁰; twenty-eight times greater than that of Mercury, Conv. ii. 14⁹²⁻⁸; five and a half times less than that of the Sun, Conv. iv. 8⁵⁶⁻⁸ [Sole]; its circumference (20,400 miles), Conv. iii. 5⁸⁰⁻¹⁰⁷; A.T. §§ 3¹⁶, 23¹⁰; its centre, Inf. xxxiv. 107; Conv. ii. 7¹⁰⁷; iii. 3¹¹; A.T. §§ 3⁶, 12¹⁶, 13⁷, ⁴⁶; *lo mezzo Al quale ogni gra-*

vezza si raduna, Inf. xxxii. 73–4; *il punto Al qual si traggon d'ogni parte i pesi*, Inf. xxxiv. 111; coincident with the centre of the universe, A. T. §§ 3[6], 12[16]; the point to which all weights are attracted, Inf. xxxii. 73–4; xxxiv. 111; the distance from the circumference of the Earth to its centre 3,250 miles, Conv. ii. 7[106–8]; if the movement of the *Primum Mobile* were to be suspended, the Sun and planets would be invisible from the Earth for half their revolutions, Conv. ii. 15[132–57]; the Pythagorean theory that the Earth is a star, and that there is a 'counter-Earth', and that both of them revolve, also that the central place in the universe is occupied, not by the Earth, but by Fire, Conv. iii. 5[29–37] [**Pittagora**]; the Platonic theory, as set forth in the *Timaeus* (40), as to the position of the Earth in the centre of the universe, and as to its motion, which is axial but not orbital, and very slow, on account of the grossness of its substance, and of its immense distance from the revolving heaven with which its revolution keeps time, Conv. iii. 5[45–52] [**Platone**]; these theories rejected by Aristotle, who held (in the *De Coelo*) that the Earth is fixed immovably as the centre of the universe, and has consequently neither orbital nor axial motion, Conv. iii. 5[53–65].

D.'s statement (Par. ix. 118–19) that the shadow of the Earth extends as far as the sphere of Venus, where it comes to a point, is based upon what Alfraganus says in his chapter on the eclipse of the Moon (cap. xxviii); he there states that the shadow (which, as he explains, owing to the fact that the Sun is larger than the Earth, must be conical, thus terminating in a point) is projected to a distance equal to 268 half-diameters of the Earth, i. e. $3250 \times 268 = 871,000$ miles. The least distance of Venus herself from the Earth Alfraganus puts at 542,750 miles; her greatest distance he puts at 3,640,000, giving a mean of 2,091,375 miles (cap. xxi). According to these *data* the Earth's shadow would project $871,000 - 542,750 = 328,250$ miles beyond Venus, when she was nearest to the Earth; and would fall short of her by $3,640,000 - 871,000 = 2,769,000$ miles, when she was furthest off. The calculation as to the least distance of Venus from the Earth is mentioned by D. in the *Convivio* (ii. 7[104–8]).

D. was also indebted to Alfraganus (cap. 8) for the *data* as to the diameter and circumference of the Earth. The measurement of the circumference of the Earth is not stated directly by D., but is indicated in his calculations as to the relative positions of Rome and of his two imaginary cities *Maria* and *Lucia*, Conv. iii. 5[80–107]. He places *Maria* at the N. Pole at 2,700 miles from Rome, and *Lucia* at the S. Pole at 7,500 miles from Rome; further he gives the distance between *Maria* and *Lucia* (i. e. the half-circumference of the Earth), in whatever direction the measure be taken, as 10,200 miles; whence we get 20,400 miles as the measurement of the whole circumference.

The relative proportions of the

diameters of the Earth, the Sun, and Mercury were likewise derived by D. from Alfraganus (Capp. 22, 24).

Terra, Quaestio de Aqua et. [*Quaestio de Aqua et Terra.*]

Terra Santa. [Palestina.]

Teruccio Donati], son of Manetto Donati, and brother of Gemma, D.'s wife; he was a member of a religious order and bachelor of divinity, and was probably the correspondent whom D. addresses as 'Pater', Epist. ix. 2^{22}, 4^{41}; in this case the nephew referred to (§ 2^{13-14}) would be Niccolò, son of Foresino (or Forese) Donati, another brother of Gemma's. [Niccolò Donati.]

Tervisina, Marchia. [Marca Trivisiana.]

Terzo Cielo. [Venere, Cielo di.]

Tesauro de' Beccheria. [Beccheria.]

Teseo, Theseus, son of Aegeus, whom he succeeded as King of Athens. In his youth he went of his own accord as one of the seven young men whom, with seven maidens, the Athenians were obliged to send every year to Crete as tribute to the Minotaur; by the help of Ariadne, daughter of Minos, who fell in love with him, he slew the monster; he then carried off Ariadne from Crete, but abandoned her at Naxos on his way home. He was a close friend of Pirithous, King of the Lapithae, whom he aided in their fight with the Centaurs. Accompanied by Pirithous he attempted to carry off Proserpine from the lower world; but the attempt was unsuccessful, Pirithous being

slain, and Theseus himself being kept prisoner, until he was eventually released by Hercules. On his return the Athenians refused to receive him as their king, whereupon he retired to Scyros, and was there slain by Lycomedes, the king of the island.

D. mentions Theseus in connexion with his descent to Hell, and escape thence, Inf. ix. 54; his fight with the Centaurs, Purg. xxiv. 121–3 [Centauri]; he is referred to as *il duca d'Atene*, in connexion with his slaying of the Minotaur and Ariadne's love for him, Inf. xii. 17–20 [Arianna : Minotauro].

Tesifone, Tisiphone, one of the Furies; placed by D. with Megaera and Alecto to guard the entrance to the City of Dis, Inf. ix. 48. [Erine.]

Tesoro, the *Trésor* of Brunetto Latini; recommended to D. by the author, on parting from him (in Round 3 of Circle VII of Hell), as his chief claim to immortality, Inf. xv. 119–20. [Brunetto Latini.]

Li Livres dou Tresor, which is Brunetto's most important work, was written for the most part during his exile in France, between 1262 and 1266; it is a sort of encyclopaedia, compiled from various sources, in French prose, and is divided into three parts; the first treats of universal history (that of Italy being brought down to the execution of Conradin after the battle of Tagliacozzo), the origin of the universe, astronomy, geography, and natural history; the second treats of 'vices and virtues'; the third treats of rhetoric and politics, with especial reference to the constitution and government of the cities of Italy. The work, the popularity of which in the Middle Ages is attested by the numerous MSS. of it, in spite of its great length, was translated into Italian during Brunetto's lifetime (this version being one of the first books printed in Italy).

Tessa (i. e. Contessa), name of the wife of Simone Donati, and mother of Forese Donati; mentioned by D. in his *tenzone* with Forese, *monna Tessa*, Son. liv. 2.

Testamento, Nuovo. [**Bibbia.**]

Testamento, Vecchio. [**Bibbia.**]

Teti, Thetis, one of the Nereids, daughter of Nereus and Doris; she was wedded to Peleus, by whom she became the mother of Achilles. Virgil, addressing Statius (in Purgatory), mentions her as being 'delle genti tue' (i. e. mentioned in the *Thebaid* or *Achilleid*) among the famous women of antiquity in Limbo, Purg. xxii. 112 [**Antigone : Limbo**]; she is referred to as *la madre (di Achille)*, in connexion with her removal of Achilles to Scyros, Purg. ix. 37 [**Achille : Schiro.**]

Teucri, name by which the Trojans were sometimes called, as being the descendants of Teucer, first king of Troy; Virgil's use of the name quoted (*Aen.* viii. 136), Mon. ii. 3[75]; (*Aen.* i. 235), Mon. ii. 9[85]. [**Troiani.**]

Teutonici. [**Tedeschi.**]

Tever, -ero. [**Tevere.**]

Tevere, river Tiber, which rises in the Etruscan Apennines about twenty miles E. of the source of the Arno, and flows past Rome into the Tyrrhenian Sea, which it enters by two mouths near Ostia; referred to as *Tevero*, Purg. ii. 101; Par. xi. 106; *Tever*, Inf. xxvii. 30; *Tevere*, Conv. iv. 13[130]; *Tiberis*, Mon. ii. 4[68]; Epist. vii. 7[139]; viii. 10[149]; its source in the Apennines, Inf. xxvii. 30 [**Apennino** [1]]; its mouth, where the souls destined for Purgatory collect, Purg. ii. 101, 103; the mountain of La Vernia, situated between its source and that of the Arno, Par. xi. 106 [**Alvernia** [2]]; the inhabitants of Lower Italy described as *i Latini dalla parte di Tevere*, as distinguished from those of Upper Italy, *dalla parte di Po*, Conv. iv. 13[129–30]; Cloelia's exploit in swimming across it from Porsena's camp, Mon. ii. 4[65–9] [**Cloelia**]; the Emperor Henry VII urged by D. to come and destroy the noxious beast (i. e. Florence), which drinks not of Po, nor of Tiber, but of Arno, Epist. vii. 7[139–41]; the Roman Cardinals adjured by their love for the sacred river with which they had been familiar from their childhood, Epist. viii. 10[149].

Thebaidos, *Thebaid* of Statius; quoted as *Thebaidos*, Conv. iii. 11[166]; *Tebana Storia*, Conv. iv. 25[61]; *Libro di Tebe*, Conv. iv. 25[80]. [**Stazio.**]

D. quotes from it twice directly, the passages quoted being more or less freely translated :—Conv. iii. 8[94–5] (*Theb.* i. 47) [**Edipo**]; Conv. iii. 11[167–9] (*Theb.* v. 609–10) [**Archemoro : Isifile**]; it is quoted indirectly, Conv. iv. 25[60–5] (*Theb.* i. 397 ff., 482–97) [**Adrasto : Polinice : Tideo**]; Conv. iv. 25[80–8]

(*Theb.* i. 529–39) [**Aceste**[2] : **Argia : Deifile**]; Conv. iv. 25[109–16] (*Theb.* i. 671–81) [**Adrasto : Edipo : Polinice**].

D. was also indebted to the *Thebaid* for details as to the following:—the Furies, Inf. ix. 38–42 (*Theb.* i. 103 ff.) [**Erine**]; the celestial messenger, Inf. ix. 80–90 (*Theb.* ii. 2 ff.); Capaneus, Inf. xiv. 51–60 (*Theb.* ii. 599–600, x. 883 ff.) [**Capaneo**]; Hypsipyle, Inf. xviii. 92 (*Theb.* v. 240 ff., 404–85; vi. 142); Purg. xxii. 112 (*Theb.* iv. 717–84); Purg. xxvi. 94–5 (*Theb.* v. 541 ff., 720–22); Conv. iii. 11[165–9] (*Theb.* iv. 785–92; v. 499 ff.) [**Isifile**]; Amphiaraus, Inf. xx. 31 ff. (*Theb.* vii. 794 ff., viii. 1 ff.) [**Anfiarao**]; the funeral pyre of Eteocles and Polynices, Inf. xxvi. 52–4 (*Theb.* xii. 429–32) [**Eteocle**]; Briareus, and the overthrow of the Giants, Inf. xxxi. 98; Purg. xii. 28–33 (*Theb.* ii. 595 ff.) [**Briareo**]; Tydeus and Menalippus, Inf. xxxii. 130–1; xxxiii. 76 (*Theb.* viii. 739 ff., 757) [**Menalippo**]; the necklace of Harmonia, Purg. xii. 50–1 (*Theb.* ii. 265 ff.) [**Armonia**]; the Theban worshippers of Bacchus on the banks of Ismenus and Asopus, Purg. xviii. 91–3 (*Theb.* ix. 434 ff.) [**Asopo**]; Statius' indebtedness to the *Aeneid*, Purg. xxi. 94–9 (*Theb.* xii. 816–17) [**Stazio**]; his invocation of Clio, Purg. xxii. 58 (*Theb.* i. 41; x. 630) [**Cliò**]; the simile of the rowers, Par. xxv. 133–5 (*Theb.* vi. 799–801, in some edd. 774–6); the simile of the bough bending before the breeze, Par. xxvi. 85–7 (*Theb.* vi. 854 ff., in some edd. 829 ff.).

Theophilus, name of the person addressed by St. Luke at the beginning of his Gospel (i. 3) and of the Acts (i. 1); St. Luke's words to him touching Christ's sayings and doings (*Acts* i. 1), quoted, Mon. iii. 9[137–9].

Thessalia, Thessaly, division of Greece, bounded on the N. by Macedonia, on the W. by Mt. Pindus, and on the E. by the Aegean; towards the S. of it is the territory of Pharsalia, in which is situated Pharsalus, the scene of the defeat of Pompey by Julius Caesar, B. C. 48.

In his Letter to the Princes and Peoples of Italy D. indicates Tuscany under the name of Thessaly, and covertly threatens Florence with the fate of Pompey at Pharsalus, Epist. v. 3[46–9]. [**Farsaglia**[1].]

Thessalonicenses, Epistola ad], St. Paul's Epistle to the Thessalonians; quoted, Mon. iii. 1[22] (1 *Thessal.* v. 8).

[**Thestylis**], name (borrowed from Virgil, *Ecl.* ii. 10, 43) of a character in the Eclogues addressed to D. by G. del Virgilio, supposed to represent a friend of the writer, Ecl. R. 59.

Thomas. [**Tommaso**[2].]

Thomas Faventinus. [**Faenza, Tommaso da.**]

Thuscia. [**Tuscia.**]

Tiberis. [**Tevere.**]

Tiberius, Tiberius Claudius Nero, adopted son and successor of Augustus, Roman Emperor, A.D. 14–37; referred to as *Tiberius Caesar*, Mon. ii. 13[46–7]; *Tiberius*, Mon. ii. 13[55]; *Caesar*, Epist. v.

10[159]; *il terzo Cesare* (D. regarding Julius Caesar as the first Roman Emperor), Par. vi. 86; the Emperor Justinian (in the Heaven of Mercury), referring to the fact that Christ was crucified under Tiberius, says that all the deeds that ever were or would be done under the auspices of the Roman Eagle shrink into insignificance beside the supreme event which took place during the reign of Tiberius, for to the Roman Eagle under him was granted the glory of avenging the sin of Adam, Par. vi. 82—90; Christ judged not by Herod, but by Pilate, as the deputy of Tiberius, Mon. ii. 13[45—58]; Epist. v. 10[159]. [**Romani** [1].]

Tideo, Tydeus, son of Oeneus, King of Calydon; being forced to fly from Calydon on account of a murder he had committed, he took refuge with Adrastus, King of Argos, who gave him his daughter Deiphyle to wife, by whom he became the father of Diomed. He accompanied Adrastus on the expedition of the Seven against Thebes, and was there wounded by Menalippus, whom he succeeded in slaying, though the wound he had received was mortal; as he lay upon the ground Minerva appeared to him with a remedy, which was to make him immortal, but, finding him engaged in gnawing the head of Menalippus (which had been brought to him by Amphiaraus with the design of defeating the object of the goddess), she turned away in horror and left him to die.

D. compares Ugolino gnawing the head of the Archbishop Ruggieri in Circle IX of Hell to Tydeus

gnawing that of Menalippus, Inf. xxxii. 130-2 [**Menalippo : Ugolino**]; his adventures with Polynices at the court of Adrastus, as narrated by Statius in the *Thebaid*, Conv. iv. 25[60—4, 78—88] [**Adrasto**].

Tifeo, Typhoeus (otherwise called Typhon), hundred-headed monster who attempted to acquire the sovereignty of gods and men, but was quelled by Jupiter with a thunderbolt, and buried in Tartarus under Mt. Aetna, the eruptions of which were supposed to be caused by his struggles to regain his liberty.

D. refers to Typhoeus as Typhon, coupling him with Tityus (after Lucan, *Phars*. iv. 595-6), *Tifo*, Inf. xxxi. 124 [**Tizio**]; Charles Martel (in the Heaven of Venus), referring to the eruptions of Mt. Aetna, says that they are due, not to the struggles of Typhoeus (cf. Ovid, *Metam*. v. 346-53), but to the presence of nascent sulphur, Par. viii. 67-70; Typhoeus is mentioned incidentally in connexion with Cupid, Conv. ii. 6[123] (where D. mistranslates *Aen*. i. 664-5).

Tifo. [**Tifeo.**]

Tignoso, Federico. [**Federico Tignoso.**]

Tigri, Tigris, river of Asia, which rises in the mountains of Armenia, and flows into the Persian Gulf, after being joined by the Euphrates; the two rivers are mentioned together, Purg. xxxiii. 112—13. [**Eufrates.**]

Timbreo, Thymbraeus, epithet of Apollo, derived from Thymbra in the Troad, where there was a celebrated temple dedicated to him. D. mentions Apollo by this name in connexion with the defeat of the Giants, he being portrayed in Circle I of Purgatory, together with Jupiter, Mars, and Minerva, as surveying their scattered limbs after the failure of their attack upon Olympus, Purg. xii. 31–3. [**Giganti.**]

Timeo [1], Timaeus, Pythagorean philosopher of Locri in S. Italy, reputed teacher of Plato, who introduces him as chief speaker in the dialogue called from him the *Timaeus*; the Platonic theory, as propounded by him (*Tim.* 41–2), as to the relation of the soul to the stars, Par. iv. 49–60. [**Platone**: *Timeo* [2].]

Timeo [2], *Timaeus* of Plato, dialogue in which the Pythagorean philosopher Timaeus discourses of the origin of things down to the creation of man; after assuming at the outset that the universe, being corporeal, had a beginning, and was made after an everlasting pattern, he proceeds to treat of the work of mind in creation, the effects of necessity, the general and specific attributes of bodies, the principles of physiology, and the outlines of pathology and medicine.

The *Timaeus*, is the only one of Plato's works mentioned by D., or of which he shows any special knowledge. A Latin translation of this treatise by Chalcidius (c. Cent. v) rendered it accessible to mediaeval students who could not read it in the original Greek; and it was probably from this source that the mediaeval knowledge of Plato was mainly derived, at any rate until about the beginning of Cent. xiii. D. may, of course, have been acquainted at first hand with Chalcidius' translation of the *Timaeus*, but it is more likely that his knowledge of it was derived from Aristotle, Albertus Magnus, and St. Thomas Aquinas, all of whom constantly quote it.

D. mentions the *Timaeus* by name in connexion with the Platonic theory as to the position and motion of the Earth (*Tim.* 40), Conv. iii. 5^{45-52} [**Terra** [2]]; he refers to it, by the mention of Timaeus, the chief speaker in the dialogue, Par. iv. 49 [**Timeo** [1]]; he was also indebted to the *Timaeus*, directly or indirectly, for the (Platonic) doctrine of separate souls (*Tim.* 69) (the source of his information in this case being probably the *Summa contra Gentiles*, ii. 58, of St. Thomas Aquinas), Purg. iv. 5–6; for the theory as to the relation of souls to stars (*Tim.* 41–2), Par. iv. 22–4, 49–50; Conv. ii. 14^{33}; iv. 21^{17-18}; and for the theory as to the phenomena of vision (*Tim.* 45), Conv. iii. 9^{99-103} [**Platone**].

Timotheum, Epistola ad, St. Paul's Epistle to Timothy; quoted, Mon. ii. 11^{68-70} (2 *Tim.* iv. 8).

Tiralli, Tyrol (formerly an independent 'county'), mountainous district drained by the Inn and the Etsch (Adige), forming the southernmost province of the Austrian Empire; mentioned by Virgil in his description of the site of Mantua, in connexion with the Lago di Garda, which he says lies at the foot of the Tyrolese Alps, the barrier between Italy and Germany, Inf. xx. 61–3. [**Benaco.**]

Tiranni, Tyrants; placed, together with Murderers and Robbers, among the Violent in Round 1 of Circle VII of Hell, Inf. xi. 34–6; xii. 103–39; their punishment is to be immersed up to their eyebrows in Phlegethon, the boiling river of blood, Inf. xii. 103–5 (the Murderers being immersed up to their necks, vv. 116–17, and the Robbers up to their waists, vv. 121–2) [Violenti]. *Examples*: Alexander the Great (or Alexander of Pherae) [Alessandro²]; Dionysius of Syracuse [Dionisio¹]; Ezzelino III of Romano [Azzolino¹]; Obizzo II of Este [Obizzo]; Attila, King of the Huns [Attila]; and (probably) Pyrrhus, King of Epirus [Pirro²].

Tiresia, Tiresias, famous soothsayer of Thebes. According to the story he once separated with his staff two serpents which he found coupled in a wood, whereupon he was changed into a woman for seven years; at the expiration of this period he found the same two serpents and struck them again, whereupon he was changed back into a man. Subsequently, Jupiter and Juno having differed as to which of the two sexes experienced the greater pleasure, the question was referred to Tiresias, as having belonged to both sexes, and he decided in favour of woman, which coincided with the opinion of Jupiter; Juno thereupon in anger struck him with blindness, but Jupiter, by way of compensation, endowed him with the gift of prophecy. (Ovid, *Metam.* iii. 316–38.)

D. places Tiresias among the Soothsayers in Bolgia 4 of Circle VIII of Hell (Malebolge), and refers to the story (which he got from Ovid, *Metam.* iii. 323–31) of his metamorphosis into a woman and back again into a man, Inf. xx. 40–5 [Indovini].

The daughter of Tiresias referred to by Virgil in his enumeration of those who are with him in Limbo is Manto the prophetess, Purg. xxii. 113. [Manto.]

Tirrhenum Aequor. [Tyrrenum Mare.]

Tisbe, Thisbe, maiden of Babylon, who was in love with the youth Pyramus; D. mentions her in connexion with the latter, Purg. xxvii. 37. [Piramo.]

Tisrin primo, the former of the two Syrian months *Tixryn*; in recording the death of Beatrice (which took place in June, 1290) D. says she died in the ninth month of the year according to the Syrian usage, their first month being 'Tisrin primo', corresponding to our October, V. N. § 30⁴⁻⁶.

D. is anxious to prove that the number *nine* is intimately connected with the day, month, and year of Beatrice's death. To bring in this number in the case of the month he has recourse to the Syrian calendar, in which (as he learned from Alfraganus) the first month corresponds to our October, so that June, our sixth month (in which Beatrice died), corresponds to the *ninth* month according to the Syrian usage. [Alfergano: Arabia.]

Titan, Titan, i. e. the Sun, so called by the Roman poets as being the son of Hyperion, one of the

Titans ; of the Sun itself, Ecl. ii. 2
[Sole]; metaphorically, of the
Emperor Henry VII, whom D.
calls *Titan pacificus*, Epist. v. 1[10];
Titan praeoptatus, Epist. vii. 1[19]
[Arrigo [2]].

Tito, Titus, son and successor of
Vespasian, Roman Emperor, A.D.
79–81 ; he served under his father
in the Jewish wars, and when Vespasian was proclaimed Emperor and
returned to Italy in 70 he remained
in Palestine in order to carry on the
siege of Jerusalem, which he captured, after a siege of several months,
in September of that year ; in the
following year he returned to Rome
and celebrated the conquest of the
Jews in a triumph with his father.

Titus is mentioned by Statius (in
Purgatory) as *il buon Tito*, Purg.
xxi. 82 ; and by the Emperor
Justinian (in the Heaven of Mercury), Par. vi. 92 ; in both these
passages reference is made to the
destruction of Jerusalem by Titus,
which D. says was the vengeance
upon the Jews for the crucifixion of
Christ (cf. Orosius, *Hist.* vii. 3, § 8)
(Purg. xxi. 82–4), whereby in its
turn the sin of Adam was avenged
(Par. vi. 92–3).

Tito Livio. [Livio.]

Titone, Tithonus, son of Laomedon, who was loved by Aurora,
and by her intercession was made
immortal. Aurora, as the goddess
of dawn, is represented in mythology
as rising at the close of each night
from the couch of her spouse
Tithonus, and ascending to heaven
from the ocean to herald the approach
of day.

Tithonus is mentioned in the

much disputed passage where D.
speaks of *la concubina di Titone*,
Purg. ix. 1 ; the most generally
accepted opinion is that D. refers,
not to the Aurora of the Sun (i.e.
the *wife* of Tithonus), but to the
Aurora of the Moon, which he indicates by describing her as the
concubine of Tithonus, and by quali-
fying the latter, not as her *spouse*,
but as her *lover* ('amico', v. 3);
the meaning then would be that the
Aurora before moonrise was lighting
up the Eastern sky (*vv.* 1–3), the
time indicated in the passage (*vv.*
1–9) being shortly after 8.30 p.m. ;
if, on the other hand, *la concubina di
Titone* be taken to mean the Aurora
of the Sun, the true dawn, the time
indicated would be a little after
3 a.m.

Titus Livius. [Livio.]

Tityrus, name (borrowed from
Virgil, *Ecl.* i. 1, 4, 13, &c.) under
which D. figures in his poetical
correspondence with Giovanni del
Virgilio, Ecl. i. 6, 24, 46; ii. 7,
12, 25, 29, 44, 45, 64, 88; Ecl.
R. 11, 26, 72, 87, 95. [*Egloghe* [2].]

Tizio, Tityus, one of the Giants,
who, for having attempted to outrage
Diana, was hurled by Jupiter down
to Tartarus, where he lay out-
stretched on the ground covering
nine acres, while a vulture eternally
preyed upon his liver (*Aen.* vi. 595–
600; *Metam.* iv. 456–8).

Virgil, having requested Antaeus
to place D. and himself upon the ice of
Cocytus, prays him not to send them
down to where Tityus and Typhoeus are (cf. Lucan, *Phars.* iv.
595–7), Inf. xxxi. 124 [Tifeo].

Toante], Thoas, son of Jason and Hypsipyle, brother of Euneos; he and his brother are referred to as *due figli*, Purg. xxvi. 95. [**Euneo.**]

Tobia, Tobias, name given in the Vulgate to the Jew who was healed of his blindness by the angel Raphael, and who in the English version is called Tobit, the son being called Tobias in both versions (*Tob.* ii. 1–10; xi. 7–13; xii. 12–15).

D. refers to the archangel Raphael as *l'altro che Tobia rifece sano*, Par. iv. 48 [**Raffaelle**].

Tolomea, name given by D. to the third of the four divisions of Circle IX of Hell, where Traitors are punished, Inf. xxxiii. 124 [**Inferno**]; here are placed those who have been traitors to their guests and companions, Inf. xxxiii. 91–157 [**Traditori**]. *Examples*: Frate Alberigo de' Manfredi [**Alberigo, Frate**]; Branca d'Oria [**Branca**]. D. assigns to Tolomea the grim 'privilege' (perhaps suggested by *Psalm* lv. 15, and *Luke* xxii. 3) of receiving damned souls while those to whom they belong are still alive upon earth, their bodies meanwhile being tenanted by fiends from hell, Inf. xxxiii. 124–35.

The name of this division is derived, according to some, from Ptolemy, King of Egypt, who murdered Pompey [**Tolommeo** 2]; but it is more probably named after Ptolemy, son of Abubus, the captain of Jericho, who treacherously murdered Simon the Maccabee and two of his sons at a banquet he made for them, B.C. 135. (1 *Maccab.* xvi. 11–17).

Tolomei, Pia de'. [**Pia, La.**]

Tolommeo [1], Ptolemy (Claudius Ptolemaeus), famous mathematician, astronomer, and geographer, born in Egypt c. A.D. 100, died c. 180. His two most famous works are the Μεγάλη Σύνταξις τῆς Ἀστρονομίας, 'the Great Composition of Astronomy', commonly known as the *Almagest*, and the Γεωγραφία, 'Geography'; he also wrote a treatise `De Judiciis Astrologicis*. All these works were translated into Latin, and were thus accessible to mediaeval students who were ignorant of Greek. D.'s knowledge of the *Almagest* was doubtless derived for the most part at second hand from the *Elementa Astronomica* of Alfraganus, which is to a great extent based upon that work. [**Alfergano.**]

D. places Ptolemy, together with Euclid, among the great philosophers of antiquity in Limbo, Inf. iv. 142 [**Limbo**]; his opinion that the movable heavens are nine in number, V.N. § 30$^{16-18}$; Conv. ii. 3$^{49-52}$; his reason for assuming the existence of a ninth heaven being the necessity to account for the diurnal motion from E. to W. of the other eight heavens (taken from the *De Coelo et Mundo* of Albertus Magnus), Conv. ii. 3$^{36-45}$ [***Coelo, De*** 2]; his description of the planet Jupiter as a star of temperate complexion, holding a middle place between the frigidity of Saturn and the fieriness of Mars, Conv. ii. 14$^{198-202}$ (*De Jud.* i. 4) [**Giove** 3]; his contention that errors in astronomy are to be imputed not to the science itself, but to the inefficiency of the observer, Conv. ii. 14$^{249-53}$ (*De Jud.* i. 1);

his opinion as to the nature of the Milky Way, Conv. ii. 15[77] (*Almag.* viii. 1) [**Galassia**]; his saying that the aspect of terrestrial things is similar to that of celestial things, A.T. § 21[29–31].

Tolommeo[2], Ptolemy XII, King of Egypt, B.C. 51–47, eldest son of Ptolemy Auletes; by his father's will the sovereignty was left jointly to him and his sister Cleopatra, but the latter was expelled after sharing the throne for about three years. Cleopatra, however, collected an army, invaded Egypt, and with the help of Julius Caesar defeated her brother, who was drowned while attempting to escape. Ptolemy had been accessory to the murder of Pompey, who fled to Egypt after the battle of Pharsalia (B.C. 48), and was stabbed in the back just as he was stepping ashore. Ptolemy had his head cut off and sent to Caesar, but the latter, to show his abhorrence of the deed, caused the murderers to be put to death.

Ptolemy is mentioned by the Emperor Justinian (in the Heaven of Mercury) in connexion with the exploits of the Roman Eagle, the allusion being to Caesar's defeat of him in the Alexandrian war, Par. vi. 69; Lucan's invective against him (*Phars.* viii. 692–4) for his murder of Pompey, Mon. ii. 9[68–74].

Tolosa, Conte di, Count of Toulouse (i. e., probably, Raymond V, Count of Toulouse, 1148–1194, who was one of the great patrons of the troubadours); mentioned, together with the King of Castile and the Marquis of Mont-

ferrat, on account of his liberality, as *il buono Conte di Tolosa*, Conv. iv. 11[125–8].

Tolosano, native of Toulouse, city of SW. France, on the Garonne; the poet Statius, by an error, described as a native of Toulouse, Purg. xxi. 89. [**Stazio.**]

Tomma. [**Tommaso**[2].]

Tommaso[1], St. Thomas the Apostle; his festival (Dec. 21) is mentioned by Cacciaguida (in the Heaven of Mars), in connexion with the Marquis Hugh of Brandenburg, 'il gran barone', Par. xvi. 128–9. [**Ugo di Brandimborgo.**]

Tommaso[2], St. Thomas Aquinas, famous scholastic theologian and philosopher, who was of noble descent, was born c. 1227 at Rocca Sicca, the castle of his father, the Count of Aquino, in the NW. corner of Campania. He received his early education at the Benedictine monastery of Monte Cassino, which was close to his home, and afterwards studied for six years at the University of Naples, which he left at the age of 16. In his next year he became a Dominican, and shortly after was sent to study under Albertus Magnus at Cologne. In 1245 he accompanied Albertus to Paris, and remained with him there for three years, during which he took a prominent part in the controversy between the University and the Begging Friars as to the liberty of teaching, being chosen to defend his Order against the famous Guillaume de St. Amour, the champion of the University, whom he successfully confuted [**Sigieri**]. In 1248 he returned with Albertus to Cologne, where he began his career as a teacher. In 1257 he was created doctor of theology by the Sorbonne (at the same time as his friend St. Bonaventura), and began to lecture on that subject in Paris, where he speedily acquired a great reputation. After lecturing in Rome and Bologna, and again in Paris, in 1272 he returned to his native country, at the instance of Charles I of Anjou, to assume the office of professor at the University of Naples, having previously refused the Archbishopric of Naples and the abbacy of Monte Cassino. In January, 1274, he was summoned by Gregory X to attend the Council of Lyons; though ill at the time, he set out on the journey, but died, after lingering for some weeks, at the Cistercian monastery of Fossa Nuova, near Terracina on the borders of Campania and Latium, March 7, 1274 (a groundless suspicion, which was shared by D., being entertained that he had been poisoned at the instance of King Charles).

Within fifty years of his death (in 1323, two years after D.'s death) Thomas Aquinas, who during his lifetime had been known as the Angelic Doctor, was canonized by Pope John XXII.

The most important of the numerous works of Aquinas is the *Summa Theologica*, in which he attempted to present a condensed summary, not only of theology, but of all known science. To this work, though he never quotes it by name, D. was deeply indebted, its influence being perceptible throughout his writings.

Among the other works of Aquinas, besides numerous scriptural commentaries, are the *Summa Catholicae Fidei contra Gentiles* (several times quoted by D.), and commentaries upon the *Ethics*, the *Physics*, *Metaphysics*, *De Anima*, *De Interpretatione*, *Posterior Analytics*, and other treatises of Aristotle. He also helped to make, or superintended, a new Latin translation of Aristotle from the Greek direct (all previous ones having been made through the medium of Arabic versions)—probably the so-called *Antiqua translatio* (as opposed to the *Nova translatio* made by Argyropylus in Cent. xv) printed in the collected editions of his works—which there is good reason to suppose is the one habitually made use of by D., and which corresponds to what he calls la *Nuova traslazione*, his *Vecchia traslazione* (Conv. ii. 15$^{63-8}$) being the Arabic-Latin version. [**Aristotile.**]

St. Thomas Aquinas is mentioned as *Tommaso*, Purg. xx. 69; Par. xiv. 6; Conv. ii. 15^{125}; iv. 8^3, 15^{125}; *Tomma*, Par. xii. 110; *Fra Tommaso*, Par. xii. 144; *Fra Tommaso d'Aquino*, Conv. iv. 30$^{26-7}$; *Thomas d'Aquino*, Par. x. 99; *Thomas*, Mon. ii. 4$^{5, 17}$; he is referred to as *il coreggier* (i.e. the wearer of the leathern girdle characteristic of the Dominicans), Par. xi. 138; his death at the hands of Charles of Anjou (according to the mediaeval belief), Purg. xx. 69; his commentary on the *Ethics* of Aristotle, quoted, Conv. ii. 15$^{125-8}$; iv. 8$^{3-6}$; his *Summa Contra Gentiles*, quoted, Conv. iv. 15$^{125-30}$; Mon.

ii. 4^{5-8}, $^{15-18}$; referred to, Conv. iv. 30^{24-30}; his definition of a miracle, Mon. ii. 4^{6-8}, $^{15-18}$. [**Gentiles, Summa Contra.**]

D. places St. Thomas, among the spirits of great theologians and others who loved wisdom (*Spiriti Sapienti*), in the Heaven of the Sun, together with his master, Albertus Magnus, and his friend, St. Bonaventura, Par. x. 99; xii. 110, 144; xiv. 6; *un* (*sole*), Par. x. 82; *lumiera*, Par. xi. 16; *benedetta fiamma*, Par. xii. 2; *luce*, Par. xiii. 32; *vita*, Par. xiv. 6 [**Sole, Cielo di**]; addressing D., St. T. informs him that he was a Dominican, that the spirit at his side is that of his old master Albertus, and that he himself is Thomas Aquinas, Par. x. 82–99; he then names ten other spirits who are their companions (*vv.* 100–38); and, after a pause, proceeds to relate the life of St. Francis of Assisi (Par. xi. 13–139) [**Francesco**[2]].

Tommaso d'Aquino. [**Tommaso**[2].]

Tommaso da Faenza. [**Faenza, Tommaso da.**]

Toppo, Il, name of a ford (apparently across a branch of the Chiana), near Arezzo, where a Sienese force was cut to pieces by the Aretines in 1288; mentioned by Jacomo da Sant' Andrea (in Round 2 of Circle VII of Hell) in connexion with Lano of Siena, who was among the slain on this occasion, Inf. xiii. 121. [**Lano.**]

Torino. [**Taurinum.**]

Torquato[1], Titus Manlius Torquatus, celebrated Roman hero, who was twice Dictator (B.C. 353, 349), and three times Consul (B.C. 347, 344, 340); he owed his surname of Torquatus to an incident in the war against the Gauls, when he slew in single combat a gigantic Gaul, from whose dead body he removed the neck-chain (*torques*), which he placed around his own neck. During the war with the Latins in B.C. 340, when he was Consul, he and his colleague, P. Decius Mus, before the decisive battle, issued an edict that no Roman should engage in single combat with a Latin, on pain of death; this command was violated by young Manlius, the consul's son, who, though he defeated his opponent, was condemned to death by his father, and executed by the lictor in the presence of the Roman army (Livy, vii. 10; viii. 6–7).

Torquatus is mentioned by the Emperor Justinian (in the Heaven of Mercury) in connexion with the exploits of the Roman Eagle, Par. vi. 46; his condemnation of his son, Conv. iv. 5^{118-21}; referred to as 'il glorioso Torquato' in connexion with his descendant, Lucius Manlius Torquatus, Conv. iv. 6^{112-14}. [**Torquato**[2].]

Torquato[2], Lucius Manlius Torquatus, adherent of Pompey during the civil war, who after the battle of Pharsalia fled to Africa, where he was slain, B.C. 46. He was a man of great learning, and in early life was a friend of Cicero, who introduces him as an Epicurean in the *De Finibus* (i. 5).

D. mentions him as an Epicurean (doubtless on the authority of Cicero), and as a descendant of the great hero, Titus Manlius Torquatus, Conv. iv. 6[111—14]. [Torquato[1].]

Torso, Tours, on the Loire, capital of the old province of Touraine; mentioned by Forese Donati (in Circle VI of Purgatory) in connexion with Pope Martin IV, who was a Frenchman, and treasurer of St. Martin of Tours, Purg. xxiv. 23. [Martino[2].]

Tosa, Cianghella della. [Cianghella.]

Tosa, Della. [Tosinghi.]

Toscana, Tuscany, province of N. Italy, of which the Mediterranean forms the W. boundary, its capital being Florence. It was at one time a marquisate and imperial fief, but after the death of the Countess Matilda in 1115, who bequeathed it as part of her inheritance to the Church, the possession of it was disputed by the Pope and the Emperor, and in the course of the struggle between them the principal cities gradually asserted their independence, forming republics, the chief of which were Florence, Pisa, Siena, Arezzo, Pistoja, and Lucca.

D. speaks of it as *Toscana*, Inf. xxiv. 122; Purg. xi. 110; xiii. 149; xiv. 16; Conv. iv. 11[77]; *Thuscia*, V. E. i. 6[35]; *Tuscia*, V. E. i. 10[51, 75]; Epist. i. *tit.*; ii. 2[34]; vi. *fin.*; vii. 3[49], *fin.*; the native country of Vanni Fucci of Pistoja, Inf. xxiv. 122; of Provenzano Salvani of Siena, Purg. xii. 110; of Sapia of Siena, Purg. xiii. 149; drained by the Arno, Purg. xiv. 16 [Arno]; divided from the Genoese territory by the Macra, Par. ix. 89–90 [Macra]; Falterona one of its mountains, Conv. iv. 11[77] [Falterona]; D. a native of, V. E. i. 6[35—6] (cf. Inf. x. 22; xxiii. 76, 91; xxxii. 66; Purg. xiv. 103, 124; xvi. 137; Par. xxii. 117); on the right side of Italy if the Apennines be taken as the dividing line (from N. to S.), V. E. i. 10[51]; the dialects within its borders vary, as for instance at Siena and Arezzo, V. E. i. 10[75—6]; included in the jurisdiction of the Bishop of Ostia as papal legate, Epist. i. *tit.* [Nicholaus]; the Roman (i. e. imperial) court in, Epist. ii. 2[33—4]; D.'s letters to the Florentines and to the Emperor Henry VII, dated from, Epist. vi. *fin.*; vii. *fin.*; Henry VII reproached with neglecting it, Epist. vii. 3[49—50].

Toscano. [Toschi.]

Toschi, inhabitants of Tuscany, Inf. xxii. 99; *gente Tosca*, Inf. xxviii. 108; *Toscano*, Par. ix. 90; *Tuscani*, V. E. i. 13[16, 44]; Epist. ii. 1[19]; *Tusci*, V. E. i. 10[64], 13[1, 13, 33, 45], 19[18]; Epist. vi. 5[141]; vii. *tit.*; Ciampolo offers to show D. and Virgil either Tuscans or Lombards (probably as a sort of ironical compliment to their respective native lands) who are with himself in Bolgia 5 of Circle VIII of Hell (Malebolge), Inf. xxii. 99; the dialect of the Tuscans different from that of the Spoletans on the one hand, and that of the Genoese on the other, V. E. i. 10[63—5]; their infatuation in claiming it to be the Italian vulgar tongue, V. E. i. 13[1—13]; their claim disposed of by an examination of the various Tuscan dialects, V. E. i. 13[13—32]; their dialect a debased form of speech,

V. E. i. 13$^{32-3}$; and by no means worthy to rank as the illustrious vulgar tongue of Italy, V. E. i. 13$^{39-44}$; the remarks as to their dialect applicable to that of the Genoese, V. E. i. 13$^{44-6}$; their dialect abandoned by their most illustrious poets in favour of the Italian vulgar tongue, V. E. i. 19$^{16-18}$; the Conti Guidi the noblest of the Tuscans, Epist. ii. 1^{19}; the Florentines the most vainglorious of the Tuscans, Epist. vi. 5^{141}; greeting of peace-loving Tuscans to the Emperor Henry VII, Epist. vii. *tit.*; the overbearing character of the Tuscans, *Tuscana tyrannis*, Epist. vii. 4^{77}.

Tosco, Tuscan; D. addressed as a Tuscan by Farinata degli Uberti (in Circle VI of Hell), Inf. x. 22; by Catalano de' Catalani (in Bolgia 6 of Circle VIII of Hell), Inf. xxiii. 91; by Camicione de' Pazzi (in Circle IX of Hell), Inf. xxxii. 66; by Guido del Duca (in Circle II of Purgatory), Purg. xiv. 103, 124; Guglielmo Aldobrandesco spoken of by his son (in Circle I of Purgatory) as 'un gran Tosco', Purg. xi. 58; D.'s native air, 'l'aer Tosco', Par. xxii. 117;—the Tuscan dialect, Purg. xvi. 137; *parola Tosca*, Inf. xxiii. 76; *Tuscana loquela*, V. E. i. 13$^{39-40}$;—the Tuscans, *Toschi*, Inf. xxii. 99; *gente Tosca*, Inf. xxviii. 108; *Tuscana tyrannis*, Epist. vii. 4^{77}. [**Toschi.**]

Tosinghi], noble Florentine family, said to have been a branch of the Visdomini, together with whom they are alluded to by Cacciaguida (in the Heaven of Mars) as being patrons of the Bishopric of Florence, the revenues of which they enjoyed during the vacancy of the see, Par. xvi. 112–14. [**Visdomini.**]

The Visdomini and Tosinghi lived in the Porta san Piero (Vill. iv. 10), were Guelfs (v. 39), and were among those who took refuge in Lucca after the battle of Montaperti (vi. 79); when the Guelfs subsequently split up into Bianchi and Neri, some of the family took one side, some the other (viii. 39).

To the family of the Tosinghi is said to have belonged the notorious Cianghella, Par. xv. 128. [**Cianghella.**]

Totila, last Ostrogothic King of Italy, 541–553, who, after conquering N. Italy, Sardinia, and Sicily, and taking Rome, was finally defeated and slain by Justinian's general, Narses, at the battle of Taginae in Umbria, 553. His siege of Florence in 542 gave rise probably to the tradition that Florence was destroyed by Attila, with whom he was confused. [**Attila.**]

D. figures Charles of Valois under the name of Totila, V. E. ii. 6^{48}. [**Carlo**^{4}.]

Traditori], Traitors; placed in Circle IX (the lowest) of Hell, Inf. xi. 64–6; xxx. 11–xxxiv. 69 [**Inferno**]. This Circle consists of a vast gloomy pit (*pozzo*, Inf. xxxi. 32, 42; *pozzo scuro*, xxxii. 16), the mouth of which is guarded by Giants [**Giganti**]; its bottom consists of an immense lake of ice formed by the frozen waters of the river Cocytus [**Cocito**]; this lake is in four divisions (the boundaries of which are not defined); in the first, which is named *Caina* (after Cain, the first murderer), are placed those who have betrayed their kindred, Inf. xxxii. 16–69 ; these are immersed in the ice up to their necks, with their faces turned downwards, and their eyes blinded with frozen tears, Inf. xxxii. 20–1, 31–7, 47–8 [Caina]; in the second division, which is named *Antenora* (after Antenor of Troy), are placed those who have betrayed their country, Inf. xxxii. 70–xxxiii. 90; these, like those in Caina, are immersed up to their necks in the ice, with their faces bent down, Inf. xxxii. 77–8, 97, 100–5 [Antenora]; in the third division, which is named *Tolomea* (after Ptolemy of Jericho), are placed those who have betrayed their guests and companions, Inf. xxxiii. 91–157; these are likewise fixed in the ice up to their necks, but they are on their backs, with their faces turned upwards, so that their tears, freezing as they gush forth, form masks of ice over their eyes, Inf. xxxiii. 93–9 [Tolomea]; in the fourth and last division, which is named *Giudecca* (after Judas Iscariot), are placed those who have betrayed their benefactors, Inf. xxxiv. 1–69; these, with the exception of Judas, Brutus, and Cassius, for whom a special torment is reserved in the jaws of Lucifer, are completely immersed in the ice, in various postures, some being recumbent, some erect, some upside down, and some bowed double, Inf. xxxiv. 11–15 [Giudecca : Lucifero].

Traiano, Trajan (M. Ulpius Trajanus), Roman Emperor, A. D. 98–117; mentioned in connexion with the story, which D. sees depicted among the examples of humility in Circle I of Purgatory, of how, as he was setting out for the wars, a poor widow stopped him, and demanded redress for the death of her son, and how, when he tried to put her off, she constrained him to accede to her demand, Purg. x. 73–96 [Superbi]; he is referred to, in the same connexion, as 'il Roman principato, il cui valore Mosse Gregorio alla sua gran vittoria' (*vv.* 74–5), the allusion being to the tradition that, at the intercession of Gregory the Great, Trajan's soul was delivered from hell; he is placed in the Heaven of Jupiter among the spirits of those who loved and exercised justice (*Spiriti Giudicanti*), Par. xx. 44–7, 106–17 [Giove, Cielo di]; he is referred to, in allusion to the story of the widow, as 'Colui che . . . La vedovella consolò del figlio' (*vv.* 44–5); and, in connexion with the legend as to his salvation through the prayers of Gregory, as *anima gloriosa* (*v.* 112). [Gregorio.]

Tramontana. [Settentrione².]

Transformatione Rerum, De. [*Rerum Transformatione, De.*]

Transmutatione Rerum, De. [*Rerum Transmutatione, De.*]

Transtiberinus, Trasteverine, belonging to the farther bank of the Tiber ; in his Letter to the Italian Cardinals D. alludes, as is supposed, to the Cardinal Francesco Gaetani, as the adherent of the Trasteverine faction, 'Transtiberinae sectator factionis', Epist. viii. 10¹⁶⁵⁻⁶. 'The Trasteverine faction' was the party of the Guelfs, and included the Orsini and the Gaetani, as opposed to the Ghibelline party, with whom the Colonnesi were identified, and whose headquarters were on the left bank of the Tiber. Francesco Gaetani was a nephew of Boniface VIII, by whom he was made a Cardinal in 1295; he was a staunch supporter of Boniface in his contest with the Colonnesi, and after the death of the former he continued to follow out his policy; he died in 1317.

Traversara, Casa, Traversari family, powerful Ghibelline house of Ravenna, where they first came into prominence about the middle of Cent. x; they are mentioned by Guido del Duca (in Circle II of Purgatory), together with the Anastagi, as being (in 1300) on the brink of extinction, Purg. xiv. 107–8; the most distinguished member of the family appears to have been Pier Traversaro (c. 1145–1225), whom Guido had already mentioned, Purg. xiv. 98 [**Traver·saro, Pier**].

Traversaro, Pier, member of the powerful Traversari family of Ravenna, born c. 1145, died 1225; he was of great influence and authority in Ravenna, with the history of which he was closely identified for nearly fifty years; he was several times (1181, 1189, 1196) Podestà of the city, an office which was filled by members of his house at least ten times in the forty years between 1180 and 1220. Piero, whose family were by tradition adherents of the Empire, was a staunch Ghibelline and enjoyed the confidence of the Emperor Frederick II. Among his own adherents were Guido del Duca of Bertinoro (Purg. xiv. 81), and the Mainardi of the same town (Purg. xiv. 97). In 1170 he and Arrigo Mainardi (Purg. xiv. 97) were taken prisoners by the Faentines while fighting against them on behalf of Forlì and Ravenna; in 1212 he was among those selected by Pope Innocent III to support Frederick of Sicily (afterwards Emperor) against the excommunicated Emperor, Otto IV; in 1216 he unsuccessfully contested with the Conti Guidi (a daughter of whose house he had married) the possession of certain castles in the Casentino, and was taken prisoner; two years later (1218), with the help of the Mainardi, he made himself master of Ravenna, which he held until his death (1225). Piero was a munificent patron of the troubadours, among his protégés being Aimeric de Pegulhan (V. E. ii. 6⁶⁴). He was succeeded in the lordship of Ravenna by his son Paolo, who, deserting the traditions of his family, became a Guelf. Paolo died at Ravenna in 1240, and with him departed the power and splendour of the ' domus Traversariorum ', the representatives of which were finally expelled from Ravenna by the Polenta family, who in 1310 entered into possession of all that was left of their inheritance.

Pier Traversaro is mentioned by Guido del Duca (in Circle II of Purgatory), together with his contemporary Arrigo Mainardi, among the worthies of Romagna, Purg. xiv. 98 [**Guido del Duca**]; the

Traversari family is mentioned as being (in 1300) without heirs, Purg. xiv. 107–8 [**Traversara, Casa**].

Trentino, belonging to Trent; *il Trentino pastore*, the Bishop of Trent, mentioned, together with the Bishops of Brescia and Verona, in connexion with a place at the N. extremity of the Lago di Garda where their three dioceses meet, Inf. xx. 67–9. [**Benaco : Trento**.]

Trento, Trent (Trient), on the Adige (Etsch), capital of Italian or S. Tyrol; mentioned in connexion with the broken ground caused by a great landslip in the valley of the Adige below the city, Inf. xii. 5; coupled with Turin and Alessandria della Paglia as being on the confines of Italy, and consequently incapable of preserving a pure dialect owing to the introduction of foreign elements, *Tridentum*, V. E. i. 15⁶¹⁻⁴.

The catastrophe mentioned by D. (Inf. xii. 4–6), as having diverted the course of the Adige on the Italian side of Trent, almost certainly refers to what is popularly known in the neighbourhood as the *Slavini di Marco*, the result of an enormous landslip which took place about the year 883 opposite Mori, some twenty miles S. of Trent, between Roveredo and Ala, and deflected the Adige considerably. The cause of the catastrophe is discussed by Albertus Magnus in his *De Meteoris* (iii. 6), which may perhaps account for D.'s mention of it, as he was familiar with that treatise [*Meteora* ²].

Trespiano, village of Tuscany, to the N. of Florence, about three miles from the Porta San Gallo; Cacciaguida (in the Heaven of Mars)

laments that it and Galluzzo were included within the Florentine territory, Par. xvi. 53–4.

Tribaldello. [**Tebaldello**.]

Tridentum. [**Trento**.]

Trinacria, name used by Virgil and other Roman poets for Sicily, which is said to have been so called from the triangular shape of the island (cf. Servius on *Aen*. iii. 384).

D. speaks of Sicily by this name, Par. viii. 67; V. E. i. 12¹⁵; ii. 6⁴⁸; *Trinacrida*, Ecl. ii. 71. [**Cicilia**.]

There appears to be a special significance in the use of the term *Trinacria* in the first of these passages, in which Charles Martel, eldest son of Charles II of Naples, is repreᵈ sented as saying (in the Heaven of Venus) that if he had lived he would have been Count of Provence (Par. viii. 58–60), King of Apulia (*vv.* 61–3), and King of Hungary (*vv.* 64–6); and he adds (*vv.* 67–75) that his descendants would have ruled in 'Trinacria', had it not been for the misgovernment of his grandfather, Charles of Anjou, which led to the massacre known as the 'Sicilian Vespers' and the expulsion of the French from Sicily [**Carlo** ³]. At the time Charles Martel is supposed to be speaking (i. e. in 1300), the King of Sicily was Frederick II of Aragon (1296–1337), a member of the rival house, which had dispossessed the Angevins. After the failure of Charles of Valois' expedition against the island in 1302, he was forced to conclude an ignominious peace with Frederick, who was confirmed in the sovereignty of Sicily by the title of 'King of Trinacria' (this title having been adopted, doubtless, instead of that of ' King of Sicily ', because the latter would have implied sovereignty over both the Sicilies, i. e. over Naples and Apulia, which remained in the hands of the Angevins, as well as over the island of Sicily), and it was by the title of ' King of Trinacria ' that Frederick was recognized by Boniface VIII in the treaty of Anagni in the following year (June 12, 1303). The employment, therefore, by Charles Martel of this particular name for Sicily lends an additional sting to his (partly prophetic) utterances in rebuke of his house; and it can hardly be doubted that D. introduced it with that intention.

Trinacrida. [Trinacria.]

Trinità, the Holy Trinity, V.N. § 30⁴¹; Conv. ii. 6⁷³; iv. 5²²; *tre Persone,* Purg. iii. 36 ; Par. xiii. 26 ; xxiv. 139 ; Conv. ii. 6⁶⁰ [**Dio**|: **Cristo: Spirito Santo**].

Tristano, Tristan of Lyonesse, hero of the old French Romance, who came by his death through his love for Yseult ; he is placed by D., together with Paris of Troy, in Circle II of Hell, among those who met their death through love, Inf. v. 67. [**Lussuriosi.**]

Tristan, the nephew of King Mark of Cornwall, by whom he was brought up, having been wounded by the poisoned sword of Morhoult, brother of the Queen of Ireland, who came to Cornwall to demand tribute of King Mark, went to Ireland to be cured of his wound ; there he met the king's daughter Yseult, whom later he was sent to fetch as the bride of his uncle Mark. On the journey they partook of a love philtre which Yseult's mother had prepared for her and King Mark, whereupon they loved each other ' at once and for ever '. When they arrived in Cornwall, Yseult managed to substitute her maiden Brangian for herself on the bridal night ; and she and Tristan continued to meet until at last they were discovered together in Yseult's chamber by King Mark, who mortally wounded Tristan with a poisoned sword. As he lay upon his deathbed Tristan begged Mark to allow him to see Yseult once more before he died ; Mark consented, and Yseult reached Tristan in time to receive his dying embrace, the vehemence of which caused her heart to break, and she died upon his breast.

There exists an old Italian version of the prose *Tristan,* made in Tuscany in Cent. xiii; but D. was no doubt familiar with this romance in the *langue d'*oïl, as he was with the *Lancelot du Lac* and the *Morte d'Arthur.* [*Lingua Oil.*]

Trivia, ' goddess of the three ways ', term applied by Virgil, and other Latin poets, to Diana (whose temple was frequently placed where three roads met), and hence by D. to the Moon, Diana being goddess of the Moon, Par. xxiii. 26. [**Diana**¹ : **Luna.**]

Trivio, Trivium, the three liberal arts (viz. grammar, logic, and rhetoric), which constituted the first portion of the mediaeval academical curriculum; mentioned, with the *Quadrivium,* Conv. ii. 14⁵⁶. [*Quadrivio.*]

Trivisiana, Marca. [**Marca Trivisiana.**]

Trivisiani, inhabitants of the town and March of Treviso (the town being in the centre of the modern province of Venetia, at the confluence of the Piavesella and the Sile, some twenty miles due N. of Venice), V. E. i. 10⁶⁹, 14³⁰; coupled with the inhabitants of the March of Ancona as *utriusque Marchiae viri*, V. E. i. 19¹⁹; the peoples of the March, referred to by Cunizza (in the Heaven of Venus) as *la turba presente, Che Tagliamento e Adice richiude*, Par. ix. 43–4 [**Marca Trivisiana**]; their dialect, coupled with that of the Venetians as being distinct from those of the Lombards and of the inhabitants of Aquileia, V. E. i. 10⁶⁸⁻⁷⁰; condemned, together with those of the Veronese, Vicentines, Paduans, and Brescians, as harsh, especially in a woman's mouth, one of their peculiarities being a fondness for consonantal endings in *f*, V. E. i. 14²⁰⁻³⁵; abandoned by their most illustrious poets in favour of the Italian vulgar tongue, V. E. i. 19¹⁶⁻¹⁹.

Troade], Troad, territory of Troy, forming the NW. angle of Mysia, in NW. of Asia Minor; referred to by the Emperor Justinian (in the Heaven of Mercury) as the place whence the Roman Eagle took its origin (the Romans being regarded as descended from the Trojans), the district itself being indicated by the mention of Antandros, the Simois, and the tomb of Hector, Par. vi. 6, 67–8. [**Antandro: Simoenta.**]

Troia, city of Troy, which after a ten years' siege was taken and destroyed by the Greeks, Aeneas and a remnant of the Trojans escaping to Italy, where they laid the foundations of the Roman Empire; mentioned in connexion with the departure of Aeneas for Italy, Inf. i. 74; Conv. iv. 5⁴⁸ (cf. Inf. xxvi. 59–60; Par. vi. 6, 67–8) [**Enea**]; Sinon the Greek, who induced the Trojans to admit the wooden horse within their walls, Inf. xxx. 98, 114 [**Sinone**]; its fall and destruction, Purg. xii. 61; Mon. ii. 3³⁴⁻⁵ (cf. Inf. xxx. 13–15); its capture by the Greeks the starting-point of Livy's history of Rome, Mon. ii. 3³²⁻⁵; referred to as *Ilion*, Inf. i. 75; Purg. xii. 62 [**Ilion**]; *Pergama*, Epist. vi. 4¹⁰⁴ [**Pergama**]; Virgil's reference to it as 'Iliaca urbs' (*Aen.* viii. 134), quoted, Mon. ii. 3⁷³; its territory referred to, Par. vi. 6, 67–8 [**Troade**].

Troiani, Trojans; driven from the Strophades by the Harpies, Inf. xiii. 10–12 [**Arpie: Strofade**]; the wars of their descendants the Romans in Italy, Inf. xxviii. 9–10; their pride and presumption punished at the fall of Troy, Inf. xxx. 13–15; their history one of the favourite themes of the Florentine women of old, Par. xv. 124–6; and the subject of romances in the *langue d'oïl*, V. E. i. 10¹²⁻¹⁸ [***Lingua Oil***]; Juno's hostility to them, V. N. § 25⁷⁴⁻⁵ [**Giuno**]; Aeneas (correctly, Hector) apostrophized by Virgil as 'the light and hope of the Trojans', Conv. iii. 11¹⁵⁸⁻⁶⁰ [**Enea**]; the aged Trojans left by Aeneas with Acestes in Sicily, Conv. iv. 26⁹⁴⁻⁶ (cf. Purg. xviii. 136–7) [**Aceste¹**]; their Penates the subject of contention between the two peoples sprung from them in Italy, viz. the Romans and the Albans, Mon. ii. 11²²⁻⁷ [**Albani**: **Romani**¹]; a strain of Trojan blood in the Lombards, notwithstanding their barbarian origin, Epist. v. 4⁵⁰⁻²[**Lombardi**¹: **Longobardi**]; Virgil's references to them as 'Teucri', quoted, Mon. ii. 3⁷⁵, 9⁸⁵ [**Teucri**]; referred to as the founders of the Roman race, 'il gentil seme de' Romani', Inf. xxvi. 60; the descent of the Romans from them, Inf. xxvi. 60; xxviii. 10; Par. xv. 126; Mon. ii. 11²²⁻⁴ [**Romani**¹].

Troiano, Trojan; *furie Troiane*, i. e. the furies which drove Hecuba of Troy out of her wits, Inf. xxx. 22 [**Ecuba**]; the Trojan Rhipeus, Par. xx. 68 [**Rifeo**]; *l'alto sangue Troiano*, i. e. the blood of the Trojans which ran in the veins of the Romans, Conv. iv. 4¹⁰³⁻⁵; *Troiana radix*, i. e. the Trojan stem whence sprang the Romans and the Albans, Mon. ii. 11²²⁻³ [**Romani**¹: **Troiani**].

Troja, -ani, -ano. [**Troia, -ani, -ano**.]

Troni, Thrones, one of the Angelic Hierarchies; described by Cunizza (in the Heaven of Venus) as mirrors reflecting the mind of the Deity to the lower intelligences, Par. ix. 61–2; mentioned by Beatrice (in the Crystalline Heaven) as ranking last in the first (i. e. highest) Hierarchy, the Cherubim and Seraphim ranking above them, Par. xxviii. 104–5; in the *Convivio* D. states that the first (i. e. lowest) Hierarchy is composed of Angels, Archangels, and Thrones, the third place in the third (i. e. highest)

Hierarchy being occupied by the Powers, Conv. ii. 6⁴³⁻⁶ [**Gerarchia**]; according to this arrangement they preside over the Heaven of Venus, Conv. ii. 6¹⁰⁹; according to the other, over the Heaven of Saturn [**Paradiso**¹]; their number not great, but at least three, corresponding to the three movements of the Heaven of Venus, Conv. ii. 6¹²⁶⁻³⁶ [**Venere, Cielo di**].

Tronto, river of Central Italy, which rises in the Apennines, flows NE. past Ascoli, and enters the Adriatic about a mile below Porto d'Ascoli; mentioned by Charles Martel (in the Heaven of Venus) as the NE. limit of the kingdom of Naples, Par. viii. 63 [**Ausonia**: **Napoli**].

Tullio. [**Cicero**.]

Tullio, Servio. [**Servio Tullio**.]

Tullo. [**Hostilius**.]

Tupino, stream in N. of Umbria, which rises in the Apennines and flows S. past Nocera and Foligno into the Tiber; mentioned by St. Thomas Aquinas (in the Heaven of the Sun) in his description of the situation of Assisi, Par. xi. 43–5. [**Ascesi**.]

Turbia, La Turbie, village at the W. extremity of the province of Liguria, in the present department of Alpes-Maritimes, about a mile and a half from the coast, above Monaco; mentioned by D., together with Lerici (at the E. extremity of Liguria), in connexion with the rugged and precipitous nature of the country between those two points in his day, Purg. iii. 49. [**Lerici**.]

Turchi, Asiatic Turks; mentioned, together with the Tartars, in connexion with the brilliancy of the colouring and design of the cloths (famous in the Middle Ages) manufactured by them, Inf. xvii. 17.

Turni, followers of Turnus, i. e. the Rutulians, Epist. vii. 5⁹⁸ [Rutuli.]

Turno, Turnus, King of the Rutulians at the time of Aeneas' arrival in Italy; he fought against the latter because Latinus, King of Latium, gave his daughter Lavinia to be the wife of Aeneas, after having promised her to Turnus. During the war Turnus slew Pallas, son of Evander, who was fighting for Aeneas, and afterwards appeared in battle wearing his belt; when he and Aeneas met in single combat, and Turnus, being vanquished, begged for his life, Aeneas, who was about to spare him, caught sight of the belt of Pallas, and, maddened at the sight, rushed upon Turnus, and ran him through with his sword.

Turnus is mentioned, together with Camilla, and Nisus and Euryalus, as having died for Italy, Inf. i. 108; his prayer to Aeneas for life, and acquiescence in his marriage to Lavinia, as narrated by Virgil (*Aen.* xii. 936–7), Mon. ii. 3¹¹⁰⁻¹⁵ [Enea : Lavinia]; his single combat with Aeneas, who would have spared his life, had it not been for the belt of Pallas, as Virgil testifies (*Aen.* xii. 887–952), Mon. ii. 11⁸⁻²¹. [Pallante : Rutuli.]

Turnus. [Turno.]

Tuscani, Tuscanus. [Toschi : Tosco.]

Tusci, Tuscia. [Toschi : Toscana.]

Tyberis. [Tevere.]

Tyrrenum Mare. [Mare Tyrrenum.]

U

Ubaldin dalla Pila. [Pila, Ubaldin dalla.]

Ubaldini, powerful Ghibelline family of Tuscany, whose head-quarters were in the Mugello (the upper valley of the Sieve) to the N. of Florence, several members of which are mentioned by D., viz. the famous Cardinal, Ottaviano degli Ubaldini (Inf. x. 120) [Cardinale, Il]; his elder brother, Ubaldino dalla Pila (Purg. xxiv. 29) [Pila, Ubaldin dalla]; and his two nephews, the Archbishop Ruggieri of Pisa (Inf. xxxiii. 14) [Ruggieri, Arcivescovo] and Ugolino d'Azzo (Purg. xiv. 105) [Azzo, Ugolino d'].

Ubaldini, Ottaviano degli. [Cardinale, Il.]

Ubaldini, Ruggieri degli. [Ruggieri, Arcivescovo.]

Ubaldo, St. Ubaldo Baldassini, born 1084, Bishop of Gubbio, 1129–1160; before he was made a Bishop he lived as a hermit upon a hill near Gubbio, in N. Umbria, on which the Chiascio rises.

St. Thomas Aquinas (in the Heaven of the Sun) mentions him in connexion with his description of the situation of Assisi, Par. xi. 44. [Ascesi: Chiassi [2].]

Ubbriachi], noble Florentine family, a member of which is placed among the Usurers in Round 3 of Circle VII of Hell, being referred to by the mention of the arms of the family, viz. on a field gules a goose argent, Inf. xvii. 62–3. [Usurai.]

The Ubbriachi lived in the Sesto d'Oltrarno (Vill. v. 39); they were Ghibellines (vi. 33), and were among those expelled from Florence in 1258 (vi. 65).

Uberti, powerful Ghibelline family of Florence; mentioned by D. together with the Visconti of Milan as typical instances of noble houses, Conv. iv. 20[38-41]; Cacciaguida (in the Heaven of Mars) speaks of them (without naming them) as having been of importance in his day and as having been brought low through their pride, referring to them as *quei che son disfatti Per lor superbia,* Par. xvi. 109–10.

To this house belonged the great Ghibelline captain, Farinata degli Uberti (Inf. x. 32), to whose patriotism it was owing that the city of Florence was saved from destruction after the battle of Mont-aperti, when the majority of the victorious party were for razing it to the ground. [Farinata.]

The Uberti, like the Lamberti (with whom they are coupled by Cacciaguida), are said to have been of German origin, and to have come to Florence in Cent. x with the Emperor Otto I (Vill. iv. 1). In 1177 they headed a rising against the government (v. 9); and eventually they became the leaders of the Ghibelline party in Florence, and as such were among those who were expelled in 1258 (v. 39; vi. 33, 65); so deeply were they hated (cf. Inf. x. 83–4), that the Guelfs, after razing their houses to the ground, decreed that the site on which they had stood should never again be built upon (viii. 26), and it remains to this day the Great Square (Piazza della Signoria) of Florence.

Uberti, Farinata degli. [Farinata.]

Ubertin Donato. [Donato, Ubertin.]

Ubertino da Casale], Ubertino d'Ilia da Casale, leader of the so-called Spiritualists in the Franciscan Order, who opposed the relaxations of discipline introduced by Matteo d'Acquasparta as General of the Order; he was born in 1259, and entered the Franciscan Order in 1273; after spending nine years as lecturer in the University of Paris he returned to Italy, where after the death (1298) of Pier Giovanni Olivi he became head of the Spiritualists; during the pontificate of Clement V his party prevailed, but on the election of John XXII he withdrew from the Franciscan Order and entered (in 1317) that of St. Benedict; he died in 1338. Ubertino, who had been a disciple of Pier Pettinagno of Siena (Purg. xiii. 128), was the author of a mystical work (written in 1305), *Arbor Vitae Crucifixae Jesu,* the influence of which on D. may be traced in the *D. C.*, especially in the *Paradiso*.

Ubertino and Matteo are referred to by St. Bonaventura (in the Heaven of the Sun) in his lament over the degeneracy of the Order, to which he himself belonged, Par. xii. 124. [**Casale: Matteo d' Acquasparta.**]

Uberto da Romena. [**Obertus de Romena.**]

Ubriachi. [**Ubbriachi.**]

Uccellatoio, name of a hill a few miles to the N. of Florence, whence the traveller coming from Bologna in the old days used to catch the first glimpse of the city ; it is mentioned by Cacciaguida (in the Heaven of Mars) together with Montemalo, a hill outside Rome, Par. xv. 109-10 [**Montemalo**].

Ufficii, Degli. [*Officiis, De.*]

Ughi, ancient noble family of Florence (extinct in D.'s day), mentioned by Cacciaguida (in the Heaven of Mars) as having been already in their decline in his time, Par. xvi. 88.

Ugo Ciapetta. [**Ciapetta, Ugo.**]

Ugo da San Vittore, Hugh of St. Victor, celebrated mystic and theologian ; he was the son of a Saxon noble, at whose castle at Hartingam he was born c. 1097, and was educated during his early years in the monastery of Hamersleben in Saxony ; c. 1115 he removed to the abbey of St. Victor near Paris, which had recently been founded by William of Champeaux, the preceptor of Abelard, and which during Cent. xii was the head-

quarters of mysticism ; he became one of the canons-regular of the abbey, and was in 1133 appointed to the chair of theology, which he held until his death in 1141. He was the intimate friend of St. Bernard (Par. xxxi. 102), and among his pupils were Richard of St. Victor (Par. x. 131) and Peter Lombard (Par. x. 107). He was a voluminous writer, his most celebrated works being the *Summa Sententiarum*, a methodical or rational presentation of the contents of faith; the *De Eruditione Didascalica*, a sort of encyclopaedia of the sciences, viewed in their relation to theology ; the *Institutiones Monasticae*, including the treatises *De arca morali*, *De arca mystica*, and *De vanitate mundi* ; and the *De Sacramentis Fidei*, on the mysteries of the faith, comprising a complete exposition of catholic theology ; he also wrote commentaries upon various books of the Old and New Testament, and upon the *De Coelesti Hierarchia* of Dionysius the Areopagite.

D. places Hugh of St. Victor among the doctors of the Church (*Spiriti Sapienti*), in the Heaven of the Sun, where he is named by St. Bonaventura, Par. xii. 133. [**Sole, Cielo del.**]

Ugo di Brandimborgo], Marquis Hugh of Brandenburg, referred to by Cacciaguida (in the Heaven of Mars) as *il gran barone*, Par. xvi. 128 ; he is said to have come to Florence from Germany with the Emperor Otto III, and while there to have conferred knighthood on several Florentine families (viz. the Giandonati, the Pulci, the Ciuffagni, the Nerli, the Gangalandi, the Della Bella, and the Alepri); he died in Florence on the festival of St. Thomas the Apostle, and was buried in the Badia of Florence (founded by his mother in 978), where the anniversary of his death was (and is still) solemnly commemorated every year on St. Thomas' day (Dec. 21); these circumstances are referred to by Cacciaguida, Par. xvi. 127–132. [Badia.]

This ' marchese di Brandimborgo' (as Villani calls him, iv. 2) appears to be identical with Ugo, Marquis of Tuscany, 961–1001, who was son of Uberto, Marquis of Tuscany, 936–961 (natural son of Ugo, King of Italy and Count of Arles, 926–945), and of the Countess Willa (foundress of the Badia of Florence in 978, daughter of Marquis Bonifazio of Spoleto, and of Countess Waldrada, sister of Rudolf II of Burgundy, 912–937).

Ugolin d' Azzo. [Azzo, Ugolino d'.]

Ugolin de' Fantolin. [Fantolin, Ugolin de'.]

Ugolino, Conte, Count Ugolino della Gherardesca, member of a powerful Pisan family, was born c. 1230; he married Margherita dei Pannocchieschi (the family to which belonged the husband of La Pia, Purg. v. 133), by whom he had many children, among them Guelfo, Gaddo (Inf. xxxiii. 68), and Uguccione (Inf. xxxiii. 89). One of his daughters married Giovanni Visconti, head of the Pisan Guelfs, by whom she became the mother of Nino Visconti (Purg. viii. 53). His eldest son, Guelfo,

married a natural daughter of Enzio (natural son of the Emperor Frederick II), King of Sardinia, and had four sons, the two youngest being Nino il Brigata (Inf. xxxiii. 89) and Anselmuccio (Inf. xxxiii. 50). Ugolino, who was a Ghibelline by tradition, having conspired with his son-in-law, Giovanni Visconti (d. 1275), to transfer Pisa from the Ghibellines to the Guelfs, was sent into exile, but by the help of the Tuscan Guelfs he was restored (1276), and gradually got the chief power into his own hands. In 1284 he was in command of the Pisan fleet, which was totally defeated by the Genoese at Meloria (Aug.), not without suspicion of treachery or cowardice on the part of Ugolino. On his return to Pisa, however, Genoa, Florence, and Lucca having meanwhile made a league against Pisa, he was elected Podestà (Oct.); by the cession of certain strongholds to the Florentines and Lucchese (Inf. xxxiii. 85–6) in the following spring he saved Pisa from her foes, and assured his own position as leader of the Guelfs in the city, the rule of which he shared with his grandson, Nino Visconti (1285). Desirous of ridding himself of the latter, he intrigued with the Ghibelline party, at the head of which was Ruggieri degli Ubaldini, Archbishop of Pisa (Inf. xxxiii. 14), by whom he was himself betrayed, and imprisoned with four sons and grandsons in the Tower of Famine (July 1288), where they were starved to death (Feb. 1289).

D. places Ugolino, together with

the Archbishop, among the Traitors in Antenora, the second division of Circle IX of Hell (where those who had been traitors to their country or their party are punished), Ruggieri being below Ugolino, just on the confines of the next division, Tolomea (the place assigned to those who have betrayed their associates), Inf. xxxiii. 13, 85; (U. and Ruggieri) *duo*, Inf. xxxii. 125; *l'un*, v. 126; *il sovran*, v. 128; *quei*, v. 132; *quel peccator*, xxxiii. 2; as they pass on their way through Antenora, D. and Virgil see two sinners frozen one above the other in the same hole, the upper one of whom (Ugolino) is gnawing the head of the lower (Ruggieri) (Inf. xxxii. 124–32); in answer to an inquiry of D., Ugolino names himself and the Archbishop, and, after referring to his betrayal by the latter, goes on to describe the circumstances of his imprisonment, and of the death of himself and his four 'sons' (xxxiii. 10–75) [**Antenora: Tolomea : Traditori**].

Of the four 'sons' of Ugolino, mentioned by D. as sharing his imprisonment and death, two only were actually his sons, viz. Gaddo, his fourth, and Uguccione, his fifth son ; the other two, Anselmuccio and Nino il Brigata, were his grandsons, the sons of his eldest son Guelfo ; all of them, except Anselmuccio, were grown men at the time. [**Anselmuccio: Brigata, Il: Gaddo : Uguccione [1]**.]

The question has been raised as to what was the treachery of which D. supposed Ugolino to have been guilty; it is argued that it cannot

have been his conduct at the sea-fight of Meloria, since in that case the Pisans would not have appointed him Captain and Podestà of their city, as they did shortly after ; nor can it have been his cession of strongholds to the Lucchese and Florentines (though this appears to have been made a ground of accusation against him, as seems to be implied by D.'s allusion, Inf. xxxiii. 85–6), since it was only by this means that he was able to save Pisa, crippled as she was by the disaster at Meloria, from the league against her. Ugolino's real crime in D.'s eyes was probably his treachery to his grandson, Nino Visconti, a member of his own party, whom he expelled from Pisa in 1288 [**Nino [2]**]. Another view is that Ugolino is condemned by D. for having abandoned the Ghibelline party, to which he originally belonged, in order to ally himself (1275) with the Guelfs, by whose help Pisa, almost the last Ghibelline stronghold in Tuscany, was crushed, and he himself established as Guelf leader.

Ugolino della Gherardesca. [**Ugolino, Conte.**]

Ugolinus Bucciola. [**Bucciola, Ugolinus.**]

Uguccione [1], Uguccione della Gherardesca, fifth son of Count Ugolino, whose imprisonment and death he shared in 1288 in the Tower of Famine at Pisa, Inf. xxxiii. 89 ; he and his elder brother Gaddo are referred to as *figliuoi*, vv. 48, 87. [**Ugolino, Conte.**]

Uguccione [2], Uguccione de' Bagni of Pisa, grammarian of Cent. xii, author of a Latin dictionary, commonly known as *Magnae Deriva-*

tiones sive Dictionarium Etymologicum, a work which enjoyed a great reputation in the Middle Ages, as is testified by the large number of MSS. still existing; it has never been printed, but the bulk of it is embodied in the *Catholicon* (completed in 1286) of Giovanni da Genova.

Uguccione, or Huguitio Pisanus, as he was commonly styled, was a native of Pisa; little is known of his life beyond that he was born c. 1140, that he was professor of ecclesiastical jurisprudence at Bologna c. 1178, and that he was Bishop of Ferrara from 1190 till his death in 1210.

D. mentions Uguccione and his *Derivationes* in connexion with the etymology of *autore*, which, on U.'s authority, he connects with the Greek word *autentin* (i. e. αὐθέντην), Conv. iv. 6¹⁵⁻⁴⁵.

Though he only mentions Uguccione and his dictionary this once, it is certain that D. was familiar with the *Derivationes*, and that this work was one, if not the chief, source of his knowledge (such as it was) of Greek words, as well as of many of his etymologies; among the more striking instances of these may be mentioned *soave* (Conv. ii. 8³⁶), *facundo* (Conv. iii. 13⁸³⁻⁵), *adolescenza* (Conv. iv. 24³⁻⁴), *gioventute* (Conv. iv. 24⁵⁻⁶), *nobile* (Conv. iv. 16⁵⁹⁻⁷⁷), *protonoè* (Conv. ii. 4³⁸⁻⁹), *peripatetici* (Conv. iv. 6¹³⁸⁻⁴²), *Flegetonta* (Inf. xiv. 131, 134–5), *Galassia* (Conv. ii. 15⁸⁻¹⁰), *allegoria* (Epist. x. 7¹⁵⁹⁻⁶¹), *prosopopea* (Conv. iii. 9¹⁷⁻¹⁹), *filosofo* and *filosofia* (Conv. iii. 11³³⁻⁵⁴), and *comoedia* and *tragoedia* (Epist. x. 10¹⁹¹⁻²⁰¹).

D. was no doubt also indebted to Uguccione's etymology ('superauratus') of *hypocrita* for the idea of representing the hypocrites in Bolgia 6 of Circle VIII of Hell as wearing mantles which were brilliantly gilded on the outside, while within they were of lead (Inf. xxiii. 61–6); and to his etymology of *invidia* for the punishment of the envious (Purg. xiii. 47–72) [**Invidiosi**]. From U., too, D. apparently got his version of the incident to which he refers in connexion with the charge of sodomy insinuated against Julius Caesar during one of his triumphs (Purg. xxvi. 76–9). [**Cesare¹.**]

Uguccione della Faggiuola], the great Ghibelline leader, was born at the castle of Faggiuola in 1250; he was Podestà of Arezzo from 1292 to 1296, and was elected Captain-General of the Ghibellines of Romagna in 1297; on the death of the Emperor Henry VII in 1313, being then Imperial Vicar in Genoa, he accepted the lordship of Pisa; in 1314 he captured Lucca and expelled the Guelfs, and on Aug. 29, 1315, he totally defeated the Florentine Guelfs and their allies at Montecatini; in the next year, however, he was driven out from Pisa and Lucca and forced to take refuge with Can Grande at Verona; he met his death in Aug. 1320 while aiding Can Grande in an attack on Padua. To Uguccione, who by some is identified with the *veltro* of Inf. i. 101, D. is said to have dedicated the *Inferno*, and to him was addressed the letter (of doubtful authenticity) concerning D. of the Frate Ilario. His victory at Montecatini is referred to by G. del Virgilio, who speaks of him as *Arator*, Carm. 27. [**Feltro²: Veltro: Montecatini.**]

Uguccione della Gherardesca. [**Uguccione¹.**]

Ulisse, Ulysses of Ithaca, son of Laërtes, and father by Penelope of Telemachus, one of the principal Greek heroes in the Trojan war; he was concerned with Diomed in decoying the youthful Achilles away from the island of Scyros [**Achille: Schiro**], and in the theft of the Palladium, on the preservation of which the safety of the city of Troy depended [**Palladio**]; and he is supposed to have been the originator of the stratagem of the wooden horse by means of which Troy was taken [**Sinone**]. After the fall of Troy Ulysses wandered about the world for twenty years before returning to his home at Ithaca; among the adventures he met with in the course of his travels were his imprisonment in the cave of the Cyclops Polyphemus in Sicily [**Polyphemus**], his detention by Circe on the island of Aeaea [**Circe**], and his escape from the Sirens [**Sirena**].

D. places Ulysses, together with Diomed, among the Counsellors of evil in Bolgia 8 of Circle VIII of Hell (Malebolge), Inf. xxvi. 56; *Greci, v.* 75; *due dentro ad un foco, v.* 79; they are enveloped in a single flame, which is divided at the top, *foco diviso di sopra, vv.* 52–3; *fiamma cornuta, v.* 68; *fiamma, v.* 76; xxvii. 1; *foco, v.* 79; *fiamma antica, v.* 85 [**Consiglieri Frodolenti**]; in response to an appeal from Virgil to recount the manner of his death, Ulysses relates how, after

spending more than a year with Circe, he was impelled to go forth and see 'the untravelled world' (*vv.* 79–99); how he set forth with but one ship and a few faithful companions, and at last came to the narrow strait at the Pillars of Hercules, where was the limit of the habitable world (*vv.* 100–11); how he inspired his comrades to go forward with him into the unknown sea, and sailed westward for five months, until they sighted a lofty mountain in the dim distance (*vv.* 112–35); and how, in the midst of their rejoicing at the sight, a storm broke from the distant land, and, striking their vessel, whirled it round three times, and then plunged it, bows foremost, into the depths of the sea (cf. *Aen.* i. 114–17) (*vv.* 136–42).

Ulysses is mentioned again in connexion with the Siren, Purg. xix. 22 [**Sirena**]; and in connexion with his westward voyage, which is spoken of as 'il varco folle', Par. xxvii. 82–3 (cf. 'il folle volo', Inf. xxvi. 125).

Ungari, natives of Hungary; their tongue one of several into which the original language of Europe was split up, V. E. i. 8²⁹⁻³²; eastward from them a different tongue prevailed, V. E. i. 8³⁶⁻⁹. [**Ungaria.**]

Ungaria, Hungary, which in D.'s day was an independent kingdom; the first king was St. Stephen (1000–1038), and the last king of his line, Andrew III (1290–1301), was on the throne at the assumed date of D.'s vision.

Hungary is mentioned by the Eagle in the Heaven of Jupiter, the hope being expressed that it may no more be ill-treated at the hands of its kings, the reigning sovereign (in 1300) being Andrew III, Par. xix. 142–3 [**Andrea di Ungaria**]; it is referred to by Charles Martel (in the Heaven of Venus), who was titular King of Hungary in right of his mother, as *quella terra che il Danubio riga Poi che le ripe tedesche abbandona*, Par. viii. 64–6.

On the death of his mother's brother, Ladislas, in 1290 without issue Charles Martel became titular King of Hungary, and was crowned at Naples, but he never took possession of his kingdom, which was seized by Andrew III, first cousin of his mother's father, Stephen IV (V); the crown, however, eventually came to his son, Charles Robert, who reigned from 1308 to 1342. [**Carlo** [3] : **Carlo** [6] : **Table L.**]

Universo, the Universe, comprising the whole corporeal and incorporeal world, which in D.'s view consisted of ten perfectly concentric Heavens, the fixed immovable centre of which was the Earth (Conv. iii. 5[56–67]) ; the centre of the Earth, where is situated the nethermost pit of Hell (Inf. xi. 65–6 ; Par. xxxiii. 22–3) [**Inferno** [1]], was consequently the centre of the Universe (A. T. §§ 3[7], 12[16], 21[66]) [**Terra** [2]]; equally immovable was the outermost Heaven, the Empyrean, the abode of the Deity, the fitting crown of the Universe, as being the container of all things (Epist. x. 25[461–3]) [**Cielo Empireo**]; its desire towards this dwelling of the Deity lends to the next, the ninth or Crystalline Heaven, the *Primum Mobile*, so rapid a motion that in

spite of its immeasurable circumference it revolves upon its centre in a little under twenty-four hours, carrying with it in its circuit all the other eight Heavens, so that if its motion were suspended the whole of the Universe dependent upon it would be thrown into confusion (Conv. ii. 15[139–56]) [**Cielo Cristallino**] ; the next Heaven is that of the Fixed Stars, 1022 in number (Conv. ii. 15[18–22]), which receive their light from the Sun (Par. xx. 6 ; xxiii. 30 ; Conv. ii. 14[125] ; iii. 12[54–6]) ; this Heaven has a special motion of its own (independent of that imparted by the *Primum Mobile*), a retrograde motion of 1° from W. to E. in 100 years, which is shared by all the Heavens enclosed by it, viz. those of the seven planets, Saturn, Jupiter, Mars, the Sun, Venus, Mercury, and the Moon [**Cielo Stellato : Paradiso** [1]] ; the motions of the several Heavens are governed by Angels or Intelligences (Par. ii. 127–9 ; Conv. ii. 5[5–8]), a separate Order of which is assigned to each Heaven [**Gerarchia**].

The centre of the Universe, Inf. xi. 65–6 ; Par. xxxiii. 22–3 ; Conv. iii. 5[56–67] ; A. T. §§ 3[7], 12[16], 21[66] ; its circumference, A. T. § 21[66] ; 'tutto il corpo dell' universo', as distinguished from 'il mondo', the terrestrial globe, Conv. iii. 5[23] ; the whole Universe made in the likeness of God, Par. i. 105 ; of whose divine goodness it is as it were the footprint, Par. xix. 44 ; Mon. i. 8[15–16] ; the Deity described as *Re dell' universo*, Inf. v. 91 ; *Dispensatore dell' universo*, Conv. i.

3^{16}; *Imperadore dell' universo*, Conv. ii. 6^{11}, 16^{101-2}; *Chi mosse l'universo*, Canz. vii. 72; *Princeps universi*, Mon. i. 7^{14-15}; iii. 16^{13} [**Dio**]; Satan, *il mal dell' universo*, Inf. vii. 18 [**Lucifero**].

Urania, Muse of heavenly things; invoked by D., with her sisters, before he begins his account of the mystical Procession in the Terrestrial Paradise, Purg. xxix. 41. [**Muse.**]

Urbano [1], Urban I, native of Rome, succeeded Calixtus I as Bishop of Rome, 222–230. D. follows the tradition that he was martyred, and includes him among those of his immediate successors mentioned by St. Peter (in the Heaven of Fixed Stars) as having, like himself, shed their blood for the Church, Par. xxvii. 44.

Urbano [2], Pope Urban IV; Jacques Pantaléon de Court-Palais, native of Champagne, Bishop of Verdun and Patriarch of Jerusalem, elected Pope at Viterbo, Aug. 29, 1261; died at Perugia, Oct. 2, 1264; he is thought by some to be included among the Popes referred to, Inf. xix. 73–4.

Urbino, town of Central Italy, about twenty-five miles due S. of Rimini, in N. corner of the province of the Marches, which in D.'s time was part of Romagna; mentioned by Guido da Montefeltro (in Bolgia 8 of Malebolge) in his description of Montefeltro, Inf. xxvii. 29–30. [**Montefeltro.**]

Urbisaglia, ancient Urbs Salvia, once an important town, but in D.'s day, as now, a collection of ruins, in the province of the Marches,

about thirty miles S. of Ancona; Cacciaguida (in the Heaven of Mars) mentions it and Luni as instances of the decay and disappearance of once powerful cities, Par. xvi. 75.

Urbs Vetus, Orvieto, town of Central Italy, in Umbria, about twelve miles NE. of Bolsena; its dialect, as well as those of Perugia, Viterbo, and Città di Castello (or Civita Castellana), not discussed by D., as being closely connected with the Roman and Spoletan dialects, V. E. i. 13^{29-32}.

Ursus, name by which D. addresses the Cardinal Napoleone Orsini, Epist. viii. 10^{159}. [**Orsini, Napoleone.**]

Usurai], Usurers, placed among the Violent in Round 3 of Circle VII of Hell, Inf. xvii. 34–78 [**Violenti**]; their punishment is to be seated in a desert of burning sand, while flakes of fire fall upon them from above, Inf. xiv. 13–30; their faces are indistinguishable, but each one bears about his neck a money-bag on which the arms of the owner are depicted, so that D. is able to recognize them, Inf. xvii. 52–7. *Examples*: one of the Gianfigliazzi of Florence [**Gianfigliazzi**]; one of the Ubbriachi of Florence [**Ubbriachi**]; one of the Scrovigni of Padua [**Scrovigni**]; Vitaliano of Padua [**Vitaliano**]; and Giovanni Buiamonte of Florence [**Buiamonte, Giovanni**].

Utica, most important city after Carthage in ancient N. Africa, situated on the N. shore of the Carthaginian Gulf, to the W. of the mouth of the river Bagradas, and about thirty miles NW. of Carthage, in the modern Tunis. During the Third Punic War Utica sided with Rome against Carthage. It was afterwards famous as the scene of the last stand made by the Pompeian party against Caesar, and of the suicide of Cato the Younger, who hence got his surname of Uticensis.

D. mentions it in connexion with Cato's death, Purg. i. 74. [**Catone**[2].]

Uzza. [**Oza.**]

V

Valbona, Lizio da. [**Lizio.**]

Val Camonica, valley, some fifty miles in length, in NE. of Lombardy, through which the Oglio flows from its source in Monte Tonale down to Lovere, where the valley terminates and the river expands into the Lago d'Iseo ; mentioned in connexion with the situation of the mountain range from which, 'per mille fonti e più', the Lago di Garda is fed, Inf. xx. 65. [**Pennino**].

Val di Macra. [**Valdimacra.**]

Val di Pado, valley of the Po ; mentioned by Cacciaguida (in the Heaven of Mars), probably with reference to Ferrara, as the district to which his wife belonged, Par. xv. 137. [**Pado.**]

Valcamonica. [**Val Camonica**].

Valdarno], valley of the Arno ; referred to by Guido del Duca (in Circle II of Purgatory), in his description of the course of the Arno, as *valle*, Purg. xiv. 30 ; *misera valle*, *v.* 41. [**Arno.**]

Valdichiana, valley of the Chiana, in Tuscany ; mentioned in connexion with the unhealthiness of the district, which was infected with malaria, especially in the summer months, Inf. xxix. 47. [**Chiana.**]

Valdigreve, valley of the Greve, small river of Tuscany, which rises about twenty miles S. of Florence, and flows N., joining the Ema close to Galluzzo, about three miles from the Porta Romana of Florence ; mentioned by Cacciaguida (in the Heaven of Mars) in connexion with the Buondelmonti, the destruction of whose castle of Montebuono in the Valdigreve, in the course of the expansion of the city of Florence, was the cause of their taking up their residence in the city itself, Par. xvi. 66. [**Buondelmonti.**]

Valdimacra, valley of the Macra, which flows through Lunigiana, the territory of the Malaspina family [**Lunigiana : Macra**] ; mentioned in connexion with Moroello Malaspina, whom Vanni Fucci (in Bolgia 7 of Circle VIII of Hell) refers to as 'vapor di Val di Magra', Inf. xxiv. 145 [**Malaspina, Moroello**] ; and in connexion with Currado Malaspina, who (in Ante-purgatory) refers to Lunigiana as 'Val di Macra', Purg. viii. 116 [**Malaspina, Currado**[2]].

Vallatrensis, belonging to Velletri, town of Central Italy, in Latium, about twenty-five miles SE. of Rome, situated on a spur of the Alban Hills; it is the seat of the Bishop of Ostia.

The Cardinal Niccolò da Prato, who was Bishop of Ostia and Velletri, is addressed as ' Episcopus Ostiensis et Vallatrensis', Epist. i. *tit.* [**Nicholaus.**]

Vanna, familiar abbreviation of *Giovanna,* Son. xiv. 9 (V.N. § 24); Son. xxxii. 9. [**Giovanna⁴.**]

Vanni Fucci. [**Fucci, Vanni.**]

Vario, Lucius Varius Rufus, distinguished Roman poet of the Augustan age, intimate friend of Virgil and Horace, and one of the editors of the *Aeneid.* He is mentioned by Horace, in conjunction with Caecilius and Plautus (*A. P.* 54–5).

Some think that *Vario,* and not *Varro* should be read, Purg. xxii. 97–8. [**Varro.**]

Varo, Var, river of S. France (ancient boundary between Gallia Narbonensis and Italy), which rises in the Maritime Alps and flows into the Mediterranean a few miles SW. of Nice; it is mentioned by the Emperor Justinian (in the Heaven of Mercury), together with the Rhine, Isère, Saône, Seine, and Rhone, in connexion with Caesar's victories in Gaul, Par. vi. 58. [**Era.**]

Varro, Publius Terentius Varro, Latin poet, born B.C. 82; he wrote epics and satires in hexameter verse, and is mentioned by Horace together with Virgil and Varius (1 *Sat.* x. 44–6).

According to the commonly accepted reading, Varro is included,

with Terence, Caecilius, and Plautus, among the Roman poets as to whose fate Statius (in Purgatory) inquires of Virgil, Purg. xxii. 97–8. [**Vario.**]

Vascones, Gascons; mentioned by D. in his Letter to the Italian Cardinals with especial reference to the Gascon Pope, Clement V, and his following, Epist. viii. 11[186]. [**Guaschi.**]

Vaticano, Vatican hill at Rome, on the right bank of the Tiber, where stand the Church of St. Peter and the Vatican palace; as having been the reputed scene of the martyrdom of St. Peter and of numbers of the early Christians, it is held to be the most sacred quarter of all Rome; it is mentioned as such by the troubadour Folquet (in the Heaven of Venus), who, prophesying the removal of the papal see to Avignon (in 1305), declares that 'Vatican and the other elect parts of Rome' shall soon be freed from the presence of the adulterous Pope, Par. ix. 139–42.

Vecchiezza, Della. [**Senectute, De.**]

Vecchio Testamento. [**Bibbia.**]

Vecchio, Del, ancient noble family of Florence (otherwise known as the Vecchietti), mentioned by Cacciaguida (in the Heaven of Mars), together with the Nerli, as examples of the simple life of the Florentines of his day as compared with their degenerate and luxurious descendants, Par. xv. 115–17.

The Vecchietti lived in the Porta di san Brancazio (Vill. iv. 12); they were Guelfs (v. 39), and as such were expelled from Florence in 1248 (vi. 33), and went into exile in 1260 after the Ghibelline victory at Montaperti (vi. 79); and eventually sided, some with the Bianchi, some with the Neri (viii. 39).

Vegetius, Flavius Vegetius Renatus, author of an *Art of War*, a compilation from various sources, dedicated to the Emperor Valentinian II (A.D. 375–392); D. mentions him and his treatise, Mon. ii. 10²²⁻³. [*Re Militari, De.*]

Veglio di Creta, the 'old man of Crete', the image of gold, silver, brass, iron, and clay, on Mt. Ida in Crete, from which the rivers of Hell take their source, Inf. xiv. 103–20. [**Creta.**]

Veltro, Il, the 'greyhound', according to the prophecy of Virgil (addressing D. on the confines of Hell) the future deliverer of Italy, who should care not for land nor for wealth, but for wisdom and love and valour, and whose birthplace should be 'between Feltro and Feltro', Inf. i. 101–11. [**Feltro²**.]

The question as to the identity of the 'Veltro' (usually taken to be the same as the mysterious DXV of Purg. xxxiii. 43), which has exercised the ingenuity of numberless commentators from Cent. xiv to the present day, still remains unsolved.

The view most commonly held is that Can Grande della Scala is the individual intended; the chief arguments in his favour being the play upon the name *Cane* implied in *Veltro*, and the well-known high opinion of Can Grande entertained and expressed by D. (Par. xvii. 79–90). [**Can Grande della Scala.**]

Various other individuals have been suggested, e. g. the great Ghibelline leader, Uguccione della Faggiuola [**Uguccione³**]; some Pope or some Emperor (e. g. Henry VII of Luxemburg); or some indeterminate personage; or, lastly, Christ at His second coming.

Venedico Caccianimico. [**Caccianimico, Venedico.**]

Venere¹, Venus, Roman goddess of love, daughter of Jupiter and Dione, and mother of Cupid; *il tosco di Venere*, i. e. the poison of unlawful love, Purg. xxv. 132; her unintentional wounding by Cupid, Purg. xxviii. 65–6; Cupid her son, as proved by Virgil and Ovid, Conv. ii. 6¹¹⁷⁻²⁶ [**Cupido**]; *Venus*, i.e. love, the most exquisite of all pleasures, V. E. ii. 2⁷⁰⁻³; referred to as *Citerea*, Purg. xxvii. 95 [**Citerea**]; *la bella Ciprigna*, Par. viii. 2 [**Ciprigna**]; her son Cupid and her mother Dione worshipped as well as herself, Par. viii. 7–8 [**Dione**]; origin of her name as applied to the planet, Par. viii. 1–12 [**Venere²**].

Venere², planet Venus, Conv. ii. 2², 4⁴, ⁸⁸, 6¹⁰⁹, 14¹¹⁰, 15¹⁴⁸; *lo bel pianeta che ad amor conforta*, Purg. i. 19; *la stella d'amor*, Canz. xv. 4; *la stella Che il sol vagheggia or da coppa, or da ciglio*, Par. viii. 11–12 (cf. Conv. ii. 2²⁻⁵, 14¹¹⁴⁻¹⁵); *essa luce, v.* 19; *esta stella*, Par. ix. 33; *questa spera, v.* 110; *la stella di Venere*, Conv. ii. 2²; *la lucentissima stella di Venere*, Conv. ii. 4⁸⁸; *Colei, che 'l terzo ciel di sè costringe*, Son. xxviii. 12; alluded to by the name of Cytherea, Purg. xxvii. 95 [**Citerea**]; the fair Cypriote, Par. viii. 2 [**Ciprigna**]; and by the name of the mother of the goddess Venus,

Dione, Par. xxii. 144 [**Dione: Venere**[1]]; Venus the third in order of the planets, its position being between Mercury and the Sun, Par. viii. 3; Son. xxviii. 12; Conv. ii. 4[4], 6[109], 14[110]; the brightest of the planets, Conv. ii. 4[88], 14[111-13]; now a morning, now an evening star, Par. viii. 11-12; Conv. ii. 2[2-5], 14[114-15]; the star of love, Purg. i. 19; Canz. xv. 4; its motion on its epicycle, Par. viii. 3; Conv. ii. 4[78-88], 6[137] [**Venere, Cielo di**]; its least distance from the Earth equal to 167 half-diameters of the Earth (i.e. $167 \times 3250 = 542{,}750$ miles), Conv. ii. 7[104-8] [**Terra**[2]]; the period of its revolution, like that of Mercury, about one year, for half of which it would be concealed from the Earth if the motion of the *Primum Mobile* were suspended, Conv. ii. 15[148-50].

In the passage, Purg. i. 19-21, Venus is described as a morning star, whereas at Easter, 1300 (the commonly assumed date of the Vision) she was an evening star—a fact which has been used as an argument in favour of 1301 (when Venus was actually a morning star at Easter), as against 1300, as the date of the Vision. This argument, however, has been disposed of by the discovery that in the Almanac of Profacius, which there is every reason to believe was the Almanac used by D., by a curious mistake Venus is shown as a morning star at Easter in 1300.

Venere, Cielo di, Heaven of Venus; the third in D.'s conception of Paradise, Par. viii. 3; Conv. ii. 2[64], 4[4, 45, 78-9], 14[110]; *terzo cielo,*

Par. viii. 37; Canz. vi. 1; Son. xxviii. 12; Conv. ii. 2[47], 3[6], 4[4], 101, 5[2], 7[10], 13[69, 74], 14[1, 11, 47], 15[185-6] [**Paradiso**[1]]; resembles Rhetoric in two respects, Conv. ii. 14[110-22], 15[184-8]; it is presided over by the Thrones, according to the arrangement adopted by D. in the *Convivio*, Conv. ii. 2[63-5], 6[109-13], 126-7 [**Troni**]; by the Principalities, according to that adopted in the *D. C.* [**Principati**]; its sphere reached by the shadow of the Earth, which here comes to a point, Par. ix. 118-19 [**Terra**[2]]; its threefold motion, according to the demonstration of Alfraganus (capp. xvi, xvii), viz. firstly, the revolution of the planet on its epicycle, secondly, the motion of the epicycle with the rest of the heaven from E. to W. once every twenty-four hours with the motion of the Sun, thirdly, the motion of the heaven, with that of the Fixed Stars, from W. to E. one degree in 100 years, Conv. ii. 6[133-47] [**Cielo Stellato**].

In the Heaven of Venus D. places the spirits of those who were lovers upon earth (*Spiriti Amanti*), Par. viii. 38; among these he names Charles Martel of Hungary [**Carlo**[3]], Cunizza da Romano [**Cunizza**], Folquet of Marseilles [**Folco**], and the harlot Rahab [**Raab**].

Veneti. [**Viniziani.**]

Venetiae. [**Vinegia.**]

Venetianus, Venetian; *Venetianum vulgare,* the Venetian dialect, V. E. i. 14[47]. [**Viniziani.**]

Venezia. [**Vinegia.**]

Venus. [**Venere**[1].]

Vercelli, town of N. Italy, in the modern Piedmont, about fourteen miles SW. of Novara; mentioned by Pier da Medicina (in Bolgia 9 of Circle VIII of Hell) as the W. extremity of the old Lombardy, which he describes as *lo dolce piano Che da Vercelli a Marcabò dichina*, Inf. xxviii. 74–5 [**Lombardia**: **Marcabò**]; one of the Guelfic towns which opposed the Emperor Henry VII, Epist. vii. 6$^{130-1}$.

Verde, one of the principal rivers of S. Italy, the ancient Liris, now called the Liri from its source to its junction with the Sacco, and the Garigliano from there to its mouth; it rises in the central Apennines, and flowing S. and SE. past Sora, Ceprano (close to which it is joined by the Sacco), and Pontecorvo, falls into the Gulf of Gaeta about ten miles E. of Gaeta.

The Verde is mentioned by Manfred (in Ante-purgatory), in connexion with the disinterment of his body and its ejectment by command of the Pope from the limits of the Kingdom of Naples, Purg. iii. 131 [**Manfredi**]; and by Charles Martel (in the Heaven of Venus), as one of the boundaries of the Kingdom of Naples, it and the river Tronto representing the frontier with the Papal States, Par. viii. 63 [**Carlo**[3]: **Napoli**].

Some identify the Verde, not with the Garigliano, but with another river of that name, now known as the Castellano, which flows into the Tronto near Ascoli; there can be little doubt, however, as to the identity of the Verde mentioned by D. with the Garigliano, which, apparently as far back as Cent. x, bore the name of Verde between Sora

and Ceprano (close to its confluence with the Sacco).

Vergine. [**Maria**[1].]

Verona, city of N. Italy, at the W. extremity of the province of Venetia, situated on a bend of the Adige, some fifteen miles E. of the S. end of the Lago di Garda; in the middle of Cent. xiii it was under the lordship of the tyrant Ezzelino da Romano, after whose death (in 1259) it rose to great prominence under the Della Scala family, who were lords of Verona for more than a century, and whose tombs still form a striking feature of the city. D. was twice in Verona during his exile, firstly as the guest of (probably) Bartolommeo della Scala, and subsequently at the court of Can Grande. [**Dante: Scala, Della.**]

Verona is mentioned in connexion with the foot-race known as the *pallio* (which was run annually on the first Sunday in Lent, the prize for the winner being a piece of green cloth, while, by a singular custom, to the last in the race was given a cock), Inf. xv. 122; the monastery of San Zeno, Purg. xviii. 118 [**Zeno, San**]; its vicinity to Mantua, V. E. i. 15^{11}; Can Grande Vicar Imperial in, Epist. x. *tit.* [**Can Grande della Scala**]; the dissertation *De Aqua et Terra* delivered at, A. T. § 24^6 [**Quaestio**].

Veronenses, inhabitants of Verona; their dialect, different from that of their near neighbours the Milanese, V. E. i. 9$^{36-8}$; condemned, together with those of the Vicentines, Paduans, Trevisans, and Brescians, as harsh, especially in a woman's mouth, one of their peculiarities being a fondness for consonantal endings in *f*, V. E. i. 14[20-35].

Veronese, belonging to Verona; *il pastor Veronese*, Bishop of Verona, mentioned, together with the Bishops of Trent and Brescia, in connexion with a place at the N. extremity of the Lago di Garda where their three dioceses meet, Inf. xx. 67–9 [Benaco : Verona]; *clerus Veronensis*, the clergy of Verona, in whose presence the dissertation *De Aqua et Terra* was delivered, A. T. § 24[7] [*Quaestio*].

Veronica, La, image of the face of our Lord impressed upon the veil of St. Veronica, which is preserved at St. Peter's at Rome.

D. mentions it in connexion with the Jubilee of 1300, during which it was exhibited on every Friday and feast-day, Par. xxxi. 104; and refers to it (in connexion, not with the Jubilee as some suppose, but with the annual exhibition of the relic to pilgrims during Holy Week) as 'quella immagine benedetta, la quale Gesù Cristo lasciò a noi per esempio della sua bellissima figura', V. N. § 41[2-5].

According to the tradition, Veronica (or Berenice) was a pious woman of Jerusalem, who in compassion for Christ as He bore the cross to Golgotha offered Him her veil or kerchief that He might wipe the sweat from His brow; when Christ handed it back to her, the image of His face was found to be miraculously impressed upon it.

Verrucchio, castle and village about ten miles SW. of Rimini belonging to the Malatesta family; D. refers to Malatesta, first lord of Rimini, and his son Malatestino,

as 'il mastin vecchio e il nuovo da Verrucchio', Inf. xxvii. 46. [Malatesta.]

Veso, Monte. [Monte Veso.]

Vesoges, ancient King of Egypt; mentioned by D., on the authority of Orosius (*Hist.* i. 14, §§ 1–3), as having been defeated by the Scythians in his attempt at universal empire, Mon. ii. 9[35-42].

Vespro Siciliano], 'Sicilian Vespers', name given to the massacre of the French by the Sicilians at Palermo on the evening of March 30, 1282, which resulted in the transference of the sovereignty of the island of Sicily from the house of Anjou to that of the house of Aragon in the person of Peter III.

The massacre is referred to by Charles Martel (grandson of Charles I of Anjou, the reigning sovereign at the time), who says (in the Heaven of Venus) that if it had not been for the misgovernment of his grandfather, which 'provoked Palermo to cry, death, death', his descendants would have succeeded to the throne of Sicily, Par. viii. 67–75. [Carlo[3] : Trinacria.]

The immediate occasion of the rising was an insult offered by a French soldier to a Sicilian maiden, as she and her friends and a large number of the inhabitants of Palermo were on their way to attend a festival outside the city on Easter Monday, 1282; the movement quickly spread, and the spirit of revolt against the oppressive rule of the House of Anjou, which had for some time previously been carefully fostered by King Charles's enemies, led to a general insurrection and the final expulsion of the French from the island. [**Cicilia.**]

Vetus Testamentum. [*Bibbia.*]

Vicentia. [**Vicenza.**]

Vicentini, inhabitants of Vicenza; their dialect condemned, together with those of the Veronese, Paduans, Trevisans, and Brescians, as harsh, especially in a woman's mouth, one of their peculiarities being a fondness for consonantal endings in *f*, V. E. i. 14$^{20-35}$. [**Vicenza.**]

Vicenza, town of N. Italy, in Venetia, on the Bacchiglione, some thirty miles NE. of Verona; mentioned by Cunizza (in the Heaven of Venus) in connexion with the defeat of the Paduans by Can Grande, Imperial Vicar in Vicenza, close to the Bacchiglione, in June, 1312, Par. ix. 47 [**Padova**]; referred to by Brunetto Latini (in Round 3 of Circle VII of Hell) by the mention of the Bacchiglione, in connexion with Andrea de' Mozzi, Bishop of Vicenza, Inf. xv. 113 [**Bacchiglione**]; Can Grande Imperial Vicar in, *Vicentia*, Epist. x. *tit.* [**Can Grande della Scala**].

Vico, hereditary castle of the family of Vico, Prefects of Rome, situated in the neighbourhood of Spoleto, in the centre of Umbria, Conv. iv. 29^{16}. [**Manfredi da Vico.**]

Vico degli Strami. [**Strami, Vico degli.**]

Vico, Manfredi da. [**Manfredi da Vico.**]

Victore, Ricardus de Sancto. [**Riccardo.**]

Victoria, name given by the Emperor Frederick II to a fortress built by him opposite to the town of Parma on the occasion of his siege of that place in 1247–8.

D. refers to its surprise and capture by the Parmesans during Frederick's absence on a hunting expedition, Epist. vi. 5$^{126-33}$. [**Parmenses.**]

Vigliacchi], the Cowardly or worthless, those who were neutrals, and did neither good nor evil; D. represents them as being disqualified from entering Hell proper, and places them in Ante-hell, a region outside the river Acheron, where their naked bodies are tormented with gadflies and wasps, so that they stream with blood, Inf. iii. 21–69 [**Antinferno**]. *Example*: 'colui Che fece per viltate il gran rifiuto', Inf. iii. 59–60 [**Celestino**].

Vigne, Pier delle. [**Pier delle Vigne.**]

Vincislao, Wenceslas IV, King of Bohemia, 1278–1305, son and successor of Ottocar II (1253–1278); D. mentions him (by the mouth of Sordello in Ante-purgatory) together with his father, with whom he compares him unfavourably, reproaching him with leading a life of luxury and ease, Purg. vii. 100–2 [**Ottachero**]; the Eagle in the Heaven of Jupiter refers to him as *quel di Buemme*, and says that 'he never knew goodness nor willed it', Par. xix. 125 [**Buemme**]; the invasion of his dominions, 'il regno di Praga', by his brother-in-law, the Emperor Albert I, in order to force him to renounce the claim of his eldest son Wenceslas to the throne of Hungary, is alluded to, Par. xix. 115–17 [**Praga: Tables C, L**].

Vinegia, Venice, at the head of the Adriatic, the great maritime and commercial state of the Middle Ages; mentioned by the Eagle in the Heaven of Jupiter in connexion with the counterfeiting of the Venetian *grosso* by Stephen Ouros II, King of Rascia, Par. xix. 140–1 [**Rascia**]; referred to by Cunizza (in the Heaven of Venus) by the mention of the island Rialto, as the E. limit of the March of Treviso, Par. ix. 26 [**Rialto**]; on the left side of Italy, if the Apennines be taken as the dividing line (from N. to S.), *Venetiae*, V. E. i. 10⁵¹⁻⁴; her shipbuilding and Arsenal, Inf. xxi. 7–15.

D. is said to have visited Venice on a mission from Guido Novello da Polenta, his host at Ravenna, to the Doge Gian Soranzo, in the spring of 1321, and to have there contracted the illness of which he died in the following September at Ravenna. [**Dante.**]

Viniziani, Venetians; mentioned in connexion with their shipbuilding and famous Arsenal, Inf. xxi. 7; their dialect, coupled with that of the Trevisans, as being distinct from those of the Lombards and inhabitants of Aquileia, *Veneti*, V. E. i. 10⁶⁸⁻⁷⁰; not worthy to rank as the Italian vulgar tongue, V. E. i. 14³⁵⁻⁴⁰, ⁴⁷⁻⁸; a specimen of it quoted, V. E. i. 14⁴⁰. [**Vinegia.**]

Violenti, the Violent; punished in Circle VII of Hell, Inf. xii.

1–xvii. 78; this Circle, as Virgil explains to D., is divided into three Rounds (*gironi*), corresponding to the three different kinds of violence, inasmuch as a man may employ violence against God, Nature, or Art, against his own person or possessions, and against his neighbour's person or possessions, Inf. xi. 28–33; in Round 1 are placed the violent against their neighbour's person or possessions (viz. Tyrants, Murderers, and Robbers), Inf. xi. 34–9; xii. 1–139 [**Omicide: Predoni: Tiranni**]; in Round 2 are placed the violent against their own persons or possessions (viz. Suicides and Spendthrifts), Inf. xi. 40–5; xiii. 1–xiv. 3 [**Scialacquatori: Suicidi**]; in Round 3 are placed the violent against God (viz. Blasphemers), against Nature (viz. Sodomites), and against Art (viz. Usurers), Inf. xi. 46–51, 94–111; xiv. 4–xvii. 78 [**Bestemmiatori: Sodomiti: Usurai**].

Violetta, name of lady (thought by some to be identical with the Pietra of Canz. xii, xv; Sest. i, ii) addressed by D. in one of his *ballate*, Ball. ii. 1, 5 (in both of which passages the common, but erroneous, reading is *nuvoletta*). [**Pietra.**]

Virgilio, poet Virgil (Publius Virgilius Maro), born at the small village of Andes (identified with the modern Pietola), near Mantua in Cisalpine Gaul, Oct. 15, B.C. 70; he was educated as a youth at Cremona and Milan, and at the age of seventeen proceeded to Rome, where he studied oratory and philosophy. After the battle of Philippi

(B. C. 42) his property was con-fiscated, but he was compensated by an estate in Campania, and intro-duced to the friendship of Octavia-nus (afterwards Emperor Augustus). Besides the *Eclogues*, *Georgics*, and *Aeneid*, several shorter poems are attributed to him, such as the *Culex* and *Ciris*, which in mediaeval times were unhesitatingly accepted as his. Virgil died, in his fifty-first year, at Brundusium (Brindisi) on his way back from Greece, Sept. 26, B. C. 19; and was, at his own request, buried near Naples, on the road to Puteoli (Pozzuoli); his tomb within a century of his death was wor-shipped as a holy place, and through-out the Middle Ages the supposed site was regarded with superstitious reverence, Virgil himself having assumed in the popular imagination the character of a wizard and ma-gician (a view of which no trace is to be found in D.'s works).

To D., Virgil, as the poet of the Roman Empire, appealed with an authority second only to that of Scripture; his writings, which are quoted by D. more frequently than any save the Bible and Aristotle, are regarded as divinely inspired (cf. 'divinus poeta noster Virgilius', Mon. ii. 3^{28-9}), while he himself is spoken of as ' somma virtù' (Inf. x. 4), and as being the mouthpiece of the Deity (Conv. iv. 4^{115-16}; cf. Purg. xxii. 66–73). As D.'s guide through the realms of Hell and Purgatory Virgil represents human reason, the light of which suffices D. until his arrival upon the threshold of Paradise, when Virgil's place is taken by Beatrice, the

representative of divine science (Purg. xxx. 31–51).

Virgil is mentioned by name, Inf. i. 79; xix. 61; xxiii. 124; xxix. 4; xxxi. 133; Purg. ii. 61; iii. 74; vi. 67; vii. 7; viii. 64; x. 53; xiii. 79; xix. 28; xxi. 14, 101, 103, 125; xxii. 10; xxiii. 130; xxiv. 119; xxvii. 20, 118, 126; xxix. 56; xxx. 46, 49, 50, 51, 55; Par. xvii. 19; xxvi. 118; V.N. § 25^{73}; Conv. i. 3^{75}; ii. 6^{120}, 11^{38}; iii. 11^{158}; iv. 4^{115}, 24^{96}, 26^{60}; *Virgilius*, V. E. ii. 6^{80}, 8^{22}; Mon. i. 11^{3}; ii. 3^{29}; *Maro*, Epist. vii. 1^{23}; Carm. 36; he is referred to as *il Poeta*, Inf. iv. 14; v. 111; ix. 51; xii. 113; xiii. 80; xviii. 20; xxix. 121; Purg. iv. 58, 136; v. 44; x. 101; xiii. 11; xiv. 140; xix. 82; xxii. 115, 139; xxviii. 146; *l'altissimo Poeta*, Inf. iv. 80; *l'antico Poeta*, Inf. x. 121–2; *il dolce Poeta*, Inf. xxvii. 3; *lo maggior nostro Poeta*, Conv. iv. 26^{60}; *Poeta*, Mon. ii. 5^{109}; *Poeta Aeneidorum*, V. E. ii. 4^{73}; *Poeta noster*, Mon. ii. $3^{44, 63, 71, 97,}$ $^{104, 111}$, 4^{50}, $5^{97, 117}$, 7^{67}, 8^{92}, 9^{83}, 11^{20}; *divinus Poeta noster*, Mon. ii. 3^{28-9}; *noster Vates*, Mon. ii. 3^{78}; (according to some), *quel Signor del-l'altissimo canto*, *Che sopra gli altri com' aquila vola*, Inf. iv. 95–6 (where others think Homer is intended); *il nostro maggior Musa*, Par. xv. 26; *il Cantor de' Bucolici Carmi*, Purg. xxii. 57; *il Dottore*, Inf. xvi. 48; *il mio Dottore*, Inf. v. 70; xvi. 13; Purg. xxi. 22, 131; (by Francesca da Rimini addressing D.), *il tuo Dottore*, Inf. v. 123; *l'alto Dottore*, Purg. xviii. 2; *il Duca*, Inf. iii. 94; vi. 94; viii. 28; x. 37; xvi. 110;

xvii. 28 ; xviii. 75, 127 ; xxii. 64 ;
xxiii. 80, 139, 145 ; xxiv. 20, 121,
127 ; xxv. 44 ; xxvi. 46 ; xxix.
17, 94 ; xxxii. 85 ; xxxiv. 78,
133 ; il Duca mio, Inf. v. 21 ; vi.
25 ; viii. 25 ; ix. 2 ; x. 30 ; xiv.
50, 61, 91 ; xvii. 4, 79 ; xix. 121 ;
xxi. 23, 88, 98, 104 ; xxii. 46,
78 ; xxiii. 37, 73 ; xxv. 36 ; xxvi.
15, 77 ; xxvii. 133 ; xxviii. 32 ;
xxix. 86 ; xxxi. 70, 93, 131 ;
xxxiv. 9, 78 ; Purg. i. 49, 111 ;
ii. 20 ; iv. 23 ; v. 2 ; vii. 9 ; viii.
88 ; ix. 68, 107 ; x. 11 ; xii. 136 ;
xv. 118 ; xvi. 14 ; xvii. 64 ; xviii.
12 ; xx. 4 ; xxii. 101, 121 ; xxv.
118 ; il mio buon Duca, Inf. xii. 83 ;
il dolce Duca, Inf. xviii. 44 ; Purg.
vi. 71 ; il savio Duca, Inf. iv. 149 ;
Purg. xxi. 76 ; xxvii. 41 ; lo verace
Duca, Inf. xvi. 62 ; il Maestro, Inf.
vii. 37 ; ix. 58, 86 ; xi. 13 ; xiii.
28, 136 ; xvi. 90, 117 ; xxiv. 47 ;
xxix. 22 ; xxx. 131, 143 ; xxxi.
130 ; xxxiv. 62, 83, 94 ; Purg. iii.
100 ; v. 11 ; xx. 134 ; il Maestro
mio, Inf. x. 3, 115 ; xii. 64 ; xv.
97 ; xxi. 80 ; xxii. 61 ; xxiii. 49 ;
xxv. 25 ; xxviii. 47 ; xxxiv. 3, 17 ;
Purg. i. 125 ; ii. 25, 115 ; iii. 53 ;
v. 31 ; ix. 89 ; xii. 11 ; xv. 40 ;
xvi. 29 ; xvii. 11, 81 ; xxi. 118 ;
il savio mio Maestro, Inf. viii. 86 ;
il Maestro accorto, Inf. viii. 41 ; lo
buon Maestro, Inf. iv. 31, 85 ; vii.
115 ; viii. 67 ; xiii. 16 ; xviii. 82 ;
xix. 43 ; xxi. 58 ; xxix. 100 ;
Purg. xiii. 37 ; xix. 34 ; xxvi. 2 ;
il Maestro cortese, Inf. iii. 121 ; il
dolce maestro, Purg. x. 47 ; il dolce
Pedagogo, Purg. xii. 3 ; lo dolce
Padre mio, Purg. xxv. 17 ; xxvii.
52 ; lo dolce Padre, Inf. viii. 110 ;
dolcissimo Padre, Purg. xxx. 50 ;

quel Padre verace, Purg. xviii. 7 ;
lo più che Padre, Purg. xxiii. 4 ; il
mio Saggio, Purg. xxvii. 69 ; quel
Saggio, Inf. x. 128 ; il Savio, Inf.
iv. 110 ; Purg. xxiii. 8 ; lo Savio
mio, Inf. xii. 16 ; xiii. 47 ; quel
Savio gentil, che tutto seppe, Inf. vii.
3 ; la mia Scorta, Inf. xii. 54 ; xiii.
130 ; xviii. 67 ; xx. 26 ; la Scorta
mia saputa e fida, Purg. xvi. 8 ; la
buona Scorta, Purg. xxvii. 19 ; la
Guida mia, Purg. xix. 53 ; (by
Beatrice speaking of D.), Colui che
l'ha quassù condotto, Purg. xxx.
139 ; la fida Compagna, Purg. iii.
4 ; il mio Signore, Inf. viii. 20, 116 ;
Purg. vii. 61 ; ix. 46 ; xix. 85 ;
questo mio Signore, Inf. xvi. 55 ;
quel Signor, che m'avea menato, Inf.
viii. 103–4 ; il mio Conforto, Purg.
iii. 22 ; ix. 43 ; Quei, che m'era ad
ogni uopo soccorso, Purg. xviii. 130 ;
il mio Consiglio saggio, Purg. xiii. 75 ;
il Magnanimo, Inf. ii. 44 ; gran
Maliscalco, Purg. xxiv. 99 ; quella
Fonte Che spande di parlar sì largo
fiume, Inf. i. 79–80 ; il Mar di
tutto il senno, Inf. viii. 7 ; quell' Ombra gentil, per cui si noma Pietola
più che villa Mantovana, Purg. xviii.
82–3 ; he is addressed by D. as,
degli altri poeti Onore e Lume, Inf. i.
82 ; lo mio Maestro e il mio Autore,
Inf. i. 85 ; Colui, da cui io tolsi Lo
bello stile che mi ha fatto onore, Inf.
i. 86–7 ; Poeta, Inf. i. 130 ; ii. 10 ;
v. 73 ; Duca, Inf. ii. 140 ; buon Duca,
Inf. x. 19 ; Duca mio, Inf. xxix.
31 ; caro Duca mio, Inf. viii. 97 ;
Maestro, Inf. ii. 140 ; iii. 12, 32,
43, 72 ; v. 50 ; vi. 103 ; vii. 49,
67 ; xiv. 43, 130 ; xix. 31 ; xx.
100 ; xxi. 127 ; xxiii. 21 ; xxiv.
72 ; xxvi. 65 ; xxxi. 21 ; Purg. iii.

61; x. 112; xii. 118; xvi. 22; xviii. 10 ; *Maestro mio*, Inf. iv. 46 ; vii. 37; xxii. 43; xxvi. 49; xxxii. 82; xxxiii. 104; xxxiv. 101 ; Purg. iv. 36, 76; *Padre*, Purg. xiii. 34; *dolce Padre*, Purg. iv. 44 ; xv. 25; xxiii. 13 ; *dolce Padre mio*, Purg. xv. 124; *dolce mio Padre*, Purg. xvii. 82 ; *dolce Padre caro*, Purg. xviii. 13 ; *famoso Saggio*, Inf. i. 89 ; *Signore*, Inf. ii. 140; iv. 46; xix. 38 ; Purg. vi. 49 ; *dolce Signor mio*, Purg. iv. 109; *Cortese*, Inf. ii. 134; *Virtù somma*, Inf. x. 4 ; *Sol che sani ogni vista turbata*, Inf. xi. 91 ; *Luce mia*, Purg. vi. 29 ; by Beatrice as, *Anima cortese mantovana*, Inf. ii. 58 ; by Sordello as, *Gloria de' Latini*, Purg. vii. 16 ; *Pregio eterno* (*di Mantova*), Purg. vii. 18.

Virgil's parents ' Lombards ', Inf. i. 68 [**Lombardi**]; his birth ' sub Julio ', Inf. i. 70 [**Julius**]; his birthplace, Pietola near Mantua, Inf. ii. 58 ; xx. 91–9; Purg. vi. 72, 74 ; xviii. 82–3 [**Mantova : Pietola**]; his life at Rome under Augustus, Inf. i. 71 [**Augusto** [2]]; his death at Brundusium, Purg. iii. 27 ; whence his body was taken to be buried at Naples, Purg. iii. 27 ; by order of Octavianus, Purg. vii. 6 [**Brandizio : Napoli : Ottaviano**]; his previous visit to Hell to fetch a spirit at the bidding of Erichtho, Inf. ix. 22–7. [**Eriton.**]

Virgil is referred to as the author of the *Eclogues*, Purg. xxii. 55 ; Mon. i. 11[5] [***Bucolica***] ; and of the *Aeneid*, Inf. i. 73–5; xx. 113; Purg. xxi. 95–7; V. N. § 25[73–6]; Conv. i. 3[75] ; ii. 6[120] ; iii. 11[158–9]; iv. 4[115], 24[96], 26[60–70]; V. E. ii. 4[73], 8[22]; Mon. ii. 3[29], 11[15] [***Aeneis***];

he is mentioned, together with Ovid, Statius, and Lucan, as one of the ' regulati poetae ', V. E. ii. 6[79–81] ; and, together with Homer, Horace, Ovid, and Lucan, he makes up ' la bella scuola Di quei signor dell' altissimo canto ', Inf. iv. 94–5 ; he is alluded to by G. del Virgilio (with reference to Inf. iv. 88–90, 101–2), Carm. 17.

Virgil's place is in Limbo, Inf. iv. 39, 81 ; Purg. vii. 31–6; xxii. 100–14; as not having duly worshipped God, Inf. iv. 37–42 ; as having sought the truth by the light of reason only, Purg. iii. 34–45 ; and as having lacked faith, Purg. vii. 7–8 ; not for any ill-doing, but for the neglect of well-doing, Purg. vii. 25–7, 34–6. [**Limbo.**]

Virgilio, Giovanni del], poet and professor of Latin poetry at Bologna, 1318–1325 (so called, as is supposed, from his devotion to Virgil), who in a Latin poem (written in 1319) invited D. while at Ravenna to come and receive the laurel crown at Bologna, an invitation which D. declined, his answer being in the form of a Latin eclogue (Ecl. i); Giovanni sent an eclogue in reply (Ecl. R.), repeating the invitation, in response to which D. wrote a second eclogue (Ecl. ii). In this correspondence Giovanni figures under the name of *Mopsus*, Ecl. i. 6, 7, &c. [**Mopsus**], and D. under that of *Tityrus*, Ecl. i. 6, 24, &c. [**Tityrus**]; he speaks of himself (in allusion to his name) as *verna Maronis*, Carm. 36. Giovanni was the author of the epitaph on D. beginning, ' Theologus Dantes nullius dogmatis expers.' [***Egloghe*** [2].]

Virtù Cardinali, Delle Quattro. [*QuatuorVirtutibus Cardinalibus, De.*]

Virtudi, Virtues, mentioned by Beatrice (in the Crystalline Heaven), in her exposition of the arrangement of the Angelic Hierarchies, as ranking second in the second Hierarchy, between Dominions and Powers, Par. xxviii. 122–3 ; in the *Convivio* D. states that the second Hierarchy is composed of Principalities, Virtues (*Virtuti*), and Dominions, in that order, Conv. ii. 6$^{51-3}$ [Gerarchia]. They preside over the Heaven of Mars [Paradiso[1]].

Virtuti. [Virtudi.]

Virtutibus Cardinalibus, De Quatuor. [*Quatuor Virtutibus Cardinalibus, De.*]

Visconti[1], powerful Ghibelline family of Milan, of which city they were lords for many years; mentioned by D., together with the Uberti of Florence, as typical instances of noble houses, Conv. iv. 20$^{38-41}$; Galeazzo Visconti (of Milan) is referred to by Nino Visconti (of Pisa) (in Ante-purgatory) by the mention of the family arms, a viper, Purg. viii. 80 [Galeazzo : Milanese].

The Visconti of Milan appear to have been of a wholly different stock from the family of the same name at Pisa. [Visconti[2].]

Visconti[2]], powerful Guelf family of Pisa, for several centuries lords of the district of Gallura in Sardinia; to this family belonged Nino Visconti, Judge of Gallura, whom D. sees in Ante-purgatory, Purg. viii. 53. [Gallura : Nino[2] : Visconti[1].]

Visconti, Galeazzo. [Galeazzo.]

Visconti, Nino. [Nino[2].]

Visdomini], noble Florentine family, alluded to by Cacciaguida (in the Heaven of Mars), together with the Tosinghi (and, as some think, the Aliotti), as being patrons of the Bishopric of Florence, the revenues of which they enjoyed during the vacancy of the see, Par. xvi. 112–14. [Aliotti : Tosinghi.]

Visio Johannis. [*Johannis Visio.*]

Vita Nova. [*Vita Nuova.*]

Vita Nuova, D.'s *New Life,* treatise in Italian, partly in prose, partly in verse, the prose text being a vehicle for the introduction and interpretation of the poems. The latter are thirty-one in number, consisting of twenty-five sonnets (of which two are irregular), five *canzoni* (two of which are imperfect), and one *ballata* [**Canzoniere**].

In the *Vita Nuova,* which is addressed to his 'first friend', Guido Cavalcanti (V. N. § 31^{22}), D. relates the story of his love for Beatrice, whom he first saw when he was nine years old (V. N. § 2) (i.e. in 1274); when he was eighteen (i.e. in 1283), he received a greeting from her, after which he had a vision, whereon he composed the sonnet, 'A ciascun' alma presa, e gentil core' (Son. i), his earliest known poetical composition (V. N. § 3); later he records the death of Beatrice (V. N. §§ 29, 30), and his own grief thereat, and how after a time he received consolation from a young and beautiful lady (V. N. § 36$^{9-10}$), whom in the *Convivio* (ii. 2$^{8-12}$) he declares to be philosophy; he concludes with the resolve, should his life be spared, to say of Beatrice what was never said of any woman, a resolve which was carried into execution in the *Divina Commedia* (V. N. § 43⁸⁻¹¹).

The title *Vita Nuova* was given to the work by D. himself; in the *Convivio* he several times refers to it by this name, Conv. i. 1¹¹³; ii. 2⁹, 13²⁸; in the book itself he speaks of it by the Latin name *Vita Nova*, V. N. § 1⁴; there is perhaps an allusion to the title, Purg. xxx. 115; D. otherwise refers to it as *libello*, V. N. §§ 1⁷, 25¹⁰⁰, 29¹⁹; Conv. ii. 2¹³. The division of the work into chapters or sections is not due to D., and dates from the last century only.

Vitaliano, name of a Paduan, whom D. places by anticipation among the Usurers (the only one who is mentioned by name, all the others being indicated by the mention of their arms) in Round 3 of Circle VII of Hell, Inf. xvii. 68; one of them, Rinaldo degli Scrovigni, informs D. that at present he is the only native of Padua there, all the rest being Florentines, but that soon his neighbour Vitaliano will be sitting alongside of him (*vv.* 67–70). [Usurai.]

This Vitaliano has been identified by some with Vitaliano del Dente, who was Podestà of Padua in 1307; by others with Vitaliano di Jacopo Vitaliani, who is mentioned in an old Paduan chronicle (c. 1335) as having been a great usurer.

Viterbium, Viterbo, town of Central Italy, in N. of Latium, between the Lago di Bolsena and the Lago di Vico, about forty miles NW. of Rome; its dialect, as well as those of Perugia, Orvieto, and Città di Castello (or Civita Castellana), not discussed by D., as being closely connected with the Roman and Spoletan dialects, V. E. i. 13²⁹⁻³²; the murder of Prince Henry 'of Almain' at Viterbo in 1271 by his cousin, Guy de Montfort, is referred to, Inf. xii. 119–20 [**Arrigo**⁶: **Guido di Monforte**]; the Bulicame, or hot-spring, near Viterbo, is mentioned, Inf. xiv. 79 [**Bulicame**].

Vittore, Riccardo da San. [Riccardo.]

Vittore, Ugo da San. [Ugo².]

Volto, Santo. [Santo Volto.]

Votivi Mancanti, Spiriti. [Spiriti Votivi Mancanti.]

Vulcano, Vulcan, Roman god of fire, who was supposed to manufacture the thunderbolts of Jupiter in his forge beneath Mt. Aetna, his workmen being the Cyclopes; mentioned by Capaneus (in Round 3 of Circle VII of Hell) in his defiance of Jupiter, Inf. xiv. 57; and referred to as *il fabbro di Giove*, v. 52 [**Capaneo**]; regarded by the heathen as the god of fire, Conv. ii. 5⁴⁰⁻¹ [**Cyclopes**].

Vulgari Eloquentia, De. [*Eloquentia, De Vulgari.*]

X

Xerxes. [Serse.]

Z

Zabulone], Zebulun, son of Jacob and Leah ; he is among those referred to by Virgil as having been released by Christ from Limbo, *Israel co' suoi nati*, Inf. iv. 59 [Limbo].

Zama]; city in Numidia, on the borders of the Carthaginian territory, scene of the decisive victory of Scipio Africanus Major over Hannibal (Oct. 19, B.C. 202), which brought to an end the long struggle between Rome and Carthage ; the battle is alluded to, Inf. xxxi. 115–17 ; Conv. iv. 5[170-1] ; Mon. ii. 11[59-61]. [Scipione[1].]

Zambrasi, Tebaldello. [Tebaldello.]

Zanche, Michel. [Michel Zanche.]

Zebedaeus, Zebedee, fisherman of Galilee, father of the Apostles James (the Great) and John (*Matt.* iv. 21), and husband of Salome (*Matt.* xxvii. 56 ; *Mark* xv. 40) [Maria Salome] ; *filii Zebedaei*, i.e. the Apostles James and John, present at the Transfiguration of our Lord (*Matt.* xvii. 1–2), Mon. iii. 9[81-3] [Giovanni[2] : Jacopo[1]].

Zeffiro, Zephyrus, the W. wind ; mentioned by St. Bonaventura (in the Heaven of the Sun) in the description of the birthplace of St. Dominic (Calahorra in Spain), Par. xii. 46–52. [Callaroga.]

Zeno. [Zenone.]

Zeno, San, Church and Monastery of San Zeno (Bishop of Verona in Cent. iv) at Verona ; mentioned, Purg. xviii. 118 ; referred to as *quel monistero*, v. 122. D. places an Abbot of San Zeno (who has been identified with a certain Gherardo II, who was abbot, in the time of the Emperor Frederick I, from 1163 till his death in 1187) among the Slothful in Circle IV of Purgatory, Purg. xviii. 118 ; *uno spirto*, v. 113 [Accidiosi] ; in conversation with Virgil he relates that he was Abbot of San Zeno in Verona under Frederick Barbarossa (*vv.* 118–20) ; and reproaches Alberto della Scala with having put his base-born and depraved son, Giuseppe, into the monastery as Abbot (*vv.* 121–6) [Alberto della Scala].

Zenone, Zeno, of Citium in Cyprus, founder of the Stoic school of philosophy (c. B.C. 400) ; after studying at Athens under various Megaric and Academic philosophers, he opened a school of his own in the painted porch (*Stoa*) of Polygnotus, whence his pupils came to be known as Stoics.

D. places Zeno, together with Empedocles and Heraclitus, among the great philosophers of antiquity in Limbo, Inf. iv. 138 [Limbo]; mentions him together with Socrates and Seneca as having expressed a contempt for life in comparison with wisdom, Conv. iii. 14$^{84-6}$; the first of the ancient philosophers who taught that virtue is the sole end of human life, Conv. iv. 6$^{83-93}$; the founder of the Stoic school of philosophy, Conv. iv. 6$^{93-4}$; his doctrine and that of Epicurus as to the real end of human life set aside as false, that of Aristotle being the true one, Conv. iv. 22$^{27-31}$ [*Academicae Quaestiones*: Stoici].

Zita, Santa, patron saint of Lucca (originally a domestic servant), who died c. 1275 and was canonized by Nicholas III; her tomb is in one of the chapels in the Church of San Frediano at Lucca, where her body is still preserved and exhibited on her festival (April 27).

D. mentions Santa Zita to indicate the city of which she was patroness, speaking of a Lucchese magistrate (said to have been one Martino Bottaio) whom he places among the Barrators in Bolgia 5 of Circle VIII of Hell (Malebolge), as 'un degli anzian' di Santa Zita' (the 'Anziani' at Lucca answering to the 'Priori' at Florence), Inf. xxi. 38; *un peccator*, v. 35; *quei*, v. 46. [Barattieri: Bottaio, Martino.]

Zodiaco, Zodiac, a belt of the heavens eighteen degrees in breadth, extending nine degrees on either side of the Ecliptic, within which, according to the Ptolemaic system, the Moon, Mercury, Venus, the Sun, Mars, Jupiter, and Saturn perform their annual revolutions. It is divided into twelve equal parts of thirty degrees, called signs, which are named from the constellations lying within them.

D. mentions the Zodiac, Purg. iv. 64; A. T. §§ 19^{57}, 20^{61}, 21^{39}; and refers to it as *l'obliquo cerchio che i pianeti porta*, Par. x. 14; he names or refers to the following of the signs:— Aries [Ariete]; Taurus [Tauro]; Gemini [Gemelli]; Cancer [Cancro]; Leo [Leone]; Libra [Libra]; Scorpio [Scorpio]; Capricornus [Capricorno]; Aquarius [Aquario]; and Pisces [Pesci].

557

TABLES

558

LIST OF TABLES

[TABLE B]

KINGS OF ARAGON AND SICILY,
1196–1337.

PETER II, King of Aragon	1196 – 1213
JAMES I (son), King of Aragon	1213 – 1276
PETER III ᵃ (son), King of Aragon	1276 }–1285
King of Sicily	1282 }
ALPHONSO III ᵇ (son), King of Aragon	1285 – 1291
JAMES II ᶜ (brother), King of Sicily	1285 – 1296
King of Aragon	1291 – 1327
FREDERICK II ᵈ (brother), King of Sicily	1296 – 1337

ᵃ [PIETRO ³: TABLE E]   ᵇ [ALFONSO ¹.]   ᶜ [JACOMO ¹ : TABLE E]
ᵈ [FEDERICO ³ : TABLE E]

[TABLE C]

KINGS OF BOHEMIA,
1197–1346.

PREMYSL OTTOCAR I	1197–1230
WENCESLAS III (son)	1230–1253
OTTOCAR II ᵃ (son)	1253–1278
WENCESLAS IV ᵇ (son)	1278–1305
WENCESLAS V (son) ¹	1305–1306
RUDOLF, of Hapsburg ²	1306–1307
HENRY, Duke of Carinthia ³	1307–1310
JOHN ᶜ, of Luxemburg ⁴	1310–1346

¹ King of Hungary, 1301–1305.
² Eldest son of Emperor Albert I; married widow of Wenceslas IV.
³ Married elder daughter of Wenceslas IV.
⁴ Eldest son of Emperor Henry VII; married younger daughter of Wenceslas IV.

ᵃ [OTTACHERO.]   ᵇ [VINCISLAO.]   ᶜ [GIOVANNI ⁴.]

[TABLE D]

KINGS OF CASTILE AND LEON,

1126-1350.

ALPHONSO VII, King of Castile and Leon, 1126-1157 [1].

SANCHO III (son), King of Castile, 1157-1158 (brother of) FERDINAND II, King of Leon, 1157-1188.

ALPHONSO VIII [a] (son), King of Castile, 1158-1214. ALPHONSO IX (son) [2], King of Leon, 1188-1230.

HENRY I (son), King of Castile, 1214-1217.

FERDINAND III (nephew) [3], King of Castile, 1217-1230; King of Castile and Leon, 1230-1252.

ALPHONSO X [b] (son), King of Castile and Leon, 1252-1284.

SANCHO IV (son), King of Castile and Leon, 1284-1295.

FERDINAND IV [c] (son), King of Castile and Leon, 1295-1312.

ALPHONSO XI (son), King of Castile and Leon, 1312-1350.

[1] On the death of Alphonso VII the crowns of Castile and Leon were divided, his eldest son becoming King of Castile, his younger King of Leon.

[2] Married the daughter of Alphonso VIII, King of Castile, and thus brought about the re-union of the crowns of Castile and Leon in the person of his son, Ferdinand III.

[3] See previous note.

[a] [ALFONSO 2.]   [b] [ALFONSO 3.]   [c] [FERDINANDO.]

[TABLE E]

KINGS OF SICILY AND NAPLES,
1129–1343.

NORMAN DYNASTY.

ROGER I	1129–1154
WILLIAM I (son)	1154–1166
WILLIAM II [a] (son)	1166–1189
TANCRED (first cousin)	1189–1194
WILLIAM III (son) [1]	1194

SWABIAN DYNASTY.

HENRY I (Emperor Henry VI) [2] [b]	1194–1197
FREDERICK I (Emperor Frederick II) [c] (son) . . .	1197–1250
CONRAD I (Emperor Conrad IV) (son)	1250–1254
CONRAD II (Conradin) [d] (son)	1254–1258
MANFRED [3] [e] (uncle)	1258–1266

ANGEVIN DYNASTY.

CHARLES I [4] [f] (of Anjou)	1266–1282

SEPARATION OF NAPLES AND SICILY (1282).

Naples (House of Anjou).		*Sicily* (House of Aragon).	
CHARLES I [f] . .	1282–1285	PETER III [5] [1] . .	1282–1285
CHARLES II [g] (son) .	1285–1309	JAMES II [k] (son) .	1285–1296
ROBERT [h] (son) .	1309–1343	FREDERICK II [1] (brother)	1296–1337

[1] Deposed by Emperor Henry VI, who had married (1185) Constance, daughter of Roger I.

[2] See previous note.

[3] Defeated by Charles of Anjou and slain at Benevento.

[4] See previous note; driven out of Sicily after the 'Sicilian Vespers'.

[5] Assumed the crown, after the expulsion of Charles of Anjou (see previous note), in right of his wife, Constance, daughter of King Manfred.

[a] [GUGLIELMO [2].]   [b] [ARRIGO [5] : TABLE H]   [c] [FEDERICO [2] : TABLE H]
[d] [CURRADINO.]   [e] [MANFREDI.]   [f] [CARLO [1].]   [g] [CARLO [2].]
[h] [ROBERTO [2].]   [1] [PIETRO [3] : TABLE B]   [k] [JACOMO [1] : TABLE B]
[1] [FEDERICO [3] : TABLE B]

O O

[TABLE F]

KINGS OF JERUSALEM AND CYPRUS,
1186–1324

GUY OF LUSIGNAN, King of Jerusalem [1]	1186 – 1192
Lord of Cyprus [2]	1192 – 1194
AMALRIC II (brother), King of Jerusalem	1197 } – 1205
Lord of Cyprus, 1194; King . .	1197 }
HUGH I (son), King of Cyprus	1205 – 1218
HENRY I (son), King of Cyprus	1218 – 1253
HUGH II (son), King of Cyprus	1253 – 1267
HUGH III (first cousin), King of Cyprus and Jerusalem .	1267 – 1284
JOHN I (son), King of Cyprus	1284 – 1285
HENRY II [a] (brother), King of Cyprus	1285 – 1324

[1] In right of his wife, Sibylla, daughter of Amalric I, King of Jerusalem, 1162–1173.

[2] Cyprus was taken from the Greeks by Richard Cœur-de-Lion in 1191, on his way to join the third Crusade, and conferred by him on Guy of Lusignan.

[a] [ARRIGO [8].]

[TABLE G]

KINGS OF PORTUGAL,
1139–1325.

ALPHONSO I	1139–1185
SANCHO I (son)	1185–1211
ALPHONSO II (son)	1211–1223
SANCHO II (son)	1223–1248
ALPHONSO III (brother)	1248–1279
DIONYSIUS [a] (son)	1279–1325

[a] [DIONISIO [3].]

[TABLE H]

EMPERORS OF THE HOHENSTAUFEN (OR SWABIAN) LINE, 1138-1254.

CONRAD III [a]	1138-1152
FREDERICK I [b] (nephew)	1152-1190
HENRY VI [1][c] (son)	1190-1197
FREDERICK II [2][d] (son)	1212-1250
CONRAD IV [3][e] (son)	1250-1254

[1] King of Sicily and Naples, 1194-1197 ; at his death the Imperial crown was contested by Philip, Duke of Swabia (1198-1208) and Otho IV (1208-1211).
[2] King of Sicily and Naples, 1197-1250.
[3] King of Sicily and Naples, 1250-1254.

[a] [CURRADO [1].]   [b] [FEDERICO [1].]   [c] [ARRIGO [5]: TABLE E]
[d] [FEDERICO [2]: TABLE E]   [e] [TABLE E]

[TABLE J]

KINGS OF ENGLAND, 1154-1327.

HENRY II [a]	1154-1189
RICHARD I (son) [1]	1189-1199
JOHN (brother)	1199-1216
HENRY III [b] (son)	1216-1272
EDWARD I [c] (son)	1272-1307
EDWARD II (son)	1307-1327

[1] Richard I was the third son of Henry II ; William, the eldest, died in childhood ; Henry, the second son, who was crowned in his father's lifetime, and was hence known as the Young King, died in 1183 [ARRIGO [4]].

[a] [ARRIGO [9].]   [b] [ARRIGO D'INGHILTERRA.]   [c] [EDOARDO.]

[TABLE K]

KINGS OF FRANCE OF THE CAPETIAN DYNASTY,
987–1322.

HUGH CAPET [a]	987–996
ROBERT [b] (son)	996–1031
HENRY I (son)	1031–1060
PHILIP I (son)	1060–1108
LOUIS VI (son)	1108–1137
LOUIS VII (son)	1137–1180
PHILIP (AUGUSTUS) II (son)	1180–1223
LOUIS VIII (son)	1223–1226
LOUIS IX (son)	1226–1270
PHILIP III [c] (the Bold) (son)	1270–1285
PHILIP IV [d] (the Fair) (son)	1285–1314
LOUIS X (son)	1314–1316
PHILIP V (brother)	1316–1322

[a] [CIAPETTA, UGO.]   [b] [ROBERTO 1.]   [c] [FILIPPO 1.]   [d] [FILIPPO 2.]

[TABLE L]

KINGS OF HUNGARY,
1205–1342.

ANDREW II	1205–1235
BELA IV (son)	1235–1270
STEPHEN IV (V) (son)	1270–1272
LADISLAS III (IV) (son)	1272–1290
CHARLES MARTEL [a] (Titular King) (nephew) . . .	1290–1295
ANDREW III 1 [b]	1290–1301
WENCESLAS V (of Bohemia 2) (son-in-law)	1301–1305
OTHO (of Bavaria) 3	1305–1308
CHARLES ROBERT 4 [c] (Carobert)	1308–1342

1 First cousin of Stephen IV (V), seized the crown on the death of Ladislas, whose nephew, Charles Martel, was the rightful heir.
2 King of Bohemia, 1305–1306.   3 Grandson of Bela IV.
4 Son of Charles Martel.

[a] [CARLO 3.]   [b] [ANDREA DI UNGARIA.]   [c] [CARLO 6.]

[TABLE M]

KINGS OF NAVARRE (AND FRANCE),
1194–1322.

SANCHO VII	1194–1234

KINGS OF NAVARRE, COUNTS OF CHAMPAGNE.

THIBAUT I (IV)[a] (nephew)	1234–1253
THIBAUT II (V) [b] (son)	1253–1270
HENRY I (III) [c] (brother)	1270–1274
JOAN I[1] (daughter)	1274 }–1305
PHILIP IV of France[d] (1285–1314)	1284 }

KINGS OF FRANCE AND NAVARRE.

LOUIS X (son), King of Navarre	1305 }–1316
King of France	1314 }
PHILIP V (brother)	1316–1322

[1] Joan I married Philip IV of France; on her death in 1305, her son Louis became King of Navarre, and on the death of his father, in 1314, he became also King of France as Louis X, thus uniting for the first time the crowns of France and Navarre.

[a] [TEBALDO[1].]   [b] [TEBALDO[2].]   [c] [ARRIGO[7].]   [d] [FILIPPO[2] : TABLE K]

[TABLE N]

KINGS OF NORWAY,
1263–1355.

MAGNUS IV	1263–1280
ERIC II[a] (son)	1280–1299
HAKON V[b] (brother)	1299–1319
MAGNUS V[1] (grandson)	1319–1355

[1] King of Sweden, 1321–1355.

[a] [ERICO.]   [b] [ACONE[2].]

[TABLE O]

KINGS OF SCOTLAND,

1249–1329.

ALEXANDER III	1249–1286
MARGARET	1286–1290
Interregnum	1290–1292
JOHN BALIOL	1292–1296
(WILLIAM WALLACE	1296–1298)
Interregnum	1298–1306
ROBERT I (Bruce)	1306–1329

[TABLE P]

KINGS OF RASCIA [1],

1222–1321.

STEPHEN PRVOVYENCHANI	1222–1228
RADOSLAFF (son)	1228-1234
VLADISLAFF (brother)	1234–124
STEPHEN OUROS I (brother)	1240–1272
STEPHEN DRAGUTIN (son)	1272–1275
STEPHEN OUROS II (Milutin) [2][a] (brother)	1275–1321

[1] The kingdom of Servia was so called in the Middle Ages.

[2] Addressed (in 1288) by Pope Nicholas IV as 'Rex Sclavorum'; he signed himself (in 1305 or 1307) in a document still extant in the Venetian archives as 'Stephanus Urosch Rex Serbicarum terrarum et maritimarum'.

[a] [STEFANO UROSIO.]

[TABLE Q]

EMPERORS MENTIONED OR ALLUDED TO BY DANTE.

i. ROMAN EMPERORS—AT ROME.

AUGUSTUS [a]	B.C. 27–A.D. 14
TIBERIUS [b]	A.D. 14–37
NERO [c]	54–68
TITUS [d]	79–81
DOMITIAN [e]	81–96
TRAJAN [f]	98–117
CONSTANTINE [g]	306–330

ii. ROMAN EMPERORS—AT CONSTANTINOPLE.

CONSTANTINE [g]	330–337
JUSTINIAN [h]	527–565

iii. EMPERORS OF THE WEST.

CHARLEMAGNE [k]	800–814
OTTO I [l]	962–973
HENRY II [m]	1002–1024
CONRAD III [n]	1138–1152
FREDERICK I [o]	1152–1190
HENRY VI [p]	1190–1198
FREDERICK II [q]	1212–1250
RUDOLF I [r]	1272–1292
ADOLF [s]	1292–1298
ALBERT I [t]	1298–1308
HENRY VII [u]	1308–1313

iv. BYZANTINE EMPEROR.

MICHAEL I [v]	811–813

[a] [AUGUSTO [2].] [b] [TIBERIUS.] [c] [NERONE.] [d] [TITO.] [e] [DOMIZIANO.]
[f] [TRAIANO.] [g] [COSTANTINO.] [h] [GIUSTINIANO.] [k] [CARLO MAGNO.]
[l] [OTTO.] [m] [ARRIGO [3].] [n] [CURRADO [1].] [o] [FEDERICO [1].] [p] [ARRIGO [5].]
[q] [FEDERICO [2].] [r] [RIDOLFO [1].] [s] [ADOLFO.] [t] [ALBERTO [2].]
[u] [ARRIGO [v] [MICHAEL.]

[TABLE R]

POPES MENTIONED OR ALLUDED TO BY DANTE.

LINUS [a]	64 (or 67)	– 76 (or 78)
CLETUS [b]	76 (or 78)	– 88 (or 90)
SIXTUS I [c]	120	– 127
PIUS I [d]	140 (or 142)–155 (or 157)	
CALIXTUS I [e]	217	– 222
URBAN I [f]	223	– 230
SYLVESTER I [g]	314	– 335
ANASTASIUS II [h]	496	– 498
AGAPETUS I [i]	535	– 536
GREGORY I [j]	590	– 604
ADRIAN I [k]	772	– 795
LEO VIII [l]	963	– 965
BENEDICT V [m]	964	
INNOCENT III [n]	1198	– 1216
HONORIUS III [o]	1216	– 1227
INNOCENT IV [p]	1243	– 1254
ALEXANDER IV [q]	1254	– 1261
URBAN IV [r]	1261	– 1264
CLEMENT IV [s]	1264	– 1268
ADRIAN V [t]	1276	
JOHN XXI [u]	1276	– 1277
NICHOLAS III [v]	1277	– 1280
MARTIN IV [w]	1281	– 1285
CELESTINE V [x]	1294	
BONIFACE VIII [y]	1294	– 1303
BENEDICT XI [z]	1303	– 1304
CLEMENT V [aa]	1305	– 1314
JOHN XXII [bb]	1316	– 1334

[a] [LINO 1.]   [b] [CLETO.]   [c] [SISTO.]   [d] [PIO.]   [e] [CALISTO.]
[f] [URBANO 1.]   [g] [SILVESTRO 1.]   [h] [ANASTASIO.]   [i] [AGABITO.]
[j] [GREGORIO.]   [k] [ADRIANUS.]   [l] [LEO.]   [m] [BENEDETTO 3.]
[n] [INNOCENZIO 1.]   [o] [ONORIO.]   [p] [INNOCENZIO 2.]   [q] [ALESSANDRO IV.]
[r] [URBANO 2.]   [s] [CLEMENTE 1.]   [t] [ADRIANO 2.]   [u] [GIOVANNI XXI.]
[v] [NICCOLÒ 2.]   [w] [MARTINO 2.]   [x] [CELESTINO V.]   [y] [BONIFAZIO 1.]
[z] [BENEDETTO 2.]   [aa] [CLEMENTE 2.]   [bb] [GIOVANNI XXII.]

' Suole a riguardar giovare altrui.'

Purg. iv. 54.